OUR SUNDAY VISI
ENCYCLOPEDIA
CATHOL
DOCTRIN

OUR SUNDAY VISITOR'S ENCYCLOPEDIA OF CATHOLIC DOCTRINE

EDITED BY RUSSELL SHAW

Our Sunday Visitor Publishing Division
Our Sunday Visitor, Inc.
Huntington, Indiana 46750

Nihil Obstat: Rev. Michael Heintz
Censor Librorum
Imprimatur: ✠ John M. D'Arcy
Bishop of Fort Wayne-South Bend
April 17, 1997

The Nihil Obstat and Imprimatur are official declarations that a book or pamphlet is free of doctrinal or moral error. No implication is contained therein that those who have granted the Nihil Obstat or Imprimatur agree with the content, opinions, or statements expressed.

International Standard Book Number: 0-87973-746-8
Library of Congress Catalog Card Number: 96-70430

Cover artwork by Monica Watts; cover design by Rebecca Heaston

PRINTED IN THE UNITED STATES OF AMERICA

Table of Contents

Contributors

Rev. James B. Anderson teaches in the Graduate School of Theology at the University of St. Thomas, Houston. A former English secretary with the Vatican Secretariat of State, he holds a doctorate in Sacred Theology from the Pontifical Gregorian University, Rome, and is the author of *A Vatican II Pneumatology of the Paschal Mystery.*

Rev. Jordan Aumann, O.P., has taught theology at the Pontifical University of St. Thomas, Rome, and other schools. Author of several books, including *Spiritual Theology*, now in its fifth printing, he has a doctorate in Sacred Theology from the Pontifical Faculty, Salamanca, Spain, and is consultor to the Vatican Congregations for the Clergy and for Evangelization.

Rev. Christopher Buckner is pastor of St. Mary's Church, Fredericksburg, Va., and assistant to the academic director of the Catholic Distance University. He holds degrees from Hunter College, St. John's University, and Mount St. Mary's Seminary and has an advanced catechetical diploma from the Vatican Congregation for the Clergy.

Rev. Msgr. Cormac Burke is a judge of the Roman Rota, highest appeals court of the Catholic Church, and professor of anthropology at the Studium Rotale, where future rotal advocates study. A native of Ireland and a civil lawyer and canon lawyer, he has published widely on moral and pastoral theology and ecclesiology, and has lectured on five continents. His books include *Covenanted Happiness* and *Authority and Freedom in the Church.*

Rev. John Burke, O.P., is director of the National Institute for the Word of God. A network television director before becoming a Dominican, he has a doctorate in Sacred Theology from the Catholic University of America. Among his many books are *Companion to the Prayer of Christians* and *The Homilist's Guide to Scripture, Theology, and Canon Law.*

David Byers is executive director of the American Board of Catholic Missions and the Committees on Evangelization, Missions, and Science and Human Values of the National Conference of Catholic Bishops. Before joining the staff of the bishops' conference, he was at the Research Center of the Glenmary Home Missioners. He has a doctorate in English from the University of Wisconsin, and has written or edited several books and published widely in periodicals.

Rev. Romanus Cessario, O.P., is professor of systematic theology at St. John's Seminary School of Theology, Brighton, Mass. The holder of a doctorate in Sacred Theology from the University of Fribourg, he is author or coauthor of several books, including *Christian Faith and the Theological Life: The Moral Virtues and Theological Ethics* and *A Love That Never Ends: A Key to the Catechism of the Catholic Church.*

John F. Crosby is professor and chair of the philosophy department at the Franciscan University of Steubenville. He has a doctorate from the University of Salzburg, Austria, and has taught and lectured widely in the United States and other countries. He has published many articles and reviews in scholarly journals, and is preparing a book on personalist philosophy.

Rev. Joseph Augustine DiNoia, O.P., is executive director of the Secretariat for Doctrine and Pastoral Practices, National Conference of Catholic Bishops, and teaches theology at the Dominican House of Studies, Washington, D.C. Holder of a doctorate from Yale University, he is author of *The Diversity of Religions: A Christian Perspective* and edits *The Thomist*.

Richard M. Doerflinger is associate director for policy development in the Secretariat for Pro-Life Activities, National Conference of Catholic Bishops, and edits the newsletter *Life at Risk: A Chronicle of Euthanasia Trends in America*. He has an M.A. in divinity from the University of Chicago and has done doctoral studies in theology at the Catholic University of America.

Jude P. Dougherty is dean of the School of Philosophy, Catholic University of America, where he also received his doctorate. He has written or contributed to several books and edited others, and is editor of *The Review of Metaphysics* and general editor of the series *Studies in Philosophy and the History of Philosophy* published by the Catholic University of America Press.

Most Rev. John P. Foley is Titular Archbishop of Neapolis in Proconsulari and president of the Pontifical Council for Social Communications. A graduate of St. Joseph's University, St. Charles Borromeo Seminary, and the Columbia University journalism school, he edited *The Catholic Standard and Times*, Philadelphia archdiocesan newspaper, before Pope John Paul II named him to his present position.

Most Rev. Francis E. George, O.M.I., is Archbishop of Chicago. He previously served as Archbishop of Portland, Ore., and Bishop of Yakima, Wash. He has a doctorate in Sacred Theology from the Pontifical University Urbaniana, Rome, and a Ph.D. from Tulane University. A former provincial superior and vicar general of the Oblates of Mary Immaculate, he is author of *Inculturation and Ecclesial Communion* and contributor to other books and journals.

Scott Hahn teaches theology and Scripture at the Franciscan University of Steubenville. He has a doctorate in theology from Marquette University and a master of divinity degree from Gordon-Conwell Theological Seminary. He and his wife, Kimberly, are coauthors of the book *Rome Sweet Home*, and he has contributed articles to many publications.

Dennis Helming teaches at the Tenley Study Center, Washington, D.C., and previously was public affairs director of the Heights Foundation, New York. He is author of *Footprints in the Snow, The*

Examined Life, and other works, and has contributed to many periodicals. He is a graduate of Harvard University and has a doctorate in canon law from the Pontifical University of St. Thomas, Rome.

Sean Innerst is director of religious education for the Diocese of Rapid City, S.D. He has a master's degree in theology from the Franciscan University of Steubenville and is enrolled in the pontifical graduate theology program of the International Marian Research Institute. He has given many workshops and lectured widely on theological and catechetical topics.

Rev. David-Maria Jaeger, O.F.M., a native of Israel, entered the Custody of the Holy Land of the Franciscan Order of Friars Minor in 1981 and was ordained a priest in 1986. Previously he was Director of the Christianity in the Holy Land Program at the Ecumenical Institute for Advanced Theological Studies, Tantur, Jerusalem. He has a doctorate in canon law from the Pontifical Athenaeum "Antonianum" in Rome and from 1986 to 1992 taught at its Jerusalem and Rome campuses. Since 1992 he has been Judicial Vicar in the Diocese of Austin, Tex.

Rev. Frederick Jelly, O.P., is professor of theology at Mount St. Mary's Seminary. He has a doctorate in Sacred Theology from the Pontifical Faculty of the Immaculate Conception. The author *of Madonna: Mary in the Catholic Tradition*, he is preparing a book to be entitled *Preaching Christ Through Mary* and has published many scholarly and popular articles. In 1993, he was awarded the Patronal Medal for Mariological scholarship by the Catholic University of America.

George Sim Johnston is a free-lance writer living in New York. A graduate of Harvard University, he formerly was vice president for corporate finance with the firm of Salomon Brothers. His articles and reviews have been published in numerous secular and religious periodicals. Currently he is writing a book on evolution.

Rev. Msgr. Francis D. Kelly is Rector/President of Pope John XXIII National Seminary, Weston, Mass. He was a consultor to the Redaction Committee for the *Catechism of the Catholic Church* and has served as Executive Director of the Department of Religious Education of the National Catholic Educational Association. His works include *The Mystery We Proclaim: Catechesis at the Third Millennium.*

Sister Margaret John Kelly, D.C., is special assistant to the president of St. John's University, New York, and executive director of the Vincentian Center for Church and Society there. She is a former provincial superior of the Daughters of Charity National Health System — Northeast, and has been vice president of the Catholic Health Association of the United States.

Mary M. Keys teaches in the Department of Government and International Studies of the University of Notre Dame. A graduate of Boston College and the holder of a recent doctorate in political science from the University of Toronto, she was a contributor to the book *Catholicism, Liberalism, and Communitarianism.*

Rev. Lawrence A. Kutz is a chaplain at centers of the Opus Dei Prelature in the Washington, D.C., area. He previously held similar positions in California and Wisconsin. He has a degree in electrical engineering from the University of Wisconsin, Madison, and a doctorate in Sacred Theology from the Lateran University, Rome.

Very Rev. Ronald D. Lawler, O.F.M. Cap., is director of adult and family catechesis in the Diocese of Pittsburgh and former president and rector of Holy Apostles College and Seminary, Cromwell, Conn. His publications include *The Teaching of Christ: A Catholic Catechism for Adults* and *Catholic Sexual Ethics*. He has a doctorate from St. Louis University, and has taught at the Catholic University of America, the University of St. Thomas, Oxford, and St. John's University.

Patrick Lee teaches philosophy at the Franciscan University of Steubenville. The holder of a doctorate from Marquette University, he has taught there and at St. Francis de Sales College and the University of St. Thomas. He is the author of *Abortion and Unborn Human Life*, and has contributed scholarly articles to many publications.

Joyce A. Little teaches theology at the University of St. Thomas, Houston. Previously she taught at Marquette University, where she also received her doctorate in theology. Her books are *Toward a Thomist Methodology* and *The Church and the Culture War*. She also has written articles and reviews for numerous publications and has lectured widely.

Paul E. Lockey has been assistant dean of the School of Arts and Sciences at the University of St. Thomas, Houston, and has taught theology there. He is an honors graduate of the Perkins School of Theology at Southern Methodist University and received his doctorate in theology from the University of Dallas. He was editor of the volume *Studies in Thomistic Theology*.

Rev. Msgr. Richard Malone teaches theology at St. Charles Borromeo Seminary, Philadelphia. His doctorate in Sacred Theology is from the Pontifical Lateran University, Rome. He served with the Congregation for the Doctrine of the Faith and was executive director of the Committees for Pastoral Research and Practices and Doctrine of the U.S. bishops' conference.

Rev. Charles M. Mangan is vice chancellor of the Diocese of Sioux Falls, S.D., and pastor of three parishes. He has written several books, is a contributor to *Our Sunday Visitor's Catholic Encyclopedia* and *Our Sunday Visitor's Catholic Dictionary*, and has written for many periodicals. He has a licentiate in canon law from the Pontifical Gregorian University,

Rome, and is Defender of the Bond in the Second Instance, Archdiocese of St. Paul and Minneapolis.

Regis Martin is an associate professor of theology at the Franciscan University of Steubenville. He has a doctorate in Sacred Theology from the Pontifical University of St. Thomas, Rome, has written scholarly and popular articles as well as two booklets published by Franciscan Press, and is editor of an anthology of Christian devotional verse, *Images of Grace.*

William E. May teaches at the John Paul II Institute for Studies of Marriage and the Family, Washington, D.C. He is author or coauthor of many books, including *An Introduction to Moral Theology* and *Marriage: The Rock on Which the Family Is Built.* He has a doctorate from Marquette University, and in 1986 was named to the International Theological Commission by Pope John Paul.

Most Rev. James T. McHugh is Bishop of Camden and was Auxiliary Bishop of Newark. He formerly directed the family life and pro-life offices of the U.S. bishops' conference. Holder of a doctorate in Sacred Theology from the Pontifical University of St. Thomas Aquinas, he served with the Holy See delegations at the United Nations population conferences in 1974, 1984, and 1994.

Stephen F. Miletic is chairman of the theology department at the Franciscan University of Steubenville. He has been director of the National Office of Religious Education, Canadian Conference of Catholic Bishops, and provost and academic dean at the Notre Dame Catechetical Institute, Arlington, Va. He has a doctorate from Marquette University and is author of the book *One Flesh* and many articles.

Most Rev. John J. Myers is Bishop of Peoria. He has a licentiate in theology from the Gregorian University, Rome, and a doctorate in canon law from the Catholic University of America, and has been active in the Canon Law Society of America. He held pastoral and administrative positions in the Peoria diocese before being named Coadjutor Bishop in 1987 and Bishop in 1990.

Rev. Boniface Ramsey, O.P., is pastor and prior of the Dominican community at the Church of St. Vincent Ferrer, New York, and currently on leave of absence from Immaculate Conception Seminary and Seton Hall University, where he holds the rank of associate professor. He has a doctorate in Sacred Theology from the Institut Catholique, Paris, has taught at the College Dominicain, Ottawa, and has written several books, including *Beginning to Read the Fathers,* and translated others.

Robert Royal is vice president for research at the Ethics and Public Policy Center, Washington, D.C. He has a doctorate in comparative literature from the Catholic University of America, and has written or edited several books, including *Jacques Maritain and the Jews* and *A Century of Catholic Social Thought*, and contributed to several others.

Rev. Robert A. Skeris is chairman of the theology department at Christendom College. He has a doctorate in theology from the University of Bonn, and has been professor at the Pontifical Institute of Sacred Music and consultor to the Vatican Office of Pontifical Ceremonies. He has published studies in liturgy and sacred music and contributed to many periodicals.

Janet E. Smith teaches philosophy at the University of Dallas. She has a doctorate in classical languages from the University of Toronto. She is the author of *Humanae Vitae: A Generation Later* and editor of *Why Humanae Vitae Was Right: A Reader*, has written articles for many scholarly and popular publications, and has lectured widely in the United States and other countries.

Rev. Msgr. Robert A. Wister is associate professor of Church history in the school of theology of Seton Hall University. Previously he was executive director of the Seminary Department, National Catholic Educational Association. He has a doctorate in Church history from the Pontifical Gregorian University, Rome, and has published and lectured widely on Church history and seminaries.

General Editor

Russell Shaw is Washington editor of Our Sunday Visitor and an associate professor at the Pontifical Athenaeum of the Holy Cross, Rome. The author or coauthor of thirteen books and a contributor to many periodicals, he is former Secretary for Public Affairs of the National Conference of Catholic Bishops and United States Catholic Conference and former Director of Public Information of the Knights of Columbus. He is a graduate of Georgetown University.

Introduction

This encyclopedia seeks to enrich Catholics' understanding of the faith they profess and the morality that guides their lives. It is based on, complements, and makes more useful and usable the *Catechism of the Catholic Church*. While either volume can be read apart from the other, and the *Catechism* is a product of the Church's Magisterium, the reader often will find it helpful to consult the two books together.

Scholars and specialists have many theological, pastoral, and catechetical resources available to them. There also are many popular catechetical digests. This encyclopedia aims at something else. On the one hand, it does not require advanced degrees or a professional background in Church work. On the other hand, it is not written down to some imagined "popular" level — it is not a digest, not a simplified treatment. It is for serious-minded readers who, although they have not had specialized training and experience, want to know in some depth what their Church teaches and are willing to make the intellectual effort that requires.

The publication of the *Catechism of the Catholic Church* in October, 1992, was one of the most important events — many would say *the* most important event — in the life of the Church since the Second Vatican Council (1962-1965). As Pope John Paul II noted in the apostolic constitution *Fidei Depositum* accompanying the *Catechism*, Pope John XXIII, in convoking the Council, entrusted to it as its principal task "to guard and present better the precious deposit of Christian doctrine in order to make it more accessible to the Christian faithful and to all people of good will."

Vatican Council II did its work well: Its sixteen documents are a rich doctrinal storehouse. Nevertheless, the years since the Council have been marked by much confusion, controversy, and dissent, not least in relation to Church teaching. This circumstance led the extraordinary assembly of the Synod of Bishops, convoked by Pope John Paul in December, 1985, to recommend a "catechism or compendium of all Catholic doctrine regarding both faith and morals." Pope John Paul readily accepted the suggestion. The result, after years of hard work carried out under the direction of a commission of cardinals and involving extensive consultation with all the bishops of the world, was the *Catechism of the Catholic Church*.

It is a remarkable document, as the Pope observes: "a statement of the Church's faith and of Catholic doctrine, attested to or illumined by Sacred Scripture, the apostolic tradition, and the Church's Magisterium." In words that firmly fix the *Catechism*'s authority, he adds: "I declare it to be a sure norm for teaching the faith and thus a valid and legitimate instrument for ecclesial communion" (*Fidei Depositum*, 3).

Obviously this encyclopedia does not take the place of the *Catechism*, but it does make reading it a more fruitful enterprise. It expands on points of doctrine the *Catechism* discusses more or less briefly. It draws together matters whose treatment is scattered in several different places. It provides important historical background and pastoral insights that the *Catechism*, given the sort of document it is, does not undertake to provide. It is written in language that English-speaking readers may find more familiar and accessible. And it provides, as resources for readers engaged in independent study, extensive cross-references and lists of suggested readings on very many topics. All this, along with the obvious fact the encyclopedia introduces readers to a large number of highly-qualified contributors, men and women of faith — bishops, priests, religious, and laity — whose love of the Church and her teaching shines through their words and is itself deeply edifying.

* * *

The editor wishes to thank a number of people: Robert Lockwood, Greg Erlandson, and Jacquelyn Lindsey of Our Sunday Visitor, with whom the idea for the project originated and who were consistently patient and encouraging as it took shape; Henry O'Brien of Our Sunday Visitor, who shepherded the manuscript with meticulous attention to detail; Dr. Germain Grisez, who offered valuable practical suggestions at the start; and the many encyclopedia contributors who supplied helpful advice about topics to be covered and other writers to contact. Their interest and enthusiasm were greatly appreciated.

A word about abbreviations: In the interests of making the encyclopedia user-friendly, they have generally not been employed. Given the large number of references to the *Catechism of the Catholic Church*, however, its title is abbreviated throughout as CCC. "Denzinger-Schönmetzer," where it appears, refers to H. Denzinger and A. Schönmetzer, eds., *Enchiridion Symbolorum, definitionum et declarationum de rebus fidei et morum*, the most authoritative compilation of the Church's magisterial documents before Vatican Council II. The number — or numbers as the case may be — following the name (e.g., Denzinger-Schönmetzer, 1356) refers to the paragraph number of their work. (In notes from the *Catechism*, a number of abbreviations are used: for example, DS for Denzinger-Schönmetzer, CDF for the Congregation of the Doctrine of the Faith, and initials for Vatican II documents.)

The reader is reminded that historical dates, including dates of births and deaths, often are uncertain. The dates used in this volume all have authoritative support, but no effort has been made to impose an arbitrary uniformity in this matter. The same goes for the spelling of names and the like.

* * *

To close with the prayer of John Paul II introducing the *Catechism of the Catholic Church:* "May the light of the true faith free humanity from the ignorance and slavery of sin in order to lead it to the only freedom worthy of the name: that of life in Jesus Christ under the guidance of the Holy Spirit, here below and in the kingdom of heaven, in the fullness of the blessed vision of God face to face" (*Fidei Depositum*, 3).

ABORTION

Abortion is "the deliberate and direct killing, by whatever means it is carried out, of a human being in the initial phase of his or her existence, extending from conception to birth" (Pope John Paul II, encyclical *The Gospel of Life, Evangelium Vitae*, 58). It includes the disruption of pregnancy before viability (the point when a child can survive outside the womb); deliberate prevention or disruption of implantation in the mother's womb so that the embryo will die (e.g., through "morning-after pills" or other abortifacient drugs); and direct killing of an unborn child who has reached viability. The destruction or discarding of human embryos produced by fertilization outside the womb is ruled out by the same moral analysis that condemns abortion (*Evangelium Vitae*, 63).

All these forms of killing are gravely wrong, whether the killing is willed as an end in itself or as a means to some other goal. Reaffirming a tradition which dates back to the first century A.D., the Second Vatican Council condemned abortion and infanticide as "abominable crimes" (*Pastoral Constitution on the Church in the Modern World, Gaudium et Spes*, 51). Abortion is an especially deplorable form of killing because it destroys life at its most helpless and dependent stage.

As *Evangelium Vitae* points out: "The one eliminated is a human being at the very beginning of life. No one more absolutely innocent could be imagined. In no way could this human being ever be considered an aggressor, much less an unjust aggressor! He or she is weak, defenseless, even to the point of lacking that minimal form of defense consisting in the poignant power of a newborn baby's cries and tears. The unborn child is totally entrusted to the protection and care of the woman carrying him or her in the womb. And yet sometimes it is precisely the mother herself who makes the decision and asks for the child to be eliminated, and who then goes about having it done" (58).

Without minimizing in any way the grave evil of abortion, the Church recognizes that many women resort to abortion in tragic and painful circumstances which may greatly reduce their personal culpability. Others often share responsibility for the abortion: the child's father, who may openly advocate abortion or encourage it by abandoning the woman to face the problems of pregnancy alone; family and friends who pressure a woman toward abortion; and even public officials and community leaders who create a legal and social climate favoring abortion (*Evangelium Vitae*, 59).

The Church offers God's forgiveness and healing to women who have had an abortion; in many dioceses, postabortion counseling programs offer sacramental reconciliation as well as emotional and psychological help to those involved in abortion.

Under Church law, anyone who successfully performs or procures an abortion thereby incurs excommunication (Canon 1398). Like any canon imposing penalties on individuals, this is to be interpreted narrowly: It applies only to those directly involved, so that the act would not have taken place without their help, and only to those who freely acted, knowing the penalty. The purpose of this penalty is not to exclude anyone from the Church but "to make an individual fully aware of the gravity of a certain sin and then to foster genuine conversion and repentance" (*Evangelium Vitae*, 62). The Church sees a particular need today to emphasize the evil of abortion in its own legal code, since many countries have changed their civil laws to allow or even encourage abortion.

Historical Background • The Church has condemned abortion from its earliest centuries. During some periods, Church law relied on the biological knowledge of the time to distinguish between very early abortions and those performed at later stages, with a lesser penalty attached to the former. But this did not affect the moral teaching against all abortion, and canon law dropped the distinction when science demonstrated that a member of the human species begins life at conception.

The Old Testament contains no explicit condemnation of abortion. This is not because the practice was accepted in ancient Israel, but because it was so alien to a religion and culture that greeted children as a blessing and viewed sterility as a curse. Little was known at the time about human development in the womb. It is in this context that one may understand the Old Testament's single reference to *accidental* abortion. The law specifies that if a man in a fight accidentally strikes a woman and causes her to miscarry, he must pay a fine, but if the woman dies, he forfeits his life (Ex 21:22-23).

Even within the Old Testament, however, a development can be seen. Later prophetic books, the Psalms, and the Book of Wisdom show a fuller appreciation of God's loving and life-giving presence at all stages of human life, including life in the womb: "Before I formed you in the womb I knew you, and before you were born I consecrated you" (Jer 1:5; cf. Ps 22:10-11, 139:15). This fuller appreciation reaches its culmination in Jesus, who embodies God's particular regard for the weak and helpless, including young children (cf. Mk 10:13-16). In the New Testament, we see not only that the Son of God first became incarnate as an unborn child but that his herald on earth, John the Baptist, first greeted him by leaping in the womb of his own mother Elizabeth (Lk 1:44). The Incarnation gave Christians a new reason to abhor all killing, including abortion: In destroying human life, we destroy a brother or sister of Christ.

As Christianity expanded beyond its Jewish roots, an explicit position on abortion became necessary. In the Greek and Roman culture of that time, abortion and infanticide were accepted, particularly when ordered by the male head of the household. Christians' universal reaction to the practice was one of outrage. The earliest known manual of Christian practice after the New Testament, the *Didache* (or, popularly, *Teaching of the Twelve Apostles*) commanded: "You shall not kill the embryo by abortion and shall not cause the newborn to perish." In the third century, Tertullian insisted that abortion is simply "an acceleration of homicide," for "he also is a man who is about to be one, just as every fruit already exists in the seed" (*Apologeticum*, IX.8). Early Church councils often equated abortion with homicide, establishing very severe penances for any Christian resorting to the practice.

As Jerome, Augustine, and other early Church Fathers took up insights from pagan philosophy to develop a reasoned defense of their faith, they became aware of speculations by Aristotle and others regarding development in the womb. Aristotle theorized that the formative element for each child is provided by the father's semen, which requires time to develop unformed matter from the mother's menstrual blood into a specifically human form. Based on his visual study of miscarried fetuses, he thought this formative process is complete at about 40 days of development, passing through intermediate stages in which the developing being has a "vegetative" soul and then an "animal" or "sensitive" soul before being prepared to receive a specifically human or rational soul.

The Septuagint translation of the Old Testament, written by Greek-speaking Jews, reflected this theory. In this version, the above-mentioned passage from Exodus requires a fine if the miscarried child is "unformed" but the death penalty if he or she is "formed." Early Christians using this translation thought it provided biblical confirmation of Aristotle's distinction; they were unaware that the distinction had been inserted into the text by scholars familiar with that theory.

The theory of delayed animation was rejected in the law of the Eastern Church. But in the West the distinction between formed and unformed fetuses was incorporated into the codification of canon law in the twelfth century, so that only the abortion of a formed or "animated" fetus was equated with murder. At the same time, abortion at any stage was still seen as a grave sin. St. Thomas Aquinas, for example, described all abortion as a sin "against nature," observing that even brute animals instinctively care for their own young.

By the nineteenth century, the discovery of the ovum and other new knowledge undermined the scientific basis for the theory of delayed animation. It became known that the male sperm and the female ovum unite at conception to form a living being of the human species with his or her own identity. In 1869, when Pope Pius IX reordered the system of canon law, he dropped the distinction between formed and unformed fetuses. At the same time, and on the same scientific basis, the American Medical Association persuaded American legislators to drop a similar distinction from civil law and treat abortion at any stage as a crime.

Throughout these centuries, theologians debated difficult circumstances in which some thought an abortion might be justified. One seventeenth-century debate focused on whether an "unanimated" fetus could be aborted to save the mother's life or reputation. In the nineteenth century, the Vatican had to resolve a dispute about craniotomy, because some theologians thought it might be justifiable to crush the skull of a child as it was being born in order to save the mother's life. In each of these cases, the Church sympathized with people facing such harrowing situations but concluded that no circumstance can objectively give anyone a right to directly dispose of someone else's life.

After the Second Vatican Council restated the Church's condemnation of abortion in 1965, Pope Paul VI clarified the status of this teaching in 1972 by declaring that it "has not changed and is unchangeable." In 1974, the *Declaration on Procured Abortion* issued by the Congregation for the Doctrine of the Faith elaborated the teaching in the face of efforts in some countries to repeal traditional laws against abortion. Appealing to principles of natural law, the *Declaration* emphasized the right to life as a fundamental right of each human being — one that cannot be denied by any individual or society, because it flows from the inherent dignity of the human person. In 1995, Pope John Paul II appealed to this insight as well as to the universal tradition of the Church to declare solemnly that "direct abortion, that is, abortion willed as an end or as a means, always constitutes a grave moral disorder, since it is the deliberate killing of an innocent human being" (*Evangelium Vitae*, 62). The Church irrevocably judges abortion to be among those inherently evil acts that can never be justified.

Modern Debates • Modern theological attempts to carve out exceptions to this absolute norm have taken two forms.

First, some theologians propose a new theory of delayed animation, based on uncertainties about the first week or two of human development. Their proposal would chiefly affect moral judgments about *in vitro* fertilization, destructive embryo research, and "morning-after" drugs and devices, not abortions performed after an embryo has implanted in his or her mother's womb. They argue that the early embryo is not yet a human individual, because it may sometimes split into two individuals ("twinning") and even reunite again as one ("recombination"). They also point to the high rate of "natural" embryo loss at this stage, and ask whether God could intend to create and discard this many human lives.

There are serious flaws in this argument. The preponderance of scientific evidence indicates a continuum of human development from conception onward. "From the time that the ovum is fertilized, a life is begun which is neither that of the father nor the mother; it is rather the life of a new human being with his own growth. It would never be made human if it were not human already" (*Declaration on Procured Abortion*, 12). Spontaneous twinning of a human embryo to produce identical twins is very rare, and the factors determining it are poorly understood. As to the alleged high death rate of human embryos, many such losses result from incomplete or faulty fertilizations that never produced a real embryo, and many "natural" losses may actually be due to influences such as tobacco, alcohol, and environmental pollution; in any event, the fact that a group of people has a short natural life span would in no way justify directly killing any of them.

The Church acknowledges that science by itself cannot detect the presence or absence of an immortal soul. But modern scientific findings provide a sound basis for treating all human beings, from conception onward, with the dignity due to a human person. At the very least, deliberately interrupting embryonic development disrupts the process by which God was bringing a human person into the world. If one is unsure whether a very early member of the human species is a person already possessing an immortal soul, such uncertainty cannot justify directly killing that being — for to do so shows a willingness to risk murder in the event that he or she does turn out to be a person. Therefore, "from the standpoint of moral obligation, the mere probability that a human person is involved would suffice to justify an absolutely clear prohibition of any intervention aimed at killing a human embryo" (*Evangelium Vitae*, 60).

The other major objection against the teaching on abortion is one brought against the teaching on homicide generally. Some suggest that grave circumstances can justify killing the innocent when this may achieve a greater good. The Church has rejected this approach, and instead follows St. Paul's injunction in Romans 3:8 that we must not do evil that good may come of it (cf. Pope John Paul II, encyclical *The Splendor of Truth, Veritatis Splendor*, 76-83).

A different problem arises when a life may be lost as a side effect of a morally upright action performed for serious and legitimate reasons. The chemotherapy that may save a pregnant woman from life-threatening cancer may also have the effect of threatening the life of her unborn child; a child on the threshold of viability may have to be delivered early to avert an immediate threat to the mother's life. Such indirect abortion may be justified if the need is grave and the death of the child is not willed as a means to the desired end. But no circumstance can justify the direct killing of an innocent human being. This applies equally to killing the unborn child to save the mother and killing the mother to save the child — in having a right to life, all human beings are created equal.

Civil Law • Today the Church must sometimes offer its message of respect for life in a hostile environment. In many secular societies that have lost sight of the moral foundations for their laws, legal protection for the unborn is weak or nonexistent. Proposals to "liberalize" abortion laws to allow for exceptions in grave circumstances have given way to proposals to drop all laws against abortion or even to celebrate the freedom to choose abortion as a newfound fundamental "right."

In the Church's eyes, such a "right" to abortion is a profoundly misguided concept. In fact, the most fundamental of human rights is the right to life, which must belong to all — beginning with the weakest and most defenseless humans — if it is to have meaning. Abortion cannot be celebrated as an instance of freedom, since it deprives helpless humans of their freedom by depriving them of their very lives. The freedom to abort is in reality a form of license, in which the weak are placed at the mercy of the strong.

At its most basic level, government exists to prevent such injustice. A law allowing or promoting abortion therefore deserves no respect and has no moral force.

Some public officials of Catholic background claim that they cannot act to protect unborn life because this would impose their Catholic morality on others. This argument seriously distorts the Church's teaching. Catholic rejection of abortion is not a simple matter of Church discipline, like rules for fasting on Friday, or even a moral norm directed only at Catholics, like the obligation to show proper respect for the Eucharistic host. Rather, this teaching flows from the Church's basic respect for human rights and human dignity. When the Church seeks legal protection for the unborn, it seeks to promote not a Catholic society but a more human society.

Other public officials acknowledge the need to protect unborn human life, but say they must work within the bounds of what is legally and politically possible in a given time and place. The Church agrees that support for imperfect laws protecting the unborn can be valid and necessary, so long as the officials involved make clear their total opposition to abortion and their intention of improving the law as this becomes possible.

See: Body and Soul; Ensoulment; Genetic Experimentation; Homicide; Human Life, Dignity and Sanctity of; Human Person; Prenatal Diagnosis; Sexuality, Human.

Suggested Readings: CCC 2270-2273. Vatican Council II, *Pastoral Constitution on the Church in the Modern World, Gaudium et Spes*, 27, 51. John Paul II, *The Splendor of Truth, Veritatis Splendor*, 76-83; *The Gospel of Life, Evangelium Vitae*. Congregation for the Doctrine of the Faith, *Declaration on Procured Abortion*. J. Connery, S.J., *Abortion: The Development of the Roman Catholic Perspective*. J. Noonan, Jr., "An Almost Absolute Value in History," in Noonan, ed., *The Morality of Abortion*.

Richard Doerflinger

ABSOLUTE MORAL NORMS

An absolute moral norm is a specific norm that is true without exceptions. Almost everyone agrees that there are general principles that are true without exception (act out of love, act justly, and so on). There is fierce debate, however, about whether there are any *specific* exceptionless moral norms, that is, moral norms that exclude specific types of choices, such as the choice of contraception, of killing innocent people, of extramarital sex, and so on. The constant teaching of the Church is that there are certain moral absolutes, moral norms that are universally true without exceptions.

Most moral norms are nonabsolute. For example, one ought to return what is lent to one; one ought to keep one's promises. But these norms have exceptions: One should not return a gun to the per-

son who lent it if he is now insane; one should not keep a promise to meet one's friend this morning if doing so would mean neglecting one's child after a serious accident. Also, none of the specific affirmative moral norms are absolute. Our life is varied, and so there is no specific action we are required to do at all times.

However, there are some specific negative moral norms that are true without exception: One ought not to torture a child to obtain desired information; one ought not to rape. Also, although less popular in our culture: One ought not to fornicate, contracept, commit adultery, or intentionally kill innocent people. Despite their logically negative form, these absolutes are extremely important. They indicate the high respect we owe to the fundamental goods of persons that are the basis of all moral norms.

Object, Intention, Circumstances • To explain this point, natural law theorists have found it helpful to distinguish between the object of an act, its intention, and its circumstances; these are three distinct aspects of the moral act. This distinction is repeated by the *Catechism of the Catholic Church* (cf. 1749ff.). The object is the primary and most proximate thing one would honestly answer if asked, "What are you doing?" The intention and the object are distinct in this way: One chooses to do something for the sake of some end; that for the sake of which one chooses is the intention; the something one chooses is called the object of the act. So, if one lies in order to escape detection, escaping detection is the end and lying is the object. If one gives alms for the sake of appearing holy, giving alms is the object and appearing holy is the end. The circumstances are the other aspects of the act not included in the end and object: where it is done, when, with whom, with what instruments, and so on.

In order for the act to be morally good, all three (object, intention, and circumstances) must be good. A defect in any of the three makes the whole act morally evil. Thus, an otherwise good act, one that is good in its object and circumstances, may become bad because of the intention. For example, a man gives alms (object) in appropriate circumstances, but for the sake of seducing someone — a bad intention and therefore a bad act. Similarly, a married couple's choice to express their marriage sexually is a morally good object, and their intention may be good, but they may violate reasonable standards of public modesty; the circumstances make an otherwise good act bad. And, most importantly, if the intention of an act is good and circumstances are appropriate, but the object is bad, then the act is morally bad. For instance, killing an innocent person (bad object) in order to support one's family (good intention) is a morally bad act.

In the last thirty years, there has been much controversy, even within Catholic circles, on these points. Some theologians hold, against what was just said, that one cannot morally evaluate the object of the act apart from all of its circumstances, especially the foreseeable consequences. Proponents of teleological ethics, or proportionalism, argue that one may choose to destroy, damage, or impede a basic human good, such as life or truth, for the sake of bringing about a proportionate end or averting terrible consequences. So, according to them, one cannot say of any specific type of choice that it will always be morally bad; it is always possible that some circumstances might arise in which such a choice would be justified for the sake of averting bad consequences.

The Teaching of the Church • However, this position conflicts with the constant teaching of the Church from her earliest days. In his Letter to the Romans, St. Paul teaches that it is not right to say that "one may do evil that good may come from it" (Rom 3:8). Throughout the history of the Church, this has been read in its obvious sense as meaning that, as St. Augustine put it, it is never morally right to do what is intrinsically evil (*secundum se malum*) for the sake of a good end (cf. Augustine's *Against Lying*, Ch. 7).

Proportionalists have said, however, that they do not deny what St. Paul affirms. They agree with him that one may not do a *moral* evil for the sake of a good end. Still, they say, St. Paul's statement does not exclude proportionalism, namely, that one may do a *premoral* evil for the sake of a (proportionate) end.

It is true that, when St. Paul denies that "one may do *evil* that good may come from it," he means *moral* evil, not premoral or nonmoral evil. However, this scarcely helps the proportionalist cause. For St. Paul could not say that one should not do moral evil so that good may come from it unless he was presupposing that it is possible to determine, independently of what good or bad will come from an act, that it is a moral evil.

Moreover, the context shows that he is speaking precisely about a situation where an evil act apparently will bring about a great good. In this part of the letter, St. Paul argues that even out of our sins good consequences will flow, since God will take their occasion to show forth his justice. His point is that, even if that is the case, it is outrageous to say one should do evil so that good should come from it: to accuse authorized teachers of saying that is slander, Paul says (cf. Rom 3:8).

In his 1993 encyclical on moral principles *The Splendor of Truth, Veritatis Splendor*, Pope John Paul II definitively reaffirms the constant teaching of the Church: "Reason attests that there are objects of the human act which are by their nature 'incapable of being ordered' to God, because they radically contradict the good of the person made in his image. These are acts which, in the Church's moral tradition, have been termed 'intrinsically evil' (*intrinsice malum*): they are such *always and per se*, in other words, on account of their very object, and quite apart from the ulterior intentions of the one acting and the circumstances" (80).

Some critics of the Church's position regularly misreport it (perhaps unintentionally) in a way that makes it an easy target for criticism. They say the Church condemns material acts or physical behaviors independently of the quality of the act of will involved.

This is not what the Church teaches. Moral acts cannot be defined by specifying only the physical behavior. Two cases of the same physical behavior could carry out quite different choices and so be parts of different moral acts. This is why the Church defines the moral acts prohibited by moral absolutes as types of choices, and not as types of physical behavior. Contraception is the prevention of conception whether as an end or as a means, but not all conception-preventing behavior involves the choice to contracept. Lying is the saying of what one thinks is false *with the intention to deceive*. It is the *intentional* killing of innocent people that is intrinsically evil (cf. Pope John Paul II, encyclical *The Gospel of Life, Evangelium Vitae*, 57 [1995]), and so on. Pope John Paul clarified this point in *Veritatis Splendor*: "By the object of a given moral act, then, one cannot mean a process or an event of the merely physical order, to be assessed on the basis of its ability to bring about a given state of affairs in the outside world. Rather, that object is the proximate end of a deliberate decision which determines the act of willing on the part of the acting person" (78).

The basis for absolute moral norms is not difficult to understand. The basic moral criterion is that we should love God and love our neighbor as ourself. To love someone is to will what is genuinely good to him or her, and rejoice in his or her good. Loving God means rejoicing in God's goodness and also loving other persons and ourselves, since God's plan in creating is to direct persons to their fulfillment (in their human nature as well as a communion in his own divine life). So, any choice that by the nature of the case involves a suppression of our love of God, neighbor, or self, is wrong in whatever circumstances it might be made. To love God and neighbor involves willing to our neighbors and ourself their and our genuine good. As human beings, our genuine good includes bodily life and health, knowledge of truth and appreciation of beauty, friendship, integration of the various aspects of ourselves, religion, and so on. A choice that is by its nature contrary to or unduly neglectful of any of these basic and intrinsic goods of the human person is morally wrong (cf. *Veritatis Splendor*, 72).

See: Consequentialism; Deontology; Law of Christ; Moral Principles, Christian; Natural Law; Proportionalism; Teleological Ethics; Utilitarianism.

Suggested Readings: CCC 1749-1756. John Paul II, *The Splendor of Truth, Veritatis Splendor*; *The Gospel of Life, Evangelium Vitae*. G. Grisez, *The Way of the Lord Jesus*, Vol. 1, *Christian Moral Principles*, Chs. 6, 10; G. Grisez and R. Shaw, *Fulfillment in Christ*, Chs. 6, 10. J. Finnis, *Moral Absolutes: Tradition, Revision, and Truth*. W. May, *Moral Absolutes*.

Patrick Lee

ABSOLUTION

Absolution refers specifically to the forgiveness of sins. Indeed, "bishops and priests, by virtue of the sacrament of Holy Orders, have the power to forgive all sins 'in the name of the Father, and of the Son, and of the Holy Spirit' " (CCC 1461).

This power comes from Christ himself, who on numerous occasions in the Gospels told people not simply "You are forgiven" but "Your sins are forgiven." On the evening of the Resurrection, when he appeared to the disciples in the Upper Room, he told them: " 'As the Father has sent me, even so I send you.' And when he had said this, he breathed on them, and said to them, 'Receive the Holy Spirit. If you forgive the sins of any, they are forgiven; if you retain the sins of any, they are retained' " (Jn 20:19-23).

Absolution is normally given within the context of the sacrament of Penance, provided the penitent has expressed sorrow for his sins and made a purpose of amendment. He must also be willing to "do some penance," whether it is offering prayers or performing some acts of charity.

Absolution can be withheld if there is reason to believe the penitent is not contrite or has no intention of changing his lifestyle. He may have committed a sin, yet failed to have sorrow for it and only be confessing it because the Church requires this; then there is lack of contrition. Or he may be living in a sinful situation and unwilling to remove himself from that situation; such a person obviously is not expressing a purpose of amendment. Absolution is considered to be conditional if given based on the condition of the penitent's sorrow or willingness to perform some act such as restitution.

See: Confession; Contrition; General Absolution; Penance and Reconciliation, Sacrament of.

ADULT BAPTISM

Adult Baptism effects the initiation into the Christian faith of one who has attained the use of reason. Adult Baptism, rather than infant Baptism, is the common practice in areas where the Gospel has only recently been preached.

Those adults preparing for Baptism enter the catechumenate, thereby becoming disposed also to receive the sacraments of Confirmation and the Holy Eucharist that, along with Baptism, comprise the Sacraments of Initiation. There are several stages leading to full initiation that are governed by the episcopal conference (cf. Canon 851.1).

The actual ceremony of adult Baptism follows the Rite of Christian Initiation of Adults. The adult, who is to have a sponsor (Canon 872), must have demonstrated the intention to be baptized, be adequately instructed in Christian doctrine and the requirements of Christian life, and have been "tested" in the Christian life as a catechumen. Furthermore, he must be encouraged to have sorrow for his sins. For those who have completed at least their fourteenth year, Baptism is to be referred to the diocesan bishop so that he himself may confer it if he wishes (Canon 863).

For adults, Baptism remits not only original sin (as in the case of infants) but also all actual sins.

The Rite of Christian Initiation of Adults provides separate ceremonies for children and adults, even though both have attained the use of reason.

See: Baptism; Sacraments of Initiation.

ADULTERY

The sixth commandment forbids adultery. In both the Old and New Testaments adultery is condemned as a grave sin. Spouses are to have the same faithful commitment to each other that Christ has to his Church and are to be signs of the commitment to others. Adultery betrays the sacramentality of marriage and the trust of one's

spouse, it endangers the good of the children and of one's partner in adultery.

Adultery violates the pledge of total committed love that spouses make to each other on their marriage day. Indeed, in a sense, one's sexuality does not belong to oneself; it belongs more to one's spouse (or even to one's future spouse). He who "gives" away his sexual powers to another other than his spouse, is giving away what belongs to his spouse. The bond of trust so necessary to the complete self-giving that defines marriage is cruelly broken in an act of adultery. Adulterers undermine the sanctity of marriage, so necessary for the good and stability of all of society. In fact, Christ condemns even the lustful thoughts that are the precursors to adultery (cf. Mt 5:27-28).

Moreover, the adulterer endangers the well-being of his children, who need an intact household to thrive. Adultery might well lead to divorce and all the consequent trauma and suffering for all involved that follow upon divorce.

The partner in adultery is also misused, for the promises that are implicit in the sexual act cannot be honestly spoken in an adulterous act; one cannot intend to care for and love unconditionally one's partner in adultery or the offspring that may result from that action, since one has already made such promises to another.

See: Chastity; Fornication; Marriage, Goods of; Sexuality, Human.

AGNOSTICISM

The term "agnostic" was coined in the mid-nineteenth century to describe a person who holds the view that one can know nothing about the existence of God. The *Catechism of the Catholic Church* broadens the definition of agnosticism to include those who posit the existence of a transcendent being, but who deny that this existent enters into any form of personal communication or communion with the human race.

In response to what often amounts to a practical atheism, the Church in modern times has twice reaffirmed the Pauline teaching (cf. Rom 1:20) that "God, the first principle and last end of all things, can be known with certainty from the created world by the natural light of human reason" (cf. Vatican Council I, *Dogmatic Constitution on the Catholic Faith, Dei Filius*, 2; also Vatican Council II, *Dogmatic Constitution on Divine Revelation, Dei Verbum*, 6).

The natural knowledge of God provides neither an alternative nor a substitute for the gift of divine truth, which is given to us only through Jesus Christ. Still, Divine Revelation itself presumes that reason by its nature is ordered to discover certain truths about both God and the ultimate meaning of human existence. So, by ignoring the natural bent of human reason to come to a knowledge of God from creation, the agnostic easily fosters a sluggish moral spirit, which can only result in personal frustration. Since full knowledge of the truth and the actualization of authentic human freedom comes only from "the Father of lights" (Jas 1:17), agnosticism constitutes an offense against the first commandment of the Decalogue: "You shall have no other gods before me."

See: Atheism; God, Nature and Attributes of; Knowledge of God.

ANGELS

As the twentieth century drew to a close, there was an upsurge of popular interest in angels. Although having some elements of a fad and in some cases reflecting New Age preoccupations, it dealt with important matters of religious belief. At the same time, many people rejected the idea that there are such beings as angels. Setting aside scriptural testimony and religious doctrine, they dismissed this age-old belief as naïve and mythological; the testimony of the Bible was treated simply as literary convention; on the whole, to believe in angels, much less practice religious devotion to them, was considered by such persons childish and unsophisticated.

How should Catholics view this matter? Their guide is the Church's teaching authority. The existence of these free, personal beings was taught by the Fourth Lateran Council in 1215: "We firmly believe and profess without qualification that there is only one true God . . . creator of all things visible and invisible, spiritual and corporal, who, by his almighty power, from the very beginning of time has created both orders of creatures in the same way out of nothing, the spiritual or angelic world and the corporeal or visible universe."

How many and what kinds of angels there are fall in the realm of speculation. Doubtless there are myriads on myriads of them, each its own species. We know that early in their existence some of these pure spirits chose to remain in loving submission to God while others rejected that. Those who did were thereby ushered into heaven's beatific vision, while those who abused their freedom sinned, became evil, and thereby became denizens of, and recruiters for, hell.

The word "angel" designates the good spirits' divine commission: to be envoys sent to help humanity. Scripture is replete with references to these spiritual guardians. Angels are said to convey God's directives to humanity and to protect them (cf. Gn 24:7, 48:16; Ps 33:8, 90:11-13, 120:20-21; Mt 18:10), and to bring human petitions before God (cf. Tob 12:12; Rv 8:2-4). "Are they not all ministering spirits, sent for service, for the sake of those who shall inherit salvation?" (Heb 1:14).

Devotion to the angels dates far back in Judaism. It was nothing new to the first generation of Christians. After St. Peter was set free from prison by an angel (Acts 12:7-8), he went to the house of one Mary. When he knocked on the door and announced his presence, the reaction of those inside who thought him still in prison was to exclaim, "It is his angel" (Acts 12:15). The feast of the guardian angels on October 2 is among the most ancient in the Church. Many Church Fathers claim that each Christian has a guardian angel assigned to him. Most theologians agree that every person, even a non-Christian, has a guardian angel to help him or her.

God could have carried out his loving, fatherly providence without angelic assistance; however, he chose to employ them as cooperators in his plans for humanity. Angels do not intervene in human history except on the occasion of special needs.

They exercise a continual service by assisting people in the ordinary course of their lives, acting in a quiet, effective manner without external show. While grace is at hand to enable humanity to know and love God, the human mind falters and the will is weak: Who does not stand in need of the angels' aid? One of the earliest Christian documents states: "There are two angels in each person: one for righteousness and the other for evil. . . . The angel of righteousness is gentle and quiet, meek and peaceful. So, whenever this angel rises to your heart, he will at once start talking to you about righteousness, chastity, holiness, self-denial, and about every righteous deed and every glorious virtue. When all these things rise to your heart, it means that the angel of righteousness is with you" (*The Shepherd of Hermas*, mand. 6, 2).

In spite of the great perfection of their spiritual nature, further perfected by grace, the angels enjoy neither the infinite power nor wisdom of God. They cannot read the inner thoughts of men and women (cf. St. Thomas, *Summa Theologiae*, I, 57, 4 ad 3), and human beings have somehow to make known to them their needs and requests. In doing so, however, it suffices to address oneself mentally to the angels.

See: Devil and Evil Spirits; Guardian Angels.
Suggested Readings: CCC 328-336, 391-395. C. Lewis, *The Great Divorce*. M. Adler, *Angels*.

Dennis Helming

ANGLICANISM

Anglicanism is the theory of worship, belief, and practice that designates members of the Anglican Communion, which is composed of the Church of England and other similar churches throughout the world. In the United States, the Anglican Communion is referred to as the Episcopal Church in the United States.

In 1527, King Henry VIII proposed to divorce his wife, Catherine of Aragon. Failing to obtain papal support, Henry declared himself supreme head of the Church of England in 1534. Parliament encouraged him in his dissent, declaring that God in Sacred Scripture had not given any greater

jurisdiction in England to the Roman Pontiff than to any other foreign bishop.

Edward VI, Henry's son, witnessed the publication of the *Book of Common Prayer* in 1549 and 1552. A new ordinal — the book of ordination rites — was issued almost simultaneously and was noted especially for deleting, like the Lutheran text, any reference to the concept of a priesthood that offers sacrifice. The total break with Catholicism was made official in 1563 when Queen Elizabeth, Henry's daughter, promulgated the Thirty-Nine Articles obliging all British citizens, under severe penalties, to adhere to the Anglican Church.

A group of English settlers brought Episcopalianism to the United States when they landed at Chesapeake Bay on May 6, 1607. In 1789, the American Anglicans, now organized as the Protestant Episcopal Church, gathered in Philadelphia for its first General Convention. The following resolutions were then adopted: that the Protestant Episcopal Church should be free from all civil, ecclesiastical, and foreign control; that the ministry should consist of bishops, presbyters, and deacons; that the norms of church doctrine and practice should be formulated by representatives of both clergy and laity; that, unlike the Church of England, no powers should be granted to a general ecclesiastical convocation unless the individual state conventions could not adequately exercise certain powers; that there should be bishops in each state possessing seats in the General Convention.

**Principles of Anglicanism • In considering the principles of Anglicanism or Anglican theology, it is helpful to recall that the Anglican Communion attempts to combine the oftentimes divided "Catholic" and "Protestant" elements into a whole. Thus the Anglican Congress of 1954 declared the Anglican Communion to be "a fellowship of Churches at one and at the same time Catholic in seeking to do justice to the wholeness of Christian truth, in emphasizing continuity through the Episcopate and in retaining the historic Creeds and Sacraments of undivided Christendom; and Evangelical in its commission to proclaim the

Gospel and in its emphasis on personal faith in Jesus Christ as Savior."

The supreme authority in the Anglican Communion now resides in the General Synod of the Church, not in the British monarch as in times past. Both Parliament and the monarch enjoy legal governorship over the Church of England, which does not contravene the authority of the General Synod. The Archbishop of Canterbury is the symbolic head of the Anglican Communion; however, he has no power to enforce certain teaching or practice.

Tension exists within both the Anglican Communion and the Episcopal Church in the United States regarding doctrine and morality. The "high" parishes evidence an emphasis on the authority of the bishop, the structure of the church, sacramental worship, an elaborate liturgy, and the "Catholic tradition." The "low" parishes stress an evangelical flavor, maintaining the utmost importance of preaching the Gospel and a "personal," Calvinistic approach to religion. "Broad" parishes are ones where tolerance is asserted, the Christian tradition is paramount, and an affinity for "liberal" causes and values holds sway. The high parishes tend to uphold traditional Christian mores, while the broad parishes, and in some cases the low parishes, are most apt to accept current secular moral standards.

The Anglican Communion accepts Sacred Scripture as normative, the Apostles' and Nicene Creeds, the historic episcopate, and two of the seven sacraments — Baptism and the Lord's Supper — as being "ordained of Christ the Lord." Ideas concerning Jesus' presence in the Eucharist and concerning sacrifice vary greatly among Anglican parishes.

The validity of orders in the Anglican Communion had been a much-debated question in Catholic circles until Pope Leo XIII in the bull *Apostolicae Curae* (September 13, 1896) declared that Anglican orders are "null and void" because of defect in the ordination rite and in the intention of the ordaining bishops. It is true, however, that some Anglican bishops have been ordained by schismatic Old Catholic bishops and other bishops who have valid orders; thus these specific An-

glican bishops would also enjoy valid orders.

The so-called Branch Theory has found acceptance within the Anglican Communion, according to which three distinct churches — the Anglican, the Eastern Orthodox, and the Roman Catholic — comprise the true Church founded by Jesus Christ and, therefore, enjoy valid orders. While proponents acknowledge the differences among these churches, they argue that there also exists a unity among them, given their similar characteristics. The Catholic Church opposes this theory because it does not square with one of the essential marks of the Church, namely, oneness.

The English Oxford Movement of the nineteenth century had a profound impact within the Anglican Communion. Some of the clergy, especially among the younger ones, felt a deep yearning for the Church of Rome, and some did eventually leave the Anglican Communion for the Catholic Church. Prior to becoming a Roman Catholic in 1845, John Henry Newman, later a cardinal and now considered "venerable" by the Church, was one of the principal figures of the Oxford Movement, which also had influence in the United States.

Many issues and current developments affect the Anglican Communion today: the ordination of women; the role of religious communities; homosexuality; abortion; contraception; euthanasia; dissatisfaction among many Anglicans that has led some to join the Catholic Church; the continuing dialogue with the Catholic Church; etc. One may take as applicable to Anglicans the words of the *Catechism of the Catholic Church* when it says that those "who believe in Christ and have been properly baptized are put in a certain, although imperfect, communion with the Catholic Church" (838).

See: Baptism; Church, Membership in; Ecumenism; Holy Orders.

Suggested Readings: CCC 811-870. Vatican Council II, *Decree on Ecumenism, Unitatis Redintegratio.* J. Hardon, S.J., *The Protestant Churches of America.* W. Whalen, *Separated Brethren.*

Charles M. Mangan

ANIMALS

In the very first chapter of the Book of Genesis, the animals and all God's creation are examined by God and judged to be "very good" (Gn 1:31). The individual parts of creation, therefore, deserve our respect, and the integrity of creation as a whole calls for our attention, especially in light of the immense recent growth of human knowledge and technology and its impact on the environment. Animals occupy a special place in the nonhuman creation because they have senses, feel pain, and may possess simple forms of emotion. And in their own special way, the sea creatures, birds of the air, and wild and tame land animals proclaim the glory of God (cf. Dn 79-81).

The honor accorded human beings in their stewardship of creation requires that special attention be paid to the well-being of animals: "It is contrary to human dignity to cause animals to suffer or die needlessly" (CCC 2418). In the philosophy of St. Thomas Aquinas, who builds on the insight of the Greek philosopher Aristotle, human beings are thought of as rational animals. This means we share many characteristics with other animals but possess in addition a rational soul that enables us to know and choose right and wrong. Part of choosing what is right includes caring for animals in much the same way as we care for the more animal side of our own natures.

Christianity and Environmentalism • The Christian cares for animals, then, for both divine and human reasons. While Christian prudence also takes into account current environmentalist concerns about the treatment of animals, it differs from environmentalism in certain ways. For example, for some environmentalists maintaining biodiversity is an end in itself. The Christian view of creation supports that goal insofar as it can be achieved while respecting other moral demands.

The diversity of creation is valuable for other reasons than the pleasure it gives human beings. God created diverse species, and thus there are several reasons for their existence. In some instances, as we learn from Genesis, they exist for human use as well as pleasure. Advances in technology have made furs, skins, and animal products

less necessary than in the past, but there is no denying that, in the Christian view, human beings may use animals for food, clothing, and other needs. Furthermore, within reasonable limits, medical experimentation on animals to relieve human suffering is morally justifiable, since it is not just to give animals the degree of respect proper to human persons (CCC 2417-2418).

The Catholic Church has also taught that animals, through an analogy of being, tell us things about God and the spiritual life that we would find harder to imagine without concrete examples. In Exodus, for instance, God reminds the Israelites how he liberated them from slavery in Egypt: "I bore you on eagles' wings and brought you to myself" (Ex 19:4). Christ himself is referred to as the Lamb of God, not only because of his sacrifice on the cross for the forgiveness of sins, but also because he showed humility and docility to the will of the Father during his life on earth. In a different analogy, he becomes the Good Shepherd (Jn 10:11) who gives his life for his flock (the Church) and instructs St. Peter, "Feed my sheep" (Jn 21:16).

Animals may also represent evils. Though good in themselves, because God created them, they may lead us into error. Eve was deceived by the serpent in the Garden of Eden to do something God had explicitly forbidden. Christ reassures the Apostles, "What father among you, if his son asks for a fish, will instead of a fish give him a serpent?" (Lk 11:11). But even the evil serpent at times teaches a good: "Behold, I send you out as sheep in the midst of wolves; so be wise as serpents and innocent as doves" (Mt 10:16).

Pope John Paul II in the encyclical *The Hundredth Year*, *Centesimus Annus* (1991), reminds us that failure to see "in visible things the message of the invisible God who created them" stems from narrowing our vision to an impoverished consumerism and from failure to recall that we do not own creation, but are stewards of God's world. The same encyclical goes on to link disregard for the "natural habitats of the various animal species threatened with extinction" with a failure to "safeguard the moral conditions for an authentic 'human ecology' " (37-38). When man forgets his place in nature and his proper relation to other creatures, especially the animals, whose bodily existence he shares, he harms them as well as himself.

See: Creation; Environment; Stewardship.

Suggested Readings: CCC 2415-2418, 2457. John Paul II, *The Hundredth Year, Centesimus Annus*, 37-38. G. Grisez, *The Way of the Lord Jesus*, Vol. 2, *Living a Christian Life*, pp. 782-788.

Robert Royal

ANNULMENT

The term "annulment" is not exact. To annul implies to dissolve or rescind something that had really existed. A civil contract can be annulled, but not the covenant of marriage. Once a true marriage has been entered on and a real marital bond created, it can only be dissolved by death.

What can at times happen is that an *apparent* marriage was in fact never a true marital covenant, because some element essential to its constitution was missing from the start and therefore no marriage ever came into being. If this can be established, then justice demands that such a "marriage" be declared null, that is, never to have existed as a marriage at all. What the Church does in such cases is not to "annul," but to make a "declaration of nullity."

An apparent bond can be nonexistent or null for various reasons. These include objective factors, such as impediments (e.g., insufficient legal age, an existing married bond, etc.: see Canons 1083-1094); or fear induced by outside pressure that causes a person to consent to an unwanted marriage (Canon 1103). A bond could also be null because of subjective intentions, as in simulation (Canon 1101), when one (or both) of the parties excludes from his or her consent some essential element of marriage (e.g., openness to having children, the permanence of the bond, etc.), or in purposeful deceit (Canon 1098) about some personal quality objectively important to married life (such as concealment of the fact of being sterile). The

factor bringing about invalidity could also be unconscious, as when a person's psychic faculties are marked by some grave deficiency that makes him or her incapable of a free act of consent (Canon 1095).

The Role of Tribunals • In such cases, where there never was a real marriage at all, it would be unjust to hold the parties to a nonexisting bond. The matter is so important, however, that it requires a proper judicial investigation before a Church tribunal. The issue is put to the court in the form of a question: Is the nullity of this marriage — between X and Y — proved? To which the court, on the basis of the evidence gathered, answers affirmatively or negatively.

A single declaration of nullity is not sufficient. It must be confirmed by a higher court before the parties are held free from the former (apparent but invalid) bond and able to marry someone else. The "first instance" court and the "second instance" (appeal) court may give opposed decisions: say, one negative (against the nullity) and the other affirmative (in favor). Often — and automatically in some places, although not under rules operative in the United States — such cases go for a final decision to the Roman Rota, the highest appeal court of the Church. In fact, either of the parties can appeal directly to the Rota even after a first decision, whether affirmative or negative (Canon 1444).

Further, even if two concordant decisions have been given (for or against the bond), the case can always be reopened at a higher level, provided new and serious arguments are adduced or some clear indications of a possible miscarriage of justice exist (Canon 1644).

When a petition for a declaration of nullity is presented to a tribunal, it can happen that both parties favor the petition. Then normally only the petitioner will be assigned an advocate to plead his or her case. The "Defender of the Bond" is an official of the tribunal whose mission is to ensure that the arguments in favor of the validity of the marriage are not neglected; a party who opposes nullity can, however, also request or appoint an advocate. The Church takes special care to protect the "right of defense" of both parties. They must be properly informed of the grounds of nullity proposed, and allowed to give evidence and present witnesses. Each one personally (and not only his or her advocate) has a right, *before* any judgment is pronounced, to know the allegations or arguments put forward by the other side and the evidence of witnesses and experts (Canon 1598). Violation of this right invalidates the whole process and any subsequent declaration of nullity.

It is sometimes thought that pursuing a declaration of nullity is expensive, especially at the level of the Rota. This is not so. Several countries, including the United States, have an agreement with the Rota by which a sum (currently ranging from $300 to $850) to cover part of the rotal costs is paid by the diocese (not the parties). The petitioner (also the respondent, if he or she requests it) then gets the services of a rotal advocate whose fees are paid by the Rota. If a person chooses to appoint his or her own advocate, he or she will have to pay the advocate's fees, which may be high. Rotal advocates are so called because they are specially qualified to plead before the Roman Rota; they are not officials or employees of the Rota.

It is often said today that there are too many declarations of nullity. What is more certain is that there are too many broken marriages. Many of these are quite valid and therefore cannot justly be declared null. There lies the deeper problem: to keep such marriages, which began in love, from ending in failure. If the spouses pray, have recourse to the sacraments, and get sound advice, they can learn to be faithful to their free commitment to each other, to their children, to God. Canon law itself insists that before accepting a petition of nullity, whenever there seems any hope of success, the judge should try to persuade the couple to try again to make the marriage work (Canon 1678).

Grounds for Declarations of Nullity • As striking as the growth in declarations of nullity is the fact that almost all cases nowadays are pleaded and judged on the relatively new grounds of consensual incapacity: that is, that although the person intended a true marriage, he or she was not capable of real consent due to some serious defect

in his or her psychic faculties, which made it impossible (and not just difficult) for him or her to understand, freely choose, or actually carry out the essential obligations of the married state.

Since marriage is something most natural to men and women, incapacity for marrying is by any standard an extraordinary handicap. That is why only a *grave* psychic deficiency can incapacitate a person. This is clear from the terms of Canon 1095, which deals with these grounds of nullity, and from papal teaching, and is firmly established in rotal jurisprudence. In 1987, Pope John Paul II said to the Rota: "An argument for real incapacity can be entertained only in the presence of a *serious form of anomaly* which must substantially undermine the capacity of understanding and/or of willing of the contracting party."

Simple immaturity, which is not gravely abnormal for the age at which a person married, offers no argument for consensual incapacity. An equally important point, specifically stated in Canon 1095, is that the psychic anomaly in question must incapacitate a person for the *essential* obligations of marriage. Certain psychic disorders, such a claustrophobia, agoraphobia, etc., even if present in a severe degree, no doubt make married life (just as social life) more difficult; but they cannot be said to relate to any essential constitutional obligation involved in marriage.

It must further be shown that the anomaly was present at the moment of consent. A psychic disorder originating after marriage cannot invalidate the consent already validly given. The fidelity promised at consent — in good times and in bad — also covers the possibility of ensuing psychic illness. The healthier partner has the obligation to be a faithful support for the person suffering the disorder, and the latter has the right to that fidelity.

See: Divorce; Marriage, Goods of; Indissolubility of Marriage; Marriage; Marriage, Sacrament of.

Suggested Readings: CCC 1629. G. Grisez, *The Way of the Lord Jesus*, Vol. 2, *Living a Christian Life*, pp. 587-588.

Cormac Burke

ANOINTING OF THE SICK

The question of illness is one of the most pressing in life. Each sickness that we face is a small death, a reminder of not only our frailty but our mortality. As the *Catechism of the Catholic Church* puts it, "Every illness can make us glimpse death" (1500). The presence of evil in the world has perplexed, confounded, and even angered humanity from the beginning. Sickness and death are a scandal; they are the enemies of our natural happiness.

Disease and death are not moral evils, but they are the result of moral evil, of the first (or original) sin committed by Adam and Eve. Sin has such a disruptive influence in the world that its consequences are not simply spiritual, but physical as well. Sickness and death are two of these consequences. St. Paul tells us in Romans 5:12 that "sin came into the world through one man and death through sin." The *Catechism of the Catholic Church* notes, "It is the experience of Israel that illness is mysteriously linked to sin and evil" (1502).

The physical evils of sickness and death offend human consciousness because we have a deep sense that things ought to be otherwise, even more so because it is often not the sin of the one who suffers that has caused his suffering. God's original plan for us did not include disease and death, and that original state in some measure haunts every human psyche. Some claim that death is natural and should be greeted as a friend, but the natural inevitably fails to satisfy the only one of God's creatures that longs for the supernatural.

God always draws good out of evil, and so it is that our sense of loss of original integrity — physical and spiritual — often prompts us to seek that which we have lost. In short, we search for salvation from sin and death. Such is the natural root of the Messianic longing of the people of Israel. Faith in the God of the patriarchs and prophets who has the power to heal (cf. Ex 15:26) led Israel to hope for the Messianic era when "no inhabitant will say, 'I am sick,' " and "the people who dwell there will be forgiven their iniquity" (Is 33:24). Jesus appears to aim precisely at fulfilling the Old Testament Messianic expectations

and announces the coming of the kingdom of God with concomitant healings. (Cf. Is 29:18-19, 35:5-6, 61:1; Mt 11:5-6; Lk 7:16, 20-23.)

Healing in Jesus' Ministry • Just as the Messianic expectations of Israel included expected signs of physical healing, so did Jesus' announcement of the kingdom include healing (Mt 11:2-6). In like manner, the sacramental liturgy of the Church, which extends the dimensions of Christ's Incarnation (and so also his kingdom) through space and time, attends to the healing of bodies and souls as a sign that God still dwells with his people (cf. Mk 16:17-18; Mt 28:20; Rv 21:1-4). In this way, Christ brings the human story full circle, as the new Adam who brings righteousness and life to the whole human family, in distinction to the first Adam who introduced sin and death into the human condition (Rom 5:17).

It is significant that the artwork chosen to adorn the first page of that section of the *Catechism* that treats of the sacraments is a fresco from the catacombs portraying, from Mark 5:25-34, the healing of the woman with a hemorrhage. This suggests that the whole of the Church's sacramental life is aimed at healing the world of the evil of sin and its effects. To deny, as do many Protestant denominations, that the sacraments fulfill the will of God in healing us of sin and its effects is, in a very real way, to deny that the Messianic kingdom has been established by Christ. The sacramental grace that heals, elevates, and perfects our fallen human nature (in body and spirit) is one of its clearest signs. It ought to be said, however, that, although sickness does not disappear after Christ's coming, healing continues to be a sign in the present of the fullness of the coming of the kingdom in heaven.

In the sacraments that Christ has given to his Church, he seeks to perfect to the fullest degree possible every part of human life. He is Emmanuel, the God who is with us from birth to death in the sacraments. Cyprian Vagaggini states that "in the liturgy it is as much the body as it is the soul that is actor and beneficiary, each according to its own natural exigencies and potentialities, in the substantial unity of the human being." He goes on to quote in support the potent phrase from Tertullian, "the flesh is the hinge of salvation" (*Theological Dimensions of the Liturgy*, pp. 312, 316). In the sacrament of the Anointing of the Sick, Christ is with us in illness and death and makes them, like his own suffering and death, an avenue to sanctity and life eternal.

The Sacrament of Anointing • In the old rite of Anointing, called Extreme Unction, or last anointing, this ministering to body and soul as a unity was evident in the five anointings of the senses that recalled the anointings at Baptism. This echo of the baptismal rite also reinforced the connection between sin and sickness and the need for strengthening grace to combat evil from the beginning to the end of Christian life. A similar point is made in the *Catechism of the Catholic Church*, which draws attention to a symmetry between the initiation rites and the "last rites" of the Church: "Thus, just as the sacraments of Baptism, Confirmation, and the Eucharist form a unity called 'the sacraments of Christian initiation,' so too it can be said that Penance, the Anointing of the Sick and the Eucharist as viaticum constitute at the end of Christian life 'the sacraments that prepare for our heavenly homeland' or the sacraments that complete the earthly pilgrimage" (1525).

This statement closes out the section on the sacrament of Anointing of the Sick and points up the fact that the sacramental life of the Church is intended to touch and heal the whole of human life. In this sense, the sacrament of Anointing of the Sick could be seen as almost emblematic of Catholic sacramental life, for that healing which is intended by all the sacraments is not only signified and effected by this sacrament but explicitly spoken of as such. (Cf. Vatican Council II, *Constitution on the Sacred Liturgy, Sacrosanctum Concilium*, 5.)

Anointing of the Sick shows in perhaps a clearer way than any of the sacraments that the liturgy of the Church addresses the whole of the human person, body and soul. The unity of body and soul, the connection between sin and sickness, and the alternate goods of repentance and life are expressed implicitly in the declaration from

Mark's Gospel that shows at least an apostolic origin for anointing the sick for the bestowal of God's grace: "So they went out and preached that men should repent. And they cast out many demons, and anointed with oil many that were sick and healed them" (6:12-13; cf. Mk 2:5-12). While this would not have been the sacrament as such, the Council of Trent declares that the action of the Twelve, who are sent out by Jesus, points to the later institution of the sacrament of the Anointing of the Sick by the same Lord. As is the case with all the sacraments, Anointing is prefigured (Mk 6:12-13) as a sign that "the kingdom of God is at hand" (Mk 1:15) and in preparation for its actual later institution by Christ.

The clearest scriptural warrant for the Anointing of the Sick is found in James 5:14-15: "Is there any among you sick? Let him call for the elders [*presbyteros*] of the church, and let them pray over him, anointing him with oil in the name of the Lord; and the prayer of faith will save the sick man, and the Lord will raise him up; and if he has committed any sins, he will be forgiven." The Council of Trent, in pronouncing on the institution of this sacrament by Christ, cites this passage and points out that the proper matter, form, minister, and effect of the sacrament are enunciated therein. To forestall any claim that the sacrament was introduced by the Apostles, Trent and the subsequent *Roman Catechism* both cite Mark 6:12-13 as proof that anointing with oil for healing must have had its root in Christ's commission and that James was only attesting to that commission.

References to the sacrament in the writings of Christian antiquity are few but they are there. Citations from the third and fourth centuries are unclear as to what exactly is being described. The character of the sacrament as a healing of soul as well as body may account for some of the lack of clarity, but James 5:14-15 is cited in several of the half-dozen or so references. St. John Chrysostom in the late fourth century makes a clear reference to the sacrament in the context of a discussion of the powers of the priesthood, and Pope Innocent I makes a certain declaration about the sacrament of Anointing in his Letter to Decentius in 416.

The sacrament of the Anointing of the Sick, when formerly called Extreme Unction and administered only as the last of the "last rites," had come to be seen as a sign of impending death, and as such, was not always as welcomed as it should have been. This conception of Anointing as the last sacramental act of Christian life was expressed by the order in which the last rites were administered from the Scholastic period until our own: Penance, Viaticum, and Anointing. Modern reforms have restored the ancient order of Penance, Anointing, and Viaticum, and so it is that the *Catechism of the Catholic Church* calls Viaticum "the sacrament of passing over from death to life" (1524).

The Revised Rite • The rites of the sacrament were revised in 1972 with the promulgation of the apostolic constitution *Sacram Unctionem Infirmorum*, in conformity with the expressed will of the Second Vatican Council that they be brought into greater conformity with the ancient practice of the Church (cf. *Sacrosanctum Concilium*, 73-75). Evidence suggests that in the early Church Anointing of the Sick was administered more commonly to supply the grace needed to those who were struggling with serious illness. Even though the priestly administration of the sacrament was the norm from the beginning, as suggested in James 5:14-15, blessed olive oil was also used by the laity in much the same way that holy water (a sacramental) is used today to invite God's grace into a person or place.

The common ancient practice, preserved today in the blessing of oils in the Chrism Mass, required that oils be blessed by the bishop. The oils were understood as bearing a continuing presence of divine power, which was discussed in language akin to that applied to the Real Presence in the Eucharist. It is not surprising, therefore, that anointings by the laity would be practiced in a manner similar to the way in which the Eucharist was borne even by the laity to the sick, those in prison, and others who could not be present for the celebration of the sacrament. The practice of lay anointing finally fell into disuse in the Middle Ages.

The Church today encourages the celebration of this sacrament when one of the faithful "begins to be in danger of death from sickness or old age" (*Sacrosanctum Concilium,* 73). If one recovers, the sacrament may be administered again later. Someone who is ill may be anointed before a serious operation, as may the elderly when they become notably weakened with the advance of age.

This sacrament is often paired with Penance and Reconciliation and the reception of the Eucharist, either in the context of a Mass or as Viaticum, which is the last reception of Holy Communion before death. The term "viaticum" comes from the two Latin words *via tecum*, roughly meaning, "with you on the way." In this last sacrament, Christ comes to accompany us on the journey through death to heaven.

Both Eucharist and Anointing are referred to as sacraments of the living, by which is meant that they should be received in a state of grace (without serious, or mortal, sin on the soul). It is for this reason that Penance is often received before Anointing. Anointing itself, however, may bring the complete remission of all guilt and punishment for sin, even without a confession of sins, if true sorrow for sin is present in the soul and one is unable to make a complete, integral confession because of infirmity. It is understood, however, that if one should recover after reception of the sacrament of Anointing, formal Reconciliation will be sought and a full confession of serious (mortal) sins made.

The matter of the sacrament consists of an anointing with blessed olive oil. This oil is solemnly blessed by the bishop at the Chrism Mass, but a priest may bless oil within the sacrament if none of the Oil of the Infirm is otherwise available. The priest or bishop who administers the sacrament first lays his hands on the head of the sick person as an *epiclesis,* or invoking of the Spirit, and prays silently. Then he says the words, "Through this holy anointing may the Lord in his love and mercy help you with the grace of the Holy Spirit," while anointing with an inscribed cross on the forehead. The person responds,

"Amen." The minister then says, "May the Lord who frees you from sin save you and raise you up," while anointing the palms of the hands with an inscribed cross. Again the person responds, "Amen."

The graces that the sacrament supplies are comfort, peace, and the courage to face the challenges of frailty and sickness and to resist temptations to discouragement and despair. Christ grants spiritual healing and may even grant bodily healing, if this be his will, through the Anointing. Even when the sacrament was administered exclusively at the point of death, "the liturgy has never failed to beg the Lord that the sick person may recover his health if it would be conducive to his salvation" (CCC 1512).

The Church is blessed also by the reception of this sacrament by the sick in the manner suggested by St. Paul: "I rejoice in my sufferings for your sake, and in my flesh I complete what is lacking in Christ's afflictions for the sake of his body, that is, the church" (Col 1:24). In this sacrament Christ fulfills that word which he spoke, "I was sick and you visited me" (Mt 25:36). The Church is built up when her members are conformed more closely to Christ by receiving their suffering as a share in his. It may seem odd to refer to the sufferings of her members as graces for the Church, but witnesses abound to the beauty of soul represented by those who have borne even unbelievably difficult trials in union with their suffering Savior. In this way, the sick and the suffering participate in a mysterious way in the building up of the Body of Christ.

See: Burial, Christian; Death; Eucharist; Last Rites; Last Things; Penance and Reconciliation, Sacrament of; Sacrament; Sacraments of the Living; Suffering in Christian Life; Viaticum.

Suggested Readings: CCC 1499-1532. Code of Canon Law, 998-1007. Vatican Council II, *Constitution on the Sacred Liturgy, Sacrosanctum Concilium,* 5, 73-75. Paul VI, *Apostolic Constitution on the Sacrament of the Anointing of the Sick, Sacram Unctionem Infirmorum.* Sacred Congregation for Divine Worship, *Introduction to the Rite of Anointing and to the Pastoral Care of the Sick, Hominum Dolores.* N. Halligan, O.P., *The Sacraments and Their Celebration.*

Sean Innerst

ANTICHRIST

According to the mind of the Church, and in the light of the New Testament revelation, the Antichrist is anyone who knowingly stands athwart the truth about Christ, culpably refusing to accept the divine origin of his being (cf. 1 Jn 2:22) or the fact of his scandalous enfleshment as man (cf. 2 Jn 7). St. Paul, for example (cf. 2 Thes 2:3-10), predicts the coming of "the lawless one," complete with "pretended signs and wonders," whom the Lord Jesus will yet "slay with the breath of his mouth" and will utterly destroy in the day of his judgment.

This "son of perdition," as Paul calls him, "who opposes and exalts himself against every so-called god or object of worship . . . proclaiming himself to be God," is in fact the very one whose expected appearance in the last days, before the triumphant return of Christ, the Church warns us about in the *Catechism of the Catholic Church* (675). Holding out the pretense of a solution to man's predicament, which can only come "at the price of apostasy from the truth," the Antichrist will thus embody "the supreme religious deception . . . a pseudo-messianism by which man glorifies himself in place of God and of his Messiah come in the flesh."

Notwithstanding the fact that many in the early Church supposed the arrival of the Antichrist to be soon, inasmuch as they believed the demand that the Gospel be preached to the world was already fulfilled in the time of the Apostles (thus, the end could not be far off), it is not possible to date the time of the Antichrist's deception. Rather, the signs relating to the end (e.g., the appearance of false messiahs, war, earthquake, famine, and persecution of Christians as reported in Mark 13) suggest that the time of the end is ever-present. Thus, one must always observe that state of vigilance that Christ himself enjoined upon his followers, none of whom could know the hour of his appointed return: "Watch therefore — for you do not know when the master of the house will come. . . . And what I say to you I say to all: Watch" (Mk 13:35-37).

See: Ascension and Parousia; Eschaton; Millenarianism.

APOCRYPHA

The technical term apocrypha refers to forms of Jewish or Christian literature that falsely claim inspired authorship by an important Old Testament figure (e.g., Abraham, Isaiah) or New Testament Apostle, and therefore claim special privilege and status within either Judaism or Christianity. The term originates with a Greek word meaning "secret" or "hidden." In effect, apocryphal literature claims to have secret knowledge that Moses or another key Old Testament personage or Jesus did not give to those who were spiritually unable to receive it; rather, the teaching was passed on to the spiritually advanced, the spiritually mature, the gifted ones. The category "apocrypha" thus implies that the narratives transmit a revelation that is "truer" or "purer" — far superior to the canonical scriptures accepted by the main group of believers.

The purpose of apocryphal literature, against this background, is to clarify the content of the canonically approved books in light of a sect's new questions. The "new" revelation taught by a given sect is expressed in its apocryphal literature, which subsequently justifies its existence as a group. Both Old and New Testament apocryphal literature exists in a great variety of literary forms: historical narratives, apocalyptic visions, didactic sayings, gospels, acts, and epistles. Old and New Testament apocryphal literature is so vast as to constitute its own area of specialization within the field of biblical studies. Old Testament apocryphal works began circulating as early as 550 B.C., or at least their proliferation increases after this point. New Testament apocryphal literature circulated very early; it slowly died out as the mainstream Church discerned the authentic and inspired body of Scripture, over against that not inspired by the Holy Spirit.

See: Canon of Scripture; Divine Revelation; Gnosticism; Inerrancy; Inspiration; New Covenant; New Testament; Old Covenant; Old Testament; Sacred Scripture.

APOSTASY

Christ wishes us to be in communion with him and one another through his Church. There are, however, various ways in which persons can deliberately separate themselves from union with the Church.

The schismatic believes in the truth that Christ has revealed, but does not accept his will coming to us through the principal authority (held by the successors of St. Peter) instituted by Christ so as to maintain the communion of his followers. The separation of the heretic is much greater, though still partial. He or she deliberately rejects some doctrine or doctrines taught by the Church in Christ's name, as part of the deposit of faith entrusted to her.

The apostate repudiates the faith in its entirety.

Many people today have "fallen away" from the faith. Usually this is due to moral weakness; to letting oneself be influenced by bad example; to not clarifying doubts (faith being a virtue, temptations — doubts — are bound to come and need to be rejected); to a failure to read explanations of Church teaching that accurately present its content and show its beauty (every Catholic assailed by doubt should consult the *Catechism of the Catholic Church*, for instance), etc.

These people are not yet apostates, for their attitude is one of apparent indifference rather than deliberate and total rejection. Such persons very often retain a longing to find God, but have to be helped over difficulties or prejudices before there is any possibility of their returning to the fold of Christ. The attitude of practicing Catholics toward them can be decisive; it must show the affectionate concern of one whose brother or sister has had the misfortune to leave the family, and whose constant prayer is that he or she will find the way back home.

See: Church, Membership in; Faith, Act of;

Faith, Virtue of; Heresy; Religion, Virtue of; Schism.

APOSTOLATE

In essence the term "apostolate" refers to the mission of the Church to carry on the redemptive work of Jesus Christ. He sent his Apostles (the word "apostle" comes from the Greek word meaning "to be sent") into the whole world to "make disciples of all nations, baptizing them in the name of the Father and of the Son and of the Holy Spirit, teaching them to observe all that I have commanded you" (Mt 28:19-20). Consequently, the whole Church, the "pillar and bulwark of the truth" (1 Tm 3:15), "built upon the foundation of the apostles" (Eph 2:20), "is apostolic, in that she remains, through the successors of St. Peter and the other Apostles, in communion of faith and life with her origin: and in that she is 'sent out' into the whole world" (CCC 863).

The source of the apostolate is thus Christ himself, who was sent by the Father to redeem all men and, indeed, the whole of creation and to send his Spirit to sanctify all men, to make them "new" creatures (cf. Vatican Council II, *Decree on the Apostolate of the Laity, Apostolicam Actuositatem*, 3-4; CCC 864). The apostolate is rooted in the vocation of *all* Christians to holiness and to participation in the redemptive work of Christ. It flows from their identity, freely given to them and accepted by them through Baptism (cf. Vatican Council II, *Dogmatic Constitution on the Church, Lumen Gentium*, 31; Pope John Paul II, encyclical *The Splendor of Truth, Veritatis Splendor*, 66, and apostolic exhortation *The Lay Members of Christ's Faithful People, Christifideles Laici*, 10) as members of the divine family, children of God, and brothers and sisters of Christ who share in his threefold office as prophet, priest, and king (cf. *Lumen Gentium*, 31) and who are called to participate "in the salvific mission of the Church" (*Lumen Gentium*, 33). It is nourished by the sacraments, in particular the Eucharist, and the liturgy (*Lumen Gentium*, 33, 35; *Constitution on the Sacred Liturgy,*

Sacrosanctum Concilium, 10; *Apostolicam Actuositatem*, 3, 4, 10).

"The apostolate of the Church . . . and of each of her members, aims primarily at announcing to the world by word and action the message of Christ and communicating to it the grace of Christ" (*Apostolicam Actuositatem*, 6). "The work of Christ's redemption" — and carrying on that work is precisely what apostolate means — "concerns essentially the salvation of men; it takes in also, however, the renewal of the whole temporal order. The mission of the Church, therefore, is not only to bring men the message and grace of Christ but also to permeate and improve the whole range of the temporal"(*Apostolicam Actuositatem*, 5). In short, the goal of the apostolate is the evangelization and sanctification of all men and the renewal of all things in Christ the Redeemer.

"The Church," the Fathers of Vatican Council II remind us, "was founded to spread the kingdom of Christ over all the earth for the glory of God the Father, to make all men partakers in redemption and salvation, and through them to establish the right relationship of the entire world to Christ. Every activity of the Mystical Body with this in view goes by the name of the 'apostolate'; *the Church exercises it through all its members, though in different ways*" (*Apostolicam Actuositatem*, 2; emphasis added). First, we shall consider the way in which the hierarchy, that is, the College of Bishops, the successors of the Apostles, exercises apostolate under the headship and leadership of the Roman Pontiff, the successor of Peter, the prince of the Apostles. Then we shall consider the apostolate of priests, of religious, and of the lay faithful.

The Apostolate of the Hierarchy • The Church, which is the People of God, is by God's will hierarchically structured: "In order to shepherd the People of God and to increase its numbers without cease, Christ the Lord set up in his Church a variety of offices which aim at the good of the whole body" (*Lumen Gentium*, 18). Jesus himself chose his Apostles, whom he constituted in the form of a college, at the head of which he placed Peter. Since the divine mission entrusted by Christ to the Apostles was to last until the end of time (cf. Mt 28:20; *Lumen Gentium*, 20), the Apostles in turn handed over to their successors, the bishops, "with priests and deacons as helpers," "the charge of the community, presiding in God's stead over the flock of which they are the shepherds in that they are teachers of doctrine, ministers of sacred worship, and holders of office in government" (*Lumen Gentium*, 20). The College of Bishops under the headship of the Roman Pontiff — for this body has no authority at all unless united with him (cf. *Lumen Gentium*, 22) — constitutes the hierarchy of the Church and exercises its apostolate by teaching doctrine, ministering the sacraments, and governing the faithful.

The hierarchy exercises its apostolate, first of all, through its Magisterium, or teaching office, a more-than-human authority invested in the College of Bishops to carry on the mission of the Apostles to proclaim the truths of salvation in Christ's name (cf. *Lumen Gentium*, 20; *Dogmatic Constitution on Divine Revelation, Dei Verbum*, 10). Christ chose the Apostles to receive God's saving Revelation; but this Revelation was not meant for them alone but for all men and women of every age, to whom Jesus sent them to teach his redeeming truth (cf. Mt 23:20). The apostolic preaching, through which the Revelation given by Jesus was communicated to the apostolic Church, was "to be preserved in a continuous line of succession until the end of time. Hence, the Apostles, in handing on what they themselves had received, warn the faithful to maintain the traditions which they had learned either by word of mouth or by letter (cf. 2 Thes 2:15); and they warn the faithful to fight hard for the faith that had been handed on to them once and for all (cf. Jude 3). What was handed on by the Apostles comprises *everything that serves to make the People of God live their lives in holiness and increase their faith. In this way the Church, in her doctrine, life, and worship, perpetuates and transmits to every generation all that she herself is, all that she believes*" (*Dei Verbum*, 8; emphasis added).

Consequently, the College of Bishops under the headship of the Pope, the supreme teacher in the Church, primarily exercises the apostolate entrusted to it within the Church by teaching the saving truths of Revelation and the way to shape one's whole life in accord with these truths: "The bishops have by divine institution taken the place of the apostles as pastors of the Church, in such wise as whoever listens to them is listening to Christ and whoever despises them despises Christ and him who sent Christ (cf. Lk 10:16)" (*Lumen Gentium*, 20).

The members of the hierarchy also exercise their apostolate through their office as ministers of sacred worship. Although all baptized persons share in the universal priesthood of Christ, "the Lord also appointed certain men as ministers, in order that they might be united in one body in which 'all the members have not the same function' (Rom 12:4). These men were to hold in the community of the faithful the sacred power of Order, that of offering sacrifice and forgiving sins, and were to exercise the priestly office publicly on behalf of men in the name of Christ. Thus Christ sent the apostles as he himself had been sent by the Father, and then through the apostles made their successors, the bishops, sharers in his consecration and mission" (*Decree on the Ministry and Life of Priests, Presbyterorum Ordinis*, 2).

Finally, the members of the hierarchy fulfill their apostolate by governing or shepherding the people entrusted to them. The Roman Pontiff, as successor of Peter, the "rock" on which Christ founded his Church (cf. Mt 16:18), whose duty it was to strengthen his brothers in the faith (cf. Mt 16:16ff.; Jn 21:15ff.; Lk 22:32), has supreme authority in the Church's governance: He "has been granted by God supreme, full, immediate and universal power in the care of souls. As pastor of all the faithful his mission is to promote the common good of the universal Church and the particular good of all the churches" (*Decree on the Bishops' Pastoral Office in the Church, Christus Dominus*, 1).

But bishops have also "been designated by the Holy Spirit to take the place of the apostles as pastors of souls and, together with the Supreme Pontiff and subject to his authority, they are commissioned to perpetuate the work of Christ, the eternal Pastor" (*Christus Dominus*, 1). They thus "govern the particular churches assigned to them by their counsels, exhortations and example, but over and above that also by the authority and sacred power which indeed they exercise exclusively for the spiritual development of their flock in truth and holiness" (*Lumen Gentium*, 27). Although the Pope has primacy of jurisdiction over them, bishops "are not to be regarded as vicars of the Roman Pontiff; for they exercise the power which they possess in their own right and are called in the truest sense of the term prelates of the people whom they govern" (*Lumen Gentium*, 27). Zealous in promoting the sanctity of their clergy, their religious, and their laity "according to the vocation of each individual" (*Presbyterorum Ordinis*, 15), bishops are charged with encouraging and coordinating all forms of the apostolate within their dioceses (*Presbyterorum Ordinis*, 17).

The apostolate of the hierarchy, therefore, essentially consists in faithfully handing over to the whole People of God the saving truths of Revelation, that is, "everything that serves to make the People of God live their lives in holiness and increase their faith" (*Dei Verbum*, 8), in ministering the sacraments that nourish their new life in Christ, and in governing the Church.

The Apostolate of Priests • The threefold apostolic mission of the hierarchy — as the teachers, ministers, and shepherds of God's people — "was handed over in a subordinate degree to priests so that they might be appointed in the Order of the priesthood and be co-workers of the episcopal Order for the proper fulfillment of the apostolic mission that had been entrusted to it by Christ" (*Presbyterorum Ordinis*, 2).

The goal of the whole Church's apostolate, as has been seen, is the evangelization and sanctification of the entire human family, communicating to it the grace of Christ. "The principal means of bringing this about is the ministry of the word and of the sacraments," and this is "committed in a special way to the clergy" (*Apostolicam Actuositatem*, 6). Since all priests share with the

bishops the "one identical priesthood and ministry of Christ," bishops "will regard them as their indispensable helpers and advisers in the ministry and in the task of teaching, sanctifying, and shepherding the People of God" (*Presbyterorum Ordinis*, 7). It is in this that the apostolate of the clergy principally consists.

The Apostolate of Religious • Some of Christ's faithful, from the very beginning of the Church, are called to consecrate themselves to the Lord in a special way by freely dedicating themselves to God through the profession and practice of the evangelical counsels of celibate chastity, poverty, and obedience. Such persons are called "religious" (cf. *Decree on the Appropriate Renewal of the Religious Life, Perfectae Caritatis*, 1). "Religious life, as a consecration of the whole person, manifests in the Church the marvelous marriage established by God as a sign of the world to come" (Canon 607.1).

The apostolate of those called to the religious life is exercised on behalf of the entire Church. It is an apostolate that reminds us that we have not here a lasting city, for the religious way of life involves a separation of men and women from the world of secular affairs so that they can live, by anticipation, as it were, in the end time, offering themselves as a "sacrifice offered to God, so that their whole existence becomes a continuous worship of God in charity" (Canon 607.1).

There is a marvelous diversity of religious life within the Church. But all religious, that is, persons professing the evangelical counsels, "are under an obligation, in accordance with the particular vocation of each, to work zealously and diligently for the building up and growth of the whole Mystical Body of Christ and for the good of the particular churches. It is their duty to promote these objectives primarily by means of prayer, works of penance, and by the example of their lives" (*Christus Dominus*, 33; cf. *Perfectae Caritatis*, 1, 3, 8).

The Apostolate of the Lay Faithful • Pope, bishops, priests, and religious have, as has been seen, their special apostolate within the Church. But the lay faithful constitute the great majority of Christ's people. It is absolutely essential to recognize that the apostolate of the lay faithful is in no way "delegated" to them by the hierarchy, the clergy, or the religious. Their apostolate, which is unique and utterly indispensable in the Church (cf. especially *Lumen Gentium*, 31), is given to them personally by Christ himself, whose living members they become through Baptism, when they are made new creatures; when they are divinized and made members of the divine family, brothers and sisters of Jesus who can, with him, call God their Father.

The lay faithful are called to holiness and to participate fully in Christ's redemptive work, which is the essential task of the apostolate. In their own way they "share in the priestly, prophetic, and kingly office of Christ, and . . . carry on the mission of the whole Christian people in the Church and in the world" (*Lumen Gentium*, 33).

The laity exercise their apostolate both within the Church and in the world. Within the Church they properly carry out their apostolate in parishes, dioceses, and on the interdiocesan, national, and international levels (cf. *Apostolicam Actuositatem*, 10; *Christus Dominus*, 30) by engaging in catechetical instruction, liturgical worship (e.g., as lectors), and by involvement in the pastoral structure of the Church (e.g., as canonists), and so forth. However, the exercise by the lay faithful of their apostolate in ecclesial tasks must never lead to their clericalization. Pope John Paul II has forcefully made this point: "The various ministries, offices and roles that the lay faithful can legitimately fulfill in the liturgy, in the transmission of the faith, and in the pastoral structure of the Church, ought to be exercised *in conformity to their specific lay vocation*, which is different from that of the sacred ministry" (*Christifideles Laici*, 23).

But above all, as he insisted, in continuity with the teaching of Vatican Council II and Pope Paul VI (cf. apostolic exhortation *On Evangelization in the Modern World, Evangelii Nuntiandi*, 70), *the* proper place for the lay faithful to exercise their apostolate is *in the world* (cf. *Christifideles Laici*, 7, 10, 14, 17, 23). The key text here is

found in Vatican Council II's *Dogmatic Constitution on the Church, Lumen Gentium*: "Their secular character is proper and peculiar to the laity. . . . By reason of their special vocation, it belongs to the laity to seek the kingdom of God by engaging in temporal, affairs and directing them according to God's will. They live in the world, that is, they are engaged in each and every work and business of the earth and in the ordinary circumstances of social and family life which, as it were, constitute their very existence. There they are called by God that, being led by the spirit to the Gospel, they may contribute to the sanctification of the world, as from within like leaven, by fulfilling their own particular duties. Thus, especially by the witness of their life, resplendent in faith, hope, and charity, they must manifest Christ to others. It pertains to them in a special way so to illuminate and order all temporal things with which they are so closely associated that these may be effected and grow according to Christ and may be to the glory of the Creator and Redeemer" (31).

Precisely because laypeople work out their existence in the world, *"the 'world' thus becomes the place and means for the lay faithful to fulfill their Christian vocation"* (*Christifideles Laici*, 15; emphasis in original). The whole vocation of the lay faithful to holiness "implies that life according to the Spirit expresses itself in a particular way in their *involvement in temporal affairs* and in their *participation in earthly activities* (*Christifideles Laici*, 17; emphasis in original). It is through the lay faithful that Christ and his Church are made present in the world (cf. *Christifideles Laici*, 7). Consequently, their vocation to sanctify themselves and to sanctify the world "ought to be called an *essential and inseparable element of the new life of Baptism*. . . . [and be recognized as] *intimately connected to mission* and to the responsibility entrusted to the lay faithful in the Church" (*Christifideles Laici*, 17; emphasis in original).

The lay faithful must realize that their apostolate is not a part-time job, as it were, unrelated to what they do in their daily lives. Carrying out their responsibilities as husbands and wives, fathers and mothers, laborers, teachers, professionals of all sorts, etc., is an integral component of their apostolate. The Fathers of Vatican II insist: "It is a mistake to think that, because we have here no lasting city, but seek the city which is to come, we are entitled to shirk our earthly responsibilities; this is to forget that by our faith we are bound all the more to fulfill these responsibilities according to *the vocation of each one* (emphasis added; cf. 2 Thes 3:6-13; Eph 4:28). But it is no less mistaken to think that we may immerse ourselves in earthly activities as if these latter were utterly foreign to religion, and religion were nothing more than the fulfillment of acts of worship and the observance of a few moral obligations. One of the gravest errors of our time is the dichotomy between the faith which many profess and the practice of their daily lives. . . . Let there, then, be no such pernicious opposition between professional and social activity on the one hand and religious life on the other. . . . Let Christians . . . be proud of the opportunity to carry out their earthly activity in such a way as to integrate human, domestic, professional, scientific and technical enterprises with religious values, under whose supreme direction all things are ordered to the glory of God" (*Gaudium et Spes*, 43).

The fields of exercising the apostolate proper to the lay faithful are immense. Of particular importance is the apostolate exercised with the family, which is in truth a "domestic church" (cf. *Lumen Gentium*, 11; *Apostolicam Actuositatem*, 11; Pope John Paul II, apostolic exhortation on *The Christian Family in the Modern World, Familiaris Consortio*, 49-64). Today, moreover, when we are threatened by a "culture of death" (Pope John Paul II, encyclical *The Gospel of Life, Evangelium Vitae*, 7-24, [1995]), it is primarily the responsibility of the lay faithful, in exercising their apostolate, to build a "civilization of love" (cf. Pope John Paul II, *Letter to Families*), to make the home a "sanctuary of life" (cf. *Evangelium Vitae*, 92-94), and to proclaim to the world the inviolable dignity of the human person made in God's image and likeness and summoned, in Christ, to a life of holi-

ness and communion with the Divine Persons (cf. *Evangelium Vitae*, Ch. 4).

The apostolate of the lay faithful, who have the common vocation of all Christians to holiness and who, like all Christians, have each their own special vocation and indispensable role to play in carrying out Christ's redemptive work, demands of them that they seek to integrate *all they do* into their baptismal commitment to make up in their own lives what is lacking in Christ's (cf. Col 1:24). Their apostolate requires them to cleave to Christ and to shape their lives in accordance with the Sermon on the Mount, the "magna charta" of the Christian life (cf. *Veritatis Splendor*, 15), to live in *communion with Christ* every moment of every day (cf. *Veritatis Splendor*, 16), efficaciously mediating his redemptive love to the world in which they live their daily lives.

See: Baptism; Bishop; Confirmation; Consecrated Life; Evangelization; Holy Orders; Priesthood of the Faithful; Vocation.

Suggested Readings: CCC 863-865, 900, 905. Vatican Council II, *Dogmatic Constitution on the Church, Lumen Gentium*, 21, 31, 33-36, 41; *Decree on the Bishops' Pastoral Office in the Church, Christus Dominus*, especially 6, 17, 23, 25, 27, 30, 33-36, 38, 39; *Decree on the Appropriate Renewal of the Religious Life, Perfectae Caritatis*, especially 1, 3, 8, 9, 16, 18, 23; *Decree on the Apostolate of the Laity, Apostolicam Actuositatem; Decree on the Church's Missionary Activity, Ad Gentes*, especially 15, 18, 19, 21, 30, 41; *Decree on the Ministry and Life of Priests, Presbyterorum Ordinis*, especially 1, 2, 7, 8, 10; *Pastoral Constitution on the Church in the Modern World, Gaudium et Spes*, 43, 76. Paul VI, *On Evangelization in the Modern World, Evangelii Nuntiandi*, especially 6, 14, 15, 17, 18, 20-22, 24, 26, 28-37, 59-61, 66-73. John Paul II, *The Christian Family in the Modern World, Familiaris Consortio*, especially 49-64; *The Lay Members of Christ's Faithful People, Christifideles Laici; Letter to Families; The Gospel of Life, Evangelium Vitae*, especially Ch. 4. G. Grisez, *The Way of the Lord Jesus*, Vol. 1, *Christian Moral Principles*, pp. 551-572, 749-764; Vol. 2, *Living a Christian Life*, pp. 77-

130, 681-721; G. Grisez and R. Shaw, *Fulfillment in Christ*, pp. 262-275, 356-365. J. Maestri, *On the Theology of Work*. W. May, "Work, Theology of," in J. Dryer, ed., *The New Dictionary of Catholic Social Thought*. J. Boyle, Jr., "The Role of the Christian Family, Articles 17-27," W. May, "The Role of the Christian Family, Articles 49-58," and R. Levis, "The Role of the Christian Family, Articles 59-64" in M. Wrenn, ed., *Pope John Paul II and the Family*. S. Wyszynski, *All You Who Labor: Work and the Sanctification of Daily Life*.

William E. May

APOSTOLIC SUCCESSION

One of the cornerstones of Catholic ecclesiology is the doctrine of apostolic succession. Catholic understanding and expression of this truth often differentiate the Catholic understanding of the mystery of the Church from that of other Christians.

The Church has its origin in the sending of the Son by God the Father — in the "mission" of the Son: "When the time had fully come, God sent forth His Son" (Gal 4:4). The Son exercised a teaching, sanctifying, pastoral ministry — proclaiming the coming of God's kingdom, teaching a new way of life, effecting our reconciliation with the Father by his cross and Resurrection, and sending the Holy Spirit to call the new community, the Church, into being.

The Second Vatican Council tells us how this mission of Jesus was to be continued: "This sacred synod . . . teaches and declares . . . that Jesus Christ, the eternal pastor, set up the holy Church by entrusting the apostles with their mission as He Himself had been sent by the Father (cf. Jn 20:21). He willed that their successors, the bishops namely, should be the shepherds in His Church until the end of the world" (*Dogmatic Constitution on the Church, Lumen Gentium,* 18).

Thus the saving mission of Jesus, given by the Father, is perpetuated through history in the person of those who have received the apostolic office.

The Apostles themselves were concerned to choose and ordain successors to continue their work. In the Acts of the Apostles, Paul is seen instructing and praying with the leaders in the Ephesus Church: "Take heed to yourselves and to all the flock, in which the Holy Spirit has made you guardians" (Acts 20:28).

Similar concern is expressed in the Letters of Paul to Timothy and Titus, bishops of the early Church: "Do not neglect the gift you have, which was given you by prophetic utterance when the elders laid their hands upon you. . . . Take heed to yourself and to your teaching; hold to that, for by so doing, you will save both yourself and your hearers" (1 Tm 4:14, 16).

The Church expresses her faith in this reality again in the *Decree on the Pastoral Office of Bishops in the Church* of the Second Vatican Council: "The bishops, by virtue of their sacramental consecration and their hierarchical communion with the head of the college and its other members, are constituted members of the episcopal body. 'The order of bishops is the successor to the college of the apostles in their role as teachers and pastors, and in it the apostolic college is perpetuated' " (*Christus Dominus*, 4; quotation from *Lumen Gentium*, 3).

These truths are dramatically celebrated at the ordination of a bishop. At the central moment of that sacramental rite, all the attending bishops silently and dramatically, one by one, impose hands over the head of the bishop-elect, passing on the mission and power that has come down from the Father to the Son to the Apostles and their successors. Together, all the bishops then pray an ancient prayer of ordination that reminds us that the Holy Spirit is the source of this apostolic mission and authority: "Pour out upon this chosen one that power which is from you — the governing Spirit whom you gave to your beloved Son, Jesus Christ, the Spirit given by Him to the holy apostles, who founded the Church in every place."

Three Major Aspects of the Doctrine • Among others, three special aspects of apostolic succession in the mystery of the Church may be highlighted.

1. *The authoritative role of the bishops as*

teachers in the Church. The Second Vatican Council says: "Among the more important duties of bishops, that of preaching the Gospel has pride of place. For the bishops are heralds of the faith, who draw new disciples to Christ; they are authentic teachers, that is, teachers endowed with the authority of Christ, who preach the faith to the people assigned to them, the faith which is destined to inform their thinking and direct their conduct" (*Lumen Gentium*, 25).

It is the bishops' teaching office that builds up the Church as a community of faith. This aspect of their mission deserves priority over administrative and other tasks. The Apostles noted at the beginning, when facing competing demands: "We will devote ourselves to prayer and to the ministry of the word" (Acts 6:4).

2. *The sacramental role of bishops as "stewards of the mysteries of God"* (1 Cor 4:1). To the Apostles first, and through them to their successors, was entrusted the mystery of the Eucharist and the power to baptize and to forgive sins. These sacramental rites bring into the here and now the full power of Christ's paschal mystery and bring to each believer the grace of redemption. Here, in a supreme way, the apostolic succession of bishops continues the mission of Christ.

3. *The apostolic succession of the bishops manifests the mystery of the Church as both a visible institutional organization and a unified mystical communion, the Body of Christ.* The *Catechism of the Catholic Church* (815) teaches:

> The unity of the pilgrim Church is also assured by visible bonds of communion:
> — profession of one faith received from the Apostles;
> — common celebration of divine worship, especially of the sacraments;
> — apostolic succession through the sacrament of Holy Orders, maintaining the fraternal concord of God's family.

Unity and apostolicity are expressed through apostolic succession. Historically, through time, since the succession of the bishops in an unbroken chain links today's Church directly to the Apostles and Christ; and also here and now, since the necessary communion of every bishop with all members of the episcopal college and, above all, with the Roman Pontiff, the Bishop of Rome, symbolizes and effects the mystery of *communio* in the one Body of Christ.

In today's context, two further observations should be made about apostolic succession.

First, this concept places an emphasis on the "vertical" nature of the Church's divine mission, which is carried on in a special way by the bishops. This mission has a divine authority emanating from its direct share in the mission of Christ. The Apostles saw themselves first of all as servants of Christ (cf. 1 Cor l) and "ambassadors for Christ" (2 Cor 5:20).

In our times, when sociological, political, and democratic tendencies abound, it is relevant to recall that apostolic succession and those who hold it are not creatures or agents of the community but are invested with a divine mission, authority, and responsibility from Christ, to whom they are primarily accountable (cf. Jn 20:21). Pastoral charity will lead them to exercise this mission with exquisite sensitivity and care for their flock, but never in a way that compromises their teaching or responsibility.

Second, recent years have seen a wonderful resurgence of biblical awareness among Catholics. This could, however, lead to a *"sola scriptura"* attitude. *Sola scriptura* — "only Scripture" — was one of the slogans of the Protestant schism in the fifteenth century. It still lives, especially in evangelistic and fundamentalistic versions of Protestantism, where it signifies exclusive reliance on the Bible, at the expense of Tradition and the living Magisterium of the Church.

The *Catechism of the Catholic Church* (cf. 80-83) gives a timely corrective to this neo-biblicism by insisting on the living Apostolic Tradition as the chief place where Divine Revelation and truth are transmitted. The Catholic understanding of the Church, rooted in the idea of apostolic succession outlined here, sees the source of its faith and morals today as arising from the Spirit-filled Church and in the authoritative teaching of the successors of the Apostles — not in any written text alone. The Scriptures are a privileged, inspired, normative expression of this living Apostolic Tradition, but the Spirit continues to live and work in the Church, especially through the papal and episcopal Magisterium.

The *Catechism* notes: "In order that the full and living Gospel might always be preserved in the Church, the Apostles left bishops as their successors. They gave them their own position of teaching authority. Indeed, 'the apostolic preaching, which is expressed in a special way in the inspired books, was to be preserved in a continuous line of succession until the end of time' " (77; quotation from Vatican Council II, *Dogmatic Constitution on Divine Revelation, Dei Verbum,* 8).

From the beginning, the Church looked to this idea of a "living Apostolic Tradition," guaranteed by apostolic succession, in times of question, doubt, and error. A classic example is provided by St. Irenaeus (c. 130-c. 202), Bishop of Lyons in southern France, who, having to refute false teachings by the Gnostics, turned to the living Apostolic Tradition of the Church. He wrote: "It is possible, then, for everyone in any Church who may wish to know the truth to contemplate the tradition of the Apostles which has been made known throughout the whole world. And we are in a position to enumerate those who were instituted bishops by the Apostles, and their successors to our own times. . . . Since it would be too long to enumerate in such a volume as to the successions of all the churches, we point out the successions of the bishops of the greatest and most ancient church known to all, founded and organized at Rome by the two most glorious Apostles, Peter and Paul, that church which has the tradition and the faith which comes down to us after having been announced to men by the Apostles. For with this church, because of its superior origin, all churches must agree, that is, all the faithful in the whole world, and it is in her that the faithful everywhere have maintained the apostolic Tradition" (*Against Heresies,* Ch. 3).

Apostolic succession is the central and vital concept for Catholic ecclesiology. It is a Spirit-

given gift in the Church, preserving her authentic teaching and her visible communion.

See: Bishop; Church, Nature, Origin, and Structure of; Collegiality; Development of Doctrine; Divine Revelation; Faith of the Church; Heresy; Infallibility; Magisterium; Pope; Sacred Scripture; Sacred Tradition.

Suggested Readings: CCC 74-100, 857-862. Vatican Council II, *Dogmatic Constitution on the Church, Lumen Gentium,* 1-10; *Dogmatic Constitution on Divine Revelation, Dei Verbum,* 7-9. St. Francis de Sales, *The Catholic Controversy,* Pt. II, Art. II. J. Newman, *Apologia Pro Vita Sua.*

Francis D. Kelly

APPARITIONS

The words "apparition" and "vision" are sometimes used interchangeably, since they both designate the perception of a visible object. One can make a distinction, however, because apparition refers primarily to the object of one's perception, something that comes from outside the viewer; but vision refers primarily to the individual who perceives the apparition, the visionary. In either case the experience is classified in Christian spirituality as paranormal and extraordinary. Extraordinary phenomena such as apparitions and visions do not constitute an essential element of Christian holiness nor are they a proof of the holiness of the visionary. The reported apparition could just as readily be the result of hallucination or an unknown natural cause as the result of an authentically supernatural cause. And since it is not permissible simply to presume that a cause is supernatural, these cases require careful investigation and discernment.

There have always been reports of apparitions in the history of the Church, and the rapid and widespread news coverage in our day makes it appear that such cases are more numerous than ever before. But whether numerous or few in number, the Church has always been cautious in making a judgment concerning reported apparitions, and the investigation is usually a long, drawn-out process. For example, since 1830 the Church has approved seven apparitions of the Blessed Virgin Mary, all of which occurred in France. Numerous other reported apparitions, including ones in Lipa (Philippines), Akita (Japan), Medjugorje, Rwanda, and Egypt, are still under investigation at this writing. According to Father J.R. Rañada of the Archdiocesan Commission in Manila, there were 210 reported apparitions of the Blessed Virgin Mary between 1948 and 1971, but not one of them has as yet been recognized as authentic. In recent years there have been an unusually high number of reported apparitions in various parts of the world. It is safe to presume that very few of them are authentic.

Types of Apparition • There are three types of authentic apparitions of supernatural origin: corporeal, imaginative, and intellectual. The corporeal type is of two kinds: (1) the physical body or a likeness thereof is actually present and is seen with the bodily eyes, in which case the apparition would be visible to all bystanders as well; (2) an image is impressed on the eyes of the visionary but no external form is present; only the visionary sees the apparition. However, the first kind of a corporeal apparition does not mean that Christ, the Blessed Virgin, or a saint is actually present; the presumption is that the apparition is formed by rays of light, a vapor, or by the power of an angel.

An apparition is "imaginative" if the image is manifested by a phantasm on the screen of the imagination, but there is no corresponding external image. There are three possible explanations of the imaginative image: (1) it is the recall of a sense impression already received; (2) it is a new arrangement of phantasms previously acquired; or (3) it is an entirely new phantasm supernaturally infused. The imaginative apparition sometimes occurs during sleep, as Scripture relates concerning St. Joseph (cf. Mt 1:20-23, 2:13, 22), but if it occurs during waking hours, the individual is usually cast into a trance, lest other sensations cause confusion. The apparition may be a likeness of Christ, the Blessed Mother, a saint, or even one of the faithful departed.

The third type of apparition is intellectual, that is, a concept or idea supernaturally infused into the mind. The apparition may last for hours or even days, and it is accompanied by great certitude. St. John of the Cross, one of the greatest authorities on extraordinary mystical phenomena, has this to say about apparitions: "Though all these experiences may happen to the bodily senses in the way of God, we must never delight in them nor encourage them; rather, we must fly from them, without seeking to know whether their origin be good or evil. For, inasmuch as they are exterior and physical, the less is the likelihood of their being from God. That which properly and generally comes from God is a purely spiritual communication, wherein there is greater security and profit for the soul than through the senses, wherein there is usually much danger and delusion" (*Ascent of Mount Carmel*, Bk. II, Ch. 11).

Discernment of Apparitions • There are three possible causes of extraordinary or paranormal phenomena: God, the devil, and a natural cause. Therefore, one may not automatically presume that a reported vision or apparition is supernatural in origin. On the contrary, the presumption must always be that there is a natural explanation or else a diabolical power at work. Throughout the centuries the Church has established specific criteria for investigating extraordinary phenomena.

The bishop of the diocese in which the apparition is reported to have taken place has the authority and the serious obligation to begin the process of investigation. And since these reputed supernatural phenomena must be examined from various aspects, such as theological, psychological, pathological, and medical, the bishop normally sets up a commission composed of experts in those various fields.

First of all, it is necessary to obtain detailed information concerning the person who claims to have had a vision or revelation. Physical, emotional, and moral qualities of the individual are investigated in order to discern whether or not there is anything that would militate against the credibility of the reputed visionary. Second, the commission must determine whether the claims and reports of the apparition are consistent with the actual facts or whether the testimony is contradictory. Third, and very important, has the supposed apparition produced good spiritual fruits in the recipient and others? Finally, when the investigation is completed, the commission will submit one of three possible judgments to the bishop: (1) that the alleged apparition fulfills all the conditions for an authentic supernatural phenomenon — that is, it appears to be of divine origin; (2) that the alleged apparition is definitely not of supernatural origin and therefore must be presumed to have a natural or a diabolical cause; or (3) that there is not enough evidence to make a definite judgment and therefore the case must remain open as long as this uncertainty exists.

If the commission decides in favor of the supernatural origin of an apparition, the final decision will come from the Holy See. But even if the Church gives official recognition to an apparition, it remains on the level of a "private" revelation. And, as the *Catechism of the Catholic Church* points out, private revelations "do not belong . . . to the deposit of faith"; their role is to help people "live more fully by" Christ's definitive Revelation "in a certain period of history" (CCC 67). The faithful are not strictly bound to accept private revelations, although it would be somewhat irreverent not to honor the Church's approval.

See: Angels; Extraordinary Gifts; Marian Devotion; Mysticism; Private Revelation.

Suggested Readings: CCC 65-67. A. Poulain, *The Graces of Interior Prayer.* Gabriel of St. Mary Magdalen, *Visions and Revelations in the Spiritual Life.* S. Zimdars-Swartz, *Encountering Mary.*

Jordan Aumann, O.P.

ASCENSION AND PAROUSIA

The Gospels of Mark and Luke and the Acts of the Apostles report the mystery of the Lord's Ascension. The event closes the period of the Easter appearances. Luke's Gospel, considered in isolation, would seem to suggest that Jesus ascended into heaven on the very day of the Resurrection (cf. Lk 24:36-49); but if we read the entire account, we see that the evangelist wishes to synthesize the final events of Christ's life. He records further details in Acts, a completion of his Gospel, where he resumes the narrative in order to continue the history of the origins of the Church.

The witness of St. Luke makes it clear that the primitive tradition of the Church included a visible Ascension of the Lord, well separated in time from the Resurrection and not to be confused with the exaltation to heaven on Easter day. Luke describes the last departure of Christ, who had already ascended to his Father, come back several times to converse with his disciples, and now departs until the *parousia.* For Luke, the Ascension is important in relation to events still to take place: the sending of the Holy Spirit at Pentecost and the interval before the day of the final restoration (Acts 3:21). In Acts, the risen Lord explains that the period before the manifestation of the kingdom in the world is the time of the Holy Spirit and of the missionary Church (1:8).

Like the Easter appearances, the Ascension is only perceptible to the disciples who witness it. It is the final elevation of the risen One into the sphere of God; he is taken up into heavenly glory once and for all. Concluding the earthly deeds of Jesus, it also is the pledge of the final coming and its condition. It is the groundwork of the intermediate time of the Church, because it makes possible, and is the deciding cause of, the descent of the Holy Spirit, through whose coming the Gospel of the Resurrection reaches the human race, calling to conversion and offering remission of sins.

The "forty days" of Luke (Acts 1:3) correspond to the biblical symbolism of the number forty: a period of time sufficient for the attainment of the desired purpose. Time in relation to the risen Jesus undoubtedly is a different standard of measure from time as we experience it. The risen Christ is already beyond time in eternity. Inasmuch as he still operates in the world, however, the transcendent "now" is inserted into the time of the world. In the life of the Church, the kingdom is now, as it were, embryonically present.

"Meanings" of the Ascension • The first meaning of the Ascension is that Christ in his human nature passes to the state of glory with his Father and the Holy Spirit: The risen One enters the heavenly intimacy of God. This is signified by "the cloud" (Acts 1:9), a biblical sign of the divine presence. The Ascension is included in the mystery of the Incarnation as its concluding moment. As in the Incarnation he laid aside his glory as eternal Son, so in the Ascension he now receives back divine glory, which has its impact on his human nature and ours. Jesus spoke several times about his having to be lifted up — on the cross — so that believers might have eternal life (cf. Jn 3:14, 8:28, 12:32); and the lifting up on the cross is the special sign and definitive foretelling of this other "lifting up" by his ascending into heaven.

The second meaning of the Ascension is the beginning of the kingdom of the Messiah, which realizes the prophetic vision regarding the Son of Man in the Book of Daniel: "To him was given dominion and glory and kingdom that all peoples, nations, and languages should serve him: his dominion is an everlasting dominion, which shall not pass away, and his kingdom one that shall not be destroyed" (7:13-14). Christ's elevation to the right hand of the Father signifies his sharing as man in the power and authority of God. This sharing is manifested in the sending of the Paraclete, the Spirit of Truth, who brings about conversion of hearts (cf. Acts 2:37). In the power of the Spirit, the Apostles can now call Jesus Lord (cf. 1 Cor 12:3).

Jesus Christ is Lord because he possesses fullness of power in heaven and on earth. This is a kingly power "far above all rule and authority and power and dominion . . . he has put all things under his feet" (Eph 1:21-22). At the same time, it is priestly power, as the Letter to the Hebrews explains at length, commenting on Psalm 109 (110), 4: "You are a priest forever after the order of Melchizedek" (Heb 5:6). Christ's eternal priesthood implies the power to sanctify, so that he becomes "the source of salvation to all who obey him" (Heb 5:9). As Lord, too, Christ is Head of his Body, the Church. This is the central idea of the opening chapters of the Letters to the Ephesians and Colossians, for example: "He has put all things

under his feet and has made him the head over all things for the Church, which is his body, the fullness of him who fills all in all" (Eph 1:22). The redemption is the source of the authority that Christ, through the Holy Spirit, exercises over the Church. By an extension of the kingship conferred on him over the whole economy of salvation, Christ also is Lord of the entire universe. "He who descended is also he who ascended far above all the heavens, that he might fill all things" (Eph 4:10) (cf. 1 Cor 15:26; Vatican Council II, *Pastoral Constitution on the Church in the Modern World, Gaudium et Spes, 45*).

Finally, Christ is Lord of eternal life. He opens to humanity access to the Father's house by means of his cross and Resurrection. The Letter to the Hebrews assures us that Jesus Christ, the unique priest of the new and eternal covenant, "entered, not into a sanctuary made with hands . . . but into heaven itself, now to appear in the presence of God on our behalf" (9:24); "he entered . . . [through] his own blood, thus securing an eternal redemption" (9:12); and "When he had made purification for sins, he sat down at the right hand of the Majesty on high" (1:3). Jesus Christ goes to the Father's house to lead us there; without him, we could not enter. Now God himself is our "place" after this life, is the "last thing" of the creature. As Hans Urs von Balthasar tells us: "Gained, he is heaven; lost, he is hell; examining, he is judgment; purifying, he is purgatory." But this is God as he humbled himself to come to men, that is, in his Son Jesus Christ, who is the revelation of the Father, the Spirit, and himself, and therefore the essence of the last things.

The Second Coming • The full right to judge human actions and consciences definitively belongs to Christ as Redeemer of the world: The Father "has given all judgment to the Son" (Jn 5:22). He did not come to judge, however, but to save, to "give eternal life to all those you [the Father] have entrusted to him" (Jn 17:2).

The Ascension appearance to the Apostles is the starting point of the *parousia*. During the present time of the Church, the risen Lord returns in the Holy Spirit, who accomplishes the working out of the richness of the "time" of Christ. In the risen Lord, we might say, Resurrection and *parousia* coincide. For example, the account in Matthew 27 of events immediately following the death of Christ gives a vision of end-time events: earthquake, splitting of rocks, opening of graves, co-resurrection of many of the bodies of saints who had fallen asleep. The total realization of the kingdom of God in the glorious Christ is the manifestation of the Second Coming. "This Jesus who has been taken up from you into heaven shall so come, as you have seen him going into heaven" (Acts 1:11). Pope St. Leo the Great (died 461) comments: "By these words all the children of the Church were taught that they are to believe that Jesus will be seen coming again in that same body in which he ascended."

All this suggests that the *parousia* will prove to be more like Christ's Resurrection and Ascension than simply one more event in history, albeit an especially noteworthy one. Jesus turned aside questions about when it would occur because they reduced the Second Coming to an event simply within the range of time and space. Yet, since the Lord in his risen body intervenes constantly in time and history in his Church, his coming always *is* close at hand. This is the mystery of the kingdom "already now" but "not yet" in its full realization. Christ's words in the Gospel of John — "Now is the judgment" (Jn 12:31); "[T]he hour is coming, and now is, when the dead will hear the voice of the Son of God, and those who hear it will live" (Jn 5:25) — caution us against thinking of these realities as remote, far off. "I am coming soon" (Rv 22:20) — the Lord's last words in the last book of the New Testament — is more than a chronological statement; it implies the primacy of the "beyond-time" of Jesus over the time of the world. "Heaven and earth will pass but my words will not pass" (Mt 24:35; Mk 13:31; Lk 21:33). St. John Chrysostom (c. 349-407) says: "After the glory of his Ascension he will be seen as judge on the Last Day, and even now he judges all things, and at the end of the world he will come as judge of humanity." Consideration of the risen Lord and his present state supplies a qualitatively new way

of thinking about the events of the last time: Christ is Resurrection and Life (Jn 11:25) here and now for all who die in him, and he will raise us up on the last day (Jn 6:54). Love indeed is stronger than sin and death.

St. Leo the Great, preaching on the mystery of the Ascension in Rome in 450, declared: "Since the Ascension is our uplifting, and where the glory of our Head shall go, there the hope of the Body is called, let us then rejoice exceedingly with fitting joy. . . . For this day, not only are we made sure heirs of paradise, but in Christ we have already reached the heights of heaven, and obtained more abundant gifts through the ineffable favor of Christ than we lost through the envy of the devil."

See: Eschaton; Jesus Christ, God and Man; Jesus Christ, Life of; Judgment, General; Last Things; Redemption; Resurrection of Christ; Resurrection of the Dead.

Suggested Readings: CCC 659-682. Vatican Council II, *Pastoral Constitution on the Church in the Modern World, Gaudium et Spes,* 45. John Paul II, *Christological Catechesis.* Congregation for the Doctrine of the Faith, *Letter on Certain Questions Concerning Eschatology.* L. Bouyer, *The Eternal Son.* J. Ratzinger, *Introduction to Christianity,* pp. 237-251.

Richard Malone

ASSEMBLY, LITURGICAL

When the Israelites gathered at Mount Sinai to ratify the covenant with God and thus become a holy nation (Ex 19–24), that assembly (Hebrew *qahal,* Greek *ekklesia*) of the chosen people furnished the model, or pattern, for the assemblies of the new People of God, who form a kingly and priestly people (Vatican Council II, *Constitution on the Sacred Liturgy, Sacrosanctum Concilium,* 6; *Dogmatic Constitution on the Church, Lumen Gentium,* 10-11; CCC 1329, 1348).

In virtue of Baptism, all are one in Christ Jesus (Gal 3:28). Hence the assembly that most adequately manifests the nature of the Church, in the Eucharist, is one in which the faithful of every class, age, and condition are joined in a hierarchically arranged group (*Sacrosanctum Concilium*, 28), whose structure should become evident in the very arrangement of the celebration itself (*Sacrosanctum Concilium*, 14, 26). The liturgical assembly in which are gathered the living members of Christ's Mystical Body is authentically ecclesial in nature, especially the Eucharistic assembly, which, under the leadership of the priest representing the bishop, is a visible and efficacious sign of the Church, and, like her, is "one, holy, Catholic and apostolic."

Christ is always present in an assembly of the faithful gathered in his name (cf. Mt 18:20; *Sacrosanctum Concilium*, 7; Sacred Congregation of Rites, *Instruction on the Worship of the Eucharist, Eucharisticum Mysterium*, 9, 12, 16 [1967]). Currently, greater stress is laid upon the value of the assembly, or gathering of the People of God in celebration, as a sign and actual expression of the Church's faith. Through this assembly the Church appears before men and bears witness of her presence as a royal, prophetic, and priestly people, intent upon the worship of God and the renewal of the world. Celebration of the Eucharistic Liturgy in the assembly of the faithful is the chief means whereby the latter may express in their lives and manifest to others the mystery of Christ and the real nature of the true Church (*Sacrosanctum Concilium*, 2, 41).

See: Celebration, Liturgical; Church, Nature, Origin, and Structure of; Community Prayer; Liturgy.

ASSENT AND DISSENT

Faith is one of the theological virtues. Though the Christian Tradition describes the act of faith in different ways, an early definition comes from St. Augustine (354-430). In his book on the predestination of the saints (*De Praedestinatione Sanctorum*), Augustine said that "belief means to think with assent."

The term "assent" derives from the Latin verb *assentire*, which is linked etymologically to *sententia*, a word that means a way of thinking or a strong opinion. To assent, then, means to possess a clear and certain conception of one side of an implied contradiction: The person who assents to something affirms the truth of a proposition, for example, that Jesus Christ is true God and true man, so as to exclude the opposite position, namely, that Christ is only one or the other.

St. Thomas Aquinas elaborated on St. Augustine's definition. In his *Summa Theologiae*, Aquinas emphasizes that Christian belief encompasses an assent ordered to knowing what is true. "To ponder with assent is distinctive of the believer," he wrote, "for this is how the believer's act of belief is set off from all other acts of the mind concerned with the true or false" (2a2ae q. 2, art. 1). Believing assent describes the interior act of faith, that which occurs in both the heart and the mind of the person who accepts the truth of the Catholic faith. "The disciple of Christ must not only keep the faith and live on it, but also profess it, confidently bear witness to it, and spread it" (CCC 1816). The act of belief forms the basis for faith's outward expression, which we traditionally refer to as the "confession" of the faith. St. Thomas further teaches that both of these actions, which flow from the virtue of faith, express what the *Catechism of the Catholic Church*, citing Romans 1:5, calls "the obedience of faith" (143).

Adherence to God • Assent points to the absolute, religious firmness of belief in God's word. However, to think or ponder with assent does not mean that the act of faith only engages the mind. Following the clear witness of the New Testament and the theological tradition that develops out of it, the *Catechism* notes that "faith is first of all a personal adherence of man to God" (150). Still, faith begets knowledge, one "more certain than all human knowledge because it is founded on the very word of God who cannot lie" (157). God's veracity, or truthfulness, controls the theological virtue of faith in a way that distinguishes it from the virtues of theological hope and charity. So the Church has made her own the phrase of Aquinas: "Believing is an act of the intellect assenting to the divine truth by command of the will moved by God through grace" (*Summa Theologiae*, 2a2ae,

q. 2, art. 9; cited in Vatican Council I, *Dei Filius,* 3, and in CCC 155).

As Christian believers, we accept as conclusive what the true God has revealed to us. The communication of divine truth occurs in a series of historical acts wherein God has spoken to mankind, first through the patriarchs and prophets of the Old Law and now, definitively, in Christ, his "Son, whom he appointed heir of all things, through whom also he created the world" (Heb 1:2).

Because Christ, the Word made Flesh, completes the work of Revelation (cf. Vatican Council II, *Dogmatic Constitution on Divine Revelation, Dei Verbum,* 4), Christians recognize that faith entails "a free assent to the whole truth that God has revealed" (CCC 150). In other words, Christian faith is not contentless; indeed, it requires an assent to a very specific content, which expresses the economy of salvation that God has chosen to reveal. For this reason, heresy, which is a kind of infidelity, entails choosing among the ordinances of faith. The heretic, "though he intends to assent to Christ, fails in his choice of the things involved in that assent, because he chooses, not what Christ really bequeathed, but what his own mind suggests" (*Summa Theologiae,* 2a2ae, q. 11, art. 1).

Because the communion of faith requires the unity of truth, "in the Christian faith, knowledge and life, truth and existence are intrinsically connected" (Congregation for the Doctrine of the Faith, *Instruction on the Ecclesial Vocation of the Theologian,* 1 [1990]). So the Church wisely specifies for her members different degrees of assent appropriate for different levels of teaching proposed by the Magisterium.

Since the virtue of faith unites the believer immediately to God, the assent of theological faith is required whenever the ordinary and universal Magisterium proposes for belief a teaching of faith that is divinely revealed. Other truths, even if not divinely revealed, can still be proposed by the Magisterium in a definitive way. As related to the assent of faith, these truths must be firmly accepted and held. At other times, the Magisterium teaches truths that help us better to understand God's Revelation, by making explicit its content, or recalling that some teaching is in conformity with the truths of faith, or by guarding against ideas that are incompatible with these truths. In such matters, the Church asks for the religious submission of the believer's will and intellect (cf. Canon 752).

The Problem of Dissent • Whereas the Church has confronted heresy from her earliest days, the problem of dissent, which sometimes takes the form of public opposition to the Church's Magisterium, is especially the fruit of the eighteenth-century Enlightenment. Philosophical liberalism considered all forms of Church teaching heteronomous and therefore an intrusion on the freedom of inquiry that, so *les philosophes* alleged, advances the human spirit. Since rationalism makes human intelligence the highest norm for truth, it is difficult, if not impossible, to reconcile acceptance of the principle of heteronomy with Christian belief. For divine truth alone measures theological faith.

Today some theologians, who have been influenced by the principle of heteronomy, make dissent part of their discussion of the act of faith. A commonly accepted view distinguishes between a dogma and a doctrine and further asserts that, whereas dissent against a dogma amounts to an act of heresy, it is often difficult in practice to distinguish a dogma from a doctrine, even one officially taught by the Church. The saints would have found this argument bewildering. Someone like St. Thomas Aquinas would have inquired, "But why should someone want to dissent *from God*?"

The problem of dissent has become so acute that in 1990 the Congregation for the Doctrine of the Faith issued a special instruction dealing with the issue. The *Instruction on the Ecclesial Vocation of the Theologian* rejects the view that "the documents of the Magisterium . . . reflect nothing more than a debatable theology" and criticizes the " 'parallel magisterium' of theologians" that purports to operate in opposition to and in competition with the Magisterium of the pastors of the Church.

The document concludes: "The freedom of the act of faith cannot justify a right to dissent. In fact this freedom does not indicate at all freedom with regard to the truth but signifies the free self-determination of the person in conformity with his moral obligation to accept the truth. The act of faith is a voluntary act because man, saved by Christ the Redeemer and called by him to be an adopted son, cannot adhere to God unless, drawn by the Father" (Jn 6:44), he offer God the rational homage of his faith (no. 36).

See: Dissent; Divine Revelation; Economy of Salvation; Faith, Virtue of; Heresy; Magisterium; Modernism; Relativism; Religion, Virtue of; Sacred Tradition.

Suggested Readings: CCC 150, 156-159, 167, 186-189, 199-202, 512, 815, 1813-1816. Vatican Council I, *Dogmatic Constitution on the Catholic Faith*, *Dei Filius*, Chs. III-IV. Vatican Council II, *Dogmatic Constitution on Divine Revelation*, *Dei Verbum*. Congregation for the Doctrine of the Faith, *Instruction on the Ecclesial Vocation of the Theologian*. A. Dulles, S.J., *The Assurance of Things Hoped For*. R. Cessario, O.P., *Theological Faith and the Christian Life*.

Romanus Cessario, O.P.

ASSISTED SUICIDE

To perform assisted suicide is "to concur with the intention of another person to commit suicide and to help in carrying it out." In so doing, one cooperates in or even perpetrates "an injustice which can never be excused, even if it is requested" (Pope John Paul II, encyclical *The Gospel of Life, Evangelium Vitae*, 66). If it involves actual assistance in the lethal act, it bears the same moral guilt as murder, for the agent intentionally helps to cause a death.

Because each human life has inherent value, the victim's request for death does not excuse the act of assisting, nor does the victim's condition of illness or disability. The one who assists may actually bear more responsibility than the suicidal person does, for he or she is not usually suffering from the despair or other mental disturbances that can reduce personal responsibility for one's actions. Morally, then, assisted suicide is no less

wrong than euthanasia, in which one person directly kills another to end suffering.

In the ancient Hippocratic oath, physicians promised not to provide lethal drugs to help a patient commit suicide. Today many medical organizations agree with the Church in condemning assisted suicide along with euthanasia.

See: Euthanasia; Homicide; Human Life, Dignity and Sanctity of; Suicide.

ASSUMPTION OF MARY

On November 1, 1950, Pope Pius XII solemnly defined as a dogma of faith Mary's bodily Assumption into heaven. The precise words of the definition, found in the apostolic constitution *Munificentissimus Deus*, teach just what we are called to believe as a matter of divine Catholic faith: "We pronounce, declare, and define it to be a divinely revealed dogma: that the Immaculate Mother of God, the ever Virgin Mary, having completed the course of her earthly life, was assumed body and soul into heavenly glory."

The subject of this definition expresses the dogmas of Mary's Immaculate Conception, her Motherhood of God, and her perpetual virginity. Pope Pius judiciously left open to further theological investigation and discussion whether or not Mary actually experienced death before being taken up into heaven, with the phrase "having completed the course of her earthly life." The use of the passive voice, "was assumed," indicates that the mystery of the Assumption is quite distinct from Christ's Ascension. Mary was "taken up" into glory by the power of God, whereas Christ ascended by that power as it belonged to him in virtue of the hypostatic unity. The words of the solemn definition, "body and soul," teach that Mary has been glorified in her complete human personhood, and do not make a dualistic anthropology as such a necessary condition to give intelligent assent to the dogma. The concluding words, "into heavenly glory," refer to the mysterious mode of existence beyond space and time in which Mary has been reunited with her Son, our risen Lord, with whom she lives eternally in the intimate presence of the triune God, in the company of all the angels and saints. Details about the mystery of heavenly glory may be found in related doctrines of the Church concerning general eschatology, particularly the beatific vision and the bodily resurrection of all the just.

Although the dogma of the Assumption did not settle a number of questions regarding Mary's departure from this life, the testimony of Tradition does seem to favor the theological opinions that she died and was most likely buried near the Garden of Gethsemane in Jerusalem, and that, in the likeness of her Son's Resurrection, her body did not decompose after her death and burial but instead Mary was gloriously assumed intact. As in the case of Christ's Resurrection, so with Mary's Assumption, what the dogma actually defines is seen to be a reality and truth only by those with the gift of faith, who freely accept and respond to what is contained in Divine Revelation. Now let us examine how it is included in the word of God.

Dogmatic Development • When Pius XII taught that the sacred writings are the "ultimate foundation" for any considerations of the dogma on the part of the Fathers of the Church and of theologians, he referred to what is *implicitly* contained in them or, as it were, divinely insinuated and suggested in the biblical Revelation. He appeals to the intimate association between the new Eve and the new Adam in that struggle foretold in the *proto-evangelium* (cf. Gn 3:15), which led to the total victory over sin and death through Christ's redemptive mission. In *Munificentissimus Deus* he quotes from St. Paul's teaching: "When the perishable puts on the imperishable, and the mortal puts on immorality, then shall come to pass the saying that is written: 'Death is swallowed up in victory' " (1 Cor 15:54). Just as Christ's glorious Resurrection was the essential agent of this victory, so also Mary, the new Eve who had so great and indispensable a role in the struggle, should most fittingly share in the victory of her Son over sin and death through her glorification.

In appealing to the authority of the great Scholastic theologians of the thirteenth century, Sts. Albert the Great, Thomas Aquinas, and Bonaventure, Pope Pius pointed out that these doctors of the Church considered the Assumption to be "the fulfillment of that most perfect grace granted to the Blessed Virgin and the special blessing that countered the curse of Eve." In the nineteenth century, Cardinal Newman concluded that both the Immaculate Conception and the Assumption of Mary were implicit in the new Eve image. We should bear this in mind, as the Scriptures seem to have gradually yielded a fuller meaning about Mary in the post-Apostolic Tradition, particularly in the celebration of the Liturgy.

A feast called the Memorial of Mary was already being celebrated by Christians during the fifth century. In the Eastern Church, it occurred on August 15, and eventually came to be known as the *koimesis* (Greek) or *dormitio* (Latin), that is, the "falling asleep" of the Virgin Mary. According to the beliefs of the early Christians, the body "fell asleep" at death and rested until awakened in the glory of the next life. Emperor Mauricius Flavius (582-602) decreed that the liturgical feast of Mary's dormition be celebrated throughout the Byzantine Empire on August 15. Thus the feast had evolved from the early fifth-century Memorial of Mary, which celebrated all her privileges as Mother of God, to the early sixth century, with the emphasis now placed upon her dormition or death, marked by a basilica in Gethsemane, Jerusalem, where popular belief held that her tomb was located. When Mary's dormition was celebrated each year on August 15 throughout the Byzantine Empire, preachers began to proclaim more clearly her Assumption as well as her death. In the Eastern Liturgies of today, the feast is more commonly called the Assumption, or "Journey of the Blessed Mother of God Into Heaven," which truly celebrates belief in the glorification of her body in eternal life. Rome adopted the feast in the seventh century, and, under Pope St. Adrian I (772-795), its title became Assumption. The feast focused on Mary's bodily Assumption from the very beginning of its celebration in the Western Church.

Among the great Fathers of the Eastern Church, Theotknos, sixth- or seventh-century bishop of

Livias (on the left bank of the Jordan), referred to the feast as the Assumption (*analepsis* in Greek). By the eighth century the doctrine of the bodily Assumption of Mary was entirely accepted in the East and was taught there by St. Germanus of Constantinople and St. John Damascene, the great Doctor of the Assumption, who preached his three famous homilies on the feast. Clear patristic testimony is given to the dogma in the West by St. Gregory of Tours (died 593). Mention has already been made of the teaching of the outstanding Scholastics of the thirteenth century.

During the sixteenth century, the feast became the greatest of the Marian liturgical celebrations, and one of the most prominent of the Church year. Doctors of the Church named by Pius XII who promoted the doctrine are: St. Bernardine of Siena (1380-1444), St. Robert Bellarmine (1542-1621), St. Francis de Sales (1567-1622), St. Peter Canisius (1521-1597), and St. Alphonsus Liguori (1696-1787). As Pope Pius XII also pointed out, Francisco Suárez held in the sixteenth century that the Immaculate Conception and Assumption could be defined as dogmas of faith.

But the Holy Father found the strongest reason for his decision solemnly to define the Assumption of Mary as a dogma in the "outstanding agreement of the Catholic prelates and the faithful." The entire Church's faith manifested itself between 1849 and 1950, when an amazing number of petitions for a solemn definition were sent to Rome from every cell of the Mystical Body of Christ. These included 113 cardinals, 18 patriarchs, 2,505 archbishops and bishops, 32,000 priests and men religious, 50,000 religious women, and 8 million laypersons. As Pope Pius IX had done a century before in reference to the Immaculate Conception, Pius XII issued an encyclical, *Deiperae Virginis*, addressed to his brother bishops of the world and inquiring whether or not Mary's bodily Assumption was definable, and also whether their priests and people wished it to be defined at the time. The response was overwhelmingly favorable. Among the many hopes expressed for salutary results of a solemn definition of Mary's glorious bodily Assumption into heaven was the strength-

ening of faith in our own bodily resurrection. This was echoed by Vatican Council II's teaching that our heavenly Mother shines forth on earth "a sign of certain hope and comfort" (*Dogmatic Constitution on the Church, Lumen Gentium*, 68) to us who yearn to be united with her one day in the perfect Church of glory.

See: Immaculate Conception; Marian Devotion; Mary, Mother of God; Mary, Mother of the Church; Mary, Perpetual Virginity of; Resurrection of Christ; Resurrection of the Dead.

Suggested Readings: CCC 966, 972, 974. F. Jelly, O.P., *Madonna: Mary in the Catholic Tradition;* "Assumption of Mary," in J. Komonchak, M. Collins, D. Lane, eds., *The New Dictionary of Theology.* K. Healy, *The Assumption of Mary.* M. O'Carroll, C.S.Sp., "The Assumption of Our Lady," *Theotokos: A Theological Encyclopedia of the Blessed Virgin Mary.*

F.M. Jelly, O.P.

ATHEISM

Faithful to the Revelation that is made in Christ, the Church teaches that every human being is called to ultimate communion with the Blessed Trinity. The biblical teaching that man is created in the image of God (*imago Dei*) proclaims not only the truth about the origin of the human creature but also the truth about his destiny. In this life, communion with God through faith expresses the highest achievement that the human person can achieve; in heaven, the blessed enjoy the same communion with God, though they see God face to face, not as "in a mirror dimly" (1 Cor 13:12). In the *Dogmatic Constitution on the Church, Lumen Gentium*, the Fathers of Vatican Council II developed a rich teaching about the personal relationship that each member of the human race is called to enjoy with God. The universal call to holiness (*Lumen Gentium*, Ch. V) serves as a kind of apologetic for Christian belief, one based on the experience of the human heart, which the saints tell us is made for God. Subsequently, Pope John Paul II has made this theme a recurring element of his ordinary instruction. He brings us back again and again to the God who stands at the center of the human drama.

Still, many of our contemporaries "either do not at all perceive, or explicitly reject, this intimate and vital bond of man to God" (CCC 2123, citing Vatican Council II, *Pastoral Constitution on the Church in the Modern World, Gaudium et Spes*, 19). At Vatican II, the Church took a fresh look at atheism.

Human Knowledge of God • Earlier remarks by the Magisterium concerning atheism reaffirmed the classical position that man could come to a knowledge of God's existence without the aid of Revelation. Thus, Vatican Council I's *Dogmatic Constitution on the Catholic Faith, Dei Filius,* anathematizes anyone who says that the one, true God, our Creator and Lord, cannot be known with certainty from the things that have been made, by the natural light of human reason (cf. Denzinger-Schönmetzer, 3006). Of course the Church never officially included the proofs for the existence of God as developed by Thomas Aquinas and others into her official teaching, but she did encourage theologians to study these theological commentaries on Romans 1:20 as a starting point for theological investigations.

As a result, practitioners of theology, when confronted with the challenge of atheism, often explained a threefold division in the ways man can come to know about God. We move from what is common, though not innate, knowledge about God, to what can be learned by demonstration, and then on to what is revealed to those who believe. In this way, any believer is able to demonstrate that the existential situation of the atheist contradicts a truth human intelligence itself could attain, and thus atheism is founded on a position that could not be reasonably defended.

In his *Summa Contra Gentiles*, Aquinas clarifies the way that philosophical reasoning contributes to our knowledge of God: "Demonstration adds to our knowledge of God, and betters it, by enabling us to come closer to specific knowledge of him. For demonstration shows God to be unchangeable, eternal, not bodily, in no way composite, unique and so on; thus eliminating many

attributes from him and so distinguishing him in our minds from other things" (Bk. III, Ch. 39). It should be recalled that this and similar uses of demonstration in apologetics contributed to a significant number of conversion stories in the twentieth century and before.

According to the traditional understanding, apologetics is the science of developing rationally persuasive arguments that are meant to dispose a person to accept the revealed truths of the faith. Because traditional apologists considered atheism intellectually untenable, they tended to approach the phenomenon in terms of the effects of original sin, either hardness of heart or blindness of mind. Theologians in turn accounted for the actual existence of self-avowed atheists by appeal to moral weakness or to the fact that the demonstrations involved in proving the existence of God required a certain philosophical acumen. Ludwig Ott reflects this tradition: "The possibility that there are also subjectively convinced theoretical atheists is founded in the spiritual and moral weakness of man, and on the fact that the proofs for God are not immediately, but only mediately evident."

New View of Atheism • In the middle of the twentieth century, these reasons no longer seemed adequate to account for the large number of people who, even if they did not adhere to a speculative atheism, nonetheless lived as if there were no God. The Church was called upon to address a sort of practical atheism. This brand of atheism, so it appeared to the Fathers of Vatican Council II, described the condition of more than just a few members of an intellectual elite who considered it fashionable to adopt atheist airs. And so the Council addressed the reality of practical atheism, that is, atheism without speculative pretensions, as a central theme of its *Pastoral Constitution on the Church in the Modern World*.

Since many modern thinkers no longer found the old apologetic persuasive, the Council aimed to develop a personalist apologetic for the existence of God. At least, this seems to be the implicit reasoning followed by the conciliar Fathers. For a variety of reasons, which owe much to major philosophical movements in the modern period, many educated persons in the twentieth century found the so-called cosmological arguments that classical theology had used to demonstrate the existence of God singularly noncompelling. Moreover, the experience of evil, oftentimes at the hands of fellow human beings who claimed to be Christian, provided a powerful, though largely unexamined, premise in an argument that denied the existence of an all-good God.

Whatever the explanation, the fact is that at mid-twentieth century, atheism seemed an overwhelming challenge for the Christian Church. So in 1965, the Church affirmed that "atheism is to be viewed as one of the most serious of contemporary phenomena and merits close attention" (*Gaudium et Spes,* 19). (Thirty years later, that judgment perhaps should be modified in light of the wide and growing interest in interreligious dialogue.)

In *Gaudium et Spes,* the treatment of atheism appears as part of the discussion of the dignity of the human person, which is the central theme of the document's first part, "The Church and Man's Vocation." Atheism is described less as a failure to recognize God in creation and more as the result of an excessive campaign to center the philosophical enterprise on the human subject. "Some so exalt the human as to empty faith in God of all content, being apparently more preoccupied with the affirmation of the human creature than with the denial of God" (19). Treating atheism as more a moral failure than an intellectual mistake, the Council even ascribes some of the blame for the fact that so many persons do not believe in God to believers whose behavior does more to conceal than reveal the reality of God and religious faith *(Gaudium et Spes*, cf. CCC 2125).

The Council also addressed what it called "systematic atheism." Without mentioning communist governments by name, *Gaudium et Spes* describes the atheistic and antireligious suppositions of a political system "which looks especially to man's economic and social liberation for his liberation, and claims that religion of its nature is an obstacle to such liberation in raising man's hopes toward a future illusory life which would discourage him from building the earthly city" (20). In a clear reference to the practices of then-ruling totalitarian governments, the conciliar Fathers also condemn the practice of using the pressures of public authority to promote this systematic atheism.

The Council's analysis of atheism points to a new initiative to remedy this sin. The person who gives himself or herself fully to the experience of being human will realize that it is impossible to live a satisfactory human life without a personal reference to God. Application to building the human city remains a worthwhile endeavor; but the heart of the Council's analysis of a life lived without God rests on the conviction that the human heart only finds rest when it rests in God: "When the divine foundation and the hope of eternal life are missing, human dignity is seriously impaired, as frequently occurs today, and the mysteries of life and death, and of guilt and grief, remain unsolved, often resulting in man's sinking into despair" (21).

For this reason, the response to modern atheism principally should be centered neither in moral exhortations nor on intellectual arguments. Instead, atheists should be extended an invitation to listen to the preaching of the Gospel "with open hearts" (21). It is highly significant that the most frequently cited passage of *Gaudium et Spes*, and perhaps of the whole body of Vatican II texts, follows the description of the modern spiritual malaise, which it loosely calls atheism. *Gaudium et Spes*, 22, declares: "It is Christ, the last Adam, who fully discloses man to himself and unfolds his noble calling by revealing the mystery of the Father and the Father's love." The Christocentric response to atheism is of course supported by a long tradition of evangelization, which begins with the very first Christian apologists.

Response to Atheism • Atheism represents a sin against God. The *Catechism of the Catholic Church* places the sin under the first commandment of the Decalogue, describing it as a way of honoring false gods. Atheism, then, constitutes an offense against the virtue of religion, which requires the human person, as a creature, to offer to God the worship and veneration that belong to the provident source of all being as his due. It is therefore fitting that the response to the person who lives as if God did not exist should include a call to worship him in the "one mediator between God and men, the man Jesus Christ" (1 Tm 2:5).

Thus the theological anthropology of *Gaudium et Spes* invites us to discover God at the center of human existence. "For the Church knows full well that her message is in harmony with the most secret desires of the human heart" (*Gaudium et Spes*, 21). The personalist approach to apologetics responds to many important themes of twentieth-century philosophy, including the existentialist philosopher's search for ultimate meaning in human existence. At the same time, the Church continues to hold that man enjoys the metaphysical capacity to come to a knowledge of God from creation.

As a perennial witness to the Christian Tradition, Aquinas offers a succinct account of the common knowledge (not to be misconstrued as innate knowledge) about God that is to be found in all men. In the *Summa Contra Gentiles*, he writes: "An awareness of God, though not clear nor specific, exists in practically everyone. Some people think this is because it is self-evident that God exists, just as other principles of reasoning are self-evident. Others, with more truth, think that the natural use of reason leads man straight away to some sort of knowledge of God. For when men observe the sure and ordered course that things pursue by nature, they see in most cases that somebody must be producing the order they observe, since rule cannot exist without a ruler. Such a consideration, however, is not yet specific enough for one to know immediately who this ruler of nature is, or what kind of being he is, or whether only one such ruler exists. Just so, by observing the movements and actions of a human being, we see that a cause of his behavior must exist in him such as does not exist in other things, and we call this 'soul,' though without yet knowing what the soul is (whether, perhaps, it is bodily) or how it operates" (Bk. III, Ch. 38).

As a step toward bringing all persons to a complete knowledge of the truth, which can only be had through Divine Revelation, the knowledge of God available to all those reflective enough to consider the world that exists around them is a solid and sure one. Not only does atheism leave one's heart empty, but to deny the existence of God, whether speculatively or in practice, does violence to the dynamism of human intelligence. For "ever since the creation of the world his invisible nature, namely, his eternal power and deity, has been clearly perceived in the things that have been made" (Rom 1:20).

See: Agnosticism; Evil, Problem of; God, Nature and Attributes of; Human Person; Imago Dei; Knowledge of God; Original Sin; Providence; Rationalism; Religion, Virtue of; Thomas Aquinas, Thought of.

Suggested Readings: CCC 2123-2126, 2128, 2140. Vatican Council II, *Pastoral Constitution on the Church in the Modern World, Gaudium et Spes*, 19-21. St. Thomas Aquinas, *Summa Contra Gentiles*, Bk. III. M. Buckley, *Atheism*. A. Nichols, O.P., "Chesterton and the Modernist Crisis," *Chesterton Review* (May, 1989).

Romanus Cessario, O.P.

AUGUSTINIANISM

The *Dictionnaire de Théologie Catholique* treats of the theology of St. Augustine (354-430) under two distinct headings: *Augustinisme* and *Augustinianisme*. The term "Augustinism" refers to the theological doctrine of St. Augustine in general, with special emphasis on his teaching on predestination, grace, and human freedom. In this context, St. Augustine stands as the depositary of the patristic tradition of theology and the forerunner of Scholasticism. Throughout the centuries, his theological authority has been invoked by theologians as disparate as Luther, Calvin, and Jansen, St. Gregory the Great, St. Anselm, and St. Thomas Aquinas.

Theology of "Augustinism" • Strictly speaking, St. Augustine never set out to produce the system of theology that we call Augustinism. Throughout his life, he was constantly in search of truth; his prolific writings are the result of his dialogues with the leading thinkers of his day or his defenses of Catholic teaching against his opponents. Thus, St. Augustine was at once an outstanding apologist, defending Catholic teaching with consummate skill, and a creative thinker, constantly questioning and probing. His theology of grace, emerging from his disputes with the Pelagians, still dominates the Catholic teaching. Nevertheless, the error of Pelagianism has persisted in some form or other throughout the entire history of the Church.

The fundamental principle that lies at the heart of Pelagianism is the absolute autonomy of human freedom. Having given man the gift of freedom, God cannot intervene without destroying that freedom. Hence, the sole determinant of man's actions is his own free choice, whether the action be morally good or evil. Further, since a man *can* be good, he *must* be good; there is no place here for efficacy of grace or the prayer of petition.

St. Augustine responded by stating that, although created in the "state of innocence," man committed the original sin, as a result of which human nature is a fallen and weakened nature. Without God's grace, the only thing a man can do entirely on his own is sin. Fallen man still retains a restless longing for God, but without the intervention of actual grace, he cannot do the good required for justification. By and large, his state is described as *non posse non peccare* ("cannot not sin"). Unfortunately, some of St. Augustine's expressions regarding actual grace are open to misinterpretation; hence, opponents of Catholic teaching have also quoted St. Augustine as their authority.

Commenting on the many-faceted theological tradition that has St. Augustine as its author, E. Simons writes: "It is to Augustine that men have gone again and again for insight into the question of their own self-understanding, so much so that in the course of the centuries an 'Augustinian' dialogue has developed within which varying interpretations of the master and his work have been proposed, to which corresponded a varying interpretation of each period of history. It is this changing dialogue which may be referred to as a whole under the name 'Augustinianism.' The works of Augustine are, with those of Thomas Aquinas, the basis and determining influence in the acceptance

and application of classical metaphysics within the Judaeo-Christian tradition. This application, nevertheless, was accomplished in different ways at the hands of both men, and thus ever since the 13th century Augustine's influence had largely been determined by its relation to Thomism. Augustinianism refers in a narrower sense to certain philosophical and theological theses which are based upon actual or purported works of Augustine" (K. Rahner, ed., *Encyclopedia of Theology: The Concise Sacramentum Mundi*, p. 54).

Theology of "Augustinianism" • It is in this latter, narrower sense that we shall treat of Augustinianism, and precisely so far as it designates the school of theology founded by Giles of Rome (Aegidius Romanus, 1243-1316). A general chapter of 1287 imposed the teachings of this school on all the members of the Augustinian order, in spite of the fact that Giles himself insisted that freedom should be granted to theologians as long as there is no danger to the faith. The decree was never obeyed literally and universally. In time, the Thomistic influence favored by Giles of Rome gradually gave way to a stronger emphasis on the teaching authority of St. Augustine and the development of positive theology. This shift of emphasis began with Gregory of Rimini (died 1358), who has been called "the true author of Augustinianism in the 14th century," and whose influence prevailed until the sixteenth century. During this period, the fundamental doctrines of the Augustinian school can be summarized as follows.

1. Man has a natural desire to see God, and therefore he has a radical capacity to do so; but the actual attainment of the beatific vision requires grace.

2. Man was created in the state of innocence and endowed with extraordinary supernatural gifts. He has never existed in the state of "pure nature"; therefore any discussion of that possibility is purely hypothetical.

3. Because of original sin, man was deprived of the extraordinary supernatural gifts and was even wounded in his human nature. For that reason, he needs a healing grace (*gratia sanans*), and without it he cannot faithfully observe the natural

law or consistently perform acts in accord with natural morality.

4. Like the Franciscan school, the Augustinians defend the primacy of the will over the intellect, from which it follows that eternal happiness consists primarily in loving rather than in the beatific vision. It also follows from this that the precept of charity binds in a special way.

5. Because of original sin, predestination to glory is absolutely gratuitous and is antecedent to God's foreknowledge of man's merits; reprobation is an effect of divine justice in view of original sin and an individual's failure to be liberated from what St. Augustine labels the *massa corruptionis*.

6. The goal of theology is neither speculative nor practical, but affective, since it should direct the Christian to beatitude, which consists in loving. Hence, the theologian should study God as the source of glory and eternal happiness, and not exclusively *sub specie deitatis*.

A Protestant Augustinian tradition began with the Reformers. It triggered a reaction among the Augustinians to remove the authority of St. Augustine as a basis for their teachings. As a result, the traditional Augustinian teaching was repeatedly invoked during the Council of Trent (1545-1564).

Later Controversies • From the seventeenth century onward, Augustinianism is for all practical purposes a school within a school, because of the dominating influence of Cardinal Noris (1631-1704). He and his companions are sometimes referred to as *Augustinenses*, to distinguish them from the school of Giles of Rome. E. Portalié describes the teaching of Cardinal Noris as "rigid Augustinianism."

At this time Augustinians found themselves divided on questions pertaining to the interaction of grace and free will. Henry Noris, later named a cardinal, published *Historia Pelagiana* in 1673 and followed it with *Vindiciae Augustinianae*. The latter work was severely criticized as Jansenistic by theologians in France, Germany, Italy, and Spain. Nevertheless, Noris's teaching spread rapidly throughout the Augustinian order, and especially at Louvain.

Although the rigorist Augustinian doctrine of Cardinal Noris and companions was frequently denounced to the Inquisition, it was never officially condemned by the Church. In fact, *Historia Pelagiana* was examined three times by the Inquisition but not condemned. Pope Innocent XII placed Noris in charge of the Vatican Library and named him a cardinal in 1695. Forty years after his death, he was praised by Pope Benedict XIV as a "light of the Church." In 1748, the Pope authorized the teaching of three theological theories concerning the interaction of grace and human free will: the Thomistic, the Molinist, and the Augustinian.

It is true that one could possibly find points of similarity to Jansenism in the writings of rigorist Augustinians, but they defended themselves by saying their interpretation of St. Augustine's teaching was totally different. Nevertheless, proponents of a moderate Augustinianism, drawn from other schools of theology, consistently opposed the rigorist Augustinian synthesis.

Like their predecessors, the moderate Augustinians were concerned primarily with the interaction of grace and human freedom. But whereas the rigorist Augustinians held for a physical predetermination of the will by grace, thus depriving the will of self-determination, the moderates maintained that grace exerts no more than a moral influence on the will. This brought to the fore the distinction between "sufficient" grace and "efficacious" grace, a distinction that came into vogue after the Council of Trent.

In sum, theologians were left with several explanations from which to choose: for example, grace exerts a physical predetermination on the human will or only a moral predetermination (Augustinians and Thomists); the distinction between the general (sufficient) grace given to all for ordinary easy acts and a special (efficacious) grace for more difficult acts (St. Alphonsus Liguori and professors at the Sorbonne). To this day, theologians are divided on the question and it remains open, although the solution has consistently inclined toward moderate Augustinianism.

See: Beatific Vision; Freedom, Human; Grace; Heaven; Jansenism; Justification; Original Sin; Providence; Quietism.

Suggested Readings: CCC 1720-1724; 1731-1742; 1987-2011; 2548-2550. F. Cayre, *Manual of Patrology.* M. Farrelly, *Predestination, Grace and Free Will.* R. Russell, "Augustinianism," *New Catholic Encyclopedia*, Vol. 1, pp. 1063-1071. E. Simons, "Augustinianism," in K. Rahner, ed., *Encyclopedia of Theology: The Concise Sacramentum Mundi*, pp. 54-60.

Jordan Aumann, O.P.

AUTHORITY

The *Catechism of the Catholic Church* defines authority as "the quality by virtue of which persons or institutions make laws and give orders to men and expect obedience from them" (1897). While in our society authority is often cast in a negative light — as indicated by the connotation of "authoritarian regimes," for instance — in itself and independent of abuse, authority is a positive reality, rooted in divine providence and human nature. Without it, society would lack cohesion and direction. The maintenance of peace and the pursuit of a common goal would not be sustainable (think, for example, of a football team without a coaching staff, an orchestra without a conductor, a high-school class without a teacher).

Genuine authority is not lording it over others for one's personal advantage; it is rather a matter of rendering a very great service to others. Hence we speak of those in office as "public servants" and of the Pope as "the servant of the servants of God."

Church Teaching on Civil Authority • Of special importance for human life is the role of civil or political authority, which has as its task the defense and promotion of the temporal common good, most fully realized in the political community. Civil authority derives its justification or legitimacy, that which distinguishes it from mere force or power, from right reason and the pursuit of the common good. The New Testament epistles contain several indications that Christians should respect and obey civil authorities, for "[t]here is no authority except from God" (Rom 13:1). This statement of the Apostle Paul appears all the more radical, not to say disturbing, when one recalls that the reigning authority of his time was none other than the emperor Nero. Here the commentary of St. John Chrysostom, a Father of the Church, is of great help: "What are you saying? Is every ruler appointed by God? I do not say that, he [Paul] replies, for I am not dealing now with individual rulers, but with authority itself. What I say is, that it is the divine wisdom, and not mere chance, that has ordained that there should be government, that some should command and others obey" (homily; cited in Pope John XXIII, encyclical *Peace on Earth, Pacem in Terris*, 46 [1963]).

Another Church Father, St. Augustine, distinguishes between true authority, exercised for the good of the governed and the peace of the community, and corrupt authority, lusting after domination and oppression, a consequence of sin. Political life as we know it presents powerful temptations in this second direction: "You know that those who are supposed to rule over the Gentiles lord it over them" (Mk 10:42; cf. Lk 22:25). In his *City of God*, Augustine chronicles the progressive degeneration of the Romans' political motivation, from the love of freedom, to love of glory, to love of power and domination. By contrast, "[i]n the household of the just man who 'lives on the basis of faith' . . . even those who give orders are the servants of those whom they appear to command. For they do not give orders because of a lust for domination but from a dutiful concern for the interests of others, not with pride in taking precedence over others, but with compassion in taking care of others" (*City of God,* XIX, 14; cf. 12 and 15).

St. Thomas Aquinas builds on Augustine's (and Aristotle's) distinction between government of free people and mastery over slaves. Only the first sort is proper to family and political life.

St. Thomas argues that, even in the absence of original sin, civil authority or government would likely have existed among humans. This is so for two reasons. First, the social nature of man requires that some in the community direct the many and varied activities of its members to a common good, that some be vigilant for the good of the others as their principal task or job. The second reason is that, even if sin did not exist, some persons would have advanced further in wisdom and justice than others. For the good of the community, it would follow that these should govern and direct their society: "[I]f one man greatly surpassed another in knowledge and justice, it would be all wrong if he did not perform this function [of principal or director] for the benefit of others; as it says in *I Peter* [4:10], 'everyone putting the grace he has received at the disposal of each other.' So Augustine too says, in Book XIX of the *City of God*, that 'the just do not rule out of a lust to dominate, but out of the duty to look after things' (ch.14); and 'this is what the order of nature prescribes, this is how God instituted man' (ch.15)" (*Summa Theologiae*, I, 96, 4; cf. 92, 1, ad 2; 96, 3).

The Magisterium in the late nineteenth and twentieth centuries has developed this perennial teaching on authority, relating it to modern forms of political life and articulating it in terms more accessible to people today.

In Vatican II's *Pastoral Constitution on the Church in the Modern World, Gaudium et Spes*, for example, we read that "[t]he persons who go to make up the political community are many and varied; quite rightly, then, they may veer towards widely differing points of view. Therefore, lest the political community be ruined while everyone follows his own opinion, an authority is needed to guide the energies of all towards the common good — *not mechanistically or despotically, but by acting above all as a moral force based on freedom and a sense of responsibility*" (emphasis added). Political authority should respect the principle of subsidiarity and endeavor to earn the consent of the governed, without which even the wisest leadership or best constitution may be rendered ineffective. Insofar as possible, "the choice of the political regime and the appointment of rulers are left to the free decision of the citizens." Whatever concrete form civil authority takes in a given society, its central aim must always be "the formation of a human person who is cultured, peace-loving, and well disposed towards his fellow men with a view to the benefit of the whole human race" (*Gaudium et Spes*, 74).

Role of Civil Authority • The particular duties of civil authorities include working for the common good, always using means that respect the natural law and the dignity of human persons. They must ensure that legislation and institutions reflect as far a possible a "just hierarchy of values," and facilitate the citizens' exercise of freedom and responsibility. Political authority must "practice distributive justice wisely," with equity and "with a view to harmony and peace" (CCC 2236). Consequently, political authority may regulate the legitimate exercise of the right to property for the sake of the common good.

In our own day, there is an especially urgent need for civil authority to safeguard and promote marriage and the family, and to protect human life from the moment of conception until natural death. Finally, civil authority must work for peace and provide for the common defense, imposing on citizens the obligations necessary to this end. When war seems unavoidable, those in office are responsible for evaluating the circumstances at hand in light of the principles of "just war doctrine." (For a fuller exposition of these and other important functions of civil authority, see the sections of the *Catechism* listed below.)

In the endeavor to fulfill their difficult and noble mission, those invested with authority have special need of the virtue of prudence regarding the common good and the means by which it may be effectively pursued. Moreover, being among those "who by nature or office are obliged to teach and educate others," they must take particular care not to give scandal, whether in their personal conduct or by means of the customs, laws, and social structures they establish or administer (cf. CCC 2284-2287).

Citizens on their part have a duty to respect and obey just authority and its legitimate demands. They have the correlative duty to resist corrupt authority when it commands acts against the divine law, the natural moral law, or the rights of the human person.

See: Church and State; Citizenship; Civil Disobedience; Civil Law; Common Good; Natural Law; Politics; Property; Religious Liberty; Revolution; Social Justice; Subsidiarity.

Suggested Readings: CCC 1806, 1883-84, 1897-1904, 1906, 1909, 1917-1923, 1927, 1930, 2109, 2197, 2202, 2207-2211, 2229, 2234-2246, 2285, 2310, 2321, 2406, 2420, 2498-2499; Vatican Council II, *Pastoral Constitution on the Church in the Modern World, Gaudium et Spes*, 52, 59, 65-71, 73-76. Leo XIII, *Diuturnum Illud; Immortale Dei.* John XXIII, *Peace on Earth, Pacem in Terris*, Chs. III-IV. Y. Simon, *A General Theory of Authority.*

Mary M. Keys

AVARICE

When avarice shows its greedy, stingy, cold-hearted face, it provokes near-universal revulsion. That is why this capital sin or vice usually parades as frugal thrift or due provision for the future or reasonable security or even risk-taking enterprise. Ironically, there are even some fervent religionists who cultivate God just "to get ahead."

When avarice incites to serious injustice in the acquisition and retaining of wealth, it is often a grievous sin. In itself, however, and insofar as it implies simply an excessive desire of or pleasure in riches, it is commonly a venial sin (cf. CCC 2536).

Avarice, envy, covetousness, and hedonism are contemporary bedfellows associated with materialism (in its moral sense). But while materialism seems rampant today, there may be reason to think that its hold on people is not so strong as would appear at first glance. The men and women of affluent societies suffer abundantly from boredom and covert sadness. Many have tried all forms of lust and found them wanting, at least to some degree; theirs is no longer the obsessive craving for things and pleasures that drives the neophyte. Many remain wed to these false joys of course, but perhaps only because they have yet to find something to compete with, if not best, them. When the prospect of a more genuine happiness is presented to those haunted by quiet desperation, this seems likely to change.

Historically, neither the Church nor the state has done all it should to discountenance excess wealth and greed, especially by discouraging shady practices often associated with them. Avaricious, say, is the merchant who artificially creates shortages, or the business executive/owner who strives to monopolize the market, or the doctor, lawyer, or accountant who preys on the ignorant gullibility of clients (cf. CCC 2537).

The virtue opposite to, and curative of, greed and its minions is not mere frugality, although for someone with the correct intention frugality is a step in the right direction. Rather, as Dorothy Sayers insists, what drives out or preempts avarice is a cultivated taste and love for genuine values and goods, plus the liberality to share them. She prescribes a "good materialism" that prizes "earthly fruits and people's labor: good work well done."

See: Capital Sins; Cardinal Virtues; Covetousness; Detachment; Envy; Property.

B

BAPTISM

The first of the seven sacraments, Baptism is "the basis of the whole Christian life, the gateway to life in the Spirit (*vitae spiritualis ianua*), and the door which gives access to the other sacraments" (CCC 1213). Baptism (from the Greek *baptizein*) remits the guilt of original sin, that is, human nature in the fallen state resulting from the willful disobedience of Adam and Eve, and incorporates one into the Church founded by Jesus Christ. It infuses sanctifying grace into the soul of the recipient and imparts an indelible character.

Various titles are used for this sacrament. The *Catechism of the Catholic Church* mentions two: the "washing and regeneration and renewal by the Holy Spirit" and "enlightenment" (CCC 1215-1216). It also quotes St. Gregory of Nazianzus (c. 329-390), who called Baptism "gift, grace, anointing, enlightenment, garment of immortality, bath of rebirth, seal, and most precious gift."

The Old Testament offers several prefigurings of Baptism: the Spirit of God hovering over the waters at the beginning of the world; Noah's ark and the Great Flood; the journeys through the Red Sea and the Jordan River; the foretelling of the divine cleansing mentioned in Ezekiel (36:25).

Jesus began his public ministry only after having voluntarily submitted himself to the baptism offered to sinners by St. John the Baptist (which, according to the Council of Trent, did not share the same effective power that the Baptism instituted by Christ enjoys). Before ascending to his Father, Jesus exhorted the Eleven to make disciples of all people by baptizing them in the name of the Blessed Trinity (cf. Mt 28:19). Throughout the New Testament, especially in the Acts of the Apostles, there are many references to the sacrament of Baptism. In a famous passage in his Letter to the Romans (6:3-4), St. Paul draws a parallel between Christ's redemptive death and Resurrection and Baptism.

Theologians are divided as to precisely when Christ established the sacrament. St. Thomas Aquinas believed the institution occurred when Jesus was baptized in the Jordan River, while St. Bernard of Clairvaux pointed to the conversation with Nicodemus (cf. Jn 3:1-15). Hugh of St. Victor (c. 1090-1141) believed the divine mandate given before Jesus' Ascension instituted Baptism. According to St. Bonaventure, the sacrament was established in its form just before the Ascension (Mt 28:19), in its matter when Christ was baptized (Lk 3:21-22), and in its purpose when Jesus spoke about its necessity to Nicodemus (Jn 3:5).

The Celebration of Baptism • Baptism, Confirmation, and the Eucharist comprise the Sacraments of Initiation. Baptism is celebrated by washing with water, either by immersion in natural water or by pouring such water over the candidate's head, while the Trinitarian formula ("N., I baptize you in the name of the Father, and of the Son, and of the Holy Spirit") is pronounced. The requisite intention in baptizing is "to will to do what the Church does when she baptizes" (CCC 1256).

The ordinary ministers of Baptism are bishops, priests, and deacons. An "extraordinary" minister is anyone else, even someone who is unbaptized or who has deliberately rejected the faith, provided the necessary intention, form, and matter are present, and the situation is one of real necessity.

Both adults and infants may be baptized. Adults preparing to receive the sacrament are to enter into a formal period of conversion, prayer, and study, often referred to as the catechumenate. This preparation helps dispose one to receive the Sacraments of Initiation. Infants, because they are tainted with original sin, are able to receive this sacrament, and Christian parents should ensure that their children do not lack Baptism. The long-standing practice of infant Baptism has a cherished place in the Church; arguments to the contrary, especially as advanced by the Protestant Reformers of the sixteenth century, have been roundly rejected.

For an adult to be baptized, he must have the intention to receive the sacrament, be instructed adequately in the teaching of the Christian faith and the duties incumbent on the faithful, have participated in the catechumenate preparation, and be sorry for his personal sins. For an infant to be baptized licitly, at least one of the parents or a guardian must give consent, and there must be a "realistic" hope that the child will be reared in the Catholic faith. In danger of death, an infant is lawfully baptized even if its parents are opposed (Canons 865.1, 868.1-2).

Each person to be baptized is to have a sponsor. The Code of Canon Law succinctly states the sponsor's role: "To assist an adult in Christian initiation, or, together with the parents, to present an infant at the baptism, . . . [to] help the baptized to lead a Christian life in harmony with baptism, and to fulfill faithfully the obligations connected with it" (Canon 872).

Effects of Baptism • The sacrament of Baptism has many effects, especially "purification from sins and new birth in the Holy Spirit" (CCC 1262). All sins are remitted — whether original sin or actual sins (i.e., mortal and venial); the temporal and eternal punishments due to sin are also extinguished. As the Council of Trent taught, nothing that is hateful to God remains in the souls of those who have been spiritually reborn in Baptism. But certain earthly consequences of sin remain after Baptism: character flaws, death, disease, illness, suffering. A powerful reminder of our human weakness is concupiscence, that tendency to sin which plagues even the baptized.

The grace of justification is conferred through Baptism if the proper dispositions of faith and the detestation of sin are present. Justification enables one to be sanctified by the infusion of sanctifying grace, along with the three theological virtues (faith, hope, charity), the seven gifts of the Holy Spirit (wisdom, understanding, counsel, fortitude, knowledge, piety, fear of the Lord) and the moral virtues, to which the four cardinal virtues (prudence, justice, fortitude, temperance) belong. Furthermore, the recipient enjoys a claim to those actual graces essential for fulfilling all baptismal obligations. The Holy Spirit forms in the baptized the beginning of eternal glory by virtue of the twelve fruits of the Holy Spirit (charity, joy, peace, patience, kindness, goodness, generosity, gentleness, faithfulness, modesty, self-control, chastity).

"Baptism constitutes the foundation of communion among all Christians, including those who are not yet in full communion with the Catholic Church" (CCC 1271). One who has been incorporated into the Mystical Body of Christ by virtue of Baptism shares in the priesthood of Christ; he is related to the members of the Catholic Church as well as to those who belong to other Christian churches that enjoy valid Baptism.

An indelible spiritual mark, or character, imprinted on the soul configures each baptized person closely to Jesus Christ the High Priest. This is what St. Augustine, quoted by the *Catechism of the Catholic Church* (1274), calls "the seal of the Lord." Baptism, which cannot be repeated, signifies that the recipient is consecrated for Christian worship and service.

Those who have been baptized possess certain responsibilities and rights within the Church. The *Catechism of the Catholic Church* enumerates three: "To receive the sacraments, to be nourished with the Word of God and to be sustained by the other spiritual helps of the Church" (CCC 1269). Accordingly, they are also called to fulfill an essential duty, namely, to " 'profess before men the faith they have received from God through the Church' and participate in the apostolic and missionary activity of the People of God [LG 11; cf. LG 17; AG 7; 23]" (CCC 1270).

Necessity of Baptism • The necessity of Baptism has long been maintained by the Church. "The

Lord himself affirms that Baptism is necessary for salvation" (CCC 1257). The Council of Trent declared that after the Gospel was preached by Christ and promulgated by the Apostles there could be no justification without Baptism by water or at least the desire to receive it. Therefore, "Baptism is necessary for salvation for those to whom the Gospel has been proclaimed and who have had the possibility of asking for this sacrament" (CCC 1257).

The Church has a positive duty to ensure that Baptism is available to all who can receive it; she is not aware of any other means that leads to everlasting life in heaven. Theologians have taught that the necessity of Baptism for salvation is a "necessity of means" (cf. Mk 16:16; Jn 3:5) and a "necessity of precept" (cf. Mt 28:19). But Baptism by water, that is, sacramental Baptism, may in an emergency be replaced by Baptism of desire or Baptism of blood.

Baptism of desire is the explicit or implicit wish for sacramental Baptism, along with contrition for one's sins based on supernatural charity (i.e., "perfect contrition"). According to Sacred Scripture, perfect love possesses the power of justification (e.g., Lk 7:47, 24:43; Jn 14:21). Both St. Ambrose and St. Augustine defended the possibility of Baptism by desire, as did such later theologians as St. Bernard of Clairvaux and Hugh of St. Victor. It is effective by virtue of the intention of the individual to receive sacramental Baptism. Baptism of desire bestows sanctifying grace; therefore, the recipient experiences the forgiveness of original sin and actual sins, and the remission of the eternal punishments attached to sin. The subjective disposition of the individual determines how many of his venial sins are forgiven and how much temporal punishment for sin is remitted. However, Baptism of desire does not imprint the indelible character nor is it the "gateway" to the other sacraments.

Baptism of blood is the martyrdom of an unbaptized person that, because of the patient acceptance of a violent death or of an attack leading to death, constitutes the confessing of the Christian faith or the practice of Christian virtue. Christ himself contended that martyrdom, like perfect love, contains justifying power (e.g., Mt 10:32, 10:39; Jn 12:25). Fathers of the Church, namely, Tertullian and St. Cyprian, regarded martyrdom as a legitimate substitute for sacramental Baptism. Since infants may receive it, Baptism of blood operates somewhat differently than Baptism of desire. It is an objective confession of the Christian faith that confers justification and forgives original sin and actual sins, and remits the eternal punishments for sin; when the proper disposition is present, venial sins are forgiven and temporal punishments remitted. Like Baptism of desire, it does not impart the indelible mark.

Catechumens preparing for the Sacraments of Initiation who die before receiving Baptism are considered to be saved because of their explicit desire to receive the sacrament and their repentance of their sins. The Church also teaches that those persons who are ignorant of Jesus Christ and his Church but who seek the truth and who do the will of God as they sincerely know it, can and will be saved. "It may be supposed that such persons would have *desired Baptism explicitly* if they had known its necessity" (CCC 1260; emphasis in original).

Children who have died without Baptism are commended to the mercy of the Lord. Throughout the centuries, some theologians have held that there exists limbo, a condition of natural happiness devoid of the beatific vision, which is experienced by children who were not baptized. This theological opinion seems to enjoy little sway among scholars today, and limbo is not mentioned in the *Catechism of the Catholic Church*. The faithful are permitted "to hope that there is a way of salvation for children who have died without Baptism" (CCC 1261). In any case, the Church insists that children not be prevented from being baptized. Extra-sacramental means of Baptism, such as prayer and the desire for Baptism on the part of the parents and/or the Church, should be remembered.

The sacrament of Baptism is celebrated in accord with the approved liturgical rites of the Church. In the case of adults, it is administered along with the other two sacraments that form the Sacraments of Initiation: Confirmation and Holy

Eucharist. In the case of infants, Baptism in the Latin Church is celebrated alone, while Confirmation and the Holy Eucharist follow some years later. The catechumenate for adults was restored by decree of the Second Vatican Council. The liturgical rite and explanation are contained in the Rite of Christian Initiation of Adults (RCIA). The Latin Church differs significantly from the Eastern Churches concerning when Confirmation and the Holy Eucharist are received.

The actual celebration of Baptism includes gestures and words symbolizing the sacrament's reality and richness. Such actions and formulae are: the Sign of the Cross, the proclamation of the word of God, the exorcism, the anointing with the oil of catechumens, the consecration of the water used for the sacrament, the profession of faith, the renunciation of Satan and his influence, the washing with the blessed water and the pronouncing of the essential words, the anointing with sacred chrism, the clothing with the white garment, the lighting of the baptismal candle from the paschal candle, the *ephetha* prayer, the recitation of the Our Father, and the solemn blessing. In some cultures, it is the custom to take the newly baptized child to the altar of the Blessed Virgin Mary for a prayer entrusting him or her to the Mother of God.

See: Adult Baptism; Apostolate; Cardinal Virtues; Catechumen; Church, Membership in; Ecumenism; Evangelization; Faith, Act of; Gifts and Fruits of the Holy Spirit; Grace; Infant Baptism; Justification; Limbo; Priesthood of the Faithful; Redemption; Sacramental Grace; Sacraments of Initiation.

Suggested Readings: CCC 1213-1284. Vatican Council II, *Dogmatic Constitution on the Church, Lumen Gentium*, 14-17. Code of Canon Law, 849-878. *Rite of Christian Initiation of Adults.* L. Ott, *Fundamentals of Catholic Dogma*, pp. 350-360.

Charles M. Mangan

BAPTISM OF CHRIST

In the early Church, Jesus' baptism is a major mystery, along with his Incarnation, death, Resurrection, and Ascension. The Synoptics record it in detail (Mt 3:13-17; Mk 1:9-11; Lk 3:21, 22). John refers to the tradition at the beginning of his account of Christ's public life (Jn 1:29-34). For Mark the episode is the beginning of the Gospel. Luke shows Jesus in the synagogue of Nazareth at the start of his public life recalling his anointing by the Spirit at the Jordan (Lk 4:16-21). In the Acts of the Apostles, it is required that Judas's replacement be someone who had been with the disciples from the time of Jesus' baptism (Acts 1:22). Peter in his sermon to the family and friends of Cornelius mentions Jesus' baptism: "Jesus of Nazareth, whom God anointed with the Holy Spirit . . . " (Acts 10:38).

One is surprised at how central a place this event has in the New Testament, despite the scandal it must have caused: Why did the sinless One subject himself to baptism? Theologians of the earliest times were aware of the Holy Spirit's presence in Jesus from the moment of his human birth, but they attributed a different and decisive significance to his solemn anointing. The very name "Christian" derived from it: Christians were not so much Christ's followers as those who shared in his anointing. "To name Christ is to confess the whole Trinity, because it indicates the God who anointed, the Son who was anointed and that wherewith he was anointed, namely the Spirit, as we have learned from Peter in the Acts" (St. Basil, *On the Holy Spirit*, 12).

Doctrinal Significance • The early Church had to interpret the baptism so as to close out heresies: adoptionism, which held that Jesus received his Divine Sonship and became the Christ, or Anointed One, only at his baptism; Gnosticism, in which Jesus was considered one person and Christ another — the man born of Mary and the Deity that descended on him at the baptism, respectively; and Arianism, which held Jesus to need the Spirit in a way incompatible with claims to divinity. For the Fathers, Jesus' baptism was a way of speaking of his divine origins, the first full revelation of his identity. As St. Ignatius of Antioch (c. 35-c. 107) says in his *Letter to the Smyrneans:* "Son of God by God's will and power, truly born of a Virgin and baptized by John so that all righteousness might be fulfilled."

The double witness of the Father and the Spirit reveals the consubstantial mystery of the coming of the Son; Jesus' baptism is the revelation of his identity as Trinitarian communion. He will be the source of the Spirit for our consecration and mission. Against the Arians, St. Cyril of Alexandria (c. 375-444) declares that "the Savior gives us [the Spirit] anew and returns us to our ancient condition and reforms us according to his image. Through the descent of the Spirit on Jesus we permanently possess the full and complete indwelling in men of the Holy Spirit" (*Commentary on John*, 5.2).

The heresies created crises and also evoked cautions in the Fathers' teaching. The strong Greek tendency to relate everything to the metaphysics of substance and being led the Fathers to set aside the idea of any change in Christ at the time of his baptism. In this context, the question arises: How can the Word incarnate become at baptism something new, which he was not already at the moment of the Incarnation? Can one attribute importance to the history of Jesus, the concrete facts of his life, without calling into question the reality of his being perfect man and perfect Savior from the beginning?

In the new climate produced by such questions, the idea of Jesus' anointing as the work of the Holy Spirit does not disappear from theology, but is transferred from the baptism in the Jordan to the Incarnation. The function of the Holy Spirit with regard to Jesus is only that of causing his human nature, by miraculously bringing about in Mary the Incarnation of the Word. The result is a weakening of the pneumatic (Spirit-acting) dimension of Christology. There are exceptions like St. Basil (died 379), who speaks of a continuous presence of the Holy Spirit in the life of Jesus; but for the Fathers the decisive time of the coming of the Holy Spirit into salvation history is no longer Jesus' baptism but Pentecost.

With the Second Vatican Council, the mystery of the coming of the Holy Spirit on Christ has reappeared in the Church's consciousness. "The Lord Jesus, 'whom the Father has made holy and sent into the world' (Jn 10:36), has made his whole Mystical Body share in the anointing by the Spirit with which he himself has been anointed" (*Decree on the Ministry and Life of Priests, Presbyterorum Ordinis*, 2). Pope John Paul II emphasizes the Holy Spirit's activity in Jesus' life: "Jesus' baptism confirms the truth about the Messiah who comes in the power of the Holy Spirit. He came 'to baptize with the Holy Spirit,' that is, to institute the new reality of being reborn from God on the part of the children of Adam burdened with sin. Jesus Christ, the Son of God, comes into the world by work of the Holy Spirit, and as Son of Man, he fulfills completely his messianic mission in the power of the Holy Spirit. . . . [I]t is the Holy Spirit himself who reveals that Jesus is the Son of God. Thus today, thanks to the Holy Spirit, the divinity of the Son, Jesus of Nazareth, shines before the world. With this in mind, St. Paul writes, 'No one can say, "Jesus is Lord," except in the Holy Spirit' (1 Cor 12:3)" (*Christological Catechesis*, August 5, 1987).

Effects for Jesus and for Us • Scripture shows a clear purpose in Jesus' baptism and in the Spirit's descent upon him. "We are entitled to suppose that this was the moment when Jesus accepted his vocation" (C.H. Dodd). Father Raniero Cantalamessa adds, "Not because before then he had not accepted it, but because only at this point in his 'growth in wisdom and grace' as a human being it had been manifested to him in clear and concrete terms." From the baptism on, the Gospels speak more explicitly of Christ's activity in the power of the Spirit, manifested in his dealing with cases of diabolical possession; and: "If it is by the Spirit of God that I cast out demons, then the kingdom of God has come upon you" (Mt 12:28).

The sister sacraments Baptism and Confirmation come together in Christ's followers. In his baptism the eternal Son provides, as it were, a blueprint for ours. He also provides the model of the Spirit's coming upon us, to empower us for mission in the world. Mission always comes from above, and no one takes it on himself. The Spirit remains in the Son, who performs the Father's will out of his inner being and not as a response to an externally imposed law.

Baptism is also the symbol of death and resurrection, a sign of repentance for sin and its forgiveness. Christ came as Lamb of God to take on himself the sin of the world and so take it away. Baptism is a symbol of sanctification; Christ has come to sanctify the whole of creation. The act of Baptism contains in sacramental form the entire mystery of Christ, the whole purpose of his coming. Pope John Paul notes that Jesus can only give the Spirit through his death and Resurrection. Christ "brings him [the Spirit] at the price of his own 'departure'; he gives them this Spirit as it were through the wounds of his crucifixion. . . . It is in the power of this Crucifixion that he says to them: 'Receive the Holy Spirit' " (encyclical *The Lord and Giver of Life, Dominum et Vivificantem,* 24 [1986]). Christ's baptism joins his mission and the giving of the Spirit.

Christ did not need to be baptized for his own sake. As God's Son in the flesh, he committed no sin. But he came to take upon himself the sins of the world, and his baptism manifests his complete identification with us sinful creatures. By stepping into the waters of the Jordan with the others whom John was baptizing, Jesus becomes one of us — not just in our humanity but in our sinfulness, not just in our life on earth but in the fruit of our sin, death: "For our sake he [the Father] made him to be sin who knew no sin, so that in him we might become the righteousness of God" (2 Cor 5:21). Jesus enters the waters to identify with our human condition in order to heal it, and so to commit himself to his Passion and death for our salvation.

See: Baptism; Christological Controversies; Confirmation; Gnosticism; Holy Spirit; Incarnation; Jesus Christ, God and Man; Jesus Christ, Life of; Redemption.

Suggested Readings: CCC 535-537. John Paul II, *Lord and Giver of Life, Dominum et Vivificantem; Christological Catechesis.* L. Bouyer, *The Eternal Son.* R. Cantalamessa, *The Holy Spirit in the Life of Christ.*

Richard Malone

BEATIFIC VISION

It is the constant teaching of the Catholic Church that the direct vision of God, both in himself and most gloriously reflected in everyone and everything else, constitutes the principal and final end for which man was made. "For what other end do we have," asks St. Augustine in the *City of God,* "if not to reach the kingdom which has no end?" The *Catechism of the Catholic Church* says: "God put us in the world to know, to love, and to serve him, and so to come to paradise" (1721). We are beings so fashioned that nothing short of the joy of gazing upon God forever will satisfy the deepest longings of our hearts. Indeed, by God's decree, enacted on the cross, man possesses no other genuine, perduring end save that of seeing God face to face.

In what, then, will the experience of the beatific vision consist? Faith tells us that it will involve an immediate knowledge of almighty God in which the blessed soul sees him directly: clearly and openly, that is, and as he is in himself, in the mystery of his triune life. In this vision of God, says St. Thomas Aquinas, "it is necessary that a created intellect see the divine essence by means of the divine essence itself . . . seeing him in that manner in which he sees himself" (*Summa Contra Gentiles,* III, q. 51).

This is a vision, moreover, the sheer joy and delight of which will overflow the entire will and being of man; it is so sublime a prospect, declares the *Catechism,* citing St. Gregory of Nyssa, that all possible felicity will have been infinitely outstripped; inasmuch as Scripture tells us, "to see is to possess. . . . Whoever sees God has obtained all the goods of which he can conceive" (*De Beatitudinis* 6; quoted in CCC 2548). It is nothing less than full and perfect communion with God, whom we desire above all else and in whom we shall obtain the delight of all else, including those we have loved and lost on earth.

Insofar as our natures are ill-equipped to obtain that for which they finally long, however, this is a vision that only the light of divine glory, *lumen gloriae,* can confer. Thus it is a gift whose bestowal infallibly raises one to the supernatural life. But, as the *Catechism* further reminds us, quoting St. Augustine, in this unimaginably purified state, "God himself will be the goal of our desires; we shall contemplate him without end, love him without surfeit, praise him without weariness" (*City of God*, 22, 30; quoted in CCC 2550).

See: Heaven; Last Things.

BEATITUDES

"The Beatitudes are at the heart of Jesus' preaching" (CCC 1716). St. Matthew, whose Gospel is, among all the New Testament books, distinguished for its moral teaching, places the Beatitudes at the beginning of the Lord's ministry.

In Matthew, Christ begins the Sermon on the Mount with the Beatitudes (Mt 5:3-12), granting them first place in that discourse in which Jesus' moral message is most richly declared. Addressing his followers, he taught how great was the blessedness of those who were authentically his disciples. Those who lead such lives are indeed happy, and their reward will be great.

The scene Matthew draws reminds us of the scene in the Old Testament in which Moses, the chief spokesman for the Old Law, brings to the people from God the magnificent Ten Commandments on Mount Sinai (cf. Ex 34, 35). These commandments, the laws of liberty and of life, lie at the very center of the Mosaic covenant with God. The people are to keep these precepts in order to be truly God's people and to deserve a promised land on earth, in which God will be their God and protector.

Christ's Beatitudes are more sublime than the commandments. Here it is not merely a question of avoiding evil actions that are hostile to love and make peaceful life on earth impossible. Rather, the Beatitudes present a radically new vision. They call us to be new people living in new way; they invite us to live a life far more excellent than what the Decalogue requires. Those who live the Beatitudes are, already on earth, happy in the goodness and greatness of their lives, and are bearers of a better promise: They have secure confidence of possessing a better, entirely blessed homeland in heaven.

The eight Beatitudes are: (1) Blessed are the poor in spirit, for theirs is the kingdom of heaven. (2) Blessed are those who mourn, for they shall be comforted. (3) Blessed are the meek, for they shall inherit the earth. (4) Blessed are those who hunger and thirst for righteousness, for they shall be satisfied. (5) Blessed are the merciful, for they shall obtain mercy. (6) Blessed are the pure in heart, for they shall see God. (7) Blessed are the peacemakers, for they shall be called sons of God. (8) Blessed are those who are persecuted for righteousness' sake, for theirs is the kingdom of heaven.

Distinctiveness of the Beatitudes • The beatitude form is found often in Scripture (cf. Sir 25:7-11, Ps 1:1-2, Rv 22:7-14). A beatitude is the joyful declaration of an important moral truth: Blessed, truly happy, and excellent are those who live thus. Then there is a promise: Those who live so well shall surely receive a longed-for reward.

The eight Beatitudes of Our Lord praise those whose lives shine with the distinctive patterns of living that Christ exemplified and lived — forms of living that are patterns for living as his true disciples. These are the wisest and the best ways to live in this fallen and redeemed world.

In the fire of faith, hope, and love, aware of the existential conditions of the world, of the tragedy of sin, and of the saving mercy of God, the lives of those who live in this manner are different from lives praised by the great pagan moralists. The first disciples of Jesus knew that the actual world was not really understood by worldly minds; and we, too, cannot live an ordinary "sensible life." Sinners living in a broken but redeemed world, we cannot live well without generous love. Having been forgiven and loved so much, we must not be ordinary competitors for goods and dignities, seeking to make ourselves happy while having only a decent respect for justice and moderation. We who have found Christ can find ourselves only in giving away what we have and are, shaping different visions of blessedness from the dreams of those who do not know the drama of salvation and divine mercy. There is a distinctive Christian way of living, and it is very good.

Aristotle praised justice and prudence, but he

did not praise the poor and the humble. The *poor in spirit* whom Christ praises are those who have understood his poverty and no longer have a taste for deceptive riches or the praises of the world. They have realized that self-giving love is the richest form of living. To give away all one has, and is, means entering a blessed way of living like that of the Lord their teacher. Happy are they — already they taste the gladness of the kingdom of heaven that will be fully theirs.

The *meek*, too, are praised. Meekness points to the patience of the poor, a patience that marks strong and generous hearts. Christ declares that he himself was meek (Mt 11:29). He would not strike out against others to acquire what was not needed, when it was so necessary to stand witness in patient strength for what is important above all else.

To *mourn* as Christ mourned is also a blessed form of life. Tears shed not out of self-pity, but out of great love and compassion, shine in the splendor of the great caring and all-embracing love of the true disciple. The meek seek no more for themselves, because they already possess the longed-for land toward which they are journeying. Those who mourn are already comforted and know the time will come when God will wipe away the tears from every eye.

To *hunger and thirst for justice* is to have a blessed passion for justice and entire goodness of heart. The disciple does not see the goal of life as merely a balance between extremes, although there is a place for that. But the love that animates his longing for justice has another measure: loving beyond all measure. Such love is the form or soul of all Christian virtues. Those who thirst so much for what is altogether good in the presence of God shall surely be satisfied. Indeed, their very passion for justice makes their lives already blessed and excellent.

To be *merciful* is to be like the Lord, who has been merciful to us and saved us. The merciful see this broken world as it is, and know how much God loves those in need about us. Faith and love, grown strong in them, enable them to realize that to be faithful they must be far more than fair to others. Fairness would not have saved them; all need mercy to mount up to the greatness to which God calls each one. In showing mercy, they taste the blessedness of living the mercy God lives and know they shall have a mercy beyond all understanding.

The *pure of heart* shall see God. The pure of heart seek one thing; their hearts are not devious and divided and unhappy. The dishonest and pretended loves of the worldly are not theirs. With all their hearts they seek what is best: God, who is the perfect goodness their hearts were made for. They seek a God who is not far from us but dwells in every neighbor. In their singleness of heart, they see the Lord himself in all; and they know they shall see him face to face, with all those they have loved with pure love, and enter into God's overwhelming joy.

The Lord's greeting, "Peace be with you," speaks of a peace that includes every blessing. The *peacemakers* are sources of every kind of peace. A good life needs to be at peace in the world, undisturbed by disorderly passions. It needs to have peace of mind and heart, peace with others and with God. Peace is shaped in homes and in neighborhoods, in cities and among nations. Those who make peace — the poor in spirit, the merciful, the pure of heart — are above all called sons of God. For they are like the incarnate Son of God, the first of peacemakers, who is himself our peace (Eph 2:14), having made peace possible for all by the blood of his cross (Col 1:20).

The *persecuted* seem to be tragic figures rather than blessed; they do what is right and are assailed because of their very goodness. But to *suffer* persecution here seems to signify much more than being made to taste pain. It suggests having such great love that one bears the cross gladly. One may recall the beautiful story of "Perfect Love" in the *Little Flowers of Saint Francis*. Above all the gifts and graces of the Holy Spirit, Francis of Assisi declares, is that of bearing the cross with overwhelming love, glad to be able to endure all for those one loves. Such is the magnificent love of Christ crucified; and blessed indeed are those who have a share in his saving love. With this last of the Beatitudes we return in a way to the first: Like the poor in spirit, the persecuted possess the kingdom of God.

The Universal Call to Holiness • The Beatitudes were not meant only for certain elite Christians. The patterns of life they present were meant to draw all toward the excellent forms of life for which human hearts, touched by grace, long. There is great attractiveness in the heroic and holy lives lived according to the Beatitudes (cf. Pope John Paul II, encyclical *The Splendor of Truth, Veritatis Splendor*, 16).

Reflection on the Beatitudes reminds us that Christian lives cannot settle peacefully into mediocrity. God takes every Christian seriously and calls each to greatness. All are called to the perfection of charity and the generosity of holy lives (CCC 2012-2014). Few may reach the heights of greatness that some of the disciples reached. But efforts to live according to the generosity of the Gospel are a great protection to grace and hope.

Disciples are to follow Christ and become like him — and it is their happiness to become like their Master. But Christ above all was poor. "Though he was rich he became poor for our sake" (2 Cor 8:9). Christ in infinite compassion wept over Jerusalem, at Lazarus' tomb, and in his blessed Passion. Jesus thirsted for righteousness, longing with his whole heart that all might become holy. He above all others was meek and merciful; he was entirely pure in heart, and was the supreme peacemaker, for "he is himself our peace" (Eph 2:14). He is first among those bitterly persecuted: Beaten, scourged, mocked, crowned with thorns, he bore every kind of evil willingly and with burning love.

Thus the Beatitudes are first of all portraits of Christ himself (CCC 1717). They sketch the many facets of his infinite love. They point out, too, the ways in which Christ most wishes our lives to be like his. To be a Christian means being called to a life that is excellent and also truly happy. Christ repeats in every Beatitude that it is a great blessing and joy to live as he invites his friends to do. They will share his crosses and drink the cup he has drunk of; but their lives will be excellent and

glad. For they will be leading the kind of life he lived. So great and good a life already gives the disciple an excellence almost beyond praise. It promises eternal life most securely.

Those who live in the excellent ways the Beatitudes commend — in poverty of spirit, as bearers of mercy and creators of peace — will be happy. Their happiness is, as we have seen, a happiness tasted already in this world, since the greatest joy in life is that of living a truly excellent life: one dear to God and a blessing to all men. To live according to the pattern by which the Lord himself lived on earth is the great joy of his disciples.

But an eternal reward also is promised for living so glad and excellent a life. While the first and eighth Beatitudes promise the kingdom of heaven, the others speak of the promised reward in different ways: The true disciples shall be comforted, shall inherit the earth, be entirely satisfied, obtain mercy, see God, be called sons of God. Most commentators agree that these are not different rewards but speak in various ways of the magnificent reward that surpasses all our hopes: the reward that will be ours when we enter the kingdom of God in all its fullness and see God face to face, so entering into his joy and sharing his blessed rest (CCC 1720).

Christian teachers have placed the Beatitudes at the heart of the Christian message since the first days of faith. They express the vocation of the faithful; they shed light on the attitudes characteristic of Christian life. They sustain hope in the midst of trials. They invite us to taste now something of the gladness of eternal life, knowing how many disciples, having happily lived the Beatitudes, have already entered its fullness (CCC 1717).

See: Evangelical Counsels; Hope; Kingdom of God; Law of Christ; Moral Principles, Christian; New Covenant; Ten Commandments; Theological Virtues.

Suggested Readings: CCC 541-550, 1023-1029; 1716-1729, 1820-1821. Vatican Council II, *Dogmatic Constitution on the Church, Lumen Gentium*, Ch. V, "The Call to Holiness"; *Decree on the Apostolate of the Laity, Apostolicam Actuositatem*, 4. John Paul II, *The Splendor of*

Truth, Veritatis Splendor. Congregation for the Doctrine of the Faith, *Instruction on Christian Freedom and Liberation, Libertatis Conscientia,* 62. St. Thomas Aquinas, *Summa Theologiae,* I-II, q. 69. G. Grisez, *The Way of the Lord Jesus,* Vol. 1, *Christian Moral Principles,* Ch. 26. P. Hinnebusch, O.P., "The Messianic Meaning of the Beatitudes," *The Bible Today,* 59 (1972), pp. 707-717.

Ronald D. Lawler, O.F.M. Cap.

BISHOP

The word "bishop" stems from the Greek term *episkopos,* whose etymology suggests a "directing hand." The New Testament makes it clear that the Apostles established local leaders in the communities they founded. The most frequent titles used to designate these leaders are *presbuteroi* (presbyters), *episkopoi* (bishops), and *diakonoi* (deacons). Many Scripture scholars say it is difficult to determine in every detail the respective functions of these men. Catholic faith affirms that bishops are true successors of the Apostles, and that the episcopacy is a determined order in the Church. "Amongst those various offices which have been exercised in the Church from the earliest times the chief place, according to the witness of tradition, is held by the function of those who, through their appointment to the dignity and responsibility of bishop, and in virtue consequently of the unbroken succession going back to the beginning, are regarded as transmitters of the apostolic line" (Vatican Council II, *Dogmatic Constitution on the Church, Lumen Gentium,* 20).

Debated Questions • Since the end of the nineteenth century there has been some debate, fueled by studies in the history of early Christianity as well as by New Testament studies, concerning the exact nature of the ordained ministry the Apostles put in place. This debate affects the ordained ministry as a whole, but it has special implications for the office of bishop. Some present-day scholars, such as Hans Küng and Edward Schillebeeckx, argue for the position, one already advanced by Modernist theologians, that the Apostles instituted bishops and presbyters to provide leadership in the constantly growing Christian communities but not necessarily with a mind to continue their own apostolic authority as it had been received from Christ. The argument, it should be noted, is largely one of silence, that is, based on what is *not* explicitly to be found in the pages of the New Testament.

The important theological question at stake in these discussions concerns the nature of the sacrament of Holy Orders. We can put the question in this way: Do the bishop and priest share uniquely in the very priesthood of Christ, which could only be the case if Christ himself so established their unique form of participation in it; or are they only recognized Church officeholders, instituted for the sake of the organizational convenience required to maintain any well-run group? Since the question pertains to the truth of the Catholic faith, the Magisterium of the Church is the only authority competent to resolve it. The Second Vatican Council in its *Dogmatic Constitution on the Church, Lumen Gentium,* declared: "This sacred Synod teaches that by divine institution bishops have succeeded to the place of the apostles as shepherds of the Church . . . so that he who hears them, hears Christ" (20). In a preeminent way, then, the bishop acts in the Person of Christ the head and shepherd.

Another question debated by theologians before the Council was what distinguishes a bishop from a priest. Some medieval theologians held that the bishop remains a priest, though one to whom an office of jurisdiction is confided. The Church now teaches definitively that the bishop enjoys the fullness of the sacrament of Order (cf. *Lumen Gentium,* 21), from which flows his authority. One liturgical source, the Sacramentary of Verona, expresses this in a formulary used for the ordination of a bishop: "Complete in your priests the highest point of your mystery." This fullness or acme is exercised in the threefold office or *munus* of the bishop, that of sanctifying, teaching, and governing.

Office of the Bishop • Vatican II's *Decree on the Bishops' Pastoral Office in the Church,*

Christus Dominus, underscores the place of preaching the Gospel in the episcopal office: "With the courage imparted by the Spirit, they should call men to faith or strengthen them in living faith. To them they must expound the mystery of Christ in its entirety. This involves those truths ignorance of which is ignorance of Christ" (11).

As successors of the Apostles, then, bishops have been entrusted with the task of preserving, explaining, and spreading the word of God of which they are servants (cf. Vatican Council II, *Dogmatic Constitution on Divine Revelation, Dei Verbum*, 10). When this teaching is done in communion with the head and members of the College of Bishops, the Church recognizes an authentic exercise of the Magisterium of the Church's pastors. The Council explained: "The infallibility promised to the Church is also present in the body of bishops when, together with Peter's successor, they exercise the supreme Magisterium" (*Lumen Gentium*, 25).

The diocesan bishop enjoys the pastoral care of the particular church entrusted to him; in some cases, he may be assisted by a coadjutor bishop and one or several auxiliary bishops. The hierarchical communion of the Church is revealed especially in the celebration by the bishop of the Eucharist. The distinctive ceremonies prescribed for episcopal liturgies emphasize the importance of this moment in the life of the local church.

The bishop uses several insignia that are the signs of his office and rank: the pastoral ring, which symbolizes his bond or spiritual marriage to the local Church; the staff, or crozier, which is a symbol of his authority as chief shepherd of the flock; the miter (from the Greek word for turban), a shield-shaped headdress with two lappets at the back. It is the custom as well for bishops to wear pectoral crosses around their necks as signs of their special relationship to Christ and of their obligation to preach "Christ crucified" (1 Cor 1:23). The bishop is the ordinary, but not the only, minister of the sacrament of Confirmation, and he alone can confer the sacrament of Holy Orders.

Because the Bishop of Rome is the supreme visible bond of the communion of the particular churches, the lawful ordination of a bishop requires a special intervention of the Pope. Some theologians, mostly of the Reformed traditions, consider this practice an exception to what they allege was the practice of the early Church. The point is moot for the most part, since only the Anglican and, in some countries, the Lutheran communions continue the practice of ordaining bishops.

See: Apostolic Succession; Collegiality; Ecumenical Council; Episcopal Conference; Holy Orders; In Persona Christi Capitis; Magisterium; Modernism; Pope; Priesthood of Christ; Synod of Bishops.

Suggested Readings: CCC 873, 893-894, 895, 879, 888, 1142, 1536, 1555-1561. Vatican Council II, *Decree on the Bishops' Pastoral Office in the Church, Christus Dominus*. R. Brown, *Priest and Bishop*.

Romanus Cessario, O.P.

BLASPHEMY

"You shall not take the name of the Lord your God in vain," reads the second commandment. On the other hand, Jesus taught us to call God not only our Father but the equivalent of Daddy (Abba) as well (cf. Mk 14:36, Rom 8:15, Gal 4:6). With this, the Master sought to compensate for the Jewish extreme of never uttering or writing the name of Yahweh (the name God gave himself in an encounter with Moses [cf. Ex 3:13-15]). We are to be on good terms, even intimate, with God, though never forgetful of how far our transcendent God must mercifully stoop in order to bind up our self-inflicted wounds.

"Blasphemy," reads the *Catechism* (2148), "is contrary to the respect due God and his holy name. It is in itself [if deliberate] a grave sin." Neither through our commissions or omissions are we to make it easy for ourselves or others to disregard God; this misuse, says the same paragraph, "can provoke others to repudiate religion." The prohibition of blasphemy extends to: inward or outward utterances against God of hatred, reproach, or defiance; speaking ill of God; calling upon God to damn, harm, or destroy the object of one's wrath;

misusing God's name (cursing); language against Christ's Church, the saints, and holy things; and invoking God's name to cover up criminal deeds.

See: Religion, Virtue of; Sacrilege.

BOASTING

One of the most familiar characters in American literature is the braggart, for example, the "Duke" and the "Dauphin" in Mark Twain's *Huckleberry Finn*. Often, these colorful literary liars are figures of fun, expressions of the high-spirited, expansive frontier. However, their charm can blind us to the fact that real-life boasting is an offense against truth (cf. CCC 2481).

As the literary examples suggest, the moral fault is usually slight. Indeed, braggarts sometimes communicate by their manner or the sheer absurdity of their "tall tales" that they are lying, and so they are innocent of the charge of deception. However, boasting to gain an unfair advantage — exaggerating one's accomplishments on a job application, for example — can seriously damage others and is no laughing matter. Bragging can also be a sign of sinful pride; often in such cases, the person deceived is the braggart himself.

See: Lying; Truthfulness.

BODY AND SOUL

The question of body and soul has been called by a German philosopher the *Weltknoten*, which means the "knot of the world." This is supposed to express the fact that as one's philosophy of body and soul changes, so does one's entire *Weltanschauung*, or worldview. The peculiar position that man occupies between heaven and earth is at issue in the question of how body and soul come together in him.

Christian writers often say that they want to avoid any and every dualism of body and soul in their philosophy of human nature. They are right to say this, for reasons that we will give below; but at the same time it must also be said that Christians recognize, if not a dualism, then at least a duality of body and soul. This duality can already be gathered from the Genesis account of the creation of man, from which we see that man is composed of something taken from the earth and something sprung directly from God.

The Immateriality of the Soul • The early Greek philosophers were unable to conceive of nonmaterial being; even in speaking of the soul they employed material and physical categories. Plato (427-347 B.C.) worked a revolution in human thought by conceiving for the first time of immaterial being and by arguing for the first time for the immateriality of the soul. One of his main arguments, which continues to be used to this day, runs as follows.

The human intellect is capable of understanding eternal being in the form of the timelessly valid essences of things. This means that the human intellect is capable of understanding immaterial being. For since material being is signed by corruptibility and change, and is thus subject to time, eternal being can only be immaterial. But if the intellect knows immaterial being, and is in fact never so much itself as when it knows it, then the intellect must itself be immaterial: Being so deeply akin to that which is eternal and immaterial, and resonating so profoundly with it, the intellectual part of the soul must itself be immaterial.

Aristotle (384-322 B.C.) developed a variant of this argument by showing that the object of intellectual knowledge is something general or universal (e.g., what we understand is not in the first place this or that man, but rather man as such, or man in principle). Now, the universal is immaterial, matter always existing only as a concrete this or that. But man could not know the immaterial universal if his knowing were itself altogether material, for how should a concrete bodily organ be receptive to that which is universal and thus nonbodily? It follows that his knowing involves a nonbodily or immaterial principle.

St. Augustine developed an original argument that enables us almost to touch and feel the immateriality of our soul (*On the Trinity*, Bk. X). Each person, he said, experiences himself within himself in a most intimate way; each knows within himself that he suffers and loves and understands;

each knows these things by living them, by having them as his own experiences. Now, if a person were in this innermost center of himself something bodily, then he would have to experience with just this unique intimacy and inwardness that bodily thing that he was. But no one ever finds any bodily organ (like the brain) in his innermost self-presence. Whenever one thinks about a bodily organ, trying to identify one's very self with it, one can only think about it at a distance from oneself and over against oneself; try as one will, one cannot experience it within oneself. It follows that each person is something nonbodily in his innermost self.

Some will find the argument simpler still if we just point out that the inner world that each knows in himself does not take up any space. For example, the anguish that I suffer within myself does not take up any space; it does not stand in any spatial relation to other things happening in my inner life, such as my reflecting on the meaning of the suffering. Since matter, whatever else it is and does, always takes up space, the human person must have something in himself that, as it takes up no space, has no matter to it.

Notice that these last two arguments show the immateriality not just of acts of rational understanding but of all acts and experiences of persons.

Substantial Difference Between Body and Soul • But there is a famous retort to all such arguments from the side of the materialists. They say that what we call an immaterial soul is really only a kind of quality or property of the brain or of the body as a whole. Just as the beauty of a painting is not a physical something in the sense in which the colors of the painting are physical, and yet the beauty is nothing but a quality of the physical painting, so with the immaterial soul: Though immaterial, it inheres as a kind of property in the material body. If this materialistic response is correct, then we have not gone beyond a fundamentally materialistic view of the soul.

Already some ancient Greek philosophers took this refined materialist position — and already Plato and Aristotle refuted it decisively. The main Platonic argument is based on our freedom in governing our bodies. We have it in ourselves to resist the promptings of the body; for the sake of some good that we have understood, we can act in our body in such a way as to govern the body and not be governed by it. But how, Plato asks, can a dependent quality act on its own initiative against that on which it depends? Could the beauty of the painting act back on the picture so as to change the colors or to delete something in the picture? Just as beauty is too passive in relation to the elements of the painting to take any such initiative, so the soul would be too passive to take any such initiative if it were nothing but a quality of the body. But since the soul can and often does take this initiative toward the body, it is essentially more in its immateriality than just the immaterial property of the body.

But what is this "more"? Most of the great Christian philosophers have explained it in terms of the *substantiality* of the soul. For Aristotle, a substance is a being that exists on its own and in itself and not merely as a part or an attribute of another being. Thus any human being is a substantial being, since it is not a part or an attribute of any other being. But we have also to say that the human soul alone is substantial being. The immaterial soul is not a mere part or an attribute of the body or of the body-soul composite; it has just that being of its own that we call its substantiality. St. Thomas Aquinas thinks that this being-of-its-own is expressed in the fact that the soul is capable of certain activities, such as rational understanding or free choosing, which belong not to the body-soul composite but to the soul alone.

With such arguments we establish the *immaterial* substantiality of the human soul. This implies that there is *a substantial difference* between body and soul in man. On this basis, one can proceed to argue for the *immortality* of the soul, that is, for its capacity to survive the death of the body. For clearly, if the refined materialistic view of the soul were true, there could be no immortality. On the same basis, one can also argue for the impossibility of the soul being generated by the parents in the same way in which the body is generated;

an immaterial substantial soul can only be directly created by God, as the Church also teaches.

Unity of Body and Soul • It may seem that we have gone so far in asserting the difference between body and soul as to portray each human being as composed of two substances or two beings, and that we can no longer make sense of the idea that each is in fact one being. It may seem so, but it is not really so. We can in fact now proceed to affirm *that the soul is the form of the body*, and to do so not in spite of all that has been said *but rather on the very basis of it.*

This idea of the soul as form, which derives from Aristotle, has been taken by the Church into her own doctrine (Ecumenical Council of Vienne [1312], constitution *Fidei Catholicae*). To call the soul the form of the body is of course not to say that it is merely the external shape of the body, nor is it to say that it is the internal structure of the body. It is rather to say that the soul, out of the abundance of its own nonbodily life of understanding and willing and loving, "in-forms" the body, making it to be a living body, and not only a living body but a bodily expression of the soul's own more-than-bodily life. It is not enough to say that the soul acts on the body and governs it and that the body acts on the soul; such interaction between body and soul, though of course it exists, falls short of the intimate union of the two expressed by saying that the soul makes the body live and even incorporates the body into its own higher spiritual life, raising it far above the merely physical. The soul does not just use the body, though it does that too, but it also dwells in the body, is present in it, indeed exists as embodied.

Philosophers have tried to put the idea that the soul is the form of the body together with the other idea — apparently opposed to the first — that the soul has its own substantiality. They have argued that the strength and independence of being implied in substantiality *is the very source* of the soul's power to inform; but that which it informs is taken into itself in such a way that what results is one composite body-soul being. Insofar as the soul has its own substantiality, it might say of the body, "I *have* a body"; but insofar as it informs the body, incarnating itself in the body, it might say of it, "I *am* my body." St. Thomas puts the two ideas together in a single phrase when he calls the soul the *substantial form* of the body.

Christian philosophers, and they almost alone among philosophers, have gone one step further and argued that the soul is incomplete apart from its bodied state. Inspired by their faith in the creation and redemption of matter and of bodies, they have said that, while the human soul can, and in fact for a time does, exist as disembodied, in this state it suffers an unnatural mode of existence, and can be fully itself only as embodied. This leads to the result that the soul, for all its substantiality, is called by these philosophers an incomplete substance or an imperfect substance, the really complete substance being not the soul alone but the body-soul composite.

True and False Dualism • For those affirming that the soul is the form of the body there are various unacceptable versions of body-soul dualism. If, for instance, one says that the body is only an encumbrance for the soul, or if one even goes so far as to say that the soul would be pure and happy but for the body, then one has fallen into an erroneous dualism. Or if one says that the soul only *uses* the body as an instrument or uses the body as raw material, then one would have a dualism different indeed but no less erroneous. On the other hand, there is a duality of body and soul that we must affirm. To affirm the substantial difference of body and soul need have nothing to do with these dualistic excesses; far from interfering with the truth about the soul as form of the body, this affirmation underlies it.

The proper understanding of the unity of body and soul in man is all-important for maintaining Catholic sexual moral teaching. As John Paul II shows in his encyclical *The Splendor of Truth*, *Veritatis Splendor*, 48-49, dissent in contemporary moral theology comes in good measure from certain dualisms of body and soul that imply an excessively spiritualistic image of man.

In conclusion, let us guard not only against a false dualism but also against a certain rationalism. Much as philosophy can understand about body and soul in man, there always remains something impenetrable and mysterious for us about how exactly man exists between heaven and earth as an embodied spirit — about how exactly that which takes up no space can inform so intimately that which is spread out in space. According to St. Augustine, "the way in which spirits are united with bodies is altogether marvelous and cannot be understood by man — yet this [unity of body and soul] is man himself."

See: Human Person; Immortality; Sexuality, Human; Theology of the Body.

Suggested Readings: CCC 362-368. Council of Vienne, *Fidei Catholicae*, Denzinger-Schönmetzer, 902. Vatican Council II, *Pastoral Constitution on the Church in the Modern World, Gaudium et Spes*, 14. Plato, *Phaedo*. St. Augustine, *On the Trinity*, X. St. Thomas Aquinas, *Summa Theologiae,* I, qq. 75-76.

John F. Crosby

BRIDE OF CHRIST

The Church is referred to as the Bride of Christ (cf. CCC 796, 808). In the Old Testament, God's love for his people is expressed at times in terms of a husband's love for his bride (cf. Is 61:8-10, Hos 2:16-20). St. Paul intensifies the image to show the relationship between Christ and his Church: "Husbands, love your wives, as Christ loved the Church and gave himself up for her" (Eph 5:25; cf. Rv 21:2, 9).

The spousal image emphasizes certain major ecclesiological truths. It stresses the *loving and enriching* nature of the election that Christ has made of his Church. He chose her out of love, and wishes to be united to her. Through this spousal union, the Church is endowed with all of Christ's riches. Indissolubly bound to Christ, she possesses all things in common with him. United to Christ, she is also *called to be fruitful*: We are all begotten into divine life in the Church, as a result of her union with Jesus Christ. For this reason, too, we refer to the Church as our mother — "holy Mother the Church." In fact, it is hard to

feel at home in the Church unless one sees in her one's mother. Further, the image of "bride" highlights the Church's *call to be faithful* to her Spouse, as Christ is always faithful to her and to us (cf. 2 Tm 2:13).

As an image, Body of Christ stresses the extent of the union between Our Lord and his Church. Bride of Christ keeps it clear that the union, however close, is nevertheless between two.

See: Church, Nature, Origin, and Structure of; Mystical Body of Christ.

BUDDHISM

Buddha and Christ are titles, not names. Just as Jesus of Nazareth is the Christ, the Anointed One, Siddhartha Gautama is the Buddha, the Enlightened One. Jesus makes the higher claim: "I am the way, and the truth, and the life" (Jn 14:6). Siddhartha merely points the way to God, but his is an ancient and honorable path that billions have trod in deep faith.

Buddhism originated in India as a movement within Hinduism about five hundred years before the birth of Christ. A religion of peace that rejected conversion by fire and sword, it nevertheless spread to Sri Lanka in the third century B.C.; to China, Burma, and Thailand early in the Christian era; to Japan and Korea in the sixth century; and later to Tibet, Indonesia, and Southeast Asia.

Meanwhile, however, Buddhism was weakening in the land of its birth. It disappeared as a separate institution in India about the year 1200, though many scholars argue that Hinduism shows profound Buddhist influence, especially in the practice of *bhakti yoga*. In Indonesia, Islam displaced Buddhism during the Middle Ages. But Buddhism has flourished in other lands, even penetrating the West in our own time. While religious almanacs give total adherents as 335 million, the figure for China (and, since 1959, Tibet) may be understated.

Teaching of the Buddha • According to the Buddhist scriptures, Siddhartha was born a prince, surrounded by every comfort. Disturbed by the existence of sickness, decrepitude, and death, he rejected his life of pleasure, sought wisdom from Hindu masters, and eventually joined a band of ascetics. When self-mortification failed to bring peace, Siddhartha turned to meditation. Seated under the bo (or bodhi) tree one climactic night, he resisted all the temptations that Mara, the Evil One, could summon as his state of contemplation deepened. By dawn he had achieved "Awakening" (or "Enlightenment"), and became known as the Buddha.

Mara's final temptation was to persuade Siddhartha to abandon this unquiet world and slip into endless Nirvana. In rejecting it, the Buddha dedicated himself to serving and saving others. For forty years he lived the life of a mendicant preacher, proclaiming his *dharma*, his eternal truth. Before dying at the age of eighty, he established the Sangha, the community of monks and nuns who would adopt the Buddhist way as a full-time vocation. The Buddha also had many lay disciples of both sexes and all castes. Unlike contemporary Hinduism, Buddhism treated all persons as social equals, respecting only spiritual merit.

The Buddha taught his disciples to observe the middle way between sensuality and self-denial; the body was to have what it needs for health, but no more. He also gave them the Four Noble Truths. First, human life is *dukkha*; pain or misery lies at its heart. Second, the cause of this misery is the desire to act selfishly, consuming rather than communing with the rest of life, which is one. The third truth is that overcoming selfish desire will end *dukkha* and bring the aspirant to Nirvana. Finally, humanity can attain this blessed state by following the Eightfold Path.

Pilgrims who wish to set foot on this path must first observe certain precepts: They must refrain from injuring any living thing, from stealing, from sexual immorality, from lying, and from using drugs or alcohol. Having adopted this morality, they may proceed through meditation on the path's eight steps: (1) right understanding of the Four Noble Truths; (2) right aspiration, the will to seek enlightenment as life's true goal; (3) right speech directed toward truth and charity; (4) right con-

duct as outlined above; (5) right livelihood so that one's occupation, whether as monk or layman, is not a distraction from truth-seeking; (6) right effort to overcome passion and sin by earnestly pursuing the way; (7) right mindfulness so that, through long and arduous practice, the mind comes to exercise control over itself and the body (the classic *Dammapada* begins: "All we are is the result of what we have thought"); and finally, (8) right absorption or concentration, by which the mind breaks through to a blinding new experience of reality. Here it rests, where thought and object, time and eternity, personal being and Being melt together in integral vision. The self has broken its bounds; free of desire and illusion, it encounters Nirvana.

Buddhism As a World Religion • Like Jesus, the Buddha left nothing written, and his teachings defy systematization. However, his followers share certain basic beliefs. First, achieving enlightenment is not an intellectual exercise. Like Christian virtue, it can be won only by doing; the Eightfold Path must be trod, not just known. Moreover, all reality, even human reality, is constant flux. This doctrine represents Buddhism's sharpest break with Hinduism, which teaches that within each individual is an unchanging *atman,* or soul. To the Buddhist, human beings are no more than temporary arrangements of body, sensation, perception, feelings, and consciousness. Transcendent being, the Nirvana to which enlightenment gives access, lies beyond the world of sense and self. Finally, this transcendent state of being is tantamount to the godhead; Buddhists recognize no personal God.

About the time of Christ, Buddhism split into Mahayana (Great Method) and Hinayana (Little Method); the latter is more commonly known as Theravada (Way of the Elders). This division, largely a matter of emphasis, still persists. Theravada Buddhists believe that each person must follow the Path alone and that wisdom is the goal of life's search. They stress the strict observance of monastic discipline and draw a sharp distinction between monk and layman. Mahayana Buddhists hold, on the other hand, that all are invited to religious practice. To them, every individual is part of the web of life and can find help in walking the Path. The Mahayanist's spiritual ideal is thus the *bodhisattva*, the compassionate saint who, like the Buddha himself, rejects entry into Nirvana for the sake of saving others.

Given the relative loneliness and abstraction of Theravada, it is not surprising that Mahayana has won more hearts in the Buddhist world. Zen Buddhism, the school best known in the West, is an intuitive form of Mahayana associated most closely with Japan and Vietnam.

Although the spirituality of some Christian mystics is reminiscent of the meditative Eightfold Path and the Sermon on the Mount echoes Buddhism's gentleness and detachment, the difference between it and Christianity is profound. Since Buddhism considers human reality to be illusory, for example, social justice based on the dignity of the person is meaningless. Most importantly, Buddhism is not an incarnational faith centering on a God-man sent for our salvation. It lacks a formal sacramental system crowned by the Eucharist and does not recognize Jesus as the definitive revelation of God in human history.

The wide disparity among the world's great religions makes it hard to imagine a final reconciliation. However, the Second Vatican Council firmly taught that, while the Church is the ordinary means of salvation, "the plan of salvation also includes those who acknowledge the Creator" (*Dogmatic Constitution on the Church, Lumen Gentium*, 16). Pope John Paul II tirelessly promotes interreligious dialogue, inspired by the words of the *Declaration on the Relationship of the Church to Non-Christian Religions*: "The Church, therefore, urges her sons to enter with prudence and charity into discussion and collaboration with members of other religions. Let Christians, while witnessing to their own faith and way of life, acknowledge, preserve and encourage the spiritual and moral truths found among non-Christians" (*Nostra Aetate*, 2).

See: Ecumenism; Evangelization; Hinduism; Islam; Missionary Activity; Religion, Virtue of.

Suggested Readings: CCC 839-856. Vatican Council II, *Dogmatic Constitution on the Church, Lumen Gentium*, 16-17; *Declaration on the Relationship of the Church to Non-Christian Religions, Nostra Aetate*. John Paul II, *On the Permanent Validity of the Church's Missionary Mandate, Redemptoris Missio*, 94-99. "Buddhism," in G. Parrinder, ed., *World Religions*. H. Smith, "Buddhism," *The Religions of Man*.

David M. Byers

BURIAL, CHRISTIAN

Death and burial have a deeply theological significance for the Christian. A Catholic recites at least once weekly the words of the Creed, "He suffered, died, and was buried," in reference to Christ himself. In death the Christian participates directly in that central part of the paschal drama because he has been conformed to Christ in the sacraments of the Church. Death assumes a paschal significance when a Christian undergoes it, because he does so in Christ.

As profound as is this drama in which each takes the path through death that Christ has trod before, the most significant participation in the death of Christ comes at Baptism, when the symbolic drama of sacramental dying and rising has its salvific effect (cf. Rom 6:3-4, Col 2:12). In Baptism the Christian dies sacramentally, to rise to new life in grace, whereas at death the Christian dies bodily and reaps what was sown in the sacramental death at Baptism. The first death, the sacramental death, determines the character of the physical death. For this reason, the symbolism of the funeral rites — such as the sprinkling with holy water, the pall which drapes the coffin, and the paschal candle — is laden with baptismal significance.

Although the funeral liturgy is not a sacrament, it does present the aspect of a kind of sacramental participation in the paschal mystery, which has at its heart the interment of Christ himself in the Holy Sepulcher. A person who has spent a lifetime in communion with Christ in his Church engages in a participation (*koinonia*) in the death of Christ in his own death and burial. Faith tells us that, by virtue of the sanctifying grace he has received in life through the sacraments, he will also participate in Christ's Resurrection (cf. Rom 6:8). It is this participation in the Passion, death, and Resurrection of Christ that has given Christian burial its particular character.

From the beginning, Christians took up the Jewish practice of burial rather than other funereal customs, such as cremation or exposure. At the time of Christ's death, the common custom involved placing a body on a shelf or niche to await the desiccation of the flesh, after which the bones would be placed in an individual ossuary. Despite the ritual proscriptions about contact with the dead (cf. Nm 9:6ff., Lv 22:4), the Jews considered burial of the dead to be a meritorious act. Tobit lists burying the dead among his acts of charity and cites it as the primary cause for his running afoul of the pagan authorities in Nineveh (Tob 1:16-19). The Jewish appreciation for the importance of making provision for the burial of the dead has continued in Christianity, as its inclusion among the seven corporal works of mercy shows.

Christian View of the Body • The honor paid to the bodies of the deceased is consonant with the importance ascribed to the body in a Christian anthropology. Tertullian's statement that "the flesh is the hinge of salvation" is echoed and developed by Karl Adam in his reflections upon the fundamental characteristics of the Church: "She does not regard the body as a 'garment of shame,' but as a holy and precious creation of God. And she teaches that this gift is so precious and so necessary for man, that the body that is dissolved in death will one day be raised again by God, to be the ministering organ of the immortal soul." The *Catechism of the Catholic Church* likewise says: "The human body shares in the dignity of 'the image of God': it is a human body precisely because it is animated by a spiritual soul, and it is the whole human person that is intended to become, in the body of Christ, a temple of the Spirit" (364).

The Christian position is that the body ought to be treated with the utmost dignity, but its treat-

ment does not bind the soul mechanistically. In the early centuries, when Christianity was still illegal, pagans would desecrate bodies with the intention of trying to frustrate the Christian resurrection. They were apparently unaware that, while in many cultures an improper disposition of the corpse was thought to threaten the final rest of the soul, in Christianity, which values the body so highly, the respect shown does not extend to the extreme of suggesting that an improper burial — or even cremation or other destruction of the bodily remains — can thwart the will of God in regard to the resurrection and glorification of the body.

Early Christian funerals were remarkable for the level of faith represented in the reserve of the mourners. Pastoral practice encouraged the singing of psalms as an expression of hope in the midst of mourning for the dead, in contrast to the loud outcries associated with non-Christian funerals of the time. This practice continues in the Office for the Dead in the Church's Liturgy of the Hours. The offering of the Eucharistic sacrifice, still a prominent part of the full funeral liturgy, is also a practice of the greatest antiquity.

Certain other activities associated with the burial of the dead, such as that of the gravedigger (*fossor*) and pallbearers (*lecticarii*), became offices of some distinction in Latin Christianity. Further testimony to the significance of death as a portal to eternal life can be seen in the construction and adornment of the Roman catacombs. In short, the ritual and profane activity that surrounded Christian funerals gave them a solemn yet celebratory flavor that itself compelled curiosity in their pagan neighbors.

The modern funeral liturgy still expresses that kind of noble and hope-filled dignity. There are three ritual moments in the liturgy: the vigil, the funeral liturgy proper, and the rite of committal. Three ritual venues are provided for — the home, the church, and the cemetery — but the official directives allow for the flexibility necessary to accommodate the diverse conditions and customs that a universal Church encounters. Canon 1176 states the right of the Christian faithful to Christian burial and outlines the aims of the Church in her funeral rites as offering intercession for the departed, honor to the body, and solace to the living. (Strictly speaking, children who have been baptized and have died before acquiring the use of reason — therefore, before being capable of mortal sin — do not require prayers of intercession for their beatitude, which can be considered assured. Nevertheless, there is no reason not to pray more generally for and also to them, asking their intercession for us.)

See: Body and Soul; Cremation; Death; Funerals, Christian; Resurrection of the Dead.

Suggested Readings: CCC 359, 362, 364-365, 1680-1690. Code of Canon Law, 1176-1185. A. Rush, *Death and Burial in Christian Antiquity.*

Sean Innerst

C

CANONIZATION

Of all the congregations at the Vatican, the Congregation for the Causes of Saints is perhaps the least well known and the least influential in the government of the Church. Nevertheless, its work in evaluating and proposing candidates for beatification and canonization is one that, many theologians hold, constantly calls for the exercise of papal infallibility. Canonization takes place by means of a solemn papal declaration that a person is certainly with God in glory. As a result, the newly canonized saint may receive official public veneration, or cult, and the faithful may petition the saint to intercede for them with God. The Roman Catholic Church is the only church in the world that has the complicated mechanism of canonization.

Every person who reaches heaven — even a baptized infant — is a saint, but only a relatively small number have been officially declared saints by the process of canonization. For this to happen, the "cause" must be introduced in the congregation at Rome, after a thorough investigation at the local level. The first question asked is whether there is a cult of veneration for the individual under consideration. That is a basic requirement for introducing a cause at Rome; the individual must have a reputation for holiness that arouses the devotion of the faithful. From the very first century of the Church's existence, when the practice developed of venerating the martyrs, the touchstone of sanctity was always the imitation of Christ and the practice of heroic virtue. The saints were acclaimed as such by the faithful who venerated them.

Throughout the first twelve centuries of the history of the Church there was a gradual increase in the control exercised by ecclesiastical prelates over the public cult of the saints. From time immemorial there had always been "popular canonizations" and this resulted in local patron saints whose feasts were not celebrated throughout the universal Church. This practice still prevails in some dioceses and nations and in religious institutes that have their own *ordo*. As the bishops intervened more and more in the process, adding new names to the calendar of saints in the local churches, they began to demand a verification of the sanctity of the individual. But as soon as the written account of the candidate's heroic virtue was approved by the bishop, the body was transferred to an altar in a ceremony called the "translation," and this sufficed for official canonization.

In the tenth century, the Popes began to intervene in the process of canonization, thus making it possible to proclaim a saint for the veneration of the universal Church. The next step was to demand miracles as well as proof of heroic virtue, and in 1170 Pope Alexander III decreed that no one could be venerated as a saint without papal authorization. This was promulgated as canon law by Pope Gregory IX in 1234 with the publication of the *Decretals*. The canonical process became more and more stringent and bureaucratic, so that by the fourteenth century a distinction was made between *saints*, who were canonized by papal authority, and *blesseds*, who were venerated locally or in religious orders. Nevertheless, the practice of "popular canonization" still continued in many Catholic countries.

In 1588, Pope Sixtus V created the Sacred Congregation of Rites, which was authorized to conduct the process of canonization and to authenticate relics of the saints, but it was not until the seventeenth century that Pope Urban VIII specified the canonical procedures for beatification and canonization. Nevertheless, Pope Urban made an exception for those cults that had been in existence for at least a century prior to his decree. In the future, however, any unauthorized *public* veneration of a candidate for canonization would automatically disqualify that person from papal approval.

Procedures for Canonization • In 1917, the official regulations for the canonization process were incorporated into the Code of Canon Law. The investigation was carried out by responding to a series of questions.

* Does the candidate have a reputation for heroic virtue or a martyr's death?

* Have any of the faithful sought the intercession of the servant of God for divine favors?

* Of what value would the canonization of the candidate be for the Church at large?

* Is there anything in the candidate's life or writings that would be an impediment to canonization?

* Are there any potential miracles due to the candidate's intercession?

* Is there any reason why it would not be expedient to proceed with the process?

The entire process, from the introduction of the cause to its conclusion, was very complicated and lengthy. It began in the local church (or diocese) under the guidance of the bishop, to decide whether the candidate had a reputation for holiness and whether that reputation was justified. At the same time, all published and unpublished writings, including any available letters, were sent to Rome to be examined for orthodoxy.

When the cause was officially introduced at Rome, it was handed over to a consultor from the congregation, who also selected a defense lawyer. The task of the lawyer was to present a brief in defense of the cause; it was answered by the Promoter of the Faith, known as "the Devil's Advocate." This dialectic could go on for many years before the differences were resolved and the volume known as the *positio* was published. The cardinals and other officials would then study the *positio* and ultimately express their verdict. If the verdict was favorable, the congregation notified the Pope and he in turn issued his acceptance.

The cause then entered upon the phase called the apostolic process, meaning that it was now in the hands of the Holy See. The whole cause was sent back to the local diocese for an even more rigorous investigation. On being returned to Rome, there were three more exchanges between the defense and the Promoter of the Faith, at the conclusion of which the candidate was given the title Venerable. The next step was an examination of the corpse (sometimes found to be incorrupt, which is usually considered a point in favor of the cause, but not infallibly so).

The entire process thus far has been a human investigation. The Church now demands a miracle that was worked through the intercession of the Venerable. If the medical and theological authorities concur that an authentic miracle has occurred, the Pope will issue a formal decree of recognition. The stage is now set to proceed to the beatification of the Servant of God, after which another miracle is required for canonization. There are literally hundreds of Blesseds who cannot be canonized because they lack the required miracles. But once the canonization takes place, the saint is offered as an example and intercessor to the entire Church.

Recent Changes in the Process • During the Second Vatican Council, Pope Paul VI quietly established a commission of prelates, theologians, and canonists to investigate the possibility of simplifying the entire process of canonization. The work proceeded at a snail's pace until Pope John Paul II directed the cardinal prefect of the congregation to complete the task. This resulted in the promulgation of the apostolic constitution *Divinus Perfectionis Magister* in 1983.

Two of the changes in the canonization process are especially important. First, the gathering of evidence in support of a cause is entirely in the hands of the local bishop and does not require an apostolic process as well. Second, the lengthy arguments between the legal advocate and the Promoter of the Faith were abolished. The title, "Promoter of the Faith" was changed to "Prelate Theologian" and the atmosphere surrounding the work of the congregation changed from that of a courtroom to a study for research into the life and virtues of the proposed candidate.

The procedure now is as follows. At the outset the local bishop must consult with other bishops to decide whether the process should be started. He then appoints officials to investigate the life and virtues or, if necessary, the martyrdom of the candidate. Testimony may still be taken from witnesses, but the primary concern is the use of historico-critical methods for examining the life and virtues of the candidate. Published and unpublished writings, including letters, are examined by local censors to judge the orthodoxy of the material. The only intervention of the Holy See at this early stage is to issue the *nihil obstat*, which means that there is nothing in the Vatican files that would impede the cause; it may proceed.

Once all the material has been received at the Congregation for the Causes of Saints, a postulator and relator are appointed. The relator is in charge of producing the *positio*, which must contain everything that the consultors and prelates need to know about the candidate, both positive and negative. The relator then assigns someone to write the *positio*. Usually this will be a competent person from the same diocese, religious order, or at least the same country as the candidate.

When the *positio* has been received at the congregation, it is first studied by expert consultors and then passed on to a board of eight theologians. If at least six approve, the *positio* moves on to a selected group of cardinals and bishops for their approval. Finally, it is submitted to the Holy Father for his decision.

Formerly a cause for beatification and canonization could not be initiated until fifty years after the death of the candidate; now the waiting period is at least five years. Previously the number of miracles required was two for beatification and two more for canonization; in the revised process one miracle is required for beatification, unless the candidate was a martyr; for canonization one more miracle is required for both martyrs and nonmartyrs. As regards consultors and relators, any qualified person, male or female, cleric or lay, may be appointed. The difficulty lies in finding persons who have the qualifications, such as fluency in several languages besides Latin and Italian and a knowledge of theology and canon law.

See: Infallibility; Magisterium; Martyrdom; Miracles.

Suggested Readings: CCC 686-688, 823-829, 956, 1717, 2030. K. Woodward, *Making Saints.*
                                                          Jordan Aumann, O.P.

CANON LAW

The inclusion of law as an important part of the life of the Church strikes many people today as improper. After all, is not faith a matter of the Spirit and of the profound exercise of human freedom? Is it not an intimate, personal action so that it is not subject to external control? Should not the living out of such a personal undertaking be eminently free from external constraint and direction? Although such questions as these reflect important truths about the act of faith, they also reflect a view of faith and religion as a purely private act. In addition, one could even say that they reflect a Western culture that has drifted far in the direction of exalting individualism and a notion of freedom with little reference to either truth or the moral obligation flowing from it.

Law is a command issued for the right ordering of a community by the person who has authority over that community. God is the ultimate source of law, and the life of man in society is governed by the natural law written in hearts that we can discover by the use of reason (cf. Rom 2:14-15). Personal relationships in every human society are further ordered by the laws enacted by those who have this authority. God himself may make known his law, as he did among the ancient Jews in the Old Testament and as he did through his Son Jesus Christ and the Apostles in the New Testament.

Sacred Scripture itself gives witness to the importance of law in the life of God's people. Clearly in the Old Testament the law was important to people. Observing the law was closely associated with the spirituality of the Hebrew people (cf. Lv 11). At its best, their spirituality viewed the law as a great gift from God, based on his love, that his people would observe to show forth their love and their fidelity to him. At other times, observing the law would come to be viewed almost as if it were in and of itself the source of sanctification. The Pharisees in Jesus' time, for example, seem to have viewed the law from this perspective.

Jesus did not reject the law and the prophets. Rather, he indicated that he came to fulfill them (Mt 5:17). St. Paul, often quoted in his denunciations of the law, actually helped significantly to clarify its proper role. His letters make clear that the Church is not simply an unstructured community, but one in which authority is present and is to be exercised for the good of the community (1 Cor 5 and 6). In those early days, law may not have been written, but the community had public and common expectations. "Stand firm, then, brothers, and keep the traditions that we taught you, whether by word of mouth or by letter" (2 Thes 2:15).

Development of Canon Law • From the earliest days the leaders of the Church gathered and made common decisions clearly intended to direct the community (cf. Acts 15:23-29). Throughout the early years there were synods and gatherings, usually local or regional meetings but sometimes general councils, that took decisions to order the life of the Church. From these early times, the decisions of Church authorities have often been articulated in brief, concise statements called canons (ultimately from the Greek *kanon*, meaning rule or measure of action). These canons were laws, and were frequently drawn together in great collections, such as the *Dionysiana* (c. 500) or the collections of St. Isidore based on the councils of Toledo (c. 589).

In some respects the canons were not uniform. Insofar as they reflected the basic structure and doctrine of the Church, they show remarkable unity, but other matters are more variable. The style of conducting the life of the Church, for ex-

ample, reflected local cultures. The laws invariably articulated the teaching of the Church and often the ways of acting that flowed from that teaching. Consistently, the canons dealt with promoting the pastoral life of the Church by ordering the life of the clergy, of married persons, and ecclesial activity.

Canon law began to emerge as a science numbered among the sacred disciplines of the Church with the work of Gratian, who wrote his *Concordantia Discordantium Canonum* in 1140. Since that time, the study of the sacred canons has been one of the major areas of study in the life of the Church.

Canon Law in Modern Times • In modern times the law of the Latin Rite Church has become increasingly organized. After the Council of Trent, Church law was brought together by a commission of cardinals (1580-1582) into an organized collection called the *Corpus Iuris Canonici*. This collection was never officially promulgated separately, but the laws had the force that they had from their original source of promulgation. This collection served as the primary source of law for the Western Church into the twentieth century.

At the First Vatican Council (1870), some dissatisfaction was expressed with this now dated collection, and there were calls for a codification that would be similar to a technical reorganization of law such as that which had occurred under Napoleon in France. Such a codification involved formal organization, precise technical terms, and brief statements of the law itself. In 1904, Pope St. Pius X directed the undertaking of such codification. This process came to fruition in 1917, when Pope Benedict XV promulgated the Code of Canon Law. The Latin Rite Church lived under this codified law for most of the twentieth century.

On January 25, 1959, Pope John XXIII announced major initiatives for the Church. He called for a synod for the church in Rome, he called for a general council of the universal Church, and he called for a revision of the law of the Church. Pope John presided over the synod and began the Second Vatican Council. He also established in May of 1963 a commission that was to undertake the revision of the law of the Church. The work of this commission was formally begun by Pope Paul VI on October 20, 1965.

This reworking of the Code of Canon Law was to be rooted firmly in the mystery of the Church. It was to formulate in concrete terms the teaching and decisions of the Second Vatican Council. It was to be pastorally sensitive, which does not mean unstructured or not binding in conscience. The Church's richer and more complete self-understanding was to be reflected. In fact, shortly before the revised Code of Canon Law came into effect, Pope John Paul II stated that "the study of the code is a school of the Council" (November 21, 1983).

The first World Synod of Bishops in April, 1967, enunciated ten principles to guide the reworking of the Code of Canon Law. Among them were the following: The articulation of the law must remain juridic in character, that is, it must be precise and technical; the law must serve the spiritual purpose of the Church; charity, temperance, and moderation must be evident; the governing power of the diocesan bishop is to be recognized positively, since this was one of the primary emphases of the Second Vatican Council; subsidiarity is to be respected, that is, local-level legislation is to be requested and even encouraged; rights of persons are to be safeguarded; the territorial principle of organization for the life of the Church and its ministry is to be maintained, although some exceptions could be made to assist special groups of persons; and a new systematic arrangement of the law of the Church is to be sought.

The drafting process continued, with working groups of various kinds and with significant consultation, until 1980, when the first major full draft was prepared. Again, consultation was welcomed. This included a meeting of representatives of the world's bishops and various experts in October of 1981. Finally, in January of 1983, the revised Code of Canon Law for the Latin Church was promulgated, to become effective on the First Sunday of Advent of that year.

The Revised Code of 1983 • The 1983 Code is a remarkable achievement. It reflects the teaching of the Second Vatican Council, even incorporating its terminology. Some things were dropped that had been included in the 1917 code and in prior legislation: The system of benefices for clergy, for example, was eliminated; details of the process of canonization and of the organization of the Roman Curia were no longer included. Other things were added. The duties and rights of the baptized were more clearly enunciated. A much-expanded role of laypersons in the life of the Church was happily embraced. Such new institutes in the life of the Church as conferences of bishops, presbyteral councils, diocesan and parish pastoral councils, and finance councils at many levels were introduced. One finds no distinction between laywomen and laymen, with the exception of admission to certain public ministries.

There was extensive and systematic use of the threefold aspect of the mission of the Church: the teaching, sanctifying, and governing functions. All the baptized are seen to share in these functions in their own way. The role of those in Holy Orders is very clearly delineated, especially the role of the diocesan bishop.

This Code of Canon Law applies to the Latin Rite Church around the world. At the same time, it is not the only canon law in the Church. There also is a Code of Canons for the Eastern Catholic Churches. In addition, there are other laws issued by appropriate Church authorities for smaller groupings. All are canon law. The latter is termed "particular law" and is very important in the everyday life of the Church. Communities of consecrated life (religious communities) and other groups have their own properly approved laws. In addition, the bishop of each diocese regulates diocesan life by promulgating laws for that particular diocese. While these cannot contradict the general law, within its context they make provision for special circumstances that reflect the culture and time of various local churches.

Eastern Canon Law • The Latin Rite Church includes those churches that have depended primarily on the See of Rome in formulating liturgy and practices of piety and as a primary source for the articulation of Church teaching. Other churches have based their lives on venerable traditions deriving from important ancient sees such as Alexandria, Antioch, Armenia, Chaldea, and Constantinople. These churches ascribe particular significance to the early ecumenical councils and to the decisions of their patriarchs. (The Maronite Church of Lebanon presents a special case.) Although, sadly, it has not always been so, the Latin Rite Church today is increasingly recognizing the beauty, dignity, and value of these other ancient churches.

Overcoming major historical difficulties, various groups from these Eastern Rites have come into full communion with the Catholic Church during recent centuries. The Popes, as successors of St. Peter and pastors of the universal Church, have desired to maintain and promote the life of these ancient churches. This was seen as a concrete means of expressing the catholicity of the Church and the richness of her heritage. The Second Vatican Council expressed this clearly in the *Dogmatic Constitution on the Church*, *Lumen Gentium*, 23, and stated that this diversity "in no way harms her unity, but rather manifests it" (*Decree on Eastern Catholic Churches, Orientalium Ecclesiarum*, 2).

The process of bringing the law of the Eastern Churches into a code to serve their life took more than sixty years. Pius XI established a commission of cardinals to begin the process in 1929. After this commission completed its work, another commission was established in 1935 to begin the actual composition of the Code of Eastern Canon Law. Segments were promulgated as they were completed, especially by a series of apostolic letters of Pope Pius XII. This particular commission was terminated in 1972, when a Pontifical Commission for the Revision of the Code of Eastern Canon Law was established. After a long process, which included extensive consultation with the bishops of the Eastern Catholic Churches, its work was accepted by a unanimous vote of its members in November, 1988. The resulting document represents a monumental historical achievement, since it brings together in an orderly way the rich ecclesial heritage of the Eastern Rite Churches that, although they have originally shared much, also have traveled different historical paths for many centuries. The final product, Code of Canons of the Eastern Churches, was promulgated on October 18, 1990, by Pope John Paul II, Bishop of Rome, to become effective on October 1, 1991.

In keeping with the principles adopted early on by the commission, the Code of Canons for the Eastern Churches was to respect the rich heritage of these churches and to be truly Eastern so that it might support and preserve the proper discipline of the Eastern Churches. It also was to be ecumenically sensitive to Eastern Churches not in full communion with the Catholic Church. It should be juridical in nature, clearly defining and protecting the rights and obligations of persons toward one another and also toward the Church herself. It was to be pastorally sensitive, not imposing unnecessary burdens. It should respect the principle of subsidiarity, being especially open to committing many matters to the particular law of the various Eastern Churches. The organization of the Code of Canons of the Eastern Churches was seen as different from that of the Code of Canon Law for the Latin Church. It would reflect the extensive work already accomplished in service of Eastern canon law in this century. This code in its final form clearly reflects the reaching and discipline of the Second Vatican Council. It incorporates the legacy of the Eastern Churches, even while moving toward appropriate unity. It is certainly open to the Eastern Churches not in full communion with the Catholic Church.

Nature and Function of Canon Law • The canons of canon law are called sacred because they exist in service of the life of God's holy people. They are intimately connected with the concrete, historical life of this Spirit-led people. Because of their deep roots in the history of the Church, they help us remain in fundamental continuity with the Church of all ages. They help to preserve the wisdom discovered by our forebears acting under the guidance of the Holy Spirit. They offer practical guidance in being faithful to the Gospel in a variety of concrete historical circumstances. If welcomed appropriately, they can help preserve our Catholic identity.

The law of the Church accomplishes many things. It articulates concisely and clearly the beliefs of the Church, not primarily for catechetical purposes but rather as the basis for further discipline and direction found in the law. It indicates the mutual duties and rights of the baptized. Especially in its most recent expressions, it underscores the great dignity of the baptized as daughters and sons of God and helps the life of the Church to reflect more clearly the fundamental equality of all baptized persons.

Consideration of the topics treated in the law of the Church points to matters that the Church holds important. Clearly, respecting persons and their duties and rights within the Church is very important. Maintaining the purity of the Gospel proclamation and making clear who may proclaim it and teach in the name of the Church are of high priority. Worship is of great importance, especially the Sacrifice of the Mass and the sacraments. One also finds emphasis on a spirit of service, especially toward the poor, while proper care and formation in the faith for children and young people are of major consequence.

Canon law helps to maintain good order in the Church. Besides underscoring the dignity of each baptized person, the law of the Church sets down procedures and standards whereby all can know who is responsible in the Church and to whom individuals can turn to have their rights vindicated. The role of the Roman Pontiff and the offices of the Roman Curia that serve his universal ministry are briefly sketched in the code. The procedure for the selection of bishops and for a diocesan bishop to take possession of his diocese is stated, as is the basic structure of a diocese, including the duties and responsibilities of parish priests and others who serve as chaplains. It is important for people to know to which diocese and parish they belong so that they can appropriately seek the Church's ministry and expect to be served. People in general need to know who speaks for the Church. In any organization it is important that such questions be an-

swered, but especially so in a Church that is universal and finds herself existing in a great variety of cultures around the world.

The Church is not about law. Law exists to serve the life of the Church. In his apostolic constitution *Sacrae Disciplinae Leges*, by which he promulgated the revised Code of Canon Law for the Latin Church, Pope John Paul II has made this point clearly: "This being so, it appears sufficiently clear that the Code is in no way intended as a substitute for faith, grace, charisms, and especially charity in the life of the Church and of the faithful. On the contrary, its purpose is rather to create such an order in ecclesial society that, while assigning the primacy to love, grace, and charisms, it at the same time renders their organic development easier in the life of both the ecclesial society and the individual persons who belong to it."

In recent years, the unity of the Church has increasingly been described in terms of communion. This communion is the unity of men among themselves, as well as their union with God as established by Jesus Christ. It is not purely invisible. It includes also the visible and juridical relationships among Christ's faithful within the unity of the Church's profession of faith, sacramental life, and governance (cf. Canon 203). The visible unity served by canon law is in service of the invisible communion at the heart of the Church.

See: Catholic Identity; Church, Nature, Origin, and Structure of; Civil Law; Communio; Ecclesial Rights and Duties; Orthodox Churches; Pope; Rites.

Suggested Readings: CCC 771, 871-933, 1951. Vatican Council II, *Dogmatic Constitution on the Church, Lumen Gentium*, Ch. III. John Paul II, *Sacrae Disciplinae Leges*. C. Burke, *Authority and Freedom in the Church*. R. Shaw, *Understanding Your Rights and Responsibilities*.

☩ **John J. Myers**

CANON OF SCRIPTURE

The word "canon" probably derives from the ancient Greek *kanon*, which literally meant straight rod or bar and by extension signified a measure of some sort. Scholars are not unanimous as to the origins of the word, but note the existence of the concept throughout antiquity. In ancient Egyptian culture, a "canon" appears to have been an instrument used to measure something else, as in our modern yardstick. The Church uses the term in reference to Scripture to denote an authentic, and therefore authoritative, list of books that make up the inspired and revealed word of God. The basis for the particular collection of forty-six Old Testament books and twenty-seven New Testament books rests in Apostolic Tradition (cf. CCC 120).

Both Old Testament and New Testament authoritative lists developed over centuries. During the process of development, first ancient Israel and then the Church recognized which written records authentically communicated Revelation about God, creation, sin, redemption, the Church, the moral life, and so on. As the Church encountered schisms and heresy from within and external attacks from a variety of powerful foes, she drew her inspiration from the Holy Spirit and her inner strength from those books that nurtured her and sustained her supernatural ability to bear witness even to the point of death. Throughout these struggles, the Church ultimately discovered which books were inspired by the Holy Spirit and were of apostolic origin.

The idea of a canonical or authoritative body of directives was present at the very birth of Israel. Starting with the law of Moses (i.e., first five books of the Old Testament), both Israel and the Church always stood on guard over the deposit of Revelation, the holy word of God in their midst. The earliest evidence of a New Testament list of accepted books is the Muratorian Canon, discovered in 1740 but dated back to around 190. Origen in the third century was the first to use canon as a technical term referring to an authoritative list. Councils at Hippo (393) and Carthage (419) drew up canons. The Church finally "closed" the canon in the sixteenth century, at the Council of Trent. This conciliar action simply formalized what had been accepted for well over thirteen centuries.

See: Divine Revelation; Inerrancy; Inspiration;

New Covenant; New Testament; Old Covenant; Old Testament; Sacred Scripture.

CAPITAL PUNISHMENT

The state's authority to put a criminal to death for serious crimes has long been accepted by the Church. In recent decades, without denying this authority, the Church has increasingly urged governments to use nonlethal forms of punishment, and Pope John Paul II has said that the death penalty is seldom or never needed in modern society (encyclical *The Gospel of Life, Evangelium Vitae,* 55-56 [1995]).

Scriptural Background • The Old Testament takes for granted that death may be inflicted upon someone who has deliberately violated God's most fundamental laws. Among the nomadic tribes of ancient Israel, a genuine prison system was out of the question. Moreover, the laws of Israel were seen as handed down directly by God, who is Lord of life and could rightly demand a wrongdoer's death. Thus the list of crimes punishable by death resembled the list of the Ten Commandments: idolatry or apostasy (Dt 13 and 17:2-7), working on the Sabbath (Ex 31:14-15, 35:2), cursing or incorrigibly defying one's parents (Ex 21:17; Dt 21:22), murder (Ex 21:12ff.; Dt 19:11-13), adultery and other sexual sins (Lv 20:10-21), and bearing false witness against an innocent person in a capital case (Dt 19:16-21).

Offenses against persons were punished in accord with the *lex talionis,* or "law of retribution": "Life for life, eye for eye, tooth for tooth" (Dt 19:21; cf. Lv 24:17-21). Only by forfeiting one's life could one sufficiently atone for maliciously taking another's life. In cases of accidental killing, the guilty party might be able to seek refuge until the victim's family no longer sought vengeance (Dt 19:1-10).

In an especially striking act of mercy, the Lord himself protects Cain, mankind's first murderer, by placing a mark on him "lest any who came upon him should kill him" (Gn 4:15). St. Ambrose (c. 339-397) commented on this passage: "God, who preferred the correction rather than the death of a sinner, did not desire that a homicide be punished by the exaction of another act of homicide" (cf. *Evangelium Vitae*, 9). Ambrose's comment is a later Christian interpretation, but his emphasis on God's mercy for sinners can also be found in the later prophetic books of the Old Testament: "As I live, says the Lord God, I have no pleasure in the death of the wicked, but that the wicked turn back from his way and live" (Ez 33:11).

The prophetic writings also provide a different perspective on capital punishment in another way. By this time Israel's political leaders are often defying God's will, and some even try to silence God's prophets by the unjust use of the death penalty (cf. Jer 26:7-15).

In the New Testament, Jesus rebukes Israel for killing its prophets (cf. Mt 23:31). Through his crucifixion he becomes the ultimate innocent victim of capital punishment. Luke's Gospel, without questioning the just use of this penalty, shows Jesus forgiving a repentant criminal crucified beside him and promising him paradise (Lk 23:39-43). The New Testament reports the killing of the deacon Stephen by people who thought they were imposing a just sentence of death; one man who assisted, Saul of Tarsus, later converted to Christianity and was himself martyred in Rome as the Apostle Paul (cf. Acts 7:57-8:2).

Even more important than Paul's personal experience is his theology of sin and forgiveness. All people are sinners who fall under the sentence of death earned by Adam; through his death on the cross, Jesus has saved us all from the power of death (Rom 5:12-21). If we are conformed to his death, we can share in the power of his Resurrection (Phil 3:10-11).

Thus, while the New Testament casts no specific judgment on the morality of capital punishment, it intensifies the message of forgiveness and conversion found in the Old Testament's prophetic books. This message runs throughout the life and teaching of Jesus, who set himself against the *lex talionis* by teaching his followers to love their enemies and return good for evil (Mt 5:38-48).

Historical Development • The New Testament acknowledged the state's authority to use force,

teaching that civil authority "is the servant of God to execute his wrath on the wrongdoer" (Rom 13:4). The idea that government wields God-given authority received more emphasis after the emperor Constantine (c. 288-337) converted to Christianity and the new religion acquired an official role in maintaining civil order. Especially in time of war, rulers saw no way to prevent desertion from the army except by threatening the same penalty of death that soldiers feared from the enemy; and when wars claimed a religious justification, as in the Crusades, Church leaders saw all the more reason to help the state enforce order.

In the fifth century, St. Augustine (354-430) provided a theological justification for capital punishment: God has exempted such punishment from the commandment against killing, by delegating governments to preserve the common good through the enforcement of just laws (*City of God*, I, 21).

In the Middle Ages, heretics called Waldensians taught that it is gravely sinful to kill criminals condemned to death. (This opinion was based not on respect for human life but on opposition to the idea that God delegates authority to humans; this sect also reviled the human body and rejected the sacredness of marriage and the hierarchical structure of the Church.) In response, Pope Innocent III expressed what had become the generally accepted teaching: "We assert concerning the power of the state, that it is able to exercise a judgment of blood, without mortal sin, provided it proceed to inflict the punishment not in hate, but in judgment, not incautiously, but after consideration" (*Profession of Faith Prescribed to the Waldensians*, A.D. 1210).

In the thirteenth century, St. Thomas Aquinas justified capital punishment using arguments borrowed in part from Aristotle. He wrote that each human being can be seen as part of the whole organism of human society; when one part endangers the whole body, it must be amputated for the good of all. He added that while human beings have inherent dignity, criminals forfeit that dignity when they abandon the order of reason and become enslaved to their passions; society may kill them as it would kill dangerous beasts (*Summa Theologiae*, II-II, 64.2). This power could only belong to the civil authority, which has responsibility for the health of the whole community; no private person may inflict the death penalty (*Summa Theologiae*, 64.3).

Throughout this period, the use of capital punishment was also seen as beyond the purview of the Church, which wields only spiritual authority. Canon law prohibited clergy from involvement in such punishment. Interestingly, St. Thomas's explanation for this limitation was that ministers of the Gospel should imitate their Master, who returned good for evil even when attacked by others (*Summa Theologiae*, 64.4; cf. 1 Pt 2:21-23).

The teaching on capital punishment was reaffirmed in the sixteenth-century *Roman Catechism* commissioned by the Council of Trent: "The just use of this power, far from involving the crime of murder, is an act of paramount obedience to the Commandment which prohibits murder. . . . [T]he punishments inflicted by the civil authority . . . give security to life by repressing outrage and violence" (Pt. III, "The Fifth Commandment").

Here the death penalty was not embraced without reservation — it could not be used out of malice or a thirst for revenge, but only when judged to be the sole adequate means of ensuring public safety.

Modern Development • The development of a more critical assessment of capital punishment in recent times has several sources.

First, at a time when the Second Vatican Council has given new emphasis to the lay vocation and the call to holiness directed to all believers, it seems strange that only clergy should imitate Jesus by abstaining from involvement in executions. Surely the call to forgive enemies and return good for evil is addressed to all Christians.

Second, the development of the Church's social teaching has deepened her understanding of the inherent dignity of the human person — a dignity that is inalienable and hence cannot be absent even from evildoers. Nor can that dignity be sacrificed in the alleged pursuit of a social good. Contrary to Thomas Aquinas's idea, borrowed from

Aristotle, no human being can be seen simply as a part to be sacrificed for the sake of a larger organism. The Church's experience of totalitarianism in its horrendous modern forms has helped to clarify her thinking on the role of the individual in the state: "The social order and its development must constantly yield to the good of the person, since the order of things must be subordinate to the order of persons and not the other way around" (Vatican Council II, *Pastoral Constitution on the Church in the Modern World, Gaudium et Spes*, 26). With the development of modern secular democracies, the state can more readily be seen to derive its authority from the consent of the governed, not from a divine mandate giving it powers over life and death qualitatively different from those belonging to individuals and smaller groups.

Third, at a time when some modern societies seem increasingly willing to destroy even helpless and innocent life, the Church has seen a need to reemphasize the inviolability of innocent human life. The "consistent ethic of life" proposed by some on the basis of this insight seeks not to equate the convicted murderer with, for example, the helpless unborn child threatened with abortion, but to insist that respect for life should be the starting point for discussing both issues.

The development of modern prison systems has also produced workable alternatives to capital punishment capable of effectively preventing a criminal from endangering other people. From a Christian viewpoint, such alternatives take the better course of "rendering criminals harmless without definitively denying them the chance to reform" (*Evangelium Vitae*, 27).

For these reasons, several modern Popes have praised developed nations' move away from the death penalty and have sometimes urged clemency in individual cases.

Two recent developments underscore this trend. The *Catechism of the Catholic Church* says public authority should limit itself to "bloodless means" if these are "sufficient to defend human lives against an aggressor and to protect public order and the safety of persons" (CCC 2267). Pope John Paul's encyclical on human life similarly teaches that punishment "ought not go to the extreme of executing the offender except in cases of absolute necessity: in other words, when it would not be possible otherwise to defend society." He also takes the argument a step further by adding that today, "as a result of steady improvements in the organization of the penal system, such cases [where execution is needed] are very rare, if not practically non-existent" (*Evangelium Vitae*, 56).

The Holy Father's statement does not change the teaching of the *Catechism*, but applies it to the reality that modern nations can virtually always punish criminals and protect society from harm without resorting to the death penalty. The encyclical and the *Catechism* recognize an urgent need to place the power of the modern state within clear moral limits.

While the moral command "Thou shalt not kill" is often expressed as a ban on direct killing of the innocent, the root meaning of "innocent" here is "not attacking" rather than "not guilty of crime." Individuals have a right to defend those under their care from unjust attack, even using deadly force if necessary; but any deliberately lethal act beyond what is needed to stop the attack is gravely wrong, because the person's death is then willed directly instead of being the accepted but not intended side effect of a legitimate act of self-defense. Pope John Paul holds the state to this same norm against directly intended killing: If imprisonment can render murderers incapable of doing further harm, the state should not insist on a further right to directly take their lives.

One may envision undeveloped societies or a future state of the world in which penal systems are fragmented and society cannot protect its people without shedding blood. But the modern practice of the death penalty by developed industrial nations is difficult to justify. The practice is all the more ominous when, in the search for "humane" methods of execution, the state enlists medical professionals to administer lethal injections and thus violate their oath to use their medical skills only for healing.

Some secular objections to the death penalty may arise from indifference to the grave evil of violent crime, hostility to law enforcement, or psychological theories that deny personal responsibility for criminal acts. The Church's measured critique of the modern use of capital punishment has nothing in common with such views or with the Waldensian heresy. That critique rests on the same principle often used to justify the death penalty — the dignity of human life — but suggests that a fully civilized society will give witness to that dignity even in the case of the convicted murderer. The issue is not only whether some acts deserve a penalty of death but whether a society hardens itself to the taking of life by choosing to inflict that penalty when there are nonlethal alternatives.

See: Authority; Homicide; Human Life, Dignity and Sanctity of; War.

Suggested Readings: CCC 2266-2267. John Paul II, *The Gospel of Life, Evangelium Vitae*, 9, 27, 40, 55-56. St. Thomas Aquinas, *Summa Theologiae*, II-II, q. 64, a. 2-4. G. Grisez, "Toward a Consistent Natural-Law Ethics of Killing," *American Journal of Jurisprudence* (1970), pp. 67-70. J. Finnis, *Fundamentals of Ethics*, pp. 128-131.

Richard Doerflinger

CAPITAL SINS

Certain sins are called the capital sins, not because they are the most serious — indeed they are not always mortal sins — but because they often lead to other sins. They are the "heads" (Latin: *capita*) of other sins, in the sense that they provide the goals for the sake of which we are tempted to commit other, perhaps more serious, sins. They have sometimes also been called deadly sins, because they are the sources of our other sins and of our overall sinfulness. The traditional list is: pride, avarice, lust, anger, gluttony, envy, sloth.

The doctrine on the seven capital sins explains how sins typically arise, and so an examination of them can be a good diagnostic tool, to see the weaknesses and defects in our moral and spiritual life. "Capital sins" refers both to the acts and to the vices or dispositions to perform such acts.

Sin is not to be thought of as if it were the choice of an evil thing. No things are evil in their nature; evil as such is the privation or eating away of what is good. So, in sinning, one wills something that is in itself good, but one does so in an inordinate way. The sin is choosing some good in such a way as to turn away from a full respect for some other good or goods and so turn away from God's plan. Thus, one of the traditional definitions of a sin is "the willing of a changeable good in an inordinate way, so that it involves a turning away from the unchangeable God" (St. Thomas Aquinas, *Summa Theologiae*, I-II, q. 84, a. 1).

Pride is called the beginning of all sins (Sir 10:13). It involves an inordinate desire for status, for praise and reputation among others. Pride can lead to an unwillingness to depend on God or others, and thus leads to many other sins that involve exalting oneself. Pride of course is quite different from a well-ordered and genuine love of self, a type of love required of us (we are to love our neighbor *as ourselves*). Pride is the desire for a status for its own sake, rather than as a concomitant of our real situation. Having lost its essential connection with our real fulfillment, pride can even move us to desire an unrealistic and harmful independence.

The inordinate desire for wealth is *avarice*, which is called the root of all vices, since it enables one to commit the other sins (1 Tm 6:10). The inordinate desire for pleasures of food and drink is *gluttony*. The inordinate desire for sexual pleasure is *lust*.

These four are desires for goods with evils attached to them. The last three capital sins are aversions from goods, because of some difficulty or threat attached to them. Thus, *sloth* is the aversion to one's own moral or spiritual good because of the difficulties in its pursuit. *Envy* is sorrow at another's good because it is perceived as threatening one's own excellence. And *anger* is the inordinate desire for vindication or vengeance.

The capital sins have the convergent effect of producing a selfish, spiteful character, bent on one's own comfort and praise, with the result that what is genuinely good is hated because it threatens to dispel one's own or others' illusions.

The contemporary culture should be considered in assessing the way capital sins can gain a foothold in our life. In our culture the very idea of objective moral norms is thought to be intolerant. What is important in life is identified with pleasant and comfortable experiences; any obstacles to such experiences should be removed. Heaven, then, seems unreal and hell must be a fiction, an unpleasant, backward, and intolerant idea. The result is a culture in which power, wealth, and pleasure are the only intrinsically important goals.

Pride takes the form, not so much of pursuing a socially respected status, as of being "one's own true self," unencumbered by the *fiats* and commands of moral authorities. Moral truths are thought of as arbitrary rules threatening one's unique personality. Pride becomes a real effort to become one's own sovereign. Lust, the demand for finer foods and exquisite drinks and snacks, avarice (including the willingness to neglect one's children to attain the things one has come to expect), anger (e.g., at "right wing extremists"), resentment (envy) of virtuous persons dismissed as "holier-than-thous" — these have become socially acceptable dispositions in our culture.

The doctrine on the capital sins makes clear some basic truths about the moral life. First, sin involves an inordinate choice of a good. All of the things pursued in the capital sins are objects that, if pursued appropriately and wisely and in accord with the other goods of the kingdom, would be quite reasonable and morally good. Thus, a status fitting one's vocation, pleasure in healthy food and drink, pleasure in sexual acts of husband and wife that truly embody and actualize their marital communion, and so on: these are goods which it is fitting to pursue. It is the pursuit of status, pleasure, comfort, and so on *as independent from the kingdom planned by God* that is the source of sin. Sin is the shriveling of one's concern to certain objects one wants, no matter what their relation to the kingdom.

See: Concupiscence; Sin; Vices.

Suggested Readings: CCC 1865-1866. St. Thomas Aquinas, *Summa Theologiae,* Pt. I-II, q. 84. G. Grisez, *The Way of the Lord Jesus*, Vol. 1, *Christian Moral Principles,* pp. 440-442.

Patrick Lee

CARDINAL VIRTUES

There is a clear difference between a student who reaches the right answer in geometry only falteringly and with much difficulty after a great deal of time and another student skilled in geometry who reaches the conclusion surely, with ease and pleasure. Both have the ability to reach the true conclusion, but the second student has something in him that the first does not. This student has a stable disposition inclining him to reason with ease, pleasure, and sureness in the area of geometry.

Similarly, there is a difference between someone who makes the right choice, but falteringly and with difficulty, on the one hand, and a person who chooses well because he has a disposition to choose well. The person with a disposition to choose well, that is, in line with love of God and neighbor, will not only make the right choices more frequently, but he or she is more attentive to the real goods at stake, more alive to the problems and opportunities, in his or her situations. That disposition to choose well is moral virtue.

A human being is complex. A human being is composed of body and soul, and has various capacities or powers: He or she has cognitive powers (capacities to know) and appetitive powers (capacities to desire or will). Thus, the human being has sense powers and intellect, and bodily appetites (capacities to have emotions, for example, to feel inclined toward or repelled by an object), and the will (the power to will or choose). Although choosing is itself an act of the will, we choose what we have judged to be good in some way (an intellectual act); we choose things we have some bodily desires or feelings about (emotions); and we carry out our choice with or by our other powers.

Because of this complexity, the different aspects of us, our different powers, can be disposed to act together well or badly. For example, our sense appetites or capacities to have emotions may have a disposition to go their own way, independently of our judgment of what is truly good. Or one's will may be disposed to love oneself to the exclusion of the rights of other people. Such dispositions are vices; whereas the dispositions in our various powers to act well are the moral virtues.

Basis of a Virtuous Life • The cardinal virtues are the four that form the basis of a virtuous life. The term comes from the Latin word for hinges (*cardines*). They are: prudence, justice, temperance, and courage.

Prudence is a disposition to discern the morally good option. While *synderesis* is the virtue for discerning ends worth pursuing, by prudence we discern the morally right means. Everyone knows the basic moral principles, at least vaguely, on one level. For example, one knows that one should pursue and protect life, health, knowledge, and community, that one should not act against these goods, and that one should not be deterred from acting for them by mere fear of discomfort. Still, it may not be clear what choices to make here and now with respect to diet and exercise, or what school to attend, or what career to pursue, or what and how much entertainment to engage in, and so on.

Prudence, then, is the practical wisdom needed to apply general principles to such concrete situations. Like the other cardinal virtues, it comes with repeated good choices. That is, prudence is the intellectual aspect of a character built or shaped by good choices.

Justice is the disposition to will to others what is their due. We have a closer emotional attachment to ourselves and our families and others toward whom we feel affection (sometimes, as with personalities on television, persons we don't actually know) than to those outside these circles. Such affections can lead us to choose in discord with love for God and neighbor. That is, they can lead us to neglect or thwart the basic goods of other people. The disposition to choose in accord with respect for what is genuinely good in *all* persons, despite promptings toward partiality, is the virtue of justice. Justice also includes a disposition to do one's part in contributing to the common good of

CARE OF THE DYING

the various communities one participates in: the Church, political community, family, voluntary associations.

Justice toward God is the virtue of religion. As creatures, we are participants of the largest community of all, the universe. Thus, one's will is correctly disposed — is just — only if it is in line with what God wills, both to himself and to his creation. So, we should cooperate with God and bring our wills into harmony with his. This virtue, then, will involve acknowledging and rejoicing in God's own intrinsic goodness, and actively cooperating with his wise plan and will for creation.

Temperance is a disposition to direct and sometimes curb our desires for pleasure. Our desire for food, drink, comfort, and sex can lead us away from choices in line with love of every aspect of human good, and God's plan.

Finally, emotional aversion in regard to pain and evil can sometimes unreasonably deter us from pursuing good. The disposition for directing and controlling our fear is *courage*, sometimes also called fortitude.

The virtues are really the different aspects of a morally good character. The Letter to the Ephesians says: "For we are his workmanship, created in Christ Jesus for good works, which God prepared beforehand, that we should walk in them" (Eph 1:10). Since we are called to fashion (or mold), with God's grace, an upright character, in order to make of our very selves a gift to give back to the Father, virtues are not mere means to some extrinsic work or social project; they are in themselves worthy of serious attention.

See: Freedom, Human; Human Virtues; Synderesis; Theological Virtues.

Suggested Readings: CCC 1804-1811. G. Grisez, *The Way of the Lord Jesus,* Vol. 1, *Christian Moral Principles*, pp. 58-59. J. Pieper, *The Four Cardinal Virtues.*

Patrick Lee

CARE OF THE DYING

A society's attitude toward terminal illness is an important test of how civilized it is. In facing death,

people unavoidably confront their beliefs and uncertainties about the meaning of life and the prospect of life after death. This is a time when individuals may be tempted to despair (cf. CCC 1500-1501), and others around them are tempted to turn away — not only because of the burdens of caring for the dying but also because their plight reminds others of their own frailty and mortality. A civilized society will treat the dying process as part of life, and treat the dying patient as a fellow human being whose life has value and dignity.

Christians especially should promote compassionate care for the dying, because the fear and suffering associated with terminal illness may otherwise lead people to consider cutting life short through euthanasia. Church teaching rejects any directly intended ending of a patient's life by action or omission; it also calls us to give positive witness to the sanctity of life when life is at its lowest ebb. Christians who tend to the sick and dying follow the example of Jesus, who healed the sick (Mt 4:24; Mk 1:34), told his disciples to do likewise (Mt 10:8), and cited care for the sick as one way to serve him by serving "the least of these my brethren" (Mt 25:35-40; cf. CCC 1506-1509).

Today one often hears of "death with dignity" and even of a "right to die." To the extent that these phrases suggest a right to control the time and manner of one's death, even to the point of killing oneself or having oneself killed to avoid suffering, they are incompatible with human dignity. To end suffering by deliberately ending the patient's life is a "false mercy, and indeed a disturbing 'perversion' of mercy" (Pope John Paul II, encyclical *The Gospel of Life, Evangelium Vitae*, 66 [1995]). Christians must counter this approach with "the way of love and true mercy," which provides "companionship, sympathy and support in the time of trial" and respects the inherent worth of the dying patient (*Evangelium Vitae*, 67). In this context, one may truly speak of ensuring a "dignified death," and even of advancing a "right" to die peacefully with human and Christian dignity (Congregation for the Doctrine of the Faith, *Declaration on Euthanasia*, IV [1980]).

Relevant Principles • Care of the dying that embodies this way of true mercy includes several elements.

First, what the Catholic tradition has called "due proportion in the use of remedies" should be observed. Catholic morality does not demand a "therapeutic obstinacy" that subjects patients to exhausting and painful treatments in order to stave off death as long as possible. Rather, "it needs to be determined whether the means of treatment available are objectively proportionate to the prospects for improvement" (*Evangelium Vitae*, 65). Patients may refuse treatments that are useless or are disproportionately burdensome to themselves and their families; such refusal reflects not a suicidal wish but acceptance of the human condition in the face of death.

Even when aggressive life-prolonging treatment is forgone, the normal care owed to all patients because of their human dignity should be continued. This includes nursing care, hygiene, and pain management; it also includes administering food and fluids, orally or with artificial assistance, if this will support life without imposing serious burdens on the patient (Pontifical Council for Pastoral Assistance to Health Care Workers, *Charter for Health Care Workers*, 120 [1995]). In the final stage of dying, patients may lose all desire for food and be unable to benefit from it; they may need only occasional sips of water or ice chips to prevent dehydration.

Second, pain and suffering should be kept within tolerable bounds. Christians can find special meaning in suffering by choosing to participate in Christ's Passion and unite themselves with his redemptive sacrifice; but this heroic self-sacrifice cannot be demanded of everyone. Excessive pain may drain patients' moral resources, interfere with their spiritual well-being, and even tempt them to hasten their death. Patients' requests for pain relief should therefore be respected; those who cannot express their wishes can generally be assumed to want such relief (*Declaration on Euthanasia*, III).

Rarely, a means of relieving pain may also tend to suppress breathing and therefore risk hastening death. Such a means may still be used if there is no other way to provide effective pain relief; the risk of hastening death is not directly intended but is accepted as an unavoidable side effect (*Evangelium Vitae*, 65). Ordinarily it is possible to avoid such risks by carefully adjusting the dosage of pain medication to the point where pain is alleviated. It should be noted that dying patients accustomed to receiving large doses of painkilling medication often develop a resistance to it and can live comfortably with dosages lethal to other people.

Another rare problem arises when pain can only be relieved by depriving the patient of consciousness. This should not be done without a serious reason; patients generally should be helped to remain lucid so that they can meet their final moral and spiritual obligations and make their peace with loved ones and with God. Certainly caregivers must never sedate the patient simply for their own convenience or to avoid having to relate to him or her (*Charter for Health Care Workers*, 124).

Third, perhaps the most important form of care for the dying is simply the loving presence of others. Caregivers should "keep company" with patients, assuring them they have inherent worth and are not seen as burdens upon others. While lending moral support and encouraging a sense of hope, they should tell patients the truth about their condition, prognosis, and treatment options in a charitable and tactful manner (*Charter for Health Care Workers*, 125-127). They should take the time to listen and offer reassurance as patients express their fears, regrets, and anxieties.

Fourth, the patient's spiritual and sacramental needs must be met. Faith in God and his promise of eternal life offers the most profound cure for the fears and anxieties of the dying process. The dying Christian should be helped to accept and prepare for death as a necessary part of earthly life, and as the doorway to closer union with Christ.

Every opportunity should be offered for recourse to the sacraments of reconciliation and the Eucharist (CCC 1524-1525). When given just before death the Eucharist is called Viaticum, as food for the person's "passing over" to eternal life. The sacrament of Anointing of the Sick, once known as Extreme Unction, strengthens the sick person with the gift of the Holy Spirit and prepares him or her for this journey. By extending her sacramental life to dying patients, as well as by the other ways of caring mentioned above, the Church assures them that they are not alone but are valued as part of a community in Christ that transcends the power of death.

See: Anointing of the Sick; Assisted Suicide; Death; Death, Determination of; Euthanasia; Human Life, Dignity and Sanctity of; Ordinary and Extraordinary Means of Sustaining Life; Suffering in Christian Life.

Suggested Readings: CCC 1006-1014, 1499-1532, 2276-2279. John Paul II, *The Gospel of Life, Evangelium Vitae*. Congregation for the Doctrine of the Faith, *Declaration on Euthanasia*. Pontifical Council for Pastoral Assistance to Health Care Workers, *Charter for Health Care Workers*, 114-135. Catholic Health Association of the United States, *Care of the Dying: A Catholic Perspective*. T. Kopfensteiner, "What Is a Dignified Death in a Culture of Life?" in *The Living Light* (Fall, 1995).

Richard Doerflinger

CATECHESIS

The principal goal of catechesis is to foster a deeper adherence to the living Person of Jesus Christ by means of a prophetic communication of the faith's great truths in a spirit of Christ's love. The apostolic works of evangelization and catechesis are the principal means by which the Church hands on the faith to each successive generation; thus, catechesis is an essential instrument of Sacred Tradition. The Church's ongoing penetration into the mysteries of the faith is directly linked to the transmission of authentic doctrine and morals, which is one of the educational goals of authentic catechesis. For the newly converted, catechesis deepens the faith engendered by the preaching of the Gospel; for the converted sinner, catechesis strengthens the resolve to turn away from sin and seek that life which God offers us in the Church. In short, catechesis stands at the very heart of the apostolic mission of the Church.

In order to indicate the antiquity of catechetical practices initiated in the Church since Vatican Council II, this entry will take a historical overview of the development of catechesis, from the pre-Christian setting to the present. This survey deepens our appreciation for the Church's outward thrust in communicating and making live the faith that comes from the Apostles.

Catechesis in the Early Church • The term "catechesis" originates with the Greek word *katecheo* ("to resound," "to echo"), which in the New Testament signifies oral instruction or the teaching of God's law (cf. Acts 18:25; Rom 2:18; Gal 6:6). The catechetical process begins with and rests on the Person of Christ the Teacher. He taught what he received from the Father (Jn 3:13, 5:17, 8:25-27). What the Apostles received from Jesus, therefore, was a divine catechesis that they had to pass on faithfully. This process of teaching includes the transmission of doctrine or dogma (in New Testament Greek, *didaskalia*, *didache*; Latin, *doctrina*). A number of New Testament sources illustrate how the early Church taught the faith. For example, it is possible to identify catechetical sections that teach basic doctrines or moral principles (e.g., Mt 5:3-11; Lk 6:20-23; 1 Thes 4:1-5:11; 1 Cor 3:1-3; Col 3:5-15; Heb 5:12-14; 1 Pt); other passages indicate postbaptismal catechesis (Acts 8:36-38, 16:33).

The early Church's catechesis had two fundamental goals. First, the Church's teaching for Jewish converts was based on the Holiness Code of Leviticus 17-19 and on decrees such as those found in Acts 15:19-21. A good example of this kind of catechesis within late Judaism of the first century is the *Rule of the Community*, found among the Dead Sea Scrolls. This manual outlines the most basic moral requirements from the Jewish Scriptures for every member of the Qumran community.

Second, after A.D. 70 and the destruction of Jerusalem by the Romans, the mother Church was scattered to the four corners of the known world. From Jerusalem to Syria, Asia Minor, Greece, and beyond Rome, the rule of faith included doctrine and moral instructions, but now drawn from the Psalter and proverbs, along with various catalogs of virtues and vices that would have been familiar to both Hellenistic Jews (Jews living outside Palestine) and pagans living in the Greco-Roman empire. Two noncanonical examples of post-New Testament catechesis are the *Didache* and the *Epistle to Barnabas*. Both contain sections described as the "Two Ways," whose purpose is to set out the "ways of the world" and "God's ways" or "the way of life." As the canonical authority of the New Testament literature grew, the habit of reading from various collections (letters of Paul, etc.) in the liturgies become more and more the norm; the catechetical process drew from these sources in addition to the basic teachings derived from the Gospel.

Eventually, in the first few centuries after the New Testament period, the catechetical homily emerged as a dominant form of catechesis. More often than not, it was delivered by bishops who viewed their episcopacy primarily in terms of their being teachers and witnesses to Jesus Christ. Pastoral letters came to systematize very basic themes. By the fourth century, the process of catechesis included four clear stages. First, people inquiring into the faith were given a basic presentation, in the form of a panoramic overview (e.g., the two discourses by St. Augustine in his *On Catechizing the Uninstructed*). Second was the catechumenate itself, which included rites of admission, penitential practices, and more systematic exploration of the doctrines and moral principles. Third, the forty (or forty-four) days of immediate and intense preparation before Easter included specific prayers, ritual exorcisms, meditations for the examination of conscience, and so on. Fourth, after Easter the newly baptized were subject to more teaching, often based on their full participation in the mystery of the Eucharist.

It was during this period that some of the elements of the "classic catechesis" came into existence. For example, the Ten Commandments were taught universally; the Our Father rose to prominence, as did, after the First Council of Nicaea

(325), various versions of the Creed. Bishops taught on prayer, but not necessarily systematically; more often than not, they taught in response to requests from deacons, presbyters, or other catechetical associates.

During the first five centuries of our era, catechesis consisted primarily in prebaptismal teaching for adult converts. The increase in infant Baptisms and the official acceptance of Christianity in the mid-fourth century, however, significantly impacted on the practice of catechesis up to and through the medieval Church. Person-to-person formation became practically impossible, given the massive conversions to Christianity. Canon law became an important means of regulating many practical liturgical and pastoral needs that arose from the conversions. Catechesis still remained at the heart of the transmission of the Tradition, along with Sacred Liturgy and the emerging theological tradition.

From the Middle Ages to the Counter-Reformation • During and after the sixth century, increased missionary efforts throughout northern and western Europe gave rise to massive conversions, as with the Germanic tribes. It was necessary to teach newly baptized but illiterate adults the most basic elements of liturgy, doctrine, and morals. These new converts were in turn responsible for teaching their baptized children. There were many theological works from which a simple catechesis could be developed. By the eighth century, various synods decreed the memorization of at least two basic formulae — the Our Father and Creed — by every parent entering the Church and every godparent assisting the newly baptized parents. The sacred drama of salvation history, re-presented in the Easter Liturgy, was another important teaching vehicle. And so, through the liturgy and simple memorization, the Church handed on the faith from one generation to another.

Over the next five centuries, a number of great saints — bishops, monk-scholars, evangelists — developed theological handbooks, doctrinal treatises, and practical guides to living a holy way of life. These works represented a full range of catechetical material, from formal theological works to hagiographies, or lives of the saints.

Between the Renaissance and Protestant Reformation, the Western Church witnessed a resurgent interest in educational theory (e.g., Erasmus, John Colet, et al.). The content and method of catechesis varied from region to region. Thus there was no attempt systematically to regulate catechetical instruction. The Fathers of the Fifth Lateran Council (1514) directed schoolmasters to teach the divine precepts or truths, the articles of the faith (from the Creed), the seven deadly sins, and various prayer themes from popular hymnals. Here is another manifestation of the "classic catechesis."

As useful and timely as such directives were for the renewal of the Church, however, they did not come in time to forestall the consequences of abuses in the Church and the great political and cultural unrest of Europe. The Protestant Reformers were very successful in winning the popular mind. This they did by developing simple, straightforward expositions of essential matters of faith and morals. Even if their content is less than acceptable, their methods were indeed somewhat innovative, and made exceptional use of new technologies, especially the printing press.

Martin Luther (1483-1546), the Augustinian monk turned Reformer, had great success in presenting elements of faith in popular form. He was highly effective at reaching people across the whole of Germany and beyond, especially in the northern parts of Europe. In 1528, he published an outline of doctrine and morals in the old medieval form called *tabulae,* or "wall table" (chart), popular in the home. As the wars of the Reformation raged, he published his teachings in book form (1529), and from this point on the term "catechism" became synonymous with an exposition of doctrine and morals in a book organized in question-and-answer format.

The Catholic Counter-Reformation was a strong and effective response to the Protestant movement. In the sixteenth century, heroic figures like St. Peter Canisius (in Germany), Edmund Auger (France), Gaspar Astete and Martínez de Ripalda (Spain), and Dr. Laurence Vaux (England) were effective in reestablishing the faith that comes from the Apostles. After the Council of Trent, Popes Pius V and Gregory XIII approved the *Roman Catechism* — the famous catechism of the Council of Trent. The form and substance of the presentation of the Catholic faith were now fixed for the next five centuries.

During the early eighteenth century, however, and persisting to the late nineteenth century, there arose a rather sterile view of catechesis, perhaps under the spell of rationalism. The move by civil authorities to require children to attend public schools effected a shift in catechetical practice, from the parish to the school. The impact of this change is still seen in most cities in the Western Hemisphere.

Catechetics in the Modern Era • Taking an overview of catechesis since the Council of Trent, contemporary catechetical research can identify at least three basic approaches to catechetical program organization. Many other approaches exist, but we focus on the ones that most influenced catechetics.

Classic Catechetics. The earliest complete expression of classic catechetics begins with St. Augustine. It is found in the *Roman Catechism* (1565) and in the *Catechism of the Catholic Church* (1992). The classic configuration includes these four pillars: (1) the Creed — what we believe; (2) the sacraments — living what we believe; (3) the moral life — the commandments; and (4) prayer — speaking to and receiving from God. The emphasis is on knowing truth, including committing to memory the basics of the faith. The value of this type of catechesis is its doctrinal orthodoxy. It views God as the source of all truth, and the Church as the guardian of the deposit of the faith. The method is deductive and requires the memorization of formulae, often in the question-and-answer format. This approach dominated catechesis from the mid-sixteenth to the mid-twentieth centuries.

Educative Catechetics. As the title suggests, this catechetical approach focuses on the way students learn. The term "educative catechetics" is from educational psychology and could be expressed as the "student-centered" approach to catechesis. The pedagogical goal is to adjust the delivery of information and the learning environment to the intellectual, emotional, and pedagogical level of the student. This approach began within developments in German educational psychology. There are three methodological steps: presentation, explanation, and application. Among the values are the appeal to the whole person and the introduction of the idea of a systematic and organized lesson plan.

Kerygmatic Catechesis. The kerygma is nothing less than the basic announcement of the Gospel. Kerygmatic catechesis draws its content from the basic Gospel proclamation. This development was initiated by the German priest Joseph Jungmann (1889-1975). The schools of catechetics in Vienna and Munich at the turn of this century provided the stimulus. The chief influences on type of catechesis included the scriptural and liturgical renewal movements of the late nineteenth and early twentieth centuries, which culminated in the recovery of the Rite of Christian Initiation of Adults. The theological approach focuses on God as Savior and the God who loves. The Church is seen as the herald of the Good News. The chief focus is on the call to personal conversion to Jesus Christ and to discipleship.

Catechesis Based on Human Developmental Needs. The use of psychological research has opened up other approaches to catechesis, one of which begins "from below," from human experience. Psychology has established the existence of developmental stages of physiological, emotional, and cognitive growth. God is seen as the mystery at the very core of human experience. The Church is the faith community of psychologically mature and responsible persons. The strength of this approach is its aim to foster a truly personal response to grace. It uses the inductive method, which begins with human experience and seeks the presence of God therein. The catechist's chief role is to foster a sense of God's personal presence and support a personal response to that presence.

The crowning catechetical achievement for the Church of Vatican Council II was the issuance of the *Catechism of the Catholic Church* by Pope John Paul II on October 11, 1992, thirty years to the day after the opening of the Council. The *Catechism* seems destined to be a most valuable instrument of catechetical and ecumenical renewal. It will assist the catechist in bringing alive faith in the one, true, catholic, and apostolic Church. Its pattern of presenting doctrine follows the ancient teaching of Judaism and earliest Christianity: focus on God, then on human persons; God intervenes, breaks into human life and experience, and humans respond.

The authenticity of any catechesis depends on whether or not the great truths about God (the Trinity), Jesus Christ, the Church, morality, and prayer are clearly presented along with personal witness. Regardless of the pedagogical approach and the skill level of the catechist, the fundamental question to be answered never changes: Does this catechesis put the recipient in touch with the living, resurrected Person of Jesus Christ?

See: Divine Revelation; Inerrancy; New Covenant; New Testament; Old Covenant; Old Testament; Sacred Scripture; Sacred Tradition.

Suggested Readings: CCC 1-25. Vatican Council II, *Dogmatic Constitution on Divine Revelation, Dei Verbum.* John Paul II, *On Catechesis, Catechesi Tradendae*; *Fidei Depositum* on the publication of the *Catechism of the Catholic Church.* R. Bradley, S.J., *The Roman Catechism in the Catechetical Tradition of the Church.* F. Kelly, *The Mystery We Proclaim: Catechesis at the Third Millennium.* E. Kevane, gen. ed., *Teaching of the Catholic Faith Today.* J. Ratzinger and C. Schönborn, *Introduction to the Catechism of the Catholic Church.*

Stephen F. Miletic

CATECHUMEN

Baptism is the sacrament by which one becomes a Christian — a son or daughter of God, a brother or sister to Jesus Christ, and a member of God's Church. Nothing more important can occur in a person's life than to receive Baptism. It is a "second birth," a birth to a new and higher life — the life of God himself.

To be baptized in the case of an adult must be a free act, one that is consciously wanted and accompanied by at least a basic understanding of its implications. It is obviously not something to be taken lightly, to be done without thought or preparation. The Church does not permit this, nor would the person to be baptized want it. Therefore, if an adult decides to become a Christian, Baptism logically calls for a period of preparation and instruction. This period is called the catechumenate; and the person receiving instruction with the intention of being baptized is a catechumen.

Since Baptism confers such incalculable benefits and gives such strength for the whole of life, Christian parents will naturally want their children to receive Baptism as soon as possible; and this is both their duty and their right according to the law of the Church (cf. Canon 867). While no pre-Baptism instruction of an infant is possible or needed, a follow-up naturally is. The *Catechism of the Catholic Church* insists that "by its very nature infant Baptism requires a *post-baptismal catechumenate*" (1231). This is naturally first given by the parents themselves.

See: Adult Baptism; Baptism; Church, Membership in; Infant Baptism.

CATHOLIC IDENTITY

When we speak of some people as being "very human" or others as "lacking in humanity," what we mean is that the former are fulfilling the models or standards befitting human nature while the latter are falling away from them. Human nature, or "what it means to be human," is not something that each one decides for oneself or that can be changed at will. It has an objective content, given by God when he made man "in his own image" (Gn 1:27).

Man is not a self-defining being in regard to his nature. He has not the right or power to define humanity. All he can do is to achieve true human identity, fulfill his potential to be human, or frustrate it. Human nature, from which alone can flow

true human identity, is something given by God. What keeps man in God's image or increases that image in him accords with human nature, giving him greater identity as a man. What lessens, disfigures, or spoils that image contradicts human nature and identity, and can in the end make a person unidentifiable as truly human.

Content of Christian Identity • Christian identity, similarly, has an objective rather than a subjective content. The requirements for achieving true Christian identity are clearly indicated in the Scriptures. To be a Christian means to follow and imitate Jesus Christ. As Jesus himself says, this involves being ready to bear the cross in a spirit of self-denial: "If any man would come after me, let him deny himself and take up his cross and follow me. For whoever would save his life will lose it, and whoever loses his life for my sake will find it" (Mt 16:24-25); "He must increase, but I must decrease" (Jn 3:30); "It is no longer I who live, but Christ who lives in me" (Gal 2:20).

This gives us the key to Christian identity. It is achieved in the measure of one's interior identification with Christ, a paradoxical process by which one in fact becomes more distinctively oneself, just as the saints were all one with Christ, approaching him from different angles, and are so different among themselves.

The norm and condition of Christian living, of acquiring the true identity of a Christian, is just the opposite therefore of self-seeking. Vatican Council II teaches: "Man can fully discover his true self only in a sincere giving of himself" (*Pastoral Constitution on the Church in the Modern World, Gaudium et Spes*, 24). The surest way to frustrate one's true identity is self-seeking in its various forms: pride, vanity, envy, impurity, greed.

Much of modern education and professional psychological counseling is nevertheless imbued with the cult of self. To acquire real Christian identity, one must distance oneself from this philosophy. "Self-identification" and "self-definition" are formulas of individualism. As a recipe for life, they lead to frustration and loneliness. The willfully self-centered person is unrecognizable as a Christian.

This applies to all Christians, to all those who by Baptism are made members of the Body of Christ and of the People of God. But if all Christians are members of the People of God, what is the specific difference in being a Catholic? Does *Catholic* identity mean something more definite or definable than simple Christian identity? Are there external and objective standards by which Catholic identity can be determined?

Distinctiveness of Catholic Identity • With words taken directly from Vatican Council II's *Dogmatic Constitution on the Church, Lumen Gentium,* 31 and 14, the 1983 Code of Canon Law, in the opening canons of Book II on "The People of God," distinguishes between Christian and Catholic identity. *Christian* identity comes from Baptism by which one is "incorporated into Christ" (Canon 204) and so, in the words of the *Catechism of the Catholic Church*, receives "the life that originates in the Father and is offered to us in the Son" (CCC 683). *Catholic* identity is possessed by "those baptized [who] are fully in communion with the Catholic Church on this earth," being "joined with Christ in its visible structure by the bonds of profession of faith, of the sacraments and of ecclesiastical governance" (Canon 205).

Catholic identity, then, means membership in the Church, the People of God formed and sustained by the Holy Spirit. Vatican Council II says that for this People and each of her members the Spirit is "the principle of their union and unity in the teaching of the apostles and fellowship, in the breaking of bread and prayers" (*Lumen Gentium*, 13). "It is the Holy Spirit, dwelling in those who believe and pervading and ruling over the entire Church, who brings about that wonderful communion of the faithful and joins them together so intimately in Christ that He is the principle of the Church's unity" (*Decree on Ecumenism, Unitatis Redintegratio*, 2).

Catholic identity consists in being in full communion with the Catholic Church — in her visible structure as it appears on this earth — accepting and enjoying bonds which link us more specially still to Jesus Christ that are defined as the profession of the same doctrine, the share and worship in the same sacraments, and the acceptance of ecclesiastical authority and discipline (*Lumen Gentium*, 14).

Catholic identity is not something static. It should grow; it can be lost. Growth in Catholic identity means an ever fuller and more intimate bonding and union with Jesus Christ, through the faith proposed by his Church, through the sacraments she administers, and through obedience to the dispositions of governance behind which one discovers his will (Lk 10:16).

Instead of growing as a Catholic of course, the opposite can happen and one can gradually suffer a loss of Catholic identity. This can occur if a person lacks the faith to appreciate the special union with Christ effected by full and wholehearted communion with the visible Church: if he or she begins to chaff against these ecclesial bonds that join us to Christ, resenting or resisting the demands they make on our mind and will; "picking and choosing" in the faith one professes, so that it is no longer the faith of the Church; neglecting the sacraments (especially Penance and Reconciliation and the Eucharist) or receiving or administering them unworthily, or participating in or celebrating the Sacred Liturgy without due reverence; ignoring legitimate Church authority or seeking to evade dispositions of government, especially of the Holy See.

No teacher or theologian has the right to appropriate the term "Catholic" for his views or to present them to the people as Catholic on his authority. The people have the right to know whether a theologian's views are within the broad stream of Catholic thinking or outside, and it is the Church, not the individual thinker, which is competent to decide.

Loss of Catholic Identity • The Church cannot lose her identity. Despite the defects of her members, she will always be the holy Church. This is something that Jesus Christ himself has guaranteed. But each Catholic can acquire more and more solidly or gradually lose his or her identity as a Catholic. The application of this point goes beyond individual persons.

The Church is made up of things human and divine. The divine things — the sacraments, Revelation, Scripture, the Magisterium — never lose their sacred identity, even if misused by men. The Eucharistic Sacrifice always remains the *Holy* Mass, even if celebrated (with due intention) by a priest in a state of serious sin.

But many things in the Church are of purely human foundation: Catholic schools and other teaching institutions, chairs of theology, hospitals, publishing houses, newspapers, bookshops, etc. They can lose their Catholic identity, even while continuing to use the name "Catholic." In judging whether a particular institution is retaining its Catholic identity, the same tests offered by Canon 205, noted above, should be applied: union with Christ through acceptance of the Church's faith, sacraments, and ecclesiastical governance. If it happens that a particular institution shows a lack of union with Christ by failing to transmit the faith passed down to us through his Church over the centuries or if it does not heed his voice speaking through indications of Church government ("He who hears you hears me, and he who rejects you rejects me" [Lk 10:16]), then it is undoubtedly losing or has already lost its Catholic identity. A Catholic name or a Catholic past are not sufficient to guarantee a present Catholic identity. This is something to be borne in mind in choosing books or schools.

Being true to one's Catholic identity requires special courage in a world that tends more and more to look for, and even demand, identification with secular principles as a qualification for the free exercise of what it chooses to define as civic rights. It is not from the media or opinion polls, not from congresses, parliaments, or supreme court decisions, that Catholics must take their standards and their stand. It is from the Gospel. "We must obey God rather than men" (Acts 5:29).

There is no conflict between being true to one's Catholic identity and having the fullest respect for the human rights of others. On the contrary, it is precisely Catholics who keep faithful to Christ and to the identity (the principles and practice) that he calls for in his followers, who can alert their fellow citizens to the threat posed to *their* human identity — to the freedom and dignity of every single person — by many of the principles and legislative practices being proposed by modern states.

See: Assent and Dissent; Church, Membership in; Church, Nature, Origin, and Structure of; Conscience; Dissent; Ecclesial Rights and Duties; Magisterium.

Suggested Readings: CCC 836-856, 863-865. Code of Canon Law, 204-207. C. Burke, *Authority and Freedom in the Church*, pp. 60ff., 192-193.

Cormac Burke

CELEBRATION, LITURGICAL

The linguistic roots of the word group "celebration/to celebrate/celebrated" have to do with a large number or a multitude: a great assembly that comes together to salute the glory or the achievements of important events or personages. "Celebration" means a concourse or numerous assemblage of persons to keep a feast or a festival, while "to celebrate" is to go in great numbers to the solemnization of a feast, where the praises of a person or a thing are "celebrated," that is, made known by extolling them. "Celebration" and "feast" are therefore practically synonymous.

From the age of the classic Latin authors of antiquity to the language of Catholic liturgy (cf. Vatican Council II, *Constitution on the Sacred Liturgy, Sacrosanctum Concilium,* 36, 54), "to celebrate" has always signified the accomplishment of an action by a group or collective (assembly) in a manner that is out of the ordinary — that differs from the routine actions of ordinary, everyday life. Such actions are not productive in the sense of being directed toward procuring one's livelihood (activity productive in this sense results in or preserves a product, and hence signifies the accomplishment of a certain quantity of work). Celebration, on the contrary, is representational activity that produces nothing usable and serves no utilitarian purpose. It is *ritual* activity, which represents, or images, the celebrating group itself by actualizing, in a collective fashion, the totality of the group's norms.

Some common aspects of such celebratory ritual activity are: the presence of certain significantly meaningful patterns or forms; the public nature of the activity, which takes place before the group; the demonstration of membership and indeed of the group itself with all its norms, which is signified by the ritual activity; the identification of the individual with the celebrating group and its norms and traditions, which is rendered possible; and the formative and supporting influence of tradition and authority.

Liturgical celebration is a social action. In contrast to the purely interior act of mental prayer, for example, it will be accomplished in bodily forms perceptible to the senses — and in that sense is sacramental in character. The ritual activity of liturgical celebration thus brings the body to the encounter with the transcendental realm. By observing forms and patterns that evoke, for instance, the origins of the celebrating group, which can be shared by the assembled members, such ritual activity allows each individual to transcend himself; thus it can link many people in a true and enduring form of community.

Sacred Actions • Every liturgical action is a preeminently sacred action because it is an action of Christ and of his Body, which is the Church. This is true above all of the celebration of the Eucharistic Sacrifice by the People of God, assembled as the Body of Christ in fulfillment of the Lord's command to "do this in remembrance of me" (Lk 22:19). In this most sacred action of Christ and of his Church, the memorial of his death and Resurrection is celebrated, God is adored in spirit and in truth, and the Church perpetuates the saving sacrifice of her Lord while, nourished by his Body and Blood, looking forward in joyful hope to sharing in the supper of the Lamb in the heavenly kingdom (cf. *General Instruction of the Roman Missal*, 7).

In the celebration of the Eucharist, Christ is also present in the person of the presiding priest. Every authentic celebration of the Eucharist is presided over by the bishop or a presbyter who acts in the Person of Christ. The priest leads the people in prayer, in listening and responding to God's word, and offers the sacrifice through Christ in the Spirit to the Father; he proclaims the message of salvation in preaching, and he administers Holy Communion, the bread and cup of salvation. Although all the faithful indeed share in the one and same priesthood of Christ and participate in the offering of the Eucharist, it is only the ministerial priest who, in virtue of the sacrament of Holy Orders, can confect the Eucharistic Sacrifice in the Person of Christ and offer it in the name of all Christian people (Vatican Council II, *Dogmatic Constitution on the Church, Lumen Gentium*, 10, 17, 26, 28; *Constitution on the Sacred Liturgy, Sacrosanctum Concilium*, 7; *Decree on the Bishops' Pastoral Office in the Church, Christus Dominus*, 15; *Decree on the Ministry and Life of Priests, Presbyterorum Ordinis*, 2-3; Paul VI, *Mysterium Fidei*, September 2, 1965; Sacred Congregation for the Doctrine of the Faith, *Concerning the Minister of the Eucharist*, August 6, 1983).

Since liturgical celebration is so vitally important for the universal Church, for the local Church, and for each and every one of the faithful (*Sacrosanctum Concilium*, 41; *Lumen Gentium*, 11; *Presbyterorum Ordinis*, 5-6; *Christus Dominus*, 30), it follows that each celebration should be so arranged that all present, ministers and people, may take their own proper part in it, and thus be led to full, active, and conscious participation involving both body and soul. "This is what the Church desires; this is what the nature of the celebration demands; it is this to which the faithful have both the right and duty by reason of their baptism" (*General Instruction of the Roman Missal*, 1, 2-3).

The active participation of the faithful in liturgical celebrations is primarily *interior*, in the sense that by it the faithful should join their minds and hearts to what they say or hear, and cooperate with God's grace. And consequently, such active participation must also be exterior, namely, such as to manifest the internal attitude and sentiments by gestures and bodily postures, by acclamations, responses, and singing (*Sacrosanctum Concilium*, 11, 30; Sacred Congregation of Rites, *Instruction on Music in the Liturgy*, March 5, 1967, 15).

Pastors of souls, then, must have a care for the adequate instruction of their flocks so that, taking due account of their age, condition, way of life, and standard of religious culture, the faithful may be able to participate actively, both internally and externally, in the celebration of the Sacred Liturgy. For such participation is the primary and indispensable source from which the faithful are to derive the true Christian spirit (*Sacrosanctum Concilium,* 19, 14).

See: Assembly, Liturgical; Eucharist; Holy Orders; Liturgy; Mass; Priesthood of Christ.

Suggested Readings: CCC 1108, 1356-1357, 1372. *General Instruction of the Roman Missal.* A. Martimort, ed., *The Church at Prayer,* Vol. 1, *Principles of the Liturgy,* pp. 227-272. J. Pieper, *In Search of the Sacred; What Is a Feast?*

Robert A. Skeris

CELIBACY, PRIESTLY

The word "celibacy" entered the English language in the mid-seventeenth century to describe the state, either chosen or enforced, of living unmarried. Strictly speaking, then, we should distinguish between the state of celibacy and the virtue of chastity. The former requires that a person refrain from marriage and, therefore, from sexual intercourse. The latter signifies a permanent state of character that disposes a person to maintain a reasonable moderation in everything pertaining to the passion of lust. Since the sexual union of male and female legitimately transpires only within the bonds of Matrimony, the virtue of chastity tempers all movements of the flesh in the unmarried that would lead directly to conjugal union. In the sixteenth century, Erasmus observed the distinction between celibacy and chastity when he remarked that not all celibates are chaste and not all chaste persons are celibate.

The celibacy of the priest assumes that the ordained man embraces the virtue of chastity, which is a basic value of the Christian life. Even in the East, where priests and deacons, though not bishops, are allowed to marry before their ordination, the same regard for chastity ensures that married clergy give an example of conjugal chastity, which is the proper virtue of the married state. The tradition of priestly celibacy in the Western Church is a long and venerable one. In his 1967 encyclical, *Sacerdotalis Caelibatus, On Priestly Celibacy,* Pope Paul VI strongly emphasized this point at a moment when agitation for a change in the Church's discipline had reached a high point.

It should be emphasized that priestly celibacy is a discipline of the Church, not a divine command. St. Thomas Aquinas saw this clearly, and argued that clerical celibacy aims to ensure that the priest is free to devote his time and energy to the things of God. But there is no inherent contradiction between the two sacraments of Matrimony and Holy Orders, nor does the celibacy of the ordained reflect negatively on the sanctity of the married.

The Value of Celibacy • The fact that celibacy is not essential to the ordained or hierarchical priesthood does not mean priestly celibacy is a negotiable value. On the contrary, the venerable practice of celibacy represents a wisdom that the Church has enacted from earliest times. How early? The question is usually answered in two parts. First, the Spanish Council of Elvira (c. 305) prescribed permanent continence for an ordained man, but the prescription was only partially observed until the beginning of the Middle Ages. Second, in the eleventh and twelfth centuries, the program of Church reform spearheaded by Pope St. Gregory VII (1073-1085) was motivated in part by the practical concern that parishes and other ecclesiastical benefices were in danger of becoming the legacies of families, so that a concerted effort was made to enforce the celibacy of the clergy in the Latin West.

Recently, a new school of thought, represented by the work of Christian Cochini, S.J., has argued that the endorsement of priestly celibacy derives from the Apostles themselves. The text of Luke 18:28-30 provides one New Testament basis for this claim: "Truly, I say to you, there is no man who has left house or wife or brothers or parents or children, for the sake of the kingdom of God, who will not receive manifold more in this time, and in the age to come eternal life." Given the New Testament emphasis on putting all things aside to follow Christ, the Apostles, so it is argued, could easily have concluded that celibacy, or at least continence for those already married, is a requirement for Gospel ministry.

In the late seventh century, the Eastern Church pointed to the cultic service of the ordained minister, even of the sub-deacon, as a *raison d'être* for refraining from conjugal relations during those times when one was assigned to sacred duties. Theologians generally agree that this line of argumentation suggests too much the ceremonial purity of the Levitical priesthood to serve as a convincing argument for the institution of celibacy in the New Dispensation. Rather, theologians prefer to endorse celibacy in terms of the inner logic of a particular religious experience and calling.

The Second Vatican Council's *Decree on the Ministry and Life of Priests, Presbyterorum Ordinis* states that the ultimate foundation for celibacy is the "mystery of Christ and his mission" (16). By this insistence, which has been reaffirmed both by Pope Paul VI and Pope John Paul II, the Church interprets celibacy as a form of life that measures up fully to the imitation of Christ, one eminently suited to carrying on his redemptive mission. The Christological view of celibacy, moreover, helps us to appreciate the common Tradition of both Eastern and Western Christianity, which prescribes that only celibate priests can be ordained bishops.

In his 1992 apostolic exhortation *I Will Give You Shepherds, Pastores Dabo Vobis*, Pope John Paul II speaks about the specific vocation to holiness that belongs to the priest. The ordained minister must pursue this vocation energetically in order to develop the pastoral charity that remains the distinctive virtue of the priest. Priestly celibacy is best understood as part of this vocation to holiness. The Church must take seriously the counsel of St. Paul: "I want you to be free from anxieties. The unmarried man is anxious about the affairs of the Lord, how to please the Lord; but the married man is anxious about worldly affairs, how to please his wife, and his interests are divided" (1 Cor 7:32-34). While the Church affirms the

sacred and sanctifying character of marriage, the discipline of celibacy does enable a man to devote himself without reserve to the imitation of Christ and the continuation of his priestly work. It also allows the priest more time to pray, even to engage in contemplative prayer so that his instruction and his counsel will reflect divine truth.

Priestly celibacy implies a *chaste* continence, for it entails not only forgoing the venereal pleasures proper to the married state but also enduring the affective solitude that is the inescapable concomitant of living alone. The "brotherhood of holy pastors," to borrow a phrase from Cardinal Newman, can ease this circumstance in some reasonable measure. Pope John Paul II provides a more challenging answer: "The ability to handle a healthy solitude is indispensable for caring for one's interior life. Here we are speaking of a solitude filled with the presence of the Lord who puts us in contact with the Father, in the light of the Spirit" (*Pastores Dabo Vobis*, 74). Only by living this Trinitarian union can the priest love all the members of Christ's Body with the love of Christ himself.

See: Chastity; Holy Orders; In Persona Christi Capitis; Priesthood of Christ; Sexuality, Human.

Suggested Readings: CCC 1579, 1580. Vatican Council II, *Decree on the Ministry and Life of Priests, Presbyterorum Ordinis*. Paul VI, *On Priestly Celibacy, Sacerdotalis Caelibatus*. John Paul II, *I Will Give You Shepherds, Pastores Dabo Vobis*. R. Cholij, *Clerical Celibacy in East and West*.

Romanus Cessario, O.P.

CHARISMS

The Greek word for charism (*charisma*) signifies a gift freely given, as contrasted with something owed or due to an individual. The words *charis* (grace) and *chara* (joy) are from the same root, and the theological meaning common to all three terms is that they are all gifts from God. The best source for investigating biblical teaching on charisms is the letters of St. Paul.

The word "charism" refers to a variety of gifts,

beginning with the Holy Spirit, who was promised by Jesus: "I will ask the Father, and he will give you another Paraclete — to be with you always; the Spirit of truth, whom the world cannot accept" (Jn 14:16-17). It includes both ordinary and extraordinary gifts of grace; and, like grace itself, all charisms are gifts from God, to be used for the glory of God (cf. 1 Pt 5:10-11). St. Paul enumerates a variety of charisms in 1 Corinthians 4–11 and Romans 12:6-8 — for example, prophecy, wisdom, knowledge, extraordinary faith, discernment of spirits, healing, working miracles, speaking in tongues, and interpretation of tongues — and he says that charismatic gifts are given for the good of the Christian community. He likewise urges Christians not to desire and to pray for these special spiritual gifts for personal satisfaction but for the good of the Christian community (1 Cor 14:1).

In the first few centuries of the Church's existence, the charismatic gifts were very much in evidence; but the emergence over time of a certain defensiveness and bureaucratization in reaction against heresies was detrimental to charismatic activity. Nevertheless, charismatic gifts have always been evident in the Church to some degree, for example, in the founders of religious orders and in the saints whom God has raised up throughout the centuries.

In 1967, the Roman Catholic Church in the United States witnessed the emergence of Neo-Pentecostalism, a charismatic movement that gave rise to prayer groups and basic Christian communities in which some of the members experienced glossolalia (speaking in tongues) and baptism in the Spirit. However, Neo-Pentecostalism had already been introduced into some of the Protestant churches as early as 1890.

With the emergence of Scholasticism in the thirteenth century, the charismatic gifts were listed as *gratiae gratis datae*. As such, they were distinguished from *gratia gratum faciens*, which was in turn divided into actual grace and habitual or sanctifying grace. In other words, *gratia gratum faciens*, as its name indicates, is any grace that is given for the sanctification of the individual who receives it; *gratiae gratis datae* are charismatic

gifts given for the spiritual benefit of others or for the building up of the Church.

But these distinctions are not mutually exclusive. Some of the so-called *gratiae gratis datae* (e.g., stigmata, levitation, and locutions) are also listed as extraordinary mystical phenomena. Phenomena such as these seem to be a divine testimony to the sanctity of the individual mystic rather than graces for apostolate or ministry.

The charismatic element of the Church is as real today as it was in the past, although the manifestations of the Holy Spirit may not be as spectacular as in the early days of Christianity. A.G. Fuente has stated that "the Holy Spirit is no longer, as in the old economy, a prerogative of a select few. Now the Holy Spirit in all the members of the Church is a reality. . . . True, the Holy Spirit still acts in some as a charism, but as the Church becomes more and more established as a visible society, the charismatic aspect diminishes and the note of personal sanctification prevails. Charisms are always in view of the common good of the Church" ("The Action of the Holy Spirit," *Compendium of Spirituality*, Vol.1).

The Second Vatican Council stated in the *Dogmatic Constitution on the Church, Lumen Gentium:* "It is not only through the sacraments and the ministrations of the Church that the Holy Spirit makes holy the people, leads them and enriches them with his virtues. . . . He also distributes special graces among the faithful of every rank. By these gifts he makes them fit and ready to undertake various tasks and offices for the renewal and building up of the Church. . . . Whether these charisms be very remarkable or more simple and widely diffused, they are to be received with thanksgiving and consolation since they are fitting and useful for the needs of the Church. Extraordinary gifts are not to be rashly desired, nor is it from them that the fruits of apostolic labors are to be presumptuously expected. Those who have charge over the Church should judge the genuineness and proper use of these gifts . . . not indeed to extinguish the Spirit, but to test all things and hold fast to what is good (cf. 1 Th 5:12, 19-21)" (12).

It is evident from this that discernment must be exercised by the pastors of the Church and by spiritual directors. This is especially true when it is a question of the more unusual charisms that usually attract the attention of those who are drawn to the sensational. At the same time, pastors in particular should heed the words of Vatican II in the *Decree on the Apostolate of Lay People, Apostolicam Actuositatem*: "From the reception of these charisms, even the most ordinary ones, there arises for each of the faithful the right and duty of exercising them in the Church and in the world for the good of men and the development of the Church, of exercising them in the freedom of the Holy Spirit" (3).

The Pauline Charisms • Most of the ancient theologians accepted without question the enumeration of charisms given by St. Paul in First Corinthians and Romans. Modern theologians are inclined to say that St. Paul was naming the charisms that pertain to ministry in the Church, but there are other charisms (*gratiae gratis datae*) that are classified as extraordinary mystical phenomena. Indeed, for some theologians, every grace can be called a charism because every grace is a free gift from God. Here, however, we restrict our discussion to the principal charisms mentioned by St. Paul.

Faith. The charism of faith is distinct from the theological virtue of the same name, but theologians do not agree on its precise meaning. According to St. John Chrysostom, it is faith that works miracles, as mentioned by Christ (cf. Mt 17:19) and St. Paul (cf. 1 Cor 13:2). Others define it as an intrepid constancy in confessing, preaching, and defending the truths of faith, especially in times of persecution. St. Thomas Aquinas describes it as a profound certitude concerning the truths of faith and the ability to expound those truths with great exactitude and clarity (*Summa Theologiae*, I-II, 111, 4, ad 2). Some theologians distinguish the charism of faith from the theological virtue of faith and also from the gift of the Holy Spirit (understanding) that perfects faith. Francisco Suárez teaches that, whereas the theological virtue of faith is a permanent habit,

the charism of faith is a transitory movement of the Holy Spirit that results in the gift of eloquence (cf. M.J. Ribet, *La mystique divine*, III, 5, n. 6). Finally, it should be noted that the virtue of faith and the gift of understanding perfect the individual, but the charism of faith is primarily for the instruction and conversion of others. Abraham and Job are outstanding examples of the charism of faith.

Power to Express Knowledge. This special grace enables a preacher or teacher to impart knowledge of sacred truth with exactitude and clarity. St. Augustine stated that this charism pertains especially to the explanation of morality and good works. The charism of knowledge is similar to the gift of the Holy Spirit that has the same name, because they both have to do with imparting a knowledge of sacred truth and Divine Revelation. The difference lies in the fact that the gift of knowledge benefits the person who has the gift, while the charism is for the instruction of others. St. Augustine and other Fathers and doctors of the Church evidently were recipients of this charism.

Wisdom in Discourse. Wisdom has been defined as a *scientia sapida,* or savory knowledge. In Catholic teaching there are various types of wisdom: the intellectual virtue that enables one to know something in all its causes; the gift of the Holy Spirit that for some theologians is the perfection of the virtue of charity; the charism of wisdom that we are here discussing. St. Paul makes the basic distinction between the philosophical wisdom sought by the Greeks and "the wisdom of God," Christ crucified, which is "an absurdity to the Gentiles" (1 Cor 1:24). Since the charism of wisdom is a grace of service for others, it can be activated by sacred preaching, the teaching of sacred doctrine, or spiritual direction. Unlike the previous charism, it is not simply imparting knowledge, but doing so in such a way that the recipient truly feels and experiences the truth. The charism of "wisdom in discourse" was given to numerous saintly preachers and spiritual writers such as St. Teresa of Ávila and St. Francis de Sales.

Gift of Tongues. In one meaning, this can be understood in relation to sacred doctrine, as recorded in Acts 2:4-6: "They began to express themselves in foreign tongues and make bold proclamation as the Spirit prompted them. Staying in Jerusalem at the time were devout Jews of every nation under heaven. These heard the sound, and assembled in a large crowd. They were much confused because each one heard these men speaking his own language." St. Dominic and St. Vincent Ferrer also received this charism on occasion.

The word "glossolalia" is sometimes used to describe this phenomenon, but less accurately, because glossolalia usually refers to a babbling that is understood neither by the speaker nor the hearer. In that case, the phenomenon may be associated with a schizophrenic syndrome, an intense emotional seizure, or a diabolical intervention. In fact, glossolalia is one of the symptoms of diabolical possession.

If, however, the glossolalia is the result of intense religious emotion, it is a form of prayer, however frenzied or ecstatic it may seem. St. Paul says: "A man who speaks in a tongue is talking not to men but to God. No one understands him, because he utters mysteries in the Spirit" (1 Cor 14:2). Sometimes the sounds emitted are not a language at all, but simply irrational utterances or cries proceeding from strong emotion. St. Paul says: "I speak in tongues more than any of you, but in the church I would rather say five intelligible words to instruct others than ten thousand words in a tongue" (1 Cor 14:18-19).

Interpretation of Tongues. This charism comes into play when an intelligible language is spoken but it needs to be translated for the benefit of the listeners. When this occurs, St. Paul insists that it should be interpreted, "but if there is no one to interpret, there should be silence in the assembly, each one speaking to himself and to God" (1 Cor 14:28). Interpretation transforms the incident from a personal religious experience to a proclamation for the benefit of the assembly. This charism would also assist those who interpret the Scripture for others.

Prophecy. Perhaps the clearest explanation of prophecy is found in St. Paul, when he distinguishes the gift of tongues from prophecy: "A man who speaks in a tongue is talking not to men but to God. No one understands him, because he utters mysteries in the Spirit. The prophet, on the other hand, speaks to men for their upbuilding, their encouragement, their consolation. He who speaks in a tongue builds up himself, but he who prophesies builds up the church. I should like it if all of you spoke in tongues, but I much prefer that you prophesy. The prophet is greater than one who speaks in tongues, unless the speaker can also interpret for the upbuilding of the church" (1 Cor 14:2-5).

In this same chapter, St. Paul mentions "revelation" three times as something distinct from prophecy. But his meaning is clear when, after saying that no more than two or three prophets should speak, he adds: "If another, sitting by, should happen to receive a revelation, the first ones [the prophets] should then keep quiet" (1 Cor 14:29-30).

Both prophecy and revelation have to do with announcing and proclaiming divine truths for building up the Christian community. The bond of this community is love, which surpasses all charisms and is even the greatest of the three: "faith, hope and love, and the greatest of these is love" (1 Cor 13:13).

Discernment of Spirits. The precise function of this charism is to identify the cause or spirit from which certain phenomena proceed. It is possible, through study and experience, to acquire a high degree of facility in discernment, but here we are referring to an authentic charism, or *gratia gratis data*. The importance of discernment of spirits proceeds from the fact that numerous phenomena to all appearances are identical yet admit of various possible causes: natural, supernatural, or diabolical. That is why some investigators of extraordinary phenomena have mistakenly diagnosed some of the saints as hysterical or schizophrenic. St. Philip Neri and St. John Vianney are two of the saints gifted with this charism.

Gifts of Healing and Miraculous Powers. Although St. Paul mentions these two charisms as distinct, they actually overlap. Not all cures are miraculous, however, because a person with the gift of healing may use natural means to restore health. The saints who were gifted with miraculous powers were well aware that it is God, and not any human being, who works miracles. The person who has this charism is merely an instrument of God, but in that capacity can do what no purely human power can do.

At a lower level we find the charisms of the works of mercy. There is a veritable army of caring, loving Christians who have dedicated themselves to the care of the sick and dying, the poor and the orphans, the protection of slaves and prisoners, etc. It is these works of service that are most visible and most readily understood as Christian love in action.

See: Discernment; Extraordinary Gifts; Holy Spirit; Miracles; Mysticism; Private Revelation; Prophecy.

Suggested Readings: CCC 688, 799-801, 951, 2003. H. Egan, *Christian Mysticism*, pp. 320-338. L. Bermejo, *The Spirit of Life*. J. Koenig, *Charismata: God's Gifts for God's People*.

Jordan Aumann, O.P.

CHARITY

Charity is the most important element in Christian life. God first loved us; and what he most desires of us is that we should love him above all and love one another out of love for God (CCC 1822). The love Christ seeks from us is the kind described magnificently by St. Paul (1 Cor 13:1-13). This love sets us free (CCC 1828). It is a love that "the Holy Spirit pours into our hearts" (Rom 5:5).

We can love freely with this divine love, not of our own power, but because God, who seeks our love, gives us the power. When grace is first planted in our hearts, the theological virtue of charity is given to us (CCC 1813). Nothing could make our lives more excellent or rich; what God asks of us is precisely what we most need.

To be faithful to the Gospel, the catechist must always put this love in first place. The *Catechism of the Catholic Church* reminds us that in all teaching of faith, whether it concerns the Creed or the sacraments or the commandments, we should always be teaching love. We must always proclaim that every Christian activity should "spring from love, and have no other objective but to arrive at love" (*Roman Catechism*, Preface, 10; quoted in CCC 25).

Love makes strong demands. The first and greatest commandment is that we should love God; the second is that we should love one another. At the root, it is love that imposes every other real duty upon us (cf. Mt 22:40; CCC 2055). But love also makes light and easy all that otherwise might have been bitter and unsupportable.

See: Beatitudes; Grace; Law of Christ; Moral Principles, Christian; Theological Virtues.

CHASTITY

Chastity is the virtue that enables one to use one's sexual powers properly. The chaste person is in control of his or her sexual desires rather than being controlled by them. Chastity frees one from being dominated by the sexual passions. Necessary for both the married and the unmarried, chastity is rooted in deep respect for the other person, who should never be used as a means merely to satisfy one's sexual desires.

The power of sexuality allows one to make a gift of oneself to another. Again, chastity is the virtue that allows one to make proper use of that power. It requires that the act of sexual intercourse be reserved for expression of a spousal commitment to one's spouse; thus it is necessary to avoid thoughts, situations, or actions that might endanger one's chastity.

Prayer, frequent use of the sacraments, self-knowledge, and ascetical practices are all aids to preserving chastity. The achievement of chastity is generally a lifelong endeavor, especially in cultures where means of entertainment and media seem designed to arouse the sexual passions in inappropriate ways. All sexual sins are the result of a lack of the virtue of chastity or lapses in chastity.

Chastity is, to repeat, necessary for persons in the celibate state and no less necessary for those who are married. Chastity enables us to overcome the effects of original sin that made our passions disordered and cause us to desire those whom we should not, often in ways that we should not, and even to have disordered desires toward our spouses with whom we are properly united sexually. Chastity allows one to avoid viewing others, even one's spouse, as a sexual object and to have the love and friendship for others, especially one's spouse, that one ought to have. Chastity is essential for a true loving relationship with one's spouse and with others as well. There is a notable treatment of these matters in a series of audience addresses given by Pope John Paul II on Genesis.

See: Education in Human Sexuality; Purity; Sexuality, Human.

CHOICE

Choice is a particular type of act of will. Given a recognition of various appealing courses of action, choice is the will's determination and inclination to perform *this* course of action rather than *that* one.

Choice is often contrasted with intention. The latter is an act of will in relation to an end to be attained by means of some action, whereas choice is an act of will selecting this action rather than another. A choice is free if it is not determined by antecedent conditions.

Choice is an inward, spiritual act. Although one chooses to perform a physical behavior, the choice itself is not physical. Moreover, like intellectual knowledge, after one makes a choice, the choice remains (or at least an aspect of it remains) until it is reversed (repented).

Every choice is important, for in our choices we shape our characters. Still, some choices are more important than others, for some choices organize more of our lives than others do. Thus, following the American ethicist and moral theologian Germain Grisez, we can distinguish between large choices and small choices. A small choice bears upon a particular course of action, and is carried out by a single behavior. A large choice involves accepting a status, entering a relationship, or undertaking a way of life. Large choices, then, are implemented by subsequent, smaller choices. For example, the choice to become a teacher is a large choice; it is implemented by other choices stretching over many years.

A commitment is another type of choice. It can be defined as a large choice bearing upon a moral dimension of the self or upon a relationship with other people, such that it establishes a basic orientation for one's life requiring an open-ended series of choices to carry out: for example, the choice to marry or the choice to reform one's life.

See: Freedom, Human; Human Goods; Practical Reason.

CHRISTIAN WITNESS

"But you shall receive power when the Holy Spirit has come upon you; and you shall be my witnesses in Jerusalem . . . and to the end of the earth" (Acts 1:8).

In the American legal system, a *witness* generally means an *eyewitness*, one who testifies to a fact known firsthand about someone or something else. But how does one witness to Christ?

Christian witness differs from legal witness in two fundamental ways. First, since the end of the Apostolic Age, Christian witness has not been an eyewitness account. People come to the truth about Jesus Christ either (rarely) through some kind of direct illumination or (commonly) from studying Scripture and hearing the teaching of the Church. Moreover, Christian witness often is silent witness. The First Epistle of Peter says: "Always be ready to make a defense to anyone who calls you to account for the hope that is in you" (1 Pt 3:15). But the average Catholic in everyday life communicates conviction by being a certain way, by following a certain path in life. Behavior reveals belief in Jesus and the Church he founded.

Pope Paul VI's 1975 apostolic exhortation *On Evangelization in the Modern World, Evangelii Nuntiandi*, which calls evangelization "the essential mission of the Church," makes this point so clearly as to justify quoting at length: "Above all the Gospel must be proclaimed by witness. Take a Christian or a handful of Christians who, in the midst of their own community, show their capacity for understanding and acceptance, their sharing of life and destiny with other people, their solidarity with the efforts of all for whatever is noble and good. Let us suppose that, in addition, they radiate in an altogether simple and unaffected way their faith in values that go beyond current values, and their hope in something that is not seen and that one would not dare to imagine. Through this wordless witness these Christians stir up irresistible questions in the hearts of those who see how they live: Why are they like this? Why do they live in this way? What or who is it that inspires them? Why are they in our midst? Such a witness is already a silent proclamation of the Good News and a very powerful and effective one" (21).

We have all seen Christian witnesses, and most of us *are* witnesses at least part of the time. Priests and religious offer the special witness of dedicating their whole lives to the service of God and neighbor. As the *Catechism of the Catholic Church* makes clear, the countless thousands of Christian martyrs who have gone to their deaths for "the truth of the faith and of Christian doctrine" (2473) are the ultimate witnesses.

The witness of the ordinary Catholic is more subtle, but no less real. The man who attends daily Mass gives witness. So does the one who organizes a summer basketball league on inner-city playgrounds, though he may never speak of Christ, provided he visibly acts from religious motives. The woman who serves as minister of the Eucharist gives witness. So, too, the one who does *pro bono* legal work for an indigent client. The high-school senior who volunteers as a retreat leader gives witness, as does the one who shovels an elderly neighbor's sidewalk. Witness is letting your light shine.

The *Catechism* says: "The transmission of the Christian faith consists primarily in proclaiming Jesus Christ in order to lead others to faith in him" (425). The witness of the Apostles was in one respect unique, since they were "chosen witnesses of the Lord's Resurrection" (CCC 860). But the duty to give witness to Christ is a duty for all his followers, including laypeople, who by reason of Baptism and Confirmation have a right and duty, individually and in associations, "to work so that the divine message of salvation may be known and accepted by all men throughout the earth" (CCC 900).

Purposes of Christian Witness • The Second Vatican Council's *Decree on the Apostolate of the Laity, Apostolicam Actuositatem,* offers a description that, though more formal, is consistent with Pope Paul's: Lay Catholics exercise their apostolate "when they endeavor to have the Gospel spirit permeate and improve the temporal order, going about it in a way that bears clear witness to Christ and helps forward the salvation of men" (2). The first purpose of witness, then, is evangelization. By living so as to prompt the questioning Pope Paul mentions, Catholics exert a kind of moral gravity. They draw people by their example to salvation in the Church, which "increases, grows, and develops through the holiness of her faithful" (CCC 2045).

Witness has another purpose as well. The *Catechism* says, "By living with the mind of Christ, Christians hasten the coming of the Reign of God, 'a kingdom of justice, love and peace' " (2046). Hastening the reign of God includes working to improve the temporal order, a phrase now somewhat out of date. The "temporal order" (the order of time as opposed to eternity) is simply our everyday world, which individual Christians make better by acts of faith and kindness that help repair the damage sin has caused and shape reality evermore closely to God's loving intent.

The world's evil is clear enough; human history is a litany of horrors that includes, in the twentieth century alone, two major wars and countless minor ones, starvation and oppression on every side, and the murderous miseries of Nazism and Stalinism. This record need not breed despair, however. Central to Christianity is the rhythm of sin and forgiveness, suffering and redemption. Every good deed a Christian does for the love of God ennobles human existence and moves us by imperceptible degrees toward the Father. If the doctrine of the kingdom of God is to be taken seriously, a kind of quasi-evolutionary process indeed animates the universe. Hope in the ultimate victory of good prompts the Christian's untiring testimony.

Christian witness, though primarily the act of an individual, is rarely solitary; as we are social creatures, so our witness is social. The *Decree on the Apostolate of Lay People* insists that "the apostolate of married persons and of families has a special importance for both Church and civil society" (11). Given the cancerous spread of divorce in recent years, a couple witnesses most powerfully by mutual fidelity "for better or for worse," demonstrating the indissolubility of Christian marriage and providing their offspring a stable platform for growth. They also witness by educating their children in the faith, often at great personal sacrifice. A Christian family holds people in a strong, intimate, and cheerful embrace. It is a model that others will long to imitate, the living cell of any sound society.

Catholics traditionally associate the word "vocation" with priests, sisters, and brothers. In fact, however, every Christian has a vocation, a calling, a job to do.

We help build the kingdom of God most immediately through our daily work, whether that be as banker, homemaker, waiter, or parish director of religious education. Two aspects of work deserve notice, one painful, both positive. First of all, I may shape reality more closely to God's will as a direct result of my labor: by being an honest banker, a caring and efficient homemaker, a skillful and courteous waiter, a religious educator faithful to the Church.

To understand the second way that work changes the world, one must recall the Christian theme of redemption through suffering. Christ did not redeem humanity by riding a wave of popular acclaim to the top; he did it by undergoing torture and death. Without the cross there is no Resurrection. Without the Resurrection there is no redemption, and we remain condemned to die like our dogs and cats. Pope John Paul II says eloquently in his encyclical *On Human Work, Laborem*

Exercens: "[Jesus'] work of salvation came about through suffering and death on a cross. By enduring the toil of work in union with Christ crucified for us, man in a way collaborates with the son of God for the redemption of humanity. He shows himself a true disciple of Christ by carrying the cross in his turn every day in the activity he is called upon to perform" (27).

Motives for Witnessing • In the passage from *On Evangelization in the Modern World* quoted above, Pope Paul VI imagines people asking of Christians: "Why are they like this?" What, indeed, would motivate one to live a life of Christian witness in a world where "nice guys finish last" and where hypocrisy and greed gather rewards? For many, perhaps, it is a matter of honesty. They accept the Church's teaching about humanity: that the Father created us in the divine image, that Jesus Christ redeemed us from sin through his death and Resurrection, that the Holy Spirit penetrates and guides the Church toward the world's salvation, and that each of us will live forever.

These are fundamental human truths. Everything else we can say about ourselves — that we inhabit a fleck of rock spinning in a void unimaginably vast; that we share the same genetic code with all other life-forms on earth; that our moral history is one of altruism and selfishness, kindness and brutality, idealism and warfare — is secondary. People who behave consistently with this vision are Christian witnesses.

Christians also find motivation in the drive to realize the reign of God on earth. Religious utopianism, involving efforts by God's self-appointed spokesmen to impose his reign on others, is a very destructive temptation, as episodes like the Puritan revolution in England attest. But indifference to building up the kingdom has even worse consequences; it allows the ever-present evil in the human heart to flourish unchecked. The Irish poet William Butler Yeats caught the problem brilliantly in his poem *The Second Coming*: "Things fall apart; the center cannot hold; / Mere anarchy is loosed upon the world, / The blood-dimmed tide is loosed, and everywhere / The ceremony of innocence is drowned; / The best lack all conviction, while the worst / Are full of passionate intensity."

When Christian witnesses lack conviction, humanity's long slow climb into God's embrace seems to slacken and "mere anarchy" substitutes for his reign.

Since the Church is the People of God, it would seem that her witness to the world is simply the collective action of her members. This is not quite the case, however. The United States stands as a symbol of democracy not because all Americans behave democratically, but because the nation was established with a certain constitution and with certain structures, laws, and customs. In the same way, the Church as an institution witnesses to the world through what Christ founded her to be. " 'The Church, in Christ, is like a sacrament — a sign and instrument, that is, of communion with God and of unity among all men' [*LG* 1].The Church's first purpose is to be the sacrament of the *inner union of men with God*. Because men's communion with one another is rooted in that union with God, the Church is also the sacrament of the *unity of the human race*" (CCC 775).

A sacrament brings about the reality it signifies. Baptism, for example, wipes away the stain of original sin as the baptismal water washes the skin. It follows that the Church, as " 'the universal sacrament of salvation' . . . [*LG* 9 §2, 48 §2; GS 45 §1]" (CCC 776), is destined in the course of ages to gather all of humanity in communion with the Creator. It is heresy to believe there is no salvation outside the visible structures of the Roman Catholic Church. Nevertheless, the Church is uniquely witness to and instrument of God's saving power. As a sacrament, the Church must visibly express her spiritual reality, just as the baptismal water expresses cleansing. If her task is to unify the whole human race, she can never rest until all Christians are one. The unity of the Church is a pledge, a necessary first step, toward the unity of all. Thus the urgency that attaches to the work of ecumenism.

The Church also witnesses to the truth of Christ by her acts. *Lumen Gentium* says: "Henceforward

the Church, endowed with the gifts of her founder and faithfully observing his precepts of charity, humility and self-denial, receives the mission of proclaiming and establishing among all peoples the Kingdom of Christ and of God, and she is on earth the seed and the beginning of that kingdom" (5, quoted in CCC 768).

The Church seeds the kingdom of God on earth as the individual Christian does, by work and by example. She is the greatest provider of human services the world has ever seen. Her ministries of healing, of feeding, of clothing, of sheltering, of welcoming, of comforting spring from Christ's own words in the twenty-fifth chapter of Matthew's Gospel, "Come, O blessed of my Father, inherit the kingdom prepared for you from the foundation of the world; for I was hungry and you gave me food. . . ." The hospitals, the parish food pantries, the great charitable organizations, the inner-city schools, the homeless shelters, the hospices and places of warm hospitality stretching in unbroken succession for two thousand years are testimony that the reign of God, "a kingdom of justice, love and peace," is not only possible but is already here, though in embryo.

Christians nurture that embryo by the witness of lives lived "as if they could see the invisible" (*On Evangelization in the Modern World,* 76) — as if they could sense God's Holy Spirit saving the world through them. St. John's Gospel closes with these words: "This is the disciple who is bearing witness to [Jesus] . . . and we know that his testimony is true" (Jn 21:24). Unlike John, modern Christians do not have the privilege of seeing the Lord with their own eyes. Their testimony is true when they act in the bright and guiding light of faith.

See: Apostolate; Church, Nature, Origin, and Structure of; Ecumenism; Evangelization; Laity; Martyrdom; Truthfulness; Work.

Suggested Readings: CCC 758-780, 2045-2046, 2471-2474. Vatican Council II, *Decree on the Apostolate of the Laity, Apostolicam Actuositatem,* 1-14; *Dogmatic Constitution on the Church, Lumen Gentium,* 1-17, 30-42, 48-54. Paul VI, *On Evangelization in the Modern World,*

Evangelii Nuntiandi, 21. John Paul II, *On Human Work, Laborem Exercens*, 25-27.

David M. Byers

CHRISTOLOGICAL CONTROVERSIES

The first Christians were convinced that God had made himself known in the Person of Jesus, the Messiah, raising him from the dead and offering salvation to men through him, and that he had poured out his Holy Spirit on the Church. Early baptismal and other liturgical formulas (cf. Acts 2:38; Mt 28:19; Justin Martyr, *Apologia* I, 61.3) indicate their belief that Jesus participated in the divinity of God.

The early Christians believed that Jesus as Messiah went beyond the understanding of the Messiah foretold by Jewish tradition. In his real humanity he could suffer and die; he was also, as Son of God, a partaker of the reality of God himself, through whom the world was not just redeemed but created. From this conviction two questions arose: If Christ is God, how is his divinity reconciled with that of the one God, God the Father, given the traditional monotheism inherited from Judaism? And how are the divine and human dimensions reconciled in his person?

The Jews could not conceive of how the supposed divinity of the Messiah could be reconciled with the transcendence that they alone confessed in a world of idolaters. The faith of their fathers, purified and sharpened by the prophets, kept the image of the one God constantly before them. For the pagans it was the other way around. Some of them could readily accept that Jesus might be a divine being and were prepared to admit him into the company of their numerous gods. They were familiar with the notion that gods appear in human form.

The Scriptures were not precise in the formulations they used to describe Jesus. As Christianity grew, different approaches developed to explain and to reconcile his humanity and divinity. The process of development would begin with meditation on the revealed word of God and culminate in dogmatic definitions at ecumenical councils. During this process, some would err in their search for a formula to express the truths of the faith. The different formulations have been given names that try to encapsulate the essence of the particular theory or belief.

Christological Errors • *Monarchians* sought to safeguard the monotheistic conception of God. They emphasized the oneness of God or, as they called it, the *Monarchia*. They are distinguished into *Patripassianists* and *Modalists*. Noetus (flourished c.180-200) taught that Christ and the Father are the same; and the same Father is born, suffers, and dies. This doctrine attributed to the Father the Passion and death of Christ, eliminating any distinction between Father and Son. It regarded Christ as a manifestation and operation of the Father who, in the aspect of a Son, became incarnate and underwent the Passion, suffering on the cross. The adherents of this teaching are called *Patripassianists* by the Orthodox.

Noetus was condemned at a synod in Smyrna in 190. His teaching was brought to Africa by Praxeas (flourished c. 190-210), who was condemned by Tertullian (c. 160-c. 222) in 213 in his *Adversus Praxeam*. A Patripassianist community at Rome was headed by a Libyan named Sabellius (flourished c. 217-220). Sabellius reduced the distinction between the Father and the Son to simple *modes of action* or manifestations. The various Persons of the Trinity are only diverse manners or modes by which God manifests himself. In creation God is manifest as Father, in redemption as Son, and in the work of sanctification as Holy Spirit. Sabellius's followers are known as *Sabellians* or *Modalists*. He and his teachings were condemned by Pope Callistus I (217-222). Noetus, Praxeas, and Sabellius all used the phrase "One God in three Persons." But the "Persons" were distinguished only by reason, not in reality.

Adoptionists considered Christ as a mere man, albeit endowed with exceptional divine gifts; he received the Divine Spirit in his Baptism and thus was "adopted" as Son of God or else he was assumed as Son of God after the Resurrection. They thereby denied the divinity of Christ.

As they strove to preserve the oneness of God and the divinity of Christ, theologians developed theological terms to express the mystery. Novatian (c. 200-258) made clear that the distinction between the Father and the Son did not compromise the divine unity, conceived by Tertullian as a single divine substance in which Father, Son, and Holy Spirit participated. The distinction within the unity was brought out by the use of the term *prosopon*, person, attributed to the Father and the Son and, by Tertullian, to the Holy Spirit. This approach was further developed by Origen (c. 185-c. 254). Origen stressed the distinction between the Logos (the Word, the Son) and the Father, which he expressed by using the term "hypostasis," individual subsistent reality.

In polemic against the Monarchians, Arius (c. 250-336) stressed the subordination of the Logos (the Word, the Son) to the point of making the Logos distinctly inferior to the Father, extraneous to his nature, created by him for the sake of the subsequent creation of the world. The controversy generated by Arius gradually moved away from its initial Christological dimension to a more broadly Trinitarian one.

Arius's teaching was repudiated at the First General Council of the Church, held at Nicaea in 325. Nicaea described the Son of God as *homoousios*, consubstantial, of one and the same substance with the Father, God in the full sense of the term.

Not all accepted this definition. One group, known as Semi-Arians, stated that Christ was *homoiousios*, like or similar to the Father. If Christ were only "like" the Father, he would not be true God. This was rejected by the First Council of Constantinople in 381, which reaffirmed the formulation of Nicaea and added to it. The Creed of this council, the Nicene-Constantinopolitan Creed, commonly referred to as the Nicene Creed, is used in the Mass today.

The divinity of Christ having been established at Nicaea and Constantinople, the question of the union of humanity and divinity continued to be controverted.

Nestorius (c. 381-c. 451), Bishop of Constanti-nople, accepted the teaching that Christ possesses two complete and perfect natures, human and divine. On the other hand, he taught that there was a "human person" resulting from the union of the body and soul in Christ, as well as the preexisting Divine Person. He held that this human person was in some way subordinate to the Divine Person. Therefore, he concluded Mary was not the Mother of God (Theotokos) but rather the Mother of Christ (Christotokos). In 431, the Council of Ephesus condemned Nestorius and declared Mary to be truly Mother of God.

Cyril of Alexandria (c. 375-444) claimed we could speak of two natures in Christ only before the union of the human and the divine because the union produced a single nature (*monophysis*), a single subject and center of will and activity.

This formulation led to *Monophysitism*, and drew the intervention of Pope Leo I the Great (c. 400-461), whose *Tomus ad Flavianum* was the basis of the formula of the Council of Chalcedon (451) that affirmed the two natures of Christ, united but not confused, whole and complete, so that Christ is *homoousios* with the Father according to his divinity and *homoousios* with men according to his humanity. Chalcedon was rejected by the Monophysites, who today form several of the Ancient Oriental Churches.

Attempting to meet the Monophysites halfway, the theory of Monoenergism or Monothelitism developed in the seventh century. This doctrine, while affirming two natures in Christ, made his willing and acting originate not from the two natures but from the hypostasis, that is, the subject, which is single, so that a single will and a single operation, divine and human, originate from it. The condemnation of Monoenergism and Monothelitism at the Third Council of Constantinople (680-681) put to an end the Christological controversies.

See: Development of Doctrine; God, Nature and Attributes of; Heresy; Incarnation; Jesus Christ, God and Man; Mary, Mother of God.

Suggested Readings: CCC 422-486. A. Grillmeier, *Christ in Christian Tradition*.

Robert J. Wister

CHURCH AND STATE

In the ancient world, the relation of Church and State as two distinct entities was not a problem that needed resolution. Organized religion was in large part *civil* religion, intimately bound up in the life and structure of the *polis*, the political community. The gods were the gods of the city or empire; priests were most often lesser functionaries of the political authority. Even in the case of the chosen people, the law given by Yahweh encompassed political organization and religious life and worship into a unified whole.

This situation was to change, slowly, first with the dawn of Christianity, and later through important changes in political theory and practice. Christ preached a religion that transcended the merely political realm. He promulgated a New Law, foretold by the Hebrew prophets, which would be written on the hearts of men. Moreover, the new faith would be universal, or catholic, making men first of all citizens of the City of God, which cannot be contained within national boundaries.

Jesus acknowledged the legitimacy of political authority in its proper realm: "Render therefore to Caesar the things that are Caesar's" (Mt 22:21). So did his Apostles in their teaching and exhortations: "Let every person be subject to the governing authorities. . . . He who resists the authorities resists what God has appointed" (Rom 13:1-2; cf. 1 Tm 2:1-4; 1 Pt 2:13-17). Yet Peter, not Caesar, was appointed head of the Church; and what is owed to Caesar was distinguished from what is owed God. The spiritual realm was distinguished from the secular, or temporal, each with its own proper authority and role in human life.

Hence arose the challenge of how to understand the nature and function of each authority, in itself and especially vis-à-vis the other: how to harmonize their activities in the service of humanity and avoid the problem of conflicting loyalties. This is far from a purely theoretical dilemma. Rather, it is bound up with the actual life of Christians under various political regimes throughout the centuries.

Historical Overview • The early decades of the Church frequently were times of persecution, more or less bloody, by Caesar and his followers. Later, after Constantine, the tables were turned and Christianity became the official religion of the Empire, with all the benefits and dangers that status brought. Then came the various heresies and schisms, from Arianism to Donatism to the separation of the Orthodox from Rome, and the political upheavals that preceded, accompanied, and followed these ecclesial crises.

In the West, dreams of a united Christendom faded with the advent of the Reformation, followed by the havoc of the so-called Religious Wars. In the interest of civil peace, many came to share the conviction that the responsibility for deciding the religion of the people in a given country lay with the prince of that realm: *cuius regio, eius religio* — "whose region, his religion," from the Peace of Augsburg (1555).

The proto-liberalism of the English political philosopher Thomas Hobbes (1588-1679) concurred with the proponents of the above thesis in placing religion under the jurisdiction of the political sovereign, whoever he or they happened to be. His overarching goal was to establish a more rational politics and in the process to end senseless violence inflamed by religious passions run wild. John Locke (1632-1704) and others argued instead for religious toleration among the citizens of a liberal republic, although in principle allowing for intolerance of untrustworthy groups such as Catholics and atheists. The *philosophes* who inspired the French Revolution were bitterly opposed to Christianity and especially to the Catholic Church, which they regarded as in league with the reactionary and oppressive aristocracy.

The United States, the first liberal democracy started more or less from scratch, made the "anti-establishment clause" an important feature of its Constitution, ensuring that the United States would not be officially Anglican, Puritan, etc.; that no church would be favored above others at the national level; and that the religious beliefs and practices of law-abiding citizens would not be interfered with. In recent decades, however, this provision has been interpreted as erecting a "wall of separation" between religion and civic life, removing religion from the public square and relegating it almost entirely to private life.

Finally, the twentieth century has witnessed the rise (and, happily, in many cases also the fall) of Fascist and Marxist regimes, which strove to impose neopaganism or dogmatic atheism and subjected the Church to violent persecutions exceeding even the horrors of Rome's colosseum.

This is the sketchiest of overviews, focusing primarily on the development of Church-State relations in Europe and North America. Yet these developments influenced vast areas of other continents, due especially to the widespread influence of liberalism and communism. This historical experience provided material for reflection on the proper relation of Church and State, on the part of the Church herself as well as by others. Centuries of theological reflection also deepened the Church's understanding of her own identity and mission, as well as of the roles proper to her members — laity, religious, priests, bishops. This resulted in a more precise appreciation of the Church's role in relation to civil society and the temporal order. Finally, beyond the general principles governing Church-State relations as such, different forms of political culture and organization require adaptation and the specification of these principles to particular situations.

Teaching on Church and State • Addressing this question in light of the contemporary situation, the Fathers of the Second Vatican Council said: "It is of extreme importance, especially in a pluralistic society, to work out a proper vision of the relationship between the political community and the Church, and to distinguish clearly between the activities of Christians, acting individually or collectively in their own name as citizens guided by the dictates of a Christian conscience, and their activity acting along with their pastors in the name of the Church" (*Pastoral Constitution on the Church in the Modern World, Gaudium et Spes*, 76). *Gaudium et Spes*, which follows from the Council's "deep reflection on the mystery of the Church" in the *Dogmatic Constitution on the Church, Lumen Gentium* (cf. *Gaudium et Spes*, 2,

40), contains some of the most helpful treatments of our subject by the modern Magisterium. Various papal encyclicals of this century also take up aspects of the relationship between Church and State, including Pope John Paul II's encyclical *The Hundredth Year, Centesimus Annus* (1991). The *Catechism of the Catholic Church*'s section "The political community and the Church" (2244-2246) draws from this encyclical as well as from *Gaudium et Spes*.

Traditional Catholic teaching describes both the Church and the political community as "perfect" societies. That means each possesses within itself means sufficient for achieving its proper ends. The end or goal of the political community and its authority is the temporal common good or the earthly happiness for which its citizens strive as human beings. Magisterial teaching especially in the past fifty years has pointed out the insufficiency of individual nation-states to achieve this goal in isolation from the broader international community. By contrast, the Church is a spiritual society whose *raison d'être* is the salvation of souls, the spiritual or supernatural common good proper to human beings as children of God redeemed by Christ and incorporated into his Mystical Body. Hence, as the Council teaches, "[t]he Church, by reason of her role and competence, is not identified with any political community nor bound by ties to any political system. It is at once the sign and the safeguard of the transcendental dimension of the human person. *The political community and the Church are autonomous and independent of each other in their own fields*" (*Gaudium et Spes*, 76, emphasis added).

One consequence is that the clergy as such do not normally have a role in civil government. While over the centuries some churchmen have indeed sought political influence and held office — with better or worse intentions, with greater or lesser degrees of success — the Church does not seek to usurp the rightful tasks and responsibilities of political authority. In his 1939 encyclical *On the Function of the State in the Modern World, Summi Pontificatus*, Pope Pius XII took up the charge that "the activity of the Church in teaching and spreading [the doctrine of Christ], and in forming and modelling men's minds by its precepts . . . [shakes] the foundations of civil authority and usurp[s] its rights." He declared that "any such aims are entirely alien to that same Church, which spreads its maternal arms towards this world not to dominate but to serve. She does not claim to take the place of other legitimate authorities in their proper spheres, but offers them her help after the example and in the spirit of her Divine Founder Who 'went about doing good' [cf. Acts 10:38]. The Church preaches and inculcates obedience and respect for earthly authority which derives from God its whole origin" (92-94).

John Paul II explains that there can be and in fact have been "exceptional cases in which it may seem opportune or even necessary to help or supplement public institutions that are lacking or in disarray, in order to support the cause of justice and peace. Ecclesiastical institutions themselves, even at the highest level, have provided this service in the past, with all the advantages, but also with all the burdens and difficulties that this entails. . . . [M]odern political, constitutional and doctrinal development tends in another direction. Civil society has been progressively given institutions and resources to fulfill its own tasks autonomously" ("Priests Do Not Have a Political Mission," *L'Osservatore Romano*, English language edition, August 4-11, 1993, cf. *Gaudium et Spes*, 40, 76).

Recognizing the rightful jurisdiction of the state, the Church claims from civil authority the freedom to carry out her God-given mission of evangelization in the service of persons, families, and society. "The Church desires nothing more ardently than to develop itself untrammeled in the service of all men under any regime which recognizes the basic rights of the person and the family, and the needs of the common good" (*Gaudium et Spes*, 42). The Second Vatican Council's *Declaration on Religious Freedom* goes so far as to insist that "the freedom of the Church is the fundamental principle governing relations between the Church and public authorities and the whole civil order": "Among those things which pertain to the

good of the Church and indeed to the good of society here on earth, things which must everywhere and at all times be safeguarded and defended from all harm, the most outstanding surely is that the Church enjoy that freedom of action which her responsibility for the salvation of men requires" (*Dignitatis Humanae*, 13).

The respective autonomy of temporal and spiritual spheres is not absolute, however. The same men and women are members of (or related to) both the Church and political society; and both are concerned with the welfare of human beings, with facilitating their attainment of happiness and fulfillment. This points to the need for cooperation between the Church and the state "according to the local and prevailing situation." Vatican Council II goes on to observe that the Church, "being founded in the love of the Redeemer, contributes towards the spread of justice and charity among nations and within the borders of the nations themselves" while she also "respects and encourages the political freedom of the citizens" (*Gaudium et Spes*, 76; cf. Pope John Paul II, Address to the United Nations General Assembly, October 5, 1995).

The Contribution of the Church • Evangelization, the primary task of the Church, is also the principal way in which she contributes, if indirectly, to the well-being of civil society and the harmony of the international community (cf. *Gaudium et Spes*, 58 and n. 7). Through it the Church leads people to true conversion of heart, which must precede and accompany any sincere and lasting work for justice. The Church also seeks to influence citizens and civil authority through her social doctrine. This body of magisterial teaching does not propose concrete political or economic models for implementation but rather offers more general "principles for reflection," "criteria for judgment," and "guidelines for action" (cf. CCC 2423). Catholic social doctrine is rooted in truths, gleaned from reason and Revelation, regarding the nature and destiny of the human person. Noting that "[o]nly the divinely revealed religion has clearly recognized man's origin and destiny in God, the Creator and Redeemer," the *Catechism* says the Church "invites political authorities to measure their judgments and decisions against this inspired truth about God and man" (CCC 2244; cf. *Centesimus Annus,* 45-46). Finally, the Church acknowledges her duty, and therefore reserves the right, "to pass moral judgments even in matters relating to politics, whenever the fundamental rights of man or the salvation of souls requires it" (*Gaudium et Spes,* 76). Examples in the twentieth century include papal condemnations of communism and Nazism.

In carrying out her duties vis-à-vis civil society and its authority, "the only means [the Church] may use are those which are in accord with the Gospel and the welfare of all men according to the diversity of times and circumstances" (*Gaudium et Spes,* 76). This refusal to appropriate the weapons of "power politics" once prompted Soviet dictator Joseph Stalin to ask mockingly, "And how many divisions has the Pope?" It has been suggested that he received his answer, posthumously, with the events of the late 1980s and early 1990s, in which the spiritual forces of the Gospel and the Church's social teaching, under John Paul II, played a key role in defeating the vast armed forces of Stalin's successors (cf. *Centesimus Annus,* 22-29, and Address to the United Nations General Assembly, October 5, 1995).

The character of a political regime and the quality of its leadership, for their part, can contribute much to preparing good soil in which the seed of the Gospel can take root, germinate, and bear fruit. The Church has no illusions regarding prospects for establishment of some political utopia, much less a theocracy. Nevertheless, greater attention by government to justice and to the spiritual aspects of human flourishing can foster the development of human virtues, sound family life, and proper education, and thereby contribute greatly to integral human well-being. Also dependent in large measure on the political situation is the climate of civil peace in which Christians and all persons of good will can work unhindered by public institutions.

Yet, as the Second Vatican Council says, "[t]he

Church itself also recognizes that it has benefited and is still benefiting from the opposition of its enemies and persecutors" (*Gaudium et Spes,* 44 and n. 23). Even oppressive states can unwittingly contribute to the growth of the Church in holiness as well as in numbers: In the divine economy, as the Apostolic Fathers noted with some amazement, the blood of martyrs is in fact the seed of Christians.

See: Authority; Church, Membership in; Church, Nature, Origin, and Structure of; Citizenship; Civil Disobedience; Common Good; Liberation Theology; Magisterium; Politics; Religious Liberty; Social Doctrine.

Suggested Readings: CCC 2242, 2244-2246, 2256-2257, 2419-2425. Vatican Council II, *Declaration on Religious Freedom, Dignitatis Humanae*; *Dogmatic Constitution on the Church, Lumen Gentium*; *Pastoral Constitution on the Church in the Modern World, Gaudium et Spes,* especially 40-45, 73-76. Pius XII, *On the Function of the State in the Modern World, Summi Pontificatus.* John Paul II, *The Hundredth Year, Centesimus Annus,* especially I, III, V, VI; Address to the United Nations General Assembly, October 5, 1995.

Mary M. Keys

CHURCH BUILDINGS

Faith teaches the Catholic that God is present everywhere. In the words of the Apostle of the Gentiles, "the Lord of heaven and earth does not live in shrines made by man" (Acts 17:24) so that he would be enclosed by them or his activity limited to their confines. In the wide expanses of creation, he has erected for himself a temple more worthy of his infinitely sublime majesty than even the most costly shrine. And in any case, such an edifice would be much too small for him. As the kingly prophet of the Old Covenant sang: "The heavens are thine, the earth also is thine; the world and all that is in it, thou hast founded them" (Ps 89:11). How far does this faith elevate the Christian above the narrow view of the heathen, who imagines his Deity to be like a man, limited in his presence and power to the precincts of the temple that housed his image! And how this faith fills us with holy fear and reverence before the incomprehensible grandeur of God, in whose eyes the whole earth is but a footstool for his feet!

Yet, Holy Church has always erected to God sanctuaries for his earthly dwelling, which with solemn rites she dedicates as temples of God, where she is convinced that God is especially near with his blessing, and where she therefore raises her hands to him in common prayer and in the Holy Sacrifice enters the covenant of grace with him. In erecting such sacred temples, the Church was and is but following the path marked out for her by the Old Covenant, whose legacy she deepened and spiritualized. Bloody sacrifices of material objects were replaced by the one spiritual and unbloody sacrifice of the Eucharist; and with it the *mysterium* — sacrificial unity with Christ and participation in his transfigured divine love — became the very soul of the Church. That, however, implied preeminent elevation above all natural created greatness and beauty, such as even the Old Covenant itself did not possess.

Even more than in the case of the chosen people, this preeminence had to find expression in a symbolic separation and withdrawal from the realm of the purely natural. Then as now, this left a direct impression upon the *locus* of this mysterious exchange between God and his Church: upon the altar.

The Centrality of the Altar • In the eyes of the Church, the consecrated and anointed altar is a focal point of God's special presence in the Sacred Liturgy; it already contains in itself detachment from and elevation above the earth, which groans under the curse of sin. This is why the praying Church, the *ecclesia orans*, refers to the altar overshadowed by God's Spirit as the "house of God and gate of heaven" from which, as in Jacob's dream, the angels ascend and descend to man. Indeed, after the anointing with holy chrism, the Church regards the altar as a powerful symbol of Christ himself, whom "God, your God, has anointed with the oil of gladness above your fellows" (Ps 45:7) to be the kingly bridegroom of Holy Church. And where Christ is present, where the godhead is enthroned, there everything inferior, earthly, merely natural recedes into the background; here grace reigns, separates, and elevates to God on high.

Then, in the strength of the *mysterium*, the Church in the Eucharistic Sacrifice enters into sacred proximity to the Christ embodied in the altar. She experiences herself and acts, in unbroken membership of him, as his Mystical Body, which offers itself with its Head and is transfigured with him. So it is that precisely in the *mysterium*, with its characteristic of being chosen out of natural creation, the Church becomes conscious of the sharp opposition that prevails between herself and all of the world opposed to God. She can perceive quite forcefully that she is not "of this world" while recognizing at the same time that she still dwells "in this world."

At that point, even the withdrawal and separation based in and upon the altar itself no longer suffice. The *mystery* compels the Church, as it were, to give even clearer visual expression to the unique character of her supernatural calling, as well as to her own inner uniformity and firm resolution in relation to a human race that denies Christ.

Hence the Church broadens and expands the spatial separation of the altar by creating the church building as the perceptible expression — indeed, outflow — of her own most profound, God-borne nature and the sole worthy *locus* of her liturgical community life in Christ. A sacred place (*locus sacer*) is a place assigned to divine worship by the dedication or blessing prescribed in the liturgical books (Canon 1205). A place is not sacred in the sense indicated by Church law because acts of worship are celebrated there, even habitually; only liturgical dedication or blessing, as decided upon by the competent authority, renders a place sacred in this sense. This forbids the habitual use of such a *locus sacer* for profane purposes (cf. Canons 1211, 1376).

Among the principal elements of the Church's legislation pertaining to sacred places are the following. A church is a sacred building (*aedes sacra*) intended for divine worship, which the faithful have a right to attend in order to worship either publicly or privately (Canon 1214). Those who build or restore churches must observe the principles and norms of liturgy and sacred art, which in their turn reflect the Christian Tradition (Canon 1216). The holiness with which a sacred place is invested does not permit its habitual use for purposes other than the exercise or promotion of worship, piety, and religion (Canon 1210). Certain norms concerning concerts in churches were set out by the Congregation for Divine Worship in a 1987 letter *The Interest Shown in Music*.

See: Assembly, Liturgical; Celebration, Liturgical; Community Prayer; Eucharist; Liturgy; Mass; Sacred Art; Sacred Music.

Suggested Readings: CCC 1179-1186. Vatican Council II, *Constitution on the Sacred Liturgy, Sacrosanctum Concilium*, 44-46, 122-127. L. Bouyer, *Liturgy and Architecture*. K. Gamber, *The Reform of the Roman Liturgy*, pp. 121-184. J. O'Connell, "Church Building and Furnishing" in *Liturgical Studies 2*.

Robert A. Skeris

CHURCH, MEMBERSHIP IN

Under the title "Who belongs to the Catholic Church?" the *Catechism of the Catholic Church* teaches that full incorporation into the Church is possessed by those who "by the bonds constituted by the profession of faith, the sacraments, ecclesiastical government, and communion — are joined in the visible structure of the Church of Christ . . . [LG 14]" (837). This of course means that others, without being fully incorporated, still belong in some way to the Church. All of those, in fact, who have received Baptism begin to live the life of Jesus Christ and become *de facto* members of the People of God (cf. Canon 204). But non-Catholic Christians, though participating in the life of Christ, do not enjoy all the benefits or means of sanctification that Jesus wished his followers to have, for the completion of their growth in him (cf. Eph 4:12-13). The fullness of membership in the Church founded by Jesus, with all

the immense benefits it brings, belongs only to Catholics.

Membership of the Church is something to be taken advantage of, bringing as it does the right to direct access to Christ, achieved through full communion in the teaching, worship, sacraments, and organic unity of the life that he sustains and secures.

Catholics should cherish the means of grace thus offered to them. They should approach the Eucharist and the sacrament of Penance and Reconciliation, treasure the Liturgy and the sacramentals of the Church, and become familiar with the rich doctrine of their faith.

The state of "nonpracticing" members is of special concern. While their neglect is often simply due to ignorance, it means they are deprived of many graces and strengths in the struggle against sin and the devil that all of us are faced with. It is part of the work of evangelization to reach out to those who feel marginalized and alienated.

"Loss" of Membership • Can membership be lost? The character of Baptism is never effaced from the soul; it remains, even in a soul in hell. But communion with the Church, external or internal, can be lost.

While some Christians — Catholic or Protestant — lapse completely from their faith, there is an important fact to note. Catholic faith, as we have seen, affords a fuller access in itself to revealed truth and the means of grace. If, then, grace touches a Catholic who has lapsed to become aware of the extent of his loss, it is possible that the very poignancy of this awareness can spark a strong desire to return, to make up, and to recover so many wasted opportunities.

"Extra Ecclesiam, Nulla Salus" • What are we to say about those who, lacking Baptism, are not members of the Church in any of the senses explained above? Here it is necessary to clarify the meaning of an old theological principle whose interpretation has caused difficulty in the past: *Extra ecclesiam, nulla salus* (literally, "outside the Church, there is no salvation"). Some people have wished to understand this saying in the most literal sense: that is, that the person who is not formally a practicing Catholic cannot be saved. The Church has condemned such an interpretation (cf. Denzinger-Schönmetzer, 3870-3873).

This is not to say that the maxim is false. Properly understood, it is quite true. The Latin word *extra* can mean either "without" or "outside." The correct interpretation and sense of the maxim is that we cannot be saved *without* the Church. It is *through* the Church, which carries on and makes present the salvific work of Jesus Christ in the world, that all who are saved reach heaven (even if it is perhaps only there that they realize it). Those who, through no fault of their own, have never known Christ or his Church can still be saved. But their salvation, too, is the effect of Jesus working through his Church. In a positive sense, this theological principle "means that all salvation comes from Christ the Head through the Church which is his Body" (CCC 846).

But this cannot make us indifferent to the situation of those outside, saying that "no doubt they are in good faith and so can be saved." While this of course may be so, objectively such people are exposed to many more difficulties. Lacking so many sources of strength, they are weaker against the attraction of evil and the devil and more exposed to the temptation of ultimate despair (cf. Vatican Council II, *Dogmatic Constitution on the Church, Lumen Gentium,* 16). Therefore, the Church feels urged to intensify her missionary activity toward them (cf. Vatican Council II, *Decree on the Church's Missionary Activity, Ad Gentes,* 8).

That mission of the Church involves all of us. A Christian who does not understand Christ's words about being salt and light and leaven has little sense of the world's need, and of his or her own mission. Vatican Council II reserves strong words for our possible responsibility here: "Believers can thus have more than a little to do with the rise of atheism. To the extent that they are careless about their instruction in the faith, or present its teaching falsely, or even fail in their religious, moral, or social life, they must be said to conceal rather than to reveal the true nature of God and of religion" (*Pastoral Constitution on the Church in the Modern World, Gaudium et Spes,* 18).

The consciousness of what it means to be a member of Christ's Church should evoke a personal response of gratitude and increased responsibility. A living member senses his or her share in the Church's whole mission. Laypeople "in particular ought to have an ever-clearer consciousness not only of belonging to the Church, but of being the Church ... [Pius XII, Discourse, February 20, 1946: AAS 38 (1946) 149; quoted by John Paul II, *CL* 9]" (CCC 899).

See: Catholic Identity; Church, Nature, Origin, and Structure of; Communio; Ecclesial Rights and Duties; Evangelization; Missionary Activity.

Suggested Readings: CCC 836-848. Vatican Council II, *Dogmatic Constitution on the Church, Lumen Gentium,* 13-17. Pius XII, *On the Mystical Body of Christ, Mystici Corporis Christi.*

Cormac Burke

CHURCH, NATURE, ORIGIN, AND STRUCTURE OF

It is common to speak of the "mystery" of the Church. Mystery in a religious sense does not imply something closed and inaccessible but rather a reality so deep that we can always discover more to its meaning without ever exhausting it. The Church is more than she appears, and the key to grasping her full reality is faith; "it is only 'with the eyes of faith' [*Roman Catechism* I, 10, 20] that one can see her in her visible reality and at the same time in her spiritual reality as bearer of divine life" (CCC 770).

The Church is the fulfillment of the design of God the Father "to raise up men to share in his own divine life" (Vatican Council II, *Dogmatic Constitution on the Church, Lumen Gentium,* 2). It is the kingdom of God, which Christ inaugurates with his Incarnation, manifests with his words and actions, and whose elements — sacraments, primacy, apostolic college, etc. — he institutes during his life here on earth.

The opening paragraph of *Lumen Gentium* says

that "the Church, in Christ, is in the nature of sacrament"; the Church is, in other words, a sign and a means of grace. The logic of the Church is the logic of the Incarnation, of which, in her visible, structured institution, she becomes in effect a sacramental prolongation.

Christians believe that Jesus, God-become-man, is the Savior of mankind: of each individual person ("there is salvation in no one else" [Acts 4:12]). How does his saving work reach us? Prayer is the most immediate form of contact open to everyone, everywhere. Is it possible, outside prayer, for a person to have real, living, and saving contact with Christ — such, for instance, as his own contemporaries had? One feels a natural envy for those who lived in Palestine two thousand years ago, with their opportunity of meeting Jesus in the flesh, of being taught and healed directly by him. If only we had been given the privilege of living in his times; or if he had chosen to be present in ours — so that we, too, could meet him. We can! Says Pope John Paul II in his encyclical *The Splendor of Truth, Veritatis Splendor*: "In order to make this 'encounter' with Christ possible, God willed his Church" (7). The Church "wishes to serve this single end: that each person may be able to find Christ, in order that Christ may walk with each person the path of life" (John Paul II, *The Redeemer of Man, Redemptor Hominis*, 13).

Jesus Christ came to save us by his sacrifice on the cross and to lead us, having become saints, to heaven. He saves and sanctifies us through his teaching ("I am the way and the truth" [Jn 14:16]); through his sacraments ("I came that they may have life" [Jn 10:10]; "he who eats me will live because of me" [Jn 6:57]); and through the expressions of his will (it is "he who does the will of my Father" who will enter the kingdom of heaven [Mt 7:21]; "He who has my commandments and keeps them, he it is who loves me" [Jn 14:21]). He has in a very particular way entrusted his doctrine and sacraments and authority to his Church: "All authority in heaven and on earth has been given to me. Go therefore and make disciples of all nations, baptizing them in the name of the Father and of the Son and of the Holy Spirit, teaching them to ob-

serve all that I have commanded you; and lo, I am with you always, to the close of the age" (Mt 28:18-20).

So, the Church is the continuation of the presence and work of Christ: "The Church is one with Christ" (CCC 795). Faith in the Church is the natural consequence of faith in Jesus Christ.

One can distinguish different moments in the founding of the Church. Its first solemn announcement comes when Peter is chosen to be the rock on which is laid the Church's foundation (Mt 16:18): "On the rock of this faith confessed by St. Peter, Christ built his Church" (CCC 424). Then there was the commission given to the body of the Apostles collegially after Our Lord's Resurrection: "Go therefore and make disciples of all nations. . . . I am with you always" (Mt 28:19-20). And finally, on Pentecost Sunday, there is the external birth of the Church — beginning to startle the world with a forceful call to repentance, so as to receive forgiveness and salvation (Acts 2:1-4; 11; 37-40). Not only this "birth" of the Church but her continuing life-giving existence is considered to be in a particular sense the work of the Holy Spirit (cf. CCC 737). "The Church is . . . the place 'where the Spirit flourishes' [St. Hippolytus, *Trad. Ap.* 35: SCh 11, 118]" (CCC 749).

Mission and Activity • The work of the Church in spreading the spirit of the Gospel has always had a powerful effect on human society through the call (the Ten Commandments, the Beatitudes, etc.) to live justice, mutual understanding, forgiveness, and peace. The promotion of these noble human purposes is indeed part of her work; yet her mission is at the same time not political. As Vatican Council II teaches: "Christ did not bequeath to the Church a mission in the political, economic, or social order; the purpose he assigned her was a religious one" (*Pastoral Constitution on the Church in the Modern World, Gaudium et Spes*, 42; cf. CCC 549) — to sanctify, teach, and guide people on the way to heaven — though this religious mission itself, as the Council also points out, is a source of commitment to foster human community and human rights.

In her identification with Jesus Christ and his

Messianic work, the Church continues his three-fold office of priest, prophet, and king. Jesus is priest (Heb 7-8; 1 Tm 2:5; CCC 1544), he is teacher (which is the root meaning of prophet), and he is king (cf. Jn 18:36-37; CCC 664). The Church is similarly characterized as having a triple mission or *munus*: priestly, prophetic, and kingly (CCC 888-896).

That these missions are central to understanding the Church is exemplified by the structure given to the 1983 Code of Canon Law (described by Pope John Paul II as "the last document of the Second Vatican Council"). In a complete departure from the previous Code, the new Code configures the laws of the Church according to the Teaching Mission or Office (*Munus Docendi*, Bk. III), the Sanctifying Mission or Office (*Munus Sanctificandi*, Bk. IV), and the mission of ruling (*Munus Regendi*, Bk. II, Pt. II; Bks. VI and VII).

While the laity do not exercise the triple mission of Christ within the Church with full ministerial power (for which a special sacramental ordination is needed [cf. CCC 875]), their peculiar Christ-given mission is in a certain sense even more challenging. It is — on the basis of their sharing fully in the universal call to holiness (cf. *Lumen Gentium*, Ch. V) — to lead, teach, and sanctify, not the Church but *the world*, doing so "from within" (*Lumen Gentium*, 31). The proper role or mission of the laity is to make Christ and his saving truth and grace present, known, and attractive in the world.

The Church is a free community. No one is forced to belong to the Church, even though she is open — and necessary — to all. One belongs because of God's call, but also because of one's own free response. The Church is a free community, too, because only within it does one find the fullness of that Truth which "makes us free" (cf. Jn 8:32). There is a fundamental equality in this community of redeemed persons, all likewise raised to the unique status of being children of God (CCC 683). Along with this equal dignity and vocation within the Church, there is also, as in any society, a variety of functions.

Following the principle of the Incarnation, the Church is both human and divine. "The Church is both visible and spiritual, a hierarchical society and the Mystical Body of Christ. She is one, yet formed of two components, human and divine. That is her mystery, which only faith can accept" (CCC 779). The visible structure of the Church consists not so much in buildings as in persons, institutions, and actions.

Authority in the Church • The Church has a constitution given by her Founder. She is not a democracy in the sense of being an institution where authority originates with the people; authority comes, rather, from above. The Church, by the will of God, is *hierarchically* structured (CCC 874-896). Our Lord sent the Apostles to teach and rule (Mt 28:18-20; Lk 10:16). Along with the Pope, the bishops are the only teachers constituted by divine right. Their authority comes from God; they are not delegates of the clergy or the people, nor for that matter of the Pope. But the choice of each bishop pertains to the Pope. In sum, the authority of bishops is not unlimited, but its limitations come not from "below," but from "above" — from the nature of their mission and office (cf. Mt 16:18, 18:18).

Authority in the Church is both to be exercised and obeyed. In its nature and in the mode of its exercise, however, it is very different from authority in secular societies. It is important to note two peculiar characteristics of Church authority: it is *sacred* and it is a work of *service*.

It is sacred precisely inasmuch as it derives directly from Christ, and not through any democratic commission. "No one can give himself the mandate and the mission to proclaim the Gospel. The one sent by the Lord does not speak and act on his own authority, but by virtue of Christ's authority; not as a member of the community, but speaking to it in the name of Christ. No one can bestow grace on himself; it must be given and offered. This fact presupposes ministers of grace, authorized and empowered by Christ" (CCC 875).

This is why we speak of "hier-archy," which, in its Greek origin, means sacred power — "which is none other than that of Christ" (CCC 1551). It takes faith to keep the sacredness of authority before one's mind, just as, with the Blessed Sacrament, someone lacking faith discerns no more than the natural substance of bread. Authority in the Church is sacred also in that it has a special *sanctifying* effect, when accepted out of supernatural motives.

Authority in the Church is a work of service (cf. *Lumen Gentium*, 24; CCC 876). "It is entirely related to Christ and to men" (CCC 1551). It is first of all service toward Christ, carrying on his mission. Those in authority in the Church must obey God before anything or anyone else (cf. Acts 5:29), and must devote themselves to the fulfillment of his will. Church authority is also service of the people, facilitating their way to — and their return to — Christ. Therefore, the structures in the Church are not power structures, but are geared to *diakonia* and ministry (both words that literally mean service). Jesus said of himself that he "came not to be served but to serve" (Mt 20:28).

St. Thomas Aquinas teaches in his commentary on the *Sentences* of Peter Lombard that "although the Church is supported by God's gift and authority, nevertheless insofar as it is a gathering of men, in its actions some element of human imperfection appears that is not divine." The Apostles, too, had their defects, which were used by God to sanctify both them and those in regard to whom they exercised the missions given them by Christ.

Although we have a guarantee that Christ's truth is behind the solemn exercise of the Church's teaching office, it would be a mistake to look for the same guarantee in relation to the ruling office. Issues of truth are not normally involved in questions of Church discipline or government (but issues of justice could be; and Church law provides means for seeking redress if this is in fact so).

The presence of the Holy Spirit is nevertheless guaranteed to the Church in her government. This does not imply that each measure of government or discipline will always be an exercise of perfect prudence. The guarantee is, rather, that Christ's *will* (as distinct, if one wishes, from his truth) is behind measures of government, when exercised

in catholic communion; and, further, that whoever accepts such measures in faith and responds to them is in fact doing what God wants ("he who listens to you, listens to me" [Lk 10:16]).

A Means of Grace • "The gathering together of the Church is, as it were, God's reaction to the chaos provoked by sin" (CCC 761). She exists not only to save us from the dispersion of sin but to gather into one the scattered children of God (cf. Jn 11:58). She purposes to raise us to the heights of sanctity, to "the hope of sharing the glory of God" (Rom 5:2) and of attaining "the glorious liberty of the children of God" (Rom 8:21). "United with Christ, the Church is sanctified by him; through him and with him she becomes sanctifying," inasmuch as "no one can bestow grace on himself; it must be given and offered" (CCC 824, 875).

From this it follows that the natural attitude of a Christian toward the Church should be one of gratitude and love: for her teaching, guidance, goodness, richness, sacraments, saints. Our love for the Church should produce in us an attitude of grateful reverence filled with respect. St. Augustine says: "Let us love the Lord our God; let us love his Church: the Lord as our Father, the Church as our Mother."

To engage in negative criticism of the Church is not natural, just as it is not natural to criticize one's mother or one's family. One prays for the Church; one is proud of the Church. If we love the Church, we will want to bring others to her, helping them, if necessary, to overcome the prejudices they may have acquired. Our love for the Church is precisely a condition for drawing them to Christ, present in the Church with the fullness of his saving and sanctifying power.

See: Apostolic Succession; Canon Law; Church, Membership in; Communio; Holy Spirit; Infallibility; Jesus Christ, God and Man; Jesus Christ, Life of; Mystical Body of Christ; People of God.

Suggested Readings: CCC 748-945. Vatican Council II, *Dogmatic Constitution on the Church, Lumen Gentium*. C. Burke, *Authority and Freedom in the Church*.

Cormac Burke

CITIZENSHIP

Early in the fourth century A.D., when the Roman Empire was suffering the painful consequences of the barbaric invasions, Christianity was frequently blamed for the decline and impending downfall of the *patria*. After all, the new religion taught people to put their hopes in a "kingdom not of this world" and to "turn the other cheek." By doing so, it undermined the practice of civic virtue and weakened the patriotic spirit of the citizenry. Once-invincible Rome was left soft and vulnerable to outside attack.

St. Augustine set out to refute these charges in his correspondence with influential persons of his day, pagans and Christians alike, and ultimately in his great work the *City of God*. Any thoughtful person could see, argued Augustine, that Christianity teaches just the sort of virtue most conducive to the well-being of a republic: love of justice tempered with mercy; fidelity and moderation; dedication to the common good even at the cost of private pleasure, wealth, or honor. Moreover, God's grace given through the new dispensation strengthens fallen and redeemed man in the arduous practice of such virtue. Good citizenship is an integral part of the duty to love our neighbor. Yet the good *Christian* citizen is freed of the illusion that Rome — or any other earthly nation — is eternal. His virtuous deeds are ultimately directed toward fulfilling his duties to the truly Eternal City, the City of God.

The *Catechism of the Catholic Church* takes up the topic of citizenship, especially in the chapters entitled "The Human Community" (1877-1889) and "You Shall Love Your Neighbor As Yourself" and "The Fourth Commandment" (2196-2246). Due to "the communal character of the human vocation" (subhead preceding CCC 1878), human persons exist not as isolated, autonomous individuals, but rather as members of various societies, in particular the family and the political community. Charity begins at home, as popular wisdom has it, and so our obligation to love our neighbor begins (but does not end) with the other members of our particular communities. Hence the *Catechism* discusses citizenship primarily in terms of the positive responsibilities or duties of citizens. At the same time, however, the Church reminds public authorities of their grave duty to respect, facilitate, and coordinate the contributions of each and all to the common good. Such responsible participation is only possible when civil rights and liberties are upheld to the greatest extent possible.

Rights and Duties of Citizens • While the specific obligations of citizens will vary significantly among the different forms of political regime, some general requirements include the following.

Citizens should contribute to the well-being of society by responsibly performing their roles in family, profession, and various voluntary organizations. They should further participate in public life and political activity in the ways and to the extent permitted by the constitution of their nation, their talent, time, inclination, etc. Being a good citizen is not simply a question of abiding by the laws; it requires initiative and active participation, working together with legitimate authorities and fellow citizens to foster the common good "in a spirit of truth, justice, solidarity, and freedom" (CCC 2239).

Citizens have the duty to respect legitimate political authority and to obey its directives in all that pertains to the common good. This does not mean that citizens are relegated to the realm of "subjects," passive "yes-men" who have no need to think for themselves nor duty to form and follow their consciences. On the contrary, they have the duty to speak and/or act when civil authority oversteps its limits or enacts policies that seem detrimental to the community's well-being. And should authority betray its mission and command acts clearly opposed to natural or divine law, hence to the moral good of persons and community, the citizen must refuse obedience to these directives. Such "civil disobedience" should be exercised with great prudence and, in all but the most extreme situations, without recourse to violence. It is a witness to the truth that might does not simply make right, and that, when forced into an "either-or" situation, "we must obey God rather than men" (Acts 5:29; cf. CCC 2242 and Pope John Paul II, encyclical *The Gospel of Life, Evangelium Vitae*, 68-74 [1995]).

While the basic rights and duties of citizens are shared by all Christians, the Church teaches that it is not ordinarily the task of religious or "the Pastors of the Church to intervene directly in the political structuring and organization of social life" (CCC 2442). Rather, this is the proper role and responsibility of the lay faithful, together with their fellow citizens of other creeds. Laypeople are fully engaged in the world, and have as an integral part of their vocation the task of imbuing temporal activities with the spirit of the Gospel. In his postsynodal exhortation *The Lay Members of Christ's Faithful People, Christifideles Laici* (1989), Pope John Paul II urges lay Christians to take seriously their civic duties: "In order to achieve their task directed to the Christian animation of the temporal order, in the sense of serving persons and society, the lay faithful are never to relinquish their participation in 'public life,' that is, in the many different economic, social, legislative, administrative and cultural areas which are intended to promote organically and institutionally the common good. The Synod Fathers have repeatedly affirmed that every person has a right and duty to participate in public life, albeit in a diversity and complementarity of forms, levels, tasks and responsibilities. Charges of careerism, idolatry of power, egoism and corruption that are oftentimes directed at persons in government, parliaments, the ruling classes, or political parties, as well as the common opinion that participating in politics is an absolute moral danger, does not in the least justify either skepticism or an absence on the part of Christians in public life" (42).

The Holy Father further stresses that, in order to perform well their civic tasks, the laity must fight "the temptation of being so strongly interested in Church services and tasks that [they] fail to become actively engaged in their responsibilities in the professional, social, cultural and political world; and the temptation of legitimizing the unwarranted separation of faith from life, that is a separation of the Gospel's acceptance from the actual living of the Gospel in various situations in the world" (*Christifideles Laici*, 2; cf. 59-60).

St. Augustine wrote that "it is difficult not to err" in our attempts to recognize and fulfill the "duties pertaining to human society" that arise from the great commandment of love. If we as citizens are to do so, more is required than just a vague good will toward others and toward the community as a whole. The citizen must strive to acquire and practice personal virtue, including temperance, courage, or fortitude, and above all justice and prudence. He or she must receive an adequate civic education, through which to come to an understanding of the principles underlying the political society. This education should underline the strengths of one's regime, but also prudently reveal its inevitable weaknesses. In this context, Catholics should feel a special responsibility to deepen their knowledge of the Church's social teaching. In this way they will be better prepared to strive to improve their country, to make it more in accord with true justice and goodness.

This sort of civic education fosters genuine patriotism, a heartfelt but moderate attachment and gratitude to one's country, as opposed to a vicious and blinding form of nationalism. As sharers in a common human nature, we are called to be more than just citizens of a given earthly republic. We are "citizens" of what the Stoic philosophers termed cosmopolis, the universal city or community. Our patriotism and care for justice must therefore transcend national borders; our "neighbor" is our fellow human being in material or spiritual need. And, as Augustine taught so forcefully, our civic participation in this world finds its ultimate meaning in our calling to be first and foremost citizens of the City of God.

See: Authority; Cardinal Virtues; Church and State; Civil Disobedience; Civil Law; Common Good; Laity; Politics; Social Doctrine.

Suggested Readings: CCC 1900-1901, 1913-1917, 2197-2200, 2234, 2237-2243, 2248, 2255-2256, 2442. Vatican Council II, *Pastoral Constitution on the Church in the Modern World,*

Gaudium et Spes, 42-43, 52, 65, 68, 72, 74, 76. Leo XIII, *Chief Duties of Christians as Citizens, Sapientiae Christianae*. John Paul II, *On Social Concerns, Sollicitudo Rei Socialis*, 42, 47; *The Lay Members of Christ's Faithful People, Christifideles Laici*, 36-44, 59-60; *The Hundredth Year, Centesimus Annus*, 44-52. St. Augustine, *City of God*, and Letters 91, 137, 138.

Mary M. Keys

CIVIL DISOBEDIENCE

The normal course of action for Christians is one of obedience to civil authorities, when these truly seek the common good by means in accord with the natural law and respecting constitutional limits on their powers. The Second Vatican Council teaches that even when authority is corrupted, citizens should still perform whatever duties are legitimately required of them by the common good (cf. *Pastoral Constitution on the Church in the Modern World, Gaudium et Spes, 74*). Moreover, at times it may be appropriate for citizens to obey unfair laws, in order to avoid giving scandal.

However, Christians, and indeed all citizens, are obliged in conscience to refuse obedience to laws and other decrees of public authority that command acts contrary to justice and the moral order. Should Caesar's demands conflict with what is owed to God, "we must obey God rather than men" (Acts 5:29).

Where possible, such passive resistance may go hand in hand with active, positive efforts to remedy the injustice in question: "When citizens are under the oppression of a public authority which oversteps its competence . . . it is legitimate for them to defend their own rights and those of their fellow citizens against the abuse of this authority within the limits of the natural law and the Law of the Gospel" (*Gaudium et Spes*, 74; CCC 2242). Only in the most serious cases may this resistance take the form of armed conflict, which is so often ineffective and apt to provoke disorder worse than what it sets out to remedy.

See: Authority; Citizenship; Civil Law; Revolution.

CIVIL LAW

The *Catechism of the Catholic Church* has relatively little to say about civil law. Of the various types of law mentioned — eternal law, natural law, revealed or divine law, civil law, and ecclesiastical law (cf. CCC 1952) — civil law receives perhaps the sketchiest explicit treatment. Nevertheless, the *Catechism*'s sections on the moral law and civil authority do provide an overview of the Church's teaching on this important subject.

The *Catechism* emphasizes the connection between the natural moral law, or "the light of understanding placed in us by God, through [which] we know what we must do and what we must avoid . . . [St. Thomas Aquinas, *Dec. praec.* I]" (1955) and civil law (cf. CCC 1959). Aquinas, in the "Treatise on Law" of the *Summa Theologiae*, begins his consideration of human law by asking why, if men have an innate inclination and sense of obligation to do the good, we need civil law at all: "Was it useful for laws to be framed by men?"

Need for Civil Law • The answer is of course yes. While human beings have a natural capacity to acquire virtue, they need guidance and education from others in order to do so. This character formation is received especially in the family, by means of parental admonition, and also in the political community, through the various laws and customs. Moreover, given the fallen nature of man, civil law is indispensable because it is backed up by force: Those not inclined to obey for the sake of the good itself or to follow the advice of a respected parent or friend may at least do so from fear of punishment. And if they do disobey, the penalty imposed provides an opportunity for correction of the offender and restores peace and order to the community. "Therefore, in order that man might have peace and virtue, it was necessary for laws to be framed, for, as the Philosopher [Aristotle] says, 'a man is the most noble of animals if he be perfect in virtue, so is he the lowest of all if he be severed from law and justice'; because man can use his reason to devise means of satisfying his lusts and evil passions, which other animals are unable to do" (*Summa Theologiae,* I-II, 95, 1; cf. Aristotle, *Politics* I, 2).

Civil law is needed to coordinate and direct the many and varied activities of the members of a particular political community to their common good. This goal cannot be achieved without "the recognition and defense of fundamental rights, and the promotion of peace and of public morality. The real purpose of civil law is to guarantee an ordered social coexistence in true justice" (Pope John Paul II, encyclical *The Gospel of Life, Evangelium Vitae,* 71 [1995]). As laws must be made and promulgated by the competent authority of a particular country, they will vary in origin and character among different forms of government and specific regimes. Hence civil law is the properly *political* form of law as Aquinas understands it: a rule of reason issued for the common good, made and promulgated by whoever has the responsibility to care for the community.

Civil law is derived from the natural moral law in one of two general ways: by way of "conclusion" or by way of "determination" or specification (CCC 1959; cf. *Summa Theologiae,* I-II, 95, 2). An example of the first sort would be a statute prohibiting homicide, a direct conclusion drawn from the natural law precept that innocent persons are not to be harmed. The second sort of relation may be illustrated by traffic laws in the late twentieth century, appropriate to protecting human life in societies where automobiles exist and are widely used — or a law reflecting the judgment that the appropriate punishment for reckless driving is a fine of such-and-such an amount.

Limits of Civil Law • While natural moral law and civil law are thus intimately related, the scope and aim of the latter is considerably more restricted. It would be a serious mistake to conclude that civil law should prohibit and punish *all* vicious acts proscribed by the natural law. Aquinas argues that "human law is framed for a number of people, the majority of whom are not perfect in virtue. Wherefore human laws do not forbid all vices, from which the virtuous abstain, but only the more grievous vices, from which it is possible for the majority to abstain; and chiefly those that are to the hurt of others, without the prohibition of

which human society could not be maintained . . . murder, theft and suchlike" (*Summa Theologiae,* I-II, 96, 2; cf. ad 1-3).

What is most critical to grasp in this connection is that human law is not an autonomous measure of right and wrong, legitimate so long as it expresses majority opinion codified by means of agreed-upon legislative procedures (this is roughly what is taught by the legal philosophy called positivism). Rather, it is a "measured measure," a valid standard only insofar as it conforms to the basic precepts of natural law. On this point, Aquinas cites St. Augustine, who writes in *On the Free Choice of the Will* (I, 5) that "what is not just seems to be no law at all." Aquinas goes on to comment that "the force of a law depends on the extent of its justice. Now in human affairs a thing is said to be just, from being right, according to the rule of reason. But the first rule of reason is the law of nature" (*Summa Theologiae,* I-II, 95, 2).

In *The Gospel of Life, Evangelium Vitae,* Pope John Paul II reaffirms this connection as an integral part of the Church's teaching: "The doctrine on the necessary conformity of civil law with the moral law is in continuity with the whole tradition of the Church. This is clear once more from John XXIII's Encyclical [*Pacem in Terris,* II]: 'Authority is a postulate of the moral order and derives from God. Consequently, laws and decrees enacted in contravention of the moral order, and hence of the divine will, can have no binding force in conscience. . . ; indeed, the passing of such laws undermines the very nature of authority and results in shameful abuse.' This is the clear teaching of Saint Thomas Aquinas, who writes that 'human law is law inasmuch as it is in conformity with right reason and thus derives from the eternal law. But when a law is contrary to reason, it is called an unjust law; but in this case it ceases to be a law and becomes instead an act of violence' [*Summa Theologiae,* I-II, 93, 3, ad 2]. And again: 'Every law made by man can be called a law insofar as it derives from the natural law. But if it is somehow opposed to the natural law, then it is not really a law, but rather a corruption of the law' [*Summa Theologiae,* I-II, 95, 2]" (72).

Legislators must therefore strive to enact laws that are both in conformity with the moral law and appropriate to the concrete character and circumstances of the people they are intended to govern. Legislators must be conscious of the tremendous formative or deformative force of law, especially fundamental or constitutional law and the regime on which it is based. The *Catechism* reminds us that scandal of the worst kind can be provoked by "laws and institutions, by fashion or opinion." Hence, "they are guilty of scandal who establish laws or social structures leading to the decline of morals and the corruption of religious practice, or to 'social conditions that, intentionally or not, make Christian conduct and obedience to the Commandments difficult and practically impossible' [Pius XII, Discourse, June 1, 1941]" (CCC 2286).

On their side, citizens, too, have a responsibility to foster the common good, in part by working for the enactment of truly beneficial civil laws. They have the duty to obey just laws, which bind in conscience, even at the cost of personal sacrifice. And as citizens, human beings, and Christians, they must refuse formal cooperation with evil, even when that evil is honored with the name of law.

See: Absolute Moral Norms; Authority; Citizenship; Civil Disobedience; Common Good; Legalism; Natural Law; Politics; Positivism; Relativism.

Suggested Readings: CCC 1897, 1902, 1904, 1950-1952, 1957, 1959, 1976-1979, 2188, 2273, 2286. Pius XI, *On Atheistic Communism, Divini Redemptoris,* III. John XXIII, *Peace on Earth, Pacem in Terris,* II. John Paul II, *The Hundredth Year, Centesimus Annus,* 44-46; *The Splendor of Truth, Veritatis Splendor,* 97-99; *The Gospel of Life, Evangelium Vitae,* 68-74. St. Thomas Aquinas, *Summa Theologiae,* I-II, 90-92, 95-97.

Mary M. Keys

COLLEGIALITY

While Our Lord conferred his own authority fully on Peter (Mt 16:16), he also gave authority to the Apostles together, as a group or college (Mt 18:16; cf. CCC 880). In its proper ecclesial sense, colle-giality is referred to the whole body of bishops, as successors of the Apostles. Each bishop has the main mission of governing his own diocese. But also like the Apostles, as Vatican Council II points out, each bishop and all together must participate, under Peter, in the concerns of the universal Church (cf. *Dogmatic Constitution on the Church, Lumen Gentium,* 23).

Collegiality has its most formal exercise in an ecumenical council. While the Synod of Bishops is not a parallel expression of collegiality, it does tend to keep the spirit and practice of collegial collaboration strong, in service of the universal Church and the particular churches.

From a theological viewpoint, the term "collegiality" applies only among the bishops, as successors of the Apostles. It is not properly applied to the various form of *participation,* encouraged by Vatican II, by which the faithful can take part in the Church's life and mission, each according to his or her ecclesial role. In this sense, all the faithful are *co-responsible* for carrying on Christ's redemptive work.

A special spirit of participation and service should animate diocesan councils of priests (Canon 495) and parish councils (Canons 228, 536). These councils are not organs of government, any more than is the Synod of Bishops; their function is to offer advice and practical help to the persons canonically charged with the mission of being pastors of parishes or dioceses.

As chapter 3 of *Lumen Gentium* makes clear, the Church has a hierarchical constitution given by Christ. In fostering service and participation, Vatican II did not seek to introduce principles of majority rule into Church decisions. The local bishop is responsible for government within each diocese. Nevertheless, in some concrete cases, the 1983 Code of Canon Law requires him to consult the *opinion* of certain bodies, without necessarily being bound by their advice (e.g., Canons 494, 515.2, 531, 1215.2, 1222.2, 1277); and in a few especially important cases, he is bound by the decision of the College of Consultors (Canons 1277, 1292.1). A wise bishop will always want and seek the advice of wise consultors.

See: Bishop; Church, Nature, Origin, and Structure of; Ecumenical Council; Episcopal Conference; Magisterium; Synod of Bishops.

COMMANDMENTS OF THE CHURCH

The life of each one of us is worthless, and worse than worthless, if it does not end in heaven. Although Jesus our Savior has opened the gates of heaven for us, we cannot on our own discover the way there, much less follow it. It has to be signposted for us, and we need to be helped along it.

Just as we have help above all in the teaching and sacraments of the Church that Jesus founded, so we have signposts in the commandments: "My son, keep my commandments, and you will live" (Prv 7:1-2); "The steadfast love of the Lord is upon those who remember to do his commandments" (Ps 103:17-18); "If you would enter life, keep the commandments" (Mt 19:17).

The modern mood does not easily take to the idea of being commanded or having to obey. Obedience is not a popular word; yet obedience to God, and to those through whom God's will comes to us, is necessary for salvation. "Whoever does the will of my Father will enter the kingdom of heaven" (Mt 7:21).

St. Paul, speaking about the civil-pagan authority of his time, is quite clear on the duty to obey it: "Let every person be subject to the governing authorities. For there is no authority except from God, and those that exist have been instituted by God. Therefore he who resists the authorities resists what God has appointed" (Rom 13:1-2). He insists that obedience to such authority is for our own good, and should be given not mainly out of fear of punishment, but precisely as a response to the prompting of our own consciences. "Would you have no fear of him who is in authority? Then do what is good, and you will receive his approval, for he is God's servant for your good. . . . Therefore one must be subject, not only to avoid God's wrath but also for the sake of conscience" (Rom 13:3-5).

The Authority of the Church • If authorities and laws and the free response of individuals are needed in civil society, they are no less necessary in the Church. Here authority is exercised even more directly in the name of a specific commission from Jesus Christ: "Whatever you bind on earth shall be bound in heaven, and whatever you loose on earth shall be loosed in heaven" (Mt 18:18; cf. Mt 16:19); "He who hears you hears me, and he who rejects you rejects me" (Lk 10:16).

The Church, then, not only preserves and teaches the Ten Commandments of the Old Testament and the "new" commandment given directly by Jesus (cf. Jn 13:34) but has the mission and duty to give further commandments to guide us more particularly in the way of Jesus Christ. "Obey your leaders and submit to them; for they are keeping watch over your souls, as men who will have to give account" (Heb 13:17).

In expounding the commandments of the Church (cf. CCC 2041-2043), the *Catechism of the Catholic Church* says their purpose is "to guarantee to the faithful the indispensable minimum in the spirit of prayer and moral effort, in the growth in love of God and neighbor."

A particular word should be said about the first three of these commandments (Mass each Sunday and holy day, confession if in the state of mortal sin, and Communion at least once a year). They indeed mark out the *indispensable minimum* if one is to keep one's Christian life alive; less than that is bound to leave a person too weak to survive in the struggle against temptation and evil.

If a person wants not just to survive, however, but to grow in love for God and others, he or she will not be content with the minimum, especially regarding Communion and confession. Since these are the only two sacraments that can be received often, and since each sacrament gives strength as only God can give it, their frequent reception should be seen as essential to support the whole of Christian life, to ensure growth in holiness, and to keep us firmly on the path to heaven.

See: Church, Nature, Origin, and Structure of; Communio.

Suggested Readings: CCC 2030-2046.

Cormac Burke

COMMON GOOD

The *Catechism of the Catholic Church* in discussing the common good quotes the *Letter of Barnabas*, a Christian document of the late first or early second century: "In keeping with the social nature of man, the good of each individual is necessarily related to the common good, which in turn can be defined only in reference to the human person: 'Do not live entirely isolated, having retreated into yourselves, as if you were already justified, but gather instead to seek the common good together' [*Ep. Barnabae*, 4, 10; PG 2, 734]" (1905).

Echoing an ancient Christian teaching, the *Catechism* stresses the importance of the common good in its sections on the human person and society. Catholic social teaching begins from the premise, rooted in both reason and revelation, that human beings — substantial unities of body and soul, hence possessing reason and will — are by their very nature social creatures. To achieve their specific perfection and reach happiness, they must under normal circumstances participate in common goods transcending their purely individual well-being and only made possible by life in society, from the family up through the political community and the universal "cosmopolis."

Over the past three or four centuries, nevertheless, many in the modern West have progressively lost sight of the common good, focusing their attention instead almost exclusively on individual rights, autonomous life plans, and partisan interests. As Pope John Paul II has noted, in modern democracies "there is a growing inability to situate particular interests within the framework of a coherent vision of the common good. The latter is not simply the sum total of particular interests; rather it involves an assessment and integration of those interests on the basis of a balanced hierarchy of values; ultimately, it demands a correct understanding of the dignity and rights of the person" (encyclical *The Hundredth Year, Centesimus Annus*, 47 [1991]). Given this unhealthy situation, which many have called a "crisis of individualism," renewed interest in the concept of the common good has been awakened in religious, political, and academic circles.

Historical Overview • The common good first assumed prominence in political science and ethics with the work of the Greek philosopher Aristotle (384-c. 322 B.C.). In his *Politics*, Aristotle cites the extent to which a political regime seeks and procures the common good (or common advantage), the good life for all its citizens, central in determining the degree of its justice: "It is evident, then, that those regimes which look to the common advantage are correct regimes according to what is unqualifiedly just, while those which look only to the advantage of the rulers are errant . . . for they involve mastery, but the city is a partnership of free persons" (Bk. 3, Ch. 6).

The central place accorded the common good in Catholic teaching is an inheritance especially from the work of St. Thomas Aquinas, who built on its treatment by Aristotle and others such as St. Augustine. Aquinas's account of the common good is essentially teleological, bound up with the "end" (in Greek, *telos*) or purpose of human existence. When Aquinas speaks of this end of human life, he is referring to the good that perfects the human being, which affords him or her the opportunity to live happily or flourish. When a single end or goal is in some way shared by or capable of perfecting many human beings, it is in that way and to that extent their common good.

Some common goods are shared by all humans as humans because they are founded in our common human nature as such. Others are common only to members of a given nation, local community, or family. Aquinas posits a hierarchical ordering among the various human goods, according to their objective perfection and universality. The highest and most perfectly common goods are immaterial or spiritual in nature. At the top of this hierarchy is God himself, the supreme, transcendent common good of human beings.

Truth and beauty are also very high human goods, "common" in that they are in no way diminished by the participation and enjoyment of a multitude of persons. St. Augustine, in his early dialogue *On Free Choice of the Will* (*De Libero Arbitrio Voluntatis*), exhorts his readers to recognize the great value of wisdom "because the highest good is known and grasped by truth, and because this truth is wisdom" (Bk. 2, Ch. 13). And he continues: "We possess in truth . . . what we all may enjoy, equally and in common. . . . No one says to the other, 'Get back! Let me approach too! Hands off! Let me also embrace it!' All men can cling to truth, and touch it. . . . No part of truth is ever made the private property of anyone; rather, it is entirely common to all at the same time" (Bk. 2, Ch. 14).

On the practical level, as the *Catechism* notes in a Thomistic vein, "[e]ach human community possesses a common good which permits it to be recognized as such"; moreover, "it is in the *political community* that its most complete realization is found" (1910). Political society facilitates the life of justice and virtue for its citizens, as well as providing for their peace and security. Its goal is — or should be — the overarching well-being of all the citizens, and in this sense is the paramount common good on the temporal, practical plane of human existence. Pope John XXIII wrote that, correctly understood, the temporal common good "embraces the sum total of those conditions of social living, whereby men are enabled more fully and more readily to achieve their own perfection" (encyclical *Mother and Teacher, Mater et Magistra*, 65 [1961]; cf. Vatican Council II, *Pastoral Constitution on the Church in the Modern World, Gaudium et Spes*, 26).

St. Thomas stresses that the temporal common good "comprises many things" and "is produced by many actions" (*Summa Theologiae*, I-II, 96, 1). Its essential moral and intellectual requirements remain the same across cultural boundaries, but it receives its particular character in the context of a given people's customs and institutions.

Each and every member of a community has a duty, and consequently ought to have the right, to contribute to the common good according to his or her abilities and position in that society. This is *a fortiori* the case for the Catholic layperson, who should be well-formed in the Church's moral wisdom and social teaching. Those in authority have a special responsibility to ensure that the vision of the good pursued is genuine and in accord with

human dignity; to coordinate the various contributions of individuals, families, and intermediate associations with a view to the common good of all; and to enact laws that truly aim at procuring the common good, whether directly or indirectly. Citizens, and especially those in positions of authority, need to cultivate virtues such as charity, prudence, and fortitude to work for the common good with discernment and perseverance. Sound religion and religious life play a key role in fostering social peace and justice, and in contributing to the character formation citizens require to work effectively for the common good.

In giving absolute priority to one's private goods, such as wealth or health, a human being actually fails to achieve his own full *personal* good. Moreover, he harms, by omission at least, the other members of his community by hindering the full realization of their common good. Thomas Aquinas remarks that "any good or evil done to one of those constituting a society redounds to the whole society, just as an injury to the hand injures the man"; and indeed even "when someone does that which contributes to his own good or evil . . . recompense is owed to him insofar as it also affects the community according as he is a member of society" (*Summa Theologiae*, I-II, 21, 3; cf. 19, 10). Pope John Paul speaks of this phenomenon in the language of spiritual solidarity among men, which he relates to the common good: "This . . . is not a feeling of vague compassion or shallow distress at the misfortunes of so many people, both near and far. On the contrary, it is *a firm and persevering determination* to commit oneself to the *common good*, that is to say to the good of all and of each individual, because we are *all* really responsible *for all*" (encyclical *On Social Concerns, Sollicitudo Rei Socialis*, 38 [1987]; italics in original).

In parallel fashion, if a particular community — say, a given nation — were to pursue its common good in isolation from or to the detriment of the wider common good — for example, of the whole human race — this would be a form of collective selfishness, and in the long run not conducive to the true good even of that country's citizens. Our common humanity is the foundation for the universal common good of which the Church's Magisterium speaks. In his encyclical *Peace on Earth*, *Pacem in Terris*, Pope John XXIII wrote: "We must remember that, of its very nature, civil authority exists, not to confine its people within the boundaries of their nation, but rather to protect, above all else, the common good of that particular civil society, which certainly cannot be divorced from the common good of the entire human family. This entails not only that civil societies should pursue their particular interests without hurting others, but also that they should join forces and plans whenever the efforts of an individual government cannot achieve its desired goals. But in the execution of such common efforts, great care must be taken lest what helps some nations should injure others" (98-99; cf. 100, 130-141).

The political philosophy of the eighteenth-century Enlightenment generally rejected any such notions as the human person's natural sociability and orientation to various common goods, culminating in a *summum bonum*, or highest human good. Political economy was posited as existing above all to provide for the individual's comfortable self-preservation. Any remaining notion of a common good was greatly watered down or replaced by the utilitarian ethic of "the greatest good for the greatest number."

Members of political communities influenced by this political and philosophical movement were more likely to focus on safeguarding their own rights than on their duty to contribute to the common good at various levels, even at the cost of personal inconvenience. In large-scale consumer societies, as Alexis de Tocqueville (1805-1859) predicted in his great work *Democracy in America*, individualism and materialism became more acute and widespread.

Recent Church Teaching • Against this backdrop, Catholic social teaching in the nineteenth and twentieth centuries maintained a central place for the common good and recognized the importance of revitalizing it on the levels of theory and practice. But certain political events of the twentieth century mandated extreme caution and clarity when discussing the common good. In their assault against liberal democracy and capitalist economics, both Fascists and communists used appeals to the common good, however distorted, in their rhetoric.

A Ukrainian recalls the verbal tactics of a party propagandist during the terrible famine Stalin engineered in that country: "[T]he gist of his speech is as follows: a stray ant is of no account; it can become lost in its search for food; it may be mercilessly crushed by someone. . . . Who cares about a stray single ant? What really counts is the anthill. . . . So it is with human beings. . . . The collective farm is everything; the individual is nothing!" (Miron Dolot, *Execution by Hunger: The Forgotten Holocaust*, pp. 70-71). Josef Pieper, a German Catholic philosopher and student of St. Thomas, recalls his experience under the Nazi regime: "The new masters' slogan, 'the common good before the good of the individual,' which was proclaimed at all turns and like everything they took up, was quickly worn out and denatured, rapidly unmasked itself as a mere pretext and propaganda trick" (*No One Could Have Known: An Autobiography: the Early Years, 1904-1945*, p. 95).

In order to guard against misinterpretation or manipulation of the term, the Magisterium in the second half of the twentieth century emphasized the role of subsidiarity in healthy social and political life. It also stressed the common good as the good of the human *persons* comprising a given community. It is not the proper good of some organic "state," to which individual lives and fortunes may be sacrificed.

Thus: "The common good is always oriented towards the progress of persons: 'The order of things must be subordinated to the order of persons, and not the other way around' [*Gaudium et Spes* 26]. This order is founded on truth, built up in justice, and animated by love" (CCC 1912; cf. also 1881, 1892; *Gaudium et Spes*, 25; and John Paul II, Address to the United Nations General Assembly, October 5, 1995, 1 and 16-18). The *Catechism* teaches that the common good can only be attained through fostering *"respect for the person* as such," facilitating the fulfillment of his duties and protecting his proper freedoms and rights; the *"social well-being* and *development"* of the community in its material and spiritual aspects; and *"peace,"* which is "the stability and security of a just order" (CCC 1907-1909; cf. 1925).

See: Authority; Cardinal Virtues; Church and State; Citizenship; Civil Law; Human Goods; Natural Law; Politics; Social Doctrine; Subsidiarity; Teleological Ethics.

Suggested Readings: CCC 1877-1896, 1898, 1901-1903, 1905-1917, 1921, 1924-1928, 2420, 2425, 2429, 2434, 2442. Vatican Council II, *Pastoral Constitution on the Church in the Modern World, Gaudium et Spes*, 23-26, 30-31, 42-43, 73-76, 84. John XXIII, *Mother and Teacher, Mater et Magistra*, 65-67; *Peace on Earth, Pacem in Terris*, 35-38, 46-48, 53-66, 70-74, 98-100, 136-141. John Paul II, *The Hundredth Year, Centesimus Annus*, 34, 41, 47-48. M. Sherwin, O.P., "St. Thomas and the Common Good: The Theological Perspective: an Invitation to Dialogue," *Angelicum* LXX (1993), 307-328.

Mary M. Keys

COMMUNIO

Communio is the central ecclesiological idea of Vatican Council II. The opening paragraph of the *Dogmatic Constitution on the Church, Lumen Gentium*, describes the Church as "a sign and instrument of communion with God and of unity among all men" (1). The Church is a living communion, drawing people into the life of Christ. She lives by that life and communicates it. The *Catechism of the Catholic Church* says: "In the Church this communion of men with God . . . is the purpose which governs everything in her that is a sacramental means" (773). The communion of the members of the Church with Christ and one another draws its life-giving source from the sacraments, especially Baptism and the Eucharist (cf. CCC 790).

In becoming man, God has sought communion with us. "All men are called to this union with Christ, who is the light of the world, from whom we go forth, through whom we live, and towards whom our whole life is directed" (*Lumen Gentium*, 3). It is up to each one of us to respond freely to this call, to accept or neglect or reject communion with Christ. A positive response is an expression of charity: love for God that is necessarily love for all others, and so becomes an *ecclesial* charity. But charity alone is not enough to enter and live within *communio*. We also need faith, precisely an ecclesial faith: " '[T]he invisible God . . . addresses men as his friends, and moves among them, in order to invite and receive them into his own company [*DV* 2].' The adequate response to this invitation is faith" (CCC 142).

Just as one loves within the community of the Church, so also one believes within the same community. It is necessary to think with Christ and with others in Christ. Christ wants his followers to be at one, not only in charity — in love for him and for one another — but also in faith and government.

Any merely human community has a limit in time; it inevitably comes to an end in death. The Christian *communio* transcends time and death. It means oneness of heart and mind with all those who have shared the spirit of Christ throughout the ages. Hence derives the Catholic sense of Tradition as something *living*. In a certain sense, following G.K. Chesterton, we can say that Catholicism is the truest democracy because it excludes no one; it gives a vote also to those who have gone before us, who belong not to the past but to a present much more permanent than ours, who are not dead but much more living than we.

Communio cannot be lived in an exclusively spiritual or disincarnated way. In the plan of Christ, full, life-giving communion is achieved in and through the Church. It is therefore essential for each individual to maintain communion with the universal Church: by praying for others, by participating in the Church's sacramental life, especially the Eucharist, by knowing Church teaching as presented by the Magisterium, by following authoritative directives, etc.

Especially this communion is realized and maintained through one's bishop, whose "authority must be exercised in communion with the whole Church under the guidance of the Pope" (CCC 895). It follows that each bishop has a special responsibility to defend and foster *communio*: to ensure that his particular church is one with the Holy See and his people one in Catholic faith, worship, and essential discipline.

One should understand how *communio* harmonizes with the Christian philosophy of personalism, also strongly present in Vatican II. The Council is in fact both community-centered and person-centered. There is no opposition.

Personalism, as the Church presents it, is not inward-looking. Its thrust goes *out* to others, emphasizing that it is "only in a sincere giving of self that one can fully discover one's true self" (Vatican Council II, *Pastoral Constitution on the Church in the Modern World, Gaudium et Spes*, 24). Personalism understands that self-fulfillment lies in responding to values to be found outside oneself: in the world, in others, in God.

By contrast, secular individualism is opposed to *communio*, putting the individual self at the center of affairs and wishing to subordinate all else to "self-expression" or "self-fulfillment," with little or no regard for the rights and freedoms of others. It is important to be able to recognize the difference between true personalism and individualism. Individualistic approaches are incapable of renewing persons or the ecclesial community.

See: Church, Nature, Origin, and Structure of; Communion of Saints; Holy See; People of God.

Suggested Readings: CCC 748-810, 1140-1144. Vatican Council II, *Dogmatic Constitution on the Church, Lumen Gentium.*

Cormac Burke

COMMUNION OF SAINTS

Through the Church we are incorporated into Christ, and he communicates his life to each of us and through each of us to others. There is a communion, then, not just between each Christian and Christ, but between all Christians among themselves. We all share in the vitality of the same life. "The term 'communion of saints' therefore has two closely linked meanings: communion 'in holy things (*sancta*)', and 'among holy persons (*sancti*)'" (CCC 948).

" 'We believe in the communion of all the faithful of Christ, those who are pilgrims on earth, the dead who are being purified, and the blessed in heaven, all together forming one Church; and we believe that in this communion, the merciful love of God and his saints is always [attentive] to our prayers' (Pope Paul VI, *CPG* §30)" (CCC 962).

This doctrine underlines what might be called the "family" aspect of the Christian faith. God is our Father, Jesus Christ our Brother, while the Holy Spirit communicates to us the charity that unites us to the Father in the Son. Under the never-failing care of our Mother Mary, the saints are our sisters and brothers who are already definitively home and who never cease with their prayers to help the rest of us still engaged in the struggle. The *Catechism of the Catholic Church* says of the saints: "Their intercession is their most exalted service to God's plan" (2683).

Thus the communion of saints cannot be reduced to a purely horizontal or this-world level. It represents a constant union, a type of supernatural assurance society, not just between those living at any one moment, but also with those who have gone before us in the faith. They, too, are members of this family of the People of God: all the past generations of Christians and all the saints in heaven. The "Communicantes" in Eucharistic Prayer I (the Roman Canon) gives particular expression to the Communion of the Saints.

This especially consoling doctrine means no Christian is ever defenseless or alone. He or she is always accompanied and always receiving help. This help goes especially from the richer — from the saints in heaven and from those on earth who are spiritually richer — to the most needy, those who are spiritually poor. Even selfish people also receive (we are all selfish), unless they absolutely close their hearts to the gift. Only in heaven will we see how much we were helped to achieve the one goal that matters, and perhaps we shall be surprised at *who* helped us most.

Each member of the Body of Christ is spiritually fulfilled only in virtue of communion with others. One's individuality or personality is not absorbed or lost in the community (as happens in impersonal economic organisms or state systems); on the contrary, it is in this communion that one grows personally — in the measure of what one gives to others and receives from them. The saints are tributaries of the saints.

The communion of saints is like a spiritual pool to which we are all called to contribute. Our prayer and sacrifices should go out to others: the Pope, bishops, pastors — everyone, for we are all brothers and sisters. Offering one's work or spiritual struggle for others is so effective as a help to them and so pleasing to God that it should be a powerful motive in the fulfilling of everyday duties and the struggle against temptations. If we truly have the spirit of Christ, we will go to the point of praying for those who seem to do us harm, since "the intercession of Christians recognizes no boundaries" (CCC 2636; cf. 2635).

It is important to be open both to giving and receiving. The more one gives, the more one receives; by the very fact of giving, one receives. "Faith is a treasure of life which is enriched by being shared" (CCC 949); and this holds true for all other spiritual goods. On the other hand, "every sin harms this communion" (CCC 953), and not just the sinner alone.

The Church has always held that the prayers of the old, the sick, the lonely, the poor, and the handicapped have special value in God's sight and so contribute in a particular way to the Communion of the Saints.

Meditation on the "Prayers of the Faithful" said in Mass can be a great help to discover the different concerns that should be the object of our prayers and sacrifices. How we receive sacramental Communion is indicative of how we are living and sharing in the Communion of the Saints. Something would be seriously missing in our dispositions if each sacramental Communion did not inspire us not only to pray for others but also to want

to overcome any selfishness or smallness of heart that divides us from them.

See: Church, Nature, Origin, and Structure of; Communio; Heaven; Mystical Body of Christ; People of God.

Suggested Readings: CCC 946-962. Vatican Council II, *Dogmatic Constitution on the Church, Lumen Gentium.*

Cormac Burke

COMMUNITY PRAYER

The Sacred Scriptures tell us that in sharing his life with the world, our Father God has not been content to draw to himself a certain number of individuals, separately from each other, but has founded a City of God, a People of God, a kingdom of God. Therefore, the individual cannot reach either existence or development on the supernatural level unless he has a close, physical link with this community willed by God. Such, in brief, is the law of salvation in community.

The Sacred Liturgy is the worship that the Church, as Church, offers to the Most High. "The Church as Church" does not mean the lifeless skeleton of an abstract juridical person who cannot worship God because no heart beats in her breast. It means, rather, the body that, together with Christ its Head, forms one mystical person, the "whole Christ," *Christus totus* (cf. 1 Cor 12:12, etc.). The soul of this Mystical Body is the *Pneuma*, the Spirit of Christ; its head is the God-Man, Jesus Christ; the members are Christ's faithful. To say that the liturgy is the prayer of the *ecclesia orans*, the praying Church as Church, is to say that in the Sacred Liturgy the whole mystical person of the Church prays, and in and with it each member in his or her individual function within the Mystical Body of Christ.

That is why, from the very depth of its community spirit, the Sacred Liturgy so often prays only in the plural: "We praise you, we bless you, we worship you, we give you thanks"; "Lord, hear our prayer"; "Bless us, O Lord." The Sacred Liturgy unites all those praying together in Christ: "[T]hat they may all be one; even as thou, Father, art in me, and I in thee, that they also may be in us" (Jn 17:21). Thus the liturgy locates men within the great historic and cosmic context of the *oikonomia*, God's plan of salvation, which encompasses time and the world.

See: Assembly, Liturgical; Celebration, Liturgical; Church, Nature, Origin, and Structure of; Communio; Liturgy; Mystical Body of Christ.

COMMUTATIVE JUSTICE

In Catholic social doctrine, there are several dimensions to the virtue of justice. Legal justice, in this system of classification, is more than a mere reflection of positive law, which may or may not be just. Legal or universal justice judges laws, addresses common concerns, and governs a citizen's obligations to the community. Distributive justice specifies the community's obligations to distribute certain goods to the individual in just proportion to his contributions and needs. Commutative justice measures the mutual exchanges between persons in society. As such, it requires an honoring of promises and fulfilling of contracts freely agreed to by two or more parties.

Commutative justice not only involves the obligations people enter into toward one another but also the full range of moral principles. Unjust or immoral contracts are not binding. Taking advantage of others, even if the practice is not illegal, is an infraction against what we owe one another in commutative justice. Licit agreements respect individual rights and private property. They pledge us to repay debts, deliver goods promised, perform services as specified, and do all this at the right time and place.

Furthermore, commutative justice requires restitution of goods stolen or otherwise improperly acquired and reparation for any harm done. Restitution is an obligation not only of the person who wrongly acquired the goods in the first instance but of anyone who knowingly benefits along the way from the misappropriation.

Distributive and legal justice are, in a sense, based on the reciprocal obligations of commutative justice, since other forms of justice build on

what is a fair relationship between two individuals. The *Catechism of the Catholic Church* teaches that without commutative justice, "no other form of justice is possible" (2411).

See: Property; Restitution; Social Doctrine; Social Justice; Stealing; Universal Destination of Goods; Usury.

CONCUPISCENCE

In its broadest sense, concupiscence is any longing of the soul for good. In its strictest and specific sense, it is a tendency to prefer a lower, sensual good over a higher one. The *Catechism of the Catholic Church* describes it as a "movement of the sensitive appetite contrary to . . . human reason . . . [that] unsettles man's moral faculties and, without being in itself an offense, inclines man to commit sin" (2515).

The human sensitive appetite comes with one's bodily makeup and is the "hunger" for whatever preserves the corporeal self or perpetuates the species. The appetite is set in motion by its particular object's presence (sight or smell of food, for instance, or provocative bodily display) or absence (thirst, say, or exhaustion). This triggering presence or absence can be either voluntary or not. Immorality enters the picture when, in response to the appetite's insistence, especially when voluntarily whetted, one eats, drinks, rests, or sleeps either less, but usually more, than the body honestly requires for individual well-being.

Customarily, however, people equate concupiscence with the instinctive mechanism that aims at reproduction. From a moral perspective, it uniquely does *not* admit of more or less in the same sense, since its rightful use is strictly reserved to the marital state. The remainder of this entry proceeds according to this historical equating of concupiscence with genital lust.

Contrary to what some may self-servingly allege, no harm — quite to the contrary — befalls the human body or personality when, with God's help, one virtuously abstains from all voluntary sexual activity (the species is simply not added to). Nevertheless, the sexual appetite, once aroused, is vehemently insistent, and there is no dearth of involuntary stimuli. Some in their weakness and near-despair deem it impossible to keep the instinct quiescent or to turn a deaf ear to its entreaties. Concupiscence first presents itself as a prompting or inclination to partake of intense sexual delight. Provided one has not culpably sought sexual provocation, there is nothing wrong with experiencing these initial inclinations, and humans cannot normally hope or be expected to avoid them. But when humans deliberately choose not to interrupt the arousal sequence or assent to the pleasurable process by extramarital deed or desire, they author a disordered and therefore immoral action.

The Source of Concupiscence • Whence this impulse to genital gratification? The Devil? Original sin? Bad company or example? An unchaste past? Pornographic stimuli? The reproductive organs themselves? The body? Human animality? Glandular secretions? Doubtless these are all factors; but all also are antecedents or accomplices, if you will. Quoting Pope John Paul II (*Dominum et Vivificantem,* 55), the *Catechism* adds, "it is not a matter of despising or condemning the body" (2516). Then who or what is the culprit? For a deed to be seriously sinful, it must at least be a human action, but one that is spiritually deficient: I only sin when I knowingly and freely *choose* to do what is morally evil, however many and powerful the prerational and semivoluntary inducements.

If concupiscence calls for unremitting moral struggle, the *Catechism* is quick to point out that this is no unaided effort: "With God's grace [the baptized] will prevail: by the *virtue* and *gift of chastity*, for chastity lets us love with upright and undivided heart; by *purity of intention* which consists in seeking the true end of man . . . to find and to fulfill God's will in everything; by *purity of vision*, external and internal, by discipline of feelings and imagination . . . . by *prayer*" (2520).

But *how* is it that I deliberately forgo a greater good and settle for one quite limited and therefore self-depriving, regardless of how adorned it may present itself? What is the specific distortion in my spiritual world that leads me to cheat myself of a higher, much more enriching good, for which moreover I am most probably made?

Original sin and its consequences, among them spiritual disorder, are a large part of the answer. So is a serious lack of personal virtue, coupled with failure to progressively cultivate and satisfy the spiritual appetite for bliss, for goodness unbounded: in other words, the slighted, malnourished human will or heart. In the end, this appetite may yet attach itself to God as the only object capable of satisfying it; but meanwhile this blind, neglected, voracious beggar is responsible for almost all the evils, frustrations, unhappiness, and sins that human beings can devise and visit upon themselves.

How Sin Is Possible • Human beings never directly will evil as such; whatever we will is willed under the aspect of good, because we at least *think* it will make us happy. But it is entirely possible to take apparent good for real good and will the former rather than the latter. The intellect, so long as its autonomy is unhampered and its power of scrutiny is given free rein, cannot lie or deceive or, more generally, distort the truth. Yet people err, and that quite often. This is a sure sign that the ability to reason is being hampered. By what? In general, by the blind, impatient, unsatisfied, frustrated hungers of the will.

The most assured way to keep lust and the appetite for overrated pleasures alive and dominant is to turn the meddling but frustrated appetite for happiness loose on the mind. Augustine famously wrote: "You have made us, O Lord, for you, and restless will our heart be until it rests in you." When our appetite for bliss is fed something less than infinite Goodness itself, it remains unsatisfied, impatient for fulfillment, ever on the prowl. The resulting tendency to exaggerate the happiness-potential of lesser goods is what concupiscence (lust) is all about.

The Remedy for Concupiscence • The remedy is theoretically easy yet very demanding in practice. The will must freely submit itself to the intellect and diligently heed its findings. Much patient forethought and hindsight are needed. The will must belatedly submit to reason, while exacting submission of corporeal drives. In doing so, the will must stop exaggerating the quite limited goods that appeal to bodily appetites.

Even so, allowing reason — the appetite for truth — to do its job, while duly addressing genuine corporeal needs, does not yet spell human fulfillment. Even moral virtues, especially the so-called cardinal virtues and truthfulness, are necessary but insufficient conditions. Mind and will must agree that the insatiable appetite for bliss will not be satisfied by any merely temporal goods, so that it behooves us to discover whether this overarching drive can be satisfied alone by God infinite and eternal. An earnest, long-term quest to know and love God in the piecemeal fashion typical of humanity is required.

The Ascetical Struggle • To the extent people, as it were, ratify their nature by giving it what is divinely intended, they strengthen themselves against the distracting allurements of temporal or even corporeal pleasures, the stuff of lust. At least in the latter stages of this process, they can come close to replicating that control over inordinate cravings that was bestowed on Adam and Eve as part of their gift of original innocence or integrity. When the proto-parents forfeited sanctifying grace and intimacy with their Maker, they lost, both for themselves and their descendants, this preternatural gift of effortless dominion over the lower drives and appetites ensuing from their partly animal nature. Humanity's first parents consequently bequeathed lust, or concupiscence, to all their progeny, except for the exempted Virgin Mary.

Another self-cheating mechanism that makes us prone to capitulate to lust and thus to sin seriously consists of the ensemble of white lies we tell ourselves about other gratifications. When one's relatively harmless whims or wants become imperious needs, one is at risk of a descent that progresses from a weak failing to possibly venial sins and thence to mortal sins. In such a situation, the will, as it were, is divided against itself, torn between contrary objects. As long as a religious person continues to grow in his or her knowledge and love of God, the driving appetite for bliss is more or less fulfilled (though not entirely) and is therefore relatively contented and quiet, and the mind can tell

the truth; concupiscence remains, but lust is largely dormant. But when a person halfheartedly pursues God while at the same time pursuing other objects as if they were sources of supreme happiness, neither the greater good nor the lesser satisfies. Then, in its disappointment, the heart grows restive and begins to heed the importunate pleas of appetite.

This explanation sheds light on what might otherwise be a mysterious passage in Revelation: "I know your works: you are neither hot nor cold. Would that you were cold or hot! So, because you are lukewarm, and neither cold nor hot, I will spew you out of my mouth. For you say, I am rich, I have prospered, and I need nothing; not knowing that you are wretched, pitiable, poor, blind, and naked" (3:15-17). Those dedicated to guiding souls along paths of interior life that lead to God are daily aware of this saying's truth.

But why does God prefer coldness to tepidity? Since pleasures are necessarily finite both in kind and intensity, that negative discovery could lead to the wisdom of seeking happiness in God. Not so with the lukewarm. By harboring fears of the extremes of both God and sin, a lukewarm Christian can almost indefinitely oscillate between little sins and equally puny loves. The lukewarm person harvests only anguish and sterility, along with unnecessary, self-induced lust.

See: Lust; Modesty; Original Sin; Purity; Sexuality, Human; Sin.

Suggested Readings: CCC 2514-2533. M. Adler, *Desires, Right and Wrong.* G. Gilder, *Men and Marriage.* J. Pieper, *The Cardinal Virtues.* G. Vann, O.P., *Morals and Man.* D. von Hildebrand, *In Defense of Purity.*

Dennis Helming

CONFESSION

Together with his sins, three acts of the penitent make up the matter of the sacrament of Penance. These are contrition, confession, and satisfaction. "Confession to a priest is an essential part of the sacrament of Penance" (CCC 1456).

Fundamentally, confession is verbal self-accusation to another individual. Within the context of the sacrament of Penance, it involves acknowledging one's sins to a priest. As an ordained minister of the Church, the priest acts in the Person of Christ. He is thus bound under the gravest seal not to disclose or make any use of anything he has heard with regard to the penitents' lives. "This secret, which admits of no exceptions, is called the 'sacramental seal,' because what the penitent has made known to the priest remains 'sealed' by the sacrament" (CCC 1467).

Contrary to media portrayals, a priest does not frustrate the justice system in not revealing the identity of a criminal. For the knowledge a priest may acquire in this context is not intended to help the criminal justice system but rather to reconcile a sinner with God. While he may counsel the person to come forward and admit his crime, the priest's primary concern is the restoration of the right relationship between the sinner and God: He brings the mercy of God to the sinner and the repentant sinner home to God.

Two questions must be addressed: What is to be confessed? And how often one should avail oneself of the sacrament, bearing in mind that canon law states the *obligation* to confess serious sins at least once a year (Canon 989)?

What Is Confessed • Both mortal and venial sins should be confessed. "All mortal sins of which penitents after a diligent self-examination are conscious must be recounted by them in confession . . .' [Council of Trent (1551); DS 1680 (ND 1626)]" (CCC 1456). The deliberate omission of any mortal sin results in the commission of another mortal sin, sacrilege. Furthermore, if one receives Holy Communion knowingly in the state of mortal sin he commits a sacrilege (cf. CCC 1457).

While the confession of venial sins is not absolutely necessary, it is strongly recommended. The regular examination and verbal acknowledgment of even the least faults help the Christian to advance spiritually. These least faults are admitted to be indeed faults, needing correction and standing in the way of the perfection Christ demands in the Gospels.

Frequency of Confession • While the answer to the second question will vary for each individual, receiving the sacrament at least monthly, though certainly not obligatory, would strike many people as a reasonable standard of frequency. There are several reasons.

First, practically speaking, one can remember better what one has done and be more aware of small faults that continue to be obstacles to union with God and less inclined to take them for granted, assuming they are simply part of one's "character."

Second, psychologically, confession is good because it helps the person to be honest with himself. By articulating his faults, he comes to know where he has failed and thus where he needs to make progress in the spiritual life. In confessing sins, he frees himself of his past and enables a future reconciliation with God and his neighbor.

Third, it is not only beneficial to articulate one's faults but also valuable to hear the words of forgiveness. While it is true that, in the privacy of one's room and one's heart, a fervent act of contrition will bring about forgiveness from the Lord, nevertheless, as sentient beings, we depend on our senses for knowledge. Periodically it is good to hear someone say, "Your sins are forgiven, go in peace." Hearing these words of absolution provides a reassuring certitude.

Fourth, spiritually, confession is good because the penitent receives from the sacrament both sanctifying grace as well as sacramental grace. Sanctifying grace makes him holy and restores him to God's friendship. The sacramental grace of Penance not only forgives sins but also helps one to keep from committing those same sins in the future. It is, in a sense, preventative medicine.

Fifth, every sacrament is an encounter with the Lord. Reception of the sacrament of Penance provides an opportunity to spend time with the Lord in an intimate and personal way.

Among the reasons for going to confession and going often, probably the most salient is the realization that by our sins we have offended God, whom we should love above all else. In his encyclical letter on the Mystical Body, *Mystici Corporis Christi* (1943), Pope Pius XII said that by frequent confession "genuine self-knowledge is increased, Christian humility grows, bad habits are corrected, spiritual neglect and tepidity are resisted, the conscience is purified, the will strengthened, a salutary self-control is attained, and grace is increased in virtue of the Sacrament itself" (88).

Some of the faithful have been deterred from receiving the sacrament for one or more reasons: it has not been available; priests have discouraged them when they do go; the lack of anonymity due to the absence of the traditional screen.

The Church insists that priests make the sacrament available and not refuse any reasonable request for it. Moreover, in hearing confessions, priests must remember their roles as "other Christs," bringing the repentant sinner home to the Lord and the merciful Lord to the sinner. The question of anonymity has been raised with regard to the new Rite of Penance. While the practice of face-to-face confession has become common in many places, the Church, for years, has believed in the right of the individual penitent to remain anonymous. "Confessionals with a fixed grille between penitent and confessor are always located in an open area so that the faithful who wish to make use of them may do so freely" (Canon 964.2). In order to clarify this, Pope Paul VI stated at a general audience on April 3, 1974, only four months after the new Rite of Penance was promulgated: "The confessional, as a protective screen between the minister and the penitent, to guarantee the absolute secrecy of the conversation imposed on them and reserved for them, must, it is clear, remain."

Finally, there is the question of when the practice of confession should begin. Even though it is absolutely necessary only that mortal sins be confessed, the Church insists that children be admitted to the sacrament from the time they reach the age of reason (generally understood to be about seven years).

The Church has also insisted that children receive the sacrament of Penance *before* receiving their first Holy Communion. This has been true in the past and remains in effect. Both the Code of Canon Law (Canon 914) and the *Catechism of the Catholic Church* (1457) specify this. Additionally, the Sacred Congregation for the Clergy, which is responsible for catechetics, has stated: "[T]he Holy See judges it fitting that the practice now in force in the Church of putting Confession ahead of first Communion should be retained" (*General Catechetical Directory, Addendum* §5).

See: Absolution; Contrition; Penance and Reconciliation, Sacrament of; Penance in Christian Life.

Suggested Readings: CCC 1451-1454. N. Halligan, O.P., *The Sacraments and Their Celebration.* C. O'Neill, O.P., *Meeting Christ in the Sacraments.* G. Kelly, ed., *The Sacrament of Penance in Our Time.*

Christopher M. Buckner

CONFIRMATION

Baptism, Confirmation, and the Eucharist comprise the sacraments of Christian initiation. By the sacrament of Confirmation, Vatican Council II says, the baptized are "more perfectly bound to the Church" and receive the "special strength of the Holy Spirit." In consequence, "they are, as true witnesses of Christ, more strictly obliged to spread and defend the faith by word and deed" (*Dogmatic Constitution on the Church, Lumen Gentium*, 11).

By virtue of this sacrament, the baptized "continue on the path of Christian initiation" (Canon 879). In fact, the Church teaches that "Confirmation is necessary for the completion of baptismal grace [cf. *Roman Ritual*, Rite of Confirmation (OC), Introduction 1]" (CCC 1285). Unlike Baptism, however, Confirmation is not an indispensable means of attaining salvation. It is necessary insofar as it leads to the perfection of salvation.

The fact that Christ himself instituted Confirmation demonstrates the importance of its reception. The Code of Canon Law emphasizes the obligation of both the recipient and those charged with ensuring its reception. "The faithful are obliged to receive this sacrament at the appropriate time; their parents and shepherds of souls, especially pastors, are to see to it that the faithful are properly instructed to receive it and approach the sacrament at the appropriate time" (Canon 890).

Theologians have taught the possibility of "Confirmation of desire." In true necessity, the grace of this sacrament may be received through the desire for Confirmation, just as in the case of Baptism. According to St. Thomas Aquinas, Baptism of desire necessarily must — at least conceptually — precede Confirmation of desire, given that the grace of Confirmation presupposes the grace of Baptism.

Biblical and Historical Background • In his *Apologia Confessionis*, the Lutheran theologian Philipp Melanchthon (1497-1560) asserted that Confirmation was established by the Church Fathers, not God, and is therefore unnecessary. Against the Reformers, the Council of Trent (1545-1563) declared that Confirmation is a true and proper sacrament whose roots are biblical. Pope St. Pius X (1835-1914) taught, contrary to the Modernists, that Baptism and Confirmation were two distinct sacraments in the early Church.

There is significant indirect scriptural proof for the institution of Confirmation by Jesus. Prophets of the Old Testament had declared that the Messiah would be invested with the Spirit of the Lord for the carrying out of his mission. Such Old Covenant messengers as Joel (3:1-2), Isaiah (11:2, 44:3-35, 61:1), and Ezekiel (36:25-27, 39:29) testified that one of the characteristics of the Messianic era would be the outpouring of the Holy Spirit over the whole of mankind.

The *Catechism of the Catholic Church* stresses the intimate connection between Christ and the Spirit of God. "The descent of the Holy Spirit on Jesus at his baptism by John was the sign that this was he who was to come, the Messiah, the Son of God. He was conceived of the Holy Spirit; his whole life and his whole mission are carried out in total communion with the Holy Spirit whom the Father gives him 'without measure' [*Jn* 3:34]" (CCC 1286).

Christ foretold the coming of the Holy Spirit and promised the Paraclete to the Apostles (Lk 12:12, 24:49; Jn 3:5-8, 14:16ff., 14:26, 16:7-15; Acts 1:5, 8) and to all the faithful (Jn 7:37-39). The Messiah shared the Advocate on Easter Sun-

day and later on Pentecost Sunday (Jn 20:22; Acts 2:1-4). "Filled with the Holy Spirit the apostles began to proclaim 'the mighty works of God,' and Peter declared this outpouring of the Spirit to be the sign of the messianic age. Those who believed in the apostolic preaching and were baptized received the gift of the Holy Spirit in their turn" (CCC 1287).

The Apostles, through the imposition of hands, gave the gift of the Holy Spirit to the recently baptized (cf. Acts 2:38, 8:14ff.) in order to complete the grace of Baptism. St. Paul, too, communicated the Spirit through the laying on of hands to about a dozen men in Ephesus (cf. Acts 19:6).

Pope Paul VI noted the inseparable link between Baptism and Confirmation and the Church's early acknowledgment of both as being crucial to Christian instruction. "For this reason in the Letter to the Hebrews the doctrine concerning the Baptism and laying on of hands is listed among the first elements of Christian instruction. The imposition of hands is rightly recognized by the Catholic tradition as the origin of the sacrament of Confirmation, which in a certain way perpetuates the grace of Pentecost in the Church" (apostolic constitution *Divinae Consortium Naturae* [1971]).

An anointing with perfumed oil (i.e., chrism) was added to the laying on of hands by the early Church. "This anointing highlights the name 'Christian,' which means 'anointed' and derives from that of Christ himself whom God 'anointed with the Holy Spirit' [*Acts* 10:38]" (CCC 1289).

Manner of Administration, Effects • Two traditions have developed concerning the sacrament of Confirmation. In the East, Baptism and Confirmation were kept united, as is so even today. Hence, Chrismation is performed with the anointing with *myron* by the priest at the time of Baptism. In the West, however, the two sacraments were separated in time as a practical matter so that the bishop could be the celebrant of Confirmation. (Until the thirteenth century, infants were routinely confirmed in the Latin Church.)

The *Catechism of the Catholic Church* concludes that both practices are meaningful and beneficial. On the one hand, the practice in the East "gives greater emphasis to the unity of Christian initiation." On the other hand, the practice in the West "more clearly expresses the communion of the new Christian with the bishop as guarantor and servant of the unity, catholicity and apostolicity of his Church," thereby calling attention to the Church's apostolic origins (CCC 1292).

Several Fathers of the Church attest that Confirmation was separate from Baptism in the primitive Church. The testimony from Church Tradition is substantial. Tertullian (c. 160-c. 222), St. Hippolytus of Rome (c. 170-c. 236), St. Cyprian (died 258), and St. Ambrose (c. 339-397), among others, wrote about the rites and inherent meaning of the sacrament.

"The sacrament of confirmation is conferred through the anointing with chrism on the forehead, which is done by the imposition of the hand, and through the words prescribed in the approved liturgical books" (Canon 880.1). Theologians have held various views as to the essential matter of the sacrament. Some (e.g., Peter Aureoli) held that the imposition of the hands is the essential matter, while others (e.g., St. Robert Bellarmine) maintained that the anointing with chrism alone is the essential matter. The practice of the Church is clear: Both the anointing and the imposition are considered the matter for the sacrament.

The actions of anointing have a secure basis in Sacred Scripture. In the ancient world, oil was a common remedy and restorative, and sacramental anointings possess profound, rich meanings. In the early Church, prebaptismal anointing with the oil of catechumens was a sign of purification and strengthening; again, the Anointing of the Sick signifies comforting and healing. The anointings with chrism in Confirmation and ordination refer to consecration (CCC 1294).

The sacred chrism used in the sacrament of Confirmation must be consecrated by a bishop, even if the sacrament is administered by a priest (Canon 880.2). During the Chrism Mass of Holy Thursday (which may be anticipated at the dis-

cretion of the bishop), the bishop consecrates the chrism for his diocese. The consecration in some Eastern Churches is reserved to the patriarch.

Confirmation, like Baptism and Holy Orders, impresses an indelible character, or mark — the *seal* of the Holy Spirit — upon the recipients' souls, ensuring that they "share more completely in the mission of Jesus Christ and the fullness of the Holy Spirit with which he is filled, so that their lives may give off 'the aroma of Christ' [2 *Cor* 2:15]" (CCC 1294). This indelible character "marks our total belonging to Christ, our enrollment in his service for ever, as well as the promise of divine protection in the great eschatological trial" (CCC 1296).

Ordinarily, the administration of Confirmation is to occur in a church and during Mass, although "for a just and reasonable cause" the sacrament may be celebrated outside Mass and in some other suitable location (Canon 881). The Confirmation Rite in the Latin Church begins after the Liturgy of the Word, with the confirmands renewing their baptismal promises and professing the faith of the Church. Then, the bishop extends his hands over those to be confirmed, a gesture that from apostolic times has signified the gift of the Holy Spirit. He also chants or recites a prayer for the Spirit's coming.

The essential words (*form*) of the sacrament of Confirmation in the Latin Rite are: "Be sealed with the Gift of the Holy Spirit." These words are uttered by the minister as he anoints the recipient's forehead with the sacred chrism. The recipient responds: "Amen." In the Eastern Churches, following a prayer invoking the Spirit, the forehead, eyes, nose, ears, lips, breast, back, hands, and feet are anointed. The anointings are accompanied by this formula: "The seal of the gift that is the Holy Spirit." The conclusion of the Confirmation Rite is marked by the sign of peace.

The chief effect of Confirmation is the fullness of the outpouring of the Holy Spirit. Sanctifying grace is therefore increased in the recipient. Furthermore, by virtue of this sacrament he or she has access to all actual graces needed to achieve its purpose of Confirmation. The *Catechism* says: "Confirmation brings an increase and deepening of baptismal grace: it roots us more in the divine filiation which makes us cry, 'Abba! Father!' [*Rom* 8:15]; it unites us more firmly to Christ; it increases the gifts of the Holy Spirit in us; it renders our bond with the Church more perfect; it gives us a special strength of the Holy Spirit to spread and defend the faith by word and action as true witnesses of Christ, to confess the name of Christ boldly, and never to be ashamed of the Cross" (CCC 1303).

Because Confirmation is one of the sacraments that imparts an indelible character (as Baptism and Holy Orders also do), it cannot be repeated. This character is understood to perfect the common priesthood of the faithful received in Baptism, so that, as St. Thomas Aquinas says, he or she "receives the power to profess faith in Christ publicly and as it were officially" (*quasi ex officio*).

"All baptized persons who have not been confirmed and only they are capable of receiving confirmation" (Canon 889.1). Baptism is entirely valid and effective even in the case of those who do not receive Confirmation and the Holy Eucharist, yet in these circumstances the sacramental process of Christian initiation remains incomplete (cf. CCC 1206).

The Latin Church considers the appropriate age of Confirmation to be the age of discretion — that is, around seven years — "unless the conference of bishops determines another age or there is danger of death or in the judgment of the minister a grave cause urges otherwise" (Canon 891). The bishops of the United States have determined that the appropriate age for Confirmation is from seven to eighteen years.

The one to receive Confirmation must be in the state of grace and be suitably catechized. Preparation for the sacrament should be directed to more intimate union with Christ and a heightened awareness of the action, gifts, and promptings of the Holy Spirit so that those confirmed will be better able to accept and carry out the apostolic responsibilities of Christians (cf. CCC 1309). The parishes of confirmands ought to be involved in this preparation. Before being confirmed, too, individuals should receive the sacrament of Penance and devote themselves to prayer.

"As far as possible a sponsor for the one to be confirmed should be present; it is for the sponsor to see that the confirmed person acts as a true witness to Christ and faithfully fulfills the obligations connected with this sacrament" (Canon 892). The Code of Canon Law mentions several requirements for the Confirmation sponsor, which are the same as those for sponsors at Baptism (cf. Canons 874, 893). It is "desirable" that the baptismal sponsor also be the sponsor at Confirmation (Canon 893.2).

Minister of the Sacrament • The bishop is the primary minister of this sacrament, but two different practices have developed in this matter.

In the West, the ordinary minister of Confirmation is the bishop, even though for grave reasons he may give the faculty to administer the sacrament to priests (Canon 882). The appropriateness of the bishop as minister of Confirmation resides in the fact that bishops are successors of the Apostles, and Confirmation has the effect of joining its recipients more closely to the Church and to her apostolic origins and mission of witnessing to Christ.

In the East, however, the priest who baptizes also ordinarily confirms as part of the same celebration. Still, he uses sacred chrism consecrated by the patriarch or bishop, thereby reaffirming the Church's apostolic unity.

The Code of Canon Law for the Western Church and the Code of Canons of the Eastern Churches both contain specific legislation concerning the administration of the sacrament of Confirmation. Note, though, that the Church desires that any priest administer Confirmation to a baptized person, not previously confirmed, who is in danger of death; this is true even in the case of the very youngest children (cf. CCC 1314).

See: Baptism; Confirmation, Age of; Holy Spirit; Sacrament; Sacraments of Initiation.

Suggested Readings: CCC 1242, 1285-1321. Code of Canon Law, 879, 896. L. Ott, *Fundamen-*

tals of Catholic Dogma, pp. 361-370. D. Wuerl, R. Lawler, O.F.M. Cap., T. Lawler, eds., *The Teaching of Christ: A Catholic Catechism for Adults.*

Charles M. Mangan

CONFIRMATION, AGE OF

Much debate has occurred in the United States over when Confirmation should be administered. Clearly, as the *Catechism of the Catholic Church* says, each "baptized person not yet confirmed can and should receive the sacrament of Confirmation" (1306). Furthermore, the "faithful are obliged to receive this sacrament at the appropriate time" (Canon 890).

In the Latin tradition, the "age of discretion" has been regarded as the most fitting age. "But in danger of death children should be confirmed even if they have not attained the age of discretion" (CCC 1307).

In June of 1993, the members of the National Conference of Catholic Bishops of the United States approved the following statement, which received the formal *recognitio* from the Vatican's Congregation of Bishops on February 8, 1994, to be effective July 1, 1999: "The National Conference of Catholic Bishops hereby decrees that the sacrament of Confirmation in the Latin rite shall be conferred between the age of discretion, which is about the age of 7, and 18 years of age, within the limits determined by the diocesan bishop and with regard for the legitimate exceptions given in canon 891, namely, when there is danger of death or, where in the judgment of the minister grave cause urges otherwise."

See: Confirmation.

CONSCIENCE

Insoluble problems can arise if one does not get clear what conscience is. In our culture there is a tendency, first, to value authenticity (doing what *I* think or feel, rather than being directed to an extrinsic end by another), then to identify following one's conscience with achieving authenticity, and, finally, to conclude that one should follow one's own conscience *rather than* follow absolute rules or outside authority. This view is quite confused. To get clear what conscience is, its positive rights — and its limitations — is the goal of this entry.

Conscience can be spoken of as an ability, an act, or as the content of an act. Used to refer to an act, "conscience" may refer to one's awareness of *general* moral truth or to one's awareness of the rightness or wrongness of a concrete, particular act.

In his Letter to the Romans, St. Paul says: "When Gentiles who have not the law do by nature what the law requires, they are a law unto themselves, even though they do not have the law. They show that what the law requires is written on their hearts, while their conscience (*synedeisis*) also bears witness and their conflicting thoughts accuse or perhaps excuse them" (2:14-15). Here conscience is used to refer to one's awareness of the principles of God's natural law, the basic truths of morality.

Speaking of conscience as an awareness of the moral good or evil of a particular act, in a definition echoing St. Thomas Aquinas, the *Catechism of the Catholic Church* says: "Conscience is a judgment of reason whereby the human person recognizes the moral quality of a concrete act that he is going to perform, is in the process of performing, or has already completed" (1778). Conscience, then, is what one thinks about what is morally right or wrong, one's judgment about a moral matter. Thus, it may be true or false.

Conscience sometimes is confused with what some psychological systems call superego. Whereas conscience is an intellectual act, a judgment that an act is right or wrong, "superego" refers to feelings one has as a result of one's psychological development. As children we internalize the approval of certain acts and the disapproval of other acts by authority figures, usually our parents. Our feelings corresponding to this approval or disapproval are perceived as being over (*super*) our conscious desires (*ego*) and as placing a constraint on them. Thus, the superego is often the source of guilt feelings that tend to limit what one feels comfortable doing. But such feelings clearly do not necessarily correspond to objective moral truth.

One may continue to feel guilty about something one knows is morally right or, for various reasons, one may lack feelings of guilt about doing something known to be morally bad. An example illustrating the difference between conscience and superego is the feeling of guilt experienced by many Germans who resisted the Nazis. They felt guilty because they were violating their superegos, but they knew (in their conscience) that what they were doing was right.

Psychologists are quite correct, nevertheless, in saying that conscience develops. One can pick out various stages. A first stage is the child's awareness of the need to follow rules of authority instead of his own unruly impulses. Breaking the rules of authority — usually the authority of his parents — creates conflict in the child's feelings; he experiences disapproval, aloneness, or insecurity, and feelings of guilt. This is the level of superego. On a second level, usually during adolescence, the child is aware of the need to limit acting on impulse in order to align his actions with the demands of the group. Since the child is a member of several groups, there will be various and sometimes conflicting rules. This can be called the level of social convention, for on this level the child thinks of good and evil primarily in terms of social cohesiveness and fairness and their opposites. A third level of development of conscience involves the young person's awareness of real human goods and true moral principles.

These stages are of course only approximations of how people often mature. Moreover, it is clear that not all do mature. In particular, to the extent a person gives in to his unruly desires in sinful acts, and thus identifies himself with those desires, he is likely to view moral truths as arbitrary, extrinsic rules rather than as truths directing his actions to his own true fulfillment. Also, all of us may revert back to earlier levels in the development of conscience from time to time. This is to say we may be tempted at times to view moral truths as mere rules imposed by an extrinsic authority (first level) or by a group (second level).

Although psychologists like Jean Piaget and Lawrence Kohlberg distinguish levels of conscience much as is done here, they presuppose quite different notions of what a mature conscience should be, and they frequently fail to distinguish the ability to *verbalize* one's awareness of a type of right and wrong from one's ability to have the awareness to begin with.

Erroneous Conscience • Given that conscience is a judgment about the rightness or wrongness of particular acts, it is easy to see that it can be mistaken. For instance, if someone thinks euthanasia is morally right, then his judgment of conscience concerning the rightness or wrongness of *this* act of euthanasia here and now will be mistaken. It matters very much, however, how one came to have a mistaken conscience. One might or might not be at fault. Clearly, if an eight-year-old thinks stealing is morally right because he was taught that by his parents, his judgments of conscience regarding acts of stealing will be mistaken, but he is not at fault for that mistake. He has an inculpably erroneous conscience. If someone does something that is really morally wrong (or "objectively morally wrong"), but does so acting on an inculpably erroneous conscience, he does not incur moral guilt for that act.

On the other hand, suppose a professional killer thinks it is perfectly right, morally speaking, to kill people for money — "It's only business," he claims. He is obviously mistaken, that is, he has an erroneous conscience. But suppose also he thinks as he does because he has killed so many people in the past that he has grown callous to the taking of human life — he has, as it were, deadened his conscience. He has an erroneous conscience, to be sure, but he is at fault for his error. When he kills people with an undisturbed conscience, he is not without guilt. One is morally responsible for the evil deeds one does as a result of having a vincibly erroneous conscience.

Of course there are other ways of being morally responsible for an error of conscience. I might, for instance, hold that something is right or wrong largely through rationalization. Suppose I think contraception is right, but I have listened only to people who agree with me, read only theologians who will ease my conscience about what I am already doing, and sought out only those counselors who would give me the advice I want to hear. I cannot then say that my error is inculpable.

Vatican Council II briefly alludes to the distinction between inculpable ignorance and culpable error: "Yet it often happens that conscience goes astray through ignorance which it is unable to avoid, without thereby losing its dignity. This cannot be said of the man who takes little trouble to find out what is true and good, or when conscience is by degrees almost blinded through the habit of committing sin" *(Pastoral Constitution on the Church in the Modern World, Gaudium et Spes,* 16). This suggests how serious is our duty to strive to inform our conscience, that is, to learn what is moral truth.

It is sometimes said or implied that Vatican II endorsed freedom of conscience and that one therefore has a right to set aside Church teaching regarding particular moral norms. Such an idea is based on a confusion.

Nowhere does Vatican II speak of "freedom of conscience." The Council teaches that people have a moral right to follow their judgments of conscience in civil society as long as public order is not violated: This is a right in relation to the civil society. The Council's affirmation is another way of saying that the civil society has a duty not to restrict the following of conscience by citizens, unless that is necessary to preserve public order. This says nothing about how to form conscience, nor does it say or imply that one need not form one's conscience by objective moral truth and Church teaching. The *Declaration on Religious Freedom, Dignitatis Humanae,* says: "So while the religious freedom which men demand in fulfilling their obligation to worship God has to do with freedom from coercion in civil society, it leaves intact the traditional Catholic teaching on the moral duty of individuals and societies towards the true religion and the one Church of Christ" (1).

Conscience and Church Teaching • One often hears an argument such as the following: "I should follow my conscience — that much everyone admits. But that means that if my conscience conflicts with what the Church teaches or with what the leaders of the Church teach, then I should certainly follow conscience rather than the Church. In fact, this is not even different from what the Church herself now admits. For the Church in Vatican II insisted on the dignity of individual conscience."

Vatican II's teaching is illustrated in the following passage: "However, in forming their consciences the faithful must pay careful attention to the sacred and certain teaching of the Church. For the Catholic Church is by the will of Christ the teacher of truth. It is her duty to proclaim and teach with authority the truth which is Christ and, at the same time, to declare and confirm by her authority the principles of the moral order which spring from human nature itself" (*Dignitatis Humanae,* 14).

So, to invoke the Church's authority in behalf of an individualistic notion of conscience is quite inaccurate.

Second, the way of posing the issue indicated above is misleading. There is a category-mistake involved in asking, "When there is a conflict, which should I follow, the Church or my conscience?" That treats conscience as if it were a *source* of moral information, whereas conscience is one's grasp of moral truth or (at times) one's erroneous judgment about moral truth. It is as if someone were to ask, "What should I listen to, the music on the radio or my ears?"

This question — "Which should I follow, the Church or my conscience?" — also is misleading in particular instances because it presupposes that I have already determined that the Church is wrong. Conscience, as was explained above, is our best judgment about a moral action, after we have taken into consideration all of the relevant factors. So, literally speaking, if my conscience tells me that I should act contrary to Church teaching, I must already have considered the Church's teaching and set it aside. But the question should be: Is it reasonable to form my conscience in that way?

To be sure, someone sincerely convinced a particular teaching is mistaken ought not to act upon it while in that state of mind. But since the Church is the Body of Christ, and is guided into all truth by the Holy Spirit (cf. Jn 14:26), it is unreasonable to place more reliance on one's own abilities than on the judgment of the authoritative teachers of the Church, including those judgments that are not proposed infallibly. As Pope John Paul II says, "The authority of the Church, when she teaches on moral questions, in no way undermines the freedom of conscience of Christians. . . . [T]he Magisterium does not bring to the Christian conscience truths which are extraneous to it; rather it brings to light the truths which it ought already to possess" (encyclical *The Splendor of Truth, Veritatis Splendor*, 64).

Someone who thinks all physicians incompetent should not visit a physician; but to think all physicians incompetent is unreasonable to begin with and harmful as well. The basis of the authority of the leaders of the Church (promised divine assistance) is quite different from the basis of a physician's authority (his knowledge and skill). Yet, our relationships to both are quite similar. As a competent physician's judgment is a more reliable guide than my own surmises, so the judgment of the teachers of the Church on faith or morals is the most reliable guide available on matters of faith and morals. Thus the *Catechism* says: "In recalling the prescriptions of the natural law, the Magisterium of the Church exercises an essential part of its prophetic office of proclaiming to men what they truly are and reminding them of what they should be before God" (2036; cf. CCC 2037).

Important as Church teaching is, it does not do the work of conscience. The Church does not and cannot pronounce directly on every specific question with a moral dimension that arises in the course of daily life. Many such questions about how one's duties ought positively to be fulfilled can only be answered well by someone whose outlook is imbued with an appreciation of the goods of human persons, who works at being a disciple of Christ, and who has appropriated the Christian outlook into his or her own character and way of thinking.

See: Conscience and the Magisterium; Conscience Formation; Magisterium; Moral Principles, Christian; Natural Law.

Suggested Readings: CCC 1776-1802, 2032-2040. John Paul II, *The Splendor of Truth, Veritatis Splendor*, 54-63. G. Grisez, *The Way of the Lord Jesus*, Vol. 1, *Christian Moral Principles*, pp. 73-96. G. Grisez and R. Shaw, *Fulfillment in Christ*, pp. 26-37.

Patrick Lee

CONSCIENCE AND THE MAGISTERIUM

The Catholic Church firmly teaches that we have a duty to obey our informed consciences, and also a duty to accept and live by the moral teaching God gives us in his Church. The moral teachings of Catholic faith are rooted in the Scriptures (in which the basic teachings of natural law are also confirmed by Revelation), and Christ himself is our foremost moral teacher (cf. Pope John Paul II, *The Splendor of Truth, Veritatis Splendor,* 84-89). Moreover, Christ guards the proclamation of moral teaching in the family of faith (cf. Mt 28:20) through the teaching office of his Church.

In our time there have been many harmful misunderstandings of the ways in which conscience and the objective teaching of the Church are related. One often hears confused claims like these: "I know the Church teaches that abortion is always wrong, but my conscience tells me it would not be wrong for me to have one. And surely we should always follow our consciences"; or again: "The Church teaches that premarital sex is wrong [or that racist practices are wrong], but you have a right to follow your own conscience."

The Church teaches, however, that "personal conscience and reason should not be set in opposition to the moral law or the Magisterium of the Church" (CCC 2039). For when each is properly understood, conscience and the Magisterium are in no way opposed to each other.

True Rights of Conscience • It is indeed true that the firm judgments of a sincere conscience must be honored. We have a right and a duty to act in accord with the dictates of our conscience, and no one must be "forced to act contrary to his conscience" (Vatican Council II, *Declaration on Religious Freedom, Dignitatis Humanae*, 3). But this is said about the sincere judgments of a moral conscience, about honest efforts to know what is morally right and in accord with God's saving will, not about the counterfeits of conscience that we will treat below.

The Church has excellent reasons for teaching that we should act in accord with the dictates of sincere conscience. In all we say and do, we have a duty to follow faithfully what we earnestly believe to be right. God himself wishes this of us, for it is in conscience that we perceive and recognize the prescriptions of his law. The Second Vatican Council reminded us: "Deep within his conscience man discovers a law which he has not laid upon himself but which he must obey. Its voice, ever calling him to love and to do what is good and to avoid evil, tells him inwardly at the right moment: do this, shun that. For man has in his heart a law inscribed by God. His dignity lies in observing this law, and by it he will be judged" *(Pastoral Constitution on the Church in the Modern World, Gaudium et Spes,* 16).

A well-formed conscience can well be said to be a voice of God resounding in the depths of our being (*Gaudium et Spes,* 16*)*. This is not because conscience is a mysterious voice that automatically provides easy answers to every moral question. In point of fact, as the *Catechism of the Catholic Church* points out (2038-2039), conscience will not speak to us faithfully as the voice of God unless we have acquired the practice of heeding it reverently and have been concerned to form our judgments of conscience responsibly in the light of God's word.

God indeed speaks in the upright conscience. This does not mean he whispers correct answers to all our moral questions so that the explicit moral teaching of Christ in the Gospel may be ignored as we consider how we should live. Nor does it mean upright people never make errors in their judgments of conscience, for consciences do frequently make mistakes. But God enables those who seek truth to come often to true and certain judgments, which they know to be right and good, the very will of God.

Even when sincere and conscientious people make material errors in difficult cases, they have not gone entirely astray. Since they sought truth with all their hearts, and remained open to all God enabled them to know, their judgments were upright and sincere. These judgments express what they earnestly believe to be God's will, for they have been attentive to the God of truth. As Vatican II observes, they have in no way lost their dignity. For what the conscientious person seeks is certainly not some excuse to do what he deeply wishes to do (even if it is wrong); rather, he longs for the truly good.

Of course it is far from altogether good to be guided by a mistaken conscience. One might be subjectively innocent in doing unchaste or unjust deeds under the influence of a mistaken conscience, but these remain evil kinds of deeds. They can cause great harm to others and to the one who does them. The ideal is not simply a sincere conscience, but, as Pope John Paul II says, a sincere and correct conscience.

Conscience and the Teachings of Faith • In a revealed religion, the word of God is the supreme source of truth. We are more certain of the truth of God's word than of the truth of anything else we know. But the gift of faith brings with it certain duties. When Divine Revelation and faith enable us to know that God himself is teaching us, we have a duty to believe his saving word.

Now the moral teaching of Christ and his Church is a strong support to conscientious people. His word gives light to the consciences of men. He teaches sublime moral truths in the light of which we can come to entirely secure answers about how we should live. His word removes anxieties and doubts about what is really good.

Suppose a disciple of Christ, who had come to know that Christ was the very Son of God, heard from his lips the teaching that divorce and remarriage are wrong and contrary to God's original plan, and involve even adultery. If, before Christ spoke, he had believed that divorce must be an acceptable practice, he might be deeply disturbed. Yet it would hardly be coherent for such a person to ask: Should I accept what Christ says or follow my own conscience? If he believes in Christ, and knows that Christ (since he is the Son of God) most certainly speaks the truth, he would know that his conscience (i.e., the sincere moral judgment that, up until this occasion when he heard the teaching of Christ, he had considered quite true) had been in fact a mistaken conscience. Because he now knew that his earlier judgment of conscience had been mistaken, he would no longer say his conscience even now approved divorce or that he remained entirely convinced that divorce and remarriage are permissible. A believer must acknowledge: My conscience does not correct God; the word of God corrects, enlightens, heals my conscience.

Even today, Christ teaches in his Church (cf. Mt 28:20; CCC 888-892, 2030-2040), and those who recognize the teachings of Catholic faith as his, allow his word even today to enlighten and heal their consciences.

The moral teaching of the Catholic Church is deeply rooted in the Gospel and in all of Scripture. What the Church draws from the Gospels, and in all centuries and all places and circumstances bears witness to as God's certain word in moral matters, ought to be accepted by the faith with complete certainty as God's own saving message (cf. Vatican Council II, *Dogmatic Constitution on the Church, Lumen Gentium,* 25). For the Church bears witness to the moral teaching of Christ with that utter certainty that Christ wished his Church to have so that we would have a secure guide for our lives.

The Ten Commandments are a certain, central, and basic framework for Catholic moral teaching. Christ bore witness that keeping these commandments is required of those who seek eternal life (cf. Lk 10:25-28). Moreover, he taught that these commandments flow from the requirements of love (cf. Mt 22:40), so that one who does not keep them does not truly love God or neighbor. Through the centuries, the Church has taught the central message of the Ten Commandments with consistent firmness,

so that the teaching of faith in these matters is definitive and clearly binding on all.

Hence the Church does teach specific moral truths like the Ten Commandments with that entire certainty and that infallibility which Christ gives to his Church to strengthen his people in knowing and doing what he requires of them to attain everlasting life. Ordinarily, the Church does not solemnly define moral teachings, but she teaches them with the infallibility that even her ordinary teaching office can have. For, as Vatican II says, the bishops "proclaim infallibly the doctrine of Christ on the following conditions: namely, when, even though dispersed throughout the world but preserving for all that amongst themselves and with Peter's successor the bond of communion, in their authoritative teaching concerning matters of faith and morals, they are in agreement that a particular teaching is to be held definitively and absolutely" (*Lumen Gentium,* 25).

Not all the moral teachings of the Church are proposed infallibly, however. For the Pope and the bishops, as faithful teachers of Christ's ways, have the duty of applying his teaching to the changing circumstances of varying times. The Church does not do this lightly, nor does she impose burdens unless certain these correspond to Christ's word and are important for the flourishing of the faithful in his ways.

Thus the measure of certainty of Church teaching is not always that of infallibility. When the Church proposes her teachings on matters of peace and justice, and on new issues in medical ethics, she is not always proposing them as entirely infallible. She acknowledges that it may be necessary in such new questions at times to refine and make more perfect the teaching as time gives greater clarity (cf. Congregation for the Doctrine of the Faith, *Instruction on the Ecclesial Vocation of the Theologian* [1990]*).*

But even when the Church is teaching only authoritatively, not infallibly, her teaching is most secure. Christ's saying that he would be with the Church as she teaches the faithful his ways applies to this teaching also (*Instruction on the Ecclesial Vocation of the Theologian*). Though the teaching is not infallible, and may need further development, the faithful may always be secure in following it in their lives.

Some, however, argue that if authoritative teaching is not infallible, it might be wrong; and if we know that it is wrong, we need not observe it. Now, it is true that if someone were entirely sure that the teaching of some magisterial leader were wrong, that person would of course not be obliged to accept the teaching in question. This is possible in some rare kinds of cases. For example, if an individual bishop were inadvertently to propose a teaching in conflict with what the Church has infallibly taught, and if one knew the infallible teaching, one would not be required to accept the erroneous teaching. But it is not true that one may reject authoritative teaching simply because one does not like it or because, moved by the pressures of the world, one "feels" it to be wrong or finds it wrong in the light of commitments or philosophies that one recognizes may themselves be wrong.

One could of course say that the Church may be wrong in certain details caught up in her authoritative teaching; but it would be wrong to pretend that *I* am more secure and safe than the Church, and *I* clearly see just where every imperfection lies. Surely, too, it would be wrong to suggest that the Church is often and flatly wrong in her insistent moral teaching. That would amount to saying Christ does not give sound moral guidance in his Church, as faith has always most firmly, even definitively, taught that he does.

Moreover, since we believe that Christ is near to us in countless ways in the Church — touching us in his sacraments, teaching us in all the teachers of faith, present as a guide concerning how we are to live and please God — we have far better reasons to accept the simply authoritative teaching of the Church than we have to accept the moral opinions of those not appointed by Christ as teachers and shepherds of his people. That in minor respects some authoritative teaching may prove to need correction does not justify saying we have no duty to follow it. Our consciences can err also, and they at times err very gravely; yet one has a duty to follow the sincere judgment of conscience. Nor are moral teachers who reject the moral teaching of the Church secure guides for the faithful. They are not infallible, and they do not have the charism of truth that Christ gives his Church to make it a secure guide for moral life in Christ.

Following a Well-Formed Conscience • Hence the Church teaches that we should follow our consciences and should shape them by the secure teaching of Christ's Church. "In forming their consciences the faithful must pay careful attention to the sacred and certain teaching of the Church. For the Catholic Church is by the will of Christ the teacher of truth. It is her duty to proclaim and teach with authority the truth which is Christ and, at the same time, to declare and confirm by her authority the principles of the moral order which spring from human nature itself" (*Declaration on Religious Freedom,* 14).

Moral conscience is concerned with the truth, with what is really right or wrong. It is not to be confused with the merely psychological dimensions of our life sometimes called "conscience." Some, for example, mistakenly suppose that, if they do not "feel guilty" upon doing something faith forbids, their consciences are telling them such behavior is permissible. Others fancy that if they really want to do something, then their consciences clearly approve it. Still others imagine that, if their friends commonly insist it is all right to do something Catholic teaching forbids, and if they themselves feel comfortable going along with their friends' judgment, then their consciences are expressing approval. But none of these strange kinds of "conscience" reflects the conscience that faith calls us to honor. These are not judgments of what is truly good and pleasing to God, but expressions of feelings people often have in the face of the world's pressures. We have no right or duty to do simply as we feel like doing, when that is opposed to the teachings of faith.

Suggested Readings: CCC 888-892, 1776-1794, 2030-2040. Vatican Council II, *Pastoral Constitution on the Church in the Modern World,*

Gaudium et Spes, 15-16; *Declaration on Religious Freedom, Dignitatis Humanae*, 3, 14. John Paul II, *The Splendor of Truth, Veritatis Splendor*, 54-64. Congregation for the Doctrine of the Faith, *Instruction on the Ecclesial Vocation of the Theologian*. G. Grisez, *The Way of the Lord Jesus*, Vol. 1, *Christian Moral Principles,* Chs. 3, 34-35.

Ronald D. Lawler, O.F.M. Cap.

CONSCIENCE FORMATION

The purpose of the formation of conscience is to reach — or help someone else (such as one's children, one's students, the members of one's flock) reach — an awareness of moral truth by which to direct one's life to what is truly good and fulfilling. Formation is not simply a process of promulgating laws, rules, and regulations, plus, perhaps, special rules to apply in case there is doubt whether a law or rule applies: This is to view things legalistically. Rather, the goal of formation of conscience is to understand moral truth and to be able wisely to direct one's life.

One should seek the moral truth relevant to every choice one makes. Nevertheless, many people believe that some areas of their lives are outside the scope of morality. Morality, on this view, concerns only certain important areas, perhaps the private realm or the spiritual realm, while other areas, such as business, play, and so on, are morally neutral. This is a mistake. Every area of life is morally significant. St. Paul tells us: "So, whether you eat or drink, or whatever you do, do all to the glory of God" (1 Cor 10:31). We are called to integrate every area of our life with our commitment of faith, our commitment to cooperate with Jesus in redemption. We are called to extend redemption to every aspect of ourselves and of creation.

First of all, we should commit ourselves to growing in moral wisdom and to discerning, with God's grace, the moral truth concerning every aspect of our life. Second, we should pray, asking the Father to send us the Holy Spirit for wisdom and prudence (cf. Jas 1:5-6). Third, we should strive to appropriate personally the truth of the Gospel. Our awareness of basic moral truths, of the possibilities open to us, and of the application of moral truths to our own situation, will grow to the extent we become more virtuous, that is, to the extent we integrate every aspect of ourselves with our commitment of faith to cooperate with Jesus in redemption and to building up the kingdom. The more our intellect, emotions, and imagination are integrated with the commitment of faith, the more we are able easily to discern what is truly morally good — both in general and also in particular situations.

Finally, we should often ask for advice. Not because only the more educated are capable of knowing moral truth, but because all of us can easily fall into self-deception and rationalization, while consulting a sound advisor can help avoid such problems.

The prudent person is able to see what is the morally right thing to do in a given situation where someone who lacks prudence might fail to see it. In a way, virtue in itself is a guide to the moral truth for a particular situation. Virtuous inclinations point one to the morally right thing to do.

This should be carefully understood, however, since confusion on this score has led to serious mistakes. First, the point is not that prudence is a source of moral truth independent of or at odds with moral principles. Rather, prudence is the virtue of applying moral principles to concrete situations, whose exercise presupposes the truth of more general principles. Some theories of prudence in effect take a subjectivist position.

Second, though, it is a fact that if one's character has been formed by respect for moral principles, that is, the intrinsic goods of persons, then one's dispositions to various options in a particular situation are a reliable guide to the question of which one is morally right, that is, which is most consistent with a love for every basic good in oneself and in others (cf. Pope John Paul II, *The Splendor of Truth, Veritatis Splendor*, 67). In that way, when many possible actions are consistent with absolute and other general moral norms (i.e., many actions seem to be right or permissible when one looks only at universal moral norms), one's inclinations themselves can be rightfully viewed as a criterion of what one ought to do.

Role of Church Teaching • How should the teaching of the Church function in the formation of conscience? Some authors say Church teaching should be *consulted* and should be one factor among many in our decision-making, but not anywhere near the primary source. This position, however, is simply not consistent with what the Church teaches. Church teaching should not be just one factor among others to be considered; it should be primary in the formation of one's conscience.

The moral teaching of the Church is not merely a set of extrinsic rules imposed on us by clerics or even by God. The moral teachings of the Church are not rules but truths. The Pope could no more make things like contraception, abortion, and divorce and remarriage right by removing the Church's "ban" on them, than he could make the earth flat by pronouncing it so.

A consistent Catholic, then, does not look on the Church's moral teaching as if it were a burden. Such a Catholic will not look upon the Church as if she were a merely human institution whose leaders inexplicably wished to curtail the liberty of Church members. Catholics believe that Christ formed the Church and promised to be with her all days even unto the end of the world (cf. Mt 28:16), that the gates of hell would not prevail against the Church (cf. Mt 16:18), that the Holy Spirit guides the Church into all truth (cf. Jn 14:17). Our Lord continues to speak to us, in the teaching of his Church, his Body (cf. 1 Cor 12:12ff). Thus, the consistent Catholic sees the Church's teaching as a precious source of light and as the primary guide for forming his conscience.

See: Cardinal Virtues; Conscience; Conscience and the Magisterium; Faith, Act of; Legalism.

Suggested Readings: CCC 1776-1802. G. Grisez, *The Way of the Lord Jesus*, Vol. 1, *Christian Moral Principles*, pp. 82-87; Vol. 2, *Living a Christian Life*, pp. 245-304. G. Grisez and R. Shaw, *Fulfillment in Christ*, pp. 32-37.

Patrick Lee

CONSECRATED LIFE

Every baptized person is called to holiness. The reality of this universal call was a central insight of the Second Vatican Council (1962-1965), which made it the theme of the fifth chapter of its foundational *Dogmatic Constitution on the Church, Lumen Gentium*: "[A]ll Christians in any state or walk of life are called to the fullness of Christian life and to the perfection of love" (40).

Positive responses to this universal call take many different forms. Indeed, one might say that there are as many ways of responding positively as there are Christians striving to live out their personal vocations, with all their unique particularity. Still, within the general framework of the universal call, certain patterns and forms of response are clearly discernible. Among these is the way of those who formally embrace the evangelical counsels — poverty, chastity, and obedience. This is the essence of the consecrated life, of which Vatican Council II says that it "gives and should give a striking witness and example of that holiness" to which all are called (*Lumen Gentium*, 39).

The consecrated life is the way chosen by those who seek more perfectly to conform their lives to Christ's by the profession and practice of the counsels. It is the state of life "constituted by the profession of the evangelical counsels" (*Lumen Gentium*, 44); and, as the *Catechism of the Catholic Church* points out, it is "profession of these counsels, within a permanent state of life recognized by the Church, that characterizes the life consecrated to God" (915).

Vatican II points to two reasons why, generally speaking, a person undertakes this state of life shaped by the counsels: "first, in order to be set free from hindrances that could hold him back from loving God ardently and worshiping him perfectly, and secondly, in order to consecrate himself in a more thoroughgoing way to the service of God" (*Lumen Gentium*, 44). Obviously, the profession of the counsels involves renunciation, the giving up of real goods; but rather than constituting an obstacle to the development of the person, such renunciation is "supremely beneficial to that development" inasmuch as it serves freedom, the cultivation of charity, and the effort to model one's life on Christ's (*Lumen Gentium*, 46).

Consecrated Life in the Church • As the Council observes, the consecrated life traces its origins back to the very beginnings of the Church. From the start, there were "men and women who set out to follow Christ with greater liberty, and to imitate him more closely, by practicing the evangelical counsels" (*Decree on the Up-to-Date Renewal of Religious Life, Perfectae Caritatis*, 1). Over time, what the Council calls a "wonderful and wide-spreading tree" (*Lumen Gentium*, 43) grew up in the Church from this source.

The *Catechism* calls attention to the following forms of the consecrated life.

* The eremetic life — the life of hermits. "They manifest to everyone the interior aspect of the mystery of the Church, that is, personal intimacy with Christ. Hidden from the eyes of men, the life of the hermit is a silent preaching of the Lord" (CCC 921).

* Consecrated virgins. "[T]he order of virgins establishes the woman living in the world (or the nun) in prayer, penance, service to her brethren, and apostolic activity. . . . Consecrated virgins can form themselves into associations to observe their commitment more faithfully" (CCC 924).

* Religious life. "Lived within institutes canonically erected by the Church, it is distinguished from other forms of consecrated life by its liturgical character, public profession of the evangelical counsels, fraternal life led in common, and witness given to the union of Christ within the Church" (CCC 925).

* Secular institutes. "[T]he members of these institutes share in the Church's task of evangelization, 'in the world and from within the world,' where their presence acts as 'leaven in the world' " (CCC 929).

* Societies of apostolic life. The members of these institutes engage in apostolic activity and live in common in observance of their constitutions. Among them are societies whose members embrace the counsels (CCC 930).

Within the consecrated life, the life of contemplatives deserves special mention. Mem-bers of contemplative institutes "give themselves over to God alone in solitude and silence, in constant prayer and willing penance. . . . [T]hey offer to God an exceptional sacrifice of praise, they lend luster to God's people with abundant fruits of holiness, they sway them by their example, and they enlarge the Church by their hidden apostolic fruitfulness" (*Perfectae Caritatis*, 7). Monastic life similarly is a form both ancient and of continuing relevance in the Church. "The principal duty of monks is to present to the divine majesty a service at once humble and noble within the walls of the monastery. This is true whether they dedicate themselves entirely to divine worship in the contemplative life, or have legitimately undertaken some apostolic or charitable activity" (*Perfectae Caritatis*, 9).

In devoting one of its documents to the renewal of religious orders, societies of common life without vows, and secular institutes, Vatican Council II underlined the importance of the consecrated life within the mission of the Church. The *Decree on the Up-to-Date Renewal of Religious Life* says authentic renewal requires both a return to sources — "the sources of the whole of Christian life and . . . the primitive inspiration of the institutes" — and also adaptation in light of contemporary needs (*Perfectae Caritatis*, 2). Much of the history of the consecrated life since Vatican II has concerned the ongoing, and sometimes controverted, effort to observe this prescription. During this time, the Holy See has published a number of implementing documents and directives, and the consecrated life receives extensive treatment in the Code of Canon Law of 1983; while the groups themselves have made numerous changes and undertaken many initiatives.

In 1994, rounding out a series of general assemblies of the Synod of Bishops devoted to states of life (laity—1987, priesthood—1990), Pope John Paul II convened a synod assembly on the theme "The Consecrated Life and Its Mission in the Church and in the World." Among the fruits of that gathering was the postsynodal apostolic exhortation *The Consecrated Life, Vita Consecrata*, published in 1996. It repeats themes and insights of *Lumen Gentium* and *Perfectae Caritatis*, while also drawing upon the synod discussion to consider the ongoing renewal of the consecrated life in light of the past three decades' experience and current circumstances. Without attempting to summarize all of this long and complex document, it will be helpful to note some points.

Besides considering with appreciation the traditional forms of consecrated life, John Paul calls attention to the emergence of "new forms," similar to the traditional forms yet embodying a distinct inspiration and new apostolic impulses. These new forms "have not supplanted earlier ones" but exist alongside them, bearing witness to "the constant attraction which the total gift of self to the Lord, the ideal of the apostolic community and the founding charisms continue to exert" (*Vita Consecrata*, 12).

The Pope examines at some length the relationship between the universal call to holiness, which is central to the common Christian vocation shared by all the baptized, and the call to the consecrated life. "All are equally called to follow Christ," he writes, "to discover in him the ultimate meaning of their lives. . . . But those who are called to the consecrated life have a special experience of the light which shines forth from the incarnate Word. For the profession of the evangelical counsels makes them a kind of sign and prophetic statement" (*Vita Consecrata*, 15). It is in this context that, leaving aside judgments about the holiness of particular individuals, he affirms: "As a way of showing forth the Church's holiness, it is to be recognized that the consecrated life . . . has an objective superiority." Moreover, the Church "has always taught the preeminence of perfect chastity for the sake of the Kingdom [footnote reference to the Council of Trent and to the 1954 encyclical of Pope Pius XII *Sacra Virginitas*], and rightly considers it the 'door' of the whole consecrated life" (*Vita Consecrata*, 32).

Special attention, in light of contemporary circumstances, is devoted by the Pope to the role of consecrated women, some of whom were present as auditors at the synod and participated in its deliberations. Affirming the Church's debt to con-secrated women of the past and present, *Vita Consecrata* acknowledges the need for new initiatives that give full scope to the exercise of their abilities and charisms. "This will be expressed in many different works, such as involvement in evangelization, educational activities, participation in the formation of future priests and consecrated persons, animating Christian communities, giving spiritual support, and promoting the fundamental values of life and peace" (*Vita Consecrata*, 58).

If profession of the evangelical counsels makes consecrated persons a "sign and prophetic statement," it is important to grasp precisely how the counsels offer a particularly compelling Christian response to the challenges of today's secular world. *Vita Consecrata* examines this question at length.

In the face of a "hedonistic culture" exemplifying "a kind of idolatry of the sexual instinct," John Paul says, consecrated chastity offers "joyful and liberating" witness to the fact that "the power of God's love can accomplish great things precisely within the context of human love" (*Vita Consecrata*, 88). The evangelical poverty of the consecrated life is a reply to the materialistic craving for possessions and in itself is a form of service to the poor that also leads many consecrated persons to engage in direct apostolic efforts on their behalf (*Vita Consecrata*, 89-90). The evangelical obedience of the consecrated life is an affirmation of committed human freedom, in response to "notions of freedom which separate this fundamental human good from its essential relationship to the truth and to moral norms" (*Vita Consecrata*, 91).

In a "utilitarian and technocratic culture" such as that of the present day, Pope John Paul observes, it is difficult for many to grasp the meaning and relevance of the consecrated life. That only serves to underline the particular need that now exists for this way of life. "Those who have been given the priceless gift of following the Lord Jesus more closely consider it obvious that he can and must be loved with an undivided heart, that one can devote to him one's whole life. . . . What in people's eyes can seem a waste is, for the individuals captivated in the depths of their heart by the beauty and goodness of the Lord, an obvious response of love" (*Vita Consecrata*, 104).

See: Apostolate; Charisms; Christian Witness; Contemplation; Evangelical Counsels; States in Life; Vocation; Women, Ecclesial and Social Roles of.

Suggested Readings: CCC 914-945, 2053. Vatican Council II, *Dogmatic Constitution on the Church, Lumen Gentium*, Ch. V; *Decree on the Up-to-Date Renewal of Religious Life, Perfectae Caritatis.* John Paul II, *The Consecrated Life, Vita Consecrata*, 1996.

CONSEQUENTIALISM

The term "consequentialism" is closely related to two others: utilitarianism and proportionalism. An ethical theory is consequentialist if it says: Choose that action that will produce the best consequences (or least bad consequences) in the long run.

Consequentialism can be divided into two theories. *Egoistic consequentialism* says one should produce the best consequences for oneself. *Utilitarian consequentialism*, or simply *utilitarianism*, says one should produce the best consequences for people in general or for the greatest number, not just for oneself. Consequentialism denies that there are moral absolutes, that is, specific, exceptionless moral norms (e.g., one ought not intentionally to kill innocent people, one ought not to commit adultery). Consequentialists cannot say of any specific type of action that it will always be wrong, because circumstances might always arise where it would appear that this action would produce the best (or least bad) consequences in the long run.

This theory has been challenged by philosophers and theologians. Most importantly, it has been definitively rejected by Church teaching (cf. CCC 1756; Pope John Paul II, encyclical *The Splendor of Truth, Veritatis Splendor* [1993], encyclical *The Gospel of Life, Evangelium Vitae* [1995]). The true moral criterion, according to the Church's Magisterium, concerns not primarily the consequences of an action, but the openness of the will itself to the intrinsic goods of persons: "If the object of the concrete action is not in harmony with the true good of the person, the choice of that action makes our will and ourselves morally evil, thus putting us in conflict with our ultimate end, the supreme good, God himself" (*Veritatis Splendor*, 72). Thus, a choice contrary to a basic good of the person, even if done to maximize good consequences or minimize bad ones, is intrinsically morally evil.

See: Absolute Moral Norms; Deontology; Law of Christ; Natural Law; Proportionalism, Teleological Ethics; Utilitarianism.

CONTEMPLATION

In the widest sense, "to contemplate" means to gaze at something that causes delight and admiration. Contemplation is therefore an activity in which the intellect simply sees and enjoys but does not analyze or probe, while the will is stimulated to love but not to possess. In other words, in contemplation, knowledge is nondiscursive and love is unifying. On the purely natural level, contemplation reaches its perfection in the aesthetic experience of the beautiful or the intuitive, loving knowledge that is the operation of wisdom.

As applied to the practice of prayer, contemplation may be acquired (ascetical contemplation) or infused (mystical contemplation). In both cases the object of the contemplative gaze is God, because, as an act of the virtue of religion, prayer is directed to God. Acquired contemplation involves the activity of the theological virtues of faith and charity, which operate under the control of the intellect and will.

Acquired Contemplation • St. Thomas Aquinas in the *Summa Theologiae* describes natural, acquired contemplation as "the simple act of gazing at the truth." St. John of the Cross defines acquired contemplative prayer as "the loving awareness of God" (*Ascent of Mount Carmel*). Taken together, the two statements provide an accurate definition of contemplative prayer as an intuitive, loving knowledge of God, which medieval authors called *scientia sapida* (savory knowledge).

By the time the practice of mental prayer became widespread in the seventeenth century, new names were given to acquired contemplation: prayer of simplicity, prayer of simple regard, prayer of the presence of God, acquired recollection, etc. It is a type of prayer that has become extremely simplified. There is no "discursus" or examination as in meditation; the sentiments that were experienced in affective prayer are channeled into a simple loving attention to God. Actually, the prayer of simplicity is a transition from ascetical to mystical prayer.

Two points of advice are in order for souls who arrive at this transition point. First, since it is difficult at the start to practice the prayer of simplicity for long periods of time, as soon as the loving attention begins to waver, one should return to the practice of discursive meditation or affective prayer. Second, one should not even attempt to practice the prayer of simplicity until there are clear signs of being ready to move on to acquired contemplation. The signs are three in number, and they are listed by St. John of the Cross in *The Ascent of Mount Carmel*. (1) One is unable to make discursive meditation as before; now there is aridity. (2) One has no inclination or desire to fix the mind on anything else. (3) One desires only to remain alone in loving awareness of God, without any particular knowledge or understanding. All three signs must be present simultaneously, because, for example, the inability to meditate could be caused by dissipation or lack of diligence; if only the first two are present, they could be the result of some emotional or mental problem.

Infused Contemplation • Infused contemplation is supernatural in origin and in its mode of operation. For that reason it is classified as *mystical* activity and is therefore attributed to an operation of the gifts of the Holy Spirit, as is all mystical activity. Hence, most theologians of the spiritual life maintain that infused supernatural contemplation involves the operation of the virtue of faith informed by charity and the gifts of understanding and wisdom. St. John of the Cross in the *Dark Night* describes mystical contemplation as "an infused and loving knowledge of God which enlightens the soul and at the same time enkindles it with love until it is raised up step by

step unto God its Creator." In her masterly treatise *The Interior Castle*, St. Teresa of Ávila describes that "step-by-step" process from simple contemplation to the transforming union.

The mystical experience of the divine presence may be painful, as in the passive purgations, or delightful, as in ecstasy or rapture. St. Teresa describes her own experience: "It used to happen, when I represented Christ within me in order to place myself in his presence, or even while reading, that a feeling of the presence of God would come upon me unexpectedly so that I could in no way doubt that he was within me or I totally immersed in him" (*The Life*, 10, 1).

This turning within, however, is in no sense egocentric, as it is in discursive meditation. As St. Teresa stated, the individual turns inward to gaze on God dwelling within. Moreover, mystical contemplation is caused by God, it is a gift from God, but it is not a *gratia gratis data,* or charismatic gift. Mystical experience in general is within the normal development of the life of grace, because with grace and the infused virtues the Christian already receives the gifts of the Holy Spirit, which are the principles of mystical activity. Moreover, the experience is perceived as something received. That is, it is not the result of the activity of the individual; it is the Holy Spirit who acts in and through the soul. For that reason, mystical contemplation is rightly described as a "passive" experience, even though the faculties of intellect and will are activated.

From the very beginning of the monastic life, contemplative prayer was proposed as its goal. Although infused contemplation comes from God through the operation of the gifts of the Holy Spirit, certain predispositions can be fostered by the individual. Obviously, the first is the prayer of petition, so faithfully practiced by the ancient monks, especially in the East. Second, the practice and perfecting of faith, hope, and charity, as well as the moral virtues proper to one's state of life. The practice of the virtues leads to what the monks called *apatheia*, the peaceful harmony and equilibrium that make the soul receptive to God's activity. Finally, the soul needs to be nourished by the word of God through *lectio divina*, the meditative reading of Scripture. Having done these things, the individual need only "wait upon the Lord."

See: Gifts and Fruits of the Holy Spirit; Meditation; Mysticism; Prayer.

Suggested Readings: CCC 2709-2719. Congregation for the Doctrine of the Faith, *Letter to the Bishops of the Catholic Church on Some Aspects of Christian Meditation.* St. Teresa of Ávila, *The Interior Castle.* T. Dubay, *The Fire Within.* J. Aumann, *Spiritual Theology.*

Jordan Aumann, O.P.

CONTRACEPTION

It surprises many people to learn that all Christian churches were united in their opposition to contraception until as recently as the early decades of this century. It was not until 1930 that the Anglican Church went on record as saying that contraception was permissible, for grave reasons, within marriage. It was also then that Pope Pius XI issued the encyclical *Casti Connubii*, whose English title is usually given as "On Christian Marriage." There Pope Pius reiterated what has been the constant teaching of the Catholic Church: Contraception is intrinsically wrong.

This teaching of the Church went virtually unchallenged until the early 1960s, when the invention of the contraceptive pill, new fears of a population explosion, and feminism led many to become enthusiastic about birth control. Many in the Church then challenged the Church's teaching. In 1968, Pope Paul VI issued the encyclical *On Human Life, Humanae Vitae,* which repeated the constant teaching of the Church.

The core of that teaching can be found in *Humanae Vitae*: "But the Church, which interprets natural law through its unchanging doctrine, reminds men and women that the teachings based on natural law must be obeyed, and teaches that it is necessary that each and every conjugal act remain ordained to the procreating of human life" (11). The encyclical adds, "The doctrine which the *Magisterium* of the Church has often explicated is this: There is an unbreakable connection

between the unitive meaning and the procreative meaning of the conjugal act, and both are inherent in the conjugal act. This connection was established by God and cannot be broken by man through his own volition" (12).

The Church condemns contraception, since it violates both the procreative and unitive meanings of the human sexual act. Contraception diminishes an act that, by its very nature, is full of weighty meaning, meaning unique to the sexual act. To engage in an act of contracepted sexual intercourse is to engage in an act that has the potential for creating new life and the potential for creating tremendous emotional bonds between male and female, and simultaneously to undercut those potentials. Sex is for babies and for bonding; if people are not ready for babies or bonding, they ought not to be engaging in acts of sexual intercourse.

The modern age is quick to express appreciation for the unitive meaning of the sexual act, but it has little understanding of the goodness of the act's procreative meaning. It tends to treat babies as burdens and not as gifts. It tends to treat fertility as some dreadful condition that needs to be guarded against. Some speak about "accidental pregnancies," as if getting pregnant were like getting hit by a car — a terrible accident. But the truth is that if a pregnancy results from an act of sexual intercourse, that means something has gone right with the act, not that something has gone wrong.

Perhaps precisely because of the widespread availability of contraception, modern times have lost sight of the fundamental truth that those not ready for babies are not ready for sexual intercourse. Few realize that sexual intercourse, making love, and making babies are for good reason inherently connected. Sexual relations are treated casually; no great commitment to another person is implied in having sexual intercourse; babies are treated as an unwelcome intrusion on the sexual act. Contraception has enabled many to have sexual intercourse outside of marriage in relationships where babies are not welcome. Herein lies much of the explanation for the large numbers of abortions and of unwed pregnancies that plague modern society.

The Church insists that sexual intercourse and having children are intimately connected, that sexual intercourse implies a great commitment, that children are an inherent part of that commitment, and that both commitment and children are wonderful gifts.

It is important to keep in mind that fertility is a great good: To be fertile is a state of health for an adult person. It is those who are not fertile who need to be helped and who seek treatment for infertility. Women now take a "pill" to thwart their fertility, as if fertility were a disease in need of a cure; contraception treats the woman's body as though there were something wrong with it. The use of contraception suggests that God made a mistake in the way he designed the body, and we must correct his error. In an age that has become very wary of dumping pollutants into the environment, it is ironic that people are so willing to dump pollutants into their bodies. The health risks of contraception to women are considerable; the list of bad side effects is long and includes high blood pressure, strokes, and increased incidence of some forms of cancer. Some intrauterine devices went off the market because many lawsuits were lodged against their manufacturers.

Few are aware that many forms of contraception are abortifacients. They work by causing an early-term abortion. Rather than inhibiting ovulation, they prevent the fertilized egg, the tiny new human being, from implanting in the wall of the uterus. The IUD works in this fashion, as do most forms of the pill (on occasion), Norplant, and Deprovera. It is impossible to estimate the numbers of abortions caused by use of contraceptives, but they undoubtedly greatly eclipse the abortions performed in clinics.

The Wrongness of Contraception • Contraception, then, enters a note of tremendous negation into the act of sexual intercourse. But lovemaking should be a most wonderful act of affirmation, a tremendous "yes" to another person, a way of expressing to another that he or she is wonderful and completely accepted; this is conveyed by making a total gift of oneself to the other. The contracepting lover, however, says in effect: "I want to give myself to you, but not to the extent of sharing my fertility with you. I want you, but not your sperm (or your egg)!"

The words for contraception are themselves very revealing. Contraception means "against the beginning" — here, against the beginning of a new life. A contracepting couple is participating in an act designed to bring about new life, yet acting against that new life. They may put barrier methods in place for protection — "protection" against a new baby; they may use a spermicide to kill the sperm — an act hostile to life and to the male.

Our age fails to understand what a marvelous privilege it is to be able to bring forth a new human being. God chooses to bring new human life into existence through the love of spouses. The entire world was created for mankind, and God wishes to share his creation with new human souls, whom he brings into the world through the love of men and women for each other. God created the world as an act of love, and the bringing forth of new human life is, quite appropriately, the product of another kind of loving act. When a man and woman have a child together, theirs is an act that literally changes the cosmos: something has come into existence that will never pass out of existence; each human person is immortal and is destined for eternal life.

This is to say that whenever a new human life comes into existence, God performs an entirely new act of creation, for only God can create an immortal soul. In sexual intercourse, spouses provide God with an opportunity to perform his creative act. As the first words of *Humanae Vitae* state, God gives spouses the mission (*munus*) of transmitting human life. Contraception, however, says no to God; it says that those who contracept want to have the wonderful physical pleasure of sex but do not want to allow God to perform his creative act.

Contraception is wrong not only because it violates the procreative meaning of the sexual act but also because it violates the act's unitive meaning.

Pope John Paul II has been most energetic in explaining how couples do not achieve true spousal union in sexual intercourse when they use contraception. He explains that the sexual act is meant to be an act of total self-giving, whereas in withholding their fertility from one another spouses are not giving totally of themselves. He has developed an interesting line of argument in which he speaks of the "language of the body." He claims bodily actions have meanings much as words do, and that, unless we intend those meanings, we should not perform actions that express them, any more than we should speak words we do not mean. In both cases, lies are being "spoken."

Sexual union has a well-recognized meaning: "I find you attractive"; "I care for you"; "I will try to work for your happiness"; "I wish to have a deep bond with you." Yet some who engage in sexual intercourse do not mean these things; they wish simply to use another for their own sexual pleasure. They have lied with their bodies, in the same way that someone lies who says "I love you" to another simply for the purpose of obtaining some favor.

It is easy to want to have sexual intercourse with lots of people, but we generally want to have babies with only one person. One is saying something entirely different with one's body when one says, "I want only to have sexual pleasure with you," and when one says, "I am willing to be a parent with you." In fact, one of the most certain ways to distinguish simple sexual attraction from love is to ask oneself whether all that is wanted from another person is sexual pleasure or whether one wishes to have a baby with one's beloved. We generally are truly in love with those with whom we want to have babies. We want our lives totally tied up with theirs, want to become one with them in the way having a baby makes two people one: their lives intertwined even in such mundane activities as buying diapers, giving birthday parties, paying for college, planning weddings. A noncontracepted act of sexual intercourse says again just what marriage vows say: "I am yours for better or worse, in sickness and health, till death do us part." Having babies with another

means sharing a lifetime endeavor with that other person.

A sexual act open to the possibility of procreation ideally represents the kind of bond to which spouses have committed themselves. Contraceptives, however, convey the message that, while sexual intercourse is desired, there is no desire for a permanent bond with the other person. The possibility of an everlasting bond has been willfully removed from the very act designed best to express the desire for such a relationship. It reduces the sexual act to a lie.

Dissent From the Church's Teaching • It is an understatement to say that many theologians and many lay Catholics since the 1960s have refused to accept the Church's teaching on contraception. Many of those who attempt to offer a theoretical basis for rejecting the Church's teaching subscribe to the moral theory known as proportionalism. Although there are many variations, a feature common to different formulations is the idea that acts are not to be judged evil in kind, that is, per se evil. Rather, proportionalists hold that the circumstances and the consequences of an act must be taken into account in assessing an action's morality, and that in some circumstances actions deemed intrinsically immoral by the Church may morally be performed. Pope John Paul II's encyclical *The Splendor of Truth, Veritatis Splendor*, was written to clarify the fact that proportionalism is not a moral theory consistent with the Catholic Tradition and thus cannot be the basis for judging the morality of action.

The chief objection of proportionalists against *Humanae Vitae* has been that its teaching is based upon a "physicalist" view of sexual intercourse: that is, the physical value of sexual intercourse, namely procreation, is elevated above its personalist values (the lovemaking power). They have also argued, on the basis of their interpretation of the "principle of totality," that it is morally permissible for spouses to sacrifice the procreative value of the sexual act when seeking its unitive values and when seeking the good of the individual, the family, and society.

The Church's teaching against contraception,

however, is not about the nature of *biological* processes. When the Church uses the word "nature" in reference to morality, she is referring not to biology but to the essence of the human being, a being capable of intellectually grasping what is good and freely acting in accord with it. The Church does not understand animal and human sexuality to have the same meaning. Whereas animal sexuality is for *reproduction*, human sexuality is for *lovemaking*, which includes openness to the love- and life-affirming possibility of *procreation* and a commitment to the love-based responsibilities that come with bonding with one's spouse. To attempt to thwart the procreative possibility of a fertile act of sexual intercourse is to attempt to shut God out of the arena he has chosen for bringing forth new life. To attempt to render fertile acts infertile is to withhold one's life-giving power from one's sexual acts and so fail in giving of oneself completely to one's spouse. The act is lacking, then, both as a procreative and as a unitive act. Contraception violates the goods of human sexuality (not just the physical values of sexual intercourse) and thus is not worthy of human choice.

Those who argue that acts should be judged by their consequences should find reason for reconsidering their approval of contraception in the impact its widespread availability has had on society. Contraception has been a major factor allowing the so-called sexual revolution to rage, and this "revolution" has led to many unwanted pregnancies and abortions. Rather than liberating women, contraception has made them much more open to sexual exploitation by men. In fact, *Humanae Vitae*, 17, predicted a general lowering of morality, should contraception become widely available. Certainly, such a lowering can be seen in the epidemic of teenage pregnancies, venereal diseases, divorces, AIDS, etc.

Contraception, in sum, is an offense against one's body, against one's God, and against one's relationship with one's spouse; moreover, it does great damage to society. Many if not most of those who use contraceptives are not aware of the negativity written into their action. Thus, they may be subjectively not culpable. Nonetheless, they still

do wrong, and most likely they will suffer some damage to their bodies and to their relationships with God and their spouse. Catholics need to educate themselves about the Church's teaching and attempt to form their consciences in accord with it; they should realize the marvelous understanding of the purpose of human sexuality that has shaped the Church's rejection of contraception.

See: Absolute Moral Norms; Chastity; Human Person; Marriage; Natural Family Planning; Natural Law; Proportionalism; Sexuality, Human.

Suggested Readings: CCC 2360-2379. Vatican Council II, *Pastoral Constitution on the Church in the Modern World, Gaudium et Spes*, 48-51. Pius XI, *On Christian Marriage, Casti Connubii.* Paul VI, *On Human Life, Humanae Vitae.* John Paul II, *The Christian Family in the Modern World, Familiaris Consortio; Original Unity of Man and Woman; Blessed Are the Pure in Heart; Marriage and Celibacy; Reflections on Humanae Vitae; Letter to Families; The Splendor of Truth, Veritatis Splendor.* J. Smith, *Humanae Vitae: A Generation Later; Why Humanae Vitae Was Right: A Reader; Humanae Vitae: A Challenge To Love.* J. Kippley, *Sex and the Marriage Covenant.*

Janet E. Smith

CONTRITION

Together with his sins, there are three acts of the penitent that make up the matter of the sacrament of Penance. These are contrition, confession, and satisfaction. "Among the penitent's acts contrition occupies first place" (CCC 1451).

Contrition is derived from the Latin *contero*, meaning "to rub away" or "to crush." It implies a breaking of something that has been hardened. St. Thomas Aquinas explains the term's significance in moral theology: "Since it is requisite for the remission of sin that a man cast away entirely the liking for sin which implies a sort of continuity and solidity in his mind, the act which obtains forgiveness is termed by a figure of speech, 'contrition' " (*Sent.* IV, dist. xvii).

Contrition, as perfect sorrow for sins, is distinguished from attrition, which is imperfect sorrow for sins. Both attrition and contrition are gifts from God, as are all graces, since man can do no good for salvation without help from God. Contrition, the perfect hatred for sin, is motivated by the love for God who has been offended. Attrition, imperfect sorrow, arises from some other motive. This may be the fear of loss of heaven, the pains of hell, or simply the ugliness of sin. What makes contrition perfect sorrow is that "it arises from a love by which God is loved above all else" (CCC 1452).

Essential Elements • Whether sorrow be perfect or imperfect, four elements are essential. Every act must be: (1) interior, (2) supernatural, (3) universal, and (4) sovereign.

Interior. The Scriptures are replete with acts of external penance, for example, the sackcloth and ashes of Job, the weeping of the woman who washed the feet of Jesus with her tears. Yet what God desires is not merely external acts but a contrite heart that accompanies them: " 'Yet even now,' says the Lord, 'return to me with all your heart, with fasting, with weeping, and with mourning; and rend your hearts and not your garments' " (Jl 2:12-13).

Supernatural. As mentioned above, all acts of sorrow, whether they be perfect or imperfect, are prompted by the grace of God. In the Old Testament, it is God who brings about the changes in man's heart: "I will sprinkle clean water upon you . . . from all your idols I will cleanse you. A new heart I will give you, and a new spirit I will put within you; and I will take out of your flesh the heart of stone and give you a heart of flesh. And I will put my spirit within you . . . and I will deliver you from all your uncleannesses" (Ez 36:25-29).

In the New Testament, both St. Peter and St. Paul remind their audiences that it was from God the Father and the Christ whom he raised up that they were brought to repentance (cf. Acts 5:30; 2 Tm 24-25). St. Augustine in his time fought strongly against the Pelagian heresy, insisting that man could do absolutely no good without the grace of God and that contrition is positively supernatural: "That we turn away from God is our doing,

and this is the bad will; but to turn back to God we are unable unless He arouse and help us, and this is the good will."

Universal. The sorrow must apply to all mortal sins, whether they are recalled or not. Sorrow for venial sins must be interior, supernatural, and sovereign, but not always universal, since venial sins of themselves do not destroy all charity.

Concurrent with real contrition is a firm purpose of amendment. The Council of Trent declared that "this contrition contains not only a cessation from sin and the purpose and the beginning of a new life, but also a hatred of the old." At the heart of this is the traditional Catholic teaching on grace, for which repentance provides the foundation. Forgiveness, which is always accompanied by God's grace, requires sorrow of soul. Grace and sin cannot coexist. Therefore, one sin cannot be forgiven while another remains. One cannot be forgiven one sin while remaining attached to another.

Sovereign. This is a corollary of the preceding element, yet extends even further. The penitent, at the moment contrition is expressed, is asked not simply to avoid the particular sin he has confessed or even those things that may lead him to commit it, but also to express a firm will never to sin again. Without knowledge of future events, the penitent has no way of knowing what may come his way, yet he recognizes that there is no evil greater than sin. Here he takes to heart the words of Our Lord, "For what will it profit a man, if he gains the whole world and forfeits his life?" (Mt 16:26).

Attrition, or imperfect contrition, is derived from the Latin *attero,* "to rub away." Many souls in the Old Testament were brought to repentance through fear of punishment and so changed their lives. The Ninevites' response to Jonah's preaching provides one such example (cf. Jon 3:5-10). Christ himself used such methods in instructing his disciples: "And do not fear those who kill the body but cannot kill the soul; rather fear him who can destroy both soul and body in hell" (Mt 10:28). The vivid account of the destruction of Jerusalem and the Final Judgment were intended to deter his listeners from sin and encourage them to reform their lives (cf. Mt 24, 25; Mk 13; Lk 21). Within the context of the sacrament of Penance, attrition disposes the sinner to receive the grace of the sacrament that ultimately justifies him or her.

The Rite of Reconciliation • Integral to the Rite of Reconciliation is the penitent's expression of sorrow, more commonly known as the Act of Contrition. In addition to personal prayers, various formulas have been used. An analysis of one of the more frequently used provides good summary insight into this discussion.

O my God: From the beginning there is an awareness that God is the object and the one who has been offended.

I am heartily sorry: Sorrow is necessary for absolution and it must be sincere.

I detest all my sins: The contrition must be universal; there can be no offense that keeps the sinner from God.

Because of Thy just punishments: God is a God of truth and justice. He cannot judge man to be freely one with his will if by sin he has shown he is not.

But most of all because they offend Thee: The primary reason for sorrow is that God is so good, separation from him is so evil, and the punishment so just.

Who are all good: There is no good without God. Any good that exists is derived from his infinite goodness.

Deserving of all my love: To love is to seek the good. Precisely because God is all good, he is deserving of all love.

I firmly resolve: Here an explicit intention is made, a resolution that is another sign of sorrow. This begins the purpose of amendment, the intention to reform one's life.

With the help of Thy grace: Whatever good is intended cannot be done apart from and without the help of God. This both acknowledges man's helplessness without God and reminds him that God is always there to help; whatever good he does is with God's help.

To sin no more: The purpose of amendment continues; true sorrow implies a resolution not to sin again, ever.

And to avoid the near occasion of sin: The purpose of amendment concludes; there is a resolution not only to sin no more but to avoid whatever may lead one to sin.

See: Confession; Penance and Reconciliation, Sacrament of; Penance in Christian Life; Sin.

Suggested Readings: CCC 1451-1454. John Paul II, *On Reconciliation and Penance in the Mission of the Church Today, Reconciliatio et Paenitentia.* N. Halligan, O.P., *The Sacraments and Their Celebration.* C. O'Neill, O.P., *Meeting Christ in the Sacraments.* G. Kelly, ed., *The Sacrament of Penance in Our Time.*

Christopher M. Buckner

CONVERSION OF THE BAPTIZED

From the very beginning of his public ministry, Our Lord made it clear that the proclamation of his kingdom called for the response of conversion. His first call was to repentance: "The time is fulfilled, and the kingdom of God is at hand; repent, and believe in the gospel" (Mk 1:15). The word "repent" in the original Greek is *metanoeite.* It means a change of heart, a turning of the mind, and is found numerous times in the Gospels and the other books of the New Testament.

Two Conversions • Such a change or conversion is not a once-in-a-lifetime event. Two conversions typically occur in a person's life. The first and fundamental conversion takes place at Baptism. Here the candidate (if an infant, vicariously through the parents and godparents) professes faith in the Trinity and the Church, renounces sin, Satan, and all his works and empty promises. (In the Western Church, the person will have the opportunity to restate these same principles himself later, at Confirmation.) Baptism, then, is the time for a primary conversion. Salvation begins with being "born anew"; in his conversation with Nicodemus, Jesus asserted: "Truly, truly, I say to you, unless one is born of water and the Spirit, he cannot enter the kingdom of God" (Jn 3:3, 5).

The call to repentance may be addressed first

to those who do not know Christ or do not know him well; he calls them through the preaching of his Church. But this is not sufficient. Sin and failure demand an ongoing repentance. So Christ calls people through the teaching of this Church to a second conversion. Scripture recounts instances of both kinds. The conversion of Saul on the road to Damascus is an example of the first (cf. Acts 9:1-19). The repentance of Peter following his threefold denial of the Lord is an example of the second (cf. Mt 26:69-75).

Acts of penance — fasting, mortification, almsgiving, works of charity — are visible manifestations of the Christian's recourse to this ongoing conversion. Recognizing that sins come from the flesh and worldly desires, he seeks to deprive himself of these allurements and thus master them before they master him. Scripture provides many examples. The holy men and women of the Old Testament demonstrate the importance of fasting and acts of penance to atone for their own sins as well as those of their people. Moses reminds the Israelites: "When I went up the mountain to receive the tables of stone, the tables of the covenant which the Lord made with you, I remained on the mountain forty days and forty nights; I neither ate bread nor drank water" (Dt 9:9; cf. Ex 24:18).

This is how Christ himself would begin his public life, offering an example as he began to preach the Gospel of repentance. Pope Paul VI says: "Christ, who always practiced in His life what He preached, before beginning His ministry spent forty days and forty nights in prayer and fasting, and began His public mission with the joyful message: 'The kingdom of God is at hand.' . . . The kingdom of God announced by Christ can be entered only by a 'change of heart' ('metanoia'), that is to say through that intimate and total change and renewal of the entire man" (apostolic constitution *On Penance, Paenitemini*, Ch. 1 [1966]).

The *Catechism of the Catholic Church* treats the conversion of the baptized in discussing the sacrament of Penance and Reconciliation. Why is there a sacrament of reconciliation after Baptism? Because the baptized are still in need of conversion. In the Gospel, even those who had accepted Christ and followed him are still referred to by him as sinners: "Those who are well have no need of a physician, but those who are sick. Go and learn what this means, 'I desire mercy, and not sacrifice.' For I came not to call the righteous, but sinners" (Mt 9:12-13).

He had been identified as one of them: "a friend of tax collectors and sinners" (Lk 7:34). This had implications for him and for them. While he would ultimately die for all, these were the ones who would benefit from his redemptive act. They recognized who he was and would appreciate what he would do for them. Remaining in his company, they would learn what they needed to do to improve their lives.

As the three years of his public life progressed, some would drop away, unable to accept the complete message of the kingdom. The rich young man departed sad; many found the teachings on the Eucharist to be hard sayings, and these walked away, never to return (cf. Jn 6:66). But others gladly left everything for him. His disciples dropped their nets and followed him; Matthew, having left his post as tax collector, invited him into his home; Zacchaeus restored fourfold what he had wrongfully taken, and salvation came to his whole household. Still, of his own disciples, one would betray him, one would deny him, and at the most crucial moment, only one would remain by his side.

Two thousand years later, we who have been baptized in his name still stand in need of conversion, while he still comes to call sinners. Those who bear the name of Christian also bear the responsibility of identifying with him. The conversion of the baptized speaks to such people: It is relevant to the times when they do not live up to their name or do not bear it well.

Conversion, Penance, and Sin • The sacrament of Penance is one of the greatest tools the Church provides for this second conversion. Along with a daily examination of conscience and a healthy prayer life, this sacramental encounter with Christ reminds the Christian of Christ's injunction to "be perfect, as your heavenly Father is perfect" (Mt 5:48). The second conversion is not a single event. As often as our failings remind us of the frailty of our fallen human nature, so often does this conversion remind us of the grace available to conquer that weakness.

Conversion of the baptized also implies a heightened awareness of sin. In today's world, this sense of sin has been lost by many. It is fundamentally linked to the sense of God, and when one loses an awareness of God, awareness of offending him is lost as well. Misunderstandings of conscience, of human acts, and of moral responsibility inevitably follow. In his 1984 apostolic exhortation *On Reconciliation and Penance in the Mission of the Church Today, Reconciliatio et Paenitentia*, Pope John Paul II identified both social and ecclesial causes for this loss.

The social causes are: a rejection of any reference to the transcendent, in favor of the individual's aspiration to personal independence; acceptance of ethical models imposed by the general consensus, even when condemned by the individual conscience; tragic social and economic conditions that oppress a great part of humanity; and obscuring of the notion of God's fatherhood and dominion over human life.

The ecclesial causes are: replacing exaggerated attitudes of the past with other exaggerations, that is, from seeing sin everywhere to not recognizing it anywhere; a similar shift from too much emphasis on the fear of eternal punishment, to preaching a love of God that excludes any punishment; from severity in trying to correct erroneous conscience, to a respect for any conscience that excludes the duty of telling the truth; confusion caused in the consciences of the faithful by differences of opinions and teachings on Christian morals; deficiencies in the practice of sacramental penance; and routine ritualism that deprives the sacrament of its full significance and formative effectiveness.

John Paul offers three aids to restoration of a proper sense of sin: sound catechesis illuminated by the Scriptures; attentive listening and trustful openness to the Magisterium of the Church; and an evermore careful practice of the sacrament of Penance (cf. *Reconciliatio et Paenitentia*, 18).

See: Baptism; Grace; Metanoia; Penance and Reconciliation, Sacrament of; Penance in Christian Life; Sin.

Suggested Readings: CCC 1427-1429, 2581-2584. Paul VI, *On Penance, Paenitemini*. John Paul II, *On Reconciliation and Penance in the Mission of the Church Today, Reconciliatio et Paenitentia*. C. O'Neill, O.P., *Meeting Christ in the Sacraments*. N. Halligan, O.P., *The Sacraments and Their Celebration*.

Christopher M. Buckner

COOPERATION

Sometimes one's actions assist another in his morally wrong actions, without one's wanting that to be so. For example: Some of our taxes go to fund abortions; or a postman may notice that some of the mail he delivers is pornography. These and similar situations raise the following question: To what extent may we perform actions that assist the wrongdoing of others? When is it morally right to cooperate with evil?

Clearly, many instances of cooperation are morally wrong. Nazi SS officers at the end of World War II were rationalizing when they claimed they were "only following orders" in committing atrocities. But then, what are the criteria for distinguishing morally right from morally wrong cooperation?

The Church distinguishes between formal cooperation and material cooperation. Formal cooperation in a morally evil act is always morally wrong, no exceptions; material cooperation is sometimes right, although not always. In formal cooperation one shares in the action of another to the extent of intending the morally evil act. For example, if a physician prescribes contraceptive pills for use in contracepting, then he or she intends that they be taken in the manner prescribed; thus, he or she formally cooperates in the contraceptive act. Similarly, those in a Catholic hospital who decide to refer patients to other hospitals for abortions intend to facilitate their wrongdoing; their cooperation in abortion is formal. In formal cooperation both the principal (the one whose wrongdoing is assisted) and the one cooperating share in the same moral act. If the principal's act is gravely wrong, as in the examples just mentioned, so is the cooperator's act.

In material cooperation one's act assists or facilitates or makes possible another's wrongdoing, but one does not intend the wrongdoing; the wrongdoing is a side effect of one's own distinct act. For example, the postman intends to deliver what is sent through the mail; that what he delivers is pornographic, and that the recipients use it immorally rather than destroying it, is not part of his act, not intended by him.

One may cooperate with wrongdoing by omission as well as by actually doing something. This happens when one's omission facilitates or enables another's wrongdoing. In this case, too, the cooperation may be either formal or material, depending on whether the principal's evil act or its success is intended or not. For example, if the head of a Catholic high school knows of a teacher undermining the faith but does nothing, he or she at least materially cooperates.

Morally Right Or Not? • Some material cooperation is morally right and some is not. For example, the postman is surely justified in performing his job, despite the assistance it gives to the person using pornography. However, suppose a nurse working in a public hospital is ordered to assist at an abortion, assistance involving handing instruments to the physician in charge. This would be material cooperation. However, although there may be some *rare* circumstances in which the nurse might be justified in doing so, in most cases providing such material cooperation would be unjust; that is, in most cases it would violate the golden rule. Moreover, it would probably give the impression of approval and almost certainly would be a failure to bear witness to the truth about the sanctity of all human life. This latter consideration calls attention to the fact that there can be no material cooperation in a particular case if materially cooperating would give scandal: One's own seeming approval of evil might lead another or others to approve it in fact.

So, how does one distinguish between material cooperation that is morally justified and that which is not? Various points should be considered. Overall, the question concerns the rightness or wrongness of performing an act that causes bad side effects. In material cooperation, the act one does is not in itself wrong, but it causes the bad side effect of facilitating or enabling someone else's wrongdoing. There must be some reason serious enough to justify accepting this bad side effect. As with causing bad side effects in general, so here, too, the question usually is one of justice or fairness: Is my accepting this bad side effect just? If the bad side effect were happening to me, instead of to someone else, would I expect the other person to forgo the action causing the bad side effect?

All of the other considerations one can point to are subsidiary to answering this question. These other considerations include: How much harm would one suffer if one did not materially cooperate? If one refused to cooperate, would this prevent the evil action? Will the cooperation involve a risk to someone's salvation? Will this cooperation impair the witness that one should give to God's truth and love? There is no clear-cut method for arriving at an answer in every case. One must apply the golden rule and take into account the relevant principles and circumstances as best one can.

See: Absolute Moral Norms; Cardinal Virtues; Double Effect; Human Goods; Modes of Responsibility; Natural Law; Synderesis; Teleological Ethics.

Suggested Readings: CCC 1949-1960. G. Grisez, *The Way of the Lord Jesus*, Vol. 1, *Christian Moral Principles*, pp. 300-303; Vol. 2, *Living a Christian Life*, pp. 440-444.

Patrick Lee

COVETOUSNESS

Except for the last two, the Ten Commandments deal with actions, either proscribing bad ones or prescribing good ones. The ninth and tenth commandments, however, outlaw an *attitude*, a grasping, unreasonable desire to possess a neighbor's spouse or goods. Since this twisted desire often does not lead to external injustices, it can easily be overlooked. Yet, as Christ says in the Sermon on the Mount, "Every one who looks at a woman lustfully has already committed adultery with her in his heart" (Mt 5:28). The same interior pitfall applies to riches, which humans can "steal" spiritually.

The *Catechism of the Catholic Church* says covetousness is "lust of the eyes . . . a passion for riches and their attendant power." It continues: "Avarice, like fornication, originates in the idolatry prohibited by the first three prescriptions of the Law. . . . The sensitive appetite leads us to desire pleasant things we do not have . . . [these] desires are good in themselves; but often they exceed the limits of reason and drive us to covet unjustly what is not ours" (2534-2536).

Avarice and envy are called "a form of sadness" (CCC 2540). This sadness stems from a spiritual emptiness and dislocation wherein authentic earthly goods are belittled or skewed, especially those of work or family, while those of less value are overprized.

The Roots of Covetousness • The past five hundred years of Western civilization have witnessed something historically unique: the first large-scale, practically universal attempt to build a secular oasis without God, without the contemplative underpinnings that disclose the truth of persons and things. Gerald Vann sees future judges of Western civilization saying to us: "Yes, you have done mighty things and good things; you have mastered Nature; you have gained wealth and power; you can live in great comfort and travel at immense speed; your science has given great gifts to humanity. But you have forgotten the one thing necessary: You have forgotten that being is more important than doing. What is the use of being able to travel at breathless speed if you have no idea where, ultimately, you want to go, or why. . . ? Science can tell you how to do things; it cannot tell you what you ought to do, still less what you ought to be. You have gained enormously in knowledge, and therefore in power; but you have lost your vision; and where there is no vision, the people perish." Why? "Because our world has ceased to be contemplative, has forgotten how to pray."

No wonder, then, that a cramped possessiveness often befouls attitudes toward earthly goods, causing them to be more exploited than appreciated. Covetous persons may gain things, but along with them come agitation and anxiety.

Vatican Council II's central document, the *Dogmatic Constitution on the Church, Lumen Gentium*, says: "All Christ's faithful are to direct their affections rightly, lest they be hindered in their pursuit of perfect charity by the use of worldly things and by an adherence to riches which is contrary to the spirit of evangelical poverty" (42). Yet poverty, especially when it consists of circumstantially imposed privation, is not good; nor in itself is the world evil. On the contrary: At the dawn of creation, God called each of its successive parts "good" and the ensemble "very good" indeed. It is human beings who get the world wrong and therefore wrong it, themselves, and the Creator of both.

Possible tensions and even moral disorders arise when humanity fails to realize that the authentic fulfillment of material creation and of the human persons who inhabit it and use it requires being ordered to the eternal, immaterial world — to God. Covetousness, by contrast, is *dis*-orientation. "Those who want to be rich are falling into temptation and a trap. They are letting themselves be captured by foolish and harmful desires which drag men down to ruin and destruction. The love of money is the root of all evil. Some men in their passion for it have strayed from the faith, and have come to grief amid great pain" (1 Tm 6:9-10).

Plato holds that the human heart, in effect, is capable of only so much affection. The more it is squandered on lesser goods, the less remains to be invested in worthier objects, for which, and especially for whom, men and women have been created and which alone can authentically fulfill them. But people often are ambushed by the immediate and tangible, the proverbial "bird in hand." Unless they make an effort to let the world of spiritual goods speak and prove its superiority to them, they are vulnerable to the appeals of base desires. What will open humanity's spiritual eyes and ears to this hidden world, which also offers objectivity, balance, and freedom? Jesus prescribes: "Pray, lest you fall into temptation" (Mt 26:41).

The expressions of covetousness — materialism, consumerism, greed (or avarice), acquisitiveness, envy, obsession with money, and so on — though sometimes sins, are symptomatic of a more radical problem: a kind of spiritual bankruptcy, by which the soul lacks that which alone can ennoble and liberate it from inordinate cravings for creature comforts and consolations.

The *Roman Catechism* (the catechism of the Council of Trent) identifies some of those who may be more tempted to covetousness: "[M]erchants who desire scarcity and rising prices, who cannot bear not to be the only ones buying and selling so that they themselves can sell more dearly and buy more cheaply; those who hope that their peers will be impoverished, in order to realize a profit either by selling to them or buying from them . . . physicians who wish disease to spread; lawyers who are eager for many important cases and trials" (III, 37).

Persons tend to overvalue things as a result of undervaluing God. But what about those who mistakenly think their acquisitiveness, far from being a moral fault, is the fuel of progress? Is not consumer demand the motor driving free enterprise? What would happen to the economic engine and our rising life standards if I were to abstain on the sidelines? Is it not beneficial to stimulate consumer appetites? So ask the advertisers and corporate chieftains. And, as Pope John Paul II, among others, points out, the free market can be, though certainly it is not always, a source of benefits (cf. encyclical *The Hundredth Year, Centesimus Annus*, 32, 34). But as Dorothy Sayers says: "Today's Christians must get rid of the superstition that acquisitiveness is a virtue and that the value of anything is represented in terms of profit and cost, price and income." How clarifying and liberating is the first of the Beatitudes: "Blessed are the poor in spirit, for theirs is the kingdom of heaven" (Mt 5:3).

"Jesus enjoins his disciples to prefer him to everything and everyone, and bids them 'renounce all that [they have]' for his sake and that of the Gospel [*Lk* 14:33]. Shortly before his passion he gave them the example of the poor widow of Jerusalem who, out of her poverty, gave all that she had to live on. The precept of detachment from riches is obligatory for entrance into the Kingdom of heaven" (CCC 2544). Human hearts are turned away from avarice and envy by self-discipline, virtue, divine law, wisdom, prayerfulness, and the sacraments. Heeding Jesus' message "initiates [Christians] into desire for the Sovereign Good; it instructs them in the desires of the Holy Spirit who satisfies man's heart" (2541). "The Lord grieves over the rich, because they find their consolation in the abundance of goods. . . [*Lk* 6:24]. Abandonment to the providence of the Father in heaven frees us from anxiety about tomorrow" (2547).

The Savior, in giving himself unstintingly to his followers, wants to make them wealthy beyond their most expansive dreams. "Where your treasure is, there will your heart be also" (Mt 6:21). But to possess that treasure, his disciples are to use wisely and generously the goods entrusted to their stewardship. There must be self-denials in order to practice the charitable almsgiving that hurts the pocketbook. "In order to possess and contemplate God, Christ's faithful mortify their cravings and, with the grace of God, prevail over the seductions of pleasure and power. . . . Desire for true happiness frees man from his immoderate attachment to the goods of this world so that he can find his fulfillment in the vision and beatitude of God" (CCC 2548-2549).

See: Avarice; Capital Sins; Cardinal Virtues; Detachment; Envy; Property; Social Justice.

Suggested Readings: CCC 2534-2557. M. Adler, *Desires, Right and Wrong.* G. Gilder, *Wealth and Poverty.* C. Lewis, *Mere Christianity.* D. Sayers, *The Whimsical Christian.* G. Vann, O.P., *Morals and Man*; *The Heart of Man.*

Dennis Helming

CREATION

In the Nicene Creed, we profess belief in "one God, the Father, the Almighty, maker of heaven and earth, of all that is seen and unseen." Just as there is one God, so also is there one creation that includes all that is not God. Jewish monotheism led to the inescapable conclusion that we all have one Father, since one and the same God has created us all (cf. Mal 2:10).

The Christian Revelation that God is Trinitarian enables us to understand that, while creation has its source in the Father, it is also and equally the work of the Son and the Holy Spirit, though in different ways. All things are created through and for Jesus Christ, the Word of the Father (cf. Col 1:16).

In the first chapter of Genesis, God *speaks* things into existence. As the psalmist points out, "For he spoke, and it came to be; he commanded and it stood forth" (Ps 33:9). The author of the Letter to the Hebrews concurs, reminding us that "by faith we understand that the world was created by the word of God" (Heb 11:3). The Holy Spirit, who is "the Lord and giver of life," is always associated with birth and breath (*ruah*, the Hebrew word for spirit also means breath). In Genesis, "the Spirit of God was moving over the face of the waters" (Gn 1:2). In the next chapter, we are told that God "formed man of dust from the ground, and breathed into his nostrils the breath of life; and man became a living being" (Gn 2:7). The psalmist reminds us that when God sends forth his Spirit, all things are created and the earth is renewed (Ps 104:30). The Blessed Virgin Mary conceived by the power of the Holy Spirit (Lk 1:35), the Holy Spirit at Pentecost gives life to the Church (Acts 2:1-4), and our rebirth as Christians requires that we receive the Holy Spirit (Jn 3:5).

Creation "Ex Nihilo" • God is the only uncreated being. Therefore, God created things not out of some preexisting matter but "out of nothing" (*ex nihilo*). "I beseech you, my child, to look at the heaven and the earth and to see everything that is in them, and recognize that God did not make them out of things that existed" (2 Mc 7:28). "Nothing" of course is not "something" out of which God creates. To say he creates *ex nihilo* is to say that God's creative act is the source of every created being and every element in every created being. He created things neither out of anything else nor out of his own substance. He called into existence that which previously had no existence whatsoever. The Fourth Lateran Council (1215) taught that God "has all together, from the beginning of time, created from nothing both spiritual and bodily creatures, that is to say angels and the terrestrial world; then human beings who belong to both, composed as they are of both spirit and body." God also created time. The Latin expression translated in the above passage as "from the beginning of time" is *simul ab initio temporis*, which literally means "simultaneously from the beginning of time."

To say that God creates out of nothing is to reject pantheism as well as all forms of divine emanationism. It is also to reject the belief that the world has always existed. To say that God creates out of nothing is to affirm that God is transcendent, that is, different from his creation.

There is a sacred order in creation that has a sacred origin (God himself). This order is apparent in the account of the six days of creation in the first chapter of Genesis: God methodically creates in a particular sequence, culminating with the creation of man on the sixth day. As the Book of Wisdom tells us, God "has arranged all things by measure and number and weight" (Wis 11:20) and the wisdom of God "orders all things well" (Wis 8:11).

To say that things are ordered also means that they are related to one another in specific ways. They are interdependent and interrelated. Genesis speaks of the plants and trees as created to supply food for man and the animals (Gn 1:3), of the sun created to rule over the day and the moon to rule over the night (Gn 1:16), and of the garden as created for man to till (Gn 2:15). Genesis also tells us that man was made to have dominion over the earth (Gn 1:28).

The fact that God has ordered all things in such a way as to make them interdependent and interrelated means that creation has been invested by him with its own intrinsic integrity. The Second Vatican Council teaches that "by the very circumstances of their having been created, all things are endowed with their own stability, truth, goodness, proper laws and order" (*Pastoral Constitution on the Church in the Modern World, Gaudium et Spes,* 36). The acorn becomes an oak tree, for example, not because God from outside it forces it to do so, but because God has implanted within the acorn its purpose by which it becomes, by its own intrinsic principles, an oak tree. God is first and final cause of all things, but he has created within the universe a network of secondary causality by which all things achieve their various purposes from within themselves and in relationship to one another and, in so doing, become participants, as it were, in creation itself.

Creation, in other words, reflects in its own way the intellect of God. Creation is ordered, not anarchical or chaotic. This also means that creation, as it comes from the hands of God, is incomplete. It must participate in its own completion. Creation is therefore something that is both gift (from God) and achievement (by us).

Although the Church teaches that creation is relatively autonomous, she does not subscribe to deism, the belief that God created the world but then left it to its own devices, for she also teaches that creation is radically dependent on God. "In him we live and move and have our being" (Acts 17:28). Indeed, were God to withdraw his support from the world, all things would return to the nothingness out of which he called them.

Creation As Good • The Church teaches that creation is good. She therefore rejects Manichaeanism and all other forms of Gnosticism which suppose that God is opposed by another god who is evil or by some element of the cosmos, such as its materiality or temporality.

We know creation is good because God tells us that it is. In Genesis, God six times calls creation good (cf. Gn 1:4, 10, 12, 18, 21, 31). Indeed, the sixth time comes at the end of the sixth day, after his creation of man, at which point we are told that "God saw everything that he had made, and behold, it was very good" (Gn 1:31).

We also know that creation is good because its sole source is God, who is absolute goodness.

Everything God has created, whether spiritual or material, is good. Nothing God has created is, by its nature, evil. As the Council of Florence in the fifteenth century taught, "The Church asserts that there is no such thing as a nature of evil, because every nature insofar as it is a nature is good."

Creation is also good because it has been invested with meaning and purpose. One purpose is to manifest the perfection, the holiness, of God. "The heavens are telling the glory of God; and the firmament proclaims his handiwork" (Ps 19:1). Creation has a second purpose as well, for God has a "plan" or purpose for the universe, that it share in his life, goodness, and love. God is the Creator; he is not the destroyer. "I know that whatever God does endures for ever; nothing can be added to it, nor anything taken from it" (Eccl 3:14). God's plan from before creation is "to unite all things in him, things in heaven and things on earth" (Eph 1:10). Creation is, in the final analysis, good because it is centered on Jesus Christ, the God-man, in whom it is ordered toward its final end as "the new heavens and a new earth" (Is 65:17; cf. 2 Pt 3:13, Rv 21:1).

The most important thing to understand about creation is that it is an act of divine love. Every aspect of creation — its Trinitarian source, its intelligibility and order, its relative autonomy, its goodness — is a reflection of the fact that it is loved by God and brought into existence to share in his life and love. But to say that creation is an act of divine love is to say three things beyond this.

First, creation is a free act of God. This means not only that God was not forced by anyone else to create (there being no one else "before" creation except God) but also that God was not forced by any inner compulsion or need to create. As the First Vatican Council taught, he created the universe neither "to increase his blessedness nor to acquire his perfection"; rather, creation manifests his perfection and blessedness. God creates out of love, in order to share his love with all that he creates.

Second, God loves what he has created. "For

thou lovest all things that exist, and hast loathing for none of the things which thou hast made, for thou wouldst not have made anything if thou hadst hated it" (Wis 11:24). So much does God love the world that he took upon himself, in the Person of the Son, its salvation from sin and death. "For God so loved the world that he gave his only Son, that whoever believes in him should not perish but have eternal life" (Jn 3:16). Redemption, however, is not just for human beings. All of creation, as St. Paul reminds us, awaits redemption (Rom 8:18-23). All of creation both comes into existence through and is redeemed by Jesus Christ. As one Catholic theologian has recently pointed out, the implications of the Catholic faith are "that the entirety of the universe of some fifteen or twenty billion light-years' radius is created in Christ and that the whole of it is fallen in the first Adam and redeemed by the second" (Donald J. Keefe, *Covenantal Theology: The Eucharistic Order of History*, Vol. I, p. 27).

Third, creation itself participates in the freedom of God. Creation is not only ordered, it also is free. That is to say, creation is governed neither by fate nor by necessity. It is not locked into the "wheel of eternal recurrence" by which all things necessarily and fatalistically repeat themselves in some great cosmic recycling process. Acorns may necessarily give rise to oak trees, but every oak tree is unique and unrepeatable. God proclaims in Isaiah, "Behold, I am doing a new thing" (Is 43:19), but in point of fact everything that comes into existence is a "new thing" never before seen. The novelty of creation is a consequence of the freedom with which God invests it, a freedom that manifests the fact that all things are destined to union with God, not to annihilation or to meaningless repetition.

The freedom of creation is manifested fully of course only in human beings, to whom free will is given. This free will is given for the sake of love. Love cannot be coerced; it can only be given freely. In creating human beings with free will, God gives them the potential to love. He does so because he desires that they share in his love by their own free act of love. This is why, after creating man,

God can speak of creation as "very good," for in man, the image of the God who is love, is made visible the potential for that kind of love which constitutes the inner life of the Trinity itself.

See: Angels; Animals; Fatherhood of God; Freedom, Human; Gnosticism; Hierarchy; Human Race, Creation and Destiny of; Imago Dei; Manichaeism; Providence.

Suggested Readings: CC 279-354. R. Butterworth, *The Theology of Creation*. S. Jaki, *Science and Creation: From Eternal Cycles to an Oscillating Universe*. P. Schoonenberg, S.J., *Covenant and Creation*.

Joyce A. Little

CREED

A creed (from the Latin *credo*: I believe) is a summary or synthesis of the faith of the Church. Such summaries also are called professions of faith and "symbols" of faith.

The Church has composed creeds for the benefit of the faithful from the very beginning. Among these are the Athanasian Creed (also known as the *Quicumque* from its Latin beginning), the professions of faith of various councils, and in our own day the *Credo of the People of God* published in 1968 by Pope Paul VI. "None of the creeds from the different stages in the Church's life can be considered superseded or irrelevant. They help us today to attain and deepen the faith of all times by means of different summaries" (CCC 193).

Two creeds have a special place in the life of the Church. These are the Apostles' Creed and the Niceno-Constantinopolitan (or Nicene) Creed. The Apostles' Creed is so called because it sums up the faith of the Apostles; it is identified in a special way with the Church of Rome, the See of Peter. The Nicene Creed arises from the first two ecumenical councils, in 325 and 381, and is shared by both the East and the West. The exposition of the truths of Revelation in the *Catechism of the Catholic Church* is organized according to the plan of the Apostles' Creed.

See: Catechesis; Divine Revelation; Ecumenical Council; Faith of the Church; Magisterium.

CREMATION

Cremation is the act of rendering a dead body to ashes by fire. The funeral rites of Christianity have always followed the Jewish custom of burial. Although there is not a necessary connection between the practice of inhumation, or burial in the earth, and the resurrection of the body, the reverence that Christians have traditionally shown for the remains of the dead does testify to the glory of that resurrection which Christians believe the body will share with the soul in heaven.

With the advent of Christianity, the practice of cremation became uncommon in the West until a movement arose to reintroduce the practice in the late nineteenth century in Europe. The suspicion of the Church in regard to this movement may well have come as a result of the secularist and materialist movements of that century and the anti-Catholicism that often accompanied them.

The old Code of Canon Law included two canons that forbade the cremation of the dead and that denied ecclesiastical burial to those who ordered that their bodies be cremated. The revised Code of 1983 reverses this position in Canon 1176.3: "The Church earnestly recommends that the pious custom of burying the bodies of the dead be observed; it does not, however, forbid cremation unless it has been chosen for reasons which are contrary to Christian teaching."

See: Body and Soul; Burial, Christian; Death; Last Things; Resurrection of the Dead.

D

DEACON

The Acts of the Apostles provides a clear account of the New Testament origins of the order of deacon: "Now in these days when the disciples were increasing in number, the Hellenists murmured against the Hebrews because their widows were neglected in the daily distribution. And the twelve summoned the body of disciples and said, 'It is not right that we should give up preaching the word of God to serve tables. Therefore, brethren, pick out from among you seven men of good repute, full of the Spirit and of wisdom, whom we may appoint to this duty. . . . These they set before the apostles, and they prayed and laid their hands upon them" (Acts 6:1-3; 6).

Because of the service (*diakonia*) that the original deacons were asked to perform, the Church continues to regard the order of deacon as a true ordained ministry in the Church. Deacons share in the sacramental grace and character of Holy Orders, even though they are ordained not to the priesthood but to the ministry. The presence of the deacon at the altar reminds the Christian community of the servant, Jesus Christ, who tells us, "I am among you as one who serves" (Lk 22:27).

In his Letter to the Philippians the second-century bishop St. Polycarp describes deacons as "servants of God and Christ, not of men" (5.2). This means that they carry on the work of Christ, who made himself, as the Gospel says, "a servant of all" (Mk 9:35). Vatican Council II's *Dogmatic Constitution on the Church, Lumen Gentium,* which sets forth the basic truths of the Church's teaching about ordained ministry, stipulates that deacons are "dedicated to the People of God, in conjunction with the bishop and his body of priests, in the service of the liturgy, of the Gospel, and of works of charity" (29). The living out of these obligations is exemplified in the lives of the holy deacons of the early Church, St. Stephen and St. Lawrence. The witness of St. Francis of Assisi helps us further grasp the spiritual significance of the diaconate. This holy man voluntarily remained a deacon throughout his life, renouncing the dignity of the priesthood so that he could give a personal witness to Christ's littleness and servanthood.

At certain moments in the Church's history, deacons, notwithstanding their dedication to service, exercised considerable influence in ecclesiastical circles. For example, the Council of Nicaea had to forbid their distributing the Eucharist to priests, a stricture apparently correcting failures to observe the deacon's hierarchical subordination to the order of presbyters. However, abuse never takes away a right. Deacons have continued to form part of the structure of the ordained ministry, whose rudiments can be discerned within the pages of the New Testament.

The life of the Church is richer on account of the diaconal service of worship and charity. Deacons assist bishops and priests in the celebration of the divine mysteries, in the distribution of Holy Communion, in assisting at and blessing marriages, in the proclamation of the Gospel and preaching, in presiding over funerals, and through dedicating themselves to various works of charity. This last ministry accounts for the distinctive way a deacon wears the sacerdotal stole, namely, over the left shoulder, so that his right arm is always free to help others. The outer liturgical vestment of the deacon in the Western Church is called a dalmatic. This square-cut chasuble is given to the deacon at his ordination, after which the bishop hands over the book of the Gospels as a sign that the newly ordained deacon above all has been charged to proclaim the Gospel of Christ, the most important service anyone can render.

The Diaconate Today • Before the Second Vatican Council, deacons were limited in the exercise of their order. For the most part they functioned only during liturgical ceremonies, and then usually in seminaries or cathedrals. Nowadays the chance of encountering a fully functioning deacon in a parish church is much higher, thanks especially to the restoration of the permanent diaconate in the Latin Church by Pope Paul VI after Vatican II. As a notable feature of this provision, married men are eligible to seek admission to the permanent diaconate. Transitional deacons, as the seminarians who are preparing for priestly ordination are called, also frequently participate in parochial ministry as part of their formation for priestly service. Since the deacon's ministry is strengthened by the sacramental grace of Holy Orders, he is especially well suited to oversee the community's wider attempts to meet the needs of its members, especially in programs of charitable action and social welfare.

In some quarters, including the Orthodox Churches of the East, there is interest in whether women can be ordained as deacons. The exact status that the "deaconess" enjoyed in the early Church is not a matter of common agreement, although it is clear that women were dedicated to Church work. Deaconesses were especially useful during the period when adult Baptism was the norm, as they were able to assist the women catechumens during certain parts of the baptismal ceremony. In some places, especially among heterodox groups of Eastern Christians, the deaconesses later arrogated to themselves certain ministerial functions associated with service at the altar. By the eleventh century, the practice of recognizing deaconesses had come to an end.

The general assumption is that the deaconess was the nonsacramental counterpart of the deacon. The rites that inaugurated deaconesses into Church service situated the ministry of deaconess within the tradition of the holy women of Israel but not in the line of apostolic ministry. In some Protestant churches, especially since the nineteenth century, groups of deaconesses have been instituted that resemble the institutes of consecrated life in the Church.

See: Holy Orders; Ministry.

Suggested Readings: CCC 1569-1571, 1588. Vatican Council II, *Decree on the Bishops' Pastoral Office in the Church, Christus Dominus*. Paul VI, *Sacrum Diaconatus Ordinem*; *Ad Pascendum*. R. Barratt, "Rediscovering the Diaconate," *Priests and People* 2, 9 (1988).

Romanus Cessario, O.P.

DEATH

According to long-established Christian Tradition, rooted in the order of being, that is, of reality, death is the first of the four last things to which the Tradition itself directs our attention (the others, in the order given in the old Penny Catechism, include judgment, hell, and heaven). It is that event which takes place the moment the soul, having left the body for judgment, ceases to vivify the body's functions with the informing, animating principle we call life. The body thus falls away into corruption, leaving the soul to journey across the threshold of eternal life, there to await the moment when God chooses to reconstitute the original body-soul unity for all eternity.

Man is the only creature whose awareness of death, his own approaching end, allows him to ponder the mystery of Everyman's death and of the necessary and inevitable end of everything. Of all creatures made by God, man alone carries his death before him, seeing it as the final cancellation of all he might otherwise have done or become. "In death," the theologian Hans Urs von Balthasar reminds us, "we will forcefully be led from ourselves into total abandonment, because we will be commanded to abandon everything and ourselves" (*Life Out of Death: Meditation on the Easter Mystery*).

While death is not the last word, there is nevertheless a terrifying finality about man's encounter with it, insofar as it decisively brings to a close the first phase of human life, which is determinative of all that is to come. As Blaise Pascal (1623-1662) characteristically puts it in his *Pensées*, "The last act is bloody, however fine the rest of the play. They throw earth over your head and it is finished forever" (165).

Death, to repeat, is not the end of life. It is, however, the end of the road. At the point of death, man has, as it were, arrived, and there is nothing more to be done. This life, which he holds of sufferance, this being, which God has given him to shepherd, must now give way to something — to Someone — transcendent to himself. The purpose of a man's life is, after all, to get beyond life. "In my end is my beginning," says the poet T.S. Eliot. If life is a vale of soul-making, then in death man has made something of himself, and that something he must perforce remain forever after.

In what, finally, does human life consist? Does not the Wisdom literature of the Bible tell us that life is a thing as vaporous as the dew, which is driven away and disappears with the wind; that, like a field of grass dried up in the heat of the sun, its withering is a mere fact of life? And all because we must die — or, more to the point, because we alone *know* we must die. Animals do not know this, do not entertain thoughts of impending extinction. Thus death is at once the most commonplace of all happenings (what could be more banal, more drearily self-evident, than the fact of one's own death?), and at the same time the most painfully incomprehensible, the least tolerable or welcome of all the things that conspire to overtake and destroy us. Death seemingly "crushes and scatters to the four winds the little bit of meaning that has been laboriously accumulated in a life," writes von Balthasar. The basic "contradiction pervading all existence," he says, remains utterly unresolvable on the purely human level (*Life Out of Death*).

Christian View of Death • In a Christian perspective, death is never simply a phenomenon of nature; it cannot be understood as the mere cessation of bodily being. Nor can it be viewed in accents of fashionable despair made famous by writers expressing existentialist *angst*.

The Christian view of death is that it can only finally be understood in theological terms, as a datum intelligible only in the light of Divine Revelation. St. Paul explains that "sin came into the world through one man and death through sin, and so death spread to all men because all men sinned" (Rom 5:12). This is to say that death is the result of sin, the sin of Adam and Eve, the original sin, which Cardinal Newman termed "the aboriginal calamity."

If death, then, is not constitutive of man's nature, it is obvious that God, from the beginning, never intended that man should die. "For God created man for incorruption, and made him in the image of his own eternity, but through the devil's envy death entered the world, and those who belong to his party experience it" (Wis 2:23-24).

For all the harrowing finality of its eruption into the weakness of being human, for all that it shatters of the body-soul unity, death nevertheless belongs to the order of that history which God himself willed to enter and redeem. He undertook to assume our death in order precisely to deliver us from the absurdity of it.

Thus the *Catechism of the Catholic Church* explains: "The Christian who unites his own death to that of Jesus views it as a step towards him and an entrance into everlasting life" (1020). This is because when Christ died, something extraordinary happened to death, something that fundamentally changes the whole dismal equation of sin and death. "In death, God calls man to himself. Therefore the Christian can experience a desire for death like St. Paul's: 'My desire is to depart and be with Christ' [*Phil* 1:23]" (CCC 1011).

And so, for the Christian whose life is an effort to cleave to Christ — to anchor all hope in him who came to conquer sin and death — death's "victory" is only apparent. "So death will come to fetch you?" says St. Thérèse of Lisieux. "No, not death, but God Himself. Death is not the horrible spectre we see represented in pictures. The catechism teaches that death is the separation of the soul from the body; that is all. I am not afraid of a separation which will unite me forever with God."

See: Body and Soul; Burial, Christian; Funerals, Christian; Heaven; Hell; Judgment, General; Judgment, Particular; Last Things; Resurrection of the Dead.

Suggested Readings: CCC 1005-1019. Vatican Council II, *Pastoral Constitution on the Church in the Modern World, Gaudium et Spes*, 18. Congregation for the Doctrine of the Faith, *The Reality of Life After Death*, 1979. H. von Balthasar, *Life Out of Death: Meditations on the Easter Mystery*.

Regis Martin

DEATH, DETERMINATION OF

In human beings, death occurs when the soul is separated from the body. A Catholic understanding of this event has implications for the way physicians determine death.

Human beings are composed of bodies and rational souls. The same soul that enables us to perform acts of knowing and loving is also, by its nature, "the form of the human body" (Council of Vienne, A.D. 1312; cf. CCC 364). Here "form" means not just bodily shape, but a principle of organization: The soul's activity unites a collection of cells, organs, and organ systems into an integrated organism. Death occurs "when the spiritual principle which ensures the unity of the individual can no longer exercise its functions in and upon the organism, whose elements, left to themselves, disintegrate" (Pope John Paul II, address to participants in a conference on determining the moment of death, December 14, 1989).

Catholic teaching does not specify a particular way to determine the moment of death but sees this as a question of medical fact. It does insist that death be ascertained by objective and reliable means, and that people be treated with the respect due to living human persons until it is morally certain they have died.

Brain-Oriented Criteria • Until recently, the medical diagnosis of death required testing for the irreversible cessation of respiration (breathing) and circulation (heartbeat and pulse). Today such diagnosis sometimes involves testing instead for the irreversible cessation of all brain functions. There

are two reasons for this trend. First, at a time when medical technology can sustain heartbeat and breathing artificially, the point at which the human body itself becomes irreversibly incapable of performing these functions may be obscured. Second, a demand for fresh organs for transplant purposes creates an incentive to determine death quickly and reliably in patients whose vital functions are being artificially sustained.

Nonetheless there is continuity between the use of brain-oriented criteria and the older means for determining death. When death is diagnosed by testing for respiration and circulation (as it still is today for patients who are not attached to life-support machinery when they die), physicians know that the cessation of these functions is irreversible only if it has lasted long enough to deprive the brain of the oxygen it needs to survive. Patients whose breathing and heartbeat have stopped can sometimes be revived — but not if the brain stem regulating and organizing these functions has also died. Therefore, it seems reasonable to test directly for the irreversible loss of all brain functions when diagnosing death.

This is not a matter of creating a new "definition" of death. Rather, physicians can use brain-oriented criteria to test for the same event that was always known as death.

A landmark event in American acceptance of such criteria was the issuance in 1981 of the report *Defining Death* by a federal advisory group, the President's Commission for the Study of Ethical Problems in Medicine and Biomedical and Behavioral Research. That commission had consulted with the American Medical Association, American Bar Association, and National Conference of Commissioners on Uniform State Laws to produce a model statute known as the Uniform Determination of Death Act. This statute declares that a person is dead if he or she has sustained "either (1) irreversible cessation of circulatory and respiratory functions, or (2) irreversible cessation of all functions of the entire brain, including the brain stem." It adds that a determination of death must be made "in accordance with accepted medical standards." This standard has been accepted in all fifty states by statute or court rulings.

The brain death standard has also been accepted by many Catholic philosophers and theologians, and in October, 1985, was endorsed by a working group of the Pontifical Academy of Sciences. These experts believe the "lower brain," or brain stem, plays a crucial role in coordinating circulatory and respiratory functions as well as other involuntary functions of the human body. When this organizing center is irretrievably lost, they argue, there is no longer a living human organism; what remains is only the cellular life of individual organs.

Some Catholic physicians and theologians question this approach. They say it overemphasizes the integrating role of the brain stem and even tends to equate the brain with the soul. They point out that a brain-dead body still has much in common with a living body, and may remain warm and even have a beating heart for some time after brain functions cease. They also observe that "irreversible cessation" of brain functions cannot be tested for directly, but must be inferred from the absence of such functions over a period of time. Indeed, conditions such as extreme cold or barbiturate overdose may produce a cessation of brain functions that can be reversed by good medical care; and physicians are warned to rule out such reversible conditions when they diagnose death using brain-oriented criteria. The brain is such a resilient organ, and its workings so poorly understood, that moral certainty regarding brain death may be possible chiefly in cases where the structural integrity of the brain has been destroyed.

At the very least, such cautions should encourage those using brain-oriented criteria to exercise extreme care so that death will never be confused with partial or reversible losses of brain function. By its nature, death is a reality that cannot be partial or (short of a special miracle) reversible.

Recent Negative Trends • Unfortunately, recent secular trends have been in the direction of greater medical and conceptual confusion about the diagnosis of death. Medical standards for the diagnosis vary, and recommended confirmatory tests are not always performed. There are indica-

tions that this is not simply a matter of clinical carelessness. Rather, some physicians believe criteria for diagnosing brain death are arbitrary in any event and may be changed depending on the need for a quick diagnosis and transplantable organs.

Some physicians and others have proposed changing brain-death criteria and corresponding laws, so that patients who have lost only their higher brain functions can be declared dead. Such a proposal aims not at updating the standards for diagnosing death but at a radical redefinition of death to encompass people who are really only unconscious, demented, or anencephalic. Such proposals are based not on any new medical data but on a demand for transplant organs combined with a dismissive view regarding the value of unconscious people's lives.

To use such tactics to obtain vital organs from helpless patients before they are really dead, thus killing them in the process, is to practice "more furtive, but no less serious and real forms of euthanasia" (Pope John Paul II, encyclical *The Gospel of Life, Evangelium Vitae*, 15 [1995]). The Church opposes such attempts to redefine life and death for utilitarian purposes.

It is troubling that some physicians who use brain-oriented criteria to diagnose death and retrieve organs may not themselves believe that brain death is the death of the person. Even if such a physician is doing no physical harm, because the patients are in fact dead, he or she is developing the character of someone who willingly kills patients to obtain their organs (cf. CCC 1005, 2296).

See: Body and Soul; Death; Euthanasia; Human Life, Dignity and Sanctity of; Human Person.

Suggested Readings: CCC 1016, 2276-2298. John Paul II, Address to Participants in a Conference on Determining the Moment of Death (December 14, 1989) (*Origins*, Vol. 19 [1990], pp. 523-525). Pius XII, "The Prolongation of Life," Allocution to an International Congress of Anesthesiologists (November 24, 1957). Pontifical Academy of Sciences, "The Artificial Prolongation of Life and the Exact Determination of the Moment of Death" (October 30, 1985). National Conference of Catholic Bishops, Committee for Pro-Life Activities, *Resource Paper: "Definition of Death" Legislation* (April, 1983). G. Grisez and J. Boyle, *Life and Death with Liberty and Justice: A Contribution to the Euthanasia Debate*, Ch. 3. Pontifical Council for Pastoral Assistance to Health Care Workers, *Charter for Health Care Workers*, pp. 83-91, 128-129 (1995).

Richard Doerflinger

DEONTOLOGY

The term "deontology" is used in two different ways. Sometimes it refers to any theory which holds that there are moral absolutes (i.e., exceptionless moral norms). In this sense, most natural law theories, including any natural law theory appealed to in Church documents, are "deontological." Then theories which *deny* that there are moral absolutes are classified as "teleological."

More often, however, the terms "teleological ethics" and "deontological ethics" are used in different senses. Then teleology refers to any theory that bases the ethical criterion on the human good, that is, on the ends to which human beings are naturally oriented (from the Greek term *telos*); while deontological theories are considered to be those that base the ethical criterion on something other than the human good, such as universalizability (theories derived from the thought of the German philosopher Immanuel Kant [1724-1804]) or intuition of duty or "value" (intuitionist theories). If the terms "teleology" and "deontology" are used in these latter senses, then natural law ethics is teleological, while deontological ethical theories are those based on something other than the human good. Here we understand deontology in this latter sense.

Deontology and Human Goods • In this sense of the term, natural law ethics is teleological rather than deontological. For example, Pope John Paul II explains the ethical criterion in this way: "If the object of the concrete action is not in harmony with the true good of the person, the choice of that

action makes our will and ourselves morally evil, thus putting us in conflict with our ultimate end, the supreme good, God himself" (encyclical *The Splendor of Truth, Veritatis Splendor*, 72 [1993]). The Second Vatican Council explains the natural law as a set of ethical norms based on what is truly perfective of human beings: "Human activity proceeds from man: it is also ordered to him. When he works, not only does he transform matter and society, but he fulfills himself" (*Pastoral Constitution on the Church in the Modern World, Gaudium et Spes*, 35; cf. *Veritatis Splendor*, 51, 35.)

This can be understood in the following way. In choosing an action, we choose it for a reason, that is, for the sake of some benefit we think it will help realize. That benefit may itself be a way of realizing some further benefit, and so on. But the chain of benefits cannot be infinite. So there must be some ultimate reasons for my choices, some benefits that I recognize as reasons for choosing that need no further support, that is to say, that are not mere means to some further benefit. What is the character of these ultimate reasons, these ultimate benefits? Clearly, at least in many cases they are aspects of the fulfillment of ourselves and of others for whom we care. We act for the sake of health, knowledge, aesthetic experience, friendship, both in ourselves and in our children, friends, and neighbors. Indeed, it seems that every choice must be in relation to some action with a natural appeal to me, that is, which in some way fulfills the potentialities that are part of me. Why else would this action rather than other possible ones be attractive or interesting?

Thus, when we choose, we cannot help but choose for the sake of some basic good, for ourselves or others we care for. That is what is central to a choice. But if that is so, then the difference between good choices and bad choices must concern how they relate to those same basic goods.

But there is a difficulty: Is moral uprightness itself a human good or not? Is moral uprightness something that perfects a human being? If not, then morality is a mere extrinsic constraint on human actions, and one can give no reason that can appeal to human persons why one should pursue moral uprightness. In that case, deontology has all the difficulties of legalism: It reduces human action to the passing of an arbitrary test. On the other hand, suppose one admits that moral uprightness is a perfection of human persons that one should pursue. Then it is hard to see why moral uprightness should be viewed as the only human perfection appropriate to pursue. Would it not be morally upright to pursue the other dimensions of human perfection, along with moral uprightness?

The solution lies in linking moral uprightness to the human goods perfective of human persons. To say moral norms are based on human goods in no way implies that it is ever right to choose to destroy or damage a basic good for the sake of promoting "greater good" in the long run. Rather, the moral norm is that one should energetically pursue various basic human goods and always remain open to and respectful of all of them.

See: Absolute Moral Norms; Human Goods; Legalism; Natural Law; Positivism; Proportionalism; Teleological Ethics.

Suggested Readings: CCC 1949-1960. G. Grisez, *The Way of the Lord Jesus*, Vol. 1, *Christian Moral Principles*, Chs. 4-8. G. Grisez and R. Shaw, *Fulfillment in Christ*, Chs. 4-8.

Patrick Lee

DESCENT INTO HELL

The fifth article of the Apostles' Creed, "He descended into hell" — the place of the dead — brings together three truths: Christ embraced a complete solidarity with the dead of all time; through his presence in the place of the dead, Sheol, he brings the objective power of his death to those waiting in Sheol for the light of glory; in his descent into Sheol he carries his obedience to his Father to the final step of accepting the spiritual punishment for human sin. Adam's sin visited loss of the vision of God upon the human race until the Son himself made amends.

The abode of the dead to which Christ descended is not the hell of eternal damnation but the place of the dead before heaven was opened to the just. Christ's self-emptying in obedience to his Father submits his obedient human nature to this spiritual desolation — he lives the Incarnation to the full.

St. Thomas Aquinas says the Eternal Word embraced the pangs of death in conformity with the will of the Father and in this obedience was truly free among the dead. He had no guilt to bind him; he gave himself in the absolute freedom of love to his Father. He did not descend to hell as subject to punishment but to suffer the punishment of those who were there. He assumes the penalties of our sins so that we might escape them. This descent completes one phase of salvation history and opens another.

The expression of this doctrine employs language that belongs to the universal symbolism of natural man and to the Incarnation. In saying Christ descends, the Church does not intend to describe a physical motion nor does she imply the existence of some kind of pit that received the souls of the dead. This usage merely conforms to an ordinary, everyday sense of the world, according to which light and heaven are located above, while darkness and the world of the grave are below. Similarly, as St. Cyril of Alexandria (c. 375-444) observes, "God the Word . . . is said to have come down from heaven, since he is now understood to be one with his own flesh." The language of descent describes the divine initiative of love and mercy in God's work of redemption.

The New Testament speaks of Christ's descent in several places. In Matthew 12:40, Jesus himself says: "For as Jonah was three days and three nights in the belly of the whale, so will the Son of man be three days and three nights in the heart of the earth." This is the grave, or Hades. But a voracious power is forced to recognize its impotence to hold its prey: "For to this end Christ died and lived again, that he might be Lord both of the dead and of the living" (Rom 14:9). The total disabling of the enemy coincides with a forcible entry into the innermost terrain of his power.

The Lord of the Apocalypse has gained power over death and Sheol: "I died and behold I am alive forevermore, and I have the keys of death and Hades" (Rv 1:18). Christ has absolute, full power, since he was dead (he has experienced death interiorly) and now lives eternally. In the power of his cross, the power of hell is already broken, the locked door of the grave is already burst open; yet it is still necessary that Christ lie in the grave and be with the dead so that the common resurrection of the just to life can follow. With the victory of Christ, Hades is thrown into the pool of fire, the second death (cf. Rv 20:10, 14-15; 21:8).

Jesus does not descend into the abode of the dead in glory. Between dying on Good Friday and rising from the dead on Easter Sunday, Christ is dead, and the obedience that takes him into the underworld is the obedience of the dead Christ. In his soul the Son experiences the passivity, the powerlessness, of every soul in Sheol. God the Son shares humankind's final disorder — death. He sanctifies the pain of the isolation in which each one lives his death and the passage from the familiar, personal, social world to this other world.

In the time before Christ, the dead went down to Sheol (in the New Testament, "Hades," or "hell," named in Acts 2:24). Sheol is the very opposite of solidarity, for there is no living communication there. In Sheol is the pit (Is 24:22), where one lives the listless existence of a shadow. "I am numbered with those who go down into the pit . . . whom you remember no longer and who are cut off from your care. . . . Your wrath lies heavy upon me. . . . Your furies have swept over me; your terrors have cut me off" (Ps 88:4-7, 16-17).

But God supplies the hope of resurrection (cf. Ez 37; Ps 16:8-11). Sheol is perceived as an intermediate state, with two separate dwellings, for the just and for the wicked (cf. Is 66:22-24, Wis 3:1-12, Dn 12:2-3). This corresponds to what we are told in the parable of the rich man and Lazarus (Lk 16:19-31, 23, 43) regarding the place of rest for the just and the place of torment for the unjust.

Suffering in Sheol • The Fathers of the Church confronted two theological questions: Who is in Sheol and what do they suffer? The suffering is the pain of the loss of the vision of God due to Adam's sin. In the logic of unexpiated original sin, all human beings who lived before Christ, even

our holy ancestors in faith, experienced in Sheol this loss of the vision of God.

Do the just and the unjust suffer the same pain of loss? Before Christ, there was already manifest in Israel, and in hidden form among other peoples, an order of salvation, directed toward Christ, which brought grace, justice, and forgiveness of sin. Sheol, from this vantage point, takes on a conditionality: The man who already believes in God, who has faith, hope, and charity, cannot be reconciled except through Christ; yet, since he has grace, he is really waiting for Christ to complete the life of Christ in him. In this case, we must speak of something like a conditional pain of loss. Thus the only one to experience it totally was the Redeemer himself. In solidarity with the dead of all time, he took the whole experience upon himself, thereby measuring the depths of that abyss.

One can sense a similar ambiguity regarding those who before Christ suffer the pains of what we now call hell. Is the torment of Gehenna more than being deprived of the vision of God? From the parable of Lazarus and the rich man and the threat of Gehenna (cf. Mt 5:22, 5:30, 7:19, 10:28), the punishment of Gehenna is seen to include punishment for serious sins against faith, hope, or charity by those who did not know Christ.

After the Resurrection of Our Lord, punishment follows upon rejection of Christ and sin against the Holy Spirit. There are, for example, many such warnings in the Letter to the Hebrews. Thus: "How much worse punishment do you think will be deserved by the man who has spurned the Son of God, and profaned the blood of the covenant by which he was sanctified, and outraged the Spirit of grace?" (Heb 10:26-29); "See that you do not refuse him who is speaking. For if they did not escape when they refused him who warned them on earth, much less shall we escape if we reject him who warns from heaven" (Heb 12:25). But if Christ has suffered, not only for the elect but for all human beings, then he has assumed even this final no toward the salvation that comes about in him. (Purgatory in the New Testament is reserved for those already saved by and in Christ but in need of purification before they can see God's face.)

Jesus is the resurrection and the life for all after he descends into the underworld of Sheol and is raised from the dead. In his Resurrection he opens the gates of heaven for the just who had been waiting to see the face of God. In doing so, he abolishes the condition of Sheol, or Hades, as loss of the vision of the glory of God.

His uniqueness as a Person is the ground of Christ's all-embracing solidarity with and redemptive substitution for men. He is the universal Word, through, with, and for whom all things were made. He is able to communicate something of his universality to the human nature united to his Divine Person without robbing it of its particularity. The Son's vicarious act of reconciliation is both exclusive and inclusive. Insofar as the sinless God-Man does what we cannot do, it is exclusive; but insofar as he does it for us, taking our place, it is inclusive. Jesus does this as head of the human race and as head of his Body, the Church.

Hans Urs von Balthasar, drawing on the mystical experience of Adrienne Von Speyr, offers an insight into what she saw Our Lord suffer on Holy Saturday: "It is out of obedience towards his Father that he descends into hell (or 'underworld,' Hades, Sheol). Because hell is (already in the Old Covenant) the place where God is absent, where there is no longer the light of faith, hope, love, of participation in God's life; hell is what the judging God condemned and cast out of his creation; it is filled with all that is irreconcilable with God, from which he turns away for all eternity. . . . And yet this hell is a final mystery of the Father as the creator (who made allowances for the freedom of man). And so in this darkness, the incarnate Son learns 'experientially' what until then was 'reserved' for the Father. Hell, seen in this way, is, in its final possibility, a trinitarian event. On Good Friday the Father hands the key to it over to the Son" (*First Glance at Adrienne Von Speyr*, p. 66).

See: Death; Hell; Jesus Christ, God and Man; Jesus Christ, Life of; Last Things; Limbo; Purgatory; Redemption; Resurrection of the Dead.

Suggested Readings: CCC 631-635. John Paul II, *Christological Catechesis.* L. Bouyer, *The Eternal Son.*

Richard Malone

DESPAIR

The first commandment steers us away from the deliberate sin against hope that is despair: hopelessness. In the clutches of its emotional exaggeration, "man ceases to hope for his personal salvation from God, for help in attaining it or for the forgiveness of his sins"; such desperation is a diabolical lie "contrary to God's goodness, to his justice — for the Lord is faithful to his promises — and to his mercy" (CCC 2091). Human wrongdoing is so blown out of proportion that it sadly eclipses God's infinite love, pardoning patience, and unlimited understanding.

Despair is not to be confused with pessimism, dread, discouragement, or timidity. Neither is it a mere passive state or passing mood. Despair involves a positive act of the will whereby a person deliberately and completely gives up any expectation of ever reaching eternal life. Presupposed is a judgment that deems salvation as definitely out of reach. This dead-end conclusion is motivated by the emotionally wrought persuasion that one's sins are too great to be forgiven, or that it is too hard for human nature to cooperate with divine grace, or that God is unwilling to aid the weakness or pardon the offenses of his creatures.

To be sure, despair is not so bad as hatred of God or formal heresy. Still, its power for wreaking havoc in the human soul is fundamentally far greater than other sins. Hopelessness cuts off the way of escape: recourse to God's tender mercy and graceful favors. Those who pitiably fall under its spell, as a matter of fact, often surrender themselves to all sorts of self-defeating misbehavior.

All this, perhaps, because at a crucial moment the despairing person failed to reject corrosive self-pity. Christ forewarns: "Pray, lest you enter into temptation" (Lk 22:40).

See: Final Perseverance; Hatred of God; Hope; Presumption; Religion, Virtue of; Tempting God.

DETACHMENT

In the moral field, detachment is a relatively new and subtle concept, as befits changed circumstances. Historically, until the second half of the twentieth century, society had always been very bottom-heavy, economically speaking. That is to say, eking out a living as best they could, have-nots traditionally vastly outnumbered the haves: some eighteen or nineteen out of every twenty. Whether or not peasants and laborers embraced their involuntary poverty to further their Christian life, quite appropriately the teaching Church for nineteen centuries largely applied Jesus' severe warning against riches to those who could afford to surround themselves with luxuries.

When the call to enter the clerical or religious state evoked a positive response, then was the moment to renounce worldly ways and commit oneself to live the virtue and actual privations of evangelical poverty, often sealed with a vow or its approximation. Meanwhile, their pastors hoped that the disadvantaged would at least make a virtue of their straits and not overly covet others' belongings or envy those better off than themselves. (To those who may not know where their next meal is coming from, one typically does not preach poverty but abandonment to providence.) The unrepentant rich were considered spiritually at risk; now and then one of these would undergo a conversion leading him to devote much of his wealth to the Church or the poor.

So, with regard to earthly goods, the dispositions and practices commended by the Church historically have been patient tolerance of unwilled indigence, virtuous commitment to live in other-worldly circumstances akin to actual poverty, and generous almsgiving. For all practical purposes, wealth was seen as an almost insurmountable obstacle to salvation; if not an evil in itself, abundance was seen as the closest thing to it. Conversely, was not scarcity well-nigh divine, certainly Christ-like, and almost as certainly virtuous? "Money" had been branded "the root of all evil" (1 Tm 6:10). Had not, moreover, Christ uncompromisingly declared that "it is easier for a camel to pass through the eye of a needle than for a rich man to enter the kingdom of heaven" (Mt 19:24)?

The Rise of the Middle Class • In modern times, however, the phenomenon of creating and spreading wealth began in earnest, begetting a middle class that, at least in the wealthy industrialized nations, occupies two-thirds or three-fourths of the economic spectrum. Neither rich nor poor, somewhat disinclined to Church service as priest or nun, while desirous or capable only of rather modest Church support and alms, how were these newly circumstanced faithful to be coached in handling an ever larger share of secular goods?

Meanwhile, for these and other reasons the Church was moving away from a literalist interpretation of the scriptural strictures against wealth. At second glance, paupers could be consumed with greed and avarice as much as the legendary robber barons, while at least some millionaires, amid the trappings of affluence and even opulence, could equal the spirit of poverty attained by vowed religious. With respect to the commitment of the latter to a life of poverty, the Church also sadly noted that some who observed the law's letter were slow to appropriate or interiorize poverty's spirit.

Amid all these socioeconomic changes, two other factors deserve mention. As Aristotle had taught and the medieval Scholastics echoed and amplified, a certain amount of wealth, property, security, and ease fosters an authentically good life of virtue, leisure, and contemplation. This was evident as more and more people adopted a middle-class standard of living, wherein the right to private property and the freedom that goes with it impose a set of corresponding duties requiring self-discipline and a host of attitudes and actions conducive to civic peace and personal virtue.

The other development is somewhat harder to grasp. When the world was socially and politically static, there was relatively little opportunity for either ascending or descending the ladder of wealth. With the economic "pie" of fixed size, one could only grow richer at the expense of another's impoverishment. But with the advent of science and technology, and the revolution, first, in industry and somewhat later in agriculture, it became plain that the pie was not fixed. Wealth could be created, and a rising economic tide could lift all but the least seaworthy of boats.

Of course those who spurred this progress could be unconscionably greedy (thus endangering their personal salvation), but the net social effects — jobs, broadened prosperity, labor-saving technological breakthroughs, and so on — were largely beneficial to society. As Aristotle foretold, as more and more people had a vital stake in their own property, their neighborhood, their community, state, and nation (not to mention the increasingly interlocked and mutually interdependent "global village"), more and more people had access to this minimum of well-being that favors personal, familial, economic, and social goods. While civilizational progress brings in its wake a new set of challenges, including moral ones, growing numbers of citizens today nevertheless have been freed from previous time and money restraints and are able to choose how they will organize their lives and spend their time. While for some that enhanced freedom unfortunately spells license, for most it represents a situation more conducive to morality than was hand-to-mouth subsistence. Increased and more widely spread wealth may not guarantee virtue, yet it does seem to have something of the character of a condition for virtuous living.

For all these reasons, the time was definitely ripe to reformulate the Christian attitude toward prosperity and abundance in more spiritual, interior terms. Physical deprivation was no longer seen as necessarily good, just as actual wealth need not be necessarily bad. What is morally crucial is to save our deepest allegiance for what is absolutely important and so to shun idolizing money and mere things, whether actually possessed or merely desired. The moral call is for attaching the heart to God, while detaching it from creatures, however comfortable and even helpful.

Thus does the *Catechism of the Catholic Church* describe this new virtue of detachment as "poverty of heart." It says: "Jesus enjoins his disciples to prefer him to everything and everyone. . . . The precept of detachment from riches is obligatory for entrance into the Kingdom of heaven"

(2544). And the *Catechism* goes on to add: "The Lord grieves over the rich, because they find their consolation in the abundance of goods [*Lk* 6:24]. 'Let the proud seek and love earthly kingdoms, but blessed are the poor in spirit for theirs is the Kingdom of heaven' [St. Augustine, *De serm. Dom. in monte* 1, 1, 3: PL 34, 1232]. Abandonment to the providence of the Father in heaven frees us from anxiety about tomorrow. Trust in God is a preparation for the blessedness of the poor. They shall see God" (2547).

See: Avarice; Covetousness; Envy; Property; Social Doctrine; Social Justice.

Suggested Readings: CCC 2401-2449, 2544-2550. Vatican Council II, *Pastoral Constitution on the Church in the Modern World, Gaudium et Spes*, 68-72. John Paul II, *The Hundredth Year, Centesimus Annus*.

Dennis Helming

DETERRENCE

Deterrence has been defined as "dissuasion of a potential adversary from initiating an attack or conflict, often by the threat of unacceptable retaliatory damage" (National Conference of Catholic Bishops, collective pastoral letter *The Challenge of Peace*, 163 [1983]). As a military strategy, deterrence is summed up in an ancient Roman maxim, "If you want peace, prepare for war." During the Cold War, the United States and the Soviet Union acted on this maxim, maintaining an unsteady peace by threatening massive nuclear retaliation if attacked.

Yet such threats are, at best, precarious and inadequate ways to maintain peace. True peace arises from mutual respect and recognition of the rights of all people. This is expressed in another maxim: "If you want peace, work for justice."

Nuclear deterrence poses an especially serious moral dilemma, since nuclear weapons can destroy entire cities with their populations in a single attack. Such an act of war is condemned by Church teaching (cf. Vatican Council II, *Pastoral Constitution on the Church in the Modern World, Gaudium et Spes*, 80: "Every act of war directed to the indiscriminate destruction of whole cities or vast areas with their inhabitants is a crime against God and man, which merits firm and unequivocal condemnation"). Because good and evil reside primarily in the will, it is also wrong to intend such an attack, even conditionally (e.g., "If you slaughter our civilians, we will slaughter yours"). That such a threat may be made for a good cause — to prevent war altogether — does not justify an evil means. Yet a nation relying on nuclear deterrence may increase the risk of war if it shows ambivalent intentions or weakens its retaliatory forces.

Pope John Paul II voiced reluctant acceptance of nuclear deterrence as a short-term strategy in a 1982 message to the United Nations: "In current conditions 'deterrence' based on balance, certainly not as an end in itself but as a step on the way toward progressive disarmament, may still be judged morally acceptable. Nonetheless in order to ensure peace, it is indispensable not to be satisfied with this minimum which is always susceptible to the real danger of explosion." Similarly, the U.S. bishops' 1983 pastoral letter on peace expresses "a strictly conditioned moral acceptance of nuclear deterrence," while insisting that deterrence is not "adequate as a long-term basis for peace" (*The Challenge of Peace*, 186).

See: Double Effect; Freedom, Human; Human Goods; War.

DETRACTION AND CALUMNY

The old saying "If you can't say something nice, don't say anything at all" is an injunction against detraction. As the *Catechism of the Catholic Church* makes clear, detraction is nothing more or less than saying damaging things about others, "tearing people down" (cf. 2477). It is not a lie, however. If, for example, one were gratuitously to disclose the fact that Johnson is a member of the Ku Klux Klan, the evil in doing so would consist in the fact that revealing this truth detracts from Johnson's reputation. Because everyone has the right to a good name, detraction is usually an offense against justice and charity.

Obviously there are cases where it is right to disclose unflattering truths about others. Detraction does not concern such cases. To continue with our example, if Johnson were running for high office, citizens would need to be aware of his racism in order to cast their votes intelligently. In the same way, it is not detraction to report a teenager's drug use to parents or civil authorities.

Unlike detraction, which involves true statements, calumny is knowingly lying to harm another's reputation. The lie may be either blunt ("I saw him take the money") or insinuated ("Let us not be hasty in concluding that my opponent is guilty of stealing"). It can be directed at individuals or at whole groups: Racial and gender stereotypes can be a form of calumny. Like detraction, calumny can be either venially or gravely sinful, depending on circumstances. A scientist's false charge that a colleague altered data, for example, could ruin a promising career; at the same time, the lie would compound the evil of damage to reputation that simple detraction entails.

See: False Witness; Lying; Slander; Truthfulness.

DEVELOPMENT OF DOCTRINE

Jesus Christ is God made man, come to redeem us and to reveal all we have to believe and do, in order to merit salvation. "I am the truth," he said (Jn 14:6), the truth that will set us free (cf. Jn 8:32).

After the Resurrection and Ascension of Jesus and throughout the lifetime of the Apostles, the Holy Spirit continued this revealing of the truth that saves. Public Divine Revelation ended with the death of the last Apostle. There has been and will be no new Revelation added to that already given to the Church, which was commissioned by Jesus (Mt 28:18-20) to preserve this doctrine of salvation and bring it to the world, under the guidance of Peter and the other Apostles (and their successors in each age: the Pope and the rest of the episcopal college).

Christian truth thus is something *given*; it precedes us, has been handed down to us, and must be passed on by us to those who come after. All the saving doctrine revealed by Jesus Christ has been in the Church's possession from the start. All is there; but the human mind does not necessarily understand all the content and riches of this truth, nor does it necessarily grasp its practical consequences, especially in its application to apparently new moral issues.

The Church therefore possesses the truth; but, under the continuing guidance of the Holy Spirit, she can constantly enter on a fuller awareness of what she possesses, achieving a "better understanding of Revelation" (CCC 892). "Thanks to the assistance of the Holy Spirit, the understanding of both the realities and the words of the heritage of faith is able to grow in the life of the Church" (CCC 94). Reflection on these truths helped lead John Henry Newman into the Catholic Church and resulted in his classic study *An Essay on the Development of Christian Doctrine* (1845).

Need for Development • The rich content of God's truth is too great and many-faceted for the human mind to comprehend fully. Good critics, according to their talents, can gradually perceive new values in a literary or artistic masterpiece, values that had perhaps escaped earlier appreciation. Yet they were already present in the masterpiece. So, in that divine masterpiece which is the life, work, and teaching of Jesus Christ, the truths remain the same; but time, reflection, and prayer give the perspective to see new aspects or values. Growing light is cast on the same truth, and growing inspiration emanates from it.

Revelation not only offers truths to enlighten our mind ("He who *believes* and is baptized will be saved" [Mk 16:16]), it also proposes practical principles to guide our conduct ("[M]ake disciples of all nations . . . teaching them to *observe* all that I have commanded you" [Mt 28:19-20; emphasis added]). We can therefore expect development to occur not only in the area of speculative theology but also in that of principles of action. While the moral message of Christ does not change, positive or negative developments in human societies can call for new applications of this message. The problems to which the Church gives an answer

may appear to be new (in the field of demography, for instance), and the answers may therefore also appear as new; but the doctrine they reflect or are drawn from is not new. It is Christ's. Moreover, the reason why we should believe these teachings come from Christ is not new, nor is it invented by the Church. It comes from Our Lord himself: "Whoever hears you, hears me" (Lk 10:16).

God does not contradict himself. A truth cannot develop into its opposite. Hence a major rule governing genuine development of doctrine is that it must always follow a line of continuity: "in the same sense, with the same meaning" (*eodem sensu, eademque sententia* [St. Vincent of Lerins]). A "development" that *changed* the meaning of a doctrine would be a corruption, not a development.

Development of doctrine, therefore, means *our* development in understanding. Our comprehension grows; revealed truth remains as always. That it remain the same, far from making it a static message, is the condition of its being dynamic, with the capacity to transform. The "given" character of Revelation would in no way justify regarding it as something inert or lifeless. The truth of Christ, which the Church possesses, is an infinite treasure of splendor and inspiration, filled therefore with a dynamism that can change persons and societies. Each age, each Christian, faces the challenge of seizing its riches without omissions, highlighting new aspects to its beauty, and responding to the further inspiration thus discovered, acting as a reflector of these truths to others.

Since development of doctrine means a deeper and more inspiring understanding of the teaching Jesus Christ entrusted to his Church, it is a constantly enriching process. "Development" that impoverished the faith (by reducing a sense of wonder and adoration in worship, for instance) could never represent true development.

A Process Open to All • This enrichment is not just for theology; it is a process that not only scholars and experts can appreciate and take part in. Each individual Christian should be constantly growing in awareness of the beauty and power of the faith, hence drawing the inspiration to sanctify his or her daily life and work. This developing grasp of doctrine should lead not only to a more informed participation in the liturgy but also to a development in the personal devotional life of each one.

It is natural that each person be specially moved by some particular truth or truths drawn from the great treasury of Christian doctrine, putting them in a special place in his or her spiritual life: the Eucharist, the Passion of Jesus, the many motives for honoring Mary, Mother of God and our Mother, the Communion of the Saints. Each Christian is free to have, and wise to develop, a preferred area of devotion.

Nevertheless, many people with a particular devotion fail to develop their grasp of the rich doctrine behind the aspect of Christian belief that attracts them. If they deepen this grasp by appropriate reading (papal encyclicals or other documents of the Magisterium, solid and well-recommended books), their devotional life will become stronger and more constant, less dependent on feelings, and at the same time a deeper source of inspiration and consolation. To discover "the unsearchable riches of Christ" (Eph 3:8) should be the ambition of each Christian.

There is no contradiction or opposition between development of doctrine and infallibility. Infallibility relates not to the fullness of understanding of revealed doctrine, but to the truth (the freedom from error) of the Church's way of proposing it. Development means that the Church can always acquire a deeper understanding of Revelation, being protected by the charism of infallibility from misunderstanding or misrepresenting those truths entrusted to it.

See: Divine Revelation; Infallibility; Magisterium.

Suggested Readings: CCC 65-66, 94, 892. Vatican Council II, *Dogmatic Constitution on Divine Revelation, Dei Verbum*, Ch. II. J. Newman, *An Essay on the Development of Christian Doctrine.*

Cormac Burke

DEVIL AND EVIL SPIRITS

In ages when belief in a supernatural world was widespread, religious believers were perhaps too ready to see the devil at work in every malady and misfortune. Today many no longer believe in the devil and even scoff at those who do. That the devil and the other fallen angels find the current environment of disbelief favorable to their cause is a central theme of C.S. Lewis's psychological masterpiece, *The Screwtape Letters.*

It is a tenet of Catholic faith that not a few angels, abusing their freedom and disregarding the truth known to their penetrating intellects, fell into sin, becoming evil and seducers into evil. "The devil and the other demons," said the Fourth Lateran Council in 1215, "were created by God good according to their nature, but they made themselves evil by their own doing." They consequently became perpetual enemies of God and were condemned to an eternal punishment; now they unceasingly seek to entice human beings to share the same fate. The *Catechism of the Catholic Church* says the demons "radically and irrevocably *rejected* God and his reign"; their sin is unforgivable, not because God puts limits to his mercy, but rather because their fully illuminated choice was made once for all and is therefore irreformable (CCC 392; cf. 393).

The Catholic Church has always warned humanity against diabolical deception to sin. Not only have devils exercised power over humans in past ages, but, even after being overcome by Christ, they are still able to exercise the power to tempt humanity (cf. Jn 8:44, 47; 1 Pt 5:8-9; 1 Jn 3:8, 10). Scripture depicts them as free, intelligent beings. The devil speaks in tempting Christ (cf. Mt 4:3-10; Lk 4:3-13); he prompts Judas to betray Jesus (cf. Jn 13:2); he wages battle against God's kingdom by sowing cockle (cf. Mt 13:19, 25, 39; Lk 22:53); he tempts men with guile (cf. 1 Cor 7:5; 2 Cor 2:11; 1 Thes 3:5); he is the prince of this world (cf. Jn 12:31, 14:30, 16:11); he displays his power in the darkness of idolatry (cf. Acts 26:18; Col 1:13); he fosters the spread of false teachings (cf. 1 Tm 4:1). The temptation that gave rise to original sin (cf. Gn 3:1ff.) is attributed to him (cf. Wis 2:23ff.; Rv 12:9); in the Old Testament he is mainly described as the tempter of humans and as their accuser before God (cf. Job 1:6ff.; 1 Chr 21:1; Zach 3:1ff.). The First Epistle of Peter makes it clear what these powerful fiends intend: "Be sober, be watchful! For your adversary the devil, as a roaring lion, goes about seeking someone to devour. Resist him, steadfast in the faith" (1 Pt 5:8-9).

Satan is "a liar and the father of lies" (Jn 8:44). In particular, he wants human beings to deny the existence of personal sin, as many in fact do today. That is why the Church invokes St. Michael the archangel "against the wickedness and snares of the devil" (traditional prayer to St. Michael). Though his tactics may vary, the devil does not desist from his efforts to promote evil both in individuals and in society, concealing his wiles at times even under the guise of noble purposes. It may be that he does the most mischief by encouraging people to fear, distrust, and defensively keep their distance from God, their all-loving Father.

Yet Satan is but a creature, of limited might (cf. CCC 395). He cannot hinder the progressive spread and consolidation of God's kingdom. He is allowed to work in the world out of hatred for God; his action may even cause grave harm (largely spiritual, but even, indirectly, physical). Yet God in his loving providence, which ever strongly, gently, and undeterredly guides human and cosmic history, permits this diabolical activity, a permission the Church calls "a great mystery" (CCC 395); and "we know that in everything God works for good with those who love him" (Rom 8:28).

The last petition of the Our Father — "deliver us from evil" — while constituting a plea for deliverance from *all* evils (CCC 2854), also deals not with evil in the abstract, "but refers to a person, Satan, the Evil One, the angel who opposes God," whose name in Greek (*dia-bolos*) means one who "throws himself across God's plan" (CCC 2851). Through his deceits sin and death invaded the world; when Satan is definitively defeated at the end of history, all creation will be "freed from the

corruption of sin and death," as Eucharistic Prayer IV says.

See: Angels; Diabolical Possession; Freedom, Human; Original Sin; Providence; Sin.

Suggested Readings: CCC 391-395, 2851-2854. C. Lewis, *The Screwtape Letters.*

Dennis Helming

DEVOTIONS

Devotion is an affective response flowing from the virtue of religion, which is related or annexed to justice because it inclines us to render to God what is due him as Creator, governor, and final end of all things. Devotion is defined as a certain, ready will to give oneself to whatever concerns the service of God. It is an act of the will whereby a person offers himself to God, to serve him (St. Thomas Aquinas, *Summa Theologiae*, II-II, q. 81, a. 5; q. 82, a. 1 c., ad 1).

Since all Christ's faithful need to exercise their participation in his priesthood, "all Christians, in the conditions, duties and circumstances of their life and through all these, will sanctify themselves more and more if they receive all things with faith from the hand of the heavenly Father and cooperate with the divine will, thus showing forth in that temporal service the love with which God loved the world" (Vatican Council II, *Dogmatic Constitution on the Church, Lumen Gentium*, 41). The laity, consecrated to Christ and anointed by the Holy Spirit (*Lumen Gentium*, 34), have a specific mission in carrying out the Church's task of sanctification (cf. *Lumen Gentium*, 30-38; *Pastoral Constitution on the Church in the Modern World, Gaudium et Spes*, 33-39, 43; *Decree on the Apostolate of the Laity, Apostolicam Actuositatem*, 4-8).

"Devotions," actions that excite the proper disposition of will and aid in the affective response which marks *devotio*, can be exercises of piety like those the Church so strongly recommends to clerics and religious: for instance, daily mental prayer, examination of conscience and frequent confession, or the annual closed retreat. Devotions can also be concrete manifestations of private piety, worshipful acts done on one's own account as spontaneous manifestations of filial affection for our Father God. Examples might include visits to the Blessed Sacrament, recitation of the Angelus or the daily Rosary, and making the Way of the Cross.

Some of these devotions (e.g., the Angelus, the Rosary) developed as a sort of layperson's Breviary, in the sense that certain devotions embody to a high degree two basic principles of the Liturgy of the Hours: concentration upon important moments in Our Lord's life and prayer at specific moments in time. This surely helps explain why such devotions have been so widespread during the course of many centuries. Devotions must of course embody a correct theology, centering attention upon the work of salvation that comes to us from the Father, through the Son, in the Holy Spirit.

Devotions and Liturgy • The best devotions express in a simple, popular manner the religious concepts and sentiments embodied in the liturgical year. A convenient way of regarding devotions will thus proceed from their respective proximity or resemblance to the official public liturgy of the *ecclesia orans*, the praying Church. Thus some devotions imitate the liturgy in their collective expression, for example, solemn processions (as at Eucharistic congresses) or adoration of the Blessed Sacrament publicly exposed. The liturgist will never weary of recalling that, as Pope Pius XII pointed out, to be content with the "fraternal meal of the Christian community" while holding in lower esteem the presence and the action of Christ in the tabernacle, would be to belittle the importance of him who performs the sacrifice.

Other devotions will embody some particular spiritual activity by which the faithful take part in the celebration of liturgical worship. One thinks, for example, of novenas, which are nine days (three days are a "triduum") of public or private devotion and special prayer for a particular intention (cf. Acts 1:13ff.) or of May devotions to Our Lady and June devotions in honor of the Sacred Heart. Such devotions, since they foster frequent confession and proper participation in the Eucharistic Sacrifice and in the divine banquet, as well as meditation on the mysteries of our redemption and

imitation of the examples of saints in heaven, have been "approved and praised again and again by the Apostolic See and by the bishops" (Pope Pius XII, *Mediator Dei*).

Finally, some devotions are simple, spontaneous expressions of individual piety in which the soul opens itself in a personal way before God. Such pious practices are frequently propagated by preachers or missionaries, or spread by a particular religious institute, sometimes in connection with private revelations to individuals.

Devotions of this type can help to popularize certain aspects of Christian piety and make them more accessible. Most spiritual writers would agree, however, that such concentration of the interior activity of the spirit upon a concrete, partial point should be regulated intelligently and prudently so as to remain "mere optional means of obtaining true interior devotion" (*Liturgy and Spirituality*; cf. Canon 839.2). Such means will often reflect diverse points of emphasis rightly stressed by various religious orders and traditions, within the larger perspective of Catholic spirituality. But there can be no question that, according to the mind of the Church, private devotions are subordinate to the official liturgy of the praying Church, which "by its very nature is far superior to any of them" (Vatican Council II, *Constitution on the Sacred Liturgy, Sacrosanctum Concilium*, 13).

See: Eucharistic Devotion; Liturgical Year; Liturgy; Liturgy of the Hours; Marian Devotion; Prayer; Private Revelation; Religion, Virtue of; Rosary.

Suggested Readings: CCC 1140, 1178, 1378, 2628. Vatican Council II, *Constitution on the Sacred Liturgy, Sacrosanctum Concilium*, 9-13. Pius XII, *On the Sacred Liturgy, Mediator Dei*. G. Braso, *Liturgy and Spirituality*, pp. 194-208. M. Walsh, *Dictionary of Catholic Devotions*.

Robert A. Skeris

DIABOLICAL POSSESSION

Diabolical possession is a tangible proof of the existence of the devil and a visible manifestation of his power. It is for that reason the strongest argument against those who deny the existence of the devil and of evil spirits. It is, however, a very rare phenomenon and is easily simulated by certain pathological states. Discernment is as necessary for verifying diabolical possession as it is for investigating the signs of mystical experience and sanctity. Indeed, whether it be a question of mystical phenomena or diabolical infestation, the incredulous will readily diagnose the symptoms as schizophrenia, epilepsy, hysteria, paranoia, or manic depression.

If one admits the existence of the devil, one must also admit the possibility of diabolical activity in our world. This is not something in the realm of possibility; it is a fact. There are seven incidents in the Gospel that deal with diabolical possession. Three of them are passing references to exorcisms (Mt 8:32-33, 12:22; Mk 16:9; Lk 8:2). The remaining four are described in greater detail: the demoniac of Capernaum (Mk 1:21-28; Lk 4:31-37); the demoniacs of Gadara (Mt 8:28-34; Mk 5:1-20; Lk 8:26-29); the daughter of the Canaanite woman (Mt 15:21-28; Mk 7:24-30); and the epileptic demoniac (Mt 17:14-20; Mk 9:13-28; Lk 9:37-43). In the time of Christ, there was a great deal of diabolical infestation, perhaps more than at any other time in history; conversely, there were numerous charismatic gifts at the beginning of Christian evangelization.

Because of the exaggerated credulity of some Christians, the Church throughout the centuries has issued guidelines to correct abuses and to provide criteria for discernment and therapy. Documents were issued by the Council of Elvira (305), the Council of Cartagena (398), the First Council of Orange (441), the Eleventh Council of Toledo (657), the First Council of Milan (1565), the Fourth Council of Milan (1576), and the Council of Salerno (1596). (Note that these were local councils, not ecumenical councils.)

Diabolical Activity • The activity of the devil is prompted by his hatred of God; so much so that he is, in a sense, the very personification of evil and always acts for an evil purpose. St. Paul tells us: "Put on the armor of God so that you may be able to stand firm against the tactics of the devil. Our battle is not against human forces but against the principalities and powers, the rulers of this world of darkness, the evil spirits in regions above" (Eph 6:12).

Diabolical activity can be divided into two types: ordinary and extraordinary. Ordinary diabolical activity occurs when the devil incites a person to sin. It falls under the general classification of temptation, but it should be noted that not all temptations are diabolical in origin. Extraordinary diabolical activity is divided into three types: local infestation, diabolical obsession, and diabolical possession.

Local infestation occurs when the devil has direct and immediate contact with inanimate objects, plants, or animals in order to exert an evil influence or even physical harm on persons. Sometimes a specific place or locality becomes the scene of diabolical infestation.

Diabolical obsession (also called personal infestation) occurs when the devil focuses his power and activity on an individual human being. He operates from the outside, on the external or internal sense faculties, but he can never gain control of the intellect and will of the individual. Diabolical obsession may be experienced as a vehement temptation to sin or as a furious physical attack on the individual.

Diabolical possession occurs when the devil invades the body of a person and exercises despotic dominion over the organs and faculties of the individual, manipulating them as one would a puppet. His dominion, however, is restricted to the body; he cannot invade the soul or gain control over the spiritual faculties of intellect and will. Authentic instances of diabolical possession are rare; for that reason one should always look first for an explanation based on natural causes.

Two factors are involved in diabolical possession: the presence of the devil in the body of a human being and the exercise of diabolical power. As a purely spiritual being, the devil is not limited by time or place; he is where he acts. Consequently, a human being could be invaded by several devils at the same time or the devil could act upon several human beings at the same time. As regards the exercise of diabolical power in cases of possession, there are periods of calm that alternate with periods of crisis. During the period of calm, there is nothing at all to indicate the presence of the devil except, in some cases, the sudden appearance of a strange chronic illness for which there is no diagnosis and no cure. Moreover, the presence of the devil is not necessarily continuous; he may come and go.

Possession by the devil is openly manifested during the periods of crisis. There will be seizures and convulsions, blasphemy, obscene words or actions, fits of anger or irreverence. The victims usually are not conscious of what they are doing, and they have no recollection when they come out of the period of crisis. However, there have been cases when the victim was fully aware of the activity of the devil during a period of crisis and witnessed with horror the devil's manipulation of the body. But even if the victim were fully aware of the devil's activity, there is never any question of sin or moral responsibility on the part of the victim.

Principles for Discernment • The basic guiding principle for discernment is the same for the diagnosis of apparent diabolical possession and for the examination of alleged supernatural phenomena: Extraordinary phenomena cannot be attributed to the devil or to a supernatural cause until all natural causality has been excluded.

A second fundamental principle can be stated as follows: A possessed person will manifest strong revulsion and even violent hatred for anything sacred. The reason for this is that the devil has such a vehement hatred for God that he will do all in his power to keep the possessed person from anything sacred or religious. It should be noted, however, that although the possessed person will exhibit extreme agitation, violent hatred, and convulsive movements, those are not the actions of the victim, but the devil working through the possessed person. It is as if an entirely different person has emerged; and that is precisely what has happened.

This alone is not infallible proof of diabolical possession, however, because it could proceed from a pathological condition. Nevertheless, this particular symptom is always a basis for a conjecture of the possibility of diabolical possession. If it is not present, there can be no question of diabolical possession. But other signs must be verified as well, and the more numerous they are, the greater is the likelihood that one is dealing with an authentic case of possession.

The *Roman Ritual*, first published in 1614, stated that if a person exhibited a hatred and aversion to the sacred as well as certain specified symptoms, those phenomena were "indicative" of diabolical possession. The three requisite symptoms were: to speak or understand a previously unknown language (glossolalia), to identify objects at a great distance or hidden from view, and to exhibit strength far beyond the age or condition of the individual. Today, however, the verification of these three phenomena can no longer be accepted as definitive proof of diabolical possession. Advances in psychiatric and parapsychological research have shown that in many cases any one of the foregoing symptoms may have a natural but pathological explanation. This greatly lessens the diagnostic value of the symptoms listed in the *Roman Ritual*.

Still, the *Roman Ritual* did not actually state that aversion to the sacred and verification of the three phenomena could be taken as definitive proof of diabolical possession. Rather, both the *Ritual* of 1614 and the revised edition of 1952 state that "the priest should not believe too readily that a person is possessed by an evil spirit; but he ought to ascertain the signs by which a person possessed can be distinguished from one who is suffering from some illness, especially one of a psychological nature" (from the 1964 version). Moreover, after listing the three specific signs, the *Ritual* adds: ". . . and various other indications which, when taken together as a whole, build up the evidence." All of which proves that the *Ritual* does not specify any signs or phenomena as definitive proof of diabolical possession.

Because of the similarity of psychiatric, parapsychological, and diabolical phenomena, one can readily appreciate the reason for insisting that one should never attribute extraordinary phenomena to a preternatural cause as long as a natural explanation is possible. No longer can diabolical possession be asserted simply on the basis of external extraordinary phenomena.

C. Balducci, an outstanding expert in demonology, has formulated the following diagnostic criterion, based on the *Roman Ritual*: "One should not readily believe that a person is possessed, since the condition may be a simulation, a psychiatric abnormality or a so-called paranormal phenomenon. The presence in one and the same individual of the twofold phenomenology (oriented, obviously, to a strong aversion to the sacred) is a powerful indication of possession. The certainty of possession will be evident from the particular tonality of the above-mentioned manifestations; that is, a tonality that is quite distinct from the modalities that characterize phenomena that have a natural cause. The certainty of possession can be further confirmed by the presence of other phenomena that it would be difficult to classify as psychiatric or paranormal."

See: Devil and Evil Spirits; Discernment; Exorcism; Hatred of God; Temptation.

Suggested Readings: CCC 392-395, 397-398, 550. *Roman Ritual*, trans. P. Weller, pp. 636-662. C. Balducci, *The Devil*. A. Royo and J. Aumann, *The Theology of Christian Perfection*, pp. 249-259, 624-636, 651-853.

Jordan Aumann, O.P.

DISCERNMENT

Both for the direction of souls and for the investigation of extraordinary mystical phenomena, it is necessary to distinguish the various spirits or impulses under which a person may act or be acted upon. In the early days of the Church, St. Paul admonished the Christians: "Do not stifle the Spirit. Do not despise prophecies. Test everything; retain what is good" (1 Thes 5:19-21). Similarly, we read: "Do not trust every spirit, but put the spirits to a test and see if they belong to God, because many false prophets have appeared in the land" (1 John 4:1).

The purpose of discernment is precisely that: to discern with certitude whether a person is acting under his or her own individualistic spirit, the Spirit of God, or the spirit of darkness and the devil. Discernment is especially called for when it is a question of extraordinary phenomena for which there is no ready explanation. What serves as a starting point in the investigation is the fact that there are only three possible causes of the phenomena in question: God's intervention, the devil, or some natural cause. There is a strong tendency to attribute every extraordinary phenomenon directly to God or the devil, but that is much too simplistic a response. The dividing line between supernatural, natural, and diabolical is not always clearly defined, but it is possible to state some general principles that govern each of these three spirits.

Natural, Supernatural, and Diabolical • Although we do not know with certainty all that nature is capable of producing, we do know many things that nature could never possibly do. The most general norm here is the principle of contradiction, which means that a thing cannot "be" and "not be" at the same time under the same circumstances. A second guiding rule is that one may not attribute to a supernatural cause what could possibly be the result of a natural or diabolical power.

As regards the human spirit, it is manifested by the habitual inclination or behavior that characterizes an individual. Flowing from one's personal character and individual temperament, it constitutes the "spirit" of the individual. Thus, an individual who manifests a ready inclination to the practice of prayer is said to have the spirit of prayer; a person who is argumentative and rebellious is said to have a spirit of contradiction. This is something intrinsic to the individual, but it is also the motivating force of one's thoughts, tendencies, and actions. Hence, certain physiological and psychological factors must be investigated, for example, temperament, personality type, sexual differences, education, mental or emotional disorders, etc. The majority of the phenomena rejected by investigators fall into this category of hallucination or self-deception.

The Spirit of God and the diabolical spirit are extrinsic to the individual, but they work through the person. The Spirit of God operates in and through a person in such a way that the person remains free and responsible; the diabolical spirit is oppressive and tends to take complete control, as in the case of diabolical obsession or possession. The good acts performed by a person who is operating under the spirit of God are always meritorious; conversely, a person acting under the despotic power of the devil is not responsible for those actions because the individual is not in control.

It is *de fide* — a matter of faith that Catholics are obliged to hold — that the devils exist, and with God's permission they can exercise an evil influence over the faithful. Their primary activity is to lie and deceive and thus lead persons away from God. They cannot perform any authentically supernatural actions, but they can falsify mystical phenomena in order to mislead the faithful or perform amazing feats of the natural order that surpass human power.

Types of Discernment • St. Paul wrote to the Corinthians: "The Spirit we have received is not the world's spirit but God's Spirit, helping us to recognize the gifts he has given us. We speak of these, not in words of human wisdom but in words taught by the Spirit, thus interpreting spiritual things in spiritual terms. The natural man does not accept what is taught by the Spirit of God. For him, that is absurdity. He cannot come to know such teaching because it must be appraised in a spiritual way. The spiritual man, on the other hand, can appraise everything, though he himself can be appraised by no one" (1 Cor 2:12-15).

The object of discernment, as we have seen, is to identify the spirit — supernatural, human, or diabolical — from which certain sentiments, desires, and religious experiences or happenings proceed. Discernment is not restricted to the scientific investigation of the paranormal and extraordinary phenomena that sometimes occur in the spiritual life, although that is its most obvious focus. The spiritual director must also discern the spirit, and St. Ignatius Loyola in the first and sec-

ond weeks of the *Spiritual Exercises* specifies particular rules to be followed.

There are two kinds of discernment of spirits: acquired and infused. The second kind is a special charism, or *gratia gratis data,* infused by God, and as such it is infallible, since it involves inspiration from the Holy Spirit. This charism was manifested in the lives of St. Philip Neri, St. John Vianney, St. Joseph Cupertino, and St. Rose of Lima, but it is rare even among the saints. We shall therefore confine our discussion to acquired discernment.

Acquired discernment of spirits is not infallible, but it is absolutely necessary for the spiritual director, whose primary function is to guide souls along the path to greater perfection. Unless the director can distinguish and identify the spirit that prompts the client's thoughts, desires, and actions, there is danger of serious error and tragic consequences. St. John of the Cross is typical of numerous spiritual masters who insist on the importance of discernment and the need for competent spiritual directors. As its name indicates, acquired discernment can be cultivated by using the proper means.

Prayer. Since growth in holiness is primarily the work of God and his grace, the first and most important means for acquiring discernment of spirits is the practice of prayer. Although discernment is an acquired art, personal effort would avail little without the assistance of the Holy Spirit, through the infused virtue of prudence and the gift of counsel. Hence, we speak here not only of the habitual practice of mental prayer, which makes the spiritual director a prayerful person, docile to the Holy Spirit, but also the prayer of petition, asking God for the grace and wisdom necessary to guide souls along the path to perfection. And one can be confident that God will answer those prayers with the special assistance he gives to all rightly disposed souls who call upon him. This is especially true of the invocation "O God, come to my assistance; O Lord, make haste to help me."

Study. The spiritual director likewise needs a wide and deep knowledge of the theology of the spiritual life. This can be acquired only by the assiduous and systematic study of sacred doctrine. The discernment of spirits calls for professional competence in the field of spiritual theology, a quasi-professional knowledge of psychology, and a familiarity with the great masters of the spiritual life. And although each individual will follow his or her own path to holiness, the spiritual director must rise above this or that "school" of spirituality. St. John of the Cross severely criticizes those directors who try to force all souls to travel along the same path (*Ascent of Mount Carmel*, prologue and Bk. II, Ch. 18).

Personal Experience. Self-knowledge is a basic requirement for any kind of direction of others. While it is true that each person has unique traits and characteristics, there is a fundamental likeness shared by all. Consequently, unless an individual possesses self-knowledge, it will be very difficult to understand others. Conversely, knowing one's own virtues and defects provides the empathy by which one can relate to others.

Beyond self-knowledge, however, the director needs personal experience in the exercises and practices of the spiritual life. Otherwise, if deficient in one or another virtue or practice of the spiritual life, the director will not be able to guide others or even understand their problems. Hence, holiness in a spiritual director is of inestimable value in the acquisition of spiritual discernment.

Removal of Obstacles. Under this heading we place the various defective qualities that are impediments to the understanding and direction of souls. One of the greatest obstacles is a kind of pride or self-sufficiency that prevents the director from having any doubts about his own ability or from seeking advice from others. Scripture tells us that God resists the proud and gives his grace to the humble. Second, the director must strive to maintain an air of professionalism; that is, he will never become so casual and friendly that his judgment is no longer objective. Finally, the director must never act or speak precipitously or judge on purely human standards. Spiritual direction must ever be under the exercise of supernatural prudence, judging all things by God's standards.

Signs of the Various Spirits • The spirit of God always inclines us to the good; the diabolical spirit always inclines us to evil, but frequently under the appearance of good. Of itself, however, the human spirit may be inclined either to good or to evil, depending on whether it follows the laws of God or human concupiscence. There may sometimes be various and even contrary spirits at work in one and the same activity, and that makes discernment very difficult. Even in the lives of authentic mystics, it is possible that a supernatural operation could be interrupted by a purely human action or, with God's permission, by a diabolical influence. There are general guidelines that will assist in discernment, and it is also helpful to remember that even when several spirits are active, one will usually predominate. In the history of the Church, there have been numerous experts in this field; for example, St. Teresa of Ávila, St. John of the Cross, and St. Ignatius Loyola, whose works are considered classics and are available in English translation. (Some modern authors are listed in the suggested readings below.)

Signs of the Spirit of God • The following are general signs by which one can suppose that an individual is acting under a divine spirit; the diabolical spirit will be characterized by the opposite, negative characteristics.

Conformity to the Truth. God is truth and cannot inspire falsity or error. Consequently, a person prompted by a divine spirit will accept the revealed truths and follow the teaching of the Church in thought, word, and deed. This is especially important for persons who are highly educated and may have a tendency to be attached to their own opinions.

Humility and Docility. Souls that are moved by the Spirit of God respond to it with great humility and complete docility. Their total abandonment to the divine will and their spirit of obedience, flowing from a deep faith, are among the most convincing signs that the Spirit of God is at work in them.

Discretion and Gravity. In whatever pertains to religious belief and practice, truly spiritual persons display a fitting seriousness, simplicity, and sincerity. They seek the glory of God above all things and are devoted to his service.

Liberty of Spirit. These souls are not attached to anything, not even to gifts received from God; in the first place, they are ready to respond immediately to the divine will. Second, they accept everything from God's hands with gratitude and humility, whether it be a consolation or a trial. Third, while they perform all their duties with promptness and eagerness, they are ready to abandon them if duty or charity calls them elsewhere. As a result, they live their lives in a joyful spirit because they themselves are free spirits.

It is not necessary to list here the signs of the human spirit or the diabolical spirit, which will always be in opposition to the signs of the Spirit of God. What is helpful is to mention the signs that are doubtful or uncertain, as listed by John Baptist Scaramelli, S.J., in the eighteenth century. These signs demand careful attention on the part of the director because they could proceed from any one of the three spirits we have mentioned. But no one of them can be attributed to the Spirit of God until one has definitely ruled out the natural human spirit or the diabolical spirit. These are the doubtful cases listed by Father Scaramelli:

* To aspire to some other vocation, or state of life, after having made a prudent and deliberate commitment.

* To be attracted to unusual phenomena or to practices that are not in conformity with one's state in life.

* To be drawn to the unusual practices of some of the saints who acted under a special grace from God.

* To strive for sensible consolations in the practice of prayer or the exercise of the virtues.

* To experience "the gift of tears" or to concentrate excessively on the sorrowful and penitential aspects of religion.

* To have an exclusive devotion to one or another religious mystery or pious exercise.

* Extraordinary favors, such as revelations, visions, stigmata, etc., when they occur in a person of little holiness. Although the extraordinary phenomena, such as *gratiae gratis datae*, or charisms, do not necessarily presuppose sanctity in the individual who receives them, God usually grants these gifts only to his servants and friends.

To conclude, a word of warning is in order. One must exercise the greatest possible care and caution in making judgments concerning discernment of spirits. As regards anything extraordinary, when these things proceed from God, the soul experiences great fear and humility at the outset, and only later are there peace and consolation. If, on the contrary, they proceed from a diabolical spirit, they will immediately cause sensible consolation and great satisfaction, to be followed by anxiety, confusion, and a restless spirit. Any one of the cases listed as doubtful by Scaramelli could be caused by a human or diabolical spirit, or it could just as readily come from God. If a person has prayerfully and seriously chosen a state of life or mode of action, then the presumption is that it is God's will, unless there are evident and weighty reasons to change.

See: Angels; Charisms; Devil and Evil Spirits; Diabolical Possession; Divination; Exorcism; Extraordinary Gifts; Grace; Mysticism; Private Revelation; Prophecy.

Suggested Readings: CCC 798-801, 1996-2005, 2663-2679. A. Royo and J. Aumann, *The Theology of Christian Perfection*, pp. 626-635, 639-653. C. Floristán and C. Duquoc, *Discernment of the Spirit and of Spirits.* E. Malatesta, ed., *Discernment of Spirits.*

Jordan Aumann, O.P.

DISPARITY OF CULT

The *Catechism of the Catholic Church* insists on the difficulties that can arise in the case of mixed marriages (between a Catholic and a baptized non-Catholic), and even more so when there is disparity of cult (a marriage between a Catholic and a nonbaptized person). The *Catechism* goes on: "Differences about faith and the very notion of marriage, but also different religious mentalities, can become sources of tension in marriage, especially as regards the education of children. The temptation to religious indifference can then arise" (1634) — especially among the children, who will have to grow up in a secularized world without the support of a home united in faith.

Disparity of cult being a canonical impediment (1086), such a marriage cannot be validly contracted without a dispensation. This is not granted unless the Catholic party is ready to protect his or her own faith, and sincerely promises to do all in his or her power to have the children baptized and educated as Catholics (cf. Canons 1124-1125).

The *Catechism* notes that the Catholic spouse has a particular task: to work so that "the free conversion of the other spouse to the Christian faith" may come about. It adds: "Sincere married love, the humble and patient practice of the family virtues, and perseverance in prayer can prepare the non-believing spouse to accept the grace of conversion" (1637). It is logical that the Catholic spouse, while fully respecting the conscientious freedom of his or her partner, should work for this. Love makes a person want whatever is good for the loved one; and few gifts are better than the grace of freely embracing the Catholic faith.

See: Marriage; Marriage, Sacrament of; Mixed Marriages.

DISSENT

Of the truths taught by the Church as revealed by God, some are solemnly "defined" by the Magisterium in a definitive way. In other words, they are proposed, in very precise formulations, "in a form obliging the Christian people to an irrevocable adherence of faith" (CCC 88).

Many other points of Catholic teaching, while not solemnly defined in this technical sense, are also authentically proposed as revealed doctrine: expressions of what God wants us to believe or do (or avoid), in order to be saved. Examples in the moral field could be Catholic teaching on abortion or contraception. Without being defined as dogmas, these points of magisterial teaching are no less part of the Catholic faith, of the belief that necessarily distinguishes a Catholic. They should be received as such, for they too have behind them

that guarantee of Christ: "Whoever listens to you, listens to me" (cf. Lk 10:16).

Even if not the object of a solemn definition, such matters cannot therefore be considered open questions theologically. The Second Vatican Council (*Dogmatic Constitution on the Church, Lumen Gentium*, 25) and the 1983 Code of Canon Law (Canon 752) say that a "religious respect" (*obsequium*) of the will and intellect must be given to such authentic teaching. The Latin word *obsequium* does not just mean submission and does not imply mere obedience, less still of an unthinking type. The word carries overtones of the attitude that a thinking person should naturally take before what is seen to be higher than his or her own mind. It is therefore the rational acceptance of the humble person who has a minimum of faith.

The person concludes: "Even though *I* do not see the truth of this point of teaching, if the Church proposes it officially, Christ's guarantee must stand behind it. Perhaps it may be expressed — defined — in a more precise way in the future (always in the same fundamental sense), but meanwhile I offer God the rational gift of my acquiescence — of will and mind — in what the Magisterium proposes." That is the free and intelligent conclusion of the person with faith, who wants to have the mind of Christ (cf. 1 Cor 2:16) and knows it must be found in communion with the Church.

The Nature of Dissent • The Catholic who *dissents* refuses to accept something taught by the Church's solemn or ordinary Magisterium. This is different from the attitude and behavior of a theologically qualified person who privately and respectfully withholds assent from some element of teaching he or she has not yet been able to make fully his or her own, while remaining "open to deeper examination of the question" (Congregation for the Doctrine of the Faith, *Instruction on the Ecclesial Vocation of the Theologian*, 31 [1990]).To dissent is not only to substitute one's own judgment for that of the Church; it is to show a lack of understanding of Christ's presence in the Church: "He who hears you hears me, and he who rejects you rejects me" (Lk 10:16). One thereby risks losing one's Catholic identity and rendering oneself ineffective for the work of evangelization.

In the Church, there is a legitimate pluralism that should not be confused with dissent. Pluralism, working from full acceptance of the teaching of the Magisterium, suggests diverse analyses or applications of certain aspects of this doctrine, aspects on which the Church herself has given no definitive answer. It is one thing to see and present the same truth from different angles or to suggest how it can be understood or applied in varying ways, and another to hold and defend a position clearly opposed to what is taught by the Church.

"Dissent . . . is opposed to ecclesial communion and to a correct understanding of the hierarchical constitution of the People of God" (Pope John Paul II, encyclical *The Splendor of Truth, Veritatis Splendor*, 113 [1993]). One who dissents is not in living communion with the mind of Christ present in the Church's Magisterium, and is not in a proper condition to receive the sacraments. Pope John Paul says: "It is sometimes claimed that dissent from the Magisterium is totally compatible with being a 'good Catholic' and poses no obstacle to the reception of the sacraments. This is a grave error" (Address to the U.S. bishops, Los Angeles, September 16, 1987).

Dissent is not a happy position, for happiness lies in communion with others in Christ. Dissent is not a humble position; it shows an over-readiness to subject God's ways or the ways of his Church to one's own personal judgment. Dissent is an attitude not of affirmation but of negation; it tends to take away a person's peace, and can induce an aggressive mood that leads to bitterness.

A person may be tempted into real dissent and adopt it for a time. God's grace, often making itself felt through the interior tension of maintaining such a position, is always there calling him or her back to a way of humbler, more joyful, and more rational communion with God's Revelation, to a surer way of personal salvation and of apostolic service.

See: Assent and Dissent; Catholic Identity; Communio; Evangelization; Magisterium; Pluralism.

Suggested Readings: CCC 157, 162, 166-169, 181, 185, 197, 949, 1816, 2088. John Paul II, *The Splendor of Truth, Veritatis Splendor*. Congregation for the Doctrine of the Faith, *Instruction on the Ecclesial Vocation of the Theologian*. C. Burke, *Authority and Freedom in the Church*, Chs. 6-7.

Cormac Burke

DIVINATION

"All forms of *divination* are to be rejected: recourse to Satan or demons, conjuring up the dead or other practices falsely supposed to 'unveil' the future. Consulting horoscopes, astrology, palm reading, interpretation of omens and lots, the phenomena of clairvoyance and recourse to mediums all conceal a desire for power over time, history, and, in the last analysis, other human beings, as well as a wish to conciliate hidden powers. They contradict the honor, respect, and loving fear that we owe to God alone" (CCC 2116).

To prophets and others God can reveal the future. Still, a sound Christian attitude consists in trusting an all-provident God for whatever the future may bring, while diligently providing for today and a bit for the morrow.

Divination's natural cause is not hard to discover: curiosity to know the future and desire for personal gain or advantage. In every age some have sought to lift the veil, at least partially. At times the results cannot be explained on merely natural grounds, being so disproportionate or foreign to the means employed. It cannot be doubted that diviners have foretold some contingent things correctly, and magicians have produced at times superhuman effects. The very survival of divination for so many centuries would otherwise be inexplicable and its role in history an insoluble problem. On the supposition that these phenomena are not caused by God, the angels, or any purely material agent, such marvels must be the work either of demons or lost souls.

Successfully using a divining rod to find subsurface water (dousing) may be explained naturally.

See: Idolatry; Magic; New Age; Religion, Virtue of; Superstition.

DIVINE REVELATION

Christian faith is based on Divine Revelation. The most basic meaning of the phrase "Divine Revelation" refers to God's action as he reveals his person and divine plan of salvation. The *Catechism of the Catholic Church* teaches: "Through an utterly free decision, God has revealed himself and given himself to man. This he does by revealing the mystery, his plan of loving goodness, formed from all eternity in Christ, for the benefit of all men. God has fully revealed this plan by sending us his beloved Son, our Lord Jesus Christ, and the Holy Spirit" (50).

The ultimate goal of Revelation is intimate and shared life with God. But intimacy and a shared life are not possible without true knowledge of God, and knowing God includes more than intellectual head knowledge: It involves an experience of divine love in Christ. In sum, by Revelation God makes known both himself and the way to heaven. The experience of divine love makes us adoptive sons of God (like Christ, men and women receive the inheritance intended by God: grace, eternal life). Our adoption occurs in Christ, when we are incorporated into the living Body of Christ, the Church. Whatever else can be said about Divine Revelation derives from these fundamental points.

Divine Revelation is both a content (person, ideas) and a process (how we come to know the person and ideas). God reveals both his person and plan of salvation (the content) through his actions and words in time and space, that is, through history (the process). God's revealing action complements our knowledge about him and his plan. Therefore, it is always important to ask two questions about Divine Revelation: What is its content, and how did God make it known? We shall examine both the content and process in more detail.

Where content is concerned, there are three fundamental points to note when speaking about Divine Revelation. First and foremost is the mystery of the Person of God, the Divine Trinity: Father, Son, and Holy Spirit. Second, there is God's plan of salvation, what the Fathers of the Church often called the "divine economy" (CCC 236). God's plan is manifested in history by words and deeds that are recorded in Scripture, lived by the people of Israel, and fulfilled in the Church. That plan is rooted in the eternal deliberations of the Father, Son, and Holy Spirit. In effect, the plan was established before the creation of the cosmos (cf. Eph 1:4-5). This means that Scripture and the living Tradition of the Church comprise *the* source of information about God's inner self or nature and about his plan of salvation (cf. Vatican Council II, *Dogmatic Constitution on Divine Revelation, Dei Verbum,* 9; CCC 80). Third, we come to know and believe what is revealed by the Holy Spirit's grace. The experience of knowing God and believing in what God has revealed is what St. Paul calls the "obedience of faith" (Rom 1:5, 16:26; CCC 142-165). That "obedience born of the Spirit's grace and freedom" leads to the worship of God (liturgy and prayer, both private and communal) and a specific way of life (morality). The divine act of creating many sons and daughters of God in Christ, who worship and obey the living God, is the singular foundation of Sacred Tradition. The link between Scripture and Tradition is the historical process by which God creates a people who manifest his life in the here and now.

As to the process of Revelation, the following considerations are relevant. We can know only so much about God based on the operations of our intellects. For example, the mind can know right from wrong on its own; also, the natural mind can arrive at the certain conclusions that there is a god and that this god is probably kind and just. However, the natural mind cannot know that this god of the universe is God our Father in heaven, that the Father has an eternal Son, and that the Father and Son have a relationship of continuous love that is expressed in and by the Holy Spirit. God has to show us this kind of truth. And that is to say we cannot know God in any deep and personal way without Divine Revelation.

God shows us the truth about himself in progressive stages. The ultimate stage of Revelation will take place in the full presence of God, in the beatific vision. The experience of receiving and internalizing the truth about God is much like the experience of a blind man who for the first time touches the leg of an elephant: He knows he is in the presence of something big, but just how big he does not yet know. Similarly, God made use of the historical process to reveal that indeed he is a loving Father; for example, he liberated the poor and oppressed from Egypt through the leadership of Moses and Aaron (cf. CCC 2984), and the great Exodus event created the People of God and prepared the way for the Church, which fulfills and will eventually completely satisfy the intent God has for all people — intimate union with himself. But we come to ultimate knowledge about God and his divine plan of salvation only through the person and work of Jesus Christ. The historical birth and death of Jesus created the possibility for any person to receive Jesus' sonship. As we are configured to the image of Jesus, the eternal Son of God, we are configured into deeper levels of sonship by God's Fatherhood. Jesus' life in believers is the objective link to God's Fatherhood. Another historical event, Jesus' baptism in the Jordan, illustrates yet another aspect of Revelation: the existence of God as Father, Son, and Holy Spirit.

A final introductory comment about Revelation concerns its link to biblical morality. This is an age in which all truth is thought to be relative. It is common to hear people say, "What's true for you may not be true for me." Or again, "We are so unique, our circumstances so specific, truths must be applied and modified to fit our life circumstances."

Such superficial sophistication could not be further from the biblical witness about the nature of truth and morality. Biblical or covenantal morality is linked to the mystery of God's person and his salvific Revelation as Father, Son, and Holy Spirit. Since God is utterly holy, perfect, just, and good, his Revelation about the road to heaven is completely solid, absolutely good, and totally reliable. Truth stands from one generation to the next because it carries within it the stuff of God,

as it were. When God reveals a way of life (i.e., the Ten Commandments, the Beatitudes), he reveals something about his own inner life. Revelation, then, derives from the way God actually "lives," and biblical morality rests on and puts us in touch with God's inner life. Therefore, we can have full confidence in what is revealed in Scripture, especially its moral teachings, because they are sure and certain guidelines for discovering what is consistent with the inner life of God. The teachings come from and lead to heaven. And so our morality, doctrines, and worship are rooted in the mystery of God's person and lead us to God through Divine Revelation.

Natural and Supernatural Revelation • The Revelation of God's person and divine plan of salvation begin in the first book of the Bible, Genesis, and continue through to the very last book, the Book of Revelation. A quick scanning of the Bible might lead one to conclude that the divine plan was delivered to us fully developed and obvious to all concerned. A second, more careful reading of the biblical texts shows that Revelation took place over many centuries, in different stages, and under a great variety of circumstances. Each stage of Revelation is based on the previous stage and prepares for the next. Revelation is completed in Jesus Christ, who both teaches and mediates it. With this in mind, we can refer to Scripture and make a distinction between natural and supernatural revelation.

Two examples of natural revelation are the universe and human beings. For instance, the beauty found in nature suggests the existence of a benevolent and good creator. We hear a poetic echo of this reasoning in the Divine Liturgy: "All creation rightly gives you praise. . . ."

Human beings, the crown of creation, reflect another kind of natural revelation. Made in God's image (Gn 1:27), male and female point to the reality of a loving creator. Our first parents were clothed in resplendent grace and justice (CCC 54); Adam and Eve enjoyed intimate communion with God from the very beginning (CCC 54; Vatican Council II, *Dogmatic Constitution on Divine Revelation, Dei Verbum*, 3; cf. Jn 1:3; Rom 1:19-20).

Even if communion with God was not passed on to their children, our first parents did pass on a capacity to manifest the image and likeness of God.

This capacity is encountered in our great potential for doing good — good that in fact we seldom do. We are capable of heroic virtue, unselfish love, justice, and glory; yet we rarely reach such greatness. We spend our lives longing and searching for truth, beauty, love, and friendship; and yet we seldom realize our hopes. How then do we explain our ability to know right from wrong even though we tend not to do what is right? The answer is: God made us that way. Thus, by natural revelation we can know quite a bit about the nature of the Creator.

Beyond natural revelation there is supernatural Revelation, by which God discloses to us something of the mystery of his person and of his divine plan of salvation that we could not know on our own. The result is contact with eternal life, which fulfills all that we long for at the natural level. Adam and Eve knew something of this Divine Revelation by virtue of their condition before the Fall. The first sin, however, disrupted the unity between humans and God and permanently ruptured human relationships. As a consequence, the human family eventually grouped into families, tribes, and nations, all under the provident care of the angels (CCC 56-57). The covenant with Noah shows God's plan to save humanity, individual by individual, region by region, and nation by nation. Two major lessons drawn from sacred history, beginning with the Tower of Babel and ending with the covenant with Noah, are that we do not have the power to preserve unity within the human family and that national identity is not the supreme good to which all security is subordinate. The covenant with Noah is a new beginning in which we learn of God's providential care for all of humanity, protecting it from the disasters caused by its own sin.

God continued the work of uniting all of his children with the call to Abraham (CCC 59). In his great mercy, God gathered the entire human family, beginning with the faith of one man, Abraham. His descendants are the trustees of the covenantal promises made to the patriarchs. The covenant with Abraham instructs us about God's tender love and great power, about his utter holiness and invitation to intimacy. This divine pedagogy culminates in the establishment of the people of Israel, cherished above all other nations and called to be a light to other nations (CCC 60-64).

But that plan of reconciling and reuniting humanity did not stop with the creating of the ethnic, cultural, and political entity called "Israel." The creation of the people Israel is an act of divine pedagogy that set the stage for God's greatest revelation and ultimate gift — Jesus Christ, eternal Son of God (CCC 53). It is in Jesus Christ, the Eternal Word made flesh, that we find the fullness of God's revelation and through whom that fullness is mediated. By giving us his Son, God, as it were, spoke all that he had to say to us (cf. Heb 1:1-2); because of Jesus and his life and work, there is nothing more to be said about God. The New Covenant, or Gospel Law, that Jesus brought to us is perfect and complete. Therefore, there can be no more revelation about God; we have all that we need (CCC 66-67).

The Process of Revelation • Having examined a few central themes pertaining to the content of Revelation, we turn now to the broad features of the transmission process. It is as important to keep in mind that Divine Revelation is from heaven as it is to recognize that the manifestation of heavenly realities takes place through the historical process and involves real flesh-and-blood people. Our appreciation of Divine Revelation will increase as we understand that the transmission process is guided by the grace and work of the Holy Spirit.

God first reveals himself by creating the universe and then Adam and Eve. This is followed by such events as the formation of a people, the Incarnation of the eternal Son, the creation of the Church, the Ascension of Jesus, and the outpouring of the Holy Spirit at Pentecost. Now we await Jesus' Second Coming. These events spanned centuries, took place in different cultural contexts, and were originally expressed in a wide variety of languages. God used the historical, political, economic, and social conditions of a fallen world to reveal his great plan of salvation. The heavenly reality touches the very fabric of historical existence.

The historical events in which God reveals and acts are similar in two respects. First, each event necessarily expresses a step in God's plan of salvation and is an intervention of divine power. The divine power is rooted in God's superabundant life. All divine interventions are linked to each other by means of this one characteristic they all share: divine power rooted in God's Trinitarian life. Second, the words that record these events or deeds also share in the same saving power manifested in the saving deeds. Events and words have a very special relationship, an inner or essential unity (cf. *Dei Verbum*, 2). This means that both the events and the words share in God's power. The word that proclaims the saving deed contains the very same saving power found in the deed itself. The action of the Holy Spirit in the saving event is the same action of the Holy Spirit in the sacred writer who recorded the event, and it is the same action that saves when the event is proclaimed. One product of this process of transmitting and eventually recording such events is what we call Sacred Scripture.

Let us consider the transmission of Revelation from Jesus until now. Divine Revelation ends with Jesus' Ascension into heaven and the giving of the Holy Spirit. The communication of that Revelation formally concludes with the death of the last apostolic eyewitness. At this point, Revelation has a fixed content, what the Church calls the deposit of faith. However, the process of transmitting Revelation from generation to generation continues long after Jesus and the death of the last Apostle. It has been carried on by the successors of the Apostles: the men who are bishops. Each point in the transmission process receives the guidance of the Holy Spirit, which ensures the faithful proclamation and transmission of the great truths (CCC 83, 91, 93). In summary, the events and words of Scripture and the transmission process are guided by the Holy Spirit who guarantees the integrity of the message of salvation.

Power of Revelation • By way of conclusion,

let us consider the meaning of Divine Revelation for today. Divine Revelation does more than inform. It has the power to save us from sin, to transform us into the image of Christ. There is something very special about Revelation that distinguishes it from other kinds of knowledge, principally because of the nature of God.

God reveals himself as good and holy and as desirous of friendship and intimate communion with us. He invites us to share in his divine nature (CCC 51; *Dei Verbum*, 2; cf. Eph 1:9, 2:18; 1 Pt 1:4). God always sends help (i.e., grace) with his many invitations. When we accept his invitation, we have already received grace (CCC 52). It is important to see that grace is, as it were, bundled with the invitation. This is not so difficult to comprehend when we look at everyday experience. Say someone wins the local lottery. Not only is the news good in itself, its goodness may very well be measured by the amount of the winner's debt. Much the same might be said of Revelation. The grace to open up and accept Revelation is packaged with God's self-disclosure of his utter goodness. Such knowledge has a grace within it, and therefore has a power to open the mind to God and whatever his plan of salvation might be for each individual. The message of God's inherent goodness enables the believer to receive a share of divine life — to see and taste that the Lord is good — which is intimate communion with God.

Believers can receive this great life of God at the Divine Liturgy, by reading the word of God, through the sacraments, or wherever there is authentic knowledge of God. But they must have an intimate knowledge of the content of Scripture in order to ground their understanding of God.

The content and process of Divine Revelation intend the salvation of all who would accept God's invitation to friendship. The action of revealing is both a pronouncement and a grace that makes possible acceptance of the pronouncement. The Church is the primary *locus* for this ongoing grace and Revelation. In this sense, the story of Divine Revelation does not end in the first or second century when the deposit of the faith became fixed (cf. CCC 84, 97, 175); it continues even to our day. God continues to enable his chosen people — the Church, the Mystical Body of Christ — to deepen their knowledge of himself through the grace of the Holy Spirit working in individuals and especially through the Magisterium (cf. CCC 85-86). The lived knowledge of God and the experience of divine life continue in and through the Church — clergy, lay, and religious — through whom that Revelation is proclaimed to the world.

See: Fatherhood of God; Imago Dei; Inerrancy; Jesus Christ, God and Man; Knowledge of God; New Covenant; New Testament; Old Covenant; Old Testament; Sacred Scripture; Sacred Tradition.

Suggested Readings: CCC 51-100, 102, 111, 114, 145, 158, 171, 204, 234, 374, 397, 401, 410, 489, 516, 674, 688, 711, 737, 760-762, 781, 785, 839, 851, 857, 861, 871, 888-892, 1124, 1202, 1219, 1548, 1950, 1953, 1961, 1965, 1996, 2032-2041, 2060, 2518, 2569-2570, 2574, 2625, 2651, 2656, 2684, 2717, 2801, 2923. Vatican Council II, *Dogmatic Constitution on Divine Revelation, Dei Verbum.* P. Grelot and J. Giblet, "Revelation," in X. Leon-Dufour, ed., *Dictionary of Biblical Theology.*

Stephen F. Miletic

DIVORCE

A man and a woman marry because they are in love and want to share life together. They choose one another in preference to all possible others, because they think they will be happier together than with anyone else. In many cases, it works — but not always. People gradually run into difficulties, discover each other's defects, get irritated, have small quarrels and then bigger ones, feel attracted to someone else. Love and fidelity often survive the crisis and take on a more voluntary and mature form: The couple "make it." Other couples do not. Love declines and finally "dies." Then the idea of continuing in a loveless marriage appears senseless. If so, what is reasonably to be done? What is the proper thing when two people who have married no longer love each other? The logical answer might seem to be, let them divorce and be free to start over again.

Other considerations (like God's will) apart, however, does this not fail to address prior questions that contain the real issue? How can two people so in love as to marry come to be so out of love that they must separate? Is there not always an element of tragedy, which must leave behind it a taste of unhappiness for life, in putting an end to a joint venture of love? How is it possible that love "died"? Did it have to die? Could it have been saved?

Once one begins to treat divorce as a progressive or good thing, one begins to think (perhaps unconsciously) that the death of married love is an eventuality with no great importance. This is the so-called divorce mentality found in individuals and societies. Then, with an apparently easy way out ensured, marriage becomes less of a commitment, people prepare less for it; when difficulties arise, perhaps they struggle less and receive less help or encouragement from pastors and friends to keep it going. That way, their love is not likely to survive. Note that the divorce rate is higher among previously divorced persons who remarry and among the children of the divorced.

When doctors start thinking that death is the logical result of an illness or just as good an outcome as the *cure* of that illness, something has gone badly wrong with medical outlook and practice. The modern approach to divorce shares that pessimistic attitude. Since the "remedy" is at hand in divorce, who cares if love grows sick and dies? Married persons should care. Marriage counselors should care, pastors should care, and should spend themselves in helping marriages survive the pathologies they are bound to undergo and helping married people cure the infections that at times afflict love.

The Question of Love • The real question is not how long love will last or what should be done if it fails, but how love can be made to last. True love pledges itself "in good times or in bad." What is natural, though hard, is to keep at the task of loving, of *learning* to love.

This is much truer still if children have been born. The *Catechism of the Catholic Church* speaks of how children can be traumatized and torn between their parents by divorce (2385). It is natural for parents to love their children and want the best for them. The best for the children is that their parents remain together. But surely it is worse if they are always quarreling? *Were* they *always* quarreling? If they had borne in mind what they naturally owe their children, they would have avoided quarrels or at least have had the humility to make up after each quarrel, and so would have prevented them from getting worse. "For the sake of our children we will learn to get on": People can rise to great sacrifice for the sake of their children. If they do, this new effort often makes each admirable again in the eyes of the other, and so their original love can in fact find a rebirth.

The argument "Why should two people be bound together if they no longer want to be bound?" can falsify the issue of divorce. So often, it is just *one* of the two who is tempted to quit, while the other still wants to work at making a success of the marriage. When they married, a successful marriage was certainly what both wanted. But one or both have allowed themselves to go through a gradual process of ceasing to "want." There, at the start of that process, is where each has to be helped; there lies the problem.

Divorce does not make married life easier, unless one holds that it is easier to get out of the difficulties of married life by running away from them. That way, people never learn to love. Moreover, even if divorce made it easier for one side, it very often makes it much harder for the other — and always so for the children. Divorce does not make for happiness. Divorce makes for divorce.

That indissolubility is a characteristic of every true marriage is explicitly recalled by Jesus: "Have you not read that he who made them from the beginning made them male and female, and said, 'For this reason a man shall leave his father and mother and be joined to his wife, and the two shall become one'? So they are no longer two but one. What therefore God has joined together, let no man put asunder" (Mt 19:4-6). Even if human reasoning at times finds it hard to understand why "no divorce and remarriage" is God's law, trust in his wisdom, readiness to bear the cross if necessary (cf. CCC 1615), and the firm hope of gaining heaven by abiding by his will, should be sufficient to bring about determined acceptance of this divine law. If "no divorce" is Our Lord's teaching, he must provide the grace to make it possible for husband and wife either to live together despite their mutual differences or else to separate but still respect the marriage bond. Those who seek Jesus' grace through prayer and the sacraments will live up to his law and merit a special reward in heaven.

See: Annulment; Marriage, Goods of; Indissolubility of Marriage; Marriage; Marriage, Sacrament of.

Suggested Readings: CCC 1650-1651, 2382, 2384-2386. G. Grisez, *The Way of the Lord Jesus*, Vol. 2, *Living a Christian Life*, pp. 728-729. C. Burke, *Covenanted Happiness*, Chs. 3-4.

Cormac Burke

DOGMA

Dogma, as the word is used in Catholic theology, covers all the truths that the Church teaches to have been revealed by God as doctrine of salvation. Dogmas are directly proposed by the Church (by a solemn definition or by the ordinary and universal Magisterium) as truths to be believed "with divine and Catholic faith" (Vatican Council I, *Dogmatic Constitution on the Catholic Faith, Dei Filius*).

In the case of some dogmas, the human mind, understanding *what* is proposed, can grasp very little of *how* this truth can be so (e.g., the Blessed Trinity, the Real Presence). In others, the mind can achieve greater understanding of the "how" (the Resurrection of Jesus, the special role of Mary in salvation, the effects of Baptism on the soul). But in all cases, the reason for believing is not our understanding nor the discovery of any inherent proof or self-evidence. It is faith in God, who guarantees such teachings proposed in his name by his Church.

To some people "dogma" suggests something meaningless or even irrational. Far from being unintelligible or without meaning, however, dogmas of faith are so full of meaning that human minds can only grasp it in part. When it is God who speaks, it is reasonable to accept his words, even though we can only partly understand their meaning. The limited power of our minds, not the obscurity of dogmas, is why we cannot penetrate their meaning fully.

Dogmas open the mind to wider horizons and spur the will to greater ambitions. They are always liberating.

The Church is constantly propounding and explaining her dogmas, and sometimes defines them (even if this is not in the form of a solemn definition in the strict sense). To "define" means to present a saving teaching in clearer focus so that what is proposed is seen in greater richness and light: "Dogmas are lights" (CCC 89).

The appropriate response to dogma is reverence and gratitude. In practice, the "sense of the faith" (*sensus fidei*) is joyful awareness of the greatness of what has been given us.

See: Assent and Dissent; Dissent; Divine Revelation; Heresy; Magisterium; Sacred Tradition.

DOMESTIC CHURCH

The Church is the instrument of salvation. Christ lives and works in and through his Church in order to save and sanctify us, communicating his life and love and mercy, making us sisters and brothers of his, daughters and sons of God. Through the Church we enter into the "family life" of the Blessed Trinity.

It is doubly significant that the family is frequently referred to as the domestic church. The Church herself has an essentially family nature. Supernatural life begins and is nurtured in the Church, just as happens with natural life in the family. The family is in many ways like the Church in miniature, for supernatural life is also nurtured in the family. The graces of the sacrament of Matrimony are there to help the spouses realize that the family they are forming is an instrument of redemption, for themselves and for their children; and that they are called to be active collaborators with Christ in this task.

In any true family, people are humanized: They grow in human virtues and in humanity. In a Christian family, they are supernaturalized as well: Supernatural virtues and supernatural life develop in them.

People are helped to acquire a deeper sense of community — union in Christ — by worshiping together in their local church. Members of families, however, are not likely to acquire that community sense at church if they are not living it at home, in the domestic church. There, first of all, they need to sense the presence of Christ, pray to him, serve him, and love him in others.

See: Family; Marriage; Marriage, Goods of; Marriage, Sacrament of.

DOUBLE EFFECT

It is Catholic teaching that it is always morally wrong directly to will the destruction or damaging or impeding of certain basic goods, such as innocent human life, marriage, sexual fecundity, conception. However, it is not always morally wrong to perform an action that causes harm to one of these basic goods as a side effect. The principle of double effect is a set of criteria by which to determine when it is morally right to choose to perform an action that causes such a bad side effect. Such actions cause two effects, one good and the other bad. Thus the name "principle of double effect."

An example will clarify. Suppose during war some soldiers are sitting around a campfire when an enemy soldier tosses a hand grenade in their midst. A brave soldier thinks quickly and dives onto the grenade; he is killed, but his action saves all of his friends. Was his action morally right? It seems that it was not only right but heroic. However, it would not be right if it were a suicide. The explanation is that he did not *directly* or *intentionally* kill himself. He foresaw that his death would occur, but as a side effect of what he was proposing intentionally to do. His end was to save his friends, and his means was to block the shrapnel. His death did not help him attain his end at all, and so it is was not intended. We ought never, then, directly destroy a basic human good, but it is sometimes morally right to choose to do something that we foresee will cause a bad side effect.

Why is this distinction important? What we intentionally do, we take on as part of our moral identity: We are, to a certain extent, what we will. To choose an object is to direct my will toward it, and the moral part of myself is shaped toward the object willed. So, if I choose to kill, or to impede human life, I set my will against life: Until I repent, I remain a person whose very self is disposed against life. Thomas More's remark about oaths (in the well-known play *A Man for All Seasons*) holds true of all of our free choices: "When a man takes an oath, he's holding his own self in his hands. Like water. And if he opens his fingers then — he needn't hope to find himself again."

But the foreseen side effects of my action do *not* become part of my identity, even though I do have some responsibility for them. Even God, who does not directly will evil at all, does permit evil; that is, God causes only good but foresees that many of the goods that he causes will also bring about bad side effects (e.g., in causing the lion he indirectly causes the death of the lamb). Similarly, it can be morally right for us to do something that causes bad side effects.

While some instances of causing a bad side effect are morally right, clearly some other instances are not. From the fact that the bad effect is not directly willed it does not follow just by itself that the act is morally right. If someone tires of taking care of his aging parents, it would be morally wrong of him to drive them out to an isolated forest and leave them, in order to detach them from him and so avoid his responsibilities. This is so even though he might rightly claim that their deaths are a side effect, that what he directly wills is only their detachment.

There is a prior question that must be answered before one invokes the principle of double effect: Is there some substantial reason for performing an action that will have a bad side effect? If not, the action should not be performed, and there is no need to bring "double effect" into play. Suppose,

for instance, one can reach a good objective by a course of action that does not involve doing harm to some human good. In those circumstances, one should adopt that course of action, not turn to a different course of action involving such harm and subject it to analysis by double effect.

The four parts of the principle of double effect are usually stated as follows: (1) the act itself must be good or at least morally indifferent; (2) the good effect must not be attained by means of the bad effect; (3) the bad effect must not be intended; and (4) there must be a sufficient balance between the good effect and the bad effect.

For example: Suppose a pregnant woman's uterus is cancerous and, if the uterus is not removed, she will die; but if the uterus is removed, the baby will die as a result. Applying the principle of double effect, one can say that the removal of the uterus could be morally right. (1) The act itself, the removal of a pathological organ, is in itself good. (2) The good effect, the healing of the mother, is not attained by means of the bad effect: Her condition is relieved by the removal of the diseased organ, not by the baby's death. (3) The baby's death is not intended — those involved were not looking for such an opportunity. (4) There is a sufficient balance between the good effect and the bad effect, and the bad effect is not intended: The mother's life is as much at stake as the child's.

This principle is not a new moral truth. It is a summing-up of other moral truths that apply especially to situations where, whatever one does, a bad effect will result.

See: Human Goods; Human Virtues; Natural Law; Practical Reason; Synderesis.

Suggested Readings: CCC 1750-1756. John Paul II, *The Splendor of Truth, Veritatis Splendor*, 77-81. G. Grisez, *The Way of the Lord Jesus*, Vol. 1, *Christian Moral Principles*, pp. 233-236, 239-241, 307-308.

Patrick Lee

E

ECCLESIAL RIGHTS AND DUTIES

The subject of ecclesial rights can be better understood if we first consider a more familiar concept: human rights.

The term "human rights" means the various rights that pertain to each human being and that, when freely exercised, enable him or her to live in a way befitting the dignity of human nature. They comprise the rights to think, choose, and act — to live — in ways that help each one fulfill himself or herself as man or woman: to grow in humanity. Human rights depend upon human duties (we have a right to that which others have an obligation to give us) and are true rights only when they are in conformity with authentic moral norms.

One has the right to be human, not the right to be inhuman. One has the right to humanize oneself, not to dehumanize self. No one can claim the right to be whatever one likes. One has the right to be a man, but not any sort of man.

For instance, one does not have the right to be a murderous man. One has the power to be a murderer, but not the right. One has the power to be an adulterer, a liar, a thief, a slanderer. But not the right. And the reason is not only that these actions harm others but also that they harm oneself. They dehumanize one, as does any violation of human rights. Similarly, there is no right to turn oneself into a sex-obsessed or a drug-addicted individual. No one has the right to self-destruction; there is no such thing as a right to suicide. One has the power to take one's own life, just as one can take the life of another, but not the *right* to do so.

The most basic human rights are not just those to food or work or housing. The most basic are the rights to seek and find truth and goodness. These are the first human values, and if we do not find them, we gradually lose our humanity and our very freedom: "[Y]ou will know truth, and the truth will make you free" (Jn 8:32).

Human rights are grounded in the simple fact of possessing human life; they are therefore not a concession of human authorities or governments. Since life itself is a gift from God through our parents, it is in the end from God that we possess our human rights just as we do our human dignity.

These considerations as a sort of preface may help the explanation and understanding of our *ecclesial* rights: our rights, that is, as Christians and members of Christ's Church.

Rights of a Child of God • Christian life begins constitutionally with Baptism, by which the person is made a child of God. The basic rights of a Christian could therefore be described as filial rights, those of a son or daughter of God, brother or sister to Jesus Christ, "the first born among many" (Rom 8:29).

Jesus Christ has called us to the Church to save and sanctify us, that is, to become one with him by living his very life more and more, and one with others through and in him: a union and communion that are meant to reach their fulfillment after death, in unlimited joy forever in heaven. All of our ecclesial rights can be summed up in one: the right to meet Christ in his Church — in his grace, truth, and will; the right to be vivified (given life: supernatural life), to be sanctified by him, taught and led by him: to come to him and to come back to him. The main right of each of the faithful is to have access to Christ: to his saving grace, to his enlightening and freeing truth, and to his sanctifying will. And a main function of authority in the Church is precisely to protect people's rights to meet Christ.

The Second Vatican Council emphasized some of these rights (cf. *Dogmatic Constitution on the Church, Lumen Gentium*, 37; *Decree on the Apostolate of the Laity, Apostolicam Actuositatem*, 3-4, etc.). But it was left to the Code of Canon Law to spell out the basic and constitutional rights of the Christian. It is worth noting that, in doing so, the Code does not follow the error (frequent in secular history) of simply making a "Declaration of Rights" without any "Declaration of Duties." It does not overlook the relationship or correspondence between rights and duties and particularly the fact that, in the case of common rights, a right cannot exist without the existence of an equally common duty: the duty to respect others in *their* use of that same right. So, the renewed law of the Church is careful to state people's *obligations* along with proclaiming their rights. Moreover, in each case it states these obligations *before* stating their rights.

A somewhat different but no less important point is the connection between the rights of some and the duties of others. When the Code speaks of "Christian faithful," or "Christ's faithful," it refers to all of the members of the People of God, clergy as well as laypeople, all of whom share the same basic Christian rights and duties (set out in Canons 208-223). The clergy have indeed certain "powers" that laypersons do not possess, such as the power to celebrate (consecrate) the Eucharist or to forgive sins in the sacrament of Penance and Reconciliation. However, it would be a mistake to think of these powers in terms of rights or privileges. Much more than to rights, they correspond to duties — the duty of serving the people (in these cases, in the administration of the sacraments).

Certain categories of persons within the Church have a special calling and mission of service. These are the clergy, the sacred ministers ("ministry" means service). They have personally volunteered and freely pledged themselves to serve others according to the spirit of "diakonia" (which also means service) stressed by the Second Vatican Council. The consequence is that the clergy have duties that are not equally shared by the laity, but

are meant rather to serve and safeguard the rights of the laity. If all within the People of God should try to maintain a keener consciousness of their duties than of their rights, this particularly befits the clergy in fulfillment of their special mission as ministers and servants of the people.

Rights and Duties in Canon Law • Title I of Book II of the Code (Canons 208-223) details "the obligations and rights" *common* to all Christians; Title II (Canons 224-231), those that are peculiar to laypeople; and chapter 3 of Title III (Canons 273-289), those that accompany the clerical state.

While the first of these canons (208) states the equal "dignity and action" among all the Christian faithful, the next canon expresses a fundamental *obligation* of all, "to preserve their communion with the Church at all times, even in their external actions" (Canon 209). This is followed by another fundamental obligation: "to live a holy life" (Canon 210).

Communion with Christ depends, along with personal prayer and the effort to keep the commandments, on growing in the truth of Christ and in the grace he offers through his Church. So Canon 213 stresses: "Christ's faithful have the right to be assisted by their pastors from the spiritual riches of the Church, especially by the word of God and the sacraments." If the faithful have the right to this assistance, their pastors clearly have the obligation to provide it.

"The people of God are first united through the word of the living God, and are fully entitled to seek this word from their priests" (Canon 762). To the right of each Christian to hear God's word corresponds the clear obligation of those specially commissioned to teach it, who are bound to echo that word (and not just their own ideas) in teaching and preaching, and to convey the actual message or doctrine of Christ as handed down by the Church and preserved by the Magisterium. This duty is set out in Canon 768: "Those who announce the word of God to Christ's faithful are first and foremost to set out those things which it is necessary to believe and to practice for the glory of God and the salvation of all." This is to be read also in the light of Canon 760: "The mystery of Christ is to be faithfully and fully presented in the ministry of the word, which must be founded upon sacred Scripture, Tradition, liturgy and the magisterium and life of the Church."

The faithful have a right to a saving and sanctifying participation in the liturgical worship and sacramental life of the Church. There is an ecclesial right that worship and the sacraments be offered or administered according to the directives of the Church. Therefore, the Second Vatican Council lays down that, outside the proper authority, "no other person, not even a priest, may add, remove, or change anything in the liturgy on his personal initiative" (*Constitution on the Sacred Liturgy, Sacrosanctum Concilium*, 22; cf. Canon 846.1).

A small but not unimportant illustration of how ministers in the Church are at the service of the rest of the faithful is to be found in the matter of clerical garb (Canon 284). The duty of clerics to wear a distinctive form of dress corresponds to the right of the faithful to be able to *identify* those on whose services they can call, those whose vocation it is to minister to them.

"Since lay people, like all Christ's faithful, are deputed to the apostolate by baptism and confirmation, they are bound by the general obligation and they have the right, whether as individuals or in associations, to strive so that the divine message of salvation may be known and accepted by all people throughout the world" (Canon 225.1; cf. Canon 211). So, the Christian apostolate is the obligation and right, not just of priests and religious, but of everyone in the Church. As St. Thomas Aquinas says: "To teach in order to lead others to faith is the task of every preacher and of each believer" (*Summa Theologiae*, III, 71, 4 ad 3; cf. CCC 904). To do apostolate is an obligation that laypeople should always be encouraged to fulfill, just as it is a right they can never be restrained from exercising, always with due regard for public order.

Parents have the first right and duty to care for the Christian education of their children (Canon 226.2; cf. Canon 793.1). This of course begins with their Baptism. Canon 867 insists that parents are

under the obligation to have their children baptized "within the first few weeks" after birth. This also means that they have the right, insofar as their pastors are concerned, that Baptism be conferred "shortly after birth" (CCC 1250).

Rights, Violated and Claimed • Ecclesial rights are often neglected by those who possess them. It is also true that at times they are not duly respected by those in authority. Canon law provides for possible violations of rights, and for the processes by which a remedy is to be sought (cf. Canons 57, 221, 270, 1505, 1649, 1732-1739, 1745, etc.), including people's right to appeal from diocesan to metropolitan or higher courts (Canons 1438-1439).

Ecclesial or Christian rights can only be adequately exercised by those who receive and invoke them humbly. Faith and grace are free gifts of God, given to those he chooses; and this applies to ecclesial rights too. One has the rights God gives, not those one may wish to claim. The Church recognizes, proclaims, and defends ecclesial rights, but does not originate them; nor can she modify or cancel those that are constitutional or introduce new ones. This is a point to be borne in mind in relation to the question of the ordination of women. There are deeper theological issues to this matter that only the Church can decide. But one gets the whole question wrong from the outset if one thinks of it in terms of the "right to ordination." No one has the *right* to be ordained a priest; it is always a free gift from God.

A final word could be on what is at times called the "right to dissent." As explained elsewhere, if by "dissent" one simply means holding a different or minority view in matters that are not official Church teaching, that is an exercise of legitimate pluralism, not of dissent. But if dissent is used in its proper sense of refusing to accept the teaching of the Magisterium, then we are speaking of a "right" that *no* Catholic has or can have.

Every Catholic has the power to reject the teaching of the Magisterium, but not the *ecclesial right* to do so. The reason is clear. To dissent from the teaching of the Church in any important matter of faith or morals is to dissent from the mind of Christ, as it comes down to us over the ages. It is therefore to separate oneself from Christ, to lose one's communion with him, to violate, nullify, and lose one's Catholic identity.

See: Apostolate; Assent and Dissent; Canon Law; Catholic Identity; Church, Membership in; Church, Nature, Origin, and Structure of; Civil Law; Conscience; Dissent; Vocation.

Suggested Readings: CCC 871-933. Code of Canon Law, 208-231. C. Burke, *Authority and Freedom in the Church.* R. Shaw, *Understanding Your Rights and Responsibilities.*

Cormac Burke

ECONOMY OF SALVATION

The expression "economy of salvation" has gained currency in recent decades and occasionally appears in the *Catechism of the Catholic Church*, especially in sections dealing with the seven sacraments (cf. 1217-1228, 1286-1293, 1333-1344, 1539-1553, 1602-1620). That is a clue to its meaning. In Greek, "economy" means something like "plan" or "management." When applied to God, the term refers to the major manifestations to the world of his universal salvific will summed up in saying that he "desires all men to be saved and to come to the knowledge of the truth" (1 Tm 2:4).

Salvation history can be seen as divided into four successive stages, wherein God's constant determination to draw humanity to himself is operative in different human settings. These distinct phases are: (1) the original plan before the Fall; (2) the period after the Fall but before Christ's coming; (3) the time of Christ's incarnate presence in the world; and (4) the period lasting until the end of history, inaugurated by his Ascension and the Holy Spirit's descent. This is the time of Christ's sacramental and ecclesial presence.

Each of these ages is characterized by a specific set of visible and invisible divine aids. However wayward humans beings may become, their all-provident and all-resourceful God is never thwarted in making his original creative intent known and viable. Moreover, while for humans' sake God may establish certain means, such as the Church and the sacraments, he is not limited to them, and his invisible help and attraction are always present in the form of actual graces to all those who tend toward him, however gropingly.

See: Ascension and Parousia; Creation; Divine Revelation; Grace; Human Race, Creation and Destiny of; Original Sin; Providence.

ECUMENICAL COUNCIL

Ecumenical or universal councils are solemn assemblies of the bishops of the whole world, called together by the Pope and meeting under his authority and presidency. They are convened to discuss and regulate matters of Church doctrine, discipline, and pastoral matters normally in response to important events or circumstances: Essential unity may be in danger, questions may have arisen about the meaning or content of some fundamental aspects of the Church's teaching, pastoral directives may be thought necessary for a renewal of the work of evangelization, etc.

The Pope is a necessary principle and foundation of the unity, authority, and legitimacy of a universal council. "There never is an ecumenical council which is not confirmed or at least recognized as such by Peter's successor" (Vatican Council II, *Dogmatic Constitution on the Church, Lumen Gentium*, 22). A council that was without him or had not been called by him would lack the right to be termed "ecumenical."

The presence and role of the bishops is also essential for an ecumenical council. "The college of bishops exercises power over the universal Church in a solemn manner in an ecumenical council. . . . The infallibility promised to the Church is also present in the body of bishops, when together with Peter's successor, they exercise the supreme Magisterium" (CCC 884, 891).

Each ecumenical council sheds new light on the mind of Christ constantly present in the life of the Church, and so becomes a new element in the development of doctrine and another event consolidating Catholic Tradition. Thus there is a necessary connection and continuity between all the councils. Vatican Council II (1962-1965), the first ecumenical council in a century and only the second in four hundred years, was no exception. It can be fully understood and properly applied only if seen and studied in the light of earlier councils, the Magisterium, and Tradition, to which its documents make constant reference.

When an ecumenical council defines matters of belief, these definitions are infallible, for they constitute special exercises of the solemn Magisterium (cf. CCC 884), where the promised assistance of the Holy Spirit, the Spirit of Truth (cf. Jn 14:17), is fully present (cf. Acts 15:28).

See: Church, Nature, Origin, and Structure of; Collegiality; Development of Doctrine; Infallibility; Magisterium; Sacred Tradition.

ECUMENISM

The term "ecumenical" comes from the same root as "Catholic." We speak of certain Church councils as ecumenical because of their universal composition; they gather together the bishops of the whole Church. Ecumenism (or the "ecumenical movement") refers to the efforts to restore the unity among Christians that was broken especially in the eleventh century, with the separation of the Eastern Orthodox Churches, and in the sixteenth, with the emergence of Protestantism. Behind the ecumenical movement is the conviction that Christ founded one Church as the only universal means of salvation, and that therefore the split of his followers into different groups and sects cannot be his will.

Christ's will or not, these splits took place. But it is surely his will that they not be left as simple historical facts. What is important now is not just to explain them, and less still to apportion blame, but to try to repair them.

This must be first of all a matter of prayer. All Christians should imitate Christ in his petition that "there shall be one flock, one shepherd" (Jn 10:16) and his particular prayer at the Last Supper for all those who believe in him: "That they may all be one; even as thou, Father, art in me, and I in thee"

(Jn 17:20-21). In praying, offering sacrifices, and working for church unity, all Christians can be sure they are praying and working for something that God himself wants (cf. CCC 820-822).

The Role of Charity and Clarity • Apart from prayer, two principles must guide all ecumenical work if it is to be fruitful — charity and clarity: truth and love; "speaking the truth in love," as St. Paul says (Eph 4:15).

Charity embraces everyone. It is open to all, welcomes all. Charity can and should be lived without limit. There is no obstacle to it but our own personal self-centeredness. Everyone is to be loved; everyone, without exception, to be treated as a brother or sister. No person can be outside the scope of our love. Even those we consider to be in error have the right to be loved. They need it; and we also need to love them and have the duty to do so.

Faith, however, cannot embrace everything. "Faith is first of all a personal adherence to God" (CCC 150), and its object is truth as God has revealed it and entrusted it to men. Even those who are in error are to be loved, but error itself is not to be loved. Real love for those in error is first of all shown precisely in the desire to see them free from error and rejoicing in the full possession of the truth. Our Lord does not want his followers to be deceived, however sincerely, in their belief.

Therefore, ecumenical contacts and dialogue must be clear. We cannot gloss over differences; that would be a lack of truth and sincerity. And unity is not brought about by deception. While the goal of the ecumenical movement is unity, this cannot be reached as the result of compromise. No one in the ecumenical dialogue can compromise —or be asked to compromise — with what he or she is convinced is the truth.

Convictions are not an impediment to dialogue. Two persons with no convictions could have no interest in arriving at the truth. People of convictions, who in particular are convinced that Christ is God and that he wanted only one Church — one body of followers — can gradually come together.

Hence the need for clarity and sincerity in examining differences: to see not if they can be reduced to a compromise formula, but if they can be overcome by means of a deeper grasp of Christ's plan of redemption, of his Revelation, of his mind and will for his followers down the ages.

The Second Vatican Council insists that unity is a *blessing* that Our Lord wishes his followers to have and that is only to be found in full communion with the one Church he himself founded and accompanies down the ages. "Our separated brethren . . . are not blessed with that unity which Jesus Christ wished to bestow on all those to whom he has given new birth into one body. . . . For it is through Christ's Catholic Church alone, which is the universal help towards salvation, that the fullness of the means of salvation can be obtained" (Vatican Council II, *Decree on Ecumenism, Unitatis Redintegratio*, 3).

Unity is the ultimate goal of the ecumenical movement. Humanly speaking, its achievement may seem remote and almost impossible. Yet no one should doubt that if human good will joins God's will, it can be accomplished.

Official ecumenical endeavors and contacts at the local level must be under the bishop's direction. But each Catholic, by the witness of his or her love for the Church and knowledge of the Church's teachings, with a readiness to carry on a dialogue of charity and clarity with all those Christians of other denominations, is already doing a profoundly ecumenical work.

See: Anglicanism; Church, Membership in; Church, Nature, Origin, and Structure of; Orthodox Churches; Protestantism.

Suggested Readings: CCC 820-822, 836-838, 1271, 2790-2791. Vatican Council II, *Decree on Ecumenism, Unitatis Redintegratio.*

Cormac Burke

EDUCATION IN HUMAN SEXUALITY

Human beings, unlike members of other species, need much education to accomplish their goals and to act correctly. Other animals act largely from instinct, whereas human beings can act either from instinct or after thoughtful reflection and choice. As do animals of other species, human beings experience powerful sexual urges, but unlike other species, it is not appropriate for human beings to act unreflectively or impulsively on those impulses. Thus, human beings must be educated in the proper use of their sexuality.

Such an education is most directly and properly under the governance of the parents, who, the Church teaches, are the "primary educators" of their children. Since human sexual intercourse is the moral prerogative only of the married, much education in human sexuality will be part of education about marriage.

In his apostolic exhortation *The Christian Family in the Modern World, Familiaris Consortio,* published in 1981, Pope John Paul II speaks of three stages of preparation for marriage: remote, proximate, and immediate. Much of education in human sexuality is indirect, implicit, and subtle.

Remote preparation for marriage takes place from the time of a child's earliest childhood. Here is where a child begins to learn the proper "hierarchy of values." This is the time when children first begin to learn that they are unique and special and deserving of the response of love; they are also coming to learn the same about others. They learn how to share with others, to care for them, to live in community with them. They begin to learn how to interact with members of the opposite sex and to see that marriage is a special relationship and also a vocation for serving Christ. They learn much about love and sexuality from observing how their parents interact and how they speak about sexual matters.

Proximate preparation will take place during adolescence and young adulthood. During this time, young people are becoming aware of changes in their bodies and in their psyches, of tensions and excitements that enter into their relationships with members of the opposite sex. The education in human sexuality at this time must be more direct. Young people need to learn about the changes happening within them and to begin to develop a surer and deeper understanding of the demanding responsibilities of human sexuality and of love.

Young men and women need to learn how their bodies are designed so as to enable them to make complete gifts of themselves to another and partake in the awesome responsibility of bringing forth new human life. They will learn how deceptive infatuation can be, and how demanding responsible love is. They will need to learn about financial responsibilities that come with marriage and establishing a home and a family. They will often learn that, although they may feel psychologically and physically prepared for sexual activity, they are not prepared for the responsibilities that come with it.

Education in Chastity • All education in human sexuality, at this level and all levels, must be much more than explanation about physiological changes and phenomena or practical advice about avoiding pregnancy and sexual diseases. It must make clear the moral issues involved and provide young people with clear instructions and positive attitudes on how to live chaste lives. Indeed, the education in human sexuality at the stage of proximate preparation can most properly be called an education in chastity. Young people need to learn how to control their sexual impulses and put them in service of love. Males and females must both learn to view members of the opposite sex as unique persons and not as sexual objects. They should learn the importance of modesty in speech and dress and the dangers of much modern entertainment. They should learn the importance of friendship with members of their own and the opposite sex, both for their intrinsic worth and as a means for self-discovery. Young people should be taught good communication skills so that they can enjoy wholesome relationships with the opposite sex; this will help relieve them of the pressure to express themselves in irresponsible ways. Instruction in the sacraments and prayer, and encouragement to partake frequently in the sacraments of the Eucharist and Reconciliation, will help young people gain the supernatural aid of grace that will help them strengthen their resolve to be chaste and enable them to grow in self-mastery.

Immediate preparation for marriage is directed to those who are engaged to be married. It should take place in the weeks or months preceding the wedding ceremony. At this point, couples should be led to examine carefully their true suitability for each other and the compatibility of their expectations and their plans for life together. Most importantly, they should deepen their understanding and appreciation of marriage as a sacrament and as a vocation wherein they are to live lives of total self-giving and be open to new life.

Many papal documents have observed that the already-married may find it an appropriate apostolate to help with marriage preparation. Couples who are living out the demands of the sacrament in accord with the Church's teaching on sexual morality provide an important witness for those answering the vocation to marriage.

Some young people of course will not marry, either because of their life circumstances or because of a vocation to the consecrated life. They must learn that their sexuality does not go to waste because their state in life calls them to live a life of celibacy. Rather, they are called to enter into a spousal relationship with Christ. The consecrated especially are to live their celibacy as a witness to a life of love turned over to God. Rather than living a loveless existence, they will be challenged, because their hearts are more free to participate in a gratuitous love of others and to live lives of radical self-giving. Instruction in the gift of celibacy and the joys of the consecrated life should be a part of any education in human sexuality.

Sex Education • The need for sex education in the schools has become a rallying cry of those who are alarmed at the high rate of sexual activity among the young and unmarried and the inevitable consequences of teen pregnancy, abortion, unwed parenthood, premature or immature marriages, and the spread of sexual diseases. Although, in view of the threat of AIDS, more are advocating education in abstinence, "responsible sexuality" in the context of most secular sex education refers to the use of an effective contraceptive. Secular sex education programs generally advise young people not to engage in sexual intercourse until they are ready, but they do not teach about chastity or that sexual intercourse is moral only within marriage.

Much secular sex education is largely concerned with explaining the working of the sexual organs, giving an introduction to different kinds of contraceptives and their effectiveness, describing various sexual diseases and the mode of their transmission, and offering a weak exhortation to abstinence. Masturbation is typically presented as a normal and natural sexual activity, and homosexuality is presented as a natural "alternative" lifestyle. Most studies show that secular sex education programs do nothing to decrease the incidence of teenage sexual activity or to diminish the numbers of unwanted pregnancies; rather, they more often make these problems worse.

The disastrous effects of such secular sex education have led some to argue that there should be no sex education in the schools at all and that only parents should provide sex education for their children. The great advantage of such a principle would be that parents may best be able to discern when their children are ready and in need of instruction in respect to various delicate issues. The Church, however, holds that, while parents have the primary responsibility for education in all matters, especially matters of faith and morals, Catholic schools and catechetical programs are suitable agencies for assisting parents and reinforcing and completing what is begun at home. The document *Educational Guidance in Human Love*, published in 1983 by the Congregation for Catholic Education, cites the Holy Father as stating: "Sex education, which is a basic right and duty of parents, must also be carried out under their attentive guidance, whether at home or in educational centers chosen and controlled by them. In this regard, the Church reaffirms the law of subsidiarity, which the school is bound to observe when it cooperates in sex education, by entering into the same spirit that animates parents" (17). The Pontifical Council for the Family in 1995 followed up on this with a document entitled *The Truth and Meaning of Human Sexuality: Guidelines for Education Within the Family.*

The schools are to operate by the same principles, laid out above, that are to direct parents.

That is, "sex education" is truly to be an education in chastity; it is to help young people realize the gift of sexuality, the demands of love and marriage, the sacredness of marriage as sacrament and vocation, and the centrality of chastity to their sexual maturity. Schools are to choose their teachers and programs with great care.

What programs should be used in the schools and when and how it is appropriate to introduce different matters are not questions that can be answered in a universal fashion. Young people in different cultures, and even within different communities within the same culture, may be facing very different challenges and be in need of very different education at different times. For instance, a chaste young woman, raised in a household governed by parents deeply committed to their Catholic faith who monitor carefully various influences of modern culture, would most likely need a very different sex education program from a young woman who was being raised in a broken home by a mother who was not practicing her faith and was involved in a sexual relationship with a man not her spouse.

Many faithful Catholics have attempted to devise programs that will meet a wide variety of needs. Some programs involve teaching parents how to teach their children. Others have comprehensive "family life" programs that begin in the first grade and go through high school. Some teach sexually active young women how to do the charting required for the use of natural family planning, with the expectation that knowledge of their fertility will lead the young women to wait for marriage. Many schools and church groups are now sponsoring rallies in which young people make pledges to remain virgins until marriage or to cease sexual activity until then. Those who have been sexually active but who resolve to refrain from sexual activity are said to regain what is called "secondary virginity." All these programs report favorable rates of success; all of course have very strong components that teach moral principles.

Since a small mistake in the beginning of any enterprise, and especially in one's sexual life, can often have grave consequences later, it is important that the young be helped to make as few mistakes as possible about their sexuality. In a world permeated with sexual provocation, Catholics are well advised to make use of all the resources available to them so as to guide young people in gaining a proper understanding of human sexuality and acquiring the virtue of chastity.

See: Chastity; Concupiscence; Natural Family Planning; Sexuality, Human.

Suggested Readings: CCC 1622, 1632. Vatican Council II, *Pastoral Constitution on the Church in the Modern World, Gaudium et Spes,* 47-52; *Declaration on Christian Education, Gravissimum Educationis,* 1. John Paul II, *The Christian Family in the Modern World, Familiaris Consortio.* Sacred Congregation for Catholic Education, *Educational Guidance in Human Love: Outlines For Sex Education.* Pontifical Council for the Family, *The Truth and the Meaning of Human Sexuality: Guidelines for Education Within the Family.*

Janet E. Smith

END OF MAN

The Greek philosopher Aristotle (384-c. 322 B.C.) taught that the end of man, or the supreme good for man, is *eudaemonia,* which means complete well-being and is commonly translated simply as happiness. Most Christian thinkers have accepted this teaching, differing from Aristotle only on the question of what happiness consists in. Whereas he thought that it consists primarily in the development of those intellectual virtues whereby the philosopher contemplates eternal truth, they say that it consists primarily in knowing and loving God and in being known and loved by God. The *Catechism of the Catholic Church* echoes these Christian thinkers when it says that the end of man — in other words, the ultimate goal of our existence — is beatitude, which can only be a beatitude with God and in God, indeed a sharing in God's own beatitude (16, 1719).

Aristotle had tried to find the sources of human happiness by exploring human nature and in particular by exploring the soul and the rational activities of the soul whereby it is enabled to become itself fully and to thrive. Christian philosophers and theologians have attempted something similar, namely, to show why it is that human nature is made for beatitude in God and could not possibly find beatitude in anything less than God.

The Human Capacity for God • Thus they have explored the mysterious infinite hunger or infinite capacity of human persons, which was expressed by St. Augustine in his *Confessions:* "Our heart was made for you, O Lord, and it will not rest until it rests in you" (Bk. I). In our restlessness we often pursue some finite good — some real good and not just a pleasurable substitute for the good — expecting to be supremely happy in the embrace of that good. But no sooner do we attain the desired good than the old restlessness, just when we least expected it, springs up again in our inmost parts; we find that we have a capacity for good that is only stimulated but never fulfilled by possessing even the greatest finite good. This is why human beings do not fit snugly in their environment like the lower animals, but are always surpassing themselves in their efforts at knowing the world and acting in it; they are possessed of an idea of infinite good that drives them always beyond every finite attainment, so that every point of arrival becomes a point of departure. We are thus led to affirm that the human person is *capax Dei* ("capable of God") and that he reaches his ultimate end only by attaining union with that which is infinite in goodness.

One will notice that for the Christian the ultimate end of man does not consist primarily in intellectual activity, as in Aristotle; not only is the infinite good of which we are capable the object of our knowing but we also participate in it by willing and loving it and delighting in it.

For our supreme beatitude we have to encounter God as personal being. If supreme goodness were impersonal, as in Plato, we would bear a wound in ourselves that would prevent us from being happy. Cardinal Newman says that human beings "would be overpowered by despondency, and would even loathe existence, did they suppose themselves under the mere operation of fixed laws, powerless to excite the pity or the attention of Him who has appointed them." We cannot exist and thrive by living only in relation to general laws, not even if these are divine laws, but we are also made for interpersonal communion, which belongs, therefore, to our ultimate end. We can find beatitude in God only if we know him as *Deus vivens et videns* ("God living and seeing") and are known by him in our unrepeatable personhood, and know that we are known by him, and in addition know ourselves as we are known by him.

This does not mean of course that the human persons whom we love are not also important for our beatitude. They do not indeed suffice entirely for it; but since we are made for interpersonal communion with them, too, they form an indispensable part of it, especially insofar as we love them in God.

The Glory of God • Some philosophers and theologians have questioned the claim that the ultimate end of man is his beatitude, and have proposed to qualify this claim by saying that the primary ultimate end of man is the glorification of God, man's happiness in God constituting only the secondary ultimate end of man. Though with this they depart somewhat from Aristotle, they do not think of themselves as departing from the study of the end of man as it is reflected in human nature. For the human person has the capacity, the vocation, even the need to transcend himself toward good beings *by giving them what is due to them in virtue of their goodness*. He does not approach beings, and least of all other persons, only under the aspect of fulfilling himself through his relation to them; but he can transcend himself by loving them for their own sakes and in their own right. Since the human person is a being of such self-transcendence, he will in his state of supreme fulfillment first of all glorify God because God is supremely worthy, infinite in holiness, and only then will he desire God as the infinite source of his good.

One sees, then, that one can approach the ultimate end of man by studying his nature as person. His infinite capacity for good, his vocation to in-

terpersonal life, his power of self-transcendence, all indicate to us various aspects of his ultimate end. This in turn means that our ultimate end grows out of our nature and is not extrinsically added on to it.

On the other hand, the Church has always been eager to affirm the free gift-character of Christ (CCC 1722), who is the way to our beatitude. From the fact that God creates beings capable of thirst one can infer that he must also create the water they need; but we cannot reason like this from man's desire for beatitude to the necessity of the Incarnation. And yet, for all the gratuity of Christ, he does not remain extrinsic to human nature; as the Church taught at Vatican Council II, "Christ the new Adam . . . fully reveals man to himself" (*Pastoral Constitution on the Church in the Modern World*, *Gaudium et Spes*, 22). It belongs to the interpersonal nature of our beatitude that the other in whom we are happy shares himself with us freely and in a way that we can never predict, which means that our beatitude is signed by the paradox that we are fulfilled in our deepest aspirations by the love that comes from the other as an undeserved gift.

See: Beatific Vision; God, Nature and Attributes of; Heaven; Human Goods; Human Person; Human Race, Creation and Destiny of; Incarnation; Redemption.

Suggested Readings: CCC 16, 260, 356, 1716-1729. Vatican Council II, *Pastoral Constitution on the Church in the Modern World, Gaudium et Spes*, 22. St. Augustine, *Confessions*, I-IX. St. Thomas Aquinas, *Summa Theologiae,* I-II, qq. 1-5. J. Newman, "The Thought of God the Stay of the Soul," in *Parochial and Plain Sermons*, Vol. 5. D. von Hildebrand, *Transformation in Christ*.

John F. Crosby

ENSOULMENT

Ensoulment is God's infusion of an immortal soul into each human being as he or she comes into existence. This event is symbolized in the biblical account of creation, when "the Lord God formed man of dust from the ground, and breathed into his nostrils the breath of life; and man became a living being" (Gn 2:7).

A human soul does not exist before the body, but is specially created by God and infused into matter prepared to receive it. In procreation, parents truly co-create with God, calling on him to create a new and unique soul for the child to whom they both contribute.

The exact time at which ensoulment occurs is not formally defined in Catholic dogma. The Eastern Church has always held that it occurs at conception, and in the West this view was shared by many early Fathers of the Church. In the Middle Ages, Western theologians following the theories of Aristotle held that an intermediate period was needed for unformed matter from the mother to be gradually prepared by the father's semen to receive a specifically human soul. But in the nineteenth century, scientific discoveries exploded the biological theories on which this view was based.

Today the Church recognizes that "from the time that the ovum is fertilized, a life is begun which is neither that of the father nor of the mother; it is rather the life of a new human being with his own growth" (Congregation for the Doctrine of the Faith, *Declaration on Procured Abortion*, 12 [1974]). Science by itself cannot define the time of ensoulment, but it provides strong evidence that a living, developing member of the human species exists from the moment of conception. The Church does teach that each living human being should be treated with the respect due to an ensouled human person.

See: Abortion; Body and Soul; Human Life, Dignity and Sanctity of; Human Person.

ENVIRONMENT

Strictly speaking, human beings do not live in an environment — they live in a world. Animals and plants, which behave more mechanically than human beings, mostly respond to stimuli in their environment. The *human* world, however, contains not only physical processes and causes but meaning, value, freedom, knowledge and choice of right

and wrong, emotion, spirit, and the providence and presence of God.

The *Catechism of the Catholic Church* classifies some of its teaching on the environment under the term "world," but most of it appears under the even more fully Christian category "creation." The Christian concept of creation supports some contemporary concerns about the environment but repudiates others.

Since God is the author of creation, Christians believe this world is good. Some modern theologians, concerned about environmental degradation, have popularized the notion of an "original blessing" that preceded original sin. Insofar as this idea reflects the fact of God's act of creation, it is true. But it does not go very far in telling us how to act. Christians also believe that both human beings and the creation are now radically fallen. Thus, not only is evil present within each person individually and in human society generally, but, as St. Paul says, creation itself is waiting for the future glory and "will be set free from its bondage to decay" (Rom 8:21). For Christians, then, nature is an imperfect elder sister to be cherished and cooperated with, not a master to be obeyed.

Christian and Non-Christian Views • This is the sharpest dividing line that separates Christian from non-Christian views of the environment. Contemporary non-Christian environmentalism usually regards nature as a benign and balanced interplay of forces and species. In fact, as everyone living without the benefits of modern technologies has experienced, nature can also be quite brutal and unbalanced. "Natural" processes have made whole species, such as the dinosaurs, extinct. Animals from locusts to elephants can devastate entire regions. According to some modern theories, volcanic eruptions caused global famines at different times in human history, and these affected population, migration, and even politics. If the world is thought of as only a play of material forces, it is neither good nor stable.

Christians begin from a different starting point. In Genesis, we learn that the creation itself is a revelation of the glory of God. Creation is "the beginning and the foundation of all God's works"

(CCC 198) and is "inseparable from the revelations and forging of the covenant of the one God with his People" (CCC 288). The order of creation and God's providence over the world, despite the Fall, tell us some important truths about how to live: We may not regard the world itself as God, or as an evil limit on us, or as a realm to be fled, or as a mechanism created by God but left to go on functioning blindly by itself. God appears both in and beyond nature. We have responsibilities to foster the good of this world; we were set by God as stewards over his creation (cf. Gn 1:28; Lk 12:41-48).

For some extreme forms of contemporary environmentalism, the very idea that human beings have been set "over" creation is an expression of hubris that has led historically to the destruction of nature. In this view, man is just another species and has an obligation to maintain the world in the condition in which he finds it. This does not fully accord with the vision revealed in the Bible. While there is an interdependence of creatures (cf. CCC 340) and the beauty of the world reminds us of the "infinite beauty of the Creator and ought to inspire the respect and submission of man's intellect and will" (CCC 341), Genesis reflects a hierarchy, with man at the summit as a steward.

In addition, human beings are valued above other parts of creation. Jesus himself reminds his Apostles not to worry because God even watches over sparrows (cf. Mt 6:26; Lk 12:24). Having been created in the image and likeness of God, man may know and choose to foster the created order. No other creature has those powers. Man also has responsibilities that correspond to his position. He must use the goods of the earth for the common good of all, but he has the right, and even the duty, to use minerals, plants, and animals productively for his food, clothing, and other needs (cf. CCC 2457).

Respect for Creation • Man's respect for creation should include not just its present configuration but its creative dynamism. As we now know, the creation continually adds new forms of life, even as others disappear. The higher animals have slowly evolved from lower forms that millions of years ago gave no indications of where creation was heading. Creation, like the Creator and man himself, is creative.

Human beings will wish to preserve all the diversity and purity of the environment they possibly can, but they cannot entirely restrain the natural creativity of nature, including their own nature. We should not lock ourselves and our descendants into one type of technology, economics, or lifestyle. In fact, technologies seem to be growing less physically damaging to nature as their quality and power improve. Understanding nature and using such powers for the common good will call for a creative application of human will and intellect.

That wisdom includes concern for the future. One of the distinctive teachings of the Catholic Church is that the generations are bound to one another. Human technology has brought great benefits to the present age and will doubtless bring even more to future ones. But the present generation has no right to enrich itself at the expense of those who will come after. Unjust appropriation of and damage to natural resources that leave nothing for the future is a form of theft from God's bequest to our descendants and contradicts the seventh commandment (cf. CCC 2456). No one may, for example, overfish or pollute the oceans, with the excuse that future generations will have the ingenuity to discover alternative forms of food. Discerning our obligation toward future generations is not simple, but it cannot be ignored.

The human race has been passing through an era of rapid change in which some forms of technology and industry have and will continue to harm the physical, emotional, and spiritual environment. Other forms have emerged that promise to be compatible with a fuller respect for all life. Our awareness of the promise and dangers, including moral dangers, of human technical mastery of the environment has grown quickly. In earlier ages, the human race struggled to wrest what it needed from the earth's resources. Today, we can provide enough food, clothing, and shelter for everyone, but must learn to do so with a fuller awareness of the effects on air, water, land, plants, and animals — the totality of creation.

See: Animals; Creation; Evolution; Population; Science and the Church; Stealing; Stewardship; Universal Destination of Goods.

Suggested Readings: CCC 282-295, 299, 325-327, 337-344, 373, 2415-2418, 2456. John Paul II, *The Hundredth Year, Centesimus Annus*, 37-38. R. Guardini, *Letters from Lake Como on Technology and the Human Race*. R. Charles, *The Social Vision of Vatican II*, pp. 343-350.

Robert Royal

ENVY

Dorothy Sayers calls envy "the sin of the have-nots against the haves." It is a great leveler: An envious person wants to see everyone else as miserable as he or she is. Envy converts wine into water. Says St. Thomas Aquinas: "Envy makes another's good an evil to oneself, inasmuch as it lessens one's own excellence." Envy starts out asking, according to Sayers, "Why should I not enjoy what others enjoy?" But it soon descends to, "Why should others enjoy what I may not?"

The *Catechism of the Catholic Church*, perpetuating a tradition dating back at least to Origen, numbers envy among the capital sins. More properly is it a rooted inclination to sin, allied with concupiscence's trio of lusts. Born of pride, vanity, and distorted self-love, envy in turn incubates hatred, calumny, detraction, and other kinds of malevolent behavior. Culpably saddened or displeased by another's spiritual or temporal goods, someone guilty of envy immoderately desires "to acquire them for oneself, even unjustly. When it wishes grave harm to a neighbor it is a mortal sin" (CCC 2539).

In popular parlance envy is often confused with jealousy. But a jealous person is driven by a real or putative right to the exclusive possession of something. An instance of excessive jealousy is one spouse's demand that the other enjoy no pleasures that the first cannot enjoy. An envious person, however, feels lessened and humiliated when somebody is more favored than himself.

Not all jealousy or displeasure at another's fortune is necessarily bad. Jealousy can be well-founded when incited by an unjust violation of one's rights. Whenever a good befalling another is undeserved (e.g., an ill-advised job promotion), annoying to others (the youth next door is given expensive stereo equipment by his doting parents and uses it to disturb the neighbors), or morally corrosive (sudden wealth overtakes someone lacking in character to put it to good use), a moment's displeasure can be harmless; but justice perhaps may dictate corrective efforts.

Envy cunningly hides behind rights and justice, and makes seemingly plausible demands. It loves to debunk talent, privilege, and wealth, while refusing to admire, respect, or show gratitude. It leaves little room for voluntary benevolence or charity; it prefers confiscatory taxation to underwrite state beneficence. Judas might be said to be envy's patron saint: "[T]his ointment might have been sold for more than three hundred denarii, and given to the poor" (Mk 14:5).

Envy is best countered by curbing the pride, vanity, and self-love that spawn it. Fraternal charity and good will weaken the disposition to envy; indeed, that is true even of the appearances of charity, for, as C.S. Lewis suggests, the best way to cure ill will may be to act as if one liked the other. Often the feint then becomes fact.

See: Avarice; Capital Sins; Cardinal Virtues; Detachment; Human Virtues; Property; Social Doctrine.

EPISCOPAL CONFERENCE

Episcopal conferences are periodic assemblies of the bishops of one region or country jointly exercising certain pastoral offices on behalf of the Christian faithful of that territory. Already before Vatican Council II they or their equivalent existed in many countries, where bishops gathered together to discuss matters of interdiocesan interest and determine common policy. The Council recommended their establishment everywhere (*Decree on the Bishops' Pastoral Office in the Church, Christus Dominus*, 37). Their purpose is to facilitate exchanges of experience among the bishops involved, and to standardize pastoral and administrative practices so as to further the Church's mission toward the world (cf. Canon 447).

As institutions of ecclesiastical origin, the episcopal conferences are not intermediate organs of government between each diocesan bishop and the Pope. It is to the Roman Pontiff, and not to the conference, that each bishop is directly responsible. The conferences can give decrees in certain matters determined by law; in order to be binding these decrees must (along with other conditions) be approved by the Holy See (Canons 455.1 and 455.2). They cannot act in the name of all the bishops involved unless all have given their consent (Canon 455.4). Evidently, given a proper ecclesial spirit on all sides, a local bishop will not lightly ignore recommendations of the episcopal conference that contribute to true Catholic unity and legitimate diversity. It should be noted, too, that the nature and authority of episcopal conferences are today subjects of continuing theological reflection.

Advisory bodies or committees set up by an episcopal conference carry out important tasks of coordination, information, and research. However, they have no jurisdiction over the areas covered by the conference.

See: Bishop; Church, Nature, Origin, and Structure of; Collegiality; Pope.

EQUIVOCATION

The morality of equivocation can be as slippery as the practice itself. The term, which does not appear in the *Catechism of the Catholic Church*, derives from two Latin words meaning "equal speech" and refers to statements that can bear more than a single meaning. "Did you do your chores?" a mother might ask. "Yes," her son replies. "I made my bed, cleaned my room, and raked leaves." She believes he raked all the leaves; in fact he raked only half of them.

Is such a statement a lie? St. Augustine says lying consists in speaking a falsehood with the intention of deceiving. The boy clearly intends to deceive, but the words he so carefully chooses are

literally true. At best, an equivocation is a half-truth, a coward's escape from an uncomfortable situation. Since it serves the same purpose as a lie, however, it has the same moral character.

The *Catechism* notes several cases where equivocation may be justified. "The good and safety of others, respect for privacy, and the common good are sufficient reasons for being silent about what ought not to be known *or for making use of a discreet language*" (2489; emphasis added). Thus "George is not here" may be a proper response to a man seeking to do George harm, even if George happens to be in the kitchen; the speaker means "not in this room," while the hearer understands "not in the house."

See: Lying; Mental Reservation; Truthfulness.

ESCHATON

It has long been the Church's conviction, the point having crystallized in a solemn and canonical way back in the fifth century at the Council of Chalcedon, that Christ himself is the Eschaton, or Final Age: the one who, in his hypostatic union of the two natures, represents both the time of promise and its consummated glory. It is he who essentially has entered time, mystery intersecting history, and is thereupon destined to come again, at the end of time, to restore and fulfill all things in himself. "Sacred Scripture calls this mysterious renewal, which will transform humanity and the world, 'new heavens and a new earth' [2 *Pet* 3:13]. It will be the definitive realization of God's plan to bring under a single head 'all things in [Christ], things in heaven and things on earth' [*Eph* 1:10]" (CCC 1043).

We stand therefore, as members of his body the Church, inside the Eschaton (or end time), even while as pilgrims we continue to live and move within history, sustained by the hope that we may yet grow into the fullness, the *pleroma*, which is Christ. It is simply the tension, replicated in countless ways in the Christian life, of things both "already" and "not yet," of figure and fulfillment, grace and glory.

Thus, when we speak of nearness to the end, or Eschaton, it is not in the sense of time, because no one has the right to say that the end is here; only God the Father knows the day and the hour, says Christ the Son (Mt 24:36). To speak of nearness to the end pertains rather to the essence of the end that is always present. As Pope John Paul II reminds us in *Crossing the Threshold of Hope,* *"Someone exists who holds in His hands the destiny of this passing world; Someone who holds the keys to death and the netherworld* (cf. Rev 1:18); *Someone who is the Alpha and the Omega of human history* (cf. Rev 22:13). . . And this someone is Love (cf. 1 Jn 4:8, 16) — Love that became man, Love crucified and risen, Love unceasingly present among men."

The whole of Christian eschatology then becomes less a matter of knowing — as its last thing, that is, Eschaton — the finality of man, than of seeing the human face of God, the countenance worn by Christ. The very last thing to remember will not be "my" death or "my" judgment, but God as the enveloping horizon of all that is. Eschatology thus is not anything futuristic, as in some mysterious eventuality meant to unfold only after earthly life is ended. Again, as Pope John Paul puts it, *"Eschatology has already begun with the coming of Christ.* The ultimate eschatological event was His redemptive Death and His Resurrection. This is the beginning of 'a new heaven and new earth' (cf. Rev 21:1)."

Under the circumstances, when the Gospels make their horizon-shattering claim that God has raised Jesus from the grave, declaring death itself to be dead, they are making the unprecedented assertion that the Eschaton, the final age, has at last dawned. In Christ, God has turned the futility of mere human longing into the fact of divine truth and reality. Christ's death on the cross was not an absurd end but a conclusive beginning. In him the new creation and final age have begun. As T.S. Eliot says at the end of "East Coker," second of his celebrated *Four Quartets*: "In my end is my beginning" (cf. CCC 1042-1050).

See: Ascension and Parousia; Beatific Vision; Heaven; Kingdom of God; Last Things; Resurrection of Christ.

Regis Martin

ETERNITY

Frequently thought to mean "everlasting" or "time without end" and sometimes "immortality," eternity in its theological sense is an attribute of God, meaning "without beginning, succession, or end," "outside of time and space," and "the condition of creation." An idea corresponding to the idea of God as eternal is the idea of God as unchanging.

According to Catholic doctrine, the cause of time exists outside time itself, because all creation is created *ex nihilo*, out of nothing (cf. CCC 296-298). Time, as time, possesses the property of potential. Thus, time measures change, which is characterized by movement from potentiality to actualization, from potency to act, a property categorically different from that of eternity. Nothing can be present to time without taking on the potential for change; hence, it is better to say that all time is present to God, rather than that God is present to all time, since there is no duration or simultaneity in God as eternal (cf. St. Thomas Aquinas, *Summa Theologiae,* I, 14, 13). Therefore, it is a non-question to ask, "Where was God before creation?" or "What was God doing before he created the world?" Such questions imply time as the condition for their answers. As well as avoiding the inference of past or future when speaking of God's eternality, the notion of "present" must also be avoided.

See: Creation; God, Nature and Attributes of; Omnipotence; Omniscience; Process Theology; Providence.

EUCHARIST

The Greek verb *eucharistein*, from which the term "Eucharist" is derived, means to give thanks or to grant a favor. In Catholic theology, Eucharist designates the sacrament instituted by Christ at the Last Supper. There he gave thanks, consecrated the bread and wine, and gave his Body and Blood as spiritual nourishment to his Apostles. Descriptions of Christ's action can be found in Matthew 26:26-28, Mark 14:22-24, Luke 22:19-20, and 1 Corinthians 11:23-25. Matthew's account closely resembles that of Mark, while Luke's seems to depend on Paul's description.

Christ's action at the Last Supper was a fulfillment of the promise he had made previously, as recorded in St. John's Gospel: "I myself am the living bread come down from heaven. If anyone eats this bread he shall live forever: the bread I will give is my flesh, for the life of the world. . . . For my flesh is real food and my blood real drink. The man who feeds on my flesh and drinks my blood remains in me and I in him" (Jn 6:51-56).

Doctrine of the Eucharist • The Eucharist is at once a mystery, a sacrament, a sacrifice, a memorial, and a meal, and it was regarded as such very early in the history of the Church. St. Justin (died 165) was one of the earliest apologists to divulge the "secret" of the Christian liturgy. After describing the confection of the Eucharist and its distribution by the deacons at the Sunday Liturgy, he says: "And this food is called among us the Eucharist. . . . For not as common bread and common drink do we receive these, but . . . we have been taught that this food . . . is the flesh and blood of that Jesus who was made flesh" (*First Apology*, 65-a67).

Previously, St. Ignatius of Antioch (died 130) had stated that the Docetists held aloof from the reception of the Eucharist "because they do not confess that the Eucharist is the flesh of our Savior Jesus Christ" (*Letter to the Smyrneans*, 7). St. Augustine (died 430), asserted very clearly the Real Presence of Christ in the Eucharist: "The bread which you see on the altar, once it is sanctified by the word of God, is the body of Christ. And that chalice, or rather what the chalice contains, once it is sanctified by the word of God, is the blood of Christ" (Sermon 227).

Other names were used, but less frequently, to designate this sacrament: for example, the Lord's supper, table of the Lord, breaking of the bread, the unbloody sacrifice, and *agape*. St. Thomas Aquinas stated that the Eucharist has a threefold significance: (1) in relation to the past, it is the memorial of the Passion and death of Christ and is called the "Sacrifice"; (2) in relation to the present, it is the source of unity among the faithful and is called "Communion"; and (3) in relation to the future, it signifies the pathway to heaven and is called "Viaticum" (*Summa Theologiae,* I-II, 73, 4). This same teaching is summarized by St. Thomas in the Eucharistic prayer *O Sacrum Convivium*: "O Sacred Banquet, in which Christ becomes our food, the memory of his passion is celebrated, the soul is filled with grace and a pledge of future glory is given to us."

As a sacrament instituted by Christ, the Eucharist is the Body and Blood of Christ truly present under the appearances of bread and wine for the spiritual nourishment of the faithful. The Catholic doctrine on the Eucharist, officially stated by Lateran Council IV (1215), was expressed even more fully by the Council of Trent against the Protestant Reformers: "Because Christ our Redeemer said that it was truly his body that he was offering under the species of bread, it has always been the conviction of the Church of God, and this holy Council now declares again, that by the consecration of the bread and wine there takes place a change of the whole substance of the bread into the substance of the body of Christ our Lord and of the whole substance of the wine into the substance of his blood. This change the holy Catholic Church has fittingly and properly called transubstantiation" (Denzinger-Schönmetzer, 1642).

The most obvious thing about the Eucharist is that it is food and drink, a sacred meal taken at the altar, the table of the Lord. Like all the other sacraments, the Eucharist effects what it signifies, namely, spiritual nourishment through an increase of sanctifying grace. It differs from the other sacraments, however, because it contains Christ himself substantially, whereas the other sacraments contain a certain instrumental power that is a share of Christ's power (cf. *Summa Theologiae,* III, 65, 3). In other words, the sacrament of the Eucharist is completed by the very words of Consecration, whereas the other sacraments are completed by the application of the matter for the sanctification of the recipient (cf. *Summa Theologiae*, III, 73, 1, ad 3).

As regards the Real Presence of the Body and

Blood of Christ, St. Thomas Aquinas treats this at great length, and his doctrine was generally accepted by the Church (cf. *Summa Theologiae*, III, 75-77). In the administration of the sacraments, the recitation of the sacramental formula makes the material of the sacrament (e.g., the water of Baptism or the chrism of Confirmation) an instrument of divine grace; but in the Eucharist the formula (i.e., the words of Consecration) produces a transformation in the substance itself. Thus, the water of Baptism and the chrism of Confirmation remain what they are, but the bread and wine become the Body and Blood of Christ.

This constitutes the mystery of the sacrament of the Eucharist, and it is truly a *mysterium tremendum*. St. Thomas Aquinas points out that it is just as credible that the accidental properties of bread and wine can remain in the Body and Blood of Christ in the Eucharist as it is that God could form a human body in the womb of the Virgin Mary without the semen of a man (*Summa Theologiae*, III, 77, 1). And in the *Adoro Te* he exclaims: "Sight, touch, and taste in thee are each deceived; / The ear alone most safely is believed: / I believe all the Son of God has spoken, / Than truth's own word there is no truer token. / . . . / God only on the cross lay hid from view; / But here lies hid at once the manhood too, / And I, in both professing my belief, / Make the same prayer as the repentant thief."

In his sermon for the feast of the Ascension, Pope St. Leo says: "Our Redeemer's visible presence has passed into the sacraments." The Christ who is present under the appearances of bread and wine is the glorified Christ, and he is present there in Body, Blood, soul, and divinity. The words of Consecration are spoken by the celebrant of the Mass *in persona Christi*: "This is my body," "This is my blood." Instantaneously Christ is present, and, indeed, he remains present as long as the Species of bread or wine remains. Rightly does the celebrant of the Mass proclaim after the Consecration, *Mysterium fidei*. St. Bonaventure says: "There is no difficulty about Christ's presence as in a sign, but that he is truly present in the Eucharist as he is in heaven, this is most difficult. There-

fore to believe this is especially meritorious" (*Opera Omnia*, IV, 217).

St. Augustine asserts that "what since the days of antiquity was preached and believed throughout the whole Church with true Catholic faith is true, even if it is proved by no argument, explained by no words" (*Contra Julianum*).

From Trent to the Present • The opposition of the Protestant Reformers to the Eucharist concentrated on two basic Catholic doctrines: the Real Presence and the Sacrifice of the Mass. Both were defended by the Council of Trent (session thirteen, October, 1551, and session twenty-two, September, 1562).

Unlike the French and Swiss Protestants, Luther did not deny the presence of Christ in the Eucharist, but he explained it in his own way. He is reported to have said, "I don't care whether this be against nature, so long as it is not against faith." However, he did reject transubstantiation and the enduring presence of Christ in the Eucharistic species outside of Mass. He believed in the Real Presence only at the moment that the Passion and death of Christ are proclaimed and at the reception of Communion; nor did he consider the Mass to be a true sacrifice.

It took twenty years and twenty-five sessions for the Council of Trent to complete its work on the theology of the Eucharist. It reaffirmed the faith of the Church in the real and enduring presence of Christ in the Eucharist as long as the appearances of bread and wine remain. In so doing, it necessarily had to proclaim the change of the substance of bread and wine into the Body and Blood of Christ, using the expression "transubstantiation." Concerning the Mass as a sacrifice, the Council declared that at the Last Supper Jesus gave his Body and Blood to his disciples under the appearances of bread and wine; then he told them, "Do this in memory of me," thus establishing a new priesthood and a sacrifice that will last until the end of time.

The definitive statements of the Council of Trent prevailed until modern times. However, by the time the Second Vatican Council convened, the stage was set for discussions on the theology of the Eucharist. Of the various remote factors that contributed to the debates, one should acknowledge the research of the faculty of theology at Tübingen, the liturgical movement initiated by Dom Prosper Guéranger, and the decree on frequent Communion issued by Pope St. Pius X. Then, in 1947, Pope Pius XII issued his encyclical on the liturgy *Mediator Dei*, in which he called for greater participation in the Mass and the reception of Communion at Mass. At the same time, he marked the distinction between the ordained priesthood and the priesthood of the laity, the importance of personal prayer as well as public, liturgical prayer, and the validity of the celebration of private Masses.

On December 4, 1963, the Second Vatican Council issued its *Constitution on the Sacred Liturgy, Sacrosanctum Concilium*, in which the following paragraph gave rise to renewed interest and discussion of Christ's presence in the Eucharist: "Christ is always present in his Church, especially in her liturgical celebrations. He is present in the sacrifice of the Mass, not only in the person of his minister . . . but especially under the Eucharistic species. By his power, he is present in the sacraments, so that when a man baptizes, it is Christ himself who baptizes. He is present in his word, since it is he himself who speaks when the holy scriptures are read in the Church. He is present, finally, when the Church prays and sings, for he promised: 'Where two or three are gathered together for my sake, there I am in the midst of them' (Mt 18:20)" (7).

This prompted some theologians to discuss the presence of Christ in the Eucharist by starting with a consideration of his presence in the community. New terms were introduced with the intention of replacing transubstantiation, for example, "transignification" and "transfinalization." If applied literally to the Eucharist, these words meant that, without any change in their physical reality, the bread and wine become the signs in which Christ gives himself as food.

The detailed and complicated discussions on the Eucharist led to the publication of the encyclical *Mysterium Fidei* by Pope Paul VI on September 12, 1965. This was followed in 1967 by the publication of *Eucharisticum Mysterium* by the Sacred Congregation of Rites and the Consilium for the implementation of the *Constitution on the Sacred Liturgy*. While expressing appreciation for the recent discussion, the document states that "the Mass, the Lord's Supper, is at the same time and inseparably: a sacrifice in which the Sacrifice of the Cross is perpetuated; a memorial of the death and resurrection of the Lord . . . ; a sacred banquet in which . . . the People of God share the benefits of the Paschal Sacrifice" (3). The interior reality of the Eucharist is not only sanctifying grace, as in the other sacraments; it is Christ himself, Body and Blood, soul and divinity. That is why the words of Christ at the Last Supper must be taken literally: "This, my body, take and eat" and "This, my blood, drink it."

Moreover, "the mystery of the Eucharist should therefore be considered in all its fullness, not only in the celebration of Mass but also in devotion to the sacred species which remain after Mass and are reserved to extend the grace of the sacrifice" (*Eucharisticum Mysterium,* 3). From the earliest days of the Church, the Eucharist has been reserved for veneration and for Viaticum. In *Mysterium Fidei* Pope Paul VI repeated the Church's teaching on the permanent presence of Christ in the Eucharist: "It is not allowable . . . to propose and to act on the opinion according to which Christ the Lord is no longer present in the consecrated hosts left after the celebration of the sacrifice of the Mass is ended" (11).

Effects of the Eucharist • Each of the seven sacraments produces effects in the recipient that also are symbolized by the sacrament. Thus, through the baptismal washing the Christian is born again into the new life in Christ (CCC 1262-1274); through chrismation at Confirmation the candidate receives strength from the Holy Spirit to witness to Christ by word and deed (CCC 1302-1308). The Eucharist, however, is unique because it contains Christ himself, "the living bread that came down from heaven" (Jn 6:51). As a result, its first effect is to unite the recipient to Christ, as Jesus promised: "The man who feeds on my flesh and drinks my blood remains in me and I in him" (Jn 6:56).

It is the teaching of the Church that "all the effects which material food and drink have on the life of our body, maintaining and increasing life, restoring health and bringing pleasure, all these effects this sacrament has on our spiritual life" (Denzinger-Schönmetzer, 698). In other words, the Eucharist preserves and increases habitual grace in the recipient; it has the power to remit venial sins and to fortify one against mortal sins; it is a source of spiritual joy to devout souls.

There is also a social, or communitarian, aspect to the Eucharist, and this is especially evident in the relationship between the Eucharist and the Church. Jesus prayed for this at the Last Supper: "I do not pray for them alone. I pray also for those who will believe in me through their word, that all may be one as you, Father, are in me, and I in you" (Jn 17:20-21). The People of God are united in one faith and one Baptism; they are also united in Christ through the Eucharist, as St. Paul teaches: "Because the loaf of bread is one, we, many though we are, are one body, for we all partake of the one loaf" (1 Cor 10:17).

The Eucharist is thus the source for making the Church a community of believers, the People of God, and for perfecting the Church as the city of God, the new Jerusalem. The Fathers of the Second Vatican Council expressed similar sentiments in *Sacrosanctum Concilium* (47-48):

> At the Last Supper, on the night he was betrayed, our Savior instituted the eucharistic sacrifice of his Body and Blood. This he did in order to perpetuate the sacrifice of the cross through the ages until he should come again, and so to entrust to his beloved Spouse, the Church, a memorial of his death and resurrection: a sacrament of love, a bond of charity, a paschal banquet in which Christ is consumed, the mind is filled with grace, and a pledge of future glory is given to us.

> The Church, therefore, earnestly desires that Christ's faithful, when present at this mystery of faith, should not be there as strangers or si-

lent spectators. On the contrary, through a good understanding of the rites and prayers, they should take part in the sacred action, conscious of what they are doing, with devotion and full collaboration. They should be instructed by God's word, and be nourished at the table of the Lord's Body. They should give thanks to God. Offering the immaculate victim, not only through the hands of the priest but also together with him, they should learn to offer themselves. Through Christ, the Mediator, they should be drawn day by day into ever more perfect union with God and with each other so that finally God may be all in all.

More recently, in the apostolic letter *Orientale Lumen* (May 2, 1995), Pope John Paul II spoke of the relationship of the Eucharist to the *communio,* which is the Church: "In the Eucharist, the Church's inner nature is revealed, a community of those summoned to the synaxis to celebrate the gift of the One who is offering and offered: participating in the Holy Mysteries, they become 'kinsmen' of Christ, anticipating the experience of divinization in the now inseparable bond linking divinity and humanity in Christ" (10).

See: Eucharistic Devotion; In Persona Christi Capitis; Liturgy; Mass; Priest; Priesthood of Christ; Priesthood of the Faithful; Real Presence; Sacrament; Sacrifice; Viaticum.

Suggested Readings: CCC 1322-1344. Vatican Council II, *Constitution on the Sacred Liturgy, Sacrosanctum Concilium.* Pius XII, *On the Sacred Liturgy, Mediator Dei.* Paul VI, *On the Holy Eucharist, Mysterium Fidei.* John Paul II, *On the Mystery and Worship of the Eucharist, Dominicae Cenae.* Sacred Congregation of Rites, *Instruction on the Worship of the Eucharistic Mystery, Eucharisticum Mysterium.* J. Powers, *Eucharistic Theology.*

Jordan Aumann, O.P.

EUCHARISTIC DEVOTION

In his 1965 encyclical on the Eucharist, *Mysterium Fidei,* Pope Paul VI wrote: "The mystery of the

Eucharist is the heart and center of the liturgy itself" (3). The focal points of Eucharistic devotion are the Sacrifice of the Mass and the reception of Communion. But from the very beginning the Blessed Sacrament was also reserved, primarily for the administration of Viaticum and for Communion outside of Mass. This led to adoration of the Blessed Sacrament reserved on the altar, as an expression of belief in the Real Presence.

This same teaching and practice was supported by Pope Paul VI in *Mysterium Fidei*: "The Catholic Church has always offered and still offers the worship of latria to the Sacrament of the Eucharist, not only during Mass, but also by reserving consecrated hosts with the utmost care, exposing them to solemn veneration by the faithful, and carrying them in procession to the joy of the great crowds of the faithful" (56). And: "This faith also gave rise to the feast of Corpus Christi. From it have originated many practices of eucharistic devotion that, under the inspiration of divine grace, have increased from day to day and that the Catholic Church uses eagerly to show ever greater homage to Christ, to thank him for so great a gift, and to implore his mercy" (63).

Fifteen years later, on February 24, 1980, Pope John Paul II issued a letter to all the bishops, priests, and deacons of the Catholic Church under the title *Dominicae Cenae*. After stating that "the Eucharist is the *raison d'être* of the Sacrament of the Priesthood, which came into being at the moment of the institution of the Eucharist," the Pope continues:

> Indeed, since the Eucharistic mystery was instituted out of love, and makes Christ sacramentally present, it is worthy of thanksgiving and worship. And this worship must be prominent in all our encounters with the Blessed Sacrament, both when we visit our churches and when the sacred species are taken to the sick and administered to them.
>
> Adoration of Christ in this Sacrament of love must also find expression in various forms of Eucharistic devotion: personal prayer before the Blessed Sacrament, hours of adoration, periods

of exposition — short, prolonged and annual (Forty Hours) — Eucharistic benediction, Eucharistic processions, Eucharistic Congresses. A particular mention should be made at this point of the Solemnity of the Body and Blood of Christ as an act of public worship rendered to Christ present in the Eucharist, a feast instituted by my predecessor Urban IV in memory of the institution of this great mystery. All this therefore corresponds to the general principles and particular norms already long in existence but newly formulated during or after the Second Vatican Council (3).

In addition to the forms of worship of the Blessed Sacrament mentioned above, it is deserving of mention that various groups of cloistered contemplative nuns dedicate themselves to perpetual adoration of the Blessed Sacrament. There has also been a rekindling of devotion to the Blessed Sacrament among the laity, thanks to the apostolic zeal of numerous pastors and preachers who propagate this devotion throughout the country. There is a constantly increasing number of parishes in which the Blessed Sacrament is exposed for adoration twenty-four hours a day for the benefit of the parishioners, who see to it that the Eucharist is never left unattended.

Unfortunately, in 1979 and again in 1980 the Congregation for Catholic Education found it necessary to issue two instructions on spiritual and liturgical formation in seminaries, emphasizing personal and community adoration of the Blessed Sacrament in seminaries and houses of religious formation. On April 3, 1980, the Congregation for Divine Worship published *Inestimabile Donum*, as an application of Pope John Paul's letter *Dominicae Cenae*, containing the norms for Eucharistic worship.

The Holy Father had already stated in his letter to bishops, priests, and deacons: "It is our vocation to nurture, above all by personal example, every healthy manifestation of worship towards Christ present in that Sacrament of love." He then asked "forgiveness — in my own name and in the name of all of you — for everything which, for whatever reason, through whatever human weakness, and at times partial erroneous application of the directives of the Second Vatican Council, may have caused scandal concerning the interpretation of the doctrine and the veneration due to this great Sacrament" (*Dominicae Cenae*, 12).

Forms of Eucharistic Devotion • Devout Catholics have always shown special reverence to the presence of Christ in the Blessed Sacrament, both during the celebration of the Mass and when venerating the Eucharist reserved in the tabernacle. Since the Church is international and multicultural, the external signs and manifestations of reverence will vary with the culture of the people.

In some places, for example, the faithful observe a reverent silence during the Mass and kneel in adoration from the *Sanctus* until the end of Mass. Genuflection before the tabernacle has been the traditional gesture of adoration in the churches of the West, while the Catholics in the Orient and the Middle East express their reverence by a deep bow from the waist. Similarly, to stand erect may be the posture of prayer and reverence in some cultures, but in others it would be considered bad manners. In view of the principle "The sacraments are for the faithful" (enunciated by St. Thomas Aquinas), the Church has always respected and approved the cultural differences among the faithful.

In the instruction *Inestimabile Donum*, the Congregation for Divine Worship promulgated detailed liturgical directives for the celebration of Mass, Communion of the faithful, and the worship of the Blessed Sacrament reserved in the tabernacle. The following directives may serve as a suitable guide for veneration of the Blessed Sacrament, making allowance for cultural differences or particular decisions made by bishops.

In receiving Communion at Mass, the faithful may stand or kneel, according to the norms approved by the conference of bishops (11).

Public and private devotion to the Holy Eucharist outside Mass is highly recommended (20).

Regarding exposition of the Blessed Sacrament, whether prolonged or brief, processions of the Blessed Sacrament, Eucharistic Congresses, "and the whole ordering of Eucharistic piety," the pastoral indications and directives given in the *Roman Ritual* are to be observed (22).

At Benediction of the Blessed Sacrament the blessing with the Eucharist should be preceded by readings from the word of God, hymns, and public as well as silent prayer (23).

The revised Code of Canon Law (1983) recommends an annual, solemn exposition of the Blessed Sacrament at a suitable time of the year, but only if a sufficient number of people can attend and if the established norms can be observed (Canon 942).

Adoration of Christ in this sacrament of love can be expressed in various forms of Eucharistic devotion, such as personal prayer before the tabernacle, public or private holy hours, Benediction of the Blessed Sacrament, and Forty Hours Devotion. "The encouragement and the deepening of Eucharistic worship," says Pope John Paul II, "are proofs of that authentic renewal which the Council set itself as an aim. . . . The Church and the world have a great need of Eucharistic worship" (*Dominicae Cenae*, 3).

See: Devotions; Eucharist; Liturgy; Mass; Real Presence.

Suggested Readings: CCC 1378-1381, 1418. Vatican Council II, *Constitution on the Sacred Liturgy, Sacrosanctum Concilium*. John Paul II, *On the Mystery and Worship of the Eucharist, Dominicae Cenae*. Congregation of the Sacraments and Divine Worship, *Instruction Concerning the Worship of the Eucharistic Mystery, Inestimabile Donum. Roman Ritual, 10: De sacra Communione et de cultu Mysterii eucharistici extra Missam*.

Jordan Aumann, O.P.

EUTHANASIA

The word "euthanasia" comes from Greek roots meaning "good death" or "easy death" (*euthanatos*). It has come to mean "mercy killing": the direct killing of a patient, usually by a doctor, to end suffering. Especially after Nazi Germany used the word to describe its killing program for the disabled and mentally ill, "euthanasia" has come to include the killing of sick and dying people for any reason, including the most ignoble.

In theological terms, euthanasia is "an action or an omission which of itself or by intention causes death, in order that all suffering may in this way be eliminated" (Congregation for the Doctrine of the Faith, *Declaration on Euthanasia*, II [1980]). Like all direct killing of the innocent, it violates God's law and is gravely wrong.

Why Euthanasia Is Wrong • The fact that a person is already dying of natural causes in no way justifies a human decision directly to attack the basic good of human life. The dying patient is still a person of incomparable worth, made in the image and likeness of God; no one may usurp God's dominion over this person's life by intentionally causing death. Nor is such an act justified by the suffering a patient may face during illness. Suffering may place the patient and others under such duress that their judgment is impaired and their personal guilt greatly reduced; but, objectively, the act of killing is just as grave an evil.

Moral responsibility for euthanasia rests with the patient who requests it and the physician or others who perform it or help make it possible. In so acting, the patient in effect commits suicide, while those who perform or assist in the lethal act are guilty of homicide.

In the form of euthanasia called assisted suicide, a person provides lethal drugs or other means so that a patient can commit suicide; the one who assists shares responsibility for the patient's death. To concur in another person's suicidal wish and help carry it out is "an injustice which can never be excused, even if it is requested" (Pope John Paul II, encyclical *The Gospel of Life, Evangelium Vitae*, 66 [1995]).

Euthanasia is sometimes proposed in the name of mercy and compassion by those closest to the suffering patient: his or her family and physician. But this is a false mercy, because it intends the destruction of a helpless person who is in special need of love and encouragement. "True 'compassion' leads to sharing another's pain; it does not kill the person whose suffering we cannot bear.

Moreover, the act of euthanasia appears all the more perverse if it is carried out by those like relatives, who are supposed to treat a family member with patience and love, or by those such as doctors, who by virtue of their specific profession are supposed to care for the sick person even in the most painful terminal stages" (*Evangelium Vitae*, 66). Humane and life-affirming care for a patient's physical, psychological, and spiritual needs is "the way of love and true mercy" (*Evangelium Vitae*, 67).

Today, proposals for euthanasia are not confined to cases of terminal illness, and the motives behind them may lack any semblance of compassion. "As well as for reasons of a misguided pity at the sight of the patient's suffering, euthanasia is sometimes justified by the utilitarian motive of avoiding costs which bring no return and which weigh heavily on society. Thus it is proposed to eliminate malformed babies, the severely handicapped, the disabled, the elderly, especially when they are not self-sufficient, and the terminally ill." Proposals to kill severely disabled patients by harvesting their vital organs before they are really dead are "more furtive, but no less serious and real forms of euthanasia" (*Evangelium Vitae*, 15).

Other Acts and Omissions • It is important to distinguish euthanasia from other acts and omissions involving seriously ill patients.

First, while an omission of the necessities of life in order to cause death is a form of euthanasia, this is different from the legitimate withdrawal of useless or burdensome medical treatment.

Sometimes aggressive treatment is withheld or withdrawn not in order to hasten death, but because that particular treatment is not beneficial or imposes grave burdens on the patient and family. "Discontinuing medical procedures that are burdensome, dangerous, extraordinary, or disproportionate to the expected outcome can be legitimate; it is the refusal of 'over-zealous' treatment. Here one does not will to cause death; one's inability to impede it is merely accepted" (CCC 2278). If an earlier death occurs, this is tolerated as an unavoidable side effect that was foreseen but not intended.

If a means of life support is especially effective

in sustaining life and can generally be provided without serious risks and burdens, proposals to withhold or withdraw it require careful scrutiny. Thus the issue of withdrawing nutrition and hydration from vulnerable patients has prompted intense discussion. Even when their provision requires artificial assistance (e.g., so-called "tube feeding" and intravenous fluids), these means can often maintain life without imposing serious burdens on the patient. Some proposals for withdrawing such means from seriously ill or permanently disabled patients are based not on the burdens of treatment but on the alleged burden of the patient's life — in effect, death is seen as preferable to the patient's diminished condition, and nutrition and hydration are withdrawn to ensure that death occurs. To act on such a judgment is to practice euthanasia by omission.

However, even withdrawal of such basic means is not always equivalent to euthanasia. For example, patients in the final stages of dying often lose the desire to take food or water, and efforts to provide these means with artificial assistance would only cause discomfort and other burdens without significantly prolonging life. Allowing the dying process to run its course, for patients whose inevitable death is imminent in any case, is not euthanasia.

A second issue requiring careful distinctions is pain control. The doses of narcotics needed to relieve pain for patients dying of cancer or other illnesses may at times be so large as to risk hastening death by suppressing respiration. Pope Pius XII taught that narcotics which risk this side effect may be used "if no other means exist, and if, in the given circumstances, this does not prevent the carrying out of other religious and moral duties."

This teaching was affirmed in 1980 by the Vatican *Declaration on Euthanasia*, and in 1995 by Pope John Paul in *Evangelium Vitae*. "In such a case, death is not willed or sought, even though for reasonable motives one runs the risk of it: There is simply a desire to ease pain effectively by using the analgesics which medicine provides" (*Evangelium Vitae*, 65). But deliberately using

such narcotics to cause death would be euthanasia: The agent directly wills the patient's death, as an end in itself or as a means to the goal of ending suffering.

On both issues — withdrawal of treatment and use of pain control — the Catholic view reflects the "principle of double effect." Sometimes an act performed with a good intention unavoidably has two effects, the good effect that is intended and a harmful side effect that is foreseen but not intended. For a serious reason, one may perform the act despite the side effect. In short, not every act or omission that may have the effect of shortening a patient's life is euthanasia. In case of doubt, one should ask oneself: What am I seeking to achieve through this act or omission? Would my purpose still be served if the patient did *not* die as a result?

Such an examination of conscience is appropriate for all involved in these decisions, including patients themselves. The patient is the best person to judge the benefits and burdens of treatment and the need for pain relief; his or her reasonable wishes should generally be followed. However, those who help care for the patient remain moral agents with their own consciences. Health care professionals convinced that a patient is demanding euthanasia by act or omission should help the patient make decisions more responsibly; they have a right and an obligation to refuse to assist in a morally evil proposal.

Biblical and Historical Background • It is sometimes said that Scripture contains no condemnation of euthanasia. But Scripture contains the commandment "Thou shalt not kill," and suggests no exception to allow the killing of suffering or dying persons. What Scripture says about suffering and the need to trust in God's providence argues against any such exception. "Accept whatever befalls you, in crushing misfortune be patient; for in fire gold is tested, and worthy men in the crucible of humiliation" (Sir 2:4-5).

This is more than mere resignation to one's fate; it is faith in a God present in even the most anguished circumstances of life, and hope that he will help those who love him. Exemplifying this ideal is the Suffering Servant, a prophetic foreshadowing of Christ, who redeems his people by bearing their guilt without complaint (cf. Is 53). The Old Testament also teaches that God is absolute sovereign over life and death, so that it would be presumptuous for human beings to try to seize control over the time and manner of death: "Learn then that I, I alone, am God, and there is no god besides me. It is I who bring both death and life" (Dt 32:39).

These teachings are confirmed in the New Testament in the Person of Christ, who abandons himself totally to the Father's will even to the point of enduring the most painful and humiliating kind of death. From this point on, Christians can see in Jesus' Resurrection a message of hope for all who face suffering and death: The way of salvation is the way of the cross (cf. Mk 10:21).

Supporters of euthanasia have tried to portray Jesus' death as the model of a noble suicide. This is a grave misreading of the New Testament, which shows Jesus as the man who is unjustly executed by sinners and whose only concern is the will of the Father. Jesus' goal is not to ensure his own death, but to remain faithful to his mission, even at the cost of death at the hands of evildoers. The Gospels' most striking portrayal of suicide is in the story of Judas, who hangs himself in despair when he realizes what he has done in betraying his Master (Mt 27:5). His death is not seen as noble, but as the tragically fitting end of someone who has turned against God.

This contrast between martyrdom and suicide runs through early Christian thought. The Fathers of the Church praised martyrs who endured in the faith even on threat of death; but they insisted that no one should needlessly provoke such a death or seek it out for its own sake. St. Jerome wrote: "It is not ours to lay hold of death; but we freely accept it when it is inflicted by others."

Christians had to preach their message in a Greek and Roman culture that accepted, and sometimes glorified, suicide in cases of disgrace or hardship. The Stoic philosopher Seneca, who lived at the time of Christ, justified suicide as a noble act once life has seemingly lost its pleasure or meaning. The early Fathers condemned this attitude as usurping God's prerogatives over life and death. True nobility, they said, lies not in withdrawing from life but in withdrawing from the passions and temptations that distract us from God's will.

As Christians applied their faith to the practice of medicine, they took up as their own the oath of Hippocrates, which forbids all assistance in a patient's suicide. Medicine became a sacred calling among Christians, a "profession" with its own ethic dedicated to healing and not killing.

In the fifth century, St. Augustine clarified and summed up the Christian witness against euthanasia: "It is never licit to kill another: even if he should wish it, indeed if he request it because, hanging between life and death, he begs for help in freeing the soul struggling against the bonds of the body and longing to be released" (Epistle 204, 5). He condemned suicide in times of hardship, insisting that "no one should inflict a voluntary death on himself by fleeing temporal troubles, lest he fall into eternal troubles" (*City of God*, I, 26). Whatever the circumstances, he taught, suicide is nothing less than the murder of oneself.

This tradition continued through centuries of Christian reflection. It confronted its next major challenge in the twentieth century, when secular thinkers applied materialistic ideas from the Enlightenment to matters of life and death. These thinkers saw no meaning in "unproductive" lives, and developed justifications for killing the retarded, disabled, and mentally ill, justifications ultimately taken up in Nazi Germany's program for exterminating "life unworthy of life."

In 1940, the Holy See formally condemned such killing of people with psychic or physical defects; and in 1943 Pope Pius XII incorporated this condemnation into his encyclical *On the Mystical Body of Christ, Mystici Corporis Christi*, citing St. Paul's statement that "the more feeble members of the Body" may be the most important in God's eyes. Pius XII expressed "profound grief" at the killing of disabled patients in the name of the "common good": "The blood of these victims, all the dearer to our Redeemer because deserving of greater pity, 'cries to God from the earth' " (92).

In 1965, the Second Vatican Council named euthanasia among the "infamies" that "poison human society" and are "a supreme dishonor to the Creator" (*Pastoral Constitution on the Church in the Modern World, Gaudium et Spes*, 27). In 1980, the Congregation for the Doctrine of the Faith elaborated this teaching in its *Declaration on Euthanasia*. Finally, in 1995, Pope John Paul II solemnly confirmed that "euthanasia is a grave violation of the law of God, since it is the deliberate and morally unacceptable killing of a human person." He declared that "this doctrine is based upon the natural law and upon the written word of God, is transmitted by the Church's Tradition and taught by the ordinary and universal Magisterium" (*Evangelium Vitae*, 65). His declaration made it clear that this teaching is an unchangeable part of the Church's witness.

Social and Legal Debate • Several trends have made euthanasia more appealing to many in the United States. In a pleasure-loving consumer society, it is difficult to find meaning in a life that involves severe suffering, and "unproductive" people are at risk of being seen as useless and even disposable burdens on others. Modern standards of speed and efficiency have influenced the medical profession, leaving little room for the patience required to care for those who cannot be cured. Advanced medical techniques have staved off many diseases, but also prolonged some conditions that tempt patients to consider euthanasia. Most importantly, many people have lost sight of God as a loving Father who watches over us and gives our lives meaning. Maximizing individual "freedom of choice" — regardless of the nature of the choice — is defended as the highest goal of human society; the freedom to choose a quick and painless death is even called the ultimate human freedom.

These trends have led in one country to an extended experiment in legalized euthanasia. Since 1973, courts in the Netherlands have effectively instructed physicians that they will be immune from prosecution if they perform euthanasia under certain guidelines. A policy originally encompassing only persistent requests for death from hopelessly suffering and dying patients has steadily expanded so that physicians have been allowed to kill patients who were physically healthy and handicapped children who never asked for death. The Netherlands stands as a stark reminder of the slippery slope leading from supposedly limited killing to a broader culture of death.

In the United States, Oregon became the first state to legalize assisted suicide for the terminally ill in November, 1994. But the measure was enjoined by a federal court, which declared it unconstitutional in August, 1995. At this writing (1997), the U.S. Supreme Court has before it cases from the states of Washington and New York also focusing on the question of assisted suicide.

In Catholic social teaching, " 'The moment a positive law deprives a category of human beings of the protection which civil legislation ought to accord them, the state is denying the equality of all before the law. When the state does not place its power at the service of the rights of each citizen, and in particular of the more vulnerable, the very foundations of a state based on law are undermined . . .' [CDF, *Donum vitae* III]" (CCC 2273). When a state protects able-bodied people from their own suicidal wishes but exempts people with certain illnesses from such protection, it has made its own judgment that some lives are less worth living than others. In the name of freedom, it gives new power to some people to end the lives of others who are among the most vulnerable members of society. Such legal permission for the strong to kill the weak is "the death of true freedom," for it undermines the mutual trust and respect that make a free society possible (*Evangelium Vitae*, 20).

See: Assisted Suicide; Care of the Dying; Double Effect; Health Care; Homicide; Human Goods; Human Life, Dignity and Sanctity of; Natural Law; Ordinary and Extraordinary Means of Sustaining Life; Suffering in Christian Life; Suicide; Teleological Ethics.

Suggested Readings: CCC 2276-2283. John Paul II, *The Gospel of Life, Evangelium Vitae*, 15, 20, 64-67. Congregation for the Doctrine of the Faith, *Declaration on Euthanasia*. St. Augustine,

City of God, I, 17-27. D. Amundsen, "Suicide and Early Christian Values" in B. Brody, ed., *Suicide and Euthanasia*, pp. 77-153. J. Sullivan, *Catholic Teaching on the Morality of Euthanasia*. L. Gormally, ed., *Euthanasia, Clinical Practice and the Law*. R. Smith, ed., *Conserving Human Life*.

Richard Doerflinger

EVANGELICAL COUNSELS

Christ is for us the teacher of life. In the Gospels, he not only makes known the precepts of love and the importance of the Decalogue and of other commandments flowing from the precepts of love (cf. Mt 22:40) but also he offers us certain counsels. That is, he commends certain excellent ways of living for those who are able and willing to walk in them, though they are certainly not required of all. Living by these Gospel counsels enables a follower of Christ to walk in the ways of love with greater freedom and security, and with that generosity "which is never satisfied with not giving more" (CCC 1974).

Poverty, Chastity, and Obedience • Christian Tradition singles out poverty, chastity, and obedience as the central Gospel counsels. Those who are willing are invited to put aside all material possessions, to lead virginal lives for the sake of the kingdom, and to live lives of more dedicated obedience than would be obligatory.

But every Christian must have a certain detachment from material goods, a firm purity of heart, and an obedient spirit; one cannot be a serious Christian and be enslaved to earthly riches, to carnal pleasures, or to proud rejection of rightful authority. Hence, in many ways, every Christian needs to live in the spirit of the counsels (CCC 915). Those who live the counsels wisely and well in their strongest senses — owning nothing, pursuing no sexual gratifications at all, devotedly obedient in all things in lives dedicated earnestly to the service of the kingdom — should be a warm encouragement to all who seek to live Christian lives in other vocations (CCC 932).

Christ himself plainly lived a life of great poverty, of virginal chastity, and of entire obedience.

"Though he was rich, yet for your sake he became poor" (2 Cor 8:9). His advice to the rich young man was to become similarly poor: to give to the poor all he had (Mt 19:21). While Christ honored marriage, he commended a life of virginal chastity to those able and willing to so live, and he himself lived such a life. He also lived a life of heroic obedience (cf. Phil 2:8), and he invited others to walk in his steps. His disciples were not only to be obedient to the precepts common to all but to forsake all and *follow him*, doing all that would be asked of them in lives committed to seeking the kingdom of God before all else.

St. Thomas Aquinas points out that we can certainly come to everlasting life without abandoning the good things of the world as thoroughly as the counsels would commend. The commandments themselves require us to refuse to make of earthly things the end of our lives; and it is in keeping the commandments that one can come to everlasting life (Mt 19:16-17). But one will attain faithfulness to God more readily by entirely giving up the seductive attractions of the world, so far as that is possible.

Now the world seduces us by the attractions of external wealth, by carnal pleasures, and by the pride of life (1 Jn 2:16). The three Gospel counsels are radical, liberating escapes from these three central sources of temptation. One can lead an especially excellent life by imitating Christ in spurning the personal possession of all earthly goods, in renouncing all sexual pleasure, and in submitting willingly every element of one's life to the Lord, ready to accept the directions of those whom one intelligently follows in the Lord's name for the sake of serving the kingdom more generously (*Summa Theologiae*, I-II, q. 108, a. 4).

Consecrated Life and the Counsels • From the first days of the Church, many lived lives in accord with the counsels. The New Testament in many places praises those who chose to live virginal lives so as to have the freedom and inner energy to serve God's kingdom with hearts devoted entirely to that end. There were many who followed the advice that the rich young man did not accept, gladly giving all they had to the poor so that their love might be more perfect and they might serve Christ and his people with freer hearts.

Hence there are deep Gospel roots to that religious life that grew up in the Church, first in informal ways, and later in more structured but widely varied forms of consecrated life in hermitages, in monasteries, and in other forms. The Church commends the generous love that calls many to bind themselves freely to live all their lives for the family of God in poverty, chastity, and obedience (cf. CCC 914-930).

The praise of the Gospel counsels is in no way a condemnation of marriage, nor a narrow pretense that only those who live in entire poverty or in religious obedience can live sublime Christian lives. Clearly, too, it is not the case that religious, and others who keep the Gospel counsels, are naturally the best people. Those who love God and neighbor most are those dearest to God (CCC 1974).

Nor would it be possible to despise the ordinary ways of salvation and please God. Someone who despises marriage or declares all ownership of goods sinful is not pleasing God (CCC 1620). The exceptional ways of living the Gospel, as in religious life, are in fact intended to be in service of the more ordinary ways of ordinary people. The way of the counsels is meant to be a way of great love. It is not external things that are praised in praising poverty, chastity, and obedience; it is the heart that gladly gives up things one has no obligation to give up, for the sake of pursuing more intense love and serving all the friends of Christ in his kingdom.

Yet the way of the counsels really is a more excellent way of life than the path of marriage and the more ordinary patterns of life in the world. People can live precious Christian lives, married and owning many things that are used to serve the poor and be a blessing to all. But Christ rightly praised the greater generosity that would give away all to the poor and school the heart in a more intense love. Married life is the path to holiness for most good people; but for those who are called, and are able to accept it, the life of virginity for the sake of the kingdom has an even greater ex-

cellence (Council of Trent, Denzinger-Schönmetzer, 1910). While many married people and many with material possessions lead exemplary lives, the virginal way of life that Christ commended is in itself a more excellent form of life, when accepted as Christ wished it to be: as a willing sacrificing of good things for the sake of a more single-minded service of God and all his people. The consecrated life pursued by those who follow the evangelical counsels has, Pope John Paul II says, "an objective superiority" as a way that manifests the holiness of the Church and mirrors Christ's own way of life (apostolic exhortation *The Consecrated Life, Vita Consecrata*, 32).

See: Beatitudes; Celibacy, Priestly; Chastity; Consecrated Life; Law of Christ; Marriage, Sacrament of; States in Life; Vocation.

Suggested Readings: CCC 914-945, 1973-1974, 2053. Vatican Council II, *Decree on the Appropriate Renewal of the Religious Life*, *Perfectae Caritatis*; *Dogmatic Constitution on the Church*, *Lumen Gentium*, Ch. VI. John Paul II, *The Consecrated Life, Vita Consecrata*, 1996. St. Thomas Aquinas, *Summa Theologiae,* I-II, q. 108, a. 4. H. von Balthasar, *The Christian State of Life*.

Ronald D. Lawler, O.F.M. Cap.

EVANGELIZATION

While most American Catholics are familiar with evangelism, a fervent call to Christian conversion, evangelization is a relatively new term. This is hardly surprising, for the word only recently has gained currency. In 1975, Pope Paul VI issued the apostolic exhortation *On Evangelization in the Modern World, Evangelii Nuntiandi*, in which he calls Catholic evangelization "the essential mission of the Church, [which] exists in order to evangelize, that is to say, in order to preach and teach, to be the channel of the gift of grace, to reconcile sinners with God" (14). The *Catechism of the Catholic Church* identifies evangelization as part of the laity's "prophetic mission" (905). Pope John Paul II has often quoted Paul VI's declaration, emphasizing the ever-increasing need for sound evangelization.

What is this essential mission that the post-Vatican II Popes value so highly? *Evangelii Nuntiandi* offers a detailed description. Catholic evangelization is (1) a complex process made up of varied elements that (2) aims at the renewal of humanity through (3) witness, (4) explicit proclamation, (5) inner adherence, (6) entry into the community, (7) "acceptance of signs," and (8) apostolic initiative (*Evangelii Nuntiandi*, 24).

First of all, Catholic evangelization is an ongoing process involving both heart and head — quite different from the onetime acceptance of Christ as Lord and Savior that televangelists typically stress. Jesus explained the experience of becoming his disciple in dynamic terms, inviting people to take up their crosses and follow. The Church evangelizes through a constant call to holiness, which individuals can achieve only through a lifetime of loving faithfulness and moral struggle, choosing good over evil in every passing situation.

Audiences and Goals of Evangelization • In-evitably, the first objects of evangelization are practicing Catholics themselves, since one cannot share what one does not have. Unless Catholics are enthusiastic about their own faith, they will be unable to call forth faith in others. Parish evangelization committees often begin by working to revitalize the celebration of weekend Mass, bringing the worshiping community together around the Eucharist (CCC 2835). They may go on to help create an atmosphere of welcome in the parish, encourage the intensive study of Scripture, form small groups for prayer and fellowship, promote family activities, improve *Catechism*-based religious education programs for children and adults, encourage parishioners to carry their Christian commitment into workplace and marketplace, and in general give faith and Church a more prominent and conscious place in daily life.

Jesus said, "Go therefore and make disciples of all nations" (Mt 28:19). Because he died to save every human being, the Church has a solemn responsibility to be the instrument of salvation for all (CCC 767-768, 776). Millions of Americans, from prosperous suburbanites to city apartment dwellers to the citizens of quiet towns, have never heard the Catholic message or have heard it so weakly that it made little impression.

The Church presents this message to them in ways collectively called "outreach." On the parish level, the most successful and effective means of spreading the Gospel in recent years has been the Rite of Christian Initiation of Adults (RCIA), a nine-month program beginning with instruction and ending with acceptance into the Church at Easter. A host of other programs emphasizes a one-on-one invitation to faith that a parishioner might extend to an inactive Catholic (usually a family member or friend) or someone seeking a church community. At the same time, the Church is making greater use of the media, especially radio and television, to evangelize the general population.

As the Holy Father's 1995 encyclical *That All May Be One, Ut Unum Sint*, stresses, the Church is committed to the ecumenical movement and seeks the unity of all Christians. Thus, while she offers the Catholic faith to any who approach, she does not reach out aggressively to seek members from the ranks of other Christian communions. Yet the challenge to evangelize remains formidable. According to a 1994 Gallup poll, one-third of all Americans lack a religious affiliation; of the remaining two-thirds, forty-two percent say they seldom or never attend services. Inactive Catholics in the United States probably number at least twenty million, "unchurched" persons about eighty million.

The most striking phrase in Pope Paul's description of evangelization is "the renewal of humanity." Christ died on the cross and rose again with no other purpose than to *renew* humanity. St. Paul says: "For we know that Christ being raised from the dead will never die again. . . . The death he died he died to sin, once for all, but the life he lives he lives for God. So you also must consider yourselves dead to sin and alive to God in Christ Jesus" (Rom 6:9-11). Authentic conversion, which is evangelization's goal, implies renewal.

Still, individual conversion is insufficient. Personal conversion, multiplied and made visible in the outward life of the Church, naturally takes on a social (though not political) character and creates a dynamic for building God's kingdom on earth. Pope Paul says evangelization "is a question not only of preaching the Gospel in ever wider geographical areas or to ever greater numbers of people, but also of affecting and as it were upsetting . . . humanity's criteria of judgment, determining values, points of interest, lines of thought, sources of inspiration and models of life which are in contrast with the word of God and the plan of salvation" (*Evangelii Nuntiandi*, 19).

Action for social justice may inspire onlookers to wonder about the source of Catholic moral energy and so lead them to God. It also helps shape human relationships according to scriptural ideals by stressing harmony over division, trust over hostility and suspicion, worship of the one true God over the many false gods abroad in contemporary culture. Finally, social action can correct laws, customs, and systems that perpetuate evil, for example, the so-called abortion right or the racism that tears the social fabric and makes a mockery of Jesus' prayer "that all may be one."

Methods and Results of Evangelization • If conversion of minds and hearts leading to the renewal of humanity is the goal of evangelization, witness and proclamation are its primary methods. The word "witness" means "give evidence for," as a witness testifies at a trial. While roles within the Church are changing rapidly, quiet witness remains the primary tool of the lay evangelizer.

It consists simply in living according to Christian love and Christian conscience, in union with the Church. The man who attends daily Mass gives witness. So does the one who organizes a summer basketball league on inner-city playgrounds, though he may never speak of Christ. The woman who serves as extraordinary minister of the Eucharist gives witness. So, too, the one who does *pro bono* legal work for an indigent client. The high-school senior who volunteers as a retreat leader gives witness, as does the one who shovels an elderly neighbor's walk. The assumption in these latter cases is of course that these persons are known to be Christians acting out of Christian motives.

Proclamation, on the other hand, is declaring those motives. People "do good" for many reasons: benevolence, sympathy, a sense of duty, sometimes even pride or an intention to deceive. The evangelizer, whether clergy or lay, does good out of Christian conviction and does not shrink from saying so. Pope Paul insists: "There is no true evangelization if the name, the teaching, the life, the promises, the kingdom and the mystery of Jesus of Nazareth, the Son of God, are not proclaimed" (*Evangelii Nuntiandi,* 22). Because Americans often see religion as a private affair, most explicit Catholic proclamation takes the form of Sunday homilies, statements from bishops individually and collectively, and other public declarations of faith and principle. However, there is a growing movement among Catholic laity to share their faith, in the spirit of St. Peter's first letter: "Always be prepared to . . . [explain] the hope that is in you, yet do it with gentleness and reverence" (1 Pt 3:15-16).

According to Paul VI, evangelization stimulates inner adherence and entry into the community. For Catholics, the community of faith, the assembly of believers, is the Church, and Catholic evangelization leads to membership in that assembly. The evangelizer invites inactive Catholics back to the practice of their religion and those with no religion to join the Church.

Living as a Catholic, participating in the sacramental life of the Church, constitutes the "acceptance of signs" Pope Paul mentions. The primary sign is the Church herself, the instrument of salvation, the visible manifestation of the kingdom of God on earth, the leaven and salt that, in God's good time, will effect the renewal of humanity. Catholics also accept the seven signs (sacraments) of the Church, especially Baptism, Reconciliation, and the Eucharist, as divinely given aids in attaining salvation (CCC 758-780).

The final mark of evangelization is that it comes full circle; the zeal of converts is well-known. "Again, the kingdom of heaven is like a merchant in search of fine pearls, who, on finding one pearl of great value, went and sold all that he had and bought it" (Mt 13:45-46). The evangelized becomes the evangelizer, offering the pearl of faith he has received so that it may pass from hand to hand in an unbroken chain leading both back to God and forward to God.

Evangelization in America • The U.S. Catholic bishops responded to the promulgation of *Evangelii Nuntiandi* by declaring evangelization a priority and taking steps to weave it into the fabric of Church life. In 1992, they published *Go and Make Disciples: A National Plan and Strategy for Catholic Evangelization in the United States*. The plan exists to guide dioceses and parishes in reevangelizing a nation that seems to be becoming progressively less Christian. It is organized around three great goals inspired by *Evangelii Nuntiandi*: (1) to awaken Catholics' enthusiasm for the faith so that they are willing to share it with others; (2) to invite all Americans to salvation in and through the Church; and (3) to promote the dignity of the human person, the welfare of the family, and the common good so that the United States "may continue to be transformed by the saving power of Jesus Christ."

What does Catholic evangelization bring to America in pursuit of these goals? First of course the faith itself, an answer to society's frustrated spiritual longings. Polls show that some ninety percent of Americans believe in God; almost as many affirm the divinity of Jesus. As already noted, however, this religiosity does not carry over into actual practice. Many of the Protestant communions so influential in the rise of the United States are losing membership at an alarming rate. The Catholic Church continues to grow, but is experiencing a worsening shortage of clergy and religious, while internal conflict divides the faithful. In this atmosphere, many turn to biblical literalism, to exotic New Age movements, even to witchcraft and Satanism, to express their need for the transcendent.

The Church also contributes the Christian notion of love to U.S. culture. Christian love, *agape* in Greek, is not the shallow libido or sentiment that underlies much commercial advertising. It refers, rather, to an attitude of openness, respect, and benevolence toward others because they, too, are God's creatures. *Agape* is a kindly and cooperative spirit, a concern for those in need and for social justice.

Agape is thus the attitudinal basis for community. Critics of the American scene never tire of pointing out that the shared assumptions of three or four generations ago have dissolved. A once-cohesive society tends to become evermore a mere mass of unrelated individuals who happen to occupy the same space. Catholic tradition, with its powerful emphasis on the faithful as the People of God, counteracts such atomization.

While evangelization may be a new concept for contemporary Catholics, there would be no Church if missionaries, starting with St. Paul, had not carried their message of salvation in Jesus Christ "to the ends of the earth." The Church in the United States sprang from the dedication of European missionaries who, whatever their cultural limitations, walked in this great tradition. Now the past may be the future, as Pope John Paul II reminds us in his 1994 letter *As the Third Millennium Draws Near, Tertio Millennio Adveniente*: "The more the West is becoming estranged from its Christian roots, the more it is becoming missionary territory" (57). The need for Catholic evangelization can only grow.

The Holy Father presents the third millennium as a wonderful opportunity for the Church critically to examine her past, repent her mistakes, and commit herself to an evangelization new in ardor, methods, and expression. Thus refreshed and intensified, Catholic Christianity, evangelical at its core, can continue the missionary journey. "The whole of the Christian life is like a great pilgrimage to the house of the Father, whose unconditional love for every human creature . . . we discover anew each day. This pilgrimage takes place in the heart of each person, extends to the believing community and then reaches the whole of humanity" (*Tertio Millennio Adveniente*, 49).

See: Apostolate; Christian Witness; Church, Nature, Origin, and Structure of; Economy of Salvation; Ecumenism; Media of Social Communications; Missionary Activity; Social Doctrine.

Suggested Readings: CCC 758-780, 905, 2045-2046, 2853. Vatican Council II, *Decree on the Church's Missionary Activity, Ad Gentes; Decree on the Apostolate of the Laity, Apostolicam Actuositatem*, 5. Paul VI, *On Evangelization in the Modern World, Evangelii Nuntiandi.* John Paul II, *As the Third Millennium Draws Near, Tertio Millennio Adveniente*, 29-59; *That All May Be One, Ut Unum Sint.* National Conference of Catholic Bishops, *Go and Make Disciples: A National Plan and Strategy for Catholic Evangelization in the United States.* K. Boyack, C.S.P., ed., *The New Catholic Evangelization.*

David M. Byers

EVIL, PROBLEM OF

Catholic doctrine maintains that evil is the privation of the good that belongs to the nature of a thing as willed by God. A thing is evil in the absolute sense when it fails to fulfill its nature and evil in the relative sense when it interferes with the fulfillment of another in its nature. Evil is committed by individuals. God allows individual evil because he has given humans freedom.

Evil does not exist as an eternal, separate force against God. Dualistic ideas regarding God's nature are condemned in Catholicism. All created beings exist outside of God's eternity. Satan, by whatever name, is the chief fallen angel and is evil insofar as he willfully chose to oppose God. Satan is not an opposing divine force equal to God, but only an opposing creature, whose influence over others does not exceed his angelic powers. God provides humans sufficient grace to resist Satan's temptation, thus offering confirmation of his sovereignty over evil.

The problem of evil concerns this question: If God is all-knowing, all-powerful, all-present, and all-loving, how is it that God allows sin and suffering? Moral evil, sin, is not only a lack in one's nature but also is the act of willfully choosing to go against one's own good. Suffering is due to the sins of oneself or others or is due to the "natural" factors of the world. What creation would have been had sin not intervened cannot be known; surely, human life would have been different. What is known is that suffering is not a defect of God's plan nor is it due to some eternal evil force equal to God.

See: Devil and Evil Spirits; Fatherhood of God; Freedom, Human; God, Nature and Attributes of; Hell; Manichaeism; Omnipotence; Omniscience; Original Sin; Process Theology; Providence; Suffering in Christian Life.

EVOLUTION

No book has more profoundly affected the way modern man views himself than Charles Darwin's *Origin of Species*, first published in 1859. The notion that man is the product of a blind, materialist process that did not have him in mind is part of the intellectual air we all breathe. Even orthodox Catholics can get into difficulties when they try to reconcile the creation account in Genesis with what they suppose science has demonstrated about the origin of the universe and of living things.

In dealing with a theory like Darwin's, Catholics should anchor themselves in the proposition that there can be no real conflict between faith and science. The danger occurs when scientists trespass into theology or vice versa. The Galileo affair is a sobering reminder of what can happen when certain parties in the Church resist a scientific hypothesis on *a priori* biblical grounds. If the congregation of cardinals that condemned Galileo had paid more attention to Augustine and Aquinas, who both held that Scripture does not teach a system of astronomy, the disastrous split that occurred between religion and science in the seventeenth century might have been avoided.

Although it is seldom aired in public, there is a sharp debate among scientists today about almost every aspect of evolutionary theory. The controversy is not over evolution per se, but over the means by which it happened. Either life-forms came about by blind chance or they did not. Darwin's theory of natural selection is the only one available purporting to explain how *homo sapiens* and other species are exclusively the result of natural forces. This is why the debate over Darwin's theory, and not evolution itself, is so important. It is Darwin's theory, moreover, and no other, that is taught in our schools. The failure of most writing on the subject to distinguish between "evolution" and "Darwinism" simply muddles the issue.

Although his name is synonymous with the theory, the idea of the evolution of life-forms did not begin with Darwin. It had been broached by the ancient Greeks, speculated on by St. Augustine, and developed into a scientific hypothesis by the French zoologist Buffon a century before the *Origin*. Darwin's epochal contribution was to provide a plausible explanation of *how* evolution occurred, one that was purely mechanistic and dispensed with God. This was his theory of natural selection.

Natural Selection • Darwin's theory in brief is that organisms produce offspring varying slightly from their parents, and natural selection will favor the survival of those individuals whose peculiarities (sharper teeth, more prehensile claws, and similar traits) render them best adapted to their environment. Darwinian evolution, then, is a two-stage process: random variation as to raw material, natural selection as the directing force.

Once he struck on this theory, Darwin spent a great deal of time observing pigeon breeders at work near his home in Kent. The first fifty pages of the *Origin* are mainly about pigeons, which often surprises readers. Darwin noticed that through selective breeding, pigeons could be made to develop certain desired characteristics: color, wing span, and so forth. He extrapolated from these observations the notion that over many millennia species could evolve by a similar process of selection, the only difference being that the "breeder" is nature itself, sifting out the weakest and allowing the fittest to leave offspring. By this simple process, Darwin claimed, some unknown original life-form floating in the primordial soup evolved and diversified into the vast array of plants and animals we see today.

But a crucial point has to be made here, one made often by Darwin's scientific critics. What

Darwin observed in the breeding pens is *micro-evolution*. Micro-evolution denotes the small changes that occur within a species over time. Such evolution is common. People, for example, are taller today than they were a hundred years ago. The varieties of finches that Darwin saw on the Galapagos Islands are another example of micro-evolution. With no direct empirical evidence, however, Darwin claimed that over long periods of time these micro-changes could add up to *macro-evolution*, which consists of the really big jumps — from amoeba to reptile to mammal, for example. There are two places to look for verification of Darwin's theory: the fossil record and breeding experiments with animals. If the theory is correct, the fossil record should show innumerable slight gradations between earlier species and later ones. Darwin was aware, however, that the fossil record of his day showed nothing of the sort. There were enormous discontinuities between major animal and plant groups. He accordingly entitled his chapter on the subject, "On the Imperfection of the Geological Record." Enormous quantities of fossils have been dug up since, and, if anything, they make more glaring the gaps that troubled Darwin. Stephen Jay Gould, the Harvard University biologist, calls this lack of gradual change in fossil record the "trade secret" of modern paleontology.

The fossil record shows exactly what it showed in Darwin's day: Species appear suddenly in a fully developed state, and change little or not at all before disappearing (ninety-nine out of a hundred species are extinct). About 550 million years ago, at the beginning of the Cambrian era, there was an explosion of complex life-forms — mollusks, jellyfish, trilobites — for which not a single ancestral form can be found in earlier rocks. A man from Mars looking at the subsequent fossil record would say species are replaced by other species, rather than evolve into them.

What about those pictures in museums and textbooks, those charts showing how large horses gradually evolved from small ones, and so forth? These portrayals are conjectural, and they are constantly being discarded. Paleontologists, in effect, find a fossil of an extinct species and make up a scenario connecting it with a later or earlier animal; but they never find the transitional forms that Darwin's theory demands.

The famous series of pictures at the American Museum of Natural History showing the "evolution" of horses, the diminutive *eohippus* slowly changing into modern *equus*, has been quietly discarded even by orthodox Darwinists. *Eohippus* remained *eohippus*; it was followed or accompanied by numerous species of horses, some larger, some smaller. The chart is nonetheless widely reprinted in textbooks. John Bonner, a biology professor at Princeton University, calls most textbook diagrams of evolutionary descent "a festering mass of unsupported conclusions."

The ancestry of man changes as often as the weather as the few bits of "hominid" fossil are shuffled about. There have been Java Man, Piltdown Man, Nebraska Man, *Ramapithicus*, and numerous others that have been rejected for one reason or another. The two most famous figures in hominid paleontology today, Richard Leakey and Donald Johansen (discoverer of "Lucy"), are in complete disagreement over man's ancestry. *Australopithicus Afarensis* has been rendered in textbooks with faces ranging from ape to human, depending on whose side the artist is on. Richard Lewontin, professor of zoology and genetics at Harvard, sums up: "We don't know anything about the ancestors of the human species. . . . Despite the excited and optimistic claims that have been made by some paleontologists, no fossil hominid species can be established as our direct ancestor."

Scientific Criticisms • Since we do not see species changing into other species in the fossils, the only other place to look is breeding experiments. Here, too, the evidence goes against Darwin. Breeders can change the color of a pigeon or the size of a cow to some degree, but they can only go so far. In fact, all breeders have the same experience: If they try to go too far in one direction, the animal or plant either becomes sterile or reverts back to type.

The most famous breeder of all, Luther Burbank, found no evidence of the unlimited plasticity of species that Darwin's theory demands and posited a Law of Reversion to Average. Richard Goldschmidt, a leading geneticist who taught at Berkeley, spent years observing the mutations of fruit flies and concluded that biologists had to give up Darwin's idea that an accumulation of "micro" changes creates new species. If there were a thousand-point mutation in the genes of a fruit fly, a statistical impossibility, it would remain a fruit fly.

Goldschmidt published a famous list of seventeen items — including teeth, feathers, the poison apparatus of the snake, whalebone — and challenged anyone to explain how they could have evolved on a step-by-step basis. He pointed out that if natural selection were the mechanism for major changes in species, then *every* intermediate form must be useful to the organism. This problem of explaining the usefulness of incipient organs — five percent of an eye, for example — has been a persistent one for Darwinists. Otto Schindewolf, the great German paleontologist and anti-Darwinist, rejected out of hand the idea that transitional forms could be found or even imagined.

Schindewolf, who died in 1971, was largely ignored in the Anglo-Saxon countries, while Goldschmidt was subject to a savage campaign of vilification for suggesting that evolution must have involved the appearance of "hopeful monsters" — sudden genetic freaks that somehow manage to function — rather than minute gradations sifted by natural selection. But scientists like Gould now claim both men were on the right track after all, and the story of evolution is one of rapid, dramatic changes followed by long periods of stasis. In downplaying the role of natural selection, however, Gould and Stanley and other scientists are left with the problem of providing a plausible mechanism to explain how the bacteria and blue-green algae that appeared on this planet over two billion years ago randomly mutated into the highly complex fauna and flora of today. Modern genetics shows that DNA programs a species to remain stubbornly what it is. There are fluctuations around a norm, but nothing more.

Other serious problems dog classical Darwinian theory. Among them are the facts that scientists see very little "struggle for survival" in nature (many species tend to cooperate and occupy noncompeting ecological niches); that all the major body plans we see today in animals and insects appeared at once in the Cambrian era, which does not fit Darwin's model; and that many species like the lungfish have not changed at all in over 300 million years despite important shifts in their environment, which flatly contradicts the constant fine-tuning Darwin attributed to natural selection.

Darwin himself was increasingly plagued by doubts after the first edition of the *Origin*. In subsequent editions he kept backing off from natural selection as the explanation of all natural phenomena. Loren Eiseley says a "close examination of the last edition of the *Origin* reveals that in attempting to meet the objections being launched against his theory the much-labored upon volume had become contradictory. . . . The last repairs to the *Origin* reveal . . . how very shaky Darwin's theoretical structure had become."

Darwin's unproven theory nonetheless became dogma in the public mind. Still, there was sharp scientific opposition from the start. As Swedish biologist Soren Lovtrup points out, most of Darwin's early opponents, even when they had religious motives, "argued on a completely scientific basis." Most did not reject evolution, but rather Darwin's explanation of it. In the decades following Darwin's death in 1882, his theory came increasingly under a cloud. Lovtrup writes that "during the first third of our century, biologists did not believe in Darwinism." Hans Driesch in Germany, Lucien Cuenot in France, Vernon Kellog and T.H. Morgan in America, biologists and geneticists with international reputations — all rejected Darwin's theory during this period.

The Scopes case in 1925 (usually called the "Scopes trial" and sometimes referred to as the "monkey trial"), which the American popular imagination still regards as putting to rest the whole case against Darwin, took place against this background of general dissent. The scientific issues were never properly discussed; a fossil tooth was proffered as the remains of something called "Nebraska Man" (it later turned out to belong to a pig); and William Jennings Bryan made the mistake of allowing his fundamentalist beliefs to be ridiculed on the witness stand by Clarence Darrow, a kind of Village Atheist raised to the national level.

The Scopes trial proved nothing about the scientific validity of Darwin's theory, but it did plant in the American mind the notion that in the debate over evolution the only choice available is between biblical fundamentalists and Darwin. G.K. Chesterton pointed out at the time that the Catholic Church, which does not treat the Book of Genesis as a sourcebook of scientific data and does not have a serious philosophical problem with evolution (properly understood), was entirely above the fray.

Because of the obvious shortcomings in Darwin's original theory, the so-called "synthetic theory" emerged in the 1930s. This incorporated genetics, molecular biology, and complicated mathematical models. But it remained completely Darwinian in its identification of random variations preserved by natural selection as the driving force of evolution. Julian Huxley, its chief spokesman, claimed that Darwinism had "risen Phoenix-like from the ashes." But the synthetic theory had as many problems as classical Darwinism, and over the next forty years its supports fell away one by one. In 1979, Stephen Jay Gould echoed the sentiments of many scientists: "The synthetic theory . . . is effectively dead, despite its persistence as textbook orthodoxy."

The Current Situation • Where does that leave us today? "Punctuated Equilibrium," would be the reply of the average biology teacher or science columnist. This is the famous hypothesis that Gould and Niles Eldredge came up with in the early seventies, when they and other paleontologists began to insist that the gaps in the fossil record must be taken at face value. According to this theory, small groups of animals break off from the herd, migrate to peripheral locations "at the edge of ecological tolerance," and mutate very rapidly into "hopeful monsters" who then replace the old herd. Because the changes occur so quickly, there is no fossil evidence — and thus the theory can be neither proved nor disproved.

Besides the punctuationists, there are two other evolutionary camps today: those who cling to classical Darwinism, because they say there is no better explanation for the origin of species (a position that is metaphysical rather than scientific); and those who reject Darwin entirely, including a well-known group of "cladists" at the American Museum of Natural History. ("Cladistics," according to one dictionary, is the "classification of organisms based on the branchings of descendant lineages from a common ancestor.") Skepticism about Darwin's theory is more widespread among scientists than is generally supposed. For example, the theory is rejected by most French biologists, including the most eminent, the late Pierre P. Grasse, president of the French Academy of Sciences and editor of the twenty-eight volumes of the *Traité de Zoologie*, who calls Darwinism "a pseudo-science" that is "either in conflict with reality or cannot solve the basic problems." Scientists like Grasse nonetheless call themselves "evolutionists" because they recognize that all life-forms share basic characteristics such as DNA and so may be descended from a single ancestor; but they are frankly agnostic about how this happened.

The Church and Evolution • The Catholic Church has never had a problem with evolution as opposed to philosophical Darwinism, which sees man solely as the product of materialist forces. Unlike Luther and Calvin and modern fundamentalists, the Church has never taught that the first chapter of Genesis is meant to teach science. As F.J. Sheed says (*Theology and Sanity*), the creation account in Genesis "tells us of the fact but not the process: there was an assembling of elements of the material universe, but was it instantaneous or spread over a considerable space and time? Was it complete in one act, or by stages? Were those elements, for instance, formed into an animal body that (as one generation followed another) gradually evolved — not of course by the ordinary laws of matter but under the special guidance of God — to a point where it was capable of union with a spiritual soul, which God then created and infused into it? The statement in Genesis does not seem actually to exclude this, but it certainly does not say it. Nor has the Church formally said that it is not so."

Pius XII correctly pointed out in the encyclical *Humani Generis* (1950) that the theory of evolution had not been completely proved. But he did not forbid "that the theory of evolution concerning the origin of the human body as coming from preexistent and living matter — for Catholic faith obliges us to hold that human souls are immediately created by God — be investigated and discussed by experts as far as the present state of human science and sacred theology allow" (36).

In his catechesis on creation in 1986, Pope John Paul II stated about the first Book of Genesis: "This text has above all a religious and theological importance. There are not to be sought in it significant elements from the point of view of the natural sciences. Research on the origin and development of individual species in nature does not find in this description any definitive norm. . . . Indeed, the theory of natural evolution, understood in a sense that does not exclude divine causality, is not in principle opposed to the truth about the creation of the visible world, as presented in the Book of Genesis. . . . It must, however, be added that this hypothesis proposes only a probability, not a scientific certainty. The doctrine of faith, however, invariably affirms that man's spiritual soul is created directly by God. According to the hypothesis mentioned, it is possible that the human body, following the order impressed by the Creator on the energies of life, could have been gradually prepared in the forms of antecedent living beings." Pope John Paul returned to this subject in 1996, in a message to the Pontifical Academy of Sciences.

The Church's quarrel with many scientists who call themselves evolutionists is not about evolution itself, which may or may not have occurred in a non-Darwinian manner, but rather about the philosophical materialism at the root of much evolutionary thinking.

In the area of theology, the Magisterium has cautioned against teachings of the French paleontologist Pierre Teilhard de Chardin, S.J., who concocted from evolutionary theory a kind of process theology that, among other things, implicitly denies original sin and the existence of first parents of the human race who differed in kind from whatever may have preceded them. In *Humanae Generis*, Pius XII also objected to polygenism, which holds that we are descended from multiple ancestors rather than from one historical person, Adam.

The Church insists that man is not an accident; that no matter how he went about creating *homo sapiens*, God from all eternity intended that man and all creation exist in their present form. Catholics are not obliged to square scientific data with the early verses of Genesis, whose truths — and they are truths, not myth — are expressed in an archaic, prescientific Hebrew idiom; and they can look forward with enjoyment and confidence to modern scientific discoveries that, more often than not, raise fundamental questions that science itself cannot answer.

See: Body and Soul; Creation; Human Race, Creation and Destiny of; Inerrancy; Original Sin; Process Theology; Science and the Church.

Suggested Readings: CCC 337-344, 355-367. John Paul II, *Message to the Pontifical Academy of Sciences on Evolution*. R. Augros and G. Stanciu, *The New Biology*. M. Denton, *Evolution: A Theory in Crisis*. G. Himmelfarb, *Darwin and the Darwinian Revolution*. S. Jaki, *Genesis 1 Throughout the Ages*. N. Macbeth, *Darwin Retried: An Appeal to Reason*.

George Sim Johnston

EXCOMMUNICATION

Through the grace given in Baptism we are united to Jesus, living with his very life in our souls. Nothing worse can happen than to lose that union with Christ and with the Church in which he lives and communicates himself.

Venial sins do not break that communion (although, unless combated, they weaken our bonds with Christ). But serious sin deprives us of grace and the presence of the Holy Spirit. God's life is extinguished in the soul; the branch, with the sap gone from it, is dead even if still physically united to the vine, to the body of the Church. Through repentance and the sacrament of Penance and Reconciliation, the sinner can return to full life-giving participation in Christ's life and the communion of the Church.

Certain particularly grave sins incur the penalty of excommunication. Over and above the loss of grace, this involves a break with the bonds that shape and hold together our union with Christ in and through his Church. The most notable effect of excommunication is being excluded from the sacraments (Canon 1331.1.2).

Automatic excommunication follows on certain offenses: apostasy, heresy, or schism (Canon 1364); the direct violation by the priest of the seal of confession (Canon 1388); the procuring or performing of an abortion or cooperation in an abortion that is necessary to its being performed (Canon 1398). In most cases, excommunication can be imposed only after due process (Canons 1314, 1341). Canon law also notes a variety of factors that remove imputability — ignorance of the law, lack of freedom, etc. (Canon 1323) — and others that diminish it, such as imperfect use of reason and ignorance of the penalty attached to a violation; it says, "an accused is not bound by an automatic penalty . . . in the presence of any" of these (1324.3).

As with all penalties in the Church, the purpose of an excommunication is "medicinal," that is, to bring about the repentance of the sinner. Repentance makes absolution from the excommunication possible (CCC 1463). If a person repents, the excommunication will always be lifted; but until this is done, he or she is barred from receiving even the sacrament of Penance and Reconciliation, and from all the other sacraments.

Apart from excommunication imposed by law — with its external effects — one should mention the possibility of "self-excommunication," whereby a person undermines the bonds (especially those of faith and governance) binding the Christian to Christ. This can be the most dangerous and insidious form of excommunication.

See: Abortion; Apostasy; Church, Membership in; Communio; Heresy; Schism.

EX OPERE OPERATO

Literally, *ex opere operato* means "from the work having been performed." It refers to the manner in which grace is conferred through the valid administration and worthy reception of a sacrament. The term was defined by the Council of Trent at its seventh session in 1547. Central to this belief is the fact that it is Christ who is always at work through his Church as she administers the sacraments. The operating definition of a sacrament is that it is an outward sign, instituted by Christ, to give grace.

As such, the term *ex opere operato* embraces several concepts: (1) The sacrament is not just a "sign" that grace is given to an individual; rather, the actual administration of the rite confers the grace. (2) The sacrament does not merely arouse the faith of the individual and thus prepare him to receive grace in this manner. (3) The conferral of grace is not dependent on the holiness or worthiness of the minister. (4) As long as the recipient places no obstacle in the way, grace will be given. (5) The rites or rituals of the Church must be observed properly.

Sacraments are not magic but are truly the active power of Christ and the Holy Spirit at work in the Church. Grace will come through the administration of the sacraments, and fruits or benefits will be received. How *well* they are received, however, is related to the disposition of the one receiving them (cf. CCC 1128).

See: Grace; Sacrament.

EXORCISM

In ecclesiastical terminology, the word "exorcism" refers to the religious ceremony in which an authorized person commands the devil or evil spirit in the name of God to cease his activity on a person, object, or place. The authority to perform exorcisms was given by Christ to his Apostles and disciples (cf. Mt 1:1, 8; Mk 3:14-15, 6:7; Lk 9:1). In the beginning, there was no specific formula for exorcism; it consisted simply in the use of adjuration, which is a command given in the name of God for the devil to cease his activity. It was designated in Scripture as "casting out devils."

There are various forms of exorcism: (1) a ritual exorcism is used in the conferral of the sacrament of Baptism and in various blessings (cf. *Roman Ritual*); (2) a private exorcism or adjuration such as "Begone, Satan" may be used by any of the faithful under the proper conditions; and (3) an official public exorcism may be conducted only with specific authorization of the bishop. In the revision of the liturgy after the Second Vatican Council, the formula for the ritual exorcism used in Baptism is no longer an adjuration addressed to the devil but an invocation addressed to God.

The first official formula for exorcism was promulgated by the Church at the end of the fourth century, but as early as 251, during the pontificate of Pope Cornelius, the minor order of exorcist was established. From that time on, official public exorcism was restricted to priests and deacons who were duly authorized by the bishop. In succeeding centuries the Church exercised ever greater vigilance in this matter. The present legislation of the Church is based on the *Roman Ritual* promulgated by Pope Paul V in 1614, but with certain modifications.

First of all, the order of exorcist and all the minor orders were abolished in the Latin Church by Pope Paul VI in 1972. In the latest edition of the *Roman Ritual,* there are some specific regulations concerning the qualities required in the exorcist, the discernment of authentic diabolical possession, and the procedure in performing an exorcism. The formula of exorcism dates back to Alcuin in the eighth century, and there is also a formula composed by Pope Leo XIII in the nineteenth century. Unlike the sacraments, which work *ex opere operato*, exorcism is a sacramental and therefore does not infallibly produce its effect.

See: Baptism; Devil and Evil Spirits; Diabolical Possession; Sacramentals.

EXTRAORDINARY GIFTS

The term "extraordinary gifts" is used in spiritual theology to designate the unusual and mysterious phenomena that transcend the known, natural powers of the human psyche and must therefore be attributed to some preternatural or supernatural cause. Extraordinary psychosomatic manifestations sometimes occur in authentic mystics, but they do not fall within the normal range of mystical experiences. They are classified as paranormal or as epiphenomena. They are also the subject matter of parapsychology, which investigates religious and mystical phenomena as well as spiritualism, occultism, diabolism, and psychic phenomena.

In Catholic theology the spiritual life is divided into the ascetical and the mystical phases. In the former, the individual is the primary agent in cooperation with ordinary grace; in the latter, the individual is acted upon by a divine power. In the ascetical stage, the practice of the virtues predominates; in the mystical stage the gifts of the Holy Spirit are the principles of operation. The perfection of the Christian life is attained in the mystical state, when the virtue of charity reaches its full development.

The phenomena of the mystical life can be divided into those that ordinarily proceed from the activity of the gifts of the Holy Spirit (concomitant mystical phenomena) and those gifts or charisms that do not occur in the normal development of the mystical life (extraordinary mystical phenomena).

"Gratiae Gratis Datae" • The technical name for extraordinary spiritual gifts is *gratiae gratis datae* or gratuitous graces, as distinct from *gratiae gratum faciens*, meaning any graces that sanctify the individual who receives them. This distinction is crucial for a proper evaluation and discernment of extraordinary gifts because the *gratiae gratis datae* are not of themselves a proof of the sanctity of the recipient; they are not even given primarily for the recipient's benefit. St. Paul treats of *gratiae gratis datae*, or charisms, in 1 Corinthians 12:8-10 and in Romans 12:6-8. He teaches that the charismatic gifts are manifestations of the Holy Spirit for the common good (1 Cor 12:7) and that the Christians should desire these gifts for the upbuilding of the Church (1 Cor 14:1).

There are, however, other extraordinary gifts that are neither a proof of holiness nor for the common good of the Church. The discernment of these gifts is sometimes very problematic, since these extraordinary phenomena may be attributed to any one of three possible causes: nature, the devil, or a supernatural power. The basic rule for discernment was established by Pope Benedict XIV in *De Beatificatione et Canonizatione Servorum Dei*: No phenomenon is to be attributed to a supernatural power until all possible natural or diabolical explanations have been investigated and excluded. And since identically the same paranormal phenomenon may occur, for example, in diabolical possession, in an authentic mystical rapture, or in a hysterical trance, the investigator should carefully consider the effects of the extraordinary phenomenon on the recipient and others. "By their fruits you shall know them."

Experts in the field of paranormal phenomena have drawn up a series of guidelines to help in the process of discernment: (1) An extraordinary spiritual gift is not of itself an indication of the sanctity of the individual, since God could even bestow a charism on a person in mortal sin. (2) Normally it would be presumptuous to ask God for extraordinary spiritual gifts. (3) No extraordinary spiritual gift is necessary for the attainment of sanctity, nor does the Church look for such in investigating the servants of God. However, the Church does require a miracle through the intercession of the individual before proceeding to beatification and to canonization. (4) It is possible that a truly extraordinary supernatural phenomenon could coexist with neurotic or psychotic symptoms or that God could permit diabolical obsession of the gifted individual.

Extraordinary Mystical Phenomena • As has been noted, the extraordinary spiritual gifts do not fall within the classification of the concomitant mystical phenomena that normally accompany the higher degrees of infused prayer and the passive purgations. Nevertheless, they are frequently encountered in the lives of the saints, either as special graces for the good of others or apparently as testimonies from God. The following are the principal extraordinary phenomena that have been observed in the lives of saints and mystics.

Visions. A vision is the perception of an image that would otherwise be invisible. St. Augustine is the author of the classical division into corporeal (seen with bodily eyes and also called an *apparition*), imaginative (a phantasm in the imagination), and intellectual (an intelligible species impressed on the intellect). Corporeal and imaginative visions could also be the result of hallucination, some natural power, or diabolical infestation. Theologians generally assert, with St. Teresa of Ávila, that visions of Christ or Mary are "representations" and not the actual bodily presence. Corporeal and imaginative visions usually present problems of discernment, and the investigator must pay special attention to the effects produced in the visionary.

Locutions. A locution is an interior illumination by means of words or a statement. It may be auricular (words heard with the bodily ear), imaginative (flashed on the screen of the imagination, as it were), or intellectual (concepts infused immediately into the intellect). Locutions sometimes accompany a vision, and when they do, the words come from the image perceived. The locutions are generally for the instruction or consolation of the one who receives them. St. John of the Cross divides the intellectual locutions into successive locutions (in which the Holy Spirit instructs the individual through a reasoning process), formal locutions (in which the ideas and concepts are immediately infused into the intellect), and substantial locutions (in which God issues a command and the effect immediately follows). The auricular and imaginative locutions may be caused by the individual or by diabolical influence, and for that reason one should always be slow to attribute them to a supernatural cause.

Revelations. These are supernatural manifestations of hidden or as yet unknown truth for the good of the Church in general or the benefit of individuals. *Public revelation* consists of the truths of the faith contained in Scripture and Tradition, which the Church proclaims for the belief of the faithful; it ended with the death of the last Apostle. All revelations since that time are classified as *private revelations*, even if they contain material that is addressed to the entire Church. Private revelations do not belong to the deposit of faith. But if, after careful discernment, it is judged that a private revelation is authentic, then the one who received it is obliged to accept it in faith. Moreover, if the revelation contains a message for others and the revelation has been declared authentic, then those others are obliged to accept it and act upon it. The Church gives at most a *negative* approval to a private revelation, declaring that there is nothing in the revelation contrary to faith and morals. Hence, the faithful at large are free to accept or not accept the revelation, although one would expect devout Christians to act in conformity with the Church's decision.

Reading of Hearts. This phenomenon consists in a supernaturally infused knowledge of the secret thoughts or the internal state of other persons without any previous communication. Similar to this phenomenon is the ability of some gifted persons to arrive at a conjectural knowledge of the secrets of hearts. If this sort of insight is possible for certain psychically gifted individuals, all the more so is it true of angels or devils, whose intellects are far superior to our own.

Hierognosis. This is the ability to recognize immediately any person, place, or thing that is holy or blessed and to distinguish it from those that are not. This gift transcends the powers of nature because there is no way, for example, that one could ordinarily distinguish a blessed or consecrated object from those that are not. Some mystics have experienced a magnetic attraction for holy objects; the devil and those under his power have expressed hatred and revulsion when brought into contact with blessed objects.

Stigmata. The spontaneous appearance of the wounds of the crucified Christ on the body of the recipient. The stigmata are usually located on the hands, feet, and side, but sometimes there are also wounds on the head, as from a crown of thorns. The first known Christian stigmatist was St. Francis of Assisi (died 1226). In modern times (1949) there is also clinical proof that Arthur Otto Mook of Hamburg, a nonpracticing Lutheran, bore the wounds of the stigmata, much against his will. There is evidence that the marks of the stigmata can be the result of auto-suggestion, hypnosis, or fraud. Therefore, this phenomenon could be the result of natural causes, a supernatural power, or diabolical intervention. In an authentic stigmata the wounds usually appear suddenly and during ecstasy, and they never become inflamed or infected. Persons who have received this extraordinary gift have usually been individuals intensely devoted to the Passion and crucifixion of Christ.

Tears of Blood and Bloody Sweat. The effusion of blood from the eyes, as in weeping, or from the pores of the skin, especially on the face and forehead. These phenomena have traditionally been interpreted as a participation in the sufferings of Christ. They are relatively rare, although in modern times there have been numerous cases of blood or an unknown liquid flowing from sacred images. There are also cases of bloody sweat (*hematidrosis*) that are not related to religious experience but may very likely be pathological. Since these phenomena are corporeal, they could be the result of a natural cause, diabolical intervention, or a supernatural power. One should proceed with extreme caution in attempting to discern their origin and purpose. In many cases there is no satisfactory explanation.

Flames of Love. These are burning sensations in the body, usually in the vicinity of the heart, without any apparent cause except the intensity of love. The phenomenon may be experienced as a simple interior heat around the heart, a burning sensation so intense that cold applications must be used, or an actual scorching of the clothing. Until proved otherwise, it should be presumed that there is a natural explanation.

Exchange of Hearts. As the name indicates, this phenomenon consists in the extraction of the heart of a mystic and the substitution of another, presumably the heart of Christ, as is recorded of

St. Catherine of Siena and St. Michael de los Santos. Of the latter case Pope Benedict XIV stated in his eulogy that it was a "mystical and spiritual exchange."

Levitation. The suspension of a physical body in the air without any visible support and contrary to the law of gravity. This is a common phenomenon in the lives of saints and mystics, and it usually occurs during ecstasy. In fact, the experts speak of simple ascensional ecstasy, ecstatic flight, and ecstatic march in designating the various types of levitation. However, this particular phenomenon is easily falsified, as has happened in spiritualistic séances. There are also some practitioners who claim to have levitated by their own power of concentration. Finally, the devil has the power to suspend a body in the air or move it through space.

Agility. The apparently instantaneous transfer or movement of a body from one place to another without passing through the intervening space. There are numerous instances of agility in the lives of the saints, and it is a phenomenon that surpasses the powers of nature. A purely spiritual being, whether angelic or diabolical, has the property of agility, but it is impossible for a physical body to move instantaneously from one place to another. Whether the transfer is caused by a supernatural power or the devil, it is always classified as an "apparent" instantaneous transfer.

The phenomenon of agility should not be confused with *telekinesis*, which is the movement of an inanimate body through space without the aid of an agent, as when a consecrated Host floated through the air to the mouth of St. Catherine of Siena.

Bilocation. This phenomenon refers to the simultaneous presence of a physical body in two distinct places at the same moment, as recorded concerning St. Martin de Porres, St. Anthony of Padua, St. Paul of the Cross, and numerous other saints. It is physically impossible for a material body to be circumscriptively present in two distinct places at the same time. Consequently, the bilocation is only apparent; the physical body is objectively present in one location but is at the same time seen in another location by means of a representation or image of some sort. This could be effected through the ministry of an angel or by means of light rays or vapors, as likely happens in cases of corporeal visions or apparitions. It is also possible that with God's permission the devil could produce an apparent bilocation.

Compenetration of Bodies. There is testimony in the New Testament (Jn 20:19) that after the Resurrection Jesus came into the presence of the disciples even though the doors were locked. The phenomenon of compenetration of matter — a body passing through another material object — has likewise been attributed to St. Dominic and St. Raymond of Peñafort. Some theologians interpret this phenomenon as a preview of the subtlety of a glorified body.

Other Extraordinary Phenomena. Many other prodigies and extraordinary phenomena, some of them bizarre, can be found in studies on the physical manifestations of religious experience. These include *inedia* (total abstinence from nourishment far beyond the time during which life can be sustained), *mystical aureoles* (light emanating from the head, face, or body of a mystic, especially during ecstasy or prayer), and *incorruptibility* (the corpse is preserved from decomposition and may even remain soft and flexible and emit a pleasant fragrance).

See: Apparitions; Charisms; Devil and Evil Spirits; Discernment; Magic; Mysticism; Private Revelation; Prophecy.

Suggested Readings: CCC 799-801, 823-829. A. Wiesinger, *Occult Phenomena in the Light of Theology.* J. Aumann, *Spiritual Theology*, pp. 424-441. H. Thurston, *The Physical Phenomena of Mysticism.*

Jordan Aumann, O.P.

F

FAITH, ACT OF

The *Catechism of the Catholic Church* organizes its presentation of faith under two headings, "I believe" and "we believe" (cf. 141-184). "I believe," the formula used in the Apostles' Creed, signifies the personal profession of the faith made individually by each believer, while "we believe," the formula of the Nicene Creed, represents the faith of the Church as it is confessed by the bishops "or more generally by the liturgical assembly of believers" (167). One might say that the first formula emphasizes the personal freedom and responsibility that are involved in accepting and living according to God's gift of faith, whereas the second calls attention to the fact that faith and the fullness of life to which faith leads are inextricably bound up with membership in the Church.

"Believing in Jesus Christ and in the One who sent him for our salvation is necessary for obtaining that salvation": so teaches the First Vatican Council (1869-1870) in its *Dogmatic Constitution on the Catholic Faith, Dei Filius* (Denzinger-Schönmetzer, 3012). Vatican I was repeating the teaching of the Council of Trent, a teaching that also is a central element of the long Tradition of the Church articulating divinely revealed truth as it is found in many places in Scripture (cf. Mk 16:16; Jn 3:36, 6:40, etc.).

But, one might well ask, what of those sincere non-Christians who lead good lives? Is there no possibility of salvation for them? Indeed there is; yet even in the case of those who, through no fault of their own, do not know Jesus Christ and his teaching about the way of salvation, there must be at least an implicit faith in all that God has revealed, manifest in an honest openness to the truth as such a person is able to know it and in living according to that truth.

There is nevertheless something mysterious in the fact that so many people apparently live and die without the fullness of faith. There can be no doubt that God has willed that everyone should live his entire life in the knowledge of God's Revelation and with its assistance; nor is it acceptable to subscribe to the relativizing notion that, finally, all religions and indeed all ways of seeking a relationship of friendship with God are equally good. Ultimately, then, the fact that so many appear not to know and accept God's Revelation can only be understood as an expression of the power of human freedom, which can accept or reject any truth, including the truth of Revelation itself.

It is a sign also of the significance of human solidarity in both the natural and supernatural dimensions of life. For, to a significant degree, God has made individuals' faith and even their salvation contingent upon the cooperation of other human beings with God in transmitting the faith to them. This is especially the case with parents and their children.

The Freedom of Faith • Faith is a gift from God, but the act of faith is on our parts a free and personal act. It is "the free response of the human person to the initiative of God who reveals himself" (CCC 162). Hence it follows that no one should be forced to embrace or profess to embrace faith against his or her will.

This has both individual and social consequences. For individual Christian evangelizers and apologists, for example, it is a reminder that, even though efforts to present and defend faith with rational arguments are necessary and desirable, still the gift of faith remains always God's to give while the assent of faith remains always the free act of one's hearers.

On the social level, too, it is important to recognize that political society cannot be structured in such a way as to require its members to accept the truth of supernatural Revelation and live according to its supernatural demands. What can and should be required is that all live according to the humanly intelligible standards of the natural law pertaining to the pursuit of the common good and the good order of society itself: for instance, norms of behavior relevant to upholding and fostering the well-being of monogamous marriage.

Neither by physical nor psychological coercion did Jesus himself ever attempt to force people to believe in him and his message, nor did he direct his disciples to do so. But, in addition to his example and his prayer, he did energetically and unremittingly preach his message in words, exhorting, correcting, challenging, and warning his hearers as he traveled throughout Palestine and beyond. Moreover, summarizing the entire mission of the Church until the end of time, he instructed his followers: "Go therefore and make disciples of all nations, baptizing them in the name of the Father and of the Son and of the Holy Spirit, teaching them to observe all that I have commanded you" (Mt 28:19-20); and he said: "He who believes and is baptized will be saved, but he who does not believe will be condemned" (Mk 16:15). The prohibition against coercion in the area of faith should never be interpreted as a prohibition of preaching and teaching the truth of faith by every available means, with the intention of preparing the way for God's gift of faith.

As human beings freely accept the gift of faith, so also faith, once received, can be lost by free human choice. The First Letter to Timothy refers to this when it remarks: "By rejecting conscience, certain persons have made shipwreck of their faith" (1:19). Complacency, passivity, and neglect in matters of religious formation place faith at risk. It is necessary that we nourish our faith by study, especially study of the word of God, by prayer, and by striving for the perfection of charity in our lives. It is healthy to bear in mind the warning of John Henry Newman, at the conclusion of his famous essay *On Consulting the Faithful in Matters of Doctrine* (1859), that the neglect of the religious education of the laity "in the educated classes will terminate in indifference, and in the poorer in superstition."

The Knowledge of Faith • Faith is knowledge of an all-consuming kind. Clearly it includes intellectual knowledge and assent to a body of truth, but both the way and the content of this knowing go much further than mere human knowledge. Different from the natural knowledge of God (which, as it were, looks at God "from the outside"), faith, along with the other supernatural gifts, draws man into the inner life of God and to an intimate personal encounter with him in his Trinitarian life. In this sense, then, faith already is the beginning of the eternal life (cf. CCC 163). Ultimately and essentially, the act of faith, made possible by the gifts of faith and grace, is a personal surrender to God in response to his Trinitarian surrender to us. The knowledge that is peculiar to faith arises within this supernatural union.

Faith necessarily involves an assent of the intellect to all the truths revealed by God (cf. CCC 15), and especially to the truth about God himself as three Persons in one God. Central to faith also is faith in Jesus Christ, who is the fullness and completion of God's self-revelation (cf. Vatican Council II, *Dogmatic Constitution on Divine Revelation, Dei Verbum*, 4). Not only does Christ reveal God to man, however, he also, as the Council points out, "fully reveals man to himself and brings to light his most high calling" (*Pastoral Constitution on the Church in the Modern World, Gaudium et Spes*, 22); by his example and word, furthermore, he shows man what he must do to respond to this calling.

The type of assent and adherence involved in the act of faith is called obedience — "the obedience of faith" (cf. CCC 143). Although obedience also is involved in natural knowledge, in the sense that it calls for acceptance of something that is evident yet can be rejected, the very nature of the act of faith is obedience because the principal content of the faith is beyond natural intelligibility. The *Catechism of the Catholic Church*, quoting Vatican Council I, says: "What moves us to believe is not the fact that revealed truths appear as true and intelligible in the light of our natural reason: we believe 'because of the authority of God himself who reveals them, who can neither deceive nor be deceived' [*Dei Filius* 3; DS 3008]" (156).

Faith thus is personal adherence of the whole person to God who reveals himself. It involves a total commitment to live according to the truths of faith in all aspects and moments of life. And while personal and total adherence to God also is the proper conclusion of a natural knowledge of God, the quality of the adherence made possible, and required, by faith is immeasurably greater than that understood by reason alone: The supernatural gifts make possible the most sublime union of the human person with each of the three Divine Persons. Unlike much natural knowledge, which may or may not be applicable to daily life, the knowledge of the faith by its very nature requires that it be put into practice in regard to all aspects of human activity.

The Certainty of Faith • Because the content of faith is the truth revealed by God, faith has a unique certainty. Obviously, revealed truth can be obscure and mysterious: One need only think of truths of faith like the Trinity, the Incarnation, the Real Presence. Fully to penetrate and comprehend truths of this sort is beyond the capacities of human intellect.

But in this circumstance there is no basis for uncertainty and doubt. Moreover, in our pilgrimage of faith, we have the assistance of the Church and her Magisterium. Thus Vatican II says of the Pope and bishops that they are "heralds of the faith, who draw new disciples to Christ; they are authentic teachers, that is, teachers endowed with the authority of Christ, who preach the faith to people assigned to them, the faith which is destined to inform their thinking and direct their conduct; and under the light of the Holy Spirit they make that faith shine forth, drawing from the storehouse of revelation new things and old (cf. Mt

13:52)" (*Dogmatic Constitution on the Church, Lumen Gentium*, 25).

Finally, a word about the relationship of the knowledge of faith and natural knowledge, the act of faith and reason. Plainly it is desirable to know and be able to explain the rational basis for the act of faith, in order to defend the gift of faith against attack — for example, against the charge that faith is irrational or unworthy of a mature and intelligent person — and to present truths of faith persuasively to others.

This is the classic work of apologetics. It also is necessary that faith be adequately comprehensible so that its application to life may be clear.

For such reasons, then, it is necessary to seek to grow in one's understanding of the truths of faith. In this effort we can be confident that there can never be any real contradiction between true knowledge of the faith and true natural knowledge, scientific or otherwise, and that if apparent conflicts arise, they reflect either erroneous knowledge of the faith or erroneous natural knowledge. As Vatican Council I says: "Though faith is above reason, there can never be any real discrepancy between faith and reason. Since the same God who reveals mysteries and infuses faith has bestowed the light of reason on the human mind, God cannot deny himself, nor can truth ever contradict truth" (*Dei Filius*, 4).

See: Creed; Divine Revelation; Faith, Virtue of; Faith of the Church; Knowledge of God; Magisterium; Science and the Church.

Suggested Readings: CCC 142-165. St. Francis de Sales, *The Catholic Controversy*, Pt. II. G. Grisez, *The Way of the Lord Jesus*, Vol. 2, *Living a Christian Life*, Ch. 1. J. Ratzinger, *Introduction to Christianity*.

Lawrence A. Kutz

FAITH OF THE CHURCH

Christian faith deeply involves the Church founded by Christ. This is so in several ways and for several reasons.

By God's will, the fullness of the faith is given through the instrumentality of the Church, which for this reason is appropriately spoken of as a mother ("Holy Mother the Church," as the old expression puts it). Indeed, even those who, by no fault of their own, do not formally and explicitly enjoy membership in the Church are said to be saved through this same instrumentality, the Church, although in this case operating more hiddenly.

Furthermore, belief itself is an ecclesial act, as the *Catechism of the Catholic Church* points out: "The Church's faith precedes, engenders, supports, and nourishes our faith" (181). And the *Catechism* goes on to quote the third-century bishop of Carthage: " 'No one can have God as Father who does not have the Church as Mother' (St. Cyprian, *De unit.* 6: PL 4, 519)."

Inextricably linked with God's Revelation concerning himself is God's Revelation concerning the Church as Christ's Body and his will that all men and women be saved through incorporation into this Body. Here people find all the means needed for salvation; here the communion of all in God already is begun in this present life.

The Second Vatican Council teaches accordingly that God has "willed to make men holy and save them, not as individuals without any bond or link between them, but rather to make them into a people who might acknowledge and serve him in holiness" (*Dogmatic Constitution on the Church, Lumen Gentium*, 9). It adds that this People of God, this "messianic people," has as its destiny "the kingdom of God which has been begun by God himself on earth and which must be further extended until it is brought to perfection by him at the end of time" (*Lumen Gentium*, 9).

The Infallibility of the Church • Moreover, as the Council says, this holy People of God, the Church, shares in the priestly, kingly, and prophetic office of Christ himself. In reference to participation in the prophetic office, Vatican II recalls that, by divine protection, the members of the whole Church, "from the bishops to the last of the faithful" (St. Augustine), "cannot err in matters of belief [when] they manifest a universal consent in matters of faith and morals" (*Lumen Gentium*, 12).

This is the infallibility of the Church as a whole. The infallible belief of the Church, however, cannot be measured by sociological instruments such as public opinion polls. Christ sustains the infallibility of the Church by having endowed her pastors and official teachers with the charism of infallibility in matters of faith and morals. These "shepherds" of the Church — that is, the Pope and the bishops in communion with him — are called the Magisterium; and it is the task of this Magisterium, or teaching authority, "to preserve God's people from deviations and defections and to guarantee them the objective possibility of professing the true faith without error" (CCC 890).

There is only *one* faith, the faith entrusted to Christ's Church, professed and preached by her through the centuries under the guidance of the Holy Spirit and with the guarantee of the Magisterium (cf. CCC 172, 174). Those who have received the fullness of the faith have a strict obligation to profess and teach it, so as to prepare the way for others to receive this gift of God. "But how are men to call upon him in whom they have not believed? And how are they to believe in him of whom they have never heard? And how are they to hear without a preacher?" (Rom 10:14). This is the work of evangelization and catechesis for which all are responsible.

See: Catechesis; Church, Nature, Origin, and Structure of; Creed; Divine Revelation; Evangelization; Infallibility; Magisterium.

Suggested Readings: CCC 166-175. St. Francis de Sales, *The Catholic Controversy*, Pt. II. J. Ratzinger, *Introduction to Christianity*.

Lawrence A. Kutz

FAITH, VIRTUE OF

The theological virtue of faith is a supernatural gift by which God raises up human persons to participate in his own life. Before man can have faith, he must be given the virtue of faith as a gift by God; before he can respond to Divine Revelation, he must receive a new capacity by which to respond. To "have faith" means to accept the gift of faith God has freely given.

The supernatural character of faith corresponds to the supernatural character of Divine Revelation and of life lived in its light. It is not enough for man to respond to God only according to a natural understanding of God and the world. From the beginning, God planned and acted to draw human beings into his inner life — ultimately, to full and eternal intimacy with him through what we call the beatific vision. This clearly is possible only by a divine, not human, action not demanded by human nature.

Supernatural life is comprised of an array of supernatural gifts and the free human response to them. The principal gift is sanctifying grace, by which man is freed from sin, transformed and elevated to the status of an adopted child of God, and made capable of meriting eternal life. Charity (which in its perfection defines the holiness of heaven itself) and hope are among the other gifts. Faith has its specific character as the foundation and starting point for all the other gifts.

God wishes to give the gift of faith to all human beings from the very beginning of their lives. Thus the Church calls attention to the grave obligation of Catholic parents to baptize their children soon after birth. Moreover, recognition of the fact that God wishes all to receive and respond to his gift of faith ought to motivate members of the Church to participate zealously in the work of evangelization.

See: Divine Revelation; Evangelization; Faith, Act of; Faith of the Church; Grace; Infant Baptism; Knowledge of God; Theological Virtues.

FALSE WITNESS

Taken literally, the eighth commandment, "You shall not bear false witness against your neighbor" (Ex 20:16), might be thought to forbid only lies uttered in formal settings like courts of law. And indeed the commandment aimed to strengthen Israel's judicial system by labeling false testimony an offense against God as well as man. The public, premeditated character of false witness makes it a particularly obnoxious form of lying, which St. Augustine says "consists in speaking a falsehood with the intention of deceiving." To bear false witness is to lie baldly, without any of the ambiguities and mitigating circumstances that often condition false statements. It is always sinful and, if the matter is grave, gravely so.

Over the centuries, the commandment has been taken to apply to lying generally, to defamation of character ("against your neighbor"), to judging others without sufficient proof, and to the unjustified betrayal of a secret. All these evils are relational in character, as the qualification "with the intention to deceive" implies. Liars do not simply utter a falsehood ("The sky is green"); they abuse the truth in order to mislead or harm others.

As the *Catechism of the Catholic Church* points out (2475), St. Paul picks up this emphasis on human relationships, while substituting a positive injunction to truthfulness for the negative formula of the Old Testament. In words reminiscent of the eighth commandment, he draws upon the notion that believers make up the Body of Christ: "Therefore, putting away falsehood, let everyone speak the truth with his neighbor, for we are members one of another" (Eph 4:25). Rather than simply forbidding false witness, this teaching enjoins true witness to the life of Christ within us.

See: Lying; Perjury; Slander; Truthfulness.

FAMILY

The family is both fruit and school of love. It begins in the self-donation of the spouses, who chose each other as husband and wife. It comes into proper being as their marital union gives birth to their children. It is the natural setting in which the most important lesson of life — to love and grow in love — is learned.

School of Love • The family normally is the place where love is first experienced and the ability to love is acquired. The person who has not received love when he or she is young is not likely to be able to give love when older.

It is natural, as well as a duty, that parents love their children. Moreover, precisely because love means wanting what is good for the other — wanting him or her to grow — parents are naturally the first to make loving demands on children. "Love is true when it creates the good of persons and of communities; it creates that good and *gives* it to others. . . . Love is demanding. . . . Nowadays people need to rediscover this demanding love, for it is the truly firm foundation of the family" (Pope John Paul II, *Letter to Families*, 14 [1994]). Parents should not spoil their children, simply giving to them without requiring anything of them (responsibility, sincerity, loyalty).

Love always means coming out of oneself, caring for others. In the family as a school of love, the parents are the first teachers. By their perseverance in the hard but marvelous task of giving themselves, they gradually become skillful and even expert teachers. Later on, they can and should involve the older children as co-teachers of the younger.

Humility is necessary in order to love. Pride is love's worst enemy. Asking pardon — making up from the heart — is the best weapon against pride. People who do not ask one another for pardon are placing their love in danger. A husband and wife who know how to apologize to each other as often as necessary are safeguarding their own conjugal love. If they have quarreled in the presence of their children (wise parents will work their differences out privately), they should also make up before them.

Parents need to correct their children in a just way. When they have corrected unjustly or have given bad example, they should not be too proud to acknowledge this before their children and rectify. This way, far from losing face, they gain authority.

The more self-giving rules in a family, the more love is learned and communicated. That is the ideal of family life, for which God gives abundant grace. But if the parents do not take their task seriously, the end result may be far from the ideal. Selfishness is present in every family, as in every person. If selfishness rules more than love, then the family itself can become a school of selfishness.

School for Social Living • Christian anthropology resists certain modern theories that consider the ideal of growth to be the building of a nondependent personality, and so criticize the family as a narrowing experience, a focus of small interests, a limitation on self-expression. The world needs, not more self-sufficiency or more self-sufficient persons, but more persons open to others and sharing life with them, and more places where people can be accepted and loved in their insufficiency. Such is the Church; such is the family, the domestic church.

The family is the most powerful force in any society for the humanizing of persons. "The well-being of the individual person and of both human and Christian society is closely bound up with the healthy state of conjugal and family life" (Vatican Council II, *Pastoral Constitution on the Church in the Modern World, Gaudium et Spes*, 47). In God's plan, the family "is a school for human enrichment" (*Gaudium et Spes*, 52), "the first school of how to be human" (*Letter to Families*, 15), "the place where different generations come together and help one another to grow wiser and harmonize the rights of individuals with other demands of social life; as such it constitutes the basis of society" (*Gaudium et Spes*, 52).

"The family is the *original cell of social life*. . . . Authority, stability, and a life of relationships within the family constitute the foundations for freedom, security, and fraternity within society. The family is the community in which, from childhood, one can learn moral values, begin to honor God, and make good use of freedom. Family life is an initiation into life in society" (CCC 2207; cf. 2224). The family therefore stands "prior to any recognition by public authority, which has an obligation to recognize it" (CCC 2202).

Loyal family life over the years is a school for understanding, solidarity, and love; for tolerance, ability to appreciate and accept, concern for others, cooperation, generosity, a place of refuge and trust. At one extreme, there is the loyalty of not letting others down. At the other, the knowledge that one will not be rejected, however much one deserves it.

Those who truly experience family life spread a spirit of fraternity. They see, and help others see, that one's "neighbor is not a 'unit' in the human collective; he is a 'someone' who deserves particular attention and respect" (CCC 2212). No Christian family can remain closed in on itself. It needs to live solidarity toward other families and also toward those without a family (cf. CCC 2208).

Specific Family Roles • Human dignity between man and woman is identical, but sexual and family roles are not. The attempt to abolish the complementarity of roles has highly negative effects on personal, social, and spiritual life.

One of the great challenges of married life is the progression from being spouses to being parents. To become — or to avoid becoming — a parent is easy; to *be* a parent is difficult. Many parents consciously or unconsciously pass up the challenge.

Children have natural respect for their parents, unless the parents forfeit it. Looking up to God and trusting him (so difficult for many people today) is enormously facilitated by being able to look up to and believe in one's parents. Young people need a father who can in some way incarnate God's fatherliness: trustworthy authority coming from love. They have no less need of a mother who can incarnate God's motherliness: his understanding and support for our weakness, God as our loving refuge (cf. CCC 239). Parental roles have been badly misunderstood when father and mother compete to wield authority, but not to give support. It is an immense strength to family life when sexual complementarity has been well developed in the parents. Children will be much more likely to bring their problems to parents to whom they have alternative access on different grounds. They are not likely to have much confidence in parents whom they sense to be engaged in a power struggle.

The brother-sister relationship also has a social as well as a personal dimension. This is more readily seen if one adverts to the situation when such a relationship is excluded because, as happens today in one-child families, there is a boy or a girl, but no sibling to relate to. Perhaps we have not yet weighed, though we are beginning to experience, the social effects of this evermore common lack of natural domestic introduction to the experience of fraternity. The danger is increasing that the very term "fraternity" will be left with an exclusively ideological content, whose practical application to life escapes the majority of persons.

Family and Prayer • The family is a school of faith and supernatural life and love. "Parents have the mission of teaching their children to pray and to discover their vocation as children of God" (CCC 2226). This mission also is a privilege.

Father Patrick Peyton, C.S.C., champion of the family Rosary in the mid-twentieth century, popularized the saying "The family that prays together, stays together." Even more importantly, each member of such a family stays with God — or will in the end come back to him. It is not mainly a matter of formal or fixed family prayers but rather of having experienced a family where God was, as it were, a "member" in his own right, not someone to be afraid of, nor just worshiped, but *loved*! Nothing lays a firmer base for a child's own spiritual life than the discovery that this is his or her parents' attitude.

Certain practices are habitual in every normal Christian family: saying grace at meals, the Angelus. But prayers should never be compulsory. The family Rosary is a marvelous devotion, but wise parents will *allow* their children to take part (e.g., to lead just one mystery) as they begin to grow up, without ever letting them look on it as an obligation or something expected of them.

Sunday Mass is a commandment of the Church. It cannot be imposed by parents on older children. Parental preaching counts very little. Parental example counts very much. If children see their parents never missing Mass, going frequently to confession, switching off certain TV programs, the impact of the example will eventually be great.

School of Sexual Identity • A growing mistrust between the sexes is one of the most disturbing phenomena of modern times. Those who find no explanation and no apparent remedy for this may conclude that sex is a negative reality that in the end leads men and women to exploit one another. Christians reject this conclusion. "Holy Scripture affirms that man and woman are made for one another" (CCC 1605). Christians believe this but believe, too, what the *Catechism* also recalls: The first sin disrupted the harmony and ease of that original communion between man and woman, with the result that "their relations were distorted by mutual recriminations; their mutual attraction, the Creator's own gift, changed into a relationship of domination and lust" (1607).

The Church has always taught that human nature is not radically vitiated by sin. We all have a fundamental yearning for truth and goodness; but we need God's grace to fulfill those yearnings. This applies very particularly to the area of sexuality. In the measure that married love and family love, aided by grace, are made strong, they will enable men and women, boys and girls, to discover the deeper mystery and meaning of sexuality, in such a way that the sexual urge is gradually purified of self-seeking and of tendencies to exploitation or domination so that its expressions — according to each one's state — strengthen the mutual respect that should always characterize relations between the sexes.

The family's role in the development of true sexual identity extends to what is today called sex education. True sexual education does not consist simply in imparting biological knowledge. Informing young people about the physiological consequences of sexual activity apart from any moral reference (i.e., failing to inculcate the virtue of chastity) is not sexual education at all, but sexual deformation that tends to leave young people incapable of understanding the real human meaning of sexuality and of relating with respect toward the other sex.

The family is meant to be the first and most natural school of proper sexual education. It is the special role and responsibility of parents to explain to their children in good time (always *before* puberty) the dignity and difficulties of sex. Sexual education operates in a thoroughly natural fashion in a family where there are several brothers and sisters. Brother-sister, after all, is the one sexual relationship not characterized by any disturbing presence of physical attraction. In a family where proper values are maintained, this offers both boys and girls an opportunity gradually to understand and appreciate the main characteristics of sexual identity. The gradual unfolding of parent-children relations (especially father-daughter, mother-son) should also play a powerful two-way role.

Family and Evangelization • In his 1994 *Letter to Families*, Pope John Paul II said families today lack life; they "have too little 'human' life. There is a shortage of people with whom to create and share the common good" (10). Families need to have their own vitality. "Love is true when it creates the good of persons and of communities" (*Letter to Families*, 14). Family love has to be inventive so as to create the Christian and human goodness of a home, with its own distinctive personality. This can come about only with the active and creative participation of each one: parents and children; and grandparents too, since no true family excludes the aged (cf. CCC 2218). The result is a "family life" that the children, having helped to create, live by, look forward to, and probably involve their friends in. Families with such a personality are not only the best safeguard for young people against negative or destructive elements in the social atmosphere but become focal points for gradually changing and renewing society.

The Christian family has a specially great mission today. "The family is placed at the center of the great struggle between good and evil, between life and death, between love and all that is opposed to love. To the family is entrusted the task of striving, first and foremost, to unleash the forces of good, the source of which is found in Christ the Redeemer of man. Every family unit needs to make these forces their own so that . . . 'the family be strong with the strength of God' " (*Letter to Families*, 23).

See: Education in Human Sexuality; Evangelization; Marriage; Marriage, Goods of; Marriage, Sacrament of; Sexuality, Human; Women, Ecclesial and Social Roles of.

Suggested Readings: CCC 1655-1658, 1666, 2196-2233. John Paul II, *The Christian Family in the Modern World, Familiaris Consortio; Letter to Families.*

Cormac Burke

FATHERHOOD OF GOD

Christ has taught us that God wants to share the communion of Trinitarian life with us. "If a man loves me, he will keep my word, and my Father will love him, and we will come to him and make our home with him" (Jn 14:23). Far from being distant or absent, the triune God is very near, not just as the first cause who sustains all things in being, but as the sheer gift of intimate personal communion. The deepest conviction of the Catholic faith is that God's purpose in creation and in the economy of salvation is to make this personal communion a reality.

St. Paul expressed this truth with striking clarity: "God sent forth his Son . . . so that we might receive adoption as sons. And because you are sons, God has sent the Spirit of his Son into our hearts, crying, 'Abba! Father!' " (Gal 4:4-6). Thus, in a remarkable way, our share in the communion of life of the Father, Son, and Holy Spirit replicates the mutual relations of the Persons of the Blessed Trinity. Christ's sonship is the principle of our own coming to life in grace — our adoption — as sons and daughters who can speak the name of the Father in the power of the Holy Spirit. "When we cry, 'Abba! Father!' it is the Spirit himself bearing witness with our spirit that we are children of God" (Rom 8:15-16).

It follows that, when Christ used the term "Father" in speaking to God, he introduced us into the family life of the Persons of the Trinity. In a real sense, he taught us their own names for each other and thus confirmed our intimate participation in their Trinitarian life. Commenting on the Lord's Prayer, St. Cyprian wrote: "Let us pray as God our master has taught us. To ask the Father in words his Son has given us, to let him hear the prayer of Christ ringing in our ears, is to make our prayer one of friendship, a family prayer. Let the Father recognize the words of his Son. Let the Son who lives in our hearts be also on our lips." In order to grasp the significance of our ability to use the personal name Father in speaking of God, we must first consider two other senses in which the term "father" can be applied to God.

The first is metaphorical. This is perhaps the most common use of the term, and can even be found outside the ambit, or confines, of the Christian churches. It identifies God as the Creator and personal principle of the universe. Since fathers play an important role in the generation of their children, we use the term "father" as a metaphor for productions of various sorts, as when we say someone has fathered an idea or an institution. On this basis, we can say that the triune God is the Father of the created order.

While this is not a uniquely Christian way of referring to God, the biblical basis for it evokes the intimacy, concern, attention, and engagement of a good father that are characteristic of the revelation of God. The usage is metaphorical because the meaning of the term entails the limitations of human fatherhood, including bodiliness and, since both a father and a mother cooperate in human generation, sexual differentiation. Since the Christian doctrine of God excludes materiality and sexual differentiation, the application of the term to God must be metaphorical.

A second sense in which the name father can be used with respect to God is according to the rule of appropriation. This is a linguistic rule, implicit throughout Christian Revelation, according to which activities or essential attributes common to all three Persons of the Trinity can be ascribed in a special way to one or another of them. Many examples can be given, but the most common one is the practice of calling the Father, Son, and Holy Spirit, respectively, Creator, Redeemer, and Sanctifier by appropriation of common activities of the triune God in our regard, namely, creation, redemption, and sanctification.

Thus it is that the rule of appropriation permits the first Person of the Trinity to be called Father just as he can be called Creator. An activity common to the three Persons as one God can be attributed to one of them without implying that he acts independently of the other two when acting *ad extra* (externally).

The Personal Name "Father" • In comparison with these two uses of the term "father" with respect to God, the importance of the personal name Father for the first Person of the Trinity stands out in sharp relief. The personal names for God do not refer to any actions on his part with respect to creatures (as with "father" in the two senses above) but to the internal relations of the three Divine Persons. The names Father, Son, and Holy Spirit refer to God independently of the existence of a creaturely realm, and thus describe the intimate, eternal reality of the three Divine Persons as such. These personal names are known to us only because Christ revealed them and thus invited us to a share in the communion of uncreated life that is the eternal, triune God.

The personal names Father, Son, and Holy Spirit describe a familial intimacy of a particularly intense form. According to Scripture and Catholic Tradition, the "comings forth" or processions *in* God are distinct from the coming forth of things *from* God. Even though the inner-Trinitarian processions give rise to real relations in God, they do not involve creation or causation of any kind. Catholic theology has been challenged to the utmost to show how this mystery can be understood, but there is no way of gaining access to it except as invited by the triune God. We know that the first Person is the Father because the Son calls him by that name; it is the Son's personal way of speaking of the Father. The same is true of the Spirit. These names do not originate in our experience of God; their basis is the "usage" of the Persons of the Trinity themselves. Insofar as we become intimates of the Trinitarian family through the grace of Christ, we can learn to use these names as well.

Lately the suggestion has arisen that other names should be preferred to these in talking about the Trinity. Proponents of inclusive language have argued that the names Father and Son evoke an irredeemably masculinist image of God.

In addressing this complex issue, it should be noted from the start that Catholic Tradition is unanimous in rejecting the sexual and androcentric connotations of the personal names of the Father and the Son. Male characteristics can be attrib-

uted to God only metaphorically, since bodiliness is essential to such properties. It is for this reason that the name Father as applied to the triune God must be seen as metaphorical.

From this perspective, the metaphorical naming of God as "mother" is not absolutely excluded. But the difficulties posed by such usage and the almost complete absence of biblical support for it rule out the simple substitution of the name "Mother" for "Father" in the public and liturgical discourse of the Catholic community when speaking of the triune God. Even worse would be the combination "Father/Mother," since such a usage undermines the possibility of making personal reference to God. In private devotion and prayer, however, there might be a place for referring to God as "mother."

But the more fundamental objection to such substitutions arises from the very nature of Trinitarian Revelation. Since we have no uninvited basis for naming the Persons of the Trinity, we have no grounds to prefer other terms to the names we have learned from Christ. The exclusive warrant for the aptness of the names Father, Son, and Holy Spirit lies in Christ's revelation of the inner-Trinitarian life. This consideration decisively excludes the substitution of the name "Mother" for "Father" when speaking of the first Person of the Trinity.

See: Divine Revelation; God, Nature and Attributes of; Hierarchy; Holy Spirit; Jesus Christ, God and Man; Knowledge of God; Sacred Tradition; Trinity; Women, Ecclesial and Social Roles of.

Suggested Readings: CCC 198-267, 2779-2802. St. Thomas Aquinas, *Summa Theologiae*, I, 33-43. A. Kimel, ed., *Speaking the Christian God.* F. Martin, *The Feminist Question*, pp. 265-292.

J.A. DiNoia, O.P.

FINAL PERSEVERANCE

"He who endures [perseveres] to the end will be saved," said the Master (Mt 10:22). Given free will and long-standing human weakness, no one in this life can be certain that death will usher him into heaven's beatific vision.

Heaven is the culmination of a series of gratuitous favors bestowed on humanity by its Father God. We can but strive after this gratuitous prize, while longing and praying for it. Believers "rightly hope for *the grace of final perseverance and the recompense* of God their Father for the good works accomplished with his grace in communion with Jesus" (CCC 2016). Since man usually dies as he has lived, he best disposes himself for this boon by leading a godly life.

Dying in God's good graces does not necessarily imply a lifelong and unbroken fidelity to grace; indeed, it is a matter of faith that lost grace can be recovered. Rather, it is commonly understood to mean keeping oneself unstained from sin from the time of the last conversion until death. Actual perseverance "consists," says John Henry Newman, "in an ever watchful superintendence of us on the part of our all-merciful Lord, removing temptations which he sees will be fatal to us, succouring us at those times when we are in particular peril, whether from our negligence or other cause, and ordering the course of our life so that we may die at a time when he sees that we are in the state of grace" ("Perseverance in Grace," in *Discourses to Mixed Congregations*).

However, from our incapacity certainly to know and strictly to merit the great gift, we should not infer that nothing can be done toward receiving it. Saints dwell on God's great mercy in granting final perseverance, and even inveterate sinners are not to lose hope. Blessed Josemaría Escrivá said: "Don't view God as a hunter out to catch his prey off guard; rather, see him as a gardener who plucks the rose only at its most beautiful peak." God radiates sinners' dying hours with an extraordinary light; and, showing them the hideousness of sin in contrast with his own infinite beauty, he makes a final appeal to them, as we see in the moving account of the good thief on Calvary (cf. Lk 23:39-43). Only those who, even then, obstinately cling to their sin exclude themselves from paradise.

See: Despair; Presumption; Religion, Virtue of; Tempting God.

FLATTERY

Praise and flattery, often confused, are actually opposites. Honest praise is complimenting people on virtues they actually have or good they really have done. Flattery is knowingly complimenting people falsely. Telling a woman of virtuous and exemplary life she is saintly is not flattery, if sincerely meant; but the same words directed to someone whom we secretly despised and thought far from saintly would be flattery, a moral fault.

The sin of flattery is not serious unless the content of the falsehood or the attendant circumstances render it so. A man may say, "You are the most beautiful woman I have ever seen." Even if the woman is plain, he may in his passion see her as beautiful, in which case he does not flatter; or he may be teasing a friend who recognizes the exaggeration, and here, too, there is no flattery; or he may be deceiving the woman to embarrass her before others, in which case his action is wrong, but not the wrong of flattery. Finally, however, he may be attempting to deceive her so as to seduce her, in which case his flattery itself is a great evil.

The *Catechism of the Catholic Church* insists: "Every word or attitude is forbidden which by *flattery, adulation, or complaisance* encourages and confirms another in malicious acts" (2480). Here the evil of flattery consists not in being a means to our own bad ends, but in forwarding someone else's sin. Thus Milton's Satan, who persuades Eve to eat the forbidden fruit by saying she will become like God, commits the same offense as King Lear's older daughters, who flatter him to forward their political ambitions.

See: Lying; Truthfulness.

FORNICATION

Fornication is the sin committed by those who engage in acts of premarital sexual intercourse, whether these are the brief encounters of promiscuous sex, the acts of those who have lived together for a long time, or the acts of the engaged who anticipate soon being married.

Some acts of fornication are manifestly wrong, since they are loveless acts that cruelly exploit another. Promiscuous acts do not express love for another; they are directed solely to sexual pleasure. Even if the exploitation is mutual, it is wrong, for one should never risk harming another or allow oneself to be harmed, nor should one risk conceiving children one has no intent to care for.

Some of those who have sexual relations apart from marriage may avow committed love to one another, but in fact they have not made the commitments necessary to legitimate sexual involvement. In all instances, fornication is immoral, since the individuals involved have not pledged themselves to the promises implicit in the sex act; they have made no binding pledge to be faithful to each other and to care for one another; and they are endangering the well-being of any children they may conceive. Human relations are notoriously fragile and susceptible to dissolution for the weakest of motives. We need the bonds of marriage to help us be faithful to the promises implicit in sexual relations.

Many who are abandoned by their premarital lovers become less trusting and giving in future relationships. Their future marital relations may be endangered. Sexual intercourse outside of marriage is also often accompanied by contraception, which in itself suggests the *de facto* temporariness of premarital relations.

See: Chastity; Education in Human Sexuality; Marriage, Goods of; Sexuality, Human.

FREEDOM, HUMAN

Scripture and Tradition clearly affirm that human beings have free choice and are morally responsible for important actions. Indeed, this truth is fundamental to the Gospel, since Jesus died on the cross for our *sins* (which are bad free choices offending God), and we are *invited* to take up our crosses and follow Jesus. The Gospel, as both a proclamation and an invitation, makes no sense unless human beings have free choice.

The word "freedom" has several meanings. Sometimes it refers to physical freedom: the lack of physical restraints upon physical behavior. At other times freedom refers to liberty: the lack of constraints placed by an authority upon someone's actions, as when an adolescent asks for more freedom. Sometimes the word refers to political freedom: the ability of a citizen to participate in political affairs or of a nation to direct its own political affairs.

The *Catechism of the Catholic Church* is not referring to these types of freedom, but to free choice, when it succinctly defines freedom as "the power, rooted in reason and will, to act or not to act, to do this or that, and so to perform deliberate actions on one's own responsibility" (1731).

Consider an example. Suppose one morning Smith resolves to skip lunch that day, for both religious and health-conscious purposes. That afternoon, taking a walk and passing by a local pizza parlor, Smith smells the aroma of pizza wafting through the air. He immediately desires the pizza, his mouth watering. He begins to deliberate: He could go into the pizza parlor and have some pizza or he could continue to walk, keeping to his fast or diet.

There is something good or attractive about each alternative. Eating the pizza would bring him great pleasure, and, he recalls, he might meet his friends or that cute waitress while waiting for his order. On the other hand, passing up the pizza parlor on this occasion would be good both religiously and for his health. In other words, each course of action offers some distinctive good, some benefit not offered by the other. He cannot do both, so he must make up his mind: He must decide which course of action to follow. This act of "making up his mind" is an act of the will. If Smith decides to eat the pizza, but slips and falls on the way and never gets to the pizza parlor, he has still willed to do so. And although he does not perform the physical behavior to carry out his choice, he is still morally responsible for his choice.

To say that such a choice is free is to say that it is not determined by the events that preceded it. That is, under the very same conditions, he could have chosen the other option or not chosen at all. Given everything that happened to him up to the point just prior to his choice — including everything in his environment, everything in his heredity, everything in his understanding and in his character — it was still possible for him to choose the pizza or to choose to walk away. To say the choice was free is to say that all of those things together were not enough to bring it about that he should choose this rather than that or even that he should choose rather than not choose.

How, then, does a person finally will one thing rather than another? The answer is that in a free choice, the person by his own act of will directs his will toward this option rather than toward that one. The free choice is a self-determined act of will.

Determinism • The denial that there are free choices, in the sense explained above, is called determinism, while the position that there are free choices is sometimes called libertarianism (not in the same sense of course in which the word is used to refer to a particular ideological and political school).

Determinism is divided into "hard determinism" and "soft determinism." Hard determinism rejects both free choice and moral responsibility. Soft determinism, also called "compatibilism," is the position that while our choices are determined by antecedent events, we are nevertheless morally responsible for some of them. On this position, all of our actions are determined, but some are determined by extrinsic factors, while others are determined only by intrinsic factors. If an act is determined by an intrinsic factor, namely our character, then the compatibilists call it free, since it is not coerced (not forced by something outside the self). This is to say that concretely one could not help but choose as one did, given one's character, but since one was not extrinsically coerced the action was "free." The position is called "compatibilism" because it holds that universal determinism is compatible with freedom and moral responsibility. It was held by various philosophers and by the Protestant Reformers Martin Luther and John Calvin.

On this view, however, prior to any actions one has performed, one's character must have been extrinsically determined. One would not, then, be morally responsible for any of the actions or the changes in one's character that flowed from that initial character. The libertarian position — the position taught by the Church — concedes that some of one's actions may indeed be determined by one's character, and so are not directly the result of free choice. Nevertheless, the libertarian position also holds, first, that character is, most profoundly, the result of previous free choices, and so for that reason one is morally responsible for actions that flow from one's character; and, second, that some of one's actions are determined neither by extrinsic factors nor by one's character, that these actions therefore are free, and that one is directly morally responsible for them.

While there are philosophical arguments for free choice, as a matter of fact most thinkers outside the Judeo-Christian tradition have held a determinist position. In the ancient tradition in the West, neither Plato nor Aristotle seems to have had a clear notion of free choice, and both seem to have held a type of soft determinism. On the other hand, libertarianism is clearly asserted both in the Old Testament and in the New. In the Council of Trent, the Church, responding to the denial of free choice by the Protestant Reformers, definitively taught that by free choice we actively cooperate with God's grace (cf. Denzinger-Schönmetzer, 1954).

In modern culture, psychologists often assume that every aberrant behavior can be completely explained by psychic causes. Sociologists and social critics often assume that social problems could be completely eradicated by education and technological advances, forgetting that bad free choices, that is, sins, are at the root of many of the most serious social problems.

Arguments for and Against Free Choice • There exists no widespread agreement among proponents of free choice about which arguments for free choice are sound.

One approach is to claim that we are immediately aware that we have free choice. In deliberating, I seem to be directly aware that I could will this option, but that I could also will that option, and that it is up to me which to choose. However, this experience cannot by itself settle the issue. While free choice is at root a positive ability (the ability to determine for oneself one's acts of willing), still, it essentially involves the absence of something, namely, the absence of any determining conditions of one's act of choice. But the absence of something cannot be a direct object of experience. (However, direct experience does provide some evidence for free choice, and it places the burden of proof on the determinist.)

A second argument can be found in the writings of Thomas Aquinas.

Thomas argued that the will can be seen to be free in acts of choice because by one's reason or intellect one perceives something good in each alternative, but also some defect in each (at least the defect of not offering what is good in the other alternative). Since, however, the will is our ability or power to incline toward an understood good, the only object that would compel the will to incline toward it would be an object good in every respect. Now, the blessed in heaven have a direct vision of God, who is pure goodness; their will cannot reject God, since God is good in every respect, and they have a clear vision of that goodness. But every other object proposed to the will is good only in some respect, and is not good in other respects. Even union with God, for those who do not have a direct vision of God, appears good in some respects but lacking in other respects, and therefore those who are still on earth can freely reject union with God or choose something incompatible with it. Hence, having deliberated and therefore seen that an object is good in some ways but not good in others, one is free either to will it or not will it — free to will this object or some other object or course of action.

Perhaps Aquinas did not intend this argument precisely as a proof that there is a free choice, but, rather, as an explanation of how and to what extent the will is free (presupposing the existence of free choice). In any case, the argument does provide additional weight to the position that there are free choices, since it shows that the understood object of the will cannot determine the will. However, the argument does not seem to exclude the possibility of a hidden cause determining one's choices.

Another approach is to argue that the denial of free choice is self-defeating. The notion of free choice is not self-contradictory, and therefore the determinist cannot show that one is logically compelled to deny it. Rather, the determinist can only argue that the denial of free choice is the more reasonable position. Thus, in asserting the determinist position he is appealing to reasonableness; he is saying, in effect, that we ought to be reasonable. But this appeal to what we *ought* to do presupposes that we might or might not be reasonable and that it is within our power to be reasonable. This, however, is to suppose that we have free choice. Hence the very denial of free choice implicitly affirms it, and it is unreasonable to deny free choice.

On the basis of all of these arguments taken together, then, one can surely say that the preponderance of evidence favors the libertarian position.

Against Free Choice • We shall consider what seem to be the three most important arguments.

First, it is often argued that our intellectual judgment must determine our choice. We deliberate, one option appears better than the others, and therefore we are determined — compelled — to choose the option that appears best.

The answer is that in some cases no option is best in every respect or according to every consideration. It is true that if one option offers as much as the other option, plus some more, then one must choose it. This sometimes happens: When househunting, for instance, one may see that one house has every good feature that another one has, plus more. In that situation the second house cannot be chosen, since it has no distinctive attractiveness. It simply drops out of consideration.

In other situations, though, one option offers one type of benefit or good, and the other option offers a different type: eating pizza versus keeping one's diet; going to law school versus going to medical school, etc. In such situations neither option is better in every respect. Rather, each offers a distinct type of benefit not offered by the other. In those kinds of situations, there is free choice.

A second argument against free choice is a generalization from situations where unconscious motives seem determinative. In psychiatry, one often discovers that a person's actions were in fact determined by an unconscious motive, for example, the desire to escape a feared object or to be like some particular person. One can then generalize. If in several cases one's choice is determined by unconscious motives, then perhaps all those choices that seem free are actually determined by unconscious motives. Thus, people often believe that the advances in psychology and psychiatry are inimical to belief in free choice.

The argument, however, is fallacious. It supposes that unconscious motives are incompatible with free choice. But they are not. Suppose that, without being aware of it, one is attracted to a person partly because she resembles an aunt of whom one is fond, and so one's interest in inviting her to dinner is motivated, partly at least, by this unconscious circumstance. Still, this unconscious motive only explains why the option is quite attractive; it does not at all show that the option is compelling. One need not know why one is attracted to an option in order to be free to accept it or reject it.

A third objection is that everything other than God must be caused by God, since God alone is self-sufficient. Free choices are certainly entities, and therefore they, too, depend on God, that is, they must be caused to exist by God. But if God causes one's free choices, then, so the objection runs, one cannot be free. In short, God's causality is incompatible with free choice.

This raises very large issues. But at least the following can be said here. The argument wrongly supposes that we understand what God's causality is in itself. For one can know that one thing is incompatible with another only if one understands the nature of each and sees their incompatibility. We understand God's causality, however, only by analogy with other instances of causality; we do not understand its intrinsic nature. So, in effect, the argument cannot really get off the ground.

Moreover, God causes the things in this world to exist. But this causality should not be thought of as if it were a kind of shoving this way or that. To cause is not the same as to determine. The situation can perhaps best be thought of this way: God does not cause a person to will this rather than that, but God causes the whole reality of someone freely willing this over that.

Which Acts Are Free? • As this discussion has indicated, not every act of will is free. Not even every act of choice is free. Which acts, then, are free? If the explanation of free choice set out here is substantially correct, then to have free choice one must be aware of different courses of action and must see some distinct sort of benefit in each.

The will is *not* free — in the sense that one could not here and now will otherwise — in two types of cases. First, the will is not free to reject God in the beatific vision. In heaven, sin has lost its attraction. (This does not mean that there is no freedom in heaven. There is still free choice about issues other than whether to remain in communion with God or reject that communion — whether to talk to Paul now or to Peter, and so on.) Second, the will is not free if one fails to deliberate. This may be the case, for example, because one is not quite awake or because one is overcome by passion. In either case, without seeing some distinctive good in the different options, one's willing of a course of action is not free; one could not have willed otherwise. Of course one still might be indirectly morally responsible for one's action — responsible, that is, for getting into the condition in which deliberation was blocked.

By free choice we fashion who we shall be. Human persons are quite unlike rocks and trees and animals, which simply are what they are and act out, according to their predetermined nature, what they shall be. Human persons, through free choice, constitute the kinds of moral persons they shall be. When I choose one option rather than another, I shape an aspect of myself in the direction of the option chosen.

Free choice is also important for understanding interpersonal communion. Supposing two rocks could become one, they could only do so by losing their individuality. However, since by their free choices persons constitute themselves, if two persons share in a choice, they really, not just metaphorically, become one, and do so without losing their individuality. People who commit themselves to pursue a way of life together really do constitute themselves as one, a point important for understanding the act of faith and marriage.

See: Choice; Conscience; Natural Law; Passions; Providence.

Suggested Readings: CCC 1730-1742, 1987-2004. G. Grisez, *The Way of the Lord Jesus*, Vol. 1, *Christian Moral Principles*, pp. 41-72. G. Grisez and R. Shaw, *Fulfillment in Christ*, pp. 12-25.

Patrick Lee

FREEMASONRY

As a more or less publicly established organization, Freemasonry dates from the year 1717 and a meeting in a London tavern. Its imposition of secrecy from the beginning, especially on its core members, and its own obviously partial and conflicting explanations, both to its general membership and to the public, make certain knowledge of its early history and precedents very difficult to obtain. However, on the basis of the central beliefs of early members and subsequent leaders, Freemasonry can be said to be an organized continuation of several earlier secret, atheistic movements like the Rosicrucians of the latter sixteenth and early seventeenth centuries. From 1717 on, Freemasonry quickly became an identifiable place of reunion for individuals of a radical anti-Catholic and atheistic spirit, with doctrines and principles diametrically opposed to Catholicism and to any structures of civil society supportive of the Church and of natural law morality.

Pope Clement XII in 1738 issued a solemn and definitive condemnation of Freemasonry and everything related to it, absolutely prohibiting Catholics under penalty of excommunication from becoming members, facilitating its activity, or associating with it in any way; the prohibition included even receiving Freemasons into one's home. Pope Benedict XIV in 1751 solemnly reiterated Pope Clement's negative judgment. Since then the Church's Magisterium has repeated the condemnation and prohibition of Freemasonry some three hundred times, counting statements by local bishops. Solemn pronouncements have been made by the Holy See on some twenty occasions. Prior to the statement of 1983 discussed below, these include numerous pronouncements of Pope Leo XIII and the solemn codification of the prohibition of membership in Freemasonry in the Code of Canon Law of 1917 (Canon 2335).

Teaching of Pope Leo XIII • The long pontificate of Pope Leo XIII (1878-1902) was marked by an abundant and positive articulation of the fundamental truths related to the social, economic, and political situation of the rapidly changing world of the last quarter of the nineteenth century. At the same time, Pope Leo was forced to confront profoundly erroneous doctrines and movements being propagated against all religion and civil order, especially in Europe. At the center of this strictly negative reality, and taking unscrupulous advantage of people's problems and aspirations, was the widespread and diversified organization of Freemasonry. From the beginning to the end of his pontificate Leo XIII condemned and prohibited Freemasonry, its principal teachings, tactics, and actions. His most complete explanation and solemn condemnation are found in the encyclical *Humanum Genus* (1884).

Pope Leo's teaching was not dictated only by Freemasonry's activities in his day, however, but by its two-hundred-year history. He focused his attention upon the principles of Freemasonry, which had not changed during that time and which would still today have to be solemnly repudiated before Freemasonry could be thought to have changed.

Pope Leo spoke of the secrecy and concealment of Freemasons: "As a convenient manner of concealment they assume the character of literary men and scholars associated for purposes of learning. They speak of their zeal for a more cultured refinement and of their love for the poor" (*Humanum Genus*, 9). Based on numerous statements by its leaders and above all on its actions, Freemasonry's "ultimate purpose forces itself into view — namely, the utter overthrow of that whole religious and political order of the world which the Christian teaching has produced, and the substitution of a new state of things in accordance with their ideas . . . drawn from mere 'Naturalism' "(*Humanum Genus*, 10). By naturalism, it should be noted, Leo meant a system that denies the capacity of reason to reach the knowledge of God and his law. Hence Freemasonry had from the beginning "conceived a deep hatred against the Catholic Church, and has ever since increased and inflamed it" (encyclical *Officio Sanctissimo* [1887]). Freemasons, the Pope concluded, "wish to see the religion founded by God repudiated and all affairs private as well as public, regulated by the principles of naturalism alone" (encyclical *Inimica Vis* [1892]). The ultimate aim was "the destruction of all religion and reference to the true God" (*Humanum Genus*, 16). So atheists could as well be members as theists (*Humanum Genus*, 17).

The core leadership hid from many of its members Freemasonry's true purpose, tactics, decisions, and actions. While many things are public, Pope Leo said, "there are many things like mysteries which it is the fixed rule to hide with extreme care, not only from strangers, but from very many members also; such as the secret and final designs, the name of the chief leaders, and certain secret and inner meetings, as well as their decisions, and the ways and means of carrying them out" (*Humanum Genus*, 9). Candidates for membership generally were required to swear secrecy and obedience, under pain of "the direst penalties and death itself. . . . Punishment is inflicted on them not infrequently, and with so much audacity and dexterity that the assassin very often escapes the detection and penalty of his crime" (*Humanum Genus*, 9).

The morality inculcated by Freemasonry was of course divorced from religious belief (*Humanum Genus*, 19). In this spirit, it sought control of all education and cultural instruments. Denying God and eternal life, it promoted a strictly this-worldly notion of morality; and in this perspective, but also for reasons of control, Freemasonry often promoted sexual license (*Humanum Genus*, 20).

A special focus of Freemasonic propaganda and action, Pope Leo pointed out, was thus the destruction of the human and Christian notions of marriage and the family. Freemasonry promoted the notion "that marriage belongs to the genus of commercial contracts, which can rightly be revoked by the will of those who make them, and that the civil rulers of the State have power over the matrimonial bond [to the exclusion of anyone else]" (*Humanum Genus*, 21).

In political doctrine and action, Freemasonry held "that the State should be without God" (*Humanum Genus*, 22). On the one hand, it promoted the notion of the Liberal State, to be governed by the new middle class according to atheistic conceptions of unlimited freedom; on the other hand, it had prepared the way for, and in fact fostered, the radical destruction of all distinctions of property and classes as "deliberately planned and put forward by many associations of *Communists* and *Socialists*" (*Humanum Genus*, 27). Periodicals and books, institutions of education and culture often were instruments for achieving its ends (cf. encyclicals *Dall' Alto Dell' Apostolico Seggio* [1890], *Custodi Di Quella Fede* [1892]). Catholics were exhorted by the Pope to "oppose publications with publications, schools with schools, associations with associations, congresses with congresses, actions with actions" (*Custodi Di Quella Fede*). In sum, Leo XIII said: "Let us remember that Christianity and Freemasonry are essentially irreconcilable, so that enrollment in one means separation from the other" (*Custodi Di Quella Fede*).

Canon Law on Masonry • The Code of Canon Law of 1917 stated in Canon 2335: "Those who join a Masonic sect or other societies of the same sort, which plot against the Church or against legitimate civil authority, incur *ipso facto* an excommunication simply reserved to the Holy See." This canon remained in force until the new Code of Canon Law of 1983.

Canon 1374 of the 1983 Code of Canon Code, specifically indicated as replacing Canon 2335 of the old Code, does not mention Freemasonry, nor is it mentioned elsewhere in the Code. Canon 1374 states: "A person who joins an association which plots against the Church is to be punished with a just penalty; one who promotes or takes office in such an association is to be punished with an interdict." This led some to ask whether membership in Freemasonry was still automatically prohibited for Catholics. In reply, the Congregation for the Doctrine of the Faith issued a brief *Declaration on Masonic Associations*, dated the day the new Code went into effect (November 26, 1983). It states that the omission from the new code of specific mention of Freemasonry reflects "an editorial criterion which was followed also in the case of other associations likewise unmentioned inasmuch as they are contained in wider categories." And it adds: "Therefore the Church's negative judgment in regard to Masonic associations remains unchanged since their principles have always been considered irreconciliable with the doctrine of the Church and therefore membership in them remains forbidden. The faithful who enroll in Masonic associations are in a state of grave sin and may not receive Holy Communion." It continues: "It is not within the competence of local ecclesiastical authorities to give a judgment on the nature of Masonic associations which would imply a derogation from what has been decided above."

Principles of Masonry • The principles of Freemasonry are irreconcilable not only with those of Catholicism but with those common to all Christians and with authentic rationality. Leading Freemasons and critics of Freemasonry agree in substance that Freemasonry proposes a total worldview, namely, that of the so-called Ancient Wisdom or Mysteries or, more precisely, of early Gnosticism, as it has been carried to the modern period especially by the Kabbalah and Theosophy. This is a pantheistic atheism that uses all available elements in a syncretistic way, attempting to encompass everything in a notion of universal brotherhood or cosmic harmony without the true God. It combines an appeal to spiritual ideals like freedom, fraternity, and equality with the imposition of a materialistic, this-worldly pragmatism that reaches both the political order and all elements of private life. It has most commonly attempted to present itself as a "deism" that all rea-

sonable men supposedly would accept. However, like the historical phenomenon of deism in general, while appealing to reason and the god it reaches (the Great Architect, who supposedly created the world but then left it for reasonable men to run), it denies reason's ability to reach knowledge of the natural moral law and reduces all to a mystical-pragmatic imposition of laws by reasonable men.

From the beginning, and especially in Protestant countries, Freemasonry posed as the defender of Protestantism against Catholicism, in order to enlist Protestants. In so doing, it did not deceive sincere believers of the Protestant churches, many of which condemned Freemasonry almost as strongly as the Catholic Church did. This Protestant face was shown in England, although Freemasonry there also gave full access to deists and open atheists, and in Germany, especially Prussia. In France, Italy, Spain, Austria, and Catholic Germany, Freemasonry was more openly libertarian, anti-institutional, and atheistic.

In the United States, from its beginnings in the mid-eighteenth century until a series of scandals almost brought about its demise in the 1820s, Freemasonry emphasized deism. In its recovery and growth after the 1850s, it directly appealed to Protestants and fostered Protestant fear of the Catholic Church. Much of its work was carried out under the slogan of "Americanism," with the accusation that Catholics were the enemies of American democracy. Simultaneously, however, it has always promoted both an atheistic humanism and, increasingly so, a theosophical and New Age cosmic mysticism.

American Freemasons, along with others of like mind, created the Know-Nothing party in the 1850s, the Ku Klux Klan after the Civil War and again from 1915 onward, and the American Protective Association in the latter 1880s and early 1890s. All were even more anti-Catholic than they were antiblack or xenophobic. In the pursuit of the basic project of transforming the United States into a lay, or secular, state and undoing its Christian traditions, Freemasonry enlisted Protestants and Jews to forge a notion of separation of Church and State that eventually undid laws or policies sustaining basic moral law, especially in relation to marriage, sexuality, and abortion. Protestants and Others United for the Separation of Church and State (founded in 1947 and later renamed Americans United) was created by members of Scottish Rite Masonry and continuously supported by its leadership; it has worked tirelessly for the elimination of all connections between public life and religion and morality based on the Judeo-Christian tradition.

See: Atheism; Gnosticism; New Age; Rationalism; Theosophy.

Suggested Readings: CCC 285, 2123-2126. Leo XIII, *Humanum Genus.* W. Whalen, *Christianity and American Freemasonry.* P. Fisher, *Behind the Lodge Doors.* L. de Poncins, *Freemasonry and the Vatican.* C. Kelly, *Conspiracy Against God and Man.*

Lawrence A. Kutz

FUNDAMENTAL OPTION

Some of our moral choices are very broad in scope. They can be called fundamental choices or options. They are not choices to do a particular kind of action, like swearing falsely or giving alms to a poor man; rather, they are concerned with the ordering of our whole lives to all that is good, and to God.

A "decision of faith" is an instance of such a fundamental option. For example, a repentant person advancing toward adult Baptism might come to decide to commit all his life to God in a fundamental choice of faith: He might resolve to give his life faithfully to the Lord, to believe all that Christ teaches in his Catholic Church, and resolve to live in all circumstances as love of God and neighbor require (cf. Pope John Paul II, *The Splendor of Truth, Veritatis Splendor*, 65-70).

Through a positive fundamental option of this kind one formally and explicitly reorients one's whole life, from alienation from God to the "obedience of faith" (Rom 1:5). A negative fundamental option can be equally decisive. Thus someone who had lived in grace might come, after many lesser infidelities, to reorder all of his life, to cease believing in God or caring at all about living in ways that please God.

Such acts are "fundamental" in their scope and radical in their consequences. Other moral acts are acts of more specific and particular kinds. Some tendentiously call these "peripheral" acts, suggesting that they are universally of lesser moral significance; and indeed the immediate thrust and aim of such acts is not to reorient one's whole life but to accomplish a far more limited end. Thus some, but not all, fundamental option theorists hold that fundamental decisions about the whole orientation of our lives are not readily accessible to clear everyday consciousness, as the choices of particular acts are. These fundamental decisions are said to be real and extremely important personal decisions, but to take place within a deeper level of our being, not clearly accessible to our ordinary consciousness.

The Question of Mortal Sin • A question raised in recent decades has been: Can a particular and "peripheral" act, like fornication or perjury, of itself and independent of some *distinct* fundamental choice (a radical and deep decision to alter one's relationship with God, which *could* accompany the performance of a particular act), be a mortal sin and have the tragic effects of a true mortal sin?

Some have argued that the answer is no. For example, some would claim that an act of fornication is itself a "grave sin," a seriously wrong kind of deed; but of itself, even if done deliberately and with full knowledge, it does not have the tragic effects of mortal sin. Nevertheless, it could in some circumstances occasion the decisive, distinct act of a fundamental choice against God. Some would call "radical" those fundamental option theories that incorporate this revisionary teaching on mortal sin.

Different kinds of reasons have been given for this position. One set of reasons is associated with somewhat dualistic presuppositions about man identified with Immanuel Kant (1724-1804) and others. The core of a man's being, his spiritual center, such theories would say, is not closely related to his ordinary everyday choices, even choices of very important concrete matters. They argue that the radical orientation of a person toward or away from God can only be made in the core of one's being, and in a formal and free choice of precisely this sort.

Others have more pastoral reasons for denying the received teaching on mortal sin. They judge that it would seem too severe today, and hardly credible to many, to maintain the received Catholic teaching that all that is required for a true mortal sin is: that one perform a gravely wrong kind of act, with sufficient knowledge and freedom. Hence they argue that a person does not commit a mortal sin unless, in a profound way, he formally wills to turn the orientation of his life from God.

The Church has firmly rejected such suggestions. Pope John Paul II, in his apostolic exhortation *On Reconciliation and Penance in the Mission of the Church Today, Reconciliatio et Paenitentia* (1984), section 17, and in his encyclical *Veritatis Splendor* (1993), sections 65-70, has explicitly reflected on this suggestion concerning fundamental choices and mortal sin, and has reaffirmed the traditional Catholic teaching on mortal sin.

The reasons for this are decisive. The fundamental teaching of the Church on mortal sin has been taught insistently by the Church, and it has deep roots in Scripture. It has been taught by the Church with the degree of universality and firmness associated with infallible teaching of the ordinary Magisterium (cf. Vatican Council II, *Dogmatic Constitution on the Church, Lumen Gentium*, 25; CCC 2032-2035). Moreover, the Church has solemnly defined the teaching that the tragic effects of mortal sin follow not only those sins by which one explicitly turns from God (as in apostasy) but the deliberate doing of any sin that faith has identified as mortal sin (Council of Trent, cf. Denzinger-Schönmetzer, 1544, 1569).

Obedience to the commandments of God in specific matters is no peripheral matter. Christ himself taught that those who wish to have everlasting life must keep the commandments, and he referred to the specific commands of the Decalogue. Scripture reminds us: "Whoever says, 'I have come to know him,' but does not keep his commandments, is a liar" (1 Jn 2:4). The Ten Commandments, rooted as they are in precepts of love (cf. Mt 22:36-40), express not mere rules, but duties that one must honor so as to be faithful to what love firmly requires. Deliberately and knowingly to perform acts incompatible with love of God is to withdraw oneself from the love of God.

The obligations that faith teaches to be seriously binding are such as are essential for supporting the rights of men, for building a just society, for shaping hearts that live in friendship with God. Theories lacking roots in the sources of faith, and opposed to the firm teaching of Scripture and the immemorial witness of the Church, will not bring about good pastoral results for the faithful.

See: Absolute Moral Norms; Choice; Conscience; Freedom, Human; Moral Principles, Christian; Mortal Sin; Sin; Ten Commandments.

Suggested Readings: CCC 1451-1452, 1756, 1857-1867. John Paul II, *On Reconciliation and Penance in the Mission of the Church Today, Reconciliatio et Paenitentia*, 17; *The Splendor of Truth, Veritatis Splendor*, 65-70. G. Grisez, *The Way of the Lord Jesus*, Vol. 1, *Christian Moral Principles*, Ch. 16, B, C, D, and Ch. 30, I.

Ronald D. Lawler, O.F.M. Cap.

FUNERALS, CHRISTIAN

Although the Church marks the passing of her children in a funeral rite from the Order of Christian Funerals (*Ordo Exsequiarum*), the rites so used are not sacraments. The sacraments have been given to the Church by Christ as means of grace in this life, and their administration ends with the end of earthly life. For her dead the Church hopes that they behold directly *the* Sacrament that they had worshiped and received in a veiled manner in all the sacraments of the Church on earth. The Church does, however, encourage the celebration of the sacrament of the Eucharist with the funeral rites, for the repose of the dead and the comfort of the living.

From the first to the last, the sacraments of the Christian life sanctify and strengthen the soul for death, which the *Catechism of the Catholic Church* calls "the last Passover of the child of God" (1680). That same source tells us that the liturgical rites that the Church celebrates after the death of one of her own endeavor to express her "efficacious communion with *the deceased*" (1684).

The *Roman Ritual* specifies rituals for three stations, the home, the church, and the cemetery, but with the understanding that the particular customs and circumstances of each country or culture may require specific adaptations legislated by the local conference of bishops. The rites approved by the bishops of the United States in 1989 consist of three ritual moments: that of the vigil and related rites and prayers; the funeral liturgy, within or outside of Mass; and the Rite of Committal.

The vigil marks the period between the death and the funeral liturgy, or Rite of Committal if there is no funeral liturgy. As the name suggests, in the vigil the Christian community keeps watch with the family of the deceased and aids them in calling to mind through Scripture and prayer the mercy of God and the promise of his comfort. This rite may be celebrated in a home, funeral home, chapel, or in the church itself prior to the funeral.

The funeral liturgy consists of a reception of the body (if this has not occurred at the vigil), a Liturgy of the Word, the liturgy of the Eucharist, and a final commendation and farewell. The liturgy is rich in baptismal symbolism. The sprinkling with holy water suggests the Baptism by which the soul was freed from sin, and incensing recalls that the body has served as a temple of the Holy Spirit. The pall, a term once used to refer to a robe or cloak, is placed on the coffin to evoke the baptismal garment. The paschal candle stands guard — as at the Easter and baptismal liturgies — to symbolize the light of the risen Christ.

When celebrated outside of Mass the funeral liturgy consists of the other three parts: reception, Liturgy of the Word, commendation and farewell. A funeral Mass is disallowed only on holy days of obligation, the Sundays of Advent, Lent, and the Easter season, as well as Holy Thursday and the Easter Triduum. In these cases, the Mass may be transferred to a time after burial.

The final ritual moment consists of the Rite of Committal in which the body of the deceased is committed to its place of repose until the resurrection of the body at the end of time. After an opening invitation to prayer for the deceased and a brief Scripture verse, the place itself is blessed by prayer. This is followed by a prayer of committal and intercessory prayer that culminates in the Our Father. After a concluding prayer, the final act consists in a prayer of blessing over the mourners.

Prayer for the Dead • The funeral rites lay a heavy emphasis on the need to pray for the dead. The addresses to the faithful present at the ceremonies encourage prayer for the departed soul, and the intercessory prayers are precisely such. The rites also exhort the community to hope in the mercy of God that is witnessed to by such intercession. The whole theological thrust of the rites aims at awakening a lively faith in the efficacy of Christ's paschal mystery and our sacramental participation in it as members of Christ's Body. The introduction to *Ordo Exsequiarum* (1969) encourages the priest, "as the teacher of faith and the minister of comfort," to preach so as to invite faith in the Resurrection; priests are to do this in such a way that "as bearers of the tenderness of the Church and the comfort of the faith, they console those who believe without offending those who grieve" (16, 17). Grief and hope have their proper moments in the rites.

The avoidance of anything that suggests the "literary genre of funeral eulogy" (CCC 1688, quoting *Order of Christian Funerals,* 41) further highlights the Church's interest in making the paschal mystery the center of the community's reflections, as well as her distaste for human honor (cf. Jas 2:1-9). This also suggests the Church's belief that presumption should be avoided as regards the disposition of the soul after death. The Council of Trent reemphasized the teaching of the Councils of Second Lyons in 1274 and Florence in 1439, attested to abundantly in the ancient tradition of the Church (cf. 2 Mc 12:42-46, 2 Tm 1:18), that intercession should be offered for the deceased.

The Church does not judge the state of soul of

any who pass from this life except in the extraordinary cases of the canonized saints and those who die after Baptism and before the age of discretion. An informal canonizing of the dead fails to serve their best interests and tends to weaken the awareness of the faithful in the communion of the saints.

The *Catechism of the Catholic Church* puts it succinctly: "From the beginning the Church has honored the memory of the dead and offered prayers in suffrage for them, above all the Eucharistic sacrifice, so that, thus purified, they may attain the beatific vision of God. The Church also commends almsgiving, indulgences, and works of penance undertaken on behalf of the dead" (1032). The funeral rites are a particularly efficacious method of intercession as they unite the prayers of the grieving with those of the whole Church.

See: Anointing of the Sick; Burial, Christian; Communion of Saints; Death; Last Things; Resurrection of the Dead.

Suggested Readings: CCC 1680-1690. Code of Canon Law, 1176-1185. National Conference of Catholic Bishops, *Order of Christian Funerals, General Introduction*, 1-49.

Sean Innerst

G

GENERAL ABSOLUTION

The issue of general absolution is understood more clearly in the different forms in which the sacrament of Penance may be administered. Generally, there are three ways that a person may approach the sacrament.

The first and most common form is for the penitent to participate in the Rite of Reconciliation individually with the priest. This includes: individual confession of sins, an assignment of some act of penance to be performed later (also called the satisfaction), an act of contrition recited by the penitent, and individual absolution.

The second form in which the sacrament may be administered is in the context of a communal penance service. Here the faithful gather in the church. Usually a number of priests are available for confessions. A short service may include a hymn, opening prayer, Scripture reading, brief homily (this may be both an exposition of the text as well as an exhortation to the people to move them to repentance), and communal examination of conscience. This usually is followed by communal recitation of the act of contrition. The priests then go to confessional stations. At this point the opportunity is provided for individual confession and individual absolution. Unless there is individual confession and absolution, the sacrament of Penance has not been received. The Church makes it clear that a sufficient number of confessors must be available to accommodate the people.

The Third Form • The third form in which the sacrament may be administered is not used in ordinary circumstances. Commonly called "general absolution," it refers to the administration of the sacrament to a large number of people at the same time. This is *not* the same as a communal penance service and is clearly *not* to be used as such. The Code of Canon Law offers very clear guidelines.

Absolution cannot be imparted in a general manner to a number of penitents at once without previous individual confession unless:

1. the danger of death is imminent and there is not time for the priest or priests to hear the confessions of the individual penitents;

2. a serious necessity exists, that is, when in light of the number of penitents a supply of confessors is not readily available rightly to hear the confessions of individuals within a suitable time so that the penitents are forced to be deprived of sacramental grace or holy communion for a long time through no fault of their own; it is not considered a sufficient necessity if confessors cannot be readily available only because of the great number of penitents as can occur on the occasion of some great feast or pilgrimage (Canon 961.1).

The Code also stipulates that for someone validly to receive sacramental absolution given to many at one time, it is necessary that he or she not only be disposed suitably for the sacrament but also intend to confess individually any serious (i.e., mortal) sins that cannot be so confessed at the moment. The faithful are to be instructed to make an act of contrition, even in danger of death, if the time permits. Moreover, the Code insists that, when the emergency has passed, each person who has received such absolution is required to approach individual confession as soon as possible and confess any serious sins that have been remitted by general absolution (Canon 963).

The mind of the Church clearly is that the sacrament of Penance normally be received in an individual manner, that general absolution is to be used only in severe or emergency situations, and that private confession of mortal sins is still required when the emergency no longer exists. It is not to be considered an emergency when a large number of people are deliberately assembled for a penance service and not enough confessors are available. If such a group is to be assembled, the Church insists that an adequate number of confessors also be assembled. Otherwise, one is creating an "emergency" and then trying to use this extraordinary permission of the Church to deal with it. Even the stipulation of Canon 961.2 that not offering sacramental absolution would deprive the people of the sacramental grace or Holy Communion "for a long time" makes it difficult to verify these conditions.

In December, 1984, Pope John Paul II issued his apostolic exhortation *On Reconciliation and Penance in the Mission of the Church Today, Reconciliatio et Paenitentia.* The document, following a world Synod of Bishops on this theme in 1983, dealt with a number of moral issues touching on the sacrament of Penance.

The Pope took note of the increasing lack of a sense of personal sin and of confusion over the notion of "social sin." He also was concerned with misunderstandings about the sacrament of Penance and with its infrequent reception by many Catholics. In directing his attention to confusion about general absolution, he spoke in the context of the three forms, mentioned above, in which the sacrament may be celebrated.

The first form is the only normal and ordinary way of celebrating the sacrament. It cannot and must not be allowed to fall into disuse or be neglected. The second form is the same as the first in the culminating sacramental act, namely, individual confession and individual absolution of sins. The third form is exceptional. It is not merely an option to be chosen according to personal preference, but is regulated by a special discipline (cf. *Reconciliatio et Paenitentia*, 32).

In discussing general absolution, Pope John Paul cites the sections of Canon Law mentioned above. He then offers further insights into the value of integral individual confession and the dangers of abusing the permission of general absolution, concluding: "It is not in fact left to the freedom of pastors and the faithful to choose from among these forms the one considered most suitable. It remains the obligation of pastors to facilitate for the faithful the practice of integral and individual confession of sins, which constitutes for them not only a duty but also an inviolable and inalienable right, besides being something needed by the soul. . . . The sacraments and consciences, I repeat, are sacred, and both require that we serve them in truth" (*Reconciliatio et Paenitentia*, 33).

Ultimately, it is important that people have individual access to the sacrament for all the reasons that the sacrament itself is important. As for priests, it is important that they hear individual confessions so that they remain attuned to the moral problems of the real world, and have a knowledge of them that is incarnational and not just conceptual. Finally, it is important for both priest and penitent to experience a God who is rich in mercy and daily extends forgiveness to those who seek reconciliation with him.

See: Absolution; Confession; Grace; Penance and Reconciliation, Sacrament of; Sin.

Suggested Readings: CCC 1480-1484. Code of Canon Law, 961-963. Paul VI, *On Penance, Paenitemini.* John Paul II, *On Reconciliation and Penance in the Mission of the Church Today, Reconciliatio et Paenitentia*, 33.

Christopher M. Buckner

GENETIC EXPERIMENTATION

Genetic science, like other quickly developing fields of scientific knowledge, has great potential for either serving or degrading humanity. Its proper use requires moral reflection and the establishment of moral limits. "The development of technology and the development of contemporary civilization, which is marked by the ascendancy of technology, demand a proportional development of morals and ethics. For the present, this last development seems unfortunately to be always left behind" (Pope John Paul II, encyclical letter *The Redeemer of Man, Redemptor Hominis,* 15 [1979]).

Genetic experimentation is of special concern for two reasons.

First, its potential for both benefit and harm transcends that of traditional medicine, because it involves the ability to analyze and alter what are sometimes called the very building blocks of life. Efforts to map the genetic constitution of humankind, as in the U.S. government's Human Genome Project, could lead to new kinds of control over the physical, mental, and even spiritual abilities of human beings. Recent Popes have compared the destructive potential of such technology with that of nuclear weapons (cf. Pope John Paul II, "Address to Men of Science," June 2, 1980).

Second, genetics has sometimes been associated with programs of "eugenics" that devalue human beings based on racial or other genetic characteristics (Pontifical Commission "Iustitia et Pax," *The Church and Racism,* 6-7 [1988]). Techniques of artificial reproduction and genetic manipulation could become tools of "new and as yet unknown forms of racism," in which "abusive and irresponsible powers . . . seek to 'produce' human beings selected according to racial criteria or any other characteristic" (*The Church and Racism,* 16). The use of genetic knowledge must be scrutinized to prevent such abuses, which deny the inherent dignity and equality of all human beings.

The Church has welcomed new advances in genetic engineering that promise to improve food production and bring other benefits to humanity (cf. Pope John Paul II, "Biological Research and Human Dignity," 6 [October 23, 1982]).

Even in experiments on plants and animals, it is important to exercise careful stewardship over God's creation. Irresponsible efforts to control the natural environment could disrupt the careful balance that makes it a fit habitat for human beings (cf. CCC 2415). Animals in particular "must be treated as creatures of God which are destined to serve man's good, but not to be abused by him" ("Biological Research and Human Dignity," 4).

Moreover, the beneficial results of such research should be shared with all, especially with poor nations, so they can enhance the lives of all people and not become the private possession of the wealthy.

Genetic Diagnosis and Screening • Many genetic illnesses and disabilities can now be diagnosed in humans, even before birth. The moral legitimacy of such techniques depends on their risk and the intended use of the results. Such testing "is gravely opposed to the moral law when it is done with the thought of possibly inducing an abortion, depending upon the results." Parents who request the testing, specialists who perform it with this destructive intention, and relatives or others who advise such a course all share in the moral guilt of eliminating "defective" offspring in this way (Congregation for the Doctrine of the Faith, *Instruction on Respect for Human Life in Its Origin and on the Dignity of Procreation: Replies to Certain Questions of the Day, Donum Vitae,* I.2 [1987]).

Prenatal diagnosis may be morally valid if performed to anticipate the special needs of a child with disabilities and make possible better treatment and care for that child. In such a case, testing may be done with parents' informed consent "if the methods employed safeguard the life and integrity of the embryo and the mother, without subjecting them to disproportionate risks" (*Donum Vitae,* I.2).

Tragically, some modern advances in genetic diagnosis are premised on the use of selective abortion in case of a positive diagnosis. For example, "chorionic villi sampling" is now sometimes used to obtain material for prenatal testing in place of the older technique of amniocentesis, even though it poses a higher risk of causing a miscarriage; this is because the newer technique can be used earlier in a pregnancy to facilitate abortion in case a genetic defect is found. The even newer technique of "preimplantation genetic diagnosis" requires the use of *in vitro* fertilization, which poses moral problems of its own, and currently has no therapeutic application: A living embryo found to have a genetic defect through this technique is simply discarded in the laboratory.

Parents themselves can also be tested for genetic defects that they may transmit to future offspring. They may validly choose, in light of their resources and their responsibilities to each other and any existing children, to use morally acceptable means (i.e., natural family planning) to delay or even forgo conceiving children who may have severe disabilities. This must be a strictly personal decision, and is not to be swayed or imposed by outside authorities. For example, public programs encouraging or requiring sterilization to prevent the conception of handicapped children are to be condemned (Pope Pius XII, "Moral Aspects of Genetics," September 7, 1953). Parents who make a loving decision to accept children with serious disabilities should receive every support and encouragement; efforts to prevent disabling conditions must never encourage an attitude that people with these conditions are somehow less than fully human (Pope John Paul II, *The Gospel of Life, Evangelium Vitae*, 63 [1995]).

The use and confidentiality of genetic information about children and adults also present moral problems. Such information should generally be used only to inform the persons tested and assist them and their families in preserving life and health. There is a danger that such information could be used by public authorities or others to classify people by their genetic tendencies and even to discriminate against them. For example, insurance companies might refuse to provide health insurance to people shown to have a higher genetic likelihood of developing various illnesses; people more likely to develop mental illnesses could be excluded from some professions. Such actions would violate people's privacy and their right to health care, and deny their essential equality in society.

The Church insists that people not be reduced to a genetic or statistical profile but be judged by their inherent dignity and their individual gifts and talents. Pope John Paul II also praised researchers who refuse to allow their discoveries about the human genome to be patented, because such refusal emphasizes that "the human body is not an object that can be disposed of at will" and

that human genetic knowledge should not be "the property of a small group" pursuing its own interests ("The Human Person — Beginning and End of Scientific Research," October 28, 1994).

Human Genetic Therapies • Ensuring good nutrition, especially for pregnant mothers, and reducing pollution from nuclear radiation, pesticides, and industrial waste are often the best ways to prevent genetic defects or ameliorate their effects. In this sense, good public health policy and respect for the environment are good "eugenic" policies.

Some uses of genetic engineering in humans involve "somatic cell" therapy. A genetically determined malfunction in a particular kind of human body cell is corrected, using genetically altered cells from that same individual, another human being, or even another species. Such therapies affect only particular cells in a developed human body, and do not change the genetic code that the patient will pass on to future generations.

In principle, experimental therapies of this kind are similar to other treatments that change one cell or organ to benefit the whole human person (Pontifical Council for Pastoral Assistance to Health Care Workers, *Charter for Health Care Workers*, 66 [1995]). They should respect the same moral norms as human experimentation generally: They must have the goal of serving human life and human dignity; the subjects must give their consent after being fully informed of possible risks; a child or other human being incapable of giving such consent should not be subjected to an experiment unless he or she can benefit directly from it; and any risks must be minimized, and be reasonable in comparison to the expected benefits.

Even the use of cells from other species may be justified if this is medically beneficial and does not compromise the human identity of the person and of his or her future offspring (*Charter for Health Care Workers*, 88-89).

Far more problematic is "germ-line" therapy, which would alter the basic genetic constitution of an individual and of all his or her future offspring.

At present, in order to affect the genetic code

in every cell of a person's body, such therapies must be performed on early human embryos. In the present state of technology, this requires using reproductive technologies such as *in vitro* fertilization to produce embryos in the laboratory, outside the mother's body, where they can be observed and manipulated.

Use of such technologies to produce human beings is morally wrong, because the technologies divorce the creation of a new human person from its only worthy human context: the loving conjugal union between husband and wife (*Donum Vitae*, II.B). By treating the new embryo as the product of a manufacturing process, techniques like *in vitro* fertilization establish researchers in a "relationship of domination" over their embryonic subjects that "is in itself contrary to the dignity and equality that must be common to parents and children" (*Donum Vitae*, II.B). Such techniques therefore "open the door to new threats against life" that treat human embryos as mere objects: selection and discarding of "imperfect" embryos, the creation of "spare" embryos for destructive experiments, and so on (*Evangelium Vitae*, 14). Also morally wrong are efforts to produce human embryos without the union of sperm and egg (e.g., parthenogenesis) or to produce genetic "copies" of embryos by cloning (*Donum Vitae*, I.6).

Even experimental therapies to correct genetic defects in human embryos would first be used on embryos that will be discarded afterward, in order to assess harmful side effects of the experiment and forestall these from occurring in the case of children intended for live birth. In practice, then, any current genetic experimentation on human embryos would involve gravely wrong practices.

Assuming that such moral problems could someday be resolved, the basic idea of "curing" a serious genetic defect such as Down syndrome in an individual as well as all his or her descendants is not inherently wrong and may be very beneficial: "By acting on the subject's unhealthy genes, it will . . . be possible to prevent the recurrence of genetic diseases and their transmission" ("The Human Person — Beginning and End of Scientific Research"). Such efforts must be "directed to

the true promotion of the personal well-being of the individual without doing harm to his integrity or worsening his conditions of life" (*Donum Vitae*, I.3). These cautions should be taken seriously indeed, when we know so little about the side effects of altering even a single human gene.

Positive Eugenics • By contrast with such attempts at "negative eugenics" (the cure of a disease or correction of a serious defect), the Church has raised grave objections to interventions in the human genetic heritage for "positive eugenics" (the production of desired traits or supposed improvements in the human species). Such nontherapeutic experiments, "aimed at producing human beings selected according to sex or other predetermined qualities," are "contrary to the personal dignity of the human being and his or her integrity and identity." Therefore, they cannot be justified on the grounds of "possible beneficial consequences for future humanity" (*Donum Vitae*, I.6). In this context, the Church condemns "experimental manipulations of the human embryo, since the human being, from conception to death, cannot be exploited for any purpose whatsoever" ("Biological Research and Human Dignity").

Here, instead of correcting a specific defect to avert serious harm to the whole person, scientists would alter the person's natural physical or mental endowment to suit their own ideas of a better or more socially desirable human being. Thus human beings would be exploited to produce characteristics that: are merely expressions of human whim (e.g., a child of the desired sex or with enhanced physical strength); risk depriving humans of their intelligence, free will, or psychological health (e.g., efforts to produce super-geniuses or unintelligent workers); or even deprive people of their common membership in the human species (e.g., efforts to create human-animal hybrids or various kinds of "superman").

It is noteworthy that scientists seldom speak of producing a human who would truly be more human in the Christian sense — that is, "more mature spiritually, more aware of the dignity of his humanity, more responsible, more open to others, especially the neediest and the weakest, and readier to give and to aid all" (*Redemptor Hominis*, 15). Evangelization and education, not genetic manipulation, are the appropriate means for improving human consciences in these ways.

In short, the Church has voiced serious cautions about human germ-line experimentation, and insists that in any event "its finality must be the natural development of the human being" (*Charter for Health Care Workers*, 13). Clarifying the fine line between negative and positive eugenics, and many other moral issues raised by the new genetics, will be matters for further reflection in decades to come.

See: Abortion; Animals; Body and Soul; Environment; Human Experimentation; Human Life, Dignity and Sanctity of; Human Person; Racism; Reproductive Technologies; Science and the Church.

Suggested Readings: CCC 2274-2275, 2295, 2414-2418. John Paul II, addresses "Biological Research and Human Dignity" (October 23, 1982), "The Ethics of Genetic Manipulation" (October 29, 1983), "The Human Person — Beginning and End of Scientific Research" (October 28, 1994). Congregation for the Doctrine of the Faith, *Instruction on Respect for Human Life in Its Origin and on the Dignity of Procreation: Replies to Certain Questions of the Day, Donum Vitae* (1987). Pontifical Council for Pastoral Assistance to Health Care Workers, *Charter for Health Care Workers* (1995). A. Moraczewski, O.P., ed., *Genetic Medicine and Engineering: Ethical and Social Dimensions*.

Richard Doerflinger

GIFTS AND FRUITS OF THE HOLY SPIRIT

The Holy Spirit is himself *the* gift (cf. Jn 14:26), the source of all comfort and grace, proceeding from the Father and the Son. As the sanctifier and giver of gifts, the Spirit is the source of all the gracious mercies by which the triune God calls us to holiness and salvation. It is through the Spirit of God that all the ordinary gifts of the Church, the rich hierarchical and sacramental gifts, con-

stantly bear fruit in the holiness of lives. The Spirit also blesses the Church with always fresh and joyful charismatic gifts (CCC 797-801).

But there are seven gifts known most commonly as the Gifts of the Holy Spirit. These are gifts that Isaiah prophesied would dwell in their fullness in the Messiah (cf. CCC 1831): wisdom, understanding, counsel, fortitude, knowledge, piety, and fear of the Lord (cf. Is 11:2-3; piety is found in the Septuagint, the Greek translation of the Hebrew Bible, but not in the Hebrew text).

These gifts are infused also into the heart of every baptized person, every member of Christ, together with grace and the theological virtues. They are necessary for all; but the Fathers and saints speak of their growing influence on the faithful as they become more mature in holiness of life.

Early stages of Christian life are more laborious: The devout soul struggles as a boatman struggles with oars. But the gifts of the Holy Spirit help the soul that has drawn nearer to the Lord to make progress with greater ease and more fervent love: They are like sails by which the graces of the Spirit move one forward more easily. By these gifts "the soul is furnished and strengthened to be able to obey God's voice and impulse more easily and promptly" (Pope Leo XIII, encyclical *On the Holy Spirit, Divinum Illud Munus* [1897]).

Those guided by the Spirit bring forth in their lives excellent actions, more shining fruits of the Spirit's many gifts. The Church traditionally lists these twelve fruits of the Holy Spirit: charity, joy, peace, patience, kindness, goodness, generosity, gentleness, faithfulness, modesty, self-control, chastity (cf. CCC 1832; Gal 5:22-23).

See: Baptism; Grace; Holy Spirit; Theological Virtues.

GNOSTICISM

Gnosticism is the belief that *gnosis*, esoteric knowledge of divine mysteries, is reserved to an elite.

Until the middle of the nineteenth century, little was known of Gnosticism other than what was found in the writings of Church Fathers who saw it as a threat to Christianity. Some writers have regarded it as a Christian heresy, but it is essentially a form of paganism. Its Christian elements are purely superficial. Gnosticism absorbed select elements from Christianity, just as it absorbed something from each of the other religions it encountered.

The discovery and publication of several codices of Gnostic writings, beginning in 1851 and continuing into the twentieth century, expanded our knowledge of Gnosticism. In 1945-1946, a large cache of Gnostic writings was discovered in the village of Nag Hammadi in Upper Egypt. Prominent among these discoveries was the so-called *Gospel of Thomas*, an apocryphal work probably of second-century origin. Gnosticism is a hotly debated phenomenon. The publication and interpretation of Gnostic texts advances the continuing controversy over its definition.

Characteristics of Gnosticism • Gnosticism may be described as a phenomenon of religious syncretism that developed in the Mediterranean and Middle Eastern world of the second century A.D. It was based on a cosmic dualism of ancient Iranian origin and absorbed certain aspects of Egyptian and Babylonian religions. Dualistic systems identify God with light and goodness, the material world with darkness and evil. The god of the Gnostics is an alien deity, totally separate from the world of men and angels. The world was created through the fall of a higher power, *Sophia* (or wisdom). This fall brought into being the material world. The world is evil because it is separate from God and the light.

Gnosticism, when it encountered Judaism, produced an interpretation of creation in which the Creator God was replaced by a *demiurge*, a subordinate manifestation of the Deity, who did not know the light, or goodness. Thus, the material world that it created was evil. Man therefore must seek liberation from the evil world of created matter in order to ascend to God. Gnostic literature includes many figures from the Hebrew Scriptures, albeit in different roles. Gnosticism was strengthened by rituals borrowed both from mystery cults and Christianity. Never a rigorous philosophical system, its diverse origins and lack of clearly de-

fined teachings resist systematization. However, certain currents are discernible.

Among the characteristics of Gnosticism was the concept of the presence in man of a divine spark, which emanated from the divine world of light and has fallen into this world. It is destined to be liberated from matter and reintegrated into the light, the divine. The Platonic concept of the fall of the soul and its attachment to matter fits well into Gnostic thought.

The Gnostics claimed that knowledge (*gnosis*) would answer the age-old questions "Who are we?" and "Where are we going?" The Gnostic answer included several recurring themes. Man's inmost being longs for union with the unknown God. Man has been banished to an imperfect world, which is not the creation of the supreme God but of a lesser being who rules with the help of evil powers. Man can be free of their domination only if he rightly knows himself and is aware that he is separated from the perfect God. Only this knowledge makes possible his return to the upper world of light where the true God dwells. This return is "salvation." It is attained not by the power of God nor by human faith nor by cooperation with the will of God, but only by the assimilation of esoteric knowledge, *gnosis*.

Gnosticism and Christianity • The second-century world was one in which religious ideas, Eastern and Western, old and new, mixed freely. Just as Gnosticism absorbed components of Judaism, it assimilated Christian elements, and many Gnostics claimed to be Christians. About the year 160, Justin (c. 100-c. 165) mentioned men who called themselves Christians, claimed to recognize Jesus as Lord, but declared that the world had been created by an evil god. These groups, named after their leaders, were called Valentinians, Marcionites, or Basilidians. They claimed that they possessed secret knowledge revealed to the Apostles by Jesus. They regarded Jesus as a semidivine messenger from God, who only appeared to be incarnate. His Passion, death, and Resurrection were explained by a variety of interpretations. The "Gnostic Christians" considered themselves to be Christians of a higher rank, "spiritual men," who alone possessed the true interpretation of cosmic events and thus were the only ones capable of attaining to perfect knowledge of God. Others, ignorant of this knowledge, who tried to work out their salvation merely by faith and good works, remained forever on a lower level.

Christian writers who wrote anti-Gnostic works include Melito of Sardis (died c.190), Hegissipus (died c.180), Irenaeus of Lyons (c. 130-c. 202), and Tertullian (c. 160-c. 222). In opposition to the Gnostics' claim to be the sole possessors of revelation, the Christian theologians brought into the foreground the concepts of Apostolic Tradition and apostolic succession as guarantors of the true Revelation. Their writings also hastened the Church's decision regarding which books constituted the canon of Christian Scriptures.

These writers emphasized that the baptismal creeds affirmed the reality of the human birth and the Passion and death of Christ. These creeds also proclaimed the one God and Lord to be Creator of the universe, and thus rejected all Gnostic speculations about the origins of the universe. They further contrasted Christian belief in the resurrection of the body with the Gnostics' contempt for the body as radically evil.

See: Body and Soul; Canon of Scripture; Creation; Divine Revelation; Freemasonry; Manichaeism; Neoplatonism; New Age; Sacred Tradition; Theosophy.

Suggested Readings: CCC 279-314. E. Pagels, *The Gnostic Gospels.*

Robert J. Wister

GOD, NATURE AND ATTRIBUTES OF

In Catholic theology, the word "God" refers to the personal proper name of the Deity as well as the abstract noun designating the Deity. "God" (Hebrew, *El*; Greek, *Theos*; Latin, *Deus*; German, *Gott*) refers to the one who is addressed in private and public prayer, as well as the one who is the absolute, underlying power of the cosmos, of all there is.

Catholicism takes its ideas about God from two sources: the Scriptures and reason. Each has different authority, but each supports and reaffirms the other. We learn of both God's existence and his attributes through reason and from the Scriptures. These sources can never tell us about God as he knows himself; but they can contribute to our awareness, knowledge, and understanding of him.

Sometimes we can learn more about what God is by saying what he is *not*: God is not any particular thing or being, not a tree, not the world, and not you or me. Sometimes, however, God reveals himself to us in such a way that we are able to say who he is: God is love, God is beingness, God is truth. We know about God from the Scriptures because he has chosen to reveal himself to us through this medium, through words and actions and through the mind and spirit. We know about God from reason because we can deduce certain things about him from the way the world is made and from the kinds of beings we are.

We are motivated to know about God not so much for God's sake, that is, for the benefit and fulfillment of himself, as for our own sake. Such knowledge tells us who we are, from whence we came, where we go, and how we are to proceed along this way. Every ontological statement concerning God thus has an implied anthropological dimension: Every idea we have about God tells us who we are to be as humans.

The Existence of God • The question about God that occurs to most modern people is whether or not God exists. When people say, "I believe in God," they are usually making what is commonly called a faith statement. It is called a faith statement because it is held that God's existence cannot be proven in the same way that an apple, a bear, or a car is proven to exist, that is, experientially or scientifically. Yet, when we look more closely, we discover that even science rests on premises that cannot be scientifically proven but rather are philosophical in their nature. Likewise the "proof of God's existence" is demonstrated philosophically, by reason.

The Scriptures reveal the existence of the God of Abraham, Isaac, and Jacob; but that same God's existence also has been "proven" by non-Jews, non-Christians, and non-Muslims through the light of natural reason. Natural reason uses common-sense knowledge of the world and deduces the existence of God from what it perceives in the "real world." Thomas Aquinas (c. 1225-1274) developed what have come to be known as the five proofs of God. While rejecting Anselm of Canterbury's ontological argument as such, Thomas recast his use of the definition of the word "God" — meaning "that than which nothing greater can be conceived" — to mean not only something that may be a definition in human understanding, as in the imagination, but also someone shown to exist in reality apart from human imagination. In other words, God is "real"; God is not simply the term used to predicate those things in human imagination greater than which nothing else can be thought.

Aquinas's five proofs are ways of demonstrating that God exists in reality apart from human imagination. In summary, they are as follows.

1. Thomas argues that God exists from the observed fact that things in the world change or "move" (*ex motu*); that such change or movement requires for its explanation some prior mover; and that ultimately, there is a first mover, itself unmoved; and that this first mover is called God.

2. Thomas argues that God exists from the recognition that things in the universe occur by efficient causes (*ex causa efficiente*) that are themselves produced by their causes; that there cannot be an infinite series of efficient causes; and that ultimately there must be a first efficient cause, which is not the cause of itself; and that this first efficient cause is called God.

3. Thomas argues that God exists from the recognition that things are contingent (*ex contingentia mundi*); that because everything might not have existed in the first place, one sees that everything is contingent, since there was a time when neither it nor anything else actually existed; that ultimately all particular things depend for their existence on a noncontingent or necessary being; and that this necessary being is called God.

4. Thomas argues that God exists from the awareness that there is a scale of perfection (*ex gradibus*); that it is observed that things are more or less perfect according to some scale or standard of judgment; that this judgment is predicated on the idea that there is a greatest, best, or most perfect; that ultimately there is an absolute standard of judgment; and this absolute standard of judgment is what is called God.

5. Thomas argues that God exists from the awareness that there is a design of things (*ex gubernatione rerum*); that it is recognized that everything, animate or inanimate, acts in a definitive end-directed way; that one sees that things act thus through their nature (active essence); that by their nature things are designed to act thus; that there is a design to the entire cosmos in which all things appear as integrated parts of a whole; and that ultimately there must be a supreme designer or governor who is the one who has designed and governs all according to a supreme intelligence; and this supreme governor or designer is what is called God.

The principal issue in showing God to exist is not what God is, but proving the reality of what is meant when the word "God" is used: in other words, showing that "God" in fact refers to a reality to which the word points. Hence, God refers not only to the word "God" as signifying an idea; "God" also points to that reality than which nothing greater can be conceived. In strict Thomistic parlance, Thomas preferred to call "God" *ipsum esse subsistens* (literally, "subsistent being itself"). In modern parlance, "God" refers to the condition, the prior necessity, beingness itself, by which everything exists. In either case, the link is the same. Without "God" nothing would or could exist, and hence "God" is properly conceived as both the ultimate creative cause of all and the sustaining cause maintaining all that is in existence.

Attributes of God • The result of this understanding of "God" is to ascribe to God what are traditionally called the attributes of God. Because divine attributes are unique to God as the condition of all that exists, these attributes are the archetypes, or paradigms, of those same characteristics, or attributes, as they are found in creation. However, since God is radically different in nature from anything that exists in creation, the divine attributes are said to apply to God not literally or "univocally" but "analogically." The *via analogiae*, the way of analogy, is the way by which particular characteristics inferred about the Creator are drawn from his effects as they are observed in nature; human reason applies these inferred characteristics to the Creator.

When characteristics are affirmatively applied to God by analogy, they are said to describe God *cataphatically*, that is, they present a positive description. As God may be described in affirmative terms, however, so he may also be described in negative terms, that is, *apophatically*: what God is not. By apophatically describing God, the hope is to eliminate all finite characteristics from one's concept of God, thereby avoiding the idea that some attribute of God is nothing more than the superior or ultimate form of a characteristic or quality found in creation. The apophatic description of God signifies that, even after divine self-disclosure in Revelation, the divine is always unfathomable and unlike anything experienced in creation.

Certain characteristics of God may be predicated by the light of natural reason. But because, as seen above, God is the condition by which everything else exists, God must be simple, that is, not composed of parts or compounded of elements, either material or immaterial. A body is subject to time and change, and it has already been seen that God cannot change, since there is nothing prior to God to act upon him. If nothing can act upon God, then God is without potentiality, but instead God is himself actuality, that is, *actus purus*, pure act. Because God is pure act and has no body, God possesses nothing, has no-thing. If God possessed something, God would have to have received it from something prior to himself. If God possessed something, what he has could be changed, and if God could be changed, this could only be because something prior to God could act upon him. But since God is prior to all

and possesses nothing, then nothing does or can either be prior to God or can change God; thus it is seen that God cannot possess anything in the way anything created possesses something, even a characteristic of itself. But if God does not possess anything, then God must be his own essence, *ipsum esse*, his own "beingness," and hence whatever other characteristic might be predicated of him. Possessing nothing, God *is* his own characteristics in pure act. God is pure actuality, pure simplicity, pure godhead.

As unchanging, God cannot exist in time. Hence, God is said to be infinite, immutable, and eternal. Likewise, since a plurality of infinities, immutabilities, and eternalities cannot exist, God is known to be absolutely one. God is said to be absolute good, because "good" is said to be the characteristic of that which exists, since it is better that a thing should exist than not exist. God is "good" itself because without him nothing would exist, inasmuch as he is the cause of all existence, the necessary condition by which existence itself exists.

Insofar as God is prior to all things and has full actuality and knows himself without lack, and insofar as all things are created by him, and since God's knowledge is one with his will to create, God's knowledge is the cause of all things in creation, and he is said to be omniscient in regard to himself and all that exists. God is omnipotent inasmuch as he is the power that causes everything to exist. His power is without beginning or end, and he is sovereign of all that is created. God is omnipresent because God is present as the essence of all, in the sense that God causes all that exists. Because God must know each thing as it is apart from other things in the same class (even particulars) in order to create each thing (as first cause and prime mover), all things are simultaneously present to God at all times throughout all of history.

God and his attendant attributes as known by reason denote a personal God. It is natural for man to anthropomorphize such a Deity, but without God's self-disclosure through Revelation, whether or not God is truly personal could not be determined. Those characteristics of God that depict him as personal are confirmed in his revelatory self-disclosure in the written word of Scripture and in the Persons of the Trinity: the Son as fully human and the Holy Spirit as enlightening the human mind through grace. God is present by grace in the world, in that he dwells in each human soul as if it were a temple.

Without confusion or commingling, humans are united with God in the depth of their souls through the activity of their hearts and minds, and are joined with God through their faith in him as the supreme truth and their love of him as the supreme good. Such possession of God cannot be reduced to mere analogy, but is a fact, similar to the possession of God in heaven by the angels and saints. God is known by the grace of his self-revelation in Scripture. The Hebrew and Christian Scriptures abound in references to God as limitless (Is 6); as the absolute master of all that exists (Ex 3:13-14); as beyond all human comprehension (Ps 139:7-12); as invisible (Rom 1-20; Jn 1:18); as providential (Acts 17:27); as true (Jn 3:33); as faithful (1 Cor 1:9); as peace (Phil 4:9); as hope (Rom 15:13); and as merciful (Lk 1:72), just to mention a few. By the grace of God active in the Magisterium, Vatican Council I (1869-1870) declared God to be the "one, true, living God, Creator and Lord of heaven and earth, omnipotent, eternal, immense, incomprehensible, infinite in intellect and will and in every perfection . . . one unique spiritual substance, wholly simple and unchanging . . . really and essentially distinct from the world, totally blessed in himself and of himself and ineffably elevated above all things which are and can be thought of apart from him."

The God of Revelation • The God known by reason, inferring his attributes from his effects in nature, is not opposed to but also not as comprehensive as the God known in Scripture. For the God in Scripture reveals himself in concrete historical actions from which divine action is known by the grace of faith. The writers of the Scriptures record the historical events as divine free acts, breaking into history without excluding the free-

dom of humanity. For the scriptural writers, faith is prior to understanding and leads to it. St. Thomas Aquinas in his discussion on God as Trinity recorded that the consideration of God from his effects in nature leads only to a certain partial knowledge of God; this knowledge must be made complete by Divine Revelation, by God's self-disclosure to humanity in matters critical for human life in understanding who and what God is.

Thomas wrote: "It is not possible through natural reason to arrive at the idea of God as a Trinity of divine persons. . . . Through natural reason man cannot come to the idea of God except through that which is created, for creatures lead [him] to the knowledge of God as [one understands] the effect from the cause" (*Summa Theologiae*, Ia, 32, 1). Human reason may know God as the source of all things, as *primum principium*, but not as Trinity. Human reason can infer God as a unity, but not as distinct Persons. The scriptural writers emphasized that God discloses himself and his attributes through his divine actions in history, actions transmitted for all generations in the written word, aspects of the divine nature that reason might not be able to reach alone. That is to say, divine attributes such as mercy, redemptive action, absolute otherness apart from the created, faithfulness, peace, trust, and personal involvement in the world and in each human life might not be easily derived from human observation of nature; and certainly God's nature as one in three Persons can be known only through Divine Revelation. Reason serves faith in demonstrating, through philosophical discourse, that those aspects of God known through reason lend certitude to those known through Revelation by faith.

See: Atheism; Creation; Divine Revelation; Eternity; Fatherhood of God; Hierarchy; Holy Spirit; Human Race, Creation and Destiny of; Jesus Christ, God and Man; Knowledge of God; Manichaeism; Omnipotence; Omniscience; Process Theology; Providence; Rationalism; Sacred Scripture; Science and the Church; Thomas Aquinas, Thought of; Trinity.

Suggested Readings: CCC 26-141, 198-324, 2807-2827. St. Augustine, *Confessions*, I. St. Thomas Aquinas, *Summa Theologiae,* Ia, 2-32. L. Ott, *Fundamentals of Catholic Dogma.* E. Gratsch, ed., *Principles of Catholic Theology.* W. Kasper, *The God of Jesus Christ.* K. Rahner, *Foundations of Christian Faith.*

Paul E. Lockey

GRACE

"Grace is *favor*, the *free and undeserved help* that God gives us to respond to his call to become children of God, adoptive sons, partakers of the divine nature and of eternal life" (CCC 1996).

Christ came to enlarge our lives: "I came that they may have life, and have it abundantly" (Jn 10:10). Through grace we are called to the new life of Christ, to fullness of life.

Grace is saving, liberating, and redemptive. Through the gift of grace God takes away sin and heals even the human dimensions of our lives. But, above all, grace is aimed at enabling us to share in God's own life; through it we become "partakers in the divine nature" (2 Pt 1:4). We become, even in this life, sons and daughters of God, able to live far richer lives: knowing securely the most important of all truths, with lives fortified with hope, and enriched by the love God pours into our hearts.

By grace, we are made members of the very Body of Christ, united to the Son of God made man as intimately as branches to the vine, and made one with one another through our unity with the Lord. But grace points essentially toward eternal life, and all the gifts of grace are intended to lead us at length to the fullest sharing in the life of God, when we see God face to face in eternal life and so are enabled also to love one another in unbreakable love.

Grace affects every dimension of Christian life. The four pillars of catechesis are: the Creed, or the truths of faith; the sacraments; the Christian form of life; and prayer. Each of these is intimately associated with grace. Faith itself is a gift of grace: We are able to believe God, to know securely the truth of all his saving message, and to entrust our whole lives to him, only by the working of grace (cf. Eph 2:8; Vatican Council II, *Dogmatic Constitution on Divine Revelation, Dei Verbum,* 5). The sacraments by God's favor make present to our lives all the mysteries of faith, and confer upon us the saving fruits of these mysteries. The ability to live the Christian life, keeping faithfully the Ten Commandments and the commandments of love, is the fruit of grace. Prayer, too, is the work of grace, for it is only in the Spirit that we can pray fruitfully (Rom 8:26-27). Moreover, only grace makes it possible for one to live the excellent and demanding ways of Christ, and to find this not burdensome but light and easy (Mt 11:28-30).

Grace gives abundant life in various ways. It liberates us from sin and from the evils sin has brought upon the world; it heals the wounds in our nature and in the world, restoring natural things to their vigorous fullness; but, above all, it transforms our lives, drawing us nearer to God, making us truly sharers in God's own divine nature (CCC 1989-1990, 1996-1997).

Grace is meant primarily to bring us to share in God's own nature and life (cf. 2 Pt 1:4). God made us to be not simply his servants but his friends. The Father willed us to be his true sons and daughters (cf. 1 Jn 3:2) in Christ his eternal Son; the Son of God wished to take up our human nature so that we could share in his divine nature. Even in this world we are to share God's life. By grace we are even now children of God, though it does not yet fully appear what we shall be (1 Jn 3:2). Even now we experience a measure of divine life. For by faith we share in the light of God's wisdom, and by the gift of his love we share already God's inmost life.

But this new life is fully possessed only when, at the end time, Christ completes the redemption of the world, healing all wounds, and taking away every sorrow and every tear from those who have loved him (Rv 21:4). Then we shall be manifestly like God, seeing him face to face, and filled with infinite joy and life that will never cease.

Centrality of Grace • Grace thus is central to all of Catholic life. To present what faith teaches of grace is to present the whole mystery of Christ, the whole story of salvation. "For by grace you have been saved through faith, and this is not your own doing; it is the gift of God" (Eph 2:8). Grace is a personal reality: It is the gift of a God who is most near to our lives, and it creates living ties of faith, hope, and love that bind us personally to God. Grace is not some rather magical thing strangely manipulated by formal prayers and sacramental gestures, as those who look at Catholic life apart from warm personal involvement in it sometimes fancy; rather, grace shapes and strengthens the most personal relationships with the Father, Son, and Holy Spirit.

Moreover, the doctrine of grace addresses the real problems of human life. Human selfishness, cruelty, and sin clearly are very real. The world we were born into is a broken world, and we ourselves suffer from the effects of original sin. Often, indeed, the world seems to shine with great hope, but repeatedly it disappoints us; and we also disappoint ourselves and those we want to love. Our hearts crave human fulfillment, but do not reach it. We have longings for what we have no power to grasp, longings for what only the favor, or grace, of God makes possible.

The first beginnings of a Christian life are rooted in grace. We are born in original sin and born into a fallen world. The sinner has no power at all to reach out toward salvation, unless grace precedes and stirs up the will to come to God. Conversion is the first work of grace; and the fruit of conversion and justification is not only the remission of sin but also the gift of life: "the sanctification and renewal of the inner man" (Council of Trent, cf. Denzinger-Schönmetzer, 1528).

God, however, wishes not only to give his people the first gifts of grace but to enable them to grow all their lives in greater love. Christian life is personal: It is growing in friendship with Father, Son, and Holy Spirit, and in authentic love of our brothers and sisters in Christ. Those who seek to please God must use the means of grace that deepen friendship with the Lord: the sacraments, prayers, and the works of love.

Finally, though, grace aims always at eternal life in its full possession. Its purpose is always to lead the sons and daughters of God, after they have received the grace of final perseverance, to the ultimate and crowning grace of the light of glory. This crowning grace enables them to see God face to face, and so be secure forever in sharing with overwhelming richness God's life and everything good. " 'In Scripture, to see is to possess. . . . Whoever sees God has obtained all the goods of which he can conceive' [St. Gregory of Nyssa, *De Beatitudinibus* 6: PG 44, 1265A]" (CCC 2548).

The Context of Grace • We have seen what grace is and its sublime purposes. To speak adequately of grace, however, one must speak also of its source, the relationship between grace and freedom, the forms of divine grace, and how God's grace is related to merit and to divine rewards. The *Catechism of the Catholic Church* speaks of all these matters, reminding us that the whole of faith is intermingled with what we say of grace.

It is Christ who won for us all the gifts of grace. Our justification was won for us by his blessed Passion (Council of Trent, cf. Denzinger-Schönmetzer, 1528-1529), and all the gifts of grace given to sinful man are merited by their only Savior (CCC 1992). It is Christ's Holy Spirit, whom he sends to the Church and to each of his followers, who confers on us the gifts of grace (CCC 2003).

Grace and freedom go well together. God gives his grace freely, and he gives it to free persons so that they might serve him freely and gladly. It is not as though God gave us part of what we need to share his life, and we contributed part: All is the gift of God.

But God's gift is free and given to our freedom. He does not force us to faith, but invites us; he does not compel us to love with divine love, but gives us the power to do so. Those whom grace moves to faith and love do in God's power what they otherwise could not have done. But the gifts of God are gently given, and they are offered to all, since God wills all to be saved (1 Tm 2:4).

God's grace is mighty and effective. When we do not reject his grace, it achieves in us all the good that God wishes to accomplish in us. All is from God; we have nothing to give that could make us sharers in divine life or able to do things possible only through the power of God. But God graciously gives in a way that honors our freedom. Should we be unwilling to allow grace to bear fruit in us, it will not. But if we happily decline to refuse grace, his gifts flower in us. Thus freedom is not crippled, but made vigorous by grace (cf. CCC 1993; Council of Trent, Denzinger-Schönmetzer, 1525).

Merit • Following Scripture, Catholic faith teaches that all of our new life in Christ is a divine favor given without our deserving it (cf. Eph 2:8) and also that we can in a certain way merit or deserve rewards from God (cf. 2 Tm 4:7-8).

To speak of "merit" is not to forget that in this world of divine mercy man cannot absolutely deserve any rewards from God (CCC 2007). But there is a graciousness in God's whole plan of salvation. He wants us to come to blessed and everlasting life freely; he wishes us in a way to deserve possession of himself; he wishes to call us into eternal life as friends who have freely loved him and have served him with free hearts; he wishes to give himself to us as a gift we have ourselves labored to obtain and struggled devotedly to possess. All is his gift, but it is a gift he has enabled us to possess freely.

Man's merit, then, is not based on any power of his own to do deeds that require divine power; it is due to God's gift. Should we do anything noble and saving, like making personal acts of faith and of love, which by his grace we can do, we do so only because God in his mercy enables us to perform such saving acts. Yet he enables *us* to do them and permits *us* to refuse to do so. Hence he graciously counts our willing reception of grace and flourishing in it as worthy of his blessing and reward.

We are said to merit eternal life, then, because we freely do the saving deeds that God makes it possible for us to do. But all is in the context of grace. "When God crowns our merits," St. Augustine remarks, "is he not crowning precisely his own gifts?" (*Letter* 194.5.19).

Christ indeed won salvation for the whole world by his death upon the cross, but this redemption, merited for all, was not immediately applied to all. When Christ had died and risen, many who would be called to everlasting life yet lived in sin. The saving actions Christ called for were indeed precious and important. That the word of God be proclaimed, that sacraments be conferred and the Spirit be received, that we be taught to love one another and, by his grace, do the works of love — all this was most serious. The merited redemption had to be applied in the adventures of salvation history. People had to be called freely and had to respond freely. There is realism in all these adventures of grace in a world penetrated with freedom and given life by the grace of God.

St. Paul repeatedly reminds his readers of the presence and the overwhelming importance of grace, and of how closely grace binds us to the Lord: "The grace of our Lord Jesus Christ be with you" (1 Thes 5:28; cf. 2 Thes 3:18, Gal 6:18, Rom 16:20). Our salvation is the more secure because it rests, not on our own strength, but on the mercy of God. It is he who will accomplish all that is needed in us. Our faithfulness is indeed called for; but it and all else is the gift of his grace. We may need to struggle, but we can do so confidently if our trust is in the Lord, rather than in ourselves, and if (despite temptations to fall away) we permit his grace to draw us to himself (CCC 2012-2016).

Actual and Sanctifying Grace • Actual graces touch constantly the lives of those who seek to grow in the Lord. These divine interventions take many forms. By them God stirs up in our minds saving thoughts and in our hearts concern to walk in his ways. We stand always in need of actual graces, from the first beginnings of conversion through every stage along the path toward holiness (CCC 2000). Special attention is needed to grasp the impact of: the *sacramental graces* that accompany our shared, liturgical worship of the Father; the *graces of state*; and the special graces, or *charisms,* by which the Spirit of Christ heartens us toward richer lives (CCC 2003-2004). Prayer, in which the Spirit of Christ himself assists our weakness (cf. Rom. 8:26), is a continuing channel of grace.

A special form of grace that needs always to be remembered is that called "sanctifying grace," or "deifying grace" (CCC 1999-2000); it also is called "habitual grace," for it is a stable and enduring gift. Received in Baptism, this grace makes us truly sharers in the divine nature (2 Pt 1:4), as most dear sons and daughters of the Father.

Sanctifying grace is an enduring gift. Hence we speak of living in the state of grace. Over the years we should grow in sanctifying grace, becoming more alive in the Lord until the day when we are entirely fulfilled in seeing God face to face in the overwhelming love of the beatific vision. This grace can be lost only by deliberate mortal sin. We would have no power of our own to recover grace; but God's free graces do pursue the sinner. Those who, led by grace, seek to return to God and to be restored to grace by the sacrament of Reconciliation — or by perfect contrition with the will to receive that sacrament — are enabled to return to the life of grace.

Religious educators must help the faithful realize the profound importance of living always in sanctifying grace and seeking to return to it promptly if ever they lose it. Only those in the state of grace are truly on the path toward eternal life; only they can worthily receive the sacraments of the Eucharist, Confirmation, Matrimony, or Holy Orders. It is an especially grave sacrilege to receive the Eucharist while in a state of mortal sin. Those who have sinned mortally "must not receive communion without having received absolution in the sacrament of penance" (CCC 1415; cf. 2120).

Those who live in sanctifying grace are truly children of God and sharers in God's own nature. Hence, not only does God pour his love into their hearts, but the Father, Son, and Holy Spirit dwell always in those whom they have made their own by sanctifying grace. "My father will love them, and we will come to them, and make our home with them" (Jn 14:23). This is far more than the presence of God in *every* creature he has made; it is a presence of personal affection, a transforming presence. God's presence in us calls us to grow in the new life of grace, that we may more and more

taste his saving presence, as saints and mystics of every age have proclaimed (St. Teresa of Ávila, *The Interior Castle*, 7, Ch. 1).

It is true that grace cannot be immediately experienced, and one cannot know with the certainty of faith that one is in the state of grace. Still, when faith urges us to live always in sanctifying grace, and tells us how wrong it would be to receive Communion while not in grace, it is speaking of the ordinary knowledge people can have that they are or are not living in God's grace. People certainly *can* have reliable awareness that they have sinned gravely or that, after sin, they have earnestly sought repentance and have received the sacrament of Penance and Reconciliation with sincere hearts. The good fruits of a life of grace are experienced; those who seek the Lord with generous hearts grow in confidence that he dwells within them.

See: Charisms; Conversion of the Baptized; Faith, Act of; Gifts and Fruits of the Holy Spirit; Justification; Liberation From Sin; Mortal Sin; Original Sin; Redemption; Sacrament; Sacramental Grace; Sin.

Suggested Readings: CCC 774-776, 1023-1029, 1127-1129, 1987-2029, 2559-2565, 2670-2672. Vatican Council II, *Dogmatic Constitution on the Church, Lumen Gentium*, Ch. VI; *Pastoral Constitution on the Church in the Modern World, Gaudium et Spes*, Ch. III. Pius XII, *On the Mystical Body of Christ, Mystici Corporis Christi*. John Paul II, *The Lord and Giver of Life, Dominum et Vivificantem*. J. Aumann, O.P., *Spiritual Theology*. C. Journet, *The Meaning of Grace*.

Ronald D. Lawler, O.F.M. Cap.

GUARDIAN ANGELS

God told Moses: "Behold, I send an angel before you, to guard you on the way and to bring you to the place which I have prepared" (Ex 23:20). Devout pilgrims on their journey to the Church triumphant in heaven have always understood the role and presence of these invisible guards and guides. The existence of angels — free, personal spirits, who minister to humanity as God's envoys — was dogmatically declared by the Fourth

Lateran Council in 1215. Jesus himself clearly implies that an assisting angel accompanies each person when he says: "See that you do not despise one of these little ones; for I tell you that in heaven their angels always behold the face of my Father" (Mt 18:10). The feast of the guardian angels on October 2 is among the most ancient in the Church's Calendar.

These angelic guardians are entrusted above all with helping humanity come to know and love God in this life, so as to enjoy eternal happiness in heaven. Over and above these spiritual services, guardian angels also render certain material favors to incite devotion to, and reliance on, them (cf. Tob 6:2ff., 11:7-8, 15; Acts 5:19-20, 12:7ff.).

"Angel of God, my guardian dear; to whom God's love commits me here. Ever this day be at my side, to light and guard, to rule and guide." What Catholic mother has not taught her children that simple prayer? At life's end, the Church, in the liturgical prayers for the departing soul, calls on the guardian angels to lead our souls to God's presence for the particular judgment. One can also invoke and pray to the guardian angels of others in their needs. During life, each person may be assured that he or she has a guardian angel who can be trusted and treated as a lifelong friend.

See: Angels; Devil and Evil Spirits.

H

HATRED OF GOD

The bitterest sin against love is hatred. But can creatures actually detest their Maker? Certainly there are cases (total reversal of fortune, the "merciless" death of a loved one), wherein God is reviled and even cursed. However, what in fact such haters reject with abhorrence is a loathsome caricature, the very opposite of God; and they are answerable for their contributions to this reverse image.

The *Catechism of the Catholic Church* (2094) describes a kind of ladder to hatred, an irreflective but progressive falsification of divine truth. (1) Indifference stems from overlooking God's charity and ignoring his unlimited power and mercy. (2) Ingratitude is born of the mental sloth and unenlightened selfishness that look upon God's gifts as entitlements. (3) Lukewarmness arises from contradictory allegiances and a fearful spirit of calculation in the face of both divine rewards and demands. (4) "*Acedia* or spiritual sloth goes so far as to refuse the joy that comes from God and to be repelled by divine goodness" (2094). (5) Hatred of God results from proud rebellion against God's sovereignty and providence; it denies God's goodness and presumes to curse him for impinging on one's life, for outlawing sin and meting out punishments.

When enmity prompts the sinner to regret the divine perfections and to loathe God in himself, then the offense represents the pinnacle of all the miserable hierarchy of sin. Such an attitude is fairly and adequately described as diabolical. In practice, however, awareness of and consent to the hatred is often diminished by a welter of emotions. In all other sins where charity is forfeited, one's aversion from God is indirect and consequent, inasmuch as some creature is inordinately preferred to the barely known supreme goodness. But here, if indeed there can ever be full forethought and consent, the rejection is direct, total.

See: Despair; Presumption; Religion, Virtue of; Tempting God.

HEALTH CARE

Since Moses raised the serpent to form the caduceus and Isaiah predicted the miraculous power of the Messiah, healing has been linked with religion and salvation. Health has served as a paradigm for human integrity: a person in harmony with self, with others, with nature, and with God. Healing of both physical and spiritual illnesses has been integral to the ministry of the Church since Jesus sent his first disciples "to teach and to heal." It is significant that the Sermon on the Mount, which contains the blueprint for Christian discipleship, is followed in Matthew's Gospel by a report of Jesus' healing a variety of illnesses and his commissioning of the Twelve "to heal every disease and every infirmity" (Mt 10:1). The Acts of the Apostles records many miraculous healings and describes the provision of service by the deacons and holy women in the early Christian communities.

The Church Fathers referred to the care of the sick and poor as a mark of authentic Christianity. The Council of Nicaea (325) identified the need for distinct facilities for the sick, the poor, and pilgrims. In the fourth century, Emperor Constantine advanced an organizational approach to the erection of hospices and hospitals. Institutional health care developed rapidly as the monastic communities grew in number and in size. Charlemagne, crowned holy Roman emperor in 800, decreed that every monastery should provide hospitality and services to the sick and pilgrims. In the early twelfth century, the Hospitallers were freed from enclosure to provide medical service to pilgrims and crusaders. These Church institutions offered extensive treatments, served as almshouses, and provided immediate response to the pestilence and famines all too frequent in the Western world. Patron saints for health efforts appeared in Camillus de Lellis, John of God, and Francis of Assisi, who embraced Christ in the leper.

Just as the creation of monasteries provided the initial impetus to institutional care, the emergence of active communities of women religious in the post-Reformation period greatly extended opportunities for service in the growing urban areas of Europe. In France, St. Louise de Marillac prepared her seventeenth-century Daughters of Charity to provide nursing services in public hospitals, prisons, and clinics, as well as in the homes of the poor, and to establish specialized, privately-supported services for foundlings, the homeless, and the aged. She also developed standardized protocols and manuals to assure quality care that was both corporal and spiritual. Later, other apostolic communities emerged throughout Europe to provide institutional service and home care to the sick.

In modern times, the provision of health and medical care gradually became a responsibility of civil powers as well as a charitable service provided by the Church, beneficent lord, or employer. In Europe today, Church ownership of health facilities is limited, but religious staff public and private facilities and serve in the national health service programs operative in their countries. In the United States, however, where there is complete separation of Church and State, the Church maintains a parallel system of health services. Furthermore, through missionary efforts from both Europe and the United States, the Church provides health services throughout the world.

Catholic Health Care in the U.S. • While in North America Catholic hospitals were established in Mexico City and in Quebec City in the seventeenth century, the real story of Catholic health care

in the United States begins in the nineteenth century and is linked to immigration patterns and the growth of communities of women religious. Persecution by civil governments and concern for emigrants motivated many religious to leave Europe and the British Isles. Through the efforts of these religious and members of emerging native communities, health services expanded rapidly in the developing U.S. While in 1850 the country had almost 2 million Catholics and 1,344 sisters, in 1900 those numbers had risen to 12 million and 40,000. Of the 106 new communities established by 1900, 23 were founded by Americans, 8 from Canadian motherhouses, and 75 from European foundations. While not all of these religious communities provided health services as their primary ministry, the sisters responded to immediate needs and easily moved from teaching to nursing and back again as situations demanded.

The immigrant communities of women generally concentrated their efforts in the growing cities of the East where their compatriots first settled, but then moved to the West as railroads and mining expanded, and to the Midwest and North Central states for various industries. In general, the German and Polish communities established facilities in the Milwaukee-Chicago-Detroit triangle; Irish communities, while heavily concentrated in the East, established foundations in the Southwest and California as well. In following the migration patterns of the Italians, Mother Frances Xavier Cabrini's sisters opened hospitals in New York, Chicago, and the Northwest. In cities such as Philadelphia and Chicago, Catholic hospitals were set up within close proximity to address the needs of the various ethnic groups. This, as well as the fact that Catholicism developed as an urban religion, accounts for the current situation, in which several Catholic hospitals not uncommonly are found in close proximity to one another.

In Maryland, where religious tolerance was operative and the Catholic population was strong, Mother Elizabeth Seton's sisters served in public facilities as early as 1823 before establishing their own hospitals. In other locations, Catholic services and facilities had to be established because Catholics were either feared or hated, and were generally unwelcome in both public and private facilities. In light of this, it is a tribute to religious congregations that many of the founding documents of their institutions underscore their willingness to serve all and declare their refusal to discriminate by religion. In many cases, particularly outside the major cities of the East, the Catholic hospital was the first and only facility in the area.

The growth within religious congregations was paralleled by the establishment of hospitals. By 1885, 154 Catholic hospitals and a wide range of clinic services were available, particularly in the railroad, mining, and logging areas of the country. Before 1900, Mother Seton's religious progeny had expanded into five distinct communities and had established hospitals across the nation. Her Emmitsburg, Maryland, foundation alone opened hospitals in such far-flung cities as St. Louis (1828), Detroit (1845), Buffalo (1845), Mobile (1852), Los Angeles (1856), Washington (1861), Boston (1862), Chicago (1869), Indianapolis (1881), and Dallas (1895).

These religious women were lured across the nation by the prospect for service, just as the immigrants were drawn to pursue opportunity or gold. The sisters expressed their dedication through a variety of services, and they exhibited great adaptability as convents and schools were transformed into wards during major epidemics of cholera, smallpox, and influenza. Women religious also provided major health service during the Civil War and the Spanish-American War, and a contingent of sister-nurses served in Italy during World War I. Many historians have noted that the nursing care given by the sisters during wars and epidemics was a major force in reducing bigotry and bias against Catholics.

Industry, economy, and innovation have consistently characterized Catholic health care. The human endowment provided by the sisters' uncompensated services and their successful fundraising efforts provided a solid financial base for their hospitals, but even that resource was surpassed by their creativity. Several hospitals in the late nineteenth and early twentieth centuries conceived and marketed prepaid insurance plans as a means of steady income. The Catholic hospitals also have an impressive history of innovation and clinical firsts, as well as a tradition of pioneering in nursing education and facilitating medical education.

At the turn of the century the Church's ongoing commitment to excellence in service was strengthened by external and internal forces. In 1910, the Flexner report urged that education for health care workers be standardized, and shortly thereafter nursing organizations were formed. Within Catholic health care a parallel trend was emerging. In 1915, the Catholic Hospital Association (CHA) was inspired through the efforts of Father Charles B. Moulinier, S.J., regent of the Marquette University School of Medicine, Mother Esperance and Sister Madeleine, both Sisters of St. Joseph in Minnesota, and Archbishop Sebastian Messmer of Milwaukee. The mission of the organization was to provide education for sisters involved in hospital work through educational programs and an annual assembly.

Once organized, the association grew from a program of one annual meeting, to a series of conferences, to a full-blown trade association offering specialized programs and services as well as a publishing house for Catholic books and its own periodical, *Hospital Progress*. The Sister-Formation Movement, begun in the 1950s, gave further impetus to the professionalization of religious women. In the 1970s, the increasing ethical challenges facing health care providers motivated the CHA to form the Pope John XXIII Center for Medical Moral Research and Education, which subsequently assumed independent status. In the early 1980s, the Catholic Hospital Association of the United States, located in St. Louis, changed its name to Catholic Health Association in order more adequately to reflect its membership and the growing emphasis on wellness. In the 1980s, it focused attention on the leadership of religious congregations and on the laity who had assumed the major governance/management responsibilities within Catholic health care.

Current Status • As indicated, the Church in

the United States is unique within the universal Church in its maintenance of church-related systems of education, social services, and health services parallel to those offered by the public sector. While elementary and secondary education and social service have generally been sponsored at the parish or diocesan level, religious communities of women initially founded and continue to sponsor over ninety percent of the more than one thousand Catholic health facilities currently providing services in this country. (Some dioceses, particularly in the Northeast, also have significant investment in health services, and a few communities of men, such as the Alexian brothers, sponsor health facilities.)

Catholic institutions and agencies now represent about one-sixth of the overall health services provided in the U.S. In 1990, Catholic health care in the United States, with annual operating revenues of over 20 billion dollars, claimed more than 60 congregational and diocesan health care systems, 600 acute care hospitals, 100 specialty hospitals, 600 homes for the aged, nursing education programs and a variety of other community health services.

Discussions of Catholic identity and religious sponsorship of institutions dominated the last three decades of the twentieth century as a new Code of Canon Law appeared, membership in religious congregations declined dramatically, controversy over the role and value of Church institutions raged, and changes in the delivery of medical care caused contraction within the overall industry. Technological advances, legislative initiatives, judicial actions, financial constraints, and moral pluralism presented serious challenges to the Catholic ethic and to the viability of Catholic institutions. In some cases, in an effort to open the governance and management of Catholic facilities to the laity, institutions were secularized, while in other cases facilities were sold or affiliated with corporations that minimized or eliminated the Catholic character.

In the 1980s and 1990s, national concern about escalating health care costs and the shocking number of disenfranchised reached its highest peak.

Social programs from the 1960s, especially Medicare and Medicaid, had expanded health coverage greatly, but millions of Americans still lacked access or coverage for medical and health care. From the early 1980s, national and global justice issues grew in importance within the Church. Task forces and study groups on health care for the poor were developed by the Catholic Health Association, several Catholic health care systems, various state Catholic conferences, some Catholic lobbying groups, and Catholic Charities USA. Several policy statements resulting from such efforts gained national prominence in the health care reform debates of the 1990s.

While in the 1960s virtually all Catholic hospitals and long-term care facilities were governed and managed by religious, by 1990 the laity dominated in administrative and governance roles. With the same rapidity, hospitals entered into sophisticated health care systems. To compensate for the decreased presence and involvement of religious, ministry formation programs for the laity gradually were developed, and the role of "mission" services was added to the system and institutional management team. Pastoral care departments were strengthened, and a new role of parish nurse was created. Many bishops, concerned that Catholic health care would decrease within their dioceses, began to meet on a regular basis with their local administrators and sponsors. At the State Catholic Conference level, more attention was given to health care issues, especially those with ethical implications such as surrogate decision-making, reproductive technologies, withdrawal or termination of treatment, assisted suicide, human genetics, and allocation of health resources. Concern over assimilation or homogenization of Catholic values heightened as the phenomenon of joint ventures, consolidations, and mergers emerged as a critical issue of national downsizing. These networks or alliances have the potential of marginalizing Catholic facilities because of the inability of the latter to cooperate in activities and participate in structures contrary to the Church's moral teaching.

Church Leadership and Health Care • While

Vatican II remained silent on Catholic health care, the Church hierarchy in the second half of the twentieth century became increasingly vocal on health issues. In their blueprints for economic justice, both Pope John XXIII and Pope Paul VI included the individual's right to medical care and to healthful social conditions. Pope John Paul II, in his stress on personalism, consistently called attention to the ethical dimensions of care and technology and continued the reflections of Pope Pius XII, who had contributed significantly to bioethical literature in the 1940s and 1950s. Under the leadership of Pope John Paul II, the first International Congress on Catholic Health Issues took place, the Holy See's Pontifical Council for Pastoral Assistance to Health Care Workers was formed.

During the last three decades, too, the Vatican intervened in several discussions impacting Catholic health care in the United States. A controversy of the post-Vatican II period on Church ownership of property evoked a Vatican response. The Congregation for the Doctrine of the Faith also responded to specific requests of the American bishops for clarification on material cooperation and sterilization.

While in the nineteenth century individual bishops of the United States encouraged or sponsored Catholic health care in their jurisdictions, in the twentieth century the entire hierarchy has influenced health service and health policy through the state and national episcopal organizations. In 1919, the National Catholic War Council (which became the National Catholic Welfare Council — later Conference — and then in 1966, the United States Catholic Conference) approved the "Program of Social Reconstruction" authored by Father John A. Ryan, which anticipated the social justice emphasis of John XXIII and Paul VI and pointed out that health and medical benefits should be available to all. In that same year, the Catholic Hospital Association was affiliated with NCWC's Social Action Department. Later, the NCWC encouraged the development of the diocesan staff position of Bishops' Representative to Health Care, which evolved into the Diocesan Health Care Coordinator or Diocesan Director of Health

Affairs. In 1948, the National Catholic Welfare Conference formed a Bureau of Health and Hospitals in its Social Action Department. This bureau made a significant contribution in establishing the National Catholic Chaplains Association and in facilitating the publication, in 1971, of the "Ethical and Religious Directives for Catholic Health Care Facilities." These directives (approved by the bishops in 1971, amended in 1975 and again in 1994) were requested by leaders of the Catholic Health Association and emerged from a series of articles on medical ethics appearing in *Hospital Progress*. In the public advocacy area, the NCWC and its successor, the United States Catholic Conference, covered areas as various as equity for Catholic facilities, compensation for the services of religious, eligibility for federal construction funds, national health insurance, and conscience clauses.

In 1981, the bishops of the United States issued their collective pastoral letter, "Health and Health Care," which not only expressed strong support for Catholic facilities and their sponsors but also articulated six basic principles that should inform national health policy and explicated the right to health care. The bishops concluded their pastoral with the identification of four critical challenges for Catholic health care leadership: personalized patient care, medical-moral issues, prophetic role, and rights and responsibilities of workers.

Over the past few decades, many individual bishops have published pastoral letters and statements on medical-moral issues. State Catholic Conferences and the national bishops' conference direct health care efforts to policy development that respects individuals, assures universal access to quality service, and supports religious freedom. A commission composed of leaders of Catholic Charities USA, the Leadership Conference of Women Religious, the bishops' conference, the Catholic Health Association, and members of the laity was formed in the mid-1980s to seek to consolidate efforts and assure Catholic influence on health care in the United States.

See: Abortion; Anointing of the Sick; Apostolate; Assisted Suicide; Care of the Dying;

Cooperation; Death, Determination of; Euthanasia; Genetic Experimentation; Human Life, Dignity and Sanctity of; Reproductive Technologies; Science and the Church; Suffering in Christian Life.

Suggested Readings: CCC 2288-2291. J. Dolan, *The American Catholic Experience.* J. Ellis, *American Catholicism.* O. Griese, *Catholic Identity in Health Care: Principles and Practice.* United States Catholic Conference, *Justice in the Marketplace: Collected Statements of the Vatican and the U.S. Catholic Bishops on Economic Policy 1891-1984.* M. Kelly, ed., *Justice and Health Care.* B. Mitchell, ed., *The Heritage of American Catholicism: Building the American Catholic City, Parishes and Institutions.* National Conference of Catholic Bishops, "Health and Health Care: A Pastoral Letter of the American Catholic Bishops." G. Reed, "Initiatives of the American Bishops in Seeking Justice in Health Care," in *Justice and Health Care.* R. Shanahan, S.J., *The History of the Catholic Hospital Association 1915-1965.* U. Stepsis and D. Liptak, *Pioneer Healers: The History of Women Religious in American Health Care.*

Margaret John Kelly, D.C.

HEAVEN

Christian Creeds, especially those of most ancient and apostolic usage, regularly refer to God as "Creator of heaven and earth." He alone is architect and preserver of all that is, whether seen or unseen. The God who ushers the universe into being is also the one who graciously fashions an abode of perfect blessedness where his angels and saints dwell in rapturous delight with the Godhead forever.

God is thus understood, according to the Church's profession of faith, as author of both cosmos *and* covenant, of nature *and* grace. In the circumstance, man becomes beneficiary of a double blessing, of being both given and for-given by the selfsame God: given in the order of nature, of existence, and then, all creation having come to grief in sin, graced by the encounter with Christ in forgiveness, in the unimaginable order of salvation that confers heaven — "the ultimate end and ful-

fillment of the deepest human longings, the state of supreme, definitive happiness" (CCC 1024).

The Church has always made much of this point, this nexus between human nature and divine grace, seeing in it "the bond, deep within creation, that both unites heaven and earth and distinguishes the one from the other" (CCC 326). Earth, then, is man's place, the state in which sin and death engulf and destroy him; while heaven remains God's own place, the nature of which places it beyond time and space, beyond the realm where sin and suffering abound. "Heaven consists in such a relationship with God," observes Frank Sheed, "that no created nature, by its own powers, could be adequate to it."

Nevertheless, it is to this precise place and condition that all men have been called. Indeed, glints of that heavenly glory have already fallen into this world, to stir into life that necessary hunger for the "Father's house" (Jn 14:2) to which we have all been invited.

"Christian tradition uses the image of heaven," writes Joseph Ratzinger, "an image linked to the natural symbolic force of what is 'high' or 'above,' in order to express that definitive completion of human existence which comes about through the perfect love towards which faith tends." Man is a being called into existence in order that he might receive and answer another call, one intended to draw him finally home to God.

Desire for Heaven • Here, in fact, is the deepest desire of the human heart: this single indestructible longing for God, for an eternity spent in intimate, blessed communion with him. Today, Ratzinger reminds us, "we are all well aware that the word 'heaven' does not designate a place beyond the stars but something much greater and more difficult to express, namely, that God has a place for us and that God gives us eternity."

Surely among the most deeply consoling words in all of Scripture are those Our Lord speaks to his disciples: "I go and prepare a place for you . . . that where I am you also may be" (Jn 14:3). In what else is this faith grounded if not the conviction that in Christ God is great and generous enough to make room even for us? Only eternity can give time itself validity before God. "If a person's death is worthless, observes Ratzinger, "then his life is worthless too. If man is ultimately jettisoned in death, if he becomes as so much refuse, then he is, even beforehand, one of the things that humanity can jettison and can treat as such. But if man never becomes refuse, if his value is called eternity, then this value is always his and marks his whole life."

This longing and desire for heaven most clearly define the whole human project. They are evident even amid the rampant idolatries of humankind. "You have made us for yourself, O God, and our hearts remain ever restless until they find rest in You," St. Augustine declares at the beginning of his *Confessions*. Or, as Augustine puts it in an exquisite passage in the *City of God*, giving unforgettable expression to what the joys of heaven will actually consist in: "There we shall rest and we shall see; we shall see and we shall love; we shall love and we shall praise. Behold what shall be in the end and shall not end" (XXII, 30).

The Experience of Heaven • Heaven not uncommonly is likened to a vast, sumptuous feast (e.g., Mt 22:1-10; Lk 14:16-24). This is, we might say, a feast awaiting those who hunger for God, for the unending Bread of Life! Moreover, as Vatican Council II teaches regarding the destiny of all human goods, in heaven "we will find them once again, cleansed this time from the stain of sin, illuminated and transfigured" (*Pastoral Constitution on the Church in the Modern World, Gaudium et Spes*, 39). This perfect life with God — in which, to recall the *de fide* teaching of Pope Benedict XII, the blessed "see the divine essence with an intuitive vision, and even face to face, without the mediation of any creature" — certainly is heaven (CCC 1023).

In heaven we shall become like God himself, so the Scriptures tell us, because we shall see him as he is. Our souls will thus be riveted upon God forever. Whether as supreme truth, as the Dominicans taught (which means that our intellects will never come to an end of seeing him), or as supreme goodness, as the Franciscans held (which means that our wills will never come to an end of loving him), is really no great matter of dispute. In the last analy-

sis, says Ratzinger, "the point of it all is the same: God totally permeates the whole man with his plenitude and his utter openness. God is 'all in all,' and thus the human person enters upon his boundless fulfillment." As G.K. Chesterton put it in his book on Thomas Aquinas: "Whether the supreme ecstasy is more affectional than intellectual is no very deadly matter of quarrel among men who believe it is both, but do not profess even to imagine the actual experience of either."

In fact, as the *Catechism of the Catholic Church* reminds us, the whole mystery of heaven, of communion with God in Christ and each other, simply beggars all understanding and description. "Scripture speaks of it in images: life, light, peace, wedding feast, wine of the kingdom, the Father's house, the heavenly Jerusalem, paradise: 'no eye has seen, nor ear heard, nor the heart of man conceived, what God has prepared for those who love him' [1 *Cor* 2:9]" (CCC 1027).

An eternity, no less, of rest and sight, of love and praise — to sound the Augustinian note — spent in Christ's presence: This truly is heaven. And if, as the Church tells us, heaven essentially depends on being in Christ, this ineluctably includes a co-being with all those who, taken together, make up the total Body of Christ. "Heaven is a stranger to isolation," Ratzinger remarks. "It is the open society of the communion of saints, and in this way the fulfillment of all human communion." The bliss of heaven, in other words, necessarily includes both dimensions, that is, the immediate vision and love of God (vertical) *and* the knowledge and love of all others in God (horizontal). The *Catechism* says: "Heaven is the blessed community of all who are perfectly incorporated into Christ" (CCC 1026).

As pilgrims of hope we remain conscious of a desire and longing for that which no human and earthly happiness can provide. The heart of man cries out for a place of infinite and perfect repose that simply does not exist in this world. "There is," says Augustine, "a God-shaped vacuum in every man that only Christ can fill."

It is this fact, comments Henri de Lubac in his seminal work on *The Mystery of the Supernatural*, this open space only Christ can fill, that causes the pain of loss in those who ultimately refuse Christ entry. "The desire to see God cannot be permanently frustrated without an essential suffering . . . for is not this, in effect, the definition of the 'pain of the damned'?" He goes on: "And, consequently — at least in appearance — a good and just God could hardly frustrate me, unless I, through my own fault, turn away from him by choice. The infinite importance of the desire implanted in me by my Creator is what constitutes the infinite importance of the drama of human existence. . . . My finality, which is expressed by this desire, is inscribed upon my very being as it has been put into this universe by God. And, by God's will, I now have no other genuine end . . . except that of 'seeing God.' "

What, finally, is heaven but that place where a man may savor freely the taste of truth, whose flavor is like the finest honey, and the embrace that of the Bridegroom who has sought us from all eternity? "I shall know the fullness of joy, when I see your face, O Lord . . . fulfillment and endless peace in your presence," says the Evening Prayer of the Church. Or, to draw upon the Church's rich hymnographic tradition, so much of it resonant with truth that mere discourse cannot equal, there is this final stanza from the text of a nineteenth-century hymn translated from the Spanish by Christian Henry Bateman: "On heaven's joyful shore his goodness we'll adore, singing forever more, 'Alleluia! Amen!' "

See: Beatific Vision; End of Man; Last Things.

Suggested Readings: CCC 325-326, 1023-1029. R. Gleason, S.J., *The World To Come.* H. de Lubac, S.J., *The Mystery of the Supernatural.* J. Ratzinger, *Eschatology: Death and Eternal Life.* H. von Balthasar, *Credo: Meditations on the Apostles' Creed.*

Regis Martin

HEDONISM

Hedonism as a more or less systematic position is grounded in the view that pleasure is the real purpose of life, that what is intrinsically good and worthwhile in life is pleasure. Our culture tends toward hedonism, as is seen in its condoning of divorce and remarriage and its increasing approval of euthanasia.

The Gospel teaches otherwise. What is intrinsically worthwhile is what is really fulfilling and the supernatural gifts offered us. Pleasure does not make a good thing good. Rather, pleasure is the experiential aspect of possessing some real good. For example, when one learns, one enjoys the activity. It is the activity that is good and recognized as worth pursuing; the pleasure follows upon the activity but is not the reason why the activity is good.

Thus, the intrinsic goods are such things as life, health, knowledge, aesthetic experience, friendship, religion. We should pursue what is really good, taking pleasure in real goods. We ought not to be diverted from what is truly worthwhile, concentrating on pleasant experiences, and we should not let fear of pain or loss of pleasure deter us from pursuing what is really fulfilling for ourselves and others, what contributes to God's plan.

Pleasure, then, is neither good nor bad only of itself. Rather, pleasure taken in activities that are really fulfilling for oneself and for others is good. It is not wrong to perform an action because it is pleasant: for example, to eat a meal because it tastes good. But pursuing a pleasure apart from an activity that is really fulfilling — for instance, eating even when it is not healthy — is wrong.

See: Absolute Moral Norms; Human Goods; Moral Principles, Christian; Natural Law.

HELL

"To a certain degree," writes Pope John Paul II, "eschatology has become irrelevant to contemporary man, especially in our civilization" (*Crossing the Threshold of Hope,* p. 183). A persisting forgetfulness of the last things has set in, particularly as regards hell, which is surely the least palatable of all the Church's doctrines proposed for our belief. And yet at no time in her long history has the Church not affirmed either the existence of hell or the eternity of the torments awaiting those who choose to go there. What is the truth about hell — about the Church's teaching that seems so to jar and assault modern sensibility?

The Existence of Hell • Hell exists. If it did not, it would be very difficult to know what to make of the many references to hell in the New Testament. See, for instance, the passage in Matthew where Jesus, addressing those on his left at the Last Judgment, is said to declare: "Depart from me, you accursed, into the eternal fire prepared for the devil and his angels" (25:41). Elsewhere, for example, the Gospel of Mark, he speaks of Gehenna with its "unquenchable fire" (9:43). As Joseph Ratzinger remarks, there can be no quibbling here: "The idea of eternal damnation, which had taken ever clearer shape in the Judaism of the century or two before Christ, has a firm place in the teaching of Jesus, as well as in the apostolic writings. Dogma takes its stand on solid ground when it speaks of the existence of hell and of the eternity of its punishments" (*Eschatology*, p. 215).

If the founder of Christianity did not keep silence about either the certainty of the fact of hell or the real possibility of actually going there, the Church hardly can stand mute before the reality now. Indeed, asks Pope John Paul, "Is not hell in a certain sense the ultimate safeguard of man's moral conscience?" How otherwise is human freedom to be respected if it does not include the right to say no to God, even to the point of rejecting his summons to love forever? The *Catechism of the Catholic Church* is very emphatic: "Mortal sin is a radical possibility of human freedom. . . . If it is not redeemed by repentance and God's forgiveness, it causes exclusion from Christ's kingdom and the eternal death of hell, for our freedom has the power to make choices for ever, with no turning back" (1861).

It would seem, then, that the salient features of the Church's doctrine of hell are these: that hell exists; that the torments peculiar to it are precisely eternal; and that we are altogether free to take ourselves there. Man's perversity being what it is, we are at liberty to make our own hell; we do so the moment we ratify, by our choices, the refusal

to love. "He who does not love remains in death" (1 Jn 3:14). And the *Catechism*, which quotes the Johannine text, is unambiguous about the context Christ had in mind: "Our Lord warns us that we shall be separated from him if we fail to meet the serious needs of the poor and the little ones who are his brethren. . . . This state of definitive self-exclusion from communion with God [i.e., Love] and the blessed is called 'hell' " (1033).

The Nature of Hell • Jean Paul Sartre was wrong: Hell is not other people. It is being alone, absolutely and forever. This is the condition of one who, habituated to a life of sheer self-enclosure, announces forever before God: "I don't want to love. I don't want to be loved. Just leave me to myself." It is, suggests Josef Pieper, the radical posture of those who literally insist on never "giving a damn"; such an attitude of mind, forever fixated upon itself, is essentially an invitation to be damned. Not to exercise the capacity to love the other, especially the poor and the unloved, to anchor instead all one's *eros* to one's own self, this is the philosophy on which hell depends. And, to be sure, God, taking us finally at our word — that terrifying compliment paid to creatures on whom from the very start the liberty to refuse felicity had been conferred — will not stop us. We are responsible for the use we make of our liberty. If heaven reposes upon God's grace and our freedom, so, too, must hell.

"The specificity of Christianity is shown in this conviction of the greatness of man," writes Ratzinger. "Human life is fully serious. . . . The irrevocable takes place, and that includes, then, irrevocable destruction" (*Eschatology*, pp. 217-218). Indeed, it is a seriousness given palpable form in the cross of Christ. We are terrifyingly free, at the last, to declare before God, in words that echo throughout C.S. Lewis's allegory, *The Great Divorce*, "Not Thy will, but mine be done." And so it *is* done, forever; and under that weight of impacted solipsism the soul sinks into everlasting hell. "There was a door," cries the loveless, self-tormenting husband to his unloving wife in T.S. Eliot's play *The Cocktail Party*, "And I could not open it. I could not touch the handle. / Why could I not walk out of my prison? / What is hell? Hell is oneself, / Hell is alone, the other figures in it / Merely projections. There is nothing to escape from / And nothing to escape to. One is always alone."

Two questions about hell need to be addressed here: the exact nature of the sufferings inflicted and the number of those condemned to endure them. As regards the first the Church's teaching is clear: There is the pain of loss, which amounts to an eternal separation from God, "in whom alone man can have the life and happiness for which he was created and for which he longs" (CCC 1057). To be deprived of the sight of God for all eternity must be the most horrifying pain of all. Then there is the pain of sense, which, while not to be understood in a merely physical way, that is, sadistic tortures, is nevertheless not purely spiritual either, particularly not in light of the Last Judgment, when the bodies of the lost will share in the punishment of their souls. The Church, with full scriptural warrant, speaks of fire; but the image aims to capture a reality profoundly deep, as this from *The Church's Confession of Faith*, originally published by the German bishops' conference, shows: "God in his holiness is a consuming fire for evil, deceit, hate, and violence (Is 10:17). Just as heaven is God himself, won forever, so hell is God himself eternally lost. The essence of hell is *final exclusion from communion with God* because of one's own fault. Because God alone is the fulfillment of man's meaning, the loss of God in hell brings the experience and the pain of ultimate meaninglessness and despair."

Finally, though some may wish to know who in fact is in hell, the Church has no information about that and is forbidden even to speculate. Neither the number of the lost, nor the names of any whom one might imagine to be lost, have ever been revealed. "God predestines no one to go to hell; for this, a willful turning away from God (a mortal sin) is necessary, and persistence in it until the end" (CCC 1037). Who can look into a man's soul at the last and judge the worth of all that he has brought before God? Only God, who has given us no list of names, only the knowledge that hell

and damnation are possible and that we need to fear them — especially we, his putative friends, who so often are in danger of betraying him.

See: Fundamental Option; Heaven; Judgment, General; Judgment, Particular; Last Things; Limbo; Purgatory; Resurrection of the Dead; Sin.

Suggested Readings: CCC 393, 633, 1033-1037, 1056-1058, 1861. J. Ratzinger, *Eschatology*. C. Lewis, *The Great Divorce*.

Regis Martin

HERESY

The virtue of faith expresses trust in God's truthfulness. By this virtue, we accept something as true not because its truth is naturally evident to our mind, but simply because we have it on God's word, communicated to us in Scripture or Tradition as interpreted by the Magisterium, "the living teaching office of the Church" (Vatican Council II, *Dogmatic Constitution on Divine Revelation, Dei Verbum*, 10).

Faith is an act of love, precisely because it proceeds from the will rather than from the mind. The will — choosing to accept God's word — "tells" the mind to accept what the mind itself does not see. Still, it would be wrong to think that the believer has closed his eyes, as it were, and is looking into the dark. Rather, we might say, the believer is looking into the light — a light too bright for his mind to penetrate. To put it another way: Faith does not constrict the mind; it looks upon infinite horizons of truth.

Nevertheless, since the mind does not humanly see the evidence of what faith proposes to it, the possibility always remains of doubting, of withholding assent, of refusing to *see in faith*. As with all the virtues, faith, too, is subject to temptations, which take the form of doubts against what is proposed to our mind for belief.

Doubts can be voluntary or involuntary. Even doubts in small matters of faith displease God if one consents to them. More important matters may also become the object of temptations to doubt, and then an even more vigorous fight against them is required. If one voluntarily doubts (i.e., *consent-*

ing to the doubt) something clearly taught by the Church, one sins against faith and is just a step short of heresy. One commits the sin of heresy either by *obstinately remaining* in the doubt or by passing from doubt to positive and formal *disbelief*, rejecting or denying some point of truth that the Church, in the use of her divine authority, proposes to be believed.

Therefore, while temptations against faith are to be expected, they are especially dangerous and ought to be firmly resisted and rapidly rejected. Still, not every sin against faith constitutes heresy. Heresy in its strict sense is incurred by a person who formally denies and persistently rejects a truth that "must be believed with divine and catholic faith," precisely because it is proposed by the Magisterium of the Church as revealed by God (cf. Canon 751).

"Heretic" comes from a Greek word that means "picking and choosing." We can legitimately pick and choose in many contexts, but not in regard to what God has revealed. To do so would mean setting up one's own judgment as the final standard and gauge of truth in matters of salvation, and refusing to accept that Jesus Christ established his Church as possessor and teacher of his truth.

Truth, Freedom, and Conscience • A misunderstanding of conscience and particularly of the relation between truth, freedom, and conscience (cf. Pope John Paul II, encyclical *The Splendor of Truth, Veritatis Splendor*, 35-64) can lead to such an attitude.

Right from the start of the Church, one sees the Apostles expressing their concern that Christians should not get their faith wrong (cf. Gal 1:6; 1 Tm 1:19; Jas 5:19-20; 2 Pt 2:1-3; 2 Jn 8-9; Jude 3-4). Perhaps it was easier then to stray into heresy, inasmuch as the doctrines were so new and their content had not always been precisely established. Today, Christian doctrine has been clarified by twenty centuries of magisterial teaching. Yet one could hardly say that heresy no longer is a problem. Failure to know and study the teachings of the Magisterium, absence of sound catechetical instruction, casual and uninformed reading of works by unreliable authors, neglecting to consult

about doubts with those qualified to advise: These are some ways in which a person "can stray from the truth" (cf. 2 Tm 2:18).

Certain doctrinal positions, without being necessarily heretical, are hard to reconcile with the thought of the Church. While specialists in theology may perhaps hold them, at least tentatively, they would be imprudent to propagate them. Catholics who are nonspecialists do well to look to the guidance of the Magisterium in such matters.

See: Assent and Dissent; Church, Membership in; Conscience and the Magisterium; Dissent; Divine Revelation; Faith, Act of; Faith, Virtue of; Knowledge of God; Magisterium; Sacred Scripture; Sacred Tradition; Schism.

Suggested Readings: CCC 817, 2089. John Paul II, *That All May Be One, Ut Unum Sint,* 18-19. Congregation for the Doctrine of the Faith, *Instruction on the Ecclesial Vocation of the Theologian.*
                                                                    Cormac Burke

HIERARCHY

The general meaning of "hierarchy" is enormously misunderstood today by many people who think it is synonymous with "inequality." In point of fact, however, hierarchy comes from two Greek words, *hieros*, which means sacred, and *arche*, meaning beginning or first or something that has priority. Hierarchy therefore means "sacred origin." Hierarchy also means "sacred order," from the Greek word *archein*, meaning to rule or to order. The order might involve elements that are equal or elements that are unequal, since hierarchy as such signifies neither equality nor inequality but refers simply to the order itself.

Hierarchy and the Trinity • Hierarchy as sacred order applies, in the first instance, to the Trinity. The Trinitarian God is three Persons ordered to one another by the mutually dependent and noninterchangeable relations of paternity (Father), filiation (Son), and passive spiration (Holy Spirit). This divine order is most clearly reflected in the fact that the Father is the first Person of the Trinity because he begets the Son, the Son is the second

Person of the Trinity because he is begotten of the Father, and the Holy Spirit is the third Person of the Trinity because he is spirated by the Father and the Son. At the same time, the sacred ordering of the Trinity is a hierarchy of equals, inasmuch as each of the Persons possesses the fullness of the divine substance.

The Trinity is also the "sacred origin" of creation, and the order invested by God in creation is therefore a sacred order because it has a sacred origin. Three levels of this order deserve our special attention. First, there is the unequal ordering of God — Man — World. The world is ordered to man, who is given dominion over it (cf. Gn 1:28). Man, however, is ordered to God as God's image (Gn 1:27), and therefore God has dominion over man (Gn 2:16).

Second, there is that equal ordering of human beings created as male and female in the image of God (Gn 1:27) and called to become in marriage the relations of husband and wife (Gn 2:24). Here we clearly have a sacred order or hierarchy analogous to the ordering of the Trinitarian Persons to one another as dependent, noninterchangeable, yet equal relations. Sacred order at the human level is a sexually differentiated hierarchy that defines not only the order of creation but also the order of salvation in the marital union of Christ and the Church as the "great mystery" or "great sacrament" (Eph 5:31-33).

Hierarchy in the Church • Third, there is the hierarchy or sacred rule of the Church, manifested in the sacred order of Pope, bishops, priests, and deacons. Those in the hierarchy of the Church are not only ordered among themselves (bishops ordained into the fullness of sacramental priesthood, priests ordained into a share in that sacramental priesthood, deacons ordained not into priesthood but into a ministry of service to bishops and priests), they are also ordered to both Christ and the Church. The hierarchy of the Church provides our sacramental link to the Apostles and, through them, to Christ himself and those events by which he instituted the New Covenant (CCC 1120). Those in the Church hierarchy are therefore ordered to Christ, in whose threefold ministry as priest,

prophet, and king they share and to whom they are accountable. The hierarchy of the Church accordingly has to do with the "holy origin" of our faith, inasmuch as it protects the integrity of that origin. As Cardinal Joseph Ratzinger has pointed out: "Hierarchy . . . means not holy domination but holy origin. Hierarchical service and ministry is thus guarding an origin that is holy, and not making arbitrary dispositions and decisions" (*Church, Ecumenism and Politics*, p. 128).

At the same time, the clerical hierarchy, or ordained ministry, is ordered to serve those who make up the royal priesthood of the faithful (CCC 1120, 1547). This means that the hierarchy has the responsibility through preaching, teaching, and the sacraments to make present the grace and truth of Christ to all members of the Church. In this way, the hierarchy of the Church serves the holiness of the Church and all of her members.

The members in their turn are ordered to the holiness of the world. The laity are called to find "the means for permeating social, political, and economic realities with the demands of Christian doctrine and life" (CCC 899) and ultimately, as Vatican Council II teaches, to consecrate the world to God (*Dogmatic Constitution on the Church, Lumen Gentium*, 34; cf. CCC 901).

In sum, then, the Catholic faith recognizes the reality of a sacred order in God (the triune communion of three equal, noninterchangeable, mutually dependent Relations of Father, Son, and Holy Spirit), a sacred order in creation that reflects God (the marital ordering of Adam and Eve as equal, noninterchangeable, mutually dependent relations of husband and wife), and a sacred order that links God and man in the Incarnation of Jesus Christ and Christ to the Church in the relations of bridegroom and bride. The ordained hierarchy of the Church is therefore one manifestation among many of the hierarchical character or sacred ordering of God himself and of God's mystery or plan, formulated before creation and set forth in Jesus Christ, to unite all things in heaven and earth to himself (Eph 1:9-10).

Many people today oppose hierarchy in the name of equality. But hierarchy as such has nothing to do with either equality or inequality. The opposite of hierarchy is not equality; its opposite is *anarchy*, the absence of law, rule, or order.

Scripture speaks of sin as the "mystery of lawlessness" and of Satan as the "lawless one" (2 Thes 2:7, 8). The opposite of hierarchy is therefore that sin, or disobedience, which refuses to accept the hierarchy or sacred order of God's mystery or plan. Jesus Christ's obedience to the Father — which is the "sacred origin" of all things, including, in a sense, the divine order of the Trinity — is the foundation upon which the hierarchy or sacred order of the "new creation" is made possible as a reaffirmation of the original hierarchy or sacred ordering of the whole of creation.

See: Bishop; Bride of Christ; Church, Nature, Origin, and Structure of; Deacon; Fatherhood of God; Holy Orders; Imago Dei; Priest; Sexuality, Human; Trinity; Women, Ecclesial and Social Roles of; Women, Ordination of.

Selected Readings: CCC 238-255, 355-373, 874-887, 897-913, 1120, 1536-1538, 1544-1571. J. Little, "Egalitarianism versus Hierarchy," in *The Church and the Culture War: Secular Anarchy versus Sacred Order.*

Joyce A. Little

HINDUISM

The most intricate Oriental rug pales before Hinduism's shimmering variety and color. Simple domestic shrines carry on the legacy of great Ankgor Wat. The gods are Brahma the Creator and Vishnu the Preserver and Shiva the Destroyer, beautiful Durga and black-faced Kali, gods with many arms or elephant heads, the Lord of the cosmic dance. At the same time, God is one, eternal, ineffable, like a still sheet of water without ripple or horizon. In modern India, blue-suited businessmen bustle past Brahmins with shaved heads and flowing robes, while pilgrims by the thousands purify themselves in the holy Ganges. Sacred cows graze amid want. Though Hinduism may have its sinners as Christianity does, it also produces holy persons like Mohandas Gandhi and accepts those like Mother Teresa of Calcutta.

So rich and complex is the Hindu weave that no brief account can do more than name the principal threads. It is an ancient faith of unclear origin, at least three thousand years old. Although defining a Hindu orthodoxy is difficult, about 750 million people, mostly Indians, count themselves adherents. Hindus divide themselves into sects and cults (though no longer officially into castes) centered on the teaching of certain leaders and the worship of certain deities. Yet all are bound together by what one writer calls a "high tradition."

Hindu Beliefs • This tradition is remarkable for the breadth of its vision, for the vast range of human difference it embraces and tries to interpret. Like Christianity, Hinduism recognizes the superiority of spiritual to physical riches; indeed, it places even greater stress on asceticism and detachment from the world. Still, Hinduism does not reject the pleasures of the flesh. Hinduism claims that people may legitimately choose to be hedonists, though they should act prudently and avoid harming others. Fame, wealth, and power are likewise considered human goods and worthy of pursuit.

The Hindu sage knows, however, that pleasure and worldly success, being essentially private satisfactions for the ego, will eventually lose their allure. Sooner or later, the individual soul, or *jiva*, will hear a higher call. This call may lead to the religion of service, where individuals devote themselves to others or to the human community at large. Yet even this selfless dedication has limits, because human history is finite, and suffering and evil can seem insurmountable.

Spirituality in Hinduism • What remains? For the Christian, salvation, heaven, union with God. The Hindu would probably agree, though he would use different words and a different theology and cosmology. The pinnacle of the spiritual life, according to Hinduism, is to experience one's innermost soul, the *Atman*, and to realize in a flash of insight that this *Atman* participates in *Brahman*, the godhead. Beneath the mask of individual personality, beneath the heavy layers of desire for pleasure, success, even service, lies an inexpressible reality. By nature, we all seek infinite being, infinite awareness, and infinite joy. We find all three — and *shantih,* or peace — by searching within.

This search is more than a life's journey. Hinduism teaches that individual *jivas* are incarnated again and again in different organisms. In the early stages, spiritual progress is automatic, a sort of evolution. Once the *jiva* attains consciousness in a human body, however, it must earn enlightenment by clearing away the mire that cakes and obscures the light at its core. The soul must struggle for *mukti,* freedom from endless reincarnations, freedom to enter Nirvana. At any given time, different individuals will be at different stages along this spiritual journey. While some zigzag higher, others may spin a lifelong round of pleasure or become idolators and remain at a standstill. Others may actually regress for a time, burying the *Atman* deeper by their evil actions.

Thus, Hinduism's snapshot of the human race will always reveal a chaotic Babel of aspirants and slackers. Hinduism has no vision of social progress, of building the kingdom of God on earth. To the Hindu, the world is simply a stage on which the drama of individual souls plays out. The plot of each drama is ruled by *karma,* the law of moral cause and effect. Every thought or action carries consequences, driving the *jiva* higher or pushing it further into darkness. Though often described as fatalist, Hinduism assigns all responsibility to the person, which is the product of its own decisions and must win through to Nirvana by deliberate acts of will.

The Role of Yoga • It follows that, for those who have passed beyond the Path of Desire, beyond the wish for pleasure and success, Hinduism is a religion of discipline. Aspirants practice *yoga,* a word related to yoke; it prescribes a course of spiritual training. There are four *yogas* appropriate to different temperaments: that of knowledge, that of love, that of work, and that of meditation. All aim at detachment from the self and from the world's distractions. Though the West is most familiar with a diluted form of meditation, the pathway to God most congenial to the Christian spirit is *bhakti,* the *yoga* of love. We noted

earlier that the goal of the Hindu seeker is union with God. To *bhaktas,* however, this unity is not total immersion in an impersonal Oversoul, but the unity of lovers who preserve their separate identities. The Hindu classic *Bhagavad-Gita,* the Song of God, presents Nirvana as an unending act of perfect worship.

Although the goal of *bhakti yoga* may echo the Christian beatific vision, the two religions are profoundly different. Although, properly understood, Hinduism's myriad gods and goddesses are emanations of the *Brahman* and mere aids to imagination, nevertheless for many of the faithful Hinduism is polytheistic. Moreover, the Hindu sage turns inward to find God, not seeking him in nature, in other human beings, or in a transcendent person who is totally other. Most importantly, Hinduism is not an incarnational religion centering on a God-man sent for our salvation. It lacks a formal sacramental system crowned by the Eucharist and does not recognize Jesus as the definitive revelation of God in human history.

The wide disparities among the world's great religions make it hard to imagine a final reconciliation. However, the Second Vatican Council firmly taught that, while the Church is the ordinary means of salvation, "the plan of salvation also includes those who acknowledge the Creator" (*Dogmatic Constitution on the Church, Lumen Gentium,* 16). Pope John Paul II tirelessly promotes interreligious dialogue, inspired by the words of the *Declaration on the Relationship of the Church to Non-Christian Religions:* "The Church, therefore, urges her sons to enter with prudence and charity into discussion and collaboration with members of other religions. Let Christians, while witnessing to their own faith and way of life, acknowledge, preserve and encourage the spiritual and moral truths found among non-Christians" (*Nostra Aetate,* 2).

See: Buddhism; Ecumenism; Evangelization; Islam; Missionary Activity; Religion, Virtue of; Theosophy.

Suggested Readings: CCC 839-856. Vatican Council II, *Dogmatic Constitution on the Church, Lumen Gentium,* 16-17; *Declaration on the Rela-*

tionship of the Church to Non-Christian Religions, Nostra Aetate. John Paul II, *On the Permanent Validity of the Church's Missionary Mandate, Redemptoris Missio,* 94-99. "Hinduism" in G. Parrinder, ed., *World Religions.* H. Smith, "Hinduism," *The Religions of Man.*

David M. Byers

HOLY DAYS OF OBLIGATION

Today some people question whether the Catholic Church is authorized to prescribe attendance at Mass on Sundays or the eve and other so-called "days of obligation." The complaint goes more or less like this: "Is it not more in keeping with personal freedom and devotion to go on my own, say, every Tuesday?" The Church doubtless has the God-given authority to oblige the faithful to attend Mass on certain days; she has also deemed it wise that we should, at least once a week, worship together (cf. CCC 2042-2043).

To satisfy this precept, one may attend Mass "anywhere" that a "Catholic rite" is followed (CCC 2180). On designated holy days, the "faithful are obliged to participate in the Eucharist . . . unless excused for a serious reason (for example, illness, the care of infants) or dispensed by their own pastor. Those who deliberately fail in this obligation commit a grave sin" (CCC 2181).

Thus do the faithful recognize the day on which Jesus resurrected and open themselves to possible graces and inspirations from what are usually a more solemn and uplifting liturgy, better and longer homilies, and, not least, possibly more pious peers. Prayerful and expectant participation in the Sunday Mass — much more than mere hurried and distracted attendance — should prove so fruitful that people are led to participate in Mass on other days as well (cf. CCC 1384-1395, especially 1391-1392).

For the Church universal there are ten holy days of obligation in addition to all Sundays. In the United States, two of these solemnities (Epiphany and Christ's Body and Blood) are celebrated on the nearest Sunday; the feasts of St. Joseph (March 19) and Sts. Peter and Paul (June 29) are not days

of obligation in the U.S.; the other six days, when Catholics are bound to participate in Mass, are Christmas, Ascension Thursday, Mary's Immaculate Conception (feast of the national patroness, December 8), Mary the Mother of God (January 1), her Assumption (August 15), and All Saints (November 1). In the case of the last three feasts, U.S. Catholics are exempt from the obligation when the feast falls on either Saturday or Monday, although the U.S. National Conference of Catholic Bishops encourages the faithful to find personal ways of devoutly observing these exempted solemnities: preferably by choosing, if possible, to participate in the Eucharistic sacrifice. The Code of Canon Law (Canon 1246.2) also makes allowance for diocesan bishops to establish, where appropriate, special feast days of obligation for their areas, but not as a permanent fixture without the Apostolic See's authorization.

See: Lord's Day; Religion, Virtue of; Worship.

Suggested Readings: CCC 2042-2043, 2177, 2180, 2185, 2187-2188.

HOLY ORDERS

The Catholic Church centers her teaching on the sacrament of Holy Orders around the mystery of Holy Thursday. In the course of the institution of the Eucharist at the Last Supper, Jesus confides the worship of the new dispensation to the Twelve. From that moment on, the Church confesses that the Eucharist "is the principal and central *raison d'être* of the sacrament of the priesthood" (Pope John Paul II, *Dominicae Cenae* [1980]).

Most of the sixteenth-century Protestant Reformers challenged this truth of the Catholic faith. As a reply to their rejection, in both theory and practice, of a sacramental priesthood, the Council of Trent considered it necessary to issue a solemn warning: "If anyone says that by these words, 'Do this in memory of me' (Lk 22:19; 1 Cor 11:24), Christ did not institute the Apostles as priests, or did not ordain them, so that priests might offer his body and blood for themselves and for others: let him be anathema" (Council of Trent, session 22 [1562]). In this way the Church reaffirmed the biblical truth that the ministerial priesthood is at the service of the common priesthood of all believers.

The High Priestly Prayer of Jesus, as recorded in John's Gospel, places the connection between ministerial priesthood and Eucharistic mystery within the larger context of God's plan to bring the human race to a knowledge of saving truth. Jesus prays for the Twelve: "Sanctify them in the truth; thy word is truth. As thou didst send me into the world, so I have sent them into the world. And for their sake I consecrate myself, that they also may be consecrated in truth" (Jn 17:17-19). The consecration of the bishop, of the priest, and, in their own way, of deacons receives its meaning from that of Christ himself. So the *Catechism of the Catholic Church*, citing Vatican Council II's *Dogmatic Constitution on the Church, Lumen Gentium*, 11, states: "Those who receive the sacrament of Holy Orders are *consecrated* in Christ's name 'to feed the Church by the word and grace of God' " (1535). As one of the sacraments established for the service of the Church's communion, Holy Orders provides the world with men whose task is to exercise Christ's work of sanctification through word and sacrament until the end of time.

Three "Orders" Within the Sacrament • The Church recognizes three "orders" within the sacrament of Holy Orders: the order of bishops (*ordo episcoporum*), the order of presbyters, or priests (*ordo presbyterorum*), the order of deacons (*ordo diaconorum*). In Roman antiquity, the Latin word *ordo* designated a body of persons established for a specific task or function; so, for example, one can think of a governing body as an instance of a political *ordo*. Ordination, then, denotes one's incorporation into an *ordo*. While other orders of service can be envisaged, it is the practice of the Church to use the term "order" only to express the sacramental reality.

The notion must be understood analogically, for Holy Orders changes the very person of the one who is ordained. Even with the sacraments related to service in the Church, the sacramental reality can never be adequately described in terms of function alone. Here the analogy of faith operates. Thus, the *Catechism* tells us: "Ordination is also called *consecratio*, for it is a setting apart and an investiture by Christ himself for his Church" (1538). This sacramental consecration replaces all other means — such as election, designation, delegation, and institution — of establishing a person in a position of ministry. The Church holds that the act of priestly consecration effects a configuration of the ordained to Christ.

The fundamental reason for holding sacramental ordination to constitute something more than the ceremonial designation of a person to perform a specific function rests on what the Church believes about the work of grace. The sacramental action always bestows an abiding grace. Pope John Paul II summarizes this teaching in his apostolic exhortation *Pastores Dabo Vobis*, summing up the 1990 Synod of Bishops on the priesthood: "By the sacramental anointing of Holy Orders, the Holy Spirit configures [priests] in a new and special way to Jesus Christ the Head and Shepherd; he forms and strengthens them with his pastoral charity; and he gives them an authoritative role in the Church as servants of the proclamation of the Gospel to every people and of the fullness of Christian life of all the baptized" (15). Priestly ordination, then, enables ordinary men to become instruments of God's grace. This happens of course without diminishing the uniqueness of Christ's priesthood. St. Thomas Aquinas reminds us, "Only Christ is the true priest, the others being only his ministers" (*Commentary on the Hebrews*, 8:4).

Because it serves as a symbolic prefigurement of the sacrament of Holy Orders, the several ordination rites for bishops, priests, and deacons refer to the priesthood of the Old Testament, the priesthood of Aaron, and the service of the Levites. To grasp the radical difference between the ritual service of the Old Testament priests and the sacramental work of the priests of the new dispensation, we must consider what Christ himself accomplished by his life on earth, especially by his death on the cross in satisfaction for sins and by his glorious Resurrection. This theme occupies the author of the Letter to the Hebrews, who asks: "Now if perfection had been attainable through the Levitical priesthood (for under it people received the law), what further need would there have been for another priest to arise after the order of Melchizedek, rather than one named after the order of Aaron?" (Heb 7:11). By posing the question, the inspired author prepares us to recognize Christ as the priest who provides "the surety of a better covenant" (Heb 7:22). This is the new and everlasting covenant written in the blood of Christ. "The redemptive sacrifice of Christ is unique, accomplished once for all; yet it is made present in the Eucharistic sacrifice of the Church" (CCC 1545). St. Thomas Aquinas shows himself the common teacher of the Church when he writes: "Christ is the source of all priesthood: the priest of the old law was a figure of Christ, and the priest of the new law acts in the person of Christ" (*Summa Theologiae*, III, q. 22, a. 4, c.).

The ministerial or hierarchical priesthood of bishops and priests serves the communion of the Church by building up the Body of Christ. In his encyclical on the liturgy *Mediator Dei* (1947), Pope Pius XII explained: "It is the same priest, Christ Jesus, whose sacred person his minister truly represents. Now the minister, by reason of the sacerdotal consecration which he has received, is truly made like to the high priest and possesses the authority to act in the power and place of the person of Christ himself." There is something radical about the priest. So much does the sacrament of Holy Orders configure a man to Christ that even one whose personal life may lack the good character his office requires still acts in the Person of Christ. It is part of God's gracious design for the good of the Church that the "sacred power" of the priest, provided he intends to remain in conformity with what Christ wants for his Church, is always efficacious in the Church and for the People of God. The sacraments are for the good of men and the communion of the Church. This rich confidence does not mean the sacraments are magic. Rather, they are sacraments of faith. But since it is indispensable that the members of Christ's Body receive the sacraments of Christ's love, their effi-

cacy does not depend on the holiness of the one who celebrates them.

Bishops, Priests, Deacons • The three degrees of the sacrament of Holy Orders are clearly taught in the Second Vatican Council's *Dogmatic Constitution on the Church, Lumen Gentium*: "The divinely instituted ecclesiastical ministry is exercised in different degrees by those who even from ancient times have been called bishops, priests, and deacons" (28). Bishops and priests share in the priesthood of Christ; deacons, ordained to a degree of service, are meant to help and serve them.

The order of bishops embraces those who are regarded as transmitters of the apostolic line. The fullness of the sacrament of Holy Orders is conferred by episcopal consecration, and so the episcopate is called the acme of the sacred ministry. It belongs to the bishop to fulfill the Messianic roles of Christ: to sanctify, to teach, and to rule. This spiritual power comes from a gift of the Holy Spirit that constitutes bishops as true and authentic teachers of the faith and the Church's pontiffs and pastors. Because the episcopal ministry is exercised in communion with the head and other members of the episcopal college, a special intervention of the Roman Pontiff is required in order that a priest might lawfully receive episcopal consecration. While the Church encourages bishops to be solicitous for all the churches, each bishop has pastoral care of a particular Church entrusted to him. The bishop is most himself when he celebrates the Eucharist, with his priests concelebrating and the deacons assisting.

The order of priests numbers those who are the coworkers of the bishops. Though they do not possess the supreme degree of the pontifical office, priests nonetheless share in the sacerdotal dignity of the bishops, on whom they depend in the exercise of their own proper power. In virtue of the sacrament of Holy Orders, priests are consecrated in order to preach the Gospel and shepherd the faithful as well as to celebrate divine worship "as true priests of the New Testament" (*Lumen Gentium*, 28).

The priest is ordained for the Eucharist, and he is a priest precisely inasmuch as he is able to offer the sacrifice of Christ's love under the sacramental signs of bread and wine. Because this sacrifice can be celebrated only in communion with the local bishop, and through him with the bishop of Rome, the priest depends on the bishop, to whom he owes respect and obedience.

Love and respect for the Roman Pontiff, who serves as a father in the faith for the whole Church, remains a special obligation for the priest. The relationship of the priest to his bishop further includes a special relationship to all the priests of his diocese. Each presbyterium — the body of priests within the diocese — forms a unit of the "sacramental brotherhood" that the sacrament of Holy Orders creates among those who are ordained.

The order of deacons includes those who are ordained "not unto the priesthood, but unto the ministry" (*Lumen Gentium,* 29). The ordination of a deacon, which is accomplished through the laying on of hands by the bishop, but not by the other presbyters as happens at the ordination of priests, marks him with a character that cannot be removed. (The same *a fortiori* is true for the orders of bishop and priest, with each ordained man participating, as his order dictates, in the office of Christ's own priesthood.)

It belongs to the deacon to distribute Holy Communion, to assist at and to bless marriages, to proclaim the Gospel and preach, to preside at funeral services, and to dedicate himself to the ministries of charity. Since the Second Vatican Council, there again exists in the Church a permanent diaconate enabling men who are involved in these works and who are ordained to receive the strength that the sacramental grace brings.

The bishop alone can validly confer the sacrament of Holy Orders. Because the Church is bound by the choice that the Lord himself made in constituting the college of the twelve Apostles, she teaches as irreformable doctrine that only men can be candidates for the sacrament of Holy Orders. Like any grace, the grace to be a priest can be received only as an unmerited gift.

Because the priest must devote himself entirely to the study of sacred truth and to the service of charity, the practice of the Western Church is to call men of faith who are willing to remain celibate for the sake of the kingdom of heaven (cf. Mt 19:12). Exceptions to this norm, which is considered of great spiritual value for the Church, can be made in specific cases, usually to welcome into the one priesthood of Christ married men who formerly enjoyed a religious ministry in one of the churches of the Episcopal communion but now are in full communion with the Church. The Eastern Church does ordain as priests and deacons men who are married, although in East and West a man who has already received the sacrament of Holy Orders can no longer marry.

Since Vatican Council II, Catholics have unfortunately become more and more acquainted with men who have received the sacrament of Holy Orders but no longer discharge the functions or are bound by the obligations associated with ordination. When a man "leaves the priesthood," he no longer performs priestly actions, but neither does he become again, strictly speaking, a layman. The indelible character imparted by the sacrament of Holy Orders (like Baptism and Confirmation) means that, once configured to Christ as a priest, a man always remains marked by the priestly vocation and ministry. In the same way, the baptized can never completely renounce their status as God's adopted children, even if they abandon the practice of the faith and no longer participate in the life of the Church.

In the second century, St. Ignatius of Antioch (died c. 107) already testifies to the three orders that the Holy Spirit creates among those who receive sacerdotal consecration. He further describes the peace and harmony that should characterize the Christian communion, to the extent it enjoys a right relationship to the hierarchical priesthood. Ignatius interprets the sacrament of Holy Orders as an instrument of God's saving action in the world. He addresses the community at Magnesia, which he had visited on the way to Rome where he would be martyred: "I exhort you to strive to do all things in harmony with God: the bishop is to preside in the place of God, while the presbyters are to function as the council of the Apostles, and the deacons, who are most dear to me, are entrusted with the ministry of Jesus Christ" (*Letter to the Magnesians* 6, 1).

See: Bishop; Celibacy, Priestly; Deacon; Eucharist; In Persona Christi Capitis; Ministry; Priest; Priesthood in the Old Testament; Priesthood of Christ; Priesthood of the Faithful; Women, Ordination of.

Suggested Readings: CCC 1533-1600. Vatican Council II, *Dogmatic Constitution on the Church, Lumen Gentium,* Ch. III; *Decree on the Bishops' Pastoral Office in the Church, Christus Dominus.* John Paul II, *I Will Give You Shepherds, Pastores Dabo Vobis.* J. Galot, *Theology of the Priesthood.* A. Nichols, O.P., *Holy Order.*

Romanus Cessario, O.P.

HOLY SEE

The Church is universal (this is what "Catholic" literally means); the message entrusted to her is for all mankind. The fact that the Church is often called the *Roman* Catholic Church does not indicate a limitation of her universality, but is rather a condition of it. A universal mission needs a reference point and a source of guidance to ensure, along with its fidelity to the will of Christ, the genuineness of its work of evangelization in all countries and continents. That reference point lies in Rome.

Each bishop has his "see," or area of jurisdiction. The Holy See is the See of Peter and his successors as Bishop of Rome.

The Pope and bishops comprise a college or body concerned for all the churches and with "supreme and full authority over the universal Church" — power that cannot be exercised without the agreement of the Roman Pontiff, who himself has "full, supreme and universal power over the entire Church, a power which he can always exercise unhindered" (Vatican II, *Dogmatic Constitution on the Church, Lumen Gentium,* 22). The episcopal college expresses "the multifariousness and universality of the People of God; and . . . the unity of the flock of Christ, in so far as it is assembled under one head" (*Lumen Gentium,* 22; cf. CCC 880-886).

The Pope has the care of all the local churches, not only to ensure that, allowing for legitimate local variations or inculturations, the means of salvation entrusted to his Church by Christ (doctrine and sacraments) are preserved everywhere, but also to provide for administrative details that serve the good of Christ's faithful: the creation of dioceses according to demographic needs, the appointments of new bishops, etc. The Holy See is also a final court of appeal, above all through its tribunals, the Apostolic Signatura and the Roman Rota. Here any member of the faithful anywhere can turn who feels that his or her rights have not been respected by lower courts (diocesan or regional appeal courts).

The terms "Holy See" and "the Vatican" are often used as equivalent. The Vatican City State also exists as a state in its own right and has membership in the main international organs designed to promote human welfare. This enables the Holy See to intervene internationally with the force of its moral authority in defense of the dignity of the person and genuine human progress and rights.

The departments of the Roman Curia, which helps the Holy Father in his work of governing the Church, include the Secretariat of State, the Congregation for the Doctrine of the Faith, the Congregations of Bishops, of the Clergy, of Divine Worship, the Pontifical Councils for the Laity, for the Family, etc.

See: Bishop; Church, Nature, Origin, and Structure of; Collegiality; Inculturation; Pope.

HOLY SPIRIT

The Catholic Church professes her faith in the Holy Spirit as "the Lord and giver of life" (Nicene Creed). This life has its origin in the Father and is given to us through the Son. It is made our interior personal possession by the Holy Spirit. Through Baptism, the sacrament of faith, the Holy Spirit enables us personally to be reborn as children of God and sharers of divine life. This rebirth unto eternal life reveals the divine *economy* of our salvation: The eternal plan of the Triune God, which has its origin in the Father, is offered to us in the Son, and reaches its completion in the Holy Spirit (CCC 683).

The Spirit in the Divine Economy • In the eternal plan of our salvation, one discovers the link between the mystery of God's inmost life of distinct Divine Persons within the Trinity (termed *theologia*) and the economy whereby God reveals through all his works the community of Divine Persons and how they share their communal life with us (CCC 236). By creating the world and then bringing it back into union with himself by redeeming it, God reveals his own inner life. This is the teaching of St. Thomas Aquinas: that the temporal missions of the Son and the Holy Spirit are the realization of the eternal processions of the Son and the Holy Spirit (*Summa Theologiae*, I, q. 43).

In the divine economy, the missions of the Son and the Holy Spirit are distinct but inseparable (CCC 689). They both presuppose a relationship with the Father, who is the principle without a beginning, or unoriginated origin, and who sends the Son and the Holy Spirit but cannot *be* sent. In the decisive moment of the Son's redemptive Incarnation, as well as in the communication of divine life by the Holy Spirit, the Son and the Holy Spirit come in an entirely new way, even though they already have been in the world from the beginning of creation. The temporal missions of the Son and the Holy Spirit not only reveal their eternal processions in the inner life of God but, more importantly, culminate freely and efficaciously in a created effect that makes the world and humanity exist in a new relationship with them.

When the Father sends his Son, the Eternal Word, to become our incarnate Savior, he always sends his Spirit, the "breath" that underlies the Word. The visible mission of the Word made flesh always is accompanied by the Holy Spirit, who reveals the Son and disposes us to welcome him in faith (CCC 687). "No one can say 'Jesus is Lord' except by the Holy Spirit" (1 Cor 12:3). Thus the Son and the Holy Spirit are inseparably joined in their missions but remain distinct Persons (CCC 689). The Holy Spirit is the light that enables us to know the Son; or, as Hans Urs von Balthasar says,

the Spirit can best be understood as "the Unknown One beyond the Word."

The divine economy according to the New Testament is expressed by this formula: "All comes from the Father, through his Son, Jesus Christ, and in the Holy Spirit, and through the Mediation of the Son, in the Holy Spirit, all returns to the Father" (Cyprian Vagaggini, *Theological Dimensions of the Liturgy: A General Treatise on the Theology of the Liturgy*, pp. 198-199). This circular dynamic, which takes place on behalf of our salvation, can be described as a going from God and a return to God. In this broad perspective, the Father appears primarily as the one from whom and to whom all things come, the Son as the one through whom all things are created and redeemed, while the Holy Spirit is the one in whom all things are sanctified and brought together in unity. In this way, the Spirit can be described as the origin and source of our sanctification, our adoption as children of God. "But when the time had fully come, God sent forth his Son, born of a woman, born under the law, to redeem those who were under the law, so that we might receive adoption as sons. And because you are sons, God has sent the Spirit of his Son into our hearts crying, '*Abba*! Father!' " (Gal 4:4-6).

Through the Son's redeeming Incarnation, the Holy Spirit is fully revealed and given, and thus is able to be known as a Person, sharing a relation to the Father and the Son and to ourselves. When referring to the Holy Spirit in relation to ourselves, Jesus calls him the Paraclete, literally "he who is called to one's side" or "Counselor"; or perhaps it would be more correct to understand the Holy Spirit as the most intimate friend. Jesus promises this beloved companion to be with his disciples forever (Jn 14:16). What is more, he will teach them all things and bring them to a remembrance of all that Jesus said and did (Jn 14:26). For he is "the Spirit of truth, whom the world cannot receive" (Jn 14:17). Moreover, Jesus tells his disciples: "You know him, for he dwells with you and will be in you" (Jn 14:17). This teaching underlies the doctrine of the divine indwelling, namely, that the Holy Spirit is the personal presence of God's love dwelling in our hearts, producing fellowship with the Son, and making us adoptive children of the Father. "God's love has been poured into our hearts through the Holy Spirit which has been given to us" (Rom 5:5).

The Spirit in the Church's Mission • God's love, which is diffusive of itself, is personified in the Holy Spirit as the reciprocal love of the Father and the Son. As the personal expression of God's love, the Holy Spirit becomes the source and dynamic force of the Church's mission as well as her unity. When the Father desired to reveal his love personally to us, he sent the Son for our salvation. Similarly, when the Father wanted to effect within us what the Son had done and accomplished for us by his redemptive Incarnation, he sent the Holy Spirit to communicate personally his love for us. In an analogous way, by continuing the self-communication of the Father's love for us in the missions of the Son and the Holy Spirit, the Church becomes "the universal sacrament of salvation" (Vatican Council II, *Dogmatic Constitution on the Church, Lumen Gentium*, 48).

The whole purpose of God's creating, redeeming, and sanctifying the world through the missions of the Son and the Holy Spirit is to draw us into the communion of his divine life and share it. God, who is self-giving love, *agape*, gives himself more and more to bring us into a sharing of his love. As the doctrinal principles of the Second Vatican Council's *Decree on the Church's Missionary Activity, Ad Gentes*, 2-5, express, the missions of the Son and the Holy Spirit flow from "fontal or fountain-like love," the love of God the Father. When *agape* is applied to God the Father, it can best be described as love flowing from love's source. The mission of the Son and the mission of the Holy Spirit, who completes the Son's salvific work, are both the revelation and efficacious source of God the Father's love for us. Similarly, the Church's mission continues the communication of the Father's love through the Son and in the Holy Spirit. The Church, dependent upon the missions of the Son and the Spirit, becomes the very fruitfulness or harvest of the Spirit (Gal 5:22).

When the Holy Spirit visibly came in the form of tongues "as of fire" at Pentecost (Acts 2:3) so as to fill the Apostles with himself and remain with them forever, he gave birth to the Church and fulfilled the Son's promise, as given in John 14:16. Consequently, the pentecostal effusion of the Spirit means: (1) the fulfillment of the Son's promise to send the Spirit; (2) the public manifestation of the Church in the world; (3) the inauguration of the Church's universal mission of preaching the Gospel to all nations; and (4) the foreshadowing of the Church's universality, as signified in the fact that this Church of the New Covenant speaks all languages and understands and embraces all tongues in self-giving love (cf. Acts 2:5-12). The Fathers of the Church contrast Pentecost to the dispersion of Babel in Genesis 11; for the image of Pentecost overcoming the divisive confusion of Babel illustrates how the Holy Spirit restores through the Church the unity of all humanity that had been damaged by sin. The Church's mission, begun at Pentecost, is to announce, bear witness, make present, and spread the communion of the Holy Trinity, which patterns the solidarity of the whole human race (CCC 738).

With the coming of the Holy Spirit at Pentecost, the Church established during Christ's life in the call of the Apostles began her universal mission to the world. The pentecostal outpouring consecrated the Apostles for their salvific mission, just as Christ had been anointed by the Spirit for his redemptive mission, first at his conception in the womb of the Virgin Mary and also with the Spirit's descent upon him like a dove at his Baptism. This can be seen more clearly in the "Johannine Pentecost," where the risen Christ on the evening of the first Easter comes and stands among them, saying, " 'Peace be with you. As the Father has sent me, even so I send you'. . . . He breathed on them and said to them, 'Receive the Holy Spirit' " (Jn 20:21-22). This gift of the Holy Spirit to the Apostles is for the forgiveness of sins, and thus brings the universal reconciliation of all persons with God, their neighbors, and their very selves.

The Apostles courageously collaborate with the

gift of the Holy Spirit at Pentecost to inaugurate the Church's mission of salvation. The apostolic ministry, instituted by Christ, associates in an essential way with the Holy Spirit in always and everywhere carrying on the Church's salvific mission. Just as the Son needs the Holy Spirit to bring about his salvific work in the hearts of individuals, so, too, in an analogous way the Holy Spirit of Pentecost needs the cooperation of the apostolic ministry throughout history to continue the Church's mission in God's plan of salvation.

It is important to acknowledge that at Pentecost not only the Apostles but all the faithful received the Holy Spirit. All were inspired for the Church's mission, and the Holy Spirit enkindled in their hearts the same salvific mission that Christ himself pursued. This salvific mission consists most of all in a conformity to his paschal mystery, which is the way to life through death, to glory through *kenosis* (literally, the emptying of self). Thus the Holy Spirit's action is seen as that dynamic personal force of self-giving love that enables all the faithful to participate fully in the dying and rising of Christ. This dynamic initiative of the Spirit sometimes visibly anticipates apostolic action through the charisms, gifts given to the faithful by the Spirit for the common good and the building up of the Church (cf. 1 Cor 12:4-11).

The Spirit and the Son • The Catholic Church professes the mystery of the Son's Incarnation by referring to the Holy Spirit; the Nicene Creed says: "By the power of the Holy Spirit he became incarnate from the Virgin Mary, and was made man." Thus "the conception and birth of Jesus Christ are in fact the greatest work accomplished by the Holy Spirit in the history of creation and salvation: the supreme grace — 'the grace of union,' source of every other grace, as St. Thomas explains" (Pope John Paul II, encyclical *The Lord and Giver of Life, Dominum et Vivificantem*, 50 [1986]; cf. St. Thomas Aquinas, *Summa Theologiae,* IIIa, q. 2, aa. 10-12; q. 6, a. 6; q. 7, a. 13). "By the power of the Holy Spirit" Jesus became man whom the Church, in the words of the Nicene Creed, professes to be "the only Son of God eternally begotten of the Father, God from God, Light from Light,

true God from true God, begotten not made, one in being with the Father."

In the Father's plan, the Son was consecrated for his redemptive mission by the anointing of the Holy Spirit (Acts 10:38), making him to be the Christ, or Messiah (literally, Anointed One), both at his conception and at his Baptism in the Jordan. Luke 3:21-22 relates how, following his Baptism, while he was praying, the Holy Spirit descended upon him in bodily form, like a dove, and the voice of the Father was heard: "Thou art my beloved Son, with thee I am well pleased." By recounting Jesus' baptism in this way, the Synoptic Gospels emphasize Jesus' role as the servant of the Lord upon whom the Spirit rests, he who had come to "bring forth justice," to open blind eyes, to release prisoners, and to be a light to the nations according to the prophecy of Isaiah (42:1-9, 49:1-9). Even more importantly, Jesus, like the suffering servant in Isaiah, had come to make a sin offering of himself, bearing others' sins and interceding for their forgiveness (Is 53:10, 12).

Similarly, the Holy Spirit anointed Jesus for his public ministry, as the one "whom the Father consecrated and sent into the world" (Jn 10:36), and as the fulfillment of the Messianic prophecy of Isaiah (61:1-2). In Luke 4:18 Jesus cites the latter passage, proclaiming in the synagogue of Nazareth: "The Spirit of the Lord is upon me, because he has anointed me. He has sent me to preach good news to the poor, to heal the contrite of heart, to preach release to the captives and sight to the blind."

Scripture speaks of Jesus throughout his public ministry as being "full of the Holy Spirit" and at times "led by the Spirit" (Lk 4:1). The evangelist Mark tells us that, following the baptism, "the Spirit immediately drove him out into the wilderness" (Mk 1:12) to begin his temptations by Satan. All this reminds us that the reason why Christ suffered and died, rose and ascended into heaven, was to communicate to us that same Holy Spirit under whose guidance and assistance he had obediently accomplished the Father's will.

Designated by the New Testament as the Spirit of Christ, the Holy Spirit's identity is the very humility of God, since his mission is always in relation to the mission of the Son and not for himself. We must never forget, however, that the Holy Spirit is a Divine Person, just as the Father and the Son are. The Holy Spirit's mission is distinct and proper to him, for he is to effect and bring to pass within us what the Son did and accomplished for us on a single occasion in his paschal mystery. The Holy Spirit effects in us the redemption brought about by and in Christ. All this means the Spirit is not simply the energy by which the Son completes his redemptive mission in us.

The Holy Spirit has been working in relation to the Son since creation, having "spoken through the prophets," and making preparation for the Gospel in the just men and women of every time and place. The Spirit already was active in the world before Christ was glorified through his paschal mystery. After his glorification through the cross, Christ sent the Holy Spirit from the Father as he had promised: "If I go, I will send him to you" (Jn 16:7). It is important to note, however, that "the Holy Spirit proceeds from the Father" (Jn 15:26) and the Father "gives" the Spirit (Jn 14:16). Until the time of his Son's glorification, the Father sends the Holy Spirit in the name of the Son (Jn 14:26), and the Spirit bears witness to the Son (Jn 15:26). "Thus the Father sends the Holy Spirit in the power of his Fatherhood, as he has sent the Son; but at the same time he sends him in the power of the Redemption accomplished by Christ — and in this sense, the Holy Spirit is sent also by the Son" (*Dominum et Vivificantem*, 6).

The First Council of Constantinople (381) affirmed that the Spirit is a Divine Person and expanded the doctrine in the Nicene Creed (325) to profess, "We believe . . . in the Holy Spirit, *the Lord and giver of life, who proceeds from the Father, who with the Father and the Son is worshiped and glorified, who has spoken through the prophets*" (emphasis added). This constitutes the Church's great profession of faith in the Holy Spirit.

In the Latin tradition of the Nicene Creed, it is the Father who from all eternity generates the Son

and together with the Son spirates (breathes) the Holy Spirit. This theological formulation of the Latin West finds dogmatic expression in the addition to the text of the Nicene Creed, originally common to West and East, of the controversial expression *Filioque* (literally, "and the Son"). Thus the Latin tradition in the Creed came to profess that the Spirit "proceeds from the Father *and the Son (Filioque)*." It is of note that significant progress toward legitimate complementarity was made in Vatican Council II's *Decree on the Church's Missionary Activity, Ad Gentes*, 2, by the adoption of the Oriental formula: that the Holy Spirit proceeds from the Father through the Son (CCC 246-248).

See: Baptism; Baptism of Christ; Charisms; Church, Nature, Origin, and Structure of; Confirmation; Economy of Salvation; Fatherhood of God; Gifts and Fruits of the Holy Spirit; God, Nature and Attributes of; Hierarchy; Incarnation; Jesus Christ, God and Man; Jesus Christ, Life of; Sins Against the Holy Spirit; Trinity.

Suggested Readings: CCC 232-267, 683-747, 797-801. Vatican Council II, *Dogmatic Constitution on the Church, Lumen Gentium*, 2-4, 17; *Decree on the Church's Missionary Activity, Ad Gentes*, 2-5. Leo XIII, *On the Holy Spirit, Divinum Illud Munus*. Pius XII, *On the Mystical Body of Christ, Mystici Corporis Christi*. John Paul II, *The Lord and Giver of Life, Dominum et Vivificantem*; *On the Permanent Validity of the Church's Missionary Mandate, Redemptoris Missio*. J. Anderson, *A Vatican II Pneumatology of the Paschal Mystery*. Y. Congar, *I Believe in the Holy Spirit*. W. Kasper, *The God of Jesus Christ*.

James B. Anderson

HOMICIDE

Homicide is the direct and voluntary killing of an innocent human being. It is forbidden by the fifth commandment, and has been recognized throughout Church history as one of those human actions that is never justified. In 1965, the Second Vatican Council condemned "all offenses against life itself, such as murder, genocide, abortion, euthanasia and willful suicide" as crimes that dishonor the Creator (*Pastoral Constitution on the Church in the Modern World, Gaudium et Spes*, 27). In 1995, Pope John Paul II solemnly reaffirmed this tradition: "By the authority which Christ conferred upon Peter and his Successors, and in communion with the Bishops of the Catholic Church, I confirm that the direct and voluntary killing of an innocent human being is always gravely immoral" (Pope John Paul II, *The Gospel of Life, Evangelium Vitae*, 57).

Each word or phrase in the definition of homicide is important. For example, "direct and voluntary killing" involves actively willing someone's death, either as an end in itself (e.g., out of hatred) or as a means to another end (e.g., in order to gain profit or end suffering). If death is not intended, but is foreseen as the side effect of another action with its own legitimate end, the killing is indirect (e.g., an act of self-defense in which lethal force is the only means of stopping the attack). While indirect killing does not fulfill the definition of homicide, it could be morally wrong on other grounds (e.g., risking someone else's life unjustly or for an insufficiently serious reason).

In speaking of an "innocent" human being, Church teaching refers not to someone without sin but to someone who is not committing an aggression against which it is necessary to defend oneself or others. Capital punishment raises special issues in this regard, discussed below.

Only the killing of human beings constitutes homicide. Animals should not be mistreated or subjected to needless suffering, but they do not have the same right to life as humans because they were not specially created in the image and likeness of God (CCC 2417-2418). Homicide does include the direct killing of human beings of all ages and conditions, from conception to natural death. The Congregation for the Doctrine of the Faith said in 1980: "Nothing and no one can in any way permit the killing of an innocent human being, whether a fetus or an embryo, an infant or an adult, an old person, or one suffering from an incurable disease or a person who is dying. Furthermore, no one is permitted to ask for this act of killing, either for himself or herself or for another person entrusted to his or her care, nor can he or she consent to it, either explicitly or implicitly. Nor can any authority legitimately recommend or permit such an action" (*Declaration on Euthanasia*, II).

Scriptural Foundations • The central importance of God's law against homicide is clear in numerous passages of Scripture. The Old Testament tells us that the first sin of human history, after Adam and Eve's initial sin of disobedience against God, is a homicide: Cain's killing of his brother Abel out of spite and envy (Gn 4:8). When God asks Abel's whereabouts, Cain sins again by lying and denying responsibility for his kin: "I do not know. Am I my brother's keeper?" (Gn 4:9). For his crime, Cain is cursed to be unfruitful and becomes "a restless wanderer on the earth" (Gn 4:12).

After most of mankind is destroyed for its sinfulness, God forges a new covenant with Noah in which he demands an accounting for each human life: "If anyone sheds the blood of man, by man shall his blood be shed; for in the image of God has man been made" (Gn 9:6). The commandment "You shall not kill" (Ex 20:13; Dt 5:17), sometimes more precisely stated as, "The innocent and the just you shall not put to death" (Ex 23:7), is an integral part of the later covenant that Moses mediates between God and the people of Israel.

Yet the Old Testament depicts violent times and a great deal of killing. Setting aside cases of war and capital punishment, which present distinct issues, there are times when it seems the innocent are killed by God or at God's command, particularly when they are members of a group that opposes God's will or the needs of Israel (e.g., Ex 12:29; Dt 3:6; Jos 10:40). Ideas of collective guilt allowed entire peoples to be depicted as God's enemies. Yet God and God alone is seen as having the right to demand an innocent person's life (Dt 32:39), because he is the Creator and the Lord of all life. To kill the innocent on one's own authority involves a sin of pride like the first sin of Adam and Eve, usurping God's unique prerogative over life and death. Only in obedience to God's direct command could any human being take innocent life.

Even in the Old Testament, however, God increasingly is seen setting aside his right to demand the life of the innocent. He tests Abraham's obedience by commanding him to kill his son Isaac, but then stops him and tells him to sacrifice an animal instead; in context, this famous passage is a repudiation of the human sacrifice practiced in other cultures of the time (Gn 22:11). In the more profound moral view of the prophetic books, God is clearly on the side of life against death: "God formed man to be imperishable; the image of his own nature he made him. But by the envy of the devil, death entered the world, and they who are in his possession experience it" (Wis 2:23-24). We are reminded that "God did not make death, nor does he rejoice in the destruction of the living" (Wis 1:13).

The theme that death and killing are provinces of Satan recurs in the New Testament. The devil is called "a murderer from the beginning" as well as "the father of lies" (Jn 8:44), recalling Cain's double sin of murder and deception. Jesus reaffirms God's commandment against killing (cf. Mt 19:18; Mk 10:19; Lk 18:20), while deepening and broadening it to forbid the hatred and anger that lead to murder (Mt 5:21-22): "Everyone who hates his brother is a murderer, and you know that no murderer has eternal life remaining in him" (1 Jn 3:15). Jesus' renunciation of violence, and his willingness to lay down his own life to save others, become an example to all Christians (1 Jn 3:16). Because "love does no evil to the neighbor," the commandments against killing and other wrongdoing toward human beings are summed up in the positive command "You shall love your neighbor as yourself" (Rom 13:9-10; cf. Gal 5:14).

Even more profoundly, the Incarnation of the Son of God as a human being is seen as definitively uniting God with the fate of each human being. With all men and women called to be brothers and sisters in Christ, the killing of any human being would assume for Christians the heinous character of fratricide, the murder of a close relative (cf. Pope John Paul II, encyclical *The Gospel of Life, Evangelium Vitae*, 8 [1995]). The idea that one might attack humans in service to God is alien to faith in the Incarnation: "If anyone says, 'I love God,' but hates his brother, he is a liar" (1 Jn 4:20; cf. Mt 25:40). Thus, for Christians, "rejection of human life, in whatever form that rejection takes, is really a rejection of Christ" (*Evangelium Vitae*, 104; cf. Vatican Council II, *Pastoral Constitution on the Church in the Modern World, Gaudium et Spes*, 22).

Historical Background • Christianity condemned all direct killing of the innocent from its earliest centuries. In this, it distinguished itself from the surrounding pagan culture, which accepted various forms of killing: abortion, abandonment and exposure of unwanted infants to the elements, gladiatorial games, and "noble" suicide. The earliest written compendium of Christian guidance after the New Testament, known as the *Didache* (originally *Didakhai ton apostolon*, or *Instructions of the Apostles*), condemned abortion and infanticide, along with other forms of homicide, as part of the "way of death" that Christians must avoid (*Didache*, II.2; cf. *Evangelium Vitae*, 54). Defending Christians against false charges of murder and cannibalism in the late second century, Athenagoras pointed out that Christians are "altogether consistent" in avoiding all forms of violence, including abortion, infanticide, and gladiators' contests (*A Plea on Behalf of Christians*, 35). Early Church law treated murder, apostasy, and adultery as the three most serious sins, requiring a long and arduous time of repentance before the sinner could be readmitted to the Christian community (cf. *Evangelium Vitae*, 54); and a man guilty of homicide could not be ordained to the priesthood.

St. Augustine was especially influential in clarifying Christian morality on homicide. He taught that, except when a criminal is executed in accordance with a just law applying to all or when God has commanded it, "whoever kills a man, either himself or another, is implicated in the guilt of murder" (*City of God*, I, 21). He was especially forceful in stating that the commandment "You shall not kill" applies to oneself and forbids suicide (*City of God*, I, 20-27). While some early Christians were tempted to kill themselves to avoid being raped and dishonored during barbarian invasions, Augustine taught that one must not kill oneself or another innocent person here and now for any reason, even to avoid future evils (*City of God*, I, 25). He also suggested that while Christians love peace, in a sinful world they may reluctantly go to war to defend the innocent from wrongdoers (*City of God*, IV, 15).

This tradition condemning homicide continues unbroken through Christian history. As Christian reflection focused on the idea of natural law, homicide was recognized as one of those acts that are contrary to nature and morally wrong for everyone. In the thirteenth century, St. Thomas Aquinas reaffirmed that all direct killing of the innocent is gravely wrong, and provided greater clarity on the difference between direct and indirect killing. He taught that it is not homicide to use lethal force if that is necessary to defend oneself or others against an unjust aggressor; in such a case, one intends only to defend against attack, so that the death of the attacker may be foreseen as an effect of one's act but is *praeter intentionem*, or beyond one's intention (*Summa Theologiae*, II-II, 64.7). Such indirect killing is the classic example of what became known as the principle of double effect.

In the sixteenth century, the *Roman Catechism* (which was authorized by the Council of Trent) reaffirmed the commandment against homicide, emphasizing that "there is no individual, however humble or lowly his condition, whose life is not shielded by this law." This catechism also observed that a person who does not intend to kill may nonetheless be guilty of homicide if he causes death in the course of an evil act or through "negligence, carelessness or want of due precaution" (Pt. III, "The Fifth Commandment").

The Church has found it necessary to underscore this teaching at times when the surrounding culture was tempted to treat a form of homicide as noble or acceptable. For centuries, canon law denied a Church burial to those who died in the course of a duel, in order to emphasize that cur-

rent secular ideas of "honor" did not justify such private killing (cf. *Codex Iuris Canonici,* Canon 1240 [1917]). Similarly, canon law has provided for excommunication for those who successfully procure or perform an abortion, especially because contemporary civil laws fail to treat this form of homicide with the gravity it deserves (*Codex Iuris Canonici,* Canon 2350; Code of Canon Law, Canon 1398 [1983]).

In 1940, the Vatican's Holy Office (predecessor of today's Congregation for the Doctrine of the Faith) was obliged to reaffirm that any direct killing of the innocent is "contrary to the natural and the divine positive law." This was in response to a question arising from Nazi Germany's euthanasia program: whether a public authority could order the killing of "those who, although not having committed any crimes deserving of death, are, however, because of psychic or physical defects, unable to be useful to the nation but, rather, are considered a burden to its vigor and strength." In 1943, Pope Pius XII repeated this condemnation of state-ordered homicide in words recalling the sin of Cain: "The blood of these victims, all the dearer to our Redeemer because deserving of greater pity, 'cries to God from the earth' " (encyclical *On the Mystical Body of Christ, Mystici Corporis Christi*, 92; cf. Gn 4:10).

Specific Applications • Several contexts in which the issue of homicide arises deserve special mention.

Abortion has been seen as a grave sin throughout Christian history. Early abortion was not always seen as a form of homicide, because of uncertainties during some periods of Church history regarding the early embryo's membership in the human species. Beginning in the nineteenth century, modern biology has confirmed that a new member of the human species comes into existence at conception; canon law has acknowledged this reality by treating abortion at every stage as the taking of human life. Abortion is an especially heinous form of killing because it destroys innocent human life in a particularly vulnerable and helpless state (*Evangelium Vitae*, 58).

It is sometimes argued that euthanasia for the

sick or dying is justifiable, either because the victims are too physically or mentally deficient to be human persons or because the killing is motivated by a merciful desire to end suffering. The Church rejects both arguments, insisting that "as far as the right to life is concerned, every innocent human being is absolutely equal to all others" (*Evangelium Vitae*, 57). In fact, Christian morality demands special attention to defending the lives of those who are most helpless. Nor do compassionate motives excuse the objectively evil character of the act of killing.

Capital punishment has long been seen as a special case, on the grounds that the state is delegated by God with authority to protect its citizens and punish those who threaten the common good. It has always been recognized that such execution is gravely wrong if imposed on an innocent person or performed out of hatred or revenge. In this century, the Church has increasingly urged governments to move away from the use of capital punishment, especially because modern societies have nonlethal means of rendering criminals unable to do further harm.

Killing in war may be seen as indirect when a nation uses only the degree of force needed to repel an attack and defend the innocent. Catholic teaching on the "just war" condemns as homicidal any act of war that deliberately kills noncombatants. The development of nuclear weapons and other means of mass destruction has raised the question whether a nation can engage in a major war today without setting the stage for homicide on an enormous scale.

In recent decades, the Church's social teaching has emphasized that homicide is the violation of each human being's right to life — a right that must be protected above all others, because it is the condition of all others (Congregation for the Doctrine of the Faith, *Declaration on Procured Abortion*, 11 [1974]). No one can enjoy other earthly goods or even associate with other human beings if his or her life is not secure against direct attack; in this sense, the commandment against homicide is "at the basis of all life together in society" (*Evangelium Vitae*, 53).

At a time when the modern state increasingly claims authority to determine individuals' lives and subordinate their needs to the demands of the community, the Church insists that the life of each human being is uniquely precious and inviolable. No government can claim authority to kill innocent people to serve the common good, because the protection of each person's right to life is an integral part of the common good. A law that allows or demands the killing of the innocent is an unjust law that deserves no obedience (*Evangelium Vitae*, 71).

See: Abortion; Absolute Moral Norms; Capital Punishment; Deterrence; Double Effect; Ensoulment; Euthanasia; Human Goods; Human Life, Dignity and Sanctity of; War.

Suggested Readings: CCC 2259-2283. John Paul II, *The Splendor of Truth, Veritatis Splendor*, 76-83; *The Gospel of Life, Evangelium Vitae*. Congregation for the Doctrine of the Faith, *Declaration on Procured Abortion*; *Declaration on Euthanasia*. St. Thomas Aquinas, *Summa Theologiae*, II-II, 64. G. Grisez, *The Way of the Lord Jesus*, Vol. 2, *Living a Christian Life*, pp. 459-505. P. Devine, *The Ethics of Homicide*.

Richard Doerflinger

HOMILY

The evolution of the homily began when Christianity moved out of the Aramaic-speaking Jewish environment of the original witnesses to Jesus and into the Greek-speaking Greco-Roman world. Although Plato and Aristotle were known, daily life in the latter world seems to have been more directly influenced by four pagan schools of philosophy: the Cynics, the Stoics, the Epicureans, and the Skeptics. The communication of the Gospel message was very much determined by the forms of communication used by these schools: personal involvement, witness, example, sermons to large and small groups, and written letters. Because public speaking played a crucial part in the lives of the Greeks, rhetoric had the central role in education.

The Homily in the Early Church • To reach

this sophisticated society, the Church had to find new modes of communication, requiring a development of the Church herself from A.D. 70-140. Within the Church there was a transition from the preacher as a charismatic prophet to a hierarchic priest. The worship devolved from the Jewish synaxis (worship assembly) to Christian Eucharist. There was a new way of approaching the Scriptures: Both Old and New Testaments had to be considered, as the Christological heresy called Montanism was rejected. This resulted in a new exegesis, moving from Jewish allegory to Christian typology. Finally, there was a new style of preaching, from the biblical diatribe to the development of classical rhetoric.

The earliest witness to this development is Ignatius of Antioch (died c. 107), for whom both the delivery of the sermon and the offering of the Eucharistic prayer were the bishop's special prerogative at the Christian synaxis. In his preaching, the bishop interpreted the corporate faith of the believing community in the power of the spirit.

Later, Justin (died c. 165), in his *First Apology*, described the homily as being preached on Sunday after the reading of Sacred Scripture and before the Eucharist, where it is still preached today.

The oldest known homily is that of *Second Clement*, an anonymous work written in the second or third century, which develops the theme of Christ's love in a simple, direct, and unorganized manner and without concern for rhetorical style.

The homilies of Origen (A.D. 185-253) are the most ancient body of homilies that have come to us; there are about two hundred in all. Origen himself called them homilies because the word "homily" in the then-current Greek usage implied familiar conversation with a group of listeners, as opposed to a more formal rhetorical "oration."

St. John Chrysostom (350-407), the most prolific preacher-writer among Greek Fathers, wrote six hundred homilies and commentaries on Scripture. With him the homily became more rhetorical, thematic, catechetical, mystagogical, and less exegetical. His preaching, along with the preaching of the other bishops, dealt with the burning doctrinal issues of the day, and their manner of preaching revived interest in the art of rhetoric.

The Homily and the Liturgy • The homily, then, is the connecting link between the two parts of the single act of worship. It is a short sermon, integrally related to a liturgical celebration and revealing to the worshipers the present significance of the liturgical act, while drawing its content mainly from scriptural and liturgical sources.

The homily reveals the mystery of Christ as it is being celebrated by the believing community in its sacraments and liturgy. Furthermore, it seeks to unfold for the worshipers the inner meaning of the mysteries of faith and, at the same time, to explore the guiding principles of Christian life during the course of the liturgical year (cf. Vatican Council II, *Constitution on the Sacred Liturgy, Sacrosanctum Concilium*, 52, 102). In doing this, the homily contributes to the instruction by which pastors fulfill their duty to ensure that the faithful take part in the liturgy fully aware of what they are doing, actively engaged in the rite, and enriched by its effects (*Sacrosanctum Concilium*, 11).

From this it can be seen that the term "homily" indicates the function of preaching in the liturgy. Consequently, "homily" cannot be properly understood apart from the understanding of the nature and purpose of the liturgy.

The liturgy, especially the Eucharist, accomplishes the work of redemption by building up the faithful and strengthening them to preach Christ, so that the Church is lifted up as a sign of salvation to the scattered children of God (*Sacrosanctum Concilium*, 2). In particular, the purpose of the Liturgy of the Word is to nourish the people of God in a spirit of thanksgiving (Sacred Congregation of Rites, *Instruction on the Worship of the Eucharistic Mystery, Eucharisticum Mysterium*, 10 [1967]).

In the Western Church, the supplanting of Greek by Latin resulted in the development of the Latin sermon, which followed Ciceronian rhetorical principles. The purpose of the sermon, discussed by St. Augustine (427) in the fourth book of his *De Doctrina Christiana*, was to teach, please, and persuade.

The barbarian invasions from the north and the collapse of the Roman Empire led to a pessimism about life. The Latin preachers of the day saw the invasions as a punishment from God; consequently, they stressed the need for repentance and focused on the eschatological dimension of human life.

Significant Latin homilists are Quodvultdeus of Carthage (c. 437), Ambrose of Milan (died 397), Augustine of Hippo (died 430), and Pope Leo the Great (died 461) By the time of Pope Leo, the sermon had become less scriptural and more legalistic, dogmatic, and moralistic. This thrust perdured in the Western Church for centuries.

The Homily Today • The Church's contemporary understanding of the homily begins with the Second Vatican Council, which restored the word of God and its preaching to their rightful place in liturgy. Vatican II's *Constitution on the Sacred Liturgy*, *Sacrosanctum Concilium*, teaches that "the liturgy of the word and the eucharistic liturgy, are so closely connected with each other that they form but one single act of worship" (56).

Because the liturgy is an exercise of the priestly office of Jesus Christ (*Sacrosanctum Concilium*, 7), the homily is properly a function of the ordained: bishops, priests, and deacons (Canon 767.1).

With the Church's growing concern for the proper catechesis of the faithful, which the *Catechism of the Catholic Church* is designed to foster, more attention currently is being paid to the *Instruction on the Proper Implementation of the Constitution on the Sacred Liturgy, Inter Oecumenici*, 55, issued by the Sacred Congregation of Rites on September 26, 1964, which allows for a plan for preaching (a *syllabus*), provided it is closely and harmoniously linked with the principal seasons and feasts of the liturgical year.

It is important to note that the homily is not limited to the celebration of Eucharist; it is an integral part of all sacramental celebrations, which sanctify, build up the Body of Christ, and give worship to God: Baptism, Confirmation, Matrimony, etc. Although all sacraments do indeed impart grace by the power of Christ operating in

them, at the same time the preaching of the homily, along with the celebrating of the ritual acts themselves, prepares the worshipers to receive sacramental grace "to their profit, to worship God duly, and to practice charity" (*Sacrosanctum Concilium*, 59).

See: Assembly, Liturgical; Catechesis; Lex Orandi, Lex Credendi; Liturgy.

Suggested Readings: CCC 4-10, 1070-1075, 2033. Vatican Council II, *Constitution on the Sacred Liturgy, Sacrosanctum Concilium*, 9-11, 19, 24, 35, 52. J. Burke, O.P., and T. Doyle, O.P., *The Homilist's Guide to Scripture, Theology and Canon Law.* T. Carroll, *Preaching the Word. Preaching in the Patristic Age: Studies in Honor of Walter J. Burghardt, S.J.*

John Burke, O.P.

HOMOSEXUALITY

Few topics require greater sensitivity than homosexuality does. The phenomenon remains very little understood, either by professional psychologists or the general public. There is, for instance, no agreement about how common the condition is nor exactly what constitutes the "condition" of homosexuality. There are those who claim to experience sexual attraction only for members of their own sex, and such individuals may properly be designated homosexual in respect to sexual orientation; but even individuals with a strong heterosexual orientation may at some point in their lives experience sexual attraction for a member of the same sex. Moreover, there is no consensus about what might be the cause or causes of homosexuality and what might be the reversibility of the homosexual condition.

Morality of Homosexual Acts • Many in modern society would like to proclaim sexual acts between homosexuals as moral and would like homosexual unions to be recognized as legitimate alternative "life arrangements" or modes of partnership. Homosexual sexual activity, however, throughout the long tradition of Judeo-Christian thought has been considered incompatible with God's plan for human sexuality. On the basis of natural law principles, Scripture, and Tradition, the Church has taught that the proper use of sexuality is between a male and female who are married and are open to having children; sexual intercourse is meant to be an expression of love by those who are married to each other. Sexual intercourse between members of the same sex is understood to be a misuse of the gift of sexuality: It does not serve to create a bond between male and female; it cannot serve the purpose of bringing forth new life; it creates an inappropriate bond between members of the same sex.

Yet some individuals find themselves with a sexual attraction to members of their own sex. The attraction can be experienced as permanent and seemingly irreversible or as a response to a particular individual in a very particular situation. The cause of such attractions is unknown. Many claim that the homosexual condition is not chosen — that it seems to be innate or the result of certain experiences in early childhood, though all such explanations seem largely speculative and without hard scientific data to support them. The American Psychiatric Association has held varying positions, and these seem to be as much influenced by cultural and political factors as reliable scientific studies.

The argument is made that if some individuals are born with a propensity to a homosexual orientation, then we must proclaim homosexuality to be natural and normal — just one of the many variants of the human identity. Some human beings have blue eyes, some have brown, some have green: We have what we are born with and are not subject to moral evaluation on what is given to us at birth. On this analogy, some individuals are born heterosexual, others are born homosexual, and there is no ground for moral approval or disapproval of these innate conditions.

Nonetheless, were it to be proven that some individuals have a genetic determination to homosexuality, in itself this evidence would not serve to invalidate the Church's claim that homosexuality is an unnatural or disordered condition. Indeed, those who think showing that homosexuality is innate would serve to prove that homosexu-

ality is natural misunderstand what the Church means by "natural."

The word "natural" has a fairly complicated meaning within the Church's moral tradition. "Natural" does not, as some think, refer simply to what is in accord with the biological processes of man. Nor does it refer to what is innate, nor even to what is "normal." Rather, the word "natural" in the context of the Church's moral doctrine has a metaphysical meaning. The Church relies largely on the principles of Thomism to explain its moral teachings. Thomism understands all things to have essences or natures; these essences or natures are good (in fact, designed by God), and everything prospers insofar as it acts and is treated in accord with its essence, or nature. That is said to be natural which accords with what is good for human beings; that is called unnatural which is not good for human beings. Integral human nature, or human nature before it suffered the effects of original sin, was an "ordered" nature. This means that the psychic processes of the human person were ordered: There were no disordered desires, no desires to eat or drink or do anything not in accord with what is good for human nature. Before the Fall, the human person reasoned correctly about reality, and his passions quite automatically and spontaneously followed the deliberations of reason. With original sin came "fallen nature."

The condition of original sin, or fallen nature, brought with it disordered passions and desires. After the Fall, humans began to act against their nature, quite constantly and predictably. As a result of original sin, all human beings, because they are imperfect, are in an unnatural and disordered condition. It is common to the human condition, for instance, for human beings to want to eat, drink, and sleep more than is good for them. It is common to the human condition for humans to want to have sexual intercourse with those with whom they should not or when they should not or in ways that they should not. In the "natural" state (that is, the prelapsarian state, or the state of humans before the Fall), humans would only desire what was good for them. After the Fall, human beings became susceptible to innumerable unnatural and disordered desires.

The Homosexual Condition • The claim by the Church that homosexuality is "unnatural" or "disordered" has been found offensive by some, since these terms seem to suggest that homosexuals are in some special category deserving of particular censure by the Church. Yet, as the above explanation of the term "natural" establishes, any human desire for what is not good is unnatural and disordered. Thus, in this context, homosexuality is simply one more of the "unnatural" or "disordered" conditions to which humans are susceptible.

It should not be surprising if some individuals are born with a propensity to homosexual sexual attractions, for it certainly seems that individuals are born with many propensities, both good and bad: for instance, a propensity to generosity, patience, anger, irritability, or alcoholism. Part of the challenge of the moral life is to learn how to order what we find disordered in our being so that, for instance, if one has a bad temper, one needs to learn how to govern it. Some of us may acquire the orderedness or disorderedness in our psyches through childhood experiences, either good or bad, rather than through heredity. Having good and generous parents who work to impart generosity to their children, for instance, will likely assist the children in being relatively free from greed and selfishness; conversely, having lazy parents may facilitate our being lazy. Such experiences as sexual abuse may deeply scar our psyches and fill us with fears and tendencies that we in no way chose to acquire. It seems plausible that a homosexual orientation is the result of any number of factors or causes. But the fact that it may be inborn — or not the product of our own choosing — does not thereby make it a "natural" condition not subject to moral evaluation.

It is very important to note that, although the Church teaches that the homosexual condition is unnatural or disordered, she does not teach that the homosexual condition itself is sinful. This is true of any disordered propensity that may be in the human soul: Those who are irritable or hot-tempered by nature are not sinful by virtue of these temperamental traits. Sin is a result of the voluntary choices we make in response to what our passions may be driving us to do. For many, there is no moral culpability in feeling irritable or hot-tempered; rather, it is in choosing and acting irritably or out of hot temper that most sins occur. (We can, though, be morally culpable if we do nothing to overcome our temperamental propensities.) So, while individuals may have little or no responsibility for having a homosexual orientation, they can exercise moral agency in respect to their actions.

Some find fault with the analogy between innate or unchosen homosexuality and a propensity to alcoholism or any moral failing. They argue that, since our sexual orientation so deeply influences how we respond to the world (how we fulfill, for instance, our needs for intimacy), to categorize homosexuality with all other human disorders mischaracterizes the plight of the individual with a homosexual orientation. It seems right to acknowledge that the plight of the homosexual is a particularly burdensome one, that the condition of homosexuality presents challenges to the moral agent many times greater than the usual challenge of dealing with disordered passions, for human beings do have a profound need for intimacy, and most individuals will satisfy that need (insofar as possible) through marriage and family.

Moreover, there is disagreement about whether it is possible for those with exclusively homosexual attractions to change their sexual orientation. Some psychologists maintain that no permanent change is possible; others maintain that, with the help of therapy and grace, many homosexuals have been successful in entering and sustaining heterosexual marriages. The Church does not require that homosexuals seek such reorientation; rather, homosexuals are called to a life of chastity, as all Christians are.

Those with a homosexual condition have often suffered unjust censure and discrimination by members of their own families, by society at large, and by some of those who represent the Church. The prejudicial rejection of homosexuals is called homophobia. Those who are guilty of homophobia refuse to recognize the full human dignity of persons with a homosexual condition. Such prejudicial rejection is in manifest conflict with the dictates of justice and Christian charity. Indeed, much love and acceptance should be extended to those with a homosexual condition, since often they find themselves lonely and rejected.

The Celibate Homosexual • The celibate lifestyle to which persons with a permanent or irreversible condition of homosexuality (if there is such) are called need not be lonely and isolating. There are, for instance, many celibate priests, nuns, and laypeople who forgo the intimacy of marriage, sexual relations, and family. Moreover, not only those called to the consecrated life are called to celibacy. Celibacy is lived by some heterosexuals who are unsuccessful in finding a spouse or who have been abandoned by their spouses. They fulfill their needs for intimacy through a deep relationship with Christ, through friendship, and by extending their love more broadly. They often have very rich human relationships in which the lack of a sexual dimension allows other dimensions of the human person and human relations to emerge.

Some object to the claim that, since many heterosexuals successfully lead celibate lives, it should be possible for homosexuals to do the same. Some think false analogies are being drawn here between the celibacy of the consecrated life, the celibacy of unwed heterosexuals, and the celibacy of homosexuals. They note that the celibacy of those in the consecrated life is a voluntary celibacy and often wins them great respect and esteem. Also, they point out, it is possible for heterosexuals who live lives of involuntary celibacy to have some hope that their situations may change. But the celibate homosexual enjoys neither the esteem given to the consecrated individual nor the hope of the unwed heterosexual. Furthermore, as mentioned, there is a stigma attached to homosexuality that makes it very difficult for homosexuals to be open about their condition, often even with family and friends. Given the amount of both overt and subtle unjust discrimination against homosexuals, open acknowledgment of one's homosexuality is often

unwise, and thus one is denied even the comfort of self-disclosure. The isolation and alienation that can accompany the homosexual condition can therefore be extreme, and the Catholic demand that homosexuals lead celibate lives can seem unrealistic and cruel.

The cost of Christian discipleship, however, is often very high. While it must be acknowledged that, for many reasons, homosexuals are in a particularly difficult situation, others face challenges that equal or surpass theirs. For example, people with severe physical or psychological anomalies may also face lives burdened with various stigmas, be subject to much discrimination, and find establishing intimate relations extremely difficult; they, too, must learn to rely upon the Lord to meet their needs. Indeed, the Lord promises us that if we pick up our cross and carry it, we will find our burdens light.

Many Christian denominations have ministries designed to help homosexual persons live lives of chastity. Father John Harvey, O.S.F.S., a moral theologian, has founded Courage, an organization committed to helping those with a homosexual orientation draw upon prayer and the sacraments to lead chaste lives. They find that once they submit to the discipline of a committed prayerful and sacramental life, they are able to meet the demands of chastity; their testimony indicates that they find the rewards of remaining faithful to Christ's teaching and to the moral law to be great. (For more information on Father Harvey's organization, contact Courage, c/o St. Michael's Rectory, 424 W. 34th St., New York, NY 10001.)

See: Chastity; Concupiscence; Freedom, Human; Moral Principles, Christian; Natural Law; Original Sin; Sexuality, Human.

Suggested Readings: CCC 2357-2359, 2396. Congregation for the Doctrine of the Faith, *Declaration on Certain Questions concerning Sexual Ethics*; *Letter to the Bishops of the Catholic Church on the Pastoral Care of Homosexual Persons.* J. Harvey, *The Homosexual Person: New Thinking in Pastoral Care.* J. Nicolosi, *Reparative Therapy of Male Homosexuality.* E. Moberly, *Homosexuality: A New Christian Ethic.* L. Payne,

The Broken Image: Restoring Personal Wholeness Through Healing Prayer; *The Healing of the Homosexual; Crisis in Masculinity.* National Association for Research and Treatment of Homosexuality (NARTH), 16542 Ventura Blvd., Suite 416, Encino, CA 91436.

Janet E. Smith

HOPE

Hope is essential for Christian life. We have a right and a duty to be confident that God, who has loved us and called us to eternal life, will never abandon us. He will really give us all the graces we need to overcome every obstacle and finally arrive at the perfect life for which we were made (CCC 1817).

Scripture repeatedly calls us to trust entirely in God by asking, "[W]ho ever trusted in the Lord and was put to shame?" (Sir 2:10). Christ urged all to place their entire trust in him and never despair: "Fear not, little flock, for it is your Father's good pleasure to give you the kingdom" (Lk 12:32). He gladly came to sinners and, reassuring them in all their inclinations to despair, said, "Come to me, all who labor and are heavy laden, and I will give you rest" (Mt 11:28); "For this is the will of my Father, that every one who sees the Son and believes in him should have eternal life" (Jn 6:40).

At Baptism God plants in every Christian the theological virtue of hope (CCC 1813). The hope that Christians are given is a divine gift. It is not a shallow human wishing but a sure confidence that God himself gives us power to exercise. His grace calls us to make acts of hope, truthfully speaking the confidence in him that he wishes us to have. He invites all to make their lives more strong and glad by refusing ever to cease hoping in him (CCC 1818).

Authentic hope avoids despair and presumption. By despair we would deliberately refuse to believe that God is faithful and to trust that he who can save us indeed will do so (CCC 2091). Presumption would lead us to act foolishly, as if we could be saved by our own power or without

doing the things God gladly makes it entirely possible for us to do so as to reach everlasting life (CCC 2092).

See: Despair; Presumption; Redemption; Religion, Virtue of; Theological Virtues.

HUMAN EXPERIMENTATION

Scientific research can help us understand God's creation and benefit humanity. The Church therefore encourages responsible medical research. But when an experiment will involve human beings, it must respect the dignity of the human person. It would be inconsistent and morally wrong to kill or even harm human beings in an effort to serve humanity (Pope John Paul II, encyclical *The Gospel of Life, Evangelium Vitae*, 89 [1995]). In medical experimentation, as in other arenas, each human being must be respected as a person — as a uniquely precious human subject, not merely an object of research (CCC 2294-2295). In particular, because body and soul are so intimately united in the human person, the human body has inherent dignity; in the pursuit of medical knowledge one should not deprive people of their bodily integrity.

Norms for Experimentation • From these convictions on the dignity of human life arise several norms for human experimentation.

First, the experiment must have the valid goal of serving human well-being. Research involving human beings is not morally neutral; it is wrong to develop new procedures or technologies that can only violate human dignity.

Second, the subject must give his or her informed consent, after receiving all relevant information about the purpose and risks of the experiment. In the case of subjects unable to give informed consent (e.g., born and unborn children, senile or unconscious patients), their consent can be presumed only if the experiment may benefit them as individuals; the consent of parents or guardians also must be obtained.

Third, while eliminating all risk to subjects may be impossible, it must be kept to a minimum (Pontifical Council for Pastoral Assistance to Health

Care Workers, *Charter for Health Care Workers*, 78-81 [1995]). Before testing a procedure on humans, one should take every step to ensure its safety, including testing on animals if appropriate; and even animals should not be abused or subjected to needless suffering by such tests. An experiment on humans should be discontinued if the risks turn out to be greater than anticipated.

Here one can speak of allowing a *proportionate* risk, so that the experiment's risks are compared to its possible benefit. A healthy subject should not undergo an experiment expected to cause grave injury or death. While it can be generous and charitable to volunteer for research that may benefit humanity, even subjects themselves do not own their lives but have a duty to be careful stewards of life. They may not volunteer for research that will kill them or destroy the substantial integrity of their bodies. Sick persons may volunteer for experimental treatment involving greater risk, if that risk is reasonable in light of the expected benefit. For example, even if a treatment carries some risk of death, one may choose to undergo it if it offers the only way to cure or alleviate a fatal illness.

These principles apply to human beings of every age and condition, from conception to natural death. For example, experimentation on a child in the womb simply to gain medical knowledge is morally wrong, even with the parents' consent, if it would harm the life or integrity of either mother or child. As the Holy Father puts it: "The use of human embryos or fetuses as an object of experimentation constitutes a crime against their dignity as human beings who have a right to the same respect owed to a child once born, just as to every person" (*Evangelium Vitae*, 63).

The same principles apply to organ transplants from living donors, another area where one person may volunteer to undergo risk for the sake of benefit to others. A decision to donate organs can be a laudable service to human life; but one should not seriously endanger one's own life or functional integrity in the process. For example, one may legitimately donate a kidney, because people can generally live unimpaired with only one kidney.

Even after death, however, humans should not donate their brains or their gonads, because these organs ensure a human being's personal and procreative identity respectively (*Charter for Health Care Workers*, 88).

Recent Developments, Current Issues • These norms are reflected in many secular documents and legal codes on the protection of human subjects. For at least two reasons, this is not surprising. First, such norms rely on the principle of the dignity of human life, which is not an exclusively Catholic idea but is open to appreciation by all people of good will. Second, modern declarations on medical ethics have their roots in the ancient Hippocratic oath, which has played a central role in the history of medicine, precisely because the early Church adopted its norms as consistent with Christian morality. Thus the Nuremberg Code, adopted by the Allied nations' War Crimes Tribunal after World War II to prevent any repetition of the infamous Nazi medical experiments, contains similar norms, as does the World Medical Association's "Declaration of Helsinki" (1964, revised in 1975).

Tragically, nevertheless, supposedly enlightened countries like the United States have known serious violations of these norms, usually involving marginalized or unpopular classes of people who had little defense against abuse.

In the Tuskegee, Alabama, syphilis experiment of the 1930s, syphilis was deliberately left untreated in hundreds of black men, in order to observe the progress of the disease. This experiment was allowed to continue for decades with the consent of federal officials, even after effective treatments for syphilis were widely known. In the late 1950s, a similar experiment involved the observation of untreated hepatitis at Willowbrook State School, a New York home for mentally retarded children. Only recently did the federal government reveal that unconsenting Americans, including pregnant women and their unborn children, were subjected to radiation experiments of uncertain risk during the 1940s and 1950s. Since the 1970s, federal lawmakers have debated public funding for unethical experiments on unborn children, including children intended for abortion. In the 1990s, that debate focused on proposals for destructive experiments on human embryos created in the laboratory.

Such abuses will stop only when Americans recognize that protections against manipulation and abuse must apply equally to all members of the human family.

See: Genetic Experimentation; Human Life, Dignity and Sanctity of; Human Person; Prenatal Diagnosis; Science and the Church.

Suggested Readings: CCC 2292-2296. John Paul II, Address to the Pontifical Academy of Sciences, October 23, 1982. Pontifical Council for Pastoral Assistance to Health Care Workers, *Charter for Health Care Workers*, 75-91 (1995). W. May, *Human Existence, Medicine and Ethics*, Ch. 1. D. McCarthy and A. Moraczewski, O.P., eds., *An Ethical Evaluation of Fetal Experimentation: An Interdisciplinary Study.*

Richard Doerflinger

HUMAN GOODS

An understanding of human goods is essential to an understanding of morality. The basic moral norm is: Love God and love your neighbor as yourself. To love God is to rejoice in his goodness and to cooperate with his plan. To love our neighbor and love ourselves is to will what is really good for the neighbor (and thus work energetically for that good) and to will what is really good for ourselves. Thus, the basic moral criterion concerns what is really good for one's neighbor and oneself; and this is to say it concerns human goods. "Human activity proceeds from man: it is also ordered to him. When he works, not only does he transform matter and society, but he fulfills himself" (Vatican Council II, *Pastoral Constitution on the Church in the Modern World, Gaudium et Spes,* 35).

This point can be seen in another way. We can only choose what seems in itself good for us or something that will help bring about what seems in itself good. What seems good to us is something that has some natural appeal to us or is con-

nected with it (either as a means toward it or as a pleasurable aspect of it). What has a natural appeal to us is that to which we have a natural inclination; and that to which we have a natural inclination is what perfects us as human beings.

Thus, we have a natural interest in (and a natural inclination to) life, health, knowledge, friendship, and so on. By contrast, eating grass, chasing rabbits, and so on, have no natural appeal to us, and so do not occur to us as objects to be chosen. Basic human goods actualize potentialities that belong to us as human beings; they are basic reasons for acting; they are intrinsic aspects of the "full-being" of human persons.

These goods are objective. What is really good for a person is that which perfects this person or builds up this person. What is bad for the person is what diminishes this person, what deprives him or her of something he or she could have or be. If some people think sickness or ignorance is good, they are simply mistaken; if some think health or knowledge is not good, then they are mistaken. It is objectively true — that is, true even if you or I think otherwise — that health and knowledge perfect, build up, and actualize the potentialities of a person, while sickness and ignorance diminish, or take away from, a person's perfection or fulfillment.

Moreover, these goods are perfective of all human beings. They are transcultural. It is true for all human beings that health and knowledge perfect them while sickness and ignorance diminish them. This is because human beings have certain basic potentialities in common. We pick out some entities in the universe and call them "human beings" precisely because they share a complex nature in common, that is, they have certain basic potentialities in common.

The basic human goods are as follows.

Human beings are living bodily things, physical organisms. As physical organisms, human beings are perfected by *life* and *health*. As intellectual, human beings are perfected by *knowledge of truth* and *aesthetic experience*. As both bodily and intellectual, human beings are perfected or fulfilled in making and doing things for their own sake, that is, *skillful performance* or *play*.

As complex beings, human beings are fulfilled by the harmony of the different aspects of the self or *self-integration*. As persons who form relationships with other human beings, they are fulfilled by *friendship* and *society*. Harmony between one's choice and what is morally true is *practical reasonableness*. The harmony between people and God is *religion*, an important basic human good. Finally, considering human beings as masculine and feminine persons who form communities that include aspects of all of the basic goods, there is the human good of *marriage*.

Such basic human goods provide an objective standard for what is right and wrong. Pope John Paul II says: "It is in the light of the dignity of the human person — dignity which must be affirmed for its own sake — that reason grasps the specific moral value of certain goods toward which the person is naturally inclined" (*The Splendor of Truth, Veritatis Splendor*, 48). Choices respectful of every basic human good are morally good; choices that in one way or another diminish one's respect for basic human goods are morally bad.

See: Absolute Moral Norms; Deontology; Legalism; Modes of Responsibility; Natural Law; Relativism; Teleological Ethics; Ten Commandments.

Suggested Readings: CCC 1749-1756. John Paul II, *The Splendor of Truth, Veritatis Splendor.* G. Grisez, *The Way of the Lord Jesus*, Vol. 1, *Christian Moral Principles*, pp. 115-140. G. Grisez and R. Shaw, *Fulfillment in Christ,* pp. 49-59.

Patrick Lee

HUMAN LIFE, DIGNITY AND SANCTITY OF

While all God's creation is good, human life has a special dignity and sanctity. For this reason one should never intentionally destroy human life, but should protect and enhance it at every stage and in every condition.

The special status of human life is based on two truths. First, human beings are set apart from the rest of creation because they are specially created in the image and likeness of God. The Book of Genesis says this directly (Gn 1:26-27) and also expresses it symbolically in its account of man's creation. God brought forth all the rest of creation by a simple word, but fashioned man with his own hands and "breathed into his nostrils the breath of life; and man became a living being" (Gn 2:7). Human nature is blessed with free will, so that we can receive God's love and choose to love God and others in return.

Second, human beings have an eternal destiny, because all are called to eternal life with Christ. By assuming our human nature, Christ has united himself with every human person (cf. Vatican Council II, *Pastoral Constitution on the Church in the Modern World, Gaudium et Spes*, 22), so that "rejection of human life, in whatever form that rejection takes, is really a rejection of Christ" (Pope John Paul II, encyclical *The Gospel of Life, Evangelium Vitae*, 104 [1995]). Because the horizon of human life transcends this earthly existence, disrespect toward human life here and now has eternal significance.

To say human life has dignity means it has intrinsic, and not only instrumental, value: "Man is the only creature on earth that God has wanted for its own sake" (*Gaudium et Spes*, 24). Human life is good in and of itself, and not only good *for* other purposes. To say human life has sanctity is to emphasize that each human being has been specially willed into existence by God to enjoy a loving relationship with him, and therefore should be treated with reverence. St. Paul says we should treat the human body as "a temple of the Holy Spirit" (1 Cor 6:19). To mistreat bodily life on the pretext of serving some higher purpose is a kind of desecration.

Respect and reverence for human beings demand unconditional respect for human life, because life is our first and most basic gift from a loving God and the condition for enjoying his other gifts. As the Congregation for the Doctrine of the Faith said in its 1980 *Declaration on Euthanasia*: "Human life is the basis of all goods, and is the necessary source and condition of every human activity and of all society" (I). We cannot pursue other human goods or achieve worthwhile goals if we are not first assured of our very existence.

The Right to Life • From the foregoing it is clear that when we speak of human rights that demand respect from individuals and society, we must speak first of the right to life. The 1974 *Declaration on Procured Abortion* of the Congregation for the Doctrine of the Faith says: "The first right of the human person is his life. He has other goods and some are more precious, but this one is fundamental — the condition of all the others. Hence it must be protected above all others. . . . It is not recognition by another that constitutes this right. This right is antecedent to its recognition; it demands recognition and it is strictly unjust to refuse it" (11).

Because this right is inherent in simply being a member of the human family, it must belong equally to every human being. Thus: "Any discrimination based on the various stages of life is no more justified than any other discrimination. The right to life remains complete in an old person, even one greatly weakened; it is not lost by one who is incurably sick. The right to life is no less to be respected in the small infant just born than in the mature person. In reality, respect for human life is called for from the time that the process of generation begins" (*Declaration on Procured Abortion*, 12).

This right does not belong more to some than to others. "As far as the right to life is concerned, every innocent human being is absolutely equal to all others" (*Evangelium Vitae*, 57). Human beings are not equal in their strength or their ability to defend and advance their own right to life. But this only means that the strong, and society as a whole, have an obligation to protect and assist the weak and helpless in defending their right to life (cf. CCC 1935-1937).

Human life is therefore also a social good; its protection is a basic purpose for which societies and legal systems are established. "When the Church declares that unconditional respect for the right to life of every innocent person — from conception to natural death — is one of the pillars on which every civil society stands, she wants simply to promote a human state. A state which recognizes the defense of the fundamental rights of the

human person, especially of the weakest, as its primary duty" (*Evangelium Vitae*, 101).

Negative and Positive Precepts • The sanctity of life has both negative and positive implications for human action.

Negatively, we must not attack or demean human life. First and foremost is the divine commandment against homicide: "You shall not kill" (Ex 20:13; Dt 5:17). This command forbids the directly intended taking of one's own life or anyone else's, regardless of the stage or condition of his or her life.

As the Second Vatican Council observed, however, human life is attacked or demeaned in many other ways as well: "The varieties of crime are numerous: all offenses against life itself, such as murder, genocide, abortion, euthanasia and willful suicide; all violations of the integrity of the human person, such as mutilation, physical and mental torture, undue psychological pressures; all offenses against human dignity, such as subhuman living conditions, arbitrary imprisonment, deportation, slavery, prostitution, the selling of women and children, degrading working conditions where men are treated as mere tools for profit rather than free and responsible persons: all these and the like are criminal: they poison civilization; and they debase the perpetrators more than the victims and militate against the honor of the Creator" (*Gaudium et Spes*, 27).

In recent decades, the Church has warned against the devaluing of human life reflected in policies favoring capital punishment, and has urged governments wherever possible to limit themselves to "bloodless means" for defending the innocent against aggressors (CCC 2267; *Evangelium Vitae,* 56). The Church also has spoken against the misuse of modern technology to attack life or to treat human beings as mere objects, whether that technology lies in the realm of nuclear or biological warfare, genetic experimentation, or reproductive medicine.

These negative precepts against destroying or demeaning life establish "the absolute limit beneath which free individuals cannot lower themselves" if they are to respect life; but such precepts also free us to say yes to life in every sphere of human activity (*Evangelium Vitae*, 75). There is a positive obligation "to promote life actively, and to develop particular ways of thinking and acting which serve life" (*Evangelium Vitae*, 76).

In this regard, Pope John XXIII listed among basic human rights "the right to life, to bodily integrity, and to the means which are necessary and suitable for the proper development of life. These means are primarily food, clothing, shelter, rest, medical care, and finally the necessary social services" (encyclical *Peace on Earth, Pacem in Terris*, 11 [1963]).

The principle of the dignity of life therefore grounds a program of active concern for the conditions of human life, beginning with people who are most disadvantaged: "As you did it to one of these the least of my brethren, you did it to me" (Mt 25:40). Since each person has a right to necessities of life such as food, shelter, and basic health care, those with abundant means have a responsibility to share their abundance with those who need help to survive and lead lives of dignity. While there may be legitimate differences of opinion as to how best to serve these needs in a given society, deliberate failure to help provide basic assistance shows a morally culpable indifference to human life. "Feed the man dying of hunger," said one medieval maxim, "for if you do not feed him you have killed him."

A Consistent Ethic • Some recent Church documents, especially those issued by the Catholic bishops of the United States, seek to unite these negative and positive precepts in what is called a consistent ethic of life. Such an ethic does not equate all norms on respect for life or assert that all are of equal gravity; still less does it insist that each individual devote equal time to all arenas in which human life is threatened. But it does highlight the way in which respect for life undergirds a wide variety of obligations to our fellow human beings. It emphasizes, for example, that even in meeting the positive obligation to defend innocent life from attack, we must not directly intend to destroy the life of the attacker but must only do what is necessary to defend life. To Catholics who

may be tempted to accept only part of the Church's witness to life — for example, its rejection of abortion or its concern for the poor — this ethic suggests that consistency demands respect for both concerns.

A consistent commitment to human life appreciates the need for both the negative and positive precepts discussed above. A commitment to negative norms against taking life, divorced from an active commitment to promote and enhance God's gift of life, can become legalistic and hardhearted; a charitable impulse to serve the needy, divorced from the norms that forbid us to destroy life to serve our goals, becomes an abomination.

Negative precepts, such as the norm against direct killing of the innocent, are absolute in a way that does not apply to positive precepts. Such negative precepts define certain acts that are incompatible with God's law by their very nature, so that we could never turn them into ways of serving God's plan for human fulfillment. These norms apply always and everywhere, *"semper et pro semper,"* establishing a basic *minimum* by which to judge our respect for life. The positive precept to promote and enhance human life is also universal, but is not absolute in quite the same way because it is open-ended: There is no "maximum" to our positive love of God and neighbor (cf. Pope John Paul II, encyclical *The Splendor of Truth, Veritatis Splendor*, 52 [1993]). Moreover, what will best promote and enhance life in a given case may depend on circumstances, and in doing so one must not violate other people's rights or other moral norms.

In particular, the positive obligation to protect and preserve life should not be pursued to the point where it interferes with man's spiritual good. Earthly life is the first and most basic human good, but it is not the highest such good — eternal life in God is (cf. *Evangelium Vitae*, 2). Therefore, seriously ill persons are not obliged to submit to life-sustaining treatment that would impose needless suffering on them and interfere with their peace of mind and spiritual well-being. And the Church has always honored martyrs who remained faithful to the Gospel, although it would mean losing their lives (cf. *Evangelium Vitae*, 47). Their faithful witness, despite threats of death, is radically different from suicide, which involves the directly intended destruction of life. One does not show disrespect to earthly life by recognizing that faithfulness to God's word is even more important.

Albeit in a less dramatic way than martyrs, all Christians are called to fulfill their lives by dying to themselves, forgetting their selfish interests, and serving the needs of others. "Life finds its center, its meaning and its fulfillment when it is given up" (*Evangelium Vitae*, 51).

Modern Debates • The major modern objections to the Church's teaching on the sanctity of life are of three kinds.

The most radical objection is the claim that human life should be subordinated to the dictates of individual human choice. This claim is sometimes put in theological terms: If life is a gift from God, we should be allowed to do what we deem best with that gift or even return it to the giver.

This argument forgets that earthly life is the condition for our making free choices about other human goods, so that a free choice to destroy life undermines the good of freedom as well. Earthly life is very different from any ordinary gift we could possess, manipulate, or give away; this life is our own bodily reality as human persons. It is absurd to speak of ourselves as owners of this gift, as if we could somehow separate ourselves from it and declare ourselves its masters. Rather, the gift of life is the gift of ourselves — a gift over which we are called to exercise careful stewardship, not absolute dominion. Such mastery or dominion belongs only to God (cf. 1 Sm 2:6; 2 Kgs 5:7).

A second objection rests on a dualistic idea of the human person that denies inherent value to the human body, arguing that only the mind, spirit, or will has such value. In this view, people's bodily lives need not always be respected or even protected from direct attack, especially when their higher mental or spiritual activity is undeveloped, diminished, or lost.

This approach poses a serious threat to the lives of some of the most helpless human beings — the unborn, the mentally retarded or senile, the coma-tose, and the dying. Its theological error lies in denying the radical unity of the human person, composed of both body and soul. This unity is such that the body shares in the dignity of the image of God, and the soul can be considered the very "form" of the body (CCC 364-365). In the Christian view, bodily life and health should not be promoted at all costs, to the detriment of moral and spiritual goods; but life and health should always be inviolable from direct attack, and always have inherent value as the life and health of a human person. Bodily life must never be dismissed as simply "a complex of organs, functions and energies to be used according to the sole criteria of pleasure and efficiency" (*Evangelium Vitae*, 23).

A third objection concedes that the sanctity of life is a noble religious ideal, but denies that it can have meaning or real impact in a secular, pluralistic society. This approach dismisses efforts to protect innocent life in law and culture as mere impositions of denominational belief.

The Church forcefully rejects this claim. The inherent goodness of human life and its importance as the condition for enjoying all other human goods and human rights are truths of natural law that can be grasped by all people of good will (cf. *Evangelium Vitae*, 101). The need to protect the lives of all human beings can also be appreciated by reflecting on historical situations in which some category or group of human persons was denied a right to life. Such exclusions of some humans from society's protection have inevitably been condemned by history as shameful and unjust. In insisting on the defense of all human life from conception to natural death, the Church seeks to promote not so much a more "Christian" society as a society more truly human (cf. CCC 2273).

To be sure, the sanctity of life is also of great significance in Catholic doctrine. What Pope John Paul II calls "the Gospel of life" affirms natural law principles on the dignity of life, while transcending them in a vision of humanity's special role in God's redemptive plan. There is here an important link between the Church's teaching on matters of faith, on creation and the Incarnation, and her teaching on morals. The Holy Father has therefore called the Gospel of life "an integral part of that Gospel which is Jesus Christ himself" (*Evangelium Vitae*, 78).

See: Abortion; Absolute Moral Norms; Body and Soul; Capital Punishment; Deterrence; Euthanasia; Genetic Experimentation; Health Care; Homicide; Human Experimentation; Human Person; Moral Principles, Christian; Natural Law; Reproductive Technologies; Social Doctrine; Suicide; War.

Suggested Readings: CCC 355-365, 2258-2330. Vatican Council II, *Pastoral Constitution on the Church in the Modern World, Gaudium et Spes*, 23-32. John Paul II, *The Gospel of Life, Evangelium Vitae*. Congregation for the Doctrine of the Faith, *Declaration on Procured Abortion*; *Declaration on Euthanasia*. Pontifical Council for Pastoral Assistance to Health Care Workers, *Charter for Health Care Workers*. J. Bernardin et al., *Consistent Ethic of Life*. B. Ashley, O.P., *Theologies of the Body: Humanist and Christian*.

Richard Doerflinger

HUMAN PERSON

A correct understanding of the human person is not only of the greatest importance in its own right; it is also important because it underlies so many fundamental Christian teachings. This is particularly true with the moral teachings of the Church, which depend entirely on the Church's understanding of the human person. That is why John Paul II often says, in discussing some erroneous idea, that it rests ultimately on a "mistaken anthropology," that is, on some mistake about what it is to be a human person.

We can approach our personhood most readily through our moral experience. We all understand that human beings are never rightly used as mere instrumental means, but should be treated as ends in themselves. We also understand that human beings are never rightly owned as mere property, but should be recognized as individuals who each has a certain ownership of his or her own being. In understanding this, we grasp the personhood of

man; it is in virtue of our personhood that we can never be used or owned. We also come to understand why each human person is a subject of rights. To violate another's basic human rights is to invade the sphere of what is his own; a person has rights because he belongs to himself.

The Church welcomes this modern sense of personhood. In her social teaching the Church opposes the philosophy of society known as collectivism (as found, for instance, in socialism) on the grounds that it absorbs individual human beings into society in such a way as to disregard them as ends in themselves, as beings of their own, and that it thus depersonalizes them (cf. Pope John Paul II, *The Hundredth Year, Centesimus Annus*, 13). In insisting that each human being is a whole of his own and never a mere part of any collectivity, the Church seeks to vindicate the personhood of human beings.

If we consider the way in which John Paul II has explained the sexual teaching of the Church, we find the same focus on man as person. He says that by sexual intimacy outside of a marital commitment the man and woman are using each other for their gratification; he explains the immorality of fornication, and even of contraception, in large part in terms of men and women showing contempt for each other as persons.

Though this sense of the human person as end in himself has gained great currency since the eighteenth-century German philosopher Immanuel Kant, it goes back many centuries. Already the Roman jurists said of the person, *Persona est sui iuris et alteri incommunicabilis*: "A person is a being of its own and does not have its being in common with any other." The sixth-century Roman philosopher Boethius gave this definition of the person, which was accepted by almost all of the great medieval philosophers and theologians: *Persona est substantia individua naturae rationalis*: "A person is an individual substance having a rational nature." The idea of individuality in this definition corresponds to the idea of incommunicability in the earlier one, and both correspond to the idea of a being that is its own end and is not an extension or part of any other.

Uniqueness of Each Person • Let us look more closely at the note of incommunicability, which is often also expressed as the unrepeatability of each person. There is no such thing as several copies of the same person, as there are many copies of the same book. We say that a species exists in various individuals, and is not tied to any one of them; if one individual dies, the species can as well live on in another. But with persons it is otherwise: A person cannot be instantiated in multiple individuals that can replace one another; a person is inseparable from one individual. If an individual human person were to be completely destroyed, no subsequent human person could replace or could be again that person; a "hole" would be opened in the world that could never be filled. This concrete individuality or unrepeatability discloses to us in a particular way the mystery of personal being.

We now have to speak of the consciousness of human persons. Without consciousness there is no personal life and acting. Many Christian philosophers (including Karol Wojtyla — Pope John Paul) have recently given greater attention to the self-presence and the self-possession of persons, thereby exploring personal being from within. Thus many have explored the "interiority" (even the Fathers of Vatican Council II speak of this in one place) that is so expressive of persons existing on their own and not as parts of any totality; others speak of interiority in terms of "subjectivity." All are saying that it is deeply revealing of personal being that persons are not just beings existing objectively in the world next to nonpersons but also live their being from within, consciously performing it out of a center, being present to themselves in all their lives as persons.

Regarding the place of consciousness in the human person, there are two extremes to be avoided. On the one hand, one should not overestimate personal consciousness, thinking that persons *are* their consciousness, and nothing but consciousness, so that in the absence of consciousness and interiority there can be no person. No, we clearly have to distinguish between the being of the person, and the conscious acting of the person. On the other hand, persons would remain completely dormant if they had only the being of the person and never developed interiority, or subjectivity. And the philosophy of the human person would remain impoverished if one studied only or primarily the being of persons, neglecting to approach persons through their most intimate experience of themselves.

Freedom and Truth • In exploring the subjectivity of persons we are led to the freedom of persons, and so are led into the heart of personal being. In our conscious self-presence we find that we possess ourselves, are handed over to ourselves, left in the hand of our own counsel (cf. Sir 15:14), and so can make disposition of ourselves; and with this we find the freedom of ourselves as persons. We are not just acted upon by other beings, but are capable of acting through ourselves; we do not just transmit what originates outside of ourselves, but can originate activity ourselves; we are not only created by God, but in a certain sense we are also creators of ourselves (cf. Pope John Paul II, *The Splendor of Truth, Veritatis Splendor*, 71). When we live in too passive a way (as by being subject to coercion, or by being too susceptible to manipulation, or living too absorbed in our social group), then we tend to disappear as persons. It is by acting through ourselves, acting with an acting that is radically our own, that is, by living our freedom, that we show ourselves as persons, and give evidence of being ends in ourselves and beings of our own.

This is why the Church at Vatican II opposed more emphatically than ever before all forms of coercion in matters of religion (cf. *Declaration on Religious Freedom, Dignitatis Humanae*). If human beings are to be treated as persons, then they must be allowed to decide on their own about Christ and his Church; but if they are coerced into professing Christ, then they are violated as persons and their profession is worth little. It is not only the Church that renounces coercion, however. God renounces it in his way of dealing with us. He does not overpower our freedom, coercing believers into believing. He instead appeals to us in such a way that we are never so free as in believing, and thus never so alive as persons as when we believe.

The modern world would agree with most of what has just been said about freedom and autonomy. The Catholic understanding of freedom, however, parts ways with many of our contemporaries by insisting that the fullness of freedom is a *freedom grounded in truth*. There is a hierarchy of goods that we did not set up, and a law that binds us though we did not enact it. It is not a foreign law that remains outside us, for when we let our actions be judged by it, there awakens in us the dimension of conscience, which is "man's most secret core, and his sanctuary" (Vatican Council II, *Pastoral Constitution on the Church in the Modern World, Gaudium et Spes*, 16). In his encounter with the "truth about good," or the moral law, the person "quickens" in his deepest interiority. The law, then, does not do violence to the person, as so many modern thinkers fear, but engenders in him the fullness of personal life. The freedom of human persons can only be understood in relation to their *transcendence* toward the objective order of truth and good that is the norm of freedom, as John Paul II has repeatedly taught, especially in *Veritatis Splendor*, 31-64. As soon as persons depart from the moral law, they are handed over to their appetites, living at the beck and call of each latest urge, and with this they, in a sense, forfeit their birthright of freedom, though even then they retain freedom in the sense of being accountable for turning away from the moral law.

Many modern thinkers object that if the moral law is not of our making, then it is harmful for human persons, since only coercion can induce us to live in accordance with it. They overlook that the moral law is such that we are able to understand it: We can understand the goods and values on which it is based and can see for ourselves why the moral law is what it is. This understanding enables us to internalize the moral law, making it our own, willing it for ourselves, and thus needing no coercion in order to live by its commandments.

One sees why so many philosophers, beginning with the Greeks, have insisted so much on the *rationality* of man (recall Boethius, who stresses our "rational nature" in his definition of person). It is through our rationality that we gain our relation to truth, which in turn underlies our freedom.

Embodiment of Human Persons • We come now to a point in the Christian understanding of the human person that is far more important than one might at first think. We human persons are not purely spiritual, like the Divine Persons and even the angelic persons; we are incarnate persons, and ours is an embodied personhood.

The modern world, for all its materialism, also presents — surprising as this at first may seem — a great deal of false spiritualism. Many of our contemporaries think of the human body only as raw material to be used for our purposes like any other raw material. On the one hand, they do not do justice to the self-control and self-mastery to which we are called in the moral life; on the other hand, they exaggerate our freedom, ignoring its embodied character, degrading the body to a mere object of manipulation.

All of Catholic sexual morality turns on the right understanding of the embodiment of human persons (cf. *Veritatis Splendor*, 48). For if we are really incarnate persons, then our bodies command respect in all our acting, whereas if our bodies are just things that we use, then they are morally neutral, completely available to whatever manipulation we find useful. It is a remarkable fact that Christianity is the great defender of the human body against the many pagan detractors of it in the modern world; Christians understand better than non-Christians how the human body shares in the dignity of the person.

For all of the individual selfhood of each human person, it is at the same time true that persons are made for communion with one another. Although man is "the only creature on earth that God has wanted for its own sake," nevertheless he "can fully discover his true self only in a sincere giving of himself" (*Gaudium et Spes*, 24). A world in which there could be only one person would make no sense. Such a solitary person would suffer a devastating deprivation by being unable either to utter a word to another person or hear the word uttered by the other. This is why we were created as man and woman. This is why God exists as a community of Persons and not as a solitary Person.

Philosophers commonly distinguish two basic forms of interpersonal life: the "I-Thou" form and the "we" form. In the I-Thou form, persons encounter each other face to face. All the main kinds of interpersonal love unfold here, including the love between man and woman. By approaching each other in respect and in love, each mediates the other to oneself, so to say. Each is enabled or empowered to love oneself as a result of first being loved by the other.

But there is also the "we" form of interpersonal life, which occurs whenever we stand next to one another in a community. The citizens in a state are bound together in the solidarity of the we, just as all human beings are bound together in the same kind of solidarity. Christians esteem all such solidarity. They do not think of themselves as isolated selves who become bound to others only by contractual acts; they understand themselves as deeply embedded in various levels of solidarity, often without their prior consent, and as profoundly nourished as persons by some of these. The social teaching of the Church takes such solidarity seriously, deriving from it many of the responsibilities that we have toward one another. The Church also derives from it many of her teachings about the way in which good and evil do not remain shut up in individuals but spread out through the communities in which we participate, raising or depressing their moral level (cf. Pope John Paul II, apostolic exhortation *On Reconciliation and Penance in the Mission of the Church Today, Reconciliatio et Paenitentia*, 16).

Of course, as was observed above, the social teaching of the Church is also quick to recognize the chronic danger of many forms of solidarity, namely, the danger of the individual's coming to think of himself as a mere part of the social whole and thus depersonalizing himself. The ideal is what Vatican Council II called a *communio personarum*, that is, a communion among those who live closely together in such a way as to remain distinct persons and indeed to thrive as such.

The Image of God • In various respects we can discern the image of God in human persons. Traditionally, Christian philosophers have recognized in the *rationality* of persons a godlike power. In modern times they have given particular attention to the *freedom* of persons (cf. CCC 1705; *Gaudium et Spes*, 17). We belong to ourselves and possess ourselves in such a way as to image the supreme self-possession of God. He possesses himself by existing through himself and on his own; and we, who do not exist through ourselves, show forth something of God's being insofar as each of us is one's own end, a kind of whole of one's own, an unrepeatable being.

Another aspect of the image of God in us also has been stressed recently by many Christian authors: We resemble the Trinitarian God through our interpersonal communion (CCC 1702). When previous Christian thinkers spoke of the image of God in man, they typically referred to a single person and to the noblest faculties found within each person. It is a relatively new, but entirely authentic, Christian development to look for the image of God in persons who are united with each other in love. John Paul II is the first Pope to recognize an image of our Trinitarian God in the man-woman difference and in the ordering of man and woman to each other (as in his *On the Dignity and Vocation of Woman, Mulieris Dignitatem*, 7).

It is in connection with the image of God in us that Christian writers commonly speak of the incomparable *dignity* of human persons. By resembling God so strongly as to exist in his image, we share in his divine dignity and holiness. But one should at the same time remember that our dignity as persons, while grounded in God, is also intrinsic to us as human persons. It is not conferred on us from without, as if God could also withdraw it whenever he liked. This is why it can to a great extent be understood by sincere people who have not yet found Christ.

See: Body and Soul; Conscience; End of Man; Faith, Act of; Freedom, Human; Hierarchy; Human Life, Dignity and Sanctity of; Imago Dei; Natural Law; Religious Liberty; Sexuality, Human; Social Doctrine; Theology of the Body.

Suggested Readings: CCC 355-384, 1699-1761. Vatican Council II, *Pastoral Constitution on the Church in the Modern World, Gaudium et Spes*, 12-32; *Declaration on Religious Freedom, Dignitatis Humanae*, 1-8. St. Thomas Aquinas, *Summa Contra Gentiles*, III, Chs. 111-114. K. Wojtyla, *The Acting Person*. J. Crosby, *Personal Selfhood*. N. Clarke, S.J., *Person and Being*.

John F. Crosby

HUMAN RACE, CREATION AND DESTINY OF

God, who is love (cf. 1 Jn 4:8), loved both the angels and humanity into autonomous existence, thus benevolently establishing and maintaining a duality between himself and his creatures without which they could neither freely accept nor reject his reality and offer. In the divine plan, creatures are not to transcend this duality by sloughing off their creatureliness and being absorbed into the single divine reality (pantheism), as is proposed in many Oriental religions. Rather, the separate existence of God and spiritual creatures must remain if they are to be united in loving mutual adherence.

Divine love's eternal, infinite self-giving chose not to limit itself to the tri-personal Trinity, but to overflow by creating out of nothing many more personal objects of that same self-giving. God, necessarily and blissfully his own end, is humanity's origin and destiny. Unlike humans, who only love what they perceive to be good, the Creator both makes to be and makes to be good that which he freely chooses to love; and since divine love is not conditioned by any human qualities or response, it is ever-faithful, irrevocable. (Indeed, for God, to create, to conserve, and to love are but one indivisible, timeless action.) Thus God lovingly maintains humans in existence, so that he might keep pouring love out on them, both here and hereafter.

God and Human Freedom • God cannot force himself on humanity; besides doing no good, that would be the antithesis of love. If he had wanted robots, robots he would have made. But by fashioning human nature so as to make men and women capable of the self-knowledge, self-possession, and self-giving that allow them to function as independent persons, the Creator has placed himself, so to speak, at his creatures' mercy. He can only do to, with, and for them what they allow him to do. Lest he compromise their freedom, God must remain invisible, leaving humans to work out their fates. Unlike the angels — whose comprehensive, intuitive grasp of reality makes single and unalterable their choice or rejection of God — humans, with their embodied spiritual nature, must work with the partial evidence their discursive intellect can gather, an ongoing process that leaves their choices tentative, provisional, but remediable.

If God cannot overwhelm humanity, neither can he underwhelm it. For his loving plan, accommodated to the step-by-step workings of human nature and freedom, to meet with success, it must be universally viable. God cannot be so hidden that only a handful of spiritual adepts can find him. His existence and character must be luminous enough that all who wish to find him can do so (even if obscure enough that those who do not seek are not obliged to find him). St. Paul shows the way: "Ever since the creation of the world his invisible nature, namely, his eternal power and deity, has been clearly perceived in the things that have been made" (Rom 1:20). Human persons can ascend from created realities to their divine cause in a virtuous upward spiral that need never end — incremental knowledge of, and love for, God growing, as they progress upward.

That was the divine plan, and still is. No human sinning or even wholesale mutiny can invalidate God's will. While absolutely free to create or not, once God has willed humans into existence, he cannot stop loving them, however fickle, mutable, and myopic they might be. If they go astray, before death there is always time and incentive enough, along with God's superabundant, invisible help, for them to retrace their steps and begin to right themselves.

How effective was God's plan after original sin and before Christ's coming (or after it, for all those unreached by his Good News)? We cannot know who ultimately has opted for God or spurned his gracious, invisible advances. But of those unexposed to Christianity, most would seem to fall short either because they have not submitted themselves to the self-discipline of virtue or because they fall into pride.

In any case, the Epistle to the Romans says that, considering the plain clues, ignorance of God is voluntary and therefore culpable. "So they are without excuse; for although they knew God they did not honor him as God or give thanks to him, but they became futile in their thinking and their senseless minds were darkened" (1:20-21). Basing itself on the same Pauline text, the First Vatican Council declared that a supernatural Revelation wrought by the Incarnation of God's word was not absolutely necessary but relatively so, given the generally sorry state of humanity. Lest humans on their own not attain to essential truths regarding God and themselves, a supernatural mode of communication assured that these truths "can be known by all with ease, with firm certainty and with no admixture of error" (Vatican Council I, *Dogmatic Constitution on the Catholic Faith, Dei Filius*, 2).

Whatever God does, however, each person, in the austere loneliness of his or her heart of hearts, must still decide whether or not to recognize and accept the gift of God. Before humans can fully and definitively accept the Good News, they must, as it were, admit and renounce all the bad news they have generated. At the point, when God is seen as their best friend, God's whole creative project will have successfully come full circle.

See: Angels; Creation; Divine Revelation; Freedom, Human; Human Person; Knowledge of God; Original Sin; Providence; Redemption.

Suggested Readings: CCC 355-379, 1707-1709, 1718-1724, 2292-2301. Vatican Council II, *Pastoral Constitution on the Church in the Modern World, Gaudium et Spes*, 12-22. J. Pieper, *The Four Cardinal Virtues.* F. Wilhelmsen, *The Metaphysics of Love.*

Dennis Helming

HUMAN VIRTUES

Virtues are dispositions to perform good acts. Virtues orienting us to human perfection are acquired by repeated acts, and are called human or "natural" virtues. They are distinct from theological virtues, which orient us beyond human perfection to God himself and are infused by God.

In creating human persons, God wills for them a perfection or goodness appropriate to their nature. So, God wills that human beings be healthy, intelligent, morally good, perfected by community, and so on. We are called to cooperate with God's plan, and so part of our vocation is to work energetically for human goods, that is, the perfection of human life and community (cf. Vatican Council II, *Pastoral Constitution on the Church in the Modern World, Gaudium et Spes*, 34).

But God has also freely chosen to share with us more than a human perfection. He has freely chosen to invite us to share his own interior divine life. When we were conceived by our human parents, we became children of human beings and received a human nature; when we were baptized, we became children of God and received sanctifying grace, which is a participation in the divine nature. Thus God has called us not only to human perfection but, what is clearly beyond our ability to comprehend, also to a share in his own interior divine life.

Hence there are two different kinds of virtues: human or natural virtues and theological virtues. Our share in divine life, also called grace, does not negate human nature; so, specifically human perfections are not superfluous in God's kingdom. Dispositions to human actions that perfect us as human are human virtues; dispositions to communion with God in his own life are the theological virtues. Human virtues include prudence, justice, temperance, fortitude, and others. Prudence, justice, fortitude, and temperance traditionally are called "cardinal" (or "moral") virtues; they are particularly important, since they are sources of other virtues and the foundations of morally good acts. The theological virtues are faith, hope, and charity.

See: Cardinal Virtues; Grace; Kingdom of God; Theological Virtues.

HUMILITY

True humility is thoroughgoing poverty of both heart and mind. St. Teresa of Ávila simply calls it "walking in the truth." It is the correlative human effort to know both God and oneself as the two parties objectively are. As St. Augustine says, "Should I know myself, I would know you, O Lord." Only when humans acknowledge their bad news will they become ready, glad, grateful recipients of the Good News (cf. CCC 2540).

The Blessed Virgin's humility, in which she reveled with her Magnificat (Lk 1:46-55), consisted in gratefully recognizing that all her sterling qualities and endowments were pure, gratuitous gifts from God. Since she did not falsely appropriate them to herself or selfishly hoard them, she in effect gave God a free hand to continue to bedeck and engrace her. In our day, Blessed Josemaría Escrivá joked, "The best business in the world would be to buy men for what they're really worth and to sell them for what they think they're worth." If pride is fiercely competitive, however, humility inclines to fraternal charity: "Clothe yourselves . . . with humility toward one another, for 'God opposes the proud, but gives grace to the humble' " (1 Pt 5:5).

Humility is a by-product of prayerful endeavors to know Christ, joined to charitable efforts to imitate him in serving others. Without a minimum of fifteen minutes of daily mental prayer, as holy men and women and spiritual writers through the ages attest, it is almost impossible to accept and act on the creaturely truth that everything of value in one's life comes from God, and humans can lay claim only to what restricts his bountiful giving: sin, shortcoming, weakness, and imperfection. The humility born in silence begins to take wing when Christians generously occupy themselves with others' needs, while forgetting their own, as well as their rights and entitlements.

See: Capital Sins; Cardinal Virtues; Human Virtues; Pride.

HYPOSTATIC UNION

This formula means a personal union or substantial union of the divine and human natures in the one Lord, Jesus Christ. The controversies over the Trinity and over the unity of the Person of Our Lord brought to the fore the reality and terminology of "person." In grappling with vocabulary, the Church defined *hypostasis* to mean Person. From the Council of Constantinople of 381 the description of the Trinity as three *hypostases* in one *ousia* came to be interpreted as *three persons in one nature*. The role of the person will become more evident as we survey the controversies that erupted over the unity of the Lord's Person.

The Eternal Word is the Person who takes the initiative of uniting a human nature to himself. The human substance is not a person but belongs to the Person of the Word. The Son of God communicates to his humanity his own personal mode of existence in the Trinity. This allows Jesus to express for us in human terms what he has of personal freedom, of receptivity to the Father and the Spirit, and of total self-giving to the Father with the Spirit in the Trinity. All of this is important because it determines the reality of our redemption, a divine act of reconciliation performed in the Lord's human nature. His human words and deeds reveal the Eternal Trinity.

Early Controversies • The first problem concerned the proper way to understand the phrase "the Word became flesh." The Church in 381 condemned the interpretation put forward by Apollinarius of Laodicea that "flesh" only meant that the Logos assumed a physical body, not a human soul and mind, because the soul and mind were replaced by the Eternal Word. In this case Jesus would not have a complete humanity like ours; but the Church teaches that Jesus assumed a full human nature — body and soul — like ours. If he had not assumed a mind, then our soul and mind would not have been redeemed, which would be rather outrageous. The Nicene Creed safeguards this teaching by explicitly stating that Jesus was made flesh and became man: "He was incarnate of the Virgin Mary, by the power of the Holy Spirit and was made man." (It should be noted that we have no better way of avoiding confusion than by saying "man." Otherwise, we fall into the heresy of stating that he became a human person or we weaken the Incarnation by saying that he became human, which is a way of acting and not a way of being.)

The next controversy revolved around how the full human nature and the Divine Person are united. Nestorius refused Mary her title of Theotokos and called her instead Christotokos, the Mother of Christ, not the Mother of God. Nestorius had several problems at once. He could not think of the human nature as distinct from the person, but could think of it only in the very concrete and individualistic way that in fact amounted to a human person. Nestorius had problems also with the union of the human nature. He could not conceive of the union of Divine Person and human nature as anything more than a moral union of grace and will, but not a truly personal union. In this way he thought he was protecting the Divine Person of the Son from being changed or damaged through a sort of confusion with the humanity. Nestorius had taken too strong a view of the Person and the human nature, but could not grasp the strength of the unity that is contained in the phrase "the Word became flesh."

Against Nestorianism the Council of Ephesus in 431 affirmed that the Word "uniting to himself in his person the flesh animated by a rational soul, became man." The Fathers reached this conclusion by noticing in the Nicene Creed that it is the one Lord Jesus who is God from God, begotten not made, and who came down from heaven to become man, suffer, and die for us. This unity of the Lord Jesus also allows the Council to say that Mary's activity in bringing forth the Word made flesh was not restricted to the human nature but terminates in the Divine Person, who is one with his human nature. Once the Incarnation takes place, activity and passivity belong to the Divine Person, for he is the one who acts or receives the impact of an action. The great clarifying questions here are, "Who is acting, the Eternal Word?" and, "How does he act, in his human nature or in his divine nature?" The

natures define the kind of action the Person is involved in, but the Person defines the agent who is responsible for acting.

Unfortunately, this was not all understood, so that some held that in the union the Divine Person would have absorbed the human nature after the union. This is a heresy called monophysitism, or "one nature-ism." The Council of Chalcedon in 451 affirmed the union of natures in the Person, but insisted that the union preserves the natures intact without confusion or separation, and so does not lead to any diminution of the human nature. "We confess one and the same Son, Our Lord Jesus Christ, the same perfect in divinity and perfect in humanity . . . consubstantial with the Father as to his divinity, consubstantial with us as to his humanity; 'like us in all things but sin.' "

The Second Council of Constantinople spelled out against some who wanted to make the Lord's human nature a kind of personal subject who acts almost by itself, that it is the Person or hypostasis who acts. "We confess that one and the same Christ, Lord and only begotten Son, is to be acknowledged in two natures without confusion, change, division or separation. The distinction between the natures was never abolished by their union, but rather the character proper to each of the two natures was preserved as they came together in one person and one hypostasis." The Person in this case is none other than the second Person of the Trinity, the Eternal Word, who could act in his human nature, be born, be hungry or thirsty, suffer, die, and rise, and in his divine nature perform miracles, reveal the Father's will, be in contact with his Father.

Two Wills and Two Operations • The final clarity on these points was achieved by the Third Council of Constantinople (681), which asserted that the Lord Jesus has two wills, human and divine, and two operations, human and divine, and not just a divine will. Opponents played on the fact there could not be any opposition between the two wills but only cooperation, in order to try to assert only one will, the divine will. They construed the conformity to be an invasion of the divine will into the human, instead of a freely willed conformity of Jesus' human will in obedience to his Father's divine will.

Clearly, however, if Jesus had a human mind and soul but no human will, he would not have been completely human. The Catholics were faithful to Chalcedon in saying that the personal union maintains the integrity of the human will and operation. Otherwise, Jesus could not have willed and merited our salvation in his human nature; but that is why he became incarnate. This lessening of his human will would have totally undermined the working out of our redemption.

In the prayer in the Garden of Olives before his Passion, we have a glance at Jesus' human will in all its freedom. "And going a little farther, he fell on the ground and prayed that if it were possible, the hour might pass from him. And he said, 'Abba, Father, all things are possible to you, re-move this cup from me; yet not what I will, but what you will' " (Mk 14:35-36). In his prayer he struggles humanly with his Father's plan (the cup) and finally assents with his human will to accept the cup from his Father's hands. The *Catechism of the Catholic Church* devotes a special reflection to this prayer in the Garden, in which Jesus shows his obedience unto death: "By accepting in his human will that the Father's will be done, he accepts his death as redemptive" (612).

See: Christological Controversies; Incarnation; Jesus Christ, God and Man; Jesus Christ, Human Knowledge of; Jesus Christ, Life of; Mary, Mother of God; Redemption; Trinity.

Suggested Readings: CCC 252, 464-469. L. Bouyer, *The Eternal Son.* R. Kereszty, *Jesus Christ, Fundamentals of Christology.* J. Newman, *The Arians of the Fourth Century.*

Richard Malone

I

IDOLATRY

Besides polytheism itself, Scripture also often excoriates "idols, [of] silver and gold, the work of men's hands. They have mouths, but do not speak; eyes, but do not see." These mere artifacts make those who worship them empty: "Those who make them are like them; so are all who trust in them" (Ps 115:4-5). God, however, is the "living God" who gives life and intervenes in history.

Many became martyrs for not adoring "the Beast," refusing even to simulate such worship. But idolatry is not limited to past pagan worship. It ever dogs believers, especially the lukewarm. Idolatry divinizes what is not God. There is idolatry, says the *Catechism of the Catholic Church* (2212-2214), wherever creatures are revered in place of God, be they gods or demons (Satanism), power, pleasure, glamour, race, ancestors, the state, or money.

According to St. Thomas Aquinas, men were led into idolatry first by disordered affections. What consummated their idolatry was the influence of demons, who offered themselves to the worship of erring men, giving answers from idols or doing things that seemed marvelous. Ignorance of the first cause, the need of images for fixing higher conceptions, the instinct of self-preservation: these all psychologically dispose to idolatry.

Human life finds its unity and purpose in adoring the one God. "The commandment," says the *Catechism* (2114), "to worship the Lord alone integrates man and saves him from an endless disintegration. Idolatry is a perversion of man's innate religious sense. An idolater is someone who 'transfers his indestructible notion of God to anything other than God' [Origen, *Contra Celsum* 2, 40: PG 11, 861]."

See: Divination; Magic; Religion, Virtue of; Superstition.

IMAGO DEI

Only man, among all of the creatures of God, is created in the image of God (*imago Dei*). As Pope John Paul II points out, it is essential that we understand the implications of the revelation that we have been created in the image of God, because "There is no adequate definition of man but this one!" (*The Whole Truth About Man*, p. 145). Genesis says: "Then God said, 'Let us make man in our image, after our likeness; and let them have dominion over the fish of the sea, and over the birds of the air, and over the cattle, and over all the earth, and over every creeping thing that creeps upon the earth.' So God created man in his own image, in the image of God he created him; male and female he created them" (Gn 1:26-27). Although a material being and bound up with the material universe, man can never find his identity within it. To know who he is, man must look to the God whom he images, not to the dust from which he is formed.

Intellect and Will. A very long and respected tradition in Christianity (which includes St. Augustine and St. Thomas Aquinas) understands our imaging of God to be bound up with the fact that we, like God, have intellect and will, that we are able to understand, to judge, to exercise freedom, and to love. The Church has always concurred with that tradition, teaching as recently as the Second Vatican Council, for example, that "man, as sharing in the light of the divine mind, rightly affirms that by his intellect he surpasses the world of mere things" (*Pastoral Constitution on the Church in* the *Modern World, Gaudium et Spes,* 15) and that "that which is truly freedom is an exceptional sign of the image of God in man" (*Gaudium et Spes,* 17).

Dominion. Closely related to the fact that God has endowed us with intellect and will is his having given us dominion over all other living creatures. "And God blessed them, and God said to them, 'Be fruitful and multiply, and fill the earth and subdue it; and have dominion over the fish of the sea and over the birds of the air and over every living thing that moves upon the earth' " (Gn 1:28). Dominion is "lordship." By giving man dominion over the earth, God, the Lord, allows man to share in his own lordship ("You have given him rule over the works of your hands, putting all things under his feet" [Ps 8:6]). This is consistent with God's having created the visible world for human beings. They are its proper lords, for the visible world is created for and ordered to them. And they have been given intellect and will, in part at least, so that they might exercise lordship over it. Thus, "even when — as in our day — man reaches the moon, he can do this only by virtue of the first covenant, from which and thanks to which he received the prerogative of dominion" (Karol Wojtyla [Pope John Paul II], *Sign of Contradiction,* p. 23).

This view, that our imaging of God is by intellect and will, is therefore accurate, but it is also incomplete — for three reasons. First, while it offers an explanation for how each single human being images the one God, it offers no insight into how human beings might image the One God understood as a triune communion of love. Second, it does not explain why it is that the angels, also endowed with intellect and will, are not characterized in Scripture as having been created in the image of God. And, finally and most importantly, it does not take into account the revelation in Genesis which explicitly states that our imaging of God is as male and female. "So God created man in his own image, in the image of God he created him; male and female he created them" (Gn 1:27).

Male and Female. The Catholic faith has always insisted upon the social, or communal, di-

mension of human existence. We are not created as independent persons, who out of our independence may or may not choose to become related to others. We are *by nature* communal beings. As God himself declares, just before creating Eve, "It is not good that man should be alone" (Gn 2:18). The Second Vatican Council therefore taught that "Life in society is not something accessory to man himself: through his dealings with others, through mutual service, and through fraternal dialogue, man develops all his talents and becomes able to rise to his destiny" (*Gaudium et Spes,* 25).

The Catholic Church also recognizes that the communal character of human existence in some way reflects the communal character of God's existence. Christ prayed to his Father that his followers "may be one even as we are one" (Jn 17:22). The Second Vatican Council notes that here Christ implied "a certain parallel between the union existing among the divine persons and the union of the sons of God in truth and love" (*Gaudium et Spes,* 24). But how is the Trinitarian communion most concretely and specifically imaged by human beings? The opening chapter of Genesis tells us that this imaging is realized most specifically in humanity's creation as male and female. As John Paul II points out: "The fact that man 'created as man and woman' is the image of God means not only that each of them individually is like God, as a rational and free being. It also means that man and woman, created as a 'unity of the two' in their common humanity, are called to live in a communion of love, and in this way to mirror in the world the communion of love that is in God, through which the Three Persons love each other in the intimate mystery of the one divine life" (*On the Dignity and Vocation of Women, Mulieris Dignitatem,* 7).

Sacrament of God. To say that our imaging of God is bound up with our masculinity and femininity means that our bodies, just as much as our souls, participate in our imaging of God. Indeed, noting that a *sacrament* is an *outward* (or *visible*) *sign* of an invisible reality, Pope John Paul II points out that the human body "enters the definition of sacrament, being 'a visible sign of an invisible reality,' that is, of the spiritual, transcendent, divine reality" (*Theology of Marriage and Celibacy*, p. 175). Indeed, as he points out elsewhere, man constitutes the "first" sacrament, because man in his bodily existence "was created to transfer into the visible reality of the world the mystery hidden since time immemorial in God, and thus be a sign of it" (*Original Unity of Man and Woman*, p. 144). Here we begin to get some sense of why it is that the angels cannot be understood as created in the image of God, inasmuch as the angelic nature is incapable of making "visible" the invisible reality of God and his mystery or plan for our ultimate union with him.

Sexual Differentiation. Humanity's imaging of the differentiation of Persons in the Trinity is not accomplished simply by the fact that God creates two distinct persons (Adam and Eve); it also involves two distinct genders (male and female). *Adam* initially does not mean man as in "male." *Adam*, in point of fact, is simply the one taken from the earth (*adamah*). The Hebrew word for male (*ish*) does not appear in the Genesis text until the creation of Eve, at which point both *ish* and *ishshah* (female) are used for the first time. Only when the female is differentiated from Adam does Adam become male in relationship to her. When God says, "It is not good that man should be alone," he reveals that the goodness of human life is specifically bound up with this sexual differentiation.

Sexual Equality. Although Adam and Eve are sexually different, the male and the female together image God. While we might expect that, as different sexes, each brings something to that image which the other does not, what each brings is equal to what the other brings. They are created as equals.

Personhood As Relation. Man and woman are created as *persons.* What does this mean? Since human beings are created in the image of the one God who is also three Persons, we might suppose that to be a human person is analogous to being a Divine Person. In the Trinity, to be a Person is to be a subsistent *relation.* The Father is the relation of paternity, the Son of filiation, and the Holy Spirit of passive spiration. To be a person, in the Trinity,

is to be in an *ordered relationship* to other persons. The Father is Father because he is ordered to the Son as the relation of Fatherhood. The Son is Son because he is ordered to the Father as the relation of Sonship. The Holy Spirit is Spirit because he is ordered to the Father and the Son as the One who is spirated by them. Although each of the Persons is fully divine, each is radically dependent upon the others for his identity as a specific, ordered, and noninterchangeable Relation within the Trinity. We might suppose, then, that human beings as male and female are called to give themselves to one another in such a way as to enter into specific, ordered, and noninterchangeable relations with one another.

Human Personhood As Marital. According to John Paul II, to be a human person means two things: first, that one has intrinsic value and dignity, and, second, that one must *achieve* the realization of who one is through *giving oneself* to another. The Holy Father tells us: "Man — whether man or woman — is the only being among the creatures of the visible world that God the Creator 'has willed for its own sake'; that creature is thus a person. Being a person means striving towards self-realization . . . which can only be achieved 'through a sincere gift of self' " (*Mulieris Dignitatem*, 7).

Adam and Eve enjoy an equal value and dignity, because God has willed Adam for his own sake and Eve for her own sake. This cannot be said of any other "visible" (or "material") creature, for the whole of the visible material order has been created not for its own sake but for the sake of Adam and Eve. At the same time, each has been created as gift for the other. God has created Eve as *wife* for Adam, and Adam as *husband* for Eve. "Therefore a man leaves his father and his mother and cleaves to his wife, and they become one flesh" (Gn 2:24). Each can achieve full personhood therefore only by self-donation to the other in the marital relationship of husband and wife.

Two final notes should be added. First, that Adam and Eve, as male and female in marital union, image the Trinity *does not mean that God is male and female.* God is spirit and therefore should not be thought of as either male or female. The word "image" should not be identified with a "mirror image" in which there is a one-on-one relationship between the image and what is imaged. When we say that male and female image the Trinity, we mean that there is a likeness between *the relationships of Father, Son, and Holy Spirit* in the Trinity and *the relationships of husband, wife, and the bond between them* by which they become "one flesh" in marriage. Just as in God there is unity in the plurality of differentiated relationships, so also in marriage there is unity in the plurality of differentiated relationships. To speak this way also means there is a likeness between that total self-giving which is love in God and that total self-giving which is love in the marital union of husband and wife.

Second, that human beings image God in marital union should not be understood as excluding from that imaging all of those men and women who do not marry. Priests, who act in the Person of Christ, are called in celibacy to give themselves totally in service to Christ's bride, the Church. Single adults and those in religious life are called to give themselves totally to Christ. Celibacy "for the sake of the kingdom" is a sign and affirmation of the fact that in the next life no one will either marry or be given in marriage (cf. Mt 22:30), because all of us, as members of the Church, shall be united to Christ by virtue of our participation in the marital union of the Church with Christ (cf. Eph 5:31-32).

See: Animals; Body and Soul; Celibacy, Priestly; Environment; Freedom, Human; God, Nature and Attributes of; Hierarchy; Human Person; Human Race, Creation and Destiny of; Marriage, Sacrament of; Sacrament; Sexuality, Human; Stewardship; Theology of the Body; Trinity.

Suggested Readings: CCC 249-256, 355-376, 1602-1605, 1701-1706. John Paul II, *Original Unity of Man and Woman.* J. Little, "The New Evangelization and Gender," *Communio* (Winter, 1995). J. Ratzinger, "Concerning the Notion of Person in Theology," *Communio* (Fall, 1990), pp. 439-454.

Joyce A. Little

IMMACULATE CONCEPTION

Pope Pius IX on December 8, 1854, solemnly defined as a dogma of Catholic faith Mary's Immaculate Conception in the womb of her own mother, St. Ann. The precise words of the definition found in the apostolic constitution *Ineffabilis Deus* are these: "We declare, pronounce and define that the doctrine which holds that the most Blessed Virgin Mary, in the first instant of her conception, by a singular grace and privilege granted by almighty God in view of the merits of Jesus Christ, the Savior of the human race, was preserved free from all stain of original sin, is a doctrine revealed by God and therefore to be believed firmly and constantly by all the faithful" (Denzinger-Schönmetzer, 2803).

A number of important revealed truths are taught in this definition. One that the subject of Mary's preservation from original sin is the person of the Blessed Virgin, that is, her body and soul substantially united, and not her soul alone. This took place at the very beginning of her human conception, the initial instant of her existence as a human person or an embodied soul within her mother's womb.

Another revealed truth is that she is the only *human person* (her Son is a Divine Person) to have been conceived immaculately in the entire course of salvation history. Third, Mary is truly redeemed by her Son by a unique kind of redemption, usually called "preservative," whereby she was kept free from all sin, both original and actual, or personal. Finally, as a consequence, although a daughter of Adam — that is, a member of our fallen human race — she was in no way contaminated by any effect of Adam's sin.

The main reason for Mary's unique privilege of the Immaculate Conception given in Pius IX's apostolic constitution is that she was predestined by the Divine Persons of the Trinity to be the Theotokos (God-Bearer), or Mother of the Word (second Person) incarnate, that is, made flesh. Out of reverence for his infinite holiness, it was most fitting that he became hypostatically (personally) united with a human nature in the womb of a woman who was never infected by even the slightest sin: neither original sin (which would have made her a part of the human race's corporate alienation from God) nor personal, or actual, sin, even though venial (which would have impeded her love of God and neighbor). This theological reasoning applies Vatican Council II's teaching about the "hierarchy of truths" (cf. *Decree on Ecumenism, Unitatis Redintegratio*, 11) by showing the connection between the dogma of the Immaculate Conception and the primary truths of Christian faith, namely, the Blessed Trinity, the Incarnation, and the redemption (cf. *Unitatis Redintegratio*, 12).

Since 1854 there have been several reaffirmations of this dogma by the Magisterium. Pope St. Pius X issued an encyclical, *Ad Diem Illum* (1904), on the fiftieth anniversary of its definition. Pope Pius XII, in his encyclical *Fulgens Corona* (1953), repeated the entire dogmatic formula on the eve of its centenary, while declaring 1954 a Marian year in the Roman Catholic Church worldwide. He also recalled that Mary introduced herself to Bernadette of Lourdes with the words "I am the Immaculate Conception"; these apparitions occurred in 1858, just a few years after the definition of the dogma. Pius XII also related it to the dogma of Mary's Assumption, which he had solemnly defined in 1950. In the Mariological teaching of Vatican II, the references to Mary's Immaculate Conception are found in the *Dogmatic Constitution on the Church, Lumen Gentium*: "the Immaculate Virgin preserved free from all stain of original sin" (59) and "Enriched from the first instant of her conception with the splendor of an entirely unique holiness" (56).

Development of the Dogma • Although there is no explicit revelation of the Immaculate Conception in the Bible, the following are the principal scriptural texts used to support the dogma: "I will put enmity between you and the woman, and between your seed and her seed; he shall bruise your head, and you shall bruise his heel" (Gn 3:15); "and she [Elizabeth] exclaimed with a loud cry, 'Blessed are you among women, and blessed is the fruit of your womb!' " (Lk 1:42); "And he [Gabriel] came to her and said 'Hail, full of grace,

the Lord is with you' " (Lk 1:28). In *Ineffabilis Deus* Pius IX uses these three texts as the biblical basis for defining the Immaculate Conception to be a "doctrine revealed by God." Just how the dogma gradually grew out of such roots in the inspired word of God depends upon a theological theory of development. This tries to explain the various factors in the Tradition that seemed to help make clear and explicit the divine "insinuations," or suggestions, of the biblical revelation.

Noting that the earliest image of Mary after the New Testament is the "new Eve," which portrays her as most closely associated with her Son, the "new Adam" (cf. Rom 5:12-21), in re-creating the fallen human race by his redemptive activity, Cardinal Newman says this implies the Immaculate Conception as well as Mary's glorious Assumption. His total victory over sin and death, symbolized by the "serpent-devil" in Genesis 3:15 (the protoevangelium, or first announcement of the Good News of salvation, immediately after the Fall), is most fittingly shared completely with Mary. If she had been infected by original sin, even for a single instant, it would have diminished the perfection of her Son's redemptive activity, since his own Mother would have come under the dominion of Satan.

While most of the Eastern and Western Fathers of the Church taught that Mary was always free from any personal sin, even the slightest, it is not clear whether they intended to exempt her from original sin. St. Augustine's problem in this regard concerned the fact that she was not conceived virginally like her Son, but naturally through the marital act, which Augustine considered the instrument of transmitting original sin from one generation to the next.

Augustine's incomparable authority in the Western Church proved to be a serious deterrent in the development of the dogma over the centuries. Even such outstanding devotees of the Blessed Mother as St. Bernard of Clairvaux and the great Scholastics (among them Sts. Albert the Great, Bonaventure, and Thomas Aquinas) were unable to accept it as a revealed truth of faith. The main difficulty of the thirteenth-century saints and scholars was that it seemed to exempt Mary from being redeemed by her Son, the Savior of the whole world (which included his own Mother). The theological breakthrough came chiefly through John Duns Scotus (1266-1308), who was mainly responsible for introducing the notion of "preservative" redemption into the explicit consciousness of the Church. Yet there still remained another six centuries before the definition of 1854.

On February 2, 1849, Pope Pius IX issued an encyclical, *Ubi Primum*, in which he asked his brother bishops around the world to inform him about what they, their clergy, and faithful believed concerning the Immaculate Conception, and also whether or not these three groups in the universal Church wished it to be defined as a dogma. The response was overwhelmingly positive.

Reflecting upon the major influences in the historical development of the Immaculate Conception, it seems that the most significant was the *sensus fidelium*, the beliefs of the faithful, particularly as celebrated in the liturgical worship of the Church. This witness inspired the gradual extension and elevation of the feast of the Immaculate Conception (December 8) and finally helped create the theological climate in which the difficulties could be discussed and decisively settled. It was only appropriate that the voice of the faithful was heard in the response to Pius IX's encyclical and clearly set him on course to oversee the final preparations for the 1854 definition.

Examination of the dogma's historical development also reveals many other significant factors, such as the objectivity and impartiality of the Popes during the many centuries of development from the Middle Ages to modern times. Their own personal inclinations were always subordinate to the criteria for determining whether or not the Immaculate Conception is a "doctrine revealed by God and therefore to be believed firmly and constantly by all the faithful."

See: Assumption of Mary; Development of Doctrine; Divine Revelation; Dogma; Infallibility; Mary, Mother of God; Original Sin; Redemption; Sacred Tradition.

Suggested Readings: CCC 490-493. Vatican Council II, *Dogmatic Constitution on the Church, Lumen Gentium*, Ch. VIII. F. Jelly, O.P., *Madonna: Mary in the Catholic Tradition*; "Immaculate Conception" in J. Komonchak, M. Collins, D. Lane, eds., *The New Dictionary of Theology*. M. O'Carroll, C.S.Sp., "The Immaculate Conception" and "Ineffabilis Deus" in *Theotokos: A Theological Dictionary of the Blessed Virgin Mary*.

F.M. Jelly, O.P.

IMMORTALITY

Plato (427-347 B.C.) was the first great defender of the immortality of the human soul in Western philosophy. He argued that the rational part of the soul is nonbodily and nonmaterial, and that in addition the soul has a natural affinity for eternal truth, which it is capable of knowing and loving; the soul, he thought, must share in the eternity of that which fulfills it so deeply.

This and other Platonic arguments for the immortality of the soul were used by St. Augustine (354-430), but with this important difference: Plato thought that human souls need to free themselves completely from the body after death and to exist as pure spirits, whereas St. Augustine and all Christian thinkers recognize that the human body has a place in the immortal life of the soul — that each human being is immortal, not as a disembodied spirit, but as a body-soul unity. Plato teaches escape from the body; Christianity teaches the redemption of the body and the resurrection of the body.

Sometimes Christian thinkers who take seriously (as against Plato) the body-soul unity of man find it difficult to affirm that the soul lives on after death; they say that man can exist *only* as a body-soul unity, and is therefore completely destroyed at death and completely restored at the resurrection of the body. But this seems contrary to the faith of the Church. Catholics believe that the separated soul undergoes the "particular" judgment immediately after death, and also that the souls of the just have, in the interval between their death and the resurrection of the body, intercessory power. We have to say, then, that the natural condition of the soul is to be embodied, and that its final condition in the world to come is to be embodied; but that its immortality is not limited to the body, and that it will for an interval exist in a disembodied state.

See: Body and Soul; Heaven; Judgment, Particular; Neoplatonism; Resurrection of the Dead.

INCARNATION

The New Testament teaches certainly that the Word became flesh. The eternal Son of God, taking human nature from his Mother, Mary, united it to his Divine Person and lived a human existence on this earth, with all the limitations such a life entails. "The Word became flesh" (Jn 1:14) so that he could be our resurrection and life.

There are some presuppositions that apply here. These include a benevolent God who is concerned enough about his creatures to enter into this union with them. Also presupposed is a human being with the capacity for becoming one with God as required in the Incarnation. We are, moreover, dealing with the preexistence of a Divine Person who at a certain moment of time takes human flesh for our salvation. This teaching allows the Church to profess the full divinity and the full humanity of Jesus Christ. Major scriptural sources are the prologue of John's Gospel and the Letter to the Philippians 2:6-9.

Faith in the Incarnation results from the perspective that Jesus offers on his mission: "I have come not to abolish them [i.e., the law and the prophets] but to fulfill them" (Mt 5:17); "Do not think I have come to bring peace on earth" (Mt 10:34); "The Son of man came to seek and to save the lost" (Lk 19:10); "He who receives you receives me, and he who receives me receives him who sent me" (Mt 10:40; cf. Lk 9:48).

Christology and the Incarnation • The prologue of John brings out the identity and difference in speaking of God the Father and of the Word who was God and who "became flesh and dwelt among us, full of grace and truth; we have beheld his glory, glory as of the only Son of the Father. . . . No one has ever seen God; the only Son who is in

the bosom of the Father, he has made him known" (John 1:14, 18).

Here we observe the need for a "descending" Christology in order to understand the mystery of the Incarnation. The evangelist realized that without such a clear statement the Gospel would lack its proper starting point. He who in his eternal being is the cause of the becoming of creatures now begins a life of becoming on his own. For the Word incarnate, becoming marks his involvement with his creatures. To *become flesh* is a stronger term than just taking on flesh or putting on flesh. To *become* points toward an involvement of the person.

We find a similar teaching in St. Paul. Consider the Letter to the Galatians: "He [God] was pleased to reveal his Son to me in order that I might preach him to the Gentiles" (1:15-16); and, "When the fullness of time had fully come, God sent forth his Son, born of a woman, born under the law, so that we might receive adoption as sons" (4:4). This thought also appears in the Letter to the Romans: "[S]ending his own Son in the likeness of sinful flesh and for sin, he condemned sin in the flesh, in order that the just requirement of the law might be fulfilled in us, who walk not according to the flesh but according to the Spirit" (8:3).

In a powerful summary, St. Paul opposes Christ's poverty to the riches that Jesus brings us: "For you know the grace of our Lord Jesus Christ, that though he was rich, yet for your sake he became poor, so that by his poverty you might become rich" (2 Cor 8:9). Here we have clear reference to the Incarnation. Christ abandons his heavenly riches (the metaphor for glory and divine goods, the state of Christ in his divine existence as Son) and becomes poor (in his humanity) in order to procure heavenly goods for human beings.

The Preexistence of Christ • In 2 Corinthians 5:21 we find a teaching that brings together these two ideas (God sending his Son in the flesh in order to make us rich): "For our sake he made him to be sin who knew no sin, so that in him we might become the justice of God." The focus is on the cross and Resurrection, but the Incarnation is the way in which the Son can make his death and

Resurrection the source of our justice (holiness). The Incarnation allows all this to happen. He "who knew no sin" refers to the preexistence of the Son of God. He "made him sin" means that the Son embraces both the Incarnation and the cross. Paul insists on the antithesis between what Jesus was in his preexistence and what he became in time. The Incarnation allows this antithesis.

With this background we can reflect upon the pre-Pauline hymn that we find in Philippians 2:5-11, which covers this same ground. Incarnation means the voluntary humiliation that is expressed in the two degrees: (1) the state of man as servant before God, and (2) the servant's obedience to death, even death on the cross. "He emptied himself" means that Christ emptied himself, impoverished himself in his divine prerogatives. The self-stripping does not consist in abandoning the "form of God" in order to take on another form, that of a "servant"; it consists in taking on the form of a servant while continuing in the form of God. While there is no direct speculation about Jesus' preexistence, still the fact of being in the form of God with the features of God presupposes his full and total participation in the divinity of the Father. Form relates to the essence or substance in its manifestation or self-expression.

This is the reason why the Father exalts the incarnate Son and gives him the exercise of the dominion over created reality, the role of God, which he had earlier renounced. Paul does not seem to be interested in the metaphysical problem of how a Divine Person can assume a human nature. The question that interests him concerns the fact that Christ the Lord is servant, while normally we would expect him to show the divine prerogatives in his human nature.

For St. Paul, Resurrection gives Christ his sovereign functions in the kingdom of God. The risen Christ in his role as sanctifier is the Son of God, now vested with power, according to the Spirit of Sanctification. In Romans 1:4 we meet this in shortened form, Christ "according to the Spirit."

Finally, we have what St. Paul says in 2 Corinthians 5:18: "All this is from God, who through Christ reconciled us to himself and gave us the ministry of reconciliation; that is, God was in Christ reconciling the world to himself, not counting their trespasses against them, and entrusting to us the message of reconciliation." In the light of what has been noted above in St. Paul, it is clear that this means that the Son who is God came in the flesh to reconcile us with his Father. The Incarnation is the grounding of the efficacy of the cross.

This is not an exhaustive study of the Gospels and of the Pauline corpus. It is a brief attempt to suggest the agreement of Paul and John on Jesus' preexistence as the source of Church teaching on the Incarnation. The early New Testament does not "progress" in its ways of presenting the Lord, from an eschatological prophet in "Q" to the Son of God when we reach the Gospel of John. Paul emphasizes the Incarnation in various ways, followed by the Gospels including the last of these, St. John. Paul's discussion of the first Adam (cf. Gal 4:4) refers to none other than the Son of God made man. What we find in Romans, 1 and 2 Corinthians, and Galatians sets up a sure context for interpreting the second chapter of Philippians in terms of preexistence and Incarnation.

It is difficult to see any basis for the assertion by some scholars that the Incarnation does not necessarily mean the preexistence of a Divine Son who, at a certain moment of time, takes flesh. We cannot admit with J.A.T. Robinson that "one who was totally and utterly a man — and had been nothing other than a man or more than a man — so completely embodied what the meaning and purpose of God's self-expression in terms of the Word or the Spirit that it could be said of him, he was God's man or that he was God for us." The Pontifical Biblical Commission, in a statement headed *Scripture and Christology*, gives useful guidance: "The New Testament authors, precisely as pastors and teachers, bear witness indeed to the same Christ, but with voices that differ as in the harmony of one piece of music. But all these testimonies must be accepted in their totality in order that Christology, as a form of knowledge about Christ rooted and based in faith, may thrive as true and authentic among believing Christians."

The Incarnation took place without any lessening of the Person of the Son. God showed the surprising capacity of his freedom and love. "If he was also weak, this was due to his own fullness of power," St. Augustine comments in the *City of God* (VIII, 17).

The Gospels also highlight the risen Lord appearing to his disciples in his humanity. They can look at him, touch him with their hands, listen to his words. They witness his Ascension into heaven. In this way we can ascertain that the union of the eternal Son with his human nature continues in the state of glory.

See: Fatherhood of God; God, Nature and Attributes of; Hierarchy; Holy Spirit; Hypostatic Union; Jesus Christ, God and Man; Jesus Christ, Life of; Redemption; Trinity.

Suggested Readings: CCC 456-483. L. Bouyer, *The Eternal Son.* R. Kereszty, *Jesus Christ, Fundamentals of Christology.* R. Cantalamessa, *Jesus Christ, The Holy One of God.* J. Newman, *The Arians of the Fourth Century.*

Richard Malone

INCEST

Incest refers to sexual relations among members of the same family or with relatives of such close relation that marriage would not be proper.

Since God designed human sexuality to expand the loving relations we have and to bring male and female to create new families, having sexual intercourse within one's close family is a misuse of the gift of sexuality. The kinds of loving relations appropriate for members of the same family do not have sexual expression as a natural or appropriate component. Many victims of incest are young children who often suffer lifetime difficulties because of inappropriate, premature sexual relations and the betrayal of trusting relationships.

See: Sex Abuse; Sexuality, Human.

INCULTURATION

Since the age of the Apostles, St. Paul's address to the Athenians (Acts 17:22-31) has rightly been viewed as a justification for that process of judiciously combining elements of pre- or non-Christian culture with Christian Revelation that Jean Daniélou felicitously termed "cultural borrowing." (The term in Greek is *chrêsis*, in Latin *justus usus*: the utilization of pagan elements in pre-Christian thought and culture after purifying them of heathen contamination and reorienting them toward Christian faith.)

Not only the principle intimated by St. Paul and clearly enunciated by St. Justin the Martyr — but even some of their very diction — is today still germane in relation to inculturation. Thus the Second Vatican Council acknowledges that in the more widely spread non-Christian religious traditions, "elements of goodness and truth" are present "by God's Providence" (*Decree on Priestly Formation, Optatam Totius*, 16), and that "precious elements of religion and humanity" (*Pastoral Constitution on the Church in the Modern World, Gaudium et Spes*, 92) can be found among those who "acknowledge God."

Indeed, "seeds of the Word" lie hidden in many national and religious traditions (*Decree on the Church's Missionary Activity, Ad Gentes*, 11), and it is by these "seeds of the Word" and "by the preaching of the Gospel" that the Holy Spirit calls all men to Christ (*Ad Gentes*, 15). Although "a ray of that truth which enlightens all men" can be reflected in rules, teachings of ways of life, and conduct among non-Christian religions (*Declaration on the Relationship of the Church to Non-Christian Religions, Nostra Aetate*, 2), it is not only the more or less common elements already present but also the opposing or even contradictory factors that must be taken into account (*Nostra Aetate*, 2-3, *Ad Gentes*, 11).

Through a sort of secret presence of God, elements of truth and grace are found already among the Gentiles. Evangelizing activity liberates all these elements from evil defilements and restores them to Christ, who is their author. He overthrows the dominion of the devil and wards off the manifold malice of evil deeds. Therefore, all those good elements found in a germinal form in the hearts and minds of men or in the rites and cultures peculiar to particular peoples are not destroyed; on the contrary, they are healed, elevated, and perfected for the glory of God, for the humiliation of Satan, and for the beatitude of men (cf. *Ad Gentes*, 9).

The process of inculturation involves several stages. It frequently begins with adaptation or accommodation, a considerate conformation to the way of life, as far as it is not expressive of non- or anti-Christian sentiments, of the people among whom the Christians live. Assimilation can then follow, in which Christians actively adopt the habits and customs of the culture, while carefully avoiding syncretism, the artificial fusion of fundamentally incompatible religious elements. The final stage is transformation, which converts or transmutes what is good in the culture into Christian values by eliminating elements that are bound up with paganism or anti-Christian religiosity.

Theology of Inculturation • The theology of inculturation and evangelization presupposes a theology of the attitude of those within the covenant to those without. Hence the theology of inculturation should be evolved from a theology of the covenant. After the preceding covenants, the New and Eternal Covenant includes evangelization and inculturation as essential constituents, namely, as the means to extend the covenant to all Gentiles (*ad gentes*). Under the New Covenant the attitude toward other cultures takes on a new dimension. This attitude leads to the utilization (*chrêsis*) of what is found good in the culture. Though foreshadowed in the Old Covenant, this utilization is characteristic of the New Covenant.

The theological reason for practicing utilization/*chrêsis* is that all that is true and good belongs to Christ and to his Mystical Body. Utilization is analogous to conversion: Just as in a human being conversion does not destroy nature but heals and cleanses it, so *chrêsis* transforms and reorients what is found good in a culture.

However, inculturation cannot be imitated in our own day in the same way in which it was practiced in antiquity in the West. This is because the results of Western inculturation and *chrêsis*, to the extent that they were guided by the Holy Spirit and sanctioned by the Magisterium of the Church,

have to be accepted and translated. And on this basis, inculturation remains not only possible and desirable but also needful.

Inculturation essentially presupposes contemplation of the divine truth as revealed in Christ (contemplation understood as pure mental gaze on the truth, *simplex intuitus veritatis:* cf. St. Thomas Aquinas, *Summa Theologiae,* II-II, q. 180, a. 3, ad 1). It is an attempt to express the result of such contemplation in a language that has not yet been Christianized or has become de-Christianized. This inculturation, like *chrêsis*, is the Christianization, the redemption, the baptism, as it were, of non-Christian language, symbolism, art, poetry, and other literature.

Inculturation thus understood is distinct from adaptation (which is a theological procedure) and assimilation (which is a psychological means to gain confidence). While inculturation is necessary for the reason given earlier, adaptation is not. It can be very helpful, but there are also situations in which it must be dispensed with, namely, when its practice would cause disturbance instead of confidence. Adaptation as an expression of nationalism or as the adoption of symbols and customs generally known to belong essentially to the non- or anti-Christian sphere is to be rejected because it is a road leading back to paganism. The practice of inculturation, and thus the completion of the Catholic religious system, as Newman puts it, is blocked when Catholicism is deformed by "indigenization" understood as rationalistic adaptation. The introduction of pagan symbols, habits, and the like after Christianization is an offense against the religious feelings of the People of God.

See: Buddhism; Evangelization; Hinduism; Islam; Missionary Activity.

Suggested Readings: CCC 120-123, 128-130, 854, 1093-1096, 1200-1206, 1232, 2585-2589. Vatican Council II, *Constitution on the Sacred Liturgy, Sacrosanctum Concilium*, 14-19, 21, 34, 37-40. Paul VI, *On Evangelization in the Modern World, Evangelii Nuntiandi*, 1-96. John Paul II, *On the Permanent Validity of the Church's Missionary Mandate, Redemptoris Missio.* Congregation for Divine Worship and Sacraments, *Fourth*

Instruction for the Correct Implementation of the Conciliar Constitution on the Liturgy (Nos. 37-40): The Roman Liturgy and Inculturation. J. Ratzinger, "Christ, Faith and the Challenge of Cultures," *L'Osservatore Romano*, English-language edition (April 26, 1995). R. Skeris, *Christus-Orpheus: Towards a Theology of Liturgico-Musical Adaptation*; "Divini Cultus Studium" in *Musicae Sacrae Meletemata*.

Robert A. Skeris

INDEFECTIBILITY

Our Lord promised that he, with his divine power, would be with his Church always (Mt 28:18-20) and that evil or error would never overcome the Church (Mt 16:18). Good is stronger than evil; God is more powerful than the devil, although at times we may be tempted to give way to the opposite impression. God's thoughts are not how we tend to think nor are his ways our ways (cf. Is 55:8). The triumph of Jesus Christ came through, letting himself be put to death on the cross: Humanly speaking, it appeared as his failure.

God would not be all-powerful unless his power was greater than all the evil of the world put together. His mercy and love would not be infinite unless they were able to absorb and overcome all men's defects, wrong dispositions, and sins. It is God's specialty to turn evil to good.

We should therefore not be surprised to encounter personal difficulties in our Christian life or to see the Church herself experiencing adversity. Sometimes this is the adversity from the weakness of her own members, as Vatican Council II points out: "The Church . . . clasping sinners to her bosom, at once holy and always in need of purification, follows constantly the path of penance and renewal" (*Dogmatic Constitution on the Church, Lumen Gentium*, 8). Sometimes it is the adversity the Church experiences in being the object of hostility, abuse, and even persecution. "Blessed are you when men revile you and persecute you and utter all kinds of evil against you falsely on my account" (Mt 5:11). The Truth was crucified to save the world.

Certain points of faith become more basic in times of crisis and need to be held on to more firmly. The Church will never be deprived of Our Lord's presence and protection. Nor will her mission be frustrated by the indifference or hostility of men. The Church will not fail: that is what we mean by the Church's indefectibility.

We, however, each one of us individually or several as a group together, might fail. We are especially at risk if we do not maintain our supernatural outlook ("O man of little faith, why did you doubt?" [Mt 14:31]).

The result of temptations should be to increase our faith: faith in the power of God, the efficacy of the work of Jesus Christ, and the indefectibility of his Church. Thus, never losing our optimism, we will be able to help others.

See: Church, Nature, Origin, and Structure of; Infallibility; Marks of the Church.

INDISSOLUBILITY OF MARRIAGE

For centuries, men and women have repeated the vow "till death do us part," feeling that they thereby express the natural resolve of two people who are so in love as to get married. The Catholic Church continues to take these words seriously and sees them as corresponding to the fact that marriage is naturally meant to be an indissoluble union. She continues to teach the indissolubility of the marriage bond, not as a Church law applying just to the marriage of Catholics but as a law of God for all marriages.

God, the author of marriage, instituted it as indissoluble from the very start. Jesus specifically confirmed this. "Have you not read that he who made them from the beginning made them male and female, and said, 'For this reason a man shall leave his father and mother and be joined to his wife, and the two shall become one'? So they are no longer two but one. What therefore God has joined together, let no man put asunder" (Mt 19:4-6). Even if one saw no other reason in favor of indissolubility, Our Lord's teaching should be enough, at least for a Christian. We should also try to see, and to get others to see, that the indissolubility of marriage, hard as at times it may seem, is a law of love, of fulfillment, and of happiness.

The Need for Self-giving • The Second Vatican Council set forth an anthropological principle of fundamental importance: "Man can fully discover his true self only in a sincere giving of himself" (*Pastoral Constitution on the Church in the Modern World, Gaudium et Spes*, 24). The self-gift the Council has in mind is not to things but to values and above all to persons: self-giving in a spirit of service and of love. When we give ourselves so, we find ourselves. If we do not manage to give ourselves in love, we lose our self. One can "triumph" externally, in this or that job or position; inside, however, one remains closed and shrunk as a person. Life without love is the most poverty-stricken existence there is.

In saying we need to commit ourselves to others in order to fulfill ourselves, Vatican Council II directly challenged a central tenet of modern secular psychology, which insists that we ought above all to protect ourselves (i.e., not give ourselves), so as to fulfill ourselves from within. We should be skeptical about bonds, suspicious of loyalties, and avoid commitments. Self-concern or self-sufficiency, rather than self-donation, should be the ideal. It is not possible to understand or live a Christian life unless one grasps the falseness of this. Christianity sees living for oneself, caring just for one's own happiness, as the way of growing frustration, where the possibilities of any real happiness gradually die out.

Love — or, rather, learning to love — is a task we must commit ourselves to, a task that lasts a lifetime, marked by efforts and failure and starting again and again. God, who created us, knows our ways, possibilities, and needs better than we do. That is why he wants to bind us to the task of loving, even when (as is bound to happen) this becomes hard or seems impossible. It cannot be impossible; otherwise, we would be predestined to hell, the abode precisely of those who never learned to love.

We all need to give ourselves to God: to love him, as he has first loved us (cf. 1 Jn 4:19). Some people give themselves to him directly by total donation in a celibate life. The majority are called to marriage as the normal way of self-giving. For, as the Church's theology insists, marriage originates precisely in the gift of oneself to another and in the acceptance of the other's self-gift. *Gaudium et Spes* speaks of the "irrevocable personal consent by which the partners mutually give and accept one another" (48; cf. CCC 1627; Canon 1057.2). Marital self-giving and acceptance — for life — comprise the way and challenge of fulfillment and growth for the great majority.

Two people truly in love want to belong to each other, to be united. Each wants to give oneself and to receive the self of the other in return. It is a poor love that does not want to be united for life. "I'll love you and accept your love for a day . . . for five years . . . until April 22, 2025. . . ." This has more the air of a commercial transaction than a proposal of love. "I'll love you, provided you suit me; I'll give myself to you and accept you, for as long as I feel happy doing so. . . ." This sounds much more like one-sided calculation and selfish reserve than generous self-giving.

Indissolubility and Love • Marriage, in God's plan, is a great school of love. When two people marry, they pledge their love to each other; they pledge to keep loving, to love the other with his or her defects. This makes deep human sense. What sort of love would they be pledging otherwise? To love is to want the good of the other person. To want to make one's partner happy, to be prepared to sacrifice oneself to do so, is of the essence of married love. "It is natural for the human heart to accept demands, even difficult ones, in the name of love for an ideal, and above all in the name of love for a person" (Pope John Paul II, general audience, April 21, 1982).

To give oneself is not the same as to lend oneself. A person who lends, holds on to what is his; he wants to be able to take it back. Real marital love is really given. It would not be genuine if the person were to retain the right to withdraw it. "Love seeks to be definitive; it cannot be an arrangement 'until further notice' " (CCC 1646). So indissolubility is an essential property of every marriage. There cannot be any real marriage where the partners will their commitment to be temporary or subject to withdrawal.

Few would question that true human love wants to be united to the loved one forever, yet the attitude of many today remains: A permanent bond? Yes — for as long as love lasts. But not a bond without love. If love dies, it is natural that the bond dies with it.

At first sight, this might seem logical, but it has more calculation than logic to it. It follows neither the logic of God nor the logic of human love itself. Where there is love, there is confidence that the relationship can work and determination to make it work.

The meaning of indissolubility is that God, taking people at their word, wants them to be faithful. This can only be understood if one recalls that love lies essentially in the *will*; it depends on the will, not on feelings. "Love for a person" (see the Pope's words above) does not mainly mean "feelings for a person." Feelings of love are generally strong at the start of a marriage, and tend later to wane or even disappear altogether. What the Pope states to be natural are the desire and determination to remain faithful — feelings or not — to the love one freely pledged to give, for better or for worse. If one remains faithful, it is always for better.

It is human nature to want a love that lasts. If a person is moved by a sexual-sentimental instinct and nothing more, he or she can drift from one casual relationship to another and end in isolation. But people have more than a mere sexual instinct: They have a *conjugal* instinct, which spurs them (also out of a healthy fear of remaining alone) to establish relationships on a permanent basis of mutual commitment for life. As there is a human instinct to keep one's life alive, so there is a conjugal instinct to keep one's marriage alive.

Christians who understand these anthropological truths are firmer and more persuasive in their defense of indissolubility: for instance, before the frequent objection that it is harsh on the Church's part to bind two people together when this is no longer what they want. But, at least at the start, it

is seldom that both husband and wife coincide in wanting to put an end to their union. Much more frequently, one wavers, begins to center on the partner's defects, stops forgiving and asking for forgiveness, fails to pray or seek good advice in time, lets his or her heart stray elsewhere, and so in the end wants to walk out on the other.

And also, if there are children, to walk out on them. In moments of tension, parents need to remember that their children have a right to their father's and mother's fidelity. God blesses the resolution to persevere "for the sake of our children" and gives the grace to live it. If it is pursued, it can even lead to the rebirth between the spouses of a love that seemed dead.

When, therefore, a couple experience difficulties, those around them — friends, neighbors, pastors, counselors — have a special responsibility in the advice they give. If they have reflected on the meaning and importance of the indissolubility of the married bond in God's plans, their advice will be a powerful support; but thoughtless advice can be destructive of many people's happiness.

There is a major crisis today in the loss of faith in indissolubility: People want a lasting love, a permanent bond of love, but they no longer trust it. Christian married couples themselves must, and can, restore faith in God's plan for marriage.

See: Annulment; Divorce; Marriage; Marriage, Goods of; Marriage, Sacrament of.

Suggested Readings: CCC 1644-1651. G. Grisez, *The Way of the Lord Jesus*, Vol. 2, *Living a Christian Life*, pp. 574-580, 589-591, 728-729.

Cormac Burke

INDULGENCES

If purgatory is one of the most difficult Catholic doctrines for non-Catholics to understand, then the Church's teaching on indulgences must be equally difficult. One reason is that the terms "purgatory" and "indulgence" are not found in Sacred Scripture. In order to appreciate the doctrine of indulgences, it is necessary first to understand what the Church teaches about purgatory.

Among the scriptural references the Church uses in explaining her doctrine on purgatory, the clearest in found in the Second Book of Maccabees. The incident concerns the aftermath of a battle between the Jews, led by Judas Maccabeus, and the Edomites. Judas and his men, collecting the bodies of their fallen, discovered sacred tokens — amulets of the pagan idols — under their tunics. Recognizing that these men had died in sin, "they turned to prayer, beseeching that the sin which had been committed might be wholly blotted out. And the noble Judas exhorted the people to keep themselves free from sin. . . . He also took up a collection, man by man, to the amount of two thousand drachmas of silver, and sent it to Jerusalem to provide for a sin offering. In doing this, he acted very well and honorably, taking account of the resurrection. For if he were not expecting that those who had fallen would rise again, it would have been superfluous and foolish to pray for the dead. But if he was looking to the splendid reward that is laid up for those who fall asleep in godliness, it was a holy and pious thought. Therefore, he made atonement for the dead, that they might be delivered from their sin" (2 Mc 12:42-45).

The central point this passage makes is that it is good to pray for the dead. If, however, there are only a heaven and a hell, it makes no point: For if the dead are in heaven, they do not need prayers; and if they are in hell, prayers will be of no avail. There must be more than these two. At the heart of the Church's teaching on purgatory, then, is the realization that, from the time a person dies until he or she reaches heaven, both the faithful on earth and the saints in heaven can assist that person with their prayers. Thus, purgatory is directly related to the doctrine on sin and so to the effects of the sacrament of Penance.

History of the Doctrine • Beyond the reference in Second Maccabees, the Scriptures offer insights on individual conversion. Alienation from God by sinning may not necessarily be overcome by a single act of repentance. In point of fact, an act of judgment may be the cause for the final conversion of the sinner. The Scriptures also offer instances where, although a sin may be confessed

and the guilt forgiven, God still imposes punishments that are not canceled (cf. Gn 3:17-19; Nm 20:12, 27:13ff.; 2 Sm 12:10-14). If this be the case, then it cannot be said that God's forgiveness of guilt always includes as well the remission of the punishment due to those sins. Intercessory prayer is also documented in the Scriptures, with the limits set only by the providential will of God and the free will of the person for whom the prayers are being offered.

From the second century A.D. onward, there are accounts of sinners performing intense acts of penance for their sins committed after Baptism. This practice was monitored by the Church, as she regulated the penances by discipline adapted to the individual penitent. Penances could be shortened for some by the intercession of their confessors, and those awaiting martyrdom could offer their salutary acts for others.

By the Middle Ages, the practice of frequent confession led to some mitigation of penances and allowed penitents to perform "redemptory" works. In addition to the private prayers and works of individuals, the public, liturgical prayers of the Church included intercession for sinners. By the eleventh century, the Church was teaching that she could and did officially intervene on behalf of the penitent. Such intervention, replacing some of the individual's penance, was an act of intercession seen in light of the totality of the Body of Christ. These first "indulgences" were acts of jurisdiction, meaning that the real canonical penance was remitted. They were outside the sacrament of Penance, yet involved punishments due to sins that had been confessed. Here, for the first time, the penance of the individual and the intercessory work of the Church were connected. It is this which constituted indulgences as such.

Theology of Indulgences • The word "indulgence" comes directly from the Latin *indulgentia*, which means forbearance. It signifies kindness in not exacting the full penalty due. The Gospel parable of the servant whose heavy debt was forgiven (Mt 18:23-35) sheds some light.

Central to the doctrine on indulgences is the fact that every sin affects the Christian in three ways: (1) it disrupts his relationship with God; (2) it disturbs his relationships with his neighbors — the rest of the Church; and (3) it unsettles him internally. The first requires sacramental confession and absolution; the second requires restoration; the third requires that he work daily on his ongoing conversion, striving to be perfect as is his heavenly Father. The *Catechism of the Catholic Church* says: "To understand this doctrine and practice of the Church, it is necessary to understand that sin has *a double consequence*. Grave sin deprives us of communion with God and therefore makes us incapable of eternal life, the privation of which is called the 'eternal punishment' of sin. On the other hand, every sin, even venial, entails an unhealthy attachment to creatures, which must be purified either here on earth, or after death in the state called Purgatory. This purification frees one from what is called the 'temporal punishment' of sin. These two punishments must not be conceived of as a kind of vengeance inflicted by God from without, but as following from the very nature of sin. A conversion which proceeds from a fervent charity can attain the complete purification of the sinner in such a way that no punishment would remain" (1472).

To properly appreciate the Church's teaching on indulgences one must adequately understand her teaching on the communion of saints. The Scriptures testify to a life beyond this one. Based on Scripture and Sacred Tradition, the Church recognizes among the members of Christ's Mystical Body three states of existence in union with God. These states of the members, who themselves collectively comprise the communion of saints, are: the militant (or pilgrim) Church on earth, the triumphant Church in heaven, and the purgative Church awaiting glory.

Part of the responsibility of the members of the Church on earth is to pray for the Church in purgatory; those in that state will one day be saints in heaven interceding for the Church on earth. We are commonly united in prayer and also in charity. This has been a hallmark of Christians since the first days, as they have always endeavored to help one another by prayers and good works. Our Lord reminds his listeners of the fruitfulness of community prayer. St. James admonishes his audience concerning the importance of good works as evidence of an underlying faith. In short, Christians have sought to imitate the Christ whose name they bear inasmuch as he prayed, suffered, and died for others. The bond of charity that identifies Christians does not, however, cease with death but continues beyond the grave. For this reason, the members of the Church on earth pray for those who have died, and those who have reached their heavenly reward intercede with the Lord both for those still on earth and those being purified from their sins.

"For this reason," as Pope Paul VI points out, "there certainly exists between the faithful who have already reached their heavenly home, those who are expiating their sins in purgatory and those who are still pilgrims on earth a perennial link of charity and an abundant exchange of all the goods by which, with the expiation of all the sins of the entire Mystical Body, divine justice is placated. God's mercy is thus led to forgiveness, so that sincerely repentant sinners may participate as soon as possible in the full enjoyment of the benefits of the family of God" (apostolic constitution *On the Revision of Indulgences, Indulgentiarum Doctrina,* 5 [1967]).

Obtaining Indulgences • The faithful may participate in the fruits of this practice in many ways. They may obtain indulgences for themselves as well as for those who have died. In addition to their prayers, they may apply the merits of their sufferings and good works. The prayers and good works of the Blessed Virgin Mary and the saints in heaven are part of a great treasury of spiritual goods to which the contrite sinner has recourse (cf. *Indulgentiarum Doctrina,* 5).

Indulgences are said to be partial or plenary insofar as they remove either part or all of the temporal punishment due to sin, though of course only God can be absolutely certain whether and when a plenary indulgence is actually obtained, since only he knows whether a person's dispositions are adequate. However, the Church stipulates three external conditions for obtaining one: sacramental confession, Eucharistic Communion, and prayer for the intentions of the Holy Father. These three conditions may be fulfilled several days before or after the performance of the prescribed work, but it is fitting that Communion be received and the prayers for the intentions of the Supreme Pontiff be said the same day the work is performed. A single sacramental confession suffices for gaining several plenary indulgences, but Communion must be received and prayers for the Supreme Pontiff's intentions recited for the gaining of each plenary indulgence. While the condition regarding prayer is fully satisfied by reciting one Our Father and one Hail Mary, individuals are free to recite any other prayer according to their own piety and devotion toward the Supreme Pontiff. In addition to these external conditions, it also is required that all attachment to sin, even to venial sin, be absent. Instead of receiving a plenary indulgence, one may receive a partial one if these conditions are not completely satisfied.

Subsequent to the issuance of *Indulgentiarum Doctrina,* Paul VI authorized the publication of a *Handbook of Indulgences (Enchiridion Indulgentiarum),* a compendium of prayers and practices for the gaining of indulgences. Examples of practices by which one may obtain a plenary indulgence are attendance at Holy Mass, devout visits to churches or oratories, and having Masses offered for the faithful departed. The faithful who use with devotion an object of piety (crucifix, cross, rosary, scapular, or medal), properly blessed by any priest, can acquire a partial indulgence.

Prefacing the scores of exercises specified in *Enchiridion Indulgentiarum* are "Three General Grants" offered as inspiration for Christ's faithful so they may incorporate into their daily lives Christ's spirit and grow in perfection. They are:

A partial indulgence is granted to any of Christ's faithful who, in the performance of his duties and bearing the trials of life, raises his mind to God in humble confidence and adds, even mentally, some pious invocation.

A partial indulgence is granted to any of Christ's faithful who, in the spirit of penance,

freely abstains from something that is permissible and pleasing to him.

A partial indulgence is granted to any of Christ's faithful who, led by the spirit of faith, with a kindly heart expends himself or some of his possessions in the service of his brethren who are in need.

If the theology of indulgences seems abstruse, an analogy may help. Consider a situation in which a child damages family property. He recognizes the wrong he has done and, having asked forgiveness from his parent, is forgiven. But he still must pay for the property damaged. In the analogous case of an indulgence, not only is the person forgiven, he also is excused from paying the debt, as might happen were the child in the example to perform some other works of charity or make some other contributions to the family's well-being.

No one member of Christ's Mystical Body can accomplish everything alone. The many members support, and indeed need, one another. Those who are ailing are especially in need. Moreover, each Christian in his or her own life complements the Passion of Christ. St. Paul offers reflections on both aspects of indulgences: "As it is, there are many parts, yet one body. The eye cannot say to the hand, 'I have no need of you.' On the contrary, the parts of the body which seem to be weaker are indispensable, and those parts of the body which we think are less honorable we invest with greater honor, . . . But God has so adjusted the body, giving the greater honor to the inferior part, that there may be no discord in the body, but that the members may have the same care for one another. If one member suffers, all suffer together; if one member is honored, all rejoice together" (1 Cor 12:20-26). And, "Now I rejoice in my sufferings for your sake, and in my flesh I complete what is lacking in Christ's afflictions for the sake of his body, that is, the church" (Col 1:24).

See: Communion of Saints; Grace; Penance in Christian Life; Purgatory; Satisfaction.

Suggested Readings: CCC 1471-1479. Code of Canon Law, 992-997. Paul VI, *On the Revision of Indulgences, Indulgentiarum Doctrina.* J.

Hardon, S.J., *The Catholic Catechism*, Ch. XV. D. Wuerl, R. Lawler, O.F.M. Cap., T. Lawler, eds., *The Teaching of Christ: A Catholic Catechism for Adults,* pp. 427-429.

Christopher M. Buckner

INERRANCY

"Inerrancy" refers to the lack of error in a field of human endeavor (e.g., engineering, musical performance, theology). When applied to Sacred Scripture, the doctrine teaches that Scripture is free from all error regarding the truth about our salvation. The Second Vatican Council affirmed that Scripture teaches "firmly, faithfully and without error that truth which God wanted put into sacred writings for the sake of salvation" (*Dogmatic Constitution on Divine Revelation, Dei Verbum*, 11). Inerrancy, then, is a way of speaking about the utter reliability of Revelation found in Sacred Scripture. In the words of *Dei Verbum*, quoting Vatican Council I, it is through God's Revelation that those religious truths which are by their nature accessible to human reason can be known by all men "with ease, with firm certainty, and without the contamination of error" (6).

It is important to recognize that inerrancy is based on the inspired character of Scripture. In a sense, God is ultimately the guarantor of scriptural inerrancy by leading and inspiring the sacred writers, who as true and free authors wrote only what God wanted written regarding the truths about our salvation.

Scholars have always recognized that there could be errors of fact in Scripture. However, it is generally conceded that the biblical authors do not in fact assert as true what is not true. For example, the assumptions about how the universe works found in the first eleven chapters of Genesis presuppose the scientific worldview of that day, clearly in error on many facts; yet the author of Genesis never asserts that the scientific view of the world of his day is in fact true. He simply assumes that view and works with it to bring out the truth about the nature of the world, its origins, and its relationship to the human community.

See: Canon of Scripture; Divine Revelation; Inspiration; New Covenant; New Testament; Old Covenant; Old Testament; Sacred Scripture.

INFALLIBILITY

The Apostles had the immense good fortune to meet Jesus Christ; their lives and eternities were stamped by that meeting. Their faith was put to many tests, but in a moment when many abandoned him, Peter said, "Lord, to whom shall we go? You have the words of eternal life" (Jn 6:68). Peter's words were those of a man bound to Jesus by love. His faith, his fidelity, was to the Person of Jesus. That also meant fidelity to his teaching: "words of eternal life."

Scripture says forcefully that "without faith it is impossible to please God" (Heb 11:6). A practical faith is asked of us: that is, faith that endeavors to carry out the teachings of Jesus in one's personal life.

At the Last Supper, Jesus said to his Apostles: "When I go and prepare a place for you, I will come again and will take you to myself, that where I am you may be also. And you know the way where I am going." Thomas was quick to intervene: "Lord, we do not know where you are going; how can we know the way?" Jesus replied with marvelous and divine words: "I am the way, and the truth, and the life" (Jn 14:3-6). The Apostles believed Jesus, followed him as the way, held to him as the truth, and reached the life that he promised and is. With one exception, they adhered to Jesus in faith and in deeds. This is our calling too. But how can we hear and follow Jesus? Has he not provided some means by which his teaching would be preserved in its authenticity throughout the ages?

He has: by endowing his Church with the charism of infallibility. "In order to preserve the Church in the purity of the faith handed on by the apostles, Christ who is the Truth willed to confer on her a share in his own infallibility" (CCC 889). The New Testament tells of Christ's decision to set up a visible, hierarchical, teaching Church, giving authority to the Apostles (and to their successors, the bishops), accompanied by the promise of his presence and that of the Holy Spirit, and the guarantee that whatever is taught will faithfully express his mind and will. "Go and make disciples of all nations . . . teaching them to observe all that I have commanded you; and lo, I am with you always" (Mt 28:18-20); "Whatever you bind on earth shall be bound in heaven, and whatever you loose on earth shall be loosed in heaven" (Mt 18:18); "He who hears you hears me, and he who rejects you rejects me" (Lk 10:16); "When the Spirit of truth comes, he will guide you into all the truth" (Jn 16:13).

Scope, Nature, Origins of Infallibility • Infallibility is not to be confused with the charism of inspiration, nor is it to be considered a source of new revelations. What matters is to "hold fast what you have, until I come" (Rv 2:25), to "guard what has been entrusted to you" (1 Tm 6:20).

"The infallibility which the divine redeemer wished to endow his Church in defining doctrine pertaining to faith and morals, is co-extensive with the deposit of revelation" (Vatican Council II, *Dogmatic Constitution on the Church, Lumen Gentium*, 25; cf. CCC 2035). The Church lives with the life of Christ. Her faith expresses his mind, constantly clarifying itself to us through the ages. Infallibility therefore is a possession and prerogative of the entire Church. Our Lord's words "Go, teach; I am with you always" apply to the whole body of the faithful, united in belief down through the ages. But the guarantee contained in these words has been more particularly given to the Magisterium — the teaching office exercised by the bishops and the Pope. "It is this Magisterium's task to preserve God's people from deviations and defections and to guarantee them the objective possibility of professing the true faith without error. . . . To fulfill this service, Christ endowed the Church's shepherds with the charism of infallibility in matters of faith and morals" (CCC 890).

The promise of Matthew 28:18-20, "Go and make disciples of all nations. . . . I am with you always, to the close of the age," should be seen in the light of the earlier guarantee addressed to all

the Apostles: "Whatever you [plural] bind on earth shall be bound in heaven, and whatever you [plural] loose on earth shall be loosed in heaven" (Mt 18:18); and this latter promise made to the whole apostolic college should in turn be understood in the light of the prior commission made to Peter alone: "You are Peter and on this rock I will build my church; . . . and whatever you [singular] bind on earth shall be bound in heaven, and whatever you [singular] loose on earth shall be loosed in heaven" (Mt 16:18-19).

So the Second Vatican Council teaches: "The Roman Pontiff, head of the college of bishops, enjoys this infallibility in virtue of his office, when, as supreme pastor and teacher of all the faithful . . . he proclaims by a definitive act a doctrine pertaining to faith or morals. For that reason his definitions are rightly said to be irreformable by their very nature and not by reason of the assent of the Church, inasmuch as they were made with the assistance of the Holy Spirit promised to him in the person of blessed Peter himself" (*Lumen Gentium*, 25). The College of Bishops, when united in faith with the Roman Pontiff, also teaches infallibly. "The infallibility promised to the Church is also present in the body of bishops when, together with Peter's successor, they exercise the supreme teaching office" (*Lumen Gentium*, 25), either in the solemn declarations of ecumenical councils or in and through their ordinary Magisterium.

The charism of infallibility enables us to hear the voice of Christ, speaking through those whom he has appointed. It is an expression of God's mercy: to ensure that truth he has communicated remains accessible to us.

Infallibility in Belief • Infallibility in belief should be distinguished from infallibility in teaching. The latter pertains to the Magisterium alone, given the conditions indicated above. Infallibility in belief pertains to the whole Church. "The whole body of the faithful . . . cannot err in matters of belief. This characteristic is shown in the supernatural appreciation of the faith (*sensus fidei*) of the whole people when, from the bishops to the last of the faithful, they manifest a universal consent in matters of faith and morals" (*Lumen Gentium*, 12).

"By a 'supernatural sense of faith' the People of God, under the guidance of the Church's living Magisterium, 'unfailingly adheres to this faith' [*LG* 12; cf. *DV* 10]" (CCC 889). To understand properly how the whole People of God is infallible in its sense of the faith (*sensus fidei, sensus fidelium*), it must be borne in mind that the body of the faithful goes beyond limits both of place and, especially, of time. The People of God always includes those of past generations, as well as those of the present moment. The former are in fact the vast majority, and it is easier to ascertain what they believed. It is *that* belief that marks the *sensus fidelium* and points infallibly to the truth.

This should be kept in mind in evaluating sociological data about current opinion in the Church. The norm in the Church is always what God wants. It is the one faith professed by the People of God over the centuries that is infallible; and in that faith we are called to communion. The faith of our fathers is a sure reference point, linking us to the teaching of Jesus "that comes down to us from the Apostles," as Eucharistic Prayer I expresses it.

Some persons see pride at work in the Church's claim to infallibility. But the claim is not proud; it is an acknowledgment of the greatness of what God has done in and through her. Pride instead is a danger for someone who, wanting to follow Christ, nevertheless refuses to admit any infallible organ of teaching instituted by him.

Acceptance of the Church's infallibility is a key test of faith in God's providence — in this divine way of ensuring access to the message of salvation.

See: Assent and Dissent; Church, Nature, Origin, and Structure of; Divine Revelation; Faith of the Church; Magisterium; Ordinary Magisterium; Pope; Sacred Tradition.

Suggested Readings: CCC 889-891, 2035. Vatican Council II, *Dogmatic Constitution on the Church, Lumen Gentium*, 12, 22-25. C. Burke, *Authority and Freedom in the Church*, Chs. 14-16.

Cormac Burke

INFANT BAPTISM

Infant baptism is the practice whereby children who have not yet attained the use of reason are incorporated into the Church of Christ through the pouring of water and the pronouncing of the Trinitarian formula, effecting the remission of original sin. The *Catechism of the Catholic Church* says: "Born with a fallen human nature and tainted by original sin, children also have need of the new birth in Baptism to be freed from the power of darkness and brought into the realm of the freedom of the children of God, to which all men are called" (1250).

There is a long history in the Church of baptizing infants. "There is explicit testimony to this practice from the second century on, and it is quite possible that, from the beginning of the apostolic preaching, when whole 'households' received baptism, infants may also have been baptized" (CCC 1252).

The Code of Canon Law states two requirements for the licit baptism of an infant, namely, "that the parents, or at least one of them, or the person who lawfully holds their place, give their consent; that there be a realistic hope that the child will be brought up in the catholic religion" (Canon 868.1.1-2). Furthermore, the sacrament of Baptism is to be delayed if this hope is "truly lacking" and the parents are to be made aware of the reason, the provisions of particular law being respected.

The Church's legislation also covers some particular situations. Thus: "An infant of catholic parents, indeed even of non-catholic parents, is lawfully baptized in danger of death, even if the parents are opposed to it" (Canon 868.2); an abandoned infant or a foundling is to be baptized unless "diligent enquiry establishes" that it has already been baptized (Canon 870); aborted fetuses, if they are alive, "are to be baptized, in so far as this is possible" (Canon 871).

Possessing "their role as nurturers of the life that God has entrusted to them" (CCC 1251), parents would "deny a child the priceless grace of becoming a child of God were they not to confer Baptism shortly after birth" (CCC 1250). The parents present the child for the sacrament along with the baptismal sponsor or sponsors, usually appointed by the parents (cf. Canon 874.1.1).

Concerning the time for baptizing an infant, the Code of Canon Law declares: "Parents are obliged to see that their infants are baptized within the first few weeks. As soon as possible after the birth, indeed, even before it, they are to approach the parish priest to ask for the sacrament for their child, and to be themselves duly prepared for it" (Canon 867.1). "If the infant is in danger of death, it is to be baptized without delay" (Canon 867.2).

As in the case of the baptism of an adult, the Rite of Christian Initiation, specifically the Rite of Baptism, is used for the baptism of an infant.

Against the teaching of some Reformers, the Church at the Council of Trent declared definitively that the baptism of a child (infant) is both valid and licit. Catholic teaching holds that faith, since it is not the "effective cause of justification" but is rather an "act of disposition," need not be present at Baptism. The Church's faith replaces the faith that the infant cannot possess.

Because the baptism of an infant is certainly valid, these infants are full members of the Church, and after they have reached the age of reason, they are bound to fulfill the obligations of baptized members of the Catholic Church. The Council of Trent rejected the notion, propagated by Erasmus of Rotterdam, that it is for children after they have reached the age of reason to decide for themselves whether or not they intend to abide by the obligations imposed by their reception of Baptism.

See: Baptism; Church, Membership in; Original Sin; Redemption; Sponsor, Baptismal.

Suggested Readings: CCC 1250-1252. Code of Canon Law, 867-868, 870-872, 874.

Charles M. Mangan

IN PERSONA CHRISTI CAPITIS

The Latin phrase *in persona Christi capitis* means "in the Person of Christ the Head." The expression is used to describe what is distinctive about the ordained priest and to express his position in the life of the Church.

The Catholic faith teaches that priestly ordination produces a change in the very person of the man upon whom the bishop lays hands. This change, which is frequently referred to as the indelible sacramental "character" of Holy Orders, is explained in terms of the priest's spiritual configuration to Christ. Because he can act "in the Person of Christ," the ordained priest is to be seen by the faithful as "another Christ."

Pope John Paul II uses the phrase in his 1992 postsynodal apostolic exhortation *I Will Give You Shepherds* to describe the *raison d'être* of the priest: "In a word, priests exist and act in order to proclaim the Gospel to the world and to build up the Church in the name and person of Christ the Head and the Shepherd" *(Pastores Dabo Vobis,* 15). To affirm that the priests of the New Covenant act "in the Person of Christ" is part of the Church's ordinary Magisterium (cf. Vatican Council II, *Dogmatic Constitution on the Church, Lumen Gentium,* 10). The expression is found in St. Thomas Aquinas, who uses it to explain how the ordained priest participates in the one priesthood of Christ. But it reflects a truth that the Church has known from the beginning and that St. John Chrysostom expressed well when he taught that the most high and infinitely good God has not granted to angels the power with which he has invested priests.

See: Holy Orders; Priesthood of Christ.

INSPIRATION

The foundation for this doctrine rests on the propositions that Sacred Scripture is ultimately authored by God and that it contains divinely revealed realities inaccessible without divine help. The key New Testament texts are 2 Timothy 3:16-17, 2 Peter 1:19-21 and 3:15-16, and John 20:31. These texts reflect the early Christian conviction that the oral and written teachings of Jesus transmitted through the Apostles in fact communicated the sacred word of God. This divine authority meant that the inspired texts had an authority that far surpassed even the most sublime and profound teachings of even the holiest and most illuminated mystics and theologians.

The *Catechism of the Catholic Church* (105) reaffirms what St. Augustine taught (i.e., Scripture is inspired: cf. *De Genesi ad Litteram* 2.9.20, *Ep.* 82.3). This teaching was developed by St. Thomas Aquinas (*De Veritate* 1.12; a.2), formally taught at the conciliar level at Trent (session four, Scriptural Canons), reiterated in the teachings of Pope Leo XIII (*Providentissimus Deus*), Pius XII (*Divino Afflante Spiritu*), more fully stated at the First Vatican Council (*Dogmatic Constitution on the Catholic Faith*, Ch. 2, "On Revelation"), and restated in a refined way by the Second Vatican Council (*Dogmatic Constitution on Divine Revelation, Dei Verbum*, 11).

The teaching of the second-century apologist Athenagoras is instructive. Anticipating the Scholastic understanding of instrumental causality in explaining the nature of inspiration, he held that the authors of Scripture wrote what the Spirit inspired them to inscribe just as the divine flutist produces heavenly music by blowing into the earthly flute (*Legatio* 9).

See: Canon of Scripture; Divine Revelation; Inerrancy; New Covenant; New Testament; Old Covenant; Old Testament; Sacred Tradition.

INTERDEPENDENCE

In Catholic social doctrine, we all simultaneously support and are supported by others. That mutual giving and receiving in society leaves us neither wholly independent nor wholly dependent, but interdependent.

Historically, the Church embraced the idea (which was first proposed in the classical world by Aristotle and further developed in its Christian dimensions by Thomas Aquinas) that human beings are by nature social. This means that human beings cannot reach their full development — religious and moral, intellectual and emotional, political and economic — on their own; societies exist so that we may all benefit from one another's gifts. Catholicism has, therefore, tended toward greater emphasis on community, compared with Protestantism's emphasis on the individual.

In modern times, interdependence has had to be defined sharply against the background of various social movements. Thus, Catholic communitarianism denies radical individualism. But the Church has long taught that individuals, families, and other private associations have responsibilities. They therefore have the right to private property and other means necessary to carry out those responsibilities.

By contrast to socialism and even to some forms of the welfare state, Catholic social teaching seeks a balance between these relatively independent social elements and the inescapable need for human solidarity.

In recent papal thinking — particularly in Pope John Paul II's encyclicals *The Hundredth Year, Centesimus Annus* (1991) and *The Splendor of Truth, Veritatis Splendor* (1993) — greater emphasis has been placed on human freedom and economic initiative than in the past. But this recognition of the divine gift of freedom is still always linked with the necessity to use freedom to do what is right and to love, foster, and support others.

See: Property; Social Doctrine; Subsidiarity.

ISLAM

"*Allahu akbar!* / God is most great! / I testify that there is no God but Allah. / I testify that Mohammed is the prophet of Allah. / Arise and pray; arise and pray. / God is great; / There is no God but Allah!"

The haunting cry of the *muezzin*, sounded of old from the minaret, in latter days from loudspeaker or radio, symbolizes Islam to the world. The Muslim religion was born in the Arabian desert over 1350 years ago and now claims as many faithful as the Catholic Church, roughly one billion. In bursts of conquest and through peaceful means, Muslims have evangelized an equatorial belt of lands circling the globe, from Morocco in the west to Indonesia in the east. Though Islam has experienced periods of decline, it has rarely been forced into retreat and today is expanding with renewed energy in Africa, Asia, and even the Americas.

In Muslim belief, the Prophet Mohammed (also spelled Muhammad) began receiving ecstatic revelations from God on Mount Hira near Mecca about A.D. 610. These revelations, which continued periodically until his death in 632, were later gathered into the Koran, the sacred book that forms the basis for Muslim theology, spirituality, and piety. While Islam later developed a considerable body of law, tradition, and theology and a vibrant mysticism (Sufism), the Koran remains the ultimate moral authority, the centerpiece of Muslim life.

Muslims consider themselves "People of the Book" and Mohammed the "Seal of the Prophets." These phrases capture the relationship that Islam bears to Judaism and Christianity. Mohammed saw himself not as the founder of a new religion but as the last in a line of prophets to which God had progressively revealed himself. This line, drawn in part from the Old and New Testaments, includes Abraham, Moses, David, and Jesus of Nazareth. But as Islam sees it, while Judaism went astray by worshiping the law or reverting to idol worship (the Golden Calf of Sinai), and Christianity erred by deifying Christ, Islam has retained its pure faith in the one true God.

The Five Pillars • This uncompromising monotheism is the first and most fundamental of the Five Pillars of Islam. The Muslim's confession of faith is simple: "There is no God but Allah, and Mohammed is his Prophet." This famous assertion, echoing the Jewish *sh'ma* ("Hear, O Israel, the Lord your God is One"), simultaneously rejects the animist religions popular in the Arabian peninsula in Mohammed's day and proclaims the prophet's unique place in salvation history. Mohammed gave the world the Koran, calling it his "standing miracle." The word *koran* means "something to be recited"; to the believer, its 114 *surahs* are quite literally divine wisdom that Mohammed, the chosen link between God and man, recorded and made known.

The second of the Five Pillars is prayer. Five times daily, in a mosque or anywhere else they happen to be, devout Muslims are to face Mecca and prostrate themselves before God, reciting traditional prayers and verses from the Koran. Typically, the content of Muslim prayer is gratitude to God for his gifts and supplication for growth in virtue: "O Lord, grant me firmness in faith and direction. Assist me in being grateful to you and in adoring you in every good way. I ask you for an innocent heart, which shall not incline to wickedness." Punctuating the routine of everyday life with public acts of worship keeps men and women consciously in God's shadow so that they do not neglect the duty they owe him and one another.

This duty in its social aspect forms the third Pillar of Islam. Mohammed specified that all Muslims must pay *zakat*, an alms equivalent to one-fortieth their worth, for support of the poor each year. While the system has broken down in many modern Muslim states, charity remains a serious religious obligation.

Fasting during the holy month of Ramadan is the fourth Pillar. With some exceptions (travelers, the ill, etc.), good Muslims at that time abstain entirely from food and drink from daybreak to sundown, taking nourishment in moderation at night. Since the Muslim calendar (which begins in the year 622, marking Mohammed's flight [*Hegira*] from Mecca to Medina) is based on the lunar cycle, Ramadan moves through the seasons. When it falls in the blazing tropical summer, fasting from water requires courage and a steadfast faith. Yet Islam finds many virtues in the practice: It teaches self-discipline, forges a sympathetic bond with the needy, and reminds all of their utter dependence on God.

Finally, every Muslim physically and economically able to do so must make a pilgrimage (*haji*) to the Kaaba, the ancient shrine in Mecca attributed to Abraham. Once they arrive in the holy city, pilgrims don identical garments, so that all approach the shrine radically equal before God. They walk around the Kaaba shoulder to shoulder, venerate the black stone set in one of its walls, and perform a number of other rituals over a period of days. The *haji* has a sacramental quality, in that it forges, even as it symbolizes, a solidarity among Muslims in the worldwide brotherhood of Islam.

Despite the Arabs' historic reputation as fierce warriors, the ideal of Islam is indeed brotherly love, expressed in the *zakat*, the pilgrimage, and in the prayer and fasting that Muslims practice in common. Obviously, all these find echoes in Judaism and Christianity, giving weight to the Muslim insistence that all three religions belong to the same prophetic tradition. Muslims and Catholics also share many other articles of faith, including a belief in free will, sin and punishment, the Last Judgment, and an afterlife. To these may be added faith in reason. It was the Muslims, after all, who preserved and transmitted the science and philosophy of ancient Greece, bridging Europe's Dark Ages.

Differences From Catholicism • Nevertheless, the differences between Islam and Catholicism are profound. While Muslims recognize religious leaders, especially in the Sufi tradition, there is no hierarchy analogous to the Pope and bishops. Thus Islam has no mechanism for the authoritative development of doctrine and relies more strongly on law and tradition than Christianity does. Moreover, many Muslims do not separate religion from politics as Western Christians do, and favor ordering public life through some form of the *sharia*, Islamic law. Most importantly, Islam is not an incarnational religion; Mohammed was a man with a divine message, not God's own Son sent for our salvation. It lacks a formal sacramental system crowned by the Eucharist and fails to recognize Jesus as the definitive revelation of God in human history.

The wide disparity among the world's great religions makes it hard to imagine a final reconciliation. However, the Second Vatican Council firmly taught that, while the Church is the ordinary means of salvation, "the plan of salvation also includes those who acknowledge the Creator, in the first place amongst whom are the Muslims" (*Dogmatic Constitution on the Church, Lumen Gentium*, 16). Pope John Paul II is tireless in his efforts to promote interreligious dialogue, inspired by the words of the *Declaration on the Relationship of the Church to Non-Christian Religions*: "Over the centuries many quarrels and dissensions have arisen between Christians and Muslims. The sacred Council now pleads with all to forget the past, and urges that a sincere effort be made to achieve mutual understanding; for the benefit of all men, let them together preserve and promote peace, liberty, social justice and moral values" (*Nostra Aetate*, 3).

See: Buddhism; Ecumenism; Evangelization; Hinduism; Judaism; Missionary Activity; Religion, Virtue of.

Suggested Readings: CCC 839-856. Vatican Council II, *Dogmatic Constitution on the Church, Lumen Gentium*, 16-17; *Declaration on the Relationship of the Church to Non-Christian Religions, Nostra Aetate*. John Paul II, *On the Permanent Validity of the Church's Missionary Mandate, Redemptoris Missio*, 94-99. "Islam," in G. Parrinder, ed., *World Religions*. H. Smith, "Islam," *The Religions of Man*.

David M. Byers

J

JANSENISM

The term designates a spiritual and theological movement prevalent in France and The Low Countries from 1650 to 1750. The originators of Jansenist teaching were John Duvergier Hauranne (died 1643), more commonly known as Saint-Cyran because he became abbot there in 1620, and Cornelius Otto Jansen (died 1638), better known as Jansenius, professor of Scripture at Louvain and later Bishop of Ypres. At the basis of Jansenism is the age-old controversy concerning the relationship of grace, free will, and predestination. What brought Jansenism to widespread attention and prepared the way for the ensuing bitter controversy and ultimate condemnation by the Holy See, was the publication of Cornelius Jansen's three-volume work on the theology of St. Augustine.

Historical Background • Since the beginning of the Protestant Reform in the middle of the sixteenth century, theologians had wrestled with the problem of human freedom, divine grace, and predestination. The traditional teaching had been Augustinian and Thomistic, but the humanists tried to lessen the emphasis on predestination and the gratuity of grace, in order to focus more on man's freedom of choice and his ability to cooperate with grace. At Louvain, Michael Baius (died 1589) reacted defensively, asserting that as a result of original sin, man is no longer free to choose the good. All he can do is sin, until he receives the grace of justification, for which he can do nothing to dispose himself.

Leonard Lessius, a Jesuit professor at Louvain, answered Baius in 1585, stating that from all eternity God has determined that through the merits of Jesus Christ grace sufficient for justification will be given to each person at the moment decided upon by God himself. Sufficient grace then becomes "efficacious" as a result of its voluntary acceptance by the individual. Then, since God foresees man's future merits resulting from the grace accepted, he predestines man to further graces and to salvation. The doctrine of Baius had already been condemned by Pope Pius V in 1567 and by Pope Gregory XIII in 1579, but it was deeply entrenched at Louvain.

The next voice to be heard was that of Domingo Bañez (died 1604), Dominican professor at the University of Salamanca, Spain. In defense of the Thomistic teaching, he asserted that prior to any consideration of man's merits, God decrees the acts of man and the free manner in which man performs those acts. Thus, man remains free, but within the providence of God, since it would be impossible for a man to be so autonomous that he becomes the total cause of his own actions. That would make God dependent on man, at least for a knowledge of man's free actions.

In 1588, the Jesuit Louis Molina published *Concordia Liberi Arbitrii Cum Gratiae Donis* at Lisbon. To protect man's freedom without detracting from God's infallible and universal knowledge, he proposed a "conditioned" knowledge called *scientia media*. God knows from all eternity how a man will act in given circumstances and, in view of that knowledge, God offers to man a particular grace as he sees that man will react to it.

The discussion now became a controversy between the Jesuits and the Dominicans. The Holy See instituted the Roman Congregation *De auxiliis gratiae* in 1597 in order to settle the dispute, but nothing came of it. The Molinist teaching prevailed until the seventeenth century, when Augustinian teaching came back into favor and, with it, the Jansenist movement.

Cornelius Otto Jansen had been educated at Louvain, where the teaching of Baius was still a vital influence, and after a lengthy stay in France with his close friend John Duvergier de Hauranne, future abbot of Saint-Cyran, he returned to Louvain for a university career. Toward 1619 he discovered the Augustinian teaching on grace and resolved not only to follow it but to propagate it by publishing a work on it. He began the project in 1627, was ordained Bishop of Ypres in 1636, and died prematurely in 1638. The three-volume work was published by his friends in 1640 under the title *Augustinus*.

Jansen adopted the most rigid and literal Augustinian teaching, especially on the question of predestination. He explicitly rejected the modifications that St. Thomas Aquinas had made concerning man's freedom of choice. The critics accused Jansen of promoting the teaching of Calvin and Baius, asserting that Jesus did not die for all but only for the elect. The work was condemned by the Inquisition in 1641 and again by Pope Urban VIII in 1643 and by Pope Innocent X in 1653.

Antoine Arnauld, professor at the Sorbonne and brother of Mère Angélique of Port Royal, took up the defense of Jansen and was later joined by Blaise Pascal, who blamed the Jesuits for the persecution of the Jansenists. The last stubborn stronghold of Jansenism was the convent of Port Royal, where Jansenist teaching had been introduced by Saint-Cyran and the community had the support of many persons in high places. The convent was finally razed to the ground in 1709. But it was not until Pope Clement XI issued the bull *Unigenitus*, condemning one hundred propositions from the writings of the ex-Oratorian Quesnel, followed by the excommunication in 1718 of all who refused to obey, that the Jansenist controversy was finally laid to rest.

Doctrinal Points • Both Cornelius Jansen and his friend Saint-Cyran were claiming to use the teaching of St. Augustine to restore the "authentic primitive teaching" of the Church. Saint-Cyran proposed to "abolish the present state of the Church" and put a renewed Church in its place. Jansen took upon himself the reform of Catholic doctrine, and Arnauld's task was to restore the devotional and liturgical practices of the past. Both of them worked under the influence of Saint-Cyran, who was already "Calvinized."

For some reason, these reformers failed to recognize the ambivalence of some of the statements in St. Augustine's teaching. The fact that both Protestant and Catholic theologians were appealing to the authority of St. Augustine should have alerted them to the need to define their terms and make distinctions. So intent were they on the reform of the Church, however, that they ended up with a rigorous moralism that alienated them from the mainstream of Catholic life.

According to Jansenist theology, human nature was so corrupted as a result of original sin that the human person is totally incapable of choosing between good and evil. Grace alone makes it possible for the human being to choose and to act morally. Only the elect can benefit from the redemption and only the elect will be saved. The primary practice of the Christian life is the performance of penitential acts. A perfect act of contrition is required for absolution from sin, and the sacramental penance must be performed before absolution is given. Further, the worthy reception of Holy Communion requires an act of pure love of God. Saint-Cyran stopped celebrating daily Mass and claimed to find his nourishment in the words of Scripture. So great was their reverence for the Eucharist and so deep was their sense of unworthiness that Jansenists were strongly opposed to frequent Communion.

Monsignor Ronald Knox has provided us with an accurate description in his book *Enthusiasm*: "Overlooked in its cradle by the mournful faces of Saint-Cyran and Mother Angélique, Jansenism never learned to smile. Its adherents forget, after all, to believe in grace, so hag-ridden are they by their sense of the need for it."

See: Augustinianism; Confession; Eucharist; Freedom, Human; Grace; Justification; Original Sin; Protestantism; Providence.

Suggested Readings: CCC 385-412, 1322-

1485, 1420-1484, 1731-1784, 1987-2016. P. Pourrat, *Christian Spirituality*, Vol. 4, pp. 1-33; L. Bouyer, J. Leclercq, J. Cognet, *A History of Christian Spirituality*, Vol. 3. R. Knox, *Enthusiasm*. J. Aumann, *Christian Spirituality in the Catholic Tradition*, pp. 228ff.

Jordan Aumann, O.P.

JESUS CHRIST, GOD AND MAN

The *Catechism of the Catholic Church* is a catechism and for that reason is different from an exegetical study or a purely theological study. The *Catechism* is meant to be a sure guide of faith, an explanation of the rule of faith, and operates in the area of the analogy of faith, that is, bringing together sections of the New Testament to let them complement one another, so as to fill out gaps we may discover in a particular Gospel or epistle. The "analogy" also refers to the ability to extend the interpretation of Scripture by seeing it in the whole of God's plan, which now includes the Spirit-guided Church. Church teaching and the teaching of the Fathers can be helpful in the task. The focus is on declaring the teaching of the Church in order to deepen the response of faith. Exegesis helps, theology helps, but catechetics has its own distinctive goal and method, which makes uses of theology but is not the same as theology.

Catechesis offers a summary of Church teaching, and this *Catechism* offers a summary of the teaching of Vatican Council II. It aims at showing us that Revelation is a tapestry of interwoven truths inseparable from one another. Against this background, then, we can approach the *Catechism*'s presentation of Christological doctrine.

Jesus Christ is the center of our faith as the eternal Son of the Father who is also endowed with the Holy Spirit in his Incarnation. There is no Christology without the teaching on the Trinity and no teaching on the Trinity without Christology. There is no Christology without the fulfillment of the Old Testament promises and the opening of the Church, the People of God, to the whole world. Now it is by the Lamb of God that the world is reconciled. Christ accomplished the work of rec-

onciliation of mankind with his Father by his suffering and death on the cross, lived with his sense of God-forsakenness, in substitution for sinners. Rising from the dead, Jesus gives his obedience of love to the Church as the principle of her members' unity with him and with one another. His Church could not become one without an internal principle of love that says yes with Christ and in the Spirit to all that the Father wills, the Virgin Mary; nor could the Church become a reality without an external principle of unity, Peter the Rock, who was selected by the Lord in the midst of the Twelve during Jesus' public life and ministry.

The Apostles' Growth in Faith • The *Catechism* and the Apostles' Creed give us the basic rule of faith; but how did the Apostles come to this rule? How much data do we have in our Gospel sources for reconstructing the Apostles' journey of faith? From the Gospels we know their point of arrival, but it may be hard to isolate clear stages along the way. One definite clue is that they have trouble integrating the Lord's Passion and death into their view of the Messiah and Son of God. It is only after Easter, when the Lord breathes on them the Holy Spirit, that they reach the fullness of faith in the Lord Jesus. At present, scholars are convinced that the Apostles moved from an implicit faith, which they received during their period of training by Jesus, to an explicit faith after the Easter appearances.

Jesus chose twelve men to be with him and participate in his mission. He was gradually revealed to the Apostles as Son of God during his public life. Jesus accepted Peter's profession of faith, which acknowledged him to be "the Christ, the Son of the living God," for he replies to Peter that the Father in heaven has revealed this to him.

The *Catechism* states that "only in the Paschal mystery can the believer give the title 'Son of God' its full meaning" (444). It points out that "the truth of Jesus' divinity is confirmed by his Resurrection. . . . Christ's Resurrection is closely linked to the Incarnation of God's Son" (653); and on the day of Pentecost "the Holy Trinity is fully revealed" (732). Thus the Resurrection is the source of explicit faith in Jesus as Divine Son. Scholars explain that Jesus' revelation of his relationship with his Father is the source of the Apostles' implicit faith. His public life and Resurrection appearances convince them that God is Father of the Lord Jesus in an unheard-of sense: Father not only in being Creator but by his relationship to his only Son. "No one knows the Son except the Father, and no one knows the Father except the Son and anyone to whom the Son chooses to reveal him" (Mt 11:27; cf. CCC 240). For this reason the Apostles confessed Jesus to be the Word.

Jesus revealed himself as Son of God in deed and in teaching that touched on the interpretation of the Old Testament law. The miracles are signs of the kingdom that strengthen faith in the One who does the Father's works; they bear witness that he is the Son of God. Jesus teaches with a divine authority that reveals his Sonship. In Jesus, the Word of God, which had resounded on Mount Sinai to give the written law to Moses, made itself heard anew on the Mount of the Beatitudes. Jesus did not abolish the law but fulfilled it by giving its ultimate interpretation in a divine way. In presenting the definitive interpretation of the law, Jesus found himself confronted by certain teachers who did not accept his interpretation of the law, guaranteed though it was by the divine signs that accompanied it.

Jesus identified himself with the temple by presenting himself as God's definitive dwelling place among men. He identified his merciful conduct toward sinners with God's own attitude toward them. By forgiving sins, Jesus either is blaspheming (as a man who made himself God's equal) or is speaking the truth that his person really does make present and reveal God's name. Only his divine identity can justify so absolute a claim as "he who is not with me is against me" and his affirmations "Before Abraham was, I AM" and even "I and the Father are one" (Mt 12:6, 30, 36-37, 41-42; cf. CCC 590). For this reason he is accused of blasphemy and false prophecy, religious crimes that the law punished by stoning. In fact, the trial conducted by the high priests, as described in Matthew, Mark, and Luke, and through chapters 8 and 10 in John, revolves around Jesus' claim to be the kind of Messiah who is Son of God.

Christology From "Below" and From "Above" • Catechesis has to deepen the rule of faith that Jesus is Son of God and Son of Man. A Christology from below (Jesus' birth, earthly life and human teaching ministry, Passion and death — all that deals with his true humanity) is enlightened by Christology from above (direct union with and obedience to his Father, miracles, prophetic teaching, Resurrection — all that indicates his Divine Sonship). The two phases of Jesus' life belong together. For Matthias to be elected by God an Apostle to give witness to the risen Lord, he had to have lived with him during his ministry (Acts 1:21). This makes sense, since assurance supplied by the Resurrection lacks content apart from data on Jesus' earthly life, the life of him whose teaching is now assured.

Vice versa, to know and to appreciate the history of the Lord Jesus in the various moments of his earthly life, from his birth and baptism to his Passion, one needs the light of his Resurrection to know that he is the unique Person who was working out our salvation in all these events and who lives today to share salvation with us. Catechesis has to be faithful to all four Gospels and not just to isolated pieces of one or the other. That is the way in which we maintain the mystery: by keeping alive the tension of faith that embraces the Divine Son and his becoming a full human being.

The Titles of the Lord • The Creed joins Jesus' name with his three titles: (1) Christ, or the Messiah, (2) his Trinitarian title of only Son, and (3) his sovereign title of Lord. The names Jesus Christ stand for the one Person who has his identity in the history of salvation through his saving mission. The titles Only Son and Lord express his relationship with his Father lived in his mission and the fact that the Father crowns the obedient Son with the glory of the Resurrection and enthronement in heaven. The titles have become names, and call to mind the history of salvation and the rich process of revelation and salvation that took place in the life of Christ.

1. Jesus — God Saves. The name of Jesus (*God*

saves) evokes God's plan of saving activity in which he intervenes in history to save us from sin. The name Jesus given to the newborn child of Bethlehem sums up God's saving might in history as well the peak of that activity when God gave his only Son to us.

Salvation history begins with God's promise of a Savior who would overcome the evil one and gather together all men into one. Scripture and Tradition continually recall the presence and universality of sin in human history. They also tell us that God makes his grace universally available. In every nation anyone who fears God and does what is right is acceptable to God, who makes his grace available from the very beginning of human history in human consciences. God goes so far as to enter into a covenant with Israel so that she can be a many-faceted light to the nations and even bring forth his Son, Jesus Christ.

Jesus can gain universal salvation because "the very name of God is present in the person of his Son" who became man (CCC 432). Jesus alone can bring about universal and definitive salvation. This entails reconciliation, pardon for sin, and a share in the divine life of the Trinity. Jesus brings about an absolute and definitive salvation as God's only Son. God's salvific will has been realized in a definitive way in Jesus Christ, in whom "God recapitulates all of his history of salvation on behalf of men" (CCC 430). It is Jesus who, as the single source of salvation, gives validity to every other invocation and granting of salvation outside of Christianity.

Surprisingly enough, Jesus' Divine Sonship is the ground of his solidarity with all mankind. As God's Son, he is the Word through whom all things were made. Some even say that in his eternal plan of salvation, the Father created the universe with human freedom as part of it in view of his Son's assuming human nature. To his human nature the Son of God can allot something of his universality. As Word made flesh, he is the head of the human race; all things were made for him.

He is Savior as priest and victim who with his blood takes away our sins and establishes the new covenant. The blood of the Son, offered in our place

in his sacrifice of love and obedience, pleases the Father and perfectly reconciles the world with him. Jesus' humanity on the cross is the new mercy seat.

In his Resurrection from the dead, Jesus passed from death to life beyond time and space. The risen body of Jesus was filled with the power of the Holy Spirit and shared in the divine life of glory because his Father raised Jesus and constituted him eternal Lord of all things. The name Jesus now includes the power and grace of the risen Lord. Under this title, Jesus deserves our recognition, worship, and glory.

In this way Christians can use the name of Jesus to recall all the benefits of salvation: God and man in eternal covenant, creation, and redemption. Jesus is the risen one, and whoever calls upon his name welcomes the Son of God who loved him and gave himself up for him. Since we are perfectly reconciled with the Father through Jesus, official liturgical prayer to the Father closes with the name of Jesus Our Lord.

2. Christ, or Messiah: a Threefold Office. The word "messiah" means "the anointed one." This places us squarely in the midst of Israel's history. There were many famous figures who were anointed with olive oil in Israel for the mission of guiding the people: the king, the priest, and the prophet. In the history of Israel after the Exile, the three offices passed into less than sacred hands. After the return from the Exile Zerubbabel was the last of the family of David to rule in Israel, the Zadok family line of the priesthood died out, and prophecy was in short supply until the day of John the Baptist. In the century before Jesus was born, the absence of divine mediation heightened the desire for the ideal Anointed One: king, priest, and prophet promised to Israel as Redeemer.

Jesus had to transform the Messianic hope from the political, earthly kingship or priesthood in order to raise it to the level of his divine mission as Son ushering in a basically spiritual kingdom of God. In his public ministry, he renews the Messiah title by talking about himself as the Son of Man, the servant "who came not to be served but to serve and give his life as a ransom for many"

(Mk 10:45). It is only at the hour of his trial when Jesus is powerless that he can affirm his claim to the seat at the right hand of the glory (Mk 14:62). When Jesus the crucified rises from the dead, he becomes the one in whom hope is fulfilled. As a prophetic action on Palm Sunday, Jesus allows the crowd to acclaim him the Messiah — who comes, however, meek and seated on a donkey: "Hosanna to the Son of David! Blessed is he who comes in the name of the Lord!" (Mt 21:9).

As eternal Son, Jesus was the one whom the Father consecrated and sent into the world (cf. Jn 10:36). Conceived as holy in Mary's womb by the overshadowing of the Holy Spirit, he was at the same time anointed with the Holy Spirit in his human nature. At the time of his baptism by John, when "God anointed Jesus of Nazareth with the Holy Spirit and with power," his eternal Messianic consecration was revealed so that he might be shown to Israel as its Messiah.

As prophet in his teaching and miracles, as priest in his Passion and death, and as Lord in his Resurrection from the dead, Jesus realized the threefold mission expressed by the name Messiah. Guided by divine grace, Peter can rally the other eleven around Jesus by confessing, "You are the Christ, the Son of the living God." On Calvary, the good thief can grasp the truth when he says, "Jesus, remember me when you come in your kingly power" (Lk 23:42). After Pentecost, Peter can proclaim to the People of God, "Let all the house of Israel therefore know that God has made him both Lord and *Christ*, this Jesus whom you crucified" (Acts 2:36).

3. The Only Son of God. In Old Testament usage, "son of God" was used for angels and the chosen people, the children of Israel and their kings. It points to an adoptive sonship that establishes a relationship of particular intimacy between God and his creature. As a result, persons using the title son of God to indicate that Jesus was the Messiah were not necessarily saying that he was more than human, for example, the centurion at the foot of the cross. The exception to this is once again Peter, who calls Jesus "the Son of the living God," to which Jesus answers that "flesh and blood

has not revealed this to you, but my Father who is in heaven" (Mt 16:16-17). After the Resurrection this title became the common title because the Apostles used it to sum up their definitive faith now enlightened by the paschal mystery.

So Paul will write, regarding his conversion on the road to Damascus, "When he who set me apart before I was born, and called me through his grace, was pleased to reveal his Son to me, in order that I might preach him among the Gentiles. . ." (Gal 1:15-16). In the synagogues, Paul proclaimed that Jesus was the Son of God. In his Letter to the Romans, Paul calls his message "the gospel concerning his Son . . . designated Son of God in power" (Rom 1:3-4).

The Apostles' witness to Jesus' awareness of his own identity will always remain the primary testimony to which faith must turn as its point of reference. In his public life Jesus used *Son of God* only once (cf. Jn 10:36) in the process of gradual revelation. The Apostles tell us that he presented himself in a variety of ways that went beyond the limits of any formula. Noted above were some of the ways in which Jesus impresses on his disciples his transcendence.

In his public life, however, Jesus did use the title *Son* of himself, of his words and deeds. Jesus taught about his intimate relationship with the Father as Son, which gives him the ability to know the Father in a way no one else could know him (Mt 11:25-26). He also speaks of his having been sent or having come as Son: "Whoever welcomes one such child in my name welcomes me, and whoever welcomes me welcomes not me but the one who sent me" (Mk 9:37). In the Synoptics (cf. Mk 1:11) at his Baptism, a voice from heaven designates Jesus as "My Son, the beloved in whom I am well pleased." At his Transfiguration (Mk 9:2-8), a voice comes from the cloud saying, "This is my Son, the beloved. Listen to him." He also spoke of himself as the Son to the chief priests, the scribes, and the elders in the parable of the vineyard, when he described himself as the Son whom the owner of the vineyard sent last of all after sending the other servants (Mk 12:1-9). Jesus could teach us about his Father, using "Father, Abba" for his prayer but reserving the "Our Father" for his disciples. It is in the Garden of Olives that he uses the more intimate *Abba* (Mk 14:36). At his trial, to the question about his identity, "Are you the Christ, the Son of the Blessed One?" he gave the direct answer: "I am; and you will see the Son of man seated at the right hand of the Power and coming with the clouds of heaven" (Mk 14:61-62). Messiah (Christ) is being interpreted by Son of God (the Blessed One).

In the Gospel of John, we find Jesus referring to himself entirely as the Son who was sent. We can find the idea of preexistence in such texts, for example: "He whom God has sent speaks the words of God" (Jn 3:34); "I can do nothing on my own. As I hear, I judge; and my judgment is just because I seek to do not my own will, but the will of him who sent me" (Jn 5:30); "For I have come down from heaven, not to do my own will, but the will of him who sent me" (Jn 6:38). In two places we find Jesus' obedience to the Father: "Jesus then said, 'I will be with you a little while longer, and then I am going to him who sent me' " (Jn 7:33); and, more clearly, "For God so loved the world that he gave his only Son, so that everyone who believes in him may not perish but may have eternal life" (Jn 3:16). This is to be compared with John 10:34-36: "Is it not written in your law, 'I said, you are gods'? If those to whom the word of God came were called 'gods' and the Scripture cannot be annulled — can you say that the one whom the Father sanctified and sent into the world is blaspheming, because I said, 'I am God's Son'?"

We can find an overall call to faith in Jesus as Son of God in John 3:18: "Those who believe in him are not condemned, but those who do not believe are condemned already, because they have not believed in the name of the only Son of God." Finally, in the story of Thomas's encounter with the risen Lord in his crucified but glorified humanity, we reach the peak of apostolic faith: "My Lord and my God" (Jn 20:28). The risen Lord is not replaced by the Church or the Holy Spirit but is still the Savior who is present and active in our world. "Remember, I am with you always, to the end of the age" (Mt 28:20). He sends the Holy Spirit on the Church to be with her forever: "Receive the Holy Spirit."

4. Lord. In the Greek translation of the Old Testament, the Hebrew name for God, which is never pronounced, is translated as *Kyrios,* or *Lord. Lord* becomes the usual way of speaking of God. The New Testament continues to apply the full sense of the title to the Father and then applies the same title to the Son after his Resurrection. This is another way the Apostles refer to Jesus as Son of God. In John we already saw that Thomas the Apostle refers to him as Lord. In the Acts of the Apostles, we hear Peter saying that God raised Jesus and made him Lord and Messiah (Acts 2:36). In Philippians 2:10-11 we read "that at the name of Jesus every knee should bow, in heaven and on earth and under the earth, and every tongue confess that Jesus Christ is *Lord*, to the glory of God the Father" (emphasis added).

Jesus refers the title to himself in a dispute with the Pharisees about the meaning of Psalm 110 (cf. Mk 12:35-37). In John 13:13, after the washing of the feet, Jesus tells the disciples, "You call me Teacher and Lord; and you are right, for so I am."

By its use in the Gospels and at the time of the Resurrection — "It is the Lord" (Jn 21:7) — the title takes on a connotation of love and adoration that becomes the ordinary Christian way of speaking of Jesus as the Lord Jesus.

In Philippians 2:9-11, the early confession of faith affirms that the power and glory due to God the Father are also due to Jesus, because he was in the form of God. The Father manifested the sovereignty of Jesus by raising him from the dead and exalting him into his glory. "If you declare with your mouth that Jesus is *Lord*, and if you believe with your heart that God raised him from the dead, then you will be saved" (Rom 10:9); and, "No one is able to say, 'Jesus is *Lord*' except in the Holy Spirit" (1 Cor 12:3). Stephen, in Acts 7:59, prays to the Son of Man exalted in glory at the right hand of the Father: "*Lord* Jesus, receive my spirit." Official prayer in the Church will often use this title in the invitation to prayer "The Lord be with you," in the conclusion "Through

Christ Our Lord," and in the prayer of hope "*Maran atha*, Our Lord, come" (Rv 22:20).

These prayers in Acts and in Revelation express the Church's abiding faith in Jesus' Lordship over the universe and over history. "For the Lord himself, with a cry of command, with the archangel's call and with the sound of God's trumpet, will descend from heaven" (1 Thes 4:16). In Revelation 19:16, he comes as the Lord of Lords and King of Kings.

See: Ascension and Parousia; Baptism of Christ; Divine Revelation; Fatherhood of God; Hierarchy; Holy Spirit; Hypostatic Union; Incarnation; Jesus Christ, Human Knowledge of; Jesus Christ, Life of; Judaism; Judaism in Catholic Doctrine; Law of Christ; Miracles; Redemption; Resurrection of Christ; Sacred Tradition; Trinity.

Suggested Readings: CCC 422-483. L. Bouyer, *The Eternal Son.* R. Kereszty, *Jesus Christ, Fundamentals of Christology.* R. Cantalamessa, *Jesus Christ, The Holy One of God.* J. Newman, *The Arians of the Fourth Century.* J. Kelly, *Early Christian Doctrines.*

Richard Malone

JESUS CHRIST, HUMAN KNOWLEDGE OF

Becoming incarnate in time and space, the eternal Son does not lose his personal identity as eternal Son. He now lives it as the Son sent by his Father into the world.

The Gospels offer us glimpses of what this means for him as here and now he lives his relationship with his Father. We see his conformity to the Father's will, his avoidance of any independent will for himself, his neglect of his own self-honor, his zeal for his Father's glory, his allowing for the impossibility of protecting himself from arrest and death, his prayer to the Father before all the major events, his aim to reveal his Father's love and compassion for the sinner, his constant referring of his works and words to the Father. The prayer in the Garden of Olives sums it up: "Not my will but thine be done" (Mk 14:36).

Relationship of Father and Son • Instead of asking about Jesus' way of knowing, "How do his divine mind and will influence his human will and mind?" it is better to ask: "What are the relationships between the mind and will of the Son and those of the Father?" Thus we can concentrate on the eternal and intra-divine movement of the Son toward the Father and the way he expresses this in his human existence. This relationship is a better starting point than the relationship between the two natures and will answer many of the kinds of questions that arise from the relationship of the two natures.

It also helps us to maintain Christ's way of being Son in his divine nature, knowledge, self-awareness, and will. That is all very personal and the source of relationships in creation and in the Church. He expresses this by the way he speaks and acts as a human being. It seems fair to say that Jesus' personal, metaphysical, and psychological realities are in a relationship within the one Person that can be called intimate closeness and interpenetration while maintaining the distinctiveness of his natures.

Jesus' experience of himself as Son reveals for us his deep personal relationship with his Father and, as a consequence, his relational being: "That they may be one as you Father in me and I in you, that they may be one in us" (Jn 17:21). This is the foundation of his ability to speak to his "Daddy" (*Abba*), but human words and human self-awareness cannot express it exhaustively. The key way we have of exploring something of this union is by exploring the language that he uses to express his relationship with his Father. All his activities — of knowing himself, of knowing God and the world, of speaking and choosing, of raising from the dead and judging, of forgiving sins and revealing — have to be interpreted in terms of the Son's relationship with his Father. The Gospels offer us the portrait of Someone who does know who he is and who expresses this in terms of being sent into the world by his Father for our good.

Jesus' Self-emptying • Theologians and biblical scholars have drawn our attention away from an abstract view of Jesus' human knowledge —

In what perfect way should the Word made flesh know God's plan in his human nature? — to a more concrete view: What effect does the self-emptying of his glory and power have on the eternal Son's way of knowing himself as sent Son? This concrete way of viewing things can help us distinguish between the kind of knowledge Jesus had in the years of his maturity, as he approached his Passion and death, and the kind of knowledge he now enjoys in the state of glory. The state of glory presupposes a full participation in divine glory after his pain, suffering, and death are done away with in his Resurrection. The kind of knowledge that goes with the self-emptying is more akin to the development that life's temptations and tests, sufferings and death entail. This brings him closer to us in everything except sin. "Although he was a Son, he learned obedience through what he suffered" (Heb 5:8).

While it is hard for us to give a precise definition to the impact of Jesus' self-emptying, we can see that the Passion does take place in a spirit of abandonment to the Father different from the kind of total knowing and total control that we associate with the all-powerful God. "Do you think that I cannot appeal to my Father, and he will at once send me more than twelve legions of angels? But how should the scriptures be fulfilled that it should be so?" (Mt 26:53).

Jesus' self-emptying entails a limitation in his way of knowing his Father's plan. This is accompanied by a series of decisions made in obedience to the Spirit. Jesus "went down with them to Nazareth, and was obedient to them; . . . And Jesus advanced [in] wisdom and age and favor before God and man" (Lk 2:51-52); "Jesus, full of the Holy Spirit, returned from the Jordan, and was led by the Spirit for forty days in the wilderness, tempted by the devil" (Lk 4:1); "And going a little farther, he fell on the ground and prayed that, if it were possible, the hour might pass from him" (Mk 14:35).

Since Jesus came for his mission of Revelation, he certainly had from his Father the knowledge he needed to accomplish the mission. This is closely connected with his own personal awareness as the sent Son: "All things have been delivered to me by my Father; and no one knows who the Son is except the Father, or who the Father is except the Son and any one to whom the Son chooses to reveal him" (Lk 10:22). As he speaks of himself and of his Father, we glimpse the depths of this deep personal relationship expressed in the work of revealing: "Father, I thank you for having revealed these things to the little ones" (Lk 10:21).

Hans Urs von Balthasar writes: "The task given him by his Father, that is, of expressing God's Fatherhood through his entire being, through his life and death in and for the world, totally occupies his self-consciousness and fills it to the brim. He sees himself so totally as 'coming from the Father' to me, as 'making known' the Father, as the 'Word from the Father,' that there is neither room nor time for any detached reflection of the 'Who am I?' kind. 'Who he is' is exhaustively expressed in his being sent by the Father who addresses him as 'My beloved Son' (Mt 3:17) — but the Son immediately recognizes this address as a call to be a 'servant.' Insofar as, from all time, he fully embraces and affirms his mission (which does not mean that he has a total and detailed view of it), he is perfect; but the mission itself sets him upon a path, and to that extent, he is also a wayfarer" (*Theodrama*, vol. III, p. 172).

Divine "I" in Human Nature • In our reflection on the Son's relationship with his Father, we can draw on Church teaching about the Divine Person and his integral human nature and human operation. It is the Divine Person of the Word made flesh who knows himself in his humanity according to the capacity of his human nature. We can speak of his psychology because his knowing has a deeply personal and subjective aspect that can be quite like the way we know ourselves as unique and different from others. Jesus' human consciousness, as the human consciousness of the Son of God, is the awareness of his relationship with his Father and, by that route, an awareness of his own personal identity and mission. The Eternal Word, in his human consciousness, feels (or intuits) in the way that belongs to our brand of consciousness, his divine "I," that of the Son sent by the Father.

In the Gospels, we find that Jesus is aware of who he is. In the Gospel of Luke, the twelve-year-old Jesus says to Mary and Joseph: "Did you not know that I must be about my Father's business?" or: ". . . in my Father's house?" (Lk 2:49). His teaching and his prayer to the Father, the use of *Abba*, indicate that he is guided from the beginning by the intuition of his Father that penetrated his conscious states.

The substructure of Jesus' psychological life was a profound level of intuitive knowledge of his Father and of the things of God, exceeding in depth and purity what we can know of ourselves in this life or in the next. He would have formed the conviction of his absolutely singular mission in this world and that this mission could only be the complete reversal of what his people expected of their Messiah.

We can be certain that Jesus also learned from absolutely everything in his human experience and from all that was most common to us, so that what was unique to him could be revealed and take form in ways that enabled him to express himself in keeping with his mission. He learned from the children, from the lilies of the field, from the vines and trees, from Joseph, from farmers, tax collectors, and fishermen. He learned from his Mother the Scriptures and the whole religious tradition of Israel.

Jesus Knows He Is the Son • The International Theological Commission says: "Before the mystery of Jesus was revealed to men, there was already in the consciousness of Jesus a personal perception of a most sure and profound relationship with his Father. From the fact that he called God his Father, it follows by implication that Jesus was aware of his own divine authority and mission. Jesus knows and is conscious of being the Son."

John allows us to glimpse something of the process whereby the Son is initiated into the Father's mysteries. Not all the relevant passages refer solely to the Son's preexistence; they can also be interpreted as events in the earthly life of Jesus, particularly where it is said, in the present tense,

that the Father "shows the Son all that he himself is doing" (Jn 5:20).

It is not enough to say that at this point the evangelist is speaking in a received apocalyptic mode, according to which a person initiated into heavenly mysteries when in ecstasy hears and sees things he must subsequently proclaim on earth or at least write down. Jesus does not come forth as an apocalyptic figure among others, to testify to secret things and events as the prophet Daniel or Joseph in Egypt did. He testifies to himself. Jesus really understands the Word he hears from God to be identical with himself. He receives himself from the Father — both once and for all and in an eternal and temporally ever-new "now." He is the Word proceeding from the Father. And in his temporal consciousness he experiences this gift of himself (from the Father's hand) as timeless (as the absolute "I am" statements make plain).

Nothing prevents us from understanding this process as taking place through time, according to his personal maturation (cf. Lk 2:40, 52). We must maintain that such development is an unfolding of the original identity of his "I" and his mission — to be the Father's Word. The ultimate horizon can remain hidden for part of the journey. The immediate horizon is the preparation and fulfillment of Israel, seen as the program for Jesus' public ministry. The all-embracing ambiance of his consciousness remains his readiness to respond to whatever concerns the Father (even to the extent of losing all tangible contact with him, all experience of his will to forgive), his readiness to pay all that is necessary so that he may proclaim this forgiveness to men.

Once we understand his very personal way of knowing his Father, then we have the basis for speaking of other forms of knowing, such as experience-based knowledge that corresponds to what he learned from those around him. This is in total accord with his self-emptying and his nature as incarnate Son. These foster his ordinary human way of knowing that was like everyone else's. Jesus' relationship with his Father as lived in our world does not abolish his ordinary human way of knowing but enhances it.

See: Hypostatic Union; Incarnation; Jesus

Christ, God and Man; Jesus Christ, Life of; Temptation of Christ; Trinity.

Suggested Readings: CCC 471-474. International Theological Commission, *The Consciousness of Christ Concerning Himself and His Mission.* J. Guillet, *The Consciousness of Christ.* F. Dreyfus, *Did Jesus Know He Was God?*

Richard Malone

JESUS CHRIST, LIFE OF

Christ is God and Man. The faithful soul not only confesses the divinity of Jesus but also honors his sacred humanity. Theology and spiritual life must be Christ-centered. St. Teresa of Ávila says in her *Autobiography* (ch. 22): "We are not angels, we have a body. . . . In the midst of business, persecutions, of trials . . . in times of dryness, Christ is our best friend. We see Him a man like ourselves, we contemplate Him in sickness and suffering. . . . It is very profitable for us, as long as we are in this life, to consider the God-made-Man." We can never explore enough the life of Christ and his teaching. Personal and social integrity are to be found only in Christ the incarnate Son, the only mediator, by whom all creation attains its true end and comes to the Father.

In the past, theology concentrated on the ontological constitution of Jesus Christ and the interpretation of the teaching of the Council of Chalcedon (451) regarding the two natures in Christ. Later, theologians like St. Anselm (1033-1109) concentrated on the salvific nature of Jesus' death. The mysteries of the life of Christ were left to spiritual writers, who wrote lives of Christ or "contemplations" of his life. These ignored theology or took it for granted, and developed a moralizing approach that presented Jesus as exemplifying Christian virtue. They also tried to re-create a psychology of the Lord, expanding on the data of the Gospels in a way not entirely faithful to them.

Today's effort at integrating both approaches can afford a richer view of the mysteries of the life of Christ. The Gospels must be the starting point, meditated on by the Tradition of the Church and received by the communion of saints.

Jesus Reveals God • Christianity is not the observance of an abstract law or commandments but an attachment to a Person, who is the way, the truth, and the life (cf. Jn 14:6). Jesus Christ is not just a saint, a genius, or a hero whose example attracts us. He is the Son of God, the incarnate Word. What we see in him is not just some set of "values" but God himself: "He who sees me sees him who sent me" (Jn 12:45); "He who has seen me has seen the Father" (Jn 14:9). His humanity is the sacrament of God. The divine human Person of Christ will only be accepted for all that he is by supernatural faith, which we cannot give ourselves but which we receive from God. "No one can come to me unless the Father who sent me draws him" (Jn 6:44). This attraction is the work of grace.

Christ is the Son of God who reveals himself and who instructs us. Christ is our Master who has the words of eternal life (Jn 6:68). He teaches as one with authority (Mt 7:29). He lives his teaching and is our model. His authority demands our obedience: To follow Christ is to do what he orders. As a master, he asks us to obey the value he puts into practice before asking it of us. It can happen that the disciple is unable to grasp the value clearly, yet, although he has the duty to obey, his obedience is not blind, since he knows that what Christ asks is good for the very reason that he asks it of us. His values are only values in God; they represent a duty for us because they are imposed by God.

Christ our Master is our Savior. The salvation Jesus brings is not only an ethical salvation, calling for a conversion of heart and revealing our own inner law to us; it is a salvation that frees us from sin and confers a new and divine life on us. It is by his death and Resurrection that Christ has acquired us, since he was delivered up for our sins and rose for our justification (Rom 4:25). The saving action of the Lord is for the Christian the principal motive for his love of Christ. This love is not just an attachment to an ideal figure who makes an impression on us, but a response of love to the greatest love there is, which consists in Jesus' giving his life for his friends (Jn 15:13). "He loved me and gave himself for me" (Gal 2:20).

For the believer who lives his faith, obedience,

and love, Christ is not someone who belongs to the past. True, he was born in the Holy Land, lived and taught there, suffered and died at a given time; and the Gospels, without being exactly a life of Christ and without always satisfying our curiosity, report certain episodes and aspects of his historical existence. But Christ the Lord triumphed over death. The risen Lord is a living Person who lives for ever and ever (Rv 1:17-18), a divine human Person who transcends time. The events of his earthly existence are past in their historical reality, but they are forever present in their spiritual reality, the interior state of the Son of God that they express, in their efficacy and salvific power. In a true sense, Christ the Lord is born, dies, and rises *today*, as the Fathers of the Church insisted. The mysteries of the life of Christ are always present, and Christ is really contemporary with each one of us.

The "Mysteries" of Christ's Life • Each particular event in the life of Christ participates in the total mystery of his life and cannot be understood without an understanding of that fullness. Jesus' life is not so much an episode of world history as the Revelation of God in the course of historical events. God "has saved us and called us to be holy" by his own grace; this grace has already been granted to us, in Christ Jesus, before the beginning of time, but it has been revealed to us by "the appearing of our Savior Christ Jesus" (2 Tm 1:9-10).

The total mystery does not exist by itself, in some way apart from the mysteries of Jesus' life. The total mystery of Jesus is the succession of mysteries, each with its own meaning and saving effect. In concentrating on one event like the Resurrection or the Passion and death in an exclusive way, one would misrepresent the central event of the Passion and Resurrection by ignoring the rest of the life of Jesus and the rest of the Gospel.

The mystery of the Lord's life has an eschatological meaning: It reveals and brings about the beginning of the realization of the kingdom of God. In Jesus Christ's preaching and action, the kingdom becomes visible. It is entirely the work of God and revealed by God's free will to his flock,

whose members recognize in Jesus' works the signs of the beginning of the kingdom. In the Gospels, the life of Jesus is perceived as a sign; its mysteries are the unfolding of the single mystery. They belong to the category of narrative episodes, and, with the teaching of Christ, are set in the unique literary form of the Gospel.

In the New Testament, there is a theological reflection on the totality of these mysteries, of such force that at times attention to details becomes secondary. St. Paul uses the word *mysterion* for this comprehensive shifting of attention from the single to the whole, that is, the divine plan of salvation that God realized by sending his own Son.

The New Testament offers several ways of using the term "mystery" about the life of Christ. In the Synoptic tradition and preaching, we find a development of distinct mysteries where "mystery" is applicable to a particular event. Mysteries are the realization of the mystery of the kingdom of God, even if they are called the mysteries of the life of Christ.

It is necessary to avoid a double danger in dealing with Jesus' life up to the time of his Baptism. None of the Gospels wishes to present a biography of Jesus or a chronology or a history in our sense. The Gospels are the fruit of the theological and Christological preaching and the early Church's reflection on it, grounded on the solid basis of the reality of salvation history.

This is the accepted way of looking at all that deals with the presentation of the public life of the Lord and of his Passion and Resurrection. It is also true of the Infancy Gospels. The Gospels do not offer us anything that approaches a merely private life of Jesus. Jesus has a private side, from which the public, revealed life proceeds. Revelation only speaks of his private life when it is helpful for the public sign of Revelation. This makes it difficult to speak of a "hidden" and a "public" life.

The Mystery of the Incarnation • The Incarnation is the event in which the Father breaks his silence, as it were, and sends his Son, while the Word assumes our sinful flesh out of obedience to the Father's will and so comes into history in our human condition. This event is the point of contact between the divine eternity, in which the Son is with the Father and upholds the world as its Creator (cf. Jn 1:3-10; 1 Cor 8:6), and human history. The coming of the Logos into history, a coming that is the beginning of Jesus' human history as God-man, must be seen as an event and an act of the Logos, his descent and coming among us.

The Incarnation has first of all the character of an event and of a mystery in Scripture. Theological questions are secondary, in comparison with the need to proclaim the event. St. Paul considers it the chief mystery "hidden for generations and centuries but now manifested to the saints" (Col 1:26). This is clear especially in Galatians 4:4-5: "But when the time had fully come, God sent forth his Son, born of woman, born under the law, to redeem those who were under the law, so that we might receive adoption as sons." In Ephesians 3:8 we find Paul saying of the mystery that had been hidden within the eternal Trinity: "To me, though I am the very least of all the saints, this grace was given, to preach to the Gentiles the unsearchable riches of Christ, and to make all men see what is the plan of the mystery hidden for all ages in God who created all things."

St. Paul speaks first of the Father's initiative: "But when the time had fully come, God sent forth his Son, born of woman, born under the law, to redeem those who were under the law, so that we might receive adoption as sons" (Gal 4:4-5). Then he speaks of the Son's initiative: "Who being in the form of God, did not count equality with God something to be grasped" (Phil 2:6). The Letter to the Hebrews (1:1) presents with great solemnity the fact of the assumption of human existence by the Son of God: "At many moments in the past and by many means, God spoke to our forefathers through the prophets; but in our time, in the final days, he has spoken to us in the person of his Son, whom he appointed heir of all things and through whom he made all things."

It is completely the Father's free, personal choice to determine the moment when his Son will come. St. Paul speaks of the "fullness of time." God fixed this moment from all eternity. However, despite all the preparations in the Old Testa-

ment, it belongs to his will to determine the precise moment of history when his Son will assume human nature. No human power could ever determine when in the plan of God the Lord Jesus was to come. We can only know it when it happened. Even after it has taken place, we cannot explain how. We can only confess that God has power and freedom to determine within the era of Revelation, the hour and the moment when his Son will begin his human existence.

The Prologue to the Gospel of John and the Letter to the Philippians offer us a way to contemplate the divine mystery itself. They offer a clue to what happened in the divine eternity and what became at a certain moment human and earthly reality.

The Self-emptying of Christ • The Son who begins his human and historical existence has his origin proceeding entirely from his Father. The event of the Incarnation unveils for us the procession of the Son from the Father. Without ceasing to be what he is, the Son becomes what he was not yet. The Son's procession from the Father has such a fullness of obedience and attentiveness to the Father that it permits him to obey the Father in this new way.

He was to become man. He was to enter mankind and assume a human nature. That nature has been deformed by the mass of sin. This is what the Johannine word *sarx* (flesh) expresses. The Letter to the Romans says similarly that the Son was sent "in the likeness of sinful flesh and for the sake of sin" (Rom 8:3). The mystery of salvation revealed in the historical event of the Incarnation is this: God did not spare his own Son but gave him up for the sake of all of us (Rom 8:32). The Father in his omnipotence and love can send his Son into the heart of what contradicts him: He can make "him to be sin" (2 Cor 5:21) without denying his divine majesty nor his own paternal honor and love. God the Son in his filial love and by the force of his obedience can dispossess himself to the point that he becomes for us and in our place a curse for our sins (cf. Gal 3:13). He is removed from his Father in the alienation of his divine glory (Phil 2:6ff.; 2 Cor 8:9), and by adopting the existence of sinners (cf. Rom 8:3, Heb 12:2) he can die a shameful death (cf. Mt 27:46) while holding on to an indestructible confidence in him who could save him from death (cf. Heb 5:7).

The reality of this descent by the Son is not only the establishment of a bridge, by means of the hypostatic union, over the abyss that separates Creator from creatures, but also the beginning of the deeper self-emptying of his whole life, by which he lays aside his human and divine dignity. The first phase of the mystery of Jesus in human history is the beginning of the self-emptying that was voluntary on his part and led to the shame of the cross endured in the place of sinners. The coming of the Son into human history entails the necessity of his distancing himself from his Father, laying aside his equality with God, taking upon himself an existence far from God, that of man living under the curse of sin. We find here all that Jesus reveals to us of the Father's love for us.

St. Paul and St. John never tire of calling our attention to the intensity of God's love. The radical character of the Son's distancing from the Father and of the abyss into which the Father was able to plunge his Son allows us to gauge the immeasurable greatness of the love of God. St. Paul speaks of it as being his mission to "announce to the pagans the unfathomable riches of Christ . . . that he may grant you to comprehend . . . what is the length and breadth and height and depth and to know the love of Christ that surpasses all knowledge" (Eph 3:8, 18-19). At the beginning of Jesus' life it is appropriate to affirm that the love between Father and Son is the Holy Spirit, that this love is love in Person. Only because the Spirit is God can he be the link of love between Father and Son, even when the Father must send his Son into the world of sin that is in contradiction with himself (2 Cor 5:21).

The sending of the Son finds its term in Mary's womb. This is revealed as a unique divine event, Mary's virginal conception. The Lord Jesus is a preexistent Person, the Eternal Word, who draws his origin immediately from the mystery of God. He is already in existence before his human be-

ginning, and takes on human existence by being sent by the Father. The Son of God accepts with his creative power and freedom the human existence that humanity conceives for this unique member; however, this happens not by means of the procreative energy that resides in Mary but in virtue of an event that, in a new and literal way, is the conception of Something and Someone humanity could not produce of itself.

The assumption of our human nature by the Son is followed by a life that is directed to the cross. The voluntary self-emptying of Jesus plays itself out in what Jesus did and endured over the years of his life up to the end (Jn 13:1). We should not try to reduce the content of St. Paul's affirmations about the kenosis of the one who is equal to God the Father. The self-emptying of the Son of God and the adoption of the condition of slave are not just sentiments nor do they represent some sort of merely abstract share in the Fall of the sons of Adam. Rather, we have here a reality whose measure is the way in which God himself is a real being. This infant was the Son of God, and the Son of God could not be more than this infant, growing up to take on the task assigned to him as man to give his life as a ransom for the many (cf 1 Tm 2:5; Mt 26:28).

See: Ascension and Parousia; Baptism of Christ; Christological Controversies; Divine Revelation; Fatherhood of God; Holy Spirit; Hypostatic Union; Jesus Christ, God and Man; Jesus Christ, Human Knowledge of; Law of Christ; Mary, Mother of God; Nativity; Original Sin; Resurrection of Christ; Temptation of Christ; Trinity.

Suggested Readings: CCC 470-630. John Paul II, "Four Themes of Christology." L. Bouyer, *The Eternal Son.* R. Kereszty, *Jesus Christ, Fundamentals of Christology.* R. Cantalamessa, *Jesus Christ, The Holy One of God.* H. von Balthasar, *Theodrama,* Vol. 3.

Richard Malone

JUDAISM

"Judaism" can mean one or more of several things that differ more or less among themselves. These range from the religion of the Old Testament and the religion of Israel as it was concretely at the time of the birth, ministry, death, and Resurrection of Jesus, to the common cultural heritage of the Jews of today, whatever their religious beliefs or philosophical convictions. Here "Judaism" is used in the sense of being distinguished from "Christianity," that is, as referring to the "other" concrete historical religion that stands in historical and theological continuity with the religion of the Old Testament, with the religion of Israel at the time of the earthly life of Jesus.

It was over the Resurrection of Jesus that the split, which led to this counter-distinction, occurred. It separated those who professed the belief that Jesus was the risen Christ and Lord — the belief that came to be known as Christianity — from those who did not, whose belief we call Judaism, precisely as distinguished from Christianity. Each of these now mutually distinct religions possesses the common patrimony of Revelation (from the side of God) and belief (from the side of man) that had been formed and secured by the time they went their separate ways, disagreeing over who is Jesus of Nazareth.

Consequences of the Split • Yet things are not of course quite that simple. To begin with, the religion of Israel was not simply a religion in the sense in which Christianity is now a religion. It was the entire national culture, the whole cultural patrimony, of a given people, the people of Israel, the Jewish people. Also, not long after Judaism and Christianity had become mutually distinct religions, those members of the Jewish people who did believe in Jesus ceased to manifest, and to transmit, their own national and cultural heritage and identity as Israelites or Jews, while only the followers of Judaism continued to possess concretely, and to hand on from one generation to another, the specific national and cultural identity of the ancient and ever lively Jewish people.

This had all sorts of consequences. Among other things, the identity of the Jewish people came to be so closely bound up with the religion of Judaism — as counter-distinguished from Christianity — that it became incompatible, in the eyes of

most Jews, with the profession of Christianity: so much so that, in their view, to be a loyal member of his people, a Jew need not be a believer in Judaism, but may not be a believer in Christianity. Another consequence was the serious impoverishment of Christendom, with the absence from the ever-expanding number of peoples present within the worldwide Christian fellowship of any consistent community from among the Jewish people, the first recipients of Revelation.

The absence of a consistent Jewish community from the Church has, in its turn, rendered so much more precious the testimony of the actual Jewish people, principally and typically expressed in the religion of Judaism, to the record of God's dealings with humankind that is our common heritage — the Old Testament. Moreover, precisely because there is, in a sense, a somewhat greater ideal continuity between the Old Testament religion and Judaism than between the Old Testament religion and Christianity — since Christianity re-reads the Old Testament in the entirely new light of Christ — the dialogue with contemporary Judaism affords the Church a uniquely valued insight into her own beginnings, so to speak, and further back.

Too much should not be made of this, however. Judaism is not altogether the same as the religion of Israel encountered by Jesus in his earthly life. Since that time, it developed enormously, partly indeed very much in response to Christianity, seeking to distinguish itself from it evermore clearly, but also perhaps — though far less visibly — under the influence of this or that current in the Christian or "para-Christian" world.

All of this goes some way toward explaining the nature, origin, and implications of the Christian approach to the Jews, as described by the Second Vatican Council: It is "while sounding the depths of the mystery which is the Church" that the Council Fathers and all Christians necessarily encounter the Jewish people and, with them, the religion that so many of them still profess, and that has shaped the cultural patrimony all of them can claim.

Historical Background • "As holy Scripture

testifies, Jerusalem did not recognize God's moment when it came (cf. Lk. 19:42). Jews for the most part did not accept the Gospel" (Vatican Council II, *Declaration on the Relationship of the Church to Non-Christian Religions, Nostra Aetate*, 4). The events of the Redemption did not even leave a particularly profound impression on the popular memory and were soon overshadowed by the event, cataclysmic for the Jewish people, of the destruction of the temple in Jerusalem (A.D. 70) by the Romans, determined to suppress definitively the attempt by the Jewish people in the land of Israel to recover their political independence and their immunity from pagan religious coercion.

While Jewish political independence in that land would only be recovered in a stable manner in our own time, the Jewish religion recovered practically at once from the devastation of its ancient center of worship. Indeed, in a process begun half a millennium or so earlier in connection with the Babylonian exile and the return to Sion, Judaism had developed far beyond the primitive sacrificial worship of the temple, and its center of gravity was shifting significantly to the spiritual worship of the synagogue. In the synagogues, which sprang up all over the ancient world wherever there were Jewish communities, religion centered on the word of God, the Sacred Scriptures, that were read aloud, interpreted, and preached on in the assembly of worshipers. The Scriptures, especially the psalms of David, also provided the texts for the community's prayers. The disappearance of the temple in Jerusalem simply made this shift definitive and universal.

On the eve of the destruction of the temple, there were several "denominations," each claiming to constitute authentic Judaism. Afterward, however, one broad-based "denomination" rose to dominance and became practically synonymous with Judaism, not only in its own doctrinal estimation, but also, broadly speaking, historically. It is variously described as that of the *Perushim* (or "Pharisees" "in New Testament transliteration) or as Rabbinical Judaism, because of the central role the rabbis — masters or teachers — have had

within it, following the complete marginalization of the priestly caste after the cessation of temple worship.

In contrast with the literalist ("Scripture alone") Sadducees, the *Perushim* and their heirs in Rabbinical Judaism — or "mainstream" Judaism — believed profoundly in the Scriptures ("The Written Teaching") as living in and through Tradition ("The Oral Teaching"), and in Tradition as the living guardian and authoritative interpreter of Scripture. In contrast with the sectarian Essenes and others, mainstream Judaism was a religion meant for the whole people. Within it, however, were recognized different degrees of knowledge, understanding, and devotion. In contrast with apocalyptic, esoteric, and emotional religious currents that have reappeared from time to time among the Jews, mainstream Judaism is a religion of faith responding to God's Revelation. Their teachers and religious leaders freely apply their intellects to understanding what faith and revelation tell them and use their reason to interpret it.

The prodigious creativity of the rabbinical schools in the first few centuries led to two major compilations, which became, beside the Hebrew Scriptures, the foundation-documents of Judaism: the Mishnah (A.D. 200) and the Babylonian Talmud (500). These vast encyclopedias (for they are that, rather than wholly systematic treatises) set the tone for the centuries that followed, and provided a sure anchor for mainstream Judaism against the centrifugal forces that continued to arise from time to time within it.

To the extent that such forces could not simply be subdued or segregated (as were the "Scripture alone" Karaites in the Middle Ages and the bizarrely Gnostic-Messianistic Sabbatians and Frankists in the seventeenth century), mainstream Judaism embraced and absorbed them, at least partially, thus to a significant extent taming and controlling them. The latter was the case of the *Kabbalah*, an essentially Neoplatonist, Gnostic mysticism that found its way into Judaism in the Middle Ages and was renewed and reinforced in the sixteenth century. It was also the case with the cluster of religious movements, originating in eighteenth-century central-eastern Europe and known as "Hassiduth," that have emphasized the will over the intellect and promoted manifestations of emotional religious enthusiasm, in a manner not unlike neo-pentecostalist or charismatic Christians today.

Indeed, on the very wide, comprehensive, solid basis of the Mishnah and the Talmud, as the foundational and normative expressions of all Sacred Tradition, mainstream Judaism maintained an impressive consistency and unity in the different parts of the world in which Jews were dispersed, the Middle East, North Africa, all through the European continent, and beyond. Essentially, Jews anywhere were, so to speak, "in communion" with Jews everywhere, notwithstanding the complete lack of any central religious authority and any organizational or administrative link.

Enlightenment and Holocaust • Matters became notably more complicated with the eighteenth-century Jewish Enlightenment, which, continuing apace throughout the following century, too, was influenced in several ways by the general European Enlightenment and its severing of the ethical and humanistic heritage of Judeo-Christian civilization from its religious and supernatural grounding. Several things now happened. There arose movements that sought to reformulate Judaism as a religion, essentially by bringing in reason (in the Enlightenment sense) to critique the received beliefs and, even more, precepts of religion, and then by "modernizing" the material expression of religion (e.g., in dress, forms of worship) to make them accord with the dominant taste of contemporary general — that is, Gentile — society.

Thus was born in Germany the denomination known today as Reform, or Liberal, Judaism, which, in some respects, might be said to resemble Liberal Protestantism. Indeed, some on the far edge of the Reform movement did not even consider it necessary to believe in God, thereby making themselves analogs not of Liberal Protestants but of contemporary Unitarians. In reaction to such extreme manifestations of the deconstructing of Rabbinical Judaism, a notable portion of the Re-

form movement sought to recover considerable traditional ground, constituting itself Conservative Judaism. "Conservative" here denotes the relationship to the "Reformers," not to traditional Rabbinic Judaism, now called Orthodox Judaism, which regards Conservative Judaism as only slightly less heterodox than the Reform denomination.

The Jewish Enlightenment also gave rise to the Wisdom of Israel movement, which sought to reinterpret Israel's heritage in a cultural-ethical key, not tied specifically to precise religious beliefs and observances, in order to reclaim for Israel's heritage the respect due it as the very foundation of Western civilization. Then, in the second half of the last century and the beginning of the present one, an increasing number of Jews, following the trend in the general society, reasserted their communal identity as a people, irrespective of adherence to Judaism as a religion, and directed their energies to establishing a national home in their ancient land. This became the State of Israel, declared independent in 1948. Yet before they could achieve this purpose, about a third of the Jewish people worldwide had been systematically murdered (1939-1945) by Germany's Nazi regime and its collaborators in several other European nations, in what came to be known as the Holocaust, or the *Shoah* (Hebrew for "calamity").

The searing questions posed by the Holocaust for faith in the God of the Covenant; the question of whether (and to what extent) the State of Israel might be said to be "the beginning of the emergence" of Israel's Messianic redemption; the tripartite division of the followers of Judaism into Orthodox, Reform, and Conservative Jews, and the multiple subdivisions of Orthodox Judaism itself; the relationship between Judaism as a religion, on the one hand, and the Jewish people on the other, including both nonbelievers or nonpracticing Jews and modern Christian Jews — all of these are questions with which Judaism and the Jewish people now wrestle mightily, nearly two millennia after the appearance of Judaism in the precise sense defined above.

Before the Holocaust, the number of all Jews

worldwide is estimated to have been eighteen million. At present the number of Jews, considered as persons self-identified or otherwise identifiable as Jews, is estimated as thirteen million. More than two thirds have had some Jewish formation, whether expressly religious or otherwise cultural or national. It is further estimated that forty-seven percent of the world's Jews live in North America and thirty-five percent live in the State of Israel. The rest live in Europe (mostly in the former Soviet Union, in France, and in Britain), in Latin America (the largest community by far being that in Argentina), and elsewhere — in Africa, Asia, and Australia. Only a minority of Jews, albeit a significant one, are adherents of Orthodox Judaism. A majority of Jews in the United States are either unaffiliated, that is, religiously nonpracticing, or members of the Reform or Conservative movements. Still, Orthodox Judaism exerts considerable political influence in the State of Israel, where its protagonists currently (1997) constitute almost a fifth of the legislature, and its institutional expressions are prominent in Jewish affairs almost everywhere.

Jewish Teaching and Practice • The doctrine and practice of Judaism are essentially grounded in the teachings and precepts of the Old Testament — or, more correctly, the Hebrew Bible, which is somewhat shorter than the Old Testament of the Church's Bible and is paralleled by the Protestant Old Testament canon. (The sixteenth-century Protestants mistakenly concluded that the Hebrew Bible was the more ancient canon, the one that Jesus and the Apostles would have known as "Scripture." They did not realize that the Hebrew Bible, or *Masoretic* canon, was definitively adopted only some time after the Resurrection, and that it was only then that certain texts of the scriptural tradition were definitively excluded from it.) The precepts were then elaborated, to an enormous extent, in the oral Tradition, whose first and fundamental records were compiled as the Mishnah (A.D. 200) and the Babylonian Talmud (500).

While the precepts continued to receive further elaboration and refinement in successive centuries, formal doctrine was not worked out in a similarly systematic and binding manner — at any rate, not as distinct from the precepts to be observed. Indeed, Judaism as such does not have a formal dogmatic theology, organized in treatises, safeguarded by definitions, decided by a Magisterium, and so on.

Still, for practical purposes, it can be said that the twelfth-century philosopher and theologian Maimonides came close to a meaningful summary of Jewish belief in his famous Thirteen Principles of Faith. These are: (1) God exists; (2) God is one and unique; (3) God is spirit and incorporeal; (4) God is eternal; (5) God alone is to be worshiped; (6) God has spoken through the prophets; (7) Moses is the greatest of the prophets; (8) the Torah — the divine teaching, that is, Scripture as transmitted by Tradition — is divine; (9) the Torah is immutable; (10) God knows all the thoughts and deeds of human beings; (11) God rewards the just and punishes sinners; (12) God's Messiah — that is, God's Anointed, the Christ — will surely come; (13) the dead will be raised to new life.

Since the Torah is God's Revelation, the study of the Torah is the highest act of homage to the Deity, the center and culmination of the life of prayer, the way of friendship and union with God. The Hasidic wing of Orthodox Judaism seeks to temper this concentration on the intellect, which might tend to devalue the religiosity of the simple and unlettered, by emphasizing as well the possibility of access to God through purely affective prayer and forms of religious enthusiasm.

Judaism essentially conceives of the whole of life as continuous worship, designed to consecrate the world to God and to hallow God's name in the world. The seemingly unending precepts, which govern in minute detail every daily activity of the observant Orthodox Jew, are best understood as "rubrics" for this total liturgy, carried out through sacred behaviors such as Sabbath observance and through explicit prayers specifying the meaning of sacred actions and turning profane actions into acts of benediction and consecration.

Indeed, practically every action of the practicing Jew, from first opening his eyes in the morning, through his ablutions, the consumption of food and drink, commencing his daily study and work, to his lying down to sleep at night, is consecrated to God through a specific prayer or blessing. The Jew's task is to refer everything in the created order back to its origin and end in God. For example, catching sight of a beautiful, wise, or powerful person occasions a blessing, which acknowledges that all beauty, wisdom, and power belong to God and thanks him for granting a participation in them to "flesh and blood."

This "liturgy" of the whole of life is designed to sanctify time itself, an idea intimately familiar to Christians. There are the "liturgy of the hours" during the day (three major public prayers in the morning, afternoon, and evening), the Sabbath each week, and the greater and lesser liturgical feasts and seasons: most eminently, the biblical solemnities of Passover, Pentecost ("Weeks"), and Tabernacles, but also the New Year and the holiest time of all, the Day of Atonement, preceded by forty days of penitence.

Above all, Judaism is faithfulness to the one God, to hallowing his name. Where necessary, Jews are to witness to God's holiness even by undergoing martyrdom, by shedding their blood for the "sanctification of the Name." Great multitudes of Jews, on innumerable occasions, in different continents, under a great variety of oppressive rulers, have done just that, and the mission of "sanctification of the Name," whether by the consecration of one's life or by a martyr's death, is at the heart of the observant Jew's consciousness.

Jewish religion is centered on the family and, secondarily, on the local congregation. Practiced fully and faithfully, it permeates and shapes every moment and aspect of the life of its followers.

The many centuries of intense practice and reflection have generated inestimable treasures of human insight, religious devotion, and spiritual wisdom, contained in an immense body of literature.

The reformers of Judaism, from the eighteenth century to the present day, whether the liberalizers of religious doctrine and practice or the proponents of a Judaism that was not specifically reli-

gious, have always sought to extract from this massive heritage of closely intertwined teachings, legends, precepts, and prayers an essential ideal of manifest validity that would stand on its own as the ultimate message of Judaism, in the broadest sense of the term. Whatever words they might use to express it, all would eventually agree that this essence is no other than that already identified as such in the Gospels as the dual commandment of love. The nontheists among them would reduce it of course even further only to the love of neighbor. Whether such humanism can truly survive for long, severed from its ground in God, is a question that has exercised the whole of our common Judeo-Christian civilization for at least three centuries now; it deserves the most serious discussion, but that clearly belongs elsewhere.

See: Divine Revelation; Jesus Christ, God and Man; Jesus Christ, Life of; Judaism in Catholic Doctrine; Old Covenant; Old Law; Old Testament; Priesthood in the Old Testament; Sacred Scripture.

Suggested Readings: CCC 62-64, 121-123, 574-598, 707-716, 759-762, 839-840, 2568-2589. Vatican Council II, *Dogmatic Constitution on the Church, Lumen Gentium,* 16; *Declaration on the Relationship of the Church to Non-Christian Religions, Nostra Aetate.* John Paul II, *On Jews and Judaism, 1979-1986.* Commission for Religious Relations With the Jews, *Guidelines on Religious Relations With the Jews* (1974); *Notes on the Correct Way to Present Jews and Judaism in Preaching and Catechesis in the Roman Catholic Church* (1985). Committee on the Liturgy, National Conference of Catholic Bishops, *God's Mercy Endures Forever: Guidelines on the Presentation of Jews and Judaism in Catholic Preaching.* A. Bea, S.J., *The Church and the Jewish People.*

David-Maria Jaeger, O.F.M.

JUDAISM IN CATHOLIC DOCTRINE

The Catholic Church teaches that Judaism stands in a unique and unrepeatable relationship to the Christian faith and Church. The status of Judaism is radically different from that of all the other non-Christian religions of humankind. While the other religions have been formed by human beings seeking, by their natural light, to express their awareness of the numinous and relate to it, Judaism has its foundation in public Revelation, in God's Revelation under the Old Covenant made by him precisely with the people of Israel. Thus, even to the extent that it is not simply the revealed religion of the Old Covenant but a product of human religiosity, affection, and thought, Judaism is still uniquely "a response to God's revelation in the old Covenant" (CCC 839) — a response, however incomplete, to the public Revelation of God in history.

The relationship is not only genetic, as it were. The similarities, parallels, and analogies are both profound and wide-ranging. In particular, Christianity and Judaism are closely united in hope, in the "expectation of the coming (or the return) of the Messiah. But one awaits the return of the Messiah who died and rose from the dead and is recognized as Lord and Son of God; the other awaits the coming of a Messiah, whose features remain hidden till the end of time; and the latter waiting is accompanied by the drama of not knowing or of misunderstanding Jesus Christ" (CCC 840).

This intimate relationship between Christianity and the religion of Judaism is so closely intertwined with the relationship between the Church and the Jewish people that any attempt to draw a sharp distinction would be problematic. Toward the Jewish people, the first People of God, the Church has a certain reverence, as toward "elder brothers," to use an expression chosen by Pope John Paul II.

This is, in fact, the approach authoritatively taught by St. Paul, when he reminds all Christian believers that to the Jews "belong the sonship, the glory, the covenants, the giving of the law, the worship, and the promises; to them belong the patriarchs, and of their race, according to the flesh, is the Christ" (Rom 9:4-5; cf. Vatican Council II, *Declaration on the Relationship of the Church to Non-Christian Religious, Nostra Aetate*, 4, CCC 839). These are not simply past realities but, in a true sense, present and future ones as well, "for the gifts and the call of God are irrevocable" (Rom 11:29; cf. *Nostra Aetate*, 4, CCC 839).

The "Hardening" of Israel • Why, then, is it the case that "a hardening has come upon part of Israel," so that they did not acknowledge Jesus of Nazareth as Christ and Lord and still do not?

In divinely inspired and deeply moving passages of great power, in chapters 9-11 of his Epistle to the Romans, St. Paul expounds on this to his Gentile converts. No paraphrase can do justice to the rich, complex, and subtle biblical doctrine therein contained, which must be read and pondered in its entirety. That "hardening," St. Paul concludes, is a "mystery" grounded in God's salvific will for all humanity. It was thanks to that mysteriously providential "hardening" that the preaching of the Gospel burst out of the confines of the Jewish people and went forth into the whole Gentile world.

This "hardening," though, will pass. A time will come when that "part" of the Jewish people, too, like the early Apostles and disciples, will hear and believe the Gospel, so that "in the end," the Apostle confidently predicts, "all Israel will be saved." Indeed: "Together with the prophets and that same Apostle, the Church awaits the day, known to God alone, when all peoples will call on God with one voice and 'serve Him shoulder to shoulder' (Soph 3:9; cf. Is 66:23; Ps 65:4; Rom 11:11-32)" (*Nostra Aetate*, 4).

Meanwhile, of course, both Jews and Gentiles "who, through no fault of their own, do not know the Gospel of Christ or His Church, but who nevertheless seek God with a sincere heart, and, moved by grace, try in their actions to do His will as they know it through the dictates of their conscience — those too may achieve eternal salvation" (Vatican Council II, *Dogmatic Constitution on the Church, Lumen Gentium*, 16). This also is true of "those who, without any fault of theirs, have not yet arrived at an explicit knowledge of God, and who, not without grace, strive to lead a good life" (*Lumen Gentium*, 16). For the divinely revealed truth is that God our "Saviour wills all human beings to be saved" (*Lumen Gentium*, 16; cf. 1 Tm 2:4). Now, whether or not the individual thus saved knows this personally in this life, salvation is always through Christ, and "it is the duty of the Church, therefore, in her preaching to proclaim the cross of Christ as the sign of God's universal love and the source of all grace" (*Nostra Aetate*, 4).

Catholic-Jewish Dialogue • As mandated by the Second Vatican Council, the Church engages in interreligious dialogue with Jews at many levels. The Holy Father encourages and directs this dialogue especially by means of the Commission for Religious Relations With the Jews, which is attached to the Pontifical Council for Promoting the Unity of Christians. In the United States, the National Conference of Catholic Bishops maintains a corresponding office of its own.

The dialogue aims at mutual knowledge and understanding, and at probing together the common beliefs, as well as the reciprocal differences, of Judaism and Christianity. Such dialogue should be particularly effective in witnessing to the great truths already taught in the Hebrew Bible concerning the divine origin of human dignity and its implications. Thus, "Jewish and Christian tradition, founded on the Word of God, is aware of the value of the human person, the image of God. Love of the same God must show itself in effective action for the good of mankind. In the spirit of the prophets, Jews and Christians will work willingly together, seeking social justice and peace at every level — local, national, and international. At the same time, such collaboration can do much to foster mutual understanding and esteem" (Commission for Religious Relations With the Jews, *Guidelines on Religious Relations With Jews,* IV [1974]).

"In virtue of her divine mission, and her very nature, the Church must preach Jesus Christ to the world" (*Guidelines on Religious Relations With the Jews*, I). A better understanding of the religion, history, and present reality of the Jews — an understanding to be gained through study and dialogue — will help ensure that "the witness of Catholics to Jesus Christ not give offence

to Jews" (*Guidelines for Religious Relations With the Jews*, I). To this end, too, Catholics "must take care to live and spread their Christian faith while maintaining the strictest respect for religious liberty in line with the teaching of the Second Vatican Council (Declaration *Dignitatis Humanae*)" (*Guidelines for Religious Relations With the Jews*, I).

Nowadays, there is once more a small number of Jews who believe in the Gospel of Jesus Christ, the Son of God (cf. Mk 1:1) and are members of the Catholic Church, while continuing to affirm their identity as members of their own people — like Our Lord, according to the flesh, his Blessed Mother, St. Joseph, and the Apostles. Some of them live in the State of Israel, in the Diocese of Jerusalem. Led by the Bishop of Jerusalem — more precisely, the Latin Patriarch of Jerusalem — this community worships, as Jesus himself did, in Hebrew. Thus the Church of Jerusalem, the "Mother Church," is once more today an especially visible sign "that Christ who is our Peace has through his cross reconciled Jews and Gentiles and made them one in Himself (cf. Eph 2:14-16)" (*Nostra Aetate*, 4).

See: Canon of Scripture; Divine Revelation; Jesus Christ, God and Man; Jesus Christ, Life of; Judaism; Old Covenant; Old Law; Old Testament; Sacred Scripture.

Suggested Readings: CCC 62-64, 121-123, 574-598, 707-716, 759-762, 839-840, 2568-2589. Vatican Council II, *Dogmatic Constitution on the Church, Lumen Gentium*, 16; *Declaration on the Relationship of the Church to Non-Christian Religions, Nostra Aetate*. John Paul II, *On Jews and Judaism, 1979-1986*. Commission for Religious Relations With the Jews, *Guidelines on Religious Relations With the Jews* (1974); *Notes on the Correct Way to Present Jews and Judaism in Preaching and Catechesis in the Roman Catholic Church* (1985). Committee on the Liturgy, National Conference of Catholic Bishops, *God's Mercy Endures Forever: Guidelines on the Presentation of Jews and Judaism in Catholic Preaching*. A. Bea, S.J., *The Church and the Jewish People.*

David-Maria Jaeger, O.F.M.

JUDGMENT, GENERAL

According to the faith of the Church set forth in the twelve articles of the Apostles' Creed, man is faced with two "final" judgments. The first will take place immediately upon death (Particular Judgment), the second at the very end of the world (General Judgment). This latter judgment will necessarily be definitive and universal, and will occur following the resurrection of the body, whose union with the soul and disposition for all eternity will then be determined before all men by God.

No one knows the day or the hour when the Son of God shall come; it is reserved to the Father alone to fix the time (cf. CCC 1040). But at the coming of Christ in triumph at the end of time, all men will rise with their bodies to render an account of all they ever did or failed to do. "Then will the conduct of each one and the secrets of hearts be brought to light. Then will the culpable unbelief that counted the offer of God's grace as nothing be condemned" (CCC 678). Only then will the Son pronounce his final word on the meaning of all being. "We shall know the ultimate meaning of the whole work of creation and of the entire economy of salvation and understand the marvellous ways by which his Providence led everything towards its final end" (CCC 1040).

This last, or final, judgment will ineluctably be public — a social event, as it were — since it will demonstrate before the world the exact terms of divine justice and mercy. Indeed, it will unfailingly manifest to all who ever lived both the justice of God in condemning sinners and the depth of his mercy to those who are saved. The General Judgment, then, is an event destined to take place in the presence of the glorified Christ, amid all the resurrected bodies, at the very end of the world.

And in that blazing presence which is Christ, who is truth itself and to whom all judgment has been given by the Father in virtue of his redeeming work on the cross (cf. CCC 679), each human being who has ever lived will stand, the truth of his relationship to God having been laid completely bare before the world. "The Last Judgment will reveal even to its furthest consequences the good each person has done or failed to do during his earthly life" (CCC 1039). Truth will at last vanquish all that stands against it, making finally and forever clear that "if God exists, truth must be the absolutely last word" (R. Garrigou-Lagrange, O.P., *Life Everlasting*, p. 82).

See: Ascension and Parousia; Judgment, Particular; Last Things; Resurrection of the Dead.

JUDGMENT, PARTICULAR

The existence of the particular judgment as an event all men must face is affirmed by the teaching of the Church and founded on Scripture and Tradition. None may escape the necessity of having to present himself before God with all that he is and all that he has done. "And just as it is appointed for men to die once, and after that comes judgment. . ." (Heb 9:27).

It is fitting, too, that the soul confront itself in that blazing moment of awareness immediately following death, in order that the true weight of a man's worth be finally known. To defer that realization until the General Judgment at the end of history would leave the soul in unnecessary suspense about its ultimate fate.

In what will the particular judgment consist but an encounter with the living God, before whom all the dross of life is consumed in the fire of divine judgment, leaving only that which is truly lasting? A man will then know himself as he is truly known, without any possibility of error regarding the meaning of his life. The soul will see how God judges, and conscience will confirm the justice of the sentence. James T. O'Connor writes in *Land of the Living: A Theology of the Last Things* (New York, 1992): "For those who die in mortal sin, estranged from God, it will be a confirmation of all the horror of death itself. For others it will be the very beginning of their victory over the death they have just experienced."

It is because humans are free, and therefore responsible, that there must be this final reckoning of the use — and abuse — they have made of liberty and of the talents given them by God to bring perfection before eternity itself (cf. Mt 25:25-30). The crucial decision for man, then, is that final yes to God which makes the gift of divine mercy possible. The *Catechism of the Catholic Church* (679) says: "By rejecting grace in this life, one already judges oneself . . . for all eternity by rejecting the Spirit of love."

See: Judgment, General; Last Things; Purgatory.

JUSTIFICATION

"The grace of the Holy Spirit has the power to justify us, that is, to cleanse us from our sins and to communicate to us 'the righteousness of God through faith in Jesus Christ' and through Baptism" (CCC 1987).

Justification, or "making just," is a free gift of God which takes away our sins and fills us with divine life. The Holy Spirit initiates this process by moving us to conversion — from a life of sin to accepting forgiveness and righteousness from God. This begins the renewal and sanctification of our interior lives.

Justification makes possible our free cooperation with the grace of God. The Holy Spirit touches our hearts and prompts us to have faith in the Word of God. The Spirit both moves us to faith and sustains us in its continuous practice, yet all the while preserving our freedom. The sinner comes to God freely, "since he could reject [God's gift]; and yet, without God's grace, he cannot, by his own free will move himself toward justice" (Council of Trent, cf. Denzinger-Schönmetzer, 1525).

Through justification we enter into the paschal mystery of Christ. "[W]e take part in Christ's Passion by dying to sin, and in his Resurrection by being born to a new life" (CCC 1988). Thus we become members of Christ's own Body, which is the Church (cf. 1 Cor 12).

"Justification is the *most excellent work of God's love.* . . . It is the opinion of St. Augustine that 'the justification of the wicked is a greater work than the creation of heaven and earth,' because 'heaven and earth will pass away but the salvation and justification of the elect . . . will not pass away' [*In Jo. ev.* 72, 3: PL 35, 1823]" (CCC 1994; emphasis in original).

Summing up the Church's faith in our justifica-

tion by Christ, the *Catechism of the Catholic Church* says: "Justification has been merited for us . . . through Baptism. It conforms us to the righteousness of God, who justifies us. It has for its goal the glory of God and of Christ, and the gift of eternal life. It is the most excellent work of God's mercy" (2020).

Controversies About Justification • The theme of justification often appears in the epistles of St. Paul, for example, the eighth chapter of the Letter to the Romans and the third chapter of the Letter to the Galatians. Historically, in elucidating the doctrine of justification, the Church has found it necessary to resist the opposed extremes represented by Pelagianism on the one hand and classic Protestant theological thought on the other.

The Catholic theologian Charles Journet explains: "How is man's justification brought about? We recall the great sentence of St. Augustine, so often forgotten by Protestants: 'God who created thee without thee will not justify thee without thee.' . . . [W]e spoke of the cause of the good act. For Luther, it comes from God alone; for Pelagius, from man alone. Both these views misinterpret St. Augustine's doctrine: *God* does not justify thee without *thee.* God justifies thee through the assent of thy free will; justification is an act of the free will moved by God. But is that possible? Certainly, says St. Thomas, for God moves natures without doing them violence. God moves man, a free being, by actuating his free will, and God leads him from one free assent to another, if man does not frustrate his activations, to the assent of justification in which the decisive grace descends on him" (*The Meaning of Grace*, p. 63).

The sole exception concerns very young children. They are born in the state of original sin, but have not committed personal sin, so that God does not require for their justification any personal act on their part; rather, without any act of will of theirs, he bestows on them the life of grace in Baptism.

The Council of Orange (529) dealt with many of these matters in a series of propositions responding to the so-called Semi-Pelagians. These were fifth-century theologians in southern Gaul who, re-acting against what they considered to be aspects of the teaching of St. Augustine, took the view that the beginning of good human acts comes solely from human beings, while God, seeing a good act begun, empowers its completion. Against such views the Council declared, for example: "If any-one contends that in order that we may be cleansed from sin, God waits for our good will, but does not acknowledge that even the wish to be purged is produced in us through the infusion and operation of the Holy Spirit, he opposes the Holy Spirit him-self" (Denzinger-Schönmetzer, 177).

Controversy over the understanding of justi-fication and related questions came to a head once again nearly a millennium later in the Protestant Reformation. But here the challenge was quite different from that posed by Pelagianism and Semi-Pelagianism. St. Augustine had taught, "When God crowns our merits, he crowns his own gifts." But whose merits are these — ours or Christ's? Journet writes: "The Protestant pro-cedure, here as elsewhere, is to oppose instead of to subordinate. To the merits of Christ alone it opposes the merits of man alone. It pronounces for salvation by the merits of Christ alone and imputes to us the theory of salvation by the mer-its of man alone, the Pelagian view condemned by the Church as heretical. What, then, is the real Catholic doctrine? It is summed up in one sentence: our merits are from God and Christ as first cause, and from us as second cause — God gives us, in Christ, the power to assent to him" (*The Meaning of Grace*, p. 70).

The Council of Trent, in Canon 32 of its Can-ons on Justification, rejected the idea that "the good works of the man justified are in such a way that they are not also the good merits of him who is justified" (Denzinger-Schönmetzer, 842); and Pope St. Pius V in 1567 condemned the proposi-tion that "the remission of temporal punishment . . . and the resurrection of the body must properly be ascribed only to the merits of Christ" (Denzinger-Schönmetzer, 1010); surely we do not merit *without* Christ, yet our merits and their fruits can also be truly attributed to us.

The theological understanding of justification and related questions remained a focal point of controversy between Catholics and Protestants well into the twentieth century. If there remain unre-solved questions in this important area, neverthe-less it can be said that theological reflection and ecumenical dialogue have helped both parties achieve more nuanced understandings and greater mutual sympathy.

See: Augustinianism; Baptism; Faith, Act of; Freedom, Human; Grace; Liberation From Sin; Original Sin; Protestantism; Redemption; Sin.

Suggested Readings: CCC 1987-2011. C. Journet, *The Meaning of Grace*.

K

KINGDOM OF GOD

As men and women strengthened in baptism by Christ, we long for and are expected to work toward the establishment of God's kingdom on earth. This is one of three essential threads of which the Our Father is woven, that central prayer whose petitions furnish the ground and thrust of all our hope. Each of the three great petitions calls upon God for basically the same thing: that the name of God be made holy on earth as in heaven; that his kingdom take root not only in eternity but also in time; that God's will be likewise effective among men as among the members of the Trinity.

These three things — name, kingdom, will — are variations on the same reality, namely, the hidden and inner life of God, his mind and heart that long to pierce the world's darkness and sin, to awaken a renewed humanity to the hope of the new heaven and the new earth. "In this new universe, the heavenly Jerusalem," the *Catechism of the Catholic Church* tells us, "God will have his dwelling among men. 'He will wipe away every tear from their eyes, and death shall be no more, neither shall there be mourning nor crying nor pain any more, for the former things have passed away' [*Rev* 21:4]" (1044).

Indeed, Jesus' oft-repeated proclamation of the kingdom remains *the* central motif of his preaching, as witness the extraordinary frequency with which the word itself occurs in the New Testament — 122 times, of which 90 are from the lips of Christ himself. What is at stake here is not the world beyond, but God himself, in his personal activity that sets about the work of salvation everywhere. Thus the phrase "the kingdom of God" points to God's rule, his living power over the world. Jesus in his very Person *is* the mystery of the kingdom, rendered as pure gift to those who love him.

"Jesus is the Kingdom," writes Joseph Ratzinger, "not simply by virtue of his physical presence but through the Holy Spirit's radiant power flowing forth from him. In his Spirit-filled activity, smashing the demonic enslavement of man, the Kingdom of God becomes reality, God taking the government of this world into his own hands. Let us remember that God's Kingdom is an event, not a sphere. Jesus' actions, words, sufferings break the power of that alienation which lies so heavily on human life" (*Eschatology*, pp. 34-35).

Everything is intended to bear on this point, to converge upon the sheer, prodigal outpouring of divine love. Under the circumstances, "the truth which the Gospel teaches about God requires a certain *change in focus with regard to eschatology.* First of all, eschatology is not what will take place in the future, something happening only after earthly life is finished. *Eschatology has already begun with the coming of Christ.* The ultimate eschatological event was His redemptive Death and His Resurrection. This is the beginning of 'a new heaven and a new earth' (cf. Rev 21:1)" (Pope John Paul II, *Crossing the Threshold of Hope*, pp. 184-185).

The Kingdom Begun and Yet to Come • Thus the hope on which all Christians depend, that is, the irruption in time and space of the kingdom announced by Jesus, has already begun: first through the enfleshment of the Eternal Word in Christ's life, death, and Resurrection; then through the instrument of the Church, which continues that saving presence in the world, especially in her sacraments. Reflecting on Jesus' revelation of the kingdom, the *Catechism* says: "By his word, through signs that manifest the reign of God, and by sending out his disciples, Jesus calls all people to come together around him. But above all in the great Paschal mystery — his death on the cross and his Resurrection — he would accomplish the coming of his kingdom" (542). He announces a kingdom for everyone, especially the lowly, more accessible to repentant sinners than the self-righteous (CCC 543-545). He shares authority in this kingdom with the Twelve, with Peter at their head (CCC 551-553). He offers a foretaste of the fullness of the kingdom in the Transfiguration, with its manifestation of his own divine glory (CCC 554-556).

But the kingdom will never achieve lasting fullness in this world; its final consummation is something whose glorious unfolding we await in hope. As St. Paul reminds us, "In hope we were saved" (Rom 8:24); and the trajectory of that hope is aimed at a reality both present and still to come.

Nevertheless, as Ratzinger says, in its encounter with the reality of the risen Lord "Christianity knew that a most significant coming had already taken place. It no longer proclaimed a pure theology of hope, living from mere expectation of the future, but pointed to a 'now' in which the promise had already become presence. Such a present was, of course, itself hope, for it bears the future within itself" (*Eschatology*, pp. 44-45).

To persist in Christian hope is thus to live between times, amid parentheses bound by both time and eternity. It is to pine for that perfection of God's kingdom in which he will be "all in all" (1 Cor 15:28), in which the hunger and thirst for justice and peace will at last be assuaged and the liberty of the sons of God finally manifested (cf. Rom 8:19, 21), in which the Church herself will stand triumphant before God, "holy and immaculate" (Eph 5:27) forever. "Sacred Scripture calls this mysterious renewal, which will transform humanity and the world, 'new heavens and a new earth' [2 *Pet* 3:13]. It will be the definitive realization of God's plan to bring under a single head 'all things in [Christ], things in heaven and things on earth' [*Eph* 1:10]" (CCC 1043).

The long-awaited dawn of God's kingdom will thereupon confer lasting fulfillment not only upon the individual believer but upon the entire Church, including the redeemed actuality of the world and creation as well. What the evil of sin wrought in terms of enmity and estrangement from God, self, neighbor, and cosmos, the grace of the kingdom will most wonderfully overcome, miraculously reconstituting that wholeness of being which God intended from the beginning.

Thus in the final doxology of the Lord's Prayer ("For the kingdom, the power and the glory are yours, now and forever") in which the three petitions are once more taken up, the Church permanently underscores the importance of the Our Father and its vibrant relation to the coming of God's kingdom. Despite the mendacity of the devil, who falsely attributes to himself the three titles of kingship, power, and glory, "Christ, the Lord, restores them to his Father and our Father, until he hands over the kingdom to him when the mystery of salvation will be brought to its completion and God will be all in all" (1 Cor 15:24-28; quoted in CCC 2855).

We know neither the time when the kingdom will definitively arrive nor the precise way in which the world's transfiguration will take place. As Jesus himself says, "about that day or that hour no one knows, not even the angels in heaven, not even the Son; only the Father" (Mk 13:32). It is not possible for any man to know the hour. Indeed, the hour possesses us, not we the hour. All we can bring to the promised hour is that childlike and trusting surrender of self which, imitating Jesus, constantly reposes itself in hope before the Father. That and an ardent willingness to work for the promised transformation, whose foreshadowing is mysteriously evidenced by our efforts to advance his kingdom (cf. CCC 1049).

See: Beatific Vision; Eschaton; Heaven; Judgment, General; Last Things; Resurrection of the Dead.

Suggested Readings: CCC 541-556, 1042-1050, 1060, 2816-2821, 2855, 2857, 2859. J. Ratzinger, *Eschatology*.

Regis Martin

KNOWLEDGE OF GOD

Why should anyone seek to know God? What we can know of God remains a central question in every age because there is a desire for God — a God-shaped hole, as it were — at the center of our being (cf. CCC 27). Often this desire is vague. Sometimes it is only a sort of dissatisfaction with things as they are, including our own work and life, accompanied by a conviction that there is One who can satisfy our desire.

A desire yearns first to clarify its object; so we search for sources that tell us of God. For those who have been taught to believe in God through Christ early in life, the principal sources for knowledge of God are the Bible and the teachings of the Church. As people mature, however, they ask new questions about God and his ways, questions that arise from personal experience and from other sources of knowledge, such as science. Because our needs keep changing and God is infinite, satisfying the desire to know God is a lifelong project.

Preparing to Know God • The Church speaks of "natural revelation." Much as we come to know others through what they do, so we begin to know the Creator through his creation. Our experience of love in our families, for example, can provide a basis for knowing a loving God. Our sense of right and wrong can lead us to know a God who judges by standards he has placed in the human heart. Rational "proofs" for the existence of God are constructed by looking at natural phenomena and then reasoning to a cause or a formal order of things beyond finite nature.

St. Thomas Aquinas's five proofs for the existence of God (cf. CCC 32) are cases in point. Aquinas's arguments presuppose that nature is not self-explanatory, and the force of each argument depends upon agreement that the human intellect can make legitimate inferences from the seen to the unseeable, from the finite to the infinite. Because modern philosophy begins with doubt, many philosophers now would limit the reach of the intellect to what can be verified by immediate sense experience or proved by testing hypotheses in a laboratory. The First Vatican Council (1869-1870), therefore, took great pains to defend the human mind's integrity and its capacity to know spiritual as well as material realities.

Nevertheless, our "natural" knowledge of God remains quite limited. The limits become clear when we try to talk about the God of natural revelation and can do so only by using analogy. Analogical predication is like metaphor inasmuch as it rests on a comparison, in this case the comparison between God and creatures. Unlike metaphor, however, the comparison is not imaginary; analogy strives to speak truly of God. In order to be true, however, what is said of God by analogy has to be recognized, even as it is said, as so different that any resemblance to created reality is tenuous. We truly call God good, for example; yet his goodness is infinite, unlimited. In ways we cannot imagine, God is goodness itself.

Analogous predication combines and corrects two ways of speaking about God: the *via affirmativa* and the *via negativa*. Affirmatively, the human intellect holds on to the reality being predicated of God; but, negatively, the human mind also refuses to come to rest in any created reality. God is truly good, but his goodness is not that of any created thing. The power of this negation therefore depends upon the truth of what is being analogously affirmed. Even natural mystics, lost in their sense of God's transcendence, often say that God is nothing like anything else. But the force of their statements derives from their very closeness to God. Without the positive experience, the denial that God is "like" his creatures is a trivial statement.

Clarifying Our Knowledge of God • An intellect sure of its own capacity to know transcendent being can look at human beings and all other created reality and see images of God and of his attributes. This knowledge of God from nature, however, pales by comparison with God's self-revelation in history.

To move from natural phenomena to historical events in order to clarify and increase our knowledge of God, we need more than the light of natural reason; we need the gift of faith. To look at the escape of Hebrew slaves from Egypt and see a powerful God at work to save his people requires the light of faith. To look at the crucifixion of a Jewish preacher and healer and see the Son of God sent to save his people from their sins is to uncover realities that no process of natural reasoning can conclude to. Faith never contradicts reason, for the God who gives us the gift of faith also makes us intelligent and free. But faith takes us beyond reason to know a God who enters into history so that the break between Creator and creatures, caused by sin, can be healed and we can live in glory with God forever.

God's gift of faith enables us to respond to him personally. In Sacred Scripture, faith means trust in a person who speaks or acts; it also means an intellectual assent to what has been said or promised by the speaker or actor. The core content of Christian faith is heard in the apostolic proclamation that Jesus of Nazareth is risen from the dead and is therefore Lord of life and death (Rom 10:9; 1 Cor 15:11).

This is the Church's proclamation in every age. The Apostles witnessed to its truth by giving their lives, as have others since. The faith of any individual believer is surrounded by countless witnesses (Heb 12:1) who attest to the truth that Jesus is God's only-begotten Son, one with the Father in the unity of the Holy Spirit. The Church is the living witness to the Tradition that links us to Christ; she guards the written Tradition, the Bible, and reads God's word as she makes present Christ's self-sacrifice in the Eucharist.

Since faith brings us into a reality beyond nature, what we say of God from the knowledge born of faith is less limited than what we can say of him analogously from natural revelation. The personal names of God — Father, Son, and Spirit — are not adequately understood by reference to creatures. Their meaning lies in what Jesus has revealed of his own relationships in the Godhead. As believers, we call God "Father" because he is the Father of Jesus Christ; and we are in Christ by reason of Baptism. Knowing God through faith therefore transforms even our understanding of natural relationships and of God's handiwork in nature.

The certainty of faith and the insights born of faith give rise to the creeds and the defined doctrines of the Church. As believers clarify their faith and gain new insight into what God has revealed in history, doctrine develops. Doctrines accepted by the Church as genuine expressions of faith enjoy the certitude of faith; they are infallibly true. They are not external decrees of a political nature. In fact, doctrines are "infallible" before they are defined, since they cannot be defined without reference to the faith handed down from the beginning. Official definition, however, brings with it a formality that enables believers to know more clearly and surely what God himself wants them to know about him. Formal doctrinal definition by the Church's Magisterium will sometimes change the content of a believer's assent, especially if the believer had not previously recognized a particular doctrine as part of the mysteries of faith; but the quality of assent, the trust in a revealing God, remains the same.

The timely formal recognition of the truths of faith — in the early centuries, the truths about the Trinity and about the two natures, divine and human, in Jesus Christ; at the Reformation, the truths about the sacraments; today, especially in the Second Vatican Council, the truths about the Church and the nature of Revelation — that recognition is a record of the Church's response to challenges to the faith in each age. Each challenge enables the Church to clarify her faith and assists later generations of believers to come to a more developed knowledge of God. Teaching of an official nature that is less than formally doctrinal can still be part of the content of faith, but how or if a particular assertion demands the assent of faith is the subject of theological discussion, which evaluates the "standing" of various statements to see how they relate to the core teachings in the hierarchy of truths.

Deepening Our Knowledge of God • Knowledge of God that begins with an inchoate personal desire leads us to love of God. As our love of God grows deeper, he becomes more recognizably present to us in nature, in history and sacraments, and in personal spiritual experience. We know the One we love; and our love makes our knowledge co-natural to us.

The witness to personal experience of God in the writings of the great mystics like St. John of the Cross and St. Teresa of Ávila is impressive; but each believer knows moments when God has touched his or her life profoundly and left, if not clearer knowledge of who he is, then deeper trust in the Church's teachings about him and greater love for him. God shares his unfathomable riches with us in prayer; but each private spiritual experience must be judged by its coherence with the public record of God's self-revelation in Scripture and Tradition.

Obstacles to Knowing God • Sin darkens the intellect, and one's personal sinfulness can preclude knowing God as friend and lover. The "taste," the desire for God, can be smothered not only by personal sin but also by social developments that make knowing God more difficult.

First, scandals in the Church weaken the witness to God that is the Church's mission to the world. Divisions among Christians also weaken the force of the Gospel and discourage many from looking to the Church for knowledge of God. The existence of evil has always provided something of an argument against the existence of a good God; but how much more destructive of belief in God is the existence of evil among God's people.

Second, natural catastrophes (sometimes called "acts of God"), severe illness, and deep injustice can create anger in some against a God who is held responsible for the state of the world. Some might argue that, if God exists, he is insane and to be avoided rather than known.

Third, the seemingly endless distractions of a consumer-oriented culture can swallow up people and prevent their asking the questions about God that would lead to deeper understanding. We collect things and experiences and easily forget their source and ultimate goal.

Fourth, people can forget what it is to be human because of society's reducing man to the state of an animal with rights. If every human being is or should be autonomous, then any interaction, even with a God who creates and saves us, is an imposition. In this vision of what it means to be human, nature is oppressive and must be conquered or it is precious and must be preserved as a museum; always, however, it is our autonomous will that determines reality. Even God's self-revelation in history is seen as a human projection. Society's task is only to arbitrate the endless conflicts of individual rights as each person chooses which truths he or she wants to live by. In such a world, God lives a hidden life.

Fifth, a conviction that religious truth can be only opinion and that there are no ways to judge the truthfulness of religious statements encourages cynicism about religion and discourages a search for knowledge of God. Sometimes the existence of "spiritual" experience is granted, but it is never a source of knowledge about anything except the person experiencing.

Finally, in a world whose parts are evermore interconnected, various teachings about God can be compared evermore easily. While comparison of different religions can relativize all of them and stop any further search, it also can serve to distinguish the Christian's knowledge of a God beyond all myth and human invention, a God who is no stranger because we participate in being and because he has given himself for us. Any path that leads to clearer and deeper knowledge of God is worth pursuing, but the privileged routes are those that he, in his mercy, has mapped out for us.

See: Agnosticism; Assent and Dissent; Atheism; Development of Doctrine; Divine Revelation; Faith, Act of; Faith of the Church; Faith, Virtue of; God, Nature and Attributes of; Hierarchy; Infallibility; Magisterium; Mysticism; Prayer; Private Revelation; Sacred Scripture; Sacred Tradition; Thomas Aquinas, Thought of; Trinity.

Suggested Readings: CCC 26-100. F. Sheed, *God and the Human Condition*, Vol. 1: *God and the Human Mind*. J. Daniélou, *God and the Ways of Knowing*. R. Sokolowski, *The God of Faith and Reason*. A. Dulles, S.J., *The Assurance of Things Hoped For: A Theology of Christian Faith*.

✠ **Francis E. George, O.M.I.**

L

LAITY

Laos means people. The laity are "prototype" members of the People of God; each one has been divinely chosen with a specific calling and mission. The proper place of the laity is in the world. They are asked there to sanctify themselves through their ordinary work and life so that their presence, friendship, and example can lead others around them to God.

The first task for the lay Christian is to sanctify his or her ordinary secular life and work. This involves work humanly well done (with effort, study, thoroughness, generosity, sacrifice), and work done out of love for God (with purified intention, trying to overcome vanity, meanness, self-centered ambition).

Along with the search for personal holiness, each layperson has the ecclesial right and duty to exercise the Christian apostolate. Each one ought to feel the call and urge to bring Christ to those around him or her (Canon 210). A Christian "who does not work at the growth of the body (of Christ) to the extent of his possibilities must be considered useless both to the Church and to himself" (Vatican Council II, *Decree on the Apostolate of the Laity, Apostolicam Actuositatem*, 2).

The apostolate specific to laypeople, which all of them can do, is in their own secular walks of life: job, family, social, or public activities. Certain aspects of Church life (various parish activities, for instance) call for lay participation; but this type of ecclesial-structural apostolate can ordinarily engage or involve few laypersons, and for fewer still can it offer full-time outlets. The special apostolic vocation of laypeople lies in their work, and in their social and family activities.

"By reason of their special vocation it belongs to the laity to seek the kingdom of God by engaging in temporal affairs and directing them according to God's will. They live in the world, that is, they are engaged in each and every work and business of the earth and in the ordinary circumstances of social and family life that, as it were, constitute their very existence. There they are called by God that, being led by the spirit of the Gospel, they may contribute to the sanctification of the world, as from within like leaven, by fulfilling their own particular duties" (Vatican Council II, *Dogmatic Constitution on the Church, Lumen Gentium*, 31).

Laypersons are not lesser members of the Church than the clergy. The essential ecclesial rights and responsibilities of the Christian flow from Baptism, and these are possessed by laity and clergy in equal measure. Laypeople therefore are not a "long arm" of the clergy, to carry out a Christian infiltration of the world. They *are* in the world, and they have their own specific mission there, "the special duty to imbue and perfect the order of temporal affairs with the spirit of the Gospel" (Canon 225; cf. *Lumen Gentium*, 31; CCC 898, 909).

See: Apostolate; Baptism; Church, Nature, Origin, and Structure of; Communio; States in Life; Vocation.

Suggested Readings: CCC 897-913. Vatican Council II, *Dogmatic Constitution on the Church, Lumen Gentium*, Ch. IV; *Decree on the Apostolate of the Laity, Apostolicam Actuositatem*. John Paul II, *The Lay Members of Christ's Faithful People, Christifideles Laici*.

Cormac Burke

LAST RITES

"Last rites" refers to the continuous administration of the sacraments of Penance, Anointing of the Sick, and Holy Communion in the form of Viaticum to one in danger of death. As early as the ninth century, Penance, Anointing, and Eucharist as Viaticum can be found combined as the last rites of the Christian life. The custom of delaying sacramental Reconciliation developed in the Church's early history when severe public penances were imposed upon penitents. Even as private penance came to be practiced, Reconciliation was still often delayed to the end of life. The common practice of priestly visits to the sick and the administration of Anointing and Viaticum naturally became unified with the private confession of sins in a continuous set of "last rites" when an illness seemed grave. The practice of uniting the three rites at life's end also led to a conception of the Anointing of the Sick as "extreme unction" or last anointing. (It was administered last.)

The revision of the sacrament of Anointing in 1972 more clearly expresses its character as the sacrament of the sick, not just the dying, and has led to a more frequent celebration by those who need the strength and healing of the sacrament when seriously ill. The identification of Anointing only as Extreme Unction has ceased as a result, and the term "last rites" is also only rarely used. The new rites do include a continuous rite of Penance, Anointing, and Viaticum for those who are at the threshold of death.

See: Anointing of the Sick; Eucharist; Penance and Reconciliation, Sacrament of; Viaticum.

LAST THINGS

The doctrine of the last things — that is, eschatology (deriving from the Greek word *eschata*, which means outcomes or ends) — is the fruit of the Church's reflection on the meaning of death, judgment, heaven, and hell, as well as purgatory, limbo, and the end of the world. These are the mysteries that bear most directly on the final section of the Creed, namely, "the resurrection of the body, and life everlasting." To reflect on such realities is an exercise in understanding the content of Christian hope.

The theological virtue of *hope* is thus the key element, the defining feature, as it were, in the study of all that is uttermost in the Christian life (including, to be sure, all that might finally imperil that hope, that is, the risk of not attaining what hope holds out for us). If one can speak of life as a journey, as a road to be entered upon and traveled along, then it is clear that three distinct characteristics above all mark out stages of that life: that it begins, that it will end, and that, in between, there exists this present moment (which, even as I write the words, falls haplessly away). Eschatology is the study that attempts to throw light on the end; the operative virtue in piercing the mystery that presently surrounds it is hope.

But why must hope be theological? Because, like all mysteries rooted in God, hope orders and habituates one to direct participation in God's life. Moreover, God alone has the power to infuse it. And, finally, neither the existence of nor the necessity for hope can be deduced apart from Divine Revelation.

And yet, the German Episcopal Conference's well-regarded catechism says, "Hope is prototypically human; no one can live without it" (*The Church's Confession of Faith: A Catholic Catechism for Adults*, 327). One might speak of hope as a sort of hard currency man uses to negotiate his way home to God, thus enabling him to overcome the abyss separating him from eternity. Hope is very different, therefore, from desire, which merely wishes that somehow things might work out. "Hope reaches deeper and goes farther. It is an expectation that the bleak monotony and burden of everyday life, the inequality and injustice in the world, the reality of evil and suffering, will not have the last word, are not the ultimate reality" (*The Church's Confession of Faith: A Catholic Catechism for Adults*, 327). In short, hope persists in the belief that reality is forever open to something — indeed, to Someone — infinitely more. "Hope, like love," writes Josef Pieper, "is one of the very simple, primordial dispositions of the living person. In hope, man reaches 'with restless heart,' with confidence and patient expectation, toward the *bonum arduum futurum*, toward the arduous 'not yet' of fulfillment, whether natural or supernatural" (*On Hope*, p. 27).

At the very core of man's being, it would appear, is the oddly indomitable impulse for more, an irrepressibility of soul unsatisfied with mere circumstance or self, hoping thereby to make a more perfect future of each. Tomorrow enters decisively into today in order to give imaginative shape to the texture of all we think or know or feel — indeed, who we are.

Theological Hope • Real hope is neither cheap grace nor mere facile optimism; rather, as we have seen, it must be theological, always trained on God, whom we confidently and trustfully expect will provide all that he has promised us. In short, "Hope is the confident expectation of divine blessing and the beatific vision of God; it is also the fear of offending God's love and of incurring punishment" (CCC 2090). It is the virtue most characteristic of *man on the way*, in transit, in parentheses between time and eternity.

Hope thus is the virtue by which man best understands his creaturely status, the essential tension in which he exists, poised between being and nothingness, heaven and hell. And it is given to man to possess in order precisely to sustain him in his pilgrim status, and thus to thwart the two deadliest of temptations: namely, despair, which refuses any longer to hope, and presumption, which imagines that one can obtain fulfillment without it. For man to countenance either is to sin against the first commandment, which obliges us to worship and serve God alone (cf. CCC 2091-2092).

On whom, then, is our hope finally anchored? The answer is plain: Jesus the Christ, who, in the prayer he gave us, grounds the whole eschatological enterprise of Christian hope. The Our Father, as the *Catechism of the Catholic Church* teaches, "is the proper prayer of the 'end-time,' the time of salvation that began with the outpouring of the Holy Spirit and will be fulfilled with the Lord's return"; in the Eucharist especially, "the *eschatological*

character of its petitions" is clearly revealed (CCC 2771).

Holy Scripture presents us with a datum whose relevance to eschatology, the last things, cannot be overstated. Before his miraculous ascent to the Father, completing the full circuit of his prior descent into the human condition thirty-three years before, Christ essentially entrusted two promises to his Apostles, those first leaders of the infant community fashioned from his own broken and pierced body on the cross. These were, in effect: "I go to prepare a place for you, and where I am you too may be"; and, "I shall not leave you orphans, even as I leave to return to my Father in heaven" (cf. Jn. 14:2, 18). Two promises, one for eternity, the other for time, for the condition of this fallen world; two sublime gifts, as it were, committed to those Jesus loved — the gift of everlasting life and the capacity to endure even this life (while anticipating that other more glorious life across the threshold of death); and both locked in the treasury of the Church, his bride, whose keys she herself holds.

Before taking leave of his disciples, Christ is at great pains to assure them that they and the Church, and all her members to the end of time, shall be guided and shaped across the great and fearful sea of history by the breath of God's own Spirit, who will infallibly confer both comfort and counsel upon this Pilgrim People, Christ's Mystical Body.

Continuity and Discontinuity • This guarantee is first made at the Last Supper and given breathtaking expression in the fourteenth chapter of John's Gospel. It represents the loftiest charter of eschatological hope that we have, striking the necessary note of continuity between the two promises made by Our Lord. Indeed, in the *Letter on Certain Questions Concerning Eschatology*, issued in 1979 by the Vatican's Congregation for the Doctrine of the Faith, the Church precisely reminds us of this fact, stressing "the fundamental continuity, thanks to the Power of the Holy Spirit, between our present life in Christ and the future life" (8). How could it be otherwise? If charity is the law of the kingdom, then its practice in the flesh — in this world — will surely constitute the measure of one's share in future glory. In other words, admission to the place where Christ has gone will decisively turn on the extent to which we have *not* lived as orphans but rather as brothers and sisters united in a common love of Christ. St. John of the Cross says in *Dichos* 64, "At the evening of life, we shall be judged on our love" (CCC 1022).

There is also the note of discontinuity, which the Congregation for the Doctrine of the Faith is equally anxious to sound. "On the other hand," we are told, Christians "must be clearly aware of the radical break between the present life and the future one, due to the fact that the economy of faith will be replaced by the economy of fullness of life; we shall be with Christ and 'we shall see God' (cf. 1 Jn 3:2), and it is in these promises and marvelous mysteries that our hope essentially consists" (8).

How, then, are the two held together? The connecting link, the mediating principle, is Christ. Or, as St. Catherine of Siena once put it, "All the way to heaven is heaven because Christ is the Way." He is the single overarching presence, on the strength of whom Old Testament figure becomes New Testament fulfillment. He alone enables us to overcome the distance between "already" and "not yet," or, as Hans Urs von Balthasar calls it in a seminal essay, "the distinction between time of promise and time of fulfillment, in fact between the three times of mere promise (the Old Testament), of fulfilled promise along with fulfillment promised (the Church of the New Testament), and complete fulfillment (eschatology)" (in *Word and Redemption: Essays in Theology*).

Von Balthasar's thesis anticipates Vatican Council II's *Dogmatic Constitution on the Church, Lumen Gentium*, particularly chapter 7, "The Eschatological Nature of the Pilgrim Church and Her Union With the Heavenly Church." This shows how the promised consummation in glory is not only a gift for the far side of paradise but one whose mysterious unfolding may be seen even in this life. This is so because, once again, Christ, "having been lifted up from the earth, is drawing all men to himself (Jn 12:32). . . . Therefore, the

promised restoration which we are awaiting has already begun in Christ, is carried forward in the mission of the Holy Spirit, and through him continues in the Church" (*Lumen Gentium*, 48).

Pieper, in a telling passage identifying Christ as "the actual fulfillment of our hope," adduces a pair of texts from St. Augustine. Interpreting the Pauline statement in Romans, "In hope were we saved" (8:24), Augustine comments: "But Paul did not say, 'we shall be saved,' but 'we have already been saved'; yet not in fact (*re*), but in hope; he says, 'in hope were we saved.' This hope we have in Christ, for in him is fulfilled all that we hope for by his promise." And elsewhere: "As yet we do not see that for which we hope. But we are the body of that Head in whom that for which we hope is brought to fulfillment" (*On Hope*, p. 35).

So crucial is this linkage of hope to Christ, says Pieper, that for anyone not to be in Christ is to be entirely bereft of hope. Whereas, to the degree one is "in" Christ — steeped in his sacramental life, which the Church, his Body, uniquely dispenses — to that very extent one puts on Jesus' hope, to which there is literally no end or limit. One thinks of the Little Flower, St. Thérèse of Lisieux, whose boundless hope in God has become the distinctive mark, the signature, of her sanctity. She urges: "Believe in the truth of what I now say: we can never have too much trust in our dear Lord, who is so powerful and so merciful. One receives as much from him as one hopes for." And, in serene expectation of the heavenly mission she longs to receive, Thérèse declares: "All of my expectations will be more than richly fulfilled; indeed, the Lord will do something wondrous for me that will infinitely exceed even my boundless wishes" (quoted in von Balthasar, *Dare We Hope: 'That All Men Be Saved'?* p. 103).

Finally, it is God himself who remains the "last thing." Says von Balthasar: "Gained, he is heaven; lost, he is hell; examining, he is judgment; purifying, he is purgatory. He it is to whom finite being dies, and through whom it rises to him, in him. This he is, however, as he presents himself to the world, that is, in his Son, *Jesus Christ*, who is the revelation of God and, therefore, the whole essence of the last things. In this way, eschatology is . . . entirely a doctrine of *salvation*."

It is fair to ask to what extent convictions like these are operative in the lives of Christians. Do we not live for the most part in the aftermath of the "disappearance" and "death" of God — that is, modernity's own great crisis of faith and therefore of the extinction of hope? "Holy Saturday: the day God was buried; isn't this remarkably true of our day, today? Is not our century starting to be one long Holy Saturday, the day God was absent?" So wrote theologian Joseph Ratzinger in an Easter meditation in 1969.

This captures the temptation with which the Church's doctrine of the "last things" must do battle. Her task, in this and every age, is to overcome the world's indifference to God, to the eternal poetry of the transcendent that Christ entered the world in order perfectly to enflesh. The Church's mission is to lead the world (in a phrase used by John Paul II as the title of a book of personal reflections) across the threshold of hope. John Paul concedes that "people of our time have become insensitive to the Last Things. . . . To a certain degree, eschatology has become irrelevant to contemporary man." But he adds: "Faith in God, as Supreme Justice, has not become irrelevant to man; the expectation remains that there is Someone who, in the end, will be able to speak the truth about the good and evil which man does. Someone able to reward the good and punish the bad" (*Crossing the Threshold of Hope*, pp. 183ff.).

And who but God is qualified to render perfect justice either to the world he made or to all those whom he suffered to redeem? "And so it is appointed that men die once, and then comes judgment" (Heb 9:27); after which an eternity of gain or loss, heaven or hell, awaits those whom God first graciously brought into being. As the Pope says, it is Love itself to whom we present ourselves: "Before all else, it is Love that judges. God, who is Love, judges through love." It is he whom we encounter in the end, the Same who made us in the beginning, the One on whom we hope for strength and support in between.

See: Ascension and Parousia; Death; Heaven;

Hell; Hope; Jesus Christ, God and Man; Judgment, General; Judgment, Particular; Limbo; Purgatory; Redemption; Resurrection of the Dead.

Suggested Readings: CCC 1020-1060. Vatican Council II, *Dogmatic Constitution on the Church, Lumen Gentium*, Ch. VII; *Pastoral Constitution on the Church in the Modern World, Gaudium et Spes*, 38-39. Congregation for the Doctrine of the Faith, *Letter on Certain Questions Concerning Eschatology.* J. Pieper, *On Hope.* H. von Balthasar, "Some Points of Eschatology," in *Word and Redemption: Essays in Theology.*

Regis Martin

LAW OF CHRIST

This entry treats many aspects of the law of Christ. First it provides a survey of Christ's moral teaching. Then it points out that his law gives his disciples power to live excellent lives. Next it shows that Christ's moral teaching binds in conscience. (Still, it is a morality of freedom, a morality that sets his disciples free.) Finally, it recalls that Jesus is himself the law of the Gospel.

The Sublime Moral Teaching of Jesus • In the Gospels, Christ is most commonly called "Teacher." In the Sermon on the Mount (Mt 5–7), in many parables and earnest exhortations, he is clearly presenting his followers a way of living that he counts immensely important for them. Those who walk in accord with his teaching will build their lives on solid ground; to neglect his teaching is to build one's life on foundations that will not endure (Mt 7:13). Their happiness in this life and their eternal salvation require that they love God and one another sincerely, that they avoid evil deeds incompatible with love (Lk 18:20), and that they do the positive acts that love requires (cf. Mt 25:31-46).

Those who heard Christ teach cried out, "Never has anyone spoken as this man speaks" (Jn 7:40). People hung on his words, because he spoke to them with great compassion and kindness and with a wisdom that astonished them. He spoke to their inmost hopes and hearts out of his own excellent life.

When a lawyer asked Jesus, "Teacher, which is the great commandment in the law?" Jesus replied, " 'You shall love the Lord your God with all your heart, and with all your soul, and with all your mind.' This is the greatest and first commandment. And a second is like it: 'You shall love your neighbor as yourself.' On these two commandments hang all the law and the prophets" (Mt 22:36-40).

In this Jesus made two things clear. First, the commandments that we love God and love our neighbor as ourselves have first place in the moral life. Other valid moral commandments have moral force precisely because they are rooted in love. All the moral requirements that God revealed — "all the law and the prophets" — "hang on," flow from, the commandments of love.

Christ does, then, firmly teach the continuing validity of the Ten Commandments. A certain young man came to Our Lord to learn how he should live to find eternal life. He had seen Jesus, and had longed to live a life like that of Jesus, a life shining with the glory of eternal life. Jesus told the young man that if he sought eternal life, he should keep the commandments. And he made clear that he meant precisely the familiar commands of the Decalogue: "You know the commandments: 'You shall not commit adultery; You shall not murder; You shall not steal; You shall not bear false witness; Honor your father and mother' " (Lk 18:20).

St. Thomas Aquinas points out how the Ten Commandments flow from the precepts of love.

The precepts of love are the first principles in the moral vision Jesus teaches. They are the most evidently true of all precepts. But only a modest amount of reflection is needed to see how the Ten Commandments follow from them. The commandments require of us that we avoid acts incompatible with love or do actions required by love. We must love our neighbor; but one who performs acts that of their very nature harm the neighbor, clearly is not acting as love of neighbor requires. This is what the New Testament teaches: "The commandments, 'You shall not commit adultery; You shall not murder; . . . and any other command-

ment, are summed up in this word, 'Love your neighbor as yourself.' Love does no wrong to a neighbor; therefore, love is the fulfilling of the law" (Rom 13:9-10; cf. *Summa Theologiae,* I-II, q. 100, a. 3).

Other commandments are so important because they really do unfold the requirements of the precepts of love. The love that Christ teaches requires that we care about everyone. Breaking the commandments mars the world and wounds the lives of those we directly harm with our evil deeds. The Gospel makes clear that there are evil kinds of deeds that one should never deliberately do. Doing evil even to achieve good is profoundly contrary to New Testament teaching (cf. Rom 3:8). Such conduct by no means assures that the goods sought by evil deeds will be achieved; but it does directly accomplish the evil it does.

The commandments of love are not entirely new in the teaching of Jesus. The Old Law, too, taught the duty to love God with all the heart (cf. Dt 6:5), and in many rich ways it called for love of the neighbor. Still, the Old Law is imperfect in what it teaches as the meaning and measure of love.

How much God loved us, and how much one could love God, had not been fully revealed in the Old Law. In Christ alone is the right measure of love put into place. We are to seek to love God with that immense love with which Christ, our brother, loved the Father and willingly endured everything out of love for him. Christ also provides us with the new and perfect standard we are to aspire to in loving one another: "As I have loved you, so you are to love one another" (cf. Jn 15:12).

Hence Christ takes care to clarify what love requires. We are not to love only our friends and neighbors; we are not to love only those who love us and treat us well. Life does not work if love does not soar far beyond that. We must love those who do not love us, forgive those who have hurt us, show mercy to those who have done us wrong. Only thus, Jesus tells his disciples, may you be "sons of your Father who is in heaven" (Mt 5:44).

The Decalogue, too, needed to be brought to

perfection. Frequently in the Sermon on the Mount Jesus contrasts what people had once thought the commandments to mean with his more perfect explanation of them. "You have heard it said . . ." Jesus would say, presenting the precept in its familiar form. "But I say to you . . ." Jesus adds, showing that in the light of love the commandment requires more than had earlier been realized. For example, "You have heard that it was said, 'You shall not commit adultery.' But I say to you that every one who looks at a woman lustfully has already committed adultery with her in his heart" (Mt 5:27-28). The New Law, St. Thomas points out, requires more universally than the Old Law did that we avoid not only external evil acts but also wrong interior movements of the heart. It requires things that the unfaithfulness of cultures has kept hearts from realizing; and it calls us to realize that the precepts of love, from which the commandments flow, must illumine our understanding of them (*Summa Theologiae,* I-II, q. 107, a. 4, c.).

"All Christians . . . are called to the fullness of Christian life and to the perfection of love" (Vatican Council II, *Pastoral Constitution on the Church in the Modern World, Gaudium et Spes,* 40; cf. Mt 5:48; 1 Thes 4:3). We are commanded to love God with our whole hearts and to love one another as Christ has loved us. These are indeed sublime precepts. We cannot keep them perfectly in this life, even with the aid of grace. But we can grow faithfully toward the peaks to which love calls us. St. Thomas gives the example of the soldier who is commanded to do specific things and also to fight all the way to victory. He cannot fulfill the total command until victory is finally won, but he is a faithful soldier if he carries out his specific duties and does continue efforts toward victory. So we do not violate the command of entire love, if we accept it, if we keep the specific precepts that flow from it and which grace does enable us to keep, and if our hearts resolve to continue growing toward fuller love and to love's final completion in beatitude (*Summa Theologiae,* II-II, q. 44, a. 6, c.).

Christ's moral teaching does not consist only of precepts. He begins his Sermon on the Mount with a proclamation of the Beatitudes (Mt 5:2ff.). These Beatitudes recall the sublime characteristics the disciple should have. They are encouraging promises of the Lord, assuring his disciples that they shall be given the kingdom and every longed-for blessing if they allow the Lord to make them poor in spirit and merciful and pure of heart, like their master. The Beatitudes show eloquently the sort of life called for by the Christian vocation. They outline the traits needed to have happiness on this earth in the midst of trials, and to have assurance of everlasting life (CCC 1716-1717).

Living a Christian Life • The Gospel counsels are poverty, perfect chastity for the sake of the kingdom, and willing acceptance of an obedience that goes beyond keeping precepts required of all. Christ, though he was rich, willingly became poor for our sakes (2 Cor 8:9); he lived a life of generous love in a perfectly chaste and unmarried life; and, though he was Lord of all, he willingly subjected himself to obedience to others. He calls those who "would be perfect" (Mt 19:21) to profit from the assistance that the Gospel counsels offer. Observing them helps one escape more fully from burdensome obstacles that so often keep people from holy lives.

Not all are called to live the counsels in their fullest scope. But all Christians are called to live in the spirit of the counsels: to be detached from material goods, to be entirely chaste, and to have hearts prepared to live in generous obedience to the Lord (CCC 917-919, 1973-1974).

Jesus was fully aware of how difficult many thought it would be to live in his excellent ways. He conceded that such excellent living was impossible for the resources of unaided human nature: the grace and assistance of God would be necessary (cf. Mt 19:25-26).

But Jesus also assured his disciples that those who drew near to him would indeed find power to walk with gladness in his ways. "Come to me, all who labor and are heavily laden, and I will give you rest. Take my yoke upon you, and learn from me; . . . for my yoke is easy, and my burden is light" (Mt 11:28-30).

We have seen that Christ indeed teaches many difficult precepts. But his law is not fundamentally a moral system; at its heart it is not even the precepts of love. "Now that which is preponderant in the law of the New Testament, and that on which all its efficacy is based, is the grace of the Holy Spirit, which is given through faith in Christ. Consequently the new law is chiefly the grace itself of the Holy Spirit, which is given through faith in Christ" (*Summa Theologiae*, I-II, q. 106, a. 1, c.; cf. Rom 3:27, 8:2). Through this grace the love of God is poured into our hearts, giving us the desire and the power to love him and one another, and to keep all his ways. As St. Augustine said: "Love makes light and nothing of things that seem arduous and beyond our power" (*On the Words of the Lord*, Sermon 79).

Binding Precepts • Since the law of Christ is, as we shall see, a law that sets us truly free, some have argued that the law of Christ is not morally binding. There have been extreme movements at the fringes of Christianity that argued: Since Christ saves those who believe in him, true believers can with impunity break any of the commandments. Others have argued that the more difficult and distinctive precepts of Christ, the commands to forgive from the heart, to have chaste minds, not to divorce and remarry, are simply ideals, and that one does not have a strict duty to observe these.

Such views clearly contradict the constant teaching of faith, and contemporary scholarship reveals how false they are to the whole moral message of the Gospel (cf. R. Schnackenburg, *The Moral Teaching of the New Testament* [1964], Ch. 2). Christ clearly presents his precepts as binding for those who seek eternal life. So, for instance, the one who divorces and remarries "commits adultery," an offense of the sort that keeps one from the kingdom of God (cf. 1 Cor 6:9).

Moreover, as Pope John Paul II has pointed out with great force, the commandments themselves are calls to heroic living in charity. One of the signs of great love is the firm will never to act in ways that directly or deliberately dishonor God or do harm to the neighbor, no matter what one

may suffer in refusing to act against the basic duties of love. Thus, Thomas More, knowing the sacredness of an oath and the great harm done to states and to persons when public truth is undermined, knew that he had a duty even to let his life be taken from him rather than to swear falsely. Christian faith has always taught that the precepts that Christ confirmed forbid kinds of actions that are always hostile to love, always wrong, no matter how difficult it may be keep them in one's particular circumstances (cf. Pope John Paul II, encyclical *The Splendor of Truth*, *Veritatis Splendor*, 79-83, 90-94).

Freed by the Law of Christ • Though called to lead truly good lives and obliged to live as love requires, we are certainly called to a magnificent freedom in Christ. "For freedom, Christ has set us free. . . . You were called to freedom, brethren" (Gal 5:1, 13). In *Veritatis Splendor* (35-53) Pope John Paul II points out the richness of freedom in the moral life that Jesus teaches.

Christ gives freedom to our moral lives in a rich variety of ways. He frees us by teaching us the truth. Thus he enables us to escape the sad mistakes of the sinful world, and to see and taste for ourselves the goodness of his form of life, which makes life work and gives gladness to our lives.

As a teacher of life, Jesus always speaks to our freedom. He never wishes us to be forced or driven to do his will, but to do it gladly and with the free hearts that he gave us.

His commandments are never arbitrary. Rather, he teaches us a way of life that corresponds to what our own hearts naturally long for. He wants us to live in ways that call us to fulfillment in the midst of a community of love. Unlike so many persuasive forces in this world, he calls us only to live the good lives we were made to live.

Jesus also sets us free by his grace and the gift of the Spirit. He will not permit life to be too burdensome for his friends (cf. Mt 11:28-30). He promises, and is faithful to his promise, to make lives of generous love easier and more happy than foolish and sinful lives could ever be.

Christ also liberates us from the burdens of the Old Law. The enduring goodness of the moral teaching of the Old Law he honored and brought to fulfillment; but he set us free from the old burden of having heavy duties, without the presence of grace to make the task easy. He freed us from many kinds of dietary and ceremonial laws that had little point after Christ, whom such laws saluted obscurely, was fully revealed.

But Christ does not call us to false kinds of freedom, to those counterfeits of freedom that undermine true personal freedom. Some would wish to have the right to do whatever they feel inclined to do, however cruel or wrong it might be. This is not freedom, but slavery to passions and to irrational drives that would create for us bitter and broken lives. Some would pretend (in the ancient way that the tempter urged in Genesis 2) that human beings should have the freedom to determine for themselves what is good or evil: to decide, if they wish, that killing the innocent or committing adultery or swearing falsely is a good thing for them to do. But our "deciding" does not change the nature of things. Our deciding that taking arsenic would heal our diseases would not make arsenic in fact healthful for us. Similarly, "deciding" that those kinds of behavior that are really evil and opposed to love are good ones does not make them in fact good ones, nor does it enable evil acts to bless our lives. Authentic freedom is meant to enable us to choose with willing hearts good forms of living, and so shape lives really dear to us.

Jesus, the New Law • Jesus is himself the New Law. He is the perfect love of the Father, and of all his brothers and sisters. His life is a teaching of the Ten Commandments, for he faithfully avoids all that is incompatible with love. "He committed no sin; . . . when he was reviled, he did not revile in return; when he suffered he did not threaten" (1 Pt 3:22-23). He not only did no wrong; positively his life was a series of endless acts of love. He was mercy to the suffering, to the sinner, to the confused, to those who in any way "labor and are heavily laden" (Mt 11:23).

His life reveals the sublime greatness that he invites us to in the Beatitudes, for the Beatitudes paint a portrait of his own life (CCC 1717). He is, above all, the one who is poor in spirit, hungry for righteousness, meek, mourning with those who mourn, merciful, most pure in heart, maker of peace, and gentle when persecuted. In him shines all the greatness of the sublime Gospel counsels: Though he was rich, he became utterly poor, so as to be with and bless us poor ones and make us rich (cf. 2 Cor 8:9); with a perfect purity of heart he loves every person with a warm, chaste, and generous love; his obedience to the Father teaches us the strong ways of profound love.

Moreover, Jesus alone enables us to live lives of saving love. By his saving love upon the cross he won for us every grace; and it is he who sends his Holy Spirit into our hearts. He touches our life in all the sacraments, enabling us to share in the very life of God as we become one with him, the eternal Son.

Jesus is everything. As all our faith is caught up into the mystery of Jesus, and all our sacramental life ties us to him, and all prayer flows from the gifts and presence of Jesus, so all our moral life is rooted in him. He alone is sufficient.

See: Beatitudes; Evangelical Counsels; Freedom, Human; Grace; Holy Spirit; Moral Principles, Christian; Natural Law; Ten Commandments.

Suggested Readings: CCC 1691-1696, 1716-1724, 1730-1742, 1914-1974, 1987-2005, 2052-2074. Vatican Council II, *Pastoral Constitution on the Church in the Modern World, Gaudium et Spes,* 22-32; *Dogmatic Constitution on the Church, Lumen Gentium,* 39-42. John Paul II, *The Splendor of Truth, Veritatis Splendor.* G. Grisez, *The Way of the Lord Jesus,* Vol. 1, *Christian Moral Principles,* Chs. 19-25. W. May, *An Introduction to Moral Theology,* rev. ed., Chs. 2, 5, 8. R. Schnackenburg, *The Moral Teaching of the New Testament,* Ch. 2.

Ronald D. Lawler, O.F.M. Cap.

LEGALISM

Legalism is the view that moral norms are arbitrary rules rather than truths. It is, unfortunately, quite prevalent. Typically, for instance, when the Pope visits the United States, the media speak of the Church's "ban" on contraception, divorce and remarriage, homosexual acts, and so on. A "ban" is a regulation that can easily be reversed. Clearly, the Church's moral teachings are frequently understood as rules imposed on a restive laity by a restrictive hierarchy.

However, the Church's moral teachings are not changeable rules; they are truths. Thus the Pope could no more decide that contraception or homosexual acts will from now on be permissible than he could decide that from now on the earth will be flat.

Of course some Church rules are changeable: for example, the rule about the fast required prior to Holy Communion. Every community needs to make some rules that have some degree of arbitrariness and are changeable. Still, the basic moral norms concerning what is consistent with love of God, neighbor, and self are truths, not arbitrary or changeable rules.

As children, perhaps all of us tend toward legalism. Our consciences develop. Also, to the extent we identify ourselves with morally bad choices, moral norms can appear as extrinsic restrictions upon our desires.

Legalism and Moral Theory • But legalism can afflict moral theory. Indeed, most of the textbooks in moral theology in this century, before Vatican Council II, leaned in this direction. They tended to view moral theology as a code of rules to be defended and clarified, rather than as an effort to understand the rich Christian life God calls us to, centered on Christ, understood in the whole context of Scripture and all of the truths of faith. This is why the Council called for a renewal of moral theology, asking that it have a "livelier contact with the mystery of Christ and the history of salvation" and be "more nourished by scriptural teaching" (Vatican Council II, *Decree on Priestly Formation, Optatam Totius*, 16).

A legalistic theory of morality might arise in the following way. Moral norms guide choices. But directives for choosing are not theoretical truths, nor are they statements describing what exists. If, then, one thinks truths must be theoretical — that is, descriptions of what is — one will

need to appeal to something other than a truth to account for the force of obligation that obviously accompanies moral norms. And one might appeal to the will of the lawgiver as the source of moral obligation, with the result that moral norms are thought of as changeable rules.

It is important to see that theoretical truth (truth about what is the case) is not the only kind of truth. Moral norms are directives, guides for choices. Some moral propositions are true, while others are false. Directives to one's true good or fulfillment and to that of other people are true. Directives guiding one to conditions that diminish one's real good or that of others are false. Moral truth, then, is based on the objective relation between actions one can choose and one's possible fulfillment and that of others. Moral truths are not mere descriptions of that relation (in which case it might seem that they get their obligation elsewhere). Rather, they are true in a different way: as directing to the genuine fulfillment of all people.

From a legalistic standpoint it is impossible to see the real basis for any of the moral teachings of the Church. The Church will appear a stern taskmaster if moral norms are viewed as arbitrary rules. One will see no reason except stubbornness for the Church's refusal to "relax the bans" against various acts. The basis for the Church's moral teachings is, however, the real fulfillment of real human persons. The Church teaches respect for the real goods and real fulfillment of persons. The actions the Church excludes are negative, that is, actions that suppress or destroy the basic goods of persons.

Legalism bears bad fruit. Viewed as extrinsic restrictions upon desire, moral norms generate resentment. Even in those who do not rebel against apparently extrinsic and arbitrary rules, legalism greatly diminishes their participation in God's plan. Following rules thought to have no real intrinsic point is a very low level of participation.

On the other hand, those who actively share in and appreciate the real purposes of a shared project actively participate in that project in a much higher degree. God's plan is the establishing of the kingdom of God, and human persons are called actively to participate in this plan. Our actions have an intrinsic relation to the kingdom of God, for the kingdom is not a purely spiritual reality that comes only at the end as a reward for passing an arbitrary test. God's kingdom includes both communion in divine life (grace and beatific vision) and fulfillment in all human goods, including bodily as well as spiritual fulfillment (cf. Vatican Council II, *Pastoral Constitution on the Church in the Modern World, Gaudium et Spes*, 39).

See: Absolute Moral Norms; Conscience; Human Goods; Kingdom of God; Magisterium; Moral Principles, Christian; Natural Law; Positivism.

Suggested Readings: CCC 1750-1756, 2032-2040. John Paul II, *The Splendor of Truth, Veritatis Splendor*. G. Grisez, *The Way of the Lord Jesus*, Vol. 1, *Christian Moral Principles*, Chs. 12, 34. G. Grisez and R. Shaw, *Fulfillment in Christ*, Chs. 12, 34.

Patrick Lee

LEX ORANDI, LEX CREDENDI

The great St. Augustine (died 430) was still alive when, in response to theological errors today known as Pelagianism, a great discussion about the nature and operation of divine grace was agitating the Church. As part of the effort at authoritative clarification of these doctrines, there was composed in the first half of the fifth century a short catalog (*indiculus*) summarizing statements by the Church's teaching authority on the doctrine of grace. Sources quoted included papal pronouncements, the decrees of local councils subsequently approved by the Supreme Pontiff, and the expression of the Church's belief that is found in her public liturgical prayer. In marshaling support for his arguments, the author of the "Indiculus" (probably the lay theologian Prosper of Aquitaine) appealed to the priestly prayers of the liturgy that, handed down from the Apostles, are celebrated uniformly in every Catholic church throughout the world "so that the norm of prayer may establish the norm of

belief" (*ut legem credendi lex statuat supplicandi*).

This does not mean that the Sacred Liturgy is, as it were, a touchstone for testing the truths of faith in the sense that, if a certain doctrine bears fruit of holiness and piety through the sacred liturgical rites, then it ought to be approved by the Church, but otherwise it ought to be condemned (*lex orandi, lex credendi*: the law of prayer is the law of belief). Pope Pius XII offered an authoritative explanation of why this is not what the Church teaches and commands (cf. encyclical *Mediator Dei*, 1947). The worship given by the Church to God in his infinite goodness, as St. Augustine briefly and clearly puts it, "is a continuous profession of Catholic faith and an exercise of hope and of charity. . . . In the Sacred Liturgy, we openly and clearly profess the Catholic faith not only by the celebration of the divine mysteries and by the offering of the sacrifice and the administration of the sacraments, but also by reciting and singing the 'Symbol' of faith which is a special badge and touchstone, as it were, of Christians, and by reading other documents and the Sacred Scriptures written under the inspiration of the Holy Spirit. The liturgy, then, contains the whole Catholic faith, since it publicly manifests the faith of the Church."

Consequently, when there was need to define a truth divinely revealed, the Supreme Pontiffs and the councils, in the course of gathering arguments from the "theological sources," often quoted the liturgy: for instance, in the definitions of the Immaculate Conception (Pius IX) and of the Assumption (Pius XII). And, in much the same way, the Church in earlier ages, when there was doubt or controversy concerning some truth, did not hesitate to seek light from the venerable rites transmitted from antiquity. "The law of prayer is the law of faith: the Church believes as she prays. Liturgy is a constitutive element of the holy and living Tradition" (CCC 1124).

As Pius XII concludes in *Mediator Dei:* "The Sacred Liturgy does not determine or constitute in an absolute sense nor by a power of its own the Catholic faith; but rather, since it is also a profession of heavenly truths, subject to the supreme teaching authority of the Church, it can supply arguments and evidence of no little validity to clarify a particular principle of Christian doctrine."

See: Development of Doctrine; Dogma; Faith of the Church; Infallibility; Liturgy; Magisterium.

Robert A. Skeris

LIBERATION FROM SIN

Christ the Savior came to free us from sin and from all the evils that sin has brought into our world (CCC 456-457).

Sin leads to countless evils. In differing ways, death (cf. Rom 5:12; CCC 1008), wars, hatreds, enmities (cf. Jas 4:1-3), and the unjust structures that occasion both sin and a multitude of sufferings (CCC 1865-1869) are fruits of personal sin. In the completion of God's liberation through Christ, all these will be overcome for those who have loved God: "God will wipe away every tear from their eyes" (Rv 7:17).

But sin is itself the most bitter of evils. Acts of mortal sin reduce persons made to be God's friends to a tragic state of sin. A single mortal sin causes one to lose the new life in Christ that grace confers. By sin one casts away the love of God; one ceases to walk the path toward eternal life (CCC 1861).

God liberates the sinner. Through the merits of Christ, he returns the sinner to the life of grace, to love, and to the hope of eternal salvation (CCC 1987-1988).

Christ merited our liberation from sin by his blessed Passion. But his Passion did not immediately transform all sinners or complete the healing of the world. The fruits of Christ's saving work are applied in the course of the adventures of salvation, in gifts God freely gives to our freedom (CCC 1066-1068).

Christ grants liberation from sin to individual persons primarily through his sacraments. Worthy reception of the sacraments supposes that those capable of doing so approach them freely, moved by the redeeming grace of Christ (CCC 1128).

See: Death; Grace; Justification; Original Sin; Redemption; Sacrament; Sin.

LIBERATION THEOLOGY

The theology of liberation is a multifaceted movement, actually encompassing several different theologies, that emerged after Vatican Council II. In its most prominent form, it appeared to advocate political and economic revolution, often along Marxist lines, as part of the "preferential option for the poor" in Latin America and in the rest of the developing world. Owing to the demise of communism, criticism from the Magisterium, and developments within liberationist thinking itself, liberation theology has turned to more reformist and democratic paths. But as a child of the 1960s, it has also led to feminist, racial, sexual, and ecological claims to liberation. A modified notion of liberation and the preferential love for the poor has found its way into recent papal thought, and will probably lead to further theological developments.

Historical Survey • Though it quickly spread to other parts of the world, liberation theology began as a primarily Latin American phenomenon. As early as the late 1950s and early 1960s, the Brazilian Paolo Freire was teaching what he called *conscientização*, a kind of consciousness-raising that seemed to many people at the time to carry radical political significance. Freire left Brazil in 1964 after a military coup, but continued his work with a book entitled *The Pedagogy of the Oppressed.* Along with other Latin American religious figures at the time, he was seeking some other path to help the poor of the continent rather than the solutions that were promised by Western-sponsored programs for "development" but never seemed to materialize. Military coups occurred in several other Latin American countries in the 1960s and 1970s. Viewing those governments — rather implausibly — as an expression of exploitative Western capitalism, opponents began exploring socialist or Marxist alternatives.

Around the same time, the Second Vatican Council gave a new impetus to meeting the challenges presented by the poorer nations. The Council encouraged concrete engagement with the modern world and the application of Catholic social principles to specific circumstances. Even before the Council, the Church in Latin America had already inspired trade union movements, Christian Democrat parties, and new universities that were a departure from its old identification with wealthy landholders. At Vatican II, the Latin American hierarchy had the opportunity to meet yearly to discuss common problems. One of the fruits of their collaboration was a 1968 continent-wide bishops' conference held at Medellín, Colombia.

Reflecting on the deepening poverty of the region and increasing political repression, the bishops began using terms that would have wide repercussions: dependency and liberation. In their view, the poor nations were dependent on the financial operations of the developed nations. And the profit-seeking of the developed world both caused and perpetuated the economic and political oppression of the undeveloped nations. The documents produced at Medellín in some ways merely repeated, but in others distorted, themes that had already been present in Vatican II's *Pastoral Constitution on the Church in the Modern World, Gaudium et Spes.* Discerning what was in harmony with the Council in this new social thought and what presented divergences from the whole tradition of Catholic social doctrine became a central point of contention in evaluating liberation theology.

The Latin American bishops as a body were and are theologically orthodox, and most of them could not be described as liberationists in the usual sense of the term. However, one of their experts, or *periti,* at Medellín was to become the father of liberation theology as such. This was the Peruvian priest Gustavo Gutierrez. Unlike most other liberationists, Gutierrez has always maintained a somewhat open, flexible approach to social questions. He made use of the social sciences, including Marxist analysis, but he usually also recognized their limits. As dependency theory became less plausible during the 1970s and Marxism showed fatal flaws, Gutierrez would move in a more democratic, sometimes even a more strictly spiritual, direction. But his 1971 volume *A Theology of Liberation* was the most influential text

of the whole movement and set the stage for subsequent developments.

A Theology of Liberation argues that the idea of liberation, not development, best describes the aspirations of the Latin American peoples. Revolutionary "praxis" is necessary to the Christian engaged with the Latin American reality. Gutierrez points to dependency and class struggle as, not ideological constructs, but facts in the current situation. Oppression reflects "institutionalized violence" and "structures of sin." By separating religion and ethics from the public sphere, modern capitalism and democracy had handed over the people to the greed and profit-seeking of economic actors. Democratic forms only served to reinforce that oppression. The large concentration of private property in a few hands alongside the poverty of the many was an injustice that cried to heaven.

Though his language was strong, Gutierrez was ambiguous about what this all meant. He seemed to endorse, but also appeared to want to avoid "baptizing," revolution (as he would put it later). Individual Christians would have to decide in their own concrete circumstances whether the old Thomistic criteria for a just war sanctioned armed revolution. Yet the terminology Gutierrez used, though nuanced and not simply to be identified with Marxism, carried the overtones of Marxist guerrilla movements throughout the continent. Less sophisticated Christians would later have no qualms about identifying liberation with Marxist rebels in El Salvador, the Soviet-allied Sandinistas in Nicaragua, or — in extreme cases — the long-standing dictatorship of Fidel Castro. Some liberation theologians would even go so far as to mourn the passing of Leonid Brezhnev and express praise for the Soviet Union's contributions to justice around the world in its support of revolutionary movements.

Gutierrez and many other prominent liberation theologians were inevitably drawn into the polarities of the Cold War. Particularly in Latin America, where "national security" military regimes regarded almost any resistance as tantamount to Leninist subversion, liberation theology found it difficult to maintain nuances.

The bishops' meeting at Medellín in 1968 and then again at Puebla, Mexico, in 1979, for example, proclaimed the need for a "preferential option for the poor." In itself, the term merely echoed a central idea of Catholic social teaching that may be found in the New Testament as well as in papal documents by Leo XIII, Paul VI, and later John Paul II. But it became controversial because, in the context of the 1970s and 1980s, it seemed to lead straight to revolution (clearly, in other contexts, such a preference might suggest many varied approaches). And in theology, some liberationists had even begun to suggest that the option for the poor meant preferring the *iglesia popular*, or popular church, to a hierarchical Church that, in a deliberate echoing of Marxist economic teaching, was said to have appropriated the "spiritual means of production."

Liberation Theology and John Paul II • From Puebla on, the history of liberation theology is closely intertwined with the papacy of John Paul II, who was elected in 1978. In fact, because of the unexpected death of John Paul I, Puebla had to be postponed until early 1979 so that the new Pope could attend. As the only pontiff who had actually lived under both Nazi and communist tyrannies, John Paul appreciated both the promise and danger of liberation theology. During the flight to the Puebla meeting, reporters asked him what he thought of the movement. He replied: "Liberation theology, yes. But *which* liberation theology?"

Under John Paul II's leadership, the Church began at Puebla a process of clarification and redefinition of liberation theology. The Vatican continued its criticisms of capitalism and materialism in the West. But it emphasized the positive achievements of Western societies both in protecting individual rights and in encouraging economic initiative. It also asserted the value of private property to the liberty of families and to human development. This was a much needed and ultimately fruitful corrective.

For much of the 1980s, many liberationists seemed to view all democratic capitalist countries, whether the United States or nations of Europe or Asia, as the moral equivalent of tyrannies in Latin America and Africa. They showed a corresponding blind spot to communist tyrannies. Every flaw in the West seemed proof of radical evil. Far worse evils in the Soviet bloc were for the most part soft-pedaled or explained away. The Church herself was torn between people who regarded opposition to Western arms build-ups and denunciation of governments fighting Marxist rebels as part of the core of their Christian commitments, and others who regarded communism with its atheist theory and violent class struggle as a dangerous Christian heresy. Priests and nuns were being killed by military regimes in Latin America while other priests and nuns were being killed by communist governments in Eastern Europe.

Because of this turmoil, the Vatican's Congregation for the Doctrine of the Faith issued two instructions on liberation theology: the 1984 *Libertatis Nuntius (Instruction on Certain Aspects of the Theology of Liberation)* and the 1986 *Libertatis Conscientia (Instruction on Christian Freedom and Liberation)*. The first warned about false notions of liberation. The second sought to present a theologically sound and positive view of human liberty and development. Though they both dealt with worries over Marxist forms of liberation theology that existed primarily in the 1970s and early 1980s, they remain a rich guide to an authentic vision of Christ's love, redemption, and liberation from all forms of sin and enslavement.

Two CDF Instructions • The first Congregation for the Doctrine of the Faith (CDF) instruction began by recognizing the positive contributions of the new theological reflection on the liberating aspects of the Gospel. But it warned: "To discern clearly what is fundamental to this issue and what is a by-product of it, is an indispensable condition for any theological reflection on liberation." Christian liberation is primarily liberation from the "radical slavery of sin." Culture, economics, society, and politics are all in their own ways in need of liberation, but only because of a far more inclusive realm of sinfulness.

Some liberation theologians gave at least the impression that politics was the primary focus, human sinfulness being a secondary problem. In this, they were risking a kind of Pelagian belief in self-salvation. They had also borrowed analytical concepts — Marxism is clearly intended here — without sufficient caution or had adopted stances that by their very nature were difficult or impossible to reconcile with Christian faith and morals. The instruction made it clear that in no way did it wish to deter those seeking justice or to perpetuate a status quo of neutrality and indifference. In fact, it found the term "theology of liberation," for all its misuses, a "thoroughly valid term."

The chosen people's exodus from Egypt is often invoked in liberation theology as an image of how God liberated his people from political exploitation and slavery. The instruction declared this perfectly appropriate, so long as it remains clear that the God who reveals himself later on Mount Sinai has been the Liberator all along. Liberation is not brought about by the mere political efforts of man. Before all else, then, theology of liberation must be a theology, a complete and confident reflection on God and his providence.

In such a theology, justice and mercy will be extended to our neighbor, which is to say to all peoples. But it is precisely here that the theological dimension shows itself. If we begin with social revolution and denigrate the search for personal holiness, our revolution will stem from the same evil impulses that have established existing unjust structures. The result of such hubris, as Marxism had amply confirmed everywhere it had been tried, is certainly no improvement in social justice: "Millions of our own contemporaries legitimately yearn to recover those basic freedoms of which they were deprived by totalitarian and atheistic regimes which came to power by violent and revolutionary means, precisely in the name of the liberation of the people. . . . Those who, perhaps inadvertently, make themselves accomplices of similar enslavements betray the very poor they mean to help" (XI.10).

Only charity and the action of redeemed, and therefore free, persons, can produce the liberation the modern world seeks.

The instruction does not deny that scientific analysis may enter into this process. But some systems of thought, such as Marxism, involve such a total vision of the world that the ideology dominates all empirical study. In his 1971 *Octogesima Adveniens*, for example, Pope Paul VI had already warned about class struggle, in its technical Marxist sense, and the totalitarian society to which Marxism led. Such a social science was all of a piece, and very difficult to resist in its totality once certain initial assumptions are conceded.

Marxism is also atheist and presupposes that the individual is subordinate to a collectivity that is subject to no outside judgment, particularly by God. Proper human dignity, as it is owed to a being made in God's image and likeness, cannot find a place in Marxism, however well intentioned some of its followers may be. In Marxism truth itself is subject to revolutionary praxis and loses its real nature as a reflection of reality. Religion — as well as good and evil themselves — is judged solely on the basis of revolutionary value. Universal love and justice appear to be illusions in such a system, hence the injustices and terrorism perpetrated in many parts of the world in the name of compassion.

The Christian knows that man does not save himself. Therefore, any talk of human self-liberation and redemption is an illusion. Unfortunately, some within the Christian churches have sought to redefine Christianity to fit their political historicism. Faith, hope, and charity are emptied of theological content and made to serve political aims. The neighbor is no longer loved as he is, but "objective hatred, class hatred permits the class enemy simply to be eliminated." For some liberationists, the church of the poor becomes a church of the proletariat that excludes others or becomes simply the only authentic church.

Several other ecclesiological problems needed to be addressed as well. The *iglesia popular* (church of the people) could not simply be a class church in which people are to be "conscientized" to the class struggle. Nor could the institutional structure of the actual Church be regarded as a mere obstacle to an ideologically specified goal. Christian "base communities" had arisen in many places where the parish structure was weak. The

Vatican recognized the value of these small religious groups, provided that the universal nature of the Church was properly respected. Unfortunately, for some liberationists, priests in traditional parishes were viewed as class enemies and their teachings did not even have to be examined, since they were by definition expressions of the class interests of the rich. Dialogue with such a Church was likewise unnecessary to them. Politics became not just one way, but the *only* way to read the Bible. The Jesus who proclaimed that his kingdom was not of this world was thereby denied.

When sociological categories replace all others, hierarchy and people are necessarily opposed, the Eucharist becomes a symbol of popular struggle, and the unity of the Church, once represented and effected by the Sacrifice of the Altar, is destroyed. Even more tragically, a false and unrealizable utopian vision leads people to believe that, as they go about seeking justice and relief for the oppressed, they can create a lasting and perfect place for themselves in this world instead of recognizing the limits of all earthly life.

The Future of Liberation Theology • The Marxist form of liberation theology weakened with the fall of communism, while John Paul II introduced important developments in Catholic social doctrine with reflections on work, liberty, solidarity, and economic initiative in recent social encyclicals such as *On Human Work (Laborem Exercens)*, *On Social Concerns (Sollicitudo Rei Socialis)*, and *The Hundredth Year (Centesimus Annus)*. Partly as a result of the dialogue with the Vatican and partly through changes in social analysis, liberation theology has moved on to more democratic and reformist currents. At the moment, the liberation of poorer nations from crushing poverty seems less likely to result from shunning the developed world and more likely to proceed from integration into the global economy. Human liberation, however, is now one of the central features of papal thought on a variety of subjects and is closely linked with the redemption.

New liberationist creeds presenting both opportunities and problems similar to the initial form of liberation theology have been put together on the basis of feminism, homosexual rights, Third World ideologies, multiculturalism, and even environmentalism. Despite many differences among these currents and variations in the quality of the theology, they share a tendency to reduce the transcendent dimension of Christianity to a worldly struggle.

The Magisterium has established, however, that quite independent of the social dimension, which sometimes may indeed contain an important element of justice, liberation theology is not theology unless it places some overriding value — a value that relativizes all else — in God as such. The twentieth century has been marked by efforts to identify God with various worldly causes. Some critics have argued that all the surrogates for God have now been exhausted. But the liberationist current is far from finished, and the next century will probably bring with it new and unforeseen liberation theologies.

See: Authority; Church, Nature, Origin, and Structure of; Preferential Option for the Poor; Property; Social Doctrine; Social Justice.

Suggested Readings: CCC 1740-1742, 2448. Congregation for the Doctrine of the Faith, *Instruction on Certain Aspects of the Theology of Liberation, Libertatis Nuntius*; *Instruction on Christian Freedom and Liberation, Libertatis Conscientia*. G. Gutierrez, *A Theology of Liberation*. M. Novak, *Will It Liberate? Questions About Liberation Theology*. P. Sigmund, *Liberation Theology at the Crossroads: Democracy or Revolution?*

Robert Royal

LIMBO

It has never been a formally defined doctrine of the faith that such an abode of souls as limbo exists whose condition is one of eternal exclusion from the blessed company of God, albeit without any pain of loss. Nevertheless, theologians over the centuries have proposed limbo as a sort of secondary thesis, thought to be useful in shoring up the absolute importance and necessity of Baptism.

Christ said to Nicodemus: "Truly, truly, I say

to you, unless one is born of water and the Spirit, he cannot enter the kingdom of God" (Jn 3:5). In the absence of the sacrament, which remits original sin as well as personal sins and elevates the soul to the supernatural life and friendship with God, provision had to be sought for basically two kinds of men. On the one hand were those of virtuous life who died before Christ came to redeem them. These were the just men of the Old Testament, who were said to go to the "Limbo of the Fathers" to await their promised deliverance. On the other hand were those unbaptized children who died without ever having committed actual sin. These, so it was reasoned, go to the "Limbo of the Infants," from which there is no deliverance. But neither is there pain, it further was reasoned, because suffering can only be proportioned to personal guilt, of which none exists in the precincts of limbo. "They rejoice," says St. Thomas Aquinas, "because they share in God's goodness and in many natural perfections" (*De Malo*, V, 3).

Moreover, it has been held, God himself might choose to remedy the want of sacramental Baptism by other means. St. Bernard, for example, held that the unbaptized infant could aspire to heaven on the strength of his parent's faith. Both the Council of Florence and the Council of Trent teach that one cannot go to God "without the water of regeneration or the desire for it." Can it not be posited that such desire must already exist in the unbaptized infant, whom God has made for himself alone and whose natural longing for God can, by his merciful grace, bring to perfection and glory that very thirst for heaven with which we were fashioned from the first moment of our being? As the *Catechism of the Catholic Church* observes, God's merciful desire that all be saved and Jesus' tenderness toward children (cf. Mk 10:14) permit us to hope "that there is a way of salvation for children who have died without Baptism" (CCC 1261).

The *Catechism* also reminds us that "God has bound salvation to the sacrament of Baptism, but he himself is not bound by his sacraments" (CCC 1257).

See: Baptism; Heaven; Last Things.

LITURGICAL YEAR

"Do this in memory of me." This great redemptive and creative word of Our Lord on the eve of his departure gave existence and meaning to the sacrifice of the Mass, the "thanksgiving" (Eucharist), as well as to the subsequent development of the liturgical year. The sacrificial gifts of the first Christian faithful were transformed in the eternal sacrifice of Christ, rendered present again in their midst as a memorial of the blessed Passion of the Redeemer and his Resurrection from the dead.

When the common celebration of the Eucharist was very early transferred to the first day of the week, the day of the Lord's Resurrection, then the cornerstone of the entire yearly cycle of liturgical celebrations had been laid down (Vatican Council II, *Constitution on the Sacred Liturgy, Sacrosanctum Concilium*, 106). The added feasts that prepare for and carry on the saving effects of Christ's paschal mystery in time are meant to assist man in his gradual approach to God, which commences in the sacrificial mystery rendered present to us again at every Mass (*Sacrosanctum Concilium*, 102).

The gradual growth of the annual festivals associated with Easter served as a model for the development of a parallel cycle, celebrating the approach of the redemption, which began with the Redeemer's Incarnation. This series of feasts, including Advent, Christmas, and the Epiphany, marks the coming of the Lord and Savior, who only became man in order to die on the cross for mankind dead through sin. Since the Virgin Mother of God is so closely connected with the salvific deeds of Christ, and is the living image of the Church, she, too, is honored during the liturgical year in a special manner (*Sacrosanctum Concilium*, 103). And the memorial celebrations of individual saints stimulate and encourage the faithful, who celebrate in them the same paschal mystery that is the foundation of their own transfiguration in the glory to which we still aspire (*Sacrosanctum Concilium*, 104).

Pope Paul VI in February, 1969, published norms for a revised calendar for the Western Church in the motu proprio *Mysterii Paschalis*.

The revised calendar was promulgated a month later by the Congregation for Divine Worship and went into effect January 1, 1970, although full implementation was delayed pending completion of related liturgical texts. The U.S. bishops ordered it into effect in the United States in 1972.

See: Eucharist; Incarnation; Mary, Mother of God; Mary, Mother of the Church; Mass; Redemption.

LITURGY

The basic meaning of the Greek root-word from which "liturgy" derives is a purely secular one: an orderly and public service in the interest of the entire people (understood as the body politic or the national community). In the two centuries immediately preceding the birth of Christ, and hence also in the Greek translation of the Old Testament (Septuagint), the word takes on a cultic meaning also found in the New Testament. Thus, with the help of cultic, priestly vocabulary evoking a worship setting, the Letter to the Hebrews contrasts the earlier (ineffective) service rendered by humans with the uniquely effective action of God in Christ (e.g., Heb 10:1-10). Acts 13:2 mentions the common prayer of individual prophets and teachers at Antioch.

By word and example the Lord Jesus during his public life strove to encourage his disciples in the practice of prayer in common. Not only did he frequent the temple with them in order to participate in the rituals prescribed by Mosaic law, but he also gave them the words of the Lord's Prayer and at the Last Supper an exemplar of the great Eucharistic prayer, both of which even today are fundamental to the Church's public prayer.

Vatican Council II indicates that the Sacred Liturgy is the public worship of the Eternal Father performed by the Mystical Body of Jesus Christ, that is, by the Head and his members. Since every liturgical celebration is an action of Christ the Priest and of his Body, which is the Church, it is an *actio praecellenter sacra,* a sacred action surpassing all others (*Constitution on the Sacred Liturgy, Sacrosanctum Concilium,* 7).

Our earthly liturgy expresses, recalls to mind, and continually renews the paschal mystery of salvation, and thus the liturgy bears a number of characteristic notes.

* It is a public manifestation of the Church's indefectible holiness and one of the most prominent signs of her divine origin.

* It is a cry bursting forth from the heart of the Church to the Father under the impulse of the Holy Spirit.

* It is perfect praise and adoration in the Spirit and in truth, giving all honor and glory to God in Christ and through Christ.

* It is a perennially effective instrument for the purification and sanctification of men.

* It is the greatest of all pedagogical means by which the Church forms and instructs her children.

* It is luminous and richly rewarding contemplation of the complete treasury of Revelation.

* It is not only the most efficacious form of the active apostolate but also the most inclusive and yet most secure foundation of the apostolate of prayer.

* It is an excellent exercise of supernatural charity, rooted in the communion of saints to effect fully the living unity of the Church.

* It is an anticipation of the eternal praise already begun in heaven, with which it constitutes one integral worship and toward which it unceasingly tends as to its final consummation.

Properties of the Sacred Liturgy • Once this broadly inclusive understanding of the Sacred Liturgy has been grasped, its chief properties emerge into full view. Among them is the fact that all liturgy is based upon Christ the Priest and above all upon his redemptive sacrifice, which always remains present to us in the Holy Eucharist. Since the liturgy is primarily a sacred action directed toward God and performed by the Church, all its other effects of sanctifying and instructing men, though very important, are simply corollaries of this chief purpose or means for achieving it.

The worship rendered by the Church to God in the liturgy must be exterior, because the nature of man as a composite of body and soul requires it to be so and because it is a public act. But to be true and genuine, its chief element must be interior, for we must always live in Christ and give ourselves to him completely so that in him, with him, and through him the heavenly Father may be duly glorified (Pope Pius XII, *Mediator Dei*, 23-24). In the Sacred Liturgy, both of these elements must be intimately linked, else religion amounts to little more than formalism without meaning or content. The internal element is not limited to the thoughts and sentiments of the liturgical ministers or the participants in a particular celebration. Rather, it also includes the present interior life of the other members of the Church, which signifies and expresses her entire life in each truly liturgical celebration.

Thus participation in the liturgy must take place primarily at the supernatural level, meaning that it is rooted in faith, hope, and charity. Its chief strength and efficacy do not depend upon the external apparatus of effective staging or the number of the participants but rather upon the ardor with which those participants are aflame, the intensity of their spiritual life and union with God.

As a public act of the Church, liturgical worship is necessarily hierarchical and ordered, which means in practice that it is subject to the prescriptions of the competent authority. Therefore, arbitrary individual initiatives and disobedience to the legitimate prescriptions *ipso facto* change the liturgical nature of the action: It is no longer the worship of the Church, the whole Christ, but the private cult of one person or a particular group.

In the course of time, the Lord Jesus forms his Church by means of the sacraments emanating from his plenitude (Vatican Council II, *Dogmatic Constitution on the Church, Lumen Gentium*, 7, 11). Through these sacraments, the Church makes her members participants in the mystery of the death and Resurrection of Christ, in the grace of the Holy Spirit who gives her life and movement (*Sacrosanctum Concilium, 5-6; Lumen Gentium*, 7, 12, 50). As Vatican II rightly stressed, the great deeds of God on behalf of the people of the Old Covenant were but an overture to the work of Christ the Lord in redeeming mankind and giv-

ing perfect glory to God. The Savior accomplished this chiefly by the paschal mystery of his blessed Passion, Resurrection from the dead, and glorious Ascension, whereby "dying, he destroyed our death and, rising, he restored our life." For it was from the pierced heart of Christ on Golgotha that there was born "the wondrous sacrament of the whole Church" (*Sacrosanctum Concilium*, 6). The paschal mystery of Jesus Christ is the wellspring from which all the sacraments and sacramentals draw their power and efficacy (*Sacrosanctum Concilium*, 61).

The liturgy that Christ's beloved bride, his Church, celebrates on earth is a foretaste of that heavenly liturgy celebrated in the Jerusalem that is above, in the heavenly city where God will be all in all. By the design of God, the earthly liturgy makes use of sacred signs perceptible to man's senses, in order to signify the invisible divine realities by which is brought about, in the manner proper to each one, the sanctification of man (*Sacrosanctum Concilium*, 7, 33).

As an exercise of the priestly office of Christ the Lord, the liturgy has a twofold dynamism: a movement from God to men, that their sanctification be achieved; and a movement from man toward God, that he be adored in spirit and in truth (*Sacrosanctum Concilium*, 5-7). In this way the Church's worship not only fulfills but expands and transforms the natural worship offered to the Deity by men.

Liturgy and Sacraments • Although the Sacred Liturgy does not exhaust the entire activity of the Church, it is still the high point toward which the Church's activity is directed and at the same time the fount from which all her power flows (*Sacrosanctum Concilium*, 9-13). Our fathers in the faith, the first Christians, spoke of all the truths and saving events of Christian life (which are incomprehensible to purely natural man) as mysteries. The Latin for that originally Greek word is *sacramentum* — which lives on in our term "sacrament." In ancient times the word "mystery" indeed referred to secret events or hidden things shown only to the initiated. But for the men of those first Christian centuries the very word embodied the idea that through the power and grace of this mysterious event, man was raised up to God, indeed "divinized." We can therefore understand why it was chiefly the three great, mysteriously divine events of Baptism, Confirmation, and the Holy Eucharist that were regarded as mysteries. With the passage of time, this expression was applied more and more exclusively to the Eucharistic Sacrifice and banquet, and as a matter of fact the Eastern liturgies even today commonly refer to Holy Mass as "the divine mysteries."

At the very heart of the Church's liturgical life is the Holy Eucharist, sacrament and sacrifice, than which the holy Church of God possesses nothing more worthy, more holy, or more admirable because in it is contained God's greatest gift: the very wellspring and author of all grace and holiness, Christ the Lord himself (*Roman Ritual*, 1614; cf. *Sacrosanctum Concilium*, 10).

Sacraments have traditionally been defined as outward signs instituted by Christ to give inward grace. Thus a sacrament is a sign of something that is effected invisibly, but also a sign that in itself presents the possibility of indicating the invisible effect in a manner comprehensible to all. If the liturgy is the life of the Church moved by the Spirit of Christ, then the sacraments are the channels through which this life continually flows out to us. Whether it is a tiny trickle or a flood tide will depend upon the love with which we allow them to act upon us. But love always presupposes knowledge as well as leading to it; and we attain the knowledge in question here only through believing discernment of the liturgical essence of the sacraments.

Through the sacrament of Holy Orders, priests, by the anointing of the Holy Spirit, are marked with a special character that configures them to Christ the eternal High Priest in a manner enabling them to act in the Person of Christ the Head of the Mystical Body. Through the priestly ministry the spiritual sacrifice of the faithful is completed in union with the sacrifice of Christ, who is the sole mediator between God and man. That sacrifice is offered in the Eucharist through the hands of the priest in the name of the entire Church in an unbloody and sacramental manner, until the Lord himself comes (cf. *Lumen Gentium*, 10; Vatican Council II, *Decree on the Ministry and Life of Priests, Presbyterorum Ordinis*, 2).

The rites of Christian initiation, which include the catechumenate and the sacraments of Baptism and Confirmation, are plainly related to the reception of the Eucharist, the third of the sacraments of initiation. The penitential liturgy and the liturgy of the sick aim ultimately at preparing Christians to receive worthily the Body of Christ. And the rich symbolism of the sacrament of Matrimony is not without reference to the Eucharist, since marriage represents the union of Christ and the Church, of which the sacrament of the Eucharist is a figure (cf. St. Thomas Aquinas, *Summa Theologiae*, III, q. 65, a. 3).

Though the Church has neither the right nor the power to institute sacraments, she does possess the power to institute sacramentals, which are rites resembling those of the sacraments but independent of them, instituted by the Church for the supernatural benefit of the faithful. As a kindly mother, the Church supplies all the reasonable demands and needs of her children, even those of the weak and simple. Though sacramentals, such as blessings of persons, places, and things, neither obliterate mortal sin nor infuse sanctifying grace, their efficacy is nonetheless very special because it involves not only the pious acts of the individual believer but also the intercession of the Church as a whole (*Sacrosanctum Concilium*, 60-61, 79). Aside from the personal devotion of the user, sacramentals have no effects other than those for which the Church prays.

To be distinguished from sacramentals are the objects and practices of popular piety and devotion that surround and accompany the sacramental life of the Church. Among them are pilgrimages and processions, veneration of relics, praying the Rosary, making the Stations of the Cross, etc. Such expressions of Catholic piety are subject to the judgment of duly constituted authority in the Church (cf. *Sacrosanctum Concilium*, 13).

The Liturgical Year • "Pray constantly!" was the admonition of the Savior and the Apostles. How does the Church fulfill this command? Though she is spiritually present to the Lord at all times, as the Lord is always present to his Church, it is impossible to carry out literally the apostolic injunction. But the Church does fulfill it, nonetheless. In ancient times it was believed that an action repeated at equal, regularly recurring intervals of time attained a kind of earthly "eternity." Just as in nature time renews itself through the orderly succession of years and moons, and through this permanent cycle of rebirth becomes, in a sense, "eternal," so, too, an event is celebrated "eternally" by observing it on a monthly or annual basis: The *solemnitas* or annual recurrence of the event or festival becomes *aeternitas*.

On such a foundation rests the celebration of the Church's year of feasts and fasts. In it, the mysteries of salvation are re-presented regularly, at carefully calculated intervals, and thus they "eternally" become reality, until their celebration in heaven will pass over into a reality that is everlasting in the full sense of the term.

The Lord's Day is the most familiar instance of this principle. Sunday is the day on which Christ proved himself to be the Lord of life and death by arising from the tomb. It is the day on which he brought to a glorious consummation the saving action of our redemption, and that is why each Sunday becomes a new Easter for us (*Sacrosanctum Concilium*, 106). It was only logical that the annual commemoration of the actual day of Christ's Resurrection should be celebrated with very special joy and solemnity, and so the Christian Easter Sunday was born; and with it was laid the foundation stone of what we know as the Church year (*Sacrosanctum Concilium*, 102-104, 110). Other days recalling the saving deeds of the Redeemer were gradually grouped around the celebration of Easter, at first chiefly in the Holy Land and at Jerusalem, where the memory of the Savior's days on earth was especially vivid. Good Friday, Holy Thursday, and Palm Sunday arose before Easter, Pentecost, and the Ascension after it: Thus evolved the Easter cycle of feasts.

But long before this development had reached its climax, its influence contributed to the forma-tion of a second cycle of feasts grouped around the celebration of Christmas, to commemorate the coming of redemption. Though the feast of Christmas as we know it today is of Western origin, its roots lie farther eastward, chiefly in the holy places of the promised land. And these celebrations, too, culminated in the celebration of the Eucharist, in which the entire work of redemption — including its first dawning — is transfigured and rendered present.

In sum, then, the Church has fulfilled the command to pray constantly (1 Thes 5:17, Col 14:2; cf. Acts 6:4, 12:5) by praying at fixed times, even daily. Such hours of prayer make up the Liturgy of the Hours, which, like a golden coronet that frames and bears the precious jewel of the Eucharistic Sacrifice, revolves around the fixed pole of the liturgical representation of that event which forms the very central core of Christianity itself: the redeeming death and Resurrection of Christ (*Sacrosanctum Concilium*, 83).

Priests and others are specially deputed by the Church to pray the Divine Office, the public prayer of the Church, which is composed chiefly of readings from Holy Scripture (psalms, canticles, passages from the other books of the Bible) and other authors such as the Fathers of the Church and theologians (*Sacrosanctum Concilium*, 95-96, 98). The most important "hours" of prayer in the Divine Office are the morning and evening hours of Lauds and Vespers, which form the axis around which the Liturgy of the Hours rotates, the "two hinges on which the daily office turns" (*Sacrosanctum Concilium*, 89). If the faithful pray the Liturgy of the Hours together with a priest in the approved form, then that, too, is "the voice of the Bride herself addressed to her Bridegroom. It is the very prayer which Christ himself together with his Body addresses to the Father" (*Sacrosanctum Concilium*, 84).

The Sacred Liturgy is the worship ("divine service") that the mystical Christ — that is, the Church as a community in association with Christ its Head — offers to the heavenly Father. It consists in the celebration and application of the redemption that takes place through the hierarchical priesthood of the ordained and the universal priesthood of the baptized, in the form of sacramental actions. "Worthy art thou, our Lord and God, to receive glory and honor and power, for thou didst create all things, and by thy will they existed and were created" (Rv 4:11).

See: Communio; Devotions; Eucharist; Holy Orders; In Persona Christi Capitis; Liturgical Year; Liturgy of the Hours; Lord's Day; Mass; Prayer; Priesthood in the Old Testament; Priesthood of Christ; Religion, Virtue of; Sacrament; Sacramentals; Sacraments of Initiation; Worship.

Suggested Readings: CCC 1066-1112. Vatican Council II, *Constitution on the Sacred Liturgy, Sacrosanctum Concilium,* 5-20, 47-100. H. von Balthasar, "The Grandeur of the Liturgy," *Communio*, 5 (1978), pp. 344-351. D. von Hildebrand, *Liturgy and Personality.* J. Ratzinger, *The Feast of Faith: Approaches to a Theology of the Liturgy.* R. Skeris, *Divini Cultus Studium.*

Robert A. Skeris

LITURGY OF THE HOURS

In the course of the liturgical year, the Church expounds and applies the paschal mystery of Christ the Lord (Vatican Council II, *Constitution on the Sacred Liturgy, Sacrosanctum Concilium,* 102). Similarly, during any individual day the Liturgy of the Hours, as it were, "clothes" and comments upon the Mass. The Divine Office is the prayer the Church "puts round about" the Holy Sacrifice (Vatican II, *Sacrosanctum Concilium,* 83; *Decree on the Ministry and Life of Priests, Presbyterorum Ordinis,* 5; *Decree on the Bishops' Pastoral Office in the Church, Christus Dominus,* 30). Distributed as it is over suitable intervals of time during each day, it is the chief expression of that unceasing prayer which the Lord himself entrusted to his Church (*Sacrosanctum Concilium,* 86).

Since the canonical hours are intended to sanctify the day, they are arranged so that they can be related more easily to the chronological hours of the day, taking into account the circumstances of contemporary life (*Sacrosanctum Concilium,* 88). Though the arrangement that prevailed at least

from the sixth century (the era of St. Benedict) envisaged recitation of the entire Psalter each week, the completely new Liturgy of the Hours promulgated in the wake of Vatican II is based upon a scheme that distributes the Psalter over a four-week period (*Sacrosanctum Concilium,* 91, spoke of "a longer period of time"). Pope Paul VI in the apostolic constitution *Laudis Canticum* of November 1, 1970, explained the background, contents, scope, and purposes of the revised Liturgy of the Hours. Approved translations of the Latin text were developed over the next several years, with the Congregation for Divine Worship and the National Conference of Catholic Bishops setting November 27, 1977, as the date for exclusive use of the English translation in the United States. The revisions had the effect of greatly reducing the quantity of daily prayer, and in this new arrangement of the psalms, Pope Paul noted, "some few of the psalms and verses which are somewhat harsh in tone, have been omitted, not least because of the difficulties that were foreseen from their use in vernacular celebration."

The chief elements of the Liturgy of the Hours are Morning Prayer and Evening Prayer (corresponding to Lauds and Vespers, and composed of a hymn, two psalms with a canticle from the Old or New Testament, a reading and a response, canticle, intercessions, and Lord's Prayer). These are the "hinges" that support the entire Divine Office (*Sacrosanctum Concilium,* 89). The other Hours include Daytime Prayer (i.e., at midmorning, midday, or midafternoon, arranged so that those who choose to say only one Hour may select the one most suitable to the actual time of day without forfeiting anything from the monthly Psalter); Night Prayer (including an examination of conscience, to be recited before retiring); and the Office of Readings (corresponding roughly to one Nocturn of the earlier Matins, with three psalms and selections from the Bible, Church Fathers, and spiritual writers), to be said at any hour of the day or even during the night hours of the previous day.

Since it is the prayer of the *ecclesia orans,* the praying Church, not only clergy but also religious and indeed layfolk are encouraged to participate in the Liturgy of the Hours when possible (*Sacrosanctum Concilium*, 99-100).

See: Community Prayer; Liturgical Year; Liturgy; Prayer.

LORD'S DAY

For some 182,000 weeks running (by one count), the chosen people have hallowed the last day of the week, the Sabbath, by attending the synagogue and abstaining from unnecessary exertions. So did Jews heed the third commandment: "Remember the Sabbath day, to keep it holy . . . in it you shall not do any work . . . for in six days the Lord made heaven and earth . . . and rested the seventh day" (Ex 20:8-11). But for the earliest Christians (cf. Acts 20:7, 1 Cor 16:2, Rv 1:10), Sunday, the resurrected Lord's day, soon replaced the Sabbath as the time to worship God publicly and solemnly by celebrating the Eucharistic Sacrifice. Tertullian (c. 160-c. 222) is the first to mention Sunday rest expressly, but he speaks of it as already a custom: "as tradition has taught us."

So today. Says the 1983 Code of Canon Law, enshrining one of the Catholic Church's six chief precepts: "Sunday is the day on which the paschal mystery is celebrated in light of the apostolic tradition and is to be observed as the foremost holy day of obligation in the universal Church" (Canon 1246). The following law specifies: "On Sundays . . . [or the eve] the faithful are bound to participate in the Mass; they are also to abstain from those labors and business concerns that impede the worship to be rendered to God, the joy proper to the Lord's Day, or the proper relaxation of mind and body."

Servile Work • Early in the Christian era, resting from work, though traditionally upheld as a moral duty, was not codified in Church or civil law. A Council of Laodicea (c. 390) prescribed that on Sunday the faithful were to abstain from work as far as possible. An earlier edict of Constantine, the first Christian emperor, forbade judges to sit and townspeople to work on Sunday. St. Caesarius of Arles (470-543) sought to impose the whole of Jewish sabbatarian law and tradition onto the Christian Sunday observance. Such austerities were rejected as alien by the Council of Orléans (538). From the eighth century down practically to our day, the law remained relatively constant: no servile work, no public commerce, no oath-taking, no court sessions. "Servile" work was largely equated with the physical, menial but productive tasks performed mainly by servants, laborers, and farmers on the week's six other days.

The 1917 Code of Canon Law focused on suspending work and on which kinds of work were forbidden. The 1983 Code emphasizes the celebration's *purpose*, its prerequisite of leisure and its concomitant of joy. The new Code thus implicitly recognizes vast changes in the working world. What may be weekday toil for one may be another's relaxing change of pace on weekends. If the Church no longer spells out what kinds of labor are incompatible with Sunday rest, she is simply recognizing that this prudential determination, given the current difficulty of generalizing amid such complex variety, is best reached in each case by the person involved.

The need to rest in order to reflect on God is no arbitrary mandate, either of God or his vicar, the Church. Rather, it is required by human and divine conditions. It entails truthfully and justly giving to God his due and to man what he cannot do without as a spiritual being: prayerful solitude.

"Sunday," says the *Catechism of the Catholic Church*, "is a time for reflection, silence, cultivation of the mind, and meditation which furthers the growth of the Christian interior life" (2186). It is possible to attend Sunday Mass indifferently, spend the rest of the day amid newspaper and various distractions, and leave the law's spirit unfilled. Likewise contrary to the spirit of Sunday observance, though rarer, would be feverish religiosity that left spirit and body weary and unregenerated. Without a minimum of religious leisure, man can hardly begin to right either himself or his relationship with God. A psalm (45:11) says it best: "Be still and see." The implication is that unreflective, noisy busyness, even at play or indolence, is a way to spiritual blindness. On the other hand, if man is to *find* more and more of the hidden divine treasure (cf. Mt 13:44), he must *seek* (cf. Mt 7:8) evermore personally and prayerfully, even at something so public as Sunday Mass.

"The Sunday celebration of the Lord's Day and his Eucharist is at the heart of the Church's life" (CCC 2177). "The Sunday Eucharist is the foundation and confirmation of all Christian practice," the *Catechism* (2181) adds, echoing Vatican Council II.

The *Catechism* continues: "Participation in the communal celebration . . . is a testimony of belonging and of being faithful to Christ and to his Church. The faithful give witness by this to their communion in faith and charity. Together they testify to God's holiness and their hope of salvation. They strengthen one another under the guidance of the Holy Spirit" (2182).

If Sunday Mass and Communion represent a point of arrival — the full manifestation of how much man means to Jesus and what he costs the God-man — so, too, is this weekly culmination a point of departure. Duly desired and prepared in spirit at least, the hour-long Sunday liturgy, with its abundant divine helps and inspirations, is meant to overflow onto the rest of the day and the whole week. Says the *Catechism*: "God's action is the model for human action . . . [we are to see that] others, especially the poor, 'be refreshed' [*Ex* 31:17]" (2172). This is so that "those . . . [with] leisure should be mindful of their brethren who have the same needs and the same rights, yet cannot rest from work because of poverty and misery" (2186). "Sunday," the *Catechism* continues, "is traditionally consecrated by Christian piety to good works and humble service of the sick, the infirm, and the elderly. Christians will also sanctify Sunday by devoting time and care to their families and relatives, often difficult to do on other days of the week."

Yet Sunday is to be no mere religious interlude from the press of ordinary business. Christians ought to live Sunday Mass and the day's distinct program of reflection, piety, and virtue so that Sunday becomes the standard against which the rest of the week is measured. In doing so, they may also discover the desire, time, and need for Mass and Communion on more than Sunday (cf. CCC 1389, 1391-1392, 1394-1395).

See: Eucharist; Holy Days of Obligation; Liturgy; Mass; Religion, Virtue of; Servile Work; Worship.

Suggested Readings: CCC 346-348, 1166-1167, 1322-1405, 2042, 2168-2188. J. Pieper, *In Tune with the World: A Theory of Festivity*. G. Vann, O.P., *Alive to God*.

Dennis Helming

LUST

The habitual inclination (vice or capital sin) to lust is built up from both the untamed sexual appetite itself and actual surrenders to genital pleasure as a predominant aim. This greatest of all corporeal pleasures was planted by its Creator in human nature as an incentive to, and reward for, two major, inseparably linked objectives: procreating and educating children, and expressing and inducing mutual love and communion between the marital partners themselves. Within that loving and hallowed precinct, spouses should wholly give of themselves, both physically and spiritually.

But outside those bounds, Christians and non-Christians alike should do everything possible to skirt both venereal desires and actions and whatever triggers the near-tyrannical passion thereto. Every deliberate and voluntary indulgence in extramarital sex, solitary or not, is deemed a mortal sin.

Sins are not such because God and the Church declare them to be so, in this instance via the sixth and ninth commandments and the Church's doctrinal authority. Rather, such deeds and desires harm their doers' moral and even emotional well-being, and so those in authority warn against such self- and happiness-defeating actions, which plainly stunt spiritual growth.

Dorothy Sayers writes in *The Whimsical Christian* that there are two ways to fall into lust: "sheer exuberance of animal spirits, or out of sheer boredom and discontent, in search of stimulants . . . people go to bed simply because they have nothing better to do." There also is a third, more corrosive way: that of those who scoff at God and traditional morality and are determined — in fact, in their view, entitled — to prove to themselves and the world that they can so indulge with impunity. Those in the first category should be gently told to "go, and do not sin again" (Jn 8:11); those in the second need to stop sating their senses and starving their hearts and come to know real goods and moral virtues; but, besides praying for them, little or nothing can be done with sinners of the third kind, until they abjure the lie they profess.

The *Catechism of the Catholic Church* advises believers "to struggle against concupiscence of the flesh and disordered desires. With God's grace [they] will prevail . . . by the *virtue* and *gift of chastity*, . . . by *purity of intention . . . vision*, . . . [and] by *prayer*" (2520). And it adds: "So-called *moral permissiveness* rests on an erroneous conception of human freedom; the necessary precondition for the development of true freedom is to let oneself be educated in the moral law" (2526).

See: Capital Sins; Chastity; Concupiscence; Human Virtues; Modesty; Purity; Sexuality, Human; Sin; Vices.

LYING

At first glance, lying seems a simple matter. People lie when they know or sincerely believe something to be true, but declare or imply something else. "Did you rob the bank?" asks the detective. "No, I did not," replies the robber, telling a lie.

Adding more examples blurs this neat picture. A father reminds his teenage son that he has a lot of homework to do before going to Mary's house. The son answers, "Don't worry, I'll get it done," meaning he will work from midnight to two in the morning after returning from Mary's.

Did the son lie? Perhaps. He knew his father meant he should do his homework before going out and his answer would be taken as a promise to do so. Then again, perhaps not. He also knew his father would be satisfied as long as his teacher did not complain and his grades remained acceptable. In saying, "I'll get it done," he was responding truly to his father's main concern, while leav-

ing the details unspecified. In sum, he knew (a) what he meant, (b) what his father would understand, and (c) that no real harm would be done by any disparity between the two.

This kind of ambiguous answer to a question is an example of what technically is called "mental reservation." The term once was popular among Catholic moralists but is absent from the *Catechism of the Catholic Church*. Participants in stable, loving relationships (parent-child, husband-wife, employer-employee, etc.) routinely engage in vague communication, evasion, or silence in order to preserve a degree of privacy while maintaining their commitment to one another. In practice, while most people may tell few outright lies, they rather frequently operate in a gray zone where truth and falsity are not so clearly defined.

Social convention, and sometimes social necessity, condones certain forms of communicating something other than literal truth. There is a sense in which actors might be said to be liars, pretending to be something they are not. The woman who remarks, "I see you forgot to put on your makeup this morning," then laughs and adds, "April Fool!" is departing from the truth, though briefly. A bridge player who compliments her husband's play may be more polite than truthful. Our judicial system, which presumes innocence, requires that an accused criminal plead "not guilty" in order to have a trial.

The *Catechism* says, quoting St. Augustine (*De Mendacio* 4, 5): "A *lie* consists in speaking a falsehood with the intention of deceiving" (2482). We can concede that civilized society would be impossible if one could not compliment the well-meaning but incompetent cook, or treat boring people politely, or keep friends in the dark about surprise parties, or minimize conflicts in a marriage, knowing they will "blow over." Here the purpose is a harmless desire to please or to avoid giving offense, quite possibly motivated by Christian charity. These are not what is meant by lies.

The position expressed in the *Catechism* treats lying as a relational act, a communication between a speaker and a listener, rather than simply the act of an individual. In this understanding, the evil of lying has two sources. A lie is wrong, first of all, because it is "a profanation of speech" (CCC 2485). This, it should be noted, is an insight derived from natural law, and the Church has traditionally based much of her moral teaching on natural law theory. "Natural law" of course does not refer to the law of the wild or even to regularities in the way the universe works, like Newton's law of motion. The natural law concerns that which is proper to human nature and its perfection; reason can reveal its tenets. For example, Aristotle defined human beings as rational animals. Because we have the power of reflection, it is wrong, a violation of natural law, to act on instinct alone in circumstances where reasoned action is appropriate. In the same way, the basic human purpose served by speech is evidently to communicate accurately. It is therefore wrong to use speech (which of course in this context includes nonverbal as well as verbal communication) to mislead or misrepresent. In doing so, we distance ourselves from the objective order of things and from the Source of that order.

Consequences of Lying • Second, deliberately communicating something false is sinful because it violates or even destroys the community, based on trust, between myself and another person or persons. "The deliberate intention of leading a neighbor into error by saying things contrary to the truth constitutes a failure in justice and charity" (CCC 2485). Justice, because one person has a duty to respect another's human dignity, and a lie is unfair and abusive treatment: by refusing you information to which you have a right, I inhibit you from reaching sound decisions and making accurate decisions. Love, because the other is my neighbor. St. Paul says: "Therefore, putting away falsehood, let everyone speak the truth with his neighbor, for we are members one of another" (Eph 4:25).

Paul's words are a reminder that lying — and here we refer to "real" lying, not mere social convention and the like — has important consequences not only for dealings between individuals but for the health of society in general. If one could not trust one's doctor to give an honest di-agnosis, or the homebuilder to use the sound materials promised, or the witness to give accurate testimony, or the teacher to teach the Civil War as it happened, or the government to keep its word to veterans, society would soon collapse in violent chaos, the war of all against all. If Third World nations felt the United States was trying to impose coercive population policies under false pretenses, the prospect of global community would be a receding glimmer. Trust is an indispensable foundation of the social order.

Since the sin of lying is relational, involving a speaker and one or more listeners, one may ask whether it makes any difference who the listeners are. Clearly it does. The *Catechism* makes this point quite specifically (2483): "To lie is to speak or act against the truth in order to lead into error *someone who has the right to know the truth*" (emphasis added). Is a prospective employer entitled to an honest answer to the question "Were you ever imprisoned for theft?" Obviously, yes. Is the employer's secretary so entitled? Or the firm's other employees? No.

Here again, however, it is easy to pose situations where the moral judgment is less evident. Suppose I have been offered a job in a distant city, starting six months from now. My present employer suspects this and questions me. I owe it to my employer to admit that I will be leaving, so the company has time to seek a qualified replacement; but I also know he is a vengeful man who would likely fire me on the spot if I told the truth. Does his (presumed) lack of justice toward me cancel out his right to know my plans?

Keeping Secrets • Both these examples raise the general question of keeping secrets. The "right to know" comes into play when something is unknown and an argument can be made for keeping it hidden. Indeed, in certain cases, we may have a positive obligation to conceal the truth in order to preserve a secret. Textbooks in moral theology frequently pose some form of the following dilemma: An armed man comes to your door and asks the whereabouts of John Doe, whom you know is cowering in the basement. Strict truthfulness apparently requires an affirmative answer, while weightier considerations seem to point elsewhere. In this case, conscience and common sense unite to overrule a general dictum; the would-be murderer has no right to the truth.

There are legitimate disagreements among theologians in their analyses of these complex matters. Still, from the fact that one may not deliberately lead another who has a right to the truth into error, it does not necessarily follow that one can tell an untruth to someone who does not have the right.

Everyday secrets are usually not so dramatic as the foregoing example, but the "right to know" may still apply. Recall that lies are relational. A secret consists of a fact about ourselves or a third party or parties that we wish to conceal. As the case of the unjust employer shows, our responsibility to ourselves may trump the listener's right to know. More often, the need to protect another person's life, property, or good name may do so. In the latter case, justifying a departure from strict truth involves a relationship, not just between speaker and listener, but between speaker, listener, and another person. Here the speaker's duty to the third party is held to outweigh the duty to be candid with the listener, as it might, for example, if Friend A asked Friend B whether Friend C had ever had a drinking problem. It is important to note that cases like these are not decided by a process of weighing competing rights and duties against one another, then acting in violation of those deemed less weighty. The point, rather, is that we are dealing here with nonabsolute duties and rights (to communicate certain information, to know certain facts) — duties and rights that are, in technical language, defeasible in appropriate circumstances.

In most situations, it is possible to avoid revealing a secret by remaining silent or giving an evasive answer. When neither tactic is likely to work, one can give a response that is obviously partial. Public officials, for instance, frequently reply to reporters' queries on sensitive policy by saying things like, "I'm working on that" or "Yes, I agree the matter should be resolved." Because such answers clearly communicate unwillingness

to communicate, there is no lie. In some cases, though, silence or a noncommittal response would be tantamount to letting the secret out. Answering, "We don't talk about that" regarding the friend with a drinking problem might be taken as an affirmative, for example. Here an outright denial may be the only effective resort. Some moralists would say a denial in such circumstances was morally justified; others would say it was a sin; and still others would say it depended on whether the questioner did or did not have a sufficient reason for wanting to know the truth.

The Evil of Lying • Once we have allowed for all the hard cases and probed the misty ambiguities that often mark questions of truth and falsity, however, we must face the fact that actual lying is a sin, a moral evil, if it is deliberate and free. How grave an evil is a lie? Philosophers and theologians have debated this question for centuries. Plato, for example, condemned lying by individuals, but thought rulers could lie in the public interest. The consensus, even among Catholic thinkers, seems to be: "It depends."

Most, for example, would say that an innocent practical joke, one that does not violate charity, is not a sin, although the joker intends to deceive. The deceit appears to be harmless, is temporary and good-natured, and may even strengthen a friendship, especially if the victim feels free to retaliate.

What people call "white lies" are usually venial sins. Unfortunately, this category is impossible to define with any clarity. Everyone will agree that the following exchange is not gravely sinful: "Did you eat your vegetables?"; "Yes, Mom," replies the child, who in fact had put the vegetables in the garbage disposal. But opinions will differ on the morality of assuring a dying man that he will get well, or answering "I don't know" when quizzed on the whereabouts of a brother accused of a crime, or engaging in a thousand other untruths for what are considered to be good reasons. In all such cases, a conscience well formed by reason and the teaching of the Church is our best practical guide.

A lie is a mortal sin when "it does grave injury

to the virtues of justice and charity" (CCC 2484). The *Catechism* offers four tests to apply in judging a lie's seriousness. The particular circumstances in which it is told are obviously relevant. With regard to the brother accused of a crime, was the crime a felony? Is the brother armed and dangerous? Does the one who is being questioned know his brother is guilty?

The second measure is the liar's intention. Is he deliberately trying to hurt the listener? ("Oh, go ahead; the bridge has been repaired.") Third is the harm a lie's victim suffers. Falsely accusing a doctor of malpractice or charging a politician with having Mafia connections could ruin that person's career. Fourth, the nature of the truth the liar distorts must be considered. A lie that endangers a woman's physical well-being is serious, one that endangers her spiritual health even worse. One must add that, in all voluntary acts, a sin is mortal only if the sinner understands the evil being committed and wills it.

Because serious lies clearly do real harm, either moral or material, liars must do more than repent and confess their sin. They also are obliged to make restitution to those they have injured, whether this means returning money or goods obtained by fraud or rehabilitating a damaged reputation. The *Catechism* (2487) says reparation may be made secretly if a public act is impossible: for example, if revealing a lie would inevitably hurt an innocent third party. Reparation aims to restore the balance of justice, and should therefore reverse or compensate for the injustice done. The punishment, accepted and self-imposed, should fit the crime.

Ours is rapidly becoming a relativistic culture where the very concepts of truth and falsity are under fire. Whose truth? False from what perspective? Such objections are little more than sophistries where lying is concerned, since a lie is a deliberate distortion of what we believe to be true, even if we happen to be wrong. The fact that we can distinguish between fact and falsehood imposes a moral obligation to speak and act the truth in our dealings with others.

Questions about lying and its possible justification have bedeviled thinkers since humanity began taking the moral life seriously. Reginald Middleton remarks in closing "The Obligation of Veracity," an 1898 essay: "It is well to remember Aristotle's advice 'not to try to be more accurate than the nature of the subject permits.' It is easy to lay down general principles in the abstract, but the question whether they apply or not in a particular concrete case may be a very difficult one to answer." Nevertheless, Catholics are bound to strict respect for the truth in matters both common and serious. One may never deviate from the truth as such.

From one viewpoint, this is simply prudent advice. Life and literature are filled with illustrations of Sir Walter Scott's warning: "Oh, what a tangled web we weave, / when first we practice to deceive." One lie creates the need for more; the skeletons in our closets continue to rattle. In Dostoyevsky's *Crime and Punishment*, Raskolnikov is condemned to long, fruitless lying in an effort to conceal a murder. An honest life brings its own reward in peace of mind.

For Catholics and other Christians, truthfulness has a still deeper dimension. They are called to "live in the truth" as men and women who have accepted the redemption Jesus has won. St. Paul says: "Do not lie to one another, seeing that you have put off the old nature with its practices and have put on the new nature, which is being renewed in knowledge after the image of the creator" (Col 3:9). Our new nature sets us a higher standard than convenience, a wish to save face or a desire for profit. Meeting this standard may require considerable discipline, as when we pay a just debt we might have avoided by lying, and occasionally it may call for something like heroism.

See: Boasting; Conscience; Equivocation; False Witness; Flattery; Mental Reservation; Natural Law; Perjury; Rash Judgment; Secrets; Slander; Truthfulness.

Suggested Readings: CCC 2482-2567. G. Grisez, *The Way of the Lord Jesus*, Vol. 2, *Living a Christian Life*, pp. 405-418. D. Hughes, "Lying," *New Catholic Encyclopedia*, Vol. VIII.

David M. Byers

M

MAGIC

"Magic" that amounts to entertaining sleights-of-hand, optical illusions, or tricks in general — in other words, what only seems (but is not, and is not claimed to be) produced by invisible powers — falls outside the Church's concern. What is dangerous, both personally and socially, is the attempt "to tame occult powers, so as to place them at one's service and have a supernatural power over others" (CCC 2117), even when this is aimed at restoring others' health. Magic is also known by such names as sorcery, witchcraft, and even Satanism.

Gravely contrary to the virtue of religion is any attempt to work miracles, not by the power of God (something occasionally and gratuitously communicated to creatures), but by the use of hidden forces beyond human control. "These practices," the *Catechism of the Catholic Church* continues, "are even more to be condemned when accompanied by the intention of harming someone, or when they have recourse to the intervention of demons. . . . Recourse to so-called traditional cures does not justify either the invocation of evil powers or the exploitation of another's credulity." Even if born of curiosity, the performance of a magical ceremony is not sinless, as it betrays weak faith or vain superstition.

Historically, magic most flourishes when religion, reason, and civilization are in decline. It is not true that "religion is the despair of magic"; in reality, magic is but a diseased religion of those who despair of God's help but still believe in a world of spirits. The Catholic Church admits in principle that demons or lost souls can possibly interfere in the course of nature, but never without God's permission. Little is known, despite the claims of some popular literature aimed at credulous persons, about how often malignant spirits act at man's request.

The similarity of some ideas and practices in the magic of all peoples should be noted. All rely on the power of words, the utterance of a hidden name, or the mere existence of the name on an amulet or stone. When the boundary between the physically possible and the impossible was uncertain, some individuals were supposed to have gained almost limitless control over nature. With today's lessening of blind faith in the powers of science and technology, the rise in anti-intellectualism and credulity is to be expected.

See: Divination; New Age; Religion, Virtue of; Superstition; Theosophy.

MAGISTERIUM

Jesus Christ is the light of the world (Jn 8:12), the Savior of all mankind (Jn 4:42). He spent the years of his public life teaching his followers. He was their *magister*, their teacher; for them he had "the words of eternal life" (Jn 6:68).

For each person, the one really important thing is to meet Jesus, to be enlightened by him, to follow him. Despite our failures, our efforts will be fruitful if they are directed toward believing Our Lord's Revelation and doing his will.

But where can we find Jesus' teaching? How and with what certainty can we know it? The Catholic believes Christ's saving words are to be found not only in Scripture but also in Tradition. The Magisterium, or teaching authority, of the Church has as its pastoral duty "seeing to it that the People of God abides in the truth that liberates" (CCC 890).

Christ's teaching in Scripture is usually very clear. At times, nevertheless, he deliberately formulates it in parables and has to explain its meaning and application privately to his Apostles. On occasions we find the Apostles failing to understand his words or even scandalized at his teaching (Lk 18:24, Mt 19:10, etc.). When the exact meaning of a teaching or precept contained in Scripture is not clear, human minds, unaided, are likely to give it very different interpretations. If these are contradictory, they obviously cannot all be true.

For instance, when Our Lord said at the Last Supper, "Take, eat in memory of me," did he literally mean what he said? Did he really give his own Body and Blood to be eaten? Was it just a meal — or also a sacrifice that he was offering and wished to be perpetuated throughout the ages? Did Jesus want all of his followers to be able to truly eat his flesh ("Unless you eat the flesh of the Son of man and drink his blood, you have no life in you" [Jn 6:53]), as Catholics believe? Or should his work and intention be reduced to the idea of the Eucharist as a simple memorial of the last Supper, no more, the bread a mere symbol of Christ's love? After the words of Consecration in a Eucharistic celebration, is the bread (and wine) now truly the Body and Blood of Jesus Christ, with only the appearances of bread remaining, or is it still just bread that momentarily evokes Christ's love (cf. CCC 1374-1377)?

Examples could be multiplied indefinitely. Was Jesus really born of a Virgin? Did he truly rise from the dead? Is he truly God incarnate? Did he found a visible, hierarchical Church and endow it with the charism of infallibility?

Did Jesus want his teaching to be subject to contradictory interpretations? It would seem not. It makes a vast difference how one answers questions such as these. Yet knowing men as he did (cf. Jn 2:25), he also knew that by themselves they tend to interpret even the clearest truth or message in differing ways, finding it hard to agree about the truth or to hold to it firmly.

Living Presence of Christ • Thus, instead of leaving his teaching to men to make what they liked or chose of it, Jesus himself acted (and continues to act) with divine power to preserve the integrity and clarity of that teaching. Precisely to ensure that his work of salvation — doctrine, sacraments, sacrifice — should be preserved in its totality and be available without any corruption to each generation and each person, he set up his Church, "the pillar and bulwark of the truth" (1 Tm 3:15; cf. CCC 2032). He promised to be always present in his Church, ensuring that what she teaches as doctrine of salvation will be protected and guaranteed in heaven, that whoever listens to his Church will in fact be listening to Jesus himself: "All authority on heaven and on earth has been given to me. Go therefore and make disciples of all nations . . . teaching them to observe all that I have commanded you; and lo, I am with you always, to the close of the age" (Mt 28:18-20); "Whatever you bind on earth shall be bound in heaven, and whatever you loose on earth shall be loosed in heaven" (Mt 16:19; cf. Mt 18:18); "He who hears you hears me, and he who rejects you rejects me" (Lk 10:16).

What emerges from these passages is the living presence of Christ in the Magisterium of the Church, the teaching office she received from her founder. Vatican Council II teaches that "the task of giving an authentic interpretation of the Word of God, whether in its written form or in the form of Tradition, has been entrusted to the living teaching office [Magisterium] of the Church alone. Its authority in this matter is exercised in the name of Jesus Christ" (*Dogmatic Constitution on Divine Revelation, Dei Verbum*, 10).

The teaching of Jesus coming to us in the complementary sources of Scripture and Tradition, as interpreted by the Magisterium, is the heritage of each Christian. Each has a strict right in justice to receive this teaching: "The right of the faithful to receive Catholic doctrine in its purity and integrity must always be respected" (Pope John Paul II, encyclical *The Splendor of Truth, Veritatis Splendor*, 113 [1993]; cf. Canons 213, 762; CCC 2037). Similarly, the pastors of the Church, to whom the passing on of this doctrine has been specially entrusted, have a particular obligation to respect this trust and to hand on what they have received to the people they serve (cf. Canon 760). The Church has the *right* to teach and the duty.

The work of the Magisterium is not only to preserve intact the message of Christ but also to spell out how it applies to issues not mentioned in Scripture. Each age (and certainly our own) tends to bring up questions of belief and behavior that Our Lord did not explicitly deal with. Did he wish to leave us without means of knowing his mind on population questions, on drug-taking, on the right or wrong use of medical treatment that can prolong or shorten a sick person's life? No. It is the right and duty of the Magisterium to teach on just such contemporary questions "to the extent . . . required by the fundamental rights of the human person or the salvation of souls" (Canon 747.2; cf. CCC 2032).

Functioning of the Magisterium • The teaching of the Magisterium can be solemn or ordinary. Each calls on our believing response. The solemn Magisterium is usually exercised through a formal proclamation by the Pope acting as supreme pastor and teacher or by an ecumenical council teaching in union with the Pope (cf. CCC 891). The ordinary Magisterium is that exercised by the Pope alone or by the bishops teaching in communion with him, "when, without arriving at an infallible definition and without pronouncing in a 'definitive manner,' they propose . . . a teaching that leads to better understanding of Revelation in matters of faith and morals" (CCC 892).

"The Church's Magisterium exercises the authority it holds from Christ to the fullest extent when it defines dogmas, that is, when it proposes truths contained in divine Revelation or having a necessary connection with them, in a form obliging the Christian people to an irrevocable adherence of faith" (CCC 88). The definition of a dogma of faith is the highest and most guaranteed exercise of the Magisterium.

Vatican Council II in the *Dogmatic Constitution on the Church, Lumen Gentium*, 25, says that our response to the ordinary Magisterium must involve a "religious assent of mind and will" (*obsequium religiosum*). The *Catechism of the Catholic Church* notes that while this assent is dis-

tinct from the assent of faith, it "is nonetheless an extension of it" (CCC 892).

While various degrees of response to the Magisterium are possible according to the way in which it is exercised, no response is adequate unless rooted in faith. So, for instance, we believe that in the godhead there are three distinct Persons but one God (dogma of the Blessed Trinity), not because we understand how this is (we do not), but because it is a revealed truth taught as dogma by the Church's living Magisterium. Similarly, because of faith and not because of some rational argument, we believe that grace gives us a real participation in the life of God as his adopted children (doctrine of our divine filiation; cf. CCC 1997). Faith is not irrational of course, but our faith essentially is faith in God, not an analogous and merely human faith in human reasoning powers.

It is true that one could reject a proposition taught by the ordinary Magisterium without falling into heresy, strictly speaking. But one could not actively dissent from it without detriment to one's faith. At the same time, it can be possible to maintain a certain reserve, in the sense that something proposed by the Magisterium, not yet being cast in the final form of a dogmatic definition, may be subject to further, though accidental, refinements of meaning: always "in the same sense and along the same lines of understanding" (*eodem sensu, eademque sententia*: St. Vincent of Lerins). Yet the fact remains that "the freedom of the act of faith cannot justify a right to dissent" (Congregation for the Doctrine of the Faith, *Instruction on the Ecclesial Vocation of the Theologian*, 36).

Theologians and the Magisterium • In the ongoing task of probing, clarifying, and illustrating the power and beauty of the truth Christ bequeathed to us, theologians have an important role to play. They, too, are subject to the Magisterium. Indeed, humility and awareness of the greatness of the subject they are investigating and of their own human limitations lead theologians to look specially to the Magisterium for orientation in their important work.

The relationship between the Magisterium and

theological research is at times debated today. Ideally, they should "interpenetrate and enrich each other," for both are in the service of the People of God — pastors obliged to guard unity and forestall divisions, theologians responsible for "participating in the building up of Christ's Body in unity and truth" (*Instruction on the Ecclesial Vocation of the Theologian*, 40). The fundamental issue is the right of the faithful to know the mind of Christ, and in this regard it is the Magisterium's task "to preserve God's people from deviations and defections and to guarantee them the objective possibility of professing the true faith without error" (CCC 890).

St. Matthew tells us Jesus "taught as one who has authority, and not as the scribes" (Mt 7:29). Today also one would expect anyone teaching in the name of Christ to speak authoritatively, offering truths clear in their formulation and application. Teaching in Christ's name must be authoritative in a further sense. It should have the proper credentials. The matter of who "has the mind of Christ" (1 Cor 2:16) is to be decided on the basis of charismatic gifts. The Magisterium has that charismatic credential of divinely given grace. It teaches not in its own name nor as claiming more expert knowledge, but in virtue of a charism given for the sake of the whole body of the faithful.

In ways both mysterious and clear, Jesus sends his grace and light to every single person (Jn 1:9). Yet not all recognize his voice or respond to it. If we already have the good fortune to be Christians through Baptism, we need to keep our hearts and minds open to his will, like St. Paul on the road to Damascus: "Lord, what do you want me to do?" (cf. Acts 22:10); for he will speak to us in vain if we are not ready to respond.

The Church is for us both "Mother and Teacher" — *Mater et Magistra* (cf. CCC 2030-2051). Her Magisterium is a logical consequence of the Incarnation, a particular expression of Our Lord's loving promise to be "with us always" (Mt 28:20). The Magisterium is a divine gift helping us in our pilgrim way on earth to see clearly the way that is Jesus and hear clearly his words of eternal life.

See: Assent and Dissent; Catholic Identity; Church, Nature, Origin, and Structure of; Development of Doctrine; Dissent; Divine Revelation; Dogma; Faith of the Church; Heresy; Infallibility; Ordinary Magisterium; Pope; Sacred Scripture; Sacred Tradition.

Suggested Readings: CCC 85-87, 888-892, 2030-2040. Vatican Council II, *Dogmatic Constitution on the Church, Lumen Gentium*, 22-25. Congregation for the Doctrine of the Faith, *Instruction on the Ecclesial Vocation of the Theologian*. C. Burke, *Authority and Freedom in the Church*, Chs. 14-16.

Cormac Burke

MANICHAEISM

Manichaeism was a complex dualistic religion, once regarded as a Christian heresy. Although it appears variously as Manicheism, Manichaeanism, Manicheanism, and Manicheeism, we will refer to it as Manichaeism in this work. It was founded by Mani, also known as Manes or Manichaeus, who was born, according to most scholars, in Mardinu in Northern Babylonia (present-day Iraq) in A.D. 216 or 217. Mani claimed to have received, through the medium of an angel, revelations from the King of the Paradise of Lights. According to these messages, he was commissioned to be a preacher of the definitive and ultimate revelation. His teaching purported to be a synthesis of all religious systems then known.

He undertook missionary journeys in India and Persia (present-day Iran). In 241-242, he accompanied the Persian king Shapur on an expedition against the Roman emperor Gordius III. Through his preaching on this expedition, his teachings first entered Syria and other eastern portions of the Roman Empire. Encountering Christianity in these areas, his religious system absorbed various Christian elements.

Under the protection of Shapur, Mani continued his religious activity for thirty years. During the reign of Bahram I of Persia (274-277), he was imprisoned at the instigation of priests and adherents of the official Zoroastrian religion. He died in prison in 277.

Manichaeism is an extreme example of a dualistic religion. Such religions teach a radical duality and opposition between good and evil, usually described as a struggle between light and darkness. This duality is used to explain the origin of sin and evil in the world.

For Mani, the forces of light and darkness were totally separate in what he calls the First Time. Light and good are identified with knowledge, revelation, spirit, soul, and endurance; darkness and evil are shown as ignorance, matter, body, and unrest. The struggle between the two resulted in a mingling of light and darkness, good and evil. This mingling produced the present world, which he considered as the Middle Time. Ultimately, there would be a final separation of the two in the End Time.

During the Middle Time, various angels or emissaries of the light have appeared to bring true light, true wisdom, to the world. Among these were Abraham, Buddha, Zoroaster, Jesus, and Mani himself. Mani considered Jesus to have been the greatest of these messengers. For him, Jesus was a divine being who only seemed to be mortal and appeared to take the bodily form of the man of Nazareth.

Since the present world had resulted from a mingling of light and darkness, its results — matter and body — were evil. Procreation was regarded as of demonic origin. Those who would seek the light were called to a regimen of abstention and extreme asceticism. They also were required to spread the message and to seek further enlightenment. Certain foods, such as melons and fruit, were considered to be luminous, to contain light, and their consumption aided enlightenment. On the other hand, wine and meat were considered dark foods, and were to be avoided. Salvation could be obtained through a regime that freed the light from the constraints of matter and body.

The leadership of Mani's religion consisted of a supreme head, twelve teachers, and seventy-two bishops. We know very little of the activities of these leaders. They came from among the elect, preachers who practiced total abstinence from meat, wine, and sexual relations. Only the elect were the true Manichaeans. They led a wandering life, possessing only food for the day and clothes for the year. Most believers were hearers, or catechumens. Called to lesser perfection, they fasted one day a week. They could hold property and marry, but they were to abstain from procreation. They were forbidden to kill animals and were to live upright lives, avoiding fraud, perjury, sorcery, and the like. They also saw to the needs of the elect, ensuring that they were properly fed and clothed.

Manichaeism and Christianity • The emergence of Mani's teachings in Christian areas of the Roman Empire resulted in an adoption and modification of Christian practices and rituals, leading many to see Manichaeism as a sect within Christianity. Rejecting the Old Testament, Mani used the New Testament where it was useful and adopted the apocryphal *Gospel of Thomas*, the *Teaching of Addas*, and the second-century *The Shepherd of Hermas*.

Asceticism was appealing to many serious Christians disturbed by apparent laxity among fellow Christians after the end of persecution in 313 and the establishment of Christianity as the state religion of the empire in 380. Attractive because of its ascetical practices and cloaked in apparent conformity with Christian customs, Manichaeism spread quickly within the Roman Empire. In 381, Mani's adherents were considered so grave a threat that the emperor Theodosius deprived them of civil rights and placed heavy penalties on them.

St. Augustine himself was a Manichaean catechumen from 373 to 382, although later he bitterly attacked his former faith. The strength of Manichaeism can be measured by the stature of its opponents. In Antioch, John Chrysostom attacked Manichaeism; in Egypt its opponent was Serapion; in Palestine, Cyril of Jerusalem. Caesarius of Arles denounced it in France, Vincent of Lerins in Spain, and Pope Leo I in Rome. In the sixth century, Emperor Justinian issued an edict of condemnation.

In addition to its successes in the Mediterranean basin, Manichaeism spread to India, Central Asia, and as far as Tibet and China.

With Mani, dualism reached its height of eminence. Although it appeared to have died out in the first millennium, similar movements and sects later arose. Some were simply variants of dualism, while others were very close to the Manichaean doctrines. Manichaeism itself had been so pervasive and was considered to be so dangerous that many later variants of dualism were condemned as Manichaean. Among these were Paulicianism, Bogomilism, and Catharism, also known as Albigensianism. Like Manichaeism, the adherents of these movements, which flourished in several different places from the early through the late Middle Ages, also drew the wrath of the civil authorities, who saw mass movements that renounced property and marriage as subversive.

See: Augustinianism; Body and Soul; Creation; Gnosticism; Neoplatonism; New Age; Process Theology; Providence; Theosophy.

Suggested Readings: CCC 285, 299, 309-314. G. Windengren, *Mani and Manichaeism.*

Robert J. Wister

MARIAN DEVOTION

The doctrine of Vatican Council II about special devotion to Mary in the Catholic Church may be characterized as Christocentric and ecclesiotypical: that is, completely centered upon Christ and presenting Mary as the most perfect example, or archetype, of faithful discipleship in his Church. "Mary has by grace been exalted above all angels and men to a place second only to her Son, as the most holy mother of God who was involved in the mysteries of Christ: she is rightly honored by a special cult in the Church" (*Dogmatic Constitution on the Church, Lumen Gentium*, 66).

The honor of her title Mother of God has been paid to Mary from the earliest times, as is evidenced by the ancient prayer Sub Tuum Praesidium: "We fly to thy patronage, O holy Mother of God, despise not our petitions in our necessities, but deliver us from all danger, O ever glorious and blessed Virgin. Amen." This brief but confident invocation of the intercession of the Mother of God traces its origins back as early as the third or fourth century. After the Council of Ephesus (431), at which she was solemnly defined to be the "Theotokos," primarily to preserve the truth about her Son's Incarnation from the first instant of his conception in her virginal womb by the power of the Holy Spirit, devotion to her grew remarkably.

As Vatican II observes, this was devotion "in veneration and love, in invocation and imitation, according to her own prophetic words: 'all generations shall call me blessed, because he that is mighty hath done great things to me' (Lk 1:48)" (*Lumen Gentium*, 66). We are reminded here of Cardinal Newman's comment: "Her glories are not only for the sake of her Son; they are for our sakes too."

Devotion to Mary spread far and wide throughout Christendom at a time when the truth about Christ, namely, that he was God as well as man from the first instant of his human conception, necessary for our salvation, was seen to depend upon the revealed truth about her, namely, that she is the Theotokos, meaning God-Bearer, or Mother of God.

The Teaching of Vatican II • Vatican II is careful to teach that even such special Marian devotion differs essentially from that due Christ and the Trinity alone. "This cult, as it has always existed in the Church, for all its uniqueness, differs essentially from the cult of adoration, which is offered equally to the Incarnate Word, and to the Father and the Holy Spirit, and it is most favorable to it" (*Lumen Gentium*, 66). In more technical terms used by the Tradition to draw this important distinction, devotion to Mary belongs to the veneration of *dulia*, or the homage and honor owed to the saints, both angelic and human in heaven, and not to *latria*, or the adoration and worship that can be given only to the Triune God and the Son incarnate. Because of her unique relationship to Christ in salvation history, however, the special degree of devotion due to Mary has traditionally been called *hyperdulia*. While *latria* is owed to her Son by reason of unity of his divine and human natures in the Person of the Word made flesh, *hyperdulia* is due to Mary as truly his Mother (cf. St. Thomas Aquinas, *Summa Theologiae,* II-II, q. 103, a. 4; III, q. 25, a. 5).

And so the most recent ecumenical council — although highly promoting devotion to Mary, especially that which is celebrated in the liturgy — was most solicitous in preventing any excesses in the matter. The Fathers at Vatican II particularly urged theologians and preachers of the word of God to avoid both a maximalism ("all false exaggeration") and a minimalism ("too summary an attitude in considering the special dignity of the Mother of God"). Vatican II's teaching instead clearly urges: "Following the study of Sacred Scripture, the Fathers, the doctors and liturgy of the Church, and under the guidance of the Church's magisterium, let them rightly illustrate the duties and privileges of the Blessed Virgin which always refer to Christ, the source of all truth, sanctity, and devotion" (*Lumen Gentium*, 67). This Christocentric devotion to Mary is best suited to convey the true doctrine of the Church ecumenically to our separated sisters and brothers in other Christian communions.

Catholics are urged to remember "that true devotion consists neither in sterile or transitory affection, nor in a certain vain credulity, but proceeds from true faith" (*Lumen Gentium*, 67). Authentic veneration of Mary must move each member of her Son's Body, the Church, "to a filial love towards our mother and to the imitation of her virtues" (*Lumen Gentium*, 67). If Marian devotion is genuinely Christocentric, it will inevitably be ecclesiotypical, helping us become more virtuous members of the Church who, always fixing our gaze upon Christ and through him striving for closer union with the Father in the Holy Spirit, make our spiritual journey of faith in the likeness of our mother Mary. *Hyperdulia* would be short-circuited, as it were, if it terminated in Mary instead of Christ and the Triune God, to whom she always directs us until we reach the mystical marriage of our heavenly home.

Mary in Luke's Gospel • The Gospels accord-

ing to Sts. Luke and John provide the most fruitful foundations for the special devotion to Mary that developed in the Catholic tradition, both in the East and the West. Among the writers of the three Synoptic Gospels (Matthew, Mark, and Luke), Luke portrays Mary as the perfect disciple of her Son, from her "yes" (*fiat*) to God's calling her to become Mother of his Son at the Annunciation (1:26-38) to her praying together with Jesus' other disciples in preparation for the descent of the pentecostal Spirit (Acts 1:14). Discipleship for the third evangelist meant "hearing the word of God" and "keeping it."

In Luke's Gospel, especially the infancy narrative, or first two chapters, Mary gives the most excellent example of the Christian vocation to follow Christ by prayerful listening to his teaching and preaching as the word of God and by careful fulfillment of God's will through living in accord with that Divine Revelation. In narrating the events that comprise the joyful mysteries of the Rosary — Annunciation, Visitation, birth of Christ, presentation, and finding in the temple — Luke tells us twice that Mary pondered these things over and over again, treasuring them in her heart (cf. 2:19, 51). This was a continuous form of prayer practiced by Mary, as by the wisdom teachers of Israel, particularly her own Son, the greatest among them. We might even call this her "Rosary" in contemplating the mysteries of her Son, experienced by him for the sake of our redemption, including Mary's unique "preservative" redemption, the Immaculate Conception. Her prayer life, letting the word of God sink into the spiritual soil of her mind and heart, led to words (e.g., the Magnificat: Lk 1:46-55) and deeds (e.g., the Visitation: Lk 1:39-45) in keeping with the Father's holy will for her in his loving plan of salvation history.

Mary's whole spiritual journey was beautifully epitomized by Vatican II as a "pilgrimage of faith" (*Lumen Gentium*, 58). On one occasion, a woman, moved to a deep admiration of Jesus' teaching, exclaimed to him: " 'Blessed is the womb that bore you, and the breasts that you sucked!' But he said, 'Blessed rather are those who hear the word of

God and keep it!' " (Lk 11:27-28). Far from rejecting this woman's praise of his Mother, Jesus wished to focus attention upon the real reason why Mary is so praiseworthy, namely, that she is outstanding among his disciples for listening so attentively to his Father's word and putting it into practice so perfectly. This is what has made her worthy of praise, indeed of special veneration, by the rest of us, and not just the fact that she is his genetic Mother.

This grace of perfect discipleship even made her a worthy Mother of God. It should not be misinterpreted as settling a debate over which is her greatest privilege, her motherhood of God or her holiness. For Luke it was inconceivable that she be the Mother of the Lord without being made worthy of this unique honor by the gift of her fullness of grace in hearing and keeping the word of God. Finally, Luke's portrait of Mary as the perfect disciple of her Son receives its finishing touch in the Acts of the Apostles: "All these with one accord devoted themselves to prayer, together with the women and Mary the mother of Jesus, and with his brethren" (1:14). Chronologically, this is the last we hear of her in the New Testament.

Mary in John's Gospel • In the fourth Gospel, Mary appears in two main scenes: at Cana in the beginning of Jesus' public ministry and at the foot of the cross in the end of his mission on earth. Without attempting a complete exegesis of the Marian symbolism involved, we shall consider here what seems to have been particularly significant about John's Gospel as it influenced the Catholic tradition in developing its special devotion to Mary. Vatican Council II sums up this approach to John's Gospel: "In the public life of Jesus, Mary appears prominently; at the very beginning when at the marriage feast of Cana, moved with pity, she brought about by her intercession the beginning of miracles of Jesus the Messiah (cf. Jn 2:1-11). . . . Thus the Blessed Virgin advanced in her pilgrimage of faith and faithfully persevered in union with her Son unto the cross, where she stood, in keeping with the divine plan, enduring with her only begotten Son the intensity of his suffering, associated herself with his sacri-

fice in his mother's heart, and lovingly consenting to the immolation of this victim which was born of her. Finally, she was given by the same Christ Jesus dying on the cross as a mother to his disciple with these words: 'Woman, behold thy son' (Jn 19:26-27)" (*Lumen Gentium*, 58).

There seems to be progress in the formation of Mary's faith between Cana and Calvary, according to the fourth evangelist. At the wedding feast, her faith was such that she had complete confidence in her Son's resourcefulness to respond to her request that he miraculously intervene; but still it was necessary that she follow him to the foot of the cross before her faith became fully informed about the Father's will for him and her. *This* was his hour, to which he had made reference at Cana when at first apparently refusing her intercessory request to use his miraculous power and save the day by changing water into wine. And even though he did anticipate that hour at his Mother's request, the sign at Cana was only a glimpse of the glory the Father would bestow upon him on Calvary, though enough to inspire his first disciples to believe in him. Mary and the beloved disciple standing at the foot of the cross were witnesses by their complete faith in Christ to the full revelation of his glory. According to John's theology of the cross, not only were Christ's Passion and death accomplished on the cross, but also his glorification in the Resurrection, Ascension to the Father, and the sending of the pentecostal Spirit. John contemplates the paschal mystery of our redemption, as does the Father, in a single intuitive glance of love. And the relationship between Mary as the disciple-mother and the beloved disciple-son must be contemplated by us in this context, namely, that they represent the perfection of faith in the total paschal mystery of Christ, his Passion, death, and glorification, and so are a model for the faith of John's apostolic community at Ephesus.

The literal sense intended by the fourth evangelist seems to be the birth of the Christian community at the foot of the cross, with a mother-son relationship between Mary and the beloved disciple, who looks after her in the family of the faithful. This interpretation apparently has been expanded in the Catholic tradition, in which the disciple-mother begins to take care of and look after the disciple-son and all the faithful disciples in the Church represented by him. This seems to be the biblical basis of Mary's spiritual motherhood of the People of God, her adoptive motherhood "in the order of grace," according to Vatican II (cf. *Lumen Gentium*, 61, 62). As the Council's teaching clearly indicates, belief in this doctrine about Mary over the centuries has formed a solid foundation for the devotion of the Catholic faithful, who have regarded her as making intercession for them and mediating her Son's saving graces to them.

Mary in the Tradition • The new Eve image of Mary is the most ancient after the New Testament. First applied to the Church, it gradually was attributed to the "woman," who came to be contemplated as the archetype of the Church, the "mother of the new living" through Christ, the new Adam. The Fathers of the Church who most used and developed this Eve/Mary typology are St. Justin Martyr (died c. 165) and St. Irenaeus (died c. 202). By their meditations upon the Bible (particularly on the Annunciation according to Luke, in contrast to the role of the first Eve in the Fall as recounted in Genesis), they came to see a kind of antithetical parallelism between Mary and Eve, in which the differences are of greater significance than any similarities.

According to this method of meditating upon the Scriptures, as evils were perpetrated in salvation history, so they are providentially undone by counterparts of the perpetrators. As in the Fall, Adam and his helpmate in the original sin, Eve, together with the serpent-devil and the tree of the knowledge of good and evil, all play roles, so the evil was to be overcome by the new creation of Christ (new Adam) and his helpmate Mary (new Eve), who made it possible for him to redeem us through the loving faith and obedience of her *fiat* at the Annunciation responding to the good angel Gabriel, while the instrument of our redemption was to be the tree of the cross.

Through this very popular image of her as the new Eve, Mary came to be revered more and more in the Church of the Fathers as the woman who conceived Christ in her heart (*in corde* or *in mente*) by faith before she conceived him in the flesh (*in carne*) or in her womb (*in ventre*). Moreover, according to John's Gospel, the side of the new Adam was pierced with a lance while he was asleep (i.e., dead) upon the cross, "and at once there came out blood and water" (Jn 19:34). The Fathers interpreted this as symbolizing the Eucharist and Baptism, the sacraments that constitute the Church, while the "new Eve" later was to be applied to Mary seen as representing the Church as its most perfect exemplar. Again, the Fathers found a comparison by contrast between the first Eve, taken from the "rib" of the sleeping Adam, and the Church (Mary) coming forth from the side of the dead Christ. As Vatican II teaches, the Fathers "frequently claim: death through Eve, life through Mary" (*Lumen Gentium*, 56).

During the fourth century, devotion to Mary as model of consecrated virgins began to develop, especially through St. Athanasius in the East and St. Ambrose in the West. We have already seen how the Sub Tuum Praesidium prayer and the solemn definition of Mary as Theotokos, or God-Bearer, at the Council of Ephesus (431) inspired widespread devotion to Mary throughout the Church of Christ. Worthy of special note is the *Akathistos*, the most important hymn of the Greek Church, which is considered to have originated sometime during the sixth century. Still a part of the Byzantine liturgy today, this hymn is sung in praise of the Incarnation and of Mary's virginal motherhood of God incarnate. During the medieval period, it influenced the Marian litanies in form and content.

See: Assumption of Mary; Devotions; Immaculate Conception; Incarnation; Jesus Christ, God and Man; Jesus Christ, Life of; Mary, Mother of God; Mary, Mother of the Church; Mary, Perpetual Virginity of; Patrology; Redemption; Rosary; Sacred Tradition; Spiritual Exegesis.

Suggested Readings: CCC 971. Vatican Council II, *Dogmatic Constitution on the Church, Lumen Gentium*, Ch. VIII. Paul VI, *Devotion to the Blessed Virgin Mary, Marialis Cultus*. John Paul

II, *The Mother of the Redeemer, Redemptoris Mater.* H. Graef, *Mary: A History of Doctrine and Devotion.* F. Jelly, O.P., *Madonna: Mary in the Catholic Tradition.* M. Hines, "Mary" in *The New Dictionary of Catholic Spirituality.*

F.M. Jelly, O.P.

MARKS OF THE CHURCH

When we say in the Creed that we believe the Church to be one, holy, catholic, and apostolic, we are affirming fundamental features by which the Church founded by Christ can be recognized.

The Church Is One. Oneness refers both to the uniqueness and the unity of the Church. The Church founded by Christ is necessarily unique, for he founded just one Church (and it follows that the present multiplicity of Christian churches is not according to the will of Christ). He also intended that his Church be one — united and undivided (cf. Jn 10:16) — as a reflection of his own unity with his Father. He especially prayed for this (cf. Jn 17:21).

Unity is a proof and the fruit of love for Christ and of union with him, and passes through unity and communion with the Church and the Pope. It is a mark of the Church that especially needs to be loved, for all of us have an individualist spirit that tends toward separation from others and from the principles of unity or authority. "Sin and the burden of its consequences constantly threaten the gift of unity. And so the Apostle has to exhort Christians to 'maintain the unity of the Spirit in the bond of peace' [*Eph* 4:3]" (CCC 814).

Unity does not mean uniformity. In the Church, on the basis of true *communio*, there has always been a great diversity of persons, classes, cultures, forms of worship — yet all within a fundamental unity of faith and heart (cf. Acts 4:32). The type of variety introduced by the Reformation involved a rejection of the norm of unity that Christ himself gave us: obedience to the guidance of the Magisterium and the hierarchy as expressing his will. "He who hears you hears me, and he who rejects you rejects me" (Lk 10:16). It left the individual Christian on his own, with the risk of following a direction that is not Christ's. It tended, moreover, to create a diversity evermore individualistic.

Unity has to be maintained not just in faith, in the truth and charity of Christ, but also in government. Therefore, the unity willed by Jesus is broken not just by heresy but also by schism. While all Catholics must be concerned to maintain ecclesial unity (cf. Canon 209), this is a particular responsibility of bishops, along with the Pope. The *Catechism of the Catholic Church* insists that "the bishop's pastoral responsibility for his particular church" is closely connected with "the common solicitude of the episcopal college for the universal Church" (879). Ecclesial unity is powerfully fostered by periodic events such as the synods of bishops, and perhaps even more so by the *ad limina* visits to the Pope and the Roman Curia that every bishop makes once every five years.

The Church Is Holy. As the continuation of the life and work of Jesus, the Church is endowed with the holiness of Christ himself. This holiness is not to be sought first in men who, with their defects, can obscure but not destroy it; rather, it should be sought in the institutions with which Christ himself endowed the Church. The holiness of the Church is to be found:

* In her belief and doctrine. So we speak of the *Holy* Bible, *Holy* Scripture, *Sacred* Tradition. The sacredness of Tradition helps one realize the special holiness that necessarily permeates the Magisterium, by which Christ guarantees the integrity of Tradition and the new insights Tradition gradually incorporates into itself. So also it is because of his office that the Pope (whatever his personal merits or example) is rightly called *Holy* Father; God ensures that his teaching is a source of holiness for those who follow it.

* In her worship and sacraments. The sacraments are holy and make people holy (independently of the worthiness of the minister: cf. CCC 1128). The Eucharistic Sacrifice, even if celebrated by a priest living deeply in sin, is still the *Holy* Mass, and brings us fruits of holiness.

* In the government of the Church where, again despite human defects, a holy principle is at

work. That is why it is called "hierarchy" (*hieros-archos*), which means sacred power.

* In her members. Throughout the centuries, the Church's life has been marked by outstanding personal holiness in many of her members: the saints, especially Mary. If they die in God's grace, even those who have long lived in sin show the power of the redemption and bear witness to the holiness of the Church.

The Church Is Catholic. The word "catholic" means universal. The embrace of the Church extends to the whole world. The spirit and doctrine of Catholicism are open to all mankind. If freely accepted, they not only save individuals, but also raise, strengthen, and purify cultures. So each grows in strength and identity, in oneness with Christ and in a variety that becomes mutually enriching.

Catholicity is intimately connected with unity. The Church would not be catholic if she did not draw all into one. When we describe the Church as Roman Catholic, this does not indicate a catholicity less than universal but rather underlines the necessary reference point so as to remain universal. As the Pope is the Holy Father, so Rome, along with Jerusalem, is the Holy City for a Catholic.

In order to be legitimate and enriching, variety or inculturation must draw its fundamental inspiration from the overall richness of Catholicism. It should also remain open to other local incarnations of the Gospel; otherwise, these would be in danger of becoming branches separated from the vine. "In virtue of this catholicity each part contributes its own gifts to other parts and to the whole Church, so that the whole and each of the parts are strengthened by the common sharing of all things and by the common effort to attain to fullness in unity" (Vatican Council II, *Dogmatic Constitution on the Church, Lumen Gentium*, 13).

The Church Is Apostolic. "Built upon the foundation of the apostles" (Eph 2:20), who received the fullness of Revelation and of the means of salvation, the Church hands on the apostolic faith, evangelizing and sanctifying with the doctrine and authority of Christ. The bishops are the successors of the Apostles and guardians of that one faith which comes down from them. Each bishop has the responsibility to keep legitimate local interests vitally linked with the center. Continuity in episcopal succession has always been the first condition of maintaining apostolicity.

These marks are tests to identify the one Church Christ wished to found. In a certain sense, too, they are tests of whether the individual Christian is properly assimilating the spirit of Christ into his or her own life. If one loves the unity of the Church and lives and protects it, if one is living with a heart open to all and filled with confidence in the links that bind us to Christ — hierarchy, Magisterium, Tradition — then, despite personal sins and weakness, one's life is gradually being made holy.

See: Apostolic Succession; Church, Nature, Origin, and Structure of; Ecumenism; Hierarchy; Magisterium; People of God; Sacred Tradition.

Suggested Readings: CCC 811-870. Vatican Council II, *Dogmatic Constitution on the Church, Lumen Gentium*. C. Burke, *Authority and Freedom in the Church*.

Cormac Burke

MARRIAGE

Life is about getting to know and love God. Our starting point is creation, particularly the masterpiece of visible creation: the human race. Each individual human, male or female, is made in the likeness of God. Man and woman "image" God in different, though complementary, ways. Considered together in their complementarity, they give a fuller image.

Although there is no sexuality in God, his creation of man as a sexually diversified being gives a key to what God is. An understanding of what it means to be masculine or feminine is essential in order to learn from a major revelation of himself inscribed by God in creation.

Everyone needs the experience of appreciating what is masculine and what is feminine. Properly experienced and lived, this involves a deep enrichment for the human person. The experience, however, does not always enrich because it involves a challenge that may not be lived up to: a challenge of understanding and of attitude expressed in multiple relations, both in the family (brothers to sisters and vice-versa; father to daughter, mother to son, and vice-versa), as well as outside (boys to girls, men to women). Someone who fails to arrive at or is deprived of an appreciation of the typical qualities of the other sex will have a defective idea of humanity.

In a society where sexual differences are considered to be of an exclusively corporal nature, sexuality is impoverished and no longer helps people to grow in knowledge of humanity or in knowledge of God.

Sexuality has an impact on major aspects of human life and growth. Social relations need the presence of masculinity *and* femininity, in their complementary differences. A unisex society, which eventually becomes a society bereft of any true human sexuality, is one in which people's growth in humanity is severely handicapped.

While there are many different types of sexually characterized relationships in society and each is important, one stands out above all as unique in God's plan: the conjugal sexual relationship — the lifelong exclusive and open-to-life union between a man and a woman that is marriage.

Marital Consent and Purposes • "The vocation to marriage is written in the very nature of man and woman as they came from the hand of the Creator" (CCC 1603). But there must be a personal response to this vocation, as to any other. Marriage in fact begins with an act of commitment — marital consent — "by which a man and a woman, through an irrevocable covenant, mutually give and accept each other in order to establish a marriage" (Canon 1057.2). This consent must be free, mutual, and genuine; by it, each of the spouses must give of himself or herself, and accept the other, in a relationship characterized by exclusiveness ("you and you alone"), permanence ("till death do us part"), and procreativity (openness to the children with whom God may bless their union). "Marriage is based on the consent of the contracting parties, that is, on their will to give themselves, each to the other, mutually

and definitively, in order to live a covenant of faithful and fruitful love" (CCC 1662).

To understand the nature of marriage, one has to go back to its institution by God. It is striking that the Bible, in the first and second chapters of Genesis, gives *two* accounts of the creation of the sexes; together they reveal God's design for sexuality and marriage. Jesus himself, in trying to raise his Apostles' minds to a proper understanding of the original divine plan for the marital relationship, refers back to one of these accounts: "He who made them from the beginning made them male and female, and said, 'For this reason a man shall leave his father and mother and be joined to his wife, and the two shall become one.' So they are no longer two but one" (Mt 19:4-6). The words Jesus uses are taken from the second chapter of Genesis, where the creation of the sexes is presented in the context that, since it is not good for man or woman to be alone, God makes a "helper," or helpmate — a conjugal partner — for him or her (Gn 2:18-24).

Thus we find Our Lord drawing attention to what would today be termed the personalist end of marriage: the goodness that comes to the spouses, in their growth as persons, from being joined together in the conjugal bonded covenant.

Our grasp of the divine plan and purpose of marriage would remain incomplete if it were drawn only from chapter 2 of Genesis. The fullness of the plan of sexual differentiation is revealed in chapter 1 of the same book: "God created man in his own image, in the image of God he created him; male and female he created them. And God blessed them, and God said to them, 'Be fruitful and multiply' " (Gn 1:27-28). This passage describes the procreational end of marriage, just as chapter 2 (which biblical experts consider in fact to be earlier in date of composition) describes the personalist end.

These ends should not be contrasted too sharply with each other. The personalist end is an "institutional" end (it derives from the institution of marriage) just as much as the procreational end. And the procreational end, properly understood, is also personalist (having children *expresses* marital love and fulfills the spouses). In the past, the hierarchy between the ends of marriage was stressed. Today the Church prefers to emphasize their interconnection and interdependence.

The *Catechism of the Catholic Church*, in harmony with the two biblical narrations just noted, speaks of "the twofold end of marriage: the good of the spouses themselves, and the transmission of life" (2363). The two ends, taken together, reveal God's overall plan in instituting marriage. Marriage is aimed at the perfecting of the spouses — their good — by fidelity to the bond of loving companionship and help between them, a bond with physical expressions that naturally lead to the begetting of children, the most personalized fruit of their union and love.

These two institutional purposes of marriage — the good of the spouses and procreation/education of children — are intimately interlinked. By true conjugal-sexual self-donation, the spouses tend to become parents, and share in the enriching experience of self-perpetuation. By their dedication to their children, they continue to grow individually as persons and in mutual esteem. At the same time, the human race is perpetuated in a family way so that children are born of love and are raised in an atmosphere where they can receive the guidance they need: firm and affectionate, inspiring respect rather than fear.

The possibility of having children is not merely a biological consequence of the physical structure of sex. The power to procreate is a complement to human love, and a major expression and support of it. So it is totally inadequate to see human procreation solely in biological terms. Allowing for the parallels between human and animal procreation, the profound differences between them must be properly noted. Animal procreation is normally the result of a casual and transient meeting of a male and a female. Human procreation is meant to take place in the setting of a stable lifelong relationship between a man and woman. The procreation of animals serves to perpetuate each species for as long as the world lasts. Human procreation brings into existence a being with an eternal soul, destined to live forever as a child of God. The act by which

animals are conceived is no more than the satisfying of a physical urge or instinct. The conception of a human person should be the fruit of mutual self-donation, of conscious marital love, an act that signifies in a unique way the exclusive, lifelong conjugal union of husband and wife.

There is a major problem today in the fact that many people, when they marry, think their mutual love is sufficient to make their marriage "fulfilling," and look on children — one or two children — as an optional factor that may enrich their married life but might also be an obstacle to self-fulfillment. "Family planning" then becomes "happiness planning" or "fulfillment planning," adding an element of calculation to conjugal love and union unlikely to lead to the greater happiness that marriage promises.

A couple can stare the love out of each other's eyes, if they continue to look just at one another. Nature's plan is that, as romantic love wanes, they learn to look together at their children, the incarnated fruit of their union, and to center their shared attention and concerns more and more on them.

The teaching of the Second Vatican Council on the *universal* call to holiness (*Dogmatic Constitution on the Church, Lumen Gentium*, Ch. V) means that God has a particular and individual plan for every single person. He similarly has a particular plan for each married couple and for the family their love naturally tends to form. Married couples do well to reflect that God is the wisest natural family planner and the marriage counselor with the longest experience. It is predictable that a marriage without children (when children can be had) or without the number of children *God* had planned for that marriage (one child, two, ten) is not likely to be conducive to the good of the spouses, fulfilling them in the measure God had in store for them.

The Good of the Spouses • The good that God seeks to draw from marriage for each of the spouses consists not merely in possible human satisfactions, but essentially in the maturing of husband and wife by persevering in the task of loving and caring for each other and their children over a lifetime. True married love is beautiful but not easy.

All human beings have defects, and it is never easy to love a defective person. What makes it particularly hard, however, are not only the defects of others but, even more, *our own* — self-concern, pride, sensuality. We all want and need to love; but that is something very hard for us to do in any true and lasting fashion. This poor capacity for loving is our most threatening defect.

But life fundamentally is about *learning* to love; and marriage and family life are never properly understood unless seen and lived as a divine plan to help and teach people to love. That is why marriage, more than a "haven" of love, is meant to be a *school* of love. Since every marriage is the binding together of two defective persons, the basic ground rule for any marriage is learning to love one's partner with his or her defects, while being content to love with one's own defective love. Learning to love is always the big task.

It is a process that never ends. As between husband and wife, it means learning to understand, to forgive, to ask forgiveness, to avoid judgments, to keep starting again after each failure so that self-love is assumed and purified in conjugal love, and conjugal love becomes parental love.

Learning to love as parents must be a joint endeavor, where husband and wife distribute responsibilities and sacrifices, and in particular try to create a home with a distinctive family personality that comes from the active and creative participation of each one involved — parents and children. Families need to have their own vitality; there has to be "family life" that the children also help to create, live by, and look forward to. Families with such a personality are not only the best safeguard for young people against negative or destructive elements in society, but they themselves become focal points for gradually changing and renewing — humanizing — society.

In married life, husband and wife have equal dignity and rights, but different and complementary roles. Growing in love within marriage does not necessarily mean becoming more alike; more often it means becoming more distinct, each one more identified in his or her conjugal role, and so more capable of acting as complement to the other.

The ability to complement one another also implies growth on the part of each in sexual identity. If the husband does not grow in masculinity, and the wife in femininity, their union and complementarity will not grow either.

Discussing marriage "under the regime of sin," the *Catechism* speaks of how evil also is experienced "in the relationships between man and woman," which can be distorted into relationships "of domination and lust" (1606-1607). Spouses need the virtue of married chastity to preserve the purity of their love. Chastity is expressed not primarily by abstinence but rather by the effort to purify the sexual act of an overly self-centered or possessive attitude, so as to retain the tenderness of what is both a loving donation to the other as well as a spousal acceptance of him or her. For this, husband and wife need God's help: "Without his help, man and woman cannot achieve the union of their lives for which God created them 'in the beginning' " (CCC 1608).

See: Chastity; Family; Human Person; Imago Dei; Indissolubility of Marriage; Marriage Covenant; Marriage, Goods of; Marriage in the Old Testament; Marriage, Sacrament of; Sexism; Sexuality, Human; Theology of the Body.

Suggested Readings: CCC 1602-1608, 1625-1628, 1643-1654, 2360-2391. John Paul II, *The Christian Family in the Modern World, Familiaris Consortio.* G. Grisez, *The Way of the Lord Jesus,* Vol. 2, *Living a Christian Life,* Ch. 9.

Cormac Burke

MARRIAGE COVENANT

The Second Vatican Council placed special emphasis on the term "covenant" to describe the unbreakable union of husband and wife (cf. *Pastoral Constitution on the Church in the Modern World, Gaudium et Spes,* 48, 50). Even on the level of its natural institution, the indissolubility of marriage images the absolutely faithful character of God's love for humankind, a love that was to find very special expression in the covenant that, through Abraham (Gn 17:1-2) and Moses (Ex 19:5), he made with his chosen people.

When Jesus Christ raised marriage to the level of a sacrament, indissolubility took on a new significance, becoming a sign of the love — faithful to death — of Christ for his Church. Indissolubility in Christian marriage is said to acquire "a special firmness by reason of the sacrament" (Canon 1056).

The use of the term "covenant" has not delegitimized reference to marriage as a contract. Both terms are applicable, as appears from Canon 1056, which speaks of the "matrimonial covenant" in paragraph 1 and of the "matrimonial contract" in paragraph 2.

To speak of covenant draws attention to the sacred character of marriage (even on the natural level). It evokes the special fidelity that should characterize conjugal love. The use of the term "contract" stresses that marriage involves the mutual interchange of rights and duties, binding in justice. It is because these rights/obligations have a juridic nature that fundamental questions related to marriage (validity of consent, separation, custody of the children, etc.) can and should be dealt with before the appropriate ecclesiastical courts.

Marriage is unique as a contract, because its nature (including its indissolubility) is determined by God. Spouses can freely choose to marry; but, having married, they are bound to respect the sacred nature God has given to this singular contract-covenant.

See: Indissolubility of Marriage; Marriage; Marriage, Goods of; Marriage, Sacrament of; New Covenant; Old Covenant.

MARRIAGE, GOODS OF

The expression "goods" (*bona*) of marriage originated with St. Augustine (354-430), one of the leading figures in the history of Western thought. Augustine used *bona* (plural of the Latin *bonum*) in the rich and significant sense of values or blessings. It is important not to overlook this, since subsequent use down the centuries, especially in the field of Church law, has tended to narrow its meaning and make it appear to be a term of purely

technical interest just for canonists. In order to understand its scope, the context in which St. Augustine utilized it must be recalled.

Augustine lived in the declining years of the Roman Empire. After a youth in which he experienced all the unhappiness of uncontrolled sexuality, he was converted, became a great saint, and remains one of the outstanding "doctors" (teachers) of the Church. His writings on marriage make him a major exponent both of its goodness and of the danger to which the sexual instinct, also within marriage, is subject.

In his early Catholic years, he defended the greatness and dignity of marriage against the pessimism of the Manichaeans, who held material creation, including the human body (and therefore also sexuality and marriage), to be evil. Later, he combated an error at the other extreme: the pseudo-optimism of the Pelagians, who denied any disordered and selfish element in sexuality and therefore ignored the importance of married chastity and the need for grace in order to live it. (Chastity in marriage inspires husband and wife to seek to purify marital intercourse of any element of self-seeking so that it becomes wholly an act of mutual and loving self-donation.)

St. Augustine's Teaching • In St. Augustine's writings, we find constant insistence that marriage is good because of three fundamental values or goods. "Let these nuptial goods be the objects of our love: offspring, fidelity, the unbreakable bond. . . . Let these nuptial goods be praised in marriage by him who wishes to extol the nuptial institution." For him, each of the essential properties of the conjugal society — its exclusiveness, its permanence, its procreativity — is a *good* thing that gives dignity to Matrimony and shows its deep correspondence to the innate aspirations of human nature, which can therefore take glory in this goodness: "This is the goodness [*bonum*] of marriage, from which it takes its glory: offspring, chaste fidelity, unbreakable bond." He saw these values as main features of a true marital bond, underlining the natural goodness of marriage and making it something admirable and attractive to human consideration.

The three *bona* are essential properties that distinguish the marital covenant from any other type of relationship between two persons. In brief, the three goods, or *bona,* are: the *exclusive fidelity* of the marital relationship (one man with one woman: the *bonum fidei*); the *permanence* of the relationship (the unbreakable character, or indissolubility, of the marital bond: the *bonum sacramenti*); and the (potential) fruitfulness of the union (procreativity, or the openness to having children: the *bonum prolis*, or the good of offspring).

Sacramentum (in the expression *bonum sacramenti*) does not refer to the sacrament of Matrimony in its theological sense. Augustine used the word in its original Latin sense: something with a hidden or deeper meaning. The Church has always held that the unbreakable character of the marriage bond is a sign (*sacramentum*) of God's unalterable love for each human being. The *bonum sacramenti* therefore does not refer to the supernatural means of grace peculiar to Christian marriage, but to the indissolubility of the marital bond, which is an essential character of each and every marriage also on the natural level.

We can illustrate briefly why each of these essential properties of marriage is truly a *value*, in close correspondence with the nature of genuine conjugal love between man and woman. To appreciate this is all the more important today, when people's natural desire for a true marital relationship is threatened by a false idea of self-sufficiency and a growing suspicion of any form of binding commitment.

Importance of the Goods • To be afraid of committing oneself to what is worthwhile is the surest way of self-frustration. Our Lord says it is only by "losing" (i.e., giving) ourselves that we can "find" ourselves (Mt 10:39; cf. Jn 12:25). This remains a main truth of the Christian approach to life. It is expressed in a phrase of Vatican Council II that is the key to Christian personalism: "Man can fully discover his true self only in a sincere giving of himself" (*Pastoral Constitution on the Church in the Modern World, Gaudium et Spes,* 24). One can only realize oneself by giving and committing oneself to love: to the love of God and also to human love (as in marriage), as leading to God's love. Human nature is therefore made for a self-gift in love and longs for this.

If we consider the self-gift of marriage (and the *acceptance* of the self-gift of the other; cf. Canon 1057.2), we find that it is essentially characterized by the three values in which St. Augustine saw the greatness and glory of the marital commitment.

Many people today are suspicious of an exclusive relationship. Yet everyone wants to be someone very special in someone else's eyes. Hence arises the good or value of the *bonum fidei*, the commitment to a faithful and exclusive love in marriage. "You are *unique* to me" is the first truly personalized affirmation of conjugal love. It echoes the words God addresses to each one of us in the Book of Isaiah: "You are mine" (43:1). The person who does not wish to belong to someone else (in a mutual belonging) consigns himself or herself to perpetual isolation and loneliness.

Many people today also are suspicious of binding themselves forever. Yet that is what love aspires to: "I'll love you for always." "Love seeks to be definitive; it cannot be an arrangement 'until further notice' " (CCC 1646). When there is acceptance of a permanent bond of love, one enjoys the goodness of knowing one is entering a stable home or haven, that one's belonging to another — and that other's belonging to one — is lasting. People want this, and while they know it will require sacrifices, "it is natural for the human heart to accept demands, even difficult ones, in the name of love for an ideal, and above all in the name of love for a person" (Pope John Paul II, address of April 21, 1982).

Many people today, finally, are suspicious of the burdens of having children. Yet nothing can so express not only the natural desire for individual self-perpetuation but the even more vital desire of love between husband and wife to incarnate itself in a new flesh. The fruitfulness of the conjugal union fulfills man's and woman's normal longing for self-perpetuation and for the perpetuation, in offspring, of their conjugal love. "A child does not come from outside as something added on to the mutual love of the spouses, but springs from the very heart of that mutual giving, as its fruit and fulfillment" (CCC 2366).

No normal person wants to be *just one* of the wives or the husbands of another. No normal person wants to be accepted as spouse on trial or *just for a time*. No normal person marries positively *excluding children*.

To this we must of course add that, however attractive the marital commitment, it is also something demanding. Times are bound to come in each marriage where one or both spouses undergo the strain of the permanent and exclusive commitment or feel weighed down by the burden of caring for their children or experience the difficulty of observing the intimate connection God has established between love, sexuality, and procreation. It is important that they should have prepared for such difficult moments, by having frequently called to mind the beauty of generous conjugal love, the fact that marriage is a way of holiness, and the great rewards God has in store for those faithful to commitments freely assumed: "Be faithful until death, and I will give you the crown of life" (Rv 2:10). In prayer they will receive grace from God to be faithful.

Canonical Aspect • From the viewpoint of anthropology, which studies the natural character of marriage, the *bona* can be said to express the main aspects of the marital commitment two people in love naturally seek. It falls to legal science to study the juridic aspects of marriage, where the interplay of rights and obligations can give rise to questions of justice. It is logical therefore that the law of the Church has considered the *bona* from the viewpoint of the fundamental rights and obligations they involve, and the canonical consequences if they are not accepted or respected.

While the Church must faithfully uphold Our Lord's teaching that the marriage bond (once properly constituted) is indissoluble (Mt 19:8), she is also aware that not every apparent marital bond was in fact validly contracted. Then justice demands that this invalid marriage be declared never to have existed. Precisely one of the main ways in which this can happen is by the exclusion on the part of one or both parties of an essential property of marriage. If, while pronouncing the proper words of consent, a person internally excludes one of the *bona*, this is termed "simulation" (pretending to give proper consent in contradiction to one's real interior intention). If the exclusion can be proved, the Church's tribunals will declare such a "marriage" null, that is, that in fact there never was any real marriage at all.

As should be clear, a person who genuinely accepts another as spouse, but later discovers that the other only accepted him or her "on trial" or with the resolution of always excluding any possibility of children, has been seriously wronged. In justice, he or she should not be held to such a false "marriage" bond.

At the same time, while exclusion of one of the *bona* can and does occur, it is important to bear in mind how deeply *unnatural* it is, at least for a person in love. It directly contradicts the "conjugal instinct" that human love naturally inspires. It means instrumentalizing the other person, treating him or her simply as an object of a self-centered experiment in satisfaction, as a means to a temporary advantage. That is why people truly in love do not think of excluding any of these essential values of marriage but rather look to confirming their love in a singular and permanent choice of one another as husband and wife, with the hope of seeing their love become incarnate in its natural fruit, their own children.

It must be acknowledged that not only have Church tribunals studied the *bona* mainly as obligations, but much moral and pastoral reflection has dwelt on them in the same light. An unwanted and unfortunate result may have been to obscure the natural attractiveness of these goods. A true revival in understanding of marriage as a normal commitment, as a way of fulfillment, and as a supernatural vocation calls for a renewed understanding of the *positive* nature of the *bona*: of how they correspond to the innate aspirations of true conjugal love between man and woman.

See: Annulment; Augustinianism; Body and Soul; Canon Law; Indissolubility of Marriage;

Manichaeism; Marriage; Marriage Covenant; Marriage, Sacrament of; Sexuality, Human; Theology of the Body.

Suggested Readings: CCC 1643-1648, 1652-1654, 2364-2366. C. Burke, "Personalism and the *bona* of Marriage," *Studia Canonica* 27 (1993), pp. 401-412.

Cormac Burke

MARRIAGE IN THE OLD TESTAMENT

The Book of Genesis contains two accounts of the creation of the sexes and the institution of marriage. "God created man in his own image. . . ; male and female he created them. And God blessed them, and God said to them, 'Be fruitful and multiply' " (Gn 1:27-28). "Then the Lord God said, 'It is not good that the man should be alone: I will make him a helper fit for him'. . . [and God made woman]. Then the man said, 'This at last is bone of my bones and flesh of my flesh'. . . . Therefore a man leaves his father and his mother and cleaves to his wife, and they become one flesh" (Gn 2:18-24).

In these texts, the basic equality of the sexes appears, along with their complementary roles. The two institutional ends of marriage — procreation and the good of the spouses — are also indicated. The expression "the two become one flesh" presupposes a singular and inseparable union, the marriage bond being therefore exclusive by nature (one man with one woman) and breakable only by death.

Although the chosen people of the Old Testament received this revelation about the nature of marriage, they did not always observe it in practice. Procreation was given such importance that a man was allowed to have several wives. Moreover, divorce was allowed in certain instances. Jesus, against all the currents of his times, rejected divorce as contrary to the divine plan ("from the beginning it was not so" [Mt 19:8]). He insisted on the uniqueness of the marriage covenant, where two become an *inseparable* one: "Have you not read that he who made them from the beginning made them male and female, and said, 'For this

reason a man shall leave his father and mother and be joined to his wife, and the two shall become one'? So they are no longer two but one. What therefore God has joined together, let no man put asunder" (Mt 19:4-6).

See: Divorce; Indissolubility of Marriage; Judaism; Marriage; Marriage Covenant; Marriage, Sacrament of; Old Covenant.

MARRIAGE, SACRAMENT OF

Marriage was instituted by God from the start of the creation of humankind (Gn 1:27-28, 2:18-24). It represents a major part of the divine design for the good of persons — of the spouses and children — as well as of society.

For Christians, marriage is much more. It is also a sacrament, one of those "efficacious signs of grace, instituted by Christ and entrusted to the Church, by which divine life is dispensed to us, [and which] . . . bear fruit in those who receive them with the required dispositions" (CCC 1131). Marriage between Christians is therefore a source of grace. "Since it signifies and communicates grace, marriage between baptized persons is a true sacrament of the New Covenant" (CCC 1617).

It is a defined dogma of faith that marriage is one of the seven sacraments, although the exact moment when Jesus raised it to the sacramental level is not certain (as it is not certain in the case of Confirmation or Anointing of the Sick). Nevertheless, a common opinion would assign it to the wedding feast of Cana (Jn 2:1-11), sanctified by the presence of Jesus and the occasion of his first miracle. There the Church sees "the confirmation of the goodness of marriage and the proclamation that henceforth marriage will be an efficacious sign of Christ's presence" (CCC 1613).

While Matrimony does not confer a sacramental "character," as do Baptism, Confirmation, and Holy Orders (cf. CCC 1121), it does consecrate a person to and for a special way of life, and so becomes a source of continuing graces. The *Catechism of the Catholic Church* (1535), putting Matrimony alongside Holy Orders as involving a "particular consecration," quotes Vatican Council

II: "Christian spouses have a special sacrament by which they are fortified and receive a kind of consecration in the duties and dignity of their state. By virtue of this sacrament, as spouses fulfill their conjugal and family obligations, they are penetrated with the Spirit of Christ, who fills their whole lives with faith, hope and charity. Thus they increasingly advance towards their own perfection, as well as towards their mutual sanctification" (*Pastoral Constitution on the Church in the Modern World, Gaudium et Spes*, 48).

What a sacrament symbolizes or signifies is important. Still more important is that it causes, or effects, what it signifies. Naturally enough, theological reflection centers particularly on this efficacy of the sacraments: on how they sanctify, more than on what they signify. Baptism, through the symbol of cleansing by water, actually purifies the soul from sin. Dogmatic treatises on the Eucharist (leaving aside the aspect of sacrifice) dwell not just on its representative value of nourishment for the individual or of a fraternal meal, but particularly on its effect in bringing about a real participation, in the individual and the community, in the actual life of Christ. This is generally true of the other sacraments. The thought of the Church has dwelt more on what each effects than on what it signifies.

Peculiarly, this has not been the case with the sacrament of Matrimony. Theological reflection has rather centered on its sign-function — Christian matrimony as signifying a great supernatural reality (union of Christ and the Church), while paying little attention to its sanctifying effect on the spouses themselves. Given the teaching of Vatican II on the universal call to holiness (*Dogmatic Constitution on the Church, Lumen Gentium*, Ch. V; cf. CCC 2012-2013), a new emphasis seems called for.

Effects of Matrimony • A point that makes Matrimony unique among the sacraments should be noted. Only in it is a natural reality — the conjugal covenant — raised to the permanent dignity of a sacrament: The natural marital relationship is sacramentalized. Thus the highest form of human community is sanctified; and grace is conferred

so that the fruitful union of the sexes, made in the Trinitarian image of God, can infuse supernatural love into the conjugal and family relationship between Christians.

While all the sacraments are sacraments of union, Eucharist and Matrimony are specially so. The Eucharist makes each individual one with Christ. Matrimony makes two individuals one with one another, identifying them at the same time with Christ. The love and union of persons is the whole purpose of existence, its paragon being the Blessed Trinity. Christ comes to incorporate all of us into this loving union. But such a union can only be achieved for us through self-giving that entails generosity, that is, through sacrifice. If marriage is a sign of the loving union of Christ and his Church, its particular effect is to enable the spouses to achieve a similar union, of love expressed in sacrifice. Conjugal love has to be sacrificial like that of Christ, who "loved the church and gave himself up for her" (Eph 5:25).

Traditional theological reflection, in seeing marriage as a sign of the union between Christ and his Church, has tended to see the husband's role in the image of Christ and the wife's in that of the Church (cf. Eph 5:21-33). Today's Magisterium tends to stress, along with equal dignity between the spouses, their equality of dedication and sacrifice as a basis for their marital relationship and their sanctity (cf. CCC 1642).

Christians, like non-Christians, marry because they are attracted by the good things marriage promises: love, companionship, support, a stable home, children. These are great values, to be received and given. They are always threatened by individual selfishness. Today in particular, they receive no help — rather the opposite — from the atmosphere prevailing in society. Such a lifelong intimate relationship as marriage is not possible without developing an open and generous heart, a condition of human and supernatural charity. This can only be achieved with a particular help of God. The help is there; but it must be adverted to and made use of. In marrying, Christians, perhaps without realizing it, receive graces — gifts — to strengthen them to live marriage in the fullness of the conjugal commitment and so to achieve its true ends.

Marriage is a union between equals based on mutual love and complementarity. The mutuality of the sacrament is underlined by the teaching constantly followed in the Latin Church, that the spouses themselves are its ministers (cf. CCC 1623). It is important that they not lose the sense of being ministers and mediators of grace to one another, throughout the whole of their married life.

Christian marriage does not create new obligations substantially distinct from those characterizing non-Christian marriage. It simply provides the spouses with help and strength to fulfill their natural conjugal obligations and achieve their Christian goal. As Pope Pius XI teaches in his 1930 encyclical *On Christian Marriage, Casti Connubii*, spouses are "not fettered but adorned, not hampered but assisted by the bond of the sacrament." Reflection on this truth might dispel the prejudices some Catholics have against "sacramental" marriage. When marriage is considered as a means and source of grace, its demands are seen as positive, exhibiting a greatness of purpose that shows them to be worthwhile on a totally new level.

Specific Graces of Marriage • Conjugal and family self-giving are a way of achieving union with God. In loving each other and their children, married people learn to love God. So the *Catechism* says: "Charity upholds and purifies our human ability to love, and raises it to the supernatural perfection of divine love" (1827).

Like all the sacraments, Matrimony offers distinctive graces, which correspond to the peculiar aspirations, challenges, duties, and difficulties of married life. These graces certainly include the following.

First of all, there is the grace that reinforces the couple's love so that it does not give way under the difficulties of a lifelong commitment, but is strengthened and grows. "This grace proper to the sacrament of Matrimony is intended to perfect the couple's love and to strengthen their indissoluble unity. By this grace they 'help one another to attain holiness in their married life. . .' " (CCC 1641; cf. 1661).

Love means loving the other as he or she is, that is, as a real person with defects. The hardest tests of married life come when romance wanes and couples begin to discover the extent of each other's defects. The sacrament must offer special and particularly strong graces for living through such moments, learning to forgive, to ask for forgiveness, to develop the aptitude for dwelling on one's partner's positive characteristics and not becoming obsessed with those that appear negative: in a word, to keep loving one another in a truly self-sacrificial, Christ-like way.

Matrimonial grace is no doubt further specified in the way it strengthens each spouse in sexual identity and donation: helping the man develop his distinctive spousal self-gift in a masculine mode and dedication, and the woman in a feminine mode and dedication. The unity of marriage is not just indissoluble, nor simply interpersonal; it is intersexual. It calls for a growth in sexual identity, so threatened today by the tendency to belittle God's gift of sexual differences, character, and function.

A particular task of married love — for which the sacrament provides grace — is to purify the sexual relationship between husband and wife of elements of selfishness and exploitation that, in the present state of human nature, can affect it (cf. CCC 1606-1607). One effect of original sin is to make man and woman become too immediately absorbed with the physical aspects and sense attraction of sex, preventing them from reaching, "seeing," and understanding the inner meaning and real substance and value of sexual differences and complementarity, and especially from sharing in the full meaning of conjugal-sexual self-giving. The sacrament of Matrimony therefore provides special graces for living conjugal chastity.

This chastity calls for a certain strength and restraint as between husband and wife, and makes them vigilant toward the tendency not to honor the mystery of their reciprocal sexuality or not to act according to the laws their mind discovers in it: a tendency that is a temptation to use, and not to respect, the other. Little is said today of conjugal chastity, yet its absence leads to the undermining of the mutual regard that should characterize the love of the spouses, as well as of the true freedom with which their reciprocal spousal donation should be made. Marital chastity is an essential safeguard for the strength, tenderness, and permanence of conjugal love. It is not likely to be attained without the help of special graces (cf. CCC 1608).

The married couple usually and naturally become a family, for spousal love is normally meant to develop into parental love. Matrimony undoubtedly offers particular sacramental graces for the unfolding of personalities, redirection of affections, and acquisition of new abilities involved in this gradual and vital process, so powerfully geared to the maturing of persons.

It is a particular mission of parents to mediate God's paternal and maternal love. The sacrament of Matrimony should therefore grant spouses special graces to grow in parental identity and love so that each learns to be a true father or mother. A sanctified marriage means a marriage where the partners have learned to be holy spouses and holy parents.

From the purely natural viewpoint, the family, with its unique functions of humanizing and socializing, is rightly called the first vital cell of society. From the Christian point of view, married couples, along with their children, are called also to be a Gospel leaven in the world. The sacramental graces peculiar to the married state must be designed to give powerful apostolic stimulus and strength. If a couple are not aware of these graces — if they are not often reminded of them, in pre- and postmarriage preaching and catechesis — they may fail to activate them or rely on them, and so miss a large part of that Christian evangelizing mission so peculiarly theirs. Nothing can so contribute to bringing the world to God as the example of married couples living their conjugal and family life in active reliance on these graces.

Regarding this apostolic dimension, the *Catechism* places Matrimony together with Holy Orders, saying these two sacraments "are directed towards the salvation of others; if they contribute as well to personal salvation, it is through service

to others that they do so" (1534). In loving each other and their children, spouses offer a witness to generosity and faithfulness that can draw those around them powerfully to God. The *Catechism* relates conjugal fidelity to "the fidelity of God to his covenant . . . [and] of Christ to his Church. Through the sacrament of Matrimony the spouses are enabled to represent this fidelity and witness to it" (1647).

Like all other graces of the Christian life, the graces specific to the sacrament of Matrimony must be *relied on*; they must be *sought* and *prayed for*. If a married couple lives unaware of them, without invoking them constantly, it is unlikely that their married life can be happy or even survive. Couples who do rely on these graces — and constantly invoke them — will have God's special help to achieve union and happiness and eternal life.

See: Apostolate; Chastity; Concupiscence; Contraception; Divorce; Domestic Church; Family; Grace; Hierarchy; Indissolubility of Marriage; Marriage; Marriage, Goods of; Sacrament; Sexuality, Human; Theology of the Body; Women, Ecclesial and Social Roles of.

Suggested Readings: CCC 1601-1666. John Paul II, *The Christian Family in the Modern World, Familiaris Consortio*. G. Grisez, *The Way of the Lord Jesus*, Vol. 2, *Living a Christian Life*, pp. 596-615.

Cormac Burke

MARTYRDOM

Of the many powerful changes the Second Vatican Council wrought in modern Catholic spirituality, none is more important than its emphasis on the positive living by all of lives of charity. We are encouraged, for example, to reflect on God's love for us, to build a personal relationship with Jesus, and to help bring justice and peace to the earth. Inevitably, this swing of the pendulum has thrown other aspects of Christianity like sin, penance, and self-sacrifice into the shade. Martyrology, the study of those who gave their lives for the faith, lacks the prominence it had even a generation ago.

One may mourn what has been lost even while welcoming the new emphasis. Tertullian, an irascible Carthaginian theologian writing around A.D. 200, is famous for the poetic phrase "The blood of martyrs is the seed of the Church." This translation takes liberties with the Latin original that, literally rendered, reads: "We become many whenever you mow us down; the blood of Christians is seed" (*Apology*, 50). In either case, Tertullian's observation hangs on an agricultural metaphor; the verb *meto* ("mow down") refers to reaping, harvesting. Just as autumn's crop dies and seeds the spring, so new Christians rise up from the death of martyrs. Christianity, like any other system of belief, thrives on commitment, and the commitment of martyrs is inspiration for the ages.

The Meaning of Martyrdom • "Martyr" in Greek means "witness." In Scripture, it usually refers to people who testified to their faith in Jesus Christ, whether or not they suffered as a result. The association with blood came later, when witnessing to Christ could mean facing lions in the arena. Three things are required for martyrdom: The victim must die, the murderers must kill out of hatred for the Christian way of life and Christian truth, and death must be voluntary. While some theologians allow exceptions to the final criterion, as in the case of the Holy Innocents, the essence of martyrdom is imitating Christ's example both in living one's life and in giving it for a higher cause. "Therefore . . . walk in love, as Christ loved us and gave himself up for us, a fragrant offering and sacrifice to God" (Eph 5:1-2).

Martyrs, the great majority of them known to God alone, have been part of the Christian experience from the beginning. Certainly thousands died in the early Roman persecutions, and many thousands more have perished in the wars, purges, divisions, and conflicts that pockmark Christian history. The first reliable written account of a martyrdom is that of Polycarp, Bishop of Smyrna in modern-day Turkey, who was burned alive in 155. In our own time, many believe, Catholics have been martyred in Cambodia, Vietnam, El Salvador, and many other countries.

One usually thinks of martyrs as dying "for the faith," without questioning the meaning of that phrase. In reality, it covers a wide range of circumstances. U.S. Catholics are familiar both with St. Isaac Jogues, S.J., and the other "North American martyrs" and with St. Maria Goretti. The first were adult missionaries killed by the Iroquois in the 1640s while trying to plant Christianity in a pagan culture. St. Maria, on the other hand, was an eleven-year-old Italian girl stabbed to death resisting rape in 1902; she paid the ultimate price for fidelity to the religion and system of moral truth in which she had been raised. What is the common element?

Pope John Paul II's 1993 encyclical on moral theology — *The Splendor of Truth, Veritatis Splendor* — devotes a section to martyrdom, arguing that martyrs witness not just beliefs but *true* beliefs. In the case of Maria Goretti and others, furthermore, this belief concerns moral truth. The encyclical condemns theories that, by denying the existence of absolute good and evil, relativize even the commandments of God and reduce all moral assertions to mere opinions, viewpoints, and perspectives. Martyrdom, in its finality and integrity, attests to belief in the existence of a universally valid and objective moral order, since people do not willingly die for an opinion; and the honor paid by the Church to martyrs solemnly attests to her own belief in the same. "This witness [of martyrdom]," the Holy Father says, "makes an extraordinarily valuable contribution to warding off in civil society and within the ecclesial communities themselves a headlong plunge into the most dangerous crisis which can afflict man: the confusion between good and evil, which makes it impossible to build up and to preserve the moral order of individuals and communities" (*The Splendor of Truth,* 92).

Witness to Truth • The willing death of martyrs, then, has a significance beyond the welfare of the Catholic Church or even of Christianity itself. Polycarp of Smyrna going to the stake was not simply defending Christian beliefs; he was acknowledging a body of moral law to which all are accountable, whether this law is known by reason or Revelation. According to an eyewitness account of his martyrdom: "The governor then said 'I have wild beasts here. Unless you change your mind, I shall have you thrown to them.' 'Why, then, call them up,' said Polycarp, 'for it is out of the question for us to exchange a good way of thinking for a bad one. It would be a very creditable thing, though, to change over from the wrong to the right.' " By honoring martyrs in our turn, we affirm that the cause for which they died has value because it conforms to the actual will of God and the truth about humanity.

Pope John Paul II, noting the rarity of martyrdom, speaks of "a consistent witness which all Christians must daily be ready to make, even at the cost of suffering and great sacrifice. Indeed, faced with the many difficulties which fidelity to the moral order can demand even in the most ordinary circumstances, the Christian is called . . . to a sometimes heroic commitment" (*Veritatis Splendor*, 93). Consider the man who repeatedly resists the temptation to advance his career dishonestly. Consider the woman who makes an agonized decision to bear, and not to kill, her unborn child. All who struggle to uphold the moral truth the Church faithfully teaches participate in that witness that the martyr gives most fully.

Nevertheless, martyrdom has a hard, sharp clarity that no lesser sacrifice can approach. It is the argument for God and God's way to which there is no response. The *Catechism of the Catholic Church* (2474) quotes Polycarp's final prayer to illustrate his faith. Perhaps more touching, because it is more simple, is the narrator's summation: "It is to him, as the Son of God, that we give our adoration; while to the martyrs, as to disciples and imitators of the Lord, we give the love they earned by their matchless devotion to their King and Teacher. Pray God we too may come to share their company and their discipleship."

See: Absolute Moral Norms; Apostolate; Christian Witness; Moral Principles, Christian.

Suggested Readings: CCC 2473-2474. John Paul II, *The Splendor of Truth, Veritatis Splendor*, 90-94. "The Martyrdom of Polycarp," *Early Christian Writings: The Apostolic Fathers*.

David M. Byers

MARY, MOTHER OF GOD

To invoke Mary as the Mother of God is to pay her the highest honor and to call upon her with a name that Christians have been using in their prayers for some seventeen centuries. According to Vatican Council II: "From the earliest times the Blessed Virgin is honored under the title of 'Mother of God' (Theotokos), under whose protection the faithful take refuge together in prayer in all their perils and needs" (*Dogmatic Constitution on the Church, Lumen Gentium*, 66). The footnote to the text of this teaching by the Council calls our attention to the following most ancient prayer to Mary, in which she is addressed by the title Theotokos: "We fly to thy patronage, O holy Mother of God (Theotokos), despise not our petitions in our necessities, but deliver us from all danger, O ever glorious and blessed Virgin. Amen." Some scholars date the origin of the Greek version of this prayer (usually called, in Latin, the Sub Tuum Praesidium) as early as the third century; if this is correct, the title Theotokos would go back in our Catholic tradition at least as far as the century before Alexander, the Patriarch of Alexandria, who is the first to have used it in his writings in 325. It would also mean that the title was on the lips of the faithful for about two centuries before Mary's role as Theotokos was defined as a dogma at the Council of Ephesus (431). As a witness to apostolic faith about Mary, the testimony to the title's usage on that part of the teaching and believing Church is indeed very early.

The English translation of the Greek word Theotokos as Mother of God is accurate enough, but it does not really capture the richness of the original. "God-Bearer," "Birth-Giver of God," "Bringer-forth-of God," etc., have all been used in the attempt to make its meaning more clearly available in the vernacular. It is a most worthwhile theological endeavor to trace the term's origins. St. Athanasius (c. 295-373), who succeeded Alexander as Patriarch of Alexandria, used it frequently in his writings along with the members of the School of Alexandria. St. Cyril of Jerusalem (died c. 386) and Eusebius of Caesarea (c. 260-c. 340) used the title for Mary in early Christian Palestine, as did the three Cappadocians — Sts. Basil the Great (c. 330-379), Gregory Nazianzus (c. 329-c. 390), and Gregory of Nyssa (c. 335-c. 394) — during the latter half of the fourth century in Asia Minor in what is now Turkey.

The attempts to translate Theotokos into Latin have also had their limitations in the Western Church. *Mater Dei* (Mother of God), *Dei Genetrix* (She who has borne God), and *Deipera* (Birth-Giver of God) have been the most customary. Etymologically, *Deipera* comes closest to the meaning of Theotokos and is found in the Latin text of the title of chapter VIII of *Lumen Gentium*, which also refers to it in the passage from section 66 quoted above.

The Nestorian Controversy • Trying to determine the meaning of Theotokos as clearly as possible helps us grasp more profoundly the Nestorian controversy that led to its dogmatic definition at the Council of Ephesus. This crisis was primarily and essentially Christological, since it centered upon the real meaning of the dogma of the Incarnation, that is, faith in Jesus Christ as the Word made flesh, conceived and born of Mary as true God and true man. Nestorius, the Patriarch of Constantinople (died c. 451), had been asked to make a pronouncement on the aptness of Theotokos as a title for Mary. Although it had been in use at least a century and probably longer, he ruled in favor of Christotokos, "Christ-Bearer." His reasons for rejecting Theotokos were the fear that this title would make Mary appear to be a goddess who begets divinity; or that it would risk reducing the Son of God to a mere creature, as the Arian heresy (condemned by the Council of Nicaea in 325 and again by the Council of Constantinople in 381) had done during the previous century; or that it could make the human nature of Christ seem incomplete, as had the heresy of Apollinarius, who denied the incarnate Lord had a human soul (also condemned at Constantinople).

These concerns of Nestorius were based upon his problem with the so-called "communication of idioms" or what might be termed in more contemporary parlance the "mutual reciprocity of predications." This axiom in Christology asserts that whatever characteristics and experiences Christ had as human can be said of him as God, and vice versa, because his one divine personality unites both his human and divine natures. Thus God was really and truly conceived and born of the Virgin Mary, and God suffered and died for us on the cross, even though such predications can be made of the God-man only by reason of his human nature. Also, concretely, Jesus of Nazareth may be said to be almighty, but only in virtue of his divinity as hypostatically united to his humanity: that is, the subject of the predicate "almighty," which is "Jesus of Nazareth," is the Son of God (divine) and the Son of Mary or Word made flesh (human).

In fairness to Nestorius, it should be noted that this dogmatic clarity about the hypostatic unity of the divine and human natures in the one Person of God's own Son, through conception and birth of the Virgin Mary, was not defined as a dogma until the Council of Chalcedon (451) some twenty years after Ephesus — although the latter paved the way by its own dogmatic definition that Christ was true God as well as true man from the first instant of his conception in "the holy Virgin Theotokos."

New Testament Roots of the Dogma • Following the Councils of Ephesus and Chalcedon, Constantinople II (553) and Constantinople III (680-681) supplied further clarifications about the mystery of the Incarnation and so also about Mary's title as Theotokos, or Mother of God. We shall consider these later in this entry. Here, however, we need briefly to examine the continuity between the Christological affirmations of the New Testament and the dogma of the Theotokos, which is not a biblical title for Mary. It is necessary to see how the New Testament Revelation regarding the human origins (*tokos*) of Jesus from the Virgin Mary initiated a line of development in the Tradition that in time led the Church to call his Mother the Mother of God (*Theos*) in order to safeguard the mystery of the Word incarnate.

In the New Testament, a number of portraits of Christ, or Christologies, are revealed. The two with which we are here most concerned are a "conception Christology" and a "preexistence Christology."

Conception Christology is found most clearly in the infancy narratives of the Gospels of Matthew and Luke, especially in the latter's scene of the Annunciation, where we ponder these words: "And behold, you will conceive in your womb and bear a son, and you shall call his name Jesus. He will be great, and will be called the Son of the Most High; and the Lord God will give to him the throne of his father David, and he will reign over the house of Jacob for ever; and of his kingdom there will be no end . . . therefore the child to be born of you will be called holy, the Son of God" (Lk 1:31-35).

Preexistence Christology is revealed in the Prologue to John's Gospel: "In the beginning was the Word: the Word was with God and the Word was God. . . . The Word became flesh . . ." (Jn 1:1, 14).

Actually, Christ's preexistence as divine before becoming flesh, assuming a human nature from Mary in time, is also found in St. Paul (cf. 1 Cor 8:6) as well as in the Prologue of John's Gospel. But the fourth evangelist makes it abundantly clear and explicit that the same Word (Logos), who became incarnate, or flesh, is also God (Theos). Usually in the New Testament only the Father in the Triune God is called Theos. To predicate "God" of the "Word" who "was made flesh" is thus a real basis in the New Testament for calling Mary Theotokos, meaning Birth-Giver of God, or Mother of God.

After the conclusion of the New Testament era, the New Testament conception and preexistence Christologies came to be combined in Sacred Tradition. This had not been explicitly done in Scripture, but the inspired authors of the New Testament did plant the roots and lay the groundwork. Here, then, we behold an excellent example of how Sacred Tradition may develop dogmas that are rooted, but not explicitly affirmed, in Sacred Scripture.

While it is well beyond the scope of this entry to go into the manifold details of this process in the history of the ancient Christian writers and Fathers and doctors of the early Church, it can be said that the development and its definitive conclusion at Ephesus both took place under the infallible guidance of the Magisterium. When those participating in the Council of Ephesus were confronted by the Nestorian crisis, they were obliged — like the conciliar Fathers at Nicaea I about a century earlier, who were challenged to defend the apostolic faith during the Arian crisis — to search the Scriptures for answers to questions that could not be found there. To safeguard the biblical faith, that is, they had to give a response that was faithful to, but also went beyond, the Bible.

To put the matter in other terms, the Fathers at Ephesus had to do more than speak about what Christ *did* to accomplish our redemption, which had been the main intention of the inspired writers of the New Testament; they had to answer the question of who Christ *was* in accord with the very meaning of the mystery of the Incarnation. This was necessary in order to refute the objections of Nestorius against the use of the title Theotokos, objections that would inevitably have led to the rejection of the New Testament Revelation that Jesus Christ is true God and true man from the first instant of his conception in the Virgin Mary's womb. Ephesus achieved a response to the Nestorian question about Christ and his unique relationship to Mary, as Nicaea I had done in responding to the Arian question by adopting the term *Homoousion* ("consubstantial," or "One in Being with the Father") to express the coequality and coeternity of the Son with the first Person of the Blessed Trinity.

Reflecting upon such matters, one is forced to conclude that the human mind is never completely satisfied with a functional definition of any reality, that is, a definition based merely upon what it *does*. The mind instinctively reaches out to grasp what it *is*, its very being, essence, or nature that makes possible its activity. This applies not only to what we can know by reason alone but also to the supernatural truths of faith. Consequently, to the extent possible in this life (where understanding of divine mysteries can only come about by way of analogy or comparison with the objects of natural knowledge), it is logical for reason, enlightened by faith and operating through the discipline of theology, to seek understanding of the truth about Christ as true God and true man, in order to grasp the meaning and redemptive fruits of his Messianic mission.

This ontological or definitive mode of speaking, as distinct from the functional mode of the Bible, was characteristic of the early ecumenical councils of the Church, from Nicaea I in the fourth century through Constantinople III (680-681). Questions having arisen about the Holy Trinity, the Incarnation, and redemption that could not be answered by the biblical mode ("Who is the saving triune God and incarnate Word *for us*?"), it was necessary, in order to protect the truths of faith from heretical misinterpretation, to employ the conciliar or ontological mode ("Who is this God *in himself*, what are the internal relationships of the Divine Persons, and what is the definitive meaning of the dogma that one of these Persons — the Son, or Word — became one of us in the womb of the Virgin Theotokos, without in any way ceasing to be the Eternal Word or coequal Son of the Father?"). When the Council of Constantinople III defined that there are not only two natures in Christ but two wills (a human will as well as divine will) and so two operations, inseparable, undivided, and without confusion, the basic elements of faith in the mystery of the redemptive Incarnation were settled by the solemn universal Magisterium of the Church. Now the stage was set for further reflections upon the mystery in light of this definitive Christology.

The Theology of "Theotokos" • As is the case with all the articles of the Creed, St. Thomas Aquinas provides a theological reflection upon Mary's role and title as Theotokos at once faithful to the revealing word of God in Scripture and Tradition, as authentically interpreted by the Church's Magisterium, and helpful in making the mystery more intelligible to reason enlightened by faith. Frequently called the "Common Doctor" because his theology has contributed to the elucidation of all the Church's doctrines, St. Thomas provides an incisive explanation of the mystery of Mary's motherhood of God in the Christological section

of his monumental synthesis of sacred doctrine, the *Summa Theologiae* (Pt. III, q. 35, art. 4), where he asks "whether the Blessed Virgin should be called the Mother of God?" Beginning his inquiry, as always, by clearly exposing the difficulties involved in getting at the truth, Thomas raises three objections against what will be shown to be orthodox faith and right reason in the matter: First, the Scriptures do not explicitly call Mary the "mother of God," and we should not say anything about divine mysteries not contained in biblical Revelation; second, Christ is called God because of his divinity, which in no way takes its origin from Mary but only from the Father from all eternity; third, since "God" is predicated of the three Divine Persons, the title "Mother of God" would make Mary the Mother of the Father and the Holy Spirit as well as the Son.

In the part of the article designated *sed contra* ("on the contrary"), where he usually cites the authority for his teaching, Aquinas quotes St. Cyril of Alexandria, the defender of orthodoxy against Nestorius at the Council of Ephesus. His theological reasoning in the body of the article then proceeds on the basis of Chalcedonian Christology, as clearly defined in the early councils of the great Fathers of the Church. He writes: "Now to be conceived and to be born are attributed to the person or hypostasis in respect of that human nature in which it is conceived and born. Since therefore the human nature was assumed by the divine Person at the very outset of conception . . . it follows that it can truly be said that God was conceived and born of the Virgin. Now a woman is considered a man's mother when she has conceived and given birth to him. Therefore, the Blessed Virgin is truly called the mother of God."

The full meaning of "truly" (*vere*) here would seem to be that Mary is the Theotokos (*mater Dei*) in the proper sense, and not simply in an extended or metaphorical sense, because motherhood is always a relationship to the person who is conceived and born. Mary's maternal relationship to Christ is therefore precisely a relationship of motherhood to the second Person of the Blessed Trinity, the Son of God, who became incarnate in her by virginal conception at the Annunciation and was born by the virgin birth at the first Christmas. Thomas concludes the body of the article by saying that rejection of this doctrine leads to one or the other of two Christological errors: either the denial of the hypostatic unity of the divine and human natures in the one Person of the Word made flesh or else the heretical belief that Christ's human nature was conceived and born of Mary before he became the Son of God.

Thomas's reply to the first objection is that, although the New Testament does not explicitly call Mary "mother of God," still it does reveal both that Christ is God and that Mary is his Mother; this answers one of Nestorius's objections. Another is answered by Aquinas's reply to the second objection, namely, his explanation that Mary is the Mother of God, "not because (she is) the mother of the divinity, but because she is the mother of a Person who has divinity and humanity." His reply to the third objection, finally, is that, although the name "God" is commonly attributed to each of the three Divine Persons, it is necessary to determine from the context what is meant by any particular use of the name; thus, when we call Mary the Mother of God (or Theotokos), "God" here can apply only to the Son, who alone became incarnate.

Reflecting briefly upon the theological explanation of the Theotokos, we see that the notion of person (*persona* in Latin and *hypostasis* in Greek) is at the very heart of this probing of the mystery. The analogy with motherhood of human persons is helpful here. Even though through the act of procreation it is our flesh and blood that we receive from our mothers and not precisely our personhood, still we do speak of our mothers in relation to our coming into being as persons and not only in relation to the origin of our bodies. For example, we naturally say, "There is Joseph's mother" or "There is Mary's mother" rather than, "There is the mother of Joseph's body" or "Mary's body." So, analogously, even though the Son of God proceeded from Mary as her true flesh and blood, not in his divinity as coequally and coeternally from the Father, still Mary is concretely

the Mother of God in his human nature, which is really the humanity of the second Person of the Blessed Trinity. As our mothers need not be the principles of our souls in order to be maternally related to us as the persons we are, so Mary need not be the principle of the Son's divinity to be really related maternally to him as the Divine Person he is.

Also, it is a metaphysical axiom that activities and experiences are predicated of a *person*, not merely of the *part* of him or her through which he or she is acting or having the experience (e.g., it is not my mouth that speaks but *I* who speak, not my leg that was injured in an accident but *I* who was injured). This throws more light upon the application of the Christological axiom regarding "the mutual reciprocity of predicates," according to which human attributes, relationships, etc., can be predicated of God the Son: for example, that Mary is truly Mother of God because a Divine Person was conceived and born of her in his humanity wedded to his divinity.

Spiritual and Ecumenical Significance • Cardinal Newman remarks in one of his sermons that the "glories" of Mary "are not only for the sake of her Son; they are for our sakes too." Not only has Mary's title of Theotokos helped preserve the revealed truth about her incarnate Son, the Son of God; we may suppose that she has at the same time been watching over us, who must know the truth about Christ for the sake of our salvation. It is noteworthy that the solemn definition of his Christological dogma at Ephesus inspired the spread of filial devotion throughout the Catholic Church up to our own day.

After Vatican Council II, nevertheless, there did seem to be a decline in Marian devotion. Asked why he thought this had taken place, the theologian Karl Rahner said: "The special temptation that affects Christians today, Catholics and Protestants alike, is the temptation to turn the central truths of faith into abstractions, and *abstractions have no need of mothers*" (emphasis added). Mary's title as Theotokos is no mere abstraction but a concrete expression of a central truth of our faith in Christ the Son of God and Savior of the world. Today theologians seem to have moved beyond making it an abstract principle, from which all the other Marian doctrines might be deduced in a systematic Mariology; it may be interpreted as the main Marian idea, but concretely, in the context of salvation history, according to which Mary's motherhood of God incarnate is contemplated amid all of her Son's graces and the gifts of his Holy Spirit. Some of these (her Immaculate Conception and consecrated perpetual virginity) have made her a worthy Theotokos, while others have followed from her divine motherhood (her exemplary discipleship, her glorious Assumption, her spiritual maternity toward us all). With such a rich understanding of this most glorious title of Mary, we now are better prepared to pursue the ecumenical dialogue, especially with our Eastern Orthodox sisters and brothers. In its *Decree on Ecumenism* Vatican Council II teaches: "In this liturgical worship, the Eastern Churches pay high tribute, in beautiful hymns of praise, to Mary ever Virgin, whom the ecumenical synod of Ephesus solemnly proclaimed to be the holy mother of God (*Deipera, Theotokos*) in order that Christ might be truly and properly acknowledged as Son of God and Son of Man, according to the Scriptures" (*Unitatis Redintegratio*, 15). In recent years, one of the most ancient feasts (that of Mary, Mother of God) has been restored as a solemnity on January 1, the Octave of Christmas. Catholics do well to unite their hearts with those of all their fellow Christians in a special way on that day, as the presiding priest or bishop prays over the gifts: "On this feast of Mary, the Mother of God, we ask that our salvation will be brought to its fulfillment. We ask this through Christ our Lord." The fervent "Amen" — so be it — signals our petition to the heavenly Father that, through devotion to the Mother of his Son, all who are redeemed by him may come closer together in him who is the center of all unity.

See: Assumption of Mary; Christological Controversies; Development of Doctrine; Immaculate Conception; Incarnation; Jesus Christ, God and Man; Magisterium; Marian Devotion; Mary, Mother of the Church; Mary, Perpetual Virginity

of; Orthodox Churches; Sacred Tradition; Thomas Aquinas, Thought of.

Suggested Readings: CCC 484-495. Vatican Council II, *Dogmatic Constitution on the Church, Lumen Gentium*, Ch. VIII. John Paul II, *Mother of the Redeemer, Redemptoris Mater*. F. Jelly, O.P., *Madonna: Mary in the Catholic Tradition*, pp. 90-99, 142-144; "The Concrete Meaning of Mary's Motherhood," *The Way Supplement, Mary and Ecumenism* (June, 1982); "Marian Dogmas Within Vatican II's 'Hierarchy of Truth,' " *Marian Studies* (1976). D. Wuerl, R. Lawler, O.F.M. Cap., T. Lawler, eds., *The Teaching of Christ: A Catholic Catechism for Adults*, pp. 85-97.

F.M. Jelly, O.P.

MARY, MOTHER OF THE CHURCH

In his closing address to the third session of Vatican Council II on November 21, 1964, Pope Paul VI proclaimed Mary "Mother of the Church." He made clear and careful reference in doing so to the teaching of the Council's *Dogmatic Constitution on the Church, Lumen Gentium*, which dwelt upon the intimate relationship between Mary and the Church.

Pope Paul had received numerous requests from the Fathers at Vatican II that the maternal role of the Blessed Virgin Mary toward the Christian people be given very special attention. He acceded to this request, with these words: "Therefore, for the glory of the Blessed Virgin and our consolation, we declare most holy Mary Mother of the Church, that is of the whole Christian people, both faithful and pastors, who call her a most loving Mother; and we decree that henceforth the whole Christian people should, by this most sweet name, give still greater honor to the Mother of God and address prayers to her." Pope Paul also pointed out the close connection between Mary's motherhood of Christ, the Son of God incarnate, and her maternal relationship to the Church: "Mary is the Mother of Christ who, as soon as he assumed human nature in her virginal womb, took to himself as Head his Mystical Body, which is the Church.

Mary, therefore, as Mother of Christ is to be considered as Mother also of all the faithful and pastors, that is of the Church."

While the title "Mother of the Church" did not appear in the final *schema*, or draft, of chapter VIII of *Lumen Gentium*, which presents at length the Council's teaching about Mary, Paul VI's official proclamation of the title was received with joyous approval by the majority of the Fathers. Although there had been disagreement during the debate that took place on the Council floor in September, 1964, most of the Fathers wished the title restored to the *schema*; but the Council's theological commission decided it was better to express its meaning in equivalent terms, and this then was done in *Lumen Gentium*, 53: "The Catholic Church, taught by the Holy Spirit, honors her with filial affection and devotion as a most beloved mother."

This, then, was the setting for many of the Council Fathers to appeal directly to Pope Paul's intervention. His teaching about Mary's motherhood of the Church is in continuity with his predecessors in the Chair of Peter: Pope Benedict XIV, from whom Vatican II borrowed the words that express the title equivalently in *Lumen Gentium*; Pope Leo XIII, whose encyclical *Adjutricem Populi* calls Mary "Mother of the Church" in her role as the teacher and "Queen of Apostles," who learned many of the divine mysteries from her; Pope St. Pius X in *Ad Diem Illum*, which speaks of the union between the faithful and Christ their Head in Mary's womb; Pope Pius XII in *Mystici Corporis Christi*, according to which Mary has bestowed upon her Son's Mystical Body the same loving care as a mother that she bestowed upon the infant Jesus; and Pope John XXIII, who used the title five times. Pope Paul also used it several times, both before and after his proclamation, which was the principal pronouncement made to the Council assembly by the Pope as its head.

Basis in Scripture • Even before Paul VI's pronouncement, there were Catholic exegetes who discerned New Testament foundations for the title Mother of the Church, especially in the Johannine writings and the infancy narrative of Luke's Gos-

pel. The fourth evangelist states: "When Jesus saw his mother, and the disciple whom he loved standing near, he said to his mother, 'Woman, behold your son!' Then he said to the disciple, 'Behold, your mother!' And from that hour the disciple took her to his own home" (Jn 19:26-27).

The spiritual symbolism of these verses — namely, the birth of the Christian community at the foot of the cross, with a mother-son relationship between Mary and the beloved disciple, who looks after her in the Johannine Church — has been expanded in the Catholic tradition. The emphasis has been shifted from the disciple-son's care of the disciple-mother, to Mary's maternal care of him and all faithful disciples in her Son's Church or eschatological family. This is Mary's spiritual motherhood "in order of grace" according to Vatican II (cf. *Lumen Gentium*, 61, 62). The symbolism of the "Woman at the foot of the Cross" seems to complete that initiated by the "Woman at Cana," where the evangelist provides an incipient sign of Mary's role as Mother of the Church in her request that Christ intervene by providing new wine, itself a symbol of the new creation, the Church; and this inspires his first disciples to believe in him (cf. Jn 2:1-11).

Especially when read in close connection with chapters 1 and 2 of Luke's Acts of the Apostles (concerning the birth of Christ's Body the Church on Pentecost), the first two chapters of Luke's Gospel (concerning the birth of Christ) imply that Mary, in becoming Mother of Christ, already became Mother of the Church. In giving birth to the Head, she also begot the members of his Body. Of course there is a striking similarity between Mary's motherhood and the maternal character of the Church, inasmuch as both have been decreed by the Father to mediate the Son's saving graces to us. At the same time, as with any analogy, there is a significant difference, since Mary's motherhood of the whole Church, pastors as well as all the faithful, is even more profoundly an aspect of the mystery of our continuous reception of Christ's new life of grace through our heavenly mother's intercession and mediation.

The Mary-Church analogy, which views

Mary's motherhood of the Church as the most excellent exemplar (or model) of the Church's own maternal role in the order of grace, has been further developed by contemplating the meaning of the overshadowing of the Holy Spirit at the Annunciation and the descent of the same Spirit at Pentecost. At the Annunciation the Spirit makes Mary alone fruitful with the Word made flesh in Christ's virginal conception; at Pentecost, the same Divine Person transforms Mary, in the company of her Son's other faithful disciples, into the firstfruits of the redemptive Incarnation. Thanks to Mary's motherhood of Christ and her spiritual, adoptive motherhood of the Church, the whole pilgrim Church upon earth is, as it were, a mother in the order of begetting and nourishing the grace of Christ in the world.

There is much more to explore about the special relationship between Mary and the Holy Spirit, so as to penetrate more deeply the mystery behind her title Mother of the Church. So, for example, to behold more clearly Mary as the masterpiece of the new creation in the Spirit, and to meditate (as did St. Maximilian Kolbe, the Polish priest who gave his life for another Auschwitz inmate during World War II) upon the Holy Spirit as the "Uncreated Immaculate Conception" in the bosom of the Holy Trinity, is to deepen our understanding of the spiritual richness contained in this title.

The Title in Tradition • Among the Fathers of the Church, St. Augustine comes closest to teaching the truth proposed in this title. His words, in his work *On Holy Virginity*, are quoted by Vatican II: "She is clearly the mother of the members of Christ . . . since she has by her charity joined in bringing about the birth of believers in the Church, who are members of its Head" (*Lumen Gentium*, 53). During the Middle Ages, Mary was called "Mother of the Nations" and "Mother of the Christian People." Sts. Peter Damian and Bonaventure spoke of the Church, respectively, as "coming from" and "taking its origin" from Mary.

Berengaud in the twelfth century seems to have been the first to use the title in the tradition. Commenting upon Revelation 12 ("the woman clothed in the sun"), he writes: "In this passage, we can also see the woman as Blessed Mary, since she is the *Mother of the Church* because she brought forth him who is the Head of the Church" (emphasis added). The title is found in an Irish litany that can be no later than the fourteenth century. From then on, testimony in the tradition increases concerning Mary's specific maternal role regarding the Church. Some of the more important names here are Denis the Carthusian, St. Peter Canisius, J.J. Olier, M.J. Scheeben, and J.B. Terrien. Lately the Anglican theologian John Macquarrie has proposed the title as an ecumenical rallying point for Catholics, Orthodox, and Protestants as well as Anglicans.

Recent Liturgical Developments • The recent sacramentary *Collection of Masses of the Blessed Virgin Mary* contains a total of forty-six Masses, twelve of which first appeared during the Marian Year observed by the Church from Pentecost, 1987, through the Feast of the Assumption, August 15, 1988. Three are dedicated to "The Blessed Virgin Mary, Image and Mother of the Church." They merit reflection for their doctrinal implications.

The introductory comments to the first of these new Marian Masses point out that it was composed in 1974 to encourage celebrations honoring Mary during the Holy Year of Reconciliation (1975), and that there are four key events of salvation history to which the texts make reference: (1) the Incarnation of the Word (the Preface recalls that Mary nurtured the Church at its very beginning by giving birth to our Savior); (2) the Passion of Christ, during which he made his Mother our mother also (Opening Prayer, Preface, Communion Antiphon A); (3) the outpouring of the Holy Spirit at Pentecost, when Mary was united in prayer with her Son's first disciples, thus becoming the perfect model of the Church at prayer (Preface); and (4) the Assumption of Our Lady into heaven, from which she watches over the pilgrim Church on earth with a mother's love until we all are reunited there (Preface). Appropriately, the lectionary for this new collection of Marian Masses chooses as the Gospel reading that section of John which speaks of Mary at the foot of her Son's cross, where he makes her spiritual mother to us as we are represented by the beloved disciple (Jn 19:25-27); and, as the first reading, Genesis 3:9-15, 20, the story of Eve and the Fall, which also stands as the prophetic protoevangelium (or first scriptural announcement of the Good News) perfectly fulfilled in Christ, Mary, and the Church.

The second Mass under this title especially celebrates the infinite goodness of God the Father, who has given us Mary as the perfect example of every Christian virtue, particularly (as the liturgical texts bring out) in her role as model of sublime love, of faith and hope, of profound humility, of perseverance in prayer (with other disciples of her Son), of worship in spirit, and of liturgical celebration.

The third Mass, which has the title "Image and Mother of the Church," celebrates the divine love expressed in giving Mary to the Church, to contemplate in her the flawless image of the Holy Trinity or all the Church hopes to become in heaven. The names that cluster as a crown about the head of the glorious Mother of the Church are: perfect disciple of Christ; virgin unsurpassed in the purity of faith; bride united with Christ in an unbreakable bond; virginal mother by the power of the Holy Spirit, in whose likeness the Church is called to beget and nourish the life of Christ's children conceived by the same Spirit through the preaching of the Gospel and Baptism; and queen adorned with the glory of her Lord forever.

The Scripture readings for the second Mass are Acts 1:12-14 (preparing for Pentecost by persevering in prayer with Mary) and John 2:1-11 (the wedding feast at Cana). For the third Mass, the readings are Revelation 21:1-5a (the new Jerusalem, beautiful as a bride adorned to greet her husband) and Luke 1:26-38 (the Annunciation).

The Teaching of the Catechism • The *Catechism of the Catholic Church* considers this doctrine under several headings. The first (CCC 964-965) — "Wholly united with her Son . . ." — concentrates upon the fact that Mary's maternal role in the Church is inseparable and directly derived from her union with the Word incarnate. "This union of the mother with the Son in the work of

salvation is made manifest from the time of Christ's virginal conception up to His death" (*Lumen Gentium*, 57). It is most manifest at the hour of his Passion, when Mary experienced *com*-passion — "suffering with" — at its fullest and he gave her to his beloved disciple (cf. *Lumen Gentium*, 58). After his glorious Ascension, Mary "aided the beginnings of the Church by her prayers" (*Lumen Gentium*, 69); while "we also see Mary by her prayers imploring the gift of the Spirit, who had already overshadowed her in the Annunciation" (*Lumen Gentium*, 59).

The *Catechism*'s second heading is ". . . also in her Assumption," which is said to be "a singular participation in her Son's Resurrection and an anticipation of the resurrection of other Christians" (966). The third heading, ". . . she is our Mother in the order of grace," contains the most extensive treatment in the *Catechism* of Mary's motherhood of the Church. It is especially important for understanding the mystery underlying this Marian title (CCC 967-970).

Mary's perfect fidelity to the Father's will, to the requirements of her Son's redemptive mission, and to every single inspiration of the Holy Spirit has made her the Church's model of faith and charity — indeed, the archetype of the Church, which sees in Mary the most excellent example and fulfillment of all that the Church herself is called to be. Mary's cooperation through obedience, faith, hope, and burning charity in the redemptive activity of her Son, sole Savior of the human race from the beginning to the end of time, is indeed "wholly singular," as Vatican II points out (*Lumen Gentium*, 61). Consenting, uniquely and wholeheartedly, to her calling to be the "Godbearer," and filled with grace from the first instant of her Immaculate Conception so as to be the worthy Mother of God, Mary was, as it were, the necessary condition willed by the Father to make his Son and hers the one Mediator of redemption to the whole world.

No other person among the redeemed in salvation history (and Mary is truly one of us, redeemed, even though singularly so by a preservative redemption making her the firstfruits of

Christ's victory over sin and death) has been given the same role as she in making our redemption possible. How fitting it therefore is that Mary continue her motherly role in heaven by continuous intercession and by mediating her Son's saving graces to the pilgrim Church on earth. Vatican Council II does not hesitate to call her our "Mediatrix" as well as our "Advocate," "Helper," and "Benefactress" (*Lumen Gentium*, 62). Nevertheless, the Council did not see fit to encourage invoking her by the name or title of Co-Redemptrix, since that is too easily misinterpreted as making her a fellow redeemer with Christ. Even though this title can be theologically explained in such a way as to avoid such a basic misconception, still the prefix "co-" ordinarily signifies a mutually cooperative effort between or among equals, for example, co-signers in a checking account; thus the term "Co-Redemptrix" can be quite confusing. On the other hand, the prefix "con-" does not have the same ambiguity, since it can apply to one who both cooperates with and is completely dependent upon and subordinate to another or others with whom he or she is cooperating. This obviously is the sense in which Mary may be said to cooperate with her Son, the sole redeemer of the human race, though it is safer not to invoke her as co-redemptrix lest it be misinterpreted.

Finally, the *Catechism* concludes its consideration of Mary's motherhood of the Church with two substantial quotations from Vatican II regarding the relationship of her mediation in the heavenly Church to Christ's unique mediatorship in applying the fruits of his redeeming love to humankind's continuous need for them throughout history. The first passage emphasizes the complete dependence of her salutary influences upon Christ's unique mediation, so that her mediation of his graces only serves to enhance his heavenly role (cf. *Lumen Gentium*, 60). The second appeals to the analogy of creation (creatures share in the one goodness of God reflected in a variety of ways) and compares it to the manifold ways in which human ministers share in their single source, the one eternal priesthood of Jesus Christ (cf. *Lumen Gentium*, 62). Mary's motherly mediation must

be properly understood as in no way adding to or taking away from her Son's unique mediation as the risen Lord in glory; her true glory is ever to be entirely transparent to his.

See: Church, Nature, Origin, and Structure of; Communio; Communion of Saints; Development of Doctrine; Immaculate Conception; Marian Devotion; Mary, Mother of God; Mary, Perpetual Virginity of; Redemption.

Suggested Readings: CCC 964-970. Vatican Council II, *Dogmatic Constitution on the Church, Lumen Gentium*, Ch. VIII. John Paul II, *Mother of the Redeemer, Redemptoris Mater.* D. Wuerl, R. Lawler, O.F.M. Cap., T. Lawler, eds., *The Teaching of Christ: A Catholic Catechism for Adults*, pp. 194-204. M. O'Carroll, C.S.Sp., *Theotokos: A Theological Encyclopedia of the Blessed Virgin Mary.* F. Jelly, O.P., "Mary and the Church," *New Catholic Encyclopedia*, Vol. 17; *Madonna: Mary in the Catholic Tradition*, pp. 37-68, 148-162.

F.M. Jelly, O.P.

MARY, PERPETUAL VIRGINITY OF

The mystery of Mary's perpetual virginity, embracing her entire life upon earth, customarily has been contemplated in the Catholic tradition according to its three major moments: her virginal conception of Christ (*virginitas ante partum*); her virginity in parturition, or giving birth to Christ (*virginitas in*, or *durante, partu*); and her perpetual virginity (*virginitas post partum*). The usage of this triple formula to express the fullness of this mystery of our faith became standard with St. Augustine (354-430), St. Peter Chrysologus (c. 400-c. 450), and Pope St. Leo the Great, whose pontificate was 440-461.

Actually, the title "ever virgin" became very popular as a name for Mary from the latter part of the fourth century on. Over the centuries Eucharistic Prayer I (Roman Canon of the Mass) has been: "In union with the whole Church we honor Mary, the ever-virgin mother of Jesus Christ our Lord and God." This is especially noteworthy, since the mystery of Mary's perpetual virginity is a dogma of our Catholic faith by reason of being taught by the ordinary universal Magisterium of the Church and not as a consequence of a solemn definition as is the case with her motherhood of God incarnate, her Immaculate Conception, and her Assumption. (The revealed truths taught by the ordinary Magisterium are most effectively communicated in the Sacred Liturgy, particularly the Eucharistic Liturgy.)

While the virginal conception is frequently expressed by the term "virgin birth," the former expression will be used throughout this entry to avoid confusing this first moment of the mystery with the second, namely, Mary's virginity in giving birth to Christ, or her virginal parturition. Moreover, it is important to resist the tendency of many Catholics, including those who practice their faith, to confuse the virginal conception of Christ with the defined dogma of Mary's Immaculate Conception. Both dogmas are misinterpreted as a result.

Virginal Conception • Mary's virginity in conceiving Christ at the moment of her *fiat,* her wholehearted free consent to God's calling that she become the Mother of his own Son incarnate at the Annunciation, is also termed "pneumatological" conception. That is, it took place through the power of the Holy Spirit, without the cooperation of male semen in the marital act. This dogmatic aspect of our faith in the mystery of Mary's virginity received not only the testimony of the infancy narratives in Matthew (1:18-25) and in Luke (1:26-38) but also the very early witness of an Apostolic Father in the Tradition, St. Ignatius of Antioch (died c. 110). The patristic testimony to the virginal conception is constant. The faith of the earliest creeds of the Church was shaped by this witness of the Gospels according to Matthew and Luke, as well as the witness of the Fathers and ancient Christian writers: ". . . by the power of the Holy Spirit he was born of the Virgin Mary and became man."

In the rather recent past, it has been proposed that the virginal or pneumatological conception may be interpreted only as a *theologoumenon* or *Christologoumenon*, that is, purely as a theological expression or Christological symbol for our Christian faith that Jesus Christ was really divine as well as human from the first instant of his human conception in the womb of Mary. This interpretation removes historicity or facticity from the virginal conception and, especially, from the New Testament evidence for it. The Catholic tradition does not favor such an exegesis of Matthew and Luke. In fact, these texts have had the greatest influence upon the tradition's faith in the facticity of the virginal conception. As the *Catechism of the Catholic Church* clearly points out, once we have assented to its historicity, then its symbolic value and spiritual significance are especially enriching (CCC 502-507).

Numerous theological reasons of fittingness are provided by St. Augustine and St. Thomas Aquinas for the virginal conception, and these continue to be handed on in the Church's Tradition. If God had not predestined that his Son be conceived and born of a virgin, and thus St. Joseph had been his natural father, Christ's divine origins would have been obscured because God the Father would not have been Jesus' *only* Father; Mary could not have been archetype (or most excellent exemplar) of the Church, who is also a virginal mother inasmuch as she gives birth to the members of Christ's Mystical Body through the spiritual regeneration of Baptism; the virginal conception is a sign that Mary conceived Christ in her heart (*in corde*) through faith before (*priusquam*) conceiving him physically in the flesh (*in carne*), as the Fathers were fond of saying in one way or another; the virginal conception was most fitting as a safeguard of the spiritual understanding of the Incarnation as the completely gratuitous work of the sovereignly gracious and merciful God, which is why Karl Barth, the outstanding Reformed theologian of the twentieth century, held fast to it without compromise.

As we ponder God's infinite wisdom, to the extent that it can be done in this life, these theological reasons of appropriateness enable us to share in that divine wisdom and begin to see things as God does. None even implicitly suggests that the mystery insinuates a negative attitude toward the marital act. After all, Christ transformed marriage into one of the seven sacraments in his Church.

Summarizing the Catholic position, the American bishops taught in their 1973 pastoral letter on Mary, *Behold Your Mother — Woman of Faith*: "The Virgin birth is not merely a symbolical way of describing God's intervention in human history. . . . We know what God has done not only from the text of the Bible, taken in isolation, but from the Bible as read, interpreted, and understood by the living Church, guided by the Holy Spirit. Catholic belief in the Virgin birth rests not on the Scriptures alone, but on the constant and consistent faith of the Church."

Virginal Parturition • Seeing in Mary's bringing forth of Christ the fulfillment of the Old Testament prophecy in Isaiah 7:14 that a virgin would both conceive and *bear* a child, Matthew reveals in his infancy narrative (1:25) that she remained a virgin in giving birth to Jesus. In the testimony of the Fathers of the West, this came to be understood as meaning that Mary's bodily integrity remained intact and she did not experience the ordinary pangs of childbirth. The Fathers of the East emphasized the aspect of her joy and freedom from pain in giving birth to Jesus. General agreement regarding this second major moment in Mary's virginity was formalized in the one undivided Church of the Fathers in the period between 375 and 425.

In a book appearing about a decade prior to Vatican Council II, Albert Mitterer maintained that the traditional interpretation of the preservation of Mary's bodily integrity is a virtual denial of the realism of her motherhood of Jesus. In response, Karl Rahner explained his own belief that Divine Revelation does not contain physiological details, and proposed that Mary's virginal parturition signifies that she, as the Immaculate Mother of the Word made flesh, was free from all sin and concupiscence, so that every moment of her childbearing as a graced human experience must have been qualitatively distinct from the birth-giving of mothers subject to sin's consequences. His inter-

pretation seems to accord with that of the Eastern Fathers.

Perpetual Virginity • Vatican II's teaching confirms the traditional Catholic faith in the dogma that Mary remained a virgin throughout her entire life: "Joined to Christ the head and in communion with all his saints, the faithful must in the first place reverence the memory 'of the glorious ever virgin Mary, Mother of God and of our Lord Jesus Christ' " (*Dogmatic Constitution on the Church, Lumen Gentium*, 52). The same ecumenical council also lends its authority to the dogmatic status of the first two major moments in her perpetual virginity: "This union of the Mother with the Son in the work of salvation is made manifest from the time of Christ's conception up to his death"; and, ". . . then also at the birth of Our Lord, who did not diminish his mother's virginal integrity but sanctified it, the Mother of God joyfully showed her firstborn Son to the shepherds and the Magi" (*Lumen Gentium*, 57).

St. Athanasius of Alexandria (c. 295-373), the champion of the true apostolic faith about the divinity of the Son against the Arian heresy of the fourth century, gave great prominence to Mariology in his development of Christology. Most likely he was the first among the Fathers of the Church to appeal to the scene of Mary at the foot of the cross (Jn 19:25) to prove her perpetual virginity. St. Epiphanius (c. 315-403), also an Eastern Father, is responsible for introducing "ever-virgin" into the Nicene Creed of the East.

The New Testament reference to the "brothers" and "sisters" of the Lord (Mk 6:3) has been for centuries, and still is today, a rather formidable objection against Mary's perpetual virginity. St. Jerome (c. 347-420), the outstanding Scripture scholar among the Fathers and doctors of the Church, responded to the objection. Replying to a book by one Helvidius that held up the virginal conception as a model for virgins in the Church and also commended Mary's marriage with Joseph as a model to married couples, inasmuch as they had children after the birth of Christ, St. Jerome countered with the interpretation that the "sisters" and "brothers" of the Lord to whom Scripture refers were really Christ's cousins. St. Jerome, however, eventually repudiated this view, since the Greek of the New Testament did have a definite word for "cousins." But, as Pope John Paul II lately has noted, there is no such word in Hebrew and Aramaic, and "the terms 'brother' and 'sister' therefore had a far broader meaning which included several degrees of relationship" (*Marian Catechesis*, August 28, 1996). A third interpretation came from Epiphanius, who was of the opinion that these were sons and daughters of Joseph from a previous marriage. Although this would be in accord with faith in Mary's perpetual virginity, it was contrary to the beliefs of Sts. Augustine and Jerome, who both considered Joseph also to be a virgin. One might also speculate that these were children of a sister of St. Joseph, brought up with Jesus after their own father died. In any case, we can safely conclude that, as the *Catechism of the Catholic Church* says, they were "close relations of Jesus, according to an Old Testament expression" (500).

The theological reason of fittingness for Mary's perpetual virginity that has come to us in the Catholic Tradition is based upon an ecclesiotypical Mariology. In this perspective, Mary is seen as a model of the Church's virginal motherhood of begetting and nurturing life in Christ, a role that also is "perpetual" in the sense that the Church will continue to perform these functions until Christ's Second Coming.

See: Assumption of Mary; Christological Controversies; Incarnation; Immaculate Conception; Marian Devotion; Mary, Mother of God; Mary, Mother of the Church.

Suggested Readings: CCC 496-507, 510. Vatican Council II, *Dogmatic Constitution on the Church, Lumen Gentium*, Ch. VIII. John Paul II, *The Mother of the Redeemer, Redemptoris Mater.* F. Jelly, O.P., *Madonna: Mary in the Catholic Tradition.* J. McHugh, *The Mother of Jesus in the New Testament.* K. Rahner, *"Virginitas in Partu:* A Contribution to the Development of Dogma and Tradition," *Theological Investigations*, IV. W. Thompson, *Christology and Spirituality.*

                                                      F.M. Jelly, O.P.

MASS

Because the Eucharist contains the Real Presence of Jesus Christ, Body and Blood, soul and divinity, it has been acclaimed by the Second Vatican Council as "the summit toward which the activity of the Church is directed [and] the fountain from which all her power flows" (*Constitution on the Sacred Liturgy, Sacrosanctum Concilium*, 10). In 1965, Pope Paul VI issued the encyclical *Mysterium Fidei*, which began with the statement: "The mystery of the Eucharist makes present again in a unique manner the sacrifice of the Cross, which was once offered on Calvary, continuously calls it to mind, and applies its saving power for the forgiveness of those sins we commit daily" (7).

Such is the Sacrifice of the Mass, which was instituted by Christ at the Last Supper. But long before Jesus celebrated the first Mass with his Apostles, God's chosen people had been celebrating each year the Passover that marked their liberation from bondage. They did this in obedience to God's command: "This day shall be a memorial feast for you, which all your generations shall celebrate with pilgrimage to the Lord, as a perpetual institution. . . . Keep, then, this custom of the unleavened bread. Since it was on this very day that I brought your ranks out of the land of Egypt, you must celebrate this day throughout your generations as a perpetual institution" (Ex 12:14, 17).

At the Last Supper, in which Jesus once again celebrated the Passover, he instituted a new memorial liturgy that would replace forever the paschal lamb and unleavened bread of the old covenant. God had commanded the Jewish people to celebrate the Passover meal on the eve of their exodus from Egypt and to observe it henceforth as a memorial feast through all generations. Similarly, Jesus instituted the Eucharistic sacrifice on the eve of his Passion and death, and then told his followers: "Do this in memory of me" (1 Cor 11:24).

Historical Overview • Faithful to the injunction of Christ, the early Christians safeguarded the Sacrifice of the Mass with reverent care during the times of persecution. St. Luke says: "They devoted themselves to the apostles' instruction and the communal life, to the breaking of bread and the prayers" (Acts 2:42). Around the year 155, St. Justin Martyr revealed the "Christian secret" — the Sacrifice of the Mass — in a treatise addressed to the pagan emperor Antoninus Pius (138-161).

On the day called the day of the sun, all who live in the cities or in the country gather together in one place, and the memoirs of the Apostles or the writings of the prophets are read, as long as time permits. Then, when the reader has finished, the one who presides verbally instructs and exhorts those present to imitate these good things.

Then we all rise and pray. When the prayers are concluded we exchange the kiss of peace.

There is then brought to the one who presides bread and a cup of wine mixed with water. Taking them, he gives praise and glory to the Father of the universe, in the name of the Son and the Holy Spirit, and he gives thanks [in Greek, *eucharistian*] for a considerable length of time for our being accounted worthy to receive these things at his hands. When he has concluded the prayers and thanksgivings, all the people express their assent by saying: "Amen."

When he who presides has given thanks and all the people have expressed their assent, those who are called deacons give to each of those present to partake of the bread and wine mixed with water, over which the thanksgiving was pronounced, and they carry away a portion for those who are absent. And this food is called among us the Eucharist. . . .

Sunday is the day on which we all hold our common assembly, because it is the first day on which God made the world, and Jesus Christ our Savior on the same day rose from the dead (*Apologia I*, 65-67).

This general outline of the celebration of the Eucharist has remained unchanged throughout the history of the Church. The Mass has been designated by many names, each of which stresses some particular aspect: "the breaking of the bread" (Acts 2:42, 46; 20:7), "the Lord's supper" (1 Cor 11:20); *Dominicum convivium* (Tertullian); "Eucharist" (in the postapostolic era); "liturgy" (in the Eastern Churches *synaxis*). However, in the Latin Church, Mass (from *Ite, missa est*) is the term that prevailed, although in recent years the term "Eucharist" has become more widespread. As the *Catechism of the Catholic Church* notes, the word Mass (*Missa*) is a reference to "the sending forth *(missia)* of the faithful, so that they may fulfill God's will in their daily lives" (1332).

Complex Reality of the Mass • "The Mass is at the same time, and inseparably, the sacrificial memorial in which the sacrifice of the cross is perpetuated and the sacred banquet of communion with the Lord's body and blood. But the celebration of the Eucharistic sacrifice is wholly directed toward the intimate union of the faithful with Christ through communion" (CCC 1382).

This statement is fully in accord with the teaching contained in the *Instruction on Worship of the Eucharistic Mystery*, *Eucharisticum Mysterium*, issued jointly in 1967 by the Consilium for the implementation of Vatican II's *Constitution on the Sacred Liturgy* and the Sacred Congregation of Rites. The instruction states in even greater detail that the Mass is a *sacrifice* in which the sacrifice of the cross is perpetuated; a *memorial* of the death and Resurrection of the Lord; a *sacred banquet* in which the faithful share the benefits of the paschal sacrifice (*Eucharisticum Mysterium*, 3). "Consequently, the Eucharistic Sacrifice is the source and the summit of the whole of the Church's worship and of the Christian life. The faithful participate more fully in this sacrament . . . not only when they wholeheartedly offer the Sacred Victim, and in it themselves, to the Father with the priest, but also when they receive this same Victim sacramentally" (*Eucharisticum Mysterium*, 3).

Pope Pius XII had stated in his encyclical on the liturgy *Mediator Dei* (1947) that "the mystery of the most Holy Eucharist which Christ, the High Priest, instituted and commands to be continually renewed, is the culmination and center of the Christian religion" (66). In the Mass, the redemptive action of the death and Resurrection of Christ is made actually present to the faithful throughout the centuries. St. Paul stated it this way: "As often as you eat this bread and drink this cup, you proclaim the death of the Lord until he comes" (1 Cor 11:26). Accordingly, immediately after the Consecration, the celebrant proclaims, "The mystery of faith!" — *Mysterium fidei!* This *anamnesis,* or remembrance, is found in the liturgy of the entire Church, both East and West.

"In the Mass, therefore, the sacrifice and sacred meal belong to the same mystery — so much so that they are linked by the closest bond. For in the sacrifice of the Mass Our Lord is immolated when 'he begins to be present sacramentally as the spiritual food of the faithful under the appearances of bread and wine' (*Mysterium Fidei*, 34)" (*Eucharisticum Mysterium*, 2). When the Protestant Reformers denied that the Mass is a true sacrifice, the Council of Trent responded in no uncertain terms: "Should anyone say that in the Mass there is not offered a true and genuine sacrifice, or that to be offered means nothing more than that Christ is given to us to eat, *anathema sit.*" Trent continues: "Should anyone say that the sacrifice of the Mass is only one of praise or thanksgiving, or but a bare commemoration of the sacrifice offered on the cross, and not propitiatory . . . *anathema sit.*"

Since the sacred species are consumed at Communion, this is also a sacrificial aspect of the Mass.

The Mass is also a sacred meal, a *sacrificial* meal, in which the Body and Blood of Christ are offered as spiritual nourishment for the faithful. Consequently, the faithful participate more fully in the Sacrifice of the Mass when they receive Communion at Mass. Moreover, the meal aspect of the Eucharist is symbolic of the unity and love that should prevail among the People of God, and in this context we can refer to the Mass as *agape*, or love feast.

Pope John Paul II states in *Dominicae Cenae* that the Church prepares two tables for her children: the word of God and the Eucharist, the Bread of the Lord (10). In the liturgy of the Mass, the faithful first *hear* the word of God and then they *eat* the Word of God. The preaching of the word is especially necessary in the celebration of the Mass, because of the close connection between the hearing of the word and Eucharistic Communion. Indeed, the two constitute a single act of worship.

At the words of Consecration, Christ is immolated in an unbloody manner in the Sacrifice of the Mass, which re-presents and perpetuates the sacrifice of the cross. At that moment, Christ becomes sacramentally present as the spiritual nourishment of the faithful under the sacred species (cf. *Mysterium Fidei*, 34). The Church constantly invites the faithful to the table of the Lord, saying at each Mass, "This is the Lamb of God. Happy are those who are called to his supper" (*Dominicae Cenae*, 11).

The principal effect of the reception of the Eucharist is an intimate union with Christ. St. Paul further states that "because there is one bread, we who are many are one body, for we all partake of the one bread" (1 Cor 12:13). Consequently, St. Augustine salutes the Eucharist as a "sign of unity, a bond of love." Such is the significance of the Mass as a "sacrificial banquet" (St. Thomas Aquinas).

Celebration of the Mass • Since the Second Vatican Council, the liturgy of the Mass has been greatly modified; but, as we have noted, the basic structure has remained stable throughout the centuries. From the time of St. Justin Martyr (died 165), the Mass consisted of two parts: the Liturgy of the Word (readings, homily, and common petitions, followed by the kiss of peace) and the Liturgy of Sacrifice (presentation of bread and wine, prayers and thanksgiving over the gifts, reception of Communion, and collection for the poor). Through the priest, who acts in the Person of Christ and in the name of the entire Church, the Sacrifice of the Eucharist is offered in an unbloody manner. The Mass is the center of the Church's life and worship, and the celebration of the Eucharist expresses in a special way its unifying and social nature.

Pope Paul VI asserts in *Mysterium Fidei* that "the whole Church, exercising with Christ the role of priest and victim, offers the sacrifice of the Mass and the whole Church is offered in it. . . . Every Mass, even though a priest may offer it in private, is not a private matter; it is an act of Christ and of the Church. In offering this sacrifice, the Church learns to offer itself as a sacrifice for all and applies the redemptive power of the sacrifice of the Cross for the salvation of the entire world" (31-32).

Pope John Paul observes in *Dominicae Cenae* that there are people "who could participate in Eucharistic Communion and do not, even though they have no serious sin on their conscience." This is due not so much to a feeling of unworthiness as to "a lack of adequate sensitivity towards this sacrament of love. We find also in recent years that there has not been due care to approach the sacrament of penance so as to purify one's conscience before participating in Communion" (11).

In the celebration of Mass, the priest acts in the person of Christ (*in persona Christi*) and in the name of the whole Church. "In the Sacrifice of the Eucharist, [Christ] is present both in the person of the minister, 'the same now offering through the ministry of the priest who formerly offered himself on the Cross,' and above all under the species of the Eucharist. For in this sacrament Christ is present in a unique way, whole and entire, God and man, substantially and permanently. This presence of Christ under the species 'is called "real" not in an exclusive sense, as if the other kinds of presence were not real, but *par excellence*' " (*Eucharisticum Mysterium*, 9).

The fact that it is the priest and the priest alone who is deputed to consecrate the bread and wine leads to the conclusion that in so doing, the priest functions in that respect as a representative of Christ and not as a representative of the faithful. This was stated by Pope Pius XII in *Mediator Dei*, and he goes on to say: "But the conclusion that the people offer the sacrifice with the priest himself is not based on the fact that, being members of the Church no less than the priest himself, they perform a visible liturgical rite; for this is the privilege only of the minister who has been divinely appointed to this office. Rather, it is based on the fact that the people unite their hearts in praise,

impetration, expiation and thanksgiving with the prayers or intention of the priest, even of the High Priest himself" (92).

See: Eucharist; Homily; In Persona Christi Capitis; Liturgy; Priest; Priesthood of Christ; Priesthood of the Faithful; Real Presence; Sacrifice.

Suggested Readings: CCC 1322-1419. Vatican Council II, *Constitution on the Sacred Liturgy, Sacrosanctum Concilium*. Pius XII, *On the Sacred Liturgy, Mediator Dei*. Paul VI, *On the Doctrine and Worship of the Eucharist, Mysterium Fidei*. John Paul II, *On the Mystery and Worship of the Eucharist, Dominicae Cenae*. Sacred Congregation of Rites, *Instruction on the Worship of the Eucharistic Mystery, Eucharisticum Mysterium*.

Jordan Aumann, O.P.

MASTURBATION

Masturbation is the act of stimulating one's own sexual organs for the purpose of sexual pleasure. Since God designed sexuality to be a means of relating to and loving another, masturbation is a misuse of the gift of sexuality; indeed, it turns one's sexual desires back upon oneself.

There can be no giving of oneself to another in the act of masturbation, and in fact it may truncate one's growth in mature relations with others. Generally accompanied by deliberately generated sexual fantasies that reduce others to sexual objects, the act of masturbation can habituate one to view others as sexual objects and to relate to them as a means to provide one with sexual satisfaction.

Many modern psychologists argue that masturbation is an innocent act of sexual release and even recommend it as such. But while certain factors may lessen the culpability of some who masturbate, it is not an innocent act without harmful consequences, especially should it become habitual.

Some with extensive pastoral experience observe that an addiction to masturbation can cause serious difficulty throughout one's life. Often young people, perhaps especially adolescents, will engage in masturbation out of sexual curiosity or because of difficulties in controlling their sexual desires. Some individuals develop a severe and debilitating obsession with masturbation. Others resort to masturbation under certain difficult psychological or social pressures. While always objectively an intrinsically evil act, the subjective culpability of the masturbator must be judged with understanding and delicacy.

Mutual masturbation is the act of two individuals engaging in sexual stimulation that does not lead to an act of sexual intercourse. What might be legitimate sexual foreplay for the married as a prelude to the sexual act is sometimes performed by the unmarried or by the married for contraceptive purposes. This, too, is an act that violates the purpose of sexuality, which is meant to enable loving spouses to engage in an act of union that retains its procreative ordination, as well as its unitive meaning.

Often masturbation is required of males by those doing fertility testing. Even for such purposes it is not morally justified, since one is still using one's sexual powers outside the context of lovemaking with one's spouse. Other moral means are available to test sperm count and motility.

See: Chastity; Education in Human Sexuality; Sexuality, Human.

MEDIA OF SOCIAL COMMUNICATIONS

The doctrine of the Catholic Church regarding the communications media can best be summarized through the opening paragraph of Vatican Council II's 1963 *Decree on the Instruments of Social Communication, Inter Mirifica:* "Man's genius has, with God's help, produced marvelous technical inventions from creation, especially in our times. The Church, our mother, is particularly interested in those which directly touch man's spirit and which have opened up new avenues of easy communication of all kinds of news, of ideas and orientations. Chief among them are those means of communication which of their very nature can reach and influence not merely single in-

dividuals but the very masses and even the whole of human society. These are the press, the cinema, radio, television and others of like nature. These can rightly be called 'the means of social communication.' "

The interest of the Church in communications, however, did not begin with the Second Vatican Council. The mandate of Christ to his Church was to teach all nations (cf. Mt 28:19; Mk 16:15). Jesus himself preached, often citing the inspired and, indeed, written word of God in what we now call the Old Testament. The four Gospel narratives of the life of Christ, the Acts of the Apostles, the letters of Paul and other Apostles are all examples of written communication that supplemented the oral preaching of the Apostles.

In the era of modern communications, the first book printed by Johannes Gutenberg in the fifteenth century was the Bible. The Vatican has had its own newspaper, *L'Osservatore Romano,* since the nineteenth century. Guglielmo Marconi, the inventor of radio, established Vatican Radio at the request of Pope Pius XI in 1931. The Vatican Film Library was established by Pope Pius XII, but it contains treasures of cinema dating from the 1890s, including moving pictures of Pope Leo XIII in the Vatican Gardens.

Papal ceremonies have been televised since the 1950s, and the Holy See was one of the first signatories of the INTELSAT (In[ternational] Tel[ecommunications] Sat[ellite Organization]) satellite treaty. The Vatican Television Center production facility was established by Pope John Paul II in 1983. The Vatican Press Office developed out of the press service designed to keep journalists informed during the Second Vatican Council. The Council Fathers themselves, in *Inter Mirifica,* specifically asked for the establishment of a commission on social communications, for the celebration of a World Communications Day (now observed in most countries on the Sunday before Pentecost), and for the preparation of a pastoral instruction on communications.

That pastoral instruction, *Communio et Progressio,* has been called the "Magna Carta" of communications in the Church. Not only does it provide a brief theology of communications ("While he was on earth, Christ revealed himself as the Perfect Communicator," giving "his message not only in words but in the whole manner of his life," 11), but it also provides practical guidelines on such subjects as freedom of information (44-47), advertising (59-62), and the active commitment of Catholics in the media of press, cinema, radio, television, and theater (135-161).

The Pontifical Commission (now Council) for Social Communications was established by Pope Paul VI in April of 1964, just four months after Vatican Council II had called for its establishment, to continue the work of two predecessor pontifical commissions — for religious and didactic cinema and for film, radio, and television.

World Communications Day was launched in 1967 by Pope Paul, as he personally read for radio and television his first message for this celebration, entitled "Church and Social Communication." (While all subsequent messages have been signed by the Holy Father, and while they contain among them a treasury of Church teaching on the communications media, this first message was the only one read in its entirety by the Pope for the electronic media.) The themes for World Communications Day are generally announced in October preceding the May celebration, and the messages (papal and otherwise) are published on January 24, the feast of St. Francis de Sales, patron saint of journalists and writers.

Teaching on Communications • The pastoral interest of the Church in the communications media nevertheless did not begin with *Inter Mirifica* and *Communio et Progressio*. As early as 1766, Pope Clement XIII wrote the encyclical letter *Christianae Reipublicae*, on the dangers of anti-Christian writings and immoral literature.

The first encyclical letter on communications in the twentieth century was *Vigilanti Cura* in 1936, on the question of motion pictures. Pope Pius XI sent it first to the bishops of the United States and then to other bishops of the world. In it, the Pope praised the initiative of the American bishops in supporting the Legion of Decency, the Catholic film-evaluating agency, which among

other things encouraged the faithful to pledge to avoid immoral films and support good motion pictures. Two years earlier, the Vatican Secretariat of State had sent a letter to the president of the International Catholic Organization for Cinema (OCIC), founded in 1928, to express concern about the moral issues involved in a medium considered as having an even greater influence than the press on public attitudes.

In 1955, Pope Pius XII expanded on his predecessor's reflections in speeches to representatives of the Italian film industry (June 21) on film as art and to the International Union of Theater Owners and Film Distributors (October 28) on the "ideal" film. Two years later, Pius XII published the encyclical letter *Miranda Prorsus*, which not only treated film but dealt for the first time with radio and television, and foresaw the profound effect the latter would have on individuals and society in general.

Those who helped prepare the pastoral instruction *Communio et Progressio*, which was published in 1971, could not have foreseen the profound changes in technology, the political landscape, and public policy on communications that would occur in the subsequent two decades. Thus, in 1992, another pastoral instruction, *Aetatis Novae* ("At the Dawn of a New Era"), was issued by the Pontifical Council as a continuation of and supplement to the earlier document. Perhaps its most novel feature is an appendix, "Elements of a Pastoral Plan for Social Communications," in which suggestions are offered for the development of a pastoral plan for communications in every diocese and episcopal conference and for the inclusion of communications considerations in pastoral planning for the other areas of the Church's activity.

Other communications themes treated formally by the Church in recent years have included *Pornography and Violence in the Communications Media: A Pastoral Response* and *Criteria for Ecumenical and Interreligious Cooperation in Communications*, both published in 1989 by the Pontifical Council, and *Ethics in Advertising*, published by the council in 1997.

Also, the need for formation of the clergy in communications was addressed in 1986 by the Congregation for Catholic Education in its document *Guide to the Training of Future Priests Concerning the Instruments of Social Communication*; and preoccupations similar to those addressed by Pope Clement XIII in 1766 were addressed by the Congregation for the Doctrine of the Faith in the 1992 *Instruction on Some Aspects of the Use of the Instruments of Social Communication on Promoting the Doctrine of the Faith*, which is mainly a compilation of Church legislation on the question.

The comments of recent Popes regarding communications are not found only in documents that specifically treat this theme. In addition to occasional references to communications media in talks for general audiences and before the recitation of the Sunday Angelus, Popes Paul VI and John Paul II have made special mention of the importance of communications in several postsynodal apostolic exhortations.

"The Church would feel guilty before the Lord," Pope Paul VI said in *On Evangelization in the Modern World, Evangelii Nuntiandi*, "if she did not utilize these powerful means (of communication) that human skill is daily rendering more perfect." Through them, he added, the Church "proclaims 'from the housetops' the message of which she is the depositary. In them she finds a modern and effective version of the pulpit. Thanks to them she succeeds in speaking to the multitudes" (45).

Pope John Paul not only incorporated communications into three postsynodal documents — *Catechesi Tradendae* (1979), 46, *Familiaris Consortio* (1981), 76, and *Christifideles Laici* (1988), 44 — but he described the new media environment and language in his 1990 encyclical letter *On the Permanent Validity of the Church's Missionary Mandate, Redemptoris Missio,* in words that capsulize the Church's contemporary view of the means of social communications and their relevance:

> After preaching in a number of places, St. Paul arrived at Athens, where he went to the Areopagus and proclaimed the Gospel in language appropriate to and understandable in those surroundings (cf. Acts 17:22-31). At that time, the Areopagus represented the cultural centre of that learned people of Athens, and today it can be taken as a symbol of the new sectors in which the Gospel must be proclaimed.

> The first Areopagus of the modern age is the world of communication, which is unifying humanity and turning it into what is known as a "global village." The means of social communication have become so important as to be for many the chief means of information and education, of guidance and inspiration in their behavior as individuals, families and within society at large. In particular, the younger generation is growing up in a world conditioned by the mass-media. To some degree perhaps, this Areopagus has been neglected. Generally preference has been given to other means of preaching the Gospel and of Christian education, while the mass-media are left to the initiative of individuals or small groups and enter into pastoral planning only in a secondary way. Involvement in the mass-media, however, is not meant merely to strengthen the preaching of the Gospel. There is a deeper reality involved here: since the very evangelization of modern culture depends to a great extent on the influence of the media, it is not enough to use the media simply to spread the Christian message and the Church's authentic teaching. It is also necessary to integrate that message into a "new culture" created by modern communications. This is a complex issue, since the "new culture" originates not just from whatever content is eventually expressed, but from the very fact that there exist new ways of communicating with new languages, new techniques and a new psychology. Pope Paul VI said that "the split between the Gospel and culture is undoubtedly the tragedy of our time" (*Evangelii Nuntiandi*, 20), and the field of communications fully confirms this judgement (376).

The integration of Christian values and of a truly Christian culture into the language and reality of modern media, and not merely the more effective *use* of communications media as instruments of evangelization, is a task waiting to be accomplished.

See: Evangelization; Science and the Church.

Suggested Readings: CCC 2493-2499. Vatican Council II, *Decree on the Instruments of Social Communication, Inter Mirifica.* Pontifical Council for Social Communications, *Pastoral Instruction on the Means of Social Communication, Aetatis Novae.* F. Eilers, S.V.D., ed., *Church and Social Communications.* C. Martini, S.J., *Communicating Christ to the World.* P. Soukup, S.J., *Christian Communication.* W. Thorn and M. Schmoelke, *Catholic Press at the Millennium.*

✠ **John P. Foley**

MEDITATION

In the Middle Ages, it was customary to speak of four types of spiritual exercises: reading, meditation, prayer, and contemplation. The medieval work *Scala Claustralium* placed these activities on a graduated scale, although they actually alternate with one another. Spiritual reading (*lectio*) was assigned to beginners in the spiritual life; meditation (*meditatio*) was suitable for those who were more advanced; prayer (*oratio*) was an exercise for devout souls; and contemplation (*contemplatio*) was the prayer level of the perfect. Not only was a distinction made between meditation and prayer, but St. Thomas Aquinas (*Sent.* IV, 15, 4, 1) and St. Francis de Sales (*Treatise on the Love of God,* I, 6, 2) explicitly stated that meditation is at best an intermediate exercise leading to prayer. St. Teresa of Ávila (*The Interior Castle,* Fourth Mansion, I, 7) and St. Alphonsus Liguori (*Apostolic Man,* Appendix I, 7) treat of meditation as an early stage of mental prayer that leads to affective prayer and acquired recollection.

In the early monastic period, under the influence of teachers like John Cassian (c. 360-c. 432), meditation was seen as a stage on the path to contemplative prayer. Once an individual had done enough spiritual reading, it was possible to make use of meditation as a means for applying to one-self the truths pondered. This in turn led to the practice of mental prayer and eventually to a contemplative experience of God. Contemplation was posited as the goal for all who practice prayer and strive for Christian perfection.

In the fifteenth century, discursive meditation was more and more fostered as a means of reform, both for individuals and for religious communities. The Benedictine monk Luigi Barbo (died 1443) promoted the spiritual exercises in Italy, and they were so successful that they were introduced at the Benedictine monastery in Valladolid, Spain, and carried thence to Montserrat by García de Cisneros in 1492. The spiritual exercises, based on discursive meditation, were later perfected by St. Ignatius Loyola (died 1556) and promulgated widely by the Jesuits.

Although the practice of meditation was vigorously attacked by Molinos and the Alumbrados, the Church consistently defended and praised meditation as a form of mental prayer. In modern times, Pope Pius XII recommended the practice of discursive meditation by priests and the laity. St. Teresa of Ávila wrote emphatically on this point: "Meditation is the basis for acquiring all the virtues, and to undertake it is a matter of life and death for all Christians" (*The Way of Perfection,* 16, 3).

The Practice of Meditation • Discursive meditation may be described as a method of prayer in which one thinks about a religious truth, applies it to one's life here and now, and resolves to carry it into practice. The *Catechism of the Catholic Church* speaks of it this way: "Meditation is above all a quest. The mind seeks to understand the why and how of the Christian life, in order to adhere and respond to what the Lord is asking. . . . To the extent that we are humble and faithful, we discover in meditation the movements that stir the heart and we are able to discern them. It is a question of acting truthfully in order to come into the light: 'Lord, what do you want me to do?' " (CCC 2705-2706).

Meditation is a discursive type of prayer that involves the use of the practical intellect, which is oriented to living and doing and not simply to speculative knowledge. One can acquire firm convictions and better understanding through study, but St. Teresa of Ávila says that in order to profit from this exercise, "the important thing is not to think much but to love much; and so do that which best stirs you to love" (*The Interior Castle*, Fourth Mansion, I, 7).

Thus, meditation has a twofold purpose, one intellectual and the other affective and practical. The intellectual purpose is to arrive at a firm conviction concerning a supernatural truth, although this could also be obtained through study. What makes meditation a form of prayer is the affective element: the act of love that is stimulated by the deeper knowledge of supernatural truth. But love cannot be idle. By its very nature, it impels one to action. Consequently the completion and perfection of discursive meditation lies in the practical resolution that follows the consideration and application of truth to one's life. Failure to make practical resolutions is the reason why some who practice discursive meditation faithfully do not reap the benefit it can provide.

Subject Matter and Method • Another point that needs clarification has to do with the subject matter of meditation. Any topic at all that relates to the spiritual life is suitable for discursive meditation: for example, a divine attribute, an event or statement from the life of Christ, the life and virtues of the Blessed Virgin Mary or some other saint, a particular virtue, etc. The basic choice of subject matter should be determined by a person's need at a particular time or what will further promote one's holiness of life. Like all the forms of mental prayer, discursive meditation is a very personal activity, and it should be adjusted to the need of the individual. When rightly used, it is a potent factor in the formation of character and the cultivation of the virtues proper to one's state of life.

The use of the proper method is also of great importance, especially for those who are beginners in mental prayer. As an individual makes progress in prayer, passing from discursive meditation to the higher stages, there is less need for structure and method. In fact, method could then become an obstacle to further progress.

In the early centuries of monasticism and in the older religious orders, there was much less emphasis on structure and method in the practice of prayer. But in the sixteenth century, discursive meditation became very popular among devout souls, and it became necessary to construct methods of mental prayer. Many of them are still in use today. Some are very detailed and highly regimented (Ignatian, Sulpician, Salesian); others are extremely simple and more flexible (Carmelite and Louis of Granada). What all of the methods have in common are the three essential acts: consideration of a truth, application to one's life, and resolve to act upon it.

A basic rule regarding method is to select the one most beneficial and to adapt it or even discard it completely when it is no longer necessary. One will always need to practice some form of discursive meditation (think, judge, act) throughout life, but the goal of the practice of prayer is to reach contemplative prayer.

The best time for discursive meditation will depend on the individual. As a general rule, the time, place, and posture should be such as to facilitate the attention and devotion needed for fruitful meditation. Normally, it will be a time when other duties or occupations are not pressing, when one has leisure. And since this is a personal decision, it is not always possible to have a time set for an entire community. What is important, however, is regularity. Some spiritual writers suggest a prayer period first thing in the morning, before taking up one's daily tasks, or late at night, after the day's work is done.

The same flexibility should be observed regarding the duration of meditation. St. Alphonsus Liguori suggested a half hour daily for beginners; St. Francis de Sales and St. Ignatius Loyola suggested one full hour. Without specifying the duration, St. Thomas Aquinas advised that mental prayer should last as long as one experiences devotion and can be attentive, otherwise tedium and distractions set in.

Another question concerns the place and posture for mental prayer. There should be a great deal of flexibility in this regard as well, although it goes without saying that in some instances, as when meditating in common, a certain amount of uniformity is necessary. Normally, it is better to pray in a place set aside for prayer, such as a church or chapel, but any place at all will suffice. The determining factor is whether or not the surroundings are conducive to prayer. Similarly, no set posture or bodily position is required for meditation. Habit, culture, or personal preference will determine whether an individual will sit, kneel, stand, or walk. Ultimately, the posture should be one in which an individual can pray best.

See: Contemplation; Mysticism; Prayer; Prayer of Petition; Quietism; Vocal Prayer.

Suggested Readings: CCC 2697-2699, 2705-2708. Congregation for the Doctrine of the Faith, *Letter to the Bishops of the Catholic Church on Some Aspects of Christian Meditation.* St. Teresa of Ávila, *The Way of Perfection.* G. Lercaro, *Methods of Mental Prayer.* A. Squire, *Asking the Fathers.*

Jordan Aumann, O.P.

MENTAL RESERVATION

The term "mental reservation" was once widely used to defend the morality of answering a question in such a way as to preserve without formally lying a secret that the questioner has no right to know. Since a given statement may be inherently ambiguous, it is possible to deceive someone even when telling the literal truth: The speaker allows the listener to accept one meaning of his statement, while reserving to himself another, quite different, meaning.

The most common form of mental reservation is the social convention. Wanting to avoid a caller who is soliciting donations, a man says, "Tell him I'm not home." The man means he is not home *to the caller,* but permits the caller to believe he is not home at all. Such conventional uses of mental reservation are generally harmless, since the hearer, recognizing the ploy, is not truly deceived.

However, the practice of mental reservation lies open to abuse, and can serve as an easy rationalization for deliberate deception. For example, a police officer in pursuit of a criminal asks a bystander, "Did a man just run by?" The answer "I did not see anyone" would be deliberately misleading if the respondent heard footsteps but kept his back turned.

Because mental reservation can be employed for conscious deception, Catholic moral teaching on truth-telling treats it with caution. The *Catechism of the Catholic Church* does not use the term, while even half a century earlier a Catholic manual of moral theology cautioned that mental reservation was not suited for use "in the affairs of daily life" and its too-facile employment would "inevitably lead to a habit of deception and perhaps to positive lying."

See: Equivocation; Lying; Secrets; Truthfulness.

METANOIA

Metanoia and its verb form *metanoeo* are found sixteen times in the Gospels and twenty-one additional times in the rest of the New Testament. Metanoia comes from two Greek words, *meta,* which indicates a change, and *nous* ("mind"). In reference to the spiritual life, it means a turning of the mind, a change of heart. As a theological concept, metanoia signifies something beyond the initial turning to Christ in Baptism, which is the first conversion of the individual. There is a second conversion, which is continuous. Throughout the Gospels, Our Lord calls those who will listen to a conversion; thus, following him requires a daily metanoia: "If any man would come after me, let him deny himself and take up his cross *daily* and follow me" (Lk 9:23; emphasis added).

The *Catechism of the Catholic Church* says this second conversion is "an uninterrupted task for the whole Church" (1428). It is uninterrupted in that it requires a daily examination of conscience and review of one's life in relation to the Gospel and its message of repentance. It is for the whole Church in a twofold manner: First, the Church as a whole reaches out to sinners and invites them to be reconciled in Christ; second, the sinners as members affect the Church by their sins. The Pauline doctrine of the Mystical Body speaks to this issue: "For just as the body is one and has many members, and all the members of the body, though many, are one body, so it is with Christ. . . . If one member suffers, all suffer together; if one member is honored, all rejoice together. Now you are the body of Christ and individually members of it" (1 Cor 12:12, 26-27).

See: Conversion of the Baptized; Penance in Christian Life.

MILLENARIANISM

The doctrine of Millenarianism, deriving from the Latin word *mille,* which means a thousand (also called Chiliasm, from the Greek *khiliasmos*), concerns the expectation of Christ's return before the end of the world in order to reign alongside the just and the holy for a period of a thousand years.

While basing their views on the Johannine testimony of the Book of Revelation (the Apocalypse), adherents of this or that form of Millenarist thought, from Joachim of Fiore in the twelfth century to Seventh-Day Adventists today, typically seize upon one passage in particular. An angel of the Lord is said to have come down out of heaven and, laying hold of the dragon, "that ancient serpent, who is the Devil and Satan . . . bound him for a thousand years, and threw him into the pit, and shut it and sealed it over him, that he should deceive the nations no more, till the thousand years were ended. After that, he must be loosed for a little while" (Rv 20:1-5).

The Catholic Church has never countenanced any earthly expectation of God's reign, refusing the seductive simplification that within the medium of human history all the perfections of the heavenly kingdom would someday flower. Instead, she holds out the hope of definitive human fulfillment only in that self-transcending movement of history in which salvation is finally won beyond the trajectory of time, in the eternal embrace of Christ. To think otherwise, says the *Catechism of the Catholic Church,* is to invite that "supreme religious deception" which is the Antichrist, the precise form of whose deception "begins to take shape in the world every time the claim is made to realize within history that messianic hope which can only be realized beyond history through the eschatological judgment" (675-676).

See: Antichrist; Ascension and Parousia.

MINISTRY

"Minister" comes from the Latin word for servant, and denotes a person acting under the authority or as an agent of another, for example, a minister of state. Accordingly, "minister of religion" is a generic expression that includes any official, clerical or lay, who performs some service for a religious body.

One accepted usage in the Church reserves minister as the term for the appropriate person for administering the sacraments: for example, when we say that the ordinary minister of Confirmation is the bishop. In this sense of the term, anyone who confers a sacrament, including the layperson who may baptize in case of necessity, is its minister. In the past, the designation was sometimes extended to include those who assist the bishop and priests in discharging their offices, so that those who served in the sanctuary were likewise known as ministers. While the Church also designates priests as her ministers or ministers of the Gospel, common parlance in English-speaking countries still usually distinguishes between the Catholic priest and the Protestant minister. In any event, it is clear that "minister" is a broad term, applied analogically to different persons.

Ministry and Vatican Council II • The Second Vatican Council put the terms "minister" and "ministry" into a specific theological context. The Council's purpose was twofold. First, it wanted to emphasize that the Incarnation reveals the divine plan to send the eternal Son for the service of saving the human race. Christ, then, is the first minister. There is no evidence of this truth more impressive than Jesus' words and deeds on the night before he died: "When he had washed their feet, and taken his garments, and resumed his place, he said to them, 'Do you know what I have done to you? You call me Teacher and Lord; and you are right, for so I am. If I then, your Lord and teacher, have washed your feet, you also ought to wash one another's feet' " (Jn 13:12-14). Second, the Council placed the work of the laity more clearly in the theological context of Christ's ministry, and so refined the Church's teaching on the apostolate of the laity, making it more clearly a full, not simply an auxiliary, part of Christ's mission. Again, the Gospel of John establishes the basis for this claim: "I am the vine, you are the branches. He who abides in me, and I in him, he it is that bears much fruit, for apart from me you can do nothing" (Jn 15:5). The Council wished to renew the service of the laity to the Church through a renewal of their faith in their union with Christ.

To understand the Council's teaching on ministry we must recall the theological teaching on the capital grace of Christ, by which he is constituted the head of the Church. Drawing out the implications of Pope Pius XII's 1943 encyclical *Mystici Corporis Christi*, which presented the Church as the Body of Christ, the Second Vatican Council sought to fathom the meaning of St. Paul's teaching that there are a variety of gifts, but one Holy Spirit who is the divine source of these gifts. After listing some of the "manifestations of the Spirit" (1 Cor 12:7) that the baptized receive, Paul states: "All these are inspired by one and the same Spirit, who apportions to each one individually as he wills" (1 Cor 12:11). The Council's gloss on this text, in its *Dogmatic Constitution on the Church*, is: "And so amid variety all will bear witness to the wonderful unity in the Body of Christ: this very diversity of graces, of ministries and of works gathers the sons of God into one" (*Lumen Gentium*, 32). As Christ remains one with the Father, who sent him into the world, so authentic Christian ministry is directed to promoting unity among the members of the Church. Those who undertake a ministry in the Church help to extend the grace of Christ's headship in the world.

The Council's *Decree on the Apostolate of the Laity, Apostolicam Actuositatem*, canonized the use of the term "ministry" to designate whatever a baptized person does for the good of the Church: "In the Church there is diversity of ministry but unity of mission" (2). After Vatican II, "ministry"

generally replaced the earlier expression "lay apostolate" to describe the various contributions that the nonordained members of the Church make to its *communio*. Today it is not uncommon to hear some individuals referred to as heading the "ministry of music" or seeing to the "ministry to the sick" or serving as "extraordinary ministers of the Eucharist." In some cases, liturgical rites have been drawn up to install these ministers in their respective offices. This is especially true for the ministries of lector and acolyte. The Code of Canon Law, moreover, stipulates that laypeople who possess the required qualities can be admitted permanently to these ministries (cf. Canon 230.1).

The Council's *Dogmatic Constitution on the Church, Lumen Gentium*, uses the expression "sacred ministers" to refer to the ordained clergy, but it also recalls the biblical teaching that they along with the nonordained faithful form the one People of God. Although the Council documents clearly maintain the distinctiveness of the ordained and hierarchical ministry that flows from the sacrament of Holy Orders, some theologians and commentators have interpreted the Council's teaching about diversity of ministry as relativizing the distinction between ordained and nonordained ministries. In so doing, they overlook the incontrovertible teaching of the Council that the ministerial priesthood remains, as a specifically sacramental reality, at the service of the common priesthood. As *Lumen Gentium* expresses it, "That office . . . , which the Lord committed to the pastors of his people, is in the strict sense of the term a *service*" (24).

Analogical Senses of "Ministry" • Some of the confusion results from a failure to understand the analogy at work when the Council teaches that the laity share in the priestly, prophetical, and kingly office of Christ. The *Catechism of the Catholic Church* helps to clarify this point by intentionally placing the discussion of ministry under the heading "The Hierarchical Constitution of the Church" (cf. CCC 874-879). This accords with the doctrine of the Church. For example, the 1983 letter *Sacerdotium Ministeriale* authoritatively taught that apostolic succession through sacramental ordination is an essential element for the exercise of priestly ministry and thus for the bestowal of the power to consecrate the Eucharist.

Accordingly, we can say that the chief and irreplaceable participant in the ministry of Jesus Christ is the bishop, who, in the words of St. Ignatius of Antioch, is like the living image of God the Father (cf. CCC 1549). It is from the bishop, especially the Bishop of Rome, that all authentic ministry derives. The Congregation for the Doctrine of the Faith has taken strong exception to the work of the Belgian theologian Edward Schillebeeckx, O.P., including his books *Ministry: Leadership in the Community of Jesus Christ* and *The Church With a Human Face: A New and Expanded Theology of Ministry*, for failing to acknowledge this doctrinal principle. The large numbers of lay pastoral workers or associates who have begun to assist in areas of Europe where there is a shortage of ordained priests has given a certain impetus to this theological reflection. But the Church, in the voice of Pope John Paul II, has repeatedly affirmed the "absolute necessity that the 'new evangelization' have priests as its initial 'new evangelizers' " (apostolic exhortation *I Will Give You Shepherds, Pastores Dabo Vobis*, 2 [1992]).

The *Catechism* begins its teaching on ministry so as to take account of its fundamentally hierarchical nature. By way of formulating the basic theological principle of Christian ministry, the text affirms that "Christ is himself the source of ministry in the Church" (874). As to its principal expression, the power to exercise ministry of the Church comes from a special sacrament: Holy Orders enables men to minister to the People of God so that all may attain salvation.

This sacramental ministry is a collegial action, because the episcopal college and its head, the successor of St. Peter, work together for the good of the universal Church. At the same time, priestly ministry is eminently personal, because the Church's ministers, who are called personally to their vocation, always bear personal witness to the common mission of the Church and to Jesus in whose person they act.

Another misunderstanding about ministry arises when the sacred power of the priest is imagined to be the religious equivalent of the political power exercised by civil rulers. The priest, however, receives his mission and his authority from Christ; and so neither the word that priests preach nor the graces of which they are the instruments are their own. These belong to Christ, who gives his power to whom he wills.

Nevertheless, there is also a power that Christ gives to every member of the Church, and that awaits the generous response of men and women who seek to promote the reign of Christ the King. In his apostolic exhortation *The Lay Members of Christ's Faithful People, Christifideles Laici*, Pope John Paul II cites a text of Pope Pius XII, who was an effective advocate of Catholic Action: "Lay believers are in the front line of Church life; for them the Church is the animating principle of human society. Therefore, they in particular ought to have an ever-clearer consciousness not only of belonging to the Church, but of being the Church, that is to say, the community of the faithful on earth under the leadership of the Pope, the common Head, and of the bishops in communion with him. They are the Church" (cited in CCC 899). The twentieth century has witnessed a renewed involvement of the Christian laity in the sanctification of the world, especially in the social and political spheres. Blessed Josemaría Escrivá, the priest-founder of the predominantly lay organization Opus Dei, provides an outstanding example of how to encourage the Christian faithful to sanctify themselves through work in the world and apostolate.

See: Apostolate; Apostolic Succession; Evangelization; Holy Orders; In Persona Christi Capitis; Laity; Priesthood of Christ; Priesthood of the Faithful; Vocation.

Suggested Readings: CCC 874-879, 1546-1553. Vatican Council II, *Dogmatic Constitution on the Church, Lumen Gentium*, 30-42; *Decree on the Apostolate of the Laity, Apostolicam Actuositatem*. John Paul II, *The Lay Members of Christ's Faithful People, Christifideles Laici*. R. Malone, ed., *Review of Contemporary Perspec-*

tives on Ministry. T. O'Meara, *Theology of Ministry*.

Romanus Cessario, O.P.

MIRACLES

Miracles manifest God's redemptive action in time and space. People today tend to lose sight of this most basic point. Many of the reasons for this loss of insight and understanding are rooted in the nature of our culture. We shall explore some of the cultural stumbling blocks that stand in the way of our arriving via the evidence of miracles at a clear and certain faith in God and his great redemptive work. Then we shall be in a better position to understand the importance of miracles in God's plan of salvation.

We place a great deal of trust in science. What would we do without penicillin, computers, synthetic materials of all kinds? We look to scientific research to provide a miracle drug for HIV-related diseases. The technological precision required to put a group of astronauts on the moon speaks well of our ability to unravel some of nature's great mysteries. One can only marvel at the amount of information that can now be stored, manipulated, and retrieved on a laser disc not more than six inches in diameter. Few would disagree that the contributions science has made to life during the last century have been truly "miraculous."

However, our hope in scientific triumphs — good as they are — can be the very thing blinding us to something far more important: faith in the living God. Placing our hope in our own ingenuity, on what *we* can do, reveals what we think of our abilities: We are the masters of our own destiny; we alone shape our own future. This half-truth is tragic precisely because it eclipses God and has resulted in reducing nature to something akin to a clock that God once wound up and then left to its own devices.

Within this worldview, science acts almost as a religious authority, while the scientist resembles a high priest dispensing the "sacrament" of knowledge. The method and its maker (science and the scientist) reveal nature's truths, unraveling and deepening our knowledge and discovery of the "clock" made by the distant God. There may be some kind of faith in God, but he, she, or it (according to this worldview) is no longer on the scene, engaged with the world. When we place human knowledge and nobility — as awesome as these are — at the center of the universe, we displace God. God becomes an outsider to the day-to-day issues of real life. He no longer controls or even influences history, because we do. This worldview is called anthropocentric because of its exclusive focus on human beings. Its view of God is seriously defective.

"Science" and the Miraculous • This lethal mixture of a "scientific" worldview and a flawed faith in God creates many roadblocks to believing in miracles as God intended them to be understood. The scientific worldview tends to ask only one question about the miraculous: "How did this happen?" That is a perfectly normal and acceptable line of investigation of course, but it ignores another of even greater importance. In the case of a miraculous healing, for example: "What does this miracle *mean* for that person? What does it *tell* us about the nature of God, about ourselves, about God's powerful kingdom being made present, about God's divine plan of salvation?" The point is simple: Our dominant cultural penchant for — or obsession with — scientific and technical/mechanical explanations limits our ability to discover what miracles signify about God. Thus we miss the sign value of a miracle. Limiting our focus to technical and mechanical explanations of the miraculous, as important as this level of understanding is, reduces our thinking itself to the mechanical level. This mind-set seems to insulate the heart against understanding the deeper nature of miracles; it effectively inhibits our ability to praise and thank God for what he has done.

A defective faith further compounds the problem. It could lead someone to give inward assent to the fact of the miracle, to the obvious good it effects; but if one's concentration upon the gift distracts and even prevents one from focusing on the Giver, there is something defective in such faith.

The miracle reveals the riches of God's mercy, God's inner goodness, God's love, God's great power over all sin, darkness, evil, deformity, and the like. Again, an incomplete or defective faith might conclude that, although God probably had something to do with a miracle, still his involvement was fairly indirect. For example, one might speculate that a miracle resulted from the confluence of several natural causes, which God indirectly brought about while he himself remained two, three, or four steps removed from the event. A response that does not perceive the divine source from which miracles flow does not understand the essential nature of the miraculous and probably will not understand the particular importance of a given miracle. A defective faith thus tends to lose sight of the value of a miracle as "a sign of the power and presence" of God and his kingdom. Then understanding of the miraculous easily degenerates into a romanticized view common in today's contemporary popular media.

There is another difficulty. The contemporary view of the universe generally assumes that all of nature constitutes a closed system operating by laws or principles demonstrable by experimentation and observation. The expression "closed system" means that nature operates or runs by itself, under its own laws or rules, much as a clock functions by the workings of its internal springs and levers; the maker of the clock has nothing do to with its continued operating.

When, however, a miracle is interpreted in the framework of a closed system of laws (motion, gravity, etc.), the first, obvious step is to ask how the miracle happened. The next logical move is to determine which laws were altered or suspended. Then one proceeds to "explain" the miracle in terms of cause and effect. In such an approach, the "laws of nature" define and determine all possibilities, and anything outside these laws cannot be considered. Since the supernatural is above or outside the laws of nature, however, it is simply extraneous and not to be taken into consideration. There is no need for faith or God in order to "understand" the miracle, provided one places *a priori*

limits on one's inquiry in this manner. The assumption is that the scientist and scientific method hold the ultimate criteria for truth and therefore can determine the authenticity of the miracle while also accounting for it.

Miracles in the Bible • The biblical witness to miracles does not speak against science, human progress in technology, or human freedom. Rather, it bears witness to an entirely different view of the universe. It points out that the natural world is not simply a system of laws. All events, ordinary or extraordinary — including floods, famine, and plagues — are attributable to God; they manifest the powerful presence of God, who can bring both blessing and condemnation. There is no conflict between the processes of nature, the course of human actions determined by historical forces, and the action of the living God, who rules over every aspect of nature and history. Taken as a whole, the Bible ascribes to God those events that were caused by natural forces and the historical process.

It is important to remember that miracles do not occur for their own sake. Miracles, like other biblical events, teach something about God, the attributes of God, and the divine plan of salvation, as well as the nature of the events with which the miracles are associated.

The Old Testament reports several types of miracles. Of paramount importance are those miraculous events that change the course of people's lives and directly advance God's plan of salvation. Often a miracle functions to verify that the manifest will of God is being fulfilled by God and not by human agency (e.g., Lk 1-2). Any personal benefit derived from the miracle is secondary to and meaningful in the larger process of divine salvation. In effect, the miracle is a form of Divine Revelation. Quite often, a miracle supports or directly confirms an earlier promise made by God or a prophecy by one of his representatives. God's miracle makes the promise of the Word happen. A miracle should not be viewed in isolation from the divine promises, which give it its meaning. The "sign value" of a miracle is in its power to confirm what was spoken in the divine promises.

In this way, God's inner life is revealed in both word and deed, and this advances the plan of salvation.

Some examples from the Old Testament illustrate what has been said. Abraham, Jacob, and especially Moses experienced miraculous interaction and direct contact with God. In Abraham's case, the covenant he made with God was confirmed with the smoking firepot and the flaming torch, both miraculous signs of the divine presence (cf. Gn 15:17-20). Sarah's infertility and advanced years could not stop God from fulfilling his promise to Abraham: that from his seed — in spite of his age and that of Sarah — would come God's people. When Sarah becomes pregnant with Isaac, there can be no doubt about who is in charge of history and nature. Again: Moses first spoke with God at the burning bush (cf. Ex 3) that was not consumed by the fire; the burning bush that is not consumed is a miraculous confirmation of Moses' call to lead God's people out of Egyptian oppression. In each of these instances, God acts to advance his plan of salvation by means of an extraordinary intervention. It misses the point to speak of a "suspension of the laws of nature." Rather, God is simply being God, acting in a sovereign way.

A miracle should be viewed on a par with what the Bible calls "wonders" or sometimes "signs." The distinctiveness of the miracle is its manifestation of divine power. Such acts of divine power are often called "exploits" (Ex 15:11) or, in the singular, "a great deed" (Heb=*gebûrâh*; cf. Ps 106:2), "a mighty thing" (Ps 106:21), "an awesome event" (Ex 34:10), and a "marvel" (Ex 15:11; Ps 106:7). That same divine power also brings the sinful to ruin (Dt 7:17-20; Mi 7:15). All of God's works of power carry the same message: "God's love is in all that he works" (Ps 107:8; 145:9).

New Testament Miracles • The principal New Testament miracles link the Person and work of Jesus of Nazareth, the eternal Son of God, with his Father's divine salvation plan. In a manner of speaking, Gospel miracles effectively define Jesus as having a power that demonstrates that his teachings are indeed from God, that his words are indeed prophetic. His power confronts, challenges, and overcomes the evil one, whose sphere of influence and control over human life are manifested in sin, sickness, and moral darkness.

John the Baptist asks Jesus to identify himself. Jesus answers by pointing out that all miracles he performed, especially physical healing, are concrete fulfillments of prophecies made by the prophets centuries before either one of them was born (cf. Lk 7:18-23; Is 29:18-19, 35:5-6, 61:1). Jesus' great and powerful miracles are signs of the eschatological age, the age of God's Messiah, who brings in the final stage of God's kingdom (cf. Lk 11:20). There is a continuity between the Old Testament promises and their New Testament fulfillment in the life and work of Jesus. Consequently it comes as no surprise to learn that some of Jesus' miracles are directly parallel to some of those found in the Old Testament. One example is the feeding of the five thousand (Mk 6:30-44; Mt 14:13-21; Lk 9:10-17; Jn 6:1-13). This miracle is similar in detail to the feeding miracles recorded in Israel's exodus from Egypt and its forty-year sojourn in the desert. In both Testaments, God leads his people into the desert, feeds them, and creates a new nation with his covenanted people (Jn 6:31-33). In the New Testament, the feeding narrative contains "new covenant" language ("took," "blessed," "broke," "handed over") found in the Passover meal (cf. Mk 6:41, 14:22).

In short, a Gospel miracle is a sign of the power of God's kingdom, which ushers in the eschatological age. (The eschaton is the final age prior to the full consummation or perfect completion of God's divine plan of salvation first revealed to Adam and Eve at the beginning of Genesis.) The rabbis taught that this eschatological age would bring reconciliation with God and with neighbor and a return to conditions of life far better than those enjoyed by Adam and Eve. In such a view, miracles are first signs of those final moments before the eschatological age consumes the whole of God's creation. Jesus' miracles of healing and the exorcisms he performed are in fact a kind of prophetic sign that this age has indeed come upon us. The forgiveness of sins is of course the critical sign that the eschaton is upon those who hear the words of Jesus. His miraculous healing in effect "proves" his claim to having the divine power to forgive sins. And his miracles also demonstrate the reality of God seen in the Old Testament: his love, compassion, and irrevocable commitment to save his people from sin, darkness, and death.

The Bible challenges our anthropocentric worldview. It views God as *the* Creator and sustainer of the universe and also of human destiny. While the Bible clearly bears witness to the value of human freedom and the goodness of human knowledge of nature, it is equally clear about God's sovereign rule over his creation. The Bible's view of the universe begins and ends with God. Understanding of a miracle therefore must begin and end with reference to the reality of God as revealed in the Scriptures. We call this kind of biblical point of view theocentric. If we are to understand miracles and what they mean, we must make every effort to transcend the limitations otherwise imposed by twentieth-century assumptions conditioning the way we think about ourselves and about God. God uncovers his purposes through miracles. He fulfills his plan of salvation and communicates the nature of his being — that he is sovereign, awesome, faithful, just, and loving. The miracles of Jesus conclude the long process by which God's kingdom comes to reign on earth and, as it were, visibly announce the restoration of divine dominion over the natural order.

See: Divine Revelation; Inerrancy; Jesus Christ, Life of; New Covenant; New Testament; Old Covenant; Old Testament; Prophecy; Rationalism; Science and the Church.

Suggested Readings: CCC 547-550. H. Kee, *Miracle in the Early Christian World: A Study in Sociohistorical Method.* P. Grelot and J. Giblet, "Miracle," in X. Leon-Dufour, ed., *Dictionary of Biblical Theology.* "Miracle," in B. Metzger and M. Coogan, gen. eds., *The Oxford Companion to the Bible.* H. Remus, "Miracle, New Testament," in *Anchor Bible Dictionary*, IV.

Stephen F. Miletic

MISSIONARY ACTIVITY

The Catholic Church is missionary by nature. By his suffering and death on the cross Jesus flung open the doors to heaven so that every human being may be saved through "the knowledge of the truth" (CCC 851). Because in his lifetime he could announce this salvation to only a few, he established the Church in his Apostles, instructing them, "Go therefore and make disciples of all nations, baptizing them in the name of the Father and of the Son and of the Holy Spirit, teaching them to observe all that I have commanded you" (Mt 28:19). Guided by the Holy Spirit, the Church has gone her way over the centuries, sometimes with an uncertain step, but never forgetting the great work she was established to complete: "As the Father has sent me, even so I send you" (Jn 20:21; cf. CCC 857-858).

Vatican Council II's *Decree on the Church's Missionary Activity, Ad Gentes,* opens with these words: "Having been divinely sent to the nations that she might be 'the universal sacrament of salvation,' the Church, in obedience to the command of her founder (Mt 16:15) . . . strives to preach the Gospel to all men" (quoted in CCC 849). Missionary work is a particular form of evangelization, the preaching of the Good News, which forms the Church's essential task. The word "mission" derives from the Latin *mittere*, which means "to send"; missionaries are messengers whom the local or universal Church sends to those who do not know Jesus Christ or have rejected him. Missionary work is the responsibility of the whole People of God, of individual laity and lay associations as well as missionary institutes.

National church agencies often support home missions, that is, dioceses that cannot provide basic pastoral services without outside help. In the United States, the Catholic Church Extension Society, the Black and Indian Mission Bureau, and the American Board of Catholic Missions provide such assistance, collecting funds in wealthier areas and distributing them where the Church is weak in material resources. However, the classic missionary is the man or woman (most often a priest or religious) who makes a lifelong commitment and journeys "to the ends of the earth" (Acts 1:8), as American Maryknollers went to China. This is the mission *ad gentes*, "to the nations."

Nature of Missionary Work • For many centuries the missionary's task, though difficult and dangerous, was clear. He was to preach the Gospel, to improve the lives of the people (e.g., by establishing schools and hospitals), and to found new Christian communities that, in time, would take root and flourish. Since World War II, though, the concept of mission has changed markedly. Local churches — dioceses and prefectures — exist throughout the world. By and large, missionaries no longer go out alone or in small groups to establish the Church among pagans. They go, rather, as emissaries from one local church to another. Thus, an American priest might volunteer to staff a parish in Guatemala, under the authority of the Guatemalan diocesan bishop.

In 1990, Pope John Paul II published a lengthy encyclical, *On the Permanent Validity of the Church's Missionary Mandate, Redemptoris Missio*, to illuminate and explain this new missionary situation. He notes the proliferation of local churches but, as the title suggests, insists on the continuing need for the traditional missionary's services. The Holy Father stresses the Church's obligation to evangelize people in geographical and cultural areas that "lack indigenous Christian communities" or have "communities . . . so small as not to be a clear sign of a Christian presence." He singles out the young, the poor, urban dwellers, migrants, and refugees for special attention, adding that the contemporary mission *ad gentes* should be chiefly directed toward Asia (37).

Somewhat surprisingly, John Paul also speaks of reevangelizing countries with a long Christian tradition "where entire groups of the baptized have lost a living sense of the faith, or even no longer consider themselves members of the Church, and live a life far removed from Christ and his Gospel" (33). The increasingly secular tone of American society, and its disturbing fascination with sex, violence, and easy gratification, could make the United States "mission territory" in the next century.

A misinterpretation of Vatican II's call for greater Church involvement in the world has fostered the spread of an incomplete notion of mission in recent decades. Some theologians have argued that the goal of mission should be the relief of poverty and the elimination of unjust social structures, not conversion to the Catholic faith. The Pope bluntly disavows this notion, saying: "The poor are hungry for God, not just for bread and freedom. Missionary activity must first of all bear witness to and proclaim salvation in Christ, and establish local Churches which then become means of liberation in every sense" (83). The U.S. bishops had made the same point a few years earlier in their own pastoral statement on the missions, *To the Ends of the Earth*: "Often those who have not heard the Gospel are doubly poor, doubly hungry, doubly oppressed. . . . Their hunger is not only for bread and rice, but also for the Word that gives meaning to their existence" (30).

Continuing Need for Missionary Work • The Holy Father has emphasized the importance of ecumenism in preparing for the third millennium of Christianity. The second millennium began with the Great Schism of East and West — Orthodoxy and Roman Catholicism — in 1054 and at midpoint saw the Protestant Reformation. Surely a great and hope-filled drive for Christian unity should mark the new age. But how can missionaries continue working to bring groups and individuals into full union with the Church in this atmosphere? Why must everyone be Catholic? Will not other Christian churches find this zeal an insult? Can people not be saved as Orthodox, as Anglicans, as Protestants, just as they can as Muslims, Buddhists, and animists?

Indeed they can, as the *Catechism of the Catholic Church* (819) and *Redemptoris Missio* (55) explicitly state. Salvation is the work of the Spirit, who disposes as he wills. Nevertheless, the Church has been sent to all of humanity to extend Christ's saving work, a task she can never ignore. Vatican II's *Decree on Ecumenism, Unitatis Redintegratio*, says without equivocation: "For it is through

Christ's Catholic Church alone, which is the universal help towards salvation, that the fullness of the means of salvation can be obtained" (3). The Church must engage in dialogue with all Christians in a most earnest search for unity (cf. CCC 813-822). Moreover, "the Church proposes; she imposes nothing" (*Redemptoris Missio*, 39); but she is the "seed, sign and instrument" (*Redemptoris Missio*, 18) of the kingdom, which entails a solemn responsibility always to evangelize.

Sadly, the Church in the United States has lost much of its missionary impetus in recent years, despite the efforts of the Society for the Propagation of the Faith, which administers the celebration of World Mission Sunday every October, and the Holy Childhood Association, which links Catholic children in a missionary spirit with the children of other lands. According to the U.S. Catholic Mission Association, there were 9,447 American missionaries in the field in 1968. By 1992 the number had shrunk to 5,441, a forty-two percent drop. Despite a rapidly growing number of lay missionaries — 406 in 1992 — the U.S. effort seemed dispirited and confused as the third millennium approached. The relativism that treats all Christian denominations and all religions as equal instruments of salvation weighed heavily on it.

Faith and hope bid us repeat that the Church is missionary by nature. Therefore, the Church will enter into every culture, accepting what is good, purifying what is less so. If the United States no longer sends missionaries in the year 2050 or 2150, then Africa or China or South America will. In her first two thousand years, the Church has made disciples of only about twenty percent of humanity, and many are "cultural Catholics," or Catholics in name only. There is still a universe to win for Christ. "Missionary activity is nothing else, and nothing less, than the manifestation of God's plan, its epiphany and realization in the world and in history; that by which God, through mission, clearly brings to its conclusion the history of salvation" (*Ad Gentes*, 9).

See: Church, Membership in; Church, Nature,

Origin, and Structure of; Ecumenism; Evangelization; Redemption.

Suggested Readings: CCC 813-822, 849-858. Vatican Council II, *Decree on Ecumenism, Unitatis Redintegratio*; *Decree on the Church's Missionary Activity, Ad Gentes.* John Paul II, *On the Permanent Validity of the Church's Missionary Mandate, Redemptoris Missio.* National Conference of Catholic Bishops, *To the Ends of the Earth.*

David M. Byers

MIXED MARRIAGES

Many complexities and difficulties accompany mixed marriage, that is, marriage between a Catholic and a baptized non-Catholic. These difficulties, the *Catechism of the Catholic Church* says, "must not be underestimated. They arise from the fact that the separation of Christians has not yet been overcome. The spouses risk experiencing the tragedy of Christian disunity even in the heart of their own home" (1634). According to Church law, such marriages cannot be licitly contracted without the express permission of the proper authority, usually the local bishop, who is not to grant it unless the Catholic party is ready to protect his or her own faith and sincerely promises to do whatever is necessary to have the children baptized and educated as Catholics (cf. Canons 1124-1125).

God's law itself, and not just canon law, would forbid such marriages if the Catholic party is weak in his or her faith, and there is real danger that the partner may draw him or her completely away from it. There is no greater loss than the loss of faith. By the same token, there is no greater gift than the gift of faith. It is logical therefore that the very love of the Catholic party for his or her spouse — whose freedom must be fully respected — serves as an inspiration to pray and work sincerely so that both may embrace that fullness of Christ's message and gifts which are to be found in the Catholic Church.

See: Disparity of Cult; Marriage; Marriage, Sacrament of.

MODERNISM

The term "Modernism" refers to a spirit of philosophical and theological inquiry that developed in the later years of the nineteenth century. The pre-Modernist period, represented by the early critical work of the French Church historian Louis Duchesne (1843-1922), should be interpreted in light of the almost complete destruction of an active theological culture occurring in Western Europe in the wake of the French Revolution and after the period of the Napoleonic wars.

The definitive condemnation of Félicité De Lamennais in 1834 illustrates the unhappy results of working for renewal in the Church and for a Christian reform of society without the intellectual formation that comes from a complete theological education. On his deathbed, Lamennais, a brilliant French essayist, remarked that his generation of theologians "never had a father" to instruct them. The French Dominican Henri-Dominique Lacordaire, who had been an early companion of Lamennais, later pronounced his theological notions bizarre.

Because of ongoing political turmoil and other events in continental Europe during the nineteenth century, not much advance was made in establishing normative standards for Catholic theology. Even the documents of Vatican Council I (1869-1870) provided authoritative instruction only concerning Revelation and the authority of the Roman Pontiff. It is against this background of a theological vacuum, as well as the intense historical efforts to uncover the origins of Christianity, that one should approach the Modernist crisis. For while Modernism is commonly identified as a good-will attempt on the part of some nineteenth-century clerical and lay theologians to refresh Roman Catholic doctrine by appeal to then-modern notions in both philosophy and the historical and social sciences, the Modernist experience is better understood as a fledgling effort on the part of some European writers to develop a new intellectual culture for the Church. Unfortunately, the Modernists attempted to achieve this goal while lacking a sufficient acquaintance with Divine Revelation and without paying much heed to the Church's Magisterium.

History of Modernism • Scholars generally agree that it is anachronistic to use the term "Modernism" in reference to the usual list of persons included in an account of the Modernist movement. Modernism, then, was not a concerted plot to subvert the Church. The intellectuals involved did not consider themselves to be part of a planned program of renewal, even if they shared the same general cultural presuppositions of educated nineteenth-century gentlemen. Indeed, these authors worked to a large extent independently, and kept in touch mainly through the epistolary services of Baron Friedrich von Hügel (1852-1925), an important religious figure in cultured English circles. Except for the Anglo-Irish Jesuit George Tyrrell (1861-1909), most of the better known figures of the Modernist period worked in France.

It is commonly said that the publication of Maurice Blondel's *L'Action* in 1893 marks an initial moment in the crystallization of the Modernist movement. A French layman, Blondel remained a devout Catholic throughout his life, even though his philosophy of "action" fueled some of the Modernists' efforts to dissociate Catholic thought from the categories employed in a classical metaphysics of being. Blondel's "method of immanence" favored an experiential method in philosophy, which Blondel assumed would more easily lead a person to accept the truth of Christianity. Experience also dominated in the mind of Alfred Loisy (1857-1940), "the Father of Catholic Modernism," who worked in the field of biblical criticism. His relativist view of truth, based on broad philosophical reflections about the relationship of meaning to context, drew suspicion upon his 1902 book, *L'Evangile et L'Eglise*, which many held to be one of the principal targets of the condemnations in Pope Pius X's 1908 encyclical *Pascendi Dominici Gregis*. Loisy's theory of truth as essentially changeable led him to advance an evolutionary account of the Church that had the unhappy result of suggesting that full efficacy of the Church's mission must await the end time. Writing after Charles Darwin's publication in 1859 of

On the Origin of Species, the Modernists were commonly influenced by popular views about evolution. One of the few Italian Modernists, the poet and philosopher Antonio Fogazzaro (1842-1911), merited a place on the Index of Forbidden Books because of his premature efforts to reconcile the theory of evolution with Church teaching.

Nineteenth-century American pragmatism, as set forth by thinkers such as William James, influenced some Modernist authors, including the French Oratorian Lucien Laberthonnière (1860-1932). His view of "moral dogmatism" actually embodied a thoroughgoing pragmatic interpretation of religious truth. Like many Modernist authors, Laberthonnière assumed that the Kantian critique of both speculative and practical reason made it impossible henceforth to pursue theological reflection along the lines of realist metaphysics and teleological ethics, which had inspired the best of thirteenth-century Scholastic thought. Because they were captivated by popular intellectual trends, many Modernists rejected as too intellectual the efforts of some theologians to construct a new systematic theology inspired by the great medieval accomplishment of Sts. Thomas Aquinas and Bonaventure and their followers. At the same time, however, the Church was actively encouraging the renewal of Catholic theology and philosophy according to the mind and the doctrine of St. Thomas Aquinas, which Pope Leo XIII commended in his 1879 encyclical *Aeterni Patris*.

Because of its fundamentally deconstructionist program, the Modernist spirit spread quickly among the lower clergy and even among some Church officeholders. The Church recognized that the "supernatural sense of faith" belonging by right to the baptized was in danger of being replaced with tenets that, though culturally relevant, reflected more the philosophical fashions of the late nineteenth century than the teachings of the Gospel. In an effort to impress on candidates for Holy Orders and for other posts in the Church the serious danger in the Modernist mentality, the Holy See required that these clerics pronounce an "Oath against Modernism." This requirement was in effect until Vatican Council II.

Many of the specific issues that were debated in the Modernist period have now been resolved by authentic advances in theology. At the close of the twentieth century, the Church has achieved at least a general agreement about the requirements for doing Roman Catholic theology. There is a lesson to be learned from the Modernist history, and it is not that the official Church always crushes creative initiatives. Maurice Blondel, who maintained a respectful spirit toward ecclesiastical authority throughout the period when the Church was obliged to take disciplinary action against the less submissive Modernists, died with a reputation for sanctity of life; he was a daily communicant at his parish church in Aix-en-Provence. His cause for beatification is presently under discussion in Rome.

See: Divine Revelation; Evolution; Inerrancy; Knowledge of God; Magisterium; Miracles; Rationalism; Sacred Scripture; Science and the Church; Teleological Ethics; Thomism.

Suggested Readings: CCC 74-94. Pius X, *Pascendi Dominici Gregis*; *Sacrorum Antistitum*. Sacred Congregation of the Holy Office, *Lamentabili Sane Exitu*. A. Vidler, *A Variety of Catholic Modernists*. R. Haight, "The Unfolding of Modernism in France: Blondel, Laberthonnière, Le Roy," *Theological Studies* 35 (1974).

Romanus Cessario, O.P.

MODES OF RESPONSIBILITY

The modes of responsibility are the primary specifications of the basic moral criterion or first principle. One way of expressing the most general moral principle is: Love God and love neighbor. Also: One ought to choose (and otherwise will) in such a way as to respect all basic human goods, both in oneself and in others. From this moral principle one can derive very specific moral norms, such as: One ought never intentionally kill innocent human persons; or: One ought (in general) to fulfill one's promises. The modes of responsibility are implications of the first moral principle that are not as specific as these norms, but are still more specific than the first principle.

Emotions can deflect us from respect for all human goods in oneself and others. The modes of responsibility specify the various ways this can occur and prescribe against its happening. Thus, one should not be deterred from pursuing real human goods by mere felt inertia or laziness (first mode), or by individualism (second mode), or by desire for pleasure (third mode). Likewise, one should not let mere fear or aversion (as opposed to a reasonable concern for a real harm to a good) deflect one from pursuing real human goods (fourth mode).

One should not let the mere emotional attachment to oneself or other people close to one (as opposed to a real duty to oneself or others close to one) determine how one chooses, for this is to act out of partiality (fifth mode). One should not pursue the mere experience or appearance of a good, in a way that interferes with sharing in the real good — that is, one should not prefer appearances to reality (sixth mode).

One should not, out of hostility, choose to destroy, damage, or impede any intrinsic human good (seventh mode.) And, finally, one should not choose to destroy, damage, or impede one instance of an intrinsic good for the sake of another instance of an intrinsic good. That is, as St. Paul points out (cf. Rom 3:8), one should not do evil that good may come from it (eighth mode).

See: Absolute Moral Norms; Conscience; Human Goods; Natural Law; Practical Reason.

MODESTY

Modesty is allied to the cardinal virtue of temperance and, more specifically, to chastity. This moral virtue, often also called "decency," moderates and controls the impulse of sexual display and responsiveness thereto by men and women.

Such display may consist of merely conventional, social signs of gender: proclaiming one's masculinity or femininity via words, looks, modes of action or dress, and the like. This communication is normal and usually harmless. Modesty seeks to domesticate, as it were, a set of more directly sexual innuendoes or emblems that tend to excite and stimulate the genital drive. However much concrete forms of modesty may vary from one culture to another or in different historical periods, genital modesty and immodesty, decency and shamelessness are universal moral categories for humanity.

Modesty authorizes sexual display where genital fulfillment is allowed, that is, in marriage. Outside of that it excludes both things as more or less sinful, in light of intention, culpable ignorance or inadvertence, and the unchaste consequences for both parties.

Two physiological facts relevant to chastity and, more particularly, to modesty are often insufficiently stressed. Women tend to be more latent, nonphysical, and sluggish in responding to sexual stimuli; if not duly forewarned, they may overlook that what for them is innocent can affect men quite differently. It takes very little display to set masculine passion raging. And, once aroused, rare and perhaps even heroic is the man who can desist from following the sexual chain of events through to the end.

Then there is the matter of men impulsively comparing, if only visually, their respective sexual endowments, as in, say, locker-room situations. This may be relatively harmless, but it also may suffice to undo a man's resistance, perhaps at some future moment of weakness. Male immodesty of this sort not only can prey upon the lust of committed, receptive homosexuals but can have lastingly harmful consequences for young men of uncertain sexual orientation, for example, by sowing doubts as to their heterosexuality. It would appear that many cases of male homosexuality involve a sense of sexual inferiority.

A modest man thus will keep to a minimum situations of nudity among fellow men or boys and, above all, will restrain his eyes, imagination, and memory in relation to women. A modest woman will dress modestly and avoid gestures or words that might seem flirtatious.

According to the *Catechism of the Catholic Church*, modesty "protects the intimate center of the person," keeping veiled what should be; "guides how one looks at others and behaves toward them"; "inspires one's choice of clothing"; "keeps silence or reserve where there is evident risk of unhealthy curiosity"; "[protests] against the voyeuristic explorations of the human body in certain advertisements, or the solicitations of certain media that go too far in the exhibition of intimate things"; and "inspires a way of life which makes it possible to resist the allurements of fashion and the pressures of prevailing ideologies" (2521-2524).

See: Capital Sins; Chastity; Concupiscence; Human Virtues; Lust; Purity; Sexuality, Human; Sin; Vices.

MORAL PRINCIPLES, CHRISTIAN

Christian life is far more than observance of a moral code. To become Christians is to be given, as a gift, a new life in Christ. This new life is far more than a new morality. It enables us to enter into friendship with the Blessed Trinity, to love and to forgive one another, and to taste the joy of that new life in faith and hope and love that God pours into the hearts of those who accept his grace.

Yet believers, empowered by God's grace, are called to "lead a life worthy of God" (1 Th 2:12). There are works of love that we have a duty to do, and evil deeds that we must avoid. Being morally upright people is not sufficient to make us Christians; and, indeed, we are not able consistently to lead morally good lives without the help of God's grace. But a life of faith is not a lawless life. If we wish to be faithful followers of Christ, we must walk freely in the ways he points out for us.

The New Testament presents various kinds of duties that Christians have. Some things we *must not do*, for certain kinds of deliberate actions are incompatible with love. A Christian must avoid those evil kinds of acts that the Ten Commandments forbid (cf. Mt 19:16-19), and every kind of act so incompatible with love that those who do such things cannot "inherit the kingdom of God" (1 Cor 6:9; cf. Gal 5:21; CCC 2072). But faith teaches *positive duties* also: We have the duty to believe God, to trust him, and to do the works of love (cf. Jn 6:28-29; Mt 25:34-46; CCC 1965-

1968). Moreover, we are to acquire those virtues needed to give consistency and faithfulness to our lives: "Clothe yourselves with compassion, kindness, humility, meekness, and patience. . . . Above all, clothe yourselves with love" (Col 3:12, 14; cf. CCC 1810-1811).

To grow toward the perfection of love of God and one another, we are to live lives shaped by the gifts of the Holy Spirit and by the Beatitudes (cf. CCC 1716-1717, 1830-1831).

While some of the moral directives of the Gospel are not precepts but counsels (like the invitation given us to give all we have to the poor, and to live a celibate life for the sake of the kingdom [CCC 1973-1975]), it is far from true that all the Gospel's difficult and sublime precepts are merely counsels or optional ideals. However much we must suffer to guard the faith, or to keep the commandments, or to forgive those who have really hurt us, the Gospel gives us firm precepts in all these matters; but it promises also to make "light and easy" the saving burden of Christ's commandments (Mt 11:28-30).

Foundational Principles • The many moral directives taught by Catholic faith are not simply a mass of unrelated rules. All the duties faith teaches flow from simple and certain first principles. Christ teaches plainly that the greatest precepts are those of love: that we should love God with all our hearts and love our neighbor as ourselves (Mt 22:37-39). He teaches, moreover, that *all* our moral duties really flow from these two. "On these two commandments hang all the law and the prophets" (Mt 22:40; cf. CCC 2055). This means that all the positive and negative duties of the Ten Commandments, all the moral requirements spoken by all the prophets and by Christ himself — all express simply what love requires. Nothing is needed except what love makes necessary.

Still, and this, too, is crucial, love does in fact make many things necessary. For example, one who swears falsely or commits adultery is in the wrong, for whoever performs these specific kinds of acts is really failing to do what love demands.

With all Christian tradition, St. Thomas

Aquinas accepts faithfully the Gospel teaching that the two commandments of love are the first principles of moral life. One can, with a modest amount of reflection, see that all the precepts of the Decalogue are valid, because the precepts of love do imply the truth of the commandments (*Summa Theologiae,* I-II, 100, 3; CCC 1970). This is especially clear when we consider the material of the commandments in the light of what love requires, and in the light of other New Testament precepts noted below.

Contemporary Catholic moralists have done creative work in tracing out more precisely the path by which it can be shown that the saying of the Lord is true: that it really is the case that all the basic precepts of revealed religion follow necessarily from the duty to love. That means that, in a sense, love alone is required of us; but this is a meaningful and true love, a love like that spelled out in the Gospels, a love from which the Ten Commandments and many other specific precepts quite literally follow.

Other kinds of moral directives also serve as principles in Christian morality. In addition to the two precepts of love, from which all else flows, there are other Gospel principles basic to Christian morality. These clearly flow from the requirements of love and help us to see how surely a variety of universal precepts, like those of the Ten Commandments, also follow from love (cf. Rom 13:9). Thus we are taught in the Golden Rule that we should "Do to others as you would have them do to you" (Lk 6:31); that is, we should treat each person with the fairness and concern we would wish others to show us. Observance of this, Christ tells us, sums up "the law and the prophets" (Lk 16:16).

One path such golden concern must take is this: We should never deliberately do harm to anyone, for "Love does no wrong to a neighbor" (Rom 13:10). Each neighbor is a person, an image of God, a bearer of inalienable rights, one to whom we must never deliberately do evil, even as a means to benefit others. And from the fact that we should never deliberately harm our neighbor, it follows, as the commandments conclude, that we should never injure the neighbor by murder or adultery or perjury (Rom 13:9).

A variety of factors must be considered in determining whether a particular human act is a morally good or bad one. All of the essential elements that determine whether an act is good or bad must be good for the act to be simply good. First, the kind of act done must be a good kind of act (one capable of serving love of God and of neighbor). The intention for which the act is done must also be good. Moreover, the circumstances must serve the goodness of the act. That means, for example, that one must not foresee that the act (however good its kind and the intention may be) is likely to produce evil effects out of proportion to the good the act is expected to realize (CCC 1749-1756).

Moral Absolutes • Christian faith has always taught that some moral directives have no exceptions at all. It is true that many moral rules indeed have exceptions. For example, we should keep our promises, but not all promises (such as promises to help another do something evil) should be kept. For such moral rules one needs to know the motive and circumstances of the individual act before one can make a final judgment on whether it is good or bad.

But some moral rules have no exceptions. Such exceptionless rules (called moral absolutes) include: never directly kill the innocent; never commit adultery; never swear falsely. One would need only to know that an act is an act of such a kind to know that one ought not do this act. For such acts "in and of themselves, independently of circumstances and intentions, are always gravely illicit by reason of their object" (CCC 1756; cf. Pope John Paul II, *The Splendor of Truth, Veritatis Splendor,* 79-83). Performance of such acts is always incompatible with authentic personal love.

Also characteristic of Christian faith is the teaching that one may not do any evil deed in hopes that great good may come of it (cf. Rom 3:8; *Veritatis Splendor,* 80). To choose in the freedom of one's heart deliberately to do a kind of deed that is evil — a deed like slaying the innocent, or committing fornication, or swearing falsely — is to do what a good person may never do: deliberately attack a basic good, bring about a real evil in a human person. It is true that the evil brought about in such acts — death, the unwitting acceptance of falsehood, and the like — are only "physical" evils; but the *deliberate doing* of such things is a moral evil, an offense against persons whom we have a duty to love and be concerned for.

Sometimes fear is expressed that the reality of moral absolutes might press people into impossible dilemmas. So, for instance, people have a duty to guard their families or protect those they love. Might not the only way to accomplish these things in particular circumstances be by performing a deed of this kind — one that violates a moral absolute, one that faith calls intrinsically evil, such as contraception or perjury? But faith is coherent: It reminds people that they have no duty to do, and never should do, evil kinds of deeds in order to obtain goods they have some duty to reach. One may have a duty to move heaven and earth in efforts to fulfill one's duties through good acts; but one never is obliged or even permitted to do something really evil in order to achieve things that ought to be achieved. Here and now a good man has no way of achieving specific good objectives if the only means available is a bad one.

The Church always honored the martyrs who laid down their lives rather than do intrinsically evil deeds (cf. *Veritatis Splendor*, 90-94). St. Thomas More, for example, could see no other way to save his own life and to guard good things for his family, than by agreeing to swear falsely as the king demanded. But he knew he ought not swear falsely for any reasons whatever, and he had the courage not to do so. Sometimes heroism is needed to be faithful to what love requires and the saving law of God demands. But God never fails to make accessible to the faithful in difficult circumstances the measure of grace that they need to be as generous as duty requires.

Principles of Other Kinds • There are other kinds of principles underlying Christian morality, principles that are not themselves moral directives but cast light on the nature and meaning of moral principles. Some of these are spelled out with striking force in Pope John Paul II's encyclical *Veritatis Splendor* (cf. 35-45). For example, the reality of freedom (especially the freedom involved in free choice) and the truth that free human actions are of overwhelming importance are principles of Christian morality. Morality is not concerned simply with seeing to it that good deeds are done (it would be very alien to Christian morality to seek to condition or manipulate people so that they do good deeds) or that good results are produced. Rather, Christian morality is concerned primarily with freely doing deeds that are truly good; and unless human actions were free, they could not be morally important (cf. CCC 1749; *Veritatis Splendor*, 38-41).

Law is also a principle of Christian morality. But Christian morality is not a legalistic code. The divine law that gives light to our lives is not a mere act of will, not an arbitrary imposition. God does not simply command us to do or not to do certain things, without gracious concern for our freedom, our hopes, and our fulfillment. His eternal law, upon which all other just law is based, is no arbitrary precept. It is his eternal plan, which is rooted in intelligence and love, a plan that guides the whole world and each person toward authentic fulfillment. This law presses us to seek the good goals we ourselves by our very nature long for — goals we must pursue if our lives are to make sense. Grounded in this saving plan of God, the Christian moral law, natural and revealed, is not a set of arbitrary precepts: It is a guidance given by God's great love to enable us to find paths that are truly good for us and that really fulfill our lives (cf. CCC 1950).

Grace, too, is a principle of Christian moral life. For God has called us not only to some purely natural end, like human satisfaction in an entirely human community; rather, he made us to become his friends, and to have inexpressible joy in sharing his divine life. Only by God's favor, however, can we perform acts that lead to the salvation for which we were made. Moreover, in our fallen state, grace is needed to live a moral life faithfully (cf. CCC 1996).

The moral law is both a natural law and a revealed law. In fact, through Moses and the prophets, and most of all through Jesus Christ, God has made known to us the ways we are to live to please God, to fulfill the requirements of love, and to come to everlasting life.

Such Revelation was in some senses not necessary, since it is possible for people to know much of what the law requires even without Revelation. The moral law that faith calls us to observe is a law corresponding to what our own hearts need; it is a natural law, and we are naturally inclined to know it. "What the law requires is written on their hearts" (Rom 2:15).

To say this, however, is not to suggest that everyone *really* knows all that the natural law requires. Obviously many people today do not know that euthanasia, say, or divorce is morally wrong. Nevertheless, to say that the natural law is written in the heart is to say its principles are indeed accessible to all. All of us are able to know that we should do what is truly good and should avoid evil; we are able to recognize some values that are genuinely good; and we are capable of understanding for ourselves that some kinds of acts are indeed morally wrong (cf. CCC 1954-1960). From these principles of natural law accessible to all, everything really follows. Still, amid the scandals, confusions, and passions of the world, many become confused and sincerely do not know clearly how they should guide their steps.

To remedy this situation, the natural law itself is revealed by God. The Decalogue sums up its basic elements. The teaching of Christ presents the moral law with great clarity and attractiveness. The graces associated with faith in Christ give deeper assurance to those who seek to lead good lives than any other source could provide. And those who know who Christ is, and know that he teaches in the Gospels and in his Church, have the right and the duty to walk in his ways.

Because the moral law is a natural law, we can defend it intelligently even before those who have not received the gifts of Revelation and faith. Because it is a revealed law, even the simple can be certain of it in the light of faith, even when they are not intellectually prepared to defend moral truth against every sophisticated objection.

Christ As the Principle of Christian Morality • Christ himself is clearly a first principle of our moral lives. He is himself the primary teacher of the way we are to live to please God, and he is the source of the light of faith by which we can grasp with certainty the truth and goodness of his paths. Moreover, he is the source of the strength we need to walk faithfully in the ways of life. He is the goodness that makes leading an excellent moral life attractive; he is the mercy that encourages us in all trials. He is himself both the life for which we long, and the way by which we can come to life.

Christian moral life is clearly not a dogged obeying of rules. It is rooted in love, and therefore at its heart it calls for a willing pursuit of what is truly good, for ourselves and for all we love. The Bible celebrates the truly and deeply good depths of reality. It celebrates life and friendship, truth and integrity of spirit, beauty and living in a glad, playful spirit before the Lord. The elements of life that philosophers have recognized as the goals of human striving, the goods that make human life rich and great, are also celebrated by the Scriptures.

Christian morality calls us to a humane and generous pursuit of what is good. Our actions and our lives are not simply instruments by which we seek to pursue even in unworthy ways the "greatest amount" of good. In special ways we must be concerned that our actions and our lives be good. It is neither wise nor loving to pursue good effects through evil means. The world was made, not so much that we should produce endless good things here, as that we should here shape loving actions and loving lives — shape ourselves, and encourage others to live in ways that respect what is truly good. The saints did not avoid evil deeds out of a selfish desire to obtain rewards or a shallow longing to escape every criticism. They avoided evil and brought about immense good in the world because they knew that, in pursuing the goodness and generosity God required of them, their lives would also become a blessing for all. St. Thomas

More could not have foreseen how God would bring good out of the trials he endured patiently. But he knew that generous faithfulness to all God's ways would be the only secure way to fulfill his own life and bless all those whom he loved.

See: Absolute Moral Norms; Beatitudes; Cardinal Virtues; Conscience; Divine Revelation; Evangelical Counsels; Freedom, Human; Fundamental Option; Grace; Law of Christ; Legalism; Martyrdom; Natural Law; Relativism; Sin; Ten Commandments.

Suggested Readings: CCC 1749-1756, 1949-1974, 1987-2016, 2052-2074. Vatican Council II, *Pastoral Constitution on the Church in the Modern World, Gaudium et Spes*, 22, 27-32, 79. John Paul II, *The Splendor of Truth, Veritatis Splendor*. National Conference of Catholic Bishops, *To Live in Christ Jesus*. G. Grisez, *The Way of the Lord Jesus*, Vol. 1, *Christian Moral Principles*, pp. 173-204, 599-626. R. Schnackenburg, *The Moral Teaching of the New Testament*.

Ronald D. Lawler, O.F.M. Cap.

MORTAL SIN

A mortal sin is a grave violation of God's law and an act incompatible with love of God. Three conditions are required for mortal sin: First, what one chooses to do must be a gravely wrong sort of act; second, one must know that it is gravely wrong; and third, one must choose to do so with full freedom (cf. CCC 1855, 1857).

Scripture itself points out kinds of sins that are deadly, so serious that "those who do such things shall not inherit the kingdom of God" (Gal 5:21). The Ten Commandments forbid basic kinds of mortal sins. The Gospels portray the Lord telling a rich young man that if he wishes to enter the kingdom of God, he must keep the commandments: He should not kill, commit adultery, bear false witness (Mk 10:19; cf. CCC 1858). In her ordinary teaching, the Church (as in the *Catechism of the Catholic Church*) teaches the faithful the sorts of sins that are grave, or mortal, in kind.

Mortal sins are not accidental occurrences, but fully human acts. One who sins mortally knows

that what he is doing is gravely wrong and in serious opposition to God's will, and his consent is sufficiently deliberate to be a true personal choice (CCC 1859). Some mortal sins are sins of weakness; but if the agent were so driven by external or internal pressures or by pathological disorders so disruptive that he could not avoid doing the act, there would be no mortal sin (CCC 1859).

The consequences of mortal sin are tragic. It results in the loss of love of God and of grace. "If it is not redeemed by repentance and God's forgiveness, it causes . . . the eternal death of hell" (CCC 1861). Still, God calls the sinner to repentance.

See: Freedom, Human; Moral Principles, Christian; Sin; Venial Sin.

MYSTICAL BODY OF CHRIST

The Church cannot be understood just by examining her visible elements. While she is an institution, the Church also and particularly is a living *organism*, with spiritual and mystical dimensions much more important than any human analysis reveals.

"The Church is the Body of Christ. Through the Spirit and his action in the sacraments, above all the Eucharist, Christ, who once was dead and is now risen, establishes the community of believers as his own Body" (CCC 805).

This way of expressing the nature of the Church is not a mere metaphor. As a persecutor of the early Christians, Saul of Tarsus thought he was opposing an institution and discovered it was a Person: "I am Jesus, whom you are persecuting" (Acts 9:5). "I am Jesus . . .": Christ and those who make up his Church, are one. From this experience Paul developed his theology of the Body of Christ: Christ the head of the Body, and we his members (cf. Eph 1:22-23; 1 Cor 12:8-11; 2 Cor 5:14-15).

Christ — God-become-man — not only redeems us from sin but incorporates us into himself, and so we become sons and daughters of God. We really share in his human-divine life as members of his Body. As in the human body, vitality (which means union and strength) is shown in the different functions of its members, but especially in the organic connection between them, and above all in the links of each one with the head (Col 1:18).

Each Christian, then, has a personal, voluntary, organic, vital, life-giving participation in this Body. So the members of the Church do not live unconnected lives. As in a true organism, the same life circulates among them, carrying strength to each according to his or her need. To separate oneself voluntarily from that life-giving circulation is to invite death.

See: Church, Membership in; Church, Nature, Origin, and Structure of; Communio; Communion of Saints.

MYSTICISM

The word "mystical" was originally used by the people of ancient Greece to designate those who had been initiated into the secret religious rites and cult. In the New Testament, however, the mysteries were not to be kept secret but made known to all. Jesus stated: "I thank thee, Father, Lord of heaven and earth, that thou hast hidden these things from the wise and understanding and revealed them to babes" (Mk 11:25); "To you it has been given to know the secrets of the kingdom of heaven" (Mk 13:11). St. Paul saw himself and the other Apostles as "stewards of the mysteries of God" (1 Cor 4:1) and preachers of "the mystery of Christ" (Eph 3:4).

The Jewish religious thinker Philo of Alexandria (20 B.C.-A.D. 50) applied the word "mystical" to the secret and hidden meaning of God's word. Eventually the term signified the allegorical interpretation of Sacred Scripture. Origen (died 254) referred to the exegesis of Scripture as "mystical and ineffable contemplation," the result of study and experiential knowledge of God. By the time of Constantine in the fourth century, Christian writers were using the word in connection with the spiritual presence of Christ in Scripture and in the sacraments, especially the Eucharist.

In the sixth century, a Syrian monk known as the Pseudo-Dionysius wrote a treatise that was translated into Latin in the ninth century under the title *Theologia Mystica*. His writings have had a great influence on the spirituality of the Western Church.

The word "mystical" was not widely used in the Latin Church until the late Middle Ages, and then there was a shift in meaning with theologians like St. Bernard (died 1153). Mystical experience, mystical theology, and contemplation were interchangeable words. Thus, St. Bonaventure (died 1274) defined mysticism as "the raising of the mind to God through the desire of love." Jean Gerson (died 1428) described it as an experimental knowledge of God, as did St. Teresa of Ávila (died 1582). Finally, St. John of the Cross (died 1592) explicitly states that mystical theology is "that secret knowledge of God which spiritual persons call contemplation" (*Spiritual Canticle*, 27, 5).

Early in the twentieth century, there was an upsurge of interest in the psychology of religious experience as well as mysticism. We can list, for example, W.R. Inge, *Christian Mysticism* (1899); A. Thorold, *An Essay in Aid of the Better Appreciation of Catholic Mysticism* (1900); W. James, *The Varieties of Religious Experience* (1902); R.M. Jones, *Studies in Mystical Religion* (1909); A.B. Sharpe, *Mysticism: Its True Nature and Value* (1910); and E. Underhill, *Mysticism* (1910).

By far the majority of authors agree that the mystical experience is something infused, secret, intuitive, and above the ordinary operations of the virtues. It is commonly admitted today in Catholic theology that mystical experience is the result of the operation of the gifts of the Holy Spirit, which means it is an experience passively received in which the Holy Spirit is the primary agent. Moreover, since the Second Vatican Council, the Church has officially proclaimed that all persons, regardless of their state of life, are called to the perfection of charity (cf. *Constitution on the Church, Lumen Gentium*, 40).

Authentic Mysticism • In recent years, there has been a tendency to expand the definition of mystical experience to include occult, psychedelic, and parapsychological phenomena. It must be maintained that the distinctive element in the mystical experience is that it is an immediate contact with God. It is, therefore, an experience in a religious context, though not necessarily in a Christian context, since it is possible for someone outside Christianity to have an authentic mystical experience. Karl Rahner, for one, made a distinction between genuine mystical experience and paranormal phenomena.

As has been said, the first requirement for genuine mystical experience is immediate contact with God. Second, the mystical experience, like all vital activities, admits of degrees of intensity, from a minimal experience to an ecstatic union. Third, since the mystical experience is essentially a received experience, it comes from God through the operation of the gifts of the Holy Spirit. Additional descriptions can be found in the classical work *The Graces of Interior Prayer* by A. Poulain.

In Catholic theology, the term "mystical phenomena" refers either to the concomitant phenomena that normally proceed from authentic mystical activity or the truly extraordinary phenomena that are not caused by the mystical experience. Theologians of the spiritual life have generally accepted the classification of concomitant phenomena drawn up by St. Teresa of Ávila in her *Interior Castle* (Fourth to Seventh Mansions). At the outset there will be an experimental knowledge of God, accompanied by spiritual joy, absorption in God, disdain for worldly pleasures, and a desire for greater perfection. As the individual progresses in sanctity, the passive purgation of senses and spirit takes place, followed by the sleep of the faculties, divine touches, ecstasy. Ultimately the individual reaches the transforming union and is confirmed in grace. All of the above are classified as concomitant mystical phenomena, although not every authentic mystic will experience all of them.

Extraordinary phenomena are not proof of the sanctity of the individual, since they may occur as "epiphenomena," or *gratiae gratis datae*. As such, they do not proceed from the sanctity of the individual nor are they proofs of sanctity. They can be attributed to any one of three causes: God, occult natural causes, or diabolical influence. Pope Benedict XIV, writing on the norms for beatification and canonization, promulgated the following rule for discernment: No phenomenon is to be attributed to a supernatural cause until all possible natural or diabolical causality has been examined and excluded (*De Beatificatione et Canonizatione Servorum Dei*). The difficulty in discernment arises from the fact that some pathological phenomena resulting from an occult or diabolical cause appear to be identical with authentic mystical phenomena, and vice versa. Consequently, no extraordinary phenomenon can ever be accepted as proof of a genuine mystical experience.

No saint is ever canonized precisely because of some extraordinary or charismatic phenomenon. What is required for canonization is the practice of virtue to a heroic degree; as usually stated, it requires "the perfection of charity." But if an individual has reached that state, the gifts of the Holy Spirit are operative, and he or she is in the mystical state.

See: Apparitions; Canonization; Charisms; Contemplation; Discernment; Extraordinary Gifts; Holy Spirit; Prayer; Private Revelation; Spiritual Exegesis.

Suggested Readings: CCC 749, 798-801, 1845, 2003, 2682. H. Egan, *Christian Mysticism*. A. Poulain, *The Graces of Interior Prayer*. E. Underhill, *Mysticism*. K. Rahner, *The Practice of Faith*.

Jordan Aumann, O.P.

N

NATIVITY

The content of the patrimony of faith regarding the virginal conception and birth of Jesus Christ has been contested from the very beginning and this has continued in our time, relying on positions already passé. Authors have denied or expressed doubts about the historical reality of these events. In practice, they tend to see the biblical data not so much as testimony to events that really took place, but as an affirmation of faith (*theologoumenon*) about Jesus Christ, Son of God from the time of his birth. The scriptural data are considered to be a dramatization in historical and biological terms of an exclusively theological event.

It is necessary to realize the cultural biases in this position. One bias rejects the possibility of miracles. Another represents the tendency to consider marital intercourse as the source and principle of all other values. There is a mistaken use of the historical-critical method, considered as almost absolute and in isolation from other methods of analyzing Scripture. The fundamental source, however, is the undue opposition posited between faith and history, so that theological significance is uprooted from its factual base.

Many decisive reasons favor the historical-biological reality of the virginal conception and birth of Jesus, above all the authenticity of the Gospel texts of Matthew and Luke (not to speak of the various references in Paul, Mark, and John). The account and the content of the Infancy Gospels have parallels neither in biblical literature nor in extra-biblical literature. Along with the differences in the two accounts of Matthew and Luke and the differences in their sources, there is a surprising and real convergence: the principal personages are the same

— Jesus, Mary, Joseph, Herod; the announcement of the birth of Jesus is made by an angel; the name of the child is Jesus, which means savior, light for the nations, and remission of sins.

Though he is described as the Son of David, Jesus is not born of Joseph, who is the head of the family but not his father. His Mother is the Virgin Mary, who conceived him by the Holy Spirit. In order to assert that he is the Son of David, Matthew and Luke must bring to the fore Mary's marriage to Joseph. It is Joseph who brings Jesus into the family and House of David. His birthplace is Bethlehem of Judah. His unusual conception and birth in both Gospels are attributed to the transcendent intervention of God. But the account is vastly different from pagan myths that spoke of some kind of physical union of a god with a woman who was to bring forth a son. Rather, God in this manner brings about the re-creation of humanity.

The Gospel writers use the same method for their narration of these events. The Infancy Gospels use all the resources of the Old Testament, but they also go beyond and, as it were, fulfill them. As René Laurentin says, "It is no longer a matter of Scripture shedding light on an event, but rather, the Christ event now explains Scripture, giving it a meaning never before suspected. Knowledge of Jesus becomes more important than knowledge of the Book" (*The Truth of Christmas*, pp. 450-451).

From the viewpoint of history as well as meaning, there is a real *concordantia discordantium* (agreement of disagreeing accounts). The two evangelists raise the same questions about the human origin of Jesus and give the same reply: Jesus is the Son of God from the beginning, and his birth in time happened in an extraordinary way. Even though this was a fact humanly embarrassing and hardly credible for the Jewish culture (Matthew) and the pagan world (Luke) of that time, they transmitted it because it corresponded to the reality. The sources of this tradition would be above all Mary (cf. Lk 2:19, 51) and even Joseph, who is the protagonist in the sources used by Matthew. If they had wanted to make up a *theologoumenon* adapted to their time, the evangelists would have referred to a Christ descended from heaven or would have said he was the son of David through his natural father, Joseph. But they did not take the easy way. Against every kind of docetism, ancient and modern, Christianity's founding event, the Incarnation, is firmly rooted in history.

See: Christological Controversies; Divine Revelation; Incarnation; Jesus Christ, God and Man; Jesus Christ, Life of; Mary, Mother of God; Mary, Perpetual Virginity of; Sacred Scripture.

NATURAL FAMILY PLANNING

The Catholic Church's teaching on childbearing is based on the principle of responsible parenthood. The Church does not teach that couples must have as many children as their bodies can bear. Rather, the principle of responsible parenthood maintains that parents have the responsibility of doing their best to educate their children to be good Christians. For many reasons, couples may judge that in order to be responsible parents they must limit the number of children they have. The Church finds methods of natural family planning (NFP) to be a morally acceptable means of limiting family size.

Many, often including those in the media and even in the medical profession, still confuse methods of natural family planning with what has been called the rhythm or calendar method. This method was based on the principle that a twenty-eight-day cycle is a normal cycle and that ovulation occurs midway through the cycle; if a woman was irregular (and most are), the calendar method required a great deal of abstinence or was ineffective.

Modern methods of natural family planning, or NFP, do not require that a woman be regular.

Rather, NFP is a highly scientific and reliable way of determining when a woman is fertile, no matter how long or short her cycle, since it does not depend upon counting days. NFP depends upon the observation of various bodily signs that signal that ovulation is imminent or has occurred.

How NFP Works • A brief description of how NFP works will assist in assessing it as a moral practice. A woman ovulates only once a month; the egg lives within her body only twenty-four hours and is fertilizable for only twelve of those. The sperm, however, can live within a woman's body for up to five days. Thus, if a couple do not desire a pregnancy, they must abstain from sexual intercourse some five days before ovulation and for at least twenty-four hours after ovulation. (Additional days of abstinence are generally advised to ensure that sexual intercourse does not occur during the fertile period.) A woman's body near the time of ovulation begins secreting a kind of mucus that helps the sperm travel to the ovum. As the hormones shift to cause this change in mucus, a woman's body temperature rises; her cervix also undergoes various changes in anticipation of a possible pregnancy. Most women can learn easily how to read these signs and can use this information either to avoid pregnancy or help achieve it. Different methods of NFP utilize different signs or different combinations of signs for determining the period of fertility.

Spacing of children can also be assisted by practicing ecological breastfeeding. Ecological breastfeeding (feeding a child exclusively with breast milk for the first six months and on demand) delays the return of fertility after a pregnancy and thus in itself provides natural spacing of about a year-and-a-half to three years between children.

Many couples are hesitant to use NFP because they fear that it may be ineffective. Yet studies done on the effectiveness of NFP show it to be more effective than any form of contraception. Couples often express hesitation because they fear the effect of abstinence upon their conjugal relationship. This fear is compounded by the fact that few abstain from sexual intercourse before marriage, and those who do not have become unduly dependent upon intercourse as a means of expressing their love for one another; they often have trouble adjusting to the abstinence required by NFP. Couples who have abstained from sexual intercourse before marriage, however, generally have little problem with the abstinence required by NFP. For them, abstinence is not primarily deprivation; rather, it echoes the abstinence they practiced before marriage out of love and respect for one another. They return to the affectionate modes of behavior of their courtship and often speak of the resumption of sexual relations after the abstinence as a honeymoon period.

Morality of NFP • Many have a difficult time grasping why NFP is morally permissible and contraception is not; after all, both practices involve the intention to have sexual intercourse, with the simultaneous intention not to have a child. But contraception is not wrong *because* it involves such intentions. Indeed, such intentions may be perfectly moral; spouses are not acting immorally in intending to have sexual intercourse, nor are they acting immorally in not intending to have children (if this is for morally justifiable, i.e., unselfish, reasons). Those who contracept choose an immoral means of achieving their purpose of having sexual intercourse while avoiding a pregnancy, whereas those using NFP choose a moral means of achieving their end.

A passage from Pope John Paul II's 1981 apostolic exhortation *The Christian Family in the Modern World, Familiaris Consortio,* makes a clear and emphatic statement about the difference between contraception and NFP: "In the light of the experience of many couples and of the data provided by the different human sciences, theological reflection is able to perceive and is called to study further *the difference, both anthropological and moral*, between contraception and recourse to the rhythm of the cycle: It is a difference which is much wider and deeper than is usually thought, one which involves in the final analysis two irreconcilable concepts of the human person and of human sexuality. The choice of the natural rhythms involves accepting the cycle of the person, that is the woman, and thereby accepting dialogue, reciprocal respect, shared responsibility and self-control. To accept the cycle and to enter into dialogue means to recognize both the spiritual and corporal character of conjugal communion, and to live personal love with its requirement of fidelity. In this context the couple comes to experience how conjugal communion is enriched with those values of tenderness and affection which constitute the inner soul of human sexuality, in its physical dimension also. In this way sexuality is respected and promoted in its truly and fully human dimension, and is never 'used' as an 'object' that, by breaking the personal unity of soul and body, strikes at God's creation itself at the level of the deepest interaction of nature and person" (32).

Some of the features of NFP described above suggest why NFP is morally permissible whereas contraceptives are not. First, it must be noted that NFP poses no health risks; it does not violate the well-being of the body; it does not treat fertility as though it were a defect needing to be corrected. Rather, it treats fertility with respect. The analogies are often cited between contraception and the practice of bulimia (vomiting after eating) on the one hand and between NFP and dieting on the other hand. Contraceptors and bulimics both wish to engage in an act and prevent that act from attaining its natural consequences: Contraceptors want the pleasure of the sexual act but not the baby that may result; bulimics want the pleasure of food but not the consequences. By contrast, dieters and users of NFP deny themselves legitimate pleasures when they are not able to accept the consequences of those pleasures. The desire to lose weight does not require that one not eat at all; rather, one eats those foods that do not have the consequences one needs to avoid, while users of NFP avoid the time of the month that has consequences they judge it good to avoid.

Moreover, especially for those living in severe poverty, it must be counted a very great advantage of NFP that it costs virtually nothing to use, whereas many other forms of contraception are expensive. Some methods also are difficult to "reverse," whereas NFP can immediately be put to use to help achieve pregnancy just as to avoid it.

When couples are abstaining during the fertile period, they are not thwarting the act of sexual intercourse, since they are not engaging in sexual intercourse; and when engaging in sexual intercourse during the infertile period, they are not withholding their fertility, since they do not have it to give at that time. They learn to live in accord with the natural rhythms of the body. In a word, use of NFP may involve nonprocreative acts, but never, as with contraception, antiprocreative acts.

One objection to contraception is that it violates the principle that the marital act should be an act of complete self-giving. But couples who practice periodic abstinence do not fail to achieve the marital goal of complete self-giving. Those engaging in sexual intercourse during the infertile time are giving all they have to give at that time. They are not simultaneously "giving and not giving" of their sexuality (as are contraceptors who are withholding their fertility); indeed, in abstaining they are giving the gift of self-restraint.

Effects Upon Marriage • Many find it odd that periodic abstinence should be beneficial rather than harmful to a marriage. But abstinence can be another way of expressing love, as it is between those who are not married or those for whom engaging in sexual intercourse involves a significant risk. Certainly, most who begin to use NFP, especially those who were not chaste before marriage and who have used contraception, generally find the abstinence required to be a source of some strain and irritability. Abstinence, like dieting or any form of self-restraint, brings its hardships; but, like dieting and other forms of self-denial, it also brings benefits. And, after all, spouses abstain for all sorts of reasons — because one or the other is out of town or ill, for instance.

Spouses using NFP find that the method helps them learn to communicate better with each other, and abstinence gives them the opportunity to do so. As they learn to communicate their affection in nongenital ways and learn to master their sexual desires, they find a new liberation in the ability to abstain from sexual intercourse. Many find that

an element of romance reenters the relationship during the times of abstinence and an element of excitement accompanies the reuniting. They have gained the virtue of self-mastery, since now they can control their sexual desires rather than being controlled by them.

Women using NFP generally feel revered by their husbands, since their husbands do not make them use unhealthy and unpleasant contraceptives. Men using NFP generally have greater self-respect, since they have gained control over their sexual desires and can now engage in sexual intercourse as an act of love, not as an act of mere sexual urgency. A proof that NFP is good for a marriage is that, whereas in the U.S. roughly half of all marriages end in divorce (and it is safe to assume that most of these couples are contracepting), very few couples who use NFP ever divorce; they seem to bond in a deeper way than those who contracept.

Although natural family planning is a moral means of planning family size, some express concern that NFP can be used with a contraceptive mentality. This expression signifies that couples are determined to be in charge of their family size and to make their lives easier by carefully restricting it, rather than allowing God to "send" them the number of children he chooses. Although it is possible for couples to use NFP with such an attitude, using NFP is never equivalent morally to using contraception, because, whereas contraception violates the natural ordination of the sexual act, NFP does not. Couples who use NFP with a "contraceptive mentality" are guilty of having a selfish and sinful attitude rather than performing disordered actions.

Many are confused as to what would qualify as moral reasons for the use of NFP. The Church gives minimal guidance on this matter. Pope Paul VI in the encyclical *Humanae Vitae*, 10, speaks of its being moral for couples to limit family size for concerns involving their physical, economic, psychological, and social conditions. Couples are asked to be generous with God in their childbearing, but are expected to be responsible in determining how many children they have the resources to raise. Couples through prayerful reflection should seek to ensure that their decisions for postponing or ceasing to have children are not governed by principles of comfort-seeking but are truly governed by unselfish motivations. Everyone should be careful about judging the motives and situations that lead others to make their decisions.

See: Chastity; Contraception; Education in Human Sexuality; Marriage, Goods of; Sexuality, Human.

Suggested Readings: CCC 2366-2372. John Paul II, *The Christian Family in the Modern World, Familiaris Consortio.* J. and S. Kippley, *The Art of Natural Family Planning.* J. Kippley, *Sex and the Marriage Covenant: A Basis for Morality.* J. Smith, *Humanae Vitae: A Generation Later.* J. Smith, ed., *Why Humanae Vitae Was Right: A Reader*, Chs. 17-20.

Janet E. Smith

NATURAL LAW

In his Letter to the Romans, St. Paul says that those who have not heard of the law of Moses, the Ten Commandments, still know what is right and wrong, because "what the law requires is written on their hearts" (Rom 2:15). This knowledge of what is right and wrong, somehow written on our hearts, has traditionally been referred to as the natural moral law.

Natural law can be considered on many levels. It is, first of all, the objective standard for what is morally right or wrong, which human beings can know, at least to a certain extent (its basic principles), without appealing to Divine Revelation. Moreover, it is the standard by which certain actions are right and other actions are wrong for all human beings, Catholic or not, and indeed Christian or not.

For example, the Church teaches that having babies, pursuing health, pursuing truth and aesthetic experience, are good to do, whereas contraception, intentionally killing innocent human persons, lying or deliberate obfuscation of truth, are in themselves morally wrong. The first types of actions are morally good and the second types of actions are morally bad, independently of whether they are prescribed or prohibited by any civil laws or enacted Church laws. And they are so for all people, whether they have accepted Revelation or not.

Hence moral truths, which are part of the natural moral law, are quite different from changeable rules enacted by a society, whether that society be a civil society or the Church. Eating meat on Fridays used to be wrong for Catholics, not because it was thought to be against the natural moral law, but only because it was against a Church law or rule, a rule that has of course changed (except in Lent). On the other hand, things like stealing, lying, fornication, adultery, and contraception are acts that are against, not Church rules, but the natural moral law. They are not wrong because the Church said they were wrong; rather, the Church teaches that they are wrong because they are wrong, and they always *were* wrong, even before the Church taught so (i.e., before the Church was founded). Thus, the rightness or wrongness of certain actions is independent of cultural or individual viewpoints, but is in some way based on human nature itself. This is why the standard of moral right and wrong is called the *natural* moral law.

What has been said so far is part of Catholic teaching. However, Catholic thinkers do not all agree on how to explain what has been said; there are various accounts of exactly *how* human nature provides the standard for what is morally right and wrong. What follows is one understanding of that.

A Theory of Natural Law • Human beings are things of a certain kind — that is, they have a definite nature. Because of the kind of thing they are, because of their nature, they are perfected by certain objects or activities and diminished by other conditions. Thus, all human beings are perfected by life and health (since they are living, bodily beings, animals); knowledge and aesthetic experience (since they have the capacity for intelligence); play and skillful performance (since as animals with reason they can transform what is naturally given); self-integration, friendship, moral goodness itself, religion, and marriage (since they are complex and have various capacities to form relationships). On the other hand, the diminishing of these objects or activities is objectively bad for human beings: It is true for all human beings that sickness, death, ignorance, broken relationships, and so on are bad and to be avoided or remedied.

Through experience and insight into our experiences, we come to recognize that life, knowledge, friendship, and so on would be good to realize, that they are worth pursuing both for ourselves and for other human persons. Thus, when we begin to deliberate about what to do, we understand that life, knowledge, friendship, and so on are to be pursued and that their opposites are to be avoided (cf. Pope John Paul II, *The Splendor of Truth, Veritatis Splendor*, 48-50).

In understanding these goods, we understand what we can be, what would be truly perfective of us as human persons, and thus part of what God is calling us to be, since God wills our fulfillment. These fundamental goods also provide an objective standard for what is right and what is wrong. "It is in the light of the dignity of the human person — dignity which must be affirmed for its own sake — that reason grasps the specific moral value of certain goods towards which the person is naturally inclined" (*Veritatis Splendor*, 48). For, while every choice is for the sake of one or more of these goods or for some aspect of it, nevertheless we can choose either in a way that is open to all of these goods or in a way that thwarts or unduly neglects some. So, choices in line with a love and appreciation of all of these goods, both in ourselves and in all other people, are morally upright and loving choices; but choices that in some way suppress a love and appreciation of any of these goods, whether in ourselves or in others, restrict our love and resist God's directives to the fulfillment of his plan, and are morally wrong. Thus the natural moral law is summed up in the directive to love God and love our neighbor as ourselves (Mt 22:37-40; Gal 5:14; Vatican Council II, *Pastoral Constitution on the Church in the Modern World, Gaudium et Spes*, 16).

One might say that the natural law is the nature of the human person or that it is the basic moral truths themselves, based on the nature of the human person, which prescribe pursuit and respect for what is really perfective of human beings and proscribe violating or neglecting any of those goods of persons. One could also identify the natural moral law with human reason, insofar as it naturally apprehends those basic moral truths (cf. CCC 1955). In any case, the natural moral law provides an objective standard by which to determine what is right and wrong. Choices that respect every fundamental human good are morally right; choices that violate or unduly neglect a basic human good are morally wrong.

Why Natural "Law"? • Why is this standard called natural *law*? To understand this is to see that moral norms have a greater impact or significance than they would if they only specified what is reasonable. Moral norms are also directives from the Creator, the ruler of the universe. By pursuing and respecting what is truly perfective of ourselves and of other persons, we are cooperating with God's plan for his creation.

God created, not in order to fulfill some need of his, for he is perfect in his own being, but out of generosity, to communicate goodness to others. Moreover, God creates wisely, and so he has a definite plan. The plan is to communicate goodness to others. Part of that plan is for human creatures, human persons, to attain the perfection or good to which God directs them in their natures. Sub-personal creatures exist for the sake of human persons, and through human persons they also will share in the attainment of God's plan.

Our human nature (which points us to our natural perfection or to the fundamental human goods) and our reason (by which we understand that these goods are to be pursued) are both created by God. Thus, our nature and our reason together are directives from God, ordering (orienting) us to our good and to the attainment of part of God's plan. Following St. Thomas Aquinas, the *Catechism of the Catholic Church* defines law in general — a definition of law that will apply to any type of law, whether it be civil law, Church law, or some other law — as "a rule of conduct enacted by competent authority for the sake of the common good" (CCC 1951). Since God is the ruler of the whole universe, and God created our reason and human nature, those basic moral truths are rightly called natural moral law.

One can see at once that this law is by no means a mere abstract code, based on an abstract human nature. Rather, natural law refers to the basic human goods. Thus, rightly understood, natural law is personalistic: It prescribes love of and respect for every human person. The basic goods — life, knowledge, skillful performance, friendship, self-integration, and so on — are just the various aspects of the being and full-being of persons. To love someone means to will what is truly good for him or her; and to will what is truly good for human persons is to will them, and actively pursue, their true fulfillment.

The natural moral law provides the basis for absolute moral norms. Since the natural moral law is the basic moral truth that we should respect every basic good, every intrinsic aspect, of human persons, it follows that choices which inevitably close one's will to some basic human good, either in oneself or in another, are always morally wrong, no matter what the circumstances and no matter the consequences one expects to follow.

A perennial misunderstanding of the natural moral law is to think of it as being nothing more than the natural teleologies (ends) of the various parts or powers of human nature. Indeed, some thinkers have argued that the Church's positions on sexual ethics, and especially on contraception, were tied to "physicalism" or "naturalism." This is the view that the criterion for what is morally right or wrong is merely the natural pattern of man's potentialities, so that certain acts are wrong simply because they are not in line with or frustrate the natural direction of this or that given power. (However, sometimes the word "naturalism" is used in a different sense, to mean any ethical theory holding that morality is in *any* way based on human nature. In this sense of the term, naturalism is not a bad thing; in fact, it is a synonym for natural moral law.)

On the physicalist or naturalist view, contraception would be wrong simply because it goes against the natural teleology of man's sexual power. However, the natural moral law need not be understood in such an impersonalist way. The moral criterion, as we have explained it above, is not the patterns found in human nature as given, but the real goods to which human beings are naturally inclined — goods that are no less than the intrinsic aspects of the full-being of human persons. Thus, it is true that the natural moral law is in some way based on the natural teleologies found in human beings; but this is so only in the sense that choices respectful of every aspect of human persons must be respectful of the real goods that constitute their full-being. On the other hand, it is this love of the real fulfillment of human persons, not the restriction of given patterns in human nature, that is decisive for the moral criterion.

These two points were expressed succinctly by the Congregation for the Doctrine of the Faith in a document on respect for human life from which Pope John Paul quotes in the 1993 encyclical *Veritatis Splendor*: "The natural moral law expresses and lays down the purposes, rights and duties which are based upon the bodily and spiritual nature of the human person. Therefore this law cannot be thought of as simply a set of norms on the biological level; rather it must be defined as the rational order whereby man is called by the Creator to direct and regulate his life and actions and in particular to make use of his own body" (50). For example, contraception is wrong not because it goes against a natural teleology — indeed, acting against a natural teleology is not necessarily wrong — but because it involves a choice that sets one's will against new human life and closes one to the fulfillment of personal communion. It rewrites the meaning of the conjugal act, as it were, separating its unitive from its procreative aspect, with a will set against the latter.

What Is Changeable and What Is Not? • Sometimes it is objected that the idea of a natural moral law that transcends cultures is outdated, that this "classical view" must give way to the new "historically-minded consciousness." Some people argue that to believe there is an unchanging natural moral law is to imagine that there is some unchanging core of human persons called their "human nature," whereas in fact everything we can understand is historically conditioned. What, then, is changeable and what is not in the natural law?

When we think about an actual example of a basic human good, this problem turns out to be far less serious than it first appears. It has been true for all human beings in all times and in all cultures that knowledge would be a good thing for them and that health would be a good thing for them. No human being in any time or in any culture has been such that knowledge or health or friendship would not be good things, would not build up or perfect him or her. When one goes down the list of basic human goods one finds that the same is true for all.

Furthermore, there could not *be* a human being, an animal with reason and free will (the basic capacities for reasoning and freely choosing), who was not perfected by life, health, knowledge, friendship, and so on. There is a necessary connection between being an animal with reason and free will — a human being — and having the potentialities for life, health, knowledge, and the rest. That is, it is necessarily the case that every human being, no matter in what time or culture, is a being who would be fulfilled in these various ways. And so it is necessarily the case that every human being should pursue and respect these basic human goods, while the basic moral truths prescribing their pursuit are true for all cultures and all times. These parts of the natural moral law are unchangeable. Many of the conclusions derived from these basic moral truths are changeable, and there are various ways, according to different cultures and times, of pursuing and protecting the basic human goods. But the basic goods themselves are common to all cultures.

See: Absolute Moral Norms; Body and Soul; Conscience; Contraception; Deontology; Freedom, Human; Human Goods; Human Person; Human Race, Creation and Destiny of; Legalism; Modes of Responsibility; Moral Principles, Christian; Relativism; Teleological Ethics.

Suggested Readings: CCC 1949-1960. John Paul II, *The Splendor of Truth, Veritatis Splendor.* G. Grisez, *The Way of the Lord Jesus*, Vol. 1, *Christian Moral Principles*, Chs. 4-8. G. Grisez and R. Shaw, *Fulfillment in Christ*, Chs. 4-8.

Patrick Lee

NEOPLATONISM

In the strict sense, Neoplatonism designates the particular form that Platonism took on at the end of the classical era, from the third to the sixth centuries A.D. In a broad sense, it designates the philosophical currents before or after this period that offer some analogy with one or other of the characteristics of Platonism at this time. These currents dominated thought from the third century on, and, both on the metaphysical and the ethical level, provided the framework for the thought of many Fathers of the Church, both Latin and Greek.

Several centuries of preparation preceded Neoplatonism. It may be said to have started with the Old Academy that immediately succeeded Plato (c. 428-348 B.C.) and passed through Aristotle (384-c. 322 B.C.), the Stoics, Philo (c. 13 B.C.-A.D. 45 or 50), and many others.

The second century of the Christian era was a period of philosophical as well as cultural and religious syncretism. Neoplatonism combines the philosophy of Plato, the religious philosophy of Marcus Aurelius (121-180), and Greek mythology to form a new and original philosophical system.

Neoplatonism, taken in the strict sense, exhibits three principal characteristics. First, it is an exegesis of Plato's dialogues, coupled with an attempt to systematize even disparate texts by appealing to a hierarchy among levels of reality. Then it is a method of spiritual life. Finally, and notably in the case of Proclus (c. 410-485), it is a pagan theology seeking to systematize and attain a rational grasp of the revelation of the gods.

History of Neoplatonism • *Alexandria.* In the second century, at Alexandria, Ammonius Saccas (176-242) attempted to systematize Platonic thought and arrive at absolute coherence. He left no writings but was significant because he was the teacher of Plotinus (204-269). Plotinus, and many who followed him, wanted primarily to be an exegete and systematizer of Plato. His main intention was to explain and order into a coherent system the various doctrines that Plato had left scattered through his dialogues.

Plotinus taught at Rome and produced fifty-four short works that his pupil Porphyry (c. 234-c. 305) collected and arranged in a series of works called the *Enneads*. Plotinus taught that there is a Supreme Being, which is the first hypostasis and fountainhead of all things. This Being embraces in itself all reality, and yet it has no determinate nature. It is The One. From The One emerged the second hypostasis, Nous, or Mind or Intelligence; and from Nous came the third hypostasis, Soul or Demiurge.

Each contains the whole of possible reality, but under a different aspect. The One contains all things, as does the Nous, as does the Soul, and as does the sensible world; but each contains the whole of reality in its own way. In The One, all things are potentially present; in the Nous they are concentrated in an immediate intuition; in the Soul they are unfolded in rational discourse; in the sensible world, they are mutually exterior, like sensations. Matter either exists from all eternity or it derives from a higher principle that has granted it existence as a grace.

Man's soul is totally independent of his body; the body is merely the instrument of the soul. The soul produces different operations in different members of the body. Matter is remote from The One. Thus the human soul, joined to a material body, is far removed from its ultimate source. The material must be curbed so that the soul will be able to cast off the yoke imposed by the body. When it does this, it will be able to reach delight through contemplation of and union with The One. Unlike the Gnostics, Plotinus does not hold the created world in contempt, but regards it as imitative of the uncreated.

Porphyry returned to earlier traditions and held that religious revelations, too, could make the way of salvation known. In Porphyry's commentary on the *Chaldean Oracles*, he identified The One with the "Father" mentioned there. The One was thus presented as a supreme, transcendent God, endowed with intellect and will. After him came a second God, the Demiurge, and a whole hierarchy of divinities. Taken literally, these teachings were not compatible with the doctrine of Plotinus.

All later Neoplatonism can be defined as an attempt to achieve a systematization among Plotinianism, the *Chaldean Oracles,* and the Orphic Hymns of Greek mythology.

Syria. Iamblichus (c. 250-c. 330), a student of Porphyry, seeking to safeguard the transcendency of The One, multiplied the hypostases, the intervening levels of reality. The One, Nous, and Soul are each divided into three intelligible triads, and each of these into three others, and so on, until a vast multitude of intelligible beings was formed. Man must be in communion with these beings, or gods, if he is to be happy. This communication is obtained by purification through asceticism. From this school came the writings of the emperor Julian the Apostate (c. 331-363), who attempted to reconcile Neoplatonism with the cult of the sun.

Athens. Neoplatonism was almost extinguished by the beginning of the fifth century. At Athens, however, Proclus (410-485) and others constructed a vast system that sought to bring Platonism and other systems into unison. In 529, Emperor Justinian (483-565) decided to bring to an end the school at Athens, the last bastion of paganism in the now Christian Empire.

Neoplatonism and Christianity • Although early Neoplatonism was anti-Christian, from the middle of the fourth century Christian thought was strongly influenced by Neoplatonic philosophy. In the East, Basil of Caesarea (329-379) and Gregory of Nyssa (c. 335-c. 394); in the West, Ambrose (c. 339-397) and Augustine (354-430) made use of Plotinus and Porphyry, frequently without citing them. In the West, from the Middle Ages onward, Neoplatonism was accepted through the works of Ambrose and Augustine.

The influence of Neoplatonism reached its apogee at the end of the thirteenth century in the writings of German Dominican disciples of Albert the

Great (c. 1200-1280). Under this influence it passed into the mystical writings of other Germans. German Neoplatonism became one of the sources of modern thought through the work of Nicholas of Cusa (1401-1464).

The encounter between Neoplatonism and Christianity conditions the history of Western philosophy. During the patristic period, it helped provide an apt vocabulary for theology. The Trinitarian theology of Ambrose and Augustine borrowed formulas from Porphyry, enabling it to express unity in a Trinity of hypostases. The Porphyrian expressions concerning the union of the soul and the body were of equal service in the formulation of the dogma concerning the hypostatic union, that is, a union without confusion of natures.

See: Augustinianism; Gnosticism; God, Nature and Attributes of; Hypostatic Union; Patrology; Trinity.

Suggested Readings: CCC 238-260. J. Boardman, J. Griffin, O. Murray, *The Oxford History of the Classical World.*

Robert J. Wister

NEW AGE

The New Age movement is difficult to characterize because it includes so many things. Catalogs of New Age products offer a dazzling array of gods, goddesses, shamans, devas, witches, and wizards from Hindu, Buddhist, Egyptian, Viking, Native American, and other cultures. Tarot, astrology, witchcraft, magic, homeopathy, reflexology, aromatherapy, palmistry, visualization, ESP, near-death and out-of-body experiences, Tai Chi, yoga, Taoist, Zen and Edgar Cayce-style meditations, self-empowerment, consciousness-raising, and inner-child therapies all find a home under this umbrella, as do a broad array of objects such as pyramids, crystals, pentacles, unicorns, wolves, rainbows, medicine wheels, Runic wheels, earth drums, magic potions, sacred stones, lava lamps, wizard walking sticks, goddess wands, totems, and rainsticks, all of which are designed to enable the individual to experience, as one catalog puts it, "personal growth and exploration."

Nor are Christian religious symbols entirely ignored by New Age. The cross has been adopted as one symbol among many interchangeable symbols (Yin-Yang, Om, and Pentagram are others) of the "spiritual totality." Even more have angels and Gregorian chant been embraced by New Agers as apt expressions of this "new" spiritual movement: the former because they can be identified with *devas*, "a Sanskrit word for angelic beings-of-light who seek their kindred spirits here on earth," the latter because it has been found consonant with other varieties of "New Age music." Nothing, perhaps, demonstrates more the syncretic character of this movement than a New Age composition, *Gregorian Waves*, characterized as a "musical homage to the Earth Goddess Gaia, paid in the tradition of the Gregorian chant."

The movement also spans a variety of other movements, including feminism, the ecology movement, a variety of self-help and self-healing movements, and movements for global peace and a global world order. In short, there are few places, in modern societies at least, that have not felt the influence of New Age "spirituality."

Many Christians are under the impression that New Age and Christianity are compatible, if not two sides of the same coin. In point of fact, however, nothing could be further removed from Christianity than New Age spirituality. This is apparent from a brief examination of four major tenets of this movement.

Unity. The defining belief of New Age is unity. All things are thought to be ultimately the same thing. The belief that "all is one" lies at the core of New Age. This of course supposes that in the final analysis everything is "God." In short, New Age is monist, because it supposes that God is undifferentiated oneness in his own being. It is also pantheistic, since in this view of things God and the world are identical.

Pure Spirit. This movement also takes the view that only spirit is real. Time, space, materiality, limits — all are illusions, according to New Age. This follows of course from the belief that all is God. For this reason, near-death and out-of-body experiences and reincarnation are thought to be truly spiritual, inasmuch as they allow a person to transcend the limits imposed by time, space, and materiality.

The Self. The New Age movement is ultimately concerned solely with the individual human self, since the self is God. This self is a spirit that is capable of unlimited existence by transcending the illusions of space, time, and materiality. It is perfect in itself, because evil is nothing more than its ignorance of its own divinity. The self is also unrelated to other selves, since all selves are one ("all is one").

Salvation. According to New Age, the only sin or evil in the world is the false belief that space, time, materiality, and limits are real, not illusory. Salvation, therefore, or "enlightenment," as New Agers are wont to call it, comes about through realizing that "all is one" and all is spirit. This being the case, the self must turn back in upon itself to discover there the divine (cosmic) consciousness that it shares with all other selves and that will allow it to transcend all the false limits imposed by the illusions of space, time, and matter. The Om Namaha Shivaya is a popular mantra in New Age, because it means "I honor the Divine within." Ultimately, salvation consists in awakening from the "dream of separation," in which we suppose ourselves to be other than God, in order to know and act upon our own divinity.

Rejection of Christianity • In the final analysis, we have here a wholesale rejection of the Christian faith. The Trinity is rejected, because God is absolute unity, not triunity. Creation is rejected, because the world is identical to God, not different from and created by him. Man as the image of God is rejected, because man is God. The Fall is rejected, because sin and evil are illusions. Jesus Christ is rejected on several grounds. He cannot be both divine and human, because there is no difference between the two. He cannot be God incarnate, because materiality is an illusion. He cannot be the savior, because we save ourselves. His death on the cross cannot be salvific, because only knowledge (enlightenment) can save us. He cannot be resurrected, because not only the body but death also is an illusion. Repentance is rejected, for we

are already perfect and just need to see that we are. Church and sacraments are rejected, not only because materiality is an illusion but also because we cannot be a community but only a unity. The Bible, Tradition, and the Magisterium are all rejected, because all authority resides with the self, not with anything exterior to the self. Heaven, hell, and judgment are rejected, because all is God.

One critic of New Age has pointed out that this movement, which began as "a scattered revolt against Western secularism and traditional Christianity," has become "an elaborate and full-orbed assault on Western culture" (Douglas R. Groothuis, *Unmasking the New Age*, p. 46). Far from offering the hope of a real spiritual revival in the West, it has done nothing more than resurrect in new garb the ancient and apparently indestructible heresy of Gnosticism, against which the Church has time and again had to do battle. The belief that spirit is the only reality, that materiality is either evil or an illusion, and that salvation consists in enlightenment or knowledge alone continually reasserts itself in one form or another in every age of human history.

Gnosticism has a longer history than the Church and is as old as the human race. Gnosticism must always be the enemy of the Catholic faith in God as triune, in creation (including matter) as good, in Christ as God incarnate, in the self as fallen not through ignorance but through pride and disobedience, in Christ's life, death, and Resurrection as redemptive, and in the Good News as salvation not from matter but from sin. Thus does Pope John Paul II speak of the "return of ancient gnostic ideas under the guise of the so-called New Age," which "in the name of a profound knowledge of God, results in distorting His Word and replacing it with purely human words" and is therefore "in distinct, if not declared, conflict with all that is essentially Christian" (*Crossing the Threshold of Hope*, p. 90).

See: Freemasonry; Gnosticism; Magic; Neoplatonism; Theosophy.

Suggested Readings: CCC 285, 2116-2117. G. Danneels, "Christ or Aquarius?" in *Catholic International*, pp. 480-488. C. Cumby, *The Hidden Dangers of the Rainbow: The New Age Movement* and *Our Coming Age of Barbarism.* R. England, *The Unicorn in the Sanctuary: The Impact of the New Age on the Catholic Church.* D. Groothuis, *Unmasking the New Age.*

Joyce A. Little

NEW COVENANT

The Old Law, or Old Covenant, is like a fatherly instruction by God (cf. CCC 1975). Through it God guides and directs his children toward the beatific vision, the goal in this life and the next (cf. Mt 5:8; 1 Cor 13:12). God's guidance includes negative and positive prescriptions that assist us in an initial taste of the fullness of life, a foretaste of that eternal life which is everlasting union with God. God's guidance also teaches us about the common good and what keeps us from our fulfillment in God (cf. Thomas Aquinas, *Summa Theologiae,* I-II, 90, 4).

The Old Covenant thus prepares for the coming of the Messiah by pointing to the beatific vision and to God's help in achieving it. As covenant in a general sense signifies an agreement that formalizes a relationship and sets its terms, including what the parties undertake to do for one another, so "covenant" applied to the divine-human relationship covers these elements and has a unique dimension of its own. In reference to the New Covenant: Jesus Christ is the personal embodiment of the beatific vision; his Incarnation is the fullest expression of covenantal love. The New Covenant differs from the Old in that its essential focus is on Jesus, who both teaches and fulfills God's fatherly instruction.

Jesus leads the way to the New Covenant *and* empowers believers toward it. The teaching *and* the giving of power to follow the teaching are what the Old Covenant calls justice and mercy. For example, in the Old Testament we find a longing "to know the Lord" (cf. Jer 31:31). In, through, and with the Person of Jesus Christ the New Law empowers and re-creates; it introduces the beatific vision to the "heart," the inner man. The Old Law could only point to the vision; the New Law — Jesus Christ himself — empowers as it teaches,

enables as it instructs. In the New Law, Christ the Redeemer saves by the power of the Holy Spirit, who sanctifies, uplifts, and instructs; in the New Law, especially in the Beatitudes, the Old Law (divine, natural, and revealed) is perfected (cf. CCC 1965).

The essence of the New Law (or New Covenant) includes two interconnected principles of divine life. Both are revealed in the person and work of Jesus Christ. The first principle is the public, historical, and external manifestation of God's divine, hidden, and interior life. The second principle is the presence and action of the Holy Spirit within the life of the believer, which animates and re-creates the believer as the image of Christ. Both principles are fundamental to fulfilling the New Law.

Christ and the Holy Spirit • The historical ministry of Jesus Christ is a personal manifestation of the divine, hidden, and inner life of God. The Sermon on the Mount is a particularly important expression of God's inner life, which expresses how Jesus acts. If the historical ministry of Jesus makes public, and therefore available to all, the hidden thoughts of God, then the Beatitudes and the rest of the Sermon on the Mount invite us to begin living here on earth the way of life that really and ultimately exists in heaven. In this sense, the New Law perfects all previous law (cf. CCC 1965) because it teaches or instructs the believer to see that the Old Covenant is really fulfilled, completed, and brought to its highest level by the power of the kingdom of God present in and through Jesus (cf. CCC 1967). The New Law shapes and directs the practice of religion (i.e., almsgiving, prayer, fasting, seeking out the Father in heaven, etc.). It is a kind of public road map laying out the path leading to the beatific vision of God.

The second principle is the work of the Holy Spirit in the believer. This work begins deep within us and eventually manifests itself in a renewed mind that can choose the ways of God in increasing measure. It is precisely the Holy Spirit that precedes and sustains any ascent to God deep within the heart, where perfect obedience to and fulfillment of the New Law begin. This action is an inner power, built on the work of the Holy Spirit (cf. Vatican Council II, *Dogmatic Constitution on Divine Revelation, Dei Verbum*, 5). We do not live the New Covenant by our own power. Neither the power of human will nor the strength of personal character can sustain this new life (cf. CCC 1966); rather, we live it by means of the internal grace of the Holy Spirit.

Christian Charity • The supernatural principle of action within us is what the New Testament calls love (Greek=*agape*; Latin=*caritas*). This kind of love is divine love and is the foundation for any human action that pleases God and has power to elevate or transform our broken humanity. The interior principle of love shapes our perceptions of reality and our choices. The external face of the Law of the Gospel makes public the hidden path one's inner heart must travel to God.

The interior principle of the Holy Spirit's life is actually a mediation of divine life. This divine life is proclaimed by the Scriptures and nurtured and built up by the sacraments, prayer, and spiritual works. It is proclaimed as the love of God given to us in Christ (cf. Rom 5:5, 8:37). This interior principle of the Holy Spirit's action prompts, sustains, deepens, and strengthens our perfect obedience to God, which is a fulfillment of the New Law.

Thus it comes as no surprise to learn that the entire Law of the Gospel is summed up in Jesus' teaching to "love one another as I have loved you" (cf. CCC 1970, 1823; Jn 15:9, 12; 13:34). Also, if the Holy Spirit's presence and action effect and sustain divine charity, or love, within the believer, then it is divine love, and nothing else, that makes it possible for us to enter into the kingdom of heaven by perfect obedience to the New Law. Only divine love can produce such an effect in believers. Another name for this interior principle is the Law of Love.

The Law of Love builds up the life of the believer (cf. 1 Cor 13). Its power is what we call grace; it strengthens us to act; it draws us toward the New Law and makes us more willing to conform our inner life and external actions to it and to God. As a result, this law of grace moves us toward a greater realization of our twofold personal dignity — as creatures made in the image and likeness of God and as brothers and sisters of Jesus through Baptism. This ability to love God perfectly and more deeply through grace-filled obedience to God is the Law of Freedom. The Holy Spirit's work effects a *freedom from* everything that stands in the way of obedient filial love that is perfect and complete (cf. CCC 1972), and it also effects a *freedom for* our complete self-offering to God and one another in Christ.

Precepts and Counsels • Over the centuries, the Church has organized the New Covenant into two basic categories, precepts and evangelical counsels. We call the above "laws" (e.g., love, freedom) precepts. They guide and empower us in removing whatever is incompatible with divine life. They reveal our sins to us and assist the Holy Spirit in removing whatever stunts the growth of divine love within us. The evangelical counsels differ from the precepts in that they seek to remove whatever impedes the growth of divine love even though it is not contrary to that love (cf. CCC 1974; St. Thomas Aquinas, *Summa Theologiae*, II-II, 183, 3). They make clear those direct ways by which perfect love and obedience to the Father in Christ through the Holy Spirit can be accomplished, according to the actual vocation that God gives each person. In the words of the Second Vatican Council: "The Church's holiness is fostered in a special way by the manifold counsels which the Lord proposes to his disciples in the Gospel" (*Dogmatic Constitution on the Church, Lumen Gentium*, 42). Whether we are called as laypeople, religious, or clergy, God will give us what we need to experience and know the beatific vision and thus to participate in the New Covenant according to his divine call.

See: Beatific Vision; Beatitudes; Divine Revelation; Evangelical Counsels; Holy Spirit; Inerrancy; Inspiration; Jesus Christ, God and Man; Grace; Law of Christ; New Testament; Old Covenant; Old Testament; Sacred Scripture.

Suggested Readings: CCC 62, 122, 1610, 1828, 1961-1964, 2058, 2515, 2542. Vatican Council II,

Dogmatic Constitution on Divine Revelation, Dei Verbum, 6, 14, 16. M. Duggan, *The Consuming Fire: A Christian Introduction to the Old Testament,* pp. 99-136. P. Grelot and J. Giblet, "Covenant," in X. Leon-Dufour, ed., *Dictionary of Biblical Theology.* G. Mendenhall and G. Herion, "Covenant," in *Anchor Bible Dictionary,* I.

Stephen F. Miletic

NEW TESTAMENT

The entry entitled "Old Testament" elsewhere in this volume points out that the Old Testament forms an indispensable part of Christian Revelation. We shall explore the link between the two Testaments in the present entry. Because aspects of the New Testament are treated in light of the Old, the reader is encouraged to read the entry on the Old Testament first, then return to this entry.

The *Catechism of the Catholic Church* begins its treatment of the New Testament with a quotation from the Second Vatican Council, taken from the *Dogmatic Constitution on Divine Revelation, Dei Verbum,* 17: "The Word of God, which is the power of God for salvation to everyone who has faith, is set forth and displays its power in a most wonderful way in the writings of the New Testament." This calls attention to the fundamental purpose of the New Testament: to manifest the word of God, the power of God for salvation, and the necessity of having faith. From this threefold matrix unfolds the multilayered tapestry of our salvation (CCC 124).

Jesus Christ is the Word of God. All Scripture, whether the Old or New Testament, contains, expresses, and points to the Word of God in one way or another. As such, the contents proclaim the ultimate truth about God and salvation. Their focus is Jesus Christ, his actions and teachings, his death and Resurrection, and the birth of his Church under the Spirit's guidance. At the very heart of this manifestation of power and salvation are the four Gospels: Matthew, Mark, Luke, and John. Together they form the principal source of our knowledge about the life and teachings of Jesus of Nazareth, incarnate Son of God (CCC 127).

In 1964, the Pontifical Biblical Commission issued a statement on the historicity of the Gospels, saying that there are three distinguishable stages in their formation. The statement represents a crystallization of an enormous amount of solid Catholic scientific research on the origins, development, transmission, and composition of the four Gospels. The commission's statement in effect advances only the most well-grounded contributions offered by biblical scholars. It also forms a reliable guide for probing the nature of the Church's deepening knowledge of the Gospel after Jesus' Resurrection. This "three-stage" historical view is much like a musical chord sounded by a choir: The words of Jesus are not monosyllabic, singular tones; rather, they are at one and the same time his words, the words of his first Apostles, who preached Jesus' words and deepened the Church's understanding of them, and the words of the authors of the Gospels, who freely and creatively arranged the words of Jesus and the Apostles. Against this background, the music of the Good News that originates in the heart of the eternal God is heard from generation to generation through the preaching, prayer, and life of the Church, the Bride of Christ.

New and Old Testaments • The New Testament cannot be understood without reference to the Old Testament. The New Testament is hidden in the Old, and the fulfillment of the Old Testament is manifest in the New. The two Testaments are inextricably bound. Jesus is the link.

To understand the unity between the two Testaments, we need to review the basic contributions of the Old Testament to Revelation. First, it reveals the first stages of the kingdom of God by unveiling the invisible God and the way of life he intends for all his children. Second, it contains a treasure-house of prayers, wisdom about human life, and sure knowledge about God. Third, and most important for our purposes, the Old Testament prepares a path made of salvation promises that generate expectations of the Messiah.

How does this "path" actually function as such? Jesus and the first Christians read their Scriptures, what we call the Old Testament, in light of Jesus' teachings, life, death, and Resurrection. We call this kind of reading Christocentric because it seeks out reference to Christ. It is also called "typological reading" because it discerns in the Old Testament text references that share similarities with Christ's historical and divine life. In effect, God's works of salvation found in the Old Covenant prefigure Jesus' work of salvation found in the New Covenant (CCC 128).

In reading the Old Testament this way, the early Church began to grow in understanding of God's plan of salvation after the Resurrection and Ascension of Jesus, first through Jesus' own teaching and later by the teaching of the Holy Spirit. Let us take only one example. The figure of Melchizedek (cf. Gn 14:18) is most instructive. He was apparently a priest of Salem (this city would eventually be called "Jeru-salem"), a priest of the Most High God. He offered Abraham bread and wine upon the latter's return from defeating four kings. Melchizedek is mentioned in Psalm 110:4, where the king is addressed as "a priest for ever after the order of Melchizedek." The author of the Epistle to the Hebrews draws on these two passages to show how they in effect express a "form of thought," a prefigurement of the sacrificial work of God's priest, Jesus Christ (Heb 6:20; 7:1ff.). Jesus offered bread and wine to the Father at the Passover meal, while offering his Body and Blood on the cross; Jesus' eternal priesthood is foreshadowed, or prefigured, in the figure of Melchizedek.

In summary, the unity of God's divine plan of salvation is perceivable when we read the Old Testament in light of the New. The message of the New Testament, focused on the life and teaching of Jesus Christ, acts like a lens that focuses the Old Testament prefigurements (or foreshadowings) of each event in the life of Jesus. This typological correspondence between the two Testaments shows that one cannot properly understand the New Testament without reference to the Old Testament. As Pope Pius XI observed, "Spiritually we are all Semites."

See: Divine Revelation; Economy of Salvation; Inerrancy; Inspiration; Jesus Christ, God and Man; Judaism; Judaism in Catholic Doctrine; New Covenant; Old Covenant; Old Testament; Priesthood in the Old Testament; Redemption; Sacred Scripture; Spiritual Exegesis.

Suggested Readings: CCC 101-133. Vatican Council II, *Dogmatic Constitution on Divine Revelation, Dei Verbum*, 11-16, 18-19, 21-22, 24-25; *Dogmatic Constitution on the Church, Lumen Gentium*, 5, 14-15, 29, 55, 67; *Constitution on the Sacred Liturgy, Sacrosanctum Concilium*, 6-7, 16, 24, 35, 51, 92, 112; *Decree on Ecumenism, Unitatis Redintegratio*, 3, 15, 17, 21. Pontifical Biblical Commission, *The Historicity of the Gospels*; *The Interpretation of the Bible in the Church*. P. Grelot and J. Giblet, "Revelation," in X. Leon-Dufour, ed., *Dictionary of Biblical Theology*.

Stephen F. Miletic

NONVIOLENCE

Nonviolence is more than the absence of violence. It is a positive commitment to return good for evil and seek peace only by means that are themselves peaceful. Such methods have been used by both Christians (e.g., Martin Luther King) and non-Christians (e.g., Mohandas Gandhi). Christian nonviolence seeks to follow Christ by demonstrating love for enemies and enduring injustice without complaint.

Transcending the Old Testament standard of justice, "an eye for an eye and a tooth for a tooth" (Ex 21:24, Lv 24:20), Jesus urged his disciples to "turn the other cheek" when attacked (Mt 5:39; cf. Lk 6:29). At his arrest he told a disciple to put away his sword, "for all who take the sword will perish by the sword" (Mt 26:52). At the same time, he did not condemn military service as such, and the New Testament affirms public authorities' use of force (Rom 13:4).

Early Christians rejected service in the Roman army, which involved serving an unjust authority and pledging oaths to pagan gods. In each age, some Christians have rejected all use of violence. St. Francis of Assisi preached nonviolence and forbade the lay members of his Third Order to use lethal weapons.

The Church admires this form of witness to Christian charity, while also seeking to ensure defense of the weak and innocent from unjust attack. One may renounce the use of force in one's own behalf, but defending the innocent is "a grave duty for someone responsible for another's life, the common good of the family or of the State" (CCC 2265).

The Second Vatican Council praised "all who forgo the use of violence to vindicate their rights and resort to those other means of defense which are available to weaker parties, provided it can be done without harm to the rights and duties of others and of the community" (*Pastoral Constitution on the Church in the Modern World, Gaudium et Spes*, 78). The Council urged civil authorities to make humane provision for "conscientious objectors" who refuse to bear arms, "provided they accept some other form of community service" (*Gaudium et Spes*, 79).

See: Authority; Beatitudes; Capital Punishment; Common Good; Deterrence; Homicide; Human Life, Dignity and Sanctity of; Law of Christ; Moral Principles, Christian; War.

O

OCCASIONS OF SIN

An occasion of sin is any person, place, or thing that is likely to lead one into sin. So, for instance, for a reformed abuser of alcohol, casual association with old friends who drink heavily, and urge him to drink with them, is likely to be an occasion of sin.

Not all occasions of sin can be avoided, for there are many inducements to sin, and human nature is weak (cf. CCC 401, 407-409). Still, one has a duty to avoid when possible those near occasions of sin that constitute a grave danger of leading one into mortal sin. A Christian must be unwilling to allow anything to separate him from the love of Christ, as mortal sin does. Thrusting oneself unreasonably into circumstances likely to lead to mortal sin reveals a lack of concern for such love as well as a lack of appropriate love of oneself.

The repentant sinner especially is charged not to commit mortal sin again (cf. Jn 8:11). And an honest resolve not to commit sin requires a will not to enter deliberately into such circumstances without a serious reason: for example, a medical student who must study anatomical pictures, a priest hearing confessions. Hence acts of contrition frequently contain expressions like "I resolve to amend my life and to avoid the near occasions of sin."

Some occasions of grave sin can be avoided entirely. Ordinarily one need not enter bookstores that sell obscene material or attend movies likely to stir one to lust. When one simply cannot avoid an occasion of sin or when one has an important reason (in charity or duty) to confront an occasion of sin, he should try to make the likelihood of yielding to the inducement to sin more remote by prayer (cf. CCC 2846-2854) and by other realistic efforts to lessen the danger.

See: Mortal Sin; Sin; Temptation.

OLD COVENANT

The Church's Sacred Scriptures consist of the Old and New Testaments, also called the Old and New Covenants, or the Old and New Laws. Our understanding of the Old Law is rooted in the Person of Jesus Christ. Jesus taught the "New" Law; what he did and taught fulfills the Old Testament, just as the rose flower fulfills the growth pattern of the rose bush. This is especially true of the moral teachings found in the Old Covenant, which Jesus affirmed (Mt 5:17-19) and deepened (Mt 5:20).

The words "old" and "new" carry special meanings with reference to Sacred Scripture. In everyday speech, "old" evokes a negative image — defective, dated, incomplete, useless, weak; or, something to be thrown away, not as "good" as something "new"; we prefer new cars, houses, clothes, and so on. These meanings are not appropriate when we speak of the Old and New Laws. The special meaning of the Old Covenant, or Old Law, is that it prepares the way for the New Covenant, or Law of Christ. The key events — deeds and words of salvation history — recorded in the Old Testament introduce us to the reality of God, who reveals himself as the loving Creator and Father (cf. Vatican Council II, *Dogmatic Constitution on Divine Revelation, Dei Verbum*, 14). God's act of self-revelation teaches us specific ways of knowing God and understanding his great plan of salvation. Jesus' life and teachings explain, deepen, elevate, and complete that initial Old Covenant way of knowing God and understanding his plan of salvation. Without knowing that the "new" fulfills the "old," we tend to misunderstand both Testaments. In fact, the Church teaches that the new is hidden in the old and the old is manifest in the new (*Dei Verbum*, 16).

Covenant in a general sense signifies an agreement formalizing a relationship and setting its terms and conditions, including what the parties undertake to do for one another. Applied to the relationship of God and human persons, the concept obviously has unique dimensions. The permanent value of the Old Testament lies mainly in its religious teachings, in its witness to God and his attributes (also called divine perfections), and in the unfolding of God's divine plan of salvation. Thus it is by means of the Old Testament that we learn primary and fundamental truths about God, his divine plan, and ourselves. Because our roots as believers are in the Old Covenant, it would be correct to say that "spiritually we are all Semites."

The *Catechism of the Catholic Church*'s major teaching on the Old Law is concentrated in paragraphs 1961-1964. These paragraphs focus on the biblical witness as the primary source for our knowledge of God's revelation to Moses. They also provide many important instructions about God's call to each of us and the way of life that accompanies that call. We shall focus on these paragraphs in the remainder of this entry.

First and foremost, the Ten Commandments represent moral teaching that expresses an initial stage of revealed law (cf. CCC 1962). The value of revealed law is that it confirms and clarifies what natural reason can tell us about God and the nature of good and evil. A second important service provided by the moral teaching of the Old Law is that it teaches what is against the love of God and neighbor (i.e., prohibitions). A third benefit is the teaching on what we ought to do, the positive prescriptions in favor of that twofold love. These three dynamic elements are summed up in the Ten Commandments (preserved in two different forms: Ex 20:2-17, Dt 5:6-21).

The Old Law guides the formation of our consciences. First, the commandments given to Moses are like a light that helps us see the reality of God and his invitation to be his children. Second, they lay out for us a way of life consistent with God's call. Through this teaching we also discover how God safeguards and protects that call and way of life. The three characteristics of the Old Law (first stage of revealed law, prohibiting, prescribing) lay the foundations for the New Covenant: Just as the roots and stems of a plant reveal the first signs of life and hold forth a promise of life yet to come, so also the Old Law reveals the first signs of God's intent for eternal life that point to a concrete way of life and to a flowering of that way, truth, and Life, to Jesus Christ, the sweet "Rose of Sharon." It is not difficult to see, therefore, that the Old Law is utterly holy, good, and spiritual (cf. Rom 7:12, 15:4; CCC 1963; *Dei Verbum*, 14-15). The Old Law teaches us many things of great value (cf. *Dei Verbum*, 15; Rom 15:4).

Role of the Old Law • To take an image from the writings of St. Paul, the Old Law is like a tutor or teacher (cf. Col 3:24). It teaches us about the divine and supreme God; it brings us in contact with the first stages of God's kingdom. Moreover, the tutor teaches us right and wrong relative to loving God and neighbor. But the deeper and fuller meanings of its teaching are not manifest until we read those teachings within the context of Jesus' own teachings, life, death, and Resurrection. By leading us to understand right and wrong in terms of love of God and neighbor, the tutor prophetically reveals what God requires for perfect love. This revelation prepares our minds for him who is perfect love incarnate, Jesus Christ. The tutor also teaches us how sin and our tendency to cooperate with it bruise, darken, mutilate, and militate against perfect love of God and neighbor. The recognition of the depth and breadth of our brokenness due to original sin, and of the need for forgiveness and transformation, is itself a prophetic moment.

However, the tutor has limitations. It cannot make us free. It can only teach about sin and liberation, not free us from sin. The longing for freedom from our personal sins and from the sinfulness of our culture is a theme that spans the whole of the Old Testament. That theme reaches a high point in the prophets and wisdom literature. The longing is prophetic; it looks to a future time when the Old Law will be written on the heart of flesh and not a heart of stone (cf. Jer 31:31-34). The birth of Jesus Christ fulfills that longing. He takes over where the tutor leaves off.

The Old Testament pattern of liberation from slavery and bondage and arrival into the promised land has prophetic value in three respects. First, it manifests the inner life and intention of the invisible God. By that pattern we come to know God as the loving Father who created us and our world. He is the one true God, holy and loving, who frees and continues to liberate his chosen ones. Second, because the divine plan unfolds throughout the Old Testament, the whole of its narratives teaches us about God's loving disposition toward the human race. The death, Resurrection, and Ascension of Jesus Christ and the giving of the Spirit to the Church completely fulfill this divine plan and underscore the depth and breadth of God's love for us. Jesus is the New Covenant answer to the great Old Covenant hope. The Church continues that answer by being *the* sacrament to the contemporary world. Thus, from Moses to the present, there is a continuous growth in knowing God and living in his ways. Third, the Old Law also is prophetic by what it lacks — namely, the power to enable us to resist sin and love God and neighbor perfectly and continuously. The Old Covenant teaches us about God and makes us God's people, but it does not empower us to love God perfectly. To what or to whom should we turn for this empowerment? The only force that empowers us to love perfectly and continuously is found in the work of the Holy Spirit, made available to everyone through the sacraments and especially through the precious Blood of Jesus Christ, poured out for us in the perfect and eternal sacrifice of love on the cross.

In conclusion, the Old Law provides key images, symbols, typologies, ways of knowing and understanding God and ourselves at the first stage of the coming of God's kingdom. The three sections of the Old Testament (Pentateuch, Prophets, and Wisdom books) teach us about right and wrong

in terms of loving God and neighbor. The Old Covenant also sets the stage for the New Covenant and the definitive arrival of the kingdom of God in the person and work of Jesus Christ.

See: Divine Revelation; Economy of Salvation; Inerrancy; Inspiration; Jesus Christ, God and Man; Judaism; Judaism in Catholic Doctrine; Law of Christ; Liberation From Sin; New Covenant; New Testament; Old Covenant; Old Testament; People of God; Redemption; Sacred Scripture; Spiritual Exegesis; Ten Commandments.

Suggested Readings: CCC 62, 122, 1610, 1828, 1961-1964, 2058, 2514, 2542. Vatican Council II, *Dogmatic Constitution on Divine Revelation, Dei Verbum,* 6, 14, 16. M. Duggan, *The Consuming Fire: A Christian Introduction to the Old Testament,* 99-136. P. Grelot and J. Giblet, "Covenant," in X. Leon-Dufour, ed., *Dictionary of Biblical Theology.* G. Mendenhall and G. Herion, "Covenant," in *Anchor Bible Dictionary,* I.

Stephen F. Miletic

OLD LAW

The Old Law is the first stage of revealed law. When God chose the Jewish people as his own and prepared the world for the coming of Christ through them, he taught them how they should live to please him. In giving his law, he revealed to them also his own holiness and goodness, and taught them to realize their own dignity (CCC 1962, 2059).

The moral teaching of the Old Law is both majestic and incomplete. Frequently it soars to great heights in its invitation to love God with all the heart, and to love the neighbor, especially the poor and oppressed, generously. In the Ten Commandments, it provides a sublime summary of our basic duties to God and neighbor, and gives a divine sanction to the fundamental teachings of the natural law written in the hearts of men.

Christ himself confirmed the enduring validity of the Ten Commandments and taught that they truly unfolded the requirements of the precepts of love. Moreover, he taught that one must keep these commandments if one wishes to enter into eternal life

(Lk 18:18ff.). St. Paul cried out that Christ set us free from the burden of the law, but he did not mean we no longer had a duty to keep the commandments confirmed by Christ and insisted on by Paul himself in his moral teaching.

Rather, we were liberated from all that was transient in the Old Law: from a multitude of dietary and ceremonial laws that made no sense, when the Savior to whom they pointed had already come. And we were liberated from the servile status of the Old Law, when the Spirit and his love were poured into our hearts so that we could with freedom and ease live the excellent ways of God, taught imperfectly of old but perfectly in Christ.

See: Divine Revelation; Law of Christ; Liberation From Sin; Natural Law; Old Testament; Ten Commandments.

OLD TESTAMENT

The Old Testament forms an indispensable part of Christian Revelation. Its permanent value lies in its ability to reveal God, teach us about the way of life God invites us to live, and prepare our minds and hearts for the coming of God's Messiah. This collection of inspired and holy writings is sacred to three major world religions: Judaism, Christianity, and Islam. Its texts are accepted by many other religions, especially in Africa and India, as at least inspired if not revelatory. The Old Testament is clearly one of the most fascinating books to have emerged from antiquity. The common impression in popular culture today seems to be that the Old Testament is merely a book about laws, about people whose names are a challenge to pronounce, about "so and so begot so and so," and about a vengeful God. Nothing could be further from the truth.

A believer in Christ knows that all things are transformed in and through Christ. This is no less true for the "Hebrew Bible," what Christians call the Old Testament. In the Old Testament, we learn that creation itself is the product of God's creative powers. We learn that God created human life and sustains it. We learn that God is more like a loving father than a benevolent despot. We learn about

the first stages in God's great providential plan to rescue and save his people from the power of sin and death, the creation of ancient Israel, and the emergence of the prophets who announced the coming of a Messiah. In short, we learn about the nature and existence of God, our Father in heaven, about his great love for Israel and all people, and about his eternal decrees and laws, which guide us to the Messiah through whom we have access to the heavenly throne of grace.

Permanent Value for Christians • Because of such a divine pedagogy, the Old Testament is entirely and completely inspired, and therefore has a permanent value for Christians: God never revoked his Covenant with his people, Israel. The Old Testament is the true word of God. Its value is twofold. First, the Old Testament has a permanent revelatory and spiritual integrity in and of itself. It reveals the one true God and the way of life to which God invites us. Second, the Old Testament is, as it were, the first installment of Revelation in which God manifests his great salvation plan. This means that the Old Testament is the first part of a two-part message. The first part could be described as the raising of our hope for salvation. The second part of that message — what we call the New Testament — satisfies the hope first raised in the Old Testament. (The entry on the New Testament considers examples of the relationship between the two Testaments.)

The Church defends the integrity of the Old Testament for many important reasons. First and especially, because it is an indispensable part of Sacred Scripture, of Revelation (CCC 121). Its permanent value lies in its revelatory role, disclosing the reality of the invisible God. Second, it is the soil that sustains the fruits of Jesus' teachings, the principal source for Jesus', and therefore the Church's, language of prayer and worship; in it is hidden the mystery of our salvation (CCC 122).

Over the centuries the Church has defended the integrity of the Old Testament against many hostile forces. In the second century, the Church vigorously fought off the heretical teachings of Marcion (died c. 160), a powerful religious leader who had organized a sizable network of communities throughout the Roman Empire. He taught that the New Testament reveals the God of love, not of hatred or of material substance; but the God of the Old Testament was a weak "demiurge" (a being somewhere between human and divine, not fully one nor the other), not of the same dignity as the God of love. This teaching flatly contradicts the teachings found in the first few chapters of Genesis, which repeat the phrase "and God saw that it was good." Creation, material substance — these are inherently good. The Old Testament proclaims the truth about God and reality.

Other "Christian" groups wanted completely to eliminate the Old Testament, because they could not accept the image of a God who creates Adam out of the mud. For such groups, there was a radical dualism or antagonism between material and spiritual realities. The spiritual was everything, the material nothing — except evil. The public teachings of Jesus were for the spiritually inferior. The really core truths were passed on as secret knowledge — a *gnosis* — for those who were superior. These groups were called the Gnostics; the Church completely rejected them.

Often, anti-Semitic hatred grew from displaced anger in misguided Christians and individual leaders among the hierarchy. The Church has every right and obligation to repudiate such attitudes, be they within its own fold or in the general culture. Such is the seriousness with which the Church takes the Old Testament.

Unfortunately, not all Christians have followed the teachings of the universal Church. Many Christian groups have perpetuated anti-Jewish sentiments, basing their feelings and reasoning on circumstances surrounding the execution of Jesus related in the Gospels. In the propaganda and other literature produced by such misinformed groups, Pilate is often portrayed as the dupe of the Sanhedrin, frequently depicted as a murderous lot. From such a beginning, it is not difficult for someone to arrive at a supposed justification for hating the Jews, thought of as those who engineered the murder of Jesus. The Church does not and never can condone such thinking. "Spiritually we are all Semites." We receive the heritage of faith from the Old Testament, fulfilled in Jesus' life and preached faithfully by the Apostles, all good Jews to the core. To lose sight of this is to lose sight of an essential aspect of our Catholic faith.

See: Divine Revelation; Economy of Salvation; Gnosticism; Inerrancy; Inspiration; Jesus Christ, God and Man; Judaism; Judaism in Catholic Doctrine; New Covenant; New Testament; Old Covenant; Redemption; Sacred Scripture; Spiritual Exegesis.

Suggested Readings: CCC 101-133. Vatican Council II, *Dogmatic Constitution on Divine Revelation, Dei Verbum*, 11-16, 18-19, 21-22, 24-25; *Dogmatic Constitution on the Church, Lumen Gentium*, 5, 14-15, 29, 55, 67; *Constitution on the Sacred Liturgy, Sacrosanctum Concilium*, 6-7, 16, 24, 35, 51, 92, 112; *Decree on Ecumenism*, 3, 15, 17, 21. Pontifical Biblical Commission, *The Interpretation of the Bible in the Church*. P. Grelot and J. Giblet, "Revelation," in X. Leon-Dufour, ed., *Dictionary of Biblical Theology*.

Stephen F. Miletic

OMNIPOTENCE

Etymologically, omnipotence combines the Latin words *omnis* (all) and *potentia* (power); it signifies all-powerful. Omnipotence is an attribute of God.

God is all-powerful in several senses. First, God is the source of being of everything that is created, since he is the power that caused everything to be. Second, God's power is eternal, without beginning or end; all other power is temporal, that is, it has a beginning, a duration, and an end. Third, God's power is categorically different from any created power. By God's power all that is created is brought into being, sustained, and allowed to become or fail to become what it was meant to be by him. Fourth, God's power does not allow him to do anything contrary to his own nature, that is, anything irrational or evil.

Fifth, the power of God is also seen in his sovereignty over the world, in bringing the world to its intended end without violating the freedom of human beings. God interacts with the world, but as he is all-powerful, his interaction, while allowing freedom and choice, has a definitive but not strictly deterministic influence. God's sovereignty and all-powerfulness are manifest in his salvific will for the world, culminating in his work in Jesus Christ. The Church shares in God's sovereign power insofar as the Church is the instrument by which the Holy Spirit accomplishes the salvation of the world.

See: Creation; Eternity; Evil, Problem of; Fatherhood of God; Freedom, Human; God, Nature and Attributes of; Natural Law; Omniscience; Process Theology; Providence.

OMNISCIENCE

Omniscience is, etymologically, the combined Latin words *omnis* (all) and *scire* (to know). Thus it signifies "all-knowing." It is one of the attributes of God.

God is omniscient in two senses. First, God has immediate and absolute knowledge of himself. Second, God has simple, simultaneous, and perfect knowledge of all things, universally and particularly (cf. St. Thomas Aquinas, *Summa Theologiae*, I, 14; CCC 216).

God knows himself immediately, without any intermediary, for example, concepts or words, and in this aspect he is absolutely unique. God is his own knowledge of himself. His very substance is his self-awareness, and he perfectly comprehends himself, without the slightest possibility that he could learn something about himself that he does not already know. God has no potentiality to be more or better than he is, since he cannot become more perfected by his knowledge than he already is.

In one unbroken and eternal act of knowing, God has knowledge of all time and everything that ever exists in time. Everything is timelessly in God's knowledge, for what it is in itself and as it is distinct from all other things. Since God is the cause of creation and since God's knowledge is one with his will to create, God's knowledge is the cause of each and every thing's existence according to its own nature. As the source of good and of creation, God knows all good; hence, he knows the privation of good in things and thus knows evil.

See: Creation; Evil, Problem of; Fatherhood of God; Freedom, Human; God, Nature and Attributes of; Omnipotence; Process Theology; Providence.

ORDINARY AND EXTRAORDINARY MEANS OF SUSTAINING LIFE

The distinction between ordinary and extraordinary means was developed by Catholic moralists in the sixteenth century to clarify the limits of our obligation to preserve human life. While we must never intentionally cause anyone's death by act or omission, we are not obliged to cling to earthly life by every possible means. "Overzealous" medical treatment may cause more harm than good (CCC 2278).

We are obliged to use only the ordinary means of preserving life: that is, those that may effectively preserve life or provide other benefits without imposing excessive pain, expense, or other burdens on a patient and family. Extraordinary means — those that offer no significant hope of benefit or that impose excessive burdens on patient and family — may be refused by a patient or those qualified to speak in his or her name. Even when aggressive treatment is discontinued because a patient's inevitable death is imminent, the ordinary care owed to all patients because of their human dignity must be continued.

Whether the burdens of a treatment outweigh its benefits in a given case is a question involving an element of subjective judgment. This question is generally best answered by the patient, after being fully informed by medical professionals.

Pope Pius XII elaborated on this distinction in addresses on medical ethics in the 1950s. In 1980, the Vatican *Declaration on Euthanasia* reaffirmed the distinction, while noting that some prefer to speak of "proportionate" and "disproportionate" means. This alternative wording emphasizes that there is no universal list of ordinary and extraordinary treatments. Whether a treatment's burdens are disproportionate to its benefits must be assessed in each set of circumstances.

See: Assisted Suicide; Care of the Dying; Euthanasia; Human Life, Dignity and Sanctity of.

ORDINARY MAGISTERIUM

The Church as teacher — *magister* — hands on the doctrine of salvation to each generation. Her Magisterium, or teaching office, is exercised when, in the name of Jesus and with his presence and protection, she teaches truths that need to be believed and practiced (faith and morals) if one is to get to heaven: "Go and make disciples of all nations . . . teaching them to observe all that I have commanded you; I am with you always, to the close of the age" (Mt 28:18-20); "He who believes and is baptized will be saved; but he who does not believe will be condemned" (Mk 16:15-16).

The Magisterium can be "ordinary" or "extraordinary." Both express the truth revealed by God, and so call for our response. The Magisterium is sometimes exercised through a solemn proclamation of dogma by the Pope (with or without the participation of the whole Catholic hierarchy) or by an ecumenical council. The ordinary Magisterium is that exercised by the Pope alone or by the bishops teaching in communion with him, "when, without arriving at an infallible definition and without pronouncing in a 'definitive manner,' they propose . . . a teaching that leads to better understanding of Revelation in matters of faith and morals" (CCC 892).

The teaching of the ordinary Magisterium of the bishops in union with the Pope is also infallible under certain conditions (cf. Vatican Council II, *Dogmatic Constitution on the Church, Lumen Gentium,* 25), although greater light may be cast on it in consequence of the constant prayer and theological reflection that should characterize the life of the whole Church. The conditions are: that the bishops be in communion with one another and the Pope; that they teach authoritatively on a matter of faith or morals; that they agree in one judgment; and that they propose this as something to be held definitively.

See: Infallibility; Magisterium; Pope.

ORIGINAL SIN

By their proud disobedience, Adam and Eve committed a personal sin, thereby renouncing the gift of friendship with God (sanctifying grace). As parents of the whole human race, moreover, they forfeited gifts intended for their descendants, most notably sanctifying grace and the effortless self-dominion of what is called "original integrity." They lost for themselves and their issue such privileges as freedom from mortality, suffering, and ignorance. Their refusal of divine gifts makes us all, from the moment of conception, sinners destined to die, creatures somehow estranged from their loving Creator. But how and to what extent humanity can and does sin vicariously are legitimate questions.

The present treatment deals largely with the nontransmittal of sanctifying grace ("original holiness") and original integrity (or "justice") and the repercussions in our moral life. The first part attempts to summarize authentic Church teachings — what Catholics are required to believe — while the second addresses certain problems surrounding traditional terminology and exaggerated interpretations. When Adam and Eve (or "protoparents" or just "Adam") are mentioned, the reference is to the time preceding their Fall (prelapsarian), unless the context clearly implies the contrary.

Doctrine on Original Sin • Genesis, chapters 1-3, recounts the Fall. St. Paul, in his Epistle to the Romans, spells out further consequences: "[S]in came into the world through one man and death through sin, and so death spread to all men because all men sinned. . . . [B]y one man's disobedience many were made sinners" (5:12, 19). Supporting passages are found in Wisdom 2:24, Genesis 2:17 and 3:3, 19, and 1 Corinthians 15:21. The first man and woman thus transmit both death and sin to their descendants via generation, and not simply by way of the imitation of their bad example, as Pelagius (c. 350-c. 425) erroneously contended.

In keeping with his overly optimistic view of humanity's moral self-sufficiency, Pelagius also erroneously claimed that St. Augustine (354-430) had fabricated the doctrine of original sin out of remnants from his Manichaean past. In his *Contra Julianum,* however, the Bishop of Hippo invokes the testimony of eleven Church Fathers, both Greek and Roman. That this doctrine was established long before Augustine is manifested by the Church's earliest practice of baptizing infants, with the attendant exorcisms and abjuration of Satan. Yet for all his orthodoxy, in the heat of battling Pelagius, Augustine did use some expressions that could at least give the impression that Adam's transgression had essentially corrupted human nature. That was the conclusion reached by Martin Luther (1483-1546), who argued that sin is unavoidable.

Historically, less than orthodox thinkers have tended either to exaggerate or minimize the moral consequences of original sin. In the thirteenth century, St. Thomas Aquinas found the golden mean and drew distinctions that make it possible to get original sin's consequences clear. But not all his helpful teaching has been absorbed by later Catholic thinking.

The Doctrine Defined • In response to Luther's misinterpretation, the Council of Trent (session 5, Canons 1-5), building on provincial councils some thousand years before, dogmatically defined in 1546 the authentic doctrine on original sin. Its declarations can be summarized as follows: (1) By original sin "the whole Adam, body and soul," lost, both for himself and his descendants, original "justice and holiness," and "incurred death" and "God's anger," plus "bondage" to "the devil." (2) This sin is passed on "by propagation," and its sinful nature and guilt (though not all its consequences) can be blotted out (not just mercifully covered over, as in Luther), in adults and infants alike, only through Christ in Baptism. (3) "Concupiscence [lust or 'a tendency to sin'] remains in the baptized," but it cannot morally "harm those who do not consent" and, by Jesus'

grace, "manfully resist." St. Paul sometimes calls this lust itself "sin," but, Trent makes clear, "only because it is from sin and inclines to sin," not because the experience thereof is already sinful, as Luther erroneously taught.

Explaining how original sin spreads to humanity via generation, the *Catechism of the Catholic Church* further asserts that "original sin is called 'sin' only in an analogical sense: it is a sin 'contracted' and not 'committed' — a state and not an act" (404). For those not personally at fault (cf. CCC 405), it is reasonable to ask how the infraction of a distantly related third party could have left them sinners. At the same time, to satisfy the Church's dogmatic definitions and requirements, it is necessary to explain how for all of humanity, except for the Savior's exempt Mother, the privation of sanctifying grace and original integrity amounts to being born in a condition of sin, only erased by Baptism.

In the first part of the second book of his *Summa Theologiae*, Thomas Aquinas says original sin deprived Adam and his issue of original justice, or "the subjection of man's mind to God" (q. 82, a. 2), thus diminishing the "natural inclination to virtue" (q. 85, a. 1). Such deprived humans start off loving creatures somewhat more than their Creator. They must therefore exert themselves positively, virtuously, in cooperation with divine help (graces usually tied to Baptism), to set their loves right. This is analogous to the reconversion to God of a baptized person who has forfeited sanctifying grace. Had this teaching become more general, many distorted emphases would have been avoided.

The interpretative, theological problems stem from three sources. First, there is the indiscriminate claim that human nature was wounded, weakened, bent for the worse by original sin (instead of locating the negative effects in an inherited disorientation of nature more or less away from God, a greater or less relational estrangement from one's Creator). Second, there is perhaps an inadequate explanation of how this disorientation can be transmitted through generation. Third, there is a tendency to blame human lusts on original sin, rather than attributing these tensions and tendencies to sin to our native, unintegrated, but complete human condition or nature, from which the gift of original integrity has been withdrawn. Adam is blamed for what is really a personal failure to develop and strengthen human nature.

The Gifts of Grace and Integrity • To understand better what humanity lost in Adam, let us consider the conditions and consequences of God's bestowal of these original gifts. Both the divine plan for man and human nature were complete and viable without them. God was neither obliged to grant them, nor were they owed to human nature. Thanks to their nature and divine helps (actual graces), but without further gifts, men and women were more than sufficiently capacitated to know and love God and enjoy habitual friendship with him (sanctifying grace).

While not necessary, however, God's "extra" gifts did facilitate his transformative intention in regard to human beings. Especially were they beneficial to the protoparents, who, uniquely, were themselves bereft of parents.

God unilaterally invested the first pair with sanctifying grace. At the dawn of consciousness, Adam found himself oriented largely toward God, through no choice or effort of his own. In effect, the fatherly Creator gratuitously started Adam and Eve out with at least all the qualities that would otherwise have come to them through the experience of being raised by the best of parents. But they were not confirmed in grace, so to speak, as can be seen in their disobedience to God. For God to have instilled in them such an overwhelming, instinctive attraction to himself as to rule that out would have negated his whole purpose in creating them free, so that they could freely respond to him.

Finally, the Creator also unilaterally bestowed on the first pair a lust-free, harmoniously knit human nature, an unowed gift whereby human spirituality and reasonableness automatically reigned supreme. This was their original integrity.

According to the creation account in the first three chapters of Genesis, Adam initially had do-

minion over his animal instincts, appetites, and passions, without having to strive to acquire it. So, for instance, until after the first sin, the protoparents' nakedness was an occasion for neither sexual arousal nor shame. Unlike his heirs, Adam at first did not have to labor to be temperate, chaste, courageous, patient, fair and just, practically wise or prudent; he and his consort possessed these qualities by God's special, "preternatural" gift.

One might say that humanity's initial moral condition and challenge resembled those of the angels. For Adam, the definitive choice lay between only God and himself: Whom would he love more? The first couple could only go wrong, as eventually they did in imitation of their angelic predecessors, by pride or envy.

In sum: What for Adam before the Fall was a point of departure became for his posterity a far-off point of arduous arrival. But if Adam at the start was divinely capacitated in his moral life, does the withdrawal of this privilege from the rest of humanity necessarily represent a moral hindrance for them? Are we thereby more immoral or more inclined to immorality? Or is it merely the case that humanity's developmental quest now must just begin earlier than Adam's by first addressing more rudimentary moral needs? And if the latter more accurately describes our situation, then the "situation" itself is simply something over and above the fundamental moral question that faced Adam quite as much as it faces us: Love for self to the exclusion of God, or love for God to the forgetfulness of self? In both scenarios, moreover, original integrity's presence *and* absence would both seem premoral.

When postlapsarian man prefers lesser goods to greater ones or pursues them in morally faulty ways, only then, not before, does the issue of more or less serious immorality arise. The behavior in question extends all the way from small imperfections to venial and even mortal sins. Even among the latter there are gradations of malice, from mortal sins of weakness to mortal sins committed with settled determination. St. Thomas Aquinas says it is at least possible for people to resist all mortal sins; but that cannot be said of venial sin.

Whatever else original sin may have done, it is certain that God created human nature in such a way that its abuse could not fundamentally vitiate either that nature or its divine destiny. Nor could Adam's disobedience exclude the possibility that his offspring might approximate the self-dominion he effortlessly exercised by divine gift. What was lost was a privileged exemption from certain moral temptations and sins.

If, however, our protoparents were spared the lusts that predispose their descendants to sin, they were not exempt from the possibility of committing the most grievous, hidden, and least rectifiable sin of all: blinding pride (together with its frequent companion). A sense of exaggerated self-worth and independence was the undoing of the angels who fell and of the human race's parents. While capable of repentance and restoration to friendship with God, the latter nevertheless forfeited with this original sin, for both themselves and all their offspring, the privilege of original integrity.

Moral Consequences of Original Sin • Does the withdrawal of original integrity entail the inflicting of a punishment on human nature? Its removal means that, as it were, humans revert to a lower-lying but still level moral playing field, nearer the animals than the angels. The door has been opened to both new vices and virtues. Human nature is intact and adequate to the moral task, which has not been substantially changed, only enlarged and lengthened. Humans are left more humble. The need for nature-reinforcing virtue is palpable, constantly experienced.

Unlike the privation of original integrity, the privation of original holiness (or justice) somehow entails inherited, though nonpersonal, sin, at least sufficient to warrant humans' view of themselves as sinners in need of the regenerative waters of Baptism. Postlapsarian humanity entertains in its heart a mixture of loves, some contradictory. Explicitly or implicitly, love for self and love for God contend. A person who habitually places God first in his hierarchy of loves does so at God's

instigation and with his ongoing, loving assistance; this is being in a "state of (sanctifying) grace." But friendship with God and acknowledged dependence upon him are jettisoned when deliberate love for creatures (usually oneself) is given priority in some major misdeed or omission. This is to say that mortal sin, in the classical Scholastic definition, is knowing and voluntary conversion to creatures, with concomitant aversion from God.

As with original integrity, so also with original holiness, God *could* in theory bring human beings into existence even now in the state of grace. Realistically, though, one must question the workability of such a procedure. Human beings require nurture, including moral formation, from their parents as well as the adult community at large; and, starting with the immediate offspring of Adam and Eve, how useful would it have been to entrust children in a state of original holiness to the nurturing of parents who were not? And when such children, more or less malformed by the experience, came to be parents, how useful would it have been to entrust children in the state of original holiness to *them*? And so on and so on, generation by generation, down to the present day. Did it, and does it, not make better sense that all concerned be universally certain of their inherited turning-away from God, so as to be alert to their need for reconciliation with him?

These considerations may serve to counteract tendencies to exaggerate or misunderstand the consequences of original sin. Finally we are entitled to ask whether original sin is a true tragedy for the human race or something rather different. It would certainly be tragic, horribly so, if the loss of integrity and grace were irremediably permanent. But if humanity finds it easy to sin, thereby forsaking a true, trusting relationship with God, now it is likewise easy *not* to sin, provided vices, addictions, and diabolical pride have not already taken root. The all-merciful God provides omnipresent, bounteous, and insistent helps, including but certainly not limited to those that come through sacramental channels. The more one grows in the practice of the cardinal virtues, the closer one comes to the internal harmony and self-dominion gratuitously given to Adam, thereby blunting the loss of the preternatural gift bestowed on him.

To paraphrase Ronald Knox: We no longer enjoy the privilege of unlimited access to the library books in the stacks, thanks to Adam's abuse of that prerogative, but must instead request them from the librarian. That requirement does not put the "books" out of reach or vitiate the educational project, but only makes waiting to get them somewhat inconvenient — a wait that, in turn, exacerbates a tendency to impatience likewise inherited from Adam. Life's objective, procedures, and basic means remain the same; the net effect of the Fall is that humans must start their work of moral self-reclamation earlier in the process and positively direct themselves to the God whose life they are to share. If there is in the world overwhelming misery, the fault lies not so much with original sin as with the personal failures of human beings to grow, through the appropriation of both truth and goodness, into the divinized creatures God will make of them, if only they assent and cooperate.

O felix culpa! "O happy fault!" This exclamation from the Church's Easter vigil hymn *Exsultet* makes reference to the fact that Christ's redemptive, remedial coming is so much greater than the original moral illness afflicting humanity. But in a way it may also apply to the postlapsarian advantages accruing to the children of Adam and Eve.

See: Concupiscence; Freedom, Human; Human Race, Creation and Destiny of; Redemption; Sin.

Suggested Readings: CCC 355-412. A. Noyes, *The Unknown God.* F. Faber, *The Creator and the Creature.* J. Pieper, *The Four Cardinal Virtues.* C. Lewis, *The Problem of Pain.* G. Vann, O.P., *Morals Makyth Man.*

Dennis Helming

ORTHODOX CHURCHES

The Orthodox Churches, in their creeds and liturgical texts, constantly insist that they preserve the original faith handed down from the Apostles. This claim is fundamental to understanding Orthodoxy's place within the Christian world. The Orthodox Churches are as ancient as the Catholic Church; indeed, for a thousand years Christians of East and West were one. Pope John Paul II speaks of Catholic and Orthodox as the "two lungs" of the Body of Christ, twin trunks of a single tree, firmly rooted in Jesus' life and teaching.

Within Orthodoxy a distinction is made between the Eastern Orthodox Churches, which accepted the Council of Chalcedon (451), and the six "pre-Chalcedonian" Oriental bodies. Orthodoxy as a whole does not possess Catholicism's integrated structure, in which local churches are bound in loyalty to the See of Peter. To the outside observer, Orthodoxy is a colorful kaleidoscope of ethnic communions with names redolent of the Middle East, the Balkans, and the Slavic nations. There are fifteen autocephalous (literally, "self-headed") Eastern Orthodox Churches: those of the ancient patriarchates of Constantinople, Alexandria, Antioch, and Jerusalem; the later-founded patriarchates of Russia, Serbia, Romania, Bulgaria, and Georgia; and the churches of Cyprus, Greece, Poland, Albania, the Czech and Slovak Republics, and North America. The Orthodox fold also includes a number of smaller groups, including 25,000-member churches in Japan and China. Each church is governed by its own synod or council of bishops, although the Patriarch of Constantinople (the Ecumenical Patriarch) can convoke all of them to discuss matters of common interest.

This autonomy in governance does not imply a lack of unity in faith and worship. All the Orthodox communions consider themselves fully members of one great Orthodox communion, confessing the same creed, performing the same liturgy, celebrating the same sacraments, living the same spirituality. Their administrative diversity is grounded partly in history, partly in a different conception of church structure than evolved in the West. To explore these foundations is to examine Orthodoxy's separation from Catholicism as well.

Historical Background • Christianity was born and grew within the Roman Empire. By the early fourth century, the city of Rome was languishing and the emperor Constantine moved his capital to the town of Byzantium (modern Istanbul) on the Bosporus. The emperor Theodosius established Christianity as the state religion shortly thereafter.

Greek culture was dominant in the eastern part of the empire (modern Turkey and the Middle East), while Latin civilization struggled to absorb conquering barbarian tribes in the West. The Church had a similar bipolar character. Despite losses to Arab expansion, Byzantine civilization flourished in succeeding centuries. Constantinople and the great church of Hagia Sophia (Holy Wisdom) became the center of the Eastern Christian world. Greek Catholic missionaries, most notably the brothers Cyril and Methodius in the ninth century, spread the Gospel throughout Eastern Europe.

Political rivalry between the Holy Roman Empire and Byzantium, plus differences in language and culture, caused the Eastern and Western Churches to drift apart. In this climate, ecclesial structures evolved in isolation. The Church in the West, stressing Christ's confirming Peter as leader of the Twelve, developed as an international organization centered on the Bishop of Rome. The East, as already noted, stressed the autonomy of local churches gathered around their bishop. Growing tensions came to a head in 1054 when each side issued a formal condemnation (anathema) of the other. This "Great Schism" fractured the Christian world. The rift was deepened when crusaders sacked Constantinople in 1204 and enthroned a Latin patriarch. No lasting results came of the Council of Florence (1438-1445), which sought the reunion of East and West.

Today's Eastern Orthodoxy is the Eastern Christianity of Byzantium, still declaring itself to be the authentic Body of Christ from which Rome broke away a millennium ago. History has not been kind to the Orthodox; Arab and Turkish conquests subjected them to centuries of Muslim rule in the Middle East, and communist takeover exposed them to persecution in Eastern Europe. Yet they have tenaciously clung to their faith, meriting the admiration of all Christians.

Steps Toward Unity • Since the publication of the Second Vatican Council's *Decree on Ecumenism, Unitatis Redintegratio*, both parties to the schism have become increasingly aware of the need to work for the fulfillment of Jesus' prayer "that they may all be one" (Jn 17:21). The anathemas of 1054 were lifted in 1965, not long after the establishment within the Roman Curia of a Secretariat (now Pontifical Council) for Promoting Christian Unity, and the two churches have engaged in official dialogue since 1980. The *Catechism of the Catholic Church* underlines the thinness of the wall that divides Catholic and Orthodox (cf. CCC 838). Pope John Paul II often expressed hope that full communion can be achieved, notably in the 1995 apostolic letter *Orientale Lumen, Light of the East.*

Some obstacles are more cultural than theological. Orthodoxy's rejection of centralized ecclesiastical authority and its use of the vernacular in liturgy, combined with the rise of nation states, ensured that Orthodox communions would be generally coextensive with national boundaries. Only in the last two hundred years, for example, has Russian Orthodoxy significantly spread beyond Russia. Moreover, old ethnic conflicts and enmities keep Christians apart, as in the former Yugoslavia, where Serbian Orthodox and Catholic Croats have often clashed.

A thousand years of separation have also created a great psychological gulf. The sanctuaries, ceremonies, and customs of one body seem odd to the other. A sense of injured righteousness leads some Orthodox to remain aloof, while Catholics may tend to dismiss Eastern Christians as quaintly old-fashioned. In *Orientale Lumen,* Pope John Paul encourages Catholics to study Eastern liturgy and spirituality and "combat tensions" between the two groups (24).

While time and fraternal charity may eventually overcome cultural differences, strictly ecclesiastical disputes must be resolved through formal dialogue. Catholics and Orthodox share the same faith, found in Holy Scripture and Sacred Tradition and codified in the Nicene Creed promulgated by the First Council of Nicaea in the year

325 — the Creed Catholics recite at Mass. However, the Orthodox accept as authoritative only the decrees of the first seven ecumenical councils of the Church, ending with the Second Council of Nicaea in 787. All later formulations, including those of the Councils of Trent (1545-1563), Vatican I (1869-1870), and Vatican II (1962-1965), are considered to have no force. Since the Orthodox do not acknowledge the primacy of the Pope, they also disregard his doctrinal pronouncements. Thus, while the Orthodox revere Mary as Theotokos, the Mother of God, they reject the doctrines of the Immaculate Conception and the Assumption because Popes affirmed them by exercising their infallible teaching authority.

Issues in Dispute • Papal primacy is the most neuralgic issue dividing Catholics and Orthodox. Many Orthodox may be willing to accord the Bishop of Rome the first place in honor, but their heritage makes it extremely difficult to accept his juridical authority. In his 1995 encyclical *That All May Be One, Ut Unum Sint*, John Paul II insists that the primacy must be preserved as a guarantor of unity in doctrine and practice, but he suggests the possibility of interpreting it in terms that might make it acceptable to Christians separated from Rome (95).

As we have seen, both churches accept the Nicene Creed as a normative confession of Christian faith. However, a dispute arose early on about the relationships of the Persons of the Trinity. Western theologians held that the Holy Spirit proceeded from the Father and the Son, rather than through or after the Son. Eventually the Roman Church unilaterally added the word *filioque* ("and the son") to the Latin text of the Nicene Creed, much to the dismay of the Orthodox. The dispute has simmered since the ninth century.

Other differences are properly viewed as distinct patterns in the tapestry of the faith rather than cause for conflict. Unlike Protestantism, Orthodoxy observes the same seven sacraments as the Catholic Church, though it may perform and understand them differently. Generally speaking, the Orthodox in their view of the sacraments place more emphasis upon the action of the worshiping community and less upon the act of the minister. For example, there is less stress on the priestly words of consecration in celebrating the Eucharist. Baptism takes the form of triple immersion, with the emphasis more on conferring new life than on wiping away the taint of original sin. Celibacy is not considered a requirement for priestly ordination, nor are the lay and clerical states as clearly distinguished as in the Catholic Church. Most Orthodox priests and deacons are married men, though bishops must be celibate.

Orthodoxy tends to have a more practical and liturgical focus than Catholicism. While Orthodox theologians have produced compendiums of doctrine over the years — for instance, Peter Mogila's 1638 *Confession* — the content of the faith has been transmitted primarily through liturgy. This was a historical necessity; whether under Muslim or communist rule, the liturgy was the main available source of religious knowledge and experience. The exact celebration of elaborate liturgies and the tenacious preservation of their ancient forms gave Orthodox communities coherence and ensured their survival. The conservatism of the Orthodox in liturgical affairs derives naturally from these conditions.

Orthodox liturgies, which may last several hours and which stress reverence and mystery, are intended to engage the total person, intellectually, emotionally, and physically. (This holistic concept also fuels the Orthodox interest in icons, whose creation has been raised to a high art.) The Christian community exists most authentically in the lived, shared experience of worship, which, more than adherence to creeds or evangelization or work for social justice, constitutes the essence of religious identity. Each person's relationship to God is mediated and expressed through this corporate worship. The notion of an individual religious life is much weaker in Orthodox Christianity than it is in Catholicism. There is a Russian Orthodox saying: "A man can be damned alone, but he can only be saved with others."

Eastern spirituality may help explain why monasticism has played so great a role in Orthodoxy, even though religious orders never developed. The monastic tradition has roots reaching back to the third century and still survives today, though in somewhat weakened form. The famous monastic enclave of Mount Athos in Greece, which included as many as six thousand men at its peak, still counts over one thousand drawn from many lands. Over the centuries, figures like St. Symeon the New Theologian (949-1033), following the tradition of the Greek Fathers, underscored the value of the contemplative life. The profound impact holy monks had on the Orthodox masses can be glimpsed in Dostoyevsky's portrait of Father Zossima in the novel *The Brothers Karamazov.*

Orthodoxy's view of the quest for salvation stresses the idea of human divinization or participation in the life of God. In the words of St. Irenaeus, "God passed into man so that man might pass over to God." The individual achieves this through incorporation into the Church, by the action of the Holy Spirit. The feasts of the Ascension and the Transfiguration, which envisage the human Jesus in glorified state, are extremely popular expressions of this mystery.

Yearning after unity with the divine gives Orthodoxy a mystical quality sometimes lacking in Western Christianity. Thus the reunification of Eastern with Western Christianity is desirable not only to offer the world a common witness but also to deepen and broaden the Christian life by joining the best characteristics of both. Pope John Paul II says: "The words of the West need the words of the East, so that God's word may ever more clearly reveal its unfathomable riches" (*Orientale Lumen,* 28).

Catholics and Orthodox perhaps have grown comfortable in their isolation, and it will not be easy for them to sit together again at the Lord's Supper. Yet the door to full communion stands wider now than at any time since the Great Schism. Not only has the Pope pointed to a possible new approach to papal primacy, he also has tried to allay Orthodox fears that Rome seeks to impose its will, saying the communion to be sought is "that of unity in legitimate diversity" (*Ut Unum Sint,* 54). In fraternal love may lie the greatest hope for healing the ancient breach: "The Church of Christ is one. If divisions exist . . . they must be overcome. But the Church is one, the Church of Christ between East and West can only be one, one and united" (*Orientale Lumen,* 20).

See: Anglicanism; Church, Membership in; Church, Nature, Origin, and Structure of; Ecumenism; Patrology; Pope; Protestantism.

Suggested Readings: CCC 830-838. Vatican Council II, *Decree on Ecumenism, Unitatis Redintegratio.* John Paul II, *That All May Be One, Ut Unum Sint; Light of the East, Orientale Lumen.* H. Smith, "Christianity," *The Religions of Man.*

David M. Byers

P

PASSIONS

The *Catechism of the Catholic Church* defines passions as emotions or "movements of the sensitive appetite that incline us to act or not to act in regard to something felt or imagined to be good or evil" (1763). As we have knowledge on two levels, sense and intellect, so we have appetite on two levels, namely, sense appetite and will.

By sense appetite we incline toward or away from something on the basis of our sense knowledge of it. For example, I smell a pizza and without thought or deliberation have a bodily desire for it. Through understanding and will (which is a distinct appetite in our spiritual aspect) we may freely choose to act or not to act on that desire. Thus, sense appetite is distinct from the will or rational appetite.

When we have emotions or passions, the objects that give rise to them — the things themselves — in a way move us or affect us. Hence our responses are fittingly called passions or emotions. Some of the specific passions are: desire, pleasure, aversion, fear, sorrow, and anger.

Since human beings are particular kinds of animals — rational — the sense appetite is an integral part of us and belongs to a full life. However, passions or emotions also can lead us astray. So, while we should not try to eradicate our emotions, we should shape them toward what is genuinely fulfilling for ourselves and our neighbors. Some passions are voluntary and some are not. If not voluntary, then they are neither morally good nor morally bad (although one might be indirectly responsible for having a passion). If a passion is voluntary, its morality is judged by the action to which it tends: If toward morally good action, then the passion is morally good; if not, then the passion is morally bad.

See: Concupiscence; Freedom, Human; Occasions of Sin; Temptation.

PATROLOGY

Patrology, also known as patristics, is a term derived from two Greek words meaning roughly "the science of the Fathers." The Fathers in question are the Fathers of the Church, and patrology is the study of their thought. The title of Father is a somewhat popular one (unlike that of Doctor, which is officially bestowed), and it is accorded to persons who, from early in the Church's history, left to posterity some intellectual and spiritual legacy, however small, that is characterized by theological orthodoxy and that the Church has acknowledged as her own.

Patrology is a vast field because there are many Fathers, who lived during a period encompassing approximately one-third of the Church's existence, who used a number of different languages, and who were preoccupied with many different themes.

The period when the Fathers flourished reaches from the time after the composition of the New Testament, around the beginning of the second century, up until the middle of the eighth century — that is, about 650 years. Hence the patrologist must be familiar with this entire stretch of time. Nor can he content himself with knowing merely the Fathers, since patrology ideally takes into account the world in which they lived, which was the background against which they wrote their treatises and preached their homilies. This background includes the political history of the time as well as its varying intellectual currents, all of which the Fathers reacted to.

Within this single vast period there are several periods of briefer duration. The greatest of these is usually considered to lie between the middle of the fourth century and the middle of the fifth. This span of time is of particular significance, both because the issues that the Fathers dealt with then were and continue to be of extraordinary importance (e.g., the relationship of the Persons of the Trinity, the divine and human natures of Christ and their interrelationship, the nature of the Church and of the sacraments, the role of grace), and because the Fathers who dealt with them were men of a remarkable theological and spiritual caliber, whose likes would not be met again until the twelfth and thirteenth centuries, if then.

The Fathers are often divided into two major groups, Latin and Greek, in accordance with the two major languages of the Mediterranean basin in which most of them lived. The western Mediterranean was Latin-speaking, the eastern part Greek-speaking. But the literature produced by the Fathers is not restricted to Latin and Greek, although they are certainly the most important languages. The Fathers also used Syriac, Arabic, Coptic, and other languages; indeed, it may be said that at least one Syriac writer, Ephrem, is the equal of the best of his Latin and Greek counterparts. Language implies the still broader concept of culture, and hence the Fathers are representatives not only of particular languages but also of the cultures that correspond to them.

Finally, there is a great variety of themes that the Fathers addressed. A man like Augustine, whose genius was sweeping, was capable of speaking and writing with authority on virtually all the pressing theological topics of his day. A lesser figure would have been more limited in what he could handle. Some Fathers simply had no occasion to touch on more than a few topics. Thus, some concentrated on defending the faith, others on the doctrine of Christ, others on the liturgy, still others on moral instruction, and so forth.

Continuing Relevance of the Fathers • From at least the fourth century — in other words, al-

ready during the very time of the Fathers — these witnesses to Catholic teaching have had a unique status in the Church, second only to the Scriptures themselves. This is true for several reasons: their fidelity to Catholic belief, their intellectual acumen, their spiritual integrity, and their proximity to the New Testament and the first foundations of the Church. A perusal of the documents of the Second Vatican Council or of the *Catechism of the Catholic Church* demonstrates how frequently they are cited (the *Catechism* quotes Augustine nearly ninety times, which is more often than it quotes Thomas Aquinas) and, consequently, how seriously they are taken by the contemporary Church. The so-called "argument from the Fathers" has traditionally carried great weight in theological discussion. It refers to a position taken by the Fathers on a particular matter of Church teaching, and it is said that when the Fathers agree unanimously among themselves on such a matter, their position is infallible.

That the Fathers enjoy considerable prestige in the Church does not mean that everything they say is of equal value. They often speak with the prejudices of their age. They are sometimes exceedingly, even vulgarly, intolerant of opposing opinions. And, most importantly from the perspective of the modern reader, their theology is occasionally marred by the fact that the theological tools at their disposal were in a primitive state of development: They simply did not have the concepts and the vocabulary that later ages possessed. But the deficits of the Fathers are more than offset by their assets. Moreover, it is impossible to think of subsequent theological development apart from the foundations that were laid by men like Irenaeus, Tertullian, Origen, Athanasius, Basil the Great, Ephrem, Jerome, Ambrose, and Augustine, to name only some of the most notable of them.

Although Catholics may rightfully claim the Fathers for themselves, they are in fact part of the common heritage of Christianity. The Orthodox Church in particular is intensely devoted to them. The most important churches of the Protestant tradition also look to them for guidance, although they do not concede them the same place that Catholics and Orthodox do.

A revival of interest in the Fathers in the second half of the nineteenth century is partly responsible for the monumental edition of early Latin and Greek writers edited by J.P. Migne in Paris and published under the title of *Patrologia Latina* and *Patrologia Graeca*; it runs to about four hundred volumes. Since then, other editions have been published in the original languages, and as the result of up-to-date scholarship, most importantly the *Corpus Scriptorum Ecclesiasticorum Latinorum* (Vienna), the *Griechische-Christliche Schriftsteller der ersten drei Jahrhunderte* (Berlin), the *Corpus Scriptorum Christianorum Orientalium* (Louvain/ Washington) and *Sources Chrétiennes* (Paris). The Fathers have also been translated into English in various editions, such as *The Ante-Nicene Fathers*, *The Nicene and Post-Nicene Fathers* (both reprinted at Grand Rapids), *The Fathers of the Church* (New York/Washington), and *Ancient Christian Writers* (Westminster, Maryland/ New York).

See: Augustinianism; Development of Doctrine; Infallibility; Magisterium; Orthodox Churches; Sacred Tradition.

Suggested Readings: CCC 4-10, 74-95, 688. J. Quasten, *Patrology*. B. Ramsey, O.P., *Beginning to Read the Fathers*.

Boniface Ramsey, O.P.

PENANCE AND RECONCILIATION, SACRAMENT OF

For all the misunderstanding and confusion that may have accompanied the word "confession" in the past, the sacrament of Penance and Reconciliation is one of the greatest treasures and mysteries that the Church possesses. While an individual may have been hurt by the humanity of a priest here and there, consolation and healing nonetheless have been brought to countless souls through this individual sacramental encounter with Christ. Confession for many is difficult, yet the reconciliation that results is a peace the world cannot give.

The sacrament of Penance has evolved over the years. This process can be traced beginning with its scriptural origins and continuing through the faithful teaching of the Church.

The term "penance" has any one of four meanings, all closely related to reconciliation. First, it refers to a virtue, a habit by which the Christian modifies his life, directing it toward perfection by practicing certain works. Second, it refers to public acts of punishment imposed by the Church or works of personal sacrifice done in atonement for sins or for the sake of personal spirituality. Third, it refers to a work of satisfaction imposed on the penitent within the context of the sacrament of Penance. Fourth, it refers to the sacrament of Penance itself. It is this fourth and final meaning with which this entry is concerned.

Scriptural Testimony • The Scriptures contain ample references to the forgiveness of sins. Some references are in connection with Baptism, while others seem to be in preparation for the institution of the sacrament of Penance. The message of St. John the Baptist was one of repentance that included the confession of sins: "Then went out to him Jerusalem and all Judea and all the region about the Jordan, and they were baptized by him in the river Jordan, confessing their sins" (Mt 3:5-7; cf. Mk 1:5).

Jesus began his public life by preaching the need for repentance of sins: "From that time Jesus began to preach, saying, 'Repent, for the kingdom of heaven is at hand' " (Mt 4:17). Parables such as that of the Prodigal Son emphasized man's need both to seek God's forgiveness and to articulate sorrow.

Beyond preaching the need for confessing sins, the Gospels include incidents where Christ, oftentimes to the scandal of his audience, applies the parables and preaching to real-life situations. The episodes involving the paralytic man (Mt 9:2-7), the "woman who was a sinner" (Lk 7:37-50), and the woman caught in adultery (Jn 8:2-11) are three examples. These instances show clearly that Jesus had the authority to forgive sins. They also prepare the way for the time when the Lord would confer on his disciples the same power.

The Church has always held that the sacrament of Penance was instituted directly by Christ himself on the evening of the Resurrection. John 20:19-23 tells us: "On the evening of that day, the first day of the week, the doors being shut where the disciples were for fear of the Jews, Jesus came and stood among them and said to them, 'Peace be with you.' When he had said this, he showed them his hands and his side. Then the disciples were glad when they saw the Lord. Jesus said to them again, 'Peace be with you. As the Father has sent me, even so I send you.' And when he had said this, he breathed on them, and said to them, 'Receive the Holy Spirit. If you forgive the sins of any, they are forgiven; if you retain the sins of any, they are retained.' "

Five insights are worth noting from this passage. First, the disciples are gathered together: The power the Lord gives them is collective; it is given to all the disciples, not just one or two. As a result, the power to forgive sins is given to all priests. This is clearly distinguished from the power that Christ gives to Peter in Matthew 16:13-20, a passage understood to refer to papal infallibility, given exclusively to Peter as the first Pope.

Second, the disciples recognize that it is the Lord — crucified, died, and risen — who is speaking to them. Hence the authority to forgive sins comes from the Lord, not from the imagination of the disciples or the consensus of the gathering.

Third, the word "peace" used by Jesus lends an appreciation to the sacrament of Penance, which at times is referred to as the "sacrament of peace." One effect of the sacrament is the peace brought about when the individual is reconciled with God.

Fourth, Christ makes it clear that the disciples' mission is of divine origin. It comes not only from himself but from the Father as well. "As the Father has sent me, even so I send you" (Jn 20:21). As Jesus is obedient in carrying out his mission from the Father, so he asks his disciples to do the same. Equally important is the presence of the Holy Spirit at the moment: "Receive the Holy Spirit" (Jn 20:21).

Fifth, Our Lord gives the disciples not only the power to forgive sins but also the power to retain them. Implicit in this is the right to make a judgment as to what should be forgiven and not forgiven.

Our Lord had already explicitly asserted his authority to forgive sins (cf. Mk 2:5-12). He now hands on this power to his disciples and to their successors. "In imparting to his apostles his own power to forgive sins the Lord also gives them the authority to reconcile sinners with the Church. This ecclesial dimension of their task is expressed most notably in Christ's solemn words to Simon Peter" (CCC 1444; cf Mt 16:19).

Since sin ruptures one's relationship with God, it also damages one's relationship with the Church of which one is a member. Forgiveness of sins restores the sinner's friendship with God and similarly reconciles him with the Church. To "bind and loose" includes judgments excluding one from ecclesial communion and also renewing that same communion (cf. CCC 1445).

Historical Development of Penance • Forgiveness of sins was an integral part of the mission of the early Church (cf. Acts 2:37-38). The Acts of the Apostles, as well as the epistles of St. Paul and St. Peter, record this growth as the early evangelizers dealt with new Christians. Those embracing Christianity were converts, either Jews or pagan Gentiles. The *Didache,* a Christian document of the first century commonly known also as the *Teaching of the Twelve Apostles*, teaches those who assemble for the Eucharistic sacrifice: "First confess your sins, so that your sacrifice may be pure."

St. Clement of Rome (30-101), the fourth Pope, writing around the end of the first century, spoke to the people of Corinth: "Be subject to the presbyters [priests] and accept discipline to penance, bending the knee of the heart." St. Ignatius of Antioch (died 110), a bishop who wrote seven epistles during his journey from Antioch to Rome, where he was martyred, associated forgiveness from the Lord with those who do penance and are in union with their bishops: "The Lord forgives those who do penance when they return to unity with God and to the communion with the bishop." St. Polycarp (c. 75-160), Bishop of Smyrna, in his Epistle to the Philippians, admonished all members of the community to follow Christian virtue. Priests were encouraged to be gentle and merciful in judgment of sin. They had the power to make judgments: "Be gentle and merciful towards all, not strict in judgment, knowing that we are all debtors of sin."

It seems almost certain that there was private administration of the sacrament of Penance early in the Church. Leo I, Pope from 440 to 461, warned against those who demanded public acknowledgment of sins, saying: "It is sufficient that the guilt which people have on their consciences be made known to the priests alone in secret confession."

By the thirteenth century the Church felt a need to set down some general norms regarding who was to go to confession and when. In 1215, the Fourth Lateran Council stated: "Let everyone of the faithful of both sexes, after he has reached the age of discretion, devotedly confess in private all his sins at least once a year to his own priest, and let him strive to fulfill to the best of his ability penance enjoined upon him."

Serving as a simple guideline for the faithful, this statement did not restrict the reception of the sacrament to an annual occurrence but served instead as a reminder of the bare minimum necessary for those who might neglect the sacrament. Some three hundred years later, the Council of Trent, in its fourteenth session (November 25, 1551), published its document on the sacrament, devoting nine chapters to the following topics: (1) The Necessity and Institution of the Sacrament of Penance; (2) The Difference Between the Sacrament of Penance and that of Baptism; (3) The Parts and Fruits of the Sacrament; (4) Contrition and Attrition; (5) Confession; (6) The Ministry of this Sacrament and Absolution; (7) Reservation of Cases; (8) The Necessity and Fruit of Satisfaction; (9) Works of Satisfaction.

In recent times, two major aspects of the sacrament on which the Church has focused her attention have been early confession and frequent confession. Three twentieth-century Popes addressed these questions in various documents. St. Pius X in his encyclical letter *Quam Singulari* (August 8, 1910) insisted on both the sacrament of Pen-

ance and the reception of Holy Communion for children from the age of reason. He seemed careful not to separate the two sacraments.

Since Vatican II the sacrament of Penance and the sacrament of Anointing have been linked as the "Sacraments of Healing." The sacrament of Reconciliation reconciles the penitent to God and to the Church. The *Catechism of the Catholic Church* contains a significant section on the role of life-long conversion as the Christian attitude that should accompany the sacrament and be an important consequence of it. The *Catechism* notes that confession should precede First Communion and that "after having attained the age of discretion, each of the faithful is bound by an obligation faithfully to confess serious sins at least once a year" (1457).

In his encyclicals *Mystici Corporis Christi* (June 29, 1943) and *Mediator Dei* (November 20, 1947), Pope Pius XII urged both the faithful and priests to observe the practice of confession, including confession of venial sins. Moreover, he warned priests against discouraging the faithful from this practice, since that would be disastrous for the whole Body of Christ.

In 1973, Pope Paul VI insisted that children preparing for their first Holy Communion should always be admitted to the sacrament of Penance first. As part of their catechetical instruction, children should be prepared for the two sacraments individually so that they have a proper understanding of each. Nevertheless, at no time should first Holy Communion ever precede first confession. "Children must go to the sacrament of Penance before receiving Holy Communion for the first time" (CCC 1457; cf. Canon 914).

Elements of the Sacrament • The Code of Canon Law provides a summary of the Church's understanding of the sacrament of Penance and Reconciliation, indicating its relevance to the individual penitent and to his relation to the Church as a whole: "In the sacrament of penance the faithful, confessing their sins to a legitimate minister, being sorry for them, and at the same time proposing to reform, obtain from God forgiveness of sins committed after baptism through the absolution imparted by the same minister; and they likewise are reconciled with the Church which they have wounded by sinning" (Canon 959).

Besides mentioning the essential points (Penance is a sacrament, is intended for the faithful, and requires a legitimate minister), this canon calls attention to other significant matters. These include the fact that, in addition to verbal confession, both sorrow for sins and a proposal to reform are required of the penitent; that forgiveness comes from God himself *through* his minister; that sinners have wounded the Church by their sinning; and that one effect of absolution is reconciliation with the Church.

These various elements suggest why there are different names for this sacrament. Traditionally, it has been referred to as Confession. More formally, it is called the sacrament of Penance. Since the Second Vatican Council, the term "sacrament of Reconciliation" has been used. As noted, it has even been referred to as the "Sacrament of Peace."

The name, however, has not really changed nor has the sacrament. Rather, the different expressions represent ways of considering the sacrament from various aspects. When we speak of that moment in which our sins are made known to the minister of the Church, the sacrament is called Confession. When we speak of the penance the priest gives to make satisfaction for sins committed, it is referred to as the sacrament of Penance. If we consider the immediate effect of the sacrament, it is called Reconciliation. (The principal effect of the sacrament is the restoration of the sinner's relationship with God that has been ruptured by sin. Additionally, the sinner is reconciled with the other members of the Church who have been hurt by his sins.) Finally, if we consider the ultimate effect of the sacrament, it may be understood as the sacrament of Peace. Peace is the tranquility of order; when man has restored his relationship with God, his life is in right order and he is at peace with God and neighbor.

In short, the action performed by the penitent is called confession; the sacrament is called Penance; the rite (or ritual) is called Reconciliation; the effect of the sacrament is peace. In one sentence: We confess our sins in the sacrament of Penance by using the Rite of Reconciliation, and are brought to peace as a result of this. The Council of Trent summarizes all of this neatly: "But the acts of the penitent, himself, to wit, contrition, confession, and satisfaction, are as it were the matter of this sacrament. Which acts, inasmuch as they are, by God's institution, required in the penitent for the integrity of the sacrament and for the full and perfect remission of sins, are for this reason called the parts of penance. But the thing signified indeed and the effect of this sacrament, as far as regards its force and efficacy, is reconciliation with God, which sometimes, in persons who are pious and who receive this sacrament with devotion, is wont to be peace and serenity of conscience with exceeding consolation of spirit."

All of the sacraments have four essential elements: form, matter, subject, and minister. The form (or formula) is the words spoken as the sacrament is being administered. The matter is normally what is seen and felt. The subject is the one who receives the sacrament. The minister is the one who administers it.

In the sacrament of Penance, the form is the words of absolution spoken by the priest. The absolution may be conditional if it is based on the penitent's willingness to fulfill a specific condition, such as making restitution if something has been stolen. The complete formula is: "God the Father of mercies, through the death and Resurrection of his Son, has reconciled the world to himself and sent the Holy Spirit among us for the forgiveness of sins. Through the ministry of the Church may God grant you pardon and peace, and I absolve you from your sins, in the name of the Father, and of the Son, and of the Holy Spirit."

The matter of the sacrament of Penance is twofold. Remotely, it consists of the sins of the penitent; proximately, it refers to the acts of the penitent, that is, these sins are repented and confessed with a will to make satisfaction. While the matter is generally understood to be that "which is seen and felt," here it applies to that part of a sacrament with or to which something is done in order to confer grace.

To this extent, then, one perceives how the idea of "matter" applies both to the sins that are forgiven and to the three accompanying acts of the penitent: contrition (CCC 1451-1454), confession (CCC 1455-1458), and satisfaction (CCC 1459-1460). Contrition is the sorrow for the sins committed; confession is verbal self-accusation regarding sins committed; satisfaction refers to the willingness of the penitent to accept whatever penance the priest may impose, whether it be recitation of specified prayers, reading from Sacred Scripture, or performing some corporal or spiritual works of mercy.

The subject of the sacrament of Penance may be any Catholic or, under certain circumstances (cf. Canon 844.3, 844.4), other validly baptized Christian who, having reached the age of reason, has committed an actual sin since Baptism. The age of reason is generally understood to be about the age of seven years, more or less. If a child younger than seven exhibits the intellectual capacity of reason and the ability to distinguish between right and wrong, he or she should be admitted to the sacrament.

The minister of the sacrament of Penance is a validly ordained priest who acts in collaboration with the bishop. Besides all that canon law requires of him as a judge, he is also meant by the Church to be a healer. He must act with both his head and his heart, encouraging the faithful to approach the sacrament frequently and making himself available for this purpose. He can never compromise the teaching of the Church, no matter how delicate the matter or how fragile the sinner. As "the sign and the instrument of God's merciful love for the sinner" (CCC 1465), he must always remember that this merciful God would never deceive the penitent or lead him astray. The *Catechism* says: "The confessor is not the master of God's forgiveness, but its servant. The minister of this sacrament should unite himself to the intention and charity of Christ. He should have a proven knowledge of Christian behavior, experience of human affairs, respect and sensitivity toward the one who has fallen; he must love the truth, be faithful to the Magisterium of the Church, and lead the penitent with patience toward healing and full maturity. He must pray and do penance for his penitent, entrusting him to the Lord's mercy" (1466).

See: Absolution; Confession; Contrition; Conversion of the Baptized; General Absolution; Indulgences; Metanoia; Penance in Christian Life; Sacramentals; Sacraments of the Dead.

Suggested Readings: CCC 1422-1498, 2838-2845. Vatican Council II, *Decree on the Ministry and Life of Priests, Presbyterorum Ordinis*, 5. John Paul II, *On Reconciliation and Penance in the Mission of the Church Today, Reconciliatio et Paenitentia*. A. Von Speyr, *Confession*. N. Halligan, O.P., *The Sacraments and Their Celebration*. C. O'Neill, O.P., *Meeting Christ in the Sacraments*. J. Hardon, S.J., *The Catholic Catechism*, Ch. XIII. D. Wuerl, R. Lawler, O.F.M. Cap., T. Lawler, eds. *The Teaching of Christ: A Catholic Catechism for Adults,* pp. 421-434. G. Kelly, ed., *The Sacrament of Penance in Our Time*.

Christopher M. Buckner

PENANCE IN CHRISTIAN LIFE

The fifth petition of the Lord's Prayer (cf. Mt 6:9-13) provides a stark and soul-shaking consideration. It is not enough that the sinner simply asks the Lord, "Forgive us our trespasses." No one has a right to forgiveness so that, taken alone, this is a petition, a plea. The petition, however, goes further: ". . . as we forgive those who trespass against us." We not only ask God to forgive us but stipulate the measure of his forgiveness. We ask — we pray — that he forgive us to the extent, and only so far as, we have forgiven others.

Jesus has used the word "as" (in the original Greek text of the Gospel, *hos*) several times. It is a particle of comparison, which he employs to demonstrate to his audience what is expected of them. He presents a paradigm that becomes the goal in Christian life, the model of spiritual and moral perfection: "You, therefore, must be perfect, *as* your heavenly Father is perfect" (Mt 5:48; emphasis added).

The Teaching and Example of Christ • Typically, Jesus does not leave people where he finds them. He meets people on their own level, but invites them to a higher level, presenting them with a challenge. An individual can accept or reject that challenge, but he can never be the same once the Lord has confronted him. The disciples were putting their nets in order when Jesus said, "Come, follow me." Immediately they left their nets and followed him (Mt 3:18-20). The story of the rich young man (Mt 19:16-22) depicts the opposite reaction. Here is someone who was offered the opportunity to come higher, but "walked away sad."

Jesus' commandment of love embodies such an invitation to his followers (Mt 22:34-40). Asked which is the greatest commandment, he replies with an answer appealing to both the Jewish and the Greek parts of his audience. First: "You shall love the Lord your God with all your heart, and with all your soul, and with all your mind." This is nothing new to the Jews, for it goes back to Deuteronomy 6. A verse that all Jews would know from memory, it is recited daily in their prayers; thus he meets them at their level. He goes on to offer a second commandment "like it": "You shall love your neighbor as yourself." This appeals to the Greeks, as it is directly from the Golden Rule: "Do unto others as you would have them do unto you."

So far, he has said nothing new, but later he challenges them to come higher. In Matthew 25, he foretells the end of time and the Final Judgment. Speaking metaphorically, he says what will separate the sheep from the goats will be their actions toward their neighbors: Love for Christ is determined by love for neighbor. How well or badly they have treated their neighbor will determine whether they will experience eternal life or eternal fire (Mt 25:31-46).

But even this is not his final challenge. At the Last Supper, having washed the feet of his disciples, he offers them another — a new — commandment: "that you love one another; even as I have loved you, that you also love one another" (Jn 13:34).

These scriptural passages show how Our Lord challenges his followers continually to do more. They concern the commandment of love, and specifically love of neighbor. The first simply says we are to love our neighbor as much as we love ourselves. The second is somewhat more challenging: Love your neighbor as much as you love Christ. The third is the most challenging: Love your neighbor as much as Christ loves you. This commandment appropriately is given on the night of the Last Supper, when Jesus gives his Body and Blood as nourishment for his disciples; its full meaning becomes clear the next day, when he dies to save all men. It is part of the spirit of penance in Christian life to recognize that more can and must always be done. No one can say he has done enough. Christ demonstrates this by his words and actions.

The Need for Penance • An assembly of the world Synod of Bishops in 1983 reflected on the place of penance and reconciliation in Christian life and the Church's mission. Pope John Paul II in his postsynodal apostolic exhortation (1984) links penance to conversion, to repentance, and to "doing penance." He writes: "To do penance means, above all, to re-establish the balance and harmony broken by sin, to change direction even at the cost of sacrifice." And of the Church's penitential discipline he says: "Even though it has been mitigated for some time [it] cannot be abandoned without grave harm both to the interior life of individual Christians and of the ecclesial community, and also to their capacity for missionary influence" (*On Reconciliation and Penance in the Mission of the Church Today, Reconciliatio et Paenitentia*, 26).

It is no coincidence that Jesus' commandment of love comes with the institution of the Eucharist. Nor is it without significance that the Mass always begins with a penitential rite. The Eucharist and penance, specifically the sacrament of Penance, are closely related. Penance, including sacramental penance, directly prepares for the reception of the Eucharist; the Eucharist heightens awareness of the need for penance. For Catholics, the sacrament of Penance is of central importance to the more general practice of penance in Christian life. Thus, Pope John Paul II explains in one of his encyclicals: "The Christ who calls to the Eucharistic Banquet is always the same Christ who exhorts us to penance and repeats his 'Repent.' Without this constant ever renewed endeavor for conversion, partaking in the Eucharist would lack its full redeeming effectiveness and there would be a loss or at least a weakening of the special readiness to offer God the spiritual sacrifice in which our sharing in the priesthood of Christ is expressed in an essential and universal manner" (*The Redeemer of Man, Redemptor Hominis*, 20 [1979]).

People often ask why the Catholic Church has a sacrament of Penance. We are born again by water and the Spirit (cf. Jn 3:5), and this regeneration restores us to God's friendship. But the continuous call of Our Lord to conversion reminds us of our fallen human nature and our ongoing need for conversion. Baptism removes original sin and any actual sin committed up to that time, but our human nature is imperfect and is in need of repair. Baptism is the time of regeneration, of being born again; Penance is the time to grow.

According to Father Nicholas Halligan, O.P.: "Certainly, if all those who had been regenerated in Baptism had enough gratitude to God to keep forever the justice received in Baptism by his grace and bounty, there would have been no need to institute any other sacrament than Baptism for the remission of sins. But since God is rich in mercy and knows our frail structure, he has also prepared a remedy of life for those who, after Baptism, have given themselves over to the slavery of sin and to the power of the devil. The remedy is the sacrament of Penance, and through it the benefit of Christ's death is applied to those who have fallen after Baptism" (*The Sacraments and Their Celebration*, p. 81).

But are there sins that cannot be forgiven? Penitents often are concerned that their sins are so grievous the Lord will not forgive them. On the one hand, the power Christ gave his Church to forgive sins was without limitation: "Whatever you loose on earth . . ." (Mt 16:19, 18:18); "If you forgive the sins of any . . ." (Jn 20:23). He set the example by forgiving some of the most grievous of sins. Yet there are scriptural passages

that seem to suggest something different. For instance: "Therefore I tell you, every sin and blasphemy will be forgiven men, but the blasphemy against the Spirit will not be forgiven. And whoever says a word against the Son of man will be forgiven; but whoever speaks against the Holy Spirit will not be forgiven, either in this age or in the age to come" (Mt 12:31-32; cf. Mk 3:28-30; Lk 12:10).

Central here are the ideas expressed by "blasphemes" and "sins against the Holy Spirit." Refusal to give credit to the Holy Spirit for his achievements indicates, at least implicitly, a failure to accept the saving power of God's presence in the world. This leads to a failure to come to the source of life and forgiveness, Jesus himself.

The Church commonly has taught that there are six such sins against the Holy Spirit: final impenitence, obstinacy in one's sins, despair of salvation, presumption of being able to save oneself without merit or repentance, resisting or opposing the known truths of salvation, and envy of the spiritual goods possessed by another or the graces that have been received.

The operative principle behind all these sins is that they are, as it were, terminal, since they have an intrinsic tendency to continue until the end of life, and, like other sins, cannot be forgiven as long as an individual persists in them. If, however, the sinner undergoes a change of heart and repents, they are no longer terminal and can be forgiven.

In the ongoing pursuit of Christian perfection, frequent reception of the sacrament of Penance is one of the greatest treasures the Church has to offer. It is unfortunate if people do not avail themselves of this gift. This sacrament and its healing power should be received often.

See: Confession; Contrition; Conversion of the Baptized; Metanoia; Penance and Reconciliation, Sacrament of; Satisfaction.

Suggested Readings: CCC 2838-3845. John Paul II, *On the Mercy of God, Dives in Misericordia; On Reconciliation and Penance in the Mission of the Church Today, Reconciliatio et Paenitentia*. N. Halligan, O.P., *The Sacraments and Their Celebration.* C. O'Neill, O.P., *Meeting Christ in the Sacraments.*

Christopher M. Buckner

PEOPLE OF GOD

The ecclesiology of Vatican Council II centers on *communio* — the vital union of each member of the Church with Christ and of all with one another in Christ. As a more concrete way of expressing this *communio*, the Council dwells on the expression "People of God."

"People of God" recalls the whole history of salvation, the record of God's care for those he has created. The result of original sin was not only that each one was estranged from him individually but that human beings lost their natural solidarity among themselves and became fundamentally dispersed. God wished not just to save them singly, or one by one, but to gather them together into a chosen people and lead them — united under leaders designated and given by him — to the promised land (CCC 781; Vatican Council II, *Dogmatic Constitution on the Church, Lumen Gentium,* 9). The Jews in the Old Testament are a figure of the Church as the new chosen people of God, open to all mankind.

"The gathering together of the People of God began at the moment when sin destroyed the communion of men with God, and that of men among themselves. The gathering together of the Church is, as it were, God's reaction to the chaos provoked by sin" (CCC 761).

Vocation and Mission of God's People • "People of God" emphasizes the pilgrim vocation of this new chosen people, their eschatological destiny as they make their way through human history toward the promised land. It suggests the particular joy that should be theirs at being summoned and gathered together by God and belonging to him, with special claims on his love and guidance and mercy. It stresses the calling addressed to each Christian to share in a common endeavor, the radical equality of Christian dignity, and the rights and duties as well as the distinctive graces of each one.

To understand this biblical expression properly, it is important to realize that the emphasis is not just on "people" but rather on "God." What matters is God's choice: that the people are *God's.* It is he who calls them together, leads and saves them. One becomes a member of this people not by physical birth but by being "born again," through God's grace given in Baptism (cf. CCC 782).

It would be a radical misunderstanding of the biblical expression and of Vatican II's intention in using it, to suggest that the Council thereby wished to introduce a more "democratic" notion of the Church, a Church where power would ultimately and properly derive from the people. The Church, hierarchical by constitution (cf. *Lumen Gentium,* 18-29), is a people gathered under God. Authority (rather than power) or jurisdiction exercised within the people comes "from above" (cf. Jn 19:11); in its fundamental aspects it can only come from a divine commission.

One is encouraged to live a faithful Christian life by one's consciousness of the privilege and dignity of belonging to God's people: "The state of this people is that of the dignity and freedom of the children of God" (*Lumen Gentium,* 9). This consciousness helps one to exercise freedom so as to remain *within* that people as a living member. Human weakness leads us to commit sins; if these are serious, the consequence is that, though still within the community of God's people, we are no longer living with its life. Nevertheless, we can always return to that life by Penance (consider the Prodigal Son: Lk 15:11-24). Heresy, however, and dissent, too, if truly radical, rupture our living communion with Christ and his members, and involve self-exclusion from the People of God (placing a person in a situation of "ex-communion").

The growing loneliness that many people experience today, even in the Church, is ultimately due to a sense of *not belonging to a people,* of not feeling the strength of common values and a common inheritance, of not having learned to rejoice in the grace and truth of Christ. "The sons and daughters of the Church, the children of this new people, rejoice in the King, in Christ" (Heschius: cf. *Liturgy of the Hours*, Lauds, First Sunday of Ordinary Time).

The People of God is God's only in the measure of its participation in the life and the triple mission of the Son of God. It is meant to be a "people on the move," evangelizing the world of which it forms part. It is not a closed people, but is open to all those it meets, seeking to draw them to join in the pilgrimage to the promised land. Its mission is also to be salt of the earth and light of the world (CCC 782). Only a Church that is truly a united people, one in faith, charity, and ideals, one in respect for rights and in the fulfillment of obligations, one in love for lawful authority coming from God, can be "that messianic people which is a most sure seed of unity, hope and salvation for the whole human race" (*Lumen Gentium*, 9).

See: Assent and Dissent; Baptism; Catholic Identity; Church, Membership in; Church, Nature, Origin, and Structure of; Communio; Dissent; Ecclesial Rights and Duties; Excommunication; Heresy; Judaism; New Covenant; Old Covenant; Schism.

Suggested Readings: CCC 781-786. Vatican Council II, *Dogmatic Constitution on the Church, Lumen Gentium*, Ch. II. C. Burke: *Authority and Freedom in the Church*, pp. 9-39.

Cormac Burke

PERJURY

Perjury, lying under oath, is an especially flagrant and malicious form of false witness that consists in lying in a public, formal setting like a court of law. It is expressly forbidden by the eighth commandment (cf. Ex 20:16).

The evil of perjury is twofold. Not only do perjurers lie, but also they swear at the same time that their lie is true. By taking an oath, they compound the injustice of any false testimony they may knowingly utter.

Lies are gravely sinful when their matter is grave and when they are told to persons with a right to the truth. Since false testimony can wrongfully condemn a person to imprisonment

or even death, and since duly appointed officials of the judicial system must have the truth in order to judge rightly, one can conclude that perjury is a serious offense against both justice and charity.

If the oath contains the words "so help me God," perjury involves yet another dimension of offense against God. This phrase refers to our hope of salvation, which only God, through his grace ("help"), can achieve. By consciously and deliberately swearing to tell the truth "so help me God" and then reneging, perjurers renounce grace and strike a Faustian bargain with evil.

See: False Witness; Lying; Religion, Virtue of; Truthfulness.

PHENOMENOLOGY

The originator of phenomenological philosophy is universally recognized to be the German philosopher Edmund Husserl (1859-1938). It was above all his groundbreaking work *Logical Investigations* (1900) that laid out for the first time the method and the presuppositions of phenomenology and drew to Husserl his first phenomenological students.

It is often said that phenomenology is not so much a philosophical doctrine as a way of philosophizing. This is well expressed by the motto of Husserl, *Zurueck zu den Sachen selbst* ("Back to the things themselves"). The idea is to philosophize about things, not by applying doubtful models and paradigms to them or deducing how they ought to be, but rather by consulting them directly, by letting each thing that we examine in philosophy speak for itself and show itself on its own terms.

Consider, for example, how the phenomenologists will deal with the claim that animals are only a complicated kind of machine or that human persons are only a complicated kind of animal. They will say it is a mistake to begin by pressing animal life into a mechanical model or pressing personal life into an instinctual model. They will say that we ought instead to ask, with the unencumbered naïveté of a child, "What is animal life? What does it show itself to be in our immediate experience of it?" Or, "What is it to exist as person? How do we act when we act as persons?" It is just such questions that exemplify the phenomenological return to the things themselves.

The answer given to these questions by almost all phenomenologists is that animal life cannot be reduced to mechanical principles, even as personal life cannot be reduced to instinctual principles. Each of these forms of life — animal and personal — is something of its own; each is itself and is nothing else. No conceivable elaboration of mechanical principles could give us life, which represents another order of being, forever irreducible to the mechanical. No conceivable elaboration of the logic of instincts could ever yield personal being, which, through the freedom that distinguishes it, is also a fundamentally other order of being, forever irreducible to the instinctual. Modern and contemporary philosophy is full of reductionistic, "nothing-but" theories ("Man is nothing but a higher animal"); it belongs to the genius of phenomenology to resist all such reductionism, and to vindicate the uniqueness of each reality about which it reflects.

One can also say it like this: The phenomenologist is not content to have his entire relation to reality mediated by conventional ways of thinking, traditional principles, stereotypes, plausible paradigms; he wants to get beyond our way of conceiving and symbolizing reality, and to attain to reality itself — to get "back to the things themselves."

Intuition and Essence • It is not surprising that phenomenology lays a great stress on the intellectual act of *intuition*, that is, the act of directly apprehending or seeing the reality that one is trying to do justice to. Intuition forms a contrast to deducing, to constructing, to hypothesizing, as well as to imposing a paradigm on something (e.g., imposing a mechanical paradigm on life); intuition gives the mind a more immediate contact with reality than any of these. It is an act of intellectual intuition in which we grasp the uniqueness of life or of personal being.

It was only natural that the phenomenologists

would give much attention to the *object* of intellectual intuition; they identified this object with *the essences of things*. It is the essence of life and the essence of personhood that, in our examples, the phenomenologist tries to grasp in intuition. Those who would reduce life or personhood to lower levels of being falsify the essences of things. The phenomenologists recognized that it is not easy for the mind to get at essences, and so they frequently analyze the difficult discipline of *bringing to evidence* the essences at stake in a given discussion. It is no accident that in the *Logical Investigations* Husserl did battle with many of the so-called positivists and nominalists of the late nineteenth century. These were philosophers who denied the reality of essence, who in different ways tried to debunk essence. Husserl's attempt to vindicate essence against them was an all-important part of his work of laying the foundations of phenomenological philosophy.

Ever since Plato, of course, it has been known that philosophy deals with knowledge of essences. For this reason phenomenology can be viewed as a certain renewal of Western philosophy rather than as a break with it. The phenomenologists, however, gained many new insights into essence and into the kinds of essences that one tries to apprehend in philosophy. For instance, they made a point of the fact that it is not only highly general essences, such as being, matter, form, substance, that interest the philosopher but that there are also more specific essences, such as the essence of promising or of the love between man and woman, which can also be brought to evidence by the philosopher; and indeed, there are even entirely individual essences, such as the essence of a particular nation or of a particular person.

Realism and Idealism • Regarding all of these essences Husserl was in the *Logical Investigations* what one calls a philosophical *realist*, that is, he regarded them as discovered by the human mind and in no way formed or made by the human mind, in no way dependent on it. This is how all of the early phenomenologists understood Husserl; they thought he was retrieving for philosophy a realism of essence. Hence the *Logi-*

cal *Investigations* seemed to them to strike a great and liberating blow at the relativism and subjectivism of the time; if there is an order of essences independent of human devising, and if we can know something of this order, then we are capable of real knowledge of being and are not hopelessly confined to our conditioning and perspectives. And in fact in the *Logical Investigations* Husserl conducts a brilliant polemic against relativism in its various forms.

And yet in his later work Husserl abandoned his realism and developed phenomenology in an *idealist* direction, that is, in the direction of a philosophy which says that the objects of our thinking are what they are only through their being thought by us, and that they are nothing in their own right, nothing independently of being thought by us. In this later work, one finds nothing more of his polemic against relativism.

This development on the part of Husserl led to a great division within phenomenology. Most of his early disciples did not follow him away from realism; against their master, they insisted that phenomenology discovers the essences of being and in no way produces them. Thus the disciples of the early Husserl and of the later Husserl form two fundamentally opposed interpretations of phenomenology, one of them realist, one idealist (or "transcendental," as the opposite of realist phenomenology is also called).

The realist phenomenologists stress much more than the idealists the unity of phenomenology with the tradition of Western philosophy, the so-called *philosophia perennis,* or perennial philosophy. They think that phenomenology has much to contribute, for example, to the metaphysics of substance (originating in Aristotle), or to the metaphysics of evil, or to questions about the existence and nature of God. The idealist phenomenologists, by contrast, do not address these questions; even if they recognize them as valid, they think that phenomenology is so limited to the relativities of human consciousness that it can never be the source of answers to such questions. They think the very idea of a phenomenological metaphysics is impossible and self-contradictory. But the realist phenomenologists think it is entirely possible, and they understand much of their work as the attempt to explore by means of our experience the ultimate structures of being.

One sees that one does not yet know much about a philosopher as long as one knows only that he is a "phenomenologist"; one has to know how he or she stands with regard to the great divide within phenomenology.

Phenomenology and Christianity • For the reader of this encyclopedia it is particularly important to know how phenomenology stands in relation to Christianity.

Although Husserl, Jewish by origin, never underwent any conversion to Christianity, it is a very significant fact that most of his early disciples did. Adolf Reinach, Edith Stein, Dietrich von Hildebrand, Hedwig Martius, to name four of the most eminent of them, all became deeply committed believers. Von Hildebrand is known for his profound religious writings and his defense of Christian values; Edith Stein became a Carmelite nun, and is now Blessed Edith Stein. All of these converts attest that their study of phenomenology in the school of Husserl was extremely important for finding their way to Christianity. They continued to understand themselves as phenomenologists even after their conversions. By contrast, the phenomenological school of the later Husserl, including thinkers like Martin Heidegger, led to no notable conversions; nor is it difficult to understand the antagonism between Catholic Christianity and idealist (or transcendental) phenomenology. The Church cannot make friends with a philosophy that refuses metaphysics and that installs the human mind as the measure of all things.

To understand the affinity of realist phenomenology with Christianity, we have to make mention of the seminal thinker Max Scheler (1874-1928). Though more a contemporary of Husserl than a student of his, Scheler was drawn into the phenomenological movement by Husserl — the early, realist Husserl. Scheler had converted to Catholicism in his youth, and was the first to bring phenomenology to bear on specifically Christian themes. Giving particular attention to the holiness of the saints, in good phenomenological fashion he argued that Christian holiness is irreducible to moral goodness and other kinds of value; he argued that it is a realm of value all its own, which in fact ranks higher than any other value. He wrote phenomenological studies of acts such as repentance and elaborated an entire philosophy of religion. He connected the phenomenological intuition of essence with St. Augustine and the Augustinian teaching about the light of eternal truth shining above the human mind. Though Scheler was not always influential in each of the conversions of phenomenologists (as he was in the conversion of von Hildebrand), his work shows how natural it is to bring Christianity together with realist phenomenology.

It is well known that Karol Wojtyla (born 1920), who was to become Pope John Paul II, studied Scheler closely, wrote a number of studies on him, and was profoundly influenced by his phenomenology. One can see this influence in, for instance, Wojtyla's essay "Subjectivity and the Irreducible in Man," in which he distinguishes between a "cosmological" view of man and a "personalist" view, and argues that the former takes man too much as a being in nature, overstressing the likeness of man to other natural beings, whereas the latter does greater justice to that which is unique to man and makes him unlike every other being in nature. Asking how it is that the personalist approach is enabled to get at the uniqueness of man, he answers that it is by examining the "subjectivity" of persons, that is, the way in which they experience themselves within themselves. This exemplifies exactly what was mentioned above — the phenomenological appeal to immediate experience for the sake of capturing the distinctive essence of a being and so of avoiding all reductionism with regard to the being.

Wojtyla holds that this phenomenological emphasis on subjectivity entered in various ways into the teaching of Vatican Council II. For example, he sees something one-sidedly "cosmological" in an exclusive focus on the *procreative meaning* of the marital act; when one studies the act as lived

by spouses, one can bring to light, as the Council brought to light more clearly than ever before in Church teaching, the *unitive meaning* that the marital act also has. With this, according to Wojtyla, one attains to a more personalist understanding of the marital act.

Another instance of the fruitfulness of realist phenomenology for Christian thought is the philosophical work of Dietrich von Hildebrand (1889-1977). His work in aesthetics, philosophy of community, epistemology, but especially ethics and philosophy of the human person (including the philosophy of man and woman), for all its Augustinian stamp, breaks much new ground, contributing many things toward a new Christian personalism. More recently, Josef Seifert (born 1945), founder of the International Academy of Philosophy in Liechtenstein, has employed the resources of realist phenomenology in order to throw new light on central issues of Western metaphysics, especially issues in natural theology. Seifert has also overcome a one-sided focus of realist phenomenology on questions of essence, and has retrieved for it the great questions of existence.

Efforts have also been made by Christian phenomenologists to build bridges to the Thomist tradition of philosophy. Very well known are the attempts in this direction by Blessed Edith Stein (1891-1942), but perhaps those of Karol Wojtyla have yielded a more convincing work of synthesis.

See: Augustinianism; Human Person; Thomas Aquinas, Thought of; Thomism.

Suggested Readings: D. von Hildebrand, "Prolegomena" to *Ethics; What Is Philosophy?* K. Wojtyla, "Subjectivity and the Irreducible Man" in *Person and Community.* M. Scheler, *On the Eternal in Man.* J. Seifert, *Back to Things in Themselves.*

John F. Crosby

PLURALISM

Salvation comes from Jesus Christ, who alone has the words of eternal life (cf. Jn 6:68). Hence arises the vital need to accept his Revelation. "He who believes and is baptized will be saved; but he who does not believe will be condemned" (Mk 16:15-16).

The truth that saves is something given, revealed by God. It has already been given in its entirety, and so the Church teaches that there can be no new public revelation after the death of the last Apostle (cf. Vatican Council II, *Dogmatic Constitution on Divine Revelation, Dei Verbum*, 4).

Revelation is complete; doctrine does not increase. However, our understanding of doctrine can and should improve and grow; or, alternatively, it could weaken or be lost.

While all truth is in Christ, and he spoke for all times and situations, he did not directly address all subjects. Nevertheless, his teaching on every single matter connected with salvation is available to us to the end of time. Whenever an apparently new question of belief or behavior comes up or an older belief is questioned, Jesus is specially present, just as he promised: "I am with you always, to the close of the age" (Mt 28:20). So, too, is the Spirit of Truth, who "will guide you into all the truth" (Jn 16:13). To fulfill his promises, Jesus set up a hierarchically structured Church, with a special mission to represent him, with a teaching power (Magisterium) that speaks not only in his name but with his very voice: "He who hears you hears me, and he who rejects you rejects me" (Lk 10:16).

Our minds therefore have not been left on their own in the challenge of understanding the full content of Christ's Revelation and its application to new circumstances. Once the Church proposes some definitive teaching on a matter of faith or morals, the matter should be settled for a Catholic.

Nevertheless, it does not follow that there is no room for reflection and research or for differing views in matters of Church doctrine. Even when the substance of a truth of faith has been established, there always remain accidental or marginal aspects allowing different interpretations. In those, research, discussion, new proposals, and hypotheses are all legitimate, provided they really range *within*, and not outside, the terms or limits of the truth already taught.

Theological Pluralism • Pluralism — or "pluriformity" — is a broader concept than theological pluriformity alone. The Extraordinary Synod of Bishops of 1985 explained that "the one and unique Catholic Church exists in and through the particular churches. . . . Here, we have the true theological principle of variety and pluriformity in unity, but it is necessary to distinguish pluriformity from pure pluralism. When pluriformity is true richness and carries with it fullness, this is true catholicity. The pluralism of fundamentally opposed positions instead leads to dissolution, destruction, and the loss of identity" (*The Final Report*, 2).

The possibility that varying interpretations or explanations may legitimately be given to aspects of revealed truth is what we call theological pluralism or, in the Synod's terminology, pluriformity. This means that the same doctrine can be seen and appreciated in different ways or that various practical conclusions can be drawn from it. Just as the same physical object can be viewed from different angles, and quite different sketches or photos made of it, so truths of faith, while retaining their objective meaning and content, may open up different aspects of their riches in different ways to different minds.

The work of theological pluralism can gradually establish the inner connections and harmonies between theses that might at first sight seem in opposition. A mind open to pluralist possibilities will look for continuity in apparently quite radical developments in Church doctrine. As an instance: magisterial teaching on religious tolerance. The preconciliar view tended to work from the thesis that "*error* has no rights," whereas modern reflection, without contradicting that, sets out from a different principle: "Each *person* has rights," including the person in error (cf. Vatican Council II, *Declaration on Religious Freedom, Dignitatis Humanae*).

The ends of marriage might offer another example. Preconciliar teaching proposed a hierarchy of ends: procreation as the primary end, and "mutual help" and "sedation of concupiscence" as two secondary ends. Nowadays marriage is assigned two ends on an equal level: procreation/ education and the "good of the spouses" (CCC 2249, 2363; Canon 1055). Not hierarchy but interdependence of the ends is now emphasized. Whether the teaching on primary and secondary ends has been completely dropped or not, is a matter of legitimate dispute among theologians.

Pluralism and Dissent • Pluralism, fully adhering to all the doctrines proposed by the Church, suggests different interpretations of aspects that do not touch the substance of what is proposed. The true pluralist continues to look to the Magisterium, always ready to accept any indication or correction coming from that charismatic source. Dissent, at times wrongly presented as a type of pluralism, interprets a doctrine in a way that rejects or contradicts it, at least in some essential aspect.

To accept that Christ really rose from the dead with his human body, while then to offer different suggestions as to the mode of this occurrence, is pluralism. It is equally shown by those who believe in the Assumption of Mary, body and soul, to heaven, some holding that she died first (like her Son) and others that the merits of her Son preserved her from the experience of death. To question or deny the reality of the bodily Resurrection of Jesus or of the Assumption of Mary, is dissent; in these two cases it would in fact be heresy, since in each instance a defined dogma is in question.

The Magisterium always remains the common reference point for legitimate theological pluralism. Pluralism, under the Magisterium, is a blessing for the Church. It leads to the enrichment of our understanding of the wonders of the faith, never to its impoverishment.

See: Assent and Dissent; Development of Doctrine; Dissent; Divine Revelation; Magisterium.

Suggested Readings: CCC 84-95. Congregation for the Doctrine of the Faith, *Instruction on the Ecclesial Vocation of the Theologian.*

Cormac Burke

POLITICS

One of the distinctive marks of the Christian religion is its essentially transpolitical character. Unlike Islam or Judaism, Christian Revelation does not call for the establishment of any particular regime or form of government, nor for any special code of civil laws and customs (cf. Vatican Council II, *Pastoral Constitution on the Church in the Modern World, Gaudium et Spes*, 76, and CCC 2245). The New Law of Christ is above all a matter of grace, which transforms a person from within.

Hence, from the beginnings of the Church to the present, Christians have lived in the most diverse sorts of political societies, with their distinct forms of organization and characteristic ways of life. They have done so, mindful of Christ's command to "render to Caesar the things that are Caesar's, and to God the things that are God's" (Mk 12:17; cf. Mt 22:21, Lk 20:25). Political life is necessary and, at its best, noble, for Christians as for all human beings. And yet it must not be forgotten that "political options are by nature contingent and never in an entirely adequate way interpret the Gospel. . . . In particular, a political party can never be identified with the Gospel, and therefore, unlike the Gospel, it can never become an object of absolute loyalty" (Pope John Paul II, address, July 28, 1993; published as "Priests Do Not Have a Political Mission," *L'Osservatore Romano*, English edition, August 4 and August 11, 1993).

The *Letter to Diognetus*, a Christian document of the second century, expresses the situation this way: "Christians are indistinguishable from other men either by nationality, language, or customs. They do not inhabit separate cities of their own, or speak a strange dialect, or follow some outlandish way of life. . . . With regard to dress, food and manner of life in general, they follow the customs of whatever city they happen to be living in, whether it is Greek or foreign. And yet there is something extraordinary about their lives. They live in their own countries as though they were only passing through. They play their full role as citizens, but labor under all the disabilities of aliens. Any country can be their homeland, but for them, their homeland, wherever it may be, is a foreign country. Like others, they marry and have children, but they do not expose them. They share their meals, but not their wives. They live in the flesh, but they are not governed by the desires of the flesh. They pass their days upon the earth, but they are citizens of heaven. Obedient to the laws, they yet live on a level that transcends the law. . . . So noble is the position that God has assigned them that they are not allowed to desert it" (5, 6).

As this shows, the transpolitical character of Christianity should not be interpreted as apolitical or antipolitical. The great commandment of love has practical consequences; the "kingdom not of this world" cannot ordinarily be attained without striving to live this commandment to the full in this world. And in this world we are made to live not as isolated individuals, but as members of various communities, from the family up through political society and the universal human community. Hence the *Catechism of the Catholic Church* treats political life, broadly speaking, under the headings "The Human Community" and "You Shall Love Your Neighbor As Yourself." And these topics in turn merit inclusion in the *Catechism* as integral parts of our "Life in Christ" (Pt. Three).

It is true that Christ himself shunned all involvement in political affairs. The core of his Messianic mission was to free Israel, and indeed all humanity, from bondage to sin and death, not to solve socioeconomic problems nor even to liberate the chosen people from the yoke of Roman domination. And yet his teaching is not without important implications for political life.

As Pope John Paul II has explained: "[Christ] did teach a doctrine and formulate precepts that shed light not only on the life of individuals but also on that of society. In particular, Jesus formulated the precept of mutual love, which implies respect for every person and his rights; it implies rules of social justice aiming at recognizing what is each person's due and at harmoniously sharing earthly goods among individuals, families and groups. In addition, Jesus stressed the universal quality of love, above and beyond the differences

of race and nationality constituting humanity. It could be said that in calling himself the 'Son of Man,' he wanted to state, by the very way he presented his messianic identity, that his work was meant for every human person, without discrimination of class, language, culture, or ethnic and social group. Proclaiming peace for his disciples and for all people, Jesus laid the foundation for the precept of fraternal love, solidarity and reciprocal help on a universal scale. For him this clearly was and is the aim and principle of good politics" ("Priests Do Not Have a Political Mission," *L'Osservatore Romano*).

Church Teaching About Politics • To understand the Church's teaching about politics, one must first be familiar with her teaching about the human person, a substantial unity of body and soul, hence possessed of reason and will. Catholic social teaching begins from the premise, rooted in both reason and Revelation, that human beings are by their very nature social creatures. To achieve their specific perfection and to reach happiness, humans must under normal circumstances participate in common goods that transcend in some way their purely individual well-being and that are made possible only by life in society. The societies most properly corresponding to the needs of human nature are, first, the family and then the political community, characterized by the pursuit of justice and the good life for its citizens.

The Second Vatican Council sums up the nature and utility of political life as follows: "Individuals, families, and the various groups which make up the civil community are aware of their inability to achieve a truly human life by their own unaided efforts; they see the need for a wider community where each one will make a specific contribution to an even broader implementation of the common good. For this reason they set up various forms of political communities. The political community, then, exists for the common good: This is its full justification and meaning and the source of its specific and basic right to exist. The common good embraces the sum total of all those conditions of social life which enable individuals, families, and organizations to achieve complete and efficacious fulfillment" (*Pastoral Constitution on the Church in the Modern World, Gaudium et Spes*, 74; cf. Pope John XXIII, encyclical *Peace on Earth, Pacem in Terris*, 53-58 [1963]).

This notion of the common good as the end of political life derives especially from the thought of St. Thomas Aquinas, who in turn built upon its use by Aristotle and others. St. Augustine, in a famous passage of his *City of God* (Bk. XIX), sets forth peace — "the tranquility of order," rather than the mere absence of war or strife — as the goal of political life and indeed of human life in general. Augustine's understanding of peace has much in common with Aquinas's notion of common good: On the political plane, both depend upon justice and civic friendship. Moreover, both evoke a harmonious arrangement or ordering of a rich variety of persons and activities, in such a way as to foster the well-being of all rather than catering to the private satisfaction of a few.

In order for the pursuit of peace and the common good to be truly effective, a political community requires both a responsible citizenry and competent authority. This civil or political authority may be vested in laws, institutions, and individuals. Its mission is to foster justice and the flourishing of the people it serves, and consequently to repress those vices most damaging to social life. To guard against abuse of authority, it is prudent that decisions be made for the most part according to law, rather than left to the unlimited discretion of individuals who may be swayed by passion or desire for personal gain. In the context of modern political life, this "rule of law" usually goes hand-in-hand with some system of checks and balances, where each power (legislative, executive, judicial) is "balanced by other powers and by other spheres of responsibility which keep it within its proper bounds" (Pope John Paul II, encyclical *The Hundredth Year, Centesimus Annus*, 44 [1991]; CCC 1904).

Nonetheless, ultimately it is human beings who make and administer the laws, set policy, and decide cases to which laws on the books do not apply. Hence not even the best set of laws and institutions suffices to render dispensable personal virtue on the part of the governed and especially the governors.

Participation in Political Life • Political leadership, indeed public service in all its forms, is an especially noble pursuit, one that demands practical wisdom and upright intention with a view to the common good. The Second Vatican Council teaches that "[t]hose with a talent for the difficult yet noble art of politics, or whose talents in this matter can be developed, should prepare themselves for it, and, forgetting their own convenience and material interests, they should engage in political activity. They must combat injustice and oppression, arbitrary domination and intolerance by individuals or political parties, and they must do so with integrity and wisdom. They must dedicate themselves to the welfare of all in a spirit of sincerity and fairness, of love and of the courage demanded by political life" (*Gaudium et Spes*, 75). An important aspect of this courage is the fortitude to abide by the moral law, even at the cost of unpopularity or inefficiency.

Participation in political life ought to elevate a person's existence, "helping him greatly in fulfilling his calling (even his religious calling)." But it would be naïve to deny that political regimes often foster a social environment in which the human person is "turned away from the good and urged to evil" (*Gaudium et Spes*, 25). The Church therefore reminds citizens and rulers alike "that the common good touches the whole man, the needs both of his body and of his soul. Hence it follows that the civil authorities must undertake to effect the common good by ways and means that are proper to them. That is, while respecting the hierarchy of values, they should promote simultaneously both the material and the spiritual welfare of the citizens." Human beings, "composed . . . of bodies and immortal souls, can never in this mortal life succeed in satisfying all their needs or in attaining perfect happiness. Therefore all efforts made to promote the common good, far from endangering the eternal salvation of men, ought rather to serve to advance it" (*Pacem in Terris*, 57, 59).

Thus far we have focused our attention on political life within a single community, its members bound together by ties of history, language, and culture as well as by a common code of laws and set of institutions. As important as these ties are, our common human nature, with its common origin and end in God, gives rise to duties that transcend the boundaries of individual nations. We are members not just of a particular society, but also of the international community, with the corresponding obligation to contribute insofar as possible to the universal common good.

On the macro level, nations, too, are obliged to act with justice toward one another and to bear in mind the good of all when formulating policy. Otherwise, as so often happens, patriotism degenerates into collective selfishness. Even efforts to foster one nation's good may become means to facilitate the exploitation of outsiders. St. Augustine unmasks this hypocrisy with an amusing analogy: "Without justice, what are kingdoms but great robber bands? What are robber bands but small kingdoms? The band is itself made up of men, is ruled by the command of a leader, and is held together by a social pact. Plunder is divided in accordance with agreed-upon law. If this evil increases by the inclusion of dissolute men to the extent that it takes over territory, establishes headquarters, occupies cities, and subdues peoples, it publicly assumes the title of kingdom! This title is manifestly conferred on it, not because greed has been removed, but because impunity has been added. A fitting and true response was once given to Alexander the Great by an apprehended pirate. When asked by the king what he thought he was doing by infesting the sea, he replied with noble insolence, 'What do you think you are doing by infesting the whole world? Because I do it with one puny boat, I am called a pirate; because you do it with a great fleet, you are called an emperor' " (*City of God*, IV, 4).

With a view to meeting the needs of the international community in an age of increasing interdependence, recent documents of the Magisterium have encouraged the establishment of an effective global authority. This authority would need to respect the principle of subsidiarity, not seeking to usurp the proper roles of individual communities and their authorities, but focusing on problems beyond the scope of individual states (cf. *Pacem in Terris*, 80-145; *Gaudium et Spes*, 77-90; Pope John Paul II, encyclical *On Social Concerns, Sollicitudo Rei Socialis* [1987]).

Subsidiarity is also of great importance within political society proper. In carrying out its service to the common good, government should facilitate rather than absorb the proper functions of persons, families, and smaller associations. Catholic teaching on politics thus opposes individualism and emphasizes the common good, while emphatically rejecting all forms of collectivism or totalitarianism. Such regimes crush the human spirit, impeding the integral human development that is the ultimate goal and justification of political life.

See: Authority; Cardinal Virtues; Church and State; Citizenship; Civil Disobedience; Civil Law; Common Good; Family; Human Goods; Human Person; Interdependence; Property; Religious Liberty; Revolution; Social Doctrine; Social Justice; Subsidiarity; Thomas Aquinas, Thought of.

Suggested Readings: CCC 407, 1878-1986, 2210-2213, 2234-2257, 2265-2267, 2273, 2302-2317. Vatican Council II, *Pastoral Constitution on the Church in the Modern World, Gaudium et Spes*, especially 23-32, 73-90. Pius XII, *On the Function of the State in the Modern World, Summi Pontificatus*. John XXIII, *Peace on Earth, Pacem in Terris*. John Paul II, *On Social Concerns, Sollicitudo Rei Socialis*; *The Hundredth Year, Centesimus Annus*. St. Augustine, *City of God*, Bks. II, 21-22, IV-VIII, XIV, 1-4, 11-15, 28, XIX; *Letters* 91 and 138. St. Thomas Aquinas, *On Kingship to the King of Cyprus*, Bk. I; *Summa Theologiae,* I-I, 90-97, 100, 105, 1, II-II, 47, 50 (on prudence), 57-58 (on right and justice).

Mary M. Keys

POPE

Christ, present in his Church, continues to proclaim the message of redemption and to offer the means of salvation to generation after generation: "I am with you always, to the close of the age"

(Mt 28:20). He sent his Apostles and their successors to teach, guide, and sanctify in his name, promising that he would be behind their teaching ("He who hears you hears me, and he who rejects you rejects me" [Lk 10:16]) and guaranteeing those who obeyed their authority that it had a divine seal of approval placed on it: "Whatever you [plural] bind on earth shall be bound in heaven, and whatever you [plural] loose on earth shall be loosed in heaven" (Mt 18:18).

Even before Christ gave his authority to the Apostles collegially, he had given it singly to Peter, choosing him as the foundation rock of the Church — "You are Peter, and on this rock I will build my church" (Mt 16:18) — and endowing him with the fullness of the authority that he was also later to give collegially to the Twelve. As Jesus entrusted Peter with the keys of his kingdom, saying, "I will give you the keys of the kingdom of heaven," he added: "Whatever you [singular] bind on earth shall be bound in heaven, and whatever you [singular] loose on earth shall be loosed in heaven" (Mt 16:19).

As the powers given to the College of the Apostles pass on down the centuries to the bishops, their successors, so the special and extra powers given to the head of the apostolic college pass to each of Peter's successors in the See of Rome. As Vatican Council II teaches, Jesus constituted the Apostles "in the form of a college or permanent assembly, at the head of which he placed Peter" (*Dogmatic Constitution on the Church, Lumen Gentium*, 19); and, as the Council further says, "Just as, in accordance with the Lord's decree, St. Peter and the rest of the apostles constitute a unique apostolic college, so in like fashion the Roman Pontiff, Peter's successor, and the bishops, successors of the apostles, are related with and united to one another" (*Lumen Gentium*, 22). Collegially united with one another and with the Pope, "and never apart from him," bishops can exercise "supreme and full authority over the universal Church," provided it is exercised with the Roman Pontiff's agreement (*Lumen Gentium*, 22). But the Roman Pontiff also has "full, supreme and universal power over the whole Church, a power which he can always exercise unhindered" (*Lumen Gentium*, 22).

Titles of the Pope • *Vicar of Christ*. A vicar is someone who takes the place of another. Peter was not elected by the rest of the Apostles in order to preside over the Church; he was chosen by Our Lord himself to be his vicar. To be a successor of Peter, as is each Pope, is different from being a successor of the Apostles, as are all bishops. The Pope is always "Peter."

Only the Pope is the Vicar of Christ, for whom Christ specially prayed, whose faith will not fail, and who has the particular mission of confirming in the faith the whole body of Christ's followers, the brothers and sisters of Jesus Christ. "Simon, Simon, behold, Satan demanded to have you, that he might sift you like wheat, but I have prayed for you that your faith may not fail; and when you have turned again, strengthen your brethren" (Lk 22:31). "Jesus said to Simon Peter . . . 'Feed my lambs' . . . 'Feed my sheep' " (Jn 21:15-17).

Supreme Pontiff. Peter appears throughout the Gospels as the leader and spokesman of the other Apostles. His special place among them was acknowledged by all from the start. "Even among the Apostles, there was a certain distinction in power within an equality of honor, and while the choice of all was identical, to one alone preeminence was given over the others" (St. Leo the Great).

The primacy given to Peter and to each Pope as his successor cannot be reduced to one of honor. It is a primacy of rule and government over the whole flock of Jesus (cf. Jn 10:16), by which the Pope has immediate jurisdiction over each portion of the People of God, over each particular church and diocese (cf. Canons 331, 333; Vatican Council II, *Dogmatic Constitution on the Church, Lumen Gentium*, 18ff.; CCC 880-882).

He is the first teacher of the faith, with a God-given responsibility to defend it, and with special divine aid in doing so. But he is also the first ruler and legislator. The "power of the keys" entrusted to him (Mt 16:19) opens the doors of heaven for us.

The Gospels seem to make a point of not hiding Peter's defects and failures. But these did not prevent Christ from choosing him nor stop others from accepting his authority. The lesson is clear: Respect, loyalty, and obedience toward the Pope, whoever he may be, cannot depend on any impression or evidence of his human wisdom or sanctity. Christ did not guarantee to preserve the Pope from the possibility of giving bad example, but simply from that of leading people astray by his teaching.

We are not united to the Pope, and through him to Christ, unless united to what he indicates in his role as Supreme Pastor. Attachment to the Pope is a sign, test, and condition of attachment to Christ and full union with him.

Servant of the Servants of God (*Servus Servorum Dei*). Christ's purpose in bestowing special gifts on Peter was that they be considered and used not as privileges but as a means of serving others. The "higher" one is called in the Church, the greater one's mission of service in imitation of Jesus, who became the servant of all (cf. Mt 20:28). The Pope's life has to be spent in this service, always conscious of the account he will have to give to his Master.

Holy Father. Catholics (and even non-Catholics) often refer to the Pope with this affectionate title that is full of significance. The Pope is the father of this family of the Church, where Christ wishes to gather the children of God into one (cf. Jn 11:52). His position has an objective holiness in itself flowing from its divine institution; and it therefore asks of each Pope a high degree of personal sanctity.

Faith enables Catholics to grasp the extraordinary gift of God to be found in the papacy. This leads them to be united to the Pope, because they see in him Christ's representative, the "sweet Christ on earth," in the expressive words of St. Catherine of Siena.

Awareness of the unique importance of the Pope in the plans of God should lead the faithful to accompany him constantly by prayer and small mortifications for him and his intentions.

See: Apostolic Succession; Church, Nature, Origin, and Structure of; Collegiality; Hierarchy; Holy See; Infallibility; Magisterium.

Suggested Readings: CCC 552-553, 765, 834, 857, 862-863, 877-882, 891-892, 895, 937-938. Vatican Council II, *Dogmatic Constitution on the Church, Lumen Gentium*, Ch. III; *Decree on the Bishops' Pastoral Office in the Church, Christus Dominus*, 2.

Cormac Burke

POPULATION

Concern about population issues has attracted considerable international attention, particularly during the past twenty years. Among other things, this concern was heightened by the decennial population conferences sponsored by the United Nations in Bucharest in 1974, Mexico City in 1984, and Cairo in 1994.

Discussion of population growth and decline involves an analysis of births, deaths, and migration. All estimates are somewhat tenuous because they depend on local census data whose reliability varies from nation to nation and continent to continent. The United Nations Population Division attempts to compile and evaluate such data worldwide, and its estimates are fairly reliable and are the basis of most professional demographic analyses and studies.

Statistical data and comparisons regarding births, deaths, and migration are not isolated, but are studied in relation to what are called demographic variables, that is, other issues that influence or are influenced by the demographic data. Thus, an increase in population growth may result from an excess of births over deaths or an increase in immigration. But the population increase or decline is also evaluated in terms of such variables as sufficiency of food, housing, disease control, education, the overall socioeconomic condition of a country, the availability of natural resources, and the production of marketable goods, to cite just a few factors. Demography as a science concerns itself with the basic statistical data and its evaluation and analysis, whereas population studies focus on the interrelationship of the demographic data with these other factors.

So, for instance, as of the mid-1990s, the world-wide population growth rate has been declining steadily for some time and is expected to continue to do so well into the twenty-first century. The actual number of people is increasing, but at a declining rate, and at different levels in various countries. In some countries, high birth rates have increased the young population — infants and children — whereas in other countries declining death rates and a longer life span have resulted in a larger elderly population. These facts influence labor markets, educational demands, and social security systems.

Consequently, population issues have received greater attention from national governments, university centers, and at the United Nations. The UN conferences have directed attention to the formulation of population policies by governments at the national, state or regional, and city levels. These policies attempt to integrate demographic information with socioeconomic concerns. Government policies can affect migration, help decrease mortality by provision of better nutrition and health care, and help decrease fertility by, among other things, provision of family planning or birth control. Note that population control and birth control are not identical, though they are related. Population control is what governments and international agencies do to increase or limit births, deaths, or migration. Birth control or family planning is what couples do to space or limit births.

Involvement of the Church • As interest in and understanding of population issues has increased, the Catholic Church has participated in the overall study and discussion. The Church has called attention to the ethical issues related to population policy, and, having reflected on her own teaching, has developed and proposed a moral-ethical perspective for consideration by scholars and policy-makers. The roots of the Church's position are found in her teaching on the dignity of the human person and in her social doctrine, which has developed and been carefully articulated especially during the last century.

Further, the Church assumes a responsibility to draw the attention of governments and international agencies to the natural law and to concern for the common good in addressing social issues. In a special way, recent Popes, the Second Vatican Council, and especially Popes Paul VI and John Paul II have refined and specifically applied the Church's teaching on social justice and responsible parenthood to contemporary population issues. This application is found in conciliar and synodal documents, in papal addresses, and in the interventions of delegations of the Holy See to international meetings on population and socioeconomic concerns.

In the international discussions of population, two different approaches have emerged: the developmentalist approach, which emphasizes the need for socioeconomic development that eventually results in decreased birth rates; and the "family-planning-first" approach, which calls for determined efforts to decrease birth rates by easy access to all methods of contraception, including sterilization and abortion, as a precondition for assistance from developed nations or international agencies.

The Holy See, from the outset, has adopted and encouraged the developmentalist approach. It can be summarized by the following points.

1. Population policy should be part of a larger commitment to a program of social justice that enables all persons to live a fully human life, one endowed with freedom and dignity.

2. Granted that rapid population growth may at times impede the development process, governments have rights and duties, within the limits of their own competence, to try to ameliorate the population problem. This includes providing information concerning the impact of population growth, as well as legislation and programs that will help families.

3. Decisions regarding the size of the family and the frequency of births should be made by the parents, without pressure from the government. Such decisions are premised on a correctly formed conscience that respects the Church's authentic interpretation of the divine law in regard to family-planning methods. Couples

should take into account their responsibilities to God, themselves, the children they already have, and the community or society to which they belong.

4. The family is the basic social unit. It should be protected from pressures that prevent it from pursuing its legitimate goals, especially in terms of family size and the frequency of births, and should be given assistance by society in regard to education, stable social conditions, and the welfare of its members.

5. In many countries, there is a need to adopt new economic systems, new methods of farming, and new forms of social and political organization. Some antiquated customs, even those related to the family (e.g., inheritance of land, dowry systems), should be changed or abandoned if they impede the development process or conflict with human dignity and human rights.

Position of John Paul II • The position of the Holy See in regard to population includes and is integrated with the Church's teaching on sexuality, the family, and on specific methods of birth control. In a series of addresses prior to and during the International Conference on Population and Development in Cairo, 1994, Pope John Paul strongly defended the family and explained the Church's moral opposition to contraception, abortion, and sterilization. As a result of the efforts of the Holy See's delegation, as well as others, the Cairo conference did express opposition to abortion as a method of family planning.

The statements of John Paul II in 1994 expanded on the basic policy statements to include the following points.

1. The dignity of the human person and his or her God-given rights.

2. The importance of the family as the fundamental unit in society and the responsibility of governments and international organizations to assist families, particularly by providing accurate demographic information and avoiding any type of coercion regarding contraception, sterilization, and abortion.

3. The value of the child as a person and the unique rights of parents to nurture and educate their children.

4. The roles and responsibilities of women and the need to safeguard mothers from being pressured to work outside the home.

5. The need to provide support and assistance for the aging.

6. The need to find new mechanisms for socioeconomic development that respect the religious, cultural, and social dimensions of the human person and not just material progress in society.

7. The value and reliability of natural family-planning methods to enable couples to make responsible decisions regarding parenthood.

8. The positive duty of governments to create proper conditions for families to live a decent life and for couples to have a relatively large family if they so choose.

9. The rights of families as well as individuals to be respected in legislation and social policies regarding migration.

10. Expansion of the efforts of governments and international organizations to reduce morbidity and mortality, and to ensure greater access to health maintenance and primary health care.

Population issues will continue to receive attention in international agencies and at the national level. There are fundamental differences of approach and different interpretations of the implications of the accepted demographic data. The Church will continue her participation in the debates, emphasizing moral-ethical concerns.

See: Abortion; Common Good; Contraception; Family; Health Care; Natural Family Planning; Sexuality, Human; Social Doctrine; Social Justice; Sterilization.

Suggested Readings: CCC 2270-2275, 2366-2372. Vatican Council II, *Pastoral Constitution on the Church in the Modern World, Gaudium et Spes*, 87. Paul VI, *On Human Life, Humanae Vitae*, 23. John Paul II, *The Christian Family in the Modern World, Familiaris Consortio*; Address to Dr. Nafis Sadik, Secretary General of the 1994 International Conference on Population and Development. J. Kasun, *The War Against Population*. E. Beisner, *Prospects for Growth: A Biblical*

View of Population, Resources and the Future.
United Nations, *World Population Prospects: The
1992 Revision.*

☩ **James T. McHugh**

POSITIVISM

Legal positivism holds that human laws have no
higher standard than themselves by which they
can be criticized. Thus it denies the existence of
natural law.

Positivism was popular at the beginning of this
century but was thoroughly discredited by the reality of Nazism. Some very pernicious laws were
passed by the Nazis that fulfill all of the formal
requirements of human law. In fact, these laws
were established by a government that was elected
by the majority of the people. However, since these
directives were aimed at the extermination of a
portion of the citizenry, they were not true law.
That is so because they were not in any way
grounded in natural law.

To make a claim on our conscience, a law must
do more than fulfill formal requirements. It must
be consistent with natural law, that is, those directives not of human origin that transcend all
cultures. Legal positivism is mistaken.

See: Absolute Moral Norms; Civil Law; Human Goods; Natural Law; Relativism.

PRACTICAL REASON

Practical reason refers, not to a distinct cognitive
power, but to a specifically distinct type of thinking or reasoning. Practical reasoning is distinct
from speculative or theoretical reasoning. The distinction is important for understanding the basic
principles of right and wrong, which together constitute natural law.

Speculative or theoretical reasoning is thinking
or reasoning about what is the case. In this type of
thinking, one attempts to conform one's thought to
what is. Practical reasoning is thinking or reasoning about what is to be done. Both of these in turn
are distinct from *technical* or *artistic* reasoning,
which is reasoning about what is to be made.

Truth in speculative thinking consists in the
conformity of what one thinks to what is. For example, if one thinks the earth is spheroid, this
thought is true, since it conforms to the reality,
the actual earth. One could speak of truth in technical thinking as the conformity of one's directives or instructions (directives or instructions for
one's hands or one's feet, etc., depending on what
one is making) to the thing one wants to make.
"Truth" in this realm is effectiveness.

Since practical or moral thinking is distinct
from the other types, practical truth also is distinct. Practical thinking — thinking about what
to do — is an act of putting order into our acts of
will. One orders one's acts of will in relation to
what is really good or fulfilling for human persons (since human action actualizes human potentialities). Thus, practical judgments that order
acts of will in conformity to every aspect of possible human good are true moral judgments, while
those that do not (even though they may order it
to *some* human good) are false moral judgments.

See: Conscience; Freedom, Human; Human
Goods; Modes of Responsibility; Natural Law;
Passions; Synderesis.

PRAYER

The practice of prayer is a component part of every religion, however primitive, because by definition religion is based on the belief in a transcendent being on whom man is somehow dependent and who can supply man's needs. The awareness of this relationship prompts man to turn his
mind and heart to God in order to worship the
Deity and to give expression to his religious sentiments. The first and most universal form of
prayer has always been the prayer of petition.

In the Old Testament, the practice of prayer
was paramount in the lives of Abraham, Moses,
David, and the prophets. The Israelites were keenly
aware of their calling as God's chosen people, and
their own history taught them that Yahweh was in
their midst. Their prayer was always deeply rooted
in confidence that God would respond to their sacrifices and their petitions. The entire Old Testa-

ment can be seen as a history of the development of prayer among the Israelites. The final summation of their personal and community prayer can be found in the collection of the psalms known as the Psalter (CCC 2568-2589).

In the New Testament, the teaching on prayer is based on the example of Christ, who prayed publicly and privately (CCC 2598-2639). He also taught his followers how to pray when he recited for them the Our Father (Mt 6:9-13; Lk 11:2-4), which has been called "the most perfect of prayers [St. Thomas Aquinas, *STh* II-II, 83, 9]" (CCC 2763) and "the summary of the whole gospel [Tertullian, *De orat.* 1: PL 1, 1155]" (CCC 2761). Jesus also listed the requisites for prayer: faith (Lk 17:5); sincerity and humility (Mt 6:5-8); and perseverance (Lk 11:5-11).

Christian Prayer • In the early Church, prayer was usually described in terms of petition: "an appeal made to God by devout people for good things" (St. Basil); "raising the mind and heart to God to ask for suitable things" (St. John Damascene); it also is described as "speaking with God" (St. Gregory of Nyssa) and "conversation and union between God and man" (St. John Climacus). The same definition of prayer was given by St. Jerome, St. Gregory the Great, St. Augustine, St. Bruno, and, much later, St. Teresa of Ávila. What runs through all these definitions as a constant is the emphasis on the personal relationship of the individual with God. Prayer becomes less an elevation of mind and heart to a transcendent God and more an intimate relationship with a loving, condescending God. "I have called you friends, for all that I have heard from my Father I have made known to you" (Jn 15:15).

St. Bonaventure and St. Thomas Aquinas treated the prayer of petition at great length, although they also recognized all four types of prayer mentioned by St. Paul: "supplications, prayers, intercessions, and thanksgivings" (1 Tm 2:1). But long before the Scholastic theologians, there was, especially in the East, a monastic tradition of striving to fulfill the scriptural injunction to "pray constantly" (1 Thes 5:17), in which use was made of the constant repetition of ejaculatory prayers or

the name of Jesus. In the West, the Benedictine monks practiced *lectio divina*, the meditative reading of Sacred Scripture and the Fathers of the Church. The next development was the division into stages of prayer, promoted by Guigo I, a Carthusian legislator and spiritual writer: reading, meditation, prayer, and contemplation. By the sixteenth century, mental prayer (and especially meditation) had become a standard practice for devout Christians of every walk of life.

Types of Prayer • Prayer is usually divided into two types: vocal prayer and mental prayer. Thanks to the teaching of saints such as St. Teresa of Ávila, we have at our disposal a clear and reliable description of the various stages of prayer. Her two major works, *The Way of Perfection* and *The Interior Castle,* were written precisely to teach Christians how to make progress on the pathway of prayer and even reach the heights of contemplative prayer. Other saints, such as St. Francis de Sales and St. Alphonsus Liguori, have publicly acknowledged how greatly indebted they were to the teaching of St. Teresa.

Vocal prayer is prayer that can be spoken or read, and usually it is expressed by means of a formula or structure that can be memorized: for example, the Our Father, the Hail Mary, the Angelus, the Act of Contrition. The prayer of the liturgy is likewise vocal prayer, as is all public prayer, and a fuller participation in the liturgy requires that the faithful know the parts that pertain to them.

Traditionally, the four types of vocal prayer have been listed as adoration, petition, thanksgiving, and contrition. The classification applies primarily to vocal prayer, although one or another of those elements can be found in every type of prayer. The highest and most excellent type of prayer is praise and adoration, but for all types of vocal prayer it is essential to follow the admonition of St. Teresa of Ávila: "For that prayer which does not attend to the one it is addressing and what it asks and who it is that asks and of whom it asks, such I do not call prayer at all, however much one may move the lips" (*The Interior Castle*, First Mansion, I, 7).

The prayer of adoration is an act of submission to God, acknowledging that we are his creatures and it is our duty to praise and worship him. It is an act of the virtue of religion and is especially prominent in the liturgy and in the official prayers of the Church. In adoring God, we likewise praise him and rejoice in his great majesty: "O magnify the Lord with me, and let us exalt his name together!" (Ps 34:3). Moreover, in offering praise and adoration to God, we are at the same time strengthening our relationship with him. As St. Augustine is reputed to have said: "O Lord, you give me the grace to love you, and when I do, you give me the grace to love you more."

The prayer of petition may be either a private personal prayer or a public liturgical prayer, in which the petitioner asks almighty God to provide temporal or spiritual assistance. From time to time individuals have objected to the use of the prayer of petition (e.g., the Quietists, Immanuel Kant), but the Church has always approved and fostered its use. In fact, a good part of all public liturgical prayer is made up of petitions in the name of Jesus. The prayer of thanksgiving, as its name indicates, is the expression of gratitude by which the faithful give thanks to God for favors received. Finally, the prayer of contrition asks God's forgiveness for our sins and imperfections.

Liturgical Prayer • The prayers of the liturgy are the prayers of the Church, the People of God, and under this heading we find the prayers recited at Mass, in the administration of the sacraments, and in the Liturgy of the Hours. In personal private prayer the individual prays in his own name, but in liturgical prayer he prays in the name of the Church. Consequently, the power and efficacy of liturgical prayer are very great (cf. Pope Pius XII, *Mediator Dei*, I, 1). With good reason did the Fathers of the Second Vatican Council say in the *Constitution on the Sacred Liturgy* that "the liturgy is the summit toward which the activity of the Church is directed; it is also the fount from which all her power flows" (*Sacrosanctum Concilium,* 10).

No one can deny that liturgical public prayer is an excellent expression of the virtue of religion, but that does not in any way detract from the value of fervent personal prayer. Although they are distinct forms of prayer, there is no opposition between community liturgical prayer and private personal prayer; in fact, even public community prayer should come from the heart or it is not prayer at all. As St. Teresa said: "I do not say mental prayer rather than vocal prayer, for to be prayer at all it must be made with consideration" (*The Interior Castle*, First Mansion, I, 7).

Mental Prayer • The first stage of mental prayer is called discursive meditation. This type of prayer was widely propagated in the sixteenth and seventeenth centuries in Spain and in France. Outstanding among the promoters of discursive meditation were St. Teresa of Ávila, St. Ignatius Loyola, St. Francis de Sales, Louis of Granada, and García de Cisneros. The technique used in meditation is to think about some religious truth or virtue, to examine one's life in that regard, and to resolve to put it into practice. This form of mental prayer became a very successful instrument for conversion and commitment to Christ, as was shown by the popularity of the *Spiritual Exercises* of St. Ignatius.

Three basic steps are required for making a good meditation: consideration of some religious truth, its application to one's own life here and now, and a resolution to incorporate it in one's life. However, there is such a wide variety of methods for discursive meditation that any person should be able to select the one that is most beneficial. Having done that, the next question has to do with subject matter. The guiding rule here is to select what is needed at this time for one's spiritual development. If one is faithful to the method of discursive meditation and has selected the proper subject matter, there is every reason to expect great progress in virtue.

The second type of mental prayer, popularized by St. Francis de Sales, is called *affective prayer*. This is a bridge, as it were, between discursive meditation and the prayer of simplicity, and, as its name indicates, the affections predominate. Hence, it is at this stage that mental prayer becomes the language of love, whereas discursive meditation called for the exercise of the virtue of prudence. The description of mental prayer given by St. Teresa of Ávila seems to fit affective prayer: "Mental prayer, in my view, is nothing but friendly intercourse, and frequent solitary converse, with him who we know loves us" (*The Life*, 8, 5).

Affective prayer usually produces joy and spiritual consolation. This is not, however, the goal or terminus of the practice of prayer. The consolations are not meant to make the individual excessively introspective, but to act as a stimulus for greater love and generosity toward God.

The final stage or grade of prayer on the ascetical level is called by various names: prayer of simple regard, prayer of simplicity, acquired contemplation, and acquired recollection. One reason for the variety of names is that there were disagreements and arguments in the past concerning the use of the term "contemplation" for an ascetical grade of prayer. Today the argument has subsided and theologians generally admit an "acquired" contemplation. It suffices to describe contemplation as a "loving awareness of God" (St. John of the Cross), "an experiential knowledge of God which is the effect of unifying love" (Gerson), or simply "a gaze of love" (St. Thomas Aquinas).

The prayer of simplicity is the transition point from ascetical prayer to mystical prayer. It seems that the seventeenth-century bishop and spiritual writer Jacques Bossuet gave this type of prayer its name — prayer of simplicity — but St. Teresa of Ávila had previously described the same type of prayer as an acquired recollection. The discursive mental acts formerly used in meditation have been replaced by a simple intuitive gaze; the affections formerly experienced in affective prayer are now unified in a single act of love. There is no set method to be followed in the prayer of simplicity; since it is definitely a contemplative type of prayer, it tends to be more and more integrated and simplified. This in turn enables the individual to be habitually recollected, living and acting in the presence of God, thus disposing himself for infused contemplation.

Mystical Grades of Prayer • When prayer reaches the mystical level, which means it involves the operation of the gifts of the Holy Spirit, it is no longer an acquired contemplative prayer produced by the operation of the intellect and will. It is classified as a type of infused contemplation, and it admits of varying degrees of intensity, ranging from simple infused contemplation to the prayer of transforming union. In *The Interior Castle*, which is made up of seven "mansions," St. Teresa discusses the grades of mystical prayer in the last four mansions. She maintains that a large number of devout souls do reach the fourth mansion, which marks the beginning of infused mystical prayer.

It should be noted at the outset that infused contemplative prayer is within the normal development of sanctifying grace and the activity of the supernatural virtues and the gifts of the Holy Spirit. If, as the Second Vatican Council has declared in the *Constitution on the Church*, all Christians of every state of life are called to the perfection of charity, then it follows that all are called to the mystical state. The fact that, apparently, only a minority actually attains to this level of spirituality does not militate against the calling. As was taught by St. Gregory the Great, when an individual attains to the perfection of the virtues, the gifts of the Holy Spirit can become actuated in what we call the mystical state.

St. Teresa's classification and description of the grades of mystical prayer are especially trustworthy because she is writing from experience. She begins with a description of "infused recollection": "The first prayer which I experienced as supernatural . . . is an interior recollection which is experienced in the soul. . . . It wants to close the eyes and not let the soul hear or see or understand anything but that with which the soul is then occupied, namely, to be able to converse with God alone. . . . It is called recollection because in it the soul gathers together all its faculties and enters within itself with its God" (*The Interior Castle*, Fourth Mansion, 3).

The second grade of mystical prayer is the prayer of quiet, in which will is captivated by God and the individual experiences ineffable sweetness and delight. "From this recollection," says St. Teresa, "there sometimes proceeds an interior quiet and peace which are full of happiness, because the soul is in such a state it does not seem to lack anything" (*Way of Perfection*, 31).

From the prayer of quiet the soul passes on to the prayer of union, in which all the faculties of the soul are captivated, so to speak. "The faculties possess the power to occupy themselves completely with God. . . . It seems to me that this kind of prayer is very definitely a union of the entire soul with God" (*The Life*, 16-17, *passim*). At this point, the soul may begin to experience some of the concomitant mystical phenomena such as ecstasy, flights of the spirit, wounds of love, or mystical touches. The prayer of union culminates in the last two degrees of prayer, the conforming union and the transforming union, known in mystical literature as the mystical espousal and the mystical marriage.

The Necessity of Prayer • We read in the Council of Trent's *Roman Catechism*: "The necessity of prayer should be insisted upon. Prayer is a duty not only recommended by way of counsel, but also commanded by obligatory precept. . . . The Church points out the necessity of prayer in the introduction that she recites at the beginning of the Lord's prayer: 'Admonished by salutary precepts, and taught by divine instruction, we presume to say,' etc." (IV, 1, 2).

Similarly, the *Catechism of the Catholic Church* emphasizes the importance of the practice of prayer in the Christian life: "*Prayer is a vital necessity.* Proof from the contrary is no less convincing: if we do not allow the Spirit to lead us, we fall back into the slavery of sin. How can the Holy Spirit be our life if our heart is far from him?" (2744). It continues: "Prayer and the *Christian life* are *inseparable*, for they concern the same love and the same renunciation, proceeding from love; the same filial and loving conformity with the Father's plan of love; the same transforming union in the Holy Spirit who conforms us more and more to Christ Jesus; the same love for all men, the love with which Jesus has loved us" (2745).

See: Contemplation; Extraordinary Gifts; Gifts and Fruits of the Holy Spirit; Liturgy; Liturgy of the Hours; Mass; Meditation; Mysticism; Prayer of Petition; Quietism; Religion, Virtue of; Vocal Prayer; Worship.

Suggested Readings: CCC 2558-2751. Vatican Council II, *Constitution on the Sacred Liturgy, Sacrosanctum Concilium*, 5-111; *Dogmatic Constitution on the Church, Lumen Gentium*, 1-42. G. Lercaro, *Methods of Mental Prayer*. J. Aumann, *Spiritual Theology*. St. Teresa of Ávila, *The Complete Works*.

Jordan Aumann, O.P.

PRAYER OF PETITION

The prayer of petition arises from a felt need and the belief that God responds. There is no need to justify the use of prayer of petition, since it springs naturally from the recognition of God's omnipotence and the awareness of one's own insufficiency. Not only is it lawful to use the prayer of petition, but it is commanded, as we read in the New Testament: "Ask, and it will be given you; seek, and you will find; knock, and it will be opened. For every one who asks receives, and he who seeks finds, and to him who knocks it will be opened. . . . If you, then, who are evil, know how to give good gifts to your children, how much more will your Father who is in heaven give good things to those who ask him!" (Mt 7:7-11).

Need for Prayer of Petition • Nevertheless, since God knows our needs better than we do, and knows from all eternity what he will grant us, why pray? It seems unnecessary.

First of all, we do not pray to God in order to inform him of our needs, and certainly not to change his mind. The devout Christian petitions God conditionally: "If it be thy will, O Lord."

On the other hand, it is an error to think that if we simply persevere in prayer, what we ask will be granted. It is surely safe to say that some things will be given to us only if we ask; but countless other things are granted even without our asking. Finally, some things will not be granted, no matter how long and how persistently we ask for them.

Every prayer of petition is answered, but sometimes the answer is "No."

The next question concerns the things we should ask for in prayer. God plainly will not grant us anything that would be detrimental to our spiritual life or would endanger our eternal salvation. Jesus asks: "What man of you, if his son asks him for bread, will give him a stone? Or if he asks for a fish, will give him a serpent?" (Mt 7:9-10).

Is it lawful to ask God for temporal things, such as good health, success, a long life, the necessities of life? The answer given by St. Augustine and quoted by St. Thomas Aquinas in the *Summa Theologiae* is that it is lawful to pray for anything that it is lawful to desire. Consequently, as long as a person uses temporal goods virtuously, one may desire them and therefore may ask God to grant them. But we do not always know what is for our own good; therefore, we should always ask for these things if it is in accordance with God's will and for our own spiritual good.

The practice of the prayer of petition is praiseworthy because, if rightly used, it gives one an opportunity to humbly submit to God's will. It is not only praiseworthy, however; it is also a necessity in the Christian life. There are numerous testimonies to this, but it suffices to quote the opinion of St. Augustine: "God does not command impossibilities, but by commanding, he admonishes you to do what you can do and pray for what you cannot do, and assists you that you may be able" (*De Natura et Gratia*, 43, 50).

The efficacy of the prayer of petition has been promised by Christ: "Whatever you ask in prayer, you will receive, if you have faith" (Mt 21:22). It could not be otherwise, given the infinite goodness of God and the love he has for those who approach him with humility and confidence. One should pray with devotion and perseverance for the things that are necessary for salvation or that will contribute to one's spiritual perfection. There is, therefore, a hierarchy of values in the objects of prayer. First come the spiritual things necessary for Christian living and eternal salvation; then come temporal goods. This is exemplified in the petitions of the Our Father. Jesus taught us to pray

first: "Thy kingdom come; thy will be done." Then comes the petition "Give us this day our daily bread."

Intercessory Prayer • Another question is whether or not it is lawful to pray for someone other than oneself. The example of Jesus suffices for an answer. At the Last Supper he prayed for the Apostles: "I am praying for them; I am not praying for the world but for those whom thou hast given me. . . . I do not pray for these only, but also for those who believe in me through their word, that they may all be one" (Jn 17:9, 20). During the persecution in the early days of the Church, it was customary for Christians to request the prayers of others, and especially the martyrs.

In the catalog of saints, there is one who stands out above all the others as a model for intercessory prayer: St. Monica, the mother of St. Augustine. Having prayed for years for his conversion, as her life was drawing to a close, she asked her son to remember her at the altar of God. "Since Abraham, intercession — asking on behalf of another — has been characteristic of a heart attuned to God's mercy. In the age of the Church, Christian intercession participates in Christ's, as an expression of the communion of saints" (CCC 2635).

But is it lawful to address prayers to anyone other than God? What is to be said, for example, about praying to the Blessed Virgin Mary, the angels, and the saints? Or even the souls in purgatory? The answer is obviously that such prayer is permitted — indeed, strongly encouraged — since such is the practice of the Church, although there have been certain refinements in recent times. As to the basic justification for this practice, it is given succinctly by St. Thomas Aquinas: "Prayer is offered to a person in two ways: first, to be fulfilled by him, and secondly, to be obtained through him. In the first way, we offer prayer to God alone, since all our prayers ought to be directed to the acquisition of grace and glory, which God alone gives, according to Ps. 83:12: 'Grace and glory he bestows.' But in the second way we pray to the saints, whether angels or human, not that God may know our petitions through them, but that our prayers may be effective through their prayers and merits" (*Summa Theologiae*, II-II, 83, 4).

The Council of Trent not only defended the practice of praying to the saints but also of venerating their images and relics. As regards prayers to the souls in purgatory, that is a disputed question among theologians. Those who reply in the negative say that, rather than praying *to* the souls in purgatory, we should pray *for* them. Those who reply in the affirmative base their opinion on the communion of saints, for it is not likely that the souls in purgatory would be entirely ignorant of the needs of souls on earth.

See: Communion of Saints; Prayer; Purgatory; Religion, Virtue of; Vocal Prayer.

Suggested Readings: CCC 2559-2751. K. Irwin, *Liturgy, Prayer and Spirituality.* J. Aumann, *Spiritual Theology.*

Jordan Aumann, O.P.

PREFERENTIAL OPTION FOR THE POOR

Since her earliest days, the Church has exercised a ministry to the poor and oppressed. These activities derive directly from the many biblical indications of our responsibilities toward those suffering from any cause, but especially those who, because of their own misfortune or their social context, cannot care for themselves. Catholic missionary work has accordingly been accompanied by the building and operation of hospitals, schools, and economic enterprises meant to enable people to live better and to participate more fully in social and economic life.

As it grew from being an oppressed minority itself to a full-scale church, Catholicism encouraged governments and other public agents to include the most vulnerable in making public decisions. In Catholic thought, charity — in the sense of love for God and others — should give birth to justice, and the works of mercy specify the contents of that justice.

Pope Leo XIII, who inaugurated modern Catholic social doctrine with his 1891 encyclical *On the Social Question, Rerum Novarum*, warned against the growing movement toward socialism and asserted the importance of private property to individual liberty and family welfare. In the process, however, he also repeated and summed up the earlier teaching: "In protecting the rights of private individuals, special consideration must be given to the weak and the poor."

Origin of the Term • In 1968, meeting at Medellín, Colombia, the Latin American Bishops' Conference (CELAM) introduced a new formulation of the Church's commitment to the poor into modern Catholic social teaching: the preferential option for the poor. Vatican Council II had encouraged the local churches to apply universal Catholic principles to their concrete circumstances. For the Latin American bishops, facing severe underdevelopment and rapidly growing populations in the 1960s, the preferential option seemed an urgent necessity. The term spread quickly to other parts of the world.

In 1971, Pope Paul VI spoke of a "preferential respect for the poor" in *Octogesima Adveniens,* 3, without implying any specific political direction that flowed from such respect. But in Latin America the preferential option soon became associated with movements of a Marxist social bent such as liberation theology, Christian "base communities," and the *iglesia popular* (popular church). Though each of these movements was composed of various complex currents, for the most part they tended to adopt Marxist analysis and to blame Western capitalism for poverty in Latin America and elsewhere among underdeveloped countries, and the traditional Church for alleged complicity in what was regarded as exploitation.

Even among Latin American bishops, this was never the majority view of what the preferential option meant. At their 1979 meeting in Puebla, Mexico, they reaffirmed the preferential option. But under the leadership of John Paul II, the notions of preferential option and liberation developed in some different directions. The Vatican's Congregation for the Doctrine of the Faith issued two instructions in the mid-1980s that sorted out the true from the false in these ideas.

To avoid the political associations of the word "option," the *Instruction on Christian Freedom and Liberation, Libertatis Conscientia,* recast the principle as "a love of preference for the poor" (68). With the collapse of Marxism and changes in attitudes about what produces wealth and liberty in the late 1980s and early 1990s, the preferential option became a less narrowly ideological and more broadly religious concept. The *Catechism of the Catholic Church* quotes (2448) the second Congregation for the Doctrine of the Faith instruction about the need for *a preferential love* toward the poor, but places it in a very different understanding of Christian society and economics. Rather than tie the desire to lift up the poor through recourse to partisan positions or one form of social analysis, the instruction returns the discussion to broad Catholic principles of society.

Recent Developments • Both the original notion and the one later promoted by the Vatican seek to transform the condition of the poor rather than merely provide them with relief. Many advocates of the early preferential option saw transformation coming from Marxist social revolution. The later form saw the dignity of the poor as bound up with their own possibilities for free initiative and self-support.

In his encyclical *The Hundredth Year, Centesimus Annus,* Pope John Paul II developed this further with a call for a cultural revolution: "one which fosters trust in the human potential of the poor and consequently in their ability to improve their condition through work or to make a positive contribution to economic prosperity. But to accomplish this, the poor — be they individuals or nations — need to be provided with realistic opportunities" (52).

As this passage shows, in addition to its relevance for each country the preferential option also had an international dimension. During much of the 1970s, underdevelopment was explained by exploitation and "dependency" of Third World nations on First World businesses and banks. Pope John Paul did not deny that developed and undeveloped nations were related to one another; in fact, even after the dependency theory was dis-

credited among social scientists, the Pope continued to remind the First World of its human responsibilities to the poor. But he changed the social vision from the Marxist view of exploiters and exploited to a Christian notion of social interdependence.

The most recent Catholic social teaching recognizes that economic liberty is a good and even a right. But like all human freedoms and rights, it must be exercised within the proper moral framework, particularly, in this case, within a properly constituted political system and under the rule of law. The problem in Latin America and elsewhere in the world had not so much been capitalist exploitation as monopolistic manipulation of the political and legal system for personal advantage.

Furthermore, as we now know, societies are more complex than originally envisioned by most modern social theorists. All Marx's predictions failed to materialize. Workers in industrial societies became wealthier rather than proletarianized. Similarly, on an international scale, the rich nations are not rich *because* the poor nations are poor, but because they have developed faster. A development process must now occur within underdeveloped nations that will bring them to the educational and technical levels necessary to produce abundance.

As even the developed nations have learned, solidarity with the poor means more than merely providing them with welfare-style assistance. In fact, John Paul warns in *Centesimus Annus* that the "social assistance state" may actually sap personal initiative and create disincentives among the very people it intends to help. Part of the preferential option means helping the poor to become part of the society through education and training. It also means crafting economic policies that provide sufficient job opportunities and easy legal means to starting new businesses so that more people have access to economic action. The preferential option today means pursuing both traditional measures of relief where warranted and a dynamic and prosperous society that provides opportunities for all members, but especially for its weakest.

See: Interdependence; Liberation Theology; Missionary Activity; Population; Property; Social Doctrine; Social Justice; Works of Mercy.

Suggested Readings: CCC 2448. John Paul II, *The Hundredth Year, Centesimus Annus.*

Robert Royal

PRENATAL DIAGNOSIS

Today many illnesses and disabling conditions, whether due to genetic defect or other causes, can be diagnosed before birth. Prenatal diagnosis presents moral questions because the techniques themselves may pose a risk to the unborn child and because test results may be put to morally good or evil uses.

Such diagnosis is permissible with the informed consent of the parents "if the methods employed safeguard the life and integrity of the embryo and the mother, without subjecting them to disproportionate risks. But this diagnosis is gravely opposed to the moral law when it is done with the thought of possibly inducing an abortion, depending upon the results: a diagnosis which shows the existence of a malformation or a hereditary illness must not be the equivalent of a death-sentence" (Congregation for the Doctrine of the Faith, *Donum Vitae, Instruction on Respect for Human Life in Its Origin and on the Dignity of Procreation: Replies to Certain Questions of the Day,* I.2 [1987]).

Similarly, Pope John Paul II has accepted the use of prenatal diagnosis "to make possible early therapy or even to favor a serene and informed acceptance of the child not yet born." But he has condemned its use with a "a eugenic intention," which condones "selective abortion" to prevent the birth of children with disabilities. Such an attitude "presumes to measure the value of a human life only within the parameters of 'normality' and physical well-being, thus opening the way to legitimizing infanticide and euthanasia as well" (encyclical *The Gospel of Life, Evangelium Vitae,* 63 [1995]).

Tragically, some advances in prenatal diagnosis are used precisely to make selective abortion easier. One of these, preimplantation genetic di-

agnosis, involves testing human embryos in the laboratory and discarding those found "defective" instead of allowing them to implant in the mother's womb. Such selective discarding is as wrong as other forms of abortion.

See: Abortion; Genetic Experimentation; Human Life, Dignity and Sanctity of.

PRESUMPTION

The opposite of despair, presumption is misplaced hope and contrary to the first commandment (cf. CCC 2092). Usually, it is the practical failure to recognize that there can be no salvation (a God-man relationship of bilateral love) without human-divine cooperation. The boast that, unaided, we can save ourselves is as presumptuous and erroneous as the unfounded claim that God will save us without our repentant conversion. We cannot dispense with God's help; nor can he dispense us from doing our small part.

Thoughtlessly presuming upon God's unlimited power or mercy alone is by far the more common sin. It can take the form of banking on a death-bed conversion or viewing hell as totally incompatible with infinite love. Perhaps commoner still is the human tendency simply to put the question off. But can wayfarers ever hope too much in God? Presumption is grounded in a contradiction: that God do our choosing for us. The presumptuous person hopes for salvation without renouncing a contrary past, hopes for pardon without acknowledging the harmful error of his ways.

Theologians draw a sharp distinction between the attitude of one who goes on erring precisely because he counts upon pardon and one whose persistence in wrongdoing is accompanied, but not motivated, by the hope of forgiveness. The first is actual presumption of a wicked kind; the other is not such specifically. In practice, it happens for the most part that the expectation of ultimate reconciliation with God is not the cause of continuing in sinful indulgence but only accompanies it.

Those inclined to presumption should reflect for a moment on the twofold divine initiative. God, who made humans without their say, does not beatify them, either here nor hereafter, without their concurrence; yet, as with the Good Thief, bliss eternal is theirs if they ask for it and do what is necessary to receive it.

See: Despair; Final Perseverance; Hope; Religion, Virtue of; Tempting God.

PRIDE

What can one always detect with loathing in others but hardly ever in oneself? The answer of course is pride: a highly inflated sense of self-worth that uncannily camouflages itself. Therein lies its particular danger. A spiritual authority says: "If you think you're not proud, that's a sure sign that you are. But if you're convinced that you are proud, that's a sure sign you're starting to be less so."

Pride is not wrong because it seeks to steal glory from a jealous, all-powerful God, resentful that his attributes might be eclipsed. Rather, God's design is that human beings not assume cares beyond their capacities, and assign these instead to their fatherly Maker. But that is only a tiny first step. The fourteenth-century German Dominican mystic John Tauler boldly proclaimed in his *Institut:* "God has created us for so high a degree of honor, that no creature could ever have dared to imagine that God would have chosen it for so great a glory; and we ourselves are now unable to conceive how he could raise us higher than he has done. For, as he could not make us gods by nature, a prerogative that can belong to him alone, he has made us gods by grace, in enabling us to possess with him, in the union of an eternal love, one same beatitude, one same joy, one same kingdom."

Pride led to the downfall of the angels (cf. Rv 12 and *passim*). The consequences persist to our day and beyond. Adam and Eve forfeited friendship with God, sanctifying grace, and all kinds of preternatural gifts, including original integrity, when they naïvely gave in to the solicitation contained in the Serpent's promise that disobedience would make them "be like God" (Gn 3:5).

Much of the Old Testament Revelation is aimed at humbling God's chosen people so that they can see their Creator for who and what he is. Their repeated failures to read God aright are amply foretold. Only a small remnant (not only then but perhaps even now) will be faithful to God's loving, redemptive covenant. And who will they be? The prophet Zephaniah identifies them as the "humble and lowly," Yahweh's poor (Zep 3:12-14). No wonder, then, that the God-man repeatedly warned, "Whoever exalts himself shall be humbled" (Mt 23:12). The *Catechism of the Catholic Church* says pride "is contrary to love of God, whose goodness it denies, and whom it presumes to curse as the one who forbids sins and inflicts punishments" (2094).

The Nature of Pride • Pride is exorbitantly loving one's own excellence, however exaggerated; it is the queen mother, as it were, of all vices and sins. A classical moral treatise describes it as "that frame of mind whereby a man, through the love of his own worth, aims to withdraw himself from subjection to . . . God, and sets at naught the commands of superiors."

Usually of course pride does not sink to such satanic, nihilistic depths. More a child of weakness, ignorance, exaggerated self-love, and unthinkingness, pride instead manifests itself as an unwarranted sense of superiority that seeks to set God to one side while feeding on the real or apparent foibles of others. This happens when a proud person regards self as the source of his or her own comparative advantages; thinks that God bestowed these gifts in recognition of his or her personal merits; imagines that he or she has nonexistent gifts, talents, or qualities; craves to excel over others. Vainglory, ambition, and presumptuousness are pride's offspring, and serve its aims. (The latter failing means trying to do what exceeds one's capacity; it is not to be confused with the "presumption" that erroneously takes salvation for granted and is against the virtue of hope.)

Pride springs from a self-love that denies the ample evidence of personal misdeeds and of others' good qualities and deeds. There also is a true self-love that is legitimate, necessary, and even virtuous; this reflexive love is also called self-interest. Thus are humans instinctively attracted pleasurably to what benefits especially their corporal welfare and survival; they are, conversely, repelled, via fears and pains, by what threatens them. Enlightened self-interest seeks to address the superior human craving for happiness and to make that quest viable by cultivating at least the cardinal virtues. An even more enlightened self-love prompts the discovery that the greatest bliss is, paradoxically, dependent on freely and lovingly giving oneself to others. Even before that final step, self-interest, in its commitment to truth and reality, recognizes and rejoices in whatever excellence others may have.

Ignoring or using others, pride thrives on untruths that are allied to the tendency to debase and level all others and to exclude the relevance of God and ethical values from human affairs. Pride is that fallacy whereby someone thinks and wants to be independent of God (and others) and, consequently, self-sufficient (in being), self-reliant (in action), and self-seeking (morally). Every sin is fundamentally a form of pride and perverse self-love. Intellectual pride is especially pernicious and durable: It seeks futilely to remake all of reality in its own cramped, mean image and likeness. How the proud of mind bristle in their hubris when confronted by Jesus' invitations to humility: "[L]earn from me; for I am gentle and lowly in heart, and you will find rest for your souls" (Mt 11:29); "Blessed are the poor in spirit, for theirs is the kingdom of heaven" (Mt 5:3).

Pride also lies behind false philosophies and ideologies that preach the perfectibility of man with its gospel of progress and have fathered so many Utopian blueprints that soon turned to nightmares. Only somewhat less unreliable are those who seek to press religion into the building and reforming of civil society, as if it were a mere means.

C.S. Lewis calls pride "the essential vice, the utmost evil," the font of "discord" and "enmity," since each person's pride is ever contending and competing with that of all others.

Paradoxically, people who see themselves as very religious can quite easily be eaten up by pride. Here, too, is confirmed the dictum *corruptio optimi*

pessima ("the corruption of the best is the worst"). The worst of all vices — something hard to grasp because it is wholly spiritual, yet no less deadly and even satanic — can smuggle itself into an ostensibly religious life. As Lewis adds: "The devil is content to see you becoming chaste and brave and self-controlled, provided all the while a dictatorship of pride is thus being built up." In the end, pride spells the blindness of mind, the impotence of love, and the eternity of a self-made hell that not even God can undo.

See: Avarice; Capital Sins; Cardinal Virtues; Covetousness; Envy; Humility; Vices.

Suggested Readings: CCC 1866, 2094, 2540. J. Leclercq, *Christ and the Modern Conscience.* C. Lewis, *Mere Christianity.* J. Pieper, *The Cardinal Virtues.* D. Sayers, *The Whimsical Christian.* D. von Hildebrand, *Christian Ethics.*

Dennis Helming

PRIEST

In 1834, John Henry Newman, while still an Anglican clergyman at Oxford, preached a sermon on "The Christian Ministry" in which he asked "whether there is reason for thinking that Christ has, in matter of fact, left representatives behind him." Newman answered the question by his subsequent conversion to Catholicism and by seeking ordination as a priest. Despite a history of opposition that begins with the authorities of pagan Rome and continues today in a variety of anticlerical initiatives, still including some by civil governments, the Catholic priesthood remains one of the most important institutions in the world. Another nineteenth-century witness to the central place it plays in the life of the Church comes from a Frenchman, St. John Marie Vianney. The holy Curé of Ars underscored the transcendent nature of the priesthood when he reminded his faithful: "Only in heaven will we know what a priest is. If we were to know this on earth, we would die, not of grief, but of love."

Origin and Nature of the Priesthood • The priesthood derives its theological meaning from the mission of the incarnate Son. Christ is the one "whom the Father consecrated and sent into the world" (Jn 10:36) for its salvation, and consecration and mission describe the reality of the priest. Within the apostolic succession, the priest appears as a coworker of the episcopal order, one in whom the function of the bishops' ministry is exercised in a subordinate degree. However, because the priest shares in the authority by which Christ himself builds up and sanctifies and rules his Body, a special sacrament confers the priesthood. Through Holy Orders priests "by the anointing of the Holy Spirit are signed with a special character and so are configured to Christ the priest in such a way that they are able to act in the person of Christ the head": this is how the Second Vatican Council's *Decree on the Ministry and Life of Priests, Presbyterorum Ordinis,* 2, describes the Christian priesthood.

Scholars offer different explanations of how the apostleship of the original Twelve became adjusted to the local community in the early days of the Church. Study of the early Christian centuries reveals that priests were ordained to celebrate the sacraments, to teach as prophets as well as to proclaim the word and instruct others in sound doctrine, and to govern as shepherds. But from the beginning of the Church, the priest carried out these three distinct offices in dependence on the episcopate, which alone embodies the ongoing apostolic ministry in the Church. From the very beginning, priests were functioning in the churches the Apostles left behind. So we are not surprised to learn that the third-century *Traditio Apostolica* of Hippolytus already includes the ordination rite for a priest: "And when a presbyter is ordained the bishop shall lay his hand upon his head, the presbyters also touching him. And he shall pray over him according to the forementioned form" (8).

There is significance in the fact that the bishop is joined by the other presbyters in the ordination. The *presbyterium* is one throughout the world, even though a priest is ordained for the service of a particular church within it. Some authors note that the term "presbyter" literally means "elder," and that the New Testament does not specifically use the term "priest" for a Christian minister but only for Christians as a whole, as in Revelation 5:10: "And [thou] hast made them a kingdom and priests to our God." But this is a semantic difficulty, not a real one. For "in virtue of the sacrament of Holy Orders, after the image of Christ, the supreme and eternal priest, [priests] are consecrated in order to preach the Gospel and shepherd the faithful as well as to celebrate divine worship as true priests of the New Testament." This text from Vatican II's *Dogmatic Constitution on the Church, Lumen Gentium,* 28, determines the place of the priest in the Church. The power to forgive sins also forms part of the priest's role of sanctifying the Christian people.

Catholic priests are either members of the diocesan clergy or belong to a religious institute. The distinction does not affect their priesthood, for both kinds of priests belong to the one *presbyterium* of the Church. Rather, the difference relates to the way a priest lives out his priestly vocation.

Diocesan priests willingly accept the obligation of remaining celibate in order to participate in the mystery of Christ and his mission; moreover, they promise obedience to the local bishop, and, although they do not radically renounce the capacity to possess material goods, they are still expected to imitate the evangelical poverty of the Apostles. Religious priests, on the other hand, by their profession of vows, commit themselves to live in community, which is meant to bear corporate witness to the distinctive charism of the religious institute. The evangelical counsels of poverty, chastity, and obedience are embraced under a vow or solemn promise as a means to imitating the life of Jesus himself. The older monastic orders require that their members remain in a single place so that the monastery or convent itself becomes a witness to the life of the Church, whereas the mendicant friars and most later foundations, including the Jesuits, require that their members be ready to move wherever the needs of the Church require priests. There are also priests who follow an eremetical way of life, in which they devote themselves entirely to works of intercession and penance for the good of the Church; though separated from the company of men, the hermit-priest remains fully present to the Church, especially when he celebrates the Holy Sacrifice of the Mass.

In the latter years of the twentieth century, the question of whether only males can be candidates for the sacrament of Holy Orders began to attract wide attention. Two important statements of the Magisterium, *Inter Insigniores* (a declaration of the Congregation for the Doctrine of the Faith published in 1976) and Pope John Paul II's 1994 apostolic letter *Ordinatio Sacerdotalis*, have repeated the Church's reasons for not ordaining women. The texts also remind us that the Church is here bound by a decision made by Christ himself and in matters of faith and the sacraments cannot simply do what she wants.

See: Bishop; Celibacy, Priestly; Consecrated Life; Holy Orders; In Persona Christi Capitis; Ministry; Priesthood of Christ; Priesthood in the Old Testament; Women, Ordination of.

Suggested Readings: CCC 1088, 1120, 1539-1541, 1546-1553, 1567, 1591. Vatican Council II, *Decree on the Ministry and Life of Priests, Presbyterorum Ordinis; Decree on the Training of Priests, Optatam Totius.* John Paul II, *Priestly Ordination, Ordinatio Sacerdotalis* (1994). Congregation for the Doctrine of the Faith, *Inter Insigniores* (1976). John Henry Newman, "The Christian Ministry," *Parochial and Plain Sermons.* E. Walsh, *The Priesthood in the Writings of the French School: Berulle, De Condren, Olier.*

Romanus Cessario, O.P.

PRIESTHOOD IN THE OLD TESTAMENT

In the last two centuries, priesthood in the Old Testament was frequently reconstructed along strictly historical-critical lines, reflecting divergent interpretive theories about the hypothetical prehistory of the Pentateuch (the first five books of the Bible) and its underlying documents and/or traditions. In view of the utter lack of any consensus — and increasing ambivalence — among the critical theorists, an alternate approach is proposed

here, namely, a canonical interpretation of the priesthood based on the final narrative form of the Old Testament.

Accordingly, we divide the history of the priesthood into two periods: the patriarchal and the Levitical. The patriarchal period corresponds to the canonical form of the Genesis narratives, while the Levitical period begins in Exodus and lasts until the coming of Christ.

The Patriarchal Period • As narrated in Genesis, the patriarchal period (e.g., Noah, Shem, Abraham, Isaac, and Jacob) represents a distinctive form of covenantal religion that stands in marked contrast to the religion of ancient Israel subsequently established at Sinai with the Mosaic covenant. The basis for the patriarchal religion was the natural family order, most especially the patriarchal authority handed down from father to son — ideally the firstborn — often in the form of the "blessing."

This explains the absence of any separate priestly institution among the patriarchs before the Levites. Instead of a priestly caste to offer mandatory sacrifices only at designated sites, the patriarchs rear altars and present offerings at places and times of their own discretion. Practicing a form of natural religion, the patriarchs freely utilize pillars built of stones (Gn 28:11-22) and trees for worship (Gn 21:33), although these are later prohibited in the Mosaic law (Dt 16:21). At this point in salvation history, family and church are coextensive — houses are domestic sanctuaries, meals are sacrifices, hearths are altars — all because fathers and their (firstborn) sons are empowered as priests by nature.

If fatherhood is the natural and original basis of priesthood, then the essential meaning of the priestly office is traceable back to the representative role, spiritual authority, and religious service of the father in the family. Likewise, the office of kingship may be viewed as embodying the father's secular responsibilities and duties, along with his powers of leadership and governance. These are then handed on to his sons, particularly the firstborn.

During the patriarchal period, it seems to follow that "in the firstborn the dual capacity of king and priest is implicitly present" (G. van Groningen, *Messianic Revelation in the Old Testament*, p. 221). In the natural order of the patriarchal family, which God instituted at creation, therefore, we see the original covenant of royal-priestly primogeniture. The priesthood should be understood primarily as a covenant institution. As such, it embodies the father-son relation and the mediatorial role of the firstborn son — between parents and siblings — within the family.

The patriarchal archetype of royal-priesthood is Melchizedek, who is also the first person to be called a priest in Scripture (Gn 14:17-20). As priest-king of Salem (i.e., Jerusalem, 2 Chr 3:1), he offers bread and wine, and then blesses Abram (Abraham) and his men.

The biblical narratives show how sin effects a tragic rupture in man's nature — and especially the human family — from Adam's fall at the beginning of Genesis to Israel's enslavement in Egypt at the start of Exodus. First, this is graphically depicted by Genesis in a series of narrative episodes that share at least one prominent feature, namely, the hubris of disinherited firstborn sons (e.g., Cain, Ishmael, Esau, Reuben, Er, Perez, Manasseh). Second, this pattern carries over into Exodus, starting with God's declaration to Moses at the bush, "Israel is my firstborn son" (Ex 4:22). It then runs like a thread through the ten plagues, climaxing at the Passover, where Israel's firstborn sons are redeemed by the blood of the paschal lamb; hence they are consecrated to serve as priests within each of the tribes and families of Israel (Ex 19:22-24).

Likewise, God announces to Israel their unique vocation and mission to be a "holy nation and a royal priesthood" — as "elder brother" in the family of nations — which is their conditional status, that is, "if you obey my voice and keep my covenant" (Ex 19:5-6). However, when Israel worships the golden calf, this blessing is forfeited to the avenging Levites (Ex 32:25-29), ushering in a second (i.e., the Levitical) period of the priesthood. Israel's priesthood thus became a hereditary office strictly for Levites — with a limited term of twenty years (Nm 4:3) — which was assumed by the laying on of hands and anointing.

Henceforth, priestly and royal power were divided in Israel, with the former going to Levi and the latter to Judah in David's time (Ps 89:4-30). According to the New Testament, however, this is dramatically reversed with Christ's coming — as God's firstborn Son (Heb 1:6), our Paschal Victim and royal High Priest (Heb 2:2-17, 5:1-10) — and the establishment of his Church as "the assembly of the firstborn" (Heb 12:23), "a royal priesthood" (1 Pt 2:9), and the true "Israel of God" (Gal 6:16).

The Levitical Period • A careful reading of the Exodus narrative reveals that, in the aftermath of Israel's apostasy with the golden calf at Sinai, God renewed the covenant with Moses alone at first (Ex 33–34). It is then extended to Israel, but only after a tent-sanctuary was built and Aaron consecrated as high priest (Ex 35–40). Only then does God command Moses to speak — on his behalf — to "the sons of Israel" about the three main types of sacrifice (whole burnt, sin, peace), which the Levites are instructed to offer on the people's behalf according to the priestly code (Lv 1–16). Finally, the Holiness Code was given for the Levites to teach the twelve (newly laicized) tribes of Israel (Lv 17–26).

The Levitical priesthood was first instituted, then, as part of the covenant renewal program necessitated by Israel's apostasy with the golden calf, which brought about a more elaborate system of priestly mediation based upon the hierarchical order of Moses, Aaron (and his sons), the Levites, and the twelve tribes of Israel. Indeed, this same priestly hierarchy (high priest, Aaronic priests, and Levites) remains in effect, though not without some significant variations, throughout all four stages of the Old Testament canonical record: the wilderness period, the conquest and settlement, the monarchy, and the postexilic period.

In the wilderness period, the recently acquired positions of Moses and Aaron are opposed by the egalitarian dissent of Korah, a fellow Levite: "All the congregation are holy, every one of them, and the LORD is among them; why then do you exalt yourselves above the assembly of the Lord?" (Nm 16:3). Moses responds to Korah: "Hear now, you sons of Levi: is it too small a thing that the God of Israel has separated you from the congregation of Israel, to bring you near to himself, to do service in the tabernacle of the Lord, and to stand before the congregation to minister to them. . . . And would you seek the priesthood also? Thus, it is against the Lord that you and all your company have gathered together" (Nm 16:8-12). Subsequent events reveal God's judgment against Korah — he descended into Sheol (Nm 16:31-33) — while confirming Aaron's high priestly prerogatives with the budding of his rod (Nm 17:8).

Moses' response is noteworthy, since it points to four distinct aspects of the Levitical priesthood. First, their "separateness" refers to their unique holiness in Israel, and a corresponding duty to distinguish between the holy, common, and unclean (Ez 44:23). Second, their proximity to God's presence points to their position of mediation, for which they assist the Aaronic priests in offering sacrifice at the altar in the sanctuary (Ez 44:11). Third, their service in the tabernacle entailed a special responsibility to care for sacred objects (Nm 4:1-33), such as the Ark of the Covenant (Dt 31:25). Fourth, their ministry to the congregation involved teaching and ruling, along with medical care in certain cases of disease and impurity (Mal 2:7; Dt 17:7; Lv 14:2). In addition, the Levites were to receive tithes (Nm 18:21), along with forty-eight designated regions in the territories of the twelve tribes that were meant to serve as "cities of refuge" (Lv 25:32-33).

Near the start of the conquest, a bi-covenantal structure is instituted within Israel by the ratification of the Deuteronomic covenant over the twelve tribes (Jos 8:30-35). They thereby place themselves under the administrative supervision of the Levites, as Moses stipulated when he first announced the Deuteronomic covenant (Dt 27:9-26). The Levites themselves are bound by an altogether different covenant, namely, "the covenant of Levi" (Jer 33:17-26; Mal 2:4-8), which Moses made with them at Sinai after the golden calf.

Significantly, this same Levitical covenant is renewed at the end of Israel's forty years of wilderness wanderings with the grandson of Aaron, Phinehas. He is divinely awarded a "covenant of perpetual priesthood" for his righteous zeal in avenging the second generation's idolatrous worship of Baal-Peor (Nm 25:1-13). Thus, the net effect of Israel's second lapse is the imposition of the Deuteronomic covenant on the twelve tribes on the plains of Moab, where their apostasy has just occurred (Dt 3:29, 4:3). Moses appoints the Levites to enforce the provisions of the Deuteronomic covenant, according to the priestly authority divinely invested in them by the Levitical covenant. A secondary effect of this renewal of the Levitical covenant was the further narrowing of the Aaronic high priesthood to Phinehas's line of descent.

During the later settlement, this renewed covenant arrangement contributed to a series of notable changes: the condemnation and collapse of Eli's priestly house at Shiloh (1 Sm 2:27-35); the expulsion of Abiathar as high priest; and the subsequent elevation of Zadok as high priest in Jerusalem (1 Kgs 2:26-35). The common denominator is genealogical descent from Phinehas, which Zadok possessed (1 Chr 6:4-8), but Eli and Abiathar both lacked (1 Sm 22:9-20). The Zadokite high priesthood in the Jerusalem temple is a major feature of the Davidic monarchy; however, the other priests and Levites are given specialized ministries within the temple, as liturgical musicians, choristers, craftsmen, treasurers, etc. (1 Chr 9:22-34, 23:2-28). Nevertheless, it should be added that the Old Testament canonical picture is incomplete — indeed, ambiguous — at certain key points, such as the period of Josiah's reform (2 Kgs 22–23).

Role of High Priests • A somewhat idealized portrait of the high priesthood emerges in the postexilic period, stemming from Ezekiel's visions of the restoration of Jerusalem under the (Zadokite) high priest (Ez 43–45). In the absence of any royal Davidic descendants to lay hold of the throne, it is not surprising that the high priest became the undisputed leader and head in postexilic Judaism. Israel's divine vocation to be "a kingdom of priests" came to be seen as embodied and fulfilled in the (royal) figure of the postexilic high priest.

This explains Zechariah's otherwise anomalous description of the royal crowning of the high priest Joshua (Zec 6:9-13), instead of Zerubbabel, the Davidic descendant who is later recalled to Persia.

This is also reflected in the emphatic praise reserved by Ben Sira for the priestly figures from Aaron down to the high priest of his day, Simon, who is extolled as "the leader of his brothers and the pride of his people" (Sir 50:1). Likewise, later intertestamental sources depict the Messiah as combining Davidic kingship and high priestly authority (Testament of Simeon 6:5–7:2; Testament of Levi 2:10-11, 4:2–5:2, 8:2-15; cf. Ps 110:1-4). Clearly, this outlook must have contributed in some way to the Messianic expectations and views of first-century Jewish Christians, such as the author of Hebrews, who makes it the basis of his argument regarding Christ's royal high priesthood "after the order of Melchizedek" (Heb 1–7).

A Zadokite high priesthood lasted in Jerusalem until Antiochus Epiphanes deposed Onias II in 175 B.C., and replaced him with Jason (175-172). The Seleucid rulers then appointed non-Zadokites until their defeat in 153 B.C. by the Hasmoneans, whose non-Zadokite rule lasted until the Roman conquest in 37 B.C. Many scholars see this breach as a major cause for the founding of the priestly community at Qumran. In any case, the subsequent appointment of high priests was only with the approval of the Herodian kings and the authority of Rome. This lasted until the destruction of the Jerusalem temple in A.D. 70, which completely extinguished the last vestiges of the Levitical priesthood — and the Old Covenant — forever.

See: Holy Orders; Judaism; New Covenant; Old Covenant; Priest; Priesthood of Christ; Priesthood of the Faithful; Redemption; Sacrifice.

Suggested Readings: CCC 62-64, 1539-1543. G. Anderson and S. Olyan, eds., *Priesthood and Cult in Ancient Israel.* A. Cody, *A History of the Old Testament Priesthood.* T. Hennesey, "The Fatherhood of the Priest," *Thomist* 10 (1947). R. Nelson, *Raising Up a Faithful Priest: Community and Priesthood in Biblical Theology.* J. O'Brien, *Priest and Levite in Malachi.* L. Sabourin, *Priesthood: A Comparative Study.* T. Torrance, *Royal Priesthood.* A. Vanhoye, *Old Testament Priests and the New Priest.*

Scott Hahn

PRIESTHOOD OF CHRIST

At the beginning of his 1992 apostolic exhortation on the priesthood, *Pastores Dabo Vobis*, Pope John Paul II expressed an important Catholic sentiment about the priesthood of Christ. The Holy Father openly admitted that, in the period following the Second Vatican Council, the ministerial and hierarchical priesthood had become the subject of considerable, and sometimes difficult, debate within the Church. "To surmount these difficulties," he pointed out, "we have at our disposal our hope, our faith in the unfailing love of Christ, and our certainty that the priestly ministry in the life of the Church and in the world knows no substitute" (10). Because there is no replacement for the ministerial priesthood, as it has been established by the Lord himself, it is important to examine the theology that stands behind the priesthood of Christ.

Historical Background • The second half of the twentieth century is not the first time controversies over the priesthood of Christ and its various instantiations in the Church have arisen. For example, one of the major items on the theological agenda of the sixteenth-century Protestant Reformers was how one should interpret the priesthood of Christ as a spiritual gift for the Church.

On account of a cluster of theological misunderstandings, sometimes fueled by the irregular practices of poorly informed clergymen, Lutherans and other Reformers argued against the institution of Holy Orders. The Reformed churches repudiated the notion of a ministerial priesthood, existing for the benefit of the Church, and instead popularized the idea of the priesthood of the individual baptized persons who comprise the Church.

The abandonment of Mass vestments, a practice Luther himself inaugurated, and the giving of the Communion cup to the laity became two symbolic actions publicly heralding the Protestant Reform. Among other more substantial gestures, these actions clearly signaled that the Reformers intended a radical reinterpretation of the Church's understanding of the priesthood of Christ. They were largely successful, so that today a predominantly functional view of ministry prevails in most Protestant denominations.

On the Catholic side, the Council of Trent (1545-1563) initiated a reform of the clergy that bore significant fruit. Recent studies have shown that the clergy, including the residential bishops, were of a considerably higher quality during the fifteenth century in countries such as France than some earlier historians, influenced by Reformation polemics, were accustomed to admit. It comes as less of a surprise, then, that the subsequent period of Catholic Reform in the sixteenth and early seventeenth centuries was blessed by the life and ministry of many holy priests.

Notwithstanding the lived experience of these men, however, many of the controversial theological issues that the Protestant Reformers had opened up remained substantially unresolved. And notwithstanding the failure to reach a theological consensus, and as a sign of God's providential care for his Church, the truth of the Catholic faith continued to manifest itself in the life of the Church. Particularly noteworthy is the establishment of many new religious congregations of priests in the years following the Council of Trent.

The theme of the priesthood of Christ engaged a considerable amount of the theological energies of the Second Vatican Council (1962-1965). The conciliar Fathers developed ecclesiology around a reaffirmation of the universal call to holiness. By reminding the members of the Church that the only tragedy in life is not to become a saint, they gave new emphasis to the biblical teaching that all the baptized "constitute the people of God and, in their own way [are] made sharers in Christ's priestly, prophetic and royal office" (Vatican Council II, *Dogmatic Constitution on the Church, Lu-*

men Gentium, 31). Because there is no holiness for anyone outside his or her participation in Christ the Priest, the priesthood of the faithful has become a theme associated with the spirituality of the postconciliar period.

In order to make certain, however, that their insistence on the priestly status of the baptized would not obscure the reality of the ministerial priesthood, the Council Fathers, giving full recognition to the analogical character of Christ's priesthood, stipulated that an *essential* difference exists between the priesthood of the laity and the priesthood of the ordained. In other words, not every member of the Church is a priest. "The common priesthood of the faithful and the ministerial or hierarchical priesthood, though they differ in essence and not simply in degree, are nevertheless interrelated: each in its own particular way shares in the one priesthood of Christ" (*Lumen Gentium*, 10).

The Council handed over this distinction to the Church so that through a process of theological reflection we might deepen our understanding of the analogical continuity embracing both the common priesthood of the baptized and the ministerial priesthood of the ordained. For doctrinal reasons, a complete Catholic theology of the priesthood of Christ must explain how this ecclesial grace constitutes an essentially different reality when it exists in a man who has received the sacrament of Holy Orders. The key to this lies in the fact that, for the Second Vatican Council, the ordained priest is an icon of Christ.

Theology of the Priesthood of Christ • The Letter to the Hebrews provides the richest source of biblical instruction on the meaning of the priesthood of Christ. Addressing an intended audience sometimes thought to be former Jewish priests who had converted to Christianity, the author makes it his purpose to explain the superiority of Christ as an instrument of divine salvation. Christ in turn is shown to be superior to the angels (Heb 1:1-14, 2:5-18), to Moses (Heb 3:1-6), and to the Levitical priesthood (Heb 7:1-10, 18).

In brief, we can say that the Letter to the Hebrews is about mediation. And in this regard it is helpful to recall how St. Thomas Aquinas explains the priesthood of Christ as a mediation dictated by the logic of the Incarnation. Aquinas points to "downward" and "upward" movements within which Christ accomplishes the roles of the Old Testament priests. First, the priest is one who gives God's holy things to the people. A text from Malachi describes this downward movement: "For the lips of a priest should guard knowledge, and men should seek instruction from his mouth, for he is the messenger of the Lord of hosts" (2:7). The priest then is one who is able to bestow divine gifts on the people. Second, there is the upward movement. The Letter to the Hebrews, in a text alluding to the description of the Levitical priesthood, stipulates this office of the priest: "For every high priest chosen from among men is appointed to act on behalf of men in relation to God, to offer gifts and sacrifices for sins" (Heb 5:1). Of course, insofar as this definition applies to the priests of the Old Law, their sacrifices must be qualified as partial and incomplete in respect to ability to make satisfaction for sins, for only Christ fulfills this role of bringing about the forgiveness of sins in a transcendent fashion. The generic notes of Christ's priesthood are thus clear: The priest is one who gives divine gifts to men and in turn offers their gifts to God, especially as an act of atonement.

The Christian Church confesses that the incarnate Son carries out the functions of the priest in an eminent degree. First, Christ brings divine gifts to men. The Second Letter of Peter makes this point about the transformation that the grace of Christ accomplishes in those who receive it as a gracious gift. "His divine power has granted to us all things that pertain to life and godliness, through the knowledge of him who called us to his own glory and excellence, by which he has granted to us his precious and very great promises, that through these you may escape from the corruption that is in the world because of passion, and become partakers of the divine nature" (1:3-4). The divine gift Christ gives is the personal gift of grace. The Old Law, about which the prophet Malachi spoke, was proposed verbally, but the New Law is, as Aquinas puts it, "primarily the grace of

the Holy Spirit which is given to those who believe in Christ" (*Summa Theologiae,* I-II, q. 106, arts. 1-2).

Second, Christ reconciles the human race to God in a definitive way so that the foreshadowing sacrifices of the old dispensation, as well as whatever might purport to replace them, are abolished. The Letter to the Colossians makes plain the unsurpassable nature of Christ's sacrifice. The inspired author suggests a reason why Christ's sacrifice accomplished the reconciliation of God and man: "For in him all the fullness of God was pleased to dwell, and through him to reconcile to himself all things, whether on earth or in heaven, making peace by the blood of his cross" (Col 1:19-20). The reason, then, lies in the personal identity of the One who suffered and died for us. Because Christ remains the Divine Person of creation even as he undergoes death, that is, the separation of his human soul from his body, he alone is able to establish the new creation of grace.

Priesthood and "Descending" Mediation • It should be noted that in his treatment of the priesthood of Christ, St. Thomas Aquinas chooses first to identify the priest as one who bestows divine gifts on the people. The Letter to the Hebrews, however, describes the priest as one ordained by God "that he may offer up gifts and sacrifices for sins" (5:1). Why does Aquinas broaden the definition to include the "descending," man-directed mediation? The answer illuminates our understanding of the priesthood of Christ.

What is fundamentally different about Christian priesthood is that it comes into being only as a result of the divine initiative. The priests whose role in a particular society is simply to represent "religion" in an official manner can make no such claim. Even the Old Testament priests, instituted by divine command, did not enjoy the personal grace communicated in Christ. The text from Malachi quoted above, which describes the divine gifts the priests of the Old Law gave to the people, says these latter received from the priests' mouths instruction in how to live: the Old Law of commandments and precepts. These instructions, while helpful to the chosen people, were only directives, a sort of divine rule of life. St. Paul explains this in the Letter to the Romans, implicitly comparing the Old Law to a pedagogue or tutor who accompanies a young person as a mentor, pointing out to him or her the difference between the good and the bad and the true and the false (cf. Rom 2:17-21). In complete contrast to this, Christ brings to us the very life of God, not instructions about how to find God.

As a Divine Person, Christ himself is God's gift to the human race. Theologians agree that only within the mystery of this completely prior and utterly gracious divine giving can there be any possibility of an authentic human response to God's love. This is to say that the Church depends on the divine initiative, which appears as the Word made flesh, in order to accomplish her mission of reconciling man to God. Indeed, only because Christ himself is first a divine gift given to the world does his once-and-for-all sacrifice achieve for us the effect it does.

A truly Catholic theology of Christ's priesthood therefore does not make pretentious claims about what man can do for God. On the contrary, the priesthood of Christ reveals what God has done for us, making all the baptized "partakers of the divine nature" (2 Pt 1:4). The baptized form a priestly people because, once incorporated into Christ, they are able to join in Christ's perfect worship of the Father. All the members of Christ the Priest are made capable of sharing in the fruits of Christ's sacrifice: Their godly image is both restored and brought to perfection. The priesthood of Christ is a way of explaining the value and the efficacy of the intervention of the Word in the religious activity of a sinful human race, as this is revealed in the Scriptures.

The logic of the Incarnation implies that no grace can be given in or to the Church outside the one mediation of Christ; in this sense, every grace is Christic. But Christ imparts this grace in a fully personal way. Wanting to remain personally present to the members of his Body, he ordained that other men, beginning with the Apostles, carry out the mission he had received from God. As the Second Vatican Council expressed it, Christ ap-pointed some members as ministers who would have the sacred power of Order within the company of the faithful, to offer sacrifice and to forgive sins, and who would publicly discharge their priestly function in the name of Christ (cf. *Decree on the Ministry and Life of Priests, Presbyterorum Ordinis*, 2).

Configuration to Christ • Over the course of her history, the Church has developed a way of expressing the personal configuration with Christ that the ordained man enjoys. The special character of Holy Orders is itself a grace of course; and a theological reason can be assigned to explain why a special sacrament is required to ready men to serve as mediators of the one Mediator. Recall that the priesthood of Christ cannot be understood apart from the fact that Christ comes forth from God as a divine gift to the world. The efficacy of what he does during his life, especially in the course of his Passion, when he most shows forth his high-priestly character, depends on his remaining a Divine Person. And although the priests of the New Law plainly remain men of flesh and blood, nevertheless they require a special configuration to Christ so that they can serve as instruments of his one mediation.

Pope John Paul II describes the identity of the priests of the New Covenant in *Pastores Dabo Vobis* in a way that makes clear the relationship of the ordained priest to the Person of Christ. "In the Church and on behalf of the Church, priests are a sacramental representation of Jesus Christ, the Head and Shepherd, authoritatively proclaiming his Word, repeating his acts of forgiveness and his offer of salvation, particularly in Baptism, Penance and the Eucharist, showing his loving concern to the point of a total gift of self for the flock. . . . In a word, priests exist and act in order to proclaim the Gospel to the world and to build up the Church in the name and person of Christ the Head and Shepherd" (15). Like Christ, the priest is a man for others. But his ability to fulfill that task rests, at a radical level, on the sacramental configuration he receives in Holy Orders. The language of theology refers to this as the "character" of the priest.

With reference to holiness, the ministerial priesthood exists for the sake of the perfection of the whole Body of Christ. Since the priesthood of Christ finds expression in the common priesthood of the faithful and the ministerial or hierarchical priesthood, however, both priests and laity can look forward to the same blessed hope. The whole Church awaits the coming of the Lord Jesus Christ as the true end of its life and worship. "Since all these things are thus to be dissolved, what sort of persons ought you to be in lives of holiness and godliness, waiting for and hastening the coming of the day of God?" (2 Pt 3:11-12).

See: Baptism; Holy Orders; In Persona Christi Capitis; Jesus Christ, God and Man; Laity; Ministry; Priesthood in the Old Testament; Priesthood of the Faithful; Vocation; Women, Ordination of.

Suggested Readings: CCC 1544-1553. Vatican Council II, *Dogmatic Constitution on the Church, Lumen Gentium,* 10; *Constitution on the Sacred Liturgy, Sacrosanctum Concilium,* 33; *Decree on the Bishops' Pastoral Office in the Church, Christus Dominus,* 11; *Decree on the Ministry and Life of Priests, Presbyterorum Ordinis,* 2, 6. Pius XII, *On the Sacred Liturgy, Mediator Dei.* John Paul II, *I Will Give You Shepherds, Pastores Dabo Vobis.* St. Thomas Aquinas, *Summa Theologiae,* III, q. 22. A. Nichols, O.P., *Holy Order.*

Romanus Cessario, O.P.

PRIESTHOOD OF THE FAITHFUL

The priesthood of the faithful is the participation of the baptized in the priesthood of Christ by virtue of their having received Baptism. While there is only one priesthood of Christ, it is possible to participate in it in two distinct modes: the ministerial priesthood and the priesthood of the faithful. Those who have been ordained belong to the former; those who have been baptized but not ordained belong to the latter.

The *Catechism of the Catholic Church* says: "The whole community of believers is, as such, priestly. The faithful exercise their baptismal priesthood through their participation, each according to his own vocation, in Christ's mission

as priest, prophet, and king. Through the sacraments of Baptism and Confirmation the faithful are 'consecrated to be . . . a holy priesthood' [*LG* 10 §1]" (1546).

The faithful offer glory, sacrifice, and worship to the almighty God with Christ the priest as their head. Baptism enables the baptized to be consecrated to Jesus through the power of the Holy Spirit. It is primarily through their participation in the Eucharist that the lay faithful give to God all they are and possess.

Vatican Council II teaches: "For all their works, prayers, and apostolic undertakings, family and married life, daily work, relaxation of mind and body, if they are accomplished in the Spirit — indeed even the hardships of life if patiently borne — all these become spiritual sacrifices acceptable to God through Jesus Christ. In the celebration of the Eucharist, these may most fittingly be offered to the Father along with the body of the Lord." Proceeding thus, the Council adds, "the laity consecrate the world itself to God" (*Dogmatic Constitution on the Church, Lumen Gentium,* 34).

Christ's sacrifice perpetuated in each Mass is the offering to the Father of everything Jesus has; and here the lay faithful join with the ordained priest in offering all they have to God. Their unity with Jesus, initiated in Baptism, is expressed and brought to perfection by their participation in the celebration of the Eucharistic Sacrifice.

Ordained and Baptismal Priesthoods • The ministerial priesthood and the priesthood of the faithful are rooted in the one priesthood of Christ; however, a crucial distinction exists between the two. Although they are "ordered one to another," yet they differ essentially and not solely in degree (*Lumen Gentium,* 10). The *Catechism* explains the critical difference: "While the common priesthood of the faithful is exercised by the unfolding of baptismal grace — a life of faith, hope, and charity, a life according to the Spirit — the ministerial priesthood is at the service of the common priesthood" (1547).

It is incumbent on priests, especially, to instruct the faithful to offer the Divine Victim, Jesus Christ, to God the Father in the Eucharistic Sacrifice —

the center of the assembly of believers over which the priest presides — and with Christ to offer their entire lives (cf. Vatican Council II, *Decree on the Ministry and Life of Priests, Presbyterorum Ordinis*, 5). The ministerial priesthood's aim is to assist in the "unfolding" of the baptismal grace of each member of the priesthood of the faithful. "The ministerial priesthood is a *means* by which Christ unceasingly builds up and leads his Church. For this reason it is transmitted by its own sacrament, the sacrament of Holy Orders" (CCC 1547).

The lay faithful, as members of the universal priesthood of the faithful, "seek the kingdom of God by engaging in temporal affairs and directing them according to God's will" (*Lumen Gentium*, 31). They possess a right and duty, either individually or in association with others, to seek to make the message of salvation known and accepted by all; in the absence of such efforts by the laity, the apostolate of the Church's pastors cannot be fully effective (*Lumen Gentium*, 33).

The Catholic faithful share in the threefold office of Christ as priest, prophet, and king. The priestly or sanctifying office is illustrated when they participate in Mass and present to God the Father the gift of themselves along with the gift of the Son through the power of the Holy Spirit. This office is demonstrated, too, by parents, by their conjugal life, and by seeing to the Christian education of their children (cf. CCC 902).

The ministries of lector and acolyte are open to laypersons who possess the requisite characteristics. Moreover, in case of need (e.g., the lack of ministers), laypeople who are not lectors or acolytes can perform certain of their functions, including liturgical reading, presiding over liturgical prayers, conferring Baptism, and distributing Holy Communion.

The lay faithful fulfill their prophetic mission when they evangelize by preaching the Gospel through words and actions and by teaching the faith. They participate in the kingly office when they cooperate with the Church's pastors in the service of the ecclesial community. It is important also to note that the Church exhorts laypeople to confront and seek to correct the errors in society:

"Moreover, by uniting their forces let the laity so remedy the institutions and conditions of the world when the latter are an inducement to sin, that these may be conformed to the norms of justice, favoring rather than hindering the practice of virtue. By so doing they will impregnate culture and human works with a moral value" (*Lumen Gentium*, 36).

The Church protects the rights and encourages the fulfillment of the duties of the laity, including those that pertain to their participation in the priesthood of the faithful. Canons 224-231 of the Code of Canon Law enumerate some of these.

See: Apostolate; Baptism; Ecclesial Rights and Duties; Holy Orders; Laity; Ministry; Priesthood of Christ; Vocation; Women, Ecclesial and Social Roles of.

Suggested Readings: CCC 897-913, 1544-1547. Vatican Council II, *Dogmatic Constitution on the Church, Lumen Gentium*, 10, 31-36; *Decree on the Ministry and Life of Priests, Presbyterorum Ordinis*, 2, 5. Code of Canon Law, 207, 224-231, 298-329. G. Grisez, *The Way of the Lord Jesus*, Vol. 1, *Christian Moral Principles*, pp. 553-555, 791-793.

Charles M. Mangan

PRIVATE REVELATION

As used in theological discourse, the word "revelation" may designate God's intervention in human history, by which he imparts supernatural truths to be believed on the authority of God revealing, or it may refer to the body of truths that are the object of our faith, as when we speak of the truths of Revelation. The truths thus revealed have been placed in the custody of the Church instituted by Jesus Christ, and as such they constitute what is known as public Revelation. It is also known as the deposit of faith, because God's Revelation was brought to completion in Jesus Christ. All who accept Christ in faith must likewise accept all the truths handed down in the twofold source of Revelation: Sacred Scripture and Tradition.

It is commonly said that public Revelation

ended with the death of the last Apostle; but the closing of public Revelation does not mean that God has withdrawn into an eternal silence. On the contrary, the history of the Church is replete with examples of private revelation. In modern times the question of private revelation must be addressed because so many persons, both Christian and non-Christian, are seeking some kind of contact with the supernatural and transcendent. Indeed, some religious denominations claim to have been founded by persons who received private revelations, among them the Mormons and the Seventh-Day Adventists.

The Catholic Church admits the possibility of private revelations and has even approved some of them: for example, the revelations made to St. Margaret Mary Alacoque, St. Bernadette at Lourdes, and the children at Fátima. On the other hand, the official position of the Catholic Church has always been one of extreme caution and even doubt when passing judgment on private revelations.

Types of Private Revelation • Private revelations are communications made to individuals by the Lord, the Blessed Virgin Mary, or some other messenger from the world beyond this one. Experts in the field usually classify them into three types: a declarative statement, as when St. Bernadette heard the words, "I am the Immaculate Conception"; a conditioned statement, such as the promises made to St. Margaret Mary Alacoque; or a denunciatory revelation, which is usually a threat of future punishment and hence a conditional prophecy.

The first thing that must be said about private revelations is that the only persons obliged to believe them are the ones who are convinced that they are supernatural in origin. Theologians dispute whether this would involve an act of supernatural faith or be simply an act of human faith. But if an individual is personally certain that a revelation is from God, then it would seem that the recipient should accept it with an act of the supernatural virtue of faith.

As regards other persons, the general principle is that one is free to accept or reject private revelations. Pope Benedict XIV stated that persons other than the recipient who accept a private revelation will do so simply on *human* faith, after making a prudent decision that the revelation is probable. If, however, a private revelation has received ecclesiastical approval, bearing in mind the great caution exercised by the investigators, it would be audacious not to accept the decision of the Church.

Nevertheless, it is true that private revelations are very susceptible to error. Even for people in good faith, there is always the danger of misinterpreting the message or reading into it something purely subjective and personal. For instance, numerous mystics have written treatises on the life of Christ, based on private revelation: for example, St. Bridget, Mary of Agreda, Anna Katherine Emmerich, and Maria Valtorta. There is great discrepancy in many of the details. The volumes written by Maria Valtorta, entitled *The Poem of the Man-God*, have been widely circulated in recent years. It should be noted, however, that this work was condemned by the Holy Office in 1959; and Cardinal Joseph Ratzinger, Prefect of the Congregation for the Doctrine of the Faith, stated again in 1985 that the condemnation by the Church still applies to the second edition of the treatise (cf. B. Groeschel, *A Still, Small Voice*, fn. 10, p. 58).

Rules for Discernment • Prudence dictates that before giving assent to any private revelation, one should exert every effort to discern whether or not it is worthy of credence. The rules for discernment are based on the authoritative teaching of masters of the spiritual life such as St. Teresa of Ávila and St. John of the Cross. Nor do we neglect the input from the study of paranormal and religious psychology, which has made great strides in modern times, thanks to the pioneer work of men like William James.

The first thing to be noted is that private revelations are extraordinary phenomena, or *gratiae gratis datae*, and as such they are not essential for salvation or Christian holiness. Neither are they a proof of the holiness of the individual who receives them. Margaret Mary Alacoque, for example, was not canonized a saint because she had received private revelations concerning devotion to the Sacred Heart or because she was the instrument chosen by God to spread this devotion throughout the world. She was declared a saint because she had reached perfection in the love of God and of neighbor. The essence of Christian holiness is the fulfillment of the twofold precept of charity given by the Lord (Mt 22:35-40). Everything else should be seen either as a means to greater perfection or the fruit of perfect love.

Second, since public Revelation was brought to its completion in Jesus Christ, no new public revelation can be expected until the Second Coming of Christ (cf. Vatican Council II, *Dogmatic Constitution on Divine Revelation, Dei Verbum*, 4). Nevertheless, the history of the Church contains numerous cases of private revelation, whether given for the good of the individual or for the good of others in the Church. In every case, however, the private revelation must be understood and interpreted in the light of the Revelation made by Christ and proclaimed by his Church. As noted above, Pope Benedict XIV stated that private revelations approved by the Church can elicit from us only *human* faith. They do not in any way bind the faithful by an act of the theological virtue of faith. The reason is that even when the Church approves a private revelation, the content of the revelation is not guaranteed to be infallibly true. Even some of the saints, for example, Catherine of Siena and Joan of Arc, made mistakes in interpreting some of the details in their revelations.

If a person is firmly convinced that a given private revelation is authentically divine in origin, that individual is obliged to believe it. It is possible, however, that a person who receives a private revelation, however holy that person might be, could make a mistake in interpreting or applying the revelation. There is no gift of infallibility here. As for the approval by Church authorities, this is usually given only after a commission of experts has studied the matter and submitted its findings to the proper authorities. According to Father P. De Letter, between 1931 and 1950 twenty-two private revelations were investigated;

two were approved (Beauraing and Banneux), six were left undecided, and the remaining fourteen were rejected (cf. *New Catholic Encyclopedia*, Vol. 12, p. 446).

The rules for discernment can be summarized as follows: (1) Any revelation that is contrary to the public teaching on faith or morals must be rejected. (2) Any teaching contrary to the common teaching of theologians or that claims to settle an argument among schools of theology is gravely suspect. (3) If some part or detail of a private revelation turns out to be false or erroneous, it is not necessary to reject the entire revelation. (4) The fact that a prophecy comes true is not a proof that the revelation was from God; it could have been due to some other factor. (5) Private revelations that are very detailed or treat of useless matter or mere curiosity should be ignored. (6) The person who receives the revelation should be carefully examined as regards physical and mental health, moral character, obedience, and humility. (7) Carefully examine the immediate fruits that are produced by the revelation.

See: Apparitions; Devil and Evil Spirits; Discernment; Extraordinary Gifts; Prophecy.

Suggested Readings: CCC 65-67, 124, 157. A. Poulain, *The Graces of Interior Prayer*. B. Groeschel, *A Still, Small Voice*.

Jordan Aumann, O.P.

PROBABILISM

Probabilism is a theory about how to resolve doubts of conscience regarding law. It says that when one is in doubt about whether a law applies, if there is a solidly probable opinion that it does *not* bind, then one may act as if there were no such law. It is abbreviated in the slogan "A doubtful law does not oblige." It has sometimes been invoked to justify dissent from the Magisterium on specific moral issues.

Probabilists of the past, however, always assumed that a teaching clearly proposed by the Magisterium is not doubtful, and so this method does not apply to such questions. The context of probabilism, moreover, was a legalistic view of morality. It was thought of as a body of somewhat arbitrary rules, and so a law did not seem to bind if it had not been sufficiently promulgated. However, once we see that morality essentially concerns moral truth directing us to what is really fulfilling and away from conditions that really harm, it seems more reasonable to say that when doubts exist, we should follow the option more probably true ("probabiliorism").

The Church has not insisted on which of various proposed methods of resolving doubts should be followed. However, the Church has excluded laxism (the idea that a person may always adopt the most permissive option) and rigorism (a person must always adopt the strictest opinion).

See: Absolute Moral Norms; Choice; Conscience; Freedom, Human; Legalism; Magisterium; Positivism.

PROCESS THEOLOGY

Process theology is a view of reality, including the notion of the divine, by which everything exists "in process." The concept of process stresses the idea of becoming, rather than being or substance: A thing is what it is becoming. Exactly what it ultimately will be cannot now be fully known, because nothing now exists as it really is meant to be, but only as it is becoming.

The English philosopher Alfred North Whitehead (1861-1947), acknowledged father of modern process thought, held that the traditional theistic idea of God as the unchanging Absolute sacrificed biblical, Hebraic relational, and concrete aspects of the idea of God for static and abstract Greek philosophical ideas. The absolute perfection of God created a problem for Whitehead: If God made everything and in its midst devised human freedom, yet he himself is not influenced by or in any way changed by what occurs in the world, then how is God "involved" in the world? And how does he will a perfect completion for the world according to his providential will without violating human freedom?

Whitehead suggested the problem be resolved by viewing reality as constituting processes that coextensively network with all other events and influences. God exists in time and is only perfect and ultimate relative to all other things. He is primordially God insofar as he brings all other things into actuality, though not via the traditional notion of creation. Correspondingly, the achievement of other beings enters into God's life and contributes to his reality.

Whitehead defined the nature of anything as referring to the manner by which it relates to everything else. Divine nature, then, while not dual, is bipolar: primordial in that God's existence only depends on himself, consequent in that God is actualized relative to the rest of reality. God and creation exist in dialectical tension, as it were, mutually influencing each other. Hence, everything is free and "in process," with nothing, not even God, having any predetermined end.

From a Catholic perspective, the flaw in Whitehead's view lies in its sacrificing God's omnipotence and providential will. Scripture reveals God to be omniscient and necessarily all-powerful, determining the purpose and teleology — the end — of creation. In process theology, however, God no longer is in control but is subject even to evil influences, suffering with humanity to bring good out of evil. God no longer knows what anything will be in the future. If everything is in process, the ability to know anything "in the future" is lost. No thing is what it is, but only becoming what it will be, which is unknown.

For Catholicism, all things exist because of their stable form in God's mind predetermining what a thing will be. Absolutes and ultimates are found in God and hence exist. Humanity can know moral certitudes and norms of conduct that, when acted upon, enable a person to align more perfectly with God's will. In Catholicism, then, freedom is a capacity for realizing, actualizing, the good that God wills an entity to be, even though free choice also allows a thing to deprive itself of achieving its good. God is involved in the world by his providential will for the good, and his gift of free choice of the will to humanity prevents history from being predestined.

See: Eternity; Evil, Problem of; God, Nature

and Attributes of; Omnipotence; Omniscience; Providence.

Paul E. Lockey

PROPERTY

Some people believe the Christian ideal excludes the notion of private property. For them, Christ's counsel to the rich young man applies to all: "Sell what you possess and give to the poor, and you will have treasure in heaven; and come, follow me" (Mt 19:21). We know that in the early days of the Church "all who believed were together and had all things in common" (Acts 2:44). Furthermore, the Church maintains that God's creation is "the original gift of the earth to the whole of mankind" (CCC 2403). Nonetheless, property is an important element in Catholic social doctrine, and the seventh commandment, "Thou shall not steal," presupposes that private property belongs to some people by right and cannot justly be taken away.

Catholic teaching on property strikes a balance between two principles. First, created goods are intended by God for the benefit of all. The division of property under different legal systems among individuals, families, tribes, corporations, or nations can never cancel the primacy of the universal destination of goods. But, second, private property protects the freedom of persons, contributes to their dignity, and enables them to meet the needs of those for whom they have a responsibility. The seventh commandment, therefore, "requires respect for the universal destination of goods and respect for the right to private property" (CCC 2401).

This balance is often described as the social dimension or social mortgage on private property. Property cannot be used to the detriment or neglect of others in need. At the same time, historical experience shows that where property rights, properly understood, are not respected, other rights crucial to the dignity of the human person are not respected either. No society in history has for very long kept a perfect balance between these two demands of justice. But all societies must undertake the difficult task of protecting individual property and the common good.

Historical Survey • The Old Testament provides many examples of private property justly held, both household goods and land. The seventh and tenth commandments attest to the regulation of external and internal attitudes toward property. Inequality of wealth in itself was not regarded as unjust and, as in the case of Abraham, might actually be regarded as a sign of God's approval. However, wealth tending toward monopoly or vast landholdings that excluded the poor from productive enterprises provoked prophetic denunciations.

In the New Testament, Christ associates with rich people, and he and St. Paul remind them of their obligations to the poor. But rarely does Christ advise anyone to abandon private property. The rich young man of the Gospel seems to have fulfilled the law in its general injunctions, but he remained unsettled in his heart. For people like him or for those entirely devoting themselves to God's service in various ministries, forsaking private property may be a means to an end. Otherwise, the early Church seems to have relied on wealthy members to provide meeting places and support for its activities in various cities.

Among the great early figures of the Church such as Clement of Alexandria (c. 150-c. 215), Cyprian (210-258), Ambrose (c. 340-397), Jerome (c. 343-420), and Augustine (354-430), the dangers of wealth were emphasized. In an ideal world before the Fall, some thought, property would not have existed. Religious communities in particular were encouraged to hold things in common. Especially as the Church became a full moral agent in society instead of an embattled sect, however, temperate use of property in a fallen world seemed a good stance between the sinful impulse toward limitless acquisition of things and political enslavement under state ownership and disposition of persons. Such a use requires a legal system that both governs in the name of the common good and permits access to material goods for all.

St. Thomas Aquinas gave a different interpretation that has become the classic Catholic expression of how property is to be regarded. Thomas, unlike the early Fathers, thought property a natural human institution for using God's gift of creation, in the sense that property is a lawful addition to the state of nature that leads to human good. He seems to believe that private property would have existed even had there been no Fall, since property helps man (who is both body and spirit) express and realize his full nature.

Private property, says Thomas, is necessary to human life for three reasons. First, people are more careful in procuring what they need for themselves if they alone are responsible rather than a large number of workers. Second, greater order results when an individual fulfills a particular task. Confusion stems from expecting everyone in a community to bear vague responsibility for each thing. Third, greater peace reigns when each person is content with his own. Thomas observes that "quarrels arise more frequently where there is no division of the things possessed," presumably a reference to religious communities (*Summa Theologiae*, II-II, q. 66, a. 2).

In using private possessions, each person is to treat them not as his own but as common. People may buy, sell, or give away what belongs to them as they wish. But these universal features of the market must always have a concern for the good of all. In some circumstances, it might be extrapolated, access to the market will distribute goods in a way that is roughly just. In other circumstances, laws may be needed to prevent fraud, monopoly, destitution, etc. St. Thomas even allows (*Summa Theologiae*, II-II, q. 66, a. 7) that in absolute need it is permissible to steal, since the goods that are private still retain their universal destination for all. But such cases are rare; all other possibilities must be exhausted, and there must be respect for all moral laws.

In the nineteenth and twentieth centuries, modern industrial conditions called for some further developments in the notion of property and its social responsibilities. The great age of industrialization seemed to be leading toward an impoverishment and exploitation of wage workers. Industrial workers living in cities began to outnumber traditional agricultural workers, who more and more left the land as industrialization also made farming more productive with far fewer hands. The resulting social dislocation received poignant literary treatment from writers such as Dickens, Balzac, and Zola. Some solution to what appeared to be the excessive concentration of capital in a few hands and the growing misery of workers seemed demanded.

In many instances, the national state seemed the logical instrument. The older medieval notions of the social dimension of property had been somewhat weakened and, in a few cases, denied by early modern capitalist thinkers. Though this history is complex, there is a common confidence in the good effects of private property per se in writers as different as Hobbes, Locke, Rousseau, Hume, and Mill. One way to read the history of socialism and communism is as a moral reaction to the imbalances thought to have emerged from capitalist industrialism. Since only the national state seemed in a position to meet the growing economic crisis, the state had to take over what Marx called the "means of production" in order to restore social responsibility to property.

Since the collapse of Marxism in the late twentieth century, the notion of state ownership of the means of production or extensive state direction of economies to guarantee the common good has fallen into disrepute. In theory, some industries may have to be owned by the state in order to fulfill common obligations or protect against too great an accumulation of private power. But, given the demonstrated ability of modern market democracies to produce wealth and care for the poor without resort to tyranny, the presumption today is in favor of responsible private ownership under the proper legal conditions.

Recent Church Teaching • The Church was instrumental in developing some idea of how both property and social responsibility might be exercised in modern conditions. The great modern tradition of Catholic social doctrine, beginning with Pope Leo XIII's 1891 encyclical *On the Social Question, Rerum Novarum*, attacked head-on the exploitation of workers by a small group of owners. Leo argued, with Aquinas, that property was a good necessary to the full development of the human person, and that therefore workers, too, needed a just wage sufficient to care for their families and other dependents. In what seemed a bold stance at the time —largely at the prodding of American Catholics — he declared the right to form labor unions to be a natural right that deserved state protection. All this was meant to reorient the Marxist claim of the inevitable class struggle between capital and labor toward a Catholic vision of the complementarity of rights and duties for both owners and workers in the just society.

Pius XI took a further step in this direction with his *On the Fortieth Year, Quadragesimo Anno.* Issued in 1931, the fortieth anniversary of Leo's earlier encyclical, *Quadragesimo Anno* faced a very different situation than the one that had existed toward the end of the nineteenth century. Then, revolutionary movements were brewing in several parts of the world. By the 1930s, communism was established in Russia, Fascism took root in Italy and Spain, and Nazism had come to power in Germany. Each was a response — a disastrously wrong one, in Pius XI's view — to some of the problems Leo had foreseen.

Property must always be recognized as having a social dimension, argued Pope Pius, but that did not give the state the right to usurp all decision-making functions. Thus he introduced the notion of subsidiarity into papal analyses. Briefly, subsidiarity means that the level of society that is closest to a social issue and capable of dealing with it should do so. Decentralization of governments was important to prevent totalitarianism, whether of the communist or Fascist type. But even more important, said Pius, was the need to empower subsidiary institutions such as families, neighborhoods, and private organizations. Each of these institutions had a God-given freedom and responsibility. To remove power from them and place it in the hands of the state was contrary to the divine order.

In the 1980s, a similar principle emerged during the collapse of the Soviet bloc. Social theo-

rists began to see that "civil society" — that is, private institutions controlling property, productive enterprise, and expenditures — was not only freer than totalitarian systems but, properly formed and understood, might actually restore a better balance between the empowerment of subsidiary institutions and the social dimension of the uses of property.

A special problem had arisen in the modern world over the nature of property held by the modern corporation, which is often not only a large national entity but an influential international one. This problem itself has been changing with changing conditions in technology, communications, and international trade. But a few general principles may be examined here.

Contrary to some modern social criticism, there is nothing inherently wrong with the establishment of a corporation as a legal person to achieve certain social and economic ends. Such practices have roots going back to the medieval and even ancient worlds, and they permit the coordinated and legal action of large charitable causes as well as business enterprises. Nor does the large accumulation of capital in an enterprise present a moral problem per se. The moral questions about corporations arise from two large factors. First, does the relatively weak and distant ownership of stockholders, who are dependent on managers for information and action, allow for a proper moral control of property? Second, are powerful corporations, operating sometimes across several continents, properly regulated so that any negative effects on society of otherwise legitimate business activities get legal attention and redress?

Some of these questions have relatively simple answers. A factory that is excessively polluting the environment may be required, either by its stockholders or by government, to take measures to reduce pollution or compensate the community for the damage. This means that reasonable laws (i.e., laws not so strict that the pursuit of unrealistic standards of environmental purity renders economic activity impossible) must exist to enforce the social dimension of the industrialized use of property.

A more complex situation arises when corporate property extends over several nations. In such instances, not only are environmental regulations more difficult to establish and enforce because of the multiple jurisdictions, but variations in local working conditions and wages also raise complicated issues. In a country like the United States, there are strict laws about child labor, a minimum wage, safety conditions, and so forth. In many developing countries, child labor, to take one example, is not in itself exploitative but is an economic necessity. Also, local wages are naturally less than in developed nations; and any attempt to require equal wages in developed and undeveloped societies would mean no new economic enterprises would be introduced into poorer nations.

The standard Catholic belief in the social dimension of property should provide some guidance, even if it is incapable of always finding a single answer to these complexities. Shareholders and managers have an obligation to consider in prudence how they may best combine a wish to make productive and beneficial use of unoccupied labor with the moral requirement to foster quality education, better hygiene, higher standards of living, and fuller respect for all dimensions of worker development. Such considerations are not simple. They must be guided by prudence as well as justice and charity.

The Duties of Christians • In our time, then, the possession of property calls for some searching moral analysis and personal effort. For the most part people who own moderate amounts of property and use it productively and legally are performing a public service, whether they create goods, provide services, or offer jobs to others. They should not be hampered in their activity unless public authorities can demonstrate a serious social evil arising from their possession and use of property that calls for a serious social response. It has been the experience of the past two centuries that economic liberty leads to societies that are prosperous and free at the same time, if moral values are respected.

Pope John Paul II pointed out in *The Hundredth Year, Centesimus Annus,* his 1991 encyclical on the centenary of Leo's first social encyclical, that distinctions are required when we try to determine whether any given "capitalist" system of property is fulfilling universal human moral requirements in our time. He states: "If by 'capitalism' is meant an economic system which recognizes the fundamental and positive role of business, the market, private property and the resulting responsibility for the means of production, as well as free human creativity in the economic sector, then the answer is certainly in the affirmative. . . . But if by 'capitalism' is meant a system in which freedom in the economic sector is not circumscribed within a strong juridical framework which places it at the service of human freedom in its totality, and which sees it as a particular aspect of that freedom, the core of which is ethical and religious, then the reply is certainly negative" (42).

Few Christians today must personally make decisions on that scale. They must be aware of them, however, in their political decisions and personal acts. For those in the prosperous developed countries, the parable of the rich man and the beggar Lazarus (Lk 16:19-31) may have great relevance.

Christ nowhere in the parable condemns the rich man for possessing wealth. He seems to have acquired it in ways that Christ thinks do not need comment. But his use of his possessions — for feasting and fine clothing — while the poor man languished at his gate, sent him to hell. In our time, we would consider charity in such circumstances good, but even better helping Lazarus to find productive work, acquire property, and realize dignity of his own. Our problem is magnified in that often the poor man is distant in another country and we can do little. Yet our obligations remain, and we must make sure that our possessions, even when justly acquired and rightly used, do not make us complacent and blind to those to whom, in justice and charity, we owe a debt in our use of property.

See: Common Good; Detachment; Evangelical Counsels; Liberation Theology; Social Doctrine; Stealing; Stewardship; Subsidiarity; Universal Destination of Goods; Work; Works of Mercy.

Suggested Readings: CCC 2401-2449. Vatican Council II, *Pastoral Constitution on the Church in the Modern World, Gaudium et Spes,* 69-72. Leo XIII, *On the Social Question, Rerum Novarum.* John Paul II, *On Social Concerns, Sollicitudo Rei Socialis; The Hundredth Year, Centesimus Annus.* St. Thomas Aquinas, *Summa Theologiae,* I-II, q. 105, aa. 2-3 and II-II, q. 66. R. Charles, *The Social Teaching of Vatican II,* pp. 299-312. M. Novak, *The Catholic Ethic and the Spirit of Capitalism.*

Robert Royal

PROPHECY

The prophet does not speak from himself but from another; he does not speak for himself but for others. The prophet is a mediator between God and man; he is a proclaimer of God's word to others.

When we hear the word "prophecy," we normally think immediately of predicting things to come. But the primary meaning of prophecy is to speak in God's name, to proclaim God's message. The element of prediction has always been closely connected with prophecy, but often it was simply a matter of proclamation or warning and admonition. In the Old Testament, we notice how often the prophet would say: "It is Yahweh who speaks"; in the New Testament readings the lector concludes with "The word of the Lord."

Understood in this way, prophecy is a *gratia gratis data,* which means it is a charism, a special gift of grace received for the benefit of the community. The very nature of prophecy as proclamation or speaking in God's name gives evidence that it is for the community and not for the individual.

St. Paul speaks about the gift of prophecy in Ephesians 4:7-11 and 1 Corinthians 12:28. In the early Church, the prophets were highly esteemed because they performed a special service for the Christian community. Later, due to the excesses of Montanus (c. 172) and some charismatic individuals, the role of the prophets was greatly diminished. Origen (died 254) lamented in his day that there were no more prophets.

The function of prophecy did not totally disappear, however. What continued was a strain of prophecy that was ecstatic, in the mystical tradition fostered by Origen, St. Gregory of Nyssa, St. Augustine, the Pseudo-Dionysius, and St. Gregory the Great. Because of their outstanding virtues, the ancient prophets were models for the monks of the early Church, but unfortunately some of the monks confused the gift of prophecy with the gifts of the Holy Spirit, thus making it a proof of personal holiness. This led to the heresy of Messalianism, which was condemned at the Council of Ephesus in 431.

A second development of the prophetic tradition is found in the prophet's role as preacher and interpreter of Scripture. In this context the prophetic function can be attributed to the great theologians such as St. Augustine, St. Anselm, St. Thomas Aquinas, and St. Bonaventure. And understanding the work of theologians to be the proclamation of the word of the Lord, the prophetic function can be applied to the Fathers and doctors of the Church, as well as to theologians throughout the centuries. In like manner, the great preachers have also performed a prophetic function in the Church.

Prophetic Function in the Church • St. Thomas Aquinas described prophecy as a social charism of knowledge for instructing mankind in the truths necessary for salvation (*De Veritate,* 12, 2). It involves an illumination of the intellect so that the prophet can transmit the sacred doctrine. Prophecy is therefore an inspiration as well as a revelation. The end product is transmission of knowledge, and on the part of the prophet it does not require anything more than imparting the message.

In the *Dogmatic Constitution on the Church, Lumen Gentium,* the Second Vatican Council declared that all the members of the Church share in the prophetic function of Christ (cf. 123), but the office and function of prophecy belong primarily to bishops (cf. 25). The latter are the principal ministers of the word, and hence they should be in the forefront for preaching and teaching sacred doctrine (cf. Vatican Council II, *Decree on the Bishops' Pastoral Office in the Church, Christus Dominus).*

What precisely can the laity do with the prophetic function? They are first and above all to bear witness by their lives (Eph 6:12). Moreover, in the measure that they have the competence, they are called upon to evangelize by word as well as by deed, as was stated by the Second Vatican Council in the *Decree on the Apostolate of the Laity, Apostolicam Actuositatem*: "The true apostle is on the lookout for occasions announcing Christ by word, either to unbelievers to draw them towards the faith, or to the faithful to instruct them, strengthen them, incite them to a more fervent life" (6).

There have been cases of authentic mystics who have received the charismatic gift of prophecy, enabling them to reveal some sacred truth or give some message for the good of the Church. An example is St. Margaret Mary Alacoque, who was commissioned by God to deliver the message concerning devotion to the Sacred Heart of Jesus. The gift of prophecy as an extraordinary mystical phenomenon is a *gratia gratis data*, and it is classified as a private revelation. As such, it does not belong to the deposit of faith entrusted to the Church.

Therefore, in giving a negative approval to a private revelation, the Church simply declares that there is nothing in the revelation or prophecy that is contrary to Scripture or the teaching of the Church. The content may be considered credible, but not infallibly so. The person who receives the prophecy or private revelation is obliged to act upon it, if it has been judged to be authentic; but no one else is obliged to anything more than a pious belief. Still, it would be reprehensible to ridicule or totally reject a private revelation after the Church had given its negative approbation, as at Lourdes or Fátima. Prior to that, however, one should bear in mind the following rules for discernment: (1) Any prophecy or revelation contrary to the Church's teaching on dogma or morals must be rejected. (2) An authentic prophecy or revelation may contain some detail that is false, due to human error. (3) The local bishop has the responsibility to investigate and make a judgment on any prophecy or revelation. He in turn should be alert to the fruits produced in the individual who received the revelation and in the faithful in general.

See: Apostolate; Catechesis; Charisms; Discernment; Evangelization; Extraordinary Gifts; Mysticism; Private Revelation.

Suggested Readings: CCC 64, 436, 702, 715, 717-719, 785, 875, 888-892, 904-907. K. Rahner, *Visions and Prophecies: Quaestiones Disputatae 10*, trans. C. Henkey and R. Strachan. Y. Congar, *Lay People in the Church*, trans. E. Gallagher. J. Aumann, *Spiritual Theology*. A. Poulain, *The Graces of Interior Prayer*.

Jordan Aumann, O.P.

PROPORTIONALISM

The constant teaching of the Church is that there are certain choices that are always morally bad: for example, to choose intentional killing of innocent people, contraception, adultery, fornication. Proportionalism denies this teaching. Proportionalism is the position that, at least in some cases, one may choose to destroy, damage, or impede a basic good such as innocent human life, marriage, or new human life, for the sake of bringing about the best or least bad proportion of good in relation to bad.

The term "proportionalism" was originated by the American moral theologian Germain Grisez, after theologians dissenting from the Church's position on moral absolutes (specific, exceptionless moral norms) objected to being called consequentialists. The latter, they protested, hold that *only* the consequences of an act are morally significant, and they did not hold that.

Grisez argued that what is distinctive about the view of these theologians, and what makes it mistaken, is the position that one arrives at moral norms by comparing the proportion of good and bad in alternatives for choice and judging that to be obligatory which seems to offer the greater good or lesser evil. Proportionalism focuses the issue on the primary logical difficulty in this position. For it is in principle impossible to reach an objective judgment about the proportion of good to bad in alternatives in any situation where there truly is a free choice to be made, since different sorts of good are always at stake, and there is no rational basis for the calculation proportionalism would require.

See: Absolute Moral Norms; Consequentialism; Deontology; Human Goods; Natural Law; Teleological Ethics; Utilitarianism.

PROSTITUTION

Prostitution is the selling of sexual acts. It represents a grave misuse of the gift of sexuality, which is itself meant to be a gift to another to whom one has pledged lifetime fidelity.

Many of those who engage in prostitution were victims of sexual abuse in their youth or are attempting to earn money to support a drug addiction or to escape poverty. Sometimes children are sold into prostitution by adults, which is clearly a horrendous offense against the innocence of children. Those who make use of prostitutes are often further exploiting the already grievously exploited; all are being unchaste, and some are also betraying their spouses.

Some argue that prostitution is a legitimate enterprise for women who have no marketable skills. Such an argument fails to see that those who engage in prostitution are reduced to being used as instruments and are not loved as human beings who have intrinsic dignity.

See: Sexuality, Human.

PROTESTANTISM

Protestantism got its name by accident. At the Diet of Speyer, Holy Roman Emperor Charles V, joined by the Catholic princes of the territories that would become modern Germany, decreed Lutheran worship restricted to the lands where it already existed. A handful of Lutheran princes and fourteen free cities protested, solidifying the movement the Augustinian priest Martin Luther (1483-1546) had launched twelve years before in 1517. The broad traditions it would generate (Anglican, Anabaptist, Congregationalist, Lutheran, Methodist, Reformed), the intellectual and spiritual impulses it would inspire (pietism, orthodoxy, evangelicalism, fundamentalism, pentecostalism), and the hundreds of denominations and sects into which it would eventually splinter — all, to the general world, are "Protestant."

But the label would never have stuck if it were not appropriate. When Luther posted his famous ninety-five theses at Wittenberg, he was certainly protesting aspects of medieval Catholicism. Many who followed him did so for principled reasons: They thought of themselves as Reformers and called their movement the Reformation. The new ideas spread with remarkable speed, winning millions of adherents across northern and western Europe in a few decades. Nationalist sentiment and the rise of humanism helped nourish this new Protestant sapling, but the Church itself was its seedbed.

Luther was not formally condemned until after the Diet of Worms (1521), where he refused to recant his teachings. Even then, an open break with Rome might have been avoided; the Augsburg Confession of 1530, which codified Lutheran belief, was intended to build bridges. But the fire of reform was burning out of control. The unity of Christianity, first broken when Eastern Orthodoxy separated from Roman Catholicism, was shattered by the Reformation. Only in the twentieth century has the ecumenical movement begun to heal these wounds in the Body of Christ.

Luther's Views of Catholicism • Luther's principal objections to the Catholicism of his day, which have defined Protestantism in most of its expressions, affected both theology and ecclesial structure. The byword of the Reformation was "justification by faith alone" or "justification by grace through faith." Luther taught that no one can win heaven through his own efforts. This is doctrinally unexceptional of course; the difficulty arises from Luther's dismissal of the efficacy of human efforts to cooperate in God's redeeming work, which in turn reflects his view of human nature as radically corrupted by original sin. Only God has the power to justify us, that is, to render us capable of salvation despite bearing the stain of both original and personal sin. God does so through the grace Jesus Christ won by his death on the cross. Christ's merit suffices for us when we turn to him with our whole being and are converted. Then God looks upon us not as the sinners we remain but as disciples of his Divine Son.

But how are we to know God and make the necessary act of faith? In Luther's view, Scripture and Scripture alone provides the link between Creator and fallen humanity. The Bible presents the marvelous story of our salvation in Jesus Christ. When we hear this story and recognize it as applying to ourselves, accepting Jesus as Our Lord and Savior, we enter the circle of the elect. Creeds, Tradition, and the teaching of the Church can help guide us in faith and morality, but the word of God as found in the Bible remains the final authority.

These two doctrines have profound implications for the Church, especially as it existed in the sixteenth century. The immediate cause of Luther's rebellion was the system of indulgences, by which individuals received remission of the punishment due to sin and even, in some cases, pardon from sins themselves. This system was obviously open to abuse, and Church officials did sell indulgences, using the proceeds to enrich themselves, build cathedrals, and even finance public works. Luther's doctrine attacked the assumptions underlying indulgences: namely, that the Church acts on God's behalf on earth, even in matters of divine grace. If the individual can turn to God by an act of simple faith, inspired by reading the Bible under the guidance of the Holy Spirit, the Church's unique role in the plan of salvation is extinguished. Indeed, to rely on the Church's teachings and sacraments is a form of idolatry, putting the human before the divine. One's approach to God must be direct and personal.

As a practical matter, Luther also had to deny papal infallibility and the binding character of most ecumenical councils. Had he admitted that Popes and councils had a teaching authority superior to his own, he would have had to submit to it. Luther extended this denial by asserting another core doctrine of Protestantism, "the priesthood of all believers." All Christians are absolutely equal in matters of worship and service; the distinction between priests and laity has no basis in the will of Christ.

The priesthood of all believers was a powerful spur to the spread of Protestantism. Early leaders convinced secular rulers that they were justified in assuming headship of the Church in their lands and reforming it. Reform typically meant suppressing the Catholic Mass, assigning the powers of the hierarchy to ministers and civil government, reformulating doctrine according to an agreed profession of faith, and abolishing religious orders and priestly celibacy. In this way, whole cities and territories became Protestant overnight, by proclamation.

A fundamental change in sacramental doctrine was Luther's last major act of rebellion. Catholicism had traditionally recognized seven sacraments as means of conferring grace, all ordinarily performed or witnessed by clergy. Lutheranism set the pattern for most Protestant churches by reducing the number to two, arguing that Holy Scripture clearly attests only to Baptism and the Eucharist. Moreover, Reformers agreed in rejecting the doctrine of transubstantiation, which holds that, when a priest speaks the words of consecration in the Mass, the bread and wine become the Body and Blood of Christ. The practical result, along with reliance on the authority of the Bible, was a revolution in worship. Protestant services were conducted in the vernacular, not Latin; they de-emphasized the sacramental sacrifice in favor of preaching the word; they recast the presider as prayer leader rather than priest; and they rejected liturgical ritual in favor of simplicity.

Development of Protestantism • From a Catholic perspective, Protestantism was a profound rejection of the sacramental/hierarchical system transmitted from ancient times. The Reformers denied clergy and Church the power to supply the means of grace, to reconcile people to God by forgiving sin, and to rule in spiritual affairs. Catholicism could not accommodate so fundamental and broad-based an assault upon its faith and practice, and what began as reform inevitably became separation. By 1560, just forty years after Luther's condemnation, much of northern Europe was Protestant, and the Council of Trent was launching the Catholic Counter-Reformation, aimed at reinforcing Catholic identity and both reforming and stabilizing the Church. The lure of self-righteous violence soon sealed the division in blood. Hundreds of thousands perished in the terrible religious wars of the sixteenth and seventeenth centuries defending the holy cause, whether Protestant or Catholic. It has been suggested that the rise of modern atheism can be traced in large part to revulsion against the horrors to which the internal conflicts of Christianity gave rise.

This sketch of the Reformation's roots makes a complex story deceptively simple; for example, the Anglican Church and certain Lutheran denominations, far from renouncing hierarchy, kept the office of bishop. The subsequent history of Protestantism is also hugely complex, and we can do no more here than highlight some major chapters in its development.

The Reformation began to splinter almost immediately. Independently of Luther, Ulrich Zwingli (1484-1531) spread reform in Switzerland in the 1520s. After his death in battle against Catholics in 1531, Zwingli's followers preached an extreme version of Protestantism, reducing the Eucharist to a simple memorial of Christ's death, setting up a theocracy in the city of Zurich, and falling out with the Lutherans. Zwingli's circle was the fountainhead from which the radical stream of the Reformation was to flow, generating such dissimilar ecclesial communities as the Baptists, Quakers, and Mennonites. To a greater or lesser degree, these groups tried to re-create the early Church, stressing membership based on personal choice rather than infant Baptism, simplicity in worship and style of life, and withdrawal from the world. The best-known American representatives of this tradition in its purest form are the Amish.

Into the theological and ecclesiological gap between Lutheranism and Zwinglianism stepped John Calvin (1509-1564), a Frenchman forced into exile in Switzerland. His *Institutes of the Chris-*

tian Religion, first published in 1536, was enormously influential as a clear and comprehensive synthesis of reformed doctrine. Calvin took justification by faith to its harsh but logical conclusion: If God alone can save and God knows all things, he must knowingly create some people to be saved and others to be damned. This is the famed Calvinist doctrine of predestination. Calvin merged Church and State in Geneva, where he held sway for twenty years, preaching that the saved can be identified by three signs: profession of faith, a strictly moral life, and a love of the sacraments. By 1550 Calvinism was the strongest form of Protestantism, having spread to France (where the Protestants were known as Huguenots), parts of Germany, and the Netherlands. John Knox (c. 1513-1572) brought a Calvinist faith to Scotland, founding the Reformed, or Presbyterian, Church.

The Reformation crossed the English Channel by another route as well. In 1534, Henry VIII, angered by the Pope's refusal to grant an annulment of his first marriage, rejected Rome and declared himself supreme head of the Church of England (i.e., the Anglican Church). After his death, Queen Mary briefly restored Catholicism, but Anglicanism was made the state religion under Elizabeth I, who reigned from 1558 to 1603. Doctrine was codified in the Thirty-Nine Articles, and worship was regulated by the *Book of Common Prayer*.

Internal strife proved to be as much a mark of English as of European Protestantism. Protestant-Catholic fighting in the sixteenth century gave way to disputes between Anglicans and Puritans in the seventeenth, as the latter tried to carry reform further than the established church wished. The Puritans were Calvinist in theology, minimalist in liturgy, and congregationalist in church organization. Their opposition to the Church of England, which had retained many of the forms of its Catholic past (a hierarchy, a common creed, a fixed and elaborated liturgy), culminated in the English Civil War, which brought Oliver Cromwell's short-lived Puritan Commonwealth to power in 1649. After restoring the monarchy, and then ensuring that it would remain in Protestant hands through the "Glorious Revolution," Englishmen settled into a grudging toleration of differing views, as long as they were not Catholic views.

In Germany, the seventeenth century saw the rise of pietism within the Lutheran Church under the inspiration of theologians like Johann Arndt and Philip Spener. Pietism, an approach to religion rather than a separate creed, quickly won adherents across the Protestant world. Reacting against intellectualism and formalism, it stressed personal piety, "heart-religion" that inspired the believer to repent, be born again, and put on new life in Christ. Pietist divines encouraged all Christians to read and study the Bible, to serve their neighbors in love, and to cultivate a lively spirituality. The movement has had a profound impact on the subsequent development of Protestantism and, arguably, on Catholicism after the Second Vatican Council.

It was at a service of the pietest Moravian Brethren in 1738 that John Wesley (1703-1791) had the conversion experience that ultimately led to the founding of the Methodist Church. The Age of Enlightenment, with its naïve belief in the power of reason to resolve all problems, posed a severe challenge to traditional religion. Deists responded by jettisoning everything in their faith that smacked of miracle or mystery. Within the Protestant world, Methodists and other evangelical Christians resisted this rationalist tide and eventually found more comfortable cultural waters with the rise of Romanticism at century's end.

The evangelicals' moral earnestness, echoing that of the Puritan settlers of New England, is one of the principal features of American Protestantism. In the colonies, prominent divines like George Whitefield (1714-1770) and Jonathan Edwards (1703-1758) preached the need for an emotional conversion and experience of salvation. Their appeal fell on fertile ground in isolated, hardscrabble frontier towns and squalid cities, triggering a series of revival movements in the mid-1700s known collectively as the Great Awakening. The evangelical impetus, which left the Baptist and Methodist communions dominant in the southern United States, has never flagged, though it has become considerably more sophisticated. The Reverend Billy Graham, perhaps the best-known American Protestant of the late twentieth century, stands in the line of revivalist preachers.

Protestantism in Modern Times • Despite its vitality, evangelicalism was not the only driving force as Protestantism entered the nineteenth century. On both sides of the Atlantic, a liberalism that tended more to accommodate the modern world than to correct it gained ground. The movement resulted most prominently in scholarship treating the Bible as a work of literature rather than an inspired book ("historical" or "higher" criticism), and in a relaxed attitude toward doctrinal differences (visible, for example, in Unitarianism). The major Protestant denominations all became worldwide bodies through missionary efforts in Europe's colonies. Finally, some Protestant thinkers began emphasizing the "social gospel," applying Christ's words on justice and love to the conditions spawned by the rise of industrialism.

The founders of the Reformation would be astounded by the variety characterizing Protestantism today. In the United States alone, the range of those who call themselves Protestants includes pentecostalists whose religion is emotional and charismatic, liberals unconcerned with doctrine, fundamentalists intent on defending biblical inerrancy, according to their understanding, and "high" Lutherans and Episcopalians loyal to traditional confessions of faith. Ecclesial structure runs the gamut from independent crossroads churches to parish systems under a well-structured hierarchy. Liturgy, sometimes even within the same denomination, can be elaborate or simple; it can strictly stress preaching or give greater prominence to the communion rite. Finally, modern Protestant theology displays a tendency to branch along ideological and cultural lines, giving birth to feminist or liberation or African-American or "story" theology. An observer might be forgiven for believing that some Protestant groups stand further from one another than they do from the Catholicism they all reject.

Although fracture and dissent continue to mark modern Protestantism, another tendency also is visible. The ecumenical movement among Protestants began with the World Missionary Conference in 1910 and led to the founding of the World Council of Churches in 1948. Certain divisions among communions of similar heritage have been healed in the past few decades: Most Congregational groups came together in the United Church of Christ, a series of mergers produced the United Methodist Church, and most recently three Lutheran bodies formed the Evangelical Lutheran Church in America.

The ecumenical impulse is forging ties with the non-Protestant world as well. After the Second Vatican Council's *Decree on Ecumenism* declared restoring unity among all Christians to be one of the Council's "principal concerns" (*Unitatis Redintegratio,* 1), the Catholic Church and many mainstream Protestant churches began a cautious, respectful rapprochement. Definite progress has been made in theological dialogue, in shared work for social justice, and in common prayer, given public prominence through the annual Week of Prayer for Christian Unity.

As the second millennium began, the Great Schism of 1054 separating East from West destroyed Christianity's corporate unity. Midway through the millennium, the Reformation further divided the Western Church, and the shock of that earthquake is still opening new faults. Does the ecumenical movement offer hope that the third millennium will reverse the sad religious history of the second so that "they may all be one" as Jesus prayed (Jn 17:21)? In 1995, Pope John Paul II issued an encyclical whose title, *Ut Unum Sint*, repeats this prayer. God having entrusted the fullness of the means of salvation to the Catholic Church, John Paul says that "the division among Christians is a serious reality which impedes the very work of Christ" (98).

See: Anglicanism; Augustinianism; Church, Membership in; Church, Nature, Origin, and Structure of; Divine Revelation; Ecumenism; Eucharist; Faith, Act of; Grace; Holy Orders; Indulgences; Justification; Magisterium; Original Sin;

Orthodox Churches; Priesthood of the Faithful; Real Presence; Redemption; Sacrament; Sacred Tradition.

Suggested Readings: CCC 813-822. Vatican Council II, *Decree on Ecumenism, Unitatis Redintegratio.* John Paul II, *That All May Be One, Ut Unum Sint.* H. Smith, "Christianity," in *The Religions of Man.*

David M. Byers

PROVIDENCE

Divine providence is the plan God has in mind for accomplishing the ultimate goal of his activity in creating purely spiritual persons (angels) and a physical universe with embodied persons in it. The fundamental pcint is that, in creation, God is acting in an intelligent and purposeful manner. Since God was not forced to create anything, but did so freely and with an ultimate purpose in view, he must have a plan to accomplish this purpose. Divine providence is the name that Catholic teaching has given to this plan.

Scripture is replete with references to God's providence even when the term itself does not appear. God's loving concern, his free creation, his intelligent ordering of the universe, his immediate engagement and encompassing power, his subjection of evil forces — these are strands that run through the entire fabric of biblical Revelation. The witness of the Fathers of the Church, especially St. Augustine (354-430) in the West and St. John Damascene (c. 675-c. 749) in the East, has been crucial to the emergence of the developed doctrine of divine providence in Catholic tradition. In Western theology, the classical statement of the doctrine is to be found in the writings of St. Thomas Aquinas (c. 1225-1274).

Especially important to the formal development of the doctrine have been religious and philosophical ideas that run directly counter to the biblical and patristic testimony: chiefly, fatalism and determinism in late antiquity; Manichaeism and its offshoots in the fourth, fifth, and later centuries; deism in the eighteenth century; and materialism, naturalism, and nihilism in the nineteenth and twentieth centuries. In varying degrees, these positions either deny the reality of providence outright or drastically attenuate its scope. The most complete magisterial correction of these positions is to be found in the documents of Vatican Council I (1869-1870), especially in the *Dogmatic Constitution on the Catholic Faith, Dei Filius*.

The Doctrine of Providence • If we consider ordinary human activities, we can begin to grasp what Catholic faith in divine providence involves. From the simplest to the most complex, our activities usually have some ends in view. An athlete who sets for himself the goal of running a marathon race will surely need a training and dietary regimen in order to realize his goal; an architect who receives a commission to build a skyscraper will not get very far without a detailed design. The successful outcome of these and countless other activities requires the development of realistic plans. But, in themselves, plans are not enough. A training regimen does not make a marathoner: He has to implement the plan through daily practice runs, disciplined eating habits, and so on. What is more, we often need the cooperation of other persons to achieve our goals: No matter how detailed her plan, the architect cannot construct a building on her own. In addition, sometimes things happen that interfere even with our best-laid plans. A bout of flu or a sprained ankle would be considerable setbacks for any potential marathoner, no matter how highly motivated and disciplined he might be.

In the first place, then, the Catholic doctrine about divine providence affirms that God has a purpose in view in creating things visible and invisible, and, moreover, that he has not left us completely in the dark as to the nature of this purpose. Because God has revealed his purposes, Christians believe we have an answer to such haunting questions as "What is the meaning of life?" and "Why is there something rather than nothing?" Everything that exists, we confess, exists for God's glory. In contrast to the many creaturely examples we could give, God's activity can have no other object than himself. Unlike human beings, God cannot improve by setting goals for himself or attaining ends other than himself. God's glory *is* God's purpose.

But — and here lies a deep mystery — God has revealed to us through his only Son that his glory is the endless bliss of Trinitarian communion and, furthermore, that he wants to share this communion with created persons — the angels and us. The uncreated Persons of the Blessed Trinity — Father, Son, and Holy Spirit — want to have the company of created persons in eternal glory. The world was created for this, for "the love that never ends" (*Roman Catechism*, Preface, 10). It is the deepest conviction of the Christian faith that everything God does has this overarching purpose in view. This fundamental conviction furnishes the starting point for all reflection on the doctrine of divine providence.

If God has a purpose in view for the universe, then he must have a plan. Divine providence refers, in the first place, to this plan as it exists in God himself. Aquinas supplied the classic statement of this truth when he stated in his *Summa Theologiae* (I, 22.1) that providence is "the plan, pre-existing in the divine mind, that orders things to their end" (*ratio ordinis rerum in finem in mente divina praeexistens*). To say the plan is in God does not mean that anything in God needs planning: As we saw, God in himself is the ultimate goal. Rather, providence refers to the eternal plan for the universe that God has in mind.

While providence has also been commonly understood to refer to the implementation of the divine plan in time, theologians have, for the sake of precision, given the name "divine governance" to the temporal execution of God's plan. Catholic theologians have commonly discerned two distinct moments in this divine providential governance of the universe: God's preservation of all things in being (*conservatio*) and God's concurrence with all things in activity (*concursus*).

Divine Causality • Our reflection on ordinary human activities prepares us to expect that the doctrine of divine providence will involve both a plan *and* its implementation. But we can also see that something very much more radical is involved when the causality we have in view is God's. The implementation of the divine plan requires God's constant and immediate involvement in the very existence and activity of everything in the created order. To put the matter bluntly, if God stopped paying attention to the world and to us, everything and everyone would simply cease to function and, indeed, to exist. This is what it means to say that God is a transcendent universal cause: Nothing escapes or falls outside the scope of God's purpose and his providence.

Here, the contrast between the divine agency and ordinary human agents must be maintained with utter clarity in order to avoid the mistakes of thinking either that God's causality is on a par with our own, or that it competes with our causality, or that it renders our own actions and purposes meaningless, or that there are no real causes operating in the universe. Precisely as transcendent universal cause of the being and activity of creatures, God's providential governance of the universe makes our free activity possible. It is not that we do our part and God does his: We would not have a part and we would not be able to play the part we have without God's intense and permanent engagement with us all the time. God's causality embraces and empowers the diverse sorts of causality in the universe by making it possible for each created agent to act according to its nature: determined, physical agents acting necessarily according to preestablished patterns, and intelligent, deliberative human and angelic agents acting freely. Here we should note the beauty and complexity of divine providence. In his goodness, God shares the dignity of being a real cause with creaturely agents.

It follows that God is not in competition with human freedom; he is the cause of it. How could it be otherwise? If the purpose of God's plan is to share the communion of Trinitarian life with creaturely persons, then his providence must encompass the real possibility that they can embrace this communion precisely as persons. It would run counter to the divine purpose for creaturely persons to be compelled to accept the invitation of divine communion. Divine providence creates the possibility and the conditions for realizing the di-

vine purpose, that is, for human beings on their pilgrim's way (*in statu viae*) to come to a share in the love that never ends.

Predestination refers to that element in the eternal plan of divine providence that concerns our movement toward this goal of communion. "For those whom he foreknew he also predestined to be conformed to the image of his Son, in order that he might be the firstborn among many brethren. And those whom he predestined he also called; and those whom he called he also justified; and those whom he justified he also glorified" (Rom 8:29-30). According to Catholic doctrine, God freely resolves from all eternity to call certain persons to beatitude and therefore to endow them with the grace necessary for salvation. While it may be true that some are chosen and some are not, that is not the point of the doctrine of predestination. Rather, its point is that the bliss of Trinitarian communion can be enjoyed only by those (which could mean all or many, rather than a few) whom God predestines. There is no creaturely enjoyment of bliss without the eternal divine decree ordaining it.

On the other hand, according to Catholic doctrine, reprobation is a nonelection to eternal bliss, according to which God declines to prevent (as will be explained further below) the moral failures or unrepentant guilt of certain persons. At the Councils of Orange and Trent, the Church has condemned the teaching, sometimes called "double predestination," that reprobation is a positive predetermination to sin and an unconditional predestination to damnation. The point of the element of reprobation in the doctrine of predestination is to embrace the possibility of an actual failure on the part of some creaturely persons to attain the eternal bliss that, as the purpose of God's plan in creating the universe, is the divinely willed end for all creaturely persons.

This line of reflection leads to a difficult question. Despite the most carefully conceived and faithfully executed training regimen, a bad injury can ruin an athlete's chance of successfully competing in a marathon race. Can God's providence be similarly thwarted? A moment's reflection shows that the answer must be no. Since God is the first cause of everything that exists, nothing can escape his providence and nothing can thwart it. This does not mean that nothing ever goes wrong in the universe. But it does mean that even things' and persons' going wrong can be embraced by divine providence. How can this be?

The Problem of Evil • What we are really asking here is: How can the existence of evil be reconciled with the divine plan in its conception and execution? A long tradition of Catholic doctrine and theology helps us to make some headway with this vexing question by introducing some important distinctions.

In the first place, Catholic theologians have insisted that, although evil is real enough, it is not something in itself. Following St. Augustine — who, in his struggle with Manichaeism, established the framework for Catholic reflection on this issue — we must say that, strictly speaking, evil is the lack of a quality or state that should exist in a particular entity or situation. In order to make this point and at the same time to insist that evil is not just any sort of negation, Catholic theologians customarily describe evil as a privation, the lack of something that should be present. Thus, blindness is an evil for an oriole but not for a baseball. Similarly, for human beings it is not an evil but a natural limitation that they cannot fly through the air at will, though it is an evil when they behave badly by failing to seek the genuinely good. For this reason, the Church has insisted that there is no such thing as pure or personified evil, not even in the fallen angels. God permits to these beings a certain scope of activity within his providential governance of the universe, but their devilry can never overcome or thwart his purposes.

A further distinction brings us closer to the field of our own experience of evil. With respect to evil as it affects us, theologians have commonly distinguished between bad things that happen to us (physical evils) and bad things that we do (moral evils). There are many forms of physical evils that we endure as inhabitants of a sometimes unpredictable cosmos: earthquakes, hurricanes, epidemics, and the like. Despite their destructive potential, these events are often simply the result of the interaction of natural forces. Moral evils, on the other hand, are the result of bad choices and actions on the part of free agents (the angels and us). They are of two kinds: bad deeds and habits (*malum culpae,* or guilt), and the suffering and pain incurred by these (*malum poenae,* or punishment).

With these distinctions in place, we are in a better position to respond to the question about the place of evil with respect to the divine plan and governance of the universe. Catholic theology has insisted that, since he is perfectly good, God cannot be the direct cause of any evil. It is true that he permits physical evils that occur as a matter of course in the universe. As Aquinas points out in the *Summa Theologiae,* "defects and death are against the natures of particular things but part of the universal plan of nature" (I, 22.2). It follows that God's permission of physical evils could never undermine the total perfection of the universe. In this sense, they do not fall outside of his providence. But what about moral evils?

Sin seems to contradict God's goodness even more blatantly than the worst physical evil. For this reason, Catholic theologians say that God sometimes declines to prevent bad deeds (*malum culpae*), but that he permits the purification of repentant sinners and the punishment of the incorrigibly wicked (*malum poenae*). When we affirm that neither of these sorts of moral evil can thwart the overall plan of divine providence, we must recall that, within this plan, God permitted the Passion and death of his only Son as his definitive resolution of the harm of sin and punishment in the world. Christ's death and Resurrection make the forgiveness of sin possible, and give meaning to the redemptive suffering that we experience as purification.

It was with the paschal mystery in view that St. Augustine argued — and Aquinas followed him in this — that all physical evils are de facto experienced by us as *malum poenae* (or punishment) and purification. In the world of sin and redemption after the cross and Resurrection, there are no morally neutral evils. Augustine's point here is often misunderstood as a kind of gloomy pessimism. In fact, it has considerable existential force when one considers the horrendous human suffering associated with many physical evils. In the wisdom of God's providence, every one of us — sinner and justified alike — lives in a spiritual environment defined by the paschal mystery. In this perspective, the sufferings we experience because of physical evils have a clear moral and redemptive value, not in themselves, but because of our union with Christ crucified. Moreover, no evils can crush us because Christ has definitively overcome them all. In the end, it is only in the perspective of Christ that we can see the truth that no evil can thwart the divine purpose and plan.

The doctrine of divine providence should stir and confirm in every Christian heart a deep and unshakable confidence in God. Our hope that the history of this yet unfinished and still unfolding plan will have a happy final chapter rests, not on wishful thinking, but on the immutable promises of the triune God.

See: Angels; Creation; Divine Revelation; Economy of Salvation; Evil, Problem of; Freedom, Human; God, Nature and Attributes of; Human Race, Creation and Destiny of; Justification; Manichaeism; Omnipotence; Omniscience; Process Theology; Redemption; Suffering in Christian Life; Trinity.

Suggested Readings: CCC 302-314. Vatican Council I, *Dogmatic Constitution on the Catholic Faith, Dei Filius.* St. Thomas Aquinas, *Summa Theologiae,* I, 22; 103-119. M. Farrelly, *Predestination, Grace and Free Will.* R. Garrigou-Lagrange, O.P., *Providence.* C. Lewis, *The Problem of Pain.*

J.A. DiNoia, O.P.

PURGATORY

It has ever been the teaching of the Catholic Church, evidence for which is scattered across the centuries of her experience, that purgatory exists and that it is appropriate it should. Purgatory is the place or condition wherein the souls of the just undergo that purifying fire that renders them fit for God and the joys of eternal life.

The doctrine of purgatory finds support in the Scriptures. There are both Old and New Testament references (cf. especially 2 Mc 12:39-45, 1 Cor 3:15, and 1 Pt 1:7). The *Catechism of the Catholic Church* (1031) quotes St. Gregory the Great, Pope from 590 to 604: "As for certain lesser faults, we must believe that, before the Final Judgment, there is a purifying fire. He who is truth says that whoever utters blasphemy against the Holy Spirit will be pardoned neither in this age nor in the age to come. From this sentence we understand that certain offenses can be forgiven in this age, but certain others in the age to come." The Church's belief also is manifest in the constant and universal practice of prayer and penance that the faithful have always offered up for the dead. In addition, the doctrine was given definitive ecclesial expression at the First Council of Lyons (1245), the Second Council of Lyons (1274), and the Council of Florence (1438-1445).

Later, the Council of Trent (1545-1563) addressed the Protestant errors of Luther, Calvin, and Zwingli, including their disavowal of the existence of purgatory. Indeed, they disavowed the whole intercessory enterprise on behalf of the dead, including the Sacrifice of the Mass, whose propiatory nature they denied. Against this background the Church once again, in summary form, recast her ancient understanding of the reality and importance of purgatory.

The Doctrine of Purgatory • What, then, is the content of Catholic belief concerning the condition of the "poor souls," that is, those detained for a time in a state of purgation — "aided by the suffrages of the faithful," to cite Trent, "and chiefly by the acceptable sacrifice of the altar" — yet destined eventually for everlasting life with God? To begin with, this is a teaching rooted in the twofold recognition of divine justice and mercy.

On the one hand, the order of justice requires reparation on the part of all who violate it. And if reparation is not made before death, then surely it must be made after, in the refining fire that burns away the accumulated dross of sin, whether unrepented venial sin and/or the temporal punishment due to mortal sin repented of and forgiven. If God be perfect justice, then to stand before him without shame we must exist in a certain relation to justice. Failing that, suffering proportionate to the penalty of sin is necessary to bring us to that condition. Some law of expiation must accordingly be found and applied. Hence the praise of 2 Maccabees for the Jewish military leader Judas Maccabee, who "made atonement for the dead, that they might be delivered from their sin" (2 Mc 12:45).

We are dealing here, says Romano Guardini, not with souls immutably fixed at the hour of their death in a state of either unambiguous evil or perfection, but rather with those "whose intention has not penetrated sufficiently below the surface to reach the settled resistance beneath and the depths filled with evil and impurity . . . whose whole life is riddled with omissions and bears in itself the ravages of wrongdoing."

Thus the underlying Christian view of purgatory clearly emerges. It is not, as Joseph Ratzinger reminds us, "some kind of supra-worldly concentration camp where man is forced to undergo punishment." That would be arbitrary and unworthy of God. "Rather is it the inwardly necessary process of transformation in which a person becomes capable of Christ, capable of God and thus capable of unity with the whole communion of saints."

The doctrine of purgatory is therefore grounded in great wisdom and consolation. "It emphasizes the sanctity and majesty of God," says Father Reginald Garrigou-Lagrange, "since nothing soiled can appear before him. It fortifies our sense of justice. It manifests the disorder, often unperceived, of venial faults." In fact, he suggests, a lively faith in purgatory carries with it salutary purgation here on earth.

The Mercy of God • On the other hand, the doctrine of purgatory is equally anchored to the recognition of divine mercy. Justice, in other words, will be tempered by the mercy whose mediation reaches the sinner even in his sin. Purga-

tory is simply another name for that mercy. And while we are saved by the fullness of the faith to which our lives give assent, the burden of sin, beneath which so many of us nevertheless labor, forces us to acknowledge a heap of "wood, hay, stubble" — St. Paul's image in his Letter to the Corinthians (1 Cor 3:12). Observes Ratzinger: "Man is the recipient of the divine mercy, yet this does not exonerate him from the need to be transformed. Encounter with the Lord *is* this transformation. . . . Purgatory follows by an inner necessity from the idea of penance, the idea of the constant readiness for reform which marks the forgiven sinner."

In what does the pain of purgatory consist? Is it purely spiritual — or might there not be sensible suffering as well, redolent of the fire that Paul describes, when Christ, assessing the worth of each man on the fearful Day of the Lord, will bring everything to light: "Because it will be revealed with fire, and the fire will test what sort of work each one has done. . . . If any man's work is burned up, he will suffer loss, though he himself will be saved, but only as through fire" (1 Cor 3:13, 15)? Surely the ordeal by fire refers to Christ himself and to his coming precisely as purifying presence.

And the chief pain of souls consigned to purgatorial fire? Is it not simply the delay of that beatific vision for which man was first created?

The sufferings of those in purgatory therefore are actually greater than any we can imagine in this life. Notwithstanding, the soul remains immeasurably compensated in prospect of that hope of heaven whose joys infallibly await. "Souls in Purgatory unite great joy with great suffering. One does not diminish the other," reports St. Catherine of Genoa, who endured such pains while on earth. "No peace is comparable to that of the souls in Purgatory, except that of the saints in Heaven. On the other hand, the souls in Purgatory endure torments which no tongue can describe and no intelligence comprehend, without special revelation" (*Treatise on Purgatory*).

See: Communion of Saints; Heaven; Hell; Indulgences; Last Things; Limbo; Prayer of Petition.

Suggested Readings: CCC 1030-1032. R. Guardini, *The Last Things.* R. Garrigou-Lagrange, O.P., *Everlasting Life.* J. Ratzinger, *Eschatology.*

Regis Martin

PURITY

Yesterday's endless classifications of pure and impure desires and actions, with their twin dangers of scrupulosity and legalism, have been, mostly happily, consigned to the past. But the need for a sound theology, to which Pope John Paul II has notably contributed, and for personal training and counseling regarding virtue in general and chastity in particular (a kind of formation admittedly difficult to find, especially by laypeople) is perhaps more pressing today, as a consequence of pervasive sexual shamelessness and exploitation, and rampant commercialization of sex.

Moreover, given today's widespread resistance to institutional, authoritative religion, especially when it impinges on certain lifestyles, perhaps an even greater need now is for soundly reasoned arguments in support of chastity and modesty. It is necessary to see that unchasteness runs counter to truly enlightened self-interest and that satisfaction of the human appetite for happiness ultimately demands whatever curbs are required on the sexual instinct in order to convert it into an apt vehicle for incarnating genuine, loving self-giving.

The *Catechism of the Catholic Church* goes a long way in recasting chastity as a "joyful affirmation" instead of a seemingly endless list of joyless prohibitions (cf. 2517-2527). The Catholic Church has come to see chastity as one of the best ways for believers to capacitate themselves for love. If, indeed, love is the wholly free gift of self, chastity should be viewed as the liberating and virtuous effort to reclaim oneself from unthinking, compulsive, and happiness-depriving behaviors, acknowledgment of which is the first step in becoming a self-owning person. "Purity of heart brings freedom from widespread eroticism and avoids entertainment inclined to voyeurism and illusion" (CCC 2525). Purity "enables us to see *according to* God" (CCC 2519).

How to be chaste? There are many traditional ways, both natural and supernatural. Among the former are curbing the eyes, memory, and imagination; working hard and well, even to the point of fatigue; cultivating ambitious, absorbing interests and ideals, plus the means thereto; responsible and full use of time; crowding out both daydreaming and self-pity; discharging the duties and debts of sound friendships; courageously fleeing from the first signs of temptation and occasions of sin; exerting oneself to give good example and exercising apostolic leadership; committing oneself to live the cardinal virtues; avoiding stimulants, erotic or even suggestive reading, TV, or movies, plus sexually or emotionally arousing situations or experiences in general; modesty and decency, especially in dress and grooming; self-discipline in food, drink, rest, and sleep; little practices of self-denial whereby men and women wean themselves from semiautomatic indulgence in pleasures and pain-avoiding reactions.

These human means need to be supplemented and reinforced by abundant supernatural help. In the general state of sin-weakened nature, complete chastity is all but impossible for the average person without humbly seeking God's grace. Frequent and medicinal (devotional) use of the sacrament of Penance, with the greatest possible and detailed truthfulness and an effective and concrete purpose of amendment, cannot be recommended too highly. Devout and conscientious attendance at Mass, with its tender, healing embrace of the Divine Physician in the Eucharist, should be a frequent, even daily, practice. Also indispensable is a life of prayer: eking out at least fifteen daily minutes to commune quietly and recollectedly with Jesus and Mary, his Mother and ours; also, contemplatively reciting the Rosary.

A person who earnestly seeks to fall madly in love with God, as we are bid in the chief of all commandments and by Christ's own beckoning, incarnate sojourn among humanity, will find therein all the bliss that can be had here on earth, and all that is necessary to quiet otherwise wanton bodily drives and appetites.

See: Capital Sins; Cardinal Virtues; Chastity;

Concupiscence; Education in Human Sexuality; Human Virtues; Lust; Modesty; Occasions of Sin; Sexuality, Human.

Suggested Readings: CCC 2514-2527. Paul VI, *On Human Life, Humanae Vitae.* John Paul II, *The Christian Family in the Modern World, Familiaris Consortio; Letter to Families.* Pontifical Council for the Family, *The Truth and Meaning of Human Sexuality.* G. Grisez, *The Way of the Lord Jesus,* Vol. 2, *Living a Christian Life,* pp. 633-680.

Q

QUIETISM

In general, Quietism is a spiritual teaching that exaggerates the passivity of the soul in its relationship with God and, as a consequence, rejects as unnecessary or even harmful any activity on the part of the individual in the higher stages of the spiritual life. Specifically, Quietism is the heterodox spiritual doctrine that was propagated chiefly by Michael Molinos (died 1696) and made great inroads in Spain, Italy, and France in the seventeenth century. It was condemned by Pope Innocent XI with the promulgation of the constitution *Coelestis Pastor* in 1687.

The exaggerated state of passivity, which is the predominant characteristic of Quietism, has always been the heresy that threatens mysticism and contemplative prayer. As early as the fifth century, the Messalians in Asia Minor promoted the practice of continual prayer in a state of total spiritual indifference and passivity. In the thirteenth century, the monks of Mount Athos were given the name "hesychasts," which means quietists, because they were thought to be infected with that same disease. Meanwhile, in the West, the revival of the theology of the Pseudo-Dionysius (unknown author of four influential treatises of the early sixth century) in the works of Meister Eckhart (died 1327) and of the unknown author of *The Cloud of Unknowing* served to focus attention on mystical questions, and especially on the prayer of quiet and the state of total abandonment to God. John Ruysbroeck (died 1381), one of the greatest masters of true mystical quietude, vigorously denounced the exaggerations of some of the promoters of mystical quietude.

The origins of the Quietism that was condemned by Pope Innocent XI in 1687 are complicated and uncertain. The Alumbrados appeared in southern Spain in 1575 and were condemned by the Inquisition in 1623. Their teaching called for the abandonment of the practice of vocal prayer in favor of mental prayer, in which all mental concepts, including meditation on the sacred humanity of Christ, had to be rejected. They likewise taught that when a soul reaches the state of perfection, it is exempted from the practice of the virtues, in favor of the state of mystical quietude.

A more immediate influence on the Quietism of the seventeenth century is found in the writing and teaching of John Falconi (died 1638) of Spain, Francis Malaval (died 1719) of France, and the Spaniard Molinos, who was the most energetic and influential propagator of Quietism in Italy. It is interesting to note, however, that there is no heretical teaching in the chief work by Molinos, *Guía Espiritual* (*A Spiritual Guide*, published in 1675), which went through twenty editions in six years. The condemnation of Molinos was issued in 1687, after a two-year investigation of his letters, conferences, and spiritual direction. Actually, the heresy of Quietism was not dealt a death blow until 1699, and then only after Pope Innocent XII had settled the controversy between Jacques Bossuet and François Fénelon in France over what has been called "semiquietism."

Quietist Teaching • In the seventeenth century, there was a great deal of enthusiasm for the practice of mental prayer, and especially the more passive types of prayer such as those referred to as the prayer of simple regard and the prayer of quiet. It became quite fashionable, especially in France, to become a member of a prayer group, to have a spiritual director, and to discuss mystical questions at great length. Contemplative prayer was promoted as something within the reach of all, and the Quietists used the terminology of St. Teresa of Ávila to expound their doctrine.

The mystical teaching of the Quietists drew a vehement reaction from the Jesuits, who considered methodical meditation to be the normal type of mental prayer, while mystical contemplative prayer was classified as an extraordinary gift given to a chosen few. In this they were opposed by the Carmelites, Dominicans, and Oratorians, who taught that mystical experience and contemplative prayer are the logical result of growth in grace and charity.

The Quietists in turn accused the Jesuits of being enemies of the mystical life and incapable of understanding the higher states of prayer. And when the Jesuits Bell'huomo and Segneri severely criticized the teaching of Molinos in his *Guía Espiritual*, their own books were placed on the Index. The condemnation of the teaching of Molinos in *Coelestis Pastor* by Pope Innocent XI does not even mention the *Guía Espiritual*, because the condemned statements were drawn from other sources.

The Quietists, therefore, were not condemned for their teaching on mystical contemplative prayer as a gift within the normal development of the life of grace and charity. That had always been the traditional teaching of Catholic theology. The error of the Quietists lay elsewhere, namely, in exaggerating the passivity and receptivity of the mystical experience to such an extent that the mystical silence and quiet becomes what Ruysbroeck called a "false idleness" in which the individual forgets self and God and every kind of activity. This is a direct denial of the obligation to cooperate with God's grace, and it places the soul in a psychological and spiritual vacuum.

Once the foregoing principle is accepted and carried to its logical conclusions, its error becomes evident. This is precisely what happened when Quietism took root in France and was propagated by Madame Guyon (died 1717) and her spiritual director Father Lacombe (died 1715). Now the catchwords are "disinterested love" and "passive prayer." The disregard of self and the abandonment to God must be so complete that one no longer performs any act of virtue, no longer recites vocal prayers, no longer forms the concepts needed for meditation, no longer makes an examination of conscience.

Madame Guyon went so far as to write in her book *Les Torrents Spirituels*: "If one whose will is lost and, as it were, swallowed up and transformed in God were reduced by necessity to doing sinful deeds, he would do them without sinning." Even a temptation to sin must be tolerated and not resisted; nor should one have any desire for salvation and eternal happiness. Once an individual reaches the higher levels of mystical life and passive contemplation, there is no longer any need to be preoccupied with Jesus Christ; that would be a distraction from one's total absorption in God.

Evelyn Underhill, in her well-known study *Mysticism*, has given a very balanced statement concerning the state of quiet and passivity: "The true condition of quiet, according to the great mystics, is at once active and passive: it is pure surrender, but a surrender which is not limp self-abandonment, but rather the free and constantly renewed self-giving and self-emptying of a burning love."

See: Contemplation; Meditation; Mysticism; Prayer; Vocal Prayer.

Suggested Readings: CCC 2709-2719. P. Pourrat, *Christian Spirituality*, Vol. 4, pp. 101-260. R. Knox, *Enthusiasm.* J. Dupré and D. Saliers, *Christian Spirituality: Post-Reformation and Modern,* pp. 121-142. J. Aumann, *Christian Spirituality in the Catholic Tradition*, pp. 232-240.

Jordan Aumann, O.P.

R

RACISM

The term "racism" covers a variety of attitudes that discriminate against people on the basis of real or imagined physical characteristics. It presumes that the human race is easily categorizable into racial types and that those types regularly display differences in intelligence or behavior. In the modern world, racism has often led to unequal treatment of people who are citizens of the same country. Segregation in the United States and apartheid in South Africa were two such cases. As such, racism is unjust, offends deeply against the equality of all people before God, and is "contrary to God's intent" (Vatican Council II, *Pastoral Constitution on the Church in the Modern World, Gaudium et Spes*, 29).

It is important, however, to distinguish between the kind of in-group and out-group feeling that anthropologists and sociologists have found to be a feature of all human communities, and racism proper. Most human beings tend to associate with people they see as similar to themselves, whether the similarity stems from social position, religion, ethnic background, or custom. In some circumstances, people also see racial differences as constituting groups. In itself, this is not necessarily sinful or wrong. But racial self-grouping, like other forms of grouping, runs the risk of regarding those outside the group as not just different or alien, but as morally or socially inferior. When that judgment unjustly results in harmful discrimination toward individuals or whole groups on the basis of assumed racial inequalities, it becomes a serious evil.

History of Racism • Racism seems to have been largely a modern development. In the ancient world, people noticed differences in physical characteristics and tended to regard their own ways as superior to those of others. But that judgment was not based on race. A good deal of group chauvinism also marks tribal societies and some larger nations, wherein even terms in the language tend to designate the in-group as superior to the out-group. Some social systems, such as the caste system in India, assigned people unjust and unequal roles. But these were not racial categories, since people of different "racial" characteristics were to be found in the various castes. Though it has some analogues in all cultures, the modern kind of racial discrimination seems not to have occurred anywhere in the world prior to the sixteenth century.

During the Age of Discovery, Europeans came into contact with widely differing cultures they had never encountered before. Some, like the Aztecs and Incas, displayed a relatively high degree of civilization. Others, including many African and Native American tribes, seemed to be at a relatively primitive level. The European reaction to the less developed cultures was not always negative. In some instances, particularly in North America, a myth arose of the "noble savage," who was imagined to live a healthy life in harmony with nature in vast forests far from the corrupting influences of overrefined civilizations. The word for "race" in many European languages at the time had a kind of cultural meaning rather than a biological or evaluative designation.

Racism has often been confused with the slavery that the Europeans began to practice in the New World around the same time. Slavery, however, has been a near-universal phenomenon in human history and was present in many pre-Columbian societies in the Americas long before the Europeans arrived. But racism played no part in Native American slavery. The relative absence of slavery during the Christian Middle Ages in Europe has been more the exception than the rule in human societies. Even when Christians began capturing slaves in Eastern Europe (the name "slave" derives from the general term Slavs), the kind of slavery they practiced was similar to that practiced in almost all previous societies. Slaves had restricted social liberty, but they were still regarded as human beings with moral dignity and souls. Up until the sixteenth century, slavery seems to have little or nothing to do with racism as racism came to be understood later.

Some serious debates occurred over the status of the Native American peoples, particularly in Spain. Theologians such as the Dominican Francisco de Vitoria (c. 1483-1546), preachers like Bartolomé de Las Casas (1474-1566), and several Popes all raised strong moral objections to the enslavement of native peoples. In Spain, popular opinion itself rose up against enslavement of Indians early in the sixteenth century when they began arriving on the Spanish docks. Unfortunately, this widespread moral reaction had little effect on the practice of Spaniards in the New World, but it did lead historically to much greater intermarriage and integration of native and Spanish peoples in Latin America than in North America.

There was no comparable outcry, however, about enslavement of African blacks. Yet the universal Christian belief that all people had moral dignity and immortal souls mitigated African slavery in some instances. In Latin America, people brought from Africa as slaves suffered discrimination and social injustice, but they did not suffer anything like the racism that grew up in British and Dutch colonies. Those nations had less direct experience of slavery and laws governing slaves than did the Spanish and Portuguese, and this left them more open to developing theories of inferiority and superiority that constituted true racism.

Slavery in the United States, for example, might be better thought of as a correlative or even a precursor of racism rather than racism's result. Blacks themselves had long enslaved other blacks in Africa, and, at least initially, blacks brought to the New World to work were only regarded as replacements for Native Americans decimated by European diseases or as extra labor for clearing and developing land. The ideology of race that justified the treatment of slaves as less than human followed later. Sadly, the Christian churches in North America did little to prevent the growth of racism or, until the nineteenth century, the practice of slavery.

Racist Theory • Paradoxically, it was during the eighteenth-century Enlightenment — when Europe thought reason and the rights of man were triumphing over religious "superstitions" — that the myth of racial superiority seems to have gotten its first full formulation. Philosophers such as Hume, Kant, and Hegel differed in many ways, but they agreed in finding what they regarded as the meager accomplishments of African, Native American, and other peoples as evidence for their inherent inferiority to Europeans and advanced civilizations. In fact, Kant seems to have been the first to have used the term "race" in its modern sense: that is, a primarily biological grouping of human beings.

In many ways, the attempts to classify human beings were just a natural extension of science to the human species. Human beings do display physiological differences that may broadly be sorted into groups. In a reaction against racism, some have claimed that these physiological differences are unimportant. A better balanced view is that, while such differences are important, probably even shaping the reception of culture among some groups, individuals and groups show such vast variation, and the interplay of human culture and physiological endowment is so complex, that any hope of scientifically isolating a genetic factor as the single cause of differences among human groups is doomed to failure on scientific grounds.

Tests, for example, show differences in average intelligence among various racial groups. The very same tests, however, also show variations *within* racial groups, related to geographic location, cultural background, and education. There are also substantial fluctuations within groups, ethnic as well as racial, over time. Under the circumstances, it appears that, while any given person may be born with greater or lesser mental abilities, human beings are generally so responsive to their environments that circumstances far outweigh genetic differences in affecting group performances.

Modern Racism • But all this was still unknown as the rise of Western science and technology stimulated racial studies. The French and Germans, who were in many ways the leaders of the Enlightenment, also took the lead in the development of racial categorization. The natural scientist Count Georges-Louis Leclerc Buffon (1707-1788) sketched a theory of forms in nature that, though not the theory of evolution as Darwin would develop it, nevertheless set the stage for the notion of higher and lower animals, including separation of the human species into different races.

The most influential popularizer of the idea that physical or racial differences are directly correlated with evolutionary differences in intelligence and moral behavior was not a scientist but a diplomat. Count Joseph Arthur de Gobineau (1816-1882) wrote a massive, four-volume *Essay of the Inequality of the Human Races*, which appeared in France between 1853 and 1855. Portions of this work were immediately translated and published in America, where they exercised a powerful influence. More ominously, Houston Stewart Chamberlain (1855-1927), a pro-German Englishman, transmitted Gobineau's claims to Germany, where racial theories were applied not only to Caucasians, Negroids, and Mongoloids, but to "Aryans" and "Semites."

Gobineau was the composer Richard Wagner's son-in-law, and both helped make Aryanism and anti-Semitism popular notions and, later, Nazi mainstays. Like earlier racism, Nazi racism saw African blacks as not as highly evolved as white Europeans. But Nazi racism also created the myth of a pure Aryan supposedly found in parts of Europe and superior to non-Aryans. In this view, even

so-called white Europeans of "impure" stock were inferior. Slavs, for example, were regarded as mere worker units by Hitler. But the most notorious category of non-Aryans for the Nazis, a group of people neither racially or culturally very distinguishable from the Germans themselves, became the single most important target of Aryan genocidal fury: the Jews.

The Aryan myth could only be maintained by ingenious lies. Jesus Christ, whom many Nazis were unprepared to call a member of an inferior race, had to be reinvented by theorists such as Alfred Rosenberg, who through a tortured set of historical and "scientific" arguments, claimed that Jesus was not a Jew. In fact, said Rosenberg, Christ was not even a Semite, but an Aryan. By this means, not only was Christianity's founder saved from possessing impure blood, but Christianity itself could be reconfigured as a pure Aryan institution with no dependence on Jews or Judaism.

The Catholic Church in Europe responded to this imposture. Pope Pius XI's 1937 encyclical *With Burning Care, Mit Brennender Sorge*, called for a repudiation of anti-Semitism. Other statements went further. The following year, Pius made a point of connecting the Catholic faith with the faith of "our Father Abraham," and in an address said even more pointedly, "Spiritually we are Semites." Contrary to many claims, the Church was quite active in protecting Jews from Nazi racist persecution. In fact, the chief rabbi of Rome converted to Catholicism after World War II in gratitude for what the Vatican had done for the Jewish people.

Racism has had other political uses in the twentieth century. In an infamous 1975 resolution at the United Nations, Arab and Soviet bloc states took advantage of Cold War divisions in international opinion to declare that Zionism was racism. The racial differences, as scientists might understand them, between most Israelis and most Arabs in the Middle East is quite small. But by using the term "racism," Israel's opponents were able to enlist the near-universal moral consensus against all forms of racism in an attempt to score political points.

In recent years in the United States, charges of racism have been raised again as people debate whether persistently lower scores by American blacks on intelligence tests stem from genetic or cultural factors or whether high crime and illegitimacy rates among blacks show some biological inability to live productive lives in society. There is no good scientific evidence that human beings show variations in behavior of this kind that correlates closely with race. Until we live in societies with far more equitable treatment of all groups, we cannot pay very much attention to speculative theories about innate capacities.

Our shared equality before God does not mean we will all show equal success in society, nor that all groups will have proportionate representation in every sector of the work and educational forces. But racism is something other than an assertion of natural human differences in ability. Racism denies that there are universally common human traits and purposes. It represents an extreme form of scientism, in that it makes certain tendencies inherited in our bodies determinative of other human factors such as will, education, intelligence, and soul. It is also an extreme form of historicism, in that it suggests different races will have different, and simply incommensurable, morals, religions, and mentalities. Majority racism has sometimes given rise to minority racism, whereby previously oppressed groups assert the superior or uncriticizable value of their own culture and roots. All of this clearly tends to a fragmenting of the human species and a denial of a common human nature given to us by God across time, space, culture, and genetic endowment.

By its very nature, Catholicism is a religion instructed by its founder, Jesus Christ, to go forth and make disciples of *all* nations (Mt 28:19). No one is or can be excluded from God's universal love and redemptive intent. Furthermore, Catholics must not only look at all human beings as ultimately destined for God but must see all as coming from God, their Creator and common Father. Racism profoundly denies both the origin and end of human life as these are revealed in the Bible.

See: Evolution; Human Person; Imago Dei; Judaism; Judaism in Catholic Doctrine; Science and the Church; Slavery; Social Doctrine.

Suggested Readings: CCC 356-361. Vatican Council II, *Pastoral Constitution on the Church in the Modern World, Gaudium et Spes*, 29. Paul VI, *On the Progress of Peoples, Populorum Progressio*, 63; *The Eightieth Anniversary, Octogesima Adveniens*, 16. L. Hanke, *Aristotle and the American Indians.* M. Ashley-Montagu, *Man's Most Dangerous Myth.* R. Benedict, *Race: Science and Politics.* T. Gossett, *Race: The History of an Idea in America.* L. Poliakov, *The Aryan Myth.*

Robert Royal

RAPE

Rape is forcing another to have sexual relations. It is a severe sin against the gift of sexuality. God designed sexuality to be a source of love between a man and a woman who freely commit themselves to each other in a lifetime loving union. Rape is a violation of the free will of another and of another's sexuality; it is a sin against both justice and chastity.

A violent act that abuses the most intimate physical and psychological parts of the person, rape leaves deep psychological scars on the victim. Rape can happen in dating situations as well as being the random act of a stranger. Especially evil are forcible sexual acts with children, that is, sexual abuse and incest, since these are generally performed by individuals to whom the children have been entrusted.

See: Incest; Sex Abuse; Sexuality, Human.

RASH JUDGMENT

A more apt name for rash judgment might be "rash condemnation." Rash judgment does not refer to judgments in general, nor are we being judgmental in believing something good about someone. Rash judgments are by definition negative evaluations that harm another person's honor and good name.

To be rash, such judgments must be unsubstantiated. The *Catechism of the Catholic Church* says we are guilty of rash judgment when we believe another guilty of a moral fault "without sufficient foundation" (2477). Running a defamatory TV advertisement about an opposition candidate in a political campaign is an example of calumny; believing the ad without proof is rash judgment. Malicious gossip about coworkers is detraction; believing the rumors without investigating them is rash judgment. We are perhaps most vulnerable to rash judgment when we hear something unpleasant about someone we do not like in the first place. Smith may readily accept the statement that "Jones is a fool" if Jones has just won the girl Smith wanted.

Doubts and suspicions do not constitute judgments. Instinctively hurrying away when approached by a stranger on a dark, lonely street may be simple prudence. To be sinful, a judgment must be deliberate and must be made on what are known to be invalid grounds. This is an aggressive act that robs people of our good opinion (even if privately) without just cause. While rash judgment is usually not gravely sinful, it can have grave consequences. The man who wrongly believes his wife is unfaithful, for example, can end a marriage and ruin many lives.

See: False Witness; Slander; Truthfulness.

RATIONALISM

Rationalism represents a philosophical outlook that affirms human reason to be the sole and ultimate authority for establishing truth claims. As a spirit dominant in many parts of the Western world since the early eighteenth century, rationalism specifically declares that theological or religious tenets possess no authority in rational discourse.

In the Catholic Church, rationalists argued that the assent of faith and the practice of religion should be limited to what human reason can establish as worthy of acceptance. In the mid-nineteenth century, Pope Pius IX first condemned the nefarious influence that rationalism had achieved in Catholic circles, with the encyclical letter *Qui Pluribus* (1846). Vatican Council I later repeated

its censure in the form of an anathema: "If anyone says that human reason is so independent that faith cannot be commanded by God: let him be anathema."

In his treatise on faith (*Summa Theologiae,* 2a2ae, q. 2, art. 3, ad 1), St. Thomas Aquinas rejects the rationalist error on the basis of man's call to ultimate communion with the Blessed Trinity. "The nature of man being dependent upon a higher nature, natural knowledge is not enough for our fulfillment, rather a certain supernatural knowledge is needed" so that we can reach our goal, which is to share in the divine goodness itself.

While the Church rejects rationalism, she does not, on that account, encourage a fundamentalist approach to faith. Again, Aquinas offers the best expression of the tradition: "God never proposes through the Apostles and prophets anything that is contrary to what reason indicates, although he does propose what exceeds the power of reason to comprehend" (*De Veritate* q. 14, art. 10, ad 7). As Blaise Pascal (1623-1662) famously remarked: "The heart has its reasons which the reason does not understand."

See: Agnosticism; Atheism; Divine Revelation; Faith, Act of; Freemasonry; Knowledge of God; Modernism; Science and the Church; Thomas Aquinas, Thought of.

REAL PRESENCE

Christ instituted the sacrament of the Eucharist at the Last Supper (Mk 14:22-25; Lk 22:14-20). Not wishing to leave his disciples entirely alone after his Ascension, he chose bread and wine to be the sacramental signs of his Body and Blood. The Church has always proclaimed belief in the Real Presence of Christ in the Eucharist under the appearances of bread and wine, a presence that remains as long as the sacramental signs of bread and wine remain.

Belief in the Real Presence • Belief in the Real Presence dates from the earliest days of the Christian era. St. Ignatius of Antioch, St. Peter's successor as Bishop of Antioch, wrote against the

Docetists, who denied the Real Presence of Christ in the Eucharist. St. Justin, writing around the year 150, was one of the earliest theologians to give a detailed description of the liturgy of the Eucharist. He closes his comments with the following confession of faith from the *First Apology* (65-67): "This food is called among us the Eucharist, of which no one is allowed to partake but the person who believes that the things which we teach are true, and who has been washed with the washing that is for the remission of sins and unto regeneration, and who is living as Christ has enjoined." He goes on: "For not as common bread and common drink do we receive these, but in like manner as Jesus Christ our Savior, having been made flesh by the Word of God, had both flesh and blood for our salvation, so likewise we have been taught that the food which is blessed by the prayer of his Word, and from which our flesh and blood by transmutation are nourished, is the flesh and blood of that Jesus who was made flesh."

Other staunch defenders of the Real Presence of Christ in the Eucharist are St. Irenaeus (died 202), St. Cyprian (died 258), and St. Cyril of Jerusalem (died c. 386), who stated: "And so we consume these [consecrated species] with perfect certainty that they are the body and blood of Christ, since under the appearance of bread the body is given to us, and the blood under the appearance of wine, so that when you have taken the body and blood of Christ, you become participators in his very body and blood" (*Mystagogical Catechesis*, 4, 1-3).

For the first fifteen hundred years of the Church's existence there was a firm belief in the dogma of the Real Presence. Even Berengarius of Tours (died 1088), who at the outset denied this teaching, ultimately accepted the statement in the profession of faith that the bread and wine "are substantially changed into the true, proper and life-giving flesh and blood of our Lord Jesus Christ." After the Protestant Reformation, the Council of Trent issued two definitive statements concerning the Real Presence: "After the consecration of the bread and wine, our Lord Jesus Christ, true God and man, is truly, really and substantially contained under the perceptible species of bread and wine." And: "If anyone denies that the body and blood, together with the soul and divinity, of our Lord Jesus Christ, and therefore, the whole Christ, is truly, really and substantially contained present in the sacrament of the most holy Eucharist, but says that Christ is present in the Sacrament only as in a sign or figure, or by his power, let him be anathema."

The presence of Christ in the Eucharist under the appearances of bread and wine is clearly revealed in the New Testament, whose authors are reliable witnesses of what Jesus said and did. Thus, in the sixth chapter of the Gospel according to St. John, in the discourse on the bread of life, we read the astonishing revelation made by Jesus: "I myself am the living bread come down from heaven. If anyone eats this bread he shall live forever; the bread I will give is my flesh, for the life of the world."

At this the Jews quarreled among themselves, saying, "How can he give us his flesh to eat?" Thereupon Jesus said to them: "Let me solemnly assure you, if you do not eat the flesh of the Son of man and drink his blood, you have no life in you. . . . For my flesh is real food and my blood real drink. The man who feeds on my flesh and drinks my blood remains in me, and I in him" (Jn 6:53-56).

The promise of the sacrament of the Body and Blood of Christ was fulfilled at the Last Supper, according to the Scriptures. The authors of the Synoptic Gospels and St. Paul are in complete agreement in stating that Jesus consecrated bread with the words "This is my body," and did the same with the cup of wine with the words "This is my blood." Then he told the Apostles to eat and drink and to do likewise in memory of him (Mt 26:26-29, Mk 14:22-25, Lk 22:15-20, 1 Cor 11:23-25). St. Paul completes his description of the institution of the Eucharist with these words: "Every time, then, you eat this bread and drink this cup, you proclaim the death of the Lord until he comes" (1 Cor 11:26).

In each celebration of the Sacrifice of the Mass, the faithful are reminded that the Eucharist is "the mystery of faith." St. John Chrysostom told the Christians of his day: "Let us submit to God in all things and not contradict him, even if what he says seems to contradict our reason and intellect. . . . Let us act in this way with regard to the mysteries, not limiting our attention to those things which can be perceived by the senses, but instead holding fast to what he says. For his word can never deceive."

For the believing Christian, the Real Presence of Christ in the Eucharist is indisputable. Thus, St. Paul asks: "Is not the cup of blessing we bless a sharing in the blood of Christ? And is not the bread we break a sharing in the body of Christ?" (1 Cor 10:16).

Transubstantiation • Christ is present in the Church in many ways — in her faith, preaching, and teaching; in her prayer and worship; in her liturgical actions; in her works of mercy; in the faithful as members of the Mystical Body. But Christ is present in a unique way in the Eucharist. Pope Paul VI stated in the encyclical *On the Holy Eucharist, Mysterium Fidei* (1965): "The presence of Christ in the Eucharist is called the real presence not to exclude the other kinds as though they were not real, but because it is real *par excellence*, since it is substantial, in the sense that Christ whole and entire, God and man, becomes present" (39). The manner of his Eucharistic presence cannot be explained in physical terms because it transcends the natural limitations and dimensions of space and quantity.

When Jesus instituted the sacrament of the Eucharist at the Last Supper with the words "This is my Body" and "This is my Blood," and when the priest at Mass says those same words, the bread and wine are changed into the Body and Blood of Christ. However, unlike other substantial changes, the Body and Blood of Christ already exist even before the change takes place. Christ is in a glorified state, and he does not leave heaven to become consubstantial with the bread and wine of the Eucharist. Rather, the bread and wine are instantaneously changed into the Body and Blood of Christ. After the words of Consecration, nothing substantial remains of the bread or wine; they have been

completely replaced by Christ's already existing Body and Blood. This change has been described in theology and in councils of the Church as transubstantiation, meaning that the entire substance of bread and of wine has been changed into the entire substance of his Body and Blood.

Theologians from the second century onward had discussed the type of change that occurs at the Consecration of the bread and wine in the Mass. They all consistently professed their belief in the personal presence of Christ in the Eucharist under the appearances of bread and wine. Various words were used to designate the change: transfiguration (St. Ambrose), transformation (St. Cyril and St. John Chrysostom), and by the seventh century St. John Damascene taught that the bread and wine are not mere "figures" but are transmuted or converted into the Body and Blood of Christ.

In the ninth century, Paschasius Radbertus stated clearly the Catholic teaching on the Real Presence, but in the eleventh century theologians once again had to defend the doctrine against Berengarius of Tours. The Roman Council of 1079 officially declared that the bread and wine are substantially changed into the Body and Blood of Christ. Berengarius publicly professed his faith in the substantial change of the bread and wine into Christ's Body and Blood, and promised that he would no longer teach anything contrary to this doctrine of the faith.

The term "transubstantiation" seems to have been introduced into the theological vocabulary before 1145 by Roland Bandinelli, who later became Pope Alexander III. By 1150 it was commonly used by the professors at the University of Paris, and eventually it found its way into official documents of the Church, such as the profession of faith drawn up by the Fourth Lateran Council in 1215. Thus it was not, as Luther erroneously maintained, an invention of St. Thomas Aquinas (died 1274), although he used the term: "This conversion is not like any natural change, but it is entirely beyond the powers of nature and is brought about purely by God's power. . . . The complete substance of the bread is converted into the complete substance of Christ's body, and the complete substance of the wine into the complete substance of Christ's blood. Hence this change . . . can be called by a name proper to itself: *transubstantiation*" (*Summa Theologiae*, III, 75, 4).

The word "transubstantiation" appears in documents of the Fourth Lateran Council in 1215, the Second Council of Lyons in 1274, and the Council of Florence in 1439.

Martin Luther (died 1546) rejected the term "transubstantiation" in favor of "consubstantiation," meaning that the glorified Body and Blood of Christ are present in and together with the bread and wine. The Swiss Reformer Ulrich Zwingli (died 1531) viewed the Eucharist as merely a figure or sign of Christ's presence; the communicant receives the Body and Blood of Christ spiritually but not really. John Calvin (died 1564) denied both transubstantiation and consubstantiation. Yet another expression was used by Osiander (died 1552), namely "impanation." His explanation was that the substance of bread and wine remain together with the substance of Christ; the result is a kind of hypostatic union. The theological reasoning was as follows: If the Word could assume and be united to a human nature in Christ, then it is also possible that Christ could unite to himself the substance of bread and wine.

The teaching of the Catholic Church was stated by the Council of Trent in 1551: "Because Christ our Redeemer said that it was truly his body that he was offering under the species of bread, it has always been the conviction of the Church of God, and this holy Council now declares again, that by the consecration of the bread and wine there takes place a change of the whole substance of the bread into the substance of the body of Christ our Lord and of the whole substance of the wine into the substance of his blood. This change the holy Catholic Church has fittingly and properly called transubstantiation."

In speaking of obedience to the Magisterium of the Church regarding the theology of the Eucharist, Pope Paul VI stated in *Mysterium Fidei*: "Not only the integrity of the faith, but also its proper mode of expression must be safeguarded, lest, by the careless use of words, we introduce false notions about the most sublime realities. We must religiously respect the rule of terminology; after centuries of effort and under the protection of the Holy Spirit the Church has established it and confirmed it by the authority of Councils; that norm often became the watchword and the banner of orthodox belief. Let no one arbitrarily, or under the pretext of new science, presume to change it. The dogmatic formulas are open to clearer and plainer explanation. . . . But that is in continuity with the sense the formulas had originally, so that, as the understanding of the faith increases, its truth remains the same" (23-25).

The Mystery of the Real Presence • The series of treatises on the theology of the Eucharist that led to the publication of *Mysterium Fidei* by Pope Paul in 1965 was for the most part ecumenical in tone. Theologians were seriously trying to find a terminology that would express a theology acceptable to both Protestant and Catholic factions. In the course of the discussion, some experts stressed the importance of an understanding of the totality of the scriptural context rather than concentrating on the Words of Institution or starting from a particular philosophical system. Many theologians today assert that transubstantiation does not mean the destruction of one substance and its replacement by another, as when wood turns to ashes. Rather, by one act of his omnipotence, God converts the substance of bread and of wine into the Body and Blood of Christ.

What makes this change even more of a mystery is the fact that the sensible qualities of bread and wine remain after the transubstantiation. The consecrated bread still looks like bread and tastes like bread, and the consecrated wine still looks like wine. But the Body, Blood, soul, and divinity of Christ are present under those appearances. We can know only through faith that Christ is sacramentally but truly present, and our faith is rooted in the words and deeds of Christ. The *Catechism of the Catholic Church* cites the Council of Trent (1551) and Pope Paul (*Mysterium Fidei,* 39) in saying that in the sacrament of the Eucharist "the body and blood, together with the soul and divinity, of our Lord Jesus Christ and, therefore, *the whole Christ is truly, really, and substantially* contained. . . . It is a *substantial* presence by which Christ, God and man, makes himself wholly and entirely present" (CCC 1374).

We can summarize Catholic teaching on the Real Presence as follows: It is of faith that the entire Christ — Body, Blood, soul, and divinity — is present under the appearances of bread and wine and under each of the species. The words of Consecration designate the Body and Blood separately — "This is my body" and "This is my blood" — but the Christ who becomes present is the immortal, glorified Christ (Rom 6:9). As was pointed out by the Council of Trent, by natural concomitance, the body, blood, and soul are present in a living human being; by supernatural concomitance, the hypostatic union of Christ's human nature and his divinity are likewise present under the Eucharistic species. This is the reality that exists in the Eucharist (cf. St. Thomas Aquinas, *Summa Theologiae*, III, 76, 1, ad 1).

This does not mean, however, that the glorified Christ leaves heaven in order to be present in the Eucharist. And since the normal quantitative extension of a body is suspended, there is no problem with the fact that the sacramental presence is contained entirely in every piece of the Host or on numerous altars at the same time. Further, the Real Presence remains as long as the species of bread and wine remain (Denzinger-Schönmetzer, 1654). Consequently, the Church has always distributed the Eucharist to the faithful outside of Mass when circumstances dictate and has approved of veneration of the Eucharist reserved in the tabernacle.

The object of faith is not doctrinal propositions but the reality and authority of God revealing. The basis for belief in the Real Presence is the declaration of Christ himself: "This is my body; this is my blood."

If the Eucharist is nothing more than a sign or a memorial, there is no need for postulating the Real Presence. And if the Mass is only a gathering of the faithful in order to experience themselves as a community, this does not require a sacramental Real Presence. But the faith expressed by the Synoptic Gospels and St. Paul refers to a sacrificial action and a sacramental reality, proclaiming the death of the Lord until he comes. Here we proclaim the mystery of faith.

See: Eucharist; Eucharistic Devotion; Mass; Sacrifice.

Suggested Readings: CCC 1373-1381. Vatican Council II, *Constitution on the Sacred Liturgy, Sacrosanctum Concilium*, 47-58. Pius XII, *On the Sacred Liturgy, Mediator Dei*. Paul VI, *On the Doctrine and Worship of the Eucharist, Mysterium Fidei*, 46-55. John Paul II, *On the Mystery and Worship of the Eucharist, Dominicae Cenae*. C. O'Neill, *New Approaches to the Eucharist*.

Jordan Aumann, O.P.

REDEMPTION

The goal of the Incarnation is the paschal mystery — the cross and Resurrection — suffered for us and for our salvation, for our atonement. There is no single synthesis or concept that captures the rich meaning of the Lord Jesus' saving Passion. The theology of the atonement expressed here is that of Hans Urs von Balthasar. His starting point is a rich understanding of the covenantal relationship that God established with the human race; this is the premise for the plan of reconciliation. God is faithful to his covenant, and the Lord Jesus comes to fulfill the covenant made with our fathers in the faith. He lives to renew it with us in his flesh when his "hour" — the hour his Father had set — finally comes. Outside of the covenantal relationship we could not imagine why the Son of God willed to endure the Passion.

The first two aspects of the atonement show its source in the acts of the Father and of the Son: the act of giving on the part of both, and the Son's exchange of place with us in the Incarnation. The third and fourth aspects express the goal of the atonement, namely, our liberation from sin and death, from the guilt of the law, from the powers of evil, and our admittance into the divine life of the Blessed Trinity. The fifth aspect is the source from which all else proceeds: the life of love among Father, Son, and Spirit.

The Acts of Father and Son • The Father gives us his Son and, with him, all good things (cf. Rom 8:32); God delivers up his Son (Mt 17:22-23, 20:18-19).

The Son allows himself to be handed over. At the heart of this obedient letting things happen, there is active consent, deliberate action. "I lay down my life of my own accord" (Jn 10:17-18). He is the priest who surrenders himself (Heb 2:14ff.), the lamb who is given up for the sins of the world (Jn 1:29). The words of the institution of the Eucharist show that Jesus' own personal self-surrender is prior to any human action to send him to death, and this self-surrender seals the final and definitive covenant (Mt 26:28; 1 Cor 11:25).

Given up for us, he becomes "sin" (2 Cor 5:21) and a "curse" (Gal 3:13) so that we might become the righteousness of God and receive the promised Spirit as sons in the Son. He who was rich becomes poor for our sakes so that we might become rich through his poverty (2 Cor 8:9). On his body, our sin and hostility are condemned (Rom 8:3; cf. Eph 2:14). The "Lamb of God who takes away the sins of the world" (Jn 1:29) may also refer to the Suffering Servant who bears our sins (Is 53:4) or to the Passover lamb (or to the scapegoat: cf. Lv 16:7ff.). The Lord Jesus takes our sins on himself so that he can take them away. On the basis of this exchange of place, we are already "reconciled to God" (Rom 5:18) in advance of our own consent, "while we were yet sinners." In the Garden of Olives, we admire Jesus' willing obedience to his Father: "Take this cup from me, but not what I will but what you will" (Mk 14:36ff.); we admire the sacrifice of love and obedience that makes up for our pride and disobedience.

Fruits of Reconciliation • The fruit of the event of reconciliation can be seen, first of all, as the liberation from all the negativity that besets us: from slavery to sin (Rom 7; Jn 8:34), from the devil (Jn 8:44; 1 Jn 3:8), from the "world powers" (Gal 4:3; Col 2:20), from the power of darkness (Col 1:13), from the law (Rom 7:1), from the "law of sin and death" (Rom 8:2), and finally from the wrath to come (1 Thes 1:10). This liberation re-

calls the ransoming of the house of Israel from the house of slavery in Egypt. It takes place by paying a high "price" (the blood of Christ: 1 Cor 6:20; 7:23; 1 Pt 1:18ff.) or the "ransom" (Mk 10:45). In cultic terms, it is a propitiation (Rom 3:25) producing an eternal redemption (Heb 9:12). Without the shedding of blood there is no forgiveness (Heb 9:22); that is to say, death has to intervene (Heb 9:15).

The loosing of bonds takes place through the Holy Spirit and imparts to us God's Holy Spirit, who cries *Abba* (Father) in us, assuring us that we share a sonship with the Lord Jesus and have access to the Father (Gal 4:6ff.; Rom 8:10ff.). We are admitted to the divine life of the Trinity. The Holy Spirit restores the likeness to God in us (this is Jesus himself) and gives us the capacity to love as the Persons of the Trinity love. God's purpose is to enable us by grace to share in Christ's Sonship (Eph 1:5ff.) by becoming "members of his Body" (1 Cor 12; Eph 4–5). The Holy Spirit gives us the freedom of the sons of God (Gal 5:13; cf. Jn 8:31ff.).

It is God's merciful love that brings about the whole action of reconciliation. On the basis of the love of the Father (Rom 8:39) and of Christ (Rom 8:35), the Son was given up "for us all" (Rom 8:32) by the Father. God so loved the world that he gave up his only begotten Son (Jn 3:16). He has mandated his Son to lay down his life for his sheep (Jn 10:15). It is God's gracious initiative that moves to restore and fulfill the covenant and "all righteousness" (Mt 3:15). This initiative takes into account the human malice and sin of those who handed the Lord Jesus over to death.

All of the aspects above must be taken together. None should diminish the importance of the others if the full force of the work of atonement is to be maintained. The history of theology bears this out. The Reformation emphasized a theology of the exchange of places that did not do justice to the aspect of the Father's and Son's free self-giving. Today the theology of liberation in some of its forms neglects these two aspects and the aspect of liberation from sin. In our times, too, we have had a theology that emphasized reconciliation and mercy at the expense of self-giving and of Christ's redemptive "exchange" with us. Other errors arise from other exaggerated emphases.

The Significance of the Incarnation • The premise for the Son's action is his reality as Divine Person and human being. The agent is a Divine Person. It is as man in his human nature that he suffers for us, yet he who suffers and dies is God. Because he is God, his sufferings have an inclusiveness, breadth, and depth that no ordinary man's can have. His very uniqueness as the God-man allows his relationships with men as head and second Adam. It is as man, but because he is God, that he is able to substitute himself for us and take upon himself the unbearable burden of the whole world's guilt. For this reason and no other, he can give a share in his once-for-all cross to his fellow human beings, with whom he is in deeper solidarity than any other man could ever be with another.

Jesus' act of self-giving and of exchange is exclusive, in that as the Son of God made man he can do something we could not do for ourselves; and it is inclusive because as human being he is our head. The uniqueness of Christ's Trinitarian Person is the ground of his all-embracing solidarity with and substitution for men.

The Lord Jesus is the universal Word through whom all things were made. He is able to communicate something of this universality to the human nature united to his Divine Person without robbing it of its particularity.

Mankind in its very being has been put in a new situation by the sinless Son's ability to substitute himself for us. The sinner is too self-enclosed within the prison of selfishness to be capable of putting himself in the place of his brethren in thought or in reality; and in any case no mere man, not even a great saint, can bear away the vast load of the world's sin. Only one Person can: the One who lives in divine distance in relation to the Father, that is, the Son, who even as man is God.

It is not a question of the sinless one identifying himself with the "no" of sin itself; Jesus is always a pure loving "yes" to the Father, and so his vicarious experience of sin's darkness cannot be like that of God-hating sinners. But the unlikeness does not lessen his pain. He suffers more deeply, more intensely, than any sinful human being could. Our Lord identifies himself with sinful mankind as *suffering* sin, not as *committing* it. All the pains merited by human wickedness he lovingly takes upon himself, not as punishment but as expiation and satisfaction. This takes place within the relationships of the divine hypostases, a depth no creature can ever have any sense of. It is sin's unfamiliarity that causes the sin-bearing Lamb such pain. He sees the *peccatum mundi* for what it is: God-offending and man-destroying. The Crucified One suffers in our place our interior estrangement from God and our experience of God's darkness; indeed, it is so painful because it is undeserved. He suffers something deeper than any ordinary man can, because only the Son knows in truth who the Father is and what it means to go without him, to have lost him apparently forever.

The Mystery of the Exchange of Places • The Fathers of the Church love to emphasize the "exchange" formulas. Thus Athanasius: The Logos became man so that we might become divinized. St. Gregory Nazianzen: "What was not assumed, was not redeemed." St. Augustine: "He had no power of himself to die for us: he had to take from us our mortal flesh. This was the way in which, though immortal, he was able to die. . . . Accordingly, he effected a wonderful exchange with us, through mutual sharing: we gave him the power to die, he will give us the power to live. . . . In taking upon himself the death that he found in us, he has most faithfully promised to give us life in him, such as we cannot have of ourselves. He loved us so much that, sinless himself, he suffered for us sinners the punishment we deserved for our sins."

The work of redemption is a work of sheer love and mercy on the part of the Persons of the Trinity. Referring to earlier theologies, which spoke of the Father punishing his Son, von Balthasar says of Jesus' initiative: "Nor can we say that God the Father 'punishes' his suffering Son in our place. It is not a question of punishment, for the work accomplished here between Father and Son with the cooperation of the Holy Spirit is utter love, the purest love possible. So too, it is a work of the purest spontaneity, from the Son's side as from the side of the Father and of the Spirit. God's love is so rich that it can also assume this form of darkness, out of love for our dark world" (*You Crown the Year With Your Goodness*, p. 85). C.S. Lewis comments: "Before I became a Christian I was under the impression that the first thing Christians had to believe was one particular theory as to what the point of this dying was. According to that theory God wanted to punish men for having deserted and joined the Great Rebel, but Christ volunteered to be punished instead, and so God let us off. . . . What I came to see is that neither this theory nor any other is Christianity. The central Christian belief is that Christ's death has somehow put us right with God and given us a fresh start. Theories as to how it did this are another matter" (*Mere Christianity*, p. 53).

If we are to follow biblical Revelation, then, we must not divide the Son of God, in the exercise of his mission, into the one who carries out his mission on earth and the one who remains unaffected in heaven. For he *is* one — he is the eternal Son dwelling in time. The event by which he consents to be transferred from the form of God into the "form of a servant" and the "likeness of men" (Phil 2:6) affects him as eternal Son. It does not matter whether we say that eternity enters into time or that eternity takes a particular "time" and its temporal contents into itself: Neither statement explains how such a process is possible. We can call it kenosis, self-emptying (as in Phil 2), but this does not imply some mythological alteration in God. It can express one of the infinite possibilities available to free, eternal life: namely, that the Son, who has everything from the Father, commits to the Father's keeping "the form of God" he has received from him, in order to concentrate on the mission that is one mode of his procession from the Father, is forsaken by the Father on the cross. Yet this "infinite distance" that recapitulates the sinner's alienation from God will remain forever

the highest revelation known to the world of the "separation" (distinction of origin and of Persons within the eternal being of God) between the Father and the Son in the Holy Spirit.

The "Wonderful Exchange" in the Fathers and St. Thomas • St. Irenaeus (130-202) says of Christ that he gave his soul for our soul, his flesh for our flesh, pouring out the Spirit of the Father in order to achieve union and communion between God and man. For the Greek Fathers, the exchange has to include the exchange that takes place in the Passion. In Christ's cross and Resurrection, as it were, the whole of human nature is crucified and co-risen. St. Cyril of Alexandria says Christ's cry on the cross is uttered in the name of all human nature; it is not for himself but for us that he entreats the mercy of God.

Part of the total exchange is the exchange of death and life, of perdition and rescue. In Western theology, Jesus truly fulfills the universal mission entrusted to him in that the exchange becomes a real exchange of places. This is not possible if it is simply some ordinary man who suffers on others' behalf; it is only possible if this human suffering is taken on by a Divine Person, who enters into humanity's desperate situation in relation to God, in order to transform it into a situation full of hope.

It is fashionable today to critique the "satisfaction theory" of St. Anselm (1033-1109). The idea that reconciliation with God can be brought about by a historical act is said to be not only anthropomorphic but false, since the Father does not send the Son to be reconciled with the world through the Son's cross but simply out of merciful love for the world (cf. Jn 3:16). Anselm is aware of this. But he sees the inseparable relationship of divine righteousness and love and the necessity that the new order in the relationship between God and humanity should be a work performed within the world by a divine human being. This need flows from the covenant, in which the partners are pledged to satisfy certain common obligations toward each other. Those who seek to undermine Anselm's intuition falsify the mission of Jesus, by reducing it to a mere symbolic illustration of something that is the case anyway: "God's attitude is always one of solidarity with man."

The mission of Jesus is concerned with reconciling the world with God (2 Cor 5:18ff.) and reconciling the tension in mankind between the individual person and the sinful human nature he inherits. Therefore, Jesus has to take the initiative on behalf of humanity. This cannot be from outside, as if *for us* meant simply "for our benefit" — it must take place from inside. He must really take upon himself the personal and social situation of the sinner. *For us* means "in our place."

St. Thomas Aquinas's view of Christ's representation builds on Anselm, emphasizing that Christ is united concretely as head with the human members of his body. This develops Augustine's teaching. Christ's mission on our behalf is more than a work, a suffering, undertaken to spare others the punishment they deserved (as Protestants emphasize). It involves his *co*-working and his *co*-suffering with those estranged from God.

In this way, the second Adam opens up an area of Christian mission in which we can have a share in his salvific work and suffering for the world. This completion of "what is lacking in Christ's sufferings for the sake of his body, the Church" (Col 1:24) takes place in faith, but it can also be experienced by those with mystical graces. It is God's secret to know how the sufferings of mankind are drawn into the work of atonement, as the first Adam's place is taken by the second Adam and his Church.

In developing the "head-members" interpretation, governed by the eminence of the head and the superabundance of merit and grace that extends to the members, something more can be added. The personal, freely willed acceptance by the head of the guilt of the members is presupposed by his effective representative action. This is essential if the head-body relationship is to exist. On the one hand, the Redeemer takes the entirety of human nature upon himself, which links him organically with all who are to be redeemed; on the other hand, his personal constitution makes him super-meritorious for the benefit of all.

The Eucharist helps us see these two elements as connected. He who gives us his Body and Blood does so in an exchange: He gives back to us what he has taken from us and transformed into himself. As an act of thanksgiving to the Father, the Eucharist shows that the Father is the Lord of the Eucharistic banquet. In the Holy Spirit, he permits Christ the head to give himself to his members. The Eucharist also underlines the life-giving power of the body and the abiding meaning of the Incarnation in Jesus' mission for man's sake. The corporal becomes spiritual, and the body becomes the bearer of the Spirit. Christ came as Redeemer of men, but he does not merely remit our guilt. He came to offer the fullness of all divine goods, summed up as our "adoption as sons," which the Father gives when he surrenders his only Son for our sake. Since he has done this, "will he not also give us all things with him?" (Rom 8:32).

See: Eucharist; Hierarchy; Incarnation; Jesus Christ, God and Man; Jesus Christ, Life of; Liberation From Sin; Mass; New Covenant; Old Covenant; Original Sin; Priesthood of Christ; Resurrection of Christ; Sacrifice; Thomas Aquinas, Thought of.

Suggested Readings: CCC 456-478, 571-655. H. von Balthasar, *Theodrama*, Vol. IV, pp. 240-270; *You Crown the Year With Your Goodness*, pp. 76-86. J. Saward, *The Mysteries of March*, pp. 39-54.

Richard Malone

RELATIVISM

Ethical relativism is the denial that there are objective moral truths. Rather, in this view, what is ethically right is relative to what people feel or think. Individual relativism, sometimes also called "subjectivism," holds that what is ethically right is relative to what the individual thinks or feels. "If you think it's right, then it's right for you," says the subjectivist. Cultural relativism holds that what is right is relative to what a group, culture, or society thinks or feels. Thus, a cultural relativist might say, "Well, I am personally opposed to killing old people, but in some cultures that is perfectly right."

Our culture is saturated with relativism, which can be seen especially on television, perhaps quintessentially on afternoon talk shows. The attractions of relativism are real. First, many people think the only way to be tolerant of others is by being relativistic. Second, it may seem that a claim to know real, absolute truth is arrogant.

Despite its attractions, relativism is profoundly mistaken. If relativism were true, one could not criticize any action or opinion. One could voice dislike, but not assert that the action or opinion departed from any standard that everyone should recognize. Most people see that there are at least some actions concerning which it is absurd to say this: for example, the actions of a Hitler or of an Idi Amin. If relativism were right, one could not say that what Hitler did was wrong. One could dislike it, but would have to say that if Hitler thought it was right, it was right for him.

Critique of Relativism • Even the act of arguing for relativism shows one implicitly realizes that it is false. For someone who argues for relativism hopes his audience will be reasonable; and in arguing for relativism, he is supposing that it is better to be reasonable than not, better to be clear than to be confused. Thus he implicitly recognizes the objective worth of reasonableness and clarity in his very act of denying any objective values. Therefore, relativism is self-inconsistent.

One need not be a relativist in order to be tolerant. A person is tolerant if he tolerates, that is, lets be, something he thinks is bad. More specifically, a person is tolerant if he refrains from using force to make people agree with him. Clearly, one can hold that certain things are true without using force to make people agree. And one can think certain things are bad without using violent means to destroy those who do or cause these things. Indeed, one of the things a person might think is objectively true is that one should not use force to make people agree with one. On the other hand, being a relativist does not guarantee that one will be tolerant. We are all familiar with those who suppress the positions of others who hold there is absolute moral truth.

It is not intolerant, however, for the state or for individuals to protect the weaker from the stronger who might try to abuse them in various ways. This is a duty of the state and often of parents, friends, or those in a position to help those being violated.

There is an objective standard of what is morally right and morally wrong. It has been true for all human beings, in all times and in all cultures, that knowledge would be a good thing for them, that health would be a good thing for them, etc. No human beings, in any time or culture, have been such that knowledge or health or friendship would not be good things, would not build them up or perfect them. Going down the list of basic human goods, one finds the same to be true for all of them.

Furthermore, there could not be a human being, an animal with reason and free will (the basic *capacities* for reasoning and freely choosing), that was not perfected by life, health, knowledge, friendship, and so on. There is a necessary connection between being an animal with reason and free will — a human being — and having the potentialities for life, health, knowledge, and so on. It is necessarily the case that every human being, no matter of what time or culture, is a being that would be fulfilled in these various ways. And so it is necessarily the case that every human being should pursue and respect these basic goods. The basic moral truths prescribing their pursuit are true for all cultures and for all times. These parts of the natural moral law are unchangeable.

Many of the conclusions derived from these basic moral truths are changeable. There are various ways, according to different cultures and times, of pursuing and protecting the basic human goods, but the basic goods themselves are common to all cultures. And so the love of human persons, which means willing to them their genuine good, has the same basic requirements in all cultures.

See: Absolute Moral Norms; Conscience; Human Goods; Natural Law; Subjectivism.

Suggested Readings: CCC 1777-1802, 1949-1960. G. Grisez and R. Shaw, *Beyond the New Morality.*

Patrick Lee

RELIGION, VIRTUE OF

The word "religion" is already telling. *Re-* means again. The rest of the word means tie, as in ligament. So religion has to do with reconnecting or bonding anew. Man tends to forget or overlook his created origin, dependency, and nature. Religion is the progressive curing of the divine-human relationship.

The virtue of religion has its start in the human search for meaning, an inquiry into what man, the universe, and any Supreme Being might signify (cf. CCC 26).

In assembling clues to what lies beyond the senses, the inquirer can turn to four complementary sources. First, by reflecting on himself, he acquires a perception of self-insufficiency that leaves him more receptive to what God may have to say or do: "Faced with God's fascinating and mysterious presence, man discovers his own insignificance" (CCC 208; 2097 speaks of the creature's "nothingness"). Then, the Creator reveals himself to man naturally through creation, much as authors show themselves through their writings. Supernaturally, moreover, God can unveil himself via extraordinary interventions in history: the miracle-certified doings and sayings of patriarchs, prophets, and, above all, the God-man. Finally, man can know God experientially (even mystically), when to those who trustingly believe and hope in him, God evermore proves his goodness.

At first, the more man discovers about God, the more exalted, aloof, different, and hopelessly distant he seems: immense, majestic, eternal, infinite, all-pure. Human misdeeds (violating both human nature and express divine commands) make the chasm seem more unbridgeable. But why should an all-blissful and utterly self-sufficient Supreme Being create in the first place and, perhaps even more remarkable, sustain such miscreants in existence? Every possible motive for doing so can be discarded but love (cf. 1 Jn 4:8): God unilaterally loves humanity into being; but now only so that he can continue to love man with the latter's grateful assent (cf. CCC 239). By hiddenly sustaining and enriching him, God is, to paraphrase St.

Augustine, even more tenderly interior and intimate to man than man is to himself.

Accordingly, the *Catechism of the Catholic Church* opens with these words: "God, infinitely perfect and blessed in himself, in a plan of sheer goodness freely created man to make him share in his own blessed life. For this reason, at every time and in every place, God draws close to man. He calls man to seek him, to know him, to love him, with all his strength." Man can further discover that the divine qualities disclosed by God's creative initiative are the very ones played out in a finite key in both time and space by the Word incarnate (cf. CCC 280, 282).

Thus, man learns or believes that God is a most benevolent Creator resembling nothing so much as an all-loving father. Not only does he generously make man but so fashions human nature that it can be fulfilled only by participating in his bounteous life as well ("created by God and for God," CCC 27). Divine largesse is endless. There is but one condition: Man is to recognize God's generosity and lovingly answer in kind. Man, says Vatican II in its *Pastoral Constitution on the Church in the Modern World*, "cannot live fully according to truth unless he freely acknowledges that love and entrusts himself to his Creator" (*Gaudium et Spes*, 19). Moreover, so loved, man is soon prompted to echo God's utterly free self-giving with God's other estranged children, his newfound brothers and sisters.

The Duty to Know God • That man's notion of God can and ought to grow is confirmed by "progressive" revelation (cf. CCC 486). The first of the commandments entrusted to Moses (and the basis for religion) largely puts forth a single Deity's exclusive claims to recognition and obedience: "I am the Lord your God, who brought you out of the land of Egypt. . . . You shall have no other gods before me. You shall not make for yourself a graven image . . . you shall not bow down to them or serve them; for I the Lord your God am a jealous God . . . but showing steadfast love to . . . those who love me and keep my commandments" (Ex 20:2-6). That man is commanded therein to love God almost seems an afterthought, as is true in most of the Old

Testament. Emphasized rather is the duty to honor, fear, praise, revere, and serve God, a duty still embodied today in the Old Covenant offshoots of both monotheistic Judaism and Islam. In the more explicit New Testament, however, Christ both develops and ranks God's many commands: "You shall love the Lord your God with all your heart, and with all your soul, and with all your mind. This is the great and first commandment. And a second is like it, You shall love your neighbor as yourself" (Mt 22:37).

Now what may have begun as a kind of lonely stab in the dark can eventually rise to the fullest possible union and identification with God, both now and in future life. Here, too, is confirmed that whoever "seeks . . . finds" (Mt 7:8). This whole charity-crowned process encompasses much more than the virtue of religion. The latter looks more to the initial steps of the larger human project, to uncovering the towering reality of God and his attitude toward his creatures. "God's first call and just demand is that man accept him and worship him" (CCC 2084). Only of God can it rightfully be said, "To know him is to love him," and man can only say this when his acquaintance with God has advanced. In its freedom, humanity can still resist. Yet the more man knows about God, the more inclined he will be to adhere lovingly to him.

How far one brings the mind into conformity with these realities determines whether religion ever moves beyond being a mere contract for mutual services between two parties with apparently diverse agendas. It seems that for most people most of the time, whether within the Judeo-Christian tradition or not, religion has been, sadly, a superficial compact: placating God just enough to get by, both here and hereafter. But humanity could have gone more deeply into the Creator-creature relationship or that of Redeemer and sinner. Then it would have discovered, not a severe divine taskmaster, whose wrath mounts as our misdeeds accumulate, but a God who mercifully loves humanity. It should not be thought, however, that God's endless love for man is soft, sentimental, indulgent. To get humans to renounce their self-defeating ways, God's love

sometimes must visit them with corrective suffering. Much like a good parent, God may have no alternative but to discipline his errant, obstinate children.

In many ways, one might say, the virtue of religion resembles the fourth commandment writ large, recognizing God as a most loving, though invisible, Father in the most total and radical sense possible. Moreover, God desires, not blindly obedient robots, but responsive children who choose to know and love him; hence he can neither overwhelm nor underwhelm them. Clues to his existence and qualities must be luminous and abundant enough so that those who seek him can indeed find him; yet his reality must be obscure enough so that those who care not to find him will not be forced to do so. This is not to say that positive and negative clues are to be found in equal numbers, though that may seem the case before the fact. To the degree one honestly searches convergent evidence as to God's reality accumulates to such a preponderant extent that to reject it would be irrational.

Again like a good parent, God must leave life's outcome in his children's fickle and uncertain hands. Otherwise, what his human creatures do would not truly be their own free doing, but the product of his behind-the-scenes manipulation (as with the properties and instinctive behavior of animals, plants, and inorganic matter). God thus makes possible man's self-ruling capacity and autonomy, which allow human persons to claim these decisions and deeds as truly their own, for which each can and must personally and inalienably answer. Humans might wish to slough off personal freedom and responsibility and thereby drain behavior of meaning and consequences. But God requires truthful acknowledgment of human responsibility for human misdeeds and omissions. In the divine plan, this admission of self-privation in effect opens the door to forgiveness.

Since the divine decision to create man was sovereignly independent of how human beings might react and correspond, God is not fazed or deterred by the human failure to correspond to such selfless self-giving. How man relates to God in no way can or does affect how God so freely, yet immutably, has chosen to behave toward humanity. God's love for man is immortal, eternal, ever-faithful, irrevocable. Ever so patiently, furthermore, God grounds even the human capacity to act counter to his loving designs and overtures. For each of his children, however refractory, God ever harbors the highest of hopes, the greatest of expectations.

The Religious Quest • God's love is so real and all-pervasive that it must make itself invisible, as it were, lest the human response be less than voluntary. It is man's job — the business of religion — to make divine love "visible" by piecing together the mosaic. Man grows acquainted with his Cause by studying the progressively discovered effects of the divine overflow: existence, talents, opportunities, graces, lights, helps, good impulses, providence, and the like. A human being is nothing if not a seeker: his the pilgrimage ever inward and upward.

The more man learns about God, the more he comes to know himself; and, according to Augustine: "The more I know myself, the more I know you, O Lord." Human bad news highlights and exalts the Good News of God's unconditional love for his prodigal sons and daughters. As man advances into his divine filiation, there arise in him such appropriate creaturely attitudes as adoration, praise, thanksgiving, petition, desires to atone, amend, vows and promises, sacrifice (cf. CCC 2096-2103). The *Catechism* (2099) again quotes Augustine: "Every action done so as to cling to God in communion of holiness, and thus achieve blessedness, is a true sacrifice." Man's self-deflation increasingly discloses a God whom he can never believe, hope in, or love too much — for man can never exhaust the infinite storehouse of divine beauty, goodness, truth, and unending being.

Offenses Against Religion • Besides the general failure to settle the God question, there are other ways for man to deny God his due, though most of these skewed practices are less tempting to our "enlightened" age (cf. CCC 2110-2117).

The reality of the Creator and the first commandment alike forbid polytheism, superstition, idolatry, divination, sorcery, and magic. The latter three all involve dealing with occult powers, most notably Satan and his minions, in a sinful attempt to obtain power over creatures or the future. Superstition in our day sometimes takes the form of attributing an importance in some way magical to the mere external performance of otherwise lawful religious actions.

A child's righting of its relationship with its parents (the fourth commandment) provides an analogy, and most probably a necessary preliminary, to man's rectifying his relationship with God. A child who does not recognize everything its parents have freely and, ideally, gratuitously done and do for it (this will be almost entirely invisible to the unthinking child) can hardly escape the centripetal orbit woven by its immature and disorderly self-love. It can hardly not take for granted parents' services and self-privations, as if they were so many rights and entitlements of its own.

Only acknowledging the huge truth of its accumulated "debts" to its parents can usher realism into the child's cramped ego-trap. A child may not be able, nor even be expected, to repay its parents fully, but the willful failure to acknowledge the fundamental and concrete truth of largely one-sided parental giving cannot help but vitiate, falsify, all the child's other relationships, especially with its much more loving and disinterested heavenly Father. Many people today leave unfulfilled, and even unrecognized, the first commandment, which enshrines the primacy of God's creative love and sovereign lordship. May not much of the reason be their failure to satisfy the much more palpable claims arising from their indebtedness to parents?

Since man is here not only to know and love God but also out of brotherly fellowship to make him known and loved, this irreplaceable personal religion is also to overflow onto one's social dealings and even into the public forum. "Man's vocation is to make God manifest by acting in conformity with his creation 'in the image and likeness of God'" (CCC 2085). Were man, hypothetically, to ratify truly and fully the God-ward vocation inscribed in his God-given nature, loving good example alone, with its attendant joy, would eloquently and persuasively suffice as God's megaphone and invitation. Even in the best of cases, however, man generates comparatively few good deeds. A person can apostolically try to make up for this lack by personally giving witness to his discoveries of how and who God truly is, especially to those at his side and others who may inquire or otherwise show themselves receptive.

In these and many other ways can one herald the liberating, glad tidings of the Good News. So, with Augustine, one should manifest gratitude to God for having made him *capax Dei*: hungry for the infinite, in both mind and heart: "You have made us for you, O Lord, and restless will our hearts be until they rest in you."

See: Agnosticism; Atheism; Blasphemy; Fatherhood of God; Freedom, Human; God, Nature and Attributes of; Holy Days of Obligation; Idolatry; Knowledge of God; Lord's Day; Magic; Prayer; Sacrifice; Sacrilege; Servile Work; Simony; Superstition; Worship.

Suggested Readings: CCC 2083-2117. M. Adler, *How to Think about God.* G. Chesterton, *The Everlasting Man.* C. Dawson, *Religion and Culture.* F. Faber, *The Creator and the Creature.* P. Kreeft, *Heaven.* J. Newman, *A Grammar of Assent.* J. Pieper, *Leisure, the Basis for Culture; On Hope.* G. Vann, *Alive to God.*

Dennis Helming

RELIGIOUS LIBERTY

The right to religious freedom is among the most widely affirmed and deeply valued human and civil liberties in our time. We rightly regard it as one of the most precious blessings of our liberal democratic heritage. Yet it also is a right often misunderstood.

When the Church supports religious liberty, she does not thereby sanction a right to believe whatever one wishes, to choose whatever religion happens to suit one's fancy, or to choose no religion at all. Nor is it implied that one religion is as good or as true as the next. What is at stake is the right of persons and communities to be free from societal, and especially governmental, compulsion regarding religious belief, life, and worship. This is the application to religious life of a principle frequently expressed in the tradition of the Church: that, as Pope John Paul II puts it, "freedom consists not in doing what we like, but in having the right to do what we ought" (homily in Oriole Park at Camden Yards, Baltimore, October 8, 1995).

The most thorough treatment of this subject by the modern Magisterium is found in the Second Vatican Council's *Declaration on Religious Freedom, Dignitatis Humanae.* This important document forms the basis of the topic's treatment in the *Catechism of the Catholic Church* ("The social duty of religion and the right to religious freedom," CCC 2104-2109, presented as part of the explanation of the first commandment).

As the *Declaration*'s Latin title suggests, the Council stresses the requirement of "the principle of religious liberty," rightly understood, for the dignity of the human person and the fulfillment of the human vocation: "The Vatican Council declares that the human person has a right to religious freedom. Freedom of this kind means that all men should be immune from coercion on the part of individuals, social groups and every human power so that, within due limits, nobody is forced to act against his convictions nor is anyone to be restrained from acting in accordance with his convictions in religious matters in private or in public, alone or in associations with others. The Council further declares that the right to religious freedom is based on the very dignity of the human person as known through the revealed word of God and by reason itself. This right of the human person to religious freedom must be given such recognition in the constitutional order of society as will make it a civil right" (*Dignitatis Humanae,* 2; cf. CCC 1907).

Moral Foundations of Religious Liberty • The dignity of the human person, a being "endowed with reason and free will, and therefore bearing personal responsibility," lies precisely in the capacity to direct oneself toward the final end of human life: knowledge and love of God. As the Council says, human beings are "impelled by their very nature and bound by a moral obligation to seek the truth, especially religious truth." They also are "bound to adhere to the truth once they come to know it and direct their whole lives in accordance with the demands of truth." However, this obligation cannot be satisfied in a way in keeping with human nature without "both psychological freedom and immunity from external coercion." It follows that the right to religious freedom is grounded "not in the subjective attitude of the individual but in his very nature"; and for this reason the right "continues to exist even in those who do not live up to their obligation of seeking the truth and adhering to it" (*Dignitatis Humanae*, 2). And the Council adds that "everybody has the *duty* and *consequently the right* to seek the truth in religious matters so that, through the use of appropriate means [free inquiry with the help of teaching and instruction, communication and dialogue], he may prudently form judgments of conscience which are sincere and true" (*Dignitatis Humanae*, 3, emphasis added).

The Council further notes that Divine Revelation confirms these conclusions drawn from rational reflection on human nature. Christ and his Apostles after him, while stressing the duty of individuals to seek and adhere to revealed truth, nevertheless refused to coerce their hearers into belief. From the earliest times, the Church has taught that such coercion is as wrong as it is counterproductive: One can force a person to his knees, but a genuine act of faith or worship cannot be compelled from without (cf. *Dignitatis Humanae*, 10). During his 1995 visit to the United Nations and the United States, Pope John Paul II told an interfaith gathering: "Religious tolerance is based on the conviction that God wishes to be adored by people who are free: a conviction which requires us to respect and honor the inner sanctuary of conscience in which each person meets God. The Catholic Church wholly supports this conviction" (greeting in Baltimore cathedral, October 8, 1995).

The right to religious liberty is not absolute, however. When its exercise threatens the just peace and stability of civil society; when the practices of some religious cult harm persons physically or mentally; when some invoke religious liberty to justify discrimination or as a tool to deny others the full rights of citizenship — in these and similar cases the competent civil authority must seek fair and upright means to defend the temporal common good against such abuses.

Role of Civil Authority • Beyond redressing abuses and adopting a position of neutrality, civil authority has an eminently positive role to play with regard to religious liberty. It must "recognize and look with favor on the religious life of the citizens" (*Dignitatis Humanae*, 3). Public authority must "undertake to safeguard the religious freedom of all the citizens in an effective manner by just legislation and other appropriate means. It must help create conditions favorable to the fostering of religious life so that the citizens will be really in a position to exercise their religious rights and fulfill their religious duties and so that society itself may enjoy the benefits of justice and peace, which result from man's faithfulness to God and his holy will" (*Dignitatis Humanae*, 6).

Yet when rulers of a given nation attempt to dictate the religious beliefs for the nation, to control or curtail the religious life of the citizens, they decisively overstep the boundaries of their this-worldly competence. Doctrines such as the *cuius regio, eius religio* of post-Reformation Europe plagued by religious wars are seriously mistaken. (The phrase, meaning "whose region, his religion," comes from the Peace of Augsburg [1555].) By contrast, Pope John Paul quotes with admiration a ruler of that time who withstood such confusion: "At a time in Western history when heretics were being tried and burned at the stake, the last Polish king of the Jagiellon dynasty [declared]. . . 'I am not the king of your consciences' " (*Crossing the Threshold of Hope*, p. 154).

The Pope's reference to heretic-burning is a sad reminder of those periods in history when certain Protestants and Catholics, including some in positions of political and even ecclesiastical authority, sought to compel belief by means ranging from social discrimination to physical force. Vatican Council II stresses that even in such dark times characterized by confused and/or malicious practice, it "always remained the teaching of the Church that no one is to be coerced into believing" (*Dignitatis Humanae*, 12). This doctrine is also evident in certain magisterial documents of the nineteenth century, which present a more restrictive view of religious liberty as a civil right. The teaching of *Dignitatis Humanae* is thus correctly understood as a development of Catholic doctrine, not a departure from outmoded Church teaching.

As a consequence of the social nature of the human person, both religious duties and the right to religious freedom apply not only to individuals but also to families, associations, and various forms of communities (cf. CCC 2105-2106; *Dignitatis Humanae*, 3-5). Of particular importance is the role of the family in the religious upbringing of children. The parental right in this area, which follows from their grave obligation as primary educators of their offspring, must be recognized and respected. The Second Vatican Council explains: "Every family . . . has the right freely to organize its own religious life in the home under the control of the parents. These have the right to decide in accordance with their own religious beliefs the form of religious upbringing which is to be given to their children. The civil authority must therefore recognize the right of parents to choose with genuine freedom schools or other means of education. Parents should not be subjected directly or indirectly to unjust burdens because of this freedom of choice. Furthermore, the rights of parents are violated if their children are compelled to attend classes which are not in agreement with the religious beliefs of the parents or if there is but a single compulsory system of education from which all religious instruction is excluded" (*Dignitatis Humanae*, 5).

The Council reserves some of its strongest language for its defense of the liberty of the Church within civil society: "Among those things which pertain to the good of the Church and indeed to the good of society here on earth, things which must everywhere and at all times be safeguarded and defended from all harm, the most outstanding surely is that the Church enjoy that freedom of action which her responsibility for the salvation of men requires. This is a sacred liberty with which the only-begotten Son of God endowed the Church. . . . Indeed it belongs so intimately to the Church that to attack it is to oppose the will of God. The freedom of the Church is the fundamental principle governing relations between the Church and public authorities and the whole civil order" (*Dignitatis Humanae*, 13). This freedom pertains to the Church as an institution, as a spiritual authority, and as a community of believers enjoying the same rights of conscience as their fellow citizens.

Violations of Religious Liberty • Various political regimes of the twentieth century committed gross violations against religious liberty: refusing the faithful the right to worship in public and often even in private; removing all religious education from the schools; forcefully propagating atheism; preventing those known to be believers or adherents of faiths other than that officially endorsed by the state from receiving a full education or advancing in their professions. The list of abuses could be extended indefinitely.

The people of the United States are fortunate not to have suffered the worst sort of open persecutions and to have freedom of belief, worship, and assembly guaranteed in the Constitution. Even here, however, many citizens are justly disturbed by trends such as the virtual removal of religion from the public schools, and the heavy financial burden placed on parents seeking to give their children a religious education in private or parochial schools.

Moreover, our secularized society, characterized by an individualistic outlook and an inordinate pursuit of wealth and comfort, may have an adverse impact on religious freedom in ways more dangerous for being more subtle. This sort of political culture tends to breed indifference and superficiality, in religious matters as in other important areas of life. These can do even more to undermine religion than open hatred for Christianity and violent persecution can do.

Moreover, there is some evidence that the founders of liberal democracy had this watering-down of religion as a concrete goal. Note this revealing passage in the 1748 treatise *Spirit of the Laws* by the French Enlightenment thinker Montesquieu (1689-1755): "[A] more sure way to attack religion is by favor, by the commodities of life, by the hope of wealth; not by indignation, but by what makes men lukewarm, when other passions act on our souls, and those that religion inspires are silent. A general rule: with regard to changes in religion, invitations are stronger than penalties" (Bk. 25, Ch. 12). Thomas Jefferson privately expressed his confident expectation that "the present generation will see Unitarianism become the general religion of the United States." It is not surprising, then, that Pope John Paul II urged Americans to acknowledge and meet "[t]he challenge facing you . . . to increase people's awareness of the importance for society of religious freedom; to defend that freedom against those who would take religion out of the public domain and establish secularism as America's official faith" (greeting in Baltimore cathedral).

In a situation of greater freedom, and consequently of less societal or governmental support for religious belief and life, it is necessary that people of religious conviction feel a corresponding increase in personal responsibility to seek and live by the truth, and to do their part to help create a culture truly open — not merely indifferent — to religion. Catholics have an obligation to pay careful attention to the teaching authority (Magisterium) of the Church in forming their consciences. They must endeavor to become men and women with the moral and intellectual backbone to counter the prevailing tide of lukewarmness and materialism. "For this reason this Vatican Council urges everyone, especially those responsible for educating others, to try to form men with a respect for the moral order who will obey lawful authority and be lovers of true freedom — men, that is, who will form their own judgments in the light of truth, direct their activities with a sense of

responsibility, and strive for what is true and just in willing cooperation with others. Religious liberty therefore should have this further purpose and aim of enabling men to act with greater responsibility in fulfilling their obligations in society" (*Dignitatis Humanae*, 8). Ultimately, religious liberty should open a path to the fullness of truth that, as John Paul observes throughout his encyclical on moral principles *The Splendor of Truth, Veritatis Splendor* (1993), alone can make people truly free.

See: Authority; Church and State; Civil Law; Conscience; Conscience and the Magisterium; Conscience Formation; Development of Doctrine; Freedom, Human; Freemasonry; Politics; Religion, Virtue of.

Suggested Readings: CCC 2104-2109, 2136-2137. Vatican Council II, *Declaration on Religious Freedom, Dignitatis Humanae*. John XXIII, *Peace on Earth, Pacem in Terris*, 14, 28-36.

Mary M. Keys

REPRODUCTIVE TECHNOLOGIES

God loves each and every human life, no matter the method of a baby's conception. He loves those conceived through the loving embrace of husband and wife, those conceived out of wedlock, those conceived through an act of rape, and those conceived in a petri dish. Obviously, though, not all acts that lead to the conception of new life are equally moral: Not all are in accord with human dignity. Many of the new reproductive technologies, such as artificial insemination, *in vitro* fertilization, surrogate motherhood, and cloning, involve procedures that violate human goods.

Many argue that the Church should not oppose any method that helps married couples fulfill one of the deepest desires of their hearts and one of the defining elements of marriage: having babies. While the Church has approved many modern medical techniques that assist couples in overcoming infertility and hopes modern medical science will find additional moral means, she nonetheless judges that some methods are simply incompatible with the moral parameters surrounding childbearing. Those moral parameters are that the human dignity of all life must be respected and that the goods of marriage must be respected.

First it must be noted that, however natural and good it is that spouses desire children, it cannot be said that they have a "right" to children. Children are a gift from God. God chose to have new life brought forth through the loving embrace of spouses. He wanted life to be the result of an act of love by those committed to loving each other and the life that may be conceived as the result of their loving acts. All human life is in profound need of being loved, and babies are especially in need of being loved by their parents. God's design is to have children lovingly conceived and cared for by loving parents. Many children are denied much that would enhance their upbringing, but we ought to strive to make certain that our actions not lead to difficulties for the children we bring into this world.

Moral and Immoral Methods • The principle the Church uses to distinguish moral from immoral methods is that moral methods assist nature, whereas immoral methods replace or substitute for the conjugal act that should be the source of new life. The justification for this principle is found in the Church's natural law theory of morality, which sees God as the author of nature and the human person as a creature who is given the ability to live freely in accord with nature or to violate nature. "Nature" here does not refer simply to the biological laws of nature; rather, it refers to the whole nature of the human person. The institution of marriage is a natural institution in that it meets natural needs of the human person on both the physical and spiritual levels. The conjugal act represents the total self-giving of spouses, and since children are the result of and the most incarnational representation of that total self-giving, it is appropriate that children come to be only through an act of conjugal sexual intercourse.

Some of the procedures developed by modern medical science do respect and assist nature. For instance, fertility drugs may help a woman who does not regularly ovulate to release an egg or eggs to be fertilized. Should she become pregnant, the pregnancy is directly the result of an act of sexual intercourse and only indirectly the result of technology. Corrective surgery for blocked fallopian tubes or for anomalies in the male reproductive organs may also enable those to conceive who have had difficulty doing so. In all moral use of reproductive technologies, the procedures simply restore the body to its normally functioning state. Conception is not the direct result of a technical intervention; the technical intervention makes it possible that conception be the direct result of an act of conjugal intercourse, and such is in accord with God's will for the bringing forth of new life.

Some methods, however, violate the unitive meaning of the sexual act. Methods such as artificial insemination, *in vitro* fertilization, and surrogacy require the collection of sperm. Generally, semen is collected through an act of masturbation, an act that is considered intrinsically immoral. Yet, even were it possible to collect the semen by a morally permissible means, artificial insemination, *in vitro* fertilization, and surrogacy nonetheless require that a technician's skill be substituted for the act of sexual intercourse as the direct cause of the conception of the child. In these methods, the child is not a result of the loving union of the spouses but of a technician's skillful manipulation of "reproductive material." For this reason, these methods are considered to be immoral.

The confusion of parenthood that comes with some reproductive technologies is reflected in a court case involving a woman who had had some of her husband's semen frozen. After they divorced, she decided to use some of the semen to have herself impregnated through artificial insemination. After the baby was born, she sued her former husband, the biological father, for child support. He contested, claiming that he was not the legal father of the child. The court decided that the lab technician was the legal father, since the lab technician was most directly responsible for the impregnation of the woman.

In addition to requiring the immoral acts of masturbation and of replacing a technician's skill for the act of sexual intercourse, the above-mentioned methods are immoral in other ways. Often the reproductive "material" used in these procedures does not belong to the parents of the child being conceived: Sperm from a man other than a woman's husband or ova from a woman other than the woman herself may be used. Such use of "alien" reproductive material violates the sanctity of marriage and of childbearing, for the child is no longer the result of a loving act of the spouses but is the result of an exchange of genetic material of those who have made no loving commitment to each other.

Indeed, it is possible now for women, married or unmarried, heterosexual or homosexual, to purchase sperm from sperm banks and to select with some specificity what sort of genes they would like their baby to have. There is virtually no oversight of the distribution of the semen. One individual man could be anonymously fathering dozens or hundreds of children through semen donations; such children may be in some danger of marrying a half-brother or half-sister some day. In a famous legal case, a doctor who worked at an infertility clinic used his own semen and fathered many children with his patients. Women long past natural childbearing age have had babies through these reproductive technologies. They purchase ova from a female donor and are impregnated through *in vitro* fertilization.

Reproduction vs. Procreation • The bringing forth of a new human life is more properly termed "procreation" than "reproduction." Many modern reproductive technologies treat the child being conceived more as a product and object than as a precious gift from God. Whereas "reproduction" suggests that a repeatable product is being produced, "procreation" reflects the involvement of God in the act of bringing forth new life, and it suggests the unrepeatable uniqueness of each human being. The term "procreation" calls attention to the fact that spouses are cooperators with God in bringing forth new human life; each human life is the result of a new creative act of God, who supplies a unique, newly created, immortal soul for each individual conceived.

Many of these techniques do not accord the embryos produced the dignity of human beings. For instance, many reproductive technologies involve the fertilization of several embryos and selective implantation of only a few; the unselected embryos are disposed of or frozen for future use. Clearly, any procedure that involves the creation of new life that is going to be "disposed of" or "used" is not compatible with innate human dignity. All current techniques for *in vitro* fertilization involve the creation of excess embryos. These procedures allow for selective termination of life carrying undesirable genetic material. People who know themselves to be carriers of defective genetic material sometimes use *in vitro* fertilization rather than an act of sexual intercourse to conceive their children, precisely so that they can have the *conceptus* examined for genetic anomalies and, if defective, discarded.

Surrogacy is a reproductive technology that involves one woman carrying a child for another, who may have fertility problems, health problems, or some other reason for not wanting to carry a child to term. The surrogate will often be fertilized by artificial methods with the sperm of the other woman's husband or will be impregnated with the *conceptus* produced from the other's ova and her husband's sperm through *in vitro* fertilization. This method shares all the disvalues of artificial insemination and *in vitro* fertilization, as well as a few more. The surrogate is generally paid for her services, generally at much less than the minimum wage, and thus the practice stands to exploit poor women. Indeed, the practice of surrogacy verges closely on the practice of baby-selling. A contract is signed beforehand, and the baby conceived is often treated like a product; many contracts require amniocentesis and abortion should the baby be deformed in some fashion. Famous court cases have confirmed the view that women bond strongly with the babies in their wombs and have difficulty abiding by the terms of a contract that requires them to give the baby away.

Cloning is another procedure that creates a new human life outside of the act of conjugal sexual intercourse. The nucleus of a mature but unfertilized egg is removed from the woman and replaced with a nucleus obtained from a specialized somatic cell of an adult organism. An unlimited number of genetically identical individuals could be produced through this process. It is not yet perfected for human beings but seems within the realm of possibility. In addition to many of the disvalues mentioned above, cloning would open up another Pandora's box of possibilities difficult if not impossible to control. It will be possible to create clones of individuals who will then have a ready supply of "spare parts." It will be possible to clone those we think have special talents or beauty, in the attempt to create a kind of a perfect society.

These reproductive technologies, along with abortion, already have served greatly to diminish the value of human life. At one time, the medical profession expressed great horror at the Nazi regime for experimentation on human beings, particularly on embryos; but now government funding is provided for experimentation on the excess embryos produced through *in vitro* fertilization, all in the name of science. The government up to now has stopped short of permitting funding of projects that involve the creation of embryos for the express purpose of experimentation, but it has not made the procedure itself illegal.

Medical "advances" such as abortion, contraception, and the new reproductive technologies, all developed in the name of compassion, have made it possible to separate sexuality and baby-making. In the resulting "brave new world," sexuality and childbearing are far removed from their natural and proper meaning and human life itself has come to have little value in the eyes of many.

See: Body and Soul; Genetic Experimentation; Human Experimentation; Human Life, Dignity and Sanctity of; Human Person; Science and the Church; Sexuality, Human.

Suggested Readings: CCC 2373-2377. Congregation for the Doctrine of the Faith, *Instruction on Respect for Human Life in Its Origin and on the Dignity of Procreation: Replies to Certain Questions of the Day, Donum Vitae.* A. Kimbrell, *The Human Body Shop: The Engineering and*

Marketing of Life. The Pope John Center, *Reproductive Technologies, Marriage, and the Church.*

Janet E. Smith

RESTITUTION

Commutative justice, which governs exchanges between persons, specifies that a free mutual transaction should result in an equality of things exchanged or a restitution of balance. For most exchanges, the price or bartering fulfills commutative justice. But anyone who fails to live up to an agreement or who steals or knowingly benefits from goods stolen from another must make restitution.

As such, it is a form of reparation, making amends to another for wrongs done. It is not enough simply to repent of the wrong and restore the article in some instances. Harm done owing to the lack of the article, especially if this extends over a long time, must also be repaired. If one has stolen money, restitution requires the return not only of the sum taken but also, where relevant, of a sum equal to the interest the money would have earned, calculated at a realistic rate. The *locus classicus* for restitution in the New Testament is the statement of Zacchaeus, the man who climbs the sycamore tree and later says to Jesus, "If I have defrauded anyone of anything, I restore it fourfold." Jesus answers, "Today salvation has come to this house" (Lk 19:8-9).

See: Commutative Justice; Property; Stealing.

RESURRECTION OF CHRIST

"On the third day he rose again according to the Scriptures." The bodily Resurrection of Christ is a dogma of faith. It also is a fact, an event that took place historically and was verified.

The oldest witness to the Resurrection is found in 1 Corinthians 15:3-8. This is in the area of historical fact. St. Paul speaks of the living tradition of the Resurrection, which he had learned after his conversion. He speaks of eyewitnesses, specific individuals known to the believers, most of them still living when he writes: twelve Apostles,

Peter, James, and more than five hundred persons. His witness is based on a fact of experience. In Acts 1:22, the Apostles of the Jerusalem community use the same argument when choosing Matthias to complete the number of the Twelve: Matthias had to be a witness not only to Jesus' public life but also to his Resurrection.

We cannot accept the hypothesis that the Resurrection was merely an interpretation of Christ's state after his death (i.e., a state of life and not of death). Nor can we accept the hypothesis that speaks of the influence that Christ after his death still exercises on his disciples. These ideas show a prejudice against the fact, reducing it to a product of the Jerusalem community, a product of the faith of the Apostles from before or after Easter. But the pre-Easter faith of the Apostles was subjected to the extreme test of the Master's Passion and death, as he had foretold (cf. Lk 22:31-32). The shock was so great that at least some of the disciples did not initially believe the news of his Resurrection (cf. Lk 24:9-11) so that the Lord had to persuade them. Jesus must convince them that it is really he, telling them to touch him and see for themselves, "for a spirit has not flesh and bones as you see that I have" (Lk 24:39). In John 20:24-29, Thomas is amazed and incredulous at the news from the other Apostles. His difficulty in admitting the Resurrection without having personally experienced the presence of the living Jesus, and then his yielding in the presence of the proofs offered him by Jesus himself, confirm the evidence of the Gospels about the reluctance of the Apostles to admit the Resurrection.

Their faith comes under the action of divine grace from the direct experience of the reality of the risen Christ. It is Jesus himself who, after the Resurrection, seeks out the disciples in order to give them a sense of the reality and to dispel the opinion or fear that it was a question of a ghost and they were victims of an illusion. In fact, he established direct contact with them through touch, as in the case of Thomas and in the meeting described in Luke. He invites them to verify that the risen body in which he comes to them is the very same that was tortured and crucified.

That body possesses new properties, having become spiritual and glorified, and no longer subject to the limitations of material beings and of the human body. But it is authentic and real. In his material identity, there is proof of Christ's Resurrection. The meeting on the road to Emmaus shows in a particularly vivid way that conviction about the Resurrection matured in the minds of the disciples through contact with the risen Christ (cf. Lk 24:15-21). Sadness and disappointment give way to a total transformation. The certainty of the Resurrection made them, as it were, new men.

Historical Event Transcending History • At the dawn of the third day after Jesus' burial by Joseph of Arimathea, the tomb was found empty. The women who went to the tomb encountered an angel who said to them: "You seek Jesus who was crucified; he is not here. He has risen as he said" (Mt 28:5-6).

There are three reasons why this event transcends history. First, no one saw the Resurrection. Certainly Christ's body was no longer in the tomb. No one was an eyewitness of the event itself. No one could say how it had happened in its physical reality. Second, the senses could not perceive the interior essence of the passage to another life. It is this transhistorical feature of the Resurrection that must especially be considered if we are to understand to some extent the mystery of that historical, but also transhistorical, event. Third, Christ did not simply return to earthly life, like those whom he had raised from the dead during his public ministry: Lazarus, the daughter of Jairus, the son of the widow of Naim. In his risen body, Christ passed from death to another life beyond space and time. This risen body of Jesus was filled with the power of the Holy Spirit and shared in the divine life of glory. He is now the "heavenly man" (1 Cor 15:47). In this sense, Christ's Resurrection eludes the criteria of simple empirical observation. In his contacts with others after the Resurrection, this real dimension of his humanity conceals another life that is now his and that withdraws him from ordinary earthly life and plunges him into mystery.

The Resurrection takes place through the power of the Father, who had raised Christ his Son (Acts 2:32) and introduced his humanity — even his body — into the communion of the Trinity. St. Paul insists that this is a manifestation of the power of God through the work of the Spirit, who in raising Jesus placed him in the glorious sphere of Lord (*Kyrios*), where he definitively merits the name Son of God that belonged to him from eternity.

Other texts speak of the Resurrection as taking place through Christ's own power (the active voice of the verb *aneste:* "he rose"). This active dimension is found in Christ's predictions. Thus John 10:17-18: "I lay down my life, that I may take it up again . . . I have the power to lay it down and I have the power to take it up again"; 1 Thessalonians 4:14: "We believe that Jesus died and rose again"; Acts 17:3: ". . . it was necessary for the Christ to suffer and to rise from the dead."

The Resurrection Is the High Point of Revelation • The Resurrection was first of all the confirmation of all that Jesus had done and taught. It was the divine seal stamped on his words and life. He had indicated to his disciples and adversaries this definitive sign of truth. If this word and promise of his are revealed as true, then all his other words and promises possess the power of truth that does not pass away. No stronger, more decisive, and more authoritative proof could have been imagined or asked for.

The truth of Christ's divinity is confirmed by the Resurrection. "When you have lifted up the Son of man, then you will know that I am he" (Jn 8:28). This reverses the condemnation by the Sanhedrin of the great blasphemy, the charge for the death sentence: that he proclaimed himself the Son of God. The Resurrection confirms the truth of his divine identity and justifies the self-attribution of the "name" of God, which he made before the pasch: "Before Abraham was, I am" (Jn 8:58).

In the Upper Room, Jesus had asked the Father to reveal that the Christ-Son was his eternal Son: "Father, the hour has come, glorify your Son that the Son may glorify you. . . . Glorify me in your presence with the glory that I had with you before the world was made" (Jn 17:1, 5).

Paul assimilates the ideas of the glory of Christ's Resurrection and his eternal Divine Sonship, fully revealed in the victorious conclusion of his Messianic mission. For Paul, in the opening verses of Romans, from the very moment of his conception and birth Jesus was the eternal Son of God become Son of Man. In the Resurrection, this Divine Sonship was shown forth in all its fullness through the power of God, who restored Jesus to life by the work of the Holy Spirit (cf. Rom 8:11) and constituted him in the glorious state of *Kyrios* so that Jesus merits under a new Messianic title the recognition, worship, and glory of the eternal Son of God. Paul spells this out in his preaching (e.g., Acts 13:32-34; cf. Ps 2:7). For Paul, the Resurrection completes the manifestation of the content of the Incarnation; it is the fullness of Revelation.

Saving Power of the Resurrection • The saving power of the Gospel has two aspects: death for liberation from sin and resurrection to open the way to a new life. A variety of elements can be distinguished within the deep internal unity of these two aspects.

The risen Christ is the source of a new life for everyone. "Father, glorify your Son that the Son may glorify you since you have given him power over all flesh, to give eternal life to all whom you have given him" (Jn 17:1-2). Jesus embraces his disciples, to whom he had promised, "I live and you will live" (Jn 14:19) — share in my life, which will be revealed after the Resurrection. All must become one by sharing in God's glory in Christ. The new life consists in victory over the death caused by sin and a sharing in the divine life of grace (cf. Eph 2:4-5, 1 Pt 1:3).

This new life according to the Spirit manifests the adoption as sons (Gal 4:4-5). Divine adoption through the Holy Spirit makes man like the only begotten Son: "All who are led by the Spirit of God are sons of God" (Rom 8:14; cf. Gal 4:6-7). This freedom from slavery is not a legal but a real gift of divine life.

John 6:54 and 6:61-62 make it clear that those who receive the Eucharist partake of the Body and Blood of the glorified Christ. St. Paul expresses this in the First Letter to the Corinthians 15:20-22 and 53-54.

The definitive victory over death won by Christ is shared by him with humanity to the extent it receives the fruits of redemption. Thanks to this process, down the centuries a new people of the redeemed, a new humanity, is formed, gathered in the Church, the true community of the Resurrection. This takes place in a sphere of indescribable spirituality, which transcends the power of human comprehension and operation. It is a mysterious process of spiritualization, which at the moment of our resurrection will affect also our bodies through the power of that same Holy Spirit who brought about Christ's Resurrection. In expectation of that final fulfillment, the risen Christ dwells in the hearts of his disciples as a source of sanctification in the Holy Spirit, of divine life and sonship, of future resurrection.

See: Baptism; Divine Revelation; Eucharist; Holy Spirit; Jesus Christ, God and Man; Jesus Christ, Life of; Miracles; Redemption; Resurrection of the Dead.

Suggested Readings: CCC 638-658. W. Pannenberg, *Jesus God and Man.* H. von Balthasar, *Mysterium Paschale.* I. de la Potterie, *The Hour of Jesus.*

Richard Malone

RESURRECTION OF THE DEAD

Concerning the Church's teaching on the subject of man's final end, the purpose for which God first called man into existence, all the creeds of Christendom and many of the Church councils, particularly from the seventh through the fourteenth centuries, unite in the most solemn and firm conviction that God wills the whole man, body and soul, to enter into eternal life.

To speak thus of man — the totality, that is, of his being — wedded finally together following the Last (or General) Judgment, is to include both man's relation to the world and to other men, relations necessarily expressed in and through the body. Man is not, in other words, a dis-incarnate being, a figure whose evident enfleshment in time

and space can be construed as some sort of mistake. Horror of the flesh is not a characteristic of the Christian vision of man. How could it be in a religion whose founder and chief protagonist came in the flesh? To believe otherwise, St. John tells us in his Second Letter, is the work of the Antichrist (v. 7).

Hope, then, for the resurrection of the human body is not an extraneous or accidental addition to Christian faith. Belief in a bodily resurrection is a constitutive feature of Christian faith, an intrinsic consequence of that belief itself.

The Apostles' Creed "culminates in the proclamation of the resurrection of the dead on the last day and in life everlasting" (CCC 988). The hope of Christianity from the beginning lies in the promise that God will someday raise the dead to new life. "But if there is no resurrection of the dead," warns St. Paul, "then Christ has not been raised; if Christ has not been raised, then our preaching is in vain and your faith is in vain" (1 Cor 15:13-14).

Jewish Belief in Afterlife • While it took many centuries to arrive at belief in the resurrection of the body, the Old Testament anticipated the New Testament faith in bodily resurrection in statements about God's great power over life and death. He "lead[s] men down to the gates of Hades and back again" (Wis 16:13; see also 1 Sm 2:6). God restores us to life (cf. Ps 30:3). Passages such as Isaiah 25:8 ("Your dead shall live; their bodies shall rise") hint at what will become a New Testament teaching. A greater degree of explicitness is seen in 2 Maccabees 7:9-13, 12:41-45, and Daniel 12:2-3. At the time of Christ, the Pharisees believed in the resurrection of the body, but the Sadducees did not. "Some Sadducees who say there is no resurrection came to him . . ." (Mk 12:18; cf. Acts 23:8).

Christ and Resurrection • Of those who would deny the power of resurrection that Christ commands — which, moreover, he *is* — Jesus bluntly asks, "Is not this why you are wrong, that you know neither the scriptures nor the power of God?" (Mk 12:24). Belief in the resurrection, he tells them, depends on faith in God, who "is not

God of the dead, but of the living" (Mk 12:27). What is being affirmed here is that God himself and the unending intimacy of communion he offers are life. To belong to God, to strengthen one's whole being in his, is to obtain an indestructible life. Paradise itself opens in Christ; the glory and salvation thereof are trained on his Person. "The bond with Jesus is, even now, resurrection. Where there is communion with him, the boundary of death is overshot here and now," says Cardinal Joseph Ratzinger.

Thus the pivotal equation of faith — acceptance of Christ equals life everlasting — becomes a truth inscribed upon his very Person. And the infinitely consoling words spoken to Martha, the sister of Lazarus whom Jesus has gone to Bethany to awaken from the sleep of death, are equally addressed to us when we, like Martha, acknowledge the living God in whom the dead are raised. When Jesus says, "Your brother will rise again," Martha replies that she knows this because she believes in the resurrection promised all pious Jews on the last day. Jesus answers, "I am the resurrection and the life; he who believes in me, though he die, yet shall he live, and whoever lives and believes in me shall never die" (Jn 11:23-26).

Here is the deepest point of entry into the Christian mystery, namely, because Christ rose from the dead, we, too, are destined to rise again. "We shall rise like Christ, with him, and through him" (CCC 995), for he is life itself, eternal life that he shares with the Father before all ages, and resurrection is the gift vouchsafed to those who believe, those whom he delights to have return with him to the origin and spring of all life. "His life," says theologian Adrienne Von Speyr, "is inwardly informed by the resurrection principle, that is, the relationship to that divine reality, that higher world to which his prayer journeyed. Since he gives his life to all, since his life pulsates in all who live, he also imparts his resurrection in the same way."

In his book *Crossing the Threshold of Hope*, Pope John Paul II is asked to reflect on the meaning of salvation that so implicates the Christian at the profoundest level in the drama of his religion.

Very simply, the Holy Father answers: "To save means to liberate from *radical, ultimate* evil," of which the two principal examples of course are death and damnation. But thanks to Christ's Resurrection, none of us need fear either one; neither that "final engulfment in the abyss of death," nor yet the still greater evil that is "God's rejection of man, that is, *eternal damnation* as the consequence of man's rejection of God" (p. 70).

It is only God, then, who saves, "and he saves the whole of humanity in Christ. *The very name Jesus, Jeshua ('God who saves')* bespeaks this salvation" (*Crossing the Threshold of Hope*, p. 70). Leave out the Christological connection and at one stroke the entirety of the Christian doctrine concerning resurrection is reduced to myth.

"Christian faith is more than the option in favor of a spiritual ground to the world," says Ratzinger. "[I]ts central formula is not 'I believe in something,' but 'I believe in Thee.' It is the encounter with the human being Jesus, and in this encounter it experiences the meaning of the world as a person" (*Introduction to Christianity*, p. 47). In the confrontation with Christ in which the whole drama of a man's faith consists, one sees in him the very presence of the eternal in this world. "Thus faith is the finding of a 'You' that bears me up and amid all the unfulfilled — and in the last resort unfulfillable — hope of human encounters gives me the promise of an indestructible love which not only longs for eternity but guarantees it" (*Introduction to Christianity*, p. 48).

The Reality of Resurrection • The *Catechism of the Catholic Church* reminds us that "incomprehension and opposition" have often been the world's reaction to faith. On this it cites St. Augustine, who held that "[o]n no point does the Christian faith encounter more opposition than on the resurrection of the body [*En. in Ps.* 88, 5: PL 37, 1134]" (CCC 996). In fact, shortly after the martyrdom of St. Ignatius of Antioch, the force of the equation had already crystallized. In one of his famous letters Ignatius writes: "For it was for our sakes that he suffered all this, to save us. And he genuinely suffered, as even he genuinely raised himself. It is not as some unbelievers say, that his Passion was a sham. It's they who are a sham! Yes, and their fate will fit their fancies — they will be ghosts and apparitions."

If salvation is a gift offered to all, then it can hardly bypass the body. For our human flesh has been assumed by Christ, taken up into the Godhead itself, and redeemed in the event of the cross. Thus the body, too, is bound for glory, for that promised destiny of which Christ first blazed the trail. "This hope," writes Hans Urs von Balthasar, "insane in view of decay and the grave, and also contradictory to all experience, hangs on one fact: Christ's Resurrection" (*Credo: Meditations on the Apostles' Creed*, p. 95).

Just when the miracle of resurrection will take place — or, for that matter, how it will happen — is futile to try to unpuzzle. Those who ask, St. Paul says, are "foolish" (cf. 1 Cor 15:35ff.).

However, it is in the deep mystery of the Holy Eucharist that one is granted that intimation of a final transfiguring glory to which we have all, in Christ, been called. Quoting St. Irenaeus, the *Catechism* invites the faithful to compare the change wrought by Christ in the Holy Eucharist to the transformation our bodies await when Christ descends on the last day to summon all the dead: "Just as bread that comes from the earth, after God's blessing . . . is no longer ordinary bread, but Eucharist, formed of two things, the one earthly and the other heavenly: so too our bodies, which partake of the Eucharist, are no longer corruptible, but possess the hope of resurrection [*Adv. haeres.* 4, 18, 4-5: PG 7/1, 1028-1029]" (CCC 1000). All salvation thus turns on the flesh, to recall Tertullian's momentous phrase (cf. CCC 1015), and it is precisely in this flesh that our final resurrection takes place. This is the faith of the Church; this is the ground of her hope.

See: Body and Soul; Death; Heaven; Human Person; Judaism; Judgment, General; Last Things; Resurrection of Christ.

Suggested Readings: CCC 988-1019. R. Gleason, S.J., *The World To Come.* J. Ratzinger, *Eschatology: Death and Eternal Life.* A. Von Speyr, *The Mystery of Death.*

Regis Martin

REVOLUTION

The term "revolution" commonly refers to the violent overthrow of a political regime or government, carried out by part or all of the citizenry. It is always a most serious matter, destroying the peace, however imperfect, of a political community, and creating an atmosphere of mistrust and hatred that may not be overcome for generations. Hence the decision to begin or to join such armed resistance is subject to the strictest moral guidelines, essentially the same as those of Catholic just war doctrine.

Revolution is legitimate only on the following terms: there has been a serious and prolonged violation of justice on the part of the authorities; all possible means of correcting the situation short of violence have been attempted and failed; the revolt will not itself be the cause of even greater misery and disorder; there are reasonable chances of success; and no better solution can be foreseen by prudent persons (cf. CCC 2243 with 2309).

If even one of these conditions is not met, it is gravely wrong to take up arms or to urge others to do so. If the conditions are met, then, as St. Thomas Aquinas suggests, it is the corrupt authorities themselves who are really guilty of sedition and revolt against the common good of their communities. Therefore, if the rebellion is carried out with proportionate means and right intention, it is in fact praiseworthy as the "deliver[ance] of a community from tyrannical rule" (*Summa Theologiae,* II-II, 42, 2).

See: Authority; Civil Disobedience; Civil Law; Common Good; Politics; War.

RITES

The English word "rite" (Latin *ritus,* whence *ritualis*) signifies a practice (*mos*) or an approved usage (*approbata consuetudo*) "rightly" accomplished, that is, according to religious observances and usages. Broadly speaking, rite today refers to the liturgical functions of one of the great liturgical families, such as the Roman "rite" or the Byzantine "rite." But in the strict sense a rite is the ensemble of formulae, actions, and practical norms to be followed in carrying out a determined liturgical function; and in that sense we speak, for instance, of the rite of infant Baptism. A particular book of such rites is called a "ritual" (*rituale*). A canonically recognized rite (cf. Vatican Council II, *Decree on Eastern Catholic Churches, Orientalium Ecclesiarum*, 2) is a group of the faithful who, organically united in the Holy Spirit by faith, sacraments, and government, are held together by their hierarchy.

Man's social activity is by nature of two basic types. Productive activity is directed toward securing one's livelihood, and it signifies the accomplishment of a certain amount of labor. It results in or preserves a product that generally possesses value for barter or exchange. Ritual actions, on the other hand, produce nothing "usable," for they are representational activity that is unaffected by utilitarian or economic considerations. The chief content of ritual activity is the social actualization of the totality of a social group's existing norms, thus imaging or representing the social group itself. Among the characteristics of such ritual activity are the fact that it contains certain patterns or forms that are richly meaningful; that it is conducted in public; that it renders possible an identification of the individual with the social group, its norms and traditions; and that it is molded and supported by tradition and authority.

Rite and Worship • Hence it is but natural that the formal, patterned aspect of cult or worship has come to be called "rite." In her formal public worship, the Catholic Church has always taken to heart what God himself prescribed for the Israelite temple when he spoke to Moses on Mount Sinai: "See that you make [it] after the pattern . . . which is being shown you on the mountain" (Ex 25:40). For the *ekklesia* of the New Covenant, the mountain of the showing, is Golgotha, where the Church was born like a new Eve from the side of the dying Redeemer, the second and everlasting Adam: *ex corde scisso nascitur Ecclesia*, from the pierced heart of Christ is born the Church. It was on Calvary that the Church became witness and co-offerer of the one sacrifice that the only-begotten incarnate Son of God offered to his Father for the sins of the world.

On the evening before he accomplished his own bloody offering, Christ gave the form and manner in which that all-sufficient sacrifice of the one everlasting High Priest was to be rendered present for all succeeding generations. It was given to his disciples, under the outward appearances of bread and wine. And so in the liturgy of the praying Church, that "image" lives on, that "pattern" that was shown to the Church on the hilltop near the Holy City.

Through the course of succeeding centuries the model (or pattern), while unchanging at its central core, has been given a great variety of forms and settings in which it has been mounted or encased like the precious legacy it is. These settings have varied according to places and peoples, their customs and languages and ethnic differences. After the faith come "rites" (cf. Pope Paul VI, *On Evangelization in the Modern World, Evangelii Nuntiandi*, 63-64, [1976]).

Tendencies toward local differentiation were strong even in the earliest days of the Church, when texts fixed in writing were rare, communication between various churches spasmodic and irregular, and local needs highly diversified. Writing around the year 400, St. Augustine testifies that, while there was unity in the Church upon essential matters, yet other things varied, including ritual practices. With the appearance of the earliest written texts (perhaps in the wake of the so-called Edict of Milan after 313), some prayer traditions receded into the background while others came to dominate the public worship of various regions. There gradually emerged the classical "shape of the Eucharist," with the different regional variants still evident today (Vatican Council II, *Constitution on the Sacred Liturgy, Sacrosanctum Concilium*, 4). Chief among these are four great families.

* Syrian, subdivided on the basis of formal criteria into an East Syrian group, including the Chaldean and Malabar rites, and a West Syrian filiation, embracing the Syrian, Armenian, Maronite, and Malankar rites, in addition to those

frequently subsumed under the category of "Byzantine": the Bulgarian, Greek, Georgian, Melchite, Rumanian, Russian, Serbian, Ukrainian, and Italo-Albanian rites.

* Egyptian, formerly centered upon Alexandria and represented today by the Coptic and Ethiopian rites.

* Gallican, which formerly flourished in Gaul, Ireland, and Scotland, and is now found in local rites of Spain (Mozarabic) and Lombardy ("Ambrosian" at Milan).

* Roman, the rite of the Western Church, which has now become predominant, even in most of the religious orders that had preserved, in various forms, more ancient ritual variations.

See: Church, Nature, Origin, and Structure of; Inculturation; Liturgy; Mass; Worship.

Suggested Readings: CCC 1200-1209. P. Bradshaw, *The Search for the Origins of Christian Worship: Sources and Methods for the Study of Early Liturgy.* A. King, *The Rites of Eastern Christendom.*

Robert A. Skeris

ROSARY

This extra-liturgical, or private, Marian devotion has been most popular among a vast variety of groups within the Church. The learned and uneducated, the wealthy and poor, contemplatives and active apostles, clergy, religious, and laity have all found the vocal prayers and meditations upon the mysteries of the Rosary an inspiring means of growth in the spiritual life and Christian discipleship. Sts. Peter Canisius (1521-1597), Louis Marie Grignon de Montfort (1673-1716), Alphonsus Liguori (1696-1787), Pope St. Pius V (1504-1572), and Popes from Leo XIII to John Paul II have contributed significantly to its spread.

The entire Rosary consists of the recitation of fifteen decades of Hail Marys. Each decade begins with the Our Father and ends with the doxology, and is accompanied with a meditation upon a mystery of our redemption by Mary's Son. The complete Rosary comprises fifteen mysteries: five joyful, contemplating the beginning of our redemption in the Incarnation, namely, the Annunciation, the Visitation, the Nativity, the presentation, and the finding of the Child in the temple; five sorrowful mysteries that direct our loving attention to the redemptive Passion and death of Christ — the agony in the garden, the scourging, the crowning with thorns, the carrying of the cross, and the crucifixion; and the five glorious mysteries concentrating upon the Resurrection and Ascension, the sending of the Holy Spirit at Pentecost, the Assumption, and the coronation of Mary. When "praying the Rosary" the ordinary practice has been to recite one cycle (or set) of mysteries; this is the requirement for gaining a plenary indulgence under the usual conditions on any particular day. Pope St. Pius V established the devotion's traditional form, which has been called the "Dominican Rosary."

Historical Development • Toward the end of the twelfth century, the first half of the Hail Mary as we know it today started to assume the spiritual significance of the Our Father and the Creed as a prayer that all the faithful should know, while the Rosary began to take shape in a Psalter of a hundred fifty Hail Marys. Meditation upon the mysteries began to develop with the addition to each psalm of a phrase referring to Jesus and Mary. Eventually the psalms were omitted, and the phrases became little lives of the Mother and Son extending from the Annunciation to their glorification.

Some time between 1410 and 1439, Dominic of Prussia, a Carthusian monk, helped popularize the devotion by linking fifty Hail Marys with fifty such phrases. *Rosarium* (a rose garden) was used to designate this collection of the fifty points of meditation, and so the name "Rosary" began to be the official title of the devotion. The rose, a symbol of joy, was fittingly applied to Mary, the "Cause of our joy" in bringing us Christ. Henry of Kalkar, another Carthusian, divided the fifty Hail Marys into decades, with an Our Father between each. By the first part of the fifteenth century the essential elements of the Rosary were in place.

Before it could become a popular form of prayer for all, the Rosary had to be simplified. In

1483, *Our Dear Lady's Psalter*, a book on the Rosary by a Dominican, makes reference to the same fifteen mysteries as today, except that the fourteenth combines the coronation with the Assumption while the fifteenth is the Last Judgment. Blessed Alan de la Roche, a Dominican, in 1470 founded the Confraternity of the Psalter of Jesus and Mary, forerunner of the Rosary Confraternity whereby the Rosary became a devotion of the universal Church. The papal bull of 1569 *Consueverunt Romani Pontifices*, frequently called the "Magna Carta" of the Rosary, firmly established the devotion in the Church. It involves an intimate unity of mental and vocal prayer, whose meditative aspect was a requisite for gaining the indulgences attached to it.

Praying the Rosary • In 1974, Pope Paul VI issued *Marialis Cultus*, an apostolic exhortation for the right ordering and development of Marian devotion. Reflecting upon the numerous spiritual advantages of the Rosary as a "compendium of the entire Gospel" (*Marialis Cultus*, 42), a prayer covering the principal salvific events in the life of Christ and having therefore a clear Christological orientation, Pope Paul emphasizes the contemplative character of the Rosary: "By its nature the recitation of the Rosary calls for a quiet rhythm and a lingering pace, helping the individual to meditate on the mysteries of the Lord's life as seen through the eyes of her who was closest to the Lord. In this way the unfathomable riches of these mysteries are unfolded" (*Marialis Cultus*, 47).

The "soul" of the Rosary, as it were, lies in pondering the mysteries of Redemption over and over, treasuring them in our hearts as Mary did when they were actually unfolding before her contemplative gaze (cf. Lk 2:19, 51). The repetition of the vocal prayers is the "body" of the Rosary, not unlike background music while one reads. The Rosary is a relatively relaxing form of prayer, designed to be a good preparation for other forms of prayer, for example, more intense participation in liturgical celebrations or the purely interior prayer of quiet in mental prayer.

Pope Paul VI says of the relationship between the Rosary and the Eucharistic Liturgy: "In fact meditation on the mysteries of the Rosary, by familiarizing the minds and hearts of the faithful with the mysteries of Christ, can be an excellent preparation for the celebration of those same mysteries in the liturgical action and can also become a continuing echo thereof. However, it is a mistake to recite the Rosary during the celebration of the liturgy, though unfortunately this practice still persists here and there" (*Marialis Cultus*, 48). But the Rosary can be a preparation for a more fervent participation in the Holy Sacrifice of the Mass and encounter with Christ in Holy Communion, as well as "a continuing echo thereof," to the extent it helps one cooperate with the sacramental graces of the Eucharist.

See: Devotions; Marian Devotion; Mary, Mother of God; Mary, Mother of the Church; Meditation; Prayer; Vocal Prayer.

Suggested Readings: CCC 971, 2673-2679, 2705-2708. Vatican Council II, *Dogmatic Constitution on the Church, Lumen Gentium*, Ch. VIII. Paul VI, *Devotion to the Blessed Virgin Mary, Marialis Cultus*. F. Jelly, O.P., *Madonna: Mary in the Catholic Tradition*. F. William, *The Rosary: Its History and Meaning*.

F.M. Jelly, O.P.

S

SACRAMENT

Although the term "sacrament" is not found in the Scriptures, there is scriptural authority for these specific vital moments in the Church's life. Over the course of history, the Church has developed her theology on the sacraments, basing this on both Sacred Scripture and Sacred Tradition. While at various times the term has been defined differently, the Church has understood some common aspects of this concept.

The sacraments have long been understood to be efficacious signs of grace. To say sacraments are efficacious means more than that they are effective — for while "effective" means that something happens, "efficacious" means that what was intended to happen will always happen, provided the individual recipient of the sacrament puts no obstacle in the way. The *Catechism of the Catholic Church* says: "Celebrated worthily in faith, the sacraments confer the grace that they signify. They are *efficacious* because in them Christ himself is at work: it is he who baptizes, he who acts in his sacraments in order to communicate the grace that each sacrament signifies" (1127).

"Sacrament" in the Tradition • The notion of this kind of sign goes back to the Fathers of the Church. They saw it to be a complex reality of two parts, one visible and the other invisible. The visible was the external aspect, referred to in Greek as the *mysterion* and in Latin as the *signum, figura,* or *sacramentum.* The invisible was the internal aspect, the Holy Spirit producing grace in the individual recipient. The primary focus of the early Church was on Baptism and the Eucharist. The grace produced was either that of new birth (Baptism) or of nourishment (the Eucharist).

The term "sacrament," first used by Tertullian (c. 160-c. 222), was understood generically to include many factors in the economy of salvation that had a sacred meaning. It was also applied specifically to Baptism, the Eucharist, and Confirmation. Tertullian speaks of the flesh being "washed . . . anointed . . . nourished." Other Latin Fathers who wrote on this topic were St. Irenaeus and St. Cyprian, while Greek Fathers include St. Gregory of Nyssa and St. John Chrysostom.

St. Augustine (354-430) pursued the theology of the topic by far the furthest. Using principles of Greek philosophy, he began with the simple notion of a sign as something that imprints a twofold image on the senses. The first is its own distinctive image; the second is a further reality that comes from the mind of the beholder. He then applied this to the realm of the sacred, concluding that a *sacred* sign must lead one to a sacred or religious reality. In any sacrament, there must be two necessary ingredients: matter and form. The matter is what is seen and felt. The form (or formula) is the words spoken. For instance, simply pouring water over an individual's head is meaningless as a sign; but when the words "I baptize you . . ." are spoken, they give direction and meaning to, or "inform," the matter. Grace comes from this now sacred sign because it is Christ himself who is at work.

In addition to the matter and form, every sacrament must also have a minister and a subject, one who gives the sign and one who receives. For each of these there is a fundamental requirement: The individual subject must be properly disposed, and the minister must intend to do what the Church does or wants done. St. Augustine and later writers such as Peter Lombard (c. 1100-1160) went to great lengths to emphasize the fact that the worthiness or unworthiness of the minister is not a factor. He is exactly that, a minister, and he assumes a subordinate role.

In the thirteenth century, St. Thomas Aquinas (1225-1274), following earlier writers, also understood the sacraments clearly as a kind of sign: "But now we are speaking of sacraments in a special sense, as implying the habitude of sign: and in this way a sacrament is a kind of sign" (*Summa Theologiae*, IIIa, 60, 1). He continues: "Properly speaking a sacrament, as considered by us now, is defined as being the 'sign of a holy thing so far as it makes men holy' " (IIIa, 60, 2).

For many of St. Thomas's predecessors, the sacraments and their consequent graces were seen as remedies for sin. Taking this one step further, he saw the sacraments as being directly connected to the Incarnation and the entire paschal mystery. His treatise on the sacraments comes immediately after that on the Passion and Resurrection of the Lord. It is not simply that God conveys his graces to man; rather, the Word made flesh came among his people and directly, physically, through his humanity touched their human activities. Beyond this, the sacraments are all intimately interwoven with the Church, the Mystical Body of Christ. It is through the sacraments that new life is given and wounds are healed; the members develop, and the whole body is renewed.

The sacraments are also part of the prayer life of the Church. Before discussing the sacraments, St. Thomas had covered the whole of the moral life, which included the virtues. Of the moral virtues, the virtue of justice, specifically as it relates us to God, is called the virtue of religion. This includes acts of adoration, worship, prayer, and sacrifice. To this extent, then, the sacraments build up the Body of Christ, as the members of that Body strengthen one another in their communal act of worship.

Sacraments and Faith • All of this requires an exercise of faith, by both the individual and the community as a whole. The time-honored expression *lex orandi, lex credendi* means that what we profess in our creeds we carry out in our liturgy. Conversely, the prayer life is an external-

ization of the faith of both the individual and the whole community (CCC 1123-1124). This is seen most especially in the Holy Eucharist. Worthy reception of Holy Communion presupposes an act of faith on the part of the communicant. Hence the formula "The Body of Christ" expects from the recipient the response "Amen" — "I believe" — when he receives the sacrament. Minimally, the person must believe that this is really and truly Body of Christ and nothing less. The "Amen" also is an externalization of the communion that exists between the members of the faithful who approach the sacrament. Indeed, all three of the theological virtues are involved in the sacraments, as faith is deepened, hope is strengthened, and charity is perfected.

Three hundred years after St. Thomas, the Council of Trent authorized the famous *Roman Catechism*. Having given some background to various interpretations, both sacred and profane, of the word "sacrament," that *Catechism* then proceeds to say what the faithful must be taught regarding what constitutes a sacrament: "But of the many definitions, each of them sufficiently appropriate, which may serve to explain the nature of a Sacrament, there is none more comprehensive, none more perspicuous, than the definition given by St. Augustine and adopted by all scholastic writers. A Sacrament, he says, is a sign of a sacred thing; or, as it has been expressed in other words of the same import: A Sacrament is a visible sign of an invisible grace, instituted for our justification."

Vatican Council II gives this overview: "The purpose of the sacraments is to sanctify men, to build up the Body of Christ, and, finally, to give worship to God. Because they are signs they also instruct. They not only presuppose faith, but by words and objects they also nourish, strengthen, and express it. That is why they are called 'sacraments of faith.' They do, indeed, confer grace, but, in addition, the very act of celebrating them most effectively disposes the faithful to receive this grace to their profit, to worship God duly, and to practice charity" (*Constitution on the Sacred Liturgy, Sacrosanctum Concilium*, 59).

The new Code of Canon Law (1983), which

continues the use of the word "sign" and in reference to sacraments states that one of the effects is grace or holiness, points out: "The sacraments of the New Testament, instituted by Christ the Lord and entrusted to the Church, as they are the actions of Christ and the Church, stand out as the signs and means by which the faith is expressed and strengthened, worship is rendered to God and the sanctification of humankind is effected" (Canon 840).

The *Catechism of the Catholic Church* echoes these statements: "The sacraments are efficacious signs of grace, instituted by Christ and entrusted to the Church, by which divine life is dispensed to us. The visible rites by which the sacraments are celebrated signify and make present the graces proper to each sacrament. They bear fruit in those who receive them with the required dispositions" (CCC 1131).

Theological Analysis • "Christ instituted the sacraments of the new law. There are seven: Baptism, Confirmation (or Chrismation), the Eucharist, Penance, the Anointing of the Sick, Holy Orders and Matrimony" (CCC 1210).

The Church teaches that there are exactly seven distinct sacraments, neither more or less. These are referred to as the "sacraments of the New Law" to distinguish them from sacraments of the Old Law. The sacraments of the Old Law were Jewish rituals performed before Christ's Passion and include such practices as offerings, sacrifices, and circumcision. Peter Lombard felt so strongly about the sacraments causing grace that he refused to use the term "sacrament" in referring to those observances of the Old Law. St. Thomas, however, had no problem with doing so. He resolved the dilemma by making a distinction. The sacraments of the New Law have sanctifying power present in them drawn from Christ and his Passion, while those of the Old Law were real sacraments insofar as they were physical signs prefiguring the redemptive act of Christ. Those who lived before Christ could use these "sacraments" to demonstrate their faith in the coming Christ and his redemptive work. Hence they would ultimately receive the fruits of the Redemption.

The ecumenical Council of Florence (1439) made this distinction: "They [the seven sacraments of the New Law] are very different from the sacraments of the Old Law. For these latter did not confer grace but were only a figure of the grace to be conferred by the Passion of Christ; but our sacraments both contain grace and confer it on those who receive them worthily."

"The seven sacraments touch all the stages and all the important moments of Christian life" (CCC 1210). Here the *Catechism* refers to St. Thomas and the analogy he draws between the natural life and the spiritual life, between the organic physical life and the sacramental life (cf. *Summa Theologiae*, IIIa, 65, 1). The sacraments are intended to achieve two ends: the perfection of man by worshiping God and the remedy of man by counteracting the harmful effects of sin. Man is perfected in two ways: as an individual and in his relationship to the whole social community. In respect to his own person, he is perfected as he achieves the fullness of life or by overcoming the various obstacles to this fullness such as sickness. With regard to the first, he makes progress in three ways: through generation, growth, and nutrition. He overcomes the obstacles by healing and by restoration to a former state of strength. With regard to the community as a whole, his perfection is accomplished in two ways: first, by having authority over a community maintaining peace and order; second, by way of natural propagation.

Against this background it is easy to see how, as the *Catechism of the Catholic Church* says, the seven sacraments encompass the full range of Christian life and "give birth and increase, healing and mission to the Christian's life of faith" (1210). We speak therefore of the sacraments of Christian Initiation — Baptism, Confirmation, Eucharist (CCC 1212); the sacraments of Healing — Penance and the Anointing of the Sick (CCC 1421); and the sacraments at the Service of Communion — Holy Orders and Matrimony (CCC 1534-1535).

Sacraments as "Signs" • It is in the nature of a sign to point to some reality other than itself. In order for a sign to be valid and valuable as a sign, it must be both visible and intelligible, able to be seen and understood.

Signs can be classified into three categories. First are what are called natural signs, signs that arise from nature itself. For example, smoke is a sign of fire; it points to fire, and it may lead us to the fire, but it is not the fire itself.

Signs of the second type are artificial, or man-made, signs. These are more along the lines of concepts that society has agreed upon. For instance, a red light or red flag is a sign of potential danger. There is nothing dangerous about the color red in itself. Rather, society has adopted it as a convention.

Signs of the third type are supernatural or divinely instituted signs, and these are the sacraments. The primary difference between this type of sign and the first two is that the sacraments are efficacious: What is intended to be accomplished is accomplished. Whereas natural and artificial signs merely point to a reality, the sacraments not only point to a reality but also, as it were, "take you there."

If natural and artificial signs are needed to point to things that are visible, then all the greater is the need for signs that point to that which is invisible. The Church teaches that sacraments are signs of grace, and grace is an invisible reality necessary for daily life as well as eternal salvation. The effect of the sacraments, when properly received, is always grace. The sacraments are efficacious signs because they were instituted by Christ, not a human person. Thus a summary definition of a sacrament is: "An outward sign instituted by Christ to give grace." A sacrament is a visible sign of an invisible reality.

Validity and Effects • For the valid administration of each sacrament there are four required elements: form, matter, subject, and minister. The first two constitute the visible or external sign. The form (or formula) refers to the words spoken as the sacraments are being administered. The matter refers to the materials used, along with the accompanying gestures.

The sign is given by one person to another. The subject is the one who receives the sacrament, and the minister is the one who administers it. All of the sacraments have an "ordinary" minister (ordinary in that he functions in ordinary circumstances). Three of the sacraments — Baptism, Confirmation, and Holy Communion — also may have an "extraordinary" minister, who functions in the absence or lack of sufficient ordinary ministers. Note that in the case of the Eucharist, or Holy Communion, the extraordinary minister is solely for the administration of the sacrament and not its confection.

Only a bishop may administer all seven sacraments. The priest acts as an ordinary minister for Baptism, Penance, Holy Communion (for both its confection and administration), and Anointing of the Sick. He may witness marriages for the Church and act as an extraordinary minister for Confirmation. The deacon is an ordinary minister for Baptism and Holy Communion (for its administration but not for its confection) and may witness marriages for the Church with the permission of the pastor. All baptized Christians who validly enter into marriage administer the sacrament of Matrimony to each other. Certain Catholics who have been approved by their pastor and appointed by the bishop may act as ministers of Holy Communion.

The subject of the sacrament varies, depending on which sacrament is in question. For example, the subject for Baptism potentially is any human being, alive (or presumed alive) and nonbaptized, who either himself expresses the desire to be baptized or on whose behalf, in the case of an infant, the desire is expressed by parents or other responsible parties. The subject for the sacrament of Holy Orders is a male, baptized and confirmed as a Catholic, who is free from any impediments. In Matrimony, both parties must be baptized Christians (in order for it to be a sacrament) who are free to marry.

As we have seen, "celebrated worthily in faith, the sacraments confer the grace that they signify" (CCC 1127). The principal effect of each sacrament is grace, for it is grace alone that sanctifies. Each sacrament confers sanctifying grace whereby the individual either is justified (if in sin) or increases in the life of grace. Through this growth in the life of grace the individual is increasingly configured to Christ, who confers that grace through his minister.

Over and above this sanctifying grace, a special sacramental grace is conferred. This sacramental grace is understood as a divine assistance to help the individual subject achieve the end toward which the particular sacrament is ordered. In Baptism, for example, the sacramental grace helps the person to be a good Christian; in Matrimony, it helps the person to lead a good married life. All of this of course presupposes that the individual places no obstacle in the way and cooperates freely with God's grace (cf. CCC 1129; *Summa Theologiae*, IIIa, 62, 3).

Three of the sacraments, Baptism, Confirmation, and Holy Orders, confer a special character (or an indelible mark) on the soul that can be received only once. A very vivid image is the Greek term *sphragis*, which in its literal sense refers to a custom in ancient times whereby a shepherd, having acquired a new sheep, would take a pair of sharp shears and cut a mark in the sheep's ear. The mark had two characteristics: It was unique (no two shepherds had the same mark) and it was indelible. The purpose was to identify the shepherd's own sheep: He could locate them wherever they were, and so provide for them and protect them from danger.

As the early Church developed her theology on the sacraments, she adopted this term to refer to the mark placed on the individual's soul in these three sacraments. The image of the shepherd continues, too, as we envisage Christ the Good Shepherd watching over those who have been marked by these sacraments and providing for them. As the *Catechism of the Catholic Church* explains: "This configuration to Christ and to the Church, brought about by the Spirit, is indelible; it remains for ever in the Christian as a positive disposition for grace, a promise and guarantee of divine protection, and as a vocation to divine worship and to the service of the Church" (1121; cf. 698).

It is important always to see the sacraments in relation to the Church. The *Catechism* says: "The sacraments are 'of the Church' in the double sense that they are 'by her' and 'for her.' They are 'by the Church,' for she is the sacrament of Christ's action at work in her through the mission of the Holy Spirit. They are 'for the Church' in the sense that 'the sacraments make the Church' [St. Augustine, *De civ. Dei*, 22, 17: PL 41, 779; cf. St. Thomas Aquinas, *STh* III, 64, 2 *ad* 3], since they manifest and communicate to men, above all in the Eucharist, the mystery of communion with the God who is love, One in three persons" (1118).

See: Ex Opere Operato; Grace; Judaism; Lex Orandi, Lex Credendi; Liturgy; Ministry; Priesthood of Christ; Religion, Virtue of; Sacramental Grace; Sacramentals; Sacraments of Initiation; Sacraments of the Dead; Sacraments of the Living; Sacrifice; Worship.

Suggested Readings: CCC 1113-1134. Vatican Council II, *Constitution on the Sacred Liturgy, Sacrosanctum Concilium*, 6-7, 59-61; *Dogmatic Constitution on the Church, Lumen Gentium*, 10-11. Paul VI, *On the Mystery of the Holy Eucharist, Mysterium Fidei*. Sacred Congregation for the Sacraments and Divine Worship, *Instruction on Certain Norms Concerning the Worship of the Eucharistic Mystery, Inaestimabile Donum*. J. O'Connor, *The Hidden Manna*. N. Halligan, O.P., *The Sacraments and Their Celebration*. C. O'Neill, O.P., *Meeting Christ in the Sacraments*. A. Nichols, O.P., *The Holy Eucharist*. J. Hardon, S.J., *The Catholic Catechism*, Ch. XIII.

Christopher M. Buckner

SACRAMENTAL GRACE

Sacraments are outward signs instituted by Christ to give grace. With the valid and fruitful reception of each sacrament comes grace in different aspects. There is first of all sanctifying grace, which sanctifies the recipients or, for those already in the state of grace, increases their holiness. Actual grace is given at that moment or later as divine assistance may be required. Finally, a special sacramental grace is conferred.

Over and above the sanctifying grace, sacramental grace is a special grace given to realize whatever purpose the sacrament is ordered to accomplish. For example, in the sacrament of Matrimony the couple receive sanctifying grace, which makes them holy; they receive actual grace, which is given to strengthen them at one particular moment or another; and, finally, the sacramental grace of Matrimony helps them to lead a good married life.

Baptism makes the recipient a Christian and marks the beginning of the recipient's commitment to Christ and his Church. In Baptism, the sacramental grace is special assistance to help him lead a good Christian life. Confirmation marks one out as an adult member of the Church and indicates a willingness to serve Christ and be ready to die for him. So, in Confirmation the sacramental grace strengthens the baptized to profess the faith and evidence it as an adult member of the Church. Likewise, the sacramental grace of Holy Orders is principally to be the official and ordained agent of divine worship and to live accordingly as a deacon, priest, or bishop.

In the sacrament of Penance, in addition to receiving sanctifying grace, which restores him to God's friendship and makes him holy again, the penitent also receives a special sacramental grace that not only forgives his sins but also helps him to keep from committing them in the future (cf. CCC 1996-2005).

See: Grace; Sacrament.

SACRAMENTALS

The concern of the Church for her people is not only for their salvation but also for their personal sanctification. This sanctification is accomplished in many ways, and most notably through the public prayer life of the Church, the liturgy, and the sacraments.

In addition, the Church provides many other ways for people to grow in holiness. These are called sacramentals. Generally speaking, a sacramental is an object or action that the Church uses after the manner of sacraments, in order to achieve through the merits of the faithful certain effects, mainly of a spiritual nature. The Code of Canon Law says: "Somewhat in imitation of the sacraments, sacramentals are sacred signs by which spiritual effects especially are signified and are obtained by the intercession of the Church" (Canon 1166).

Sacramentals include times and places, words and actions, objects and gestures. They derive their benefit not only from the individual who uses them but also from the intercessory prayer of the Church. They differ from sacraments in three ways.

The first difference is that sacraments are outward signs instituted by Christ to give grace. Sacramentals were not instituted by Christ but rather by the Church.

The second difference is the manner in which grace may be received from the use of sacramentals. Sacraments confer grace *ex opere operato*, literally, "from the work having been performed." Assuming the individual does not place an obstacle in the way, the grace comes from the performance of the sacramental action itself. The conferral of grace in the administration of a sacrament does not depend on the worthiness of the minister. The grace that comes from the use of sacramentals depends on the fervor and devotion of the one who uses them.

The third difference is in the grace received. Sacraments confer both sanctifying grace and sacramental grace when they are received. Such is not the case with sacramentals. They do not confer sanctifying grace immediately; rather, they dispose the individual to receive it and cooperate with it. Moreover, the different graces are received in proportion to the various purposes of each sacramental.

These three differences together present us with a composite picture of a sacramental. It is true that Our Lord instituted the seven sacraments, yet he did not dictate the manner or ritual for their administration. Rather, he left it to his Church to determine these rites. The exact mingling of the water and wine, the triple immersion or infusion of baptismal water, the quality or condition of other elements, as well as the time and place for the ceremonies — all these belong to the Church to determine.

Additionally, to enhance the celebration of these sacraments the Church over the centuries has seen fit to add lights, candles, incense, blessings, etc. All of this is done with the intention of stimulating the devotion of the faithful and increasing their faith.

Since it is the devotion of the faithful that is involved here, the grace of sacramentals does not come from the actions having been performed (*ex opere operato*). Instead, the grace depends on the action of the one who uses them. The expression used to describe this, *ex opere operantis*, means, literally, "from the work of the doer." Clearly, however, this is not *efficacious* (as is the case with sacraments), since the Church cannot confer sanctifying grace nor can she institute any efficacious signs to cause grace: Grace comes from God alone. Through her mission to sanctify the world, the Church encourages the faithful to use whatever means are available to deepen their faith, provided these are in harmony with the teachings of the Church and are not contrary to anything that has been revealed by God or that is part of the Divine Liturgy.

Various Forms of Sacramentals • Sacramentals may be divided into four general categories: (1) ceremonies — these are the rites typically associated with the administration of each of the seven sacraments as well as other rituals and cultural practices; (2) independent religious actions — exorcisms, blessings, and consecrations; (3) the religious use of blessed objects; (4) the blessed objects themselves. (This list is not all-inclusive or comprehensive but simply takes note of some sacramentals used most commonly in the Church today.)

Ceremonies. First and foremost, "ceremonies" pertains to the rites that accompany the administration of individual sacraments. The rites are not the same as the sacraments themselves but rather the rituals the Church has developed that surround the actual form and matter of the sacraments. "Ceremonies" also refers to other ceremonies that the Church encourages, especially those pertaining to the Eucharist such as exposition and Benediction of the Most Blessed Sacrament, the Forty Hours

devotion, a holy hour spent in adoration. Finally, there are those devotions pertaining to the Blessed Mother and the saints, such as novenas.

Independent Religious Actions. "Among sacramentals *blessings* (of persons, meals, objects, and places) come first" (CCC 1671). Praising God, they always invoke the name of Jesus and usually include making the Sign of the Cross over those objects to be blessed. Blessings may be permanent in that they are done once. These would include the consecration of a person who is set apart for a special office in the Church or of a thing set apart as belonging to God and to be used for sacred purposes only, especially within liturgical rites (cf. CCC 1672).

The strongest form of a blessing is that commonly referred to as exorcism. It is a prayer in which the name of Jesus Christ is invoked publicly and authoritatively so "that a person or object be protected against the power of the Evil One and withdrawn from his dominion" (CCC 1673).

Exorcisms may be performed simply, as in the Rite of Baptism, or solemnly, in the case of demonic possession. The latter is done only with the permission of the bishop, and the case is examined carefully. The priest who performs the exorcism prays and fasts and must follow diligently the rules established by the Church. Care is taken to avoid sensationalism.

Blessed Objects. These include objects that are aids for fostering devotion to God and the saints. Among them are statues, religious paintings, the rosary, scapular, medals, holy water, and the three holy oils (oil of the catechumens, oil of the sick, and sacred chrism).

The Use of the Objects. Not only are the objects sacramentals, but their actual use is considered a sacramental as well. Thus, such things as wearing a medal or cross, reciting the Rosary, carrying blessed palms, pious displaying of paintings, statues, or other religious art, and the use of holy water are all considered to be sacramentals.

See: Devotions; Eucharistic Devotion; Ex Opere Operato; Exorcism; Grace; Marian Devotion; Rites; Rosary; Sacrament; Sacramental Grace.

Suggested Readings: CCC 1667-1679. Vatican

Council II, *Constitution on the Sacred Liturgy, Sacrosanctum Concilium*, 13, 60-63. J. Hardon, S.J., *The Catholic Catechism*, pp. 548-559.

Christopher M. Buckner

SACRAMENTS OF INITIATION

The three of the seven sacraments that lead the faithful into the "fullness" of the Catholic life — Baptism, Confirmation, and the most Holy Eucharist — are referred to as the sacraments of Christian initiation because they "lay the *foundations* of every Christian life" (CCC 1212).

The seven sacraments, instituted by Jesus Christ, are often divided into three categories: the three sacraments of Christian initiation (Baptism, Confirmation, Holy Eucharist); the two sacraments of healing (Penance, Anointing of the Sick); and the two sacraments at the service of Communion and the mission of the faithful (Holy Orders, Matrimony).

The *Catechism of the Catholic Church*, quoting Pope Paul VI in *Divinae Consortium Naturae*, presents a brief summary of the nature and purpose of the sacraments of initiation, both collectively and individually. "The sharing in the divine nature given to men through the grace of Christ bears a certain likeness to the origin, development, and nourishing of natural life. The faithful are born anew by Baptism, strengthened by the sacrament of Confirmation, and receive in the Eucharist the food of eternal life. By means of these sacraments of Christian initiation, they thus receive in increasing measure the treasures of the divine life and advance toward the perfection of charity" (CCC 1212). Hence, one is enabled through these three sacraments to fulfill the Church's (and the individual's) mission, commanded by Christ himself, to "go and make disciples of all the nations" (Mt 28:19).

Baptism, Confirmation, Eucharist • Baptism, through the washing with water and the pronouncing of the Trinitarian formula, effects the remission of original sin (and, in the cases of children who have attained the age of reason and of adults, actual sin) and incorporation into the Church, the Mystical Body of Christ. This sacrament "is the basis of the whole Christian life, the gateway to life in the Spirit (*vitae spiritualis ianua*), and the door which gives access to the other sacraments" (CCC 1213).

Confirmation, by the anointing with sacred chrism on the forehead of the recipient and the verbalizing of the approved formula by the bishop or by a priest who has been delegated the requisite faculty to confirm, fortifies one to become an *adult* Catholic, ready and willing to proclaim the name of Christ and his holy Gospel far and wide. It "is necessary for the completion of baptismal grace" and assists the baptized to be "more perfectly bound to the Church." Those confirmed "are enriched with a special strength of the Holy Spirit," are "true witnesses of Christ," and are "more strictly obliged to spread and defend the faith by word and deed" (CCC 1285).

The most Holy Eucharist, which is both sacrifice and sacrament, is the completion of Christian initiation. By the enunciation of the correct words by a duly ordained priest or bishop over the valid matter of bread and wine approved by the Church, the real, true, and substantial Body, Blood, soul, and divinity of Jesus Christ become present. "Those who have been raised to the dignity of the royal priesthood by Baptism and configured more deeply to Christ by Confirmation participate with the whole community in the Lord's own sacrifice by means of the Eucharist" (CCC 1322). Jesus left us "the Eucharistic sacrifice of his Body and Blood . . . in order to perpetuate the sacrifice of the cross throughout the ages until he should come again, and so to entrust to his beloved Spouse, the Church, a memorial of his death and resurrection: a sacrament of love, a sign of unity, a bond of charity, a Paschal banquet 'in which Christ is consumed, the mind is filled with grace, and a pledge of future glory is given to us' [*SC* 47]" (CCC 1323).

The sacraments of initiation are administered and received according to the normative liturgical books approved by the Apostolic See. There exist various rites for the celebration of these sacraments, whether they are celebrated all at once (in the case, for example, of adults who are catechumens preparing for Baptism and reception into the Catholic Church, usually at the Easter Vigil on Holy Saturday) or in stages (as in the case of infants who are baptized shortly after birth but who do not receive the Holy Eucharist and are not confirmed until later).

In 1972, during the pontificate of Pope Paul VI, the Rite of Christian Initiation of Adults — prescribed by the Second Vatican Council — was approved. A second *editio typica* was published in 1985 by the authority of Pope John Paul II.

The Rite "includes not only the celebration of the sacraments of Baptism, Confirmation, and the Eucharist, but also all the rites belonging to the catechumenate" (Congregation for Divine Worship, decree *Christian Initiation of Adults*, 2). The Second Vatican Council, in response to many requests, mandated the restoration and revision of the Church's centuries-old catechumenate and directed that it be adapted to local traditions.

The phrase "sacraments of initiation" was first used in the nineteenth century and is readily accepted today by theologians, canonists, and pastoral associates. Church law clearly accepts this understanding by asserting, "The sacraments of Baptism, Confirmation, and the Most Holy Eucharist are so interrelated that they are required for full Christian initiation" (Canon 842.2).

See: Baptism; Catechumen; Confirmation; Eucharist; Sacrament.

Suggested Readings: CCC 1210-1419. A. Bouley, O.S.B., ed., *Catholic Rites Today: Abridged Texts for Students. The Rites of the Catholic Church.*

Charles M. Mangan

SACRAMENTS OF THE DEAD

Some sacraments can be both validly and fruitfully received in the state of sin, and these are "sacraments of the dead." They are distinguished from "sacraments of the living."

The sacraments of the dead are Baptism and Penance. Both confer sanctifying grace or restore it. Baptism removes original sin; in the case of an adult, it also removes all actual sin committed during the person's life. The sacrament of Penance, when properly received, removes all actual sin committed since the last worthy reception of Penance.

The sacrament of Anointing of the Sick may be considered in some way to belong to this category as well. It may be received in the state of grave sin and it is possible for a person to be restored to God's friendship by its reception. Ideally, though, it should be preceded by sacramental confession. In either case, the sacrament is received validly and fruitfully, supposing there is attrition or at least a disposition to repent on the part of the recipient. Because it should be received in the state of grace nevertheless, it is usually considered a sacrament of the living.

See: Anointing of the Sick; Baptism; Grace; Penance and Reconciliation, Sacrament of; Sacrament; Sacraments of the Living.

SACRAMENTS OF THE LIVING

"Sacraments of the living" is a term sometimes used to refer to those sacraments that must be received in the state of grace if they are to be received fruitfully. They are distinguished from the "sacraments of the dead." The "state of grace" means that one possesses sanctifying grace and is in right relationship with God.

Specifically, the sacraments of the living are Confirmation, Holy Eucharist, Matrimony, and Holy Orders. If Confirmation, Matrimony, and Holy Orders are not received in the state of grace — that is, the recipient is in the state of mortal sin — they are still received validly: a person is still confirmed, married, or ordained. However, the person does not receive the graces that accompany the sacrament. When the person goes to confession and is restored to the state of grace, the graces are received retroactively.

In the case of Holy Communion, someone who knowingly receives the sacrament in the state of mortal sin still receives the Eucharist truly but commits a grave sin in so doing. This is a sin of sacrilege. When the person seeks reconciliation with the Lord through the sacrament of Penance, he is required to confess not only the other mortal sin or sins he has committed but also this additional sin of sacrilege.

The sacrament of Anointing of the Sick is different in this regard. It may be received fruitfully in the state of mortal sin, since one of its effects is forgiveness of sin. The Rite of Anointing, however, is not automatic in its effect. When administered to someone in the state of sin, attrition, or at least a disposition to repent, is presumed on the part of the recipient. Obviously it is more advantageous that it be received in the state of grace.

See: Adult Baptism; Anointing of the Sick; Baptism; Confirmation; Eucharist; Grace; Holy Orders; Infant Baptism; Marriage, Sacrament of; Sacrament; Sacraments of the Dead.

SACRED ART

One of the essential characteristics of art is its affinity with religion, which in certain ways renders artists interpreters of God's infinite perfections and, in particular, of the beauty and harmony of God's creation (cf. Pope Pius XII, Allocution to Italian Artists, April 8, 1952).

If this be true for art in general, it is even more true of religious art: art that serves religion, art that is inspired and promoted by religion, art that turns to religion for its themes and subjects — and such art has always existed. The fact of this relationship between art and religion (and hence the reality of a religious art) becomes questionable only when the two attempt to exclude each other and confine themselves to their own separate spheres. Though born in the age of the so-called Enlightenment, this problem is still a pressing one in the present age. The connection of art and liturgy must be viewed in the broader context of the relationship of art to religion.

A work of art manifests the creative spirit of the artist, some part of whose inner life penetrates and marks his or her work. There is an analogy between God's creativity and the artist's creative talent, since both are, in a sense, life-giving, though of course God creates extra-divine entities out of nothing by his will alone, whereas the artist

needs matter already created and ready to be formed with the help of implements. The work of art is a new and different expression of something quite familiar, created according to the pattern engraved in the artist's mind and soul by the Divine Creator.

The artist serves as God's particular tool, whose supreme task is to present and reveal to his fellow men the infinite in definite form, the timeless in the time-bound, the permanent in the temporary, the essential in the accidental, the eternal ideas of God in the ephemeral matter of this world. When a work of art succeeds in transforming heavy and opaque terrestrial substance into a transparent showcase of God's eternal ideas materialized in this world, then it automatically becomes a message of God, a road sign pointing to him. The stronger the impact of the creative talent, the clearer is the message, the wider the road.

Art and Worship • Vatican Council II uses the term "sacred art" (*ars sacra*), which, though more specific than "religious art," is somewhat more inclusive than the term "liturgical art," which applies to the objects (e.g., sacred vessels, vestments, books) or to the organization and decoration of space used for worship (e.g., architecture, painting, sculpture, stained glass). Sacred art is the highest manifestation of religious art (Vatican Council II, *Constitution on the Sacred Liturgy, Sacrosanctum Concilium*, 122); it is the art that serves the official worship of the Church by providing for use at worship things that are worthy signs and symbols of supernatural realities.

The Church has not adopted any particular artistic style for her exclusive use. Rather she allows free access to the sacred precincts of the temple for styles from every epoch, provided they evince the reverence and honor due the holy rites performed in sacred buildings (*Sacrosanctum Concilium*, 123). Since sacred art furnishes the "implements" and places of worship used for the celebration of the liturgical rites, it is to that extent conditioned by the ministerial task it must fulfill, a task that can be at once symbolical and instrumental. Thus it is clear that the Church has always claimed the right to pass judgment on sacred art, and to decide which works are in fact to be regarded as suitable for sacred use (cf. Sacred Congregation of the Holy Office, *Instruction De Arte Sacra*, June 30, 1952). Plainly, artists and architects must have both the skill and the will to find in religion the inspiration of methods and plans best adapted to the needs of divine worship (cf. Pope Pius XII, encyclical *Mediator Dei*, 1947).

One of these needs is surely that of exciting in the worshipers sentiments of piety and devotion. The Church, mother and teacher, created in the course of almost two thousand years an artistic patrimony, including a proper and high artistic liturgical language with which she speaks to souls and souls speak to God. "It is not lawful for Christian artists to ignore such a language; they must learn it and respect it, so as worthily to express their conceptions. It is not the Church for art, but rather art for the Church" (Circular of the Holy Office, February 25, 1947). As Pius XII reminded us, it is not easy for men to pass from the sensible to the spiritual, to raise themselves from imperfect beauty to preeminent Beauty. But the effort needs to be made, because souls ennobled, elevated, and prepared by truly sacred art are thus better disposed to receive the religious truths and the grace of Christ the Lord (cf. Pope Pius XII, Allocution to Italian Artists, April 8, 1952).

Since the Sacred Liturgy should be celebrated with the greatest possible perfection, churches and oratories, church furnishings and vestments should be examples of genuine sacred art, including modern art (Sacred Congregation of Rites/Consilium, *Instruction Inter Oecumenici*, September 26, 1964). Sacred art is at bottom a pastoral art, at the service of the praying community while expressing genuine Catholic truth in the vesture of beauty. This effectively rules out "the gaudy, the ornamental, the petty, the ostentatious" and "all stereotyped commercial imitations" abusively termed sacred art (*The House of God: Sacred Art and Architecture*).

See: Celebration, Liturgical; Church Buildings; Liturgy; Sacred Music.

Suggested Readings: CCC 2500-2503, 2513.

Vatican Council II, *Constitution on the Sacred Liturgy, Sacrosanctum Concilium*, 122-127. T. Day, *Where Have You Gone, Michelangelo?* R. Graber, "Religion and Art" in *Sacred Music and Liturgy Reform after Vatican II*. R. Seasoltz, *The House of God: Sacred Art and Architecture*.

Robert A. Skeris

SACRED MUSIC

Cultic song — sacred music (*musica sacra*) in the strict sense of the term — is narrower in meaning than the broader concept of "ritual music" or "ecclesiastical chant" or devotional "church music," and it is plainly different from the even wider category of music that is simply "religious" in its general inspiration or tendency. *Musica sacra* (sacred music), or cultic song, is both sung prayer and prayerful song: those holy words that are offered to God together with the cultic action itself, being sung as part of the very ritual of worship.

Song in Christian worship is prayer that is simultaneously intensified and enhanced by increased fervor and devotion. It is by no means a decorative adjunct or a mere ornament but rather, according to words that Vatican Council II quoted from Pope St. Pius X, a "necessary or integral part of the solemn liturgy" (*Constitution on the Sacred Liturgy, Sacrosanctum Concilium*, 112). Sacred music, in other words, is a part of the whole that shares in the basic meaning of that total action and serves its fundamental purpose, namely, the glory of God and the sanctification of the faithful (*Sacrosanctum Concilium*, 112). It is a "necessary" part and not merely a peripheral addition, for it belongs integrally to worship, to the full and complete form of sacred ritual action — at least, whenever that sacred action makes use not only of signs and symbols but also of words.

Music and the Liturgy • Sacred music plainly has a ministerial function (*munus ministeriale*) to fulfill in the Sacred Liturgy (*Sacrosanctum Concilium*, 112). As was pointed out in the *aula* of St. Peter's during Vatican II, sacred music is a handmaid of the liturgy (*ancilla liturgiae*) from the standpoint of its behavior (*quoad actionem*), but not from the standpoint of its nature (*quoad naturam*). In regard to its nature, sacred music is and will remain "a necessary and integral part of the solemn liturgy."

Sacred music will fulfill its task and "function as a sign" the more meaningfully, the more intimately it is linked to the liturgical action (*Sacrosanctum Concilium*, 112). And the liturgical action to which sacred music is so intimately linked is in fact an *actio praecellenter sacra*, that is, a sacred action surpassing all others (*Sacrosanctum Concilium*, 7). In accordance with this clear statement of Catholic teaching, therefore, one demand must be made of singing and music in liturgy as an integral part of worship: They must be holy. *Sacred* music is called for, which means in practice that it must be free from all that is profane, both in itself and in the manner of performance (St. Pius X, *motu proprio Tra le Sollecitudini*, November 22, 1903; Sacred Congregation of Divine Worship, *Instruction Liturgicae Instaurationes*, September 5, 1970). Such sacred music significantly contributes to the glory of God and the sanctification of the faithful by its winning expression of prayerfulness, by its promotion of solidarity through unanimous congregational participation at specified times, and by enriching the Divine Liturgy with heightened solemnity (*Sacrosanctum Concilium*, 112).

It has become clear that what is needed here is not one-sided emphasis on "active" physical (and vocal) "participation" by everyone present in every part of the sacred rite. Active participation (cf. *Sacrosanctum Concilium*, 14) means chiefly the interior participation whereby the faithful make their own sentiments of mind and heart match what they say and hear, and cooperate with divine grace (*Sacrosanctum Concilium*, 11; Sacred Congregation of Rites, Instruction *Musicam Sacram*, March 5, 1967). Hence the faithful are also to be taught "that they should raise their mind to God through interior participation as they listen to the singing of ministers or choir" (*Musicam Sacram*). It goes without saying that these interior sentiments will also be expressed outwardly (*Sacrosanctum Concilium*, 30).

The treasure of immeasurable value, greater than even that of any other art, which is the musical tradition of the Church universal (*Sacrosanctum Concilium*, 112), is to be preserved and fostered with very great care (*Sacrosanctum Concilium*, 114). In present usage, the term "sacred music" includes Gregorian chant, sacred choral music (polyphony) both ancient and modern, sacred music for instruments such as the organ and other approved instruments, and sacred music for congregational hymnody (*Musicam Sacram*). When a choral (polyphonic) setting of the chants for the ordinary of the Mass is used, these chants may be sung by the choir alone in the customary way, that is, either *a cappella* or with instrumental accompaniment. The congregation, however, must not be altogether left out of the singing for the Mass (*Musicam Sacram*, 34).

The Church acknowledges Gregorian chant as proper to the Roman liturgy and therefore states that, other things being equal, it should be given pride of place (*principem locum obtineat*) in liturgical services (*Sacrosanctum Concilium*, 116). What makes Gregorian chant "liturgical" to such a great degree is the unity between text and music that the chant exemplifies so perfectly. The melody is at the service of the word: It adapts itself both to the accentual structure of the text and to its liturgical function. A truly sacred music must, so to speak, be ready to serve as the body in which the spirit contained in the words manifests itself in sound. It can rightly be called the "sonic vesture of the liturgy." Today, such a music is frequently regarded as superfluous in a world governed by technology and economics; and that constitutes its grandeur as well as its misery.

See: Assembly, Liturgical; Liturgy; Mass; Prayer; Sacred Art; Worship.

Suggested Readings: CCC 1156-1158, 1191. Vatican Council II, *Constitution on the Sacred Liturgy, Sacrosanctum Concilium*, 112-121. Sacred Congregation of Rites, Instruction *Musicam Sacram*. Pius XII, *Musicae Sacrae Disciplina*. T. Day, *Why Catholics Can't Sing*. J. Ratzinger, *The Feast of Faith: Approaches to a Theology of the Liturgy*, pp. 97-126. R. Skeris, *Crux et Cithara*,

73-84, 108-121, 129-155, 156-203, 214-222; *Divini Cultus Studium,* pp. 177-241.

Robert A. Skeris

SACRED SCRIPTURE

Sacred Scripture begins in the mind of God. Its creative power is unleashed by the action of God's living word, encountered in both Scripture and Sacred Tradition. In Scripture, God speaks his divine words by means of human language (CCC 101-104; Vatican Council II, *Dogmatic Constitution on Divine Revelation, Dei Verbum*, 13). In Scripture, one sees the mystery of Jesus' Incarnation foreshadowed in the fact that God's holy and divine word is expressed in and united to common and ordinary human words. This analogy between Scripture and the Incarnation suggests why the Church venerates the Bible, without being a "religion of the book." It venerates the Person of the living Word, the source of free worship of the living God. This analogy also prepares us for the veneration of the Body and Blood of Christ (CCC 103). The Church draws nurture and strength from the Bread of Life, taken from the one table of God's word and Christ's Body (CCC 101-104; *Dei Verbum*, 21, 24).

Understanding Scripture • A healthy and balanced understanding of Sacred Scripture always includes two fundamental perspectives: the heavenly or eternal and the historical. "Balance" means that we never lose sight of the double-sided fact that Scripture did not, as it were, drop out of the heavens and that it contains more than mere human words — it is the word of God. Viewing Scripture from a historical perspective, we note that God speaks to his people over many centuries and through many different languages (principally in Hebrew, Aramaic, and Greek). From an eternal or divine perspective, however, we agree with St. Augustine: God speaks only one Word. From eternity there can be only one syllable because there is no past, present, or future. God speaks that monosyllabic Word most fully in and through the Person of Jesus Christ (Heb 1:1-3). The power of this insight leads us to see that only one Divine

Word — the Eternal Word, the eternal Son of God, Jesus Christ — is present throughout all of Scripture (CCC 102). That presence of God's one Eternal Word, uttered only once and present throughout, is the fundamental unifying point of Sacred Scripture; here all things come from Christ and point to Christ.

The Holy Spirit inspired the authors of Scripture to record words and deeds that God wanted us to know for the sake of our salvation (CCC 107; *Dei Verbum*, 11). The saving power and eternal security brought by these words and deeds are not guaranteed by the biblical authors' purely human abilities; rather, Scripture's power to mediate God's saving power and to proclaim authentically the truths of the faith is grounded in the work of the Holy Spirit. And yet the biblical authors were true authors in the sense that they were free to select, organize, order, shape, and compose the substance of Scripture. In freedom, they wrote down exactly what God wanted us to know for the sake of our salvation. The Bible witnesses to the double mystery of our human freedom and God's divine and provident plan of salvation, which cannot be undermined by human weakness or even angelic rebellion.

If the word of God permeates every word of Sacred Scripture, and if each and every one of the biblical authors freely composed his materials and wrote under the guidance of the Holy Spirit exactly what God wanted us to know for our salvation, then God's word is present in both the Old and New Testaments, in all their books, whole and entire (CCC 105; *Dei Verbum*, 11). As we have seen, the one Word unifies all of Scripture. It follows that every part of the Old and New Testaments forms and communicates an integral part of God's divine plan of salvation. No one part is "less inspired" than any other. The Gospels, preeminent over all of Sacred Scripture, are the privileged witness to the words and deeds of the Savior. God's great plan of salvation, from his promise to Adam and Eve (Gn 3:15) to the Savior's Second Coming, is expressed in all of Scripture.

The inspired character of Sacred Scripture tells

us something about the process of interpreting it. If God is the author, it follows that any authentic interpretation must be the work of the Holy Spirit. Christ himself initiated this way of interpreting Scripture by opening the minds of the disciples to understanding how all of it relates to his Person and Messianic mission (cf. Lk 24:25). The Christian interpretation of Scripture is ultimately God interpreting himself. Through the work of the Holy Spirit, Christ assists each generation of believers in interpreting the Bible by opening their minds to understanding it (CCC 108). In this way, Scripture is interpreted in the Spirit in which it was written (CCC 111; *Dei Verbum*, 12).

The Church offers three broad principles that must guide the interpretation of Scripture. First, we interpret each passage in light of the unified witness of all. This approach guards against unbalanced interpretations that harm the Church's earthly pilgrimage to the Father. Second, we read each passage in light of the wisdom of the Fathers of the Church and the Sacred Liturgies, in order to be formed by the living memory of God's word. Third, we read each passage in light of the "analogy of faith." This expression refers to the great truths and doctrines of the faith taught as found in the Creed and magisterial pronouncements. The links between Sacred Scripture and the great truths unveil the inner unity of faith; it is a single piece, an organic and integrated whole. Such knowledge significantly broadens and deepens our understanding of what God actually communicates in Scripture (CCC 109-114).

Two Senses of Scripture • In addition to the above guidelines, the Church distinguishes between two senses of Sacred Scripture: the *literal* and the *spiritual* (CCC 115). The literal sense of a passage is determined through knowledge of the text's original language and its literary form and through the historical circumstances of both its author and intended recipients. The spiritual sense can be divided into three main categories: allegorical, moral, and anagogical (cf. CCC 117).

The *allegorical* sense brings out the relationship between the events in the Old Testament and their fulfillment in the New. For example, ancient Israel's crossing of the Red Sea is a prefigurement (or type) of Christ's victory on the cross and Resurrection and a prefigurement (or type) of our escape from the hold of original sin by means of sacramental Baptism. In this way, many — but not all — of the actions in the Old Testament establish or prefigure what is to be revealed in the New Testament. The typological link between the two Testaments by means of prefigurement exhibits the richness and vastness of Sacred Scripture.

The *moral* sense of a passage instructs us on what we ought to do, on what God's justice, love, and mercy require of his children (cf. 1 Cor 10:11). We learn of God's will through the law of Moses and even more deeply in Jesus' Beatitudes. The instruction of Scripture is like a lamp to our feet, leading us to love God's law day and night (Ps 119). Examples of the moral sense are those stories in Scripture written to show the presence or lack of moral standards, through heroic acts of virtue or violent or deceitful acts of utter depravity.

The *anagogical* sense (Greek: *anagoge*, "elevation, lifting up") raises our minds to the heavenly realities, showing us the eternal significance hidden in the temporal and limited words of men. For example, in Revelation 21:1–22:5 the Church is a sign of the heavenly Jerusalem, which we long to see at the end of this age.

The collection of books we call Sacred Scripture is only a handful of the many religious works produced by various Jewish and Christian groups. From the hundreds of available writings, the Church discerned that the forty-six books of the Old Testament and the twenty-seven books of the New Testament would form the final and authoritative list of sacred books. The final decree that closed the authoritative list of Old and New Testament books was issued at the Council of Trent some fifteen centuries after the death of Christ; however, the canon of Sacred Scripture was more or less stable by the end of the first half of the second Christian century. The basis for selecting the particular books found in our Bible is the Apostolic Tradition: The preaching and teaching of the Apostles guided the Church's selection of authentic writings, which eventually became the collection we call the New Testament.

The Old Testament was the early Church's only "bible." When the first Christians went to pray and hear readings from Scripture at the synagogue, when Jesus himself read and taught from Scripture, it was from the Old Testament; the promises of God that Jesus fulfills are from the Old Testament. For these reasons, the Old Testament is permanently valid and an indispensable part of Sacred Scripture (CCC 121). The Old Testament is the true word of God, even if it contains imperfect and provisional matters. The Old Testament's enormous value ranges from providing an initial divine pedagogy to the preparation-in-prophecy for the coming of Christ (CCC 122; *Dei Verbum*, 15). Thus it initiates, as it were, a progressive revelation in the lives of Christians that leads to our knowledge of and an encounter with the living Savior.

The New Testament also can be understood from "above" and from "below." First, the word of God is displayed most powerfully in the New Testament (CCC 124; *Dei Verbum*, 17). It hands on the ultimate truth of God's Revelation. The central focus of the New Testament is the Person of Jesus Christ. By focusing on his acts, teachings, Passion, and glorification, as well as the Church's beginnings under the life and power of the Spirit, the New Testament is the preeminent witness to the reality of the living God.

The Four Gospels and the One Gospel • The Church teaches that there are three basic stages in the formation of the Gospel (CCC 126). The first is *Jesus' life and teaching*. This level refers to the historical events in Jesus' life. The Gospels merely give us summaries of his teachings and the key events in his life. There is no book large enough to capture and express all of his wonderful words and deeds (cf. Jn 21:25). The memory of Jesus formed the foundation of the first apostolic preaching, which comprises the second historical level, that of the *oral tradition*. This level concerns the preaching and teaching of the Apostles, who transmitted Jesus' words and deeds to the next generation of believers. The Apostles were enlightened

by the Holy Spirit to see and preach the truth about Jesus Christ. As they began to die, there was need to record, in a systematic fashion, the apostolic preaching and teaching — the very memory of Jesus' great words and deeds of salvation. The systematic recording of his words and deeds is the final historical level of Gospel tradition, referred to as *the written Gospel*, the text as we now have it. The authors of the Gospels functioned in complete and authentic freedom when they chose to preserve only certain elements from the apostolic memory of Jesus Christ handed down either orally or in written form. Other elements of the Gospels were synthesized or interpreted in light of the Church's current circumstance. Regardless, we always are told the honest truth about Jesus Christ (*Dei Verbum,* 19). These three levels are coordinated into one polyphonic chord, orchestrated by the Holy Spirit and making up the one true Gospel of Jesus Christ.

The fourfold Gospels are, in a sense, really one Gospel because they bear witness to one saving truth, namely, Jesus Christ. The four Gospels hold a preeminent place over all the other books of Sacred Scripture because they bear witness to Jesus Christ, the central truth of the whole of Scripture. The relationship between the Old and New Testaments is hidden within the mystery of Jesus Christ. For example, the Old Testament speaks of the high priest of Jerusalem during David's time as having no beginning and as offering bread and wine. This mysterious figure bears a striking resemblance to Jesus Christ, the Eternal Word, who is the Alpha and the Omega, the beginning and the end, the first and the last, who offered bread and wine at his last Passover meal, which is our first and only Eucharistic feast. The Old Testament clearly plays a necessary role in shaping our imagination and anticipation regarding the Messiah, who will be king and priest — and, as we find in the New Testament, sinless victim; the Old Testament seems to create an outline of what we later discover is the Messiah. This kind of relationship between the Testaments is called typology. Through it we learn how the New Testament is hidden in the Old and how the Old Testament manifests and is manifested in the New. With St. Jerome, we can say, "Ignorance of the Scriptures is ignorance of Christ" (CCC 133).

See: Canon of Scripture; Divine Revelation; Inerrancy; Inspiration; New Covenant; Old Covenant; New Testament; Old Testament; Sacred Tradition; Spiritual Exegesis.

Suggested Readings: CCC 101-133. Vatican Council II, *Dogmatic Constitution on Divine Revelation, Dei Verbum,* 11-16, 18-19, 21-22, 24-25; *Dogmatic Constitution on the Church, Lumen Gentium,* 5, 14-15, 29, 55, 67; *Constitution on the Sacred Liturgy, Sacrosanctum Concilium,* 6-7, 16, 24, 35, 51, 92, 112; *Decree on Ecumenism, Unitatis Redintegratio,* 3, 15, 17, 21. Pontifical Biblical Commission, *The Interpretation of the Bible in the Church.* P. Grelot and J. Giblet, "Revelation," in X. Leon-Dufour, ed., *Dictionary of Biblical Theology,* pp. 499-505.

Stephen F. Miletic

SACRED TRADITION

Sacred Tradition expresses the normative, historical record of God's creative and salvific interaction with the world. This record is a privileged moment of grace, most evident in the history of biblical Israel and the Church. It is authoritatively taught and transmitted through the Magisterium of the Church.

The word "tradition" means handing on or handing down something to another. This term emphasizes a process or means by which something happens. Thus, tradition is the means by which Revelation and grace are mediated. The term refers to the concrete, historical, and personal means by which Revelation is taught, internalized, and lived out. The term "sacred" refers to the content or the ultimate source of what is handed on, namely, the divine life of God.

If Sacred Tradition carries, transmits, hands on, or mediates Divine Revelation, its content originates in the eternal and divine life of God. It expresses Revelation from on high, suitable for transforming life here below and for leading to eternal life in the hereafter. As such, the process

of transmission is more than a communication of ideas: It is the means by which Divine Revelation is made available to each generation of believers.

The Church's dogmatic and theological tradition organizes Sacred Tradition into the following elements: the word of God, the liturgy, the Fathers of the Church, the Magisterium. Each element contains something of the others and so represents a mini-mosaic of the whole. Woven together, these four elements form a fabric yielding a deeper vision of both the content and the process of receiving and living Revelation.

Heaven Joined to Earth • It is essential not to lose sight of the heavenly and earthly dimensions of Sacred Tradition. Without clarity on this point, our view of it could easily lapse into being so "heavenly" as to be "no earthly good" or else we might reduce what is sacred and transcendent to being merely a product of the historical process (cf. CCC 91-93).

The very substance of Sacred Tradition, like that of Sacred Scripture, begins in the eternal life of God, which is present to but outside the created order. This statement is based on one of God's divine perfections or attributes, namely, omniscience ("all knowing"). God has simultaneous knowledge of all events, past, present, and future. God "views" things as if they were all in the present, as one gazes at a work of art on the canvas: There is no past or future, the whole picture is simultaneously present. The divine plan of redemption comes to us through the passing of time, but it is not viewed this way from God's eternal point of view; for God, the plan of salvation is perfect, already complete, already fulfilled.

This eternal plan issuing from the mind and heart of the Father, timeless and hidden from the ages, finds its historical expression within time and space, and is completed in the Person and work of Jesus Christ. The connection between heaven and earth, then, is within his Person and work. He, personally and historically, is the link binding heaven to earth forever, bonding the spiritual with the material. He therefore is our model for understanding how the divine, invisible, immaterial reality of God's being can be eternally bonded to material creation. Jesus is the basis for receiving Divine Revelation through Sacred Tradition and for the sacredness of the latter.

In this sense, we can say that the very core of Sacred Tradition is divine, heavenly — a divine quality of essence radiating through the historical process and mediating divine life through material reality. The sacraments are but one example of this deeply mysterious, concrete, and utterly unfathomable mystery. There is a kind of image that helps us understand the relationship between the heavenly and earthly dimensions of Sacred Tradition in a flower and the wonderful scent it communicates: The flower's beauty attracts our eyes; then, having captivated us by its beauty, the flower further delights us with a captivating scent, which adds a new dimension of beauty not initially perceived. Flower and scent are inseparable, even though one is visible and the other not.

Sacred Tradition and the Word of God • The Church teaches that Sacred Tradition and Sacred Scripture form one sacred deposit of God's word (cf. Vatican Council II, *Dogmatic Constitution on Divine Revelation, Dei Verbum*, 9; CCC 80). Both flow from the same "divine well-spring" and come together to form a unity that moves toward the same goal (*Dei Verbum*, 9). We need to probe the relationship between Sacred Tradition and Sacred Scripture in order better to understand the two distinct ways or modes in which they express God's word.

The mode of transmitting God's word within Sacred Tradition is principally oral, beginning with Jesus Christ's own teaching and preaching. By teaching and preaching about the kingdom of God, Jesus "handed over" (the technical meaning of "tradition") his teaching to the Apostles. They in turn handed over what they received to apostolic men, who in turn handed over the faith to the next generation of leaders, namely, the first bishops; and so on (*Dei Verbum*, 9; cf. Vatican Council II, *Dogmatic Constitution on the Church, Lumen Gentium*, 20). Eventually, these teachings were organized into systematic narratives; the letters of some of the Apostles were organized and transmitted as distinct bodies of literature, and

formed what the Church would eventually call the New Testament.

The content of what was handed over in this manner has a technical name: It is what the theological tradition calls the "sacred deposit" of the faith, the *depositum fidei*. This deposit contains doctrine that God wants us to know for the sake of our salvation — that is, for the sake of entering into full and complete union with him, beginning here on earth and realized more fully in heaven. A second aspect concerns the "faith which is deposited within us" — the handing on of a way of life designed by and built upon the grace and work of the Holy Spirit in the hidden, inner life of the believer. The Church "hands over" the faith in both senses: the deposit of truth and a work of grace helping us to live the way of life that God intends under the guidance of the Holy Spirit.

The second mode of communicating the word of God is through its revelatory, inspired, and inerrant written expression within Sacred Scripture. It is fair to say that Sacred Scripture is the normative expression of Divine Revelation the Church had already lived. This means that Sacred Tradition came before Sacred Scripture. The Church's life under the Spirit's guidance was known and lived in Jesus' day by a few and was more universally lived within the Church after Pentecost — well before there was a New Testament. Thus, before there is a New Testament there is within the Church a deposit of the faith (doctrine) and an ongoing and living faith experience (inner grace to yield to God's great truths). The link between the word of God in Sacred Tradition and Sacred Scripture is inseparable; they come from the same source — God. Sacred Tradition is the womb or matrix from which emerges the New Testament.

Sacred Tradition and the Liturgy • The Church's liturgical tradition constitutes another essential element of Sacred Tradition (cf. CCC 1124). Both the process and content of Revelation are communicated through our liturgical practices. Through the Church's witness to repentance, the divine forgiveness of sins, and her universal life of prayer we find a witness to the ongoing vitality and effectiveness of Divine Revelation as a power that extends Christ's redemptive work throughout history until he comes again in glory. Through the liturgy, especially of the sacraments, we come into touch with the throne of God in heaven and his great power to transform even the most lowly human life.

Considered in terms of process, the authority to bind and forgive and the authority to teach on faith and morals with the charism of certain truth are passed on by means of episcopal ordination, which takes place within the Church's liturgical prayer. Through the imposition of hands and the words of consecration the charism of truth is handed on. This action realizes Jesus' promise to be with the Church until the end of time. By means of episcopal ministry, then, the charism of truth remains with the Church, even in her darkest hours of crisis and confusion.

Another way in which liturgy hands on Divine Revelation pertains to the liturgical gestures and words, which are drawn from Sacred Scripture. When we begin our prayer in the name of the Trinity and with the Sign of the Cross, it is as if we were calling to mind biblical truths and biblical stories. To do such action and speak such language is to wash the soul with a language that, although completely human, is nonetheless from heaven. Our prayer language has a power to open us up to the eternal Father, Son, and Holy Spirit, who are recognized as beckoning us to a deeper human life rooted in heaven. The liturgical words and deeds effect the sacred mysteries within the sacraments, making present to us here and now the realities to which Sacred Scripture points. In this way, the liturgy continues to present the sacred mysteries of salvation, recorded in Sacred Scripture and lived out in sacred history.

There is an intimate connection between our liturgical prayer and our dogmatic beliefs — they are linked as water is to wine. A theological phrase that expresses this principle is *lex orandi, lex credendi* (the "rule of prayer" is our "rule of faith"). The content of liturgy expresses the content of the deposit of faith; the content of faith is found in the content of liturgy. The liturgical life of the Church disposes us to the saving mysteries by making the graces of salvation available to us in tangible, concrete sacramental signs.

This double rule finds further confirmation in the charism of truth given the whole Body of Christ, the Church. Theologians speak of the *sensus fidei* (literally, "the sense of the faith") to refer to a supernatural sense of the faith that is a result of the inner work of the Holy Spirit within the life of the whole of the people of God — from the bishops to the last of the faithful — when they manifest a universal consent in matters of faith and morals (cf. *Lumen Gentium*, 12; CCC 92). The purpose of the supernatural sense of the faith is to adhere to what God has revealed, penetrate that Revelation more deeply with right judgment, and apply the Revelation more fully in daily life (CCC 93). And so the "rule" is not a dead law to which slavish obedience is required. Rather, the "rule" is really a way of life that supernaturally deepens our natural life through the liturgical and sacramental mediation of grace.

Together these two principles (rule of prayer/ faith and the "sense of the faith") function as anchors that steady the Church's gaze into the beatific vision of God, who lives in unapproachable light.

Sacred Tradition and the Magisterium • It is not enough to pray enlightened prayers and experience grace. The mind also must come to understand and penetrate the substance of Revelation. In order to guide the mind toward truth, Christ established through the Apostles what we today call the Magisterium. They in turn hand this gift of truth to their successors, the bishops. This process of transmission was established in order to secure a certain and truthful knowledge of God that was without error.

The Magisterium is the teaching office of the Church, whose role is to safeguard the deposit of faith and morals that guides the Church's journey to God. This teaching office is exercised at two levels, the extraordinary (Scripture, councils, infallible papal pronouncements) and ordinary (e.g., a local bishop's pastoral letter, sacramental preaching, etc.). One of the principal reasons for defining doctrines is so that the truths of Revelation are not lost by being so completely reinterpreted that they cease to have any connection with their original expressions. When it defines dogma, the Church acts with the authority of Christ himself (CCC 88) and follows the guidance of heaven (cf. Mt 16:17).

There are practical reasons why God established an infallible teaching office for the Church. First, while all people have the potential to know the fullness of the truth, they do not always agree on what constitutes that fullness. There is a need for a fuller, deeper, and more prophetic grasp of truth, driven neither by politically correct trends nor by a compromised agenda. Only God can effect such a vision of truth, which he promises to give through the Magisterium. Second, there is a vital and organic link between dogma and the spiritual life. As John 8:31-32 makes abundantly clear, to know Christ is to know truth and so to be set free from that which binds and oppresses ("Jesus then said to the Jews who had believed in him, 'If you continue in my word, you are truly my disciples, and you will know the truth, and the truth will make you free' "). Truth lights up the path of faith and makes it secure; grace sustains us on that path; God's love poured out in our hearts further confirms the intellectual content of truth (CCC 88-89). Through the teachings of the Magisterium we come to know truth, and through grace that knowledge empowers us to love God and neighbor as ourselves. The intimate connection between the teaching office (the Magisterium) and our spiritual life is a necessary foundation for preserving the unity of the one, true, catholic, and apostolic Church.

Sacred Tradition and the Fathers of the Church • It is from the Fathers of both the Western (Latin-speaking) and Eastern (Greek-speaking) Church that we have received our great theological, liturgical, and catechetical traditions. Led by the Spirit of Truth and the needs of each generation, the Fathers proclaimed the Gospel, presenting the truth faithfully, explaining it clearly, making the Good News more widely known throughout the Eastern and Western Roman empires.

For example, great catechetical traditions were developed by such powerful figures as St. Cyril of Jerusalem, St. John Chrysostom, St. Ambrose, and St. Augustine, to mention only a few. Through the work of such men and of many holy women, the Church grew in her understanding of the truths of the faith, deepened in her own faith, and increased in her ability to transmit the faith intact and in the fullness of the Spirit of Love and Truth. The organizational pattern of the *Catechism of the Catholic Church* attests to the patristic model of catechesis, which sought to explain the Church's beliefs, morals, sacraments, and prayer.

In summary, God's word, the liturgy, the Magisterium, and the Fathers of the Church manifest like elements in a brilliant mosaic the unfathomable love of God and his desire for many sons and daughters in and through the Person and work of Jesus Christ. These four elements are like four pillars that sustain each generation of the Church, enabling her boldly to proclaim the wisdom of God in Christ to the whole cosmos (cf. Eph 3:10). Through Sacred Tradition we gain access to the ongoing mystery of salvation, witnessed to in Sacred Scripture and lived out in the life of every believer who has been given the Holy Spirit through God's merciful acts of love and kindness.

See: Apostolic Succession; Catechesis; Divine Revelation; Inerrancy; Infallibility; Lex Orandi, Lex Credendi; Liturgy; Magisterium; New Covenant; New Testament; Old Covenant; Old Testament; Ordinary Magisterium; Patrology; Sacrament; Sacred Scripture.

Suggested Readings: CCC 55, 74-81, 83-84, 95, 97, 113, 120, 142-175, 638, 1124. Vatican Council II, *Dogmatic Constitution on the Church, Lumen Gentium*, 12, 20-21; *Dogmatic Constitution on Divine Revelation, Dei Verbum*, 10-16, 18-19, 21-22, 24-25. Y. Congar, O.P., *The Meaning of Tradition*. P. Grelot and J. Giblet, "Revelation," in X. Leon-Dufour, ed., *Dictionary of Biblical Theology*.

Stephen F. Miletic

SACRIFICE

By the virtue of religion we relate to God as our first principle and ultimate end and render to him what is due (St. Thomas Aquinas, *Summa Theologiae*, II-II, 81, 1). The internal and principal acts of religion are devotion and prayer; sacrifice is listed among the external acts of religion (*Summa Theologiae*, II-II, 85). Sacrifice can be described as the offering of a visible or sensibly perceptible object to God in order to acknowledge his dominion over us and our subjection and obedience to him.

To qualify as a true and authentic sacrifice, the external act must be the expression of an internal act of sacrifice, and the offering must be made to God alone. Seen in this context, religious sacrifice is a fulfillment of the first commandment of God: "I, the Lord, am your God, who brought you out of the land of Egypt, that place of slavery. You shall not have other gods besides me" (Ex 20:2). The traditional catechetical formula is: "I am the Lord your God: you shall not have strange gods before me."

Sacrifice involves offering something tangible to God. As we have noted, there must first of all be an internal submission to God and then the external action or rite as an expression of one's faith and obedience. Hence, St. Augustine says, "Every action done so as to cling to God in communion of holiness, and thus achieve blessedness, is a true sacrifice."

Sacrifice in the Old Testament • Various statements in the Old Testament testify to the primary importance of the internal disposition in offering sacrifice. Samuel asks: "Does the Lord so delight in holocausts and sacrifices as in obedience to the command of the Lord? Obedience is better than sacrifice, and submission than the fat of rams" (1 Sm 15:22). David confessed that he could obtain forgiveness not by a purely external ritual of sacrifice but by the interior disposition of repentance: "For you are not pleased with sacrifices; should I offer a holocaust, you would not accept it. My sacrifice, O God, is a contrite spirit; a heart contrite and humbled, O God, you will not spurn" (Ps 51:18-19).

The Old Testament describes a variety of sacrificial rituals, sometimes as acts of adoration and sometimes as expressions of thanksgiving for benefits received, atonement for sin, or petitions to God for temporal or spiritual needs. Normally, the victim or the thing offered to God was destroyed in some way or completely set aside from human use. Thus, in a holocaust the victim was cremated; in a sacrificial meal, food and drink were consumed; sometimes oil or wine was poured into the ground. This was done to show that what was offered to God in sacrifice could not be taken back for human use.

Sacrifice is the central and most excellent of all the external acts of the virtue of religion, which is itself the highest of all the moral virtues. The primary purpose of sacrifice is to give a visible sign of our recognition of God's dominion over us and our submission to him. It is offered to God alone.

But the sacrifices of the Old Law were only a foreshadowing of what was to come. "Since the law has only a shadow of the good things to come, and not the very image of them, it can never make perfect those who come to worship by the same sacrifices that they offer continually each year" (Heb 10:1).

"But when Christ came as high priest of the good things which have come to be . . . he entered once for all into the sanctuary, not with the blood of goats and calves but with his own blood, thus obtaining eternal redemption. For if the blood of goats and bulls and the sprinkling of a heifer's ashes can sanctify those who are defiled so that their flesh is cleansed, how much more will the blood of Christ, who through the eternal spirit offered himself unblemished to God, cleanse our consciences from dead works to worship the living God" (Heb 9:11-14).

Sacrifice in the New Testament • Christ is therefore "mediator of a new covenant"; he takes away the sins of many by his sacrifice (Heb 9:15, 26). Unlike the priests of the Old Law, who offered "again and again those same sacrifices which can never take away sins, . . . Jesus offered one sacrifice for sins and took his seat forever at the right hand of God" (Heb 10:11-12).

Christ's offering of himself for the sins of mankind is the unrepeatable sacrifice that brings redemption once and for all. Consequently, those who accept Christ as their High Priest can approach him with confidence as heirs of the kingdom (Heb 10:19-22). Jesus has a priesthood that does not pass away. Therefore, he is always able to save those who approach God through him, "since he always lives to make intercession for them" (Heb 7:24-25).

In this context St. Paul writes: "We know that Christ, raised from the dead, dies no more; death no longer has power over him. As to his death, he died to sin once and for all; as to his life, he lives for God" (Rom 6:9-10).

The symbol of the sacrifice of Christ and, indeed, of our redemption, is the cross. The sacrifice of Christ is a sacrifice of atonement; it is also a sacrifice of petition, asking forgiveness and mercy of the heavenly Father. "It pleased God to make absolute fullness reside in him, and by means of him, to reconcile everything in his person, both on earth and in the heavens, making peace through the blood of his cross" (Col 1:19-20).

Christ's sacrifice is an expiation and a propitiation that moves the heavenly Father to look with favor on sinful humanity and restore it to a state of grace, and ultimately to glory. But there can be no sacrifice without a priest, and in this case Christ is the sole High Priest. He is also the victim offered in sacrifice (Heb 9:11-18; Col 1:22-23).

Jesus Christ, the Word made flesh, has made superabundant satisfaction for the sins of the world by his death on Calvary. All this was foretold in Isaiah, chapters 52 and 53; and this is Catholic belief, as stated by the Council of Trent: "When we were enemies, Christ, because of his great charity with which he loved us, merited justification for us by his holy passion on the tree of the cross and satisfied God his Father for us." St. Paul says that "the gift is not like the transgression. For if by that one person's transgression the many died, how much more did the grace of God and the gracious gift of the one person Jesus Christ overflow for the many" (Rom 5:15).

During the Last Supper, Christ told his Apostles clearly that he was offering his life as an immolation and a sacrifice for sin: "This is my body, which

will be given for you. . . . This cup is the new covenant in my blood, which will be shed for you" (Lk 22:19-20). It is, therefore, of Catholic faith that Christ offered a true and perfect sacrifice to his heavenly Father. The Council of Trent stated: "Jesus Christ, a perfect priest, offered himself to God his Father on the altar of the cross, to bring about by his death eternal redemption."

Numerous passages in the Gospels refer to Christ's death as a true sacrifice (e.g., Mt 16:21, 20:28; Jn 6:52, 10:10-15, 17:19). The same doctrine is found in St. Thomas Aquinas, who bases his theological proof on the teaching of St. Augustine: "A sacrifice properly so called is something done for that honor which is properly due to God, in order to appease him. . . . But Christ offered himself up for us in the Passion: and this voluntary enduring of the Passion was most acceptable to God, as coming from charity. Therefore it is manifest that Christ's Passion was a true sacrifice" (*Summa Theologiae*, III, 48, 3).

The Eucharist As Sacrifice • In the early Church, there was also widespread recognition of the Eucharist as a true sacrifice: for example, the *Didache*, chapter 14; St. Justin, *Dialogus cum Tryphone*; Hippolytus, *Apostolic Tradition; Didascalia Apostolorum* of the Syriac tradition; and works of Tertullian and St. Cyprian.

The contrary teaching of the Protestant Reformers in the sixteenth century elicited a solemn definition from the Council of Trent. The first chapter of the decree on the Sacrifice of the Mass affirms that Christ offered himself on the cross once and for all for the redemption of mankind and that he left to his Church the visible, unbloody sacrifice that commemorates and perpetuates the sacrifice on the cross. Then the Council solemnly affirms that the Mass is a true and proper sacrifice and cannot be restricted to a Communion service (Denzinger-Schönmetzer, 1751).

Chapter 2 of this same decree declares that the Mass is the unbloody immolation of Christ; only the manner of offering distinguishes it from the sacrifice on the cross. Consequently, the Mass has a propitiatory value that benefits the living and the dead. However, the sacrifice of the Mass does not in any way detract from the unique efficacy of the sacrifice of the cross.

The foregoing declarations were accepted without dissent by the Fathers of the Council. What was disputed, however, was whether or not the Last Supper could be considered an authentic sacrifice, since it preceded the sacrifice of the cross. This in turn gave rise to questions about the propitiatory value of the Last Supper. The Council did not decide the matter, nor did it designate the ritual action that completes the Sacrifice of the Mass. This second point was not officially settled until 1947, when Pope Pius XII issued his encyclical on the liturgy, *Mediator Dei*, and declared that the Sacrifice in the Mass is completed with the separate consecrations of the bread and the wine.

Pope Pius likewise restated the traditional teaching that the Mass is a true sacrifice wherein Christ, by an unbloody immolation, offers himself as a victim to the eternal Father, as he had done on Calvary (*Mediator Dei*, 68). The minister is the same insofar as the priest has the power of performing this liturgical action *in persona Christi*. Finally, the Body and Blood of Christ are both really present in the Eucharistic species, while the unbloody immolation of Christ in the Mass is symbolized by the separation of the species (*Mediator Dei*, 70).

As *Mediator Dei* makes clear, the Eucharist as sacrifice does not *repeat* the sacrifice of the cross — Christ died only once — nor is it merely a *remembrance* of Calvary. It is a sacrament instituted by Christ, who clearly designated its matter and formula. Since the sacraments effect what they signify, the Body and Blood of Christ become present under the appearances of bread and wine at the words of Consecration and remain present thereafter.

Theologians generally agree that for the Eucharist to be a true sacrifice, the separate Consecration of the bread and the wine suffices. What is still problematic is how the sacrifice of the cross, which happened thousands of years ago, is present in the Eucharistic sacrifice. Various opinions are put forth by theologians; but the Consilium set up

to implement the *Constitution on the Liturgy* of Vatican Council II states simply that the Mass is "a sacrifice in which the Sacrifice of the Cross is perpetuated" (*Instruction on the Worship of the Eucharistic Mystery, Eucharisticum Mysterium*, 1 [1967]). Christ, we repeat, died only once and for all, but his sacrifice is perpetuated in the Consecration of bread and wine ("Do this in memory of me") and applied to souls in the sacred banquet of Communion. It also states that in the Mass "the sacrifice and sacred meal belong to the same mystery — so much so that they are linked by the closest bond" (*Eucharisticum Mysterium*, 3).

Sacrament and Sacrifice • As we have seen in the Letter to the Hebrews, "we have been sanctified through the offering of the body of Jesus once for all" (10:10). However, Christ continues to function as priest and victim in order to apply the effects of redemption to souls until the end of time. His redemptive sacrifice is made present and visible in the sacramental signs of the Eucharist: the consecrated species of bread and wine. The act by which all this takes place is the Eucharistic sacrifice, popularly called the Sacrifice of the Mass. St. Thomas points out that for those who receive the Eucharist at Mass, it is both sacrament and sacrifice, but for those who do not receive it, it is a sacrifice offered for their salvation (*Summa Theologiae*, III, 79, 7).

The Council of Trent touched on this matter in the following declaration: "For it is one and the same victim; it is the same now offering himself, by the ministry of the priests, who offered himself then on the cross, only the mode of offering being different. And by this unbloody offering, we receive most richly of the fruits of that bloody one. . . . Wherefore, it is justly offered, according to the tradition of the apostles, not only for the sins, penalties, satisfactions and other necessities of the faithful in this life, but also for the dead in Christ, who have not yet attained complete purification" (Denzinger-Schönmetzer, 1743).

Pope Paul VI stated in his *Credo of the People of God*: "We believe that the Mass, celebrated in the person of Christ by the priest in virtue of the power of orders and offered by him in the name of

Christ and the members of Christ's Mystical Body, is truly the sacrifice of Calvary made present sacramentally on our altars" (24).

The words of the institution of the sacrament of the Eucharist indicate that it is both a sacrament and a sacrifice. Moreover, it is sacrificial under two aspects: as a re-presentation of the sacrifice of Christ on the cross, and as a sacred meal in which the consecrated bread and wine are consumed (Communion). As to the first aspect, Pope Paul VI states in his encyclical on the Eucharist *Mysterium Fidei* (1965): "The mystery of the Eucharist makes present again in a unique manner the sacrifice of the cross, which was once offered on Calvary, continuously calls it to mind, and applies its saving power for the forgiveness of those sins we commit daily" (27). Concerning Communion, the encyclical quotes St. Paul's admonition to the Corinthians not to partake of pagan sacrifices because they are now partakers at the table of the Lord: "The cup of blessing that we bless, is it not a participation in the blood of Christ? The bread that we break, is it not a participation in the body of Christ?" (1 Cor 10:16).

"Both sacrifice and sacrament," says Pope Paul, "form inseparable parts of the same mystery. The Lord is immolated in an unbloody manner in the sacrifice of the Mass, which presents anew the sacrifice of the cross and applies its saving power, at the moment when through the words of consecration he begins to be sacramentally present as the spiritual food of the faithful under the appearances of bread and wine" (34).

The Eucharist has, therefore, three aspects that are distinct but inseparable: the Eucharist as the re-presentation of the sacrifice of Christ on Calvary; the sacrificial sacrament that is received in Communion; and the permanent sacrament of the Eucharist reserved on our altars. In relation to the faithful, the central action of the Eucharist is found in the Sacrifice of the Mass, a cultic meal. Various liturgical documents of the Church have repeatedly insisted that "the whole of liturgical life gravitates about the Eucharistic Sacrifice and the other Sacraments" (Pope John Paul II, apostolic letter of December 4, 1988).

See: Eucharist; Eucharistic Devotion; In Per-

sona Christi Capitis; Jesus Christ, God and Man; Justification; Mass; New Covenant; Old Covenant; Priesthood in the Old Testament; Priesthood of Christ; Real Presence; Redemption; Religion, Virtue of; Sacrament; Worship.

Suggested Readings: CCC 1356-1381, 2099-2100. Vatican Council II, *Constitution on the Sacred Liturgy, Sacrosanctum Concilium,* 47-57. Paul VI, *On the Doctrine and Worship of the Eucharist, Mysterium Fidei,* 26-55. Sacred Congregation of Rites, *Instruction on the Worship of the Eucharistic Mystery, Eucharisticum Mysterium,* 1-9.

Jordan Aumann, O.P.

SACRILEGE

If man is bound to revere God and his name, so, too, does the first commandment bid humans to hold sacred whatever comes from or pertains to their Creator, Redeemer, and Sanctifier. "Sacrilege," says the *Catechism of the Catholic Church* (2120), "consists in profaning or treating unworthily the sacraments and other liturgical actions, as well as persons, things or places consecrated to God." Reverence for things divine also has a social dimension: Silence, good taste, high standards of dress and grooming, generosity, decorum, respect and "good manners" in and around divine worship doubtless help people duly to turn toward God in mind and heart.

Each of the sacraments is a privileged, grace-filled encounter with God, especially when man receives him at Communion. Continues the *Catechism*: "Sacrilege is a grave sin especially when committed against the Eucharist, for in this sacrament the true body of Christ is made substantially present for us." It is sacrilegious for a person "conscious of [unpardoned] grave sin" to receive Communion (cf. Canon 916).

Laypeople should not forget, nor should priests, that all clerics, however affable and accessible, are God's envoys and should be treated accordingly. The issue is not the virtuousness or lack thereof of the individual, but the sacred character of the office. Also, every Catholic church where the Blessed

Sacrament is reserved in the tabernacle is God's home. While Catholics might not doff their shoes, like Muslims, they suitably leave casualness and informality at the stoop (cf. CCC 1387). On this it is instructive to recall Jesus' just rage in driving abusers from the temple in Jerusalem (cf. Mt 21:12-13, Mk 11:15-17, Jn 2:13-17).

See: Blasphemy; Religion, Virtue of.

SATISFACTION

One speaks of *sacramental* penance to distinguish it from other meanings of the word "penance," that is, the sacrament itself, the virtue of penance, and public acts of penance determined by the Church. It is also called satisfaction. That term is derived from the Latin *satisfacere*, which itself is composed of two Latin words, *satis* ("enough") and *facere* ("to do" or "to make"). The *Catechism of the Catholic Church* teaches: "Absolution takes away sin, but it does not remedy all the disorders sin has caused. Raised up from sin, the sinner must still recover his full spiritual health by doing something more to make amends for the sin: he must 'make satisfaction for' or 'expiate' his sins" (1459; cf. 1473, 2412, 2487). Satisfaction refers to the willingness of the penitent to accept whatever penance the priest may impose in the sacrament and includes the actual performance of that penance. Taking into account the situation of the penitent and seeking the penitent's spiritual good, it usually consists of prayers, reading Sacred Scripture, or some corporal or spiritual work of mercy (CCC 1460; cf. 618, 2447).

Some find it difficult to understand how it is possible to "make up" for sins simply by saying three Hail Marys or performing some act of penance or work of charity. Since any sin offends against the infinite God, no prayer or work of ours could atone for even the slightest sin. But the sacramental penance or satisfaction provides an opportunity for the sinner to do something so as to participate in some way in the redemptive act of Christ, which has already atoned for our sins. St. Paul says: "Now I rejoice in my sufferings for your sake, and in my flesh I complete what is lacking in Christ's afflictions for the sake of his body, that is, the church" (Col 1:24).

Colman E. O'Neill, O.P., writes of satisfaction: "There is . . . nothing ludicrous about the trifling penance imposed in confession. Any penance, no matter how severe, would be trifling, would be infinitely inadequate, in comparison with the offense. The three Hail Marys or the round of the beads are simply token damages; it is the Church's appeal to the Passion of Christ that makes the sinner's act of repentance feasible" (*Meeting Christ in the Sacraments,* pp. 286-287).

See: Absolution; Confession; Contrition; Penance and Reconciliation, Sacrament of; Penance in Christian Life; Sin; Suffering in Christian Life.

SCHISM

Under the title "Who belongs to the Catholic Church?" the *Catechism of the Catholic Church* notes that fullness of Catholic communion depends on maintaining "the bonds constituted by the profession of faith, the sacraments, ecclesiastical government, and communion" (837).

Catholic communion is ruptured, and one separates oneself from full life-giving participation in the Church, not only by heresy but also by schism. While heresy involves the formal denial of a point of doctrine taught by the Church's Magisterium as revealed truth, schism as such implies a refusal to accept the central or supreme governing authority of the Church; it is not preserving "unity or communion under the successor of Peter" (CCC 838; cf. 2089).

Schism can be express or implicit. Certain attitudes involve what might be termed incipient schism, insofar as they substantially involve a rejection of Church authority, even while acceptance of doctrine often is formally proclaimed.

Those who follow schismatic trends thus separate themselves more and more from the full union with Christ that he himself made conditional on being united with his Church. His words "Whoever listens to you listens to me, and whoever rejects you rejects me" (Lk 10:16) apply to government and discipline as well as to doctrine. They indicate the condition for remaining in life-giving communion not only with Christ's truth but also with his will, on which our salvation and sanctification likewise depend.

See: Apostasy; Church, Membership in; Church, Nature, Origin, and Structure of; Communio; Heresy.

SCIENCE AND THE CHURCH

The condemnation of Galileo over 350 years ago cast a long-lived shadow on the Church that is only now beginning to lighten. That condemnation, for "vehement suspicion of heresy" in teaching that the earth revolves around the sun, has echoed down the centuries mostly as myth. It is true that the Holy Office's verdict, based on too literal a reading of Scripture, was an abuse of power. But, as always, there were mitigating circumstances: misunderstandings, personality conflicts, the duty to protect received truth against a brash and troubling dissenter. Most importantly, Galileo could not prove his case; the evidence he cited for the heliocentric system was suggestive but inconclusive. Thus the authorities did not act out of blind superstition, nor were they the enemies of human progress.

Galileo became a symbol of the "war between religion and science" because, in the centuries that followed, the two disciplines developed apart from, and sometimes in conscious opposition to, each other. The Church at times has been guilty of ignoring or attacking scientific assertions, even when well-grounded. Too often, religious leaders have tried to evade uncomfortable scientific conclusions by appealing to the Bible and claiming the higher authority of faith. Even today, fundamentalist proponents of "creation science" continue to fight a rearguard action against the theory of evolution, a stance that mainstream Christian churches either never adopted or have long abandoned.

Not all the mistakes have been on one side, however. Many respected scientists, both past and present, have dismissed religion as irrelevant fancy, accepting Thomas Henry Huxley's overwrought claim for empiricism: "There is but one kind of knowledge, and but one method of acquiring it." Nineteenth-century positivists and twentieth-century atheists have treated science not as a way of explaining the wonders of God's creation but as a way of explaining the creation without God. (In this entry, "science" refers to the classic empirical disciplines, most prominently physics, chemistry, and biology.)

This historical tension, perhaps unavoidable but certainly unfortunate, has kept the Galileo affair alive. Today, however, change is in the air. The scientific and religious communities seem progressively willing to admit the limits of their methods and their wisdom. Moreover, the ethical pressure that advances in science and technology are bringing to bear on society makes both sides more inclined toward collaboration. Nuclear weapons, threats to the global environment, invasive communications, artificial intelligence, genetic engineering — all these raise philosophical and moral questions that science has no means of answering but Christianity has been mulling for centuries. The ingredients for partnership, however uneasy, are in place.

There is widespread agreement within the Catholic Church that the tension between religion and science must end, for the good of all (CCC 159). The problem received some attention at the Second Vatican Council (cf., e.g., the *Pastoral Constitution on the Church in the Modern World, Gaudium et Spes*, 62), and John Paul II's pontificate is remarkable for his openness to science and his eagerness to heal old wounds. In 1979, the Holy Father publicly admitted that the Church had treated Galileo unjustly. Shortly thereafter, he appointed a special commission that exonerated the pioneer scientist. Then, in 1988, he issued a major statement on the importance of creating a mutually reinforcing harmony between the two disciplines. Speaking of the search for "areas of common ground," he said: "It is crucial that this common search based on critical openness and interchange should not only continue but also grow and deepen in its quality and scope. For the impact [science and religion have] and will continue to have, on the course of civilization and on the world itself, cannot be overestimated, and there is so much that each can offer the other."

Christianity's Role in Science • From a historical perspective, the Church has every reason to seek reconciliation with the world of science, since Christianity provided a cultural medium that nourished and strengthened science in its youth. Ancient Greece is usually considered the cradle of science; did it not produce Aristotle, Euclid, Archimedes, and Ptolemy? However, Greek science made slow and irregular progress, and it faded with the general decline of Greek learning after the second century A.D.

By contrast, the mathematically- and experimentally-based science that emerged like a thunderclap in the early seventeenth century transformed Western civilization so profoundly that a medieval man like Chaucer, brought forward to our century, would hardly recognize his surroundings. This prodigy shows no signs of exhaustion; it is vital, exuberant. Our great-grandchildren will probably live in a world we would find significantly alien.

How can Christianity claim credit for helping launch this phenomenon? Unlike the great Eastern religions — empirical science did not develop to any degree in China, India, or Japan — Christianity holds that the physical universe is the conscious creation of an intelligent Deity. Nature is therefore coherent, it makes sense, it is according to plan. Moreover, man is the rational being whom God made in his image and "gave dominion" over the rest of creation. In the Christian mirror, humanity sees reflected a creature equipped with superior intellect to probe, to comprehend, and to subdue (in the benign sense of "develop") the earth. The faith of the Christian, though always humble before the word of God as transmitted through the Church, is *fides quaerens intellectum*, a faith seeking understanding of the world as it is.

Such an inquiring faith should respond eagerly to the scientific enterprise. Indeed, before the dawn of the modern scientific era, Christianity did so. Medieval scholars, most notably St. Thomas Aquinas in his *Summa Theologiae*, forged a grand synthesis of theology, incorporating also the best scientific thought from the ancient world, the "natural philosophy" of Aristotle. Combining insights from faith, reason, and observation, St. Thomas tried to describe created reality in its totality.

Relevance of the Synthesis • The Thomistic synthesis may be impossible to imitate in our own day, given the complexity and rapid change that characterize modern science. Nevertheless, it can serve as a point of reference in describing the interaction between religion and science.

The synthesis has three fundamentally important implications for us. First, we must understand it as a model rather than a rigid orthodoxy. Theology owes intellectual loyalty to science itself, not to a particular scientific explanation of how things work. Now that Aristotelian ideas about the material world have been superseded, modern science must supply the terms. As science develops an evermore adequate account of nature and its laws, Catholic theology must reflect this new knowledge. In Pope John Paul's words: "Just as Aristotelian philosophy, through the ministry of such great scholars as St. Thomas Aquinas, ultimately came to shape some of the most profound expressions of theological doctrine, so can we not hope that the sciences of today . . . may invigorate and inform those parts of the theological enterprise that bear on the relation of nature, humanity and God?"

The second implication of the medieval synthesis challenges the current bias in contemporary culture toward the relativization, if not outright denial, of religious truth. There would be no point in reconciling science and faith unless the Church believed she could make objectively true statements about the world. Christianity is an incarnational religion, grounded in physical reality through the Word made flesh. It therefore aims, no less than science, to paint reality accurately.

One must immediately add that the content and method of religious truth-seeking are radically different from scientific content and method. Science focuses on the quantifiable aspects of things perceptible to the aided or unaided senses. It leaves aside our relationship to God and one another, salvation, humanity's place in the universe, the purpose of human life, and our ultimate destiny. It is silent regarding matters of the spirit. The intuitive conviction that there is more to us than biology — our sense of mystery, our sense of incompleteness, our experience of ourselves as free moral agents — lie outside its scope. The *Catechism of the Catholic Church* observes: "Science and technology are ordered to man, from whom they take their origin and development; hence they find in the person and in his moral values both evidence of their purpose and awareness of their limits" (2293).

Historically, science's area of competence has grown with the expansion of knowledge and the increasing sophistication of its tools. It is therefore extremely imprudent to attribute unexplained natural phenomena to divine action, arguing, for example, that God must have miraculously created life on earth because scientists cannot show how life could evolve from nonlife. Next year or next century, some enterprising biologist may discover the chemical pathways by which an organism comes to replicate itself, and then this "religious" assertion will be discredited.

Of course it is equally imprudent for scientists to argue that they will eventually be able to explain everything and that therefore religion has no place. This, after all, is an expression of faith, not a scientific assertion. Better by far for both disciplines to respect their mutual limitations. In a 1994 address to the Pontifical Academy of Sciences, John Paul II remarked: "The scientific community is ceaselessly called to keep the factors in order, situating scientific factors within the framework of an integral humanism [that takes] into account the metaphysical, ethical, social and juridical questions that conscience faces."

If scientific and religious statements are both objective in their own ways, they can also be complementary and mutually illuminating. This complementarity is the third and final implication of the Thomist synthesis. Pope John Paul II lays great stress on it in his 1988 statement: "As dialogue and common searching continue, there will be growth towards mutual understanding and a gradual uncovering of common concerns. . . . In

the process we must overcome every regressive tendency to a unilateral reductionism, to fear, and to self-imposed isolation. What is critically important is that each discipline should continue to enrich, nourish and challenge the other to be more fully what it can be and to contribute to our vision of who we are and who we are becoming."

The theory of evolution has occasioned the bitterest battles between science and religion in the past century. The Church's sources of knowledge — Scripture, Tradition, theological and moral reasoning — can supply no data for an independent judgment on evolution. Obviously, however, the Church can join with evolutionary biologists to make complementary observations about human life and dignity, our tendency toward evil, the beginnings of life, the nature of consciousness, the goal of human evolution, and many other fascinating subjects. While no one would pretend that the insights of religion and science fit together as neatly as pieces in a jigsaw puzzle or that they exhaust what can be said on a given topic, both represent valid and valuable contributions. Wisdom lies nearer the confluence of science and religion than with either one alone.

Improving the Relationship • Although science and religion can develop a respectful and supportive relationship, the way forward is studded with difficulties. Three centuries of suspicion, defensiveness, and mistrust have created a formidable psychological barrier. As we have seen, however, there are many signs of hope, at least at the level of the universal Church. Not only has John Paul II regularly spoken of the need for reconciliation, he has given new prominence to the Pontifical Academy of Sciences and the Vatican Observatory. Carrying on a tradition he established as Archbishop of Cracow, he has hosted a number of conferences where theologians, philosophers, and others discuss such topics as God's action in the world.

The Church in the United States, unfortunately, has not been in the forefront of change. The science faculties of Catholic colleges and universities have not traditionally been strong. The handful of Catholic organizations in the religion/science field are dwarfed by the American Scientific Affiliation, an evangelical Protestant group. There is little specifically Catholic reflection on even the most controversial subjects, such as the objectivity of religious truth or the moral implications of advances in the science and technology of human genetics.

In 1995, however, the National Conference of Catholic Bishops took a small but significant step with the publication of *Science and the Catholic Church*, a brief statement intended to dispel the Galileo myth and promote greater interchange with the scientific community. The bishops called for collaboration on the philosophical and practical levels, noting that science and religion must "make room for one another" in the modern world. *Science and the Catholic Church* applied the perspective of the Holy Father's 1988 statement to the American context and reached a similar conclusion. "Contemporary American culture," the bishops said, "owes much to the spirit and practice of scientific humanism: practicality, optimism, that famous 'can-do' attitude. . . . The Church . . . offers an essential complement: reflection, meditation, self-examination, historical perspective, recognition of mystery, knowledge of one's place in the whole. The two disciplines ought to be mutually enriching."

It is impossible to predict the future of interaction between religion and science because the field is so new, but improved relations seem destined to last. Perhaps science had to break away from established authority in order to develop its proper autonomy; Galileo's rebellion may have been inevitable. Now science is in the ascendant and need fear no undue interference from organized religion. At the same time, the Church, while continuing to teach the truth about humanity and its God, need not fear the truth that science contributes. No longer stern parent and upstart child, they can enjoy a mature and fruitful dialogue.

The alternative is unhealed fragmentation in human knowledge, as science and religion pursue their paths alone, and ongoing alienation between humanity's expanding power and its ability to use that power for good. Nuclear weapons were cre-

ated in the maelstrom of wartime emergency, when ordinary standards of morality seemed not to apply. It is a tribute to mankind's ability to right itself, and to the intense moral scrutiny to which these weapons have been subjected, that they have never been used again. A range of other scientific and technological advances, most notably the rise of human genetics, cries out for similar scrutiny.

Not only does the Catholic Church have a responsibility to assist in this analysis, her efforts will forward the essential work of evangelization. The Church can bring Christ to the nations only if she possesses a sympathetic understanding of the modern world, so profoundly shaped by science. The Holy Father's 1988 statement contains these striking lines: "Science can purify religion from error and superstition; religion can purify science from idolatry and false absolutes. Each can draw the other into a wider world, a world in which both can flourish." The remark echoes Albert Einstein's more pungent aphorism: "Science without religion is lame, religion without science is blind."

See: Atheism; Evolution; Media of Social Communications; Miracles; Rationalism; Superstition; Thomas Aquinas, Thought of; Truthfulness.

Suggested Readings: CCC 2293-2294. Vatican Council II, *Pastoral Constitution on the Church in the Modern World, Gaudium et Spes*, 36, 57-62. John Paul II, "Message," in R. Russell et al., eds., *Physics, Philosophy and Theology: A Common Quest for Understanding*. National Conference of Catholic Bishops, *Science and the Catholic Church*. S. Jaki, *The Origin of Science and the Science of Its Origin*. R. Russell et al., eds., *John Paul II on Science and Religion: Reflections on the New View from Rome*.

David M. Byers

SECRETS

"Three may keep a secret, if two of them are dead." Benjamin Franklin's aphorism in *Poor Richard's Almanac* is amusing, but, were it also true, Christians could not carry out an important duty. If husbands and wives held no secrets together or kept nothing secret from their children; if lawyers told all they knew; if General Motors knew Ford's plans or France knew Russia's, both personal relationships and the common good would suffer. Because divulging secrets can cause great mischief, the *Catechism of the Catholic Church* says: "Truthfulness keeps to the just mean between what ought to be expressed and what ought to be kept secret: it entails honesty and discretion" (2469).

Three Classes of Secrets • The *Catechism* distinguishes three classes of secrets, as is common in Christian ethics. First of all, it states unequivocally that the seal of confession can never be broken, no matter what the consequences (CCC 2490). As the Code of Canon Law says, the sacramental seal is "inviolable" (Canon 983.1). The secrets a priest knows from the confessional are a sacred trust, and nothing can dispense him from his obligation to the penitent. The blood of martyred priests over centuries has sanctified this bond and made it one of the most deeply felt and faithfully observed facets of Catholic practice.

Natural secrets, the second type, are those to which the retort "None of your business" rightfully applies. They are private matters: ordinarily, the state of one's health, one's hopes and desires, one's strategies and plans, flights of fancy, and turnings of the heart. We all have private worlds from which we may rightfully exclude others for a good reason or no reason except the maintaining of our privacy. As long as what is private does no harm to someone else, we may innocently hide it. A prospective employer is entitled to an honest answer to the question "Were you ever imprisoned for theft?" — but the secretary or the firm's other employees are not.

As the foregoing suggests, in certain cases we may have a positive obligation to conceal the truth in order to preserve a secret. Textbooks in moral theology frequently pose some form of the following dilemma: An armed man comes to your door and asks about John Doe, who you know is cowering in the basement. Strict truth-telling would require revealing John's presence, while weightier considerations suggest silence or an evasive answer. Conscience and common sense prevail, and

the secret is safe. Everyday secrets are usually not so dramatic. Nevertheless, our right to legitimate privacy and freedom, our responsibility to ourselves, or the need to protect another person's life, property, or good name often oblige us to keep them.

The *Catechism*, alert to the conditions of modern life, extends the obligation to respect personal dignity to the media. Unless revealing private flaws (corruption in public officials is an example) serves some compelling public good, those in the media trample individual rights by doing so (CCC 2492). No less than individuals, the media must refrain from invading privacy.

Natural secrets are ones we learn simply in the course of everyday life, by knowing people, by "hearing things," sometimes by less innocent means like listening to gossip or prying. The third class of secrets consists of information we gain under explicit or implicit promise of confidentiality. Most frequently, such secrets reflect sharing among intimate friends ("This is just between you and me"). They are also a necessary part of many professional relationships. A legal system based on the principle that persons accused of crimes are presumed innocent until proven guilty would be inconceivable without the attorney-client privilege. The practice of psychotherapy would quickly end if doctors disclosed the details of therapy. Contracts, partnerships, treaties, alliances: All would be compromised in a world without professional secrets.

Generally speaking, the moral gravity of wrongfully divulging a secret depends on the harm done. Letting the guest of honor know that a surprise party is in the works is a lesser offense than broadcasting the fact that someone has a history of mental instability. In the same way, giving out information gained under promise of confidentiality is usually more seriously sinful than revealing natural secrets, because it adds betrayal of trust to the damage. The friend who violates a confidence not only does harm, she proves herself no friend; the soldier who turns traitor not only causes bloodshed, he fails in his public duty.

May an important secret ever be told? Yes, but

only if there is no other way to avoid serious harm to the person who confided the secret, the person to whom it was confided, or a third party (CCC 2491). Say, for example, that an acquaintance lets it slip that he is embezzling company funds. The duty to see justice done outweighs the obligation to preserve confidentiality. A psychiatrist might learn in the course of therapy that a patient harbors serious homicidal fantasies toward her. She may betray the patient's trust to protect her own life.

Catholics are to adhere to the truth: "Put false ways far from me; and graciously teach me thy law!" (Ps 119:29). Where secrets are concerned, though, the way of truth is sometimes murky, since to be true to one's commitments one must occasionally withhold the truth. Where moral uncertainties arise, the best guide is a conscience formed by intelligence, sensitivity, and the teaching of the Church. In the end, "God shall bring every deed into judgment, with every secret thing, whether good or evil" (Eccl 12:14).

See: Equivocation; Lying; Martyrdom; Media of Social Communications; Mental Reservation; Truthfulness.

Suggested Readings: CCC 2469, 2490-2492. G. Grisez, *The Way of the Lord Jesus*, Vol. 2, *Living a Christian Life*, pp. 405-418.

David M. Byers

SEMINARY

A seminary is a place where candidates are prepared for ordination to the priesthood.

In the first fifteen hundred years of the Church's life, training of future priests was varied and, in some cases, haphazard. Many diocesan priests were ordained after little more than a brief period of instruction under the direction of a local priest. Others studied at cathedral schools such as those at York, Paris, and Seville. Religious priests usually received their training at monastic schools. Thomas Aquinas received his early education at the Benedictine abbey of Monte Cassino. A few priests studied at the great medieval universities. The strength or weakness of their education depended on the individual institutions.

Catholic seminaries as we know them are the creation of the Council of Trent's decree *Cum Adolescentium Aetas*, promulgated in 1563, and the reforms initiated by the Second Vatican Council's *Decree on Priestly Formation, Optatam Totius*. Trent legislated that the candidate for diocesan priesthood was to pursue studies in Scripture, the rubrics, and dogmatic, moral, and pastoral theology. He was to assist daily at Mass, and go to confession once a month and to Holy Communion according to the advice of his spiritual director.

Early seminaries provided spiritual formation and pastoral education but did not teach theology. Theological education was left to the universities. As seminaries opened in small towns where there was no university, however, they began to offer theological instruction. But although Trent urged that every diocese establish a seminary, this was an impossible task.

Religious orders trained their candidates in "houses of study" that differed from diocesan seminaries. The character of each order determined the method, the content, and the length of training. The preparation of religious included periods of discernment such as postulancy and novitiate. Their training was often much longer than that of diocesan clergy.

Seminaries in the United States • At the invitation of Bishop John Carroll, the first seminary for the training of diocesan priests in the United States, St. Mary's Seminary in Baltimore, was established in 1791 by Sulpicians fleeing the aftermath of the French Revolution. As the American Church grew, the number of seminaries multiplied.

Seminaries founded to train diocesan priests owe their existence to the initiative of an individual bishop such as James Roosevelt Bayley in Newark; to the Sulpicians or Vincentians, religious orders whose mission includes the training of diocesan priests; to Benedictine monasteries, such as St. Meinrad in Indiana, which have chosen the training of diocesan priests as their particular apostolate; and to groups of priests, such as those who founded Mount St. Mary's in Emmitsburg, Maryland, and individual priests such as Father

Joseph Jessing, who founded the Pontifical College Josephinum in Ohio. The characteristics of the individual foundations contributed to the particular institution's ethos, which in many instances perdures to this day.

Religious order seminaries in the United States owe their existence to similar pioneering spirits. Each order has a unique spirit, or "charism," as well as one or more specific apostolates. The diverse apostolates of religious orders and congregations necessitated individual and separate seminaries, where the candidates would not only be trained for the order's work but also, very importantly, imbued with its spirit, its charism.

While the foundation of these seminaries was in many ways random, in fact entrepreneurial in some cases, the majority benefited from systems in place within the Church. They followed the outline of a course of studies and a basic philosophy of education and formation that evolved from the sixteenth-century Council of Trent for the diocesans, and from the history and traditions of particular religious orders for their own members. The Third Plenary Council of Baltimore (1884) attempted to standardize seminary training in the United States by promulgating norms regarding the length and content of the curriculum.

In 1965, the Roman Catholic seminaries in the United States reached the peak of their enrollment and were riding high on the enthusiasm generated by the Second Vatican Council and the continuing growth of the Catholic Church here. The 169 theological seminaries served 8,916 students (5,461 studying for the diocesan priesthood, 3,455 for religious communities). The theology students, moreover, were just the tip of the iceberg. There were 41,041 seminarians in minor seminaries, 164 of these seminaries conducting college-level programs and 189 with high-school programs. At this moment in history the Catholic seminaries had, like the Catholic Church herself, passed through a period of unprecedented institutional expansion. They were about to embark on a long period of renewal, change, experimentation, evaluation, and consolidation.

Seminaries and Vatican Council II • The Sec-

ond Vatican Council's *Decree on Priestly Formation, Optatam Totius*, called for a renewal of seminary studies. In 1969, four years after the close of the Council, the Congregation for Catholic Education published the *Ratio Fundamentalis Institutionis Sacerdotalis*, or *The Basic Plan for Priestly Formation*. The *Basic Plan* called on each nation to adapt the plan to its own exigencies. Within the United States, the direction of the renewal was assumed by the bishops' Committee for Priestly Formation, established in 1966 by the National Conference of Catholic Bishops. A major role of this committee is the drafting and revision of the *Program of Priestly Formation*. Four editions of this *Program* (1971, 1976, 1981, and 1993) have been approved up to now by the NCCB and by the Congregation for Catholic Education.

The *Program of Priestly Formation* set binding norms for seminary education in the United States at all levels: high school, college, and graduate theology. It established a program that includes spiritual, intellectual, and pastoral formation.

The period following the Second Vatican Council transformed the seminaries and their programs. One aspect of the renewal resulted in major institutional reorganization. The majority of religious-order seminaries coalesced into collaborative institutions, while, with few exceptions, the diocesan seminaries maintained their separate and independent character.

The religious, social, and cultural transformation of the American landscape impelled the seminaries to further modifications. The number of seminarians declined. In particular, the high-school and college programs experienced sharp curtailments in enrollment, and many closed. The number of older applicants, many of whom had pursued careers in established professions, prompted the establishment of Pope John XXIII National Seminary in Weston, Massachusetts, for "adult vocations." Responding to the changing needs of the Church, many seminaries admitted lay students for a variety of programs, academic and pastoral. The faculty, formerly composed exclusively of priests, became more diverse, including laypersons and religious sisters.

When the third edition of the *Program of Priestly Formation* was published in 1981, a period of rapid and dramatic change had been completed. Since the Second Vatican Council, institutions essentially new in structure and in programs had been created. That year, Cardinal William Baum, Prefect of the Congregation for Catholic Education, announced a "papal visitation," an ecclesiastical assessment of the seminaries of the United States. The director of the visitation was Bishop John Marshall of Burlington, Vermont. It was based upon the recently approved third edition of the *Program of Priestly Formation* and was carried out by visiting teams composed of bishops and seminary personnel. From 1982 to 1986, each seminary was visited by a team that examined the spiritual, academic, and pastoral programs, and also the seminary's administration and structure.

In 1986, at the conclusion of the visitation, Cardinal Baum affirmed the diocesan seminaries as "generally satisfactory." He added: "Some, in fact, are excellent, a few have one or more serious deficiencies, and the majority are serving the Church well." A similar letter, in 1988, praised college seminaries while lamenting their declining enrollment.

In 1990, a letter jointly issued by Cardinal Baum and Cardinal Jerome Hamer, O.P., of the Congregation for Institutes of Consecrated Life and Societies of Apostolic Life addressed the results of the visitations of the religious seminaries, the unions and clusters and independent institutions. While in general this letter emphasized the same themes as Cardinal Baum's letter regarding the freestanding diocesan seminaries, it also noted that the previous arrangement, in which the entire priestly formation program was in one institution, had given way to study centers providing academic training and houses of formation providing spiritual formation.

In 1990, the world Synod of Bishops, an assembly in Rome of representative bishops convened by Pope John Paul II, considered "The Formation of Priests in the Circumstances of Today." The preparation for the synod involved consultation with rectors and bishops throughout the world.

In 1992, Pope John Paul II issued an apostolic exhortation entitled *Pastores Dabo Vobis*, reflecting on priestly formation. These events, the Vatican visitation, and specific consultations, combined to influence the 1993 edition of the *Program of Priestly Formation*.

Seminary Formation Today • Roman Catholic seminaries are accredited educational institutions. The high-school and college seminaries are accredited by appropriate state and regional associations. The theological seminaries and schools are accredited as graduate-level institutions by regional accrediting agencies and as professional graduate schools by the Association of Theological Schools of the United States and Canada. At the completion of their training, seminarians receive the degree of Master of Divinity. In some instances, they receive the Licentiate in Sacred Theology.

Almost all seminary professors hold doctoral degrees in their area of specialization. A large number are active participants in scholarly societies. Spiritual directors and field-education directors participate in similar national organizations. Seminary administrators and faculty meet annually at the convention of the Seminary Department of the NCEA (National Catholic Educational Association) and at the biennial meeting of the ATS (Association of Theological Schools) of the United States and Canada.

The traditions of the Church and the directives of the Holy See are an essential part of seminary identity and affect the execution of their mission. The relationship of the seminaries with the Holy See, the National Conference of Catholic Bishops, diocesan bishops, and religious superiors is regulated by canon law. However, like all institutions of human construct, they are subject to the vagaries of their contemporary culture, its strengths and weaknesses.

In 1993, there were 11 high-school seminaries enrolling 1,183 students; college seminaries numbered 46, with 1,389 seminarians. The 46 theological seminaries had an enrollment of 3,131 seminarians (2,377 studying for the diocesan priesthood, 754 for religious communities).

In former years, the majority of seminarians entering the theological seminaries had already attended high-school or college seminaries. As more candidates came from a variety of educational and cultural backgrounds, however, the seminaries established "pretheology" programs to prepare them for theological studies. The 1992 edition of the *Program of Priestly Formation* affirmed this and required that most applicants, even those already holding bachelor's degrees, spend one or two years in preparatory programs before studying theology. In addition to academic credentials, a candidate for a seminary must be sponsored by a bishop or religious superior. Recommendations from pastors and community leaders, as well as psychological assessment, are integral parts of the application procedure.

The changing racial and ethnic composition of the Church in the United States is reflected in the seminaries and in their programs. Most seminaries offer ESL (English as a Second Language) programs. St. Vincent DePaul Seminary in Boynton Beach, Florida, offers classes in both English and Spanish. A number of seminaries also offer special programs geared to ministry to Latino Catholics.

The seminary program has several components. The goal of the seminary is to unite "human, spiritual, intellectual, and pastoral formation into an integral program of priestly formation" (*Program of Priestly Formation*, 249 [4th edition, 1993]). The seminarian is "challenged to a life of integral human growth and development, as well as a life of supernatural virtue" (*Program of Priestly Formation*, 278). Spiritual formation focuses on daily celebration of the Eucharist, the Liturgy of the Hours, and frequent celebration of the sacrament of Penance. This is augmented by retreats and conferences on spiritual themes. Individual spiritual direction is an essential component.

Intellectual formation is directed to "the education of a priest who is theologically informed and solidly grounded in the wisdom of the Church. . . . Such an education should be pastorally oriented, ecumenically sensitive, and personally appropriated by the individual seminarian. It should also be relevant to the world in which the Gospel is preached" (*Program of Priestly Formation*, 339). Programmatically, it consists of courses in Scripture, dogmatic theology, moral theology, historical studies, canon law, spirituality, liturgy, homiletics, and pastoral studies.

Pastoral formation aims at helping the seminarian to become "a shepherd . . . looking for solutions on the basis of honest motivations of faith and according to the theological demands inherent in pastoral work" (*Pastores Dabo Vobis*, 58). This is achieved in theological field education, which promotes learning through active engagement in pastoral life. It is refined through theological reflection on the implications of various pastoral situations. Some diocesan seminarians spend a full year away from the seminary in a supervised parish assignment. Many religious communities include even longer periods of pastoral engagement as part of their programs.

In the course of his training, the seminarian is periodically evaluated in all areas of formation by faculty and pastoral supervisors. These evaluations constitute the basis of the decision concerning ordination by the bishop or religious superior.

Certain distinctions between diocesan and religious seminaries remain, although it is not uncommon to find religious order candidates at many diocesan seminaries. Most of the diocesan seminaries, as noted above, are "freestanding," conducting the spiritual, intellectual, and pastoral components of the program within one institution. The largest freestanding diocesan seminaries are the University of St. Mary of the Lake in Mundelein, Illinois, St. Charles Seminary in Philadelphia, and Mount St. Mary's in Emmitsburg.

Several diocesan seminaries are "university-related," that is, the intellectual and pastoral formation takes place under the auspices of a Catholic university and the spiritual formation in a seminary residence, usually on the university campus. Examples are the Saint Paul Seminary of the University of St. Thomas in St. Paul, Minnesota, and Immaculate Conception Seminary of Seton Hall University in South Orange, New Jersey. Diocesan seminarians also study in Europe. Those who attend the Pontifical North American College in Rome are enrolled in Roman universities and those at the American College in Leuven, Belgium, attend the Universities of Leuven and Louvain.

The great majority of candidates for priesthood in religious communities live in houses of their particular community, where they receive spiritual formation. They attend study centers such as Washington Theological Union in Silver Spring, Maryland, Catholic Theological Union in Chicago, Illinois, the Graduate Theological Union in Berkeley, California, and Weston School of Theology in Cambridge, Massachusetts.

See: Holy Orders; Ministry; Priest; Vocation.

Suggested Readings: CCC 1562-1568. John Paul II, *I Will Give You Shepherds*, *Pastores Dabo Vobis*. National Conference of Catholic Bishops, *Program of Priestly Formation*, 4th ed. J. Ellis, "A Short History of Seminary Education," in J. Lee and L. Putz, eds., *Seminary Education in a Time of Change*. J. Ellis, ed., *The Catholic Priest in the United States: Historical Investigations*. C. Kauffman, *Tradition and Transformation in Catholic Culture: The Priests of Saint Sulpice in the United States from 1791 to the Present*. J. White, *The Diocesan Seminary in the United States: A History from the 1780s to the Present*.

Robert J. Wister

SERVILE WORK

Given the considerable social and occupational changes in recent years, the *Catechism of the Catholic Church* no longer speaks of abstaining from "servile work" ("work befitting a slave or servant") as part of the mandatory rest on Sundays and other holy days of obligation. Rather, "the faithful are to refrain from engaging in work or activities that hinder the worship owed to God, the joy proper to the Lord's Day, the performance of works of mercy, and the appropriate relaxation of mind and body" (2185).

The aim is clearly that of "worshipful rest": switching from one's regular job to other pursuits,

especially spiritual, that usher in a relaxing change of pace. A professional gardener, for example, may find such rest in writing letters, while a journalist may do the same in working in the garden. Family needs or important social service (zoo attendants, restaurant employees) "can legitimately excuse from the obligation of Sunday rest," but the faithful should see to it that exceptions do not become the rule, leading "to habits prejudicial to religion, family life, and health" (2185). Those who must work on Sundays and other holy days "should still take care to set aside sufficient time for leisure" and religion (2187).

Public authorities are obliged to ensure citizens a time for rest and divine worship. Employers have a similar duty toward their employees. For example, domestic help, except in special circumstances, should be given the day off. Retail businesses in sound financial shape should likewise remain closed on Sunday unless providing a needed service to which some people have access only on that day.

As St. Augustine wrote: "The charity [love] of truth seeks holy leisure," the better to know and love God. Yet because Sunday is "made for man" (Mk 2:27) — and not vice versa — "the necessity of charity," continues Augustine, "accepts just work," lest our Sunday devotion or rest deprive others of what they, too, require.

See: Lord's Day; Religion, Virtue of; Worship.

SEX ABUSE

Sex abuse is understood to be any sexual misconduct by adults toward children or young people entrusted to their care. This abuse can leave deep scars on young people and haunt them into their adult years. It can impair greatly their ability to have healthy and happy sexual lives, and can even be the source of psychological ills connected with sexual perversion and crime. Many sexual abusers were abused when they were young. It is a tremendous abuse of adult responsibility and a grave moral wrong. The offense is further aggravated, moreover, when perpetrated by someone in a position of trust — for example, a counselor, clergyman, or physician — against someone who has trusted in him.

See: Sexuality, Human.

SEXISM

Sexism is easy to define but difficult to apply. Sexism is unjust discrimination toward a person or persons on the basis of gender. The difficulty of applying this definition in a particular case, however, rests on the difficulty in judging what constitutes *unjust* discrimination. If, on the one hand, males are superior to females or vice versa, there would be no injustice in discrimination toward those who are inferior. If, on the other hand, there is no serious differentiation between male and female, such that anything a man may do, a woman may also do and vice versa, then of course all discrimination would qualify as unjust. But if male and female are equal and yet there is also a substantial difference between them, then forms of discrimination consonant with that difference would not be unjust.

Is there a significant differentiation between male and female, such that the two sexes are not simply interchangeable in who they are and what they are capable of doing? Nature clearly does differentiate between the two sexes, at least insofar as males are excluded from conceiving, bearing, and giving birth to children. But does the difference extend any further than this?

The Catholic faith holds that male and female are equal *and* that there is a significant difference between them, both in the order of creation and in the order of salvation. According to Genesis, man is created in the image of God as male and female (Gn 1:27). Each equally images God, yet the sexual differentiation itself is crucial precisely because it is bound up with the way man images God (Gn 1:27). Furthermore, the primary female sphere of influence and responsibility is marriage, family, and the realm of personal relationships, whereas the primary male sphere of influence and responsibility is work and the world (Gn 3:16-19). The first covenant God offers to mankind, through Adam and Eve, is rooted in this sexual differentiation.

The order of salvation revealed and instituted by Christ does not eliminate this differentiation but rather builds upon it. The "great mystery" of the New Covenant is the marital union of the male Christ, the bridegroom, with his female bride, the Church (Eph 5:31-32). Indeed, Christ saves us as the bridegroom who dies for the sake of his Church (Eph 5:25). As Pope John Paul II has pointed out, "Christ has entered this history and remains in it as the Bridegroom who 'has given himself' " (*On the Dignity and Vocation of Women, Mulieris Dignitatem*, 25).

Woman and Motherhood • The woman is defined in her very being as mother. We are told to call no man father (Mt 23:9), but women are defined as mothers — Eve as mother of all the living (Gn 3:20) and Mary as the Mother of God (Councils of Ephesus, Chalcedon). "Motherhood implies from the beginning a special openness to the new person; and this is precisely the woman's part" (*Mulieris Dignitatem*, 18). Motherhood is the indispensable foundation of all human life, because "the history of every human being passes through the threshold of a woman's motherhood" (*Mulieris Dignitatem*, 19). Hence, "in God's plan, woman is the one in whom the order of love in the created world of persons takes first root" (*Mulieris Dignitatem*, 29). Thus the woman's special sphere of responsibility is that of marriage and family.

That this is her primary sphere does not mean a woman has no right to pursue a job or career. It does, however, mean that a woman's marriage and family should never be sacrificed to that career. It also means, as Pope John Paul II has noted, that "while it must be recognized that women have the same right as men to perform various public functions, society must be structured in such a way that wives and mothers are *not in practice compelled* to work outside the home, and that their families can live and prosper in a dignified way even when they themselves devote their full time to their own family" (*The Christian Family in the Modern World, Familiaris Consortio*, 23). This in turn mandates that "the work of women in the home be recognized and respected by all in its irreplaceable value" (*Familiaris Consortio*, 23).

Thus discrimination that favors a woman in her role as wife and mother by ensuring, for example, that she is not forced to work outside the home would not be sexist or unjust, but simply consonant with the order God has created.

By the same token, the fact that the husband and father should, in the ordinary course of events, be the head of the family, responsible in his work for its economic and social well-being, does not mean his role *within* the family should be denied or diminished. It is therefore important that "efforts must be made to restore socially the conviction that the place and task of the father in and for the family is of unique and irreplaceable importance" (*Familiaris Consortio, 25*). At the same time, however, "equal pay for equal work" should be resisted when this means without qualification paying all people the same for the same work, regardless of marital status, family obligations, or other relevant differences. The family is the basic cell of society, and the head of the family (usually a man, but sometimes a woman) should be paid a family wage. The principle of equal pay for equal work is literally unjust, because it supposes that the financial obligations of the person working do not matter at all; and that is simply another way of saying the family does not matter, children do not matter, a person's monetary commitments to others do not matter. It results in the unjust impoverishment of women and children and in the unjust practice of compelling wives and mothers to go to work outside the home to help support their families.

Finally, whether one considers denying women access to the ordained priesthood unjust or not will depend in large part upon whether one views ordination as a personal right or a privilege. The Church holds that no one, man or woman, can lay claim to ordination as a right. Analysis of the question of ordaining women necessarily focuses upon the maleness of Christ. The fact that the New Covenant is the marital union of Christ the bridegroom with his bride the Church suggests that his maleness is indeed significant. Such at least has always been the faith and practice of the Church.

This does not mean women are inferior to men.

It simply points to the fact that, where male and female are concerned, there are two ways of living out the vocation of love. "The Bridegroom is the one who loves. The Bride is loved: it is she who receives love, in order to love in return" (*Mulieris Dignitatem*, 29). Indeed, the fact that women should submit to their husbands as the Church submits to Christ (Eph 5:24) does not imply inferiority, since men are instructed to love their wives as Christ loves the Church (Eph 5:25). Rather, it allows us "to hazard the idea that the wife's 'submission' to her husband, understood in the context of the entire passage (5:22-23) of the letter to the Ephesians, signifies above all the 'experiencing of love' " (Pope John Paul II, *Theology of Marriage and Celibacy*, p. 211).

See: Bride of Christ; Cardinal Virtues; Family; Hierarchy; Imago Dei; Sexuality, Human; Social Justice; Theology of the Body; Women, Ecclesial and Social Roles of; Women, Ordination of.

Suggested Readings: CCC 355, 369-372, 383, 772-773, 796, 808, 1577-1578, 1807, 1928, 2207, 2434. John Paul II, *On the Dignity and Vocation of Women, Mulieris Dignitatem; The Mother of the Redeemer, Redemptoris Mater; The Christian Family in the Modern World, Familiaris Consortio; Original Unity of Man and Woman.* G. Gilder, *Men and Marriage.* W. Ong, S.J., *Fighting for Life.* K. Stern, *The Flight From Woman.*

Joyce A. Little

SEXUALITY, HUMAN

One of the fundamental elements of human nature is sexuality. We are all either male or female, and that identity plays a foundational role in our response to life.

Human sexuality is not at all on the order of animal sexuality. The sexual acts of animals are purely physical; they are solely for the reproduction of the species. To the question "Why did God create male and female of other species?" the answer is simply, "So that they could reproduce." The sexual acts of humans, on the other hand, are not simply physical but engage the entirety of the human person: the physical, psychological, and spiritual. Thus human sexual acts must respect the values of all these realms.

Human beings have a profound need for intimacy with others, for getting to know and love others on a deep plane and for allowing others to know and love them. Unlike the offspring of animals, whose successful upbringing does not require that their parents be committed spouses, human children do need the unconditional love of parents devoted to each other as spouses. Whereas animals *reproduce*, humans *procreate*; whereas most animals "mate" for as long as it takes to conduct the sexual act, humans desire and need stable and loving relationships, both for their own well-being and for the well-being of their children.

When asked in reference to human beings, the question "Why did God make two sexes?" provokes an answer far different from that appropriate for other species. Again, for other animals sexual differences are merely instrumental to reproduction; but humans are divided into sexes for the further reason that they may thereby more perfectly image God. God himself is a community, a loving union of three Persons; he made us in his image; we are to be a loving community as well.

Sexuality is foundational to man's being a loving community. Male and female are to love each other with a unitive love, one that unites them in the community that is marriage. Thus unitive love is also a creative love: A new life, a new person to love, may issue from this love. Two become one flesh most literally in the procreation of a new life. Father, mother, and child as family are a kind of trinity, a loving union that is the basis of all community.

The Unitive Meaning • Pope John Paul II in his writings on human sexuality speaks of the "nuptial meaning of the body." He observes that the very physiology of the human person indicates that we are incomplete in ourselves: We need another of the opposite sex; we need a spousal relationship to complete ourselves. Our very physiology indicates that we are meant to make gifts of ourselves to another and to receive an-

other. The most natural way of achieving that spousal union and of making a gift of oneself to another is to marry. Those who are called to the religious life or to the single life will meet their need for a spousal relationship in their relationship with Christ, and will make a more extensive, if less intensive, gift of themselves in their apostolates to others.

God made us to love and to be loved. We flourish when loved by others; we grow and expand in loving others. One's sexual attractions and powers can contribute greatly to one's ability to love and to respond to love, but they must be put in service of love and made subordinate to its demands. Sexual attraction leads us to have a powerful interest in another person; it motivates us to reach out to another, to seek his or her company, to get to know him or her. It has the potential of leading us to develop a deep and abiding love for that person.

Initially the attraction may be physical; but since humans are a union of body and soul, to let the physical attraction govern our behavior toward another would be to reduce the other to an object. Human beings are a unity of body and soul; they are *persons*, who have a dignity and worth of their own; they deserve to be respected and loved; they deserve not to be used. Human beings are capable of discerning and respecting the worth and value of others, and it is a part of their dignity neither to misuse others nor to allow themselves to be misused by others.

This latter tendency of human beings — that is, to reduce each other to sexual objects — is rooted in original sin. Because of original sin, our sexual desires are disordered; most, if not all, human beings at some time are tempted to have sexual relations with those with whom they should not or in ways that they should not; they are tempted to violate the norms of sexual morality. These temptations are a result of original sin, and since sexual pleasures are so powerful and the human need for intimacy so great, it is easy for individuals to succumb to sexual temptation. For this reason, the need to understand the basis of the morality of sexual ethics is crucial, as is habituation in the virtue of chastity.

Sexual morality is based on the principle that the human person is never to be used as an object. The dignity of the human person requires that both the acting person and the person on the receiving end of the action behave in ways appropriate to creatures able to discern what is true and good and free to act in accord with what is true and good. Humans are able to understand what goods are attached to sexuality and are free to discipline themselves to respect those goods.

To be loving and responsible, to be disciplined about one's sexuality, means that one must not engage in sexual relations without being prepared for the likely consequences of those relations. Sexual relations create deep and abiding bonds with another individual; indeed, willingness to engage in sexual intercourse should mean that one desires a special relationship and special bonds with another. The nakedness of the sexual act signifies the complete self-giving appropriate to the act; it also suggests the extreme vulnerability of those who entrust themselves to another in this act. The self-giving must be genuine; the vulnerability must be protected. Only the promises made in marriage provide the context in which such total self-giving is appropriate and in which one should risk such vulnerability. Indeed, one could say that sexual acts contain implicit promises. One of these is the promise to be true to the bond that is created by, and is appropriate to, the sexual act.

The Procreative Meaning • Also implicit in the sexual act is the promise to care lovingly for any children conceived by the act. Not only does sexuality allow humans to overcome their constitutional solitude, to find union with another (which, because to a great extent it meets the human need for intimacy, is deeply satisfying), it also allows them to participate in the awesome act of helping to bring forth a new human life. In addition to the creating of bonds, sexual relations also have as a possible and natural outcome, the creating of new human life.

The "trinity" that the human being images is most fully realized when the spousal union brings forth new human life. Because God is a lover, he is also a creator; his love overflows into the creation of new beings. As *Humanae Vitae* states, "God has entrusted to spouses the extremely important mission of transmitting human life" (1). God created the whole universe so that new beings might be able to share in the unimaginable riches of his being. He created human beings to share eternal bliss with him. Thus, he desires new human life and has chosen to entrust its bringing forth to spouses.

Nor is the bringing forth of a new human life a momentary act. Responsible parents must devote themselves to the proper education and upbringing of their children. They are to create a family, wherein new life is welcome and cherished, and the gifts of individuals with different talents and interests are nourished. The family is both the cell of society and a domestic church. Here the family members learn to exist as a community, to share and to worship together. The family has a special obligation to foster hospitality and reach out to those in need of a warm, loving home environment; these may include the elderly, the handicapped, the abandoned, and the poor. The family is a school of love.

Sins Against Sexuality • The sixth and ninth commandments deal with sexuality. Although explicitly they forbid only adultery, implicitly they forbid all sexual misbehavior. But why would God have chosen adultery as the sexual sin to forbid explicitly, thereby indicating that all other sexual sins are logically included under that umbrella? This conveys a clear message: that sexuality belongs within marriage and not outside it. It belongs within marriage because, again, it has the twofold power of creating bonds and babies, goods that can be properly respected only within marriage. Adultery is a violation of the good of bonding that sexuality brings; it also is a violation of the good of children, for one cannot do justice to the task of rearing children conceived with one's partner in adultery. In short, adultery and all other sexual sins are sins against fidelity: the fidelity owed to one's spouse (one's sexuality belongs only to one's spouse) and the fidelity owed one's children (all sexual acts should be in accord with the good of procreation).

Every sin is a violation not only of a human good (here, sexuality) but also of human virtue. The *Catechism of the Catholic Church* makes it clear that sins against the good of sexuality are sins against the virtue of chastity. Chastity is the virtue of self-mastery that enables one to control one's sexual desires so that one does not desire those whom one should not desire, nor desire one's spouse in an improper fashion.

But not only do all sins violate human goods and human virtues, all are also acts of injustice against God, acts against Love Itself. God has given human persons the great gift of sexuality that drives them to seek loving, intimate relationships and enables them to participate in the profoundly meaningful and satisfying work of raising a family. To misuse one's sexuality is thus to misuse one of God's great gifts; it is to be ungrateful for what one has been given, to act in an unloving way toward others, toward oneself, and toward God.

The Catholic Church worked out her understanding of human sexuality in the midst of a culture with many distorted views of the good of human sexuality. Ritual prostitution, infanticide, homosexual behavior, promiscuity, and a disdain for the procreative power of sexuality, among other sexual aberrations, were practiced, and even philosophically justified, by elements in pagan society. Christ elevated marriage to a sacrament and to a vocation, a means of serving God. Christianity placed human sexuality on a very high plane; it expected men and women to respect each other's dignity and to join in a harmonious loving union. Today, a true Christian understanding of sexuality stands as a sign of contradiction to the sexual practices of most modern cultures by reason of its demands that sexuality be subordinated to the dignity of the human person, to fidelity, and to the good of children, and that it be enjoyed in an unselfish fashion.

See: Adultery; Body and Soul; Chastity; Contraception; Domestic Church; Education in Human Sexuality; Family; Homosexuality; Human Goods; Human Person; Imago Dei; Marriage; Marriage, Goods of; Marriage, Sacrament of; Natural Family Planning; Sexism.

Suggested Readings: CCC 369-373, 1601-1658, 2331-2400. Vatican Council II, *Pastoral Constitution on the Church in the Modern World, Gaudium et Spes*, 48-51. Pius XI, *On Christian Marriage, Casti Connubii*. Paul VI, *On Human Life, Humanae Vitae*. John Paul II, *The Christian Family in the Modern World, Familiaris Consortio; Letter to Families*. C. Burke, *Covenanted Happiness*. R. Lawler, J. Boyle, W. May, *Catholic Sexual Ethics*. K. Wojtyla, *Love and Responsibility*.

Janet E. Smith

SIMONY

Simony is so called because the magician Simon, envious of the spiritual powers at work in the Apostles, sought to buy from them the "secret" that would enable him to work similar wonders (cf. Acts 8:9-24). Thus, according to the Code of Canon Law (Canon 848), simony is unlawful "buying or selling of spiritual things."

Forbidden therefore is commerce in such things as relics, sacred images, vessels and vestments, indulgences, sacramentals, exorcisms, sacraments, and so forth. In past times, it was not uncommon for money to be paid in exchange for admission to at least the minor grades of Holy Orders, since membership in the clerical state offered access to endowed clerical posts (benefices) and finally to a regular source of income. Simony was a grave problem in the Church in the ninth to eleventh centuries. The eleventh century reform movement, identified especially with Pope St. Gregory VII (1073-1085) had the rooting out of simony as a major objective. Canon law severely punished such simoniacal behavior, and its strictures, together with social changes, largely put a stop to the practice. Christ himself spelled out the relevant principle: "You received without pay, give without pay" (Mt 10:8; cf. Is 55:1).

But Jesus also taught that "the laborer deserves

his food" (Mt 10:10). Thus it falls to bishops to determine suitable "offerings" to be given on the occasion of sacramental services rendered. The above-cited canon adds: "The minister should ask nothing for the administration of the sacraments beyond the offerings defined by the competent authority, always being careful that the needy are not deprived of the help of the sacraments because of their poverty."

See: Blasphemy; Religion, Virtue of; Sacrilege.

SIN

Sin is a major concept in Christian catechesis. "The Bible speaks of sin often, almost on every page," X. Leon-Dufour writes. Sin is discussed frequently in the *Catechism of the Catholic Church* also, because much of what is central to faith cannot be grasped without understanding sin. Moreover, to walk in Christ's ways we need to understand well the malice of sin. It has disastrous effects in human life, but the world often makes sinful deeds seem very attractive.

The central mystery of Jesus cannot be understood without realizing what sin is. For his very name means Savior, and he came into this world to save us from our sin. It is impossible to understand the great love of his blessed Passion without realizing that he died precisely for *our* sins. Neither can we appreciate the greatness of the new life to which he calls us in the Resurrection if we have not reflected on our sinfulness. Our entire human condition is unintelligible until we understand sin and its effects. A world that denies sin loses its grip on God: It cannot believe that a world burdened with so many evils could have been made by and be ruled by a God of boundless love, wisdom, and power.

The *Catechism* speaks of sin when speaking of the fall of men and of angels, of Providence and the mystery of evil, of Christ the Savior, in explaining the sacraments through which Christ heals our sinful condition, and when speaking of the new life of grace accessible to us when Christ frees us from our sins. It speaks of sin when it speaks of the last things: of the merciful cleansing of purgatory, of the overwhelming mercy of eternal life with God, and of the "lamentable reality of hell." Certainly, in this broken world, we are not able to understand ourselves or how much God has loved us until we begin to understand the mystery of sin.

The *Catechism* speaks of sin most forcefully in speaking of the moral life. The focus of Christian living is on doing the works of love. But realistic teaching of Christ's ways requires that we speak as he did. We not only encourage people by presenting the vision of walking in ways of love but also strengthen them in avoiding the gravest enemy of love and of the life of grace: deliberate sin, and especially mortal sin.

Christ certainly spoke often and frankly about sin. The New Testament frequently makes clear the pressing problem sin presents for us and the importance of rejecting sin (e.g., Eph 3:5-7). The most distinctive teachings of Christian morality, such as the duty to forgive even those unworthy of forgiveness, and to love even those who harm us, cannot be understood, as the parables of Jesus suggest, unless we really know how truly and deeply we are ourselves sinners and in need of a mercy we do not deserve (cf. Mt 18:23-25).

Reality of Sin • Some seek to dismiss the very idea of sin, and to explain it "as merely a developmental flaw, a psychological weakness, a mistake, or the necessary consequence of an inadequate social structure" (CCC 387). But the testimony of Scripture and the unbearable burden of human malice that we experience do not allow us to reduce sin to such factors. Men and women are free and responsible in many of their actions, and only too often they deliberately do evil deeds. They often seek even to avoid the obvious truth, to avoid "light," because their deeds are evil (cf. Jn 3:20). Moral evil in fact becomes pervasive in the world, and the source of every kind of sorrow and pain.

The many terms Scripture uses for sin reveal different aspects of its reality. In the Old Testament, for example, the word *hatta* is very commonly used for sin. It implies a "falling short of the mark." This is no innocent mistake or misstep: It is a deliberate failure to walk in God's ways.

Another term often used for sin is *pesha*, which suggests defiance or a revolt: In abandoning what the Lord calls us to, we set ourselves personally against God. Again, *awon* is often used for sin. This word connotes iniquity or guilt, recalling the way sin distorts the sinner's inner being.

New Testament expressions for sin include *Hamartia, anomia*, and *adikia. Hamartia*, like the Old Testament *hatta*, sees sin as a casting aside of God's norms for human life. *Anomia*, or "lawlessness," is used to stress that spirit of rebellion and contempt for God's law found in sin. *Adikia*, "injustice," emphasizes that sin is a refusal to live in the justice God makes accessible to us. Sin is also called *skotos* ("darkness") and *pseudos* ("falsehood") in the New Testament, to reveal that it resists the light God offers us and the truth he proclaims in Christ.

All that Scripture says of sin — and its fearful descriptions of so many malicious human sins throughout salvation history and their tragic consequences — makes clear that sin is indeed an act of "disobedience, a revolt against God . . . thus 'love of oneself even to contempt of God' [St. Augustine, *De civ. Dei* 14, 28: PL 41, 436]" (CCC 1850). Sin is often defined as " 'an utterance, a deed, or desire contrary to the eternal law' [St. Augustine, *Contra Faustum* 22: PL 42, 418; St. Thomas Aquinas, *STh* I-II, 71, 6]" (CCC 1849). But it must be remembered that sinful violations of God's eternal law are deliberate, and that his law is no arbitrary command. Rather, his law, given to us because he loves us, supplies us with light to guide our lives in ways that guard all that is good and, as it were, make life work.

In the first pages of Scripture, we read of the account of the first human sin (cf. Gn 3:1-11). Though our first parents were friends of God, and lived joyfully before him, they encountered in the garden a seductive voice, the presence of Satan. He who had once been an angel, but had deliberately and irrevocably turned against God and against the paths of love and of grace, led them to the fatal but deliberate choice. Their sin was not only a personal sin but one that affected all mankind and all human history.

The consequences of that sin are revealed in all the subsequent pages of Scripture. The proliferation of sin, the penetration of sin and its bitterness into all dimensions of human life, its becoming embedded in the very structures of society, bringing its pain and sorrow into all the corners of human life — these consequences make us realize how important it is for us to turn earnestly away from deliberate sin.

A Contrite Heart • Christian remembrance of sin is far from self-righteous. One who acknowledges sin in the spirit of the Scriptures is concerned not so much with others' sins but with his or her own. A repentant people acknowledges its own sins, and asks for mercy. "O Lord, . . . you are just in all you have done; all your deeds are faultless, all your ways right. . . . For we have sinned and transgressed . . . and we have done every kind of evil" (Dn 3:26-29). The individual repentant sinner is unwilling to prefer himself to anyone. "This saying is sure and worthy of full acceptance, that Christ Jesus came into the world to save sinners — of whom I am the foremost" (1 Tm 1:15).

But neither is remembrance of sin simply depressing for the Christian. To remember sin is to remember the infinite mercy of God (cf. 1 Tm 1:16). The believing community experiences great comfort in acknowledging its sins, and the penitential psalms have been favorite prayers of the Christian people (e.g., Ps 51, 130). Indeed, repentance is the first step in conversion of heart, in coming to earnest faith — "Repent, and believe!" (Mark 1.15) — and to confident trust in God and life in the joy of his grace.

Only a repentant community is a forgiving community. In our daily life, we experience how harsh are those who are "innocent" and self-righteous. To such people even Christ could scarcely speak at times, and we all find such self-righteous people difficult to live with. Those who cannot acknowledge their sins are enemies of peace in the community of love. Christ's parables on forgiveness manifest how deeply rooted is willingness to forgive in the recognition that we ourselves have sinned. Repentant sinners know they owe

God far more than anyone could owe them, so that they indeed have a duty to him to forgive gladly and to have mercy (Mt 18:23-35). Tranquil acknowledgment of our sins is needed to create communities of forgiveness and mercy.

Mortal Sin • It is especially important in our time to teach clearly the nature of deliberate mortal sin. Though we live in an age that tends to be forgetful of sin, mortal sin remains a fearful reality. The teacher of faith must make clear the nature of acts of mortal sin, and of the state of mortal sin. He also must make clear the consequences of mortal sin, how one must live to avoid mortal sin, and the paths one must take to find forgiveness if he or she has fallen into mortal sin. Nothing else that could happen in our lives is as tragic for us as a deliberate mortal sin.

Mortal sin is identified both by the characteristics that make it mortal and by its consequences. A mortal sin is one that by its nature is a gravely evil kind of act, an evil so grave that it is simply incompatible with the love of God. Scripture itself makes clear (e.g., 1 Jn 5:16) that some sins have the deadly consequences of mortal sin and others do not. Already in Scripture there are lists of sins mortal by their nature: "fornication, impurity, licentiousness, idolatry. . . ; those who do such things will not inherit the kingdom of God" (Gal 5:19-21). Through the centuries the Church has had "lists" of mortal sins, sins such as murder, adultery, perjury.

But to be a "mortal" sin, not only must the kind of deed done be a gravely wrong kind of act (or seriously considered such by the one who performs it), but there also must be full knowledge and deliberate consent. That is, one commits a mortal sin only if he has "knowledge of the sinful character of the act" and gives "a consent sufficiently deliberate to be a personal choice. Feigned ignorance and hardness of heart do not diminish, but rather increase, the voluntary character of sin" (CCC 1859).

Clearly, then, not just sins in which one explicitly chooses to abandon or to despise God are mortal sins; one turns against God not only by sins like blasphemy and hatred of God but also by doing any of those acts faith teaches to be mortal — acts incompatible with love of God. Thus, the Catholic faith has taught persistently in its catechesis and preaching that many of the kinds of sins seen to be common are "mortal" kinds of sins: for example, perjury, fornication, abortion, adultery. Unintentional ignorance and promptings of passions so strong that they make a free personal choice impossible can lessen responsibility so that some who do mortally sinful kinds of acts do not in fact sin mortally. Still, many mortal sins are committed, and the pastoral practices of the Church reflect this reality.

Mortal sin results in the loss of sanctifying grace; one who has committed such a sin ceases really to love God. He enters into an enduring "state of sin." Unless he is moved by God's unmerited grace to repent, mortal sin "causes exclusion from Christ's kingdom and the eternal death of hell, for our freedom has the power to make choices for ever, with no turning back" (CCC 1861).

One who has committed a mortal sin, and not repented, may not receive any sacraments except those instituted to take away sin, such as Baptism and Penance. Those in the state of mortal sin are in a special way excluded from receiving the sacrament of the Eucharist (CCC 2120; see 1 Cor 11:27-29); it would be a gravely sinful sacrilege to receive Communion while in the state of mortal sin. One who wishes to live a Christian life, but has committed a mortal sin, should, moved by grace, act promptly to find forgiveness.

Forgiveness and Avoidance of Sin • Because by mortal sin one loses God's grace and ceases to love God, he has no power to do grace-filled acts that might lead to forgiveness. Yet God is able to call one back to grace, and does earnestly call the sinner to life. Still, the paths to forgiveness are for God to determine, not us. Catholic faith teaches that the sole ordinary way to recover grace after deliberate mortal sin is through receiving Christ's sacrament of reconciliation. This requires confessing one's sins with earnest sorrow and resolving to do penance and commit grave sin no more.

Nevertheless, there are extraordinary ways of

returning to grace. Those not in their present circumstances able to receive the sacrament of reconciliation can receive forgiveness even of the gravest sins by sincere acts of a perfect kind of contrition: that is, by a sorrow rooted in the love of God, when this sorrow is associated with a resolution to come to sacramental confession as soon as possible. Those who do not know of the necessity of the sacrament may receive forgiveness by acts of perfect contrition, which would implicitly involve a willingness to do all the Lord requires.

Since mortal sin is an evil with such bitter consequences, the teacher of faith must instruct people in ways of avoiding it. Often people travel the path to mortal sin by the way of venial sins. Venial sins are less serious than mortal sin because they are less evil kinds of acts: such as impatient words or somewhat selfish acts, acts that are neither in the service of love nor simply incompatible with love of God and neighbor. Or, sin can be venial, even if the act is of a gravely sinful kind, if one is less guilty because he acted without sufficient knowledge or freedom.

Those who wish to avoid mortal sin should avoid venial sin and the occasions of sin. They should seek positively to be faithful to the Christian vocation: to prayer, to acts that nourish love of God and neighbor, to growth in virtue, to forgiveness of others, and to patience in trials. Our Christian vocation is a call to greatness of heart, to an ever greater love of God and a service of him with the whole heart; and a life spent in earnest pursuit of Christian holiness is the most secure defense against falling into mortal sin.

Christ has conquered sin and death. No one who, moved by grace, comes to Christ with all one's heart, need tremble before the dangers of sin. Catholic faith teaches that God gives us power to escape sin if we are faithful to prayer and to his gifts of grace. Nor do the efforts needed to overcome sin make life too burdensome. For the New Law of Christ, which leads us along the ways of life, is not merely a matter of commandments and of exhortations to reject sin. His New Law is essentially the gift of the Holy Spirit, and of divine love; and "love makes light and easy things that would otherwise seem burdensome and beyond our power" (St. Augustine, *On the Words of the Lord*, Sermon 70).

See: Concupiscence; Conscience; Freedom, Human; Fundamental Option; Grace; Hell; Human Race, Creation and Destiny of; Law of Christ; Liberation From Sin; Moral Principles, Christian; Mortal Sin; Natural Law; Occasions of Sin; Original Sin; Penance and Reconciliation, Sacrament of; Purgatory; Redemption; Ten Commandments; Venial Sin.

Suggested Readings: CCC 309-314, 385-412, 430-435, 456-457, 598-618, 1263-1264, 1441-1467, 1510, 1520, 1846-1869, 1949-1974. Vatican Council II, *Pastoral Constitution on the Church in the Modern World, Gaudium et Spes*, 13, 27-32, 79. John Paul II, *On Reconciliation and Penance in the Mission of the Church Today, Reconciliatio et Paenitentia*, 14-18. G. Grisez, *The Way of the Lord Jesus*, Vol. 1, *Christian Moral Principles*, pp. 311-457. X. Leon-Dufour, *Dictionary of Biblical Theology*, 2nd ed., "Sin," pp. 550-554.

Ronald Lawler, O.F.M. Cap.

SINS AGAINST THE HOLY SPIRIT

Several kinds of sins are called sins against the Holy Spirit in Scripture. St. Thomas Aquinas (*Summa Theologiae*, II-II, q. 14, aa. 1-2), following St. Augustine, lists these sins as: initial impenitence, obduracy in sin, presumption, rejection of the known truth, envy of the grace of others, and final impenitence. All of these strike against the very springs of forgiveness, since they involve rejection of the graces and gifts by which the Spirit calls us to mercy.

Scripture presents these sins against the Holy Spirit as especially serious sins, pointing out that "whoever blasphemes against the Holy Spirit never has forgiveness, but is guilty of an eternal sin" (Mk 3:29).

Catholic faith, aware of scriptural teaching on the unlimited scope of God's mercy, and of examples in Scripture of mercy shown to those who had been impenitent or had sinned against the light, knows that even such sins are absolutely forgivable by God (cf. CCC 1864). But faith is also aware of the special seriousness of such sins, and why they are called, in a sense, "unforgivable," since they shape in us attitudes that tend to harden the heart in resisting grace and so to reject forgiveness (cf. CCC 1864).

Pastoral wisdom therefore warns against such sins with a special earnestness. Still, it presses no one toward despair, but calls even those who have sinned in such obstinate ways to seek persistently for divine forgiveness.

See: Despair; Final Perseverance; Holy Spirit; Penance and Reconciliation, Sacrament of; Presumption; Religion, Virtue of; Sin.

SITUATION ETHICS

This ethical theory was made popular in the 1950s by the Episcopalian minister Joseph Fletcher. According to the theory, the only universal moral norm is, "Love God and neighbor"; what one should do in the concrete depends on the circumstances or concrete situation. On this theory, then, all other moral norms — "Do not commit adultery," "Do not intentionally kill innocent people," etc. — are only general guides, not exceptionless moral truths.

Situation ethicists argued that belief in moral absolutes (specific, exceptionless moral norms) was nothing more than rule worship or legalism, valuing abstract universal rules above concrete, particular persons.

Although situation ethics is no longer popular among philosophers and theologians (at least, not as explicitly articulated), its basic idea seems to live on in confusions among many laypeople, teachers, and pastors. Thus, it is important to note that moral absolutes are not based on mere abstract rules but on the implications of real love of real human persons. Certain types of choices are always wrong, precisely because they are incompatible with love of God and neighbor — they inevitably diminish or suppress love of God and neighbor. For example, intentionally killing the innocent closes one's will to the intrinsic and personal good of innocent human life.

Situation ethics, sometimes referred to by the expression "the new morality," was critiqued at some length by Pope Pius XII in his allocutions of April 18, 1952, and February 2, 1956.

See: Absolute Moral Norms, Human Goods; Law of Christ; Legalism; Natural Law; Practical Reason; Proportionalism; Relativism.

SLANDER

Broadly speaking, slander is synonymous with calumny: knowingly lying to harm another person's reputation. In legal language, however, slander refers to spoken assault, while the use of written, printed, or graphic communication to defame is called libel. In either case, slanderers mean to rob victims of their good name. This is sinful because, as the *Catechism of the Catholic Church* makes clear, "everyone enjoys a natural right to the honor of his name and reputation and to respect" (2479). A sound reputation is as much a possession, and as important for happiness, as marketable job skills or a kind heart. To slander one's neighbor is to take something of real value; it is an offense against justice and charity.

Whether slander is gravely or venially sinful depends on its content. For example, one could repeat a false rumor that Mrs. Brown had told Mrs. Smith that Mrs. Jones was carrying on an affair. Unless one thereby intended serious injury to Mrs. Brown (by implying grave wrongdoing on her part or otherwise seeking to harm her), this arguably would represent trivial gossip as applied to her but a very serious slander as applied to Mrs. Jones. Some slanders are so malicious as to merit the description "character assassination" and require efforts on the part of the slanderer to repair the damage, if any, to the reputation of the slandered party.

As Jesus' life shows, Christians will often suffer slander for their beliefs. If possible, they should expose their attacker's lies. If not, they have little choice but to bear the slight patiently, taking comfort in the Lord's promise: "Blessed are you when men revile you and persecute you and utter all kinds of evil against you falsely on my account.

Rejoice and be glad, for your reward is great in heaven" (Mt 5:11-12).

See: Detraction and Calumny; False Witness; Lying; Perjury; Rash Judgment; Truthfulness.

SLAVERY

In the modern world, slavery of all kinds is universally condemned as unnatural and immoral. It is difficult for us to understand, therefore, that slavery in various forms has been a common feature of almost all societies throughout history down to quite recent times. In fact, Vatican Council II still felt it necessary to say (*Pastoral Constitution on the Church in the Modern World, Gaudium et Spes,* 30) that we must continue to combat all forms of social and political slavery (the last legal protections for slavery were probably abolished in the 1960s) and even warns (*Gaudium et Spes,* 4) that new forms of social and psychological slavery have emerged in our time.

Slavery not only has been a widely accepted social institution throughout the world, but it also gave rise to little moral protest or religious condemnation, except regarding its abuses, until the past few centuries. Christianity has had a role in curbing and ultimately eliminating slavery, primarily by emphasizing the eternal dignity and destiny of all souls. But prior to the rise of democratic ideals, servants, serfs, and slaves of some kinds were generally regarded as socially useful and licit. Both the history of slavery and recent moral developments against that practice, then, deserve careful analysis.

Slavery in the Ancient World • In Israel, as in much of the ancient world, slavery was paradoxically often a humane substitute for death. Captives taken in war, thieves, debtors, and children whose indigent parents might otherwise have left them to die by exposure made up the bulk of the slave population. That population was never very large, and scholars usually refer to such societies as slaveholding societies. ("Slave societies" properly so called, such as ancient Greece and Rome and the American South before the Civil War, show much greater economic and social dependence on the whole system of slavery.) In addition, Jewish law encouraged humane treatment of slaves and limited periods of slavery for debt to a maximum of six years — at least in theory.

The New Testament situation is slightly different than the one found in the Old Testament. Israel had by then been more influenced by Greco-Roman slave societies. But Jews in the New Testament period still had a more positive vision of manual work than did the classical world. Furthermore, while no antislavery ethic had fully emerged — indeed, given the organization of both Jewish and Roman societies, it is difficult to see how it could have — many passages in the New Testament call on Christians to recognize slaves as brothers in Christ. For example, Paul's famous statement in Galatians 3:27-28 (in Christ "there is neither Jew nor Greek, there is neither slave nor free, there is neither male nor female") did not systematically deny slavery. Nevertheless, the universally unifying human thrust eventually bore much fruit.

It is important to keep in mind that slavery has taken many forms, ranging from relatively benign servant status to full-scale chattel slavery wherein one person owns another person, who has few or no legal rights. Christianity has faced all these forms of slavery as it has faced various forms of government throughout its history. Where slavery existed, the Church usually tried to ameliorate it by encouraging the bonds created by servant/master relationships that were often barely distinguishable from family membership. Two important phases in the Church's confrontation with slavery particularly stand out: the struggle with slavery in the ancient world and the struggle over slavery as it began with the European expansion into the Americas.

Contrary to common impressions, slavery in the Roman Empire was already becoming less burdensome and harsh than under the republic. Mistreatment of slaves, even under secular Roman law, was discouraged. Christianity preached obedience to masters, but also love of master for slave. The early Church drew many slaves and ex-slaves precisely because of this stance. At the extreme, some Christians even sold themselves into slavery in order to ransom others from slavery, a practice they thought symbolic of Christ's redemption of the human race.

There were outright theological denunciations of slavery as well. St. Gregory of Nyssa rejected slavery in his homilies, and other saints tried to imagine societies without slaves. Two former slaves became Popes: Pius and Callistus in the second and third centuries. As the Church gained influence over the Empire, she tried both to improve the treatment of slaves and to protect them legally. Though the process was slow and complicated and subject to economic factors, the basic Christian belief that we are all children of God played no little role in virtually stamping out slavery in Europe by the late Middle Ages.

Slavery began to creep back in as Europe expanded her horizons after centuries of turmoil and war. Pirates and Muslim traders took slaves to North Africa as well as to Italian and Spanish ports. The term "slave," as opposed to the older Latin *servus* (commonly translated "servant"), owes its existence to the fact that many of the slaves during this period were captured in Slavic lands. This sort of slavery was less harsh than chattel slavery or the late Roman form, but it still involved brutality, sexual exploitation, and other gross injustices.

Slavery in the Americas • The largest slave problem to face Christianity, however, came with the explorations of the Americas. African states had practiced slavery and slave trading long before the arrival of white Europeans. Muslim slave traders shipped even more slaves to Islamic countries than Christians did to their own nations and to the New World. But the transatlantic voyages suddenly created a vast new market. Many of the indigenous peoples in the Caribbean had died out from European diseases transmitted unwittingly by the explorers. The missing labor force was supplied by black African slaves who were already quite resistant to both European diseases and the diseases of the New World.

This period is often presented as a massive failure of Christian morals with regard to slaves. To a great extent it was. Christians were not to take the plight of black Africans seriously in their moral reflections for several centuries. But the condition of indigenous Americans was another matter. The moral reaction against enslaving them played a role in stimulating some fresh Christian thought that is often overlooked or undervalued.

At its best, Catholic reflection on the classical and biblical teachings on slavery began to break new ground in the New World. For example, the Spanish theologians who had to deal with the enslavement of the new peoples of the Americas denied that Indians could be enslaved because they were not Christians. The school of Salamanca in Spain, most notably in the person of the Dominican theologian Francisco de Vitoria, began to elaborate what has developed into modern international law and human rights — and the modern prohibition of slavery.

The Spaniards actually ceased conquest for a time and debated the ethics of the undertaking, something never before or after done by an expanding empire. At the king's request, theologians examined the Aristotelian dictum that some people are slaves by nature. A debate at the monastery of Valladolid established once and for all that many natives were quite reasonable and capable of self-government. And even if they were not fully rational, they still, as their defender Bartolomé de Las Casas said, could be governed by others only for their own good, not for the good of the governors. Several centuries after the fact, Samuel Johnson remarked: "I love the University of Salamanca; for when the Spaniards were in doubt as to the lawfulness of their conquering America, the University of Salamanca gave it as their opinion that it was unlawful."

Spanish theory was an important and progressive step for its time, and several Popes echoed the concern for native Americans in sixteenth-century encyclicals, most notably Paul III, who in *Sublimis Deus* forbade enslaving Indians. Spanish practice, however, lagged far behind.

In the United States • The Church in the United States was a weak force both in theory and in practice during the struggle to abolish slavery. Early Catholic missionaries and European explorers had themselves been made slaves by Indian tribes. But Catholics in the colonies that would later unite to form the United States were like most Americans. In fact, Jesuits in Maryland and Catholics elsewhere were slave owners and apparently morally untroubled by the fact. The Church taught that slavery could be justified by a concern for the physical, moral, and spiritual welfare of the slaves. Except for unusual figures like the nineteenth-century convert writer and social critic Orestes Brownson, abolition hardly agitated American Catholics at all. The First Plenary Council of Baltimore, meeting in 1852, did not even mention slavery.

In August, 1862, Archbishop John B. Purcell of Cincinnati did recommend emancipation, just five months before Lincoln's Emancipation Proclamation. Probably more typical, however, was Bishop Augustine Verot, who, in a sermon at Saint Augustine, Florida, explained the biblical basis for a proper kind of slavery. Some of the reluctance to criticize may have stemmed from the fact that Catholics felt themselves outsiders in America, some from the long-standing Catholic contact with slave-holding societies. Nonetheless, despite the good beginnings made by the Spanish during the sixteenth century, when the push to abolish slavery around the world began, it came primarily from British Protestants.

Today it is common to refer to workers as wage slaves or to speak of people as enslaved by greed, materialism, pleasure, power, and prestige. While regrettable and in need of correcting, none of these situations has much in common with slavery as such. Slavery as a formal institution has almost entirely ceased to exist because of modern moral, technological, and social improvements. The human race has achieved a great victory over an evil that seems to have existed almost everywhere since man's first appearance. Our future task is to ensure that we do not fall back into age-old habits under political delusions and to continue the never-ending struggle against all forms of slavery, including slavery to sin.

See: Development of Doctrine; Human Person; Imago Dei; Racism; Social Doctrine; Work.

Suggested Readings: CCC 2414. R. Charles, *The Social Teaching of Vatican II*, pp. 28-34. M. Bloch, *Slavery and Serfdom in the Middle Ages*. L. Hanke, *Aristotle and the American Indians*. J. Hennesey, S.J., *American Catholics*, pp. 143-162.

Robert Royal

SOCIAL DOCTRINE

"Social doctrine," or the social teaching of the Church, refers to the developing body of Catholic thought about political, economic, ethical, and cultural questions as these relate to the common good. The Church has no political or economic theories per se, since these belong to the realm of human reason and experience, and remain the responsibility of laypeople. But the Church may judge social theory and practice from the standpoint of faith and morals, especially in light of the virtue of justice. During the twentieth century in particular, Catholic social doctrine has developed rapidly in response to questions posed by communism, socialism, totalitarianism, and democratic capitalism.

Historical Survey • The New Testament contains little direct commentary on social questions, though many Gospel principles can be extended to help shape a Christian framework for thinking about them. The early Church expected Christ's Second Coming within a short time and did not take much interest in public affairs. As it became clear that no one really knows how far off the end time might be, the Church began a process that has distinguished her ever since: Inspired by a vision of Christ as the Lord of all of creation, including human societies, she moved from being a socially marginalized sect to functioning as a globally involved church.

The first major step in developing a comprehensive social teaching came in the fifth century with the publication of St. Augustine's *City of God* (*De Civitate Dei*). Augustine had to reply to charges that Christian otherworldliness had led to the decline of Rome, both in personal morals and in military power. His argument was twofold. First, he pointed to defects within paganism itself as the real cause of the decline. The classical philosophers were good reasoners, but they could not correct the faults of human nature that they saw quite clearly; only God's grace, said Augustine, could do that. Next, Augustine showed how the Christian story of the Fall, redemption, and restoration could explain historical events and the proper response to them. Augustine thought the state an "unnatural" institution in that, if the human race had never fallen, the state would not have been necessary.

But the Fall had occurred, and that meant the state was necessary to curb personal vices and promote public virtues, especially the common good. States were limited in what they could achieve in this realm. The state was primarily an imperfect remedy: The Church alone could provide mankind with the fullness of truth and salvation. Yet even in the limited sphere of the state, justice was indispensable to the state's functions. Otherwise, the state reflected the sinful desire to dominate others (*libido dominandi*) and was nothing more than "a large gang of bandits" (*magnum latrocinium*).

Thus, Augustine established two principles that have remained central to subsequent Catholic social teaching: the importance of personal virtue to public life and the need to judge states and policies from a standpoint outside practical politics and economics. In other words, the city of man, though it can never be the City of God, requires good order in the soul and in the state.

In the Middle Ages, several things were added to the basic Augustinian heritage. One of the most important was the recognition of a difference not only between the two cities but between the temporal and spiritual powers. Pope Gelasius I, writing in *Duo Quippe Sunt* to the Byzantine emperor Anastasius I in the year 494, first formulated the idea. God himself had ordained distinct roles for the Church in the spiritual realm and for the state in the temporal realm (a development of Jesus' saying "Render unto Caesar the things that are Caesar's and to God the things that are God's" [Mt 22:21]). Catholic scholars have long disagreed about the implications of this doctrine. But it is clear both from the statement and subsequent medieval history that the beginnings of a kind of separation of Church and State had emerged in the Christian West.

Gelasius' teaching was probably meant to secure the autonomy of the Church. But it also gave the state a more positive role than it had in the thinking of St. Augustine. A major step in developing this insight occurred in the thirteenth century with the work of St. Thomas Aquinas. While St. Augustine had written in a time of troubled relations between Church and State, Aquinas lived in a period of generally greater harmony. He emphasized the work of the Greek philosopher Aristotle as a guide to the positive functions the state can exercise.

The State As Natural Institution • St. Thomas thought the state was a natural institution for several reasons. Human beings, though the most intelligent of earthly creatures, require the longest and most complicated nurturing among all the animals. They can only reach full development through communities and can only do certain things within properly constituted political systems.

First among these natural communities was the family, which provided an indispensable basis for both private and public good. But the state, too, is necessary, among other reasons, to make sure that families did not become merely feuding tribes. The state orders and fosters smaller groupings, without usurping their functions, in the name of the common good. In St. Thomas, then, the state is more than merely a remedy for the Fall; it is a natural expression of human nature. Catholicism's relatively communitarian bent, as compared with Protestantism's individualism, finds its deepest sources in these medieval developments.

What kind of state, though, is the best for fallen human beings? Aquinas believed that even though the Fall had corrupted the will and weakened human intellect, with grace it is still possible, if arduous, for us to know and follow the natural law. Monarchy, the rule by a wise and virtuous king, was the best form of government, but monarchy was inclined to degenerate into tyranny. And this led St. Thomas to qualify his vision. Kings rule by the consent of their subjects, he taught. It is best if they govern a mixed regime that includes a class of prominent men who can both advise and rein in the king.

Such regimes have the achievable earthly task of promoting justice, but their action and scope are limited and subordinated to the ultimate destiny of all human beings in God. As many subsequent theorists have observed, these medieval notions lie at the root of modern political concepts such as democracy, checks and balances among branches of the state, freedom of conscience, and limited government.

It would take several centuries, however, for these concepts to achieve the form in which they exist today. Some of the later Scholastic philosophers, such as Francisco de Vitoria (c. 1483-1546) and Francisco Suárez (1548-1617), developed the earliest notions of international law and universal human rights. But Augustine and Aquinas continued to dominate Catholic social teaching (as well as being recognized by secular historians of political theory) as it began to deal with the great changes produced by the modern democratic impulse of the American and French revolutions.

Modern Catholic Social Thought • With the appearance of modern democracy, the Church found herself in a difficult situation. Though Catholic social doctrine contained elements of ancient and medieval democratic thought, modern democracy — especially as it came to be practiced on the model of the French Revolution (the American Revolution produced far less Church-State tension) — was virulently and violently anti-Catholic. During the nineteenth century, this led to deep divisions and battles in France, in Germany (Bismarck's famous *Kulturkampf*, or "culture war" against Catholicism), and elsewhere. The Church had lived with many forms of government before and could have coexisted reasonably well with democracy, except for the bitter partisan feelings that had arisen on both sides during the struggles of the century.

Under the papacy of Leo XIII (1878-1903), however, a new era in Catholic social teaching began. Pope Leo promoted both a return to the work of Thomas Aquinas and an opening, based on long-standing Catholic principles, to democratic thought. Leo urged French Catholics, for example, who had often remained monarchist or opposed to republican forms, to a rallying (*ralliement*) for the Republic. As a result of Leo's initiative, in the twentieth century Catholics and democrats have come to understand that there is no necessary conflict between Catholicism and modern democracy.

Leo also was conscious that socialism, materialism, and a host of other modern problems needed urgent attention. His 1891 encyclical *On the Social Question, Rerum Novarum*, was the first of the great modern social encyclicals. In it, Leo argued that socialism, far from being the answer to the social situation of working men and women would, if implemented, claim workers as its first victims — a prophetic observation whose truth was to become evident in a matter of decades in communist nations.

Leo responded to the modern problems of industrialization, urbanization, and the plight of the worker with an updated and highly articulated restatement of the old Catholic vision of a society of different ranks and functions. Unions and just (or "family") wages seemed partial means to balancing the needs of labor and capital. These and other suggestions were aimed at preventing overcentralization and providing diverse opportunities and responsibilities for all. Modern conditions, in Leo's view, did not negate, but rather offered fresh opportunities for, the wisdom that had been accumulated in the tradition of Catholic social teaching.

Leo's heritage was developed further by Pius XI in the encyclical *On the Fortieth Year, Quadragesimo Anno*. Published in 1931, this document reflects a keen awareness of the precarious condition of the democracies in the interwar years, and of the totalitarian threats presented by German Nazism, Italian Fascism, and Russian communism. Pius XI first expressed a crucial concept that had begun appearing in Catholic social thinking just prior to the encyclical: subsidiarity. Briefly, subsidiarity reminds us that God has given freedom and responsibility to human persons and that it is a disorder and a grave evil for the state to usurp the responsibility of individuals, families, private associations, and other so-called intermediate institutions.

World War II and the rebuilding that followed it halted further developments in social teaching for some years. But in the 1960s, the Church under Pope John XXIII began a renewal, updating (*aggiornamento*), and return to sources (*ressourcement*) that looked optimistically toward the human future. In the documents of the Second Vatican Council (1962-1965), such as the *Dogmatic Constitution on the Church, Lumen Gentium*, and the *Pastoral Constitution on the Church in the Modern World, Gaudium et Spes*, the Church embraced with new enthusiasm her role as a guide for the world. And in the *Declaration on Religious Freedom, Dignitatis Humanae*, the Council stated that religious liberty was a basic human right.

In these documents and in some subsequent encyclicals such as Paul VI's *On the Progress of Peoples, Populorum Progressio*, the Church began to show a more activist confidence in the powers of government for social welfare within nations, and in international justice and development. Some Marxist elements seemed to attach themselves to this analysis, such as dependency theory, which linked the poverty and dependency of Third World economies with exploitation by the First World.

This attitude soon gave rise, particularly in Latin America, to a complex movement known as liberation theology. Accepting Marxist notions of class struggle, dependency theory, and capitalist oppression, many liberation theologians seemed to view Soviet-sponsored revolutions during the Cold War as a kind of religious crusade. At the 1968 meeting of the Latin American Bishops' Conference (CELAM) in Medellín, Colombia, a new term, the "preferential option for the poor," appeared. In some ways, this idea was merely a restatement of the old Christian principle that the weakest demand our attention. In other ways, how-

ever, it led to an opposition of a church of the poor (*iglesia popular*) to the traditional church.

With the 1978 election of the first Polish Pope, John Paul II, this and many other currents in the Church received some new orientations. Karol Wojtyla had faced both Nazism and communism in his native Poland and was no friend of either. He had also been a workingman, a writer, and a professor of modern philosophy prior to becoming Pope, and brought a rich mix of practical human experience and modern learning to modern social questions.

Recent Developments • John Paul II has given human work a special, if not entirely new, emphasis as one of the ways by which people participate in creation and reflect the image and likeness of divine intellect, will, and creativity. As a practitioner of the modern philosophical school known as phenomenology, he presented a rich description of the specifically human character of work in his 1981 encyclical *On Human Work, Laborem Exercens*. Traditionally, work had mostly been regarded as a curse after the Fall. In John Paul, work both repairs the consequences of the Fall and reflects our participation in God's creation, a high and noble calling.

Under his leadership, the Vatican Congregation for the Doctrine of the Faith issued an *Instruction on Certain Aspects of Liberation Theology* (1984) and an *Instruction on Christian Freedom and Liberation, Libertatis Conscientia* (1986). These two documents sought to sift what was good in the liberation movement from what not only was false but had been proclaimed as such since Leo XIII's inauguration of modern Catholic social teaching. The Church could not help but be in favor of authentic liberation, but in Latin America the idea of liberation seemed to have taken a Marxist turn that conflicted with several Catholic principles concerning property, the human person, and society.

John Paul II also wrote several encyclicals during and after the decline and fall of communism in Eastern Europe and the former Soviet Union that staked out some new principles or at least arrived at some new emphases. In the 1987 encyclical *On Social Concerns, Sollicitudo Rei Socialis*, for example, he began to move the Church toward a greater acceptance of markets and capitalism than had been evident earlier. In part, this stemmed from empirical evidence of the greater prosperity and freedom of democratic market systems, in part from a theoretical development in Catholic social thought that placed freedom, including economic enterprise, high on the list of human attributes.

John Paul did not entirely leave behind, however, the need for social solidarity. In fact, in *Sollicitudo Rei Socialis* he offers a definition of what he calls the *virtue* of solidarity: "This then is not a feeling of vague compassion or shallow distress at the misfortunes of so many people, both near and far. On the contrary, it is a firm and persevering determination to commit oneself to the common good; that is to say, to the good of all and of each individual, because we are *all* really responsible *for all*" (38). Within solidarity, no one is to be merely passive or active; the weaker are to take initiative and the stronger are not to insist on every advantage. The whole is to be informed and guided by Christian charity.

With *Centesimus Annus* (1991), his encyclical upon the hundredth anniversary of *Rerum Novarum*, John Paul went still further in spelling out how subsidiarity and solidarity have become the two central principles for modern Catholic social thought. The Pope puts the crucial point in the form of a question: "Can it perhaps be said that, after the failure of Communism, capitalism is the victorious social system, and that capitalism should be the goal of the countries now making efforts to rebuild their economy and is this the model that ought to be proposed to the countries of the Third World?" (42).

He responds by saying that the answer is complex. Certainly, we can say "yes" insofar as economic freedom and initiative are part of God's gift to man. But these gifts can only be properly exercised, says the Pope, if certain conditions are met: "If by 'capitalism' is meant a system in which freedom in the economic sector is not circumscribed within a strong juridical framework

that places it at the service of human freedom in its totality, and that sees it as a particular aspect of that freedom, the core of which is ethical and religious, then the reply is certainly negative." Without spelling out the details — which must be left to the responsible peoples and governments in individual countries — John Paul recapitulates the long Catholic tradition that government must respect initiative and liberty, as well as secure justice through properly ordered and responsible institutions.

The latest phase of Catholic social teaching focuses on the moral bases of democracy. Given that democratic forms and market economics at the end of the twentieth century have emerged victorious from the struggle with communism, the crises within democracies — family breakdown, illegitimacy, consumerism, drugs, moral relativism, environmental problems — present some difficult challenges. John Paul II's 1993 encyclical on moral principles *The Splendor of Truth, Veritatis Splendor,* argues that it is only by recovering the Christian view of human freedom as the power to do what is morally right, that free institutions such as democracy and market economics can be saved from their own worst excesses.

See: Augustinianism; Authority; Church and State; Common Good; Family; Liberation Theology; Natural Law; Phenomenology; Politics; Preferential Option for the Poor; Religious Liberty; Socialization; Social Justice; Subsidiarity; Thomas Aquinas, Thought of; Work.

Suggested Readings: CCC 2401-2463. Vatican Council II, *Dogmatic Constitution on the Church, Lumen Gentium; Pastoral Constitution on the Church in the Modern World, Gaudium et Spes; Declaration on Religious Freedom, Dignitatis Humanae.* Leo XIII, *On the Social Question, Rerum Novarum.* Pius XI, *On the Fortieth Year, Quadragesimo Anno.* Paul VI, *On the Progress of Peoples, Populorum Progressio.* John Paul II, *On Social Concerns, Sollicitudo Rei Socialis; The Hundredth Year, Centesimus Annus; On Human Work, Laborem Exercens; The Splendor of Truth, Veritatis Splendor.* Congregation for the Doctrine of the Faith, *Instruction on Certain Aspects of*

Liberation Theology; *Christian Freedom and Liberation*. E. Fortin, "St. Augustine" and "St. Thomas Aquinas," in L. Strauss and J. Cropsey, eds., *History of Political Philosophy*. R. and A. Carlyle, *A History of Medieval Political Theory in the West*. H. Rommen, *The State in Catholic Thought*. R. Charles, S.J., *The Social Teaching of Vatican II*. M. Novak, *The Catholic Ethic and the Spirit of Capitalism*.

Robert Royal

SOCIALIZATION

In Catholic social thought, human beings by nature tend to associate with one another, especially in families and political society. Human potential can only come to full fruition in such associations, and some essential human activities can only be carried out in common. Therefore, socialization is not, as in some modern social theories, an artificial imposition on an autonomous individual or a tradeoff of freedom for the sake of social benefits. Socialization in the Catholic sense goes to the heart of what it means to develop fully as a human person.

Individuals and subsidiary institutions, such as families and local associations, have both a right and a duty to exercise their proper functions. For most people, it is in family life and small groups that they learn responsibility and cooperation. Catholic thought sees an articulated series of institutions between the individual and the national state, which prevent excessive centralization of power (as occurred in Fascist and communist states) and provide opportunities for freedom and responsibility (sometimes stifled in democratic welfare states). The *Catechism of the Catholic Church* (1883) warns that personal freedom and initiative should not be usurped by excessive state intervention.

But the state has its own role in promoting solidarity among all the individuals and institutions and by coordinating action that can only be carried out at a national level. Proper socialization thus requires a balance of subsidiarity and solidarity. Together, these promote both the good of individuals and associations, and the common good of society.

See: Common Good; Family; Human Person; Social Doctrine; Subsidiarity.

SOCIAL JUSTICE

The term "social justice" is of relatively recent coinage in Catholic social doctrine, and its meaning remains in some dispute. The modern emphasis on society's responsibilities in justice and charity to promote the common good appears to have arisen primarily in response to industrialization, urbanization, changes in agricultural patterns, and the human dislocations they brought in their wake. Many of the welfare provisions of modern democracies, such as unemployment insurance and social security, were created to deal with those problems. Social justice has thus often been seen as in part a demand for social supports. But such demands have usually also been accompanied by a call for the reordering of social priorities, both within societies and in international relations.

Nonetheless, there is some question whether social justice, properly understood, is something more than the traditional forms of justice applied to modern problems. The Church, following Aristotle, has long taught that there are three basic types of justice: legal, distributive, and commutative. Commutative justice governs the free exchanges between individuals and, though a model for the other kinds of justice, has little to do with social questions directly — with a few exceptions. Wages, for example, though primarily a question of an agreement between individuals, also have a social dimension. If employers do not pay a just wage, workers and their dependents will be unable to live, leading to social chaos. Early modern social encyclicals, such as Pope Leo XIII's 1891 *On the Social Question, Rerum Novarum*, examined the relative duties of capital and labor in contemporary circumstances.

Welfare and social insurance issues may be viewed as falling into another traditional category, distributive justice. According to the Catholic notion of subsidiarity, the social structure closest to the level of a problem that has the capacity to deal with that problem should take the responsibility to do so. Thus, in the normal course of affairs, individuals are responsible for themselves, families for children and other dependents, private associations for their members, and so on. Subsidiarity not only aims at preventing concentration of power in the state, a danger that Pius XI's 1931 encyclical *On the Fortieth Year, Quadragesimo Anno*, saw as the road to Nazism, Fascism, and communism; subsidiarity also seeks to empower the various sectors of society to play their God-given roles in human life.

Distribution of Goods in Society • According to distributive justice, society as a whole has the responsibility to distribute goods in proportion to individual contributions and needs. Inequality in society is not itself wrong unless it becomes excessive (*Quadragesimo Anno*, 58). In fact, it would be unjust to reward equally those who contribute more and those who contribute less. But natural inequality in talents and enterprise cannot justify the exclusion, exploitation, or marginalization of anyone in society (CCC 1937), since God has destined created goods for all. A problem thus arises when the subsidiary institutions are unable or unwilling to perform their duties, and persons fall outside natural modes of distribution.

Beginning with *Quadragesimo Anno*, the term "social justice" began to be applied to the need for modern societies as a whole to respond to such situations. In modern societies, unemployment compensation, welfare and food programs, and social security and health care insurance have been established by governments because the instability of modern labor markets and breakdown of extended families seemed to put many people in considerable peril. Furthermore, the disabled and the children born to those who are unmarried or who will not work are innocents who need protection. One dimension of social justice has been to promote this welfare function and critique sinful structures of society, including an international order that shows wide differences in development (Vatican Council II, *Pastoral Constitution on the Church in the Modern World, Gaudium et Spes*,

29; cf. Pope John XXIII, encyclical *Peace on Earth, Pacem in Terris* [1963], and Pope Paul VI, encyclical *On the Progress of Peoples, Populorum Progressio* [1967]).

But social justice in these wider implications closely resembles another traditional category, legal justice. The traditional name is unfortunate, because it implies that the legal system and the laws upon which it is based are simply just. In fact, legal (or universal) justice is a wider category that judges whether the legal judgments and institutions of individual nations and international bodies are themselves just. Respect for the transcendent dignity of the human person and for the rights that flow from that dignity is the only true basis for legal authority (CCC 1930). Calls for the reordering of social priorities to help the poor and unfortunate are part of traditional legal justice. The 1971 world Synod of Bishops that considered the theme of justice in the world, while rarely using the term "social justice," nevertheless calls for a loving pursuit of justice in all areas of human life without qualification.

Content of Social Justice • Approached in its most universal form, social justice promotes the interests of the poor and marginalized, but it also calls for the creation and maintenance of a well-ordered social mainstream. The normal functionings of the economic order and the political system are needed for society even to be capable of helping its weaker members. Furthermore, social justice ideally aims at empowering all sectors to participate in society: "Society ensures social justice when it provides the conditions that allow associations or individuals to obtain what is their due, according to their nature and their vocation. Social justice is linked to the common good and the exercise of authority" (CCC 1928).

Private property and the moral and productive use thereof are important components of any just social order. When socialism and Marxism were still believed to be potentially fruitful paths, there was some weakening of appreciation for private property among many proponents of social justice. Now that it is clear that coercive state systems provide neither material goods nor political liberties, social justice is more directed toward seeking greater equity and compassion within market systems.

During the Cold War, calls for social justice often recommended reductions in military spending and corresponding increases in social spending. In some instances, that was and is a just change. But the powerful image from Isaiah, "they shall beat their swords into ploughshares, and their spears into pruning hooks" (2:4), led many to believe a simple choice between two alternatives was to be made. One of the obligations of society in legal justice, however, is to protect its members from threats, whether foreign or domestic. Despite the ethical complication of nuclear weapons and the large nuclear arsenals of the United States and other nations, legal justice demands security and freedom, as well as support for the weak and helpless.

Social justice does not, therefore, dictate that resources be redirected from military uses to social development simply because the first are destructive and the second, perhaps, constructive. Military expenditures must correspond to the threat being faced. Similarly, it would be preferable to spend money on schools rather than prisons. But how many policemen and how many teachers to hire, given limited funds, can only be decided on the basis of judgments of the need for crime prevention and incarceration on the one hand and for education and training on the other. Public safety and public education are both matters of social justice, and the poor city-dweller who enjoys neither to any great degree may be the most wronged member of a society.

In a similar way, many of the social justice questions that currently vex advanced societies require a clear and broad analysis of all social factors in light of legal justice. Should a given country reduce welfare to discourage dependency and illegitimacy — or should it increase spending for carefully targeted child support and job training? Should a national budget favor the growth of the economy or taxation for social purposes? Should modern technological innovations be stimulated to provide jobs and remain competitive with other countries — or should efforts be made to transfer industries and jobs to developing nations?

Such issues involve both social justice and the kind of prudence traditionally associated with legal justice. Social justice, then, seems to be, as one analyst has said, "a form of legal justice properly understood."

See: Civil Law; Common Good; Commutative Justice; Environment; Human Life, Dignity and Sanctity of; Human Person; Interdependence; Liberation Theology; Preferential Option for the Poor; Property; Restitution; Social Doctrine; Socialization; Stealing; Subsidiarity; Universal Destination of Goods; Usury; Work.

Suggested Readings: CCC 1929-1942. Vatican Council II, *Pastoral Constitution on the Church in the Modern World, Gaudium et Spes*, Ch. II. John Paul II, *On Human Work, Laborem Exercens*; *On Social Concerns, Sollicitudo Rei Socialis*; *The Hundredth Year, Centesimus Annus*. J. Calvez and J. Perrin, *The Church and Social Justice: The Social Teaching of the Popes from Leo XIII to Pius XII, 1878-1958*. R. Charles, *The Social Teaching of Vatican II*. J. Hoffner, *Fundamentals of Christian Sociology*. J. Pieper, *The Four Cardinal Virtues*.

Robert Royal

SOUL

"Soul" is said not of pure spirits, such as God or angels, but only of bodily beings. But it is not said only of human beings; Aristotle ascribes soul to plants and animals. Of course he recognizes the uniqueness of the human soul; in man the soul has not only vegetative powers (as plants have) and sensitive powers (as animals have) but also rational powers, which makes it akin to the pure spirits.

Ever since Plato, philosophers — including Christian philosophers — have given much attention to showing that the soul is nothing material or physical. The soul indeed presupposes a body that is ensouled or that embodies it, but it is itself nothing bodily. The philosophers have tried to establish this by showing that the soul performs activities, such as rational understanding or free choosing, which are possible only on the condition that the soul takes up no space and is thus immaterial. Recent research into the brain, especially the work of Sir John Eccles, has added intriguing empirical confirmation of the immateriality of the soul.

In addition to its *immateriality*, there is also its *substantiality*, which Plato as well as the great Christian philosophers have tried to establish. To call the soul substantial means that it does not exist just as a quality or property of the body, but has a being of its own. Obviously the substantiality of the soul has to be affirmed if one is to hold that the soul survives the death of the body, that is, hold the immortality of the soul. Plato concluded from the soul's immortality that it is in the body as in a prison. Most Christian thinkers, while also agreeing about the immortality of the human soul, take much more seriously its embodiment, even to the point of affirming that the soul exists in its proper way only as embodied.

See: Body and Soul; Human Person; Immortality.

SPIRITUAL EXEGESIS

"Spiritual exegesis" refers to the interpretation of Scripture's spiritual senses as they are derived from the literal-historical sense, in accord with the Church's tradition of reading Scripture "with its divine authorship in mind" (Vatican Council II, *Dogmatic Constitution on Divine Revelation, Dei Verbum*, 12). As such, spiritual exegesis is a true spiritual science, requiring critical and contemplative study, by which the intended meaning of the scriptural authors, both human and divine, may be discovered in two stages: first, by distinguishing the literal and spiritual senses; second, through discerning the three spiritual senses — that is, allegorical, moral (or tropological), and anagogical.

(It should be noted that in speaking of the literal sense of Scripture, Catholic tradition does not necessarily mean the same thing as fundamentalists, who understand the term in a rigid manner. Fundamentalists generally seek the "literal" meaning of a text without serious consideration of literary genres or adequate study of the figurative use of language by the human writers. Consequently, they equate the "literal sense" with a rather flat and wooden interpretation. Not surprisingly, fundamentalists also end up rejecting the classical notion of the three spiritual senses altogether.)

Spiritual exegesis is sometimes given other names: typology, allegory, *quadriga, lectio divina, sensus plenior*, patristic and/or medieval exegesis, etc. In some cases, these labels may be used pejoratively to refer to any arbitrary or fanciful interpretation of Scripture. This occasionally prompts a reaction to the opposite extreme, that of denying the validity of spiritual exegesis or even the existence of a spiritual sense.

But Jesus himself refers to Jonah (Mt 12:39), Solomon (Mt 12:42), the temple (Jn 2:19), the brazen serpent (Jn 3:14), and many other Old Testament "signs" that point to him. In addition, Paul speaks of Adam as a "type" of Christ (Rom 5:14), and interprets Abraham's two wives and sons as an "allegory" (Gal 4:21-31). Likewise, the tabernacle and its rituals are described in Hebrews as "types and shadows of heavenly realities" (8:5), and the law as a "shadow of the good things to come" (10:1). Here we see the unity of the divine economy and plan for salvation history in the correlation of the literal and spiritual senses of Scripture or what Paul calls the "letter" and the "spirit" (2 Cor 3:3-18). Very similar to the two natures of Christ, the letter (*littera*) and spirit should be neither confused nor separated but rather united, as it were, in Christ.

Foundations of Spiritual Exegesis • The practice of spiritual exegesis follows from the Church's recognition that the Old and New Testaments are "sacred and canonical" because "written under the inspiration of the Holy Spirit . . . they have God as their author." The dual authorship of Scripture means that the human writers "made full use of their powers and faculties so that, though [God] acted in them and by them, it was as true authors that they consigned to writing whatever he wanted written, and no more" (*Dei Verbum*, 11). Thus, all that the human writers intend to affirm as truth — by which the literal-historical sense may be primarily identified — is divinely preserved from error (*Dei Verbum*, 11).

However, because Scripture is uniquely inspired by God, other meanings — namely, the spiritual senses — may be conveyed by those things that are signified by the words themselves. St. Thomas Aquinas explains: "That God is the author of holy Scripture should be acknowledged, and he has the power, not only of adapting words to signify things (which human writers can also do), but also of adapting things themselves [i.e., to signify other things]" (*Summa Theologiae* I.I, 1, 10, ad 1).

Initially, the spiritual sense is not a textual sense, so much as the sense of things spoken of in the text, notably in the New Testament, where Old Testament things are interpreted in the light of their fulfillment in Christ. For example, when the Old Testament speaks of the temple, its literal-historical meaning refers to the magnificent building in ancient Jerusalem. However, since this sacred edifice was built "according to the plan" revealed in "the writing from the hand of the LORD" (1 Chr 28:19; cf. Ex 25:9), God intended it to serve not only as a place of worship but also as a sign of other higher realities. The New Testament applies it to: first, Christ's Body (Jn 2:21); second, the Mystical Body of the Church and individual believers (1 Cor 3:16-17, 6:19; 2 Cor 6:16); and third, the "heavenly dwelling" of the saints in eternal beatitude (2 Cor 5:1-2; Rv 21:9-22).

These three respectively signify the allegorical, tropological (or moral), and anagogical senses. The *Catechism of the Catholic Church* distinguishes these (117), and then explains them by citing the thirteenth-century Danish theologian Augustine of Dacia: "The Letter speaks of deeds; Allegory to faith; the Moral how to act; Anagogy our destiny" (118). In sum, the first spiritual sense is the allegorical, which applies the literal sense primarily to Christ in order to build up the virtue of faith. The second spiritual sense is the moral (or tropological), which relates the literal sense to the Christian life for the purpose of increasing the

virtue of love. The third spiritual sense is the anagogical, which applies the literal sense to our eternal state in heaven for building up the virtue of hope.

Magisterial Principles and Interpretive Guidelines • Certain principles must be observed to ensure that spiritual exegesis is critically balanced and to avoid lapses into arbitrary interpretation and fanciful excess. First, the priority of the literal-historical sense calls for careful application of literary and historical methods, including modern critical ones, "in order to discover *the sacred authors' intention*" (CCC 110). Second, the uniquely inspired nature of Scripture calls for exegetes to read it "in the Spirit," by applying three criteria set forth in *Dei Verbum*, 12, and repeated by the *Catechism*: (1) *"Be especially attentive 'to the content and unity of the whole Scripture' "* (112); (2) *"Read the Scripture within 'the living Tradition of the whole Church' "* (113); (3) *"Be attentive to the analogy of faith"* (114). (Emphases in the original.)

In its 1993 document *The Interpretation of the Bible in the Church*, the Pontifical Biblical Commission issued additional guidelines. First, noting that "one should be especially attentive to the dynamic aspect of many texts," it warns of overly rigid applications of historical criticism: "Historical-critical exegesis has too often tended to limit the meaning of texts by tying it too rigidly to precise historical circumstances. It should seek rather to determine the direction of thought expressed by the text." Second, it notes how "certain texts which in ancient times had to be thought of as hyperbole . . . must now be taken literally," particularly since "the paschal event, the death and resurrection of Jesus, has established a radically new historical context, which sheds fresh light upon the ancient texts and causes them to undergo a change in meaning." Third, attention is called to the unity and convergence of literal and spiritual senses in many texts, and how spiritual exegesis was actually used by the scriptural writers themselves, in both the Old and New Testaments. A fourth principle shows how to do spiritual exegesis with texts that do not explicitly affirm a spiritual sense, by looking for an "authentic doctrinal tradition or conciliar definition given to a biblical text."

In view of these magisterial principles and guidelines, it is clear that spiritual exegesis attempts to steer a middle way between two opposite extremes: that of historicism on the one hand, which invalidates the New Testament writers' "precritical" exegesis, and fundamentalism on the other, which tends to interpret the New Testament spiritual senses in an exclusively literalistic manner. Both extremes may be traced to the Protestant rejection of the Church's living Tradition and its normative role in guiding scriptural interpretation.

Ironically, today some Catholic exegetes seem oblivious to or simply dissent from the Church's teaching and practice, particularly on this point of the spiritual sense. For instance, J.A. Fitzmyer warns against any "return to the theory of multiple senses of Scripture that was in vogue in the middle ages," despite the teachings of the Church on this matter (CCC 115-119); he refers to the "spiritual sense" as "a sort of weasel word," and argues instead in favor of an absolute "identification of the literal sense of Scripture with the spiritual sense," since "in reality, the spiritual sense of Scripture is nothing other than the literal sense intended by the human author."

Historical Development • The first several centuries of the Christian era witnessed two very different interpretive approaches, in the schools of Antioch and Alexandria. Antioch was noted for its emphasis on Scripture's literal sense, while Alexandrians preferred the spiritual senses. The best of Antioch is reflected in St. John Chrysostom's (died 407) profound and eloquent exegetical sermons, while the mystical interpretation of the Gospel of John underwrites the Alexandrian perspective of Athanasius (died 373), most notably in his Christology. Outside of these schools, a greater degree of balance was to be found in the exegesis of such Fathers as Jerome (c. 340-c. 420) and Augustine (354-430). This balance helped to stabilize exegesis in the medieval period; while the spiritual senses predominated in the monasteries (e.g.,

Bernard of Clairvaux), the literal received considerable attention in the universities (e.g., Thomas Aquinas).

Spiritual exegesis retained widespread influence throughout the Middle Ages. Indeed, it served to integrate the classical liberal arts with the emergent Christian civilization. The unity of life and thought was rendered possible by the queenly role of theology, which primarily was done by means of scriptural exposition. Spiritual exegesis and theological vitality coincide throughout Church history, so that Newman observes at the conclusion of his study of doctrinal development: "It may be almost laid down as an historical fact that the mystical interpretation and orthodoxy will stand or fall together" (*Essay on the Development of Doctrine*).

Nevertheless, as a result of the Protestant Reformation and the eighteenth-century Enlightenment, and the consequent dissolution of the medieval synthesis, spiritual exegesis fell into neglect and disuse, even in the Church. Now, faced with the collapse of Christendom and the unrelenting onslaught of secular critical theories with their vapid exegetical methodologies, many may be tempted to place it on the growing list of those endangered Church traditions threatened with extinction. Nevertheless, there are good reasons why spiritual exegesis can be expected not only to survive but thrive on into the third millennium.

Indeed, the last four decades are witness to a rising tide of Catholic theologians and exegetes (e.g., Henri de Lubac, Hans Urs von Balthasar, Yves Congar, Jean Daniélou, Louis Bouyer, Joseph Ratzinger, Augustine Bea, Ignace de la Potterie, F.X. Durrwell), who recognize the importance and value of spiritual exegesis, and actively encourage its renewal, not simply as an antiquarian item but as a truly critical science and spiritual art.

In this regard, the pioneering work of de Lubac and von Balthasar deserves special mention. Von Balthasar observes how de Lubac's groundbreaking work demonstrated that "the theory of the senses of Scripture is not a curiosity of the history of theology but an instrument for seeking out the most profound articulations of salvation history"; for "when exegesis is understood in this way, it includes all of theology, from its historical foundation to its most spiritual summits." He concludes that "the theology of the present and of the future will have to emulate all this" (*The Theology of Henri de Lubac*).

See: Divine Revelation; Inerrancy; Inspiration; Judaism in Catholic Doctrine; New Testament; Old Testament; Sacred Scripture.

Suggested Readings: CCC 109-119. Vatican Council II, *Dogmatic Constitution on Divine Revelation, Dei Verbum*. Pius XII, *Divino Afflante Spiritu*. Pontifical Biblical Commission, *The Interpretation of the Bible in the Church*. H. de Lubac, "On an Old Distich: The Doctrine of the 'Fourfold Sense' in Scripture" in *Theological Fragments*. B. de Margerie, *An Introduction to the History of Exegesis*. M. Simonetti, *Biblical Interpretation in the Early Church*. B. Smalley, *The Study of the Bible in the Middle Ages*. T. Torrance, *Divine Meaning: Studies in Patristic Hermeneutics*.

Scott Hahn

SPONSOR, BAPTISMAL

Baptismal sponsors should be "firm believers, able and ready to help the newly baptized — child or adult — on the road of Christian life" (CCC 1255). Often called "godfather" or "godmother," the baptismal sponsor possesses a task that the *Catechism of the Catholic Church* hails as "a truly ecclesial function (*officium*)."

The Code of Canon Law offers three canons detailing the nature of and requirements for this role.

If possible, the one to be baptized should have a sponsor. For an adult, the sponsor is to help the catechumen during the Christian initiation process; while in the case of an infant or child, the sponsor, along with the parents, presents the child for Baptism and encourages the child to live a Christ-oriented life (Canon 872).

Only one sponsor of either sex is needed; however, there may be two, male and female (Canon 873).

The sponsor must be appointed by the candidate, the parents, or guardian — or even the priest or minister. He or she must be suitable and willing to fulfill the duties. The sponsor, who cannot be the mother or father of the candidate, must be at least sixteen years old, unless the diocesan bishop stipulates otherwise or unless the parish priest or minister believes that an exception is warranted. He or she must be a Catholic who has been confirmed, received the Holy Eucharist, "lives a life of faith," and does not suffer from any canonical penalty (Canon 874.1).

See: Adult Baptism; Baptism; Infant Baptism.

STATES IN LIFE

"State in life" in secular language usually refers to the type of job or work each person has, and to whether or not he or she is married or single, etc. For a Christian, the term should have a much richer meaning, for it implies a position in life that a person holds not by accident or even by simple personal preference, but essentially by a divine choice, within a plan of love drawn up by God.

In the early Church, the conviction was universal that to be a Christian was to be called to holiness, and that this was to be achieved wherever each one was already living and working: "Every one should remain in the state in which he was called" (1 Cor 7:20).

The Second Vatican Council wished to restore this sense of the fullness of the call to holiness within ordinary life. "This holiness of the Church is expressed in many ways by the individuals who, each in his or her own state of life, tend to the perfection of love, thus sanctifying others. . . . All Christians in any state or walk of life are called to the fullness of Christian life and to the perfection of love" (*Dogmatic Constitution on the Church, Lumen Gentium*, 40). Marriage, "the state of life that is sanctified by a special sacrament," is specially noted as a way of life that should lead to holiness for the spouses, for their children, and for those around them (*Lumen Gentium*, 35).

See: Church, Nature, Origin, and Structure of; Consecrated Life; Evangelical Counsels; Holy Orders; Laity; Marriage; Vocation.

STEALING

The seventh commandment prohibits taking anything that is not ours. As such, it implies that possession of property is a normal state of affairs and that infringement of the rightful possession of property harms our neighbor and contradicts the requirements of justice and love. Stealing particularly offends against the virtue of commutative justice, whereby private exchanges should occur freely between parties who regard the exchange as fair and mutually advantageous. It is also stealing, however, when we wrongly fail to return things that belong to someone else and use them for our own advantage.

In Catholic thought, there are two principal types of stealing: theft and robbery.

Theft • The distinguishing characteristic of theft is that stealing occurs secretly against the will of the person being wronged. Theft occurs in a variety of ways. A thief may simply take away the material or intellectual possessions of another person; but it is also theft when, for example, a person secretly avoids responsibilities agreed to. "Goofing off" on a job instead of returning fair work for fair pay is a form of theft. Similarly, sneaking into a theater or riding a bus without paying for the required ticket secretly harms another who depends on money returns for services rendered, and is a form of theft.

Theft may be a mortal or venial sin, depending on the importance of what is stolen. Stealing an apple from someone else's tree may be a relatively small matter if the person is wealthy (it is still an illicit offense against property, however, unless there are extenuating circumstances, as explained below). But stealing even a piece of fruit from a poor person who is living precariously may be a grave matter, less because of the physical worth of the actual object than because of its effects on the victim. Repeated small thefts, though relatively unimportant in material terms, demonstrate a settled habit, or vice, that is serious in itself.

Theft involves deception of some sort and is therefore also a sin against the commandment not to lie. Concealing the fact that we have found someone else's property, for example, passively deceives and steals from that person at the same time.

In a sense, another kind of theft occurs in some instances of what is called fraud. Fraud often involves a voluntary exchange, but like theft, it involves some deception that makes the exchange that occurs not the one that the person defrauded agrees to. St. Thomas Aquinas notes that this deception usually takes one of three forms: (1) in material, by which a lesser thing, say, silver, is substituted for a greater, say, gold; (2) in quantity, where short weight or length is given; or (3) in quality, as when something is presented as being in better condition than it is in fact (*Summa Theologiae*, II-II, q. 77, a. 2).

Though property is normally to be respected as belonging to another, in extreme circumstances the taking of another's property may be justified if immediately needed to preserve life. St. Thomas says, for example (*Summa Theologiae,* II-II, q. 76, a. 7), that a person starving or dying, with no other means for obtaining the necessities of life, may take another's property (though plainly such a person may not take property upon which the owner is dependent for his or her survival). In such circumstances, the natural law allows us to appropriate things that God has created with a "universal destination" for the good of each of his creatures. Nonetheless, the moral law still applies in these cases: We should take only what is necessary, minimize harm done, and make restitution for anything taken unjustly, if that becomes possible in the future.

We now recognize that there are also temporal aspects to theft. It may be a form of theft when a person or nation irresponsibly runs into debt, leaving to descendants an obligation they have not agreed to. In such instances, the present person or community has in effect appropriated the future earnings of another generation. The same may be said of some kinds of environmental damage. To use up resources and leave nothing for those to come or to bequeath badly polluted water, air, and soil to our descendants is to steal from them the pleasures of the earth that God has intended for all.

Robbery • The second major form of stealing is robbery. It differs from theft in that it involves the open and violent taking of what belongs to another. All stealing is a kind of harm to the person, but robbery is a graver sin than theft because it not only harms the property by which a person lives but also potentially threatens the person's bodily well-being and life itself. No actual violence need take place for robbery to have occurred if the threat of violence was sufficient to make someone unwillingly give up his goods to another. Extortion, blackmail, and other kinds of intimidation are all in their ways robbery.

A new, modern form of stealing involves what is currently called intellectual property. Electronic devices and information networks make it possible for someone to steal copyrighted materials and computer software without paying authors and publishers their fair share. Modern communications technology has made it possible to steal funds in financial accounts and illicitly acquire valuable business and technological information. These practices harm another's just possession of property and are a sin against justice and charity.

See: Commutative Justice; Environment; Lying; Property; Restitution; Stewardship; Truthfulness; Universal Destination of Goods.

Suggested Readings: CCC 2401-2449. G. Grisez, *The Way of the Lord Jesus*, Vol. 2, *Living a Christian Life*, pp. 788-834.

Robert Royal

STERILIZATION

An intentional act whose sole immediate effect is to render procreation impossible is a direct sterilization. It may be temporary or permanent, and applied to men or women. It may use castration (rendering a man impotent) or surgery designed to prevent procreation without affecting sexual potency: vasectomy for men and tubal ligation, oophorectomy (removal of the ovaries), or hysterectomy (removal of the uterus) for women. It may be performed using radiation or drugs that are ingested, injected, or implanted to suppress the ability to conceive for months at a time (e.g., Depo-Provera, Norplant).

Whatever the means used, direct sterilization is intrinsically evil (CCC 2370). The ability to procreate is a basic good of the human person, as even our civil law has recognized (cf. *Skinner* v. *Oklahoma*, 315 U.S. 535 [1942]). Procreation is not merely a biological function, for it empowers us to help create a person with an immortal soul, made in God's image and likeness and called to live with him for eternity. Suppressing this ability mutilates a healthy human faculty and shows disrespect for the life that it is designed to help create.

So close is the connection between suppressing life and suppressing the ability to create life that they have sometimes been treated together in Church law. A canon included in the universal law of the Church from the thirteenth century until 1917, known as *Si aliquis*, treated sterilization as akin to homicide. In his encyclical *The Gospel of Life*, *Evangelium Vitae* (1995), Pope John Paul II distinguishes contraception and sterilization from the greater evil of abortion; but he warns that the negative attitude toward new life embodied in a "contraceptive mentality" increases the temptation to resort to abortion if preventive methods should fail (13).

Sterilization can also be considered in the context of marriage understood as a sacrament of mutual self-giving. In their sexual union, a husband and wife make a gift to each other of their sexuality, including its procreative meaning. To intervene to suppress this meaning is to make the marital covenant less complete than it should be. This is not to say marriage is less valid among those who are infertile or beyond childbearing age; but one should not deliberately act to close off a procreative ability that would otherwise exist.

Sterilization is more gravely wrong than other contraceptive means, because it implies a more committed decision to act against the good of procreation; it is often permanent and may be irreversible.

Social Implications • Sterilization's permanence, along with the fact that it can be imposed on someone even against his or her will, makes it particularly open to abuse by governments seeking to prevent procreation by certain classes of people or to reduce population growth generally.

Such abuses were condemned in 1930 in Pope Pius XI's encyclical *On Christian Marriage*, *Casti Connubii*. Besides reaffirming the Church's longstanding teaching against contraception and sterilization, he spoke against modern "eugenics" policies that require the sterilization of people with various physical or mental deficiencies: "Public magistrates have no direct power over the bodies of their subjects; therefore, where no crime has taken place and there is no cause present for grave punishment, they can never directly harm, or tamper with the integrity of the body, either for the reasons of eugenics or for any other reason" (70).

Many people today associate eugenics policies with Nazi Germany. Yet the first modern law authorizing involuntary sterilization for eugenic reasons was enacted in 1907 in Indiana, and it was followed by many other states. In the 1924 case of *Buck* v. *Bell*, the U.S. Supreme Court upheld a Virginia law providing for sterilization of women deemed "feeble-minded." Later, at the Nuremberg war crimes trials following World War II, Nazi defendants cited such American laws and rulings to show that their own program was not unique. Not until the late 1970s did federal guidelines place restrictions on sterilization performed on mentally retarded women without their consent.

Involuntary sterilization has also been used for population control in countries like the People's Republic of China. The Second Vatican Council condemned such abuses, declaring that "the decision regarding the number of children depends on the judgment of the parents and is in no way to be left to the decrees of public authority" (*Pastoral Constitution on the Church in the Modern World*, *Gaudium et Spes*, 87). Pope Paul VI reaf-

firmed this teaching, saying: "When the most inalienable right of matrimony and procreation is taken away, human dignity is destroyed" (*On the Progress of Peoples*, *Populorum Progressio*, 37 [1967]). In reviewing the responsibilities of government authorities, Pope John Paul II taught in 1982 that "any violence applied by such authorities in favor of contraception or, still worse, of sterilization and procured abortion, must be altogether condemned and forcefully rejected" (*The Christian Family in the Modern World*, *Familiaris Consortio*, 117). Here and in other documents, the Church has condemned wealthy nations' attempts to condition economic aid upon poorer countries' willingness to implement sterilization programs.

Modern Questions • Some theologians who dissent from Church teaching on contraception also seek to justify sterilization, in cases where an unintended pregnancy could result in physical harm or other hardships to the mother. The Church's Magisterium has rejected such arguments, because sterilization is intrinsically wrong and "it is not licit, even for the gravest reasons, to do evil so that good may follow therefrom" (Pope Paul VI, *On Human Life*, *Humanae Vitae*, 14 [1968]; cf. Rom 3:8). In such cases, the Church calls married couples to consider the morally acceptable means for avoiding pregnancy through periodic abstinence, also known as NFP, or natural family planning (CCC 2370).

Two aspects of sterilization remain subjects for legitimate debate: indirect sterilization and "material cooperation."

While rejecting all direct sterilization, Church teaching permits "the use of those therapeutic means truly necessary to cure diseases of the organism, even if an impediment to procreation, which may be foreseen, should result therefrom, provided such impediment is not, for whatever motive, directly willed" (*Humanae Vitae*, 15). In such cases (for example, the removal of a cancerous uterus to prevent the spread of cancer), only the cure of a disease is intended; any sterility that may result is an indirect and unintended side effect.

In recent years, some theologians sought to

justify a procedure known as "uterine isolation" in cases where the condition of the uterus would render a future pregnancy difficult or dangerous. But in August, 1994, the Congregation for the Doctrine of the Faith replied that this is a direct sterilization, because it directly intends to suppress procreation as a means of avoiding these future medical risks; pregnancy can be avoided in such a case by the morally acceptable means of NFP. Medical advances and moral reflection will undoubtedly continue to raise questions about the meaning and limits of indirect sterilization.

Second, while Catholic hospitals must not intentionally cooperate with the provision of direct sterilizations, some theologians argue that there are circumstances when some degree of involvement constituting material cooperation may seem necessary to avoid a great evil. The variety and complexity of modern health care networks has raised new variations on this situation. Some argue that the need to compete in a health care market can create economic pressures serious enough to justify material cooperation. Such views raise difficult new questions for the Church, since any cooperation of this kind by a Catholic institution at least poses a risk of scandal and arguably is wrong in itself.

See: Contraception; Cooperation; Double Effect; Health Care; Natural Family Planning; Population; Reproductive Technologies; Sexuality, Human; Theology of the Body.

Suggested Readings: CCC 2297, 2366-2372. Pius XI, *On Christian Marriage, Casti Connubii.* Paul VI, *On Human Life, Humanae Vitae.* John Paul II, *The Christian Family in the Modern World, Familiaris Consortio*; *The Gospel of Life, Evangelium Vitae.* Pontifical Council for the Family, *Ethical and Pastoral Dimensions of Population Trends: Instrumentum Laboris.* Congregation for the Doctrine of the Faith, *Quaecumque Sterilizatio, Sterilization in Catholic Hospitals*; *Responses to Questions Proposed Concerning 'Uterine Isolation' and Related Matters.* J. Ford, G. Grisez, et al., *The Teaching of Humanae Vitae: A Defense.*

Richard Doerflinger

STEWARDSHIP

The biblical vision of man's place in creation puts him between animals and purely spiritual beings: the angels and God. Man has responsibilities over the creatures below him, but not, as some radical environmentalists have charged, because the Bible gives him the right to exploit nature. All things are God's, and man must watch over and care for all created things in honor of him.

In the Old Testament, God commands Adam and Eve, "Be fruitful and multiply, and fill the earth and subdue it" (Gn 1:28). In the New Testament, Jesus warns the disciples in a parable to be just and care for the Lord's household, because when he comes again, they will be judged for their stewardship (Lk 12:41-48).

In its fullest sense, stewardship means that all things and all actions should be directed toward glorifying God. Our labor and its fruits, our lives in our families, and our conduct toward the natural world and human society all fall under different forms of stewardship. When we choose what work to do or when to rest, how to spend money, and who will be our leaders, we should be guided not only by immediate aims but by God's Revelation about his creation and his ultimate aims for the whole world.

In recent years, the image of stewardship has been especially applied to concerns about the natural environment. This is a proper development, now that the human race has grown to the point of having a global impact on nature, with serious implications for its duties to future generations.

Stewardship, however, does not and cannot mean so great a reverence for nature that human beings do not shape and use the world around them. In fact, stewardship obliges us to make the natural world productive for the common good of all. The notion of stewardship operates within the framework of universal moral laws and can never be used to justify limits on population through contraception, abortion, and other morally illicit means.

Properly understood, stewardship should lead the Christian to recognize the full meaning of

Christ's words: "Every one to whom much is given, of him will much be required" (Lk 12:48).

See: Animals; Creation; Environment; Population; Universal Destination of Goods.

SUBJECTIVISM

Subjectivism is another term for individual relativism, that is, the position that what is morally right and wrong is relative to what an individual thinks or feels. (*Cultural* relativism holds that what is morally right is relative to the group or culture.) The subjectivist says: "If you think it is right, then it is right for you. But if I think something else is right, then that is right for me."

Subjectivism often originates in a confused notion of freedom. Many people think freedom somehow is antithetical to objective moral norms. People sometimes wish to say that true autonomy must include the freedom to determine what is right and wrong, the freedom to "create one's own values" (cf. Pope John Paul II, encyclical *The Splendor of Truth, Veritatis Splendor*, 35-37 [1993]).

This is a confused notion of freedom. We can freely choose to respond positively or negatively to what is truly good and fulfilling for ourselves and for others, but we cannot bring it about that choosing against our true good or our neighbor's is morally upright. Some choices fulfill our capacity to love God, and the true good of our neighbor and self, and other choices diminish that capacity. Such truths are not contrary to freedom; rather, they mean that our freedom has eternal significance.

See: Absolute Moral Norms; Conscience; Freedom, Human; Human Goods; Moral Principles, Christian; Natural Law; Relativism.

SUBSIDIARITY

One of the most significant concepts in twentieth-century Catholic social teaching, subsidiarity shows the importance of keeping persons and institutions from being swallowed up by the state. Subsidiarity was first formulated in Pius XI's 1931 encyclical *On the Fortieth Year, Quadragesimo Anno*, and was a response to both Fascist and communist collectivism, which were on the rise in the 1930s. But subsidiarity reflects Catholic notions about distribution of social power going back to medieval feudalism and the ancient world, and has important applications in modern democracies as well.

In Pius XI and subsequent papal thinking, subsidiarity (*subsidium*: Latin for "support") requires the state to foster personal freedom and institutions for the sake of the common good. Contrary to the organic and totalitarian theories of society, however, this does not mean that all other institutions are subject to the state. Rather, individuals and intermediate institutions should have the freedom to exercise their proper responsibilities: "Just as it is wrong to take away from individuals what they can accomplish by their own ability and effort and entrust it to a community, so it is an injury and at the same time both a serious evil and a disturbance of right order to assign to a larger and higher society what can be performed successfully by smaller and lower communities" (*Quadragesimo Anno*, 79).

In this vision, society has multiple layers of authority, and the national state exists to promote the common good through national coordination and, when no other social institution can perform a necessary social function, as the agent of last resort.

In recent years, totalitarianism and authoritarianism have receded. Subsidiarity has been invoked, particularly in John Paul II's 1991 encyclical *The Hundredth Year, Centesimus Annus*, to caution modern democracies about the dangers to family stability and individual initiative in the excesses of the welfare state. John Paul also pointed to the need for the state to foster economic enterprise instead of merely becoming a universal employer (*Centesimus Annus*, 48). The crisis of welfare systems and social programs in all the developed nations at the end of the twentieth century seems to have given the idea of subsidiarity renewed relevance.

See: Property; Social Doctrine; Socialization.

SUFFERING IN CHRISTIAN LIFE

The existence of evil, of which suffering is a consequence, is perhaps the most pressing of human questions. The evil suffered or witnessed by humanity in the twentieth century has led many even to reject the possibility of a supreme good. The Second Vatican Council document *Pastoral Constitution on the Church in the Modern World*, *Gaudium et Spes*, mentions "a violent protest against evil in the world" among the causes of the rise of atheism in our time (19).

Even among the ancients, for whom the existence of the divine was virtually a given, evil had to be accounted for. For some, its existence suggested the dualism of two principles in the universe, one supremely evil and the other supremely good. Dualism often included a kind of spatial component in which the created world was seen as a place from which one must seek escape to a better place or state. This idea of escape from evil by escape from the world — or at least the minimizing of the influence of the world of suffering — forms a part of most of the major religious and philosophical movements in human history. The fundamental nature of the problem is perhaps summed up by the modern existentialist Albert Camus, who affirmed that the only really important question is whether or not one should commit suicide.

In so saying, he forces us to recognize that the question of evil is essentially caught up with the question of the meaning of human life itself. If suffering has no meaning, then life has no meaning. Most, like the ancient Stoics or Epicureans or even most modern existentialists, choose not to push the question as far as Camus and instead try to minimize pain or maximize pleasure or otherwise take a heroic stance in the face of ultimate meaninglessness. Buddhism, rather, suggests that pain is rooted in desire and that desire is ordered toward goods that are illusory, and so solves the problem of evil in the world by insisting that there is no world. Modern atheism posits the contrary side of that conclusion in saying that there is no God who made the world.

All this points to the common human experi-

ence that suffering, sickness, anguish, and death are things that ought not to be. If there is evil, then something is missing that ought to be there, in God or in the world. That is the conclusion, for example, of a popular book with the provocative title *When Bad Things Happen to Good People,* whose author says that in the case the title suggests, either God must not be all-good or God must not be all-powerful. The writer reasons that the latter is the preferable answer. Again, the sense that something is missing that ought to be there, in God or the world, is a common feature of the human experience. That missing thing is perfection. "Why," we ask, "would a perfect God make an imperfect world?" (By this is meant a world in which there is suffering and death.)

The Question of God • First, the question of the fact and manner of God's existence has to be faced. Does he exist? Is he perfect? Those two questions really resolve into one. If God exists, then all of the so-called transcendental properties of God (truth, unity, goodness, beauty — that is, all perfections) are present in him, too. That answers the problem in one respect: God cannot be all-good and not all-powerful, too, and still be God. God is by definition infinite in all his perfections. His attributes are said to be "convertible," meaning that to say that God is perfectly good is the same thing as to say that he is perfect in *every* way, including in power, beauty, truth, etc. Simply put, each of the attributes of God contains the others. So the important question is whether this perfect God exists.

St. Thomas Aquinas summed up five ways of demonstrating God's existence in his *Summa Theologiae*. In article 3 of question 2 of Part I of the *Summa*, he presents brief descriptions of the proofs of God's existence based upon his being the source of all motion, perfection, and order, and as the uncaused cause and the one necessary being. To sum up the demonstrations, we could say that Aquinas shows that God is the only sufficient explanation for the existence of anything else in our experience. Without God, as Frank J. Sheed so aptly put it, there is no answer to the question "Why is there not nothing?"

So, if God does exist and must be perfect, why is there evil? One could also ask, "*How* can there be evil, if the perfectly good God is the source of all things?" The answer is that God is the source of the good but not the evil in all things. As the Book of Genesis shows us, all that God creates is good in itself, or ontologically good (Gn 1:31). God created a perfect, though finite, world in the beginning. The common human sense that something is missing from the world is a kind of confirmation of the original integrity, harmony, and order of all things and the absence of evil and suffering at creation's beginning. In order to experience a loss, one must first possess the thing that has been lost. Something cannot be missed that has not gone missing. The loss of original innocence and the freedom from suffering that accompanied it haunt the human spirit like a distant memory of that perfect world now gone wrong.

Human Freedom • In order to create the perfect people for this perfect world, however, God had to allow them the freedom necessary to love. Love, which is the greatest human good, cannot be exercised without human freedom (cf. CCC 1604). No one can be forced to love. Love is by its nature chosen or it is not love. Without love, the world would have been less than perfect. Without human freedom, there could be no love.

With freedom comes the possibility of sin, and with sin comes suffering — sickness, anguish, pain, and death. God did not create evil so that love could exist, but he had to *allow* for the possibility of evil so that the greatest of goods — love — could be. God did not intend or create evil, but he, as we, must occasionally allow an unintended, lesser evil in order to gain a greater, intended good. In ethics, this is called the principle of double effect.

Ironically, it is the complete ontological goodness of God's creation, including the possibility of human love, which makes the entrance of moral evil (sin) and then physical evil (pain and suffering) possible. God created a good world that, by the tragedy of human sin, became less than God had made it (cf. *Summa Theologiae,* I, q. 48, a. 5;

I, q. 49, a. 2). The world retains its ontological goodness, which is to say that its existence itself is good, but moral goodness has been reduced in man, and the physical goodness of creation generally has been marred as well. As St. Paul puts it, "creation was subjected to futility" (Rom 8:20). In respect to the human person, we would say that he retains the image of God but that his likeness to God has been reduced (cf. Gn 1:26; CCC 299, 705).

The *Catechism of the Catholic Church* states that Adam and Eve "were constituted in an original 'state of holiness and justice.' . . . As long as he remained in the divine intimacy, man would not have to suffer or die" (375-376). The rebellion of our first parents introduced sin, suffering, and death into God's good creation (cf. CCC 390). All the lamentations of the Old Testament point implicitly to this state of human affairs. "Be gracious to me, O LORD, for I am languishing; O LORD, heal me, for my bones are troubled. . . . Turn, O LORD, save my life; deliver me for the sake of thy steadfast love. For in death there is no remembrance of thee; in Sheol who can give thee praise?" (Ps 6:2, 4-5). That cry issuing from the heart of the psalmist echoes that of every man and woman facing the question of human suffering and mortality.

The Meaning of Suffering • In the story of Job, we have perhaps the fullest expression of the *mysterium iniquitatis* before Christ's coming. Suffering is shown to be connected to God's righteousness and sovereignty and yet not necessarily a judgment upon the one who suffers. In fact, the Lord requires atoning sacrifices from Job's three accusers for having taxed him with sin as the cause of his sufferings (Jb 42:7-9).

Although Job is naturally repelled by the tragedies and accusations he faces, his response is one of religious submission to the divine will. When his property is taken away and his children killed, we are told that he "fell upon the ground, and worshiped." In this, Job presents a challenge to modernity, for in the face of the greatest challenge to faith, undeserved suffering, Job worships. Yet he protests his innocence to his three accusers and is rebuked by God, who does not so much condemn Job's claims to innocence as protest the suggestion that only commutative justice is at work in human suffering.

It is not Job's deeds for which he must repent "in dust and ashes" (42:6) but the shallowness of his words. "Who is this that darkens counsel by words without knowledge?" comes the Lord's voice from the whirlwind. While Job and his accusers debate the question of his guilt or innocence, the Lord breaks in to say that God's plan runs deeper than human concepts of justice, however important they may be. God's justice includes the weightier character of righteousness, of utter holiness, something "too wonderful" to be contained in mere commutation. In this respect, Job's first response, that of worship, was the most appropriate, and it is to worship that the story returns in the last chapter (42:1-9).

In Job, we catch a glimpse of the real incomprehensibility of suffering. That is, God does not deny the importance of the question of suffering. He does not simply say, "Man, you are too small to complain to me." He says, "The thing about which you complain is bigger, that is, deeper, than you are" (cf. St. Augustine, *City of God*, XX, 2). The real gravity of the question of the suffering of the innocent is not fully revealed until God himself suffers in Christ. In Christ, one might say, God poses the scenario "when the worst thing happens to *the* best Person."

In his reflection on human suffering, *Salvifici Doloris* (1984), Pope John Paul II recalls the conciliar statement that Christ "fully reveals man to himself" (31, quoting *Gaudium et Spes*, 22). In regard to human suffering, there is no other satisfactory answer than that which Christ gives. "Christ does not explain in the abstract the reasons for suffering , but before all else he says: 'Follow me! Come! Take part through your suffering in this work of saving the world, a salvation achieved through my suffering! Through my cross!' " (*Salvifici Doloris*, 26). In Christ, the meaning of suffering is disclosed to be a salvific meaning. The paschal mystery is the greatest reversal of fortune in human history; in fact, it re-

verses human history itself. The greatest enemy of man, suffering unto death, becomes the avenue to eternity, to eternal beatitude.

"In the cross of Christ not only is the Redemption accomplished through suffering, but *also human suffering itself has been redeemed*" (*Salvifici Doloris*, 19). "Human suffering has reached its culmination in the passion of Christ. And at the same time it has entered into a completely new dimension and a new order: *it has been linked to love*" (*Salvifici Doloris*, 18). By the total offering of himself Christ reveals in all its depth the "dimension of love" in human suffering, making it possible for St. Paul to say, "I rejoice in my sufferings for your sake, and in my flesh I complete what is lacking in Christ's afflictions for the sake of his body, that is, the church" (Col 1:24). Here the whole spiritual theology of Christian mortification, understood as a share in Christ's redemptive suffering, is contained in seed.

Commenting on this mystery, John Paul II notes that "Christ *has opened His suffering to man. . . .* Man, discovering through faith the redemptive suffering of Christ, also discovers in it his own sufferings; he *rediscovers them through faith*, enriched with a new content and meaning" (*Salvifici Doloris*, 20; cf. Mt 25:35-36.)

Often in the midst of suffering, the words that were addressed to St. Paul in regard to some suffering of his are heard: "My grace is enough for you, for in weakness power reaches perfection" (2 Cor 12:9). In this, the depth of the mystery of suffering is disclosed, when it becomes clear that suffering has been transformed in Christ to *"constitute a special support for the powers of good"* (*Salvifici Doloris*, 27).

See: Atheism; Augustinianism; Buddhism; Double Effect; Evil, Problem of; Freedom, Human; God, Nature and Attributes of; Human Race, Creation and Destiny of; Manichaeism; Original Sin; Process Theology; Providence; Thomas Aquinas, Thought of.

Suggested Readings: CCC 1500-1513. John Paul II, *On the Christian Meaning of Human Suffering, Salvifici Doloris.* C. Lewis, *The Problem of Pain.* D. von Hildebrand, *The Nature of Good and Evil.* P. Kreeft, *Making Sense Out of Suffering.*

Sean Innerst

SUICIDE

Suicide is the direct killing of oneself, and is always morally wrong. Reaffirming a constant Christian tradition, the Second Vatican Council named "willful suicide" among the crimes that degrade life and dishonor the Creator (*Pastoral Constitution on the Church in the Modern World, Gaudium et Spes*, 27). Because each human life, including one's own, is precious to God, "suicide is always as morally objectionable as murder" (Pope John Paul II, encyclical *The Gospel of Life, Evangelium Vitae*, 66). St. Augustine observed that anyone who thinks it is justifiable to kill himself should also kill his neighbor, "since the Scripture says: 'Thou shalt love thy neighbor as thyself'" (Letter 204 [19], Vol. 32, p. 6).

Suicide differs from martyrdom, where the Christian remains committed to the faith even under threat of death. It also differs from the refusal of extraordinary means for preserving life. One need not always cling to one's life regardless of all other values at stake; but life is always a gift of God and a basic human good, and one should never directly attack it.

These truths may be obscured in secular societies that revere individual autonomy and view bodily life as a personal possession, to be discarded at will in times of hardship. But human life is never a mere possession — it is a divine gift over which we are called to have careful stewardship.

Christian cultures once dealt harshly with suicides in order to emphasize the gravity of the act — for example, by denying Christian burial. Today "the Church prays for persons who have taken their own lives" (CCC 2283), recognizing that suicidal people suffer from anguish or mental disturbance that can remove or reduce moral responsibility. An expressed desire for suicide is best seen as an urgent plea for help and love; Christians should respond with psychological, spiritual, and other assistance.

See: Assisted Suicide; Body and Soul; Euthanasia; Homicide; Human Life, Dignity and Sanctity of; Human Person.

SUPERSTITION

The first commandment proscribes superstition, which the *Catechism of the Catholic Church* calls a "perverse excess of religion" (2110); so does sound human knowledge of God and the universe. One dictionary defines this bogus religious expression as "a belief or practice resulting from ignorance, fear of the unknown, or trust in magic or chance," accompanied by "an irrational, abject attitude of mind toward the supernatural, nature, or God." While such a definition can cover everything from the "evil eye" to culling omens from the entrails of a female parrot beheaded on the eve of the new moon, the term is not limited to such practices as these.

Superstition "can even affect the worship we offer the true God, e.g., when one attributes an importance in some way magical to certain practices otherwise lawful or necessary. To attribute the efficacy of prayers or of sacramental signs to their mere external performance, apart from the interior dispositions that they demand, is to fall into superstition" (CCC 2111). Faulty worship of the true God is one of four forms that superstition may take, the others being idolatry (worshiping false or multiple gods or other creatures), divination (seeking from demons and lost souls knowledge of future events), and magic (attempting to tame occult powers for personal gain or for harming others). The three latter topics are covered elsewhere in this volume.

Those who refuse to believe in God, to paraphrase G.K. Chesterton, end up believing in anything. What has not served as an object of worship or an oracle for esoteric clues to the future, the occult, and the will of the gods? Stars, air, wind, water, sun, crystals, amulets, palmistry, smoke, mirrors, salt, Tarot cards, arrows, points, lines and figures, devils, abstract notions personified, necromancy, dream interpretation, philters, potions and charms to excite love, omens, lucky and unlucky days, numbers, persons, things, actions, spells, incantations, and so on — all these have been pressed into superstition's service.

Not included are the superseded medieval ordeals and "judgments of God." These so-called "vain observances" rested on the root belief that God would work a miracle rather than allow an innocent to perish or the wicked to prevail. While not exactly superstitious, ordeals came close to what is called "tempting God," and their disuse was consequently encouraged.

Superstition in part stems from ignorance of natural causes, combined with common curiosity about what lies beneath the tangible. Then, claims St. Thomas Aquinas, devils soon exploit so much gullibility. But with educational and scientific progress, superstitions do tend to fade.

The Rebirth of Superstition • Nevertheless, a countertrend set in, beginning over a century ago. Just when the afterlife was thought to have been explained away in some scientific circles, spiritism seemed to revive, not so much among the unlettered as among some leading scientists themselves. While spiritism may be a reaction to materialism, seeking to communicate with souls and sundry spirits also evidences man's restless desire to penetrate, by any means, the mystery beyond death. As if further evidence were needed, today's public seems to have an insatiable appetite for lurid accounts of so-called out-of-body experiences. A number of such books have become best-sellers. A similar itch for the supernatural may lie behind some of the many recent books about angels.

How can superstition infect worship of the true God? A layman attempting to perform the functions of an ordained priest; a pardoner (as in Chaucer's *Canterbury Tales*) selling spurious indulgences; a fanatic devotee inventing false miracles and answers to prayers to spur his favorite devotion; wholesale believers in supernatural apparitions, visions, and revelations that serve no good purpose: These are guilty of at least material superstition. Since unenlightened practices tend to spring up with great ease, the Pope and bishops are charged with determining proper devotions or at least discountenancing improper worship.

While sometimes looked at askance by non-Catholics, certain Catholic devotions associated with particular places, events, and feasts have been approved, since such ties have proved auspicious to the growth of both believers and the devotion itself. Admittedly, popular credulity has contributed to such devotions in some cases; in turn, these hallowed places, things, and times have generated legends in their turn. While charged with removing any fraud or error, Catholic authorities are generally tolerant of "pious beliefs" that have helped to further Christian piety. On the other hand, belief in alleged private revelations is permitted, though not required, when the Church permits it. In the absence of an authoritative judgment of the Church, Catholics should approach such cases with extreme caution.

See: Apparitions; Devotions; Divination; Gnosticism; Idolatry; Magic; New Age; Private Revelation; Religion, Virtue of; Tempting God; Theosophy; Worship.

Suggested Readings: CCC 2110-2122.

Dennis Helming

SYNDERESIS

Synderesis is the disposition for understanding the first principles of practical reasoning. It is a disposition all people have from the time they begin to reason about what they ought or ought not to do. Understanding the principles of practical reason is important because these principles are the basic moral truths grasped even before, or independently of, faith; they are the principles of the natural moral law.

How they are known can be understood as follows. Through experience we understand those activities that actualize our basic potentialities as opportunities it would be good to realize. For example, as a child one experiences healthy functioning and sickness. One naturally enjoys healthy functioning and naturally is repelled by sickness. This much is common to human beings and other animals. But, further, with the enjoyment and repulsion as pointers, so to speak, for one's understanding, one comes to understand health as a unitary condition and as something good to pursue and preserve: One understands health to be an end to be pursued.

Something similar occurs with other perfections of our nature. By apprehending them in experience, we understand them as goods to be pursued: knowledge, aesthetic experience, skillful performance and play, friendship or society, self-integration, moral goodness itself, religion, and marriage.

Having grasped the ends worth pursuing, we also understand that we should choose in line with a love of such goods both in ourselves and in others. That much we know by our virtue called synderesis. The virtue or disposition for discerning the right choice to make in relation to the ends understood by synderesis is prudence.

See: Cardinal Virtues; Conscience; Human Goods; Human Virtues; Natural Law; Practical Reason.

SYNOD OF BISHOPS

While Synods of Bishops have been frequent throughout the centuries, the Second Vatican Council wished to make them something regular in the life of the Church. Now, every three years or so, bishops from each country or region, chosen by their fellow bishops of the area, meet together in a synod, along with the Pope, a certain number of delegates whom he has appointed, and officials of the Roman Curia, to study some important topic of Church life and concern (e.g., family, formation of priests, evangelization, penance). Each makes his contribution freely.

After the synod, the Pope usually publishes a document called an apostolic exhortation, drawing together the ecclesial wisdom thus brought to light. Among these have been *Familiaris Consortio* (1981), on marriage and family life; *Reconciliatio et Paenitentia* (1984), on the sacrament of Penance; and *Christifideles Laici* (1988), on laypeople.

These are the ordinary general assemblies of the Synod of Bishops. Church law also makes provision for regional synods made up of the bishops of a particular country or region and "extraordinary" synodal assemblies convened by the Pope for some special purpose. Synods of these two kinds have in fact been held since Vatican II.

The Synod of Bishops serves to strengthen the participants' ecclesial bonds both with the Pope and among themselves. By means of the synod they bring their experience to the central government of the Church, learn from the experience of other areas and dioceses, and can return to their own dioceses with renewed wisdom, initiatives, and evangelizing zeal.

See: Bishop; Church, Nature, Origin, and Structure of; Collegiality; Ecumenical Council.

T

TAOISM

It is not surprising that Taoist thought, mediated through Zen Buddhism, influenced America's young rebels in the 1960s and 1970s. This religion exists or has existed in three forms: popular, mystical, and philosophical. Popular Taoism, with its shamanism and elaborate rituals, has fallen into serious decline. The mystical form, which requires withdrawal from society into a world of nature study, self-denial, and meditation, is of interest only to the most seriously religious. But philosophical Taoism presented an appealing alternative to cultural Christianity, offering a vision of harmony through free pursuit of an undefined but seemingly impressive spirituality. It opened new vistas for a generation whose catchwords were love and peace.

Taoism is a very ancient faith, emerging at about the same time as Confucianism in the sixth or fifth century B.C. Its founder, perhaps more legend than historical figure, was Lao Tzu, the Old Master. Lao Tzu's legacy to the world, the fundamental scripture of Taoism, is the *Tao Te Ching, The Way and Its Power*. Not to be confused with the Confucian *I Ching*, the *Tao Te Ching* is a slim, philosophical treatise whose haunting verses often seem to express a wisdom that transcends rational analysis: "Be bent and you will remain straight; be vacant and you will remain full."

Taoist Beliefs • Attempts to define the *Tao*, the Way, are bound to fall short, because it is by definition ineffable. Nevertheless, description can be helpful. On the broadest and most abstract level, the *Tao* is reminiscent of the reality Buddhists seek to embrace by entering Nirvana. It is the One, the Eternal, the Unmoving and Unchanging; it is the ground of all being, accessible to human knowing only through mystical insight. The *Tao Te Ching* opens by declaring: "The *Tao* which can be conceived is not the real *Tao*."

The *Tao* is not simply transcendent, however. It is also the order and vital rhythm that powers nature through its unending cycle of change. Finally, the *Tao* is living according to the cadence of the universe, in tune with the flow of things. (In the *Star Wars* movie trilogy, sages train the hero to listen to the "Force," allowing it to act through him; this is a crude, but not inaccurate, metaphor for the *Tao* as guide to behavior.)

As this implies, Taoism holds that everything in nature, including the human person, participates in the primal life-source. In order to live well, the individual must abandon the effort consciously to direct his actions and must allow himself to be borne along. Perfect behavior is *wu wei*, literally "nonaction," but more helpfully rendered "spontaneous action" or "action in accord with the universe." *Wu wei* is behavior that does not spring from self, but from the *Tao* finding concrete expression through the individual. The *Tao Te Ching* says: "By nonaction everything can be done."

Armed with some understanding of the *Tao*, one can approach another elusive Taoist concept, that of *Te*. *Te* refers to the power by which a thing manifests itself; thus *Tao Te Ching, The Way and Its Power*. (Shakespeare's Portia offers a glimpse of *Te* when she describes mercy in *The Merchant of Venice:* "The quality of mercy is not strained; it droppeth as the gentle rain from heaven.") Taoist adepts achieve *Te* by acting entirely naturally, in conformity with their own intuition of reality. Their behavior, like that of nature itself, is marked by simplicity, serenity, grace, and a cosmic rightness beyond description or compare.

Moral Implications of Taoism • And by freedom. Some argue that liberation from restraint, specifically the social rigidities of Confucianism, is the formative impulse behind Taoism. Certainly, a religion centered on a truth embedded in nature but only subjectively knowable will spurn universal moral codes as unenlightened and artificial. Taoism has even sparked rebellions against oppressive governments, most notably the Revolt of the Yellow Turbans in A.D. 184. When detached from politics, however, the freedom Taoism embraces rejects violence and is tempered by compassion and respect for others: "Triumph is not beautiful." On a higher level, the adept can seek liberation from the constraints of life as an "immortal" or achieve ultimate union with the *Tao*.

Rejection of universal moral codes implies rejection of moral absolutes. A famous Taoist parable takes as its motif the question "Who knows what is good or evil?" All values are relative, and in the end all contraries blend into one another. As noted earlier, the *Tao* is, at one and the same time, the force that drives the ceaseless change of nature and the whole that encompasses all of reality. Its unity is therefore complex, like the unity of the ocean that serenely contains and nourishes teeming, time-bound life.

Nothing better expresses this concept than the symbol of the *yin-yang* wheel, which rewards contemplation. The revolving rim represents the All; the intermingled shapes that ceaselessly change places and spin into a blur represent the apparent opposites of light (*yang*) and dark (*yin*), male and female, summer and winter, active and passive, even life and death. Taoist wisdom revels in nature but comes ultimately to a halt before the mystery of the universe and simply stands awestruck. This attitude breeds detachment, calm, even a good-humored indulgence toward pretentious people who do not understand. "He who feels punctured," says the *Tao Te Ching*, "must once have been a bubble."

While gentleness and reverence for nature echo certain strains in Western spirituality (think of St. Francis of Assisi), Taoism has little in common with Christianity. It recognizes no personal God,

no natural law discoverable by reason, no objective moral authority. Since the adept seeks a reality beyond human society, efforts to build the kingdom of God on earth seem irrelevant. Most importantly, Taoism is not an incarnational faith centering on a God-man sent for our salvation. It lacks a formal sacramental system crowned by the Eucharist and does not know Jesus as the definitive Revelation of God in history.

The wide disparity among the world's great religions makes it hard to imagine a final reconciliation. However, the Second Vatican Council firmly taught that, while the Church is the ordinary means of salvation, "the plan of salvation also includes those who acknowledge the Creator" (*Dogmatic Constitution on the Church, Lumen Gentium*, 16). Pope John Paul II tirelessly promotes interreligious dialogue, inspired by the words of the Council's *Declaration on the Relationship of the Church to Non-Christian Religions, Nostra Aetate*: "The Church, therefore, urges her sons to enter with prudence and charity into discussion and collaboration with members of other religions. Let Christians, while witnessing to their own faith and way of life, acknowledge, preserve and encourage the spiritual and moral truths found among non-Christians" (2).

See: Buddhism; Church, Membership in; Evangelization; God, Nature and Attributes of; Missionary Activity; Natural Law; Redemption.

Suggested Readings: CCC 836-856. Vatican Council II, *Dogmatic Constitution on the Church, Lumen Gentium*, 16-17; *Declaration on the Relationship of the Church to Non-Christian Religions, Nostra Aetate*. John Paul II, *On the Permanent Validity of the Church's Missionary Mandate, Redemptoris Missio*, 94-99. G. Parrinder, ed., "China," *World Religions*. H. Smith, "Taoism" and "Confucianism," *The Religions of Man*.

David M. Byers

TELEOLOGICAL ETHICS

"Teleological ethics" usually refers to ethical theories that hold that the criterion for moral rightness and wrongness lies in the consequences to be produced by the various actions open to one. According to such theories, that action is morally right which will produce the best consequences or least bad consequences in the long run, even if this means directly destroying, damaging, or impeding some fundamental human good as a means. Thus, teleological ethical theories — on the usual meaning of the term — contrast with any theory holding that there are moral absolutes, that is, that there are some specific acts one must never do, no matter what the consequences or the circumstances. Theories that maintain moral absolutes, according to this use of the term, are called "deontological."

Pope John Paul uses the term in this way in his 1993 encyclical on moral principles, *The Splendor of Truth, Veritatis Splendor*: "The teleological ethical theories (proportionalism, consequentialism), while acknowledging that moral values are indicated by reason and by Revelation, maintain that it is never possible to formulate an absolute prohibition of particular kinds of behavior which would be in conflict, in every circumstance and in every culture, with those values" (75).

Sometimes, however, the terms "teleological ethics" and "deontological ethics" are used slightly differently. Teleological ethics sometimes means any theory that bases the ethical criterion on the human good, that is, on the ends to which human beings are naturally oriented (from the Greek word *telos*, meaning end or goal). On this use of the term, deontological theories are those that base the ethical criterion on something other than the human good, such as universalizability (Kantian theories) or intuition of "value" (intuitionist theories). Natural law ethics is, in this sense of the term, teleological rather than deontological.

Pope John Paul explains the basic ethical criterion as follows: "If the object of the concrete action is not in harmony with the true good of the person, the choice of that action makes our will and ourselves morally evil, thus putting us in conflict with our ultimate end, the supreme good, God himself" (*Veritatis Splendor*, 72; cf. Vatican Council II, *Pastoral Constitution on the Church in the Modern World, Gaudium et Spes*, 35). Natural law ethics is teleological in this sense, but also it holds that there are moral absolutes. One might describe it, then, as a "nonconsequentialist teleological ethical theory." The rest of this entry uses the term "teleological ethics" to refer to theories that deny moral absolutes; they also are referred to here as proportionalist.

The Case for Proportionalism • The Church has always taught that certain actions are intrinsically evil and that one ought never choose such actions as means toward any end. The end does not justify the means; or, as St. Paul stated it, one may not do evil that good may come from it (Rom 3:8).

Proportionalists hold that an important distinction is blurred by traditional moral theologians: the distinction between premoral evil and moral evil. Premoral evil is sometimes also called physical, or ontic, evil. Premoral evil refers to nonmoral disvalue. Proportionalists agree that one ought never do a moral evil as a means toward an end. However, they hold that in some cases it is morally right to cause a premoral evil for the sake of a proportionate end. That is, they hold that it is sometimes right intentionally to destroy, damage, or impede a basic good (such as life, truth, or marriage) for the sake of attaining a proportionately greater good or lesser evil. For example, they hold that in some cases it is morally right to choose abortion or euthanasia, where these seem to offer results proportionately more good or less evil than the alternatives.

Some proportionalists say some moral norms are virtually or practically exceptionless: for example, the norms excluding rape or torture. This does not mean that such acts are intrinsically morally evil, but that circumstances cannot be imagined (at least by those theologians) in which doing such acts would be productive of the least bad consequences. On this view, situations where such actions would be right are highly unlikely but still not impossible. (Indeed, considering hostage situations, blackmail, and the like, one wonders whether this position reveals more about the limitations of these theologians' imaginations than it does about the logical implications of their ethical theory.)

Proportionalists present various arguments for their position. First, they maintain that it is really just common sense or self-evident. In conflict situations, they say, one should do the lesser evil. But is not the denial of this absurd, for would it not say that in conflict situations one should do the *greater* evil? Surely, they conclude, that must be mistaken. Second, proportionalists argue that the theological tradition has at least implicitly assumed proportionalism. For it has said that sometimes it is right to kill in self-defense or in war. And is not saying that just to say that certain killings (certain types of doing premoral evil) are justified for the sake of a proportionate end? Third, they argue, common sense also supposes proportionalism in holding that, for instance, it is morally right to spank children or give them vaccinations, for these acts involve doing premoral evil (inflicting pain or sickness) for the sake of a proportionate end.

The Case Against Proportionalism • However, these arguments do not prove the proportionalist position. First, proportionalism is far from common sense or self-evident. The opposite of the proportionalist principle "Do the lesser evil" is not "Do the greater evil." Rather, it is "Do no evil, even if one's refusal will bring bad consequences." As Pope John Paul II reminds us, the powerful sign of Christian martyrdom shows that respect for the basic goods of persons requires fidelity even to the point of death. "In raising them [the martyrs] to the honor of the altars, the Church has canonized their witness and declared the truth of their judgment, according to which the love of God entails the obligation to respect his commandments, even in the most dire of circumstances, and the refusal to betray those commandments, even for the sake of saving one's own life" (*Veritatis Splendor*, 91). If proportionalists were right, not only would the refusal of a martyr like St. Thomas More to violate goods of truth and religion be unwise, it would conflict with common sense and be self-evidently mistaken.

Second, even if the proportionalists' claim were true that traditional authors, such as the great doctors of the Church or the approved moral theologians of previous generations, had already implicitly conceded their principle, that would prove only that traditional presentations were not fully consistent. It may be that some of the arguments or expressions of traditional authors could be taken to imply the proportionalist measuring of consequences. However, when traditional authors thought explicitly about the matter, they clearly rejected any proportionalist position and affirmed the position reaffirmed by Pope John Paul and the *Catechism of the Catholic Church* (cf. 1756).

With regard to the specific issues raised by proportionalists (e.g., killing, causing pain as punishment, vaccination) one should note that the explicit explanations of these particular issues by traditional moral theologians never invoked proportionalist arguments. Their justification of self-defense, killing in war, and so on, was never that willing and doing evil were necessary to avoid terrible consequences or were justified by a proportionate end. Rather, their claim was that in these cases an intrinsic good was not intentionally destroyed or damaged.

The examples of causing pain as punishment (such as spanking) and vaccination are misleading. Pain is not itself a harm to a basic good. It is part of the functioning of a healthy organism in adverse conditions. So, intentionally causing it is not an intrinsic moral evil. One may intentionally cause a small pain, as in spanking, as a means of punishment or deterrence, since this is not to act against a basic good. By contrast, the tradition was clear that one ought never intentionally mutilate for the sake of a good end (e.g., to escape a military draft).

Similarly, vaccination involves introducing a small amount of a virus as a means to stimulate the production of antibodies. The means is the exposure to the virus, and whatever sickness or damage to healthy functioning is caused is a side effect, not a means. Thus, traditional authors never condoned willing and doing evil as a means to a good end. The tradition is not committed to an inconsistent set of moral judgments.

Logical Difficulties • There are several logical difficulties with teleological ethics. First, suppose I could save five people from certain death, but only by torturing or killing one of my children. Would it be right for me to act against one good (my child's life or health) in order to bring about an end offering proportionately greater good?

Proportionalists might agree that this would not be right. They might say that the impact on my relationship to my child is an important consequence that outweighs the other consequences. But this suggests the question: Suppose I could save six, or seven, or . . . Is there a point at which I should torture or kill my own child? Any readiness on my part to kill my child for the sake of some overall net benefit would utterly change the attitude I have now toward the child. Instead of having an unconditional love for him, I would be viewing his welfare, his life, as something to be cherished only if it fits in with the well-being of the whole, the group. In that case, my love for the whole might be unconditional, but I would be ready to exclude my child from my concern, since I would be ready to will his destruction as a means of preventing harm to the whole. But such readiness is contrary to the love we are called to have, not only for our children — although in regard to them it is perhaps easier to see the point — but for every person. We should exclude *no* person from the circle of those for whom we care or have respect. But readiness to destroy, damage, or impede some aspect of a person's real and intrinsic good is incompatible with genuine love of that person. Proportionalism makes each individual life, and its fulfillment, dispensable in relation to a larger group or whole.

Moral actions are not just physical behaviors that last but a short time. Rather, the physical behavior is morally significant just insofar as it carries out a choice or act of will. In choosing, one disposes oneself in this or that direction. While the behavior may be transitory, this shaping of oneself remains as an aspect of oneself, unless one later repents. So, if one chooses contrary to a basic human good (that is, contrary to an intrinsic

aspect of a human person), one disposes oneself against that good. Such choices diminish or suppress in oneself a love of some aspect of the intrinsic good of real human persons.

A second problem for teleological ethics is that it requires a kind of measuring of consequences that is impossible. The proportionalist says that at least in some cases one should destroy, damage, or impede a basic good for the sake of avoiding bad consequences in the long run. This presupposes that in such cases one can first calculate what the consequences of each possible action would be, then measure them against one another. For the conclusion of one's deliberation is that one action would produce the lesser evil in comparison with the others. But in any situation where there is real free choice, such measuring is impossible.

If one *could* measure the consequences against one another, one could see that one option offers everything the other one does, plus more. And if one could see that, there would no longer be any free choice: One *could not* choose the option that offered measurably less good than the other. Free choice only enters the picture when two or more options offer distinctive types of good so that no option is simply better than the others from every perspective.

For example, one option might impact badly on life or health while another may harm truth or friendship. To measure such consequences against one another, it would be necessary to measure life against truth or friendship. But these are different sorts of basic goods. They have no units in common by which it is possible objectively to measure them against one another. To do so would be like trying to determine which is longer: thirty seconds or twenty yards. There is no single measuring rod by which to compare them.

In sum, if there is a moral question, then there is free choice; and if there is free choice, then the options for choice cannot be measured against one another. But if the options cannot be measured against one another, then proportionalism cannot be applied. So, whenever there is really a moral question, proportionalism is inapplicable. It follows that proportionalism, which requires such measurement, is not a reasonable alternative to the constant teaching of the Church on basic moral standards.

As we have seen, the rejection of proportionalism has been reiterated by Pope John Paul II in the encyclical *Veritatis Splendor* as well as in the 1995 encyclical *The Gospel of Life*, *Evangelium Vitae*. Significantly, Pope John Paul teaches that the Church's teaching on moral absolutes is part of Divine Revelation: "In teaching the existence of intrinsically evil acts, the Church accepts the teaching of Sacred Scripture. The Apostle Paul emphatically states: 'Do not be deceived: neither the immoral, nor idolaters, nor adulterers, nor sexual perverts, nor thieves, nor the greedy, nor drunkards, nor revilers, nor robbers will inherit the kingdom of God' (1 Cor 6:9-10)" (*Veritatis Splendor*, 81). Those who disagree with the Pope on this question now differ with the successor of St. Peter precisely on the question of what does and what does not belong to Revelation.

See: Absolute Moral Norms; Consequentialism; Deontology; Human Goods; Natural Law; Proportionalism; Utilitarianism.

Suggested Readings: CCC 1749-1756. John Paul II, *The Splendor of Truth, Veritatis Splendor*; *The Gospel of Life, Evangelium Vitae*. G. Grisez, *The Way of the Lord Jesus*, Vol. 1, *Christian Moral Principles*, Ch. 6. G. Grisez and R. Shaw, *Fulfillment in Christ*, Ch. 6. J. Finnis, *Moral Absolutes: Tradition, Revision, and Truth*. W. May, *Moral Absolutes*.

Patrick Lee

TEMPTATION

A temptation is anything that inclines a person to commit sin.

Some temptations arise from within ourselves (cf. Jas 1:14). Our own passions and emotions incline us to long for attractive gratifications even through doing acts we know are evil. Pride also inclines us to sin. The imperfection of our very nature is a source of temptation: Our fallen state increases this disordered drive, and our past personal sins make the situation worse.

We also experience temptations from the world. Persons, places, and things can be occasions of sins to us. Even things good in themselves can be incitements in us to seek attractive goods in unreasonable ways.

Faith also recognizes Satan, once an angel, but now hostile to God and to us, as one source of temptation. In his hatred for God, he seeks to drive us toward sinful and self-destructive choices (CCC 394-395).

Temptations are not themselves sins, and no one can entirely escape temptation. In the Our Father, the Lord urges us to pray that the Father "lead us not into temptation" or allow us to be overcome by it (cf. CCC 2846). We must of course distinguish between trials and tests that are necessary for growth, and temptations that incline to sin (cf. CCC 2487). Clearly, even very good people experience temptations of many kinds; and the Gospel encourages us in our trials by presenting Christ himself as experiencing temptations, though he experienced them in perfect innocence (cf. CCC 538-540).

Moreover, Christian faith assures us that God will always give to those who seek it with all their hearts sufficient grace to overcome temptation, and to remain faithful to God (cf. CCC 2848).

See: Concupiscence; Devil and Evil Spirits; Mortal Sin; Occasions of Sin; Original Sin; Sin; Venial Sin.

TEMPTATION OF CHRIST

All three Synoptic Gospels record that, after his baptism, Jesus withdrew into the desert, and all attribute this decision to the Holy Spirit. Luke, most attuned to the Holy Spirit's activity in Jesus' life, makes a double mention of the Spirit: "Filled with the Holy Spirit, Jesus returned from the Jordan and was led by the Spirit into the desert" (Lk 4:1). There, the Synoptics relate, he was tempted by the devil. The temptations raise an immediate problem: How can he whom Matthew, Mark, and Luke present in the perfection of his Divine Sonship be tempted?

Each evangelist gives his own coloring to the episode, corresponding to the aim and character of his narrative. Matthew and Luke point out a connection between Jesus' temptations and those of Israel in the desert, implying that Jesus is the new Israel, succeeding where Israel failed. Mark alludes to the difference in outcome between the temptations of Jesus and of Adam, implying that Jesus is the new Adam. Luke inserts the genealogy of Jesus between the baptism and the temptations (3:23-38) to imply that Jesus, the Son of God who is tempted, is also son of Adam. The three accounts have a common theme: They correct a false understanding of Jesus' mission as Son. In Luke 22:31-32, Jesus tells his disciples of a confrontation with Satan, who would have sifted them like wheat; some writers think he recounted parables like this to point out the seductive character of diabolic opposition to him and his ministry.

Others see a context for these temptation scenes in the request for a sign made of him during his ministry; but his only sign was fidelity to his Father. A middle course between a literalist interpretation of these scenes and an interpretation purely in terms of parable finds their real basis in the life of Jesus in the fact of temptation that he confronted. Not only the three Synoptics but also John's Gospel reflect this tradition (6:15, 26-34; 7:1-4). The author of the Epistle to the Hebrews makes much of it, for example: "We do not have a high priest who is unable to sympathize with our weaknesses, but one who has similarly been tested [tempted] in every way as we are yet without sin" (4:15).

Satan Overcome • The scenes depict Jesus' temptations coming from outside him; they do not suggest that they proceed from any inner conflict. His mission was guided by principles that can be stated very simply: implicit obedience to the will of God ("living on every word that God utters"); trust in God that asks no proof ("You shall not put the Lord your God to the test"); and a dedicated allegiance to God that excludes all lesser claims ("Do homage to the Lord your God and worship him alone"). Jesus has tied up his adversary (cf.

Mk. 3:27) and can now carry his campaign forward into enemy territory, free of any indecision or uncertainty about his aims or the means to be employed. Jesus frees himself from Satan, to free everyone from Satan; this is the meaning of the episode in the light of the whole Gospel, which gives the impression of an irresistible advance against the demonic hold on the world. At Jesus' approach, the demons experience fright, they tremble, they beg not to be driven out, but his presence allows no escape. The people recognize a new kind of teacher: "A new teaching! With authority he commands even the unclean spirits, and they obey him" (Mk 1:27).

It is significant that the Spirit directs Christ to make his way to the desert. Jesus is led into the solitude of prayer before embarking upon his preaching mission. The purpose of his stay is contemplation, for the victory over Satan will be the fruit of prayer, and a long period of prayer precedes the struggles of the ministry. Later, too, he interrupts the activity of his public life at intervals in order to dedicate himself to prayer. "[S]o much the more the report went abroad concerning him; and great multitudes gathered to hear and to be healed of their infirmities. But he withdrew to the wilderness and prayed" (Lk 5:15-16).

Satan's defeat began where his first victory also had begun: in an individual's free will. Jesus appears to us at this moment as the new Adam, at last uttering that free "yes" for which God had created heaven and earth. A created will had expanded to welcome the will of God within itself. Jesus' power comes from within; he acts with the power and authority of God. The demons sense that he is "the Holy One of God," with the holiness of God within him that they cannot resist: "By the finger of God I cast out demons" (Lk 11:20). Peter in the Acts of the Apostles makes a strict connection between Jesus' activity against the demons and his anointing with the Holy Spirit: "God anointed Jesus of Nazareth with the Holy Spirit and power. He went about . . . healing all those oppressed by the devil" (Acts 10:38).

Death still remained under Satan's sway, but

even this he lost by rashly dragging Jesus into it. The Passion is the second episode in the great struggle between Jesus and the prince of darkness, that appointed time when the devil returns to the attack against Jesus (cf. Lk 4:13). Satan had lost all power over him in the desert, but now "through death" Jesus reduces to total impotence the one "who has the power of death, that is, the devil" (Heb 2:14).

The three temptations make clear the uniqueness of Christ's Sonship. At the very beginning of his life of preaching, he is opposed in a radical way to the devil as the "the god of this world" (2 Cor 4:4), and the devil recognizes his identity as Son in a particular way (cf. Lk 4:41, 8:28). Matthew and Luke offer a Christology in which the Son of God is at work in salvation history as Satan's opponent. Because Jesus as Son is beyond all categories, extraordinary temptations happen to him. For the Christ to be Son is much more than being Messiah.

When his temptations are scrutinized in depth, they are seen to be only remotely like ours. For example, in the temptation to accept worldly power and adore the devil as king of the world, Christ is tempted in his very attitude of Son, beloved of and abandoned to the Father. Temptation is not a sin, and to say that Christ was tempted is not in any way to call into question his freedom from sin. The temptations show us why Christ could not sin. He was in control of himself, under the guidance of his reason. But he is ultimately our model and example because he was tempted and tested and learned obedience experientially in his human nature (cf. Heb 2:17). As his emptying of glory allowed him to suffer and to die, it also allowed him to be tempted, as part of the process whereby the incarnate Son brings to human beings a fidelity in temptation that replaces our infidelity and weakness.

See: Baptism of Christ; Devil and Evil Spirits; Incarnation; Jesus Christ, God and Man; Jesus Christ, Life of; Original Sin; Redemption; Sin; Spiritual Exegesis; Temptation.

Suggested Readings: CCC 538-540. John Paul II, *Christological Catechesis*. L. Bouyer, *The Eter-*

nal Son. R. Cantalamessa, *The Holy Spirit in the Life of Christ*.

Richard Malone

TEMPTING GOD

Throughout his public life and even when dying on the cross, Jesus often was taunted by his contemporaries to prove himself, to display inarguably his divine origin. In the face of such incontrovertible evidence, so they claimed, they would then believe in him. In the parable of Dives and Lazarus (Lk 16:19-31), Christ unmasked their hard hearts, their hardness of belief: "If they do not hear Moses and the prophets, neither will they be convinced if some one should rise from the dead."

In not flatly and prosaically declaring himself to us, God is not, as it were, playing hard to get. It is necessary that he respect our freedom and ability to reason on our own. Otherwise, there would be no human contribution to the bilateral business of redemption, and consequently we would exclude ourselves.

Tempting God goes against the first commandment, on the one hand, and, on the other, all the natural evidence for God's existence and character. God's peace and self-disclosure are reserved to "men of good will" (Lk 2:14). According to the *Catechism of the Catholic Church*, "*Tempting God* consists in putting his goodness and almighty power to the test by word or deed" (2119; emphasis in the original). It implies that available clues are insufficient, either in themselves or in the face of the skeptic's superior criteria for belief.

Thus did Satan seek to persuade Jesus to hurl himself from the temple's pinnacle and, by this gesture, oblige God to intervene (cf. Lk 4:9). Jesus countered with words from Deuteronomy: "You shall not put the Lord your God to the test" (6:16). The challenge contained in such tempting of God affronts the respect and trust we owe our Creator and Lord. It always harbors doubts about divine love, providence, and power (cf. 1 Cor 10:9, Ex 17:2-7, Ps 95:9).

See: Despair; Faith, Act of; Fatherhood of God;

Final Perseverance; Hope; Knowledge of God; Presumption; Religion, Virtue of; Temptation of Christ.

TEN COMMANDMENTS

The Ten Commandments have always had a central place in the moral teaching of the Catholic Church, as among the Jewish people. The whole revealed moral teaching of the Old Law is summarized in them. They express also the essentials of the natural law, which is written in the hearts of men. People of all cultures and times are in principle capable of grasping the validity and goodness of these commandments. But this fundamental moral teaching had to be, and was, explicitly revealed. "God wrote on the tables of the Law what men did not read in their hearts," St. Augustine says (cf. CCC 1962); for, according to St. Bonaventure, "in the state of sin the light of reason was obscured and the will had gone astray" (cf. CCC 2071).

A Gift of God Himself • The Catholic Church believes that God himself revealed the Ten Commandments, as a central part of his covenant with the chosen people. In making himself forcefully known as their Lord, and with great power making clear that the commandments were indeed his own teaching to them, he revealed very clearly their profound duty to follow these precepts (cf. CCC 2050).

In revealing the commandments, God not only made known the ways people should walk to live well before him, the commandments were also a revelation of God himself (CCC 2070). In teaching these profound commandments, God made known how different he was from Baal and all the pagan gods. Worship of such gods, and life in these decadent religions, involved much lust and cruelty. God reveals his holiness and great goodness in making these sublime commands a center of his covenant with his people. Moreover, the Ten Commandments reveal man to himself. The commandments, written in our hearts, and personally revealed by God, enable every person to know the fundamental rights and the basic duties of the

human person (CCC 2070; cf. Pope John Paul II, encyclical *The Splendor of Truth, Veritatis Splendor,* 95-101).

The Ten Commandments are the centerpiece of the revealed law of God in the Old Testament. Though they were not perfectly understood in the Old Law, and were brought to their fulfillment in Christ, they were rightly counted as an immense blessing. In the midst of the passions and confusions of this world, God mercifully teaches his people precious and saving precepts, a "law of knowledge and of life" (Sir 45:5). To have the teaching of God himself as the central moral vision of their life conferred on the Jews an overwhelming dignity and blessing: "[W]hat other nation is there, that has statutes and ordinances so righteous as all this law. . . ?" (Dt 4:8).

The Ten Commandments are found in two places in the Pentateuch (the first five books of the Bible): in Exodus 20:1-17 and in Deuteronomy 5:6-21. There are slight differences between the two formulations. The Church has regularly used the Ten Commandments in her catechesis, and education in the commandments has always been a basic part of preparing adults for Baptism. Through the centuries the faithful have been given summary statements of these commandments, in varying forms, but much like this:

1. I am the Lord your God: You shall not have other gods before me. You shall not make a graven image.

2. You shall not take the name of the Lord your God in vain.

3. Remember to keep holy the Sabbath day.

4. Honor your father and your mother.

5. You shall not kill.

6. You shall not commit adultery.

7. You shall not steal.

8. You shall not bear false witness against your neighbor.

9. You shall not covet your neighbor's wife.

10. You shall not covet anything that belongs to your neighbor.

The Ten Commandments are traditionally divided into two sets, each etched into one of the two tablets of the law. The first tablet expressed the duties we owe to God, and the set of precepts found here is properly related to the first and greatest of all commandments: "You shall love the Lord your God with all your heart" (Mt 22:37). The second tablet enumerates basic duties we have to our fellow men, duties that flow from the second greatest of commandments: "You shall love your neighbor as yourself" (Mt 22:39; cf. CCC 2067).

But the ordering of the commandments and the number found in each set vary in two traditions. The Catholic tradition, with that of the Lutheran Confessions, would have the first three commandments above on the first table. But some Eastern Churches and the Reformed Protestants number the commandments differently. They divide the first commandment above into two: The first speaks only the duty of recognizing the Lord, and only he, as God, while the second forbids making or worshiping a graven image. Then the second to eighth commandments of the Catholic tradition become the third to the ninth, and the tenth commandment for them absorbs both the ninth and tenth of the earlier tradition.

Christ and the Ten Commandments • The Gospel portrays Christ himself confirming the Ten Commandments and stressing their importance for those who hope to find eternal life. A rich young man had come to Jesus, eager to share in life such as he saw shining in him. He asked Jesus which commandments he must keep to enter into eternal life (cf. Mt 19:16). Jesus tells him he must keep the well-known and ordinary commandments: "You shall not kill; You shall not commit adultery; You shall not steal; You shall not bear false witness; Honor your father and mother" (Mt 19:18-19). Pope John Paul II discusses at length this passage in St. Matthew's Gospel in the first chapter of his 1993 encyclical on moral principles, *The Splendor of Truth, Veritatis Splendor* (cf. 6-27).

Eternal life is indeed that life which we shall possess fully only in the life to come, when we shall see God face to face and enter into the joy that is his life (Mt 25:21). Yet we begin to share in eternal life even in this life. By the reception of grace, which is a sharing in God's nature and his eternal life, and by the gifts of faith, hope, and love, we are already "rescued from the power of darkness" (Col 1:13) and brought into God's wonderful light, into sharing eternal life. But to enter into eternal life, by the participation in such life that we can have now and by its fullness in eternity, we must have in our hearts the love that reveals itself in refusing, in accord with God's commandments, to do anything incompatible with love. To possess eternal life one must be faithful to the commandments of life.

In the Sermon on the Mount, Christ points out often how much more is expected of those who live by the grace of God in his kingdom, animated by the love that he pours into their hearts, than was expected in older times. "You have heard it said. . . ," Jesus tells his listeners, reminding them of what the law had formerly required; "but I say to you. . . ," and he gives more demanding precepts (cf. Mt 5:21-22, 27-28, 31-32).

Christ stresses that the Ten Commandments, and indeed all the revealed moral precepts that had been handed down, are derived from the two great commandments of love. To love God is the greatest commandment of all; but the command to love our neighbor as we love ourselves is like that first and greatest one. On these two commandments depend the whole law and the prophets. He who genuinely loves God and neighbor will fulfill the whole law and the prophets. This love is not vague or amorphous. From it follow necessarily the Ten Commandments; and one does not love if one violates the commandments. This is the sublime force of the commandments: They unfold the requirements of love.

Divine Defense of Essentials of Morality • The Ten Commandments are taught us by God himself in two ways. First, he teaches their content indirectly when, as our Creator, he gives us minds and hearts capable of discovering and knowing surely that we ought to avoid such evil deeds. He enables us to recognize how wrong, how contrary it is to all love and all fairness, to strike out against basic goods in any person. Such is the natural law, which is written in our hearts: "[W]hat the law requires is written in their hearts, while their conscience also bears witness" (Rom 2:15).

Even without Divine Revelation, one can know surely that it is wrong to slay an innocent person in order to get something one craves or escape some evil.

Though any person can know this, it is possible also for individuals to go astray. They can convince themselves — under the pressures of original sin and the sin of the world, as well as the influence of disordered passions — that if they can obtain some good they earnestly want by doing something which is in fact evil, which strikes against basic goods in another person, then it is reasonable and good to do so. In revealing himself and the Ten Commandments, however, God assures his people even more certainly of the truth of the fundamental moral precepts. Everything enabling people to know that God has revealed himself and is with them becomes also a basis for knowing with utter certainty that it is in no case permissible to do the radically evil kinds of deeds centrally forbidden by the Ten Commandments.

This is signified in the very wording of some presentations of the commandments. "Every one of you shall revere his father and his mother, and you shall keep my sabbaths: I am the LORD your God. . . . You shall not steal. . . . I am the LORD" (Lv 19:3, 12). The solemn utterance "I am the Lord" places all the authority of God against doing such base acts. It also is a teaching that what is commanded is a good and right command. It is not prescribed by cultures, nor by the power of older generations. The Lord himself, the one who is most wise and most good and true, assures us of the validity of the commandments.

Content of the Ten Commandments • All the valid moral precepts of the "law and the prophets" are *in some way* contained in the Ten Commandments. They do not explicitly mention the first and most basic moral principles: that we must love God with the whole heart and love our neighbor; yet these precepts are really present in the Ten Commandments, in the vital way in which principles are present in the conclusions from which they flow (cf. St. Thomas Aquinas, *Summa Theologiae*, I-II, q. 100, a. 3, c.). The commandments have such power, since they really do flow

from the duty to love God with the whole heart and to love the neighbor. It is the evident duty to love that gives the Ten Commandments their power.

Structure of the Ten Commandments • Thomas Aquinas points out that the Ten Commandments are not a random set of precepts but are a wonderfully structured presentation of the basic duties of human persons toward God and one another (*Summa Theologiae,* q. 100, a. 5, c.). They point out in an orderly way the basic responsibilities of God's people and of all who would lead good and noble human lives. They present first the basic, specific duties that flow from our duty to love God and then the duties that flow from our duty to love one another.

God is the Lord of the people of God — and to the sovereign a people owes fidelity, reverence, and service. Thus the first three commands, which speak of our duties to the God who has revealed himself to us, address these responsibilities. (1) We must give to no other the sovereign honor that belongs to God; to him we owe faith, hope, and love. That is, of all that calls for our belief, nothing is so decisive as the word he himself makes clear to be his own word; our trust must be in him before all else, before money and all the powers of the world; our love must go out first to him, who is most good to us, and who is the guardian of all that is good, and the Lord of all goodness in all that we love. (2) To God we owe the greatest reverence; he himself and his name are always to receive from us respectful love. (3) In memory of his countless benefits to us, service is owed to him who created us and cares for us; and in the light of faith, we owe the perfect worship of the Mass as a remembrance of the infinite love of the cross.

The precepts of the second tablet sketch out in an orderly way the duties flowing from the obligation to love one another; they guard those basic goods without which life in society cannot be lived humanly and well. (4) The first commandment on the second table speaks of the duties flowing from the duty to love those with an exceptionally strong claim to our love: duties that underlie the basic unit of the family and the elementary foundations of moral living. It points out the duties parents have toward those to whom they have given life and duties of children toward their parents. (5) Among the duties all of us owe to one another, the first is the duty to respect life itself, not deliberately to kill or indeed deliberately do any evil to the person of the neighbor, for any reason whatever. (6) But great harm is done in other ways, too — the powerful gift of sexuality needs to be governed by intelligent love. Hence it is wrong to perform intrinsically disordered acts, ignoring the purposes of sexuality and so treating it as something trivial. This corrupts human love, weakens the home, endangers children, and creates countless evils for human life. (7) The precept against stealing also guards human things, forbidding assaults on the dignity of persons through seizing their possessions. (8) The eighth commandment recalls the importance of truth for human life and protects that truth without which the greatest harms come upon persons and society. The last two commandments (9 and 10) recall the interiority of moral life. Even the deliberate coveting of those things that so basically disrupt human life and peace — lust for another's wife or deliberate setting of the heart on his property — are acts against love for persons and the peace of the family of God.

All Ten Commandments are accessible to the whole human race. For they follow, with only a modest amount of reflection, from the most basic and evident of moral principles: We should love God and neighbor and should do harm to no one (*Summa Theologiae,* q. 100, a. 3, c.).

Other moral precepts are contained in the Ten Commandments in more subtle ways. St. Thomas says they are present "as conclusions are contained in their premises" (*Summa Theologiae,* q. 100, a. 3, c.). That is to say, they follow from the commandments of love and from the Ten Commandments, but not with the clarity with which the latter follow from the former. It is not so evident that actions proscribed by these precepts, which are more difficult to know, are always incompatible with love. In fact, such derivative precepts often have exceptions: They do not concern the kind of

act that as such is always wrong. Rather, the act may be wrong in some circumstances but not in all, since it is not the kind of deed that of itself is always incompatible with love. To understand these precepts thoroughly is a more difficult matter. But even very ordinary people can come to know them well, with the assistance of the wise and the good, who cast light on more difficult moral issues for the whole community of love. For example, the morality of self-defense is not as simply spelled out as is the morality of directly killing the innocent; the latter is always wrong, but the former will be permissible or not, depending on important circumstance.

Moral Absolutes • The Ten Commandments call us to observe the most basic duties of love for God and neighbor. For that reason, in their primordial content the commandments express grave obligations. They are fundamentally immutable; they oblige always and everywhere; they have no exceptions (CCC 2072; cf. *Summa Theologiae,* I-II, q. 100, a. 8, c.). The negative duties they proclaim are moral absolutes, basic duties that form the strong central framework of a sound moral life. From these follow the other, more complex duties that have a variety of exceptions and need a certain greater wisdom to grasp correctly.

The commandments are said to express grave and exceptionless duties in their primordial content, that is, in their most basic senses, when they are grasped in their fundamental and most basic meanings. Thus, the fifth commandment reminds us forcibly that it is always wrong to "kill." Pope John Paul II spells out with great clarity why objectively it is always and in all circumstances gravely wrong deliberately to kill the innocent, even if they are old and infirm or are still in the womb (encyclical *The Gospel of Life, Evangelium Vitae,* 53-67). To choose to kill the innocent is to choose an act always incompatible with love of God and love of neighbor. The first focus of the commandments is on clear and most basic precepts like these, though they cast light also on the more difficult moral directives concerning self-defense and capital punishment; these latter are to be studied in the light of the Ten Commandments but are more complex issues than those directly addressed by the Decalogue.

Thus the Ten Commandments provide the most fundamental education in specific moral issues. They are rooted in love and are precious because they unfold the responsibilities of love. There are other moral questions more difficult than those immediately addressed by the Decalogue, but their solution also is to be sought in the light cast by the Decalogue. The study of morality through the virtues, and through reflection on basic goods and the first principles that guide our pursuit of them, in no way conflicts with the study of morality through the Decalogue. Reflection on these Ten Words of God always remains important to the Catholic teacher of morality.

See: Absolute Moral Norms; Cardinal Virtues; Divine Revelation; Human Goods; Law of Christ; Moral Principles, Christian; Natural Law; Old Law.

Suggested Readings: CCC 1749-1756, 1949-1974, 2052-2074. John Paul II, *The Splendor of Truth, Veritatis Splendor*; *The Gospel of Life*, *Evangelium Vitae*. St. Thomas Aquinas, *Summa Theologiae*, I-II, qq. 100; 106-107. P. Lee, "Permanence of the Ten Commandments: St. Thomas and His Modern Interpreters," *Theological Studies*, 42 (1981), pp. 422-443. W. May, *An Introduction to Moral Theology*, rev. ed., Chs. 2-3.

Ronald D. Lawler, O.F.M. Cap.

THEOLOGICAL VIRTUES

In giving us the theological virtues of faith, hope, and love, God makes it possible for our lives to be closely intertwined with his own. These virtues give us the power to believe God himself with a personal and living faith, to have an entire trust in him, and to love him with sincere hearts. As people redeemed by Christ the Lord, we are invited to form personal relationships with God the Father, the Son, and the Holy Spirit (cf. CCC 1812); and the most fundamental of the ties shaping our friendship with God are precisely faith, hope, and love. "So faith, hope, love abide, these three; but the greatest of these is love" (1 Cor 13:13).

The theological virtues are both like and unlike other virtues. They are not acquired in the same way natural virtues are. Natural virtues, like courage or justice, are acquired by freely performing actions that correspond to them — brave deeds, just deeds, and the like. But faith, hope, and love are gifts of God, infused into our souls with grace at Baptism. To all those to whom he gives a participation in his own life by grace, God gives the power to perform those saving acts of believing, trusting, and loving him (CCC 1813).

Still, those who come to faith in more mature years come to faith (itself entirely God's gift) through free obedience to preliminary calls and invitations of grace. In many ways, God's grace summons people to hunger for faith, to recognize signs of his reality and presence, to cry out to him for that light by which alone we can see with tranquility and certainty the saving truth and the blessed paths of life to which he calls us.

Faith and the other theological virtues are gifts of God. "By grace you have been saved through faith; and this is not your own doing, it is the gift of God" (Eph 2:8; CCC 153). Hope, too, is a divine gift. The unshakable confidence that saints have had in God is a confidence that God himself gives. They have found a Lord who has himself enabled them to realize that he is entirely worthy of absolute trust. Love of God and of neighbor is also God's gift. It is by the love that God pours into our hearts (cf. Rom 15:5) that we can have the simplicity and joy of personal and saving love.

Yet God's gifts are given to our freedom. By his grace it is we ourselves who freely believe, freely hope, freely love. Ordinary and supernatural things come together in the lived experiences of faith, hope, and love. We have reasons to believe, grounds for hope, motives for love. But the grace of God transforms all our reasonings and all our human strivings. Adults coming toward conversion are led by God's grace through many paths on the way to a living faith. When faith comes, it is not simply the end of a long journey or a long argument. It is the beginning of a new life, a gift freshly received, enabling one to be related to God in ways radically dependent on the

God who is most near to us and who has enabled us to realize that he calls us to himself (cf. CCC 154, 160).

In Christ, God has stepped into human history. The Lord himself has become our teacher and Savior; he enables us to share in his life. Our basic Christian acts of believing, trusting, and loving bind us directly to him, and derive their joy and their firmness from the fact that they are really rooted in God.

Growing in Faith, Hope, and Love • Like natural virtues, the theological virtues are ordered to action. The virtue of faith, for example, enables us in our own free acts to believe God himself, as the virtue of courage enables us to do brave things; and one can grow in faith and love, as one can grow more brave and more just. Growth in the theological virtues is entirely surrounded by grace, though it also is free. Exercising the theological virtues makes them stronger and more deeply rooted in our souls. We can do this by making free and deliberate acts of faith, hope, and love, and also by living lives animated by these virtues. As we willingly shape our lives so that we act more and more out of motives of faith, hope, and love, and do more and more generous things because of our faith, God makes the gift of faith itself stronger and more deeply rooted within us.

Faith, hope, and love relate us immediately to the Lord. Faith is not simply believing that something is true, not just having right opinions about religious matters. It is a personal tie to the living God, believing God himself (CCC 1814). Faith simply would not be possible if God had not revealed himself, did not make himself accessible, so that we could be certain it is he who speaks in the voices heard in the family of faith. He transforms the water of human argument and hopes into the wine of faith, giving us the certainty of his nearness that enables us to give ourselves to him entirely and really believe all he has revealed, in the certainty that it is he who has revealed it and called us to faith (Vatican Council II, *Dogmatic Constitution on Divine Revelation, Dei Verbum,* 5; CCC 157).

One who has come to believe God does not believe particular matters of faith simply because they are attractive or because of clever arguments proving them true. One who has come to an intelligent faith believes whatever God has revealed; for if one has found the Lord, it is certainly right to believe him. In the Gospels, we see how Christ led the Apostles to an intelligent and strong faith in himself and then rightly expected them to believe his words, because they knew he was their Lord. St. Peter was able to respond vigorously to the Lord's invitation to faith. St. Peter did not understand the Eucharist or how the stirring words of Christ could be proved true — but he knew Christ. Hence he was able to say wisely, "We have believed, and have come to know, that you are the Holy One of God" (Jn 6:69; cf. Mt 16:16, Mk 8:29; CCC 150-153).

Hope and love, too, are theological, centered directly in God. Our hope is rooted not in our knowing how to escape deep perils, but in God's revealed faithfulness. He himself has taught us that he will never forsake us, and hope is built strongly on God, who has entered our lives. The love of God is entirely grounded on the living God, who has drawn near us. It is God himself whom we love; and we love him and one another by the love that he has personally poured into our hearts. All things are anchored in God, who is stronger than all else.

See: Baptism; Beatitudes; Cardinal Virtues; Charity; Faith, Act of; Faith, Virtue of; Grace; Hope; Human Virtues; Moral Principles, Christian.

Suggested Readings: CCC 150-165, 1812-1844, 2095-2096. Vatican Council I, *Dogmatic Constitution on the Catholic Faith, Dei Filius,* Ch. III. Vatican Council II, *Dogmatic Constitution on Divine Revelation, Dei Verbum,* Ch. I. St. Thomas Aquinas, *Summa Theologiae,* I-II, q. 62. R. Garrigou-Lagrange, O.P., *The Theological Virtues.*

Ronald D. Lawler, O.F.M. Cap.

THEOLOGY OF THE BODY

By "theology of the body" we mean the teaching of Pope John Paul II, elaborated for the most part in his Wednesday audience addresses between

1979 and 1984, concerning the human body and in particular concerning its masculinity and femininity. Though this teaching can be found already in chapters 2 and 3 of his early work, *Love and Responsibility*, and though it underlies very many of his papal teachings, it finds its fullest expression in this famous series of addresses.

John Paul said that this series could be entitled "The redemption of the body and the sacramentality of marriage." The theology of the body, he says, has the particular task of providing the foundation for much that he says about the redemption of the body and about marriage as a sacrament.

We can identify the two main sources out of which the Pope develops his theology of the body. On the one hand, John Paul meditates on the word of God contained in Sacred Scripture, and especially on those passages in the Old and New Testaments dealing with man and woman (above all Gn 1—3; Mt 5:27-28, 19:3-8, 22:23-33; Mk 10:2-9, 12:18-27; Lk 20:27-38; Eph 5:21-33). The theology of the body is biblically based from beginning to end. On the other hand, John Paul constantly employs, as a kind of principle of biblical interpretation, his personalist philosophy. (Of course the distinction between these two sources of his thought is not as sharp as it may at first seem, since his personalist philosophy, too, has its biblical foundations.)

The Personalist Philosophy of John Paul • The reader is advised to consult the entry "Human Person," which presents an understanding of the human person that accords completely with the personalism of John Paul. Here we shall simply point to his favorite way of capturing the essence of his philosophy of the human person. He quotes from the Second Vatican Council's *Pastoral Constitution on the Church in the Modern World*, *Gaudium et Spes*, 24: Although man is "the only creature on earth that God has wanted for its own sake," it is nevertheless true that he "can fully discover his true self only in a sincere giving of himself." This passage expresses a fundamental polarity in the makeup of the human person.

On the one hand, God wills each human being for his or her own sake, which means that God recognizes each human person as a being of his or her own, as one who cannot exist as a mere part of some whole or as a mere instrumental means for achieving some result. Just as we should affirm human persons for their own sakes and avoid all using of them, so God, too, affirms human persons for their own sakes, and indeed he is the very last one to indulge in any using of them. The way in which he respects our freedom gives evidence of how he wills us for our own sakes.

On the other hand, each human person is made for self-donation, for communion with other persons. We are not only beings of our own, belonging to ourselves, but we are beings for others, made for interpersonal love. Since God exists as a community of three Divine Persons, it only makes sense that we, being created in the image of God, should exist, not in isolation one from another, but in the communion of love one with another. John Paul thinks this self-donation to which we are called is lived in a particularly perfect way in the spousal or conjugal self-donation of man and woman. He stresses repeatedly that self-donation is not in opposition to the belonging of each person to himself, but is rather based on it. Only because persons first belong to themselves can they give themselves away to other persons; and of course they give themselves away in such a way as never to cease belonging to themselves. John Paul never thinks of the union of persons in terms of fusion or amalgamation; rather, he stresses that persons remain distinct persons even in the most intimate union of love.

The Nuptial Meaning of the Body • So far, we have expressed this polar structure of the human person without any mention of the body. But John Paul thinks it cannot be adequately understood apart from the way in which it is embodied. He has something to say about how we experience our selfhood through the body, and it would belong to the theology of the body to say more about it. But in his own development of this theology he is above all concerned with the place of the body in the self-donation to which human persons are called.

This concern leads him beyond the general fact of our embodiment, to the more particular fact that we are embodied as man and woman. That it is not good for us to be alone, that we can find ourselves only through a sincere gift of ourselves, has its first fundamental bodily expression in our existing as man and woman; and in fact it cannot really be understood apart from the difference and complementarity of the sexes. It is as man and woman that we are first raised out of our solitude, and ordered one to another, and called to self-donation. The capacity of the masculine body and of the feminine body to serve self-donation is called by John Paul the "nuptial meaning" of the human body, a concept that stands at the heart of his theology of the body.

On this basis John Paul is led to break new ground in the theology of the image of God in man. Traditionally, one said that this image lies primarily in the rationality of man, which belongs to the soul; one left the body entirely out of that which images God. But John Paul, following a well-known teaching of Vatican II, says (cf., e.g., his document *On the Dignity and Vocation of Women*, *Mulieris Dignitatem*, 6-7) that man and woman, taken in their unity-in-difference, also image God, and in particular image the inner-Trinitarian communion of the Divine Persons. Since the man-woman distinction is by its very nature also a bodily distinction, it follows that it is not the soul alone but the body-soul union that constitutes the image of God in man. John Paul is the first Pope to teach that the body, too, shares in the image of God in man.

Obstacles to Experiencing the Nuptial Meaning • The nuptial meaning of the body has been obscured by the Fall, and as a result we often have great difficulty experiencing it. With extraordinary depth and originality, John Paul analyzes the way in which a man looks lustfully at the body of a woman and is attracted to it, yet without understanding its nuptial meaning. The body of the woman ceases to be expressive of her as person and to invite the man to spousal love. In this lustful looking, men see women — and in an analogous way women see men — as objects of con-

sumption rather than as persons to be loved in a spousal way; their look violates the personal selfhood of the other and ignores the fact that each other person is "an enclosed garden," "a fountain sealed" (expressions taken by John Paul from the Song of Songs 4:12 and applied to men and women as persons).

Women feel shame in the presence of the concupiscent look of men. Inspired by Max Scheler's study of shame, John Paul shows that there is a noble sexual shame that is a kind of "personalist instinct" whereby women protect themselves from the aggressive, concupiscent sexuality of men. His idea is that when a woman realizes she is an object of male lust, she naturally tries to subdue all that could be sexually provocative about her appearance, not because she fears or despises her sexuality, but because she wants to defuse the male concupiscence that she feels threatening her. The same woman who knows how to feel this sexual shame will have no difficulty revealing herself to the man who loves her, for he will know how to look at her so as to see the mystery of her person in her body. Of course there is also male shame, which is in many ways analogous to female shame, but John Paul gives particular attention to the shame of the woman.

It is on this basis that John Paul gave his famous Wednesday audience address of October 8, 1980, in which he provoked a firestorm of ridicule in the international press by saying that the "adultery in the heart" condemned by Jesus in the Sermon on the Mount *can be committed even by spouses within marriage*. Though some were astonished by this claim, it follows in the most obvious way from his personalistic theology of the body.

The mere fact that a man and a woman are married does not by itself make the nuptial meaning of the body evident to each of them, nor does it prevent them from looking at each other with the look that seeks selfish gratification. The most depersonalizing concupiscent looking may dominate the intimate relations of spouses; in this case, they desire each other in such a way as to do violence to each other, and the fact that they are married does nothing to prevent such violence. John

Paul teaches that marriage is not supposed to be a state of "legalized lust" but rather a state in which lust is overcome by love, and in which the selfish "sex appeal" of the body gives way to the deeper appeal of the nuptial meaning of the body.

Something else also interferes with our experience of the capacity of the body to serve self-donation. Besides the selfish concupiscence of fallen men and women, there is also the modern passion to dominate the world and everything bodily by means of technology. One looks upon the material world, and even one's own body, as nothing but raw material for human devising, as if everything bodily received its meaning from man's intentions. As a result, we become estranged from our bodies, looking at them as objects over against us; we become unable to experience our bodies sharing in our subjectivity, as John Paul puts it; we no longer recognize ourselves as embodied persons; we lose touch with the deep, personal meanings — including the nuptial meaning — that are inscribed in our body even before we act in any way on it.

The Redemption of the Body • In order to retrieve the nuptial meaning of the body from those factors that obscure our understanding of it, John Paul in his theology of the body goes back "to the beginning," that is, back to man and woman as they lived their bodily being before the Fall. This leads him to his profound analyses of the "original innocence" and the "original nakedness" of man and woman.

He says the first man and woman did not experience any shame in their nakedness because each could see in the body of the other the person of the other, and because the attraction of masculinity and femininity stood completely in the service of love. It is not just that they mastered this attraction by strong self-control and made a right use of it by their will; this would express for John Paul too extrinsic a dominion of soul over body. Rather, the person dwelt so intimately in the body that the body expressed to the other nothing but the worth and splendor of the person; bodily sexuality was completely absorbed in the energy of spousal love. With the sin of our first parents, a rupture appeared in the intimacy of the body-soul unity; the body now acquired the capacity to obscure the person as well as to reveal him or her; it could now awaken selfish, consuming desire as well as spousal love; the freedom of original nakedness gave way to the anxiety of feeling shame.

The "redemption of the body," about which John Paul has much to say in his theology of the body, refers to the restoration of the lost integrity of our being. It refers to the reintegration of bodily sexuality and personhood and to the radical "personalization" of masculinity and femininity. The redemption of the body, though it will be consummated in eternity, begins already now in time. Man and woman as they existed in the beginning, and as they will exist in the end, constitute a fundamental norm for men and women living on earth.

John Paul gives much thought to the eschatological aspects of the theology of the body. In reflecting on the fact that there will be no marriage in the world to come (cf. Mt 22:30), he asks whether the masculinity and femininity of the body will also be abolished. He answers that it will not; glorified human bodies will retain their masculinity and femininity, and they will retain their nuptial meaning, even if this meaning will not be lived out in the form of marriage. Here we have one of the keys to John Paul's thought on consecrated virginity. He affirms emphatically that the consecrated virgin does not turn away from his or her body, with all its nuptial meaning. The renunciation of marriage does not lead to a "neutering" of human beings, for the masculinity and femininity of the body and the body's nuptial meaning are more fundamental than marriage and can serve love in other than marital ways.

Contraception • But let us return to the nuptial meaning of the body as it is lived in the marital intimacy of spouses. John Paul teaches that the consummation of spousal love in the unity of one flesh is intrinsically connected with procreation. This is why marital contraception is wrong. The bodily expression of spousal love is so intimately united with possible procreation that whenever it is sterilized *it suffers as an expression of spousal love, which begins to be replaced with selfish us-*

ing. The Holy Father thinks people have such a hard time understanding this because they are so used to treating the body as raw material to be manipulated for human purposes; if they can recover a sense of their embodied personhood, they will learn to see that deep personal meanings are already inscribed in the body, and that among these meanings is a certain inseparability of the unitive and procreative meanings of marital intimacy. John Paul has also made an original use of his theology of the body to advance the Catholic understanding of NFP (natural family planning).

Pope John Paul's theology of the body is an all-important component of his personalism. Many philosophers sound like him in affirming the freedom and self-possession of persons and in affirming the fundamental rights that persons have. Some of them will even follow him in recognizing a higher truth to which our freedom is bound. But only relatively few know how to do justice to our embodied personhood and to the way in which our bodies share in our inner personal lives. With great originality, John Paul has gone further than Christians have commonly gone in appreciating the place of the body in the life of the person, and has done this without any least concession to materialism.

See: Body and Soul; Celibacy, Priestly; Chastity; Concupiscence; Consecrated Life; Contraception; Education in Human Sexuality; Evangelical Counsels; Hierarchy; Human Person; Imago Dei; Lust; Marriage; Natural Family Planning; Natural Law; Original Sin; Phenomenology; Resurrection of the Dead; Sexuality, Human; Women, Ecclesial and Social Roles of.

Suggested Readings: CCC 362-373. John Paul II, *Original Unity of Man and Woman: Catechesis on the Book of Genesis; Blessed Are the Poor of Heart: Catechesis on the Sermon on the Mount and Writings of St. Paul; The Theology of Marriage and Celibacy: Catechesis on Marriage and Celibacy in the Light of the Resurrection of the Body; Reflections on Humanae Vitae: Conjugal Morality and Spirituality.* K. Wojtyla, *Love and Responsibility.* R. Hogan and J. LeVoir, *Covenant of Love: Pope John Paul on Sexuality, Marriage,* *and Family in the Modern World*, pp. 3-62. K. Schmitz, *At the Center of the Human Drama: The Philosophical Anthropology of Karol Wojtyla/John Paul II*, Ch. 4.

John F. Crosby

THEOSOPHY

Theosophy, a term derived from the Greek *theos* (god) and *sophia* (wisdom) and thus meaning "wisdom of god," was used specifically from the Renaissance onward to designate both an epistemology (a theory of the way man knows) and a religious view radically opposed to the tradition of objective knowledge and to Catholicism. It incorporates rather completely the premises and conclusions of early Gnosticism — perhaps the epitome of militant atheism — which flourished in the first centuries of the Christian era. It was transmitted from the start of the Renaissance by hermeticism (i.e., Gnosticism wrapped in Egyptian mythology, according to a series of third-century A.D. documents translated from Greek into Latin in the middle of the fifteenth century), the Jewish Kabbalah, philosophical alchemy (not only a practice but a view of reality asserting man's ability to rule the universe through secret knowledge), and other traditions of occultism, as well as by aspects of that synthesis of much of ancient Greek philosophy, emphasizing an emanationistic and pantheistic view and a mystical epistemology, which is called Neoplatonism.

Theosophy is principally a complex form of pantheistic atheism, that is, a view rejecting the true nature of God and of his creation by obscuring the distinction between the two. It proposes to explain everything on the basis of a supposed direct experience of ultimate reality that reveals the hidden truths and laws of creation.

The term was used by Jakob Boehme (1575-1624), a German thinker sometimes called the theosophist *par excellence* for his exposition of the various versions of the long tradition of pantheistic atheism, especially hermeticism and the Kabbalah. His formulations had great influence on main currents of modern philosophy and culture, in particular German idealism — perhaps already Kant's philosophy but especially the so-called Absolute Idealism of Fichte, Schelling, and Hegel — and on modern comparative studies of mysticism that ignore the truth of God as Creator and the necessary distinction between nature and grace.

In many ways, the Kabbalah is the heart of theosophy, both as its initial source in the Renaissance and, during several centuries after, as the main stimulus for its development. The Kabbalah, from the Hebrew for "tradition," refers to a supposed unwritten tradition of secret knowledge going back to Moses. It was developed in written expositions under that name by some Jewish scholars, especially from the tenth century onward. However, there are elements in the rabbinical tradition going back to sources before Christ that expound the same view: a magico-mystical view, with great emphasis placed on language and numbers as the supposed keys to "salvation" and power over the universe.

The current usage of the word is tied to the teachings and activities of the Theosophical Society founded in New York in 1875 by Russian emigrant Madame Blavatsky (1831-1891) and others. This society and others associated with or derived from it are a manifestation of and a channel for the dominant current of pantheistic atheism in our times. While incorporating most of the esoteric ideas that Boehme in a way crystallized and much of modern philosophy developed, it has adopted fully the parallel epistemology and ontology of Far Eastern Hinduism and Buddhism. The ideas promoted by the various theosophical societies of the twentieth century give perhaps the main theoretical underpinnings and stimulus for the so-called New Age movement.

While the Magisterium of the Church has seldom used the word "theosophy" in condemning erroneous currents of thought, it can be considered as included under the headings of naturalism, pantheism, and other forms of atheism. It seems that many of the ideas condemned by Pope St. Pius X early in this century under the name of Modernism ought to be seen as the ideas of the-

osophy; and many theosophists praised Modernism as being in line with their thought. The Holy Office (now Congregation for the Doctrine of the Faith) acknowledged the word specifically in its reply of July 18, 1919, to the query "whether the doctrines, which today are called theosophical, can be in harmony with Catholic doctrine; and thus whether it is permitted to join theosophical societies, attend their meetings, and read their books, daily papers, journals, and writings." The answer was: "In the negative in all cases."

The *Catechism of the Catholic Church* does not use the term, but it can be considered as treated under the heading of atheism. Theosophy is "theoretical" atheism in the sense that it expounds a theory of atheism; it also promotes a life in accordance with its theory and is therefore not merely academic. It is a "pantheistic" atheism as contrasted with a "nihilistic" atheism in that it conceals its rejection of the true God and his plan for creation with a highly developed discourse about "God," "divinity," "transcendence," "spirituality," etc. It might be classified as "militant" atheism in the sense that it aggressively attacks the foundations and main truths of Jewish and Christian Revelation, as well as the intelligibility of creation as it is commonly understood.

Principal Teachings of Theosophy • The principal teachings of historical and present-day theosophy, contained in a voluminous and eclectic literature, are as follows.

1. First and last, it teaches that Man (considered to be one numerical entity) *is* God (or whatever word is used for ultimate reality). While many theosophists hesitate to say this clearly, others say it bluntly and insistently, while accusing Judaism and Christianity of having covered up and distorted this central truth of the "Ancient Wisdom." All the other propositions of theosophy are means for promoting this *a priori* and voluntaristic decision against God and his plan for creation.

2. Epistemologically, it asserts that the only path to the truth about reality is "experience" defined as direct contact with ultimate reality. Experience is said "to transcend" (meaning, in the theosophist use of the word, "to see the falsehood

of") all normal objective knowledge. This experience is spoken of variously as "enlightenment," "awakening," "remembering," "breaking through," "attaining full consciousness." Perhaps the most sophisticated exposition proposes passing through levels of increasingly "higher" consciousness until full consciousness is reached, probably after a considerable number of reincarnations.

The essence of this "experience" is said to be of "the consubstantially or absolute oneness of everything." Thus it is asserted that distinctions — for example, between God and creation, man and nature, man and animals, man and man, man and woman — are only for the unenlightened masses or are useful for purely pragmatic purposes. In modern expositions, in line with terminology derived from Buddhism and Hinduism, it separates what people think is their identity (the "lower" or "conventional" self) and their real self, reached through experience, which is the self of God. Experience is said to be the way to break through appearances (all normal knowledge attained through reason and Christian Revelation) to reach reality (Man is God).

3. While the absolute oneness of reality is directly or indirectly asserted, it is simultaneously somewhat covered over by expositions of complex theogonies and cosmogonies, advanced as attempts at explaining symbolically the experiences attained by the privileged few and as a concession to the unenlightened masses who hold to the conventional use of the intellect.

These expositions all follow the early Gnostic pattern of emanationistic pantheism: Denying above all the truth of creation "out of nothing" and therefore the reality of God as Creator and the law of God, it proposes Man as an outflowing from God of his very substance. This is posited as a movement by God to know himself, requiring his producing himself as an object. This object is what is called Man or Sophia or Christ or the Buddha. To explain the appearance of individuality, of matter, of evil (all of which, it says, the ignorant masses stubbornly call reality), it proceeds to talk about the "fall" of Man, either as

necessary for God as subject in order to fully know himself as object, or as some fault in God.

The most sophisticated final view presented under the notion of return to God is that of a race of individuals who have finally realized that they are the Man who is God, now understanding himself through them. Theosophists adamantly oppose any personal notion of God and therefore ultimately use the word IT.

4. Theosophy asserts that there is only one religion, the Ancient Wisdom, which theosophy transmits. All particular religions are mere forms of this religion, each provisionally adequate for certain people and certain times. With special emphasis, it says that neither Judaism nor Christianity is any more true than Buddhism or Islam or any of the ancient religions. In fact, traditional Christianity is attacked for being too tied to the previous Jewish religion and its Scriptures, and for having deformed the Christian Scriptures and the true Jesus. Jesus, it says, like the many Buddhas, was a model of "enlightenment," but no more God than anyone or anything else. Theosophy may now be the deepest underlying source of religious indifferentism, that is, the complete relativizing of all religious truth (and all other truth as well).

5. In line with its basic view that individual men and women, sexuality, etc., are illusions or at best necessary temporary evils and that the only true reality is Man, who is God, theosophy (along with the historical currents of thought it has incorporated and promotes) advances ideas of a radical communitarianism. While utopian, these also point to forced programs of socialization controlled by the theosophistic elites. Since particular moral norms are denied stable and universal validity, effectively denied also are such things as the value of individual human life, the family, and the Judeo-Christian sexual ethic. Theosophy at best encourages an undefined and undefinable humanitarianism and a criterion of pragmatic feasibility, which leaves individuals and the masses of people defenseless against power elites.

Many ideas in today's culture have been influenced deeply by or are derived from theosophy and the currents it summarizes and fosters. Some theological currents inside and outside the Catholic Church are also deeply affected by it: for example, the tendency in some theological circles to replace the traditional distinction between the natural and supernatural orders of knowledge with the notion of multiple and unending levels of greater consciousness. Perhaps, too, some ideas of prayer approach the notions of theosophical enlightenment and union. Some currents of moral theology propose notions of conscience and moral norms that border on the theosophist's rejection of all objectivity by identifying subject and object. Lastly, some treatments of the Trinity and Christology appear not unlike the emanationistic symbolism and "divine" notions of man propounded by theosophists; and some expositions of "self-denying" love seem like transliterations of the theosophical and Far Eastern notion of "transcending" (i.e., rejecting) the common view of self in favor of the realization that the real self is the Self that is God.

See: Agnosticism; Atheism; Buddhism; Creation; Freemasonry; Gnosticism; God, Nature and Attributes of; Hinduism; Knowledge of God; Modernism; Neoplatonism; New Age.

Suggested Readings: CCC 29, 285, 2123-2128, 2140. Pius IX, *Syllabus of Errors.* Leo XIII, *On the Restoration of Christian Philosophy, Aeterni Patris.* St. Pius X, *On the Doctrine of the Modernists, Pascendi Dominici Gregis.* Sacred Congregation of the Holy Office, *Condemnation of the Errors of Rosmini-Serbati, Post Obitum.*

Lawrence A. Kutz

THOMAS AQUINAS, THOUGHT OF

St. Thomas Aquinas (1224 or 1225-1274), doctor of the Church, philosopher, and theologian, is regarded as one of the intellectual giants of all ages. Although St. Thomas was primarily a theologian, his philosophy is universally studied by both Christian and non-Christian. This entry concerns primarily his philosophy. The influence of his theological thinking is noted in entries throughout this volume.

The Church has long recognized that philosophy either opens one to the Catholic faith or closes it as an intellectual option. Among the philosophies that open to the faith, none has better withstood the test of time than that of St. Thomas. In his lifetime, he was consulted by the papacy of his day, and his philosophy has been recommended by nearly every Pope since his death. It is recommended not only for its intrinsic depth and its consistency with the faith but also for its congruence with common sense and with modern science.

From the time of the Church Fathers, it has been acknowledged that natural wisdom is important not only for the defense of the faith but for an understanding and development of the truths contained within Divine Revelation. If philosophy, for example, were to teach truly that there is no evidence for the existence of God and that the whole of reality is material reality, then the teachings of Christ and his Church would have to be reinterpreted from that point of view in a purely secular way.

Without a rational foundation or support in reason, the acknowledgment of the existence of God becomes simply a matter of belief, gratuitously adopted. Acceptance of a creating, all-powerful, and benevolent God, the Alpha and Omega of the universe, would then become an unverifiable assumption, an intellectual crutch for those not willing to face up to an account of the human race that places it wholly within nature. And, where materialism is accepted as true, the teachings of the Church are usually interpreted as a kind of poetry: They are regarded as providing an occasional uplifting insight into human nature and a moral message, but not as teachings to be taken literally. This has consequences not only with respect to the way we view Christ and the Church but for morality and culture.

For such reasons as these, then, the Church not only has stressed the biblical sources of the faith and centuries of theological discussion but has placed a heavy emphasis on the study of philosophy for its role in the defense of the faith.

The Philosophy of Realism • Technically, the philosophy of St. Thomas is known as a "realism," as distinguished from philosophies called by names such as idealism, pragmatism, empiricism, and positivism. A key feature of realism is the conviction that things are the way we perceive them to be; things have structures or natures that control our thinking about them. Realism affirms that ideas are derived from, and our judgments are based on, things independent of the mind. Our thoughts are not mere conceptual schema that we for convenience impose on nature in a subjective manner. St. Thomas did not initiate this way of thought, but he did much to refine its basic tenets.

The theology of St. Thomas reflects a thorough acquaintance with Sacred Scripture and with the writings of the Church Fathers. In his philosophy, he is heavily indebted to the classical philosophy of Greece and Rome. In the course of his teaching at the fledgling University of Paris, he commented on most of the major works of Aristotle, interpreting and developing the thought of his master, whom he called "the philosopher." Aristotle reasoned to "a self-thinking intellect," "a *summum bonum*," "a first efficient cause." His analyses of human nature, of man's quest for happiness, and of the means for the acquisition of virtue were appreciated by St. Thomas, as they are by students in every age. St. Thomas made use of numerous Aristotelian distinctions as he developed a theological understanding of the Gospels and their implication. Thus we have a school of contemporary thought that bears the name Aristotelian/Thomistic.

St. Thomas also drew heavily on Latin authors, particularly Cicero and Seneca, in developing a theory of morality, law, and society, and on the Arabic commentators, principally Averroës and Avicenna. He also had a great respect for the Jewish thinker Rabbi Moses Maimonides. Important as these authors were to him, his theology was grounded primarily in the Fathers of the Church, especially St. Augustine, whom he quoted more than any other author.

St. Thomas shows clearly the compatibility of faith and reason. He stands within an intellectual tradition older than the Church itself. He is read for the natural wisdom contained in his many works, for in employing Greek and Roman cat-

egories of thought he added to them. Even more importantly, he is read for the light he continues to shed on the Catholic faith itself.

The principal works of St. Thomas include his *Summa Theologiae*, the *Summa Contra Gentiles*, the *Quaestiones Disputatae, De Veritate, De Anima, De Potentia, De Malo,* and his commentary on the *Sentences* of Peter Lombard. His philosophical legacy includes contributions to metaphysics, philosophical psychology, the philosophy of nature, political theory, and ethics.

St. Thomas is famous for the often cited "five ways" he offers in evidence of the existence of God. These are, in fact, a summary of the then-common ways of approaching God as prime mover, first efficient cause, first necessary being, self-existent being, and ultimate final cause. The five ways do not directly conclude to God's existence; rather, they generate a line of argument leading to what everyone recognizes as an appropriate predicate or aspect of divine being. Thus, having shown the existence of a prime mover, St. Thomas can say, "and this everyone understands to be God" (*Summa Theologiae*, I, q. 2, a. 3).

Knowing and Willing • From considerations of human knowing, St. Thomas shows the difference between sensory and intellectual cognition and between knowing and willing (*Summa Theologiae*, I, q. 14, aa. 1-6; I, qq. 84-89). Whereas sense knowledge is always particular and of the material aspects of things, intellectual knowledge is always of the abstract, universal, and immaterial. St. Thomas concludes from this that the human intellect is immaterial by nature and in principle capable of existing apart from matter.

The intellect is but one faculty of an immaterial soul; the will is the other. What we call the "will" is rational appetite, the power to choose goods presented not simply by the senses but by intellect as well. Those goods may be absent, abstract, or available only in a distant future, but the intellect is capable of considering them, with consequences for choice. In the presence of an unqualified good, the will responds of necessity in a positive manner. But no terrestrial good is unqualified. Human freedom, however, lies in how we allow things to be presented to us. We can manipulate our thought in such a way that a limited good appears as the unqualified good. The child may knowingly pilfer his mother's purse to buy a sweet, putting aside the impropriety of the act by concentrating only on the sensual pleasure. Thus, St. Thomas's analysis of the powers of the soul leads him to affirm the necessity of virtue, both intellectual and moral.

A virtue is simply a good habit (*Summa Theologiae*, I-II, qq. 49-54). There can be good habits of intellect and good habits of the will. Mathematical and linguistic aptitudes, for instance, are evidence of intellectual virtue, as is scientific knowledge of any sort. To behave virtuously, one needs not only a knowledge of what is fitting or suitable but also a habit of right choices. In the moral order, the ancients identified four cardinal virtues — that is, justice, prudence, temperance, and fortitude — and St. Thomas incorporates these into his moral philosophy. The virtue of religion, for example, is identified as a species of piety, one manifestation of the virtue of justice whereby we pay what is due: in the case of religion, our debt to God.

St. Thomas's reflections on human nature cohere with his thoughts about nature as a whole. The inanimate, vegetative, sensory, and rational are distinguished. All material reality is composite in character, consisting of matter (that which is determined) and form (that which makes the thing to be what it is). The form of a living material substance is called a soul. St. Thomas distinguishes between vegetative, sentient, and rational souls. Only man has a rational soul; and, because of its immaterial character, discerned from an analysis of human knowing, St. Thomas reasons that it is capable of existing apart from matter. Thus the immortality of the human soul, taught as part of the Creed, makes sense from the standpoint of natural reason.

Aquinas on Science • One important area of St. Thomas's thought, surprisingly relevant, is sometimes neglected. In discussing Aristotle's doctrine of abstraction and causality, St. Thomas has some valuable things to say about the nature of science (cf. *Commentary on the De Trinitate of Boethius*, Questions V and VI). As Aristotle taught, to understand something fully, one needs to know its essence or nature, that is, its material and formal causes, its source, and its purpose. Science, in St. Thomas's analysis, consists not simply in description but in knowing why things behave the way they do. Controlled observation and measurement are not ends in themselves. If gold is malleable, is of a certain hue, and resists corrosion, there is a reason why. To give the reason why is to establish the cause. The ancients knew well the properties of many substances, but failed to explain why those substances behaved as they do. It was left to modern science to explain why, for example, copper conducts electricity, expands when heated, is a relatively soft metal, and enters readily into combination with certain elements and not others.

St. Thomas, like Plato and Aristotle, recognized that all science is of the permanent, that is, of the universal. Though the sciences study particular things, they are not interested in the particular but in what all things of a certain kind, or class, have in common. There is no science of the particular. Nature is such that one can go from an experience of some members of a class to assertions that pertain to the class as a whole. One does not, for example, have to experience all copper to know what copper is. Thus observation can give us laws of nature that are unvarying from time to time and place to place. It is the business of the natural sciences not only to record and formulate laws of nature but to give an explanation of the phenomena those laws report by establishing the mechanisms in nature responsible for them.

St. Thomas recognized that not all science is of the same sort. The intellect's ability to abstract from the particular makes possible the natural or physical sciences. Its further ability to abstract from all but the quantitative features of the material object gives us mathematics and the possibility of mathematical physics. A third type of abstraction enables the intellect to prescind from all individual differences so as to consider what the object has in common with the whole of reality, namely, existence and the characteristics that pertain to existence.

Thus St. Thomas's analysis of change leads him to the conviction that the things of experience are contingent and ultimately dependent for their very being on self-existent being, namely, God. God is known through natural wisdom as the explanation of things that do not exist of themselves.

St. Thomas's philosophy allows him to predicate many attributes of God. Perfections found in a limited way in many are affirmed of God in an unlimited way (*Summa Theologiae*, I, q. 13, a. 2). Thus St. Thomas can speak of God's intellect and will, of his goodness, power, providence, and love, while at the same time denying that these perfections exist in God as they exist in man. They are said to be predicated in an analogous manner. Their meaning is partly the same, partly different. St. Thomas thus avoids the dual pitfalls of univocity, which would affirm "intellect" of God in the same way as it is found in man (a position leading to an anthropomorphism), and equivocity, which would deny that man is in any way similar to God (a position leading to agnosticism).

Natural Law • St. Thomas, with Aristotle, recognizes that man is a social and political animal (*De Regno*, I-14; *Summa Theologiae*, I-II, qq. 90-97). He is born into and is shaped by a culture. He lives under laws adopted by a community that, when functioning properly, seeks the common good. Here St. Thomas's conviction that nature is the handiwork of God leads him to affirm that we can determine from considerations of human nature what is suitable for man, whether taken individually or in community. Aquinas, like Aristotle, recognizes that there are certain constants in human behavior and that these can be identified. These constants are the grounds for those normative enunciations that remain the same from generation to generation or, for that matter, whenever and wherever man is found. This is the basis of his famous doctrine of natural law.

It should be clear that not everything legislated or determined to be law by a lawgiver is in fact to be treated as law. There is a distinction between moral law and civil law, and Aquinas will not give the moral force of law to enactments that clearly fly in the face of reason and experience.

St. Thomas takes for granted the compatibility of individual and community interests. Each contributes to the vitality of the other. Community does not imply holding everything in common, but it does depend on the recognition that certain goods ought to be preferred. Acknowledgment of a hierarchy of communal goods does not conflict with the recognition that individuality is the wellspring of initiative, enterprise, and responsibility. An individual's autonomy is seen as a condition for the cultivation of goods such as study, reflection, recreation, and intimacy, all important. A community is not diminished because its members cordon off certain areas of their lives. Rather, a group is strengthened by the goods that its members return to it as a result of their individual pursuits and by their participation in heterogeneous but noncontradictory communities. Community is not a total unity but rather a harmony of complementary interests.

A communal interest that can easily be overlooked is what may be called "the spiritual common good." The prince (today of course we say "the state") from his own viewpoint has a stake in the success of those structures that contribute to man's well-being as a thinking and choosing agent. Conversely, the prince must be careful not to aid and abet social forces inimical to the pursuit of personal moral virtue.

Given St. Thomas's wide-ranging intellect, there is hardly any area of life or knowledge that he did not treat, at least implicitly. The natural wisdom he inherited and advanced by his philosophical work was nevertheless always a preamble, to be perfected by his theological endeavor.

Because human nature is constant and because the basic requirements for human fulfillment do not change, St. Thomas's writings are of perennial value in the social order. Given the truth and consequent strength of his metaphysics, a metaphysics that leads us to a knowledge of God and of man's relation to God, his writings will forever be important, not only for the discipline of theology, but for the development of one's spiritual life as well.

See: Atheism; Augustinianism; Authority; Cardinal Virtues; Common Good; God, Nature and Attributes of; Knowledge of God; Natural Law; Patrology; Politics; Rationalism; Science and the Church; Seminary; Thomism.

Suggested Readings: St. Thomas Aquinas, *Summa Theologiae*, trans. Fathers of the English Dominican Province. É. Gilson, *The Christian Philosophy of St. Thomas Aquinas*; *History of Christian Philosophy in the Middle Ages.* J. Maritain, *St. Thomas Aquinas: Angel of the Schools.* R. McInerny, *Aquinas on Human Action: A Theory of Practice.* J. Weisheipl, *Friar Thomas D'Aquino: His Life, Thought and Works.*

Jude P. Dougherty

THOMISM

"Thomism," sometimes called "Neo-Thomism," refers to the doctrine of St. Thomas Aquinas (1224 or 1225-1274) as developed by modern disciples.

Since his death, Thomas has never ceased to be read, but his thought assumed new importance in the nineteenth century as the Church was forced to combat a wave of modern philosophy inimical to the Catholic faith. Various forms of empiricism and positivism, with roots in both Great Britain and the Continent, resulted either in an outright materialism that denied the existence of God or in an agnosticism that placed God beyond the range of human knowledge. For the Catholic mind, however, the truths given in Revelation complement those attainable by natural reason. Belief makes sense because there is evidence that God exists and that his nature is such that Revelation is credible.

In an effort to combat the emerging materialisms and skepticisms then dominating Europe, Pope Leo XIII urged the study of St. Thomas, in a now-famous encyclical, *Aeterni Patris* (1878). St. Thomas was recommended both as a philosopher and as a theologian, but Leo recognized that philosophy can only be fought by philosophy.

The Thomistic Movement • Although Pope Leo did not initiate the Thomistic revival, his encyclical gave impulse to a fledgling movement, and scholars throughout Europe and the Americas responded to his call. Institutes launched during his pontificate quickly became important centers of learning.

A roll call of the major scholars associated with the movement would be a lengthy one indeed. Prominent among the early contributors to the movement were faculties led by Désiré-Joseph Mercier at Louvain, Belgium, and Edward A. Pace at the Catholic University of America. The movement's almost worldwide character is noticeable from the very names of those who contributed to it: Pierre Mandonnet, Martin Grabmann, Carnelio Fabro, Reginald Garrigou-Lagrange, Leo Ward, Fulton J. Sheen, Gerard Smith, Anton Pegis, Louis DeRaymaeker, and legions of others, not to mention many still contributing.

Perhaps the most outstanding and influential of the movement's twentieth-century proponents were Jacques Maritain and Étienne Gilson. Both exercised considerable influence on Catholic higher education in North America. For at least three generations, many students enrolled in Catholic universities studied philosophy by means of the original works and commentaries of these two giants.

The essence of Thomism is its respect for antiquity and the timelessness of basic truths regarding nature, knowledge, and God. Marked by the dual confidence that nature is intelligible and that the human intellect is capable of ferreting out the secrets of nature, Thomism is at once compatible with prescientific knowledge — "common sense" — and with contemporary scientific inquiry. It insists that God is knowable by reason, apart from faith, that man is a material/spiritual being with a component, the rational soul, capable of surviving death.

Further, Thomism subscribes to a doctrine of free will that holds man responsible for his actions, as opposed to a philosophical determinism that places the emphasis on external circumstances. It incorporates a theory of natural law with emphasis on the rational character of law and the importance of personal moral virtue for family and civil life.

Thomists have made major contributions to many areas of philosophy, principally to metaphysics and philosophical anthropology, but also to social and political philosophy, to the philosophy of science, and to the philosophy of art. Because of the perennial philosophical issues it confronts, Thomism values in a special way the history of philosophy. Convinced that the ancients, no less intelligent than we, have something to say across the ages about an unchanging human nature, it values ancient reports and commentaries thereon. This sets it apart from recent trends in Anglo-American and continental philosophy, such as analytic philosophy, pragmatism, and various forms of Continental existentialism and subjectivism, which ignore the history of Western thought.

Instruction from a Thomistic point of view is especially valued by those who desire to deepen their knowledge of the Christian faith. The study of St. Thomas provides the Christian with a host of distinctions, precisions, and definitions that enable him to clarify and interpret the faith as given in the Gospels and as developed by the Fathers and doctors of the Church. It also provides the believer with intellectual tools to combat the materialism and agnosticism of the dominant secular culture.

Important journals that provide forums for the discussion of Thomism include *The Thomist, The Modern Schoolman*, and the *American Catholic Philosophical Quarterly*.

See: Agnosticism; Atheism; Freedom, Human; God, Nature and Attributes of; Human Person; Knowledge of God; Natural Law; Rationalism; Science and the Church; Seminary; Thomas Aquinas, Thought of.

Suggested Readings: J. Collins, *Three Paths in Philosophy*. É. Gilson, *The Christian Philosophy of St. Thomas Aquinas; Thomist Realism and the Critique of Knowledge*. G. McCool, S.J., *Nineteenth-Century Scholasticism: The Search for a Unitary Method; From Unity to Pluralism: The Internal Evolution of Thomism*. L. Shook, C.S.B., *Étienne Gilson*.

Jude P. Dougherty

TRINITY

Jesus Christ's revelation of God as Trinitarian is taken for granted today, but at the time it posed a serious problem for Jews and later gave rise to considerable disagreement among Christians. For the Jews, steeped in a centuries-old tradition of monotheism, Jesus' claim of divinity, not to mention his references to the Holy Spirit, could sound only heterodox (a return to the polytheism from which the Jews had so long struggled to extricate themselves) or blasphemous. Hence, his claims that "I and the Father are one" (Jn 10:30) and "Truly, truly, I say to you, before Abraham was, I am" (Jn 8:58) provoked attempts to stone him. The issue from the Jewish point of view is nowhere more dramatically displayed than in the Gospel of John, where Jesus heals the paralytic on the Sabbath: "And this was why the Jews persecuted Jesus, because he did this on the sabbath. But Jesus answered them, 'My father is working still, and I am working.' This was why the Jews sought all the more to kill him, because he not only broke the sabbath but also called God his Father, making himself equal with God" (Jn 5:16-18).

Christians accepted Jesus' revelation of God. They baptized "in the name of the Father and of the Son and of the Holy Spirit" (Mt 28:19) and they prayed that "the grace of the Lord Jesus Christ and the love of God and the fellowship of the Holy Spirit be with you all" (2 Cor 13:14). Over time, however, the need arose to understand more precisely just what these triadic formulas mean. It was then discovered that not everyone thought they mean the same thing. A few hardy souls supposed Christ to have revealed that there are three gods (tritheism). More serious was the view known variously as Sabellianism, Monarchianism, Patripassianism, or modalism, which was based on the supposition that Father, Son, and Holy Spirit refer not to real distinctions within God but simply to different ways, or "modes" (hence the name modalism), in which God relates to us. As our Creator, he is called Father; as our Redeemer, he is called Son; as our Sanctifier, he is called Holy Spirit. The most serious threat to the Church's faith was Arianism, also known as Subordinationism, the view that only the Father is God, while Jesus Christ is a mere creature, superior to us in the grace and prerogatives he enjoys from the Father, but nevertheless inferior to the Father. So persuasive was the Arian position that St. Jerome would later remark, "One day the world woke up to find itself Arian."

The fourth-century councils of Nicaea (325) and Constantinople I (381), called to combat Arianism, produced the Nicene-Constantinopolitan, or simply Nicene, Creed. This creed declares Jesus Christ, in contrast to the Arian view that he is a creature, to be "God from God, Light from Light, true God from true God, begotten, not made." It also specifies that the Son is *homoousious* (of the same substance) with the Father, a direct refutation of the Arian belief that he is *homoiousios* (of a similar substance) to the Father. This same Creed declares the Holy Spirit to be "the Lord and giver of life, who proceeds from the Father and the Son. With the Father and the Son he is worshiped and glorified."

The Dogma of the Trinity • The dogma of the Trinity is made up of three crucial elements.

First, God is one substance or being *and* three Persons. There is only one God because there is only one divine substance. The three Persons constitute one God because each is consubstantial with the other two, that is, each fully possesses one and the same divine substance. Hence, the Church rejects tritheism, the belief that the three Persons are three different gods.

Second, the Father, the Son, and the Holy Spirit are three distinct Persons within the godhead. Because all three possess the fullness of the divine substance, all three are coequal and coeternal. They are distinct from one another, in that each possesses the fullness of divinity in a way different from the other two, but they are inseparable from one another, inasmuch as they share the same

divine substance or being. Hence, the Church rejects both modalism and Arianism, which considers God to be undifferentiated unity within himself.

Third, the word "Person" with regard to the Trinity is a technical term designating three distinct subsistent relations within the Trinity: paternity (the Father), filiation (the Son), and passive spiration (the Holy Spirit). These three relations are rooted in the two acts or "processions" that make up the inner life of the Trinity. The first procession is that by which the Father eternally begets the Son; the second that by which the Holy Spirit is spirated by (proceeds from) the Father and the Son. The Persons of the Trinity are therefore differentiated from one another by virtue of the different relations they have to one another.

Many theologians have pointed out that, despite the dogma of the Trinity, most Catholics tend to ignore the differentiations within the godhead, either by treating only the Father or the Father and the Son as God (and ignoring the Holy Spirit altogether) or by treating the Father, the Son, and the Holy Spirit as though they were God in identically the same way. What we have here is a failure to appreciate the hierarchical character of the Trinity.

God As Hierarchy/Patriarchy • Hierarchy has two meanings. The first comes from the two Greek words *hieros* (meaning sacred) and *archein* (meaning to rule). Hierarchy, in this first sense, therefore means a sacred rule or order. The Trinity is a hierarchy or sacred order — for three obvious reasons. First, because each of the Persons is a distinct subsistent relation different from the other two Persons or relations, each Person is unique or singular. Each relation is different from the other two; indeed, each relation is unique because each Person enjoys a different way of relating to the other two Persons and to the divine substance itself. The Father possesses the divine substance *in himself*, the Son *as received from the Father*, the Holy Spirit *as received from the Father and the Son*. Each of the Persons fully possesses the divine substance, but each does so in a different way.

By the same token, each Person enjoys a unique relationship with the other two Persons by virtue of the fact that each is defined by his specific relation. The relation of paternity (the Father) is different from both the relation of filiation (the Son) and the relation of passive spiration (the Holy Spirit). This means that the three Persons, though inseparable, are not interchangeable or identical. The Father can do only those things appropriate to Fatherhood, the Son those things appropriate to Sonship, and the Holy Spirit those things appropriate to passive spiration. The Father, therefore, cannot do anything specifically bound up with Sonship or spiration, the Son cannot do anything specifically bound up with Fatherhood or spiration, and the Holy Spirit cannot do anything specifically bound up with Fatherhood or Sonship. This is reflected, for example, in the fact that the Father always commands, sends, and gives to the Son, whereas the Son always obeys, is sent, and receives from the Father.

Second, the three Persons of the Trinity are ordered to one another by virtue of their relations. The Father is the relation of paternity because he is ordered to the Son as Father. The Son is the relation of filiation because he is ordered to the Father as Son. The Holy Spirit is the relation of passive spiration because he is spirated by the Father and the Son and ordered to them accordingly. The three Persons are not free to choose to enter into any sort of relationship at all; they are defined as Persons by their relationship to one another, a relationship eternally rooted in the twofold procession of the Son from the Father and the Holy Spirit from the Father and the Son. Indeed, so completely are they defined by their relationship to one another that we speak of the circumincession of the Persons, by which they exist not only in distinction from one another but also in some fashion within one another.

Third, the three Persons are totally dependent on one another. Although each possesses the fullness of the divine substance, each is not and cannot be God except in relationship to the other two. Each is incomplete without the other two. This means that, while it is proper to say that the Father, for example, is God, it is not proper to say that God is just the Father.

Hierarchy also means "sacred origin," from the Greek word *arche*, meaning first or beginning or priority. Because the three Persons of the Trinity are coeternal, we cannot speak of the Trinity as having a temporal beginning. But we can speak of an ontological beginning or source of the Trinity. That source is the Father, who begets the Son and who, together with the Son, spirates the Holy Spirit, but who himself is unbegotten or ingenerate. We can speak of the Father, therefore, as the source of everything, including the Trinity itself, for he is, as some of the Church Fathers pointed out, the "unoriginated origin." He therefore enjoys priority within the Trinity (which is why he is always designated as the *first* Person of the Trinity and which also enables us to understand why Jesus tells us that "the Father is greater than I" [Jn 14:28]). Indeed, because the Trinity is a hierarchy or sacred order that has its origin in the Father, we might properly speak of the Trinity as a patriarchal hierarchy or simply a patriarchy.

Importance of the Dogma of the Trinity • The dogma of the Trinity is the central mystery of the Christian faith and the dogma that, above all others, makes the Christian faith unique among world religions. Its significance, therefore, cannot be overestimated.

First, the Trinity is a revelation that ultimate reality is constituted by both unity and plurality. We are not forced, as Christians, to choose between the undifferentiated unity of monism and the plurality of the pagan gods. God is both three and one, a unity of substance that is simultaneously a community of three Persons.

Second, God is a community of love. "God is love" (1 Jn 4:8, 16). This revelation has a twofold significance, for it tells us that God is love in himself and not just in relationship to us, and that love in the godhead is not the narcissism of self-love but love as total self-giving to another. The Father gives all he has to the Son, and the two of them in turn give all they have to the Holy Spirit. Thus are the Son and the Holy Spirit able to possess fully the one divine substance that originates in the Father.

Third, the Trinity is a revelation that personhood is bound up with relationality. To be a Person within the Trinity is to be a relation ordered to another Person or relation. There are no "rugged individualists" in the Trinity. Not even the Father can be known as a Person in his own right, but only in relationship to the Son who makes him known.

Fourth, the Trinity is a revelation of the meaning and significance of hierarchy. The ultimate reality is a sacred order. Hierarchy does not necessarily mean inequality, for the three Persons of the Trinity are both hierarchical and coequal. The opposite of hierarchy, therefore, is not equality; the opposite of hierarchy is anarchy, the absence of order. The hierarchical character of God is the guarantor of the hierarchical or ordered character of creation.

Fifth, although God is eternal and unchanging, he is not static. God's inner life is comprised of those two processions by which the Son is begotten and the Holy Spirit spirated. These processions are eternal and can be expressed only in the present tense, inasmuch as there is no "before" and "after" in God. God is unceasingly dynamic, because his inner life is unceasingly constituted by these two processions by which the three Persons are eternally ordered and related to one another.

Sixth, the two processions within the Trinity are the source of the two Trinitarian "missions" made manifest in redemption. The Father's begetting of the Son is the source for the Father's sending of the Son for our salvation. And the procession of the Holy Spirit by the Father and the Son is the source for the sending of the Holy Spirit by the Father and the Son to the Apostles and to the Church, in order that the grace and truth of Christ might be manifest throughout the world. By these two missions does God continually renew the whole of creation.

Finally, the two Trinitarian missions reveal that, because the Persons of the Trinity are unique and unrepeatable relations, noninterchangeable with one another, so also do they enjoy unique and noninterchangeable relations with us. We do not have simply one relationship with God, we have a threefold relationship with him. By the power of the Holy Spirit, we share in the Sonship of Jesus Christ, thus becoming sons and daughters of the Father, whose plan to bring all things in heaven and on earth into union with himself (Eph 1:10) is revealed and initiated by the Son and brought to completion in the Holy Spirit.

See: Christological Controversies; Eternity; Fatherhood of God; God, Nature and Attributes of; Hierarchy; Holy Spirit; Hypostatic Union; Imago Dei; Jesus Christ, God and Man; Knowledge of God; Mary, Mother of God; Providence.

Suggested Readings: CCC 232-267, 683-716, 2663-2672. E. Forman, *The Triune God: An Historical Study of the Doctrine of the Trinity.* J. Kelly, *Early Christian Doctrines.* J. Newman, *An Essay on the Development of Christian Doctrine.* G. Prestige, *God in Patristic Thought.* J. Ratzinger, *Introduction to Christianity,* Pt. 1, especially Ch. V. J. Sullivan, O.P., *The Image of God: The Doctrine of St. Augustine and Its Influence.*

Joyce A. Little

TRUTHFULNESS

St. John's Gospel tells of Jesus standing before Pontius Pilate and declaring, "For this I was born, and for this I have come into the world, to bear witness to the truth. Every one who is of the truth hears my voice." Pilate cynically replies, "What is truth?" (Jn 18:37-38).

The incident captures the Catholic Church's stance before the modern secular world. In her doctrine, based on Scripture and lived Tradition, the Church offers a body of truths: not guesses, opinions, or viewpoints, but truths. Sometimes people accept these truths, sometimes they disagree, sometimes they yawn with indifference. In an age where all claims to truth are suspect, where my truth may not be yours, however, people whom the Church addresses may well shrug and give some form of Pilate's answer. What, indeed, is the truth when "everything is relative"?

Pope John Paul II felt this issue to be so crucial that in 1993 he issued an encyclical on moral principles entitled *The Splendor of Truth, Veritatis*

Splendor. He says: "The Church has faithfully preserved what the word of God teaches not only about truths which must be believed, but also about moral action, action pleasing to God" (28). The encyclical corrects certain trends in modern theology that question the Church's competence to recognize truth and teach it authoritatively.

The Catholic Church traditionally has taken a "realist" view of truth, basing itself on the philosophy of Aristotle as interpreted by St. Thomas Aquinas. Realists argue, in line with common sense, that truth is conformity of mental images and ideas with what is "out there." If two people see a dog, one might say, "That is a dog," while the other says, "That is a fox." The first statement is true because it conforms to reality; the other is false because it does not.

Besides observing and reasoning about the physical world, one can attain truth by reasoning from abstract principles. The Church has traditionally based much of its moral teaching on natural law theory. The natural law concerns that which is proper to human nature and its fulfillment, and reason can reveal its tenets. For example, procreation plainly is one purpose of sex. It is therefore wrong to use sex only as a source of pleasure or self-expression, which involves choosing and acting against the human good of procreation.

Over the centuries, many philosophers have challenged the realist position. Plato believed the human mind could arrive at truth only by apprehending certain ideas existing in a realm apart from everyday reality. Hume and the empiricists taught that sense impressions alone provide a sound basis for knowledge; one cannot discover truth by drawing conclusions from principles. Pragmatism teaches that an idea is true to the extent that it is useful in reaching a certain goal. Finally, various "postmodern" doctrines generally referred to as deconstructionism hold that statements are so deeply conditioned by the speaker's cultural background that all are partial truths at best and none can claim to have an absolute character or to take priority over the others. There are many truths, not just one.

The Church's realist perspective, reaffirmed in *The Splendor of Truth,* allows her to assert that certain things are true, others false. This provides a rationale for developing a body of doctrine from Scripture and Tradition. Confidence in the human ability accurately to recognize and analyze reality, as well as in God's having willed to disclose aspects of reality to human beings, makes it possible for the Church to propose her teaching as objectively true, provided it is faithful to Divine Revelation.

Religion and Science • Two comparisons between religious truth in the Catholic tradition and truth as modern science understands it may be instructive. Scholars like Stanley Jaki argue that Christianity fostered the rise of modern science, since Christianity and science share similar realist assumptions. The scientific method presupposes that the universe is intelligible, that humanity can, with effort, discover true things about it. The great civilizations of Asia, where philosophical realism did not take hold, never developed the natural sciences as a systematic tool for probing reality.

The second comparison, though less precise, is still worth noting. Karl Popper and others suggest that any scientific assertion must be falsifiable, open to correction. How likely such correction may be depends on the individual case. Einstein's famous formula, $E = mc^2$, seems true for all possible frames of reference, while a particular description of solar physics may be readily subject to revision. Nevertheless, although currently accepted scientific assertions are treated as true in practice, the scientific method itself is a process operating in time, always seeking a more adequate explanation of physical phenomena.

The Church for her part defends the truth of her doctrine in every age, but recognizes at the same time that no merely human formulation of the content of Revelation is exhaustive; therefore she seeks constantly to grow in understanding the truth she holds and professes. Thus, while religion lacks the self-correcting mechanisms built into experimental science, Catholic doctrine does "develop" over time, as Cardinal Newman's 1845 *Essay on the Development of Christian Doctrine* explained and the Second Vatican Council confirmed. "This Tradition that comes from the apostles makes progress in the Church, with the help of the Holy Spirit. There is growth in insight into the realities and words that are being passed on. . . . Thus, as the centuries go by, the Church is always advancing towards the plenitude of divine truth, until eventually the words of God are fulfilled in her" (*Dogmatic Constitution on Divine Revelation, Dei Verbum*, 8).

The substantive similarities between religion and science do not negate their profound differences, most obvious among them the fact that each is competent in respect to a different body of truths. Indeed, "truth" in Scripture has a meaning radically different from its meaning in the realist tradition we have been tracing.

Truth in the Bible signifies especially fidelity to the covenant between God and Israel and, later, between God and all of humanity. To "live in the truth" is to realize that human beings are God's creatures; that Jesus Christ has redeemed us by his selfless sacrifice; that, under the guidance of the Holy Spirit, we are to act so as to have eternal life. The truth of Christ is the ultimate truth, because it is God's self-revelation and because it contemplates humanity in its spiritual and physical reality, that is, our source, the meaning of our lives, and our final destiny.

The Church teaches the spiritual realities we are to believe: that God is three Persons in One, that Jesus is really present in the Eucharist, and so on. It also serves as a guide to human behavior, delineating the "ought" as well as the "is." This doctrine's ultimate foundation is divine self-revelation in the Person of Jesus Christ, who said, "I am the way, and the truth, and the life; no one comes to the Father, but by me" (Jn 14:6). This Revelation is transmitted to us in the Scriptures and in the unbroken two-thousand-year-old Tradition that is the life of the Christian community, its saints, spirituality, councils, and teaching.

Requirements of Truthfulness • Given the Catholic view of truth, both revealed and discovered by reason, what is required of the truthful Christian? The *Catechism* (2467), quoting the

Decree on Religious Freedom, Dignitatis Humanae, 2, says: "It is in accordance with their dignity that all men, because they are persons . . . are both impelled by their nature and bound by a moral obligation to seek the truth, especially religious truth." This statement brings to mind Polonius's famous advice to his son in *Hamlet* (I, iii, 82-84): "This above all: to thine own self be true, / And it must follow, as the night the day, / Thou canst not then be false to any man."

Truthful people must avoid self-deception, being honest with themselves about their motives, their actions, and the consequences thereof. "But be doers of the word, and not hearers only, deceiving yourselves" (Jas 1:22). Of all the demands of truthfulness, this may be the most difficult, because it is the most subtle. How easy it is to tell ourselves we are acting on principle, when our real motive is pride or envy or anger! How easy to convince ourselves we are in love, only to walk away when our partners no longer satisfy. How easy to drown conscience in rationalization or sentimentality.

Once conscience is disabled, we cannot be true to God. We therefore risk mouthing empty prayers with an empty heart, since it is not we who pray but some false conception of ourselves. We risk playing at religion as if it were a charade. Finally, we run the terrifying risk of being judged on the last day, not for who we *say* we are, but in naked reality.

Shakespeare says being true to ourselves enables us to be true to others. The virtue of truthfulness requires people to speak and act so as to present themselves accurately to the world, "guarding against duplicity, dissimulation and hypocrisy" (CCC 2468). Truthfulness involves much more than not lying when asked a direct question. It takes in a range of clear-minded habits: straightforwardness, sincerity, openness, candor, earnestness, even purity of heart. Truthful Christians are as they seem. They treat others honestly as a matter of justice and of love.

The *Catechism* (2469) quotes a classic defense of honest behavior as stated by St. Thomas Aquinas in his *Summa Theologiae* (II-II, 109, 3 ad 1): "Men could not live with one another if there were not mutual confidence that they were being truthful to one another." If one could not trust the doctor to treat all patients fairly, or the homebuilder to use sound materials, or the judge to refuse bribes, or the teacher to prepare lessons carefully, or the government to protect life and liberty, society would soon collapse in violent chaos. If Third World nations felt that the United States was trying to impose coercive population policies under false pretenses, the prospect of global community would be a receding glimmer. Trust is an indispensable foundation of the social order.

Such illustrations are quite straightforward. There is truth and falsity; the moral is plain, as in a children's storybook. In fact, however, life routinely presents us with ambiguous situations, and the morality of telling the truth is often not so simple. We have noted our responsibility to treat others with justice and love, but sometimes these duties appear to conflict. The principal calls Mike's mother to say Mike was ejected from class for misbehavior. She talks the problem through with her repentant son. Later, when her husband asks, "Anything special happen today?" she answers, "No." Is this response just? Perhaps not. Is it loving, under the circumstances? Quite possibly. Making that determination would require a rather extensive knowledge of Mike's overall record of deportment, his relationship with his father, and possibly other matters that the mother-wife in the example knows quite well but a general discussion of truthfulness cannot take into account. Again: A police officer knows a pedestrian has been hit by a car and killed. The woman's husband rushes up to inquire and the officer pleads ignorance, not wanting to be the one to crush him. This may perhaps be loving behavior, but it rather clearly is unjust.

Secrets • Secrets so dramatically illustrate the difficulty of always telling the truth that some textbooks on moral theology devote separate sections to them. A frequently used example poses some form of the following dilemma: An armed and menacing man comes to your door and asks the whereabouts of John Doe, whom you know is cowering in the basement. Few if any moralists would suggest that there is a duty to disclose his whereabouts, and virtually all would say there is a duty to withhold that information; but moralists would disagree about whether or not that can be done by lying.

Everyday secrets, by and large, do not involve potential murder victims in our basements. Some secrets we are obligated to keep under most circumstances: for example, the knowledge that a certain friend was once imprisoned. Some we may be obligated to reveal: for example, that an acquaintance intends to embezzle funds. Many secrets, however, are mere matters of convenience. If I admit that the company may transfer me, my wife will be extremely upset and make my life miserable. If I question feminist orthodoxy, my sorority sisters will mock me. If it becomes known that I spent the Vietnam years in Canada, I will not get this job. Yet, keeping any of these secrets might compromise truthfulness, with uncertain moral justification.

If a great many situations are ambiguous in principle, how can we know how to behave? A lively, informed conscience is the Catholic's guide. In *The Splendor of Truth*, Pope John Paul II defines conscience as "an act of a person's intelligence, the function of which is to apply the universal knowledge of the good in a specific situation and thus to express a judgment about the right conduct to be chosen here and now" (*Veritatis Splendor*, 32). In actual experience, a well-formed conscience seems to operate by intuitively grasping, in a manner akin to imagination, the moral "fit" of a given course of action.

The Pope goes on to say: "Although each individual has a right to be respected in his own journey in search of the truth, there exists a prior moral obligation, and a grave one at that, to seek the truth and to adhere to it once it is known" (*Veritatis Splendor*, 34.) Catholics have a serious responsibility to know the Revelation of God in Jesus Christ as conveyed in and through the Church. One studies Scripture and Tradition, and the Christian doctrine deriving from them, not only because knowing the content of the faith is supremely important in itself but also to form one's conscience as a tool for discerning moral truth. Freedom of conscience, then, is emphatically not freedom to create a private, free-floating morality, to "do your own thing." It is freedom to live in harmony with the objective moral order. "If you continue in my word, you are truly my disciples, and you will know the truth, and the truth will make you free" (Jn 8:32).

Thus "the disciple of Christ consents to 'live in the truth,' that is, in the simplicity of a life in conformity with the Lord's example, abiding in his truth" (CCC 2470). In order to do so, Christians must make a decision to believe what God proposes to them in the Scriptures and the Magisterium of the Church. This faith decision is an answer to modern relativism, since by it Christians declare and affirm that some things are objectively true and that truth serves as a guide to moral action.

Their warrant for making this decision is nothing else than God's offer of salvation, presented to them in the quiet of their hearts. According to St. John, a group of disciples once reacted to Jesus' Eucharistic preaching by grumbling: "This is a hard saying; who can listen to it?" Jesus turned to the Twelve, asking if they, too, were skeptical and wanted to leave him. Peter, speaking for the others, replied: "Lord, to whom shall we go? You have the words of eternal life; and we have believed, and have come to know, that you are the Holy One of God" (Jn 6:60-69). It is faith that opens the door to truth — and to wisdom.

See: Absolute Moral Norms; Assent and Dissent; Conscience; Development of Doctrine; Divine Revelation; Knowledge of God; Lying; Magisterium; Mental Reservation; Natural Law; Relativism; Sacred Tradition; Science and the Church; Secrets; Subjectivism; Synderesis; Thomas Aquinas, Thought of.

Suggested Readings: CCC 2464-2570. Vatican Council II, *Declaration on Religious Freedom, Dignitatis Humanae; Dogmatic Constitution on Divine Revelation, Dei Verbum,* 1-10. John Paul II, *The Splendor of Truth, Veritatis Splendor.* G. Grisez, *The Way of the Lord Jesus,* Vol. 1, *Christian Moral Principles*, pp. 390-398.

David M. Byers

U

UNIVERSAL DESTINATION OF GOODS

God created the world both to show his glory and to provide the human race with the various things it needs. Each human person is God's creature and was intended by God to receive his necessary share of created goods. Though the things of the world have, through human institutions, been parceled out into various forms of property, in the last analysis even property rights and the commandment against stealing may give way to the requirements of the universal destination of goods that is God's will in creating.

The concept of the universal destination, however, must be properly understood. In recent centuries, under the impulse of ideologies such as socialism, property rights were denigrated as opposed to God's universal will. This is misleading at best and usually wrong. For the most part God's will in these matters is accomplished through the principle of subsidiarity, whereby individuals are responsible for themselves, families for children and dependents, associations for members, and so forth. A society as a whole or the world community may choose to aid those who are not being served by subsidiary institutions. But private property and subsidiarity of jurisdictions are important, both because they distribute the goods of the earth in a generally just way and because they empower individuals and human groups to play their role in God's creation.

If the universal destination meant a centralized distribution of goods, it would soon lead to totalitarianism. At absolute need, individuals or groups, or even whole societies, may have the right to appropriate property that has been unjustly kept from them and to which they have an immediate

and life-threatening need. But this can only be done if all other moral prohibitions are observed (cf. St. Thomas Aquinas, *Summa Theologiae*, II-II, q. 76, a. 7).

In recent years, the universal destination has also been used to warn about degradation of the environment, which may become, in effect, an unjust appropriation of goods God has also intended for future generations.

See: Common Good; Environment; Preferential Option for the Poor; Property; Revolution; Social Doctrine; Stealing; Subsidiarity.

USURY

In ancient and medieval societies, the taking of interest on a loan was thought to be illicit. Since the time of the ancient Greek philosopher Aristotle, money had been regarded as a medium of exchange. As such, it was consumed in economic transactions, and interest on a loan meant profit on something that, following the exchange, no longer existed, a sin against commutative justice (St. Thomas Aquinas, *Summa Theologiae*, II-II, 78, 1).

Loans, it was assumed, were made to friends for short periods, and money did not have the kind of investment purposes with which it is associated in modern economies. One who lent money could do so because he would not be using it for anything else during a certain period. So even small amounts of interest were regarded as usury, that is, an improper charge for the use.

Thus the teaching of the Fathers, councils, and Popes up to the middle of the fifteenth century condemned the act of taking profit on a loan without just title. And, as a student of the question writes, "This dogmatic teaching remains unchanged. What is a just title, what is technically to be treated as a loan, are matters of debate, positive law, and changing evaluation. . . . But the pure and narrow dogma today is the same as in 1200" (John T. Noonan, *The Scholastic Analysis of Usury*).

In modern economies, it is clear, money has investment uses and is widely productive. The Franciscan St. Bernardine of Siena (1380-1444) was perhaps the first theologian to recognize that time of use had an economic value and, at least in certain cases, might be licitly compensated. St. Antoninus (1389-1459), a Dominican of Florence, seems to have questioned whether Aristotle was correct in saying that money is naturally sterile. Money alone, he said, is sterile, but, combined with knowledge and enterprise, it is fruitful. His *Summa Moralis* examined commerce and banking, and prepared the way for modern notions of interest, which generally regard proper returns on loans taken with just title as fair.

Today, the term "usury" is usually reserved for taking excessive (i.e., unusually high for the economic conditions) interest on a loan because of someone's circumstances: The greed of the lender takes unjust advantage of the weakness or ignorance of the borrower.

See: Commutative Justice; Property; Restitution; Stealing; Universal Destination of Goods.

UTILITARIANISM

This ethical theory was first made popular in the nineteenth century in the writings of Jeremy Bentham and John Stuart Mill. The basic moral criterion, according to utilitarianism, is: Select the action that will produce the best or least bad consequences in the long run for people in general; one should maximize happiness (or well-being) and minimize unhappiness.

There are various types of utilitarianism. All say that one should maximize good consequences or minimize bad ones. But they differ, first, on what to count as a good consequence. *Hedonistic* utilitarianism counts only pleasure as an intrinsic good and only pain as an intrinsic bad. *Ideal* utilitarianism holds that there is at least one object other than pleasure that is objectively and intrinsically good. And *preference* utilitarianism counts as a good consequence the satisfaction of someone's preference, recognizing that preferences will vary among individuals. (Of course the various types of utilitarianism also differ, corresponding to their views on the good, about what to count as a bad consequence.)

Second, *act-utilitarianism* applies the principle of utility (maximize happiness) directly to all actions. *Rule-utilitarianism* applies the principle directly to rules: that is, select those rules whose following will maximize happiness.

Finally, there are still more distinctions among types of utilitarianism, depending on how one answers the following questions. For what subjects should good and bad consequences count, all possible people or only actual people? How should the distribution of the good and bad consequences make a difference (if at all) to one's judgments? Should an action that significantly harmed five percent of the population but significantly increased the average well-being of the rest be performed?

Utilitarianism has several philosophical difficulties — for example, the impossibility of knowing all the consequences of an action and the impossibility of measuring quantities of benefit and harm where essentially incommensurable human goods are concerned. It has been consistently rejected by Church teaching.

See: Absolute Moral Norms; Consequentialism; Deontology; Natural Law; Proportionalism; Teleological Ethics.

V

VENIAL SIN

Both Scripture and Tradition teach that there is a kind of sin that, while far from trivial, is not "deadly" (cf. 1 Jn 5:17; CCC 1854). Such sins do not separate us from the new life of grace or from the love of God (CCC 1855).

These less tragic sins are called venial sins. The word "venial" means forgivable. One can obtain forgiveness for such sins far more readily than for mortal sins, since the one who has committed them remains in the love of God, and so is far more disposed to find forgiveness (CCC 1875).

Sins can be venial for two kinds of reasons. First, the kind of evil act one performs may be less seriously wrong. To speak an unkind word, for example, is surely wrong; but it is not as seriously wrong as mortal kinds of sins, like murder or perjury. Again, one might sin venially even when performing a gravely wrong kind of act, if one's knowledge were so obscured or one's freedom were so hindered that in doing the act one were really not fully choosing to do such an act (CCC 1862).

Venial sins remain significant evils. For they weaken the love of God in one's heart, they impede progress in virtue, and they harm in many ways the peace of Christian life. They merit temporal punishment. Moreover, "Deliberate and unrepented venial sin disposes us little by little to commit mortal sin" (CCC 1863).

Hence the Church urges us strongly to struggle against our venial sins, and to approach the sacrament of Penance for the remission of such sins (CCC 1458; Canon 988.2).

See: Mortal Sin; Penance and Reconciliation, Sacrament of; Sin.

VIATICUM

Viaticum, called "the last sacrament of the Christian" by the *Catechism of the Catholic Church* (cf. 1524), is a Latin term that meant provisions for a journey.

From *via tecum*, which could be loosely rendered "with you on the way," it now refers to the reception of the Eucharistic species by those near death. Viaticum can be administered alone, within or outside of Mass, or in concert with Reconciliation and Anointing, according to the rites promulgated in 1972.

In speaking about Viaticum, the *Catechism* cites John 6:54: "He who eats my flesh and drinks my blood has eternal life, and I will raise him up at the last day," and goes on to say: "The sacrament of Christ once dead and now risen, the Eucharist is here the sacrament of passing over from death to life, from this world to the Father" (1524).

Reception of the Eucharist as Viaticum mysteriously connects both the Jewish Passover and the paschal mystery of Christ. The Jewish Passover includes a sacrificial, saving meal eaten "in haste" in preparation for a journey (Ex 12:11). Jesus fulfills and transforms that Passover into the memorial, saving meal of his passing over to the Father, in which we consume the Lamb who causes the angel of death to pass over us without harm (cf. Jn 13:1, 1 Cor 5:7).

The paschal symbolism of the Eucharist is perhaps clearest when the sacrament is received as Viaticum because the recipient then is most conformed to Christ in his passing over into eternal life.

See: Anointing of the Sick; Death; Eucharist; Last Rites; Last Things.

VICES

Vices are dispositions to commit sins. As repeated good actions produce virtues, dispositions to make good choices, so repeated sins produce dispositions to make bad choices: vices. Thus arise imprudence, injustice, intemperance, and cowardice — vices contrary to the four cardinal virtues.

While sin itself is a positive act, a choice to do this or that for some good or apparent good, what makes the sin a sin, what makes it evil, is its lack of due order toward love of God and neighbor. Sin is not choosing some entity evil in itself, since there are no such things (evil being a *lack* of good in a thing that ought to be there). Rather, sin is choosing to pursue some good, but in such a way as to turn away from God's plan: that is, love of God and neighbor. Thus the adulterer, the thief, even the sinner who envies the grace of others, begins with a love of some good — for example, this or that pleasure — but pursues this good in such a way as to turn away from love of God and neighbor.

Still, one can have a disposition to perform an act with such a lack in it. Choices are not just transitory events. Rather, when we choose we shape our characters in this way or that, and in the case of evil, as in the case of good, that shaping or constitution remains unless we repent. We should examine our consciences for particular sins, but also for vices, the dispositions remaining in us from past sins. Penance and self-denial are needed to reorient such aspects of ourselves unintegrated with the commitment of faith.

See: Capital Sins; Evil, Problem of; Freedom, Human; Penance in Christian Life; Sin.

VOCAL PRAYER

There are three fundamental and distinguishing elements in the Catholic religion: sacrifice, sacrament, and prayer. In sacrifice, we offer something to God, namely, the bread and wine that become the Body and Blood of Christ in the Sacrifice of the Mass; in the sacraments, we receive something from God, namely, the special graces for which each of the sacraments was instituted by Christ; and in prayer we communicate with God in thought, speech, or cultic action.

By vocal prayer is meant any form of prayer expressed in words, whether printed or spoken, silent or vocalized. Words are essential not only for communication among human beings but for giving expression to one's religious sentiments. Indeed, the sentiments or feelings may also be expressed by gestures or in rites and ceremonies, which are often used in the liturgy and the administration of the sacraments. Prayer is therefore an essential element in every religion.

Vocal prayer is also used by private individuals. It may be something that springs spontaneously from the heart or the recitation of a set formula such as the Our Father, a litany, or the Sign of the Cross. Most people begin to pray as children, when they memorize certain formulas of prayer that they never forget.

There are several good reasons why people should make use of vocal prayer: first, the recitation of a prayer formula or the singing of a hymn can readily stimulate devotion; second, the whole person can be involved in the prayer, body and soul; third, the manifestation of religious sentiments in word or gesture can be an inspiration to other persons. For this reason the public liturgical prayer of a community is usually considered to be much more powerful and to give greater glory to God than private vocal prayer.

According to St. Thomas Aquinas in the *Summa Theologiae*, public (or "common") prayer requires three conditions: the use of a formula of prayer approved by the Church, recitation or chanting of the prayer in the name of the Church, and lawful delegation to pray in the name of the Church. These conditions are met, for example, when a community of cloistered nuns chants the Liturgy of the Hours or when a priest or deacon prays the Divine Office in private.

Whether public or private prayer or vocal or mental prayer, it will be an expression of any one of the four religious sentiments traditionally listed: adoration, petition, thanksgiving, or contrition. Pope Pius XII stated in his encyclical *On the Sacred Liturgy, Mediator Dei,* that there should be no opposition between liturgical prayer and private devotions: "Unquestionably, liturgical prayer, being the public supplication of the illustrious Spouse of Jesus Christ, is superior in excellence to private prayers. But this superior worth does not at all imply contrast or incompatibility between these two kinds of prayer. Both merge harmoniously in the single spirit which animates them" (37).

Both forms of prayer are beneficial: liturgical prayer, so that one can pray with the community and in the name of the Church; private or charismatic prayer, so that one can personally communicate with God. Jesus referred to these two forms of prayer when he said: "For where two or three are gathered in my name, there am I in the midst of them" (Mt 18:20); and again, "But when you pray, go into your room and shut the door and pray to your Father who is in secret; and your Father who sees in secret will reward you" (Mt 6:6).

Vocal Prayer Formulas • The formulas used in vocal prayer are expressions of the interior religious sentiments of individual Christians. They are found in the various liturgical books approved by the Church and in the prayer books used by the faithful. The value of these formulas is that they can be used to stimulate devotion or can serve as vehicles for expressing one's religious sentiments.

Certain structured vocal prayers have become traditional in the Church and are used constantly by the faithful: the Sign of the Cross, the Glory Be, the Our Father, the Act of Contrition, the Hail Mary, the Angelus, the Hail, Holy Queen. Other formulas are used frequently in the liturgy: for example, the Confiteor, the Gloria, the Creed, the Agnus Dei, and the responses to the Prayer of the Faithful. Numerous other types of vocalized prayer are used for paraliturgical devotions: the various litanies, the Divine Praises, the Stations of the Cross, the Rosary, etc. The Church exercises great vigilance through the bishops in regard to the approval and use of vocal prayers.

"Whether prayer is expressed in words or gestures, it is the whole man who prays. But in naming the source of prayer, Scripture speaks sometimes of the soul or spirit, but most often of the heart (more than a thousand times). According to Scripture, it is the *heart* that prays. If our heart is far from God, the words of prayer are in vain" (CCC 2562).

There are several important conclusions that follow from the foregoing quotation. First, since the heart is the source of authentic prayer, prayer is best described as "the language of love." Second, even vocal prayer requires a certain degree of attention and devotion. For this, we have the teaching of Christ: "And in praying do not heap up empty phrases as the Gentiles do; for they think that they will be heard for their many words" (Mt 6:7).

The words of St. Teresa of Ávila in *The Way of Perfection* (ch. 15) are very persuasive: "In case you should think there is little gain to be derived from practicing vocal prayer perfectly, I must tell you that, while you are repeating the *Pater noster* or some other vocal prayer, it is quite possible for the Lord to grant you perfect contemplation."

See: Contemplation; Devotions; Liturgy; Liturgy of the Hours; Meditation; Prayer; Prayer of Petition; Religion, Virtue of; Rosary; Sacrament; Worship.

Suggested Readings: CCC 2598-2643, 2697-2704. Pius XII, *On the Sacred Liturgy, Mediator Dei*. K. Irwin, *Liturgy, Prayer and Spirituality*. J. Wright, *A Theology of Christian Prayer*.

Jordan Aumann, O.P.

VOCATION

"To each one of you I say therefore: heed the call of Christ when you hear him saying to you: 'Follow me!' Walk in my path! Stand by my side! Remain in my love! . . . The reason for my mission, for my journey, through the United States is to tell you, to tell everyone — young and old alike — to say to everyone in the name of Christ: 'Come and follow me!' " (Pope John Paul II, Boston, October 1, 1979).

The notion of vocation has been enlarged and enriched by the teaching of the Second Vatican Council and by subsequent reflection. Its Latin root means "to call." It is a concept that should not be ignored by any human person, since by virtue of existence itself man is called, summoned, to a specific destiny by his Creator (cf. Vatican Council II, *Pastoral Constitution on the Church in the Modern World, Gaudium et Spes*, 19). By the very fact of our existence we are called to eternity; and by his life, death, and Resurrection Jesus Christ opened up to everyone the possibility of personal union with God. The enthusiastic proclamation of the Gospel by evangelizers like Pope John Paul II has confirmed the faith of many and brought many others to an encounter with Jesus Christ. In this encounter, men and women become aware of their vocation as sons and daughters of God. This common Christian vocation is further specified through the personal vocation to which each of the baptized is called.

Every creature is unalterably related to its Creator, but God created man and woman with a destiny to eternal communion with himself. While the goal is common to all, each person's path to achieve that goal is quite particular. A person's "vocation" incorporates the entire enterprise of invitation, response, and choice of a specific way of life. It provides the focus both for life's major choices and everyday decisions. This becomes very clear in the light of Revelation. In Genesis, man is called into existence in the image and likeness of God. Later, the call of Abraham by name and his response become the biblical pattern of God's initiative and the ideal response in faith and trust. The Virgin Mary is the most perfect embodiment of the faithful response (CCC 144).

Some qualities of vocation become evident from these examples. A vocation truly does come from God. It is his initiative. But it neither destroys human freedom nor answers every question. Darkness can remain. In fact, the very working out of a vocation depends on the person's free response. The shape and quality of the response have a great deal to do with the uniqueness of each vocation.

Christian Vocation • While the Old Testament reveals God's personal care for man, it is Jesus Christ who definitively reveals the will of God and throws light on the meaning of man's existence and call. Christ is the new Adam, and in "the rev-elation of the mystery of the Father and his love, [Christ] fully reveals man to himself and brings to light his most high calling" (*Gaudium et Spes*, 22). As indicated above, each person is called to become a son or daughter of God in Jesus the Son. This new relationship is based on communion with God in Jesus Christ (Vatican Council II, *Dogmatic Constitution on Divine Revelation, Dei Verbum*, 2; *Gaudium et Spes*, 19) and in his Church, the Body of Christ in space and time (CCC 1). Communion with God, then, is at the heart of every person's vocation. It can rightfully be said that all people are called before the foundation of the world to Christian faith — to be Christians (cf. Eph 1:26). Vatican II's *Constitution on Divine Revelation* succinctly describes God's gracious, salvific call to people: "His will was that men should have access to the Father, through Christ, the Word made flesh, in the Holy Spirit, and thus become sharers in the divine nature." Indeed, he invites and receives all into his company (*Dei Verbum*, 2).

The general call for all persons becomes individualized through the Church and through the concrete circumstances of one's life. Through the word of God proclaimed by the Church and the action of God made present in the sacraments and liturgy of the Church, God touches the heart of every believer. In Baptism, for example, the new Christian is called by name and receives the gift of sharing in God's own life (CCC 2012-2016). Each person is touched by grace and enjoys a personal relationship with God, who is Father, Son, and Holy Spirit.

Those baptized in infancy must one day make a personal response to the call from Christ. The commitment must be renewed throughout life, by each person. The vocation to holiness is none other than striving to fulfill God's will by means of the grace he himself grants to us. This in turn is revealed and effected in Jesus Christ. "[I]f any one is in Christ, he is a new creation; the old has passed away, behold, the new has come" (2 Cor 5:17). Seen more technically, holiness is a result of sanctifying grace given first at Baptism: "The grace of Christ is the gratuitous gift that God makes to us of his own life, infused by the Holy Spirit into our soul to heal it of sin and sanctify it" (CCC 1999). Accordingly, the first response to the Christian's vocation is to follow Jesus (CCC 2232), which means to follow the path marked out by him. The Christian heeds the exhortation "come follow me" because Jesus sums up man's perfect response to God (Pope John Paul II, *The Splendor of Truth, Veritatis Splendor*, 6).

Following Christ is never an imposition; it is a free invitation to discover who we truly are and are called to be. In this pursuit, we must be free collaborators in God's plan (CCC 1731, 2002). Anything but a personally chosen response affronts human dignity. God has first gratuitously chosen us to share communion with him through divine adoption (Eph 1:4; *Dei Verbum*, 2). This is the inner logic of man's creation, and so for him to be most faithful to himself entails a free commitment of self to the One who calls. Rightly, then, does Vatican II's *Gaudium et Spes* indicate that "if man is the only creature on earth that God has wanted for its own sake, man can fully discover his true self only in a sincere giving of himself" (24). This gift of self finds its greatest expression in our most fundamental relationship, which is our relationship with God through Jesus Christ. Self-surrender to God in faith is at the basis of every successful search for vocation. In speaking specifically of priesthood, with clear application to any vocation, Pope Paul VI describes the heart of freedom: "There cannot be vocations unless they be free; that is, unless they be spontaneous offerings of oneself, conscious, generous, total. . . . Freedom reaches its supreme foundation: precisely that of oblation, of generosity, of sacrifice" (quoted in Pope John Paul II, *I Will Give You Shepherds, Pastores Dabo Vobis*, 36).

The universal call to holiness summons all to follow Christ and perfect themselves through their work. "The Church finds in the very first pages of the Book of Genesis the source of her conviction that work is a fundamental dimension of human existence on earth" (Pope John Paul II, *On Human Work, Laborem Exercens*, 4; cf. 25, CCC 2427-2428). Through labor — manual and intel-

lectual activity — man is called to discover himself and his dignity. The first chapters of Genesis use special imagery to recount the original condition of man prior to the Fall. Commanded as he was to be fruitful, multiply, and have dominion over the earth, his life was rooted in labor. The garden was there to be tilled and worked. In freely mingling his effort and personality with the world entrusted to him, he became co-creator in the divine plan without diminishing his utter dependence on the Creator (cf. *Laborem Exercens*, 4). It is not surprising therefore that the fullness of Christian life involves work, wherein those born anew in Baptism as daughters and sons of God freely collaborate in the Father's plan for creation and Christ's work of redemption by helping to build a "civilization of love."

The vocation to holiness grows and flourishes in the household of the Church. People are called not only to communion with God but also to communion with others. The *ekklesia*, the "people gathered by God," is the general sacrament of salvation and communion of men with God and one another (Vatican Council II, *Dogmatic Constitution on the Church, Lumen Gentium*, 1, 9, 51; CCC 542, 959).

The call to holiness is also a call to apostolate (cf. Vatican Council II, *Decree on the Apostolate of the Laity, Apostolicam Actuositatem*, 2). Baptism is the effective call to holiness because through it people are really made holy as children of God and sharers in the divine life (*Lumen Gentium*, 40). The baptismal vocation entails the mission of going into the whole world to spread the Good News of communion with God through Jesus Christ. The Church then is evangelistic by nature. All the baptized share the mission to invite others into communion with God through Christ and the Church, which carries on his mission.

Personal Callings Within the General Call • God's call to holiness does not remain generic. His call is not limited to the silent touch of grace at Baptism. The common Christian vocation to holiness takes specific forms: some permanent, some temporary for each person. Each person receives a special vocation from God that only he or she can fulfill. One of the great tasks of each Christian is prayerfully to discern the path that God intends him to follow. One discovers this path through prayer, prudent advice, and personal reflection on one's own talents. Each person's specific way of living the general call to holiness is mediated by a variety of personal factors, for example, one's natural abilities, one's successes or failures, the people and experiences that affect one's life, the opportunities that are offered and acted upon — or ignored. Once discovered, one's personal path becomes an integral part of one's relationship with God.

Single and married laity, religious, and secular priests live the common Christian vocation in special ways, but each special vocation shares certain elements: It is the Father's choice, it comes from him and is his gift, it derives from the Church, it finds fulfillment in the Church, and it is given as a service to the Church (*Pastores Dabo Vobis*, 35).

This variety of vocations in the Church is an aspect of the divine institution of the Church, by which some become sacred ministers or clerics by sacramental ordination and are distinguished from other Christian faithful or laity. From both groups persons can be called to a life of special consecration and thereby participate in a profound way in the life and holiness of the Church (Canons 204.1, 28; *Lumen Gentium,* 10, 20, 30-33; CCC 871-873).

The vast majority of Christians are lay faithful, in the single and, especially, married states (cf. CCC 871-873). They live in the midst of the ordinary affairs of work and family and social life. The specific vocation and mission of the laity is to sanctify the world by participating in its structures and endeavors (cf. *Lumen Gentium*, 31, 33, 36; *Apostolicam Actuositatem*, 2, 5; *Christifideles Laici*, 15, 36ff.). Christian marriage is a sacrament involving a special way of holiness and service. Those who have received this sacrament are called to serve the mission of the Church through an example of committed love to each other and generous, self-sacrificing commitment to the Christian formation of their family. As a sacrament, Matrimony (or Christian marriage) is a grace-filled encounter with Christ. In its love and commitment, spousal love resembles Christ's own love for the Church in its permanence, fidelity, and fruitfulness (cf. *Lumen Gentium*, 48-52).

Some among the laity forgo marriage for honorable motives (CCC 2231), without becoming consecrated as religious. They may forgo marriage to care for others, to pursue professional excellence, or for some other generous reason. There are in addition special forms of permanent commitment for laypeople, married as well as celibate, through which they dedicate themselves for the apostolic mission of renewing society from within. Participation in certain institutes such as Focolare, Opus Dei, or the Neo-Catechumenal Way, for example, would facilitate that possibility.

The Clerical Vocation • When he founded his Church, Jesus Christ called all the baptized to communion with him in holiness and to share in his mission as priest, prophet, and king. However, to some Christ addressed a special call to shepherd his people, instituting them in a variety of offices (bishops, priests, and deacons) that aim at the good of the whole body (*Lumen Gentium*, 18).

The sacrament of Holy Orders is a constant sign in the Church that it is God who takes the initiative for our salvation through Jesus Christ and the gift of the Holy Spirit. The Church finds expression as the faithful gather around those who are sent by God to proclaim the Gospel and celebrate the sacraments with the power and authority of Christ himself. She does not call herself into existence nor does she gather on her own terms. Neither do those ordained to carry on the mission of Jesus Christ as head of the Church call themselves. Rather, they are empowered by Christ and receive the mandate from those who preside over the Church in his name (CCC 874-896, 1536-1600). But they do this not for themselves but as a ministry of service for Christ and for the Church (CCC 876; *Lumen Gentium*, 24; cf. Rom 1:1, Phil 2:7, 1 Cor 9:19).

"In the Church and on behalf of the Church, priests are a sacramental representation of Jesus Christ . . . authoritatively interpreting his word, repeating his acts of forgiveness and his offer of salvation — particularly in baptism, penance and the eucharist, showing his loving concern to the point of a total gift of self for the flock, which they gather into unity and lead to the Father through Christ and the Spirit" (*Pastores Dabo Vobis*, 15). The special vocation to ministerial priesthood presupposes the universal vocation to holiness, which it reinforces with a new requirement to strive for holiness (cf. Vatican Council II, *Decree on the Ministry and Life of Priests, Presbyterorum Ordinis*, 12). To ministerial priesthood the Latin Church has attached celibacy, in imitation of Jesus Christ the eternal High Priest and as a source of total availability to serve the whole People of God. Furthermore, the sacrament of Holy Orders indelibly signs those ordained to highlight and strengthen with divine grace the permanence of this vocation. Pope John Paul II, in Philadelphia in 1979 on his first apostolic journey to the United States, spoke clearly of the permanent character of the priestly vocation: "It cannot be that God who gave the impulse to say 'yes' now wishes to hear 'no' " (homily to priests, October 4, 1979).

Promoting vocations to the priesthood is a grave ecclesial responsibility (Canon 223; *Apostolicam Actuositatem*, 11; *Presbyterorum Ordinis*, 11, etc.). It is a matter not so much of multiplying programs as it is of inviting men into fuller communion with Jesus Christ and with his Church. Moving more deeply into the mystery of the Church brings the gifts and graces from God that will sustain thriving Christian life in the community. Priests are among those gifts necessary for the life of the Church. As the Church herself, protected by the Holy Spirit, will never founder, so that same Spirit will never fail to call many men to God's service as priests.

It appears that there are common trends within successful seminarian programs. The first entails holding high standards for the priestly vocation and inviting men to measure up to it. This becomes countercultural, insofar as many people do not value the ordained priesthood enough or sufficiently hold up the ideal of a profound personal commitment to living the mystery of Christ's priesthood in and for the Church (cf. *Pastores Dabo Vobis*, 8). Other fundamental elements include a sincere devotion to the Holy Eucharist and a warm devotion to the Blessed Virgin Mary. Attending thoroughly to these basic aspects inspires well-motivated priestly vocations. In addition, an authentic fraternity among these men is generated as they come to common ground in reference to beliefs and spirituality.

Consecrated Life • From early on in the life of the Church, some Christians were inspired to follow Jesus Christ more closely by living more intensely the evangelical counsels commended by the Lord — poverty, chastity, and obedience (cf. *Lumen Gentium*, 44; CCC 914-936). According to the 1994 world Synod of Bishops on consecrated life, the witness of such persons enables the Church to be "an eloquent sign of victorious grace." Their consecrated lives enrich the Church by pointing clearly and effectively to Jesus Christ and to the kingdom of the Father, which is even now breaking forth in the life of the Church. Their total dedication to God's honor contributes to the "upbuilding of the Church and the salvation of the world" (Canon 573; *Lumen Gentium*, 42-44; *Decree on the Bishops' Pastoral Office in the Church, Christus Dominus,* 33; *Decree on the Appropriate Renewal of the Religious Life, Perfectae Caritatis*, 1).

Guided by the same Holy Spirit, Church authority has given an interpretation of the counsels and set stable forms of living that embody them through the approval of institutes of consecrated life: religious institutes, secular institutes, and societies of apostolic life (Canons 573-746). The members of such institutes, by a public consecration to holiness in response to a special divine vocation, are set apart for the service of the People of God. For the most part, they are committed to life in common (Canon 602, *Perfectae Caritatis*, 15). In some cases, this is through a life of prayer and penance in contemplative communities totally withdrawn from the world. Better known to us are those institutes whose members serve in apostolic ministries, such as teachers, social workers, health care providers, parish pastoral assistants, and missionaries.

Sharing the vision of the Second Vatican Council, as it has found rich expression in the life of the Church in succeeding decades, enables Catholics to value other vocations in the Church as well as to value their own. Experience demonstrates that those who tend to undervalue ordained ministry or consecrated life also tend to have a pessimistic view of Christian marriage. A strong, positive embracing of the high calling and genuine value of each Christian vocation fosters the balance and unity that allow the Church to enjoy the peace that is a gift of the Spirit. In the communion of the Church, all have the responsibility to affirm and support one another in their distinct vocations.

The reality of our human condition requires that we acknowledge that some persons fail in pursuit of their special vocations. A marriage partner may depart, or a priest or sister may abandon a freely assumed commitment. The Church with love and honesty holds people to be true to their vocations. Anything less would not be worthy of our trust in God's ever-present grace. At the same time, we trust in the infinite mercy of our Father God. The Church reflects this mercy in her own pastoral care insofar as the truth of our sacred mysteries and the common good of the Church allow.

The Lord Jesus calls each person to discipleship. He calls us by name. All in the Church are invited to share the life of God as adopted daughters or sons. We are called to holiness, but that does not mean that we are all called by the same path. Many are the gifts by which the Lord builds up the Church, all directed to our growth in love (Eph 4:11-16).

See: Apostolate; Baptism; Charisms; Consecrated Life; Discernment; Evangelical Counsels; Holy Orders; Laity; Marriage; Ministry; Seminary; States in Life; Work.

Suggested Readings: Vatican Council II, *Dogmatic Constitution on the Church, Lumen Gentium*, 39-44; *Dogmatic Constitution on Divine Revelation, Dei Verbum*, 2; *Decree on the Apostolate of the Laity, Apostolicam Actuositatem; Decree on the Appropriate Renewal of the Religious Life, Perfectae Caritatis; Decree on the Ministry and Life of Priests, Presbyterorum Ordinis; Decree on Priestly Formation, Optatam Totius*. John Paul II, *The Splendor of Truth, Veritatis Splendor; The Christian Family in the Modern World, Familiaris Consortio; The Lay Members of Christ's Faithful People, Christifideles Laici; I Will Give You Shepherds, Pastores Dabo Vobis; Apostolic Letter to the Youth of the World; Holy Thursday Letters to My Brother Priests; Letter to Families*.

✠ **John J. Myers**

WAR

The Bible sees peace within and among nations as the fruit of a proper relationship with God and as a sign of the coming of God's reign: "[T]hey shall beat their swords into plowshares, / and their spears into pruning hooks; / nation shall not lift up sword against nation, / neither shall they learn war any more" (Is 2:4). Yet early Israel often found itself at war, seeing its own war efforts as ordered by God to protect his people and punish evildoers who rejected his reign.

In the New Testament, Jesus begins a new order based on the inner peace that comes from God's offer of love and forgiveness for all (Jn 16:33). Jesus blesses peacemakers (Mt 5:9) and warns that "all who take the sword will perish by the sword" (Mt 26:52). Yet he knows his own message will bring conflict and division as some refuse to hear it: "I have not come to bring peace, but a sword" (Mt 10:34).

The New Testament does not condemn military service and sometimes speaks of civil authorities as legitimately wielding "the sword" to suppress evil (Rom 13:3-4). Many early Christians nonetheless renounced service in Rome's army, not least because it involved swearing allegiance to an unjust state and its pagan gods. A long tradition of Christian pacifism renounces all recourse to deadly force, in literal adherence to Jesus' example of returning only good for evil even at the loss of one's own life (cf. Mt 5:39, 1 Pt 2:23-24). But the Church has held that those who have others under their care must defend them from attack so that "legitimate defense can be not only a right but a grave duty for someone responsible for another's life, the common good of the family or of the state" (CCC 2265). True peace will never be established simply by force of arms; yet such force may sometimes be necessary to protect the innocent.

The Just War Theory • In the fifth century, when Rome was threatened by barbarian invasions, St. Augustine taught that waging war is sometimes a tragic necessity in a sinful world — "but beyond doubt it is greater felicity to have a good neighbor at peace, than to conquer a bad one by making war" (*City of God*, IV, 15). He outlined moral criteria that were developed by others and accepted by the Church as the "just war" criteria. Their intent is not to justify war but to embody the strong presumption against going to war unless all criteria are met.

First, one must have a just cause, such as the protection of basic human rights or the defense of the innocent from unjust aggression. Second, the use of force must be ordered by a competent and lawful authority with responsibility for the common good. Third, all peaceful means of resolving the conflict must be exhausted; war must be a last resort. Fourth, one must have a "right intention" in seeking to restore order and justice; even those with a just grievance cannot go to war out of hatred or a thirst for vengeance. Fifth, there must be a reasonable probability of success, and the expected benefits must be proportionate to the human and other costs of war.

These criteria relate to what is sometimes called the *ius ad bellum*, or legitimacy of going to war. Two additional criteria affirmed by Catholic teaching relate to the *ius in bello*, or moral limits during war. The first, sometimes called proportionality of means, demands that the degree of force used be reasonable in light of the military goal; one must not needlessly risk lives or cause more harm than one is trying to prevent. The second, known as the principle of discrimination or of noncombatant immunity, forbids targeting civilian populations.

The principle of discrimination is of special importance, because it is simply a restatement of the fifth commandment: Directly taking innocent human life is always wrong. This principle has led Popes beginning with Pius XII to condemn the modern theory of total warfare, which holds that any means necessary to achieve victory may be used. When the Allies engaged in obliteration bombing of Dresden and other cities to terrorize Germany and hasten the end of World War II, Catholic theologians condemned the act. Similar objections have been raised to the use of the atomic bomb on Hiroshima and Nagasaki, because the valid goal of ending the war and saving Allied soldiers' lives could not justify the evil means of directly killing many thousands of noncombatants. Such destruction cannot be defended as the kind of "indirect" killing involved in using the minimum force necessary to defeat an attacking army.

Recent Development • In light of the carnage made possible by nuclear weapons in our time, the Second Vatican Council urged "a completely fresh reappraisal of war" (*Pastoral Constitution on the Church in the Modern World, Gaudium et Spes*, 80). By this the Council did not mean that the just war criteria were obsolete, but that it is far more difficult to fulfill them in the nuclear age.

The Council solemnly reaffirmed the principle of discrimination: "Every act of war directed to the indiscriminate destruction of whole cities or vast areas with their inhabitants is a crime against God and man, which merits firm and unequivocal condemnation" (*Gaudium et Spes*, 80). Recognizing that any war between the major world powers risked a nuclear exchange that could be indiscriminately destructive, the bishops of the world pledged to "spare no effort in order to work for the moment when all war will be completely outlawed by international agreement" (*Gaudium et Spes*, 82).

Thus the near impossibility of respecting the requirements of *ius in bello* in a nuclear war ren-der it increasingly difficult to fulfill the requirements of *ius ad bellum* so as to justify going to war at all. Pope John XXIII said in 1963 that in the nuclear age "it is irrational to think that war is a proper way to obtain justice for violated rights" (encyclical *Peace on Earth, Pacem in Terris*, 127). In modern circumstances, only defense of the innocent from direct attack by an aggressor may constitute a clear "just cause" for going to war.

During the Cold War, the United States and Soviet Union maintained an unsteady peace through nuclear deterrence. Each nation stockpiled nuclear weapons and threatened the other with widespread destruction if it initiated a conflict. The Church objected to this policy on two grounds. First, such a balance of terror is a precarious and dangerous approach that may in fact touch off the devastation it tries to prevent. Second, the huge resources devoted to this arms race are thereby diverted from the constructive and humanitarian efforts that could build the foundations for genuine peace (cf. *Gaudium et Spes*, 81). Modern Popes have said that deterrence can only be justified as a temporary stance leading to mutual disarmament; some theologians have gone further, urging unilateral nuclear disarmament because a policy of threatening indiscriminate destruction is intrinsically evil.

Since the dissolution of the Soviet empire, the Church has continued to apply the just war criteria to new realities and new threats, such as abhorrent modern tendencies to see terrorism or even genocide or "ethnic cleansing" as legitimate means of waging war.

See: Absolute Moral Norms; Authority; Capital Punishment; Common Good; Deterrence; Homicide; Human Life, Dignity and Sanctity of.

Suggested Readings: CCC 2265, 2307-2317. Vatican Council II, *Pastoral Constitution on the Church in the Modern World, Gaudium et Spes*, 77-82. John XXIII, *Peace on Earth, Pacem in Terris*, 109-119. National Conference of Catholic Bishops, *The Challenge of Peace: God's Promise and Our Response*. W. Nagle, ed., *Morality and Modern Warfare*. J. Finnis, J. Boyle, G. Grisez, *Nuclear Deterrence, Morality and Realism*. D.

Hunter, "A Decade of Research on Early Christians and Military Service," *Religious Studies Review* (April, 1992).

Richard Doerflinger

WOMEN, ECCLESIAL AND SOCIAL ROLES OF

The role of women in the Church and in society is based on man's creation in the image of God as male and female (Gn 1:27). This differentiation among human beings according to gender is the only human differentiation created by God as a part of the goodness of creation. Although Adam and Eve, by their disobedience, introduced evil into the world, they did not destroy the fundamental reality of their sexual differentiation; but they did bring about a fallen world that would affect them in ways consonant with that distinction. This is apparent in the consequences God tells them they have brought upon themselves: consequences that are themselves a revelation of the fact that there are distinctly male and female spheres within the order that God has created and will ultimately redeem. The male sphere is that of work in the world, while the female sphere is bound up with being mother and spouse.

"To the woman he said, / 'I will greatly multiply your pain in childbearing; / in pain you shall bring forth children, / yet your desire shall be for your husband, / and he shall rule over you.' / And to Adam he said, / 'Because you have listened to the voice of your wife, / and have eaten of the tree / of which I commanded you, / "You shall not eat of it," / cursed is the ground because of you; / in toil you shall eat of it all the days of your life; / thorns and thistles it shall bring forth to you; / and you shall eat the plants of the field. / In the sweat of your face / you shall eat bread / till you return to the ground, / for out of it you were taken; / you are dust, / and to dust you shall return' " (Gn 3:16-19).

That the woman's role is bound up with the realm of personal relationships is affirmed in the name Eve, which means "mother of the living" (Gn 3:20).

The order of salvation does not destroy the male-female differentiation, but builds on it. The New Covenant is not just Christ, but the marital union of Christ the bridegroom with his bride the Church (Eph 5:31-32). Christ is the "new Adam" and Mary, forerunner and archetype of the Church, is the "new Eve." She, like Eve, is defined as mother — Mother of God (Councils of Ephesus and Chalcedon) and Mother of the fledgling Church (cf. Jn 19:27).

Motherhood and Women • While Scripture tells us to "call no man your father on earth, for you have one Father, who is in heaven" (Mt 23:9), Eve and Mary are named mothers. As Pope John Paul II has noted regarding human parents: "Although both of them together are parents of their child, the woman's motherhood constitutes a special 'part' in this shared parenthood, and the most demanding part. Parenthood — even though it belongs to both — is realized much more fully in the woman, especially in the prenatal period" (*On the Dignity and Vocation of Women, Mulieris Dignitatem*, 18). Motherhood therefore is the key to understanding the role of women both in the Church and in society. Recent Popes have affirmed the importance and centrality of women as mothers. Speaking in 1955 to a Catholic Action women's group, Pope Pius XII observed: "Now the sphere of woman, her manner of life, her native bent, is motherhood. Every woman is made to be a mother: a mother in the physical meaning of the word or in the more spiritual and exalted but no less real sense." And John Paul II has written: "Motherhood implies from the beginning a special openness to the new person: and this is precisely the woman's part" (*Mulieris Dignitatem,* 18). Motherhood is linked in a special way to trust, personhood, and love.

It is important to recognize that, as John Paul II puts it, "Before anyone else it was God himself, the Eternal Father, who entrusted himself to the Virgin of Nazareth, giving her his own Son in the mystery of the Incarnation" (*The Mother of the Redeemer, Redemptoris Mater,* 39). Although Mary's relationships with the Father and Christ are unique, what happened at the Annunciation and at Christmas is significant for every mother, because it brings home in a particularly vivid way the fact that every child, including the Son of God, is entrusted to a woman and can enter this world only by way of a mother. "God entrusts the human being to her in a special way" (*Mulieris Dignitatem,* 30). Trust is rooted in the relationship between a mother and her child. This trust is bound up, however, with far more than conception and birth; it is bound up with the entire well-being of the child and the mature adult he will someday become. Both Eve and Mary were recognized as bringing not just children but *men* into the world (cf. Gn 4:1, Jn 16:21). If Christ is the truth, Mary is the trust, a realm that all women as mothers share with her.

The woman also stands in a special way for the sphere of love. "In God's eternal plan, woman is the one in whom the order of love in the created world of persons takes first root" (*Mulieris Dignitatem*, 29). In the first instance, this means that woman is the matrix of all personal relations. "Of the essence of motherhood is the fact that it concerns the person. Motherhood always establishes a unique and unrepeatable relationship between two people: between mother and child, and between child and mother" (*Redemptoris Mater,* 45). In the second instance, this means that love is indissociable, or inseparable, from woman because it is indissociable from marriage, in which the bride is the one "who receives love in order to love in return" (*Mulieris Dignitatem*, 29), and also indissociable from that entrusting that is bound up with motherhood, because entrusting is "the response to a person's love, and in particular to the love of a mother" (*Redemptoris Mater*, 45).

The woman therefore enjoys a particular aptitude and responsibility for the whole realm of personal relationships on the human level. And she also bears a kind of privileged position with regard to the linking of that human world with the divine realm of personal relationships through the action of the Holy Spirit, inasmuch as it is through both Mary (at the Annunciation) and the Church (at Pentecost) that the Holy Spirit effects the union of those two realms. Thus does Pope John Paul II

insist that "the dignity of women is measured by the order of love" and that "woman can only find herself by giving love to others" (*Mulieris Dignitatem,* 29, 30). In a letter to women published shortly before a September, 1995, United Nations conference on women in Beijing, Pope John Paul, deploring "obstacles which . . . still keep women from being fully integrated into the social, political and economic life," declared: "We need only think of how the gift of motherhood is often penalized rather than rewarded even though humanity owes its very survival to this gift."

Women in the Church • Because the Church is recognized as the mother of all of the children of God and as a kind of extended family for every Christian, the woman stands for and represents the realm of the Church in a special way. The Blessed Virgin Mary, by her *fiat* at the Annunciation, bore Christ into the world, and she is, by virtue of that act, the archetype and forerunner of the Church, which continues to bear Christ into the world and to initiate, nurture, and sustain that active response to Christ that enables us to become, in her, the children of God. It is through the active ministry of the Church that the grace and truth of Christ bear fruit in this world. Therefore, as Hans Urs von Balthasar once noted, "the feminine, Marian principle is, in the Church, what encompasses all other principles, even the Petrine" (*Woman in the Church*, p. 113). Even the Petrine and apostolic authority of the Magisterium is secondary to the faith and grace of the Church, since the Pope and bishops can teach nothing not already present in the faith of the Church and can teach anything only by virtue of that grace that is sustained and nurtured by the gift of the Holy Spirit to the Church. As Pope John Paul II puts it, Mary's faith " 'precedes' the apostolic witness of the Church, and ever remains in the Church's heart, hidden like a special heritage of God's revelation. All those who from generation to generation accept the apostolic witness of the Church share in the mysterious inheritance and in a sense share in Mary's faith" (*Redemptoris Mater,* 27).

All women — married, single, or consecrated — are called to participate actively in the life of the Church. That women cannot be ordained priests does not mean they have no place in the mission of the Church. Rather, it means that "Christ looks to them for the accomplishment of the 'royal priesthood' " (*Mulieris Dignitatem*, 30). The royal priesthood of all believers, far from being secondary to the ordained priesthood, is the very reason for it, inasmuch as "the ministerial priesthood is at the service of the common priesthood. It is directed at the unfolding of the baptismal grace of all Christians" (CCC 1547).

This "unfolding of the baptismal grace" of every Christian is entrusted to the woman in a special way because each person is entrusted to her in a special way. In every role a woman assumes within the life of the Church — whether as wife, as mother, as consecrated, as single, as involved at any level of the lay apostolate — she is called upon to strengthen the life of faith and the bonds of communion among all persons within the Church. She, like Mary at the Annunciation, is called to bear children into the world, but even more, she, like Mary at Cana, is called to bring those children and all children into a relationship with Christ, guiding them to "do whatever he tells you" (Jn 2:5).

Women in Society • The role of women in society must be understood within the context of the lay apostolate, which itself is bound up with the apostolate of the Church. "The Church was founded to spread the kingdom of God over all the earth for the glory of God the Father, to make all men partakers in redemption and salvation, and through them to establish the right relationship of the entire world to Christ" (Vatican Council II, *Decree on the Apostolate of the Laity, Apostolicam Actuositatem*, 2). Everyone in the Church is called to participate in this apostolate. The primary lay apostolate lies not in the Church but in the world. If it is the role of the ordained ministry to serve all those who share in the royal priesthood of Christ, by effecting for them the grace, truth, and authority of Christ through teaching, sacraments, and governance, it is the role of the laity to take Christ out into the world. The laity are, in fact, called "to consecrate the world itself to God" (Vatican Coun-

cil II, *Dogmatic Constitution on the Church, Lumen Gentium*, 34).

Of particular import for the lay vocation is the need to renew within culture an "authentic humanism" to counter the secular humanism of our age and to oppose the "culture of death" that today surrounds us (Pope John Paul II, *The Lay Members of Christ's Faithful People, Christifideles Laici,* 38). This can only be done by restoring within society the reality and virtues of marriage and family life. "The family can and must require from all, beginning with public authority, the respect for those rights which, in saving the family, will save society" (*Christifideles Laici,* 40). As nurturers of life, women, in particular, have an important role to play in this regard.

Pope Pius XII recognized how deeply the currents of the modern world run counter to the interests of the family, and how pivotal is the role of women in reversing those currents. He told the women of Catholic Action: "The fate of the family, the fate of human relations are at stake. They are in your hands (*tua res agitur*). Every woman has then . . . the obligation, the strict obligation in conscience, not to absent herself but to go into action in a manner and way suitable to the condition of each so as to hold back those currents which threaten the home, so as to oppose those doctrines which undermine its foundations, so as to prepare, organize and achieve its restoration."

In Western societies at least, women today have come into their own, enjoying full political, social, and economic rights. The dignity of women requires that they take their rightful place in the political, social, and economic spheres of society. But it also requires that they do so in a way that protects and preserves their motherhood and the marital and family life that flow from it. Women, therefore, should ensure, in whatever walk of life, that marriage, family, and children always be given priority. That sphere, far from being merely "private" and secondary to the public world of politics, finance, and culture, is what sustains the goodness of the public sphere and guarantees its vitality. "The future of humanity passes by way of the family" (Pope John Paul II, *The Christian Family in the Modern World, Familiaris Consortio*, 86). Married women, therefore, while enjoying the right to work outside the home, should never sacrifice their homes and families to their jobs or careers, however important those might be. Wives and mothers should serve as a constant reminder to the rest of society that the work of society, at every level, is ordered to the value and dignity of the human person, and that success and achievement must always be ordered to the person's good and to those human relationships of marriage and family without which there can be no community, culture, or civilization. As mothers, both spiritual and physical, women have a special obligation to protect, defend, and speak on behalf of the unborn, the ill, the old, the handicapped, doing so in a "culture of death" that would increasingly subject the weakest and most vulnerable among us to the individualistic ethic of "control" over life and death.

All women (married, single, or consecrated) have a special responsibility, whether at home or at work, to restore the bonds of trust in the truth of Christ and in the need all of us have to give ourselves over to that truth. In today's scientific, technological atmosphere, the only truths recognized as true for everyone are the abstractions produced by scientific method. Such truths, valuable though they are, offer nothing that can sustain human beings as *persons* in an increasingly depersonalized world. Such a world has no way to understand *the truth as a Person* or the importance of the woman as mother. Abstract truth is abstract precisely because it has detached itself from the unique, the irreplaceable, the personal. It does not, therefore, as Karl Rahner once observed, require a mother. But *the truth* is a person, Jesus Christ, and Christ requires a mother. Every mother reminds us that the world of persons and the order of love take priority, even in the realm of truth. As mother, whether spiritual or physical, every woman should seek to bear into our world the truth of Christ and the order of love that the increasing relativism, cynicism, hostility, and violence of our society would deny. As Pope John Paul has observed, "Today the world is hun-

grier and thirstier than ever for that motherhood which, physically or spiritually, is woman's vocation as it was Mary's" (*L'Osservatore Romano*, January 15, 1979). And, saluting the "genius of women," he declares the need that "this genius be more fully expressed in the life of society as a whole as well as in the life of the Church" (*Letter to Women*).

See: Apostolate; Domestic Church; Family; Hierarchy; Imago Dei; Marriage; Marriage, Goods of; Mary, Mother of God; Mary, Mother of the Church; Ministry; Priesthood of the Faithful; Sexism; Sexuality, Human; States in Life; Theology of the Body; Vocation; Women, Ordination of; Work.

Suggested Readings: CCC 355-373, 487-511, 722-723, 963-975, 1546-1547, 1577, 1602-1617, 2201-2213, 2331-2335, 2392-2393. John Paul II, *The Christian Family in the Modern World, Familiaris Consortio; The Mother of the Redeemer, Redemptoris Mater; On the Dignity and Vocation of Women, Mulieris Dignitatem; Letter to Women*. L. Bouyer, *Woman in the Church*. G. von Le Fort, *The Eternal Woman*. J. Little, "The Significance of Mary for Women," *Marian Studies, XXXIX* (1988), pp. 136-158; "Mary and Feminist Theology," *Thought*, LXII (December, 1987), pp. 343-357.

Joyce A. Little

WOMEN, ORDINATION OF

In the history of the Church, the ordained priesthood has consistently been restricted to men. This restriction has been understood as reflecting the mind of Christ, who chose only men to be his Apostles. The exclusion of women, therefore, is rooted in the action of Christ and sustained in the Tradition of the Church. Clearly, why this should be so is based on the fact that the priesthood is a *sacramental office*, not just a job or function, because priests are ordained to act *in persona Christi* (in the Person of Christ) as the head and bridegroom of the Church. In order, however, to understand the significance of the relationship of Christ and the Church as bridegroom and bride, we must understand two other teachings of the Church, first, that of the Trinity, and second, that of man's creation in the image of God as male and female.

The Lesson of the Trinity • When we say that God is Trinity, we mean that God is one substance and three Persons — Father, Son, and Holy Spirit. These three Persons are subsistent *relations*. The Father is the relation of paternity (or fatherhood), the Son the relation of filiation (or sonship), the Holy Spirit the relation of passive spiration — "spiration" because he is spirated by the Father and the Son, "passive" because he does not do the spirating himself but is spirated by them. To be a person in the Trinity, therefore, is to be a relation.

These three Persons are also mutually *dependent* upon one another and mutually *ordered* to one another. The Father is Father because he has a Son, and he is ordered to the Son as Father. The Son is Son because he has a Father, and is ordered to the Father as Son. The Holy Spirit is Spirit because he is spirated by the Father and the Son, and is ordered to the Father and the Son as the One spirated by them. These Persons are therefore *noninterchangeable*. The Father, for example, cannot be the Son or Holy Spirit and cannot therefore do any of those things appropriate to filiation or spiration. (As one God, of course God *can* do all things capable of being done.) In short, the Trinity reveals to us that to be a person is to be in a dependent, ordered, noninterchangeable relation to another person or other persons.

Human beings, according to Revelation, are made in the image of God as male and female (Gn 1:27). They are made not just as male and female, however, but also as gifts to one another in the marital union of husband and wife (Gn 2:24). In other words, human beings are created to image God as *persons ordered to and dependent upon one another in the noninterchangeable relations of husband and wife*. The male is created to become bridegroom, the female to become bride. Although the Trinitarian implications of man's creation in the image of God are not apparent until the revelation given in Christ that God is Trinity, the Genesis text makes it clear that our imaging

of God is bound up with sexual differentiation and marital union.

The New Covenant not only reveals the triune character of God but also reaffirms, in the order of salvation, the marital order of creation, for the New Covenant is not just Jesus Christ, but precisely the marital union of Christ the bridegroom with his bride the Church. This union is the "great mystery," or "great sacrament," of salvation. Indeed, the author of Ephesians links this marital union with the original marital ordering of creation (Eph 5:31-32). Not only is Christ the Son of God, enjoying by virtue of his divinity a dependent, ordered, noninterchangeable relationship with the Father and Holy Spirit, he also is the bridegroom of the Church, enjoying by virtue of his humanity a dependent, ordered, noninterchangeable relationship with his bride the Church. We might, therefore, suppose that Christ is male not because God is male (there is no gender in God) but because he is *the relation of bridegroom*, which only a male can be. As Pope John Paul II has pointed out: "Christ has entered this history and remains in it as the Bridegroom who 'has given himself' " (*On the Dignity and Vocation of Women, Mulieris Dignitatem*, 25).

"In the Person of Christ" • That Christ reserved the ordained priesthood for men is, therefore, bound up with the fact that the priest receives a share in the priesthood of Christ and is called to act in the Person of Christ the bridegroom, which is the specifically male relation.

Pope John Paul II has declared that "the Church has no authority whatsoever to confer priestly ordination on women and . . . this judgment is to be definitively held by all the Church's faithful"; this is, he adds, "a matter of great importance . . . which pertains to the Church's divine constitution itself" (*Ordinatio Sacerdotalis*, 4). He is referring here to the holiness or integrity of the Church and her structures. The reservation of the ordained priesthood to men is one of the unchangeable structures of the Church because it is holy or good in itself, reflecting the mind of Christ, who reaffirms the order of creation within the order of salvation. The male priesthood is bound up with the very integrity of that order. The Church's teaching in this matter was reaffirmed yet again by the Congregation for the Doctrine of the Faith in a *Responsum* of November 18, 1995.

Two final considerations. First, the restriction of the priesthood to men does not mean that women are inferior to men. The Genesis text that makes clear the noninterchangeable character of male and female as the image of God also, and just as clearly, reveals their equality. "Here too [Gn 1:27] we find the first statement of the equal dignity of man and woman; both, in equal measure, are persons. Their constitution, with the specific dignity which derives from it, defines 'from the beginning' the qualities of the common good of humanity, in every dimension and circumstance of life. To this common good both man and woman make their specific contribution. Hence one can discover, at the very origins of human society, the qualities of communion and of complementarity" (Pope John Paul II, *Letter to Families*, 6).

The persons of the human community are equal in their humanity, just as the Persons of the divine communion are equal in their divinity.

Second, the ordained priesthood exists to serve the royal priesthood, that priesthood of all the faithful received at Baptism. In relation to her members, as well as in relation to Christ, the Church has a feminine character, and every one of us is entrusted at Baptism to the Church as mother. By the same token, every one of us is entrusted at conception to a woman as mother. We might therefore ask ourselves the question that John Paul II raises regarding the significance of women in relation to the royal priesthood: "If the human being is entrusted by God to women in a particular way, does not this mean that *Christ looks to them for the accomplishment of the 'royal priesthood'* (1 Pt 2:9), which is the treasure he has given to every individual?" (*Mulieris Dignitatem*, 30).

See: Apostolate; Bride of Christ; Hierarchy; Holy Orders; Imago Dei; In Persona Christi Capitis; Ministry; Priest; Priesthood in the Old Testament; Priesthood of Christ; Priesthood of the Faithful; Sexism; Sexuality, Human; Theology of the

Body; Trinity; Vocation; Women, Ecclesial and Social Roles of.

Suggested Readings: CCC 251-252, 254-255, 369-372, 796, 815, 830, 833, 857, 858-862, 981, 1087-1088, 1120, 1142, 1506, 1510-1511, 1536, 1539-1541, 1544-1549, 1551-1553, 1562, 1564, 1567-1568, 1576-1578, 1581, 1591, 1598. John Paul II, *Priestly Ordination, Ordinatio Sacerdotalis.* Congregation for the Doctrine of the Faith, *Declaration on the Admission of Women to the Ministerial Priesthood, Inter Insigniores.* M. Hauke, *Women in the Priesthood?* M. Miller, *Sexuality and Authority in the Catholic Church.* J. Tolhurst, ed., *Man, Woman and Priesthood.*

Joyce A. Little

WORK

For much of Christian history there has been confusion and misperception about the status of work in God's plan.

In the opening chapters of Genesis, God himself is portrayed as a kind of workman, who labors during the six days of creation, then rests on the seventh day. Shortly after, Adam is described as having been put in the Garden of Eden to cultivate and care for it (Gn 2:15), even before the Fall. Thus, human work is before all else a cooperation with and development of God's creative act. Man's having been created in the image and likeness of God appears in the use of human will and intellect to produce and order goods. Work, then, is a unique sign of human dignity and an expression of human personality.

The Bible, however, also speaks of some of the negative consequences for human work that followed the Fall: "In the sweat of your face you shall eat bread" (Gn 3:19). Since work as such preceded the Fall, it cannot be regarded merely as a punishment for sin or an evil in itself; but the painful and disturbing sides of work, like all the evils of human existence, are the result of Adam and Eve's sin. Some human work after the banishment from the garden also becomes idolatrous, in that it either denies God as the ground of all human achievement (cf. Ps 127) or seeks goods in a way that conflicts with the divine order of creation. For the most part, however, the Old Testament celebrates the fruits of the just worker. The patriarchs have wealth and many descendants because of their faith and work.

The New Testament continues this tradition but also emphasizes other elements in it. Throughout both the Old and New Testaments, God is active, working to repair the damage done by the Fall, to liberate his people from bondage to sin, and ultimately — in Christ — to redeem the human race. Human work appears in this perspective to have several dimensions. Jesus worked for thirty years in Joseph's carpenter's shop; many of the disciples are drawn from the ranks of fishermen and agricultural workers. Christ's parables sometimes refer to these workmen and their obligations toward one another and to their stewardship of creation. Yet Christ also warns about being too anxious and occupied about mere earthly goods and reminds his disciples that the more important labor is to store up treasure in heaven.

Christian Views on Work • Early Christianity expected Christ's immediate return and encouraged a relative detachment from the things of this world as a result. Every honest station in life, even that of a servant, was compatible with the Christian vocation of waiting in hope. But scholars disagree whether in the early Church these occupations themselves were seen as part of the Christian vocation. There is no doubt that working quietly so as to be a burden to no one and giving alms to the poor out of one's earnings remained duties, however near the Second Coming. In his Second Letter to the Thessalonians (3:10), St. Paul reminds those who think otherwise that whoever does not work should not eat.

As it became clear that Christ's return might be some time off, Christian theologians began to reflect on work as a contribution to the common good and a share in Christ's redemptive action. Both Greek and Roman culture had denigrated manual labor in favor of the more "liberal" activities of politics and intellectual pursuits. Christianity was influenced by this environment to some extent. But as Rome gradually collapsed during

the fourth and fifth centuries, the monasteries then being founded gave manual labor and the preservation of the goods of civilization a different status than they had in classical times, when manual labor was often associated with slavery. The dignity of all who contributed to the common life in monasteries gave work a solid social and religious status.

In the high Middle Ages, this led to further development. St. Thomas Aquinas, drawing on a distinction present in the Greek philosopher Aristotle, divides human action into two kinds: making and doing. Making is the humbler activity we usually call work, and it was less damaged after the Fall. Even without grace, says Thomas, fallen men could do simple goods such as tilling fields and building barns. The higher function of doing, which includes the characteristically human activities such as thought, politics, charity, moral action, and so forth, involve man's will and sense of good and evil more directly and were thus more damaged by the Fall. But man, precisely as man, needs the products of both manual and spiritual work.

The Protestant Reformation was largely responsible for moving work in its specifically religious dimension outside the monasteries and into the workshops and households of average Christians. Medieval Catholic guilds and other institutions had placed various occupations under the patronage of Christ, Mary, and the saints. But it was mostly from Luther and Calvin that the modern notions of work as a Christian calling got their start. Unfortunately, this impulse also led, contrary to the intentions of the Reformers, to the eventual separation of work from religious ties and, some have argued, to secularization in capitalist society.

Recent Thinking on Work • The twentieth century has witnessed a great flowering of reflection on work. Work and the social situation of workers had become acute problems with the rise of modern capitalism and industrialism. Instead of living in age-old rural communities, modern workers migrated to burgeoning cities. Agricultural workers could see famine as an act of God;

unemployed industrial workers appeared to be suffering the consequences of some fault in man. The seeming growth in the poverty of workers stimulated various proposals, including socialism, communism, and labor unions.

Pope Leo XIII, recognizing the new situation and the dangers it posed both to the physical welfare and spiritual life of industrial workers, tried to give a Catholic answer to the problem. In his 1891 encyclical *On the Social Question, Rerum Novarum*, Leo early noted that the socialist vision of man did not accord very well with Catholic anthropology and theology. Prophetically, he predicted that if socialism were established, the workers themselves would be the first to suffer from this wrong solution to their very real problems.

Catholic reflection on work and workers centered on questions of freedom, family solidarity, and the family wage in capitalist societies where work and workers were coming to be regarded as mere commodities. But political reactions to market economies could be even more worrisome. In the 1930s, facing both Nazism and communism, Pope Pius XI posited a principle of subsidiarity aimed at preventing politics and economic life from being absorbed by the state. The Church was seeking a balance between the just claims of labor and capital that would permit vibrant economic life as well as just and stable conditions for vulnerable workers.

Unlike modern conceptions of work, the Christian view does not attribute great value to mere production and consumption. Both of these must be seen within the larger framework of what is good for man and for the common good of society. Abundance and just access to material goods may become the normal condition in modern developed societies. But these societies have responsibilities to use their blessings to provide for the poor and unfortunate within their borders and the poor in underdeveloped parts of the world. And they must be concerned with the human development of the worker.

At the Second Vatican Council, the Church began another phase of such reflections. Encouraging *ressourcement* — that is, a return to the sources of Christian thought in the Scriptures and the Church Fathers — the Council developed an insight already formulated by Pope John XXIII in his 1961 encyclical *Mother and Teacher, Mater et Magistra*: Human work is "an expression of the human person." The Council and several encyclicals by Pope Paul VI began emphasizing the theme that work is both co-creation (as man cooperates with God) and a share in the redemption (as workers try to repair the consequences of the Fall). In this regard, unemployment and underemployment not only harm the worker financially but also harm him spiritually as a person.

Particularly in the writings of Pope John Paul II, who was a workingman in Poland during World War II, work has received even greater theological dignity. In his 1981 encyclical *On Human Work, Laborem Exercens*, John Paul asks every Christian to examine "the place that his work has not only in the earthly progress but also in the development of the kingdom of God" (27). In *The Acting Person*, a philosophical book written before he became Pope, Karol Wojtyla tried to lay out a complete exposition of how every human act reveals the transcendent dimension of the person who works in love with others.

Despite the positive reevaluation of work, human labor is still often marked with the pain and toil that accompany human things after the Fall. Work cannot — and should not — be romanticized or expected always to be a pleasant use of our powers or a fulfilling development of human faculties. Society may try to make work as humanly satisfying as possible, but at least for the foreseeable future many jobs in many parts of the world will remain harsh tasks. Also, as anyone who has worked on a farm, in a factory, an office, or even a rectory knows, there are internal as well as external evils that must be confronted in the pursuit of our basic needs and participation in redemption. In fact, the willingness to endure the hardship of work when necessary is one of the ways we participate in the redemptive work of Christ's cross.

See: Apostolate; Common Good; Family; Original Sin; Sexism; Slavery; Social Doctrine;

Stewardship; Subsidiarity; Suffering in Christian Life; Vocation.

Suggested Readings: CCC 2426-2436. Vatican Council II, *Pastoral Constitution on the Church in the Modern World, Gaudium et Spes*, 67. John Paul II, *On Human Work, Laborem Exercens*. R. Charles, *The Social Teaching of Vatican II*, pp. 28-34, 312-333. M. Weber, *The Protestant Ethic and the Spirit of Capitalism*. M. Novak, *The Catholic Ethic and the Spirit of Capitalism*.

Robert Royal

WORKS OF MERCY

Mercy is one of the fruits of charity and therefore proceeds from love of God and neighbor. Traditionally, the works of mercy have been divided into two categories, the spiritual and the corporal. Seven acts of charity have been identified in each category. The spiritual works of mercy are to: convert sinners, instruct the ignorant, counsel the wayward, comfort the sorrowing, bear adversity patiently, forgive offenses, and pray for the living and the dead. The corporal works lead us to: feed the hungry, clothe the naked, give drink to the thirsty, shelter the homeless, tend the sick, visit prisoners, and bury the dead.

In Catholic social doctrine, justice, too, is one of the fruits of charity, and the works of mercy provide a guide to what constitutes justice to our neighbor. Private charitable action by individuals, groups, and the Church in particular, have distinguished Christian societies from other forms throughout history. In keeping with the principle of subsidiarity, these private individuals and groups have the primary responsibility to meet the needs of the neighbor who cannot meet them himself. Subsidiarity also specifies, however, that if smaller entities are unable to carry out this work, governments, from local to international scale, may have to undertake these responsibilities as a last resort.

Charity toward others in this sense is thus not "charity" in the modern meaning, but a form of justice. After a period of rapid growth in the welfare state, developed societies are currently reex-amining how much of the works of mercy should be handled by government and how much by private association. At an international level, the responsibility of the developed to the underdeveloped nations remains a complex and urgent question.

See: Commutative Justice; Health Care; Ministry; Preferential Option for the Poor; Social Doctrine; Socialization; Social Justice; Subsidiarity; Universal Destination of Goods.

WORSHIP

Worship is reverence duly paid to God or, indirectly, to creatures he has spiritually enriched. Sovereign, absolute worship — the adoration of religion — is owed to God alone; to revere a creature in this way would be idolatry. "To adore God is to acknowledge him as God, as the Creator and Savior, the Lord and Master of everything that exists, as infinite and merciful Love" (CCC 2096).

When Catholics venerate angels or saints, relics or the cross, they honor them subordinately, for their special relationship with God. Because Mary ever-virgin was and is uniquely close to God, this supereminent saint is owed special veneration (cf. CCC 971). Properly speaking, statues or other images are not worshiped, but only the God-adorned and excellent person thus represented.

Interior adoration is all-important; God is to be hallowed "in spirit and in truth" (Jn 4:23). Neither "sacred" things nor deeds in themselves endear man to God but rather the intention with which he plies or does them. Mere repeated religious gestures or words, bereft of interior values, are sham, even superstition (cf. CCC 2111). The harshest words from Jesus' lips were the "woes" addressed to the hypocritical Pharisees (cf. Mt 23:2-36; Lk 11:39-52). But that is not to say that Christ proscribed external worship in favor of a sole "adoration of the heart," as is sometimes alleged.

Some Protestants have historically accused Catholic ceremonies of being tainted by paganism and idolatry, and have condemned them in the name of a supposedly purer Christianity, without priest, altar, or temple, in the privacy of one's mind and heart. Today, however, many Protestants value public religious services and prize preaching. Moreover, it is clear that Christ (and his Apostles) respected Jewish rituals and observed ceremonial requirements, while avoiding legalism and trappings. Instead of adoring only at Jerusalem or Garizim, Jesus told his followers to worship God everywhere, regardless of nation or tongue. Believers were to adore with true and sincere worship, which supposes and implies a pure and upright life, but in no way excludes public ritual.

Composed of soul and body, man is to express religious attitudes with both, as when he sings, genuflects, or recites prayers aloud. If man's religious spirit is to overflow onto the body, it is also true that praying with the body (reciting in unison, appropriate dress and grooming, reverent postures, gestures, and the like) reinforces the soon distracted or lagging spirit (cf. CCC 1387, 2700-2704). Humans, furthermore, are social beings, both naturally (helping one another to grow) and supernaturally (contributing to, and receiving from, a Church both visible and invisible). Those united by the same faith, sacraments, and authority should also suitably share the same public worship: whence stems the Catholic liturgy and its binding character.

While nonliturgical worship may be optional, the general duty to revere the Creator and Savior. Man is bound to acknowledge God prayerfully because of who he is and what he does (cf. CCC 2628-2643) is not. In justice, man owes God worship, something sporadically and somewhat deliberately expressed in this life and, in the next, joyously perpetuated and ecstatically amplified. The more humans come to appreciate God in and of himself, the more this homage comes "naturally" to them. Since heaven will entail the perfection of knowledge and love of God, Christians should not fear they will be bored spending eternity in praise of their triune Maker, Redeemer, and Sanctifier.

Variety of Worship • One can worship alone or in the assembly, in both cases following forms specified by the Church or other suitable forms. Worship ranges from a single, soon-ended prayer to a lifelong consecration to serve God (cf. CCC 914-933). Worship also serves as a main way for keeping the first commandment and expressing the three essential theological virtues of faith, hope, and love (cf. CCC 2084-2097). Since worship seeks to exalt and revere our hidden, transcendent God, from time immemorial humanity has pressed into service the signs and symbols of artistic ingenuity to express both divine beauty and human longings for it: painting, music, poetry, architecture, and even dance. One can, moreover, adore God by carrying out either sacred deeds (using holy water, for example) or secular actions done for his sake (offering up, say, one's diligent factory or office chores).

As the twentieth century advanced, and culminating in Vatican II's central proclamation of the universal call to holiness (cf. *Dogmatic Constitution on the Church, Lumen Gentium*, Chs. 2, 4), the awareness grew that laypersons are to sanctify themselves and thereby their families, jobs, and peers. They are to discharge, conscientiously, virtuously, and lovingly, the duties and commitments of their state in life for God's and their neighbors' sake. Strengthened in the sacraments and fortified by prayer and sacrifice, laypeople can thus turn mundane tasks into prayer.

At one time "comparative religion" was in vogue. It claimed to find precedents in natural religions and so-called mystery cults for much, if not all, of the Catholic liturgy. But, it was implied, if the latter were merely a syncretist invention, so much for its divine origin and uniqueness. It would be strange, however, if forms of religious worship were vastly different from one another, considering the universal character of human nature and its all-worthy Creator. Furthermore, behind the signs of Catholic worship, something wholly unique and divine is being *enacted*, not just commemorated or expounded. The sacraments inaugurated by Christ also *effect* via divine action what they represent.

Is there a divine guideline for worship? What is the best way for man to pray? The Apostles asked this question of Jesus, who in turn gave them the

Our Father and, later, the self-sacrificing deeds to be echoed and made really, though sacramentally, present at every Mass. In both are enshrined the four strains of praying. The Our Father, said Tertullian (c. 160-c. 222), "is truly the summary of the whole gospel"; St. Thomas Aquinas called it the "most perfect of prayers" (cf. CCC 2767-2772). In it, man first *adores*, glorifies, and praises God for being who and what he is: "Our Father, who art in heaven, hallowed be thy name." Then man *thanks* God for his largesse: "thy kingdom come, thy will be done, on earth as it is in heaven." As his needy children, God's followers *petition* him: "Give us this day our daily bread . . . and lead us not into temptation, but deliver us from evil." Recognizing that they have strayed from their Father, they also seek to *atone*: "Forgive us our trespasses,

as we forgive those who trespass against us." No wonder then that the thrice-daily custom arose among the earliest Christians of making the Lord's Prayer their own prayer.

See: Assembly, Liturgical; Church Buildings; Devotions; Eucharist; Holy Days of Obligation; Homily; Liturgy; Lord's Day; Prayer; Religion, Virtue of; Sacrament; Sacred Art; Sacred Music; Sacrifice; Superstition; Theological Virtues.

Suggested Readings: CCC 914-933, 2084-2103, 2626-2643, 2767-2772. Vatican Council II, *Dogmatic Constitution on the Church, Lumen Gentium*, especially Chs. 2, 4; *Constitution on the Sacred Liturgy, Sacrosanctum Concilium; Decree on the Apostolate of the Laity, Apostolicam Actuositatem.*

Dennis Helming

Index

Note: For a number of reasons, this index is not arranged in the conventional manner. For example, some published works, such as the papal documents, are placed as subentries under the names of the Popes to whom the documents are attributed; still other works are placed alphabetically with their authors' names following in brackets. As for individual names, some have their last names with initials for their first names, while others have their full names. The names of saints are under the heading "saints," although a few, because of their importance, may be entered in the usual manner; on the other hand, the Popes are entered alphabetically under their own names. Entries that may have both a singular and plural form are found under their singular nomenclature; still others may be classified under a general heading but include related matter — for instance, under "psychology" are included "psychological counseling, psychological systems, and psychologists." Other modifications include some cross-references that have been arbitrarily selected because of their perceived importance within the context of this volume.